# Oxford
## LEARNER'S DICTIONARY
## Business

OXFORD
UNIVERSITY PRESS

OXFORD
UNIVERSITY PRESS

Great Clarendon Street, Oxford OX2 6DP

Oxford University Press is a department of the University of Oxford. It furthers the University's objective of excellence in research, scholarship, and education by publishing worldwide in

Oxford New York

Auckland Cape Town Dar es Salaam Hong Kong Karachi Kuala Lumpur Madrid Melbourne Mexico City Nairobi New Delhi Shanghai Taipei Toronto

With offices in

Argentina Austria Brazil Chile Czech Republic France Greece Guatemala Hungary Italy Japan Poland Portugal Singapore South Korea Switzerland Thailand Turkey Ukraine Vietnam

OXFORD and OXFORD ENGLISH are registered trade marks of Oxford University Press in the UK and in certain other countries



First published 2006
2015 2014 2013
10



This dictionary includes some words which have or are asserted to have proprietary status as trade marks or otherwise. Their inclusion does not imply that they have acquired for legal purposes a non-proprietary or general significance nor any other judgement concerning their legal status. In cases where the editorial staff have some evidence that a word has proprietary status this is indicated in the entry for that word but no judgement concerning the legal status of such words is made or implied thereby

The British National Corpus is a collaborative project involving Oxford University Press, Longman, Chambers, the Universities of Oxford and Lancaster and the British Library

ISBN-13: 978 0 19 431733 7

Typeset by Oxford University Press

Printed in China

ACKNOWLEDGEMENTS

*Edited by:* Dilys Parkinson

*Cover photography:* Corbis (figures/Zefa/Guntmar Fritz); OUP (business-people/Corbis) (clock/Corbis), (businessman/Corbis)
*Advisory Board:* Dr Keith Brown, Prof Guy Cook, Dr Alan Cruse, Ruth Gairns, Moira Runcie, Prof Gabriele Stein, Dr Norman Whitney, Prof Henry Widdowson

# Guide to using this dictionary

Headword and pronunciation

★ shows that this is an important business word

Label shows the business area it is used in

Examples

Common phrases show how to use the word

★ **expense** /ɪk'spens/ *n.*
**1** (*Account.*) [C,U] money that a business spends on supplies, workers, services, etc. in order to operate: *Labour is the airline industry's biggest expense.* ◇ *marketing/sales ~s* ◇ *pension/relocation ~s*
⊙ *to* ***bear/incur*** *an ~* ♦ *to* ***cover/meet*** *an ~* ♦ *to* ***deduct sth/treat sth/write sth off*** *as an ~* ♦ *to* ***control/cut/reduce/trim*** *~s* ♦ ***big/high/large/low/unexpected*** *~s*

Help with irregular forms

Common prepositions or patterns

Help with synonyms and opposites

→ shows a related word or phrase to look at

★ **lend** /lend/ *v.* (**lent**, **lent** /lent/)
[T,I] **~ (sth) (to sb/sth)** | **~ sb sth** (about a bank or financial institution) to give money to sb on condition that they pay it back over a period of time and pay interest: *The bank refused to lend the money to us.* ◇ *They refused to lend us the money.* ◇ *Some banks have stopped lending to small businesses.* SYN LOAN → BORROW

Phrase with stress to help with pronunciation

Abbreviations

Differences between British and American English

Different meanings of a word or phrase

**ˌannual ˌgeneral 'meeting** (*abbr* **AGM**) (*BrE*) (*AmE* **ˌannual 'meeting**) *n.* [C] **1** an important meeting of the shareholders or members of a company, held once a year, to present the accounts and discuss important topics **2** a meeting of the members of any organization, held once a year

Help with spelling

Derivatives or words with similar meaning but different part of speech

**ageism** (*AmE usu.* **agism**) /'eɪdʒɪzəm/ *n.* [U] unfair treatment of people considered too old SYN AGE DISCRIMINATION ▶ **'ageist** *adj.*: *ageist attitudes* **'ageist** *n.* [C]

Idioms

Phrasal Verbs

Label shows how formal it is.

**bring** /brɪŋ/ *v.* (**brought**, **brought** /brɔːt/) IDM **bring sth into 'force** to cause a law, rule, etc. to start being used → idioms at CONTROL *n.*, QUESTION *n.* PHR V **'bring sb/sth before sb** (*fml.*) to present sb/sth for discussion or judgement: *The case will be brought before the bankruptcy judge today.* **ˌbring sth 'down** to re-

# Pronunciation and phonetic symbols

## Vowels

| | | | |
|---|---|---|---|
| iː | **see** /siː/ | ɜː | **fur** /fɜː(r)/ |
| i | **any** /ˈeni/ | ə | **ago** /əˈgəʊ/ |
| ɪ | **sit** /sɪt/ | eɪ | **pay** /peɪ/ |
| e | **ten** /ten/ | aɪ | **five** /faɪv/ |
| æ | **hat** /hæt/ | əʊ | **home** /həʊm/ (*BrE*) |
| ɑː | **father** /ˈfɑːðə(r)/ | oʊ | **home** /hoʊm/ (*AmE*) |
| ɒ | **got** /gɒt/ | aʊ | **now** /naʊ/ |
| ɔː | **saw** /sɔː/ | ɔɪ | **join** /dʒɔɪn/ |
| ʊ | **put** /pʊt/ | ɪə | **near** /nɪə(r)/ |
| uː | **too** /tuː/ | eə | **hair** /heə(r)/ |
| u | **usual** /ˈjuːʒuəl/ | ʊə | **pure** /pjʊə(r)/ |
| ʌ | **cup** /kʌp/ | | |

## Consonants

| | | | |
|---|---|---|---|
| p | **pen** /pen/ | s | **see** /siː/ |
| b | **bad** /bæd/ | z | **zoo** /zuː/ |
| t | **tea** /tiː/ | ʃ | **she** /ʃiː/ |
| d | **did** /dɪd/ | ʒ | **vision** /ˈvɪʒn/ |
| k | **cat** /kæt/ | h | **how** /haʊ/ |
| g | **get** /get/ | m | **man** /mæn/ |
| tʃ | **chin** /tʃɪn/ | n | **now** /naʊ/ |
| dʒ | **June** /dʒuːn/ | ŋ | **sing** /sɪŋ/ |
| f | **fall** /fɔːl/ | l | **leg** /leg/ |
| v | **van** /væn/ | r | **red** /red/ |
| θ | **thin** /θɪn/ | j | **yes** /jes/ |
| ð | **then** /ðen/ | w | **wet** /wet/ |

(r) shows that British pronunciation will have /r/ only if a vowel sound follows immediately. Otherwise the /r/ sound is omitted. In American pronunciation, every 'r' of the ordinary spelling is sounded.

**Stress in phrases**

The stress patterns given in this dictionary are the recommended ones, but you may hear others. For example, the stress may change when phrases are combined with other words and the main stress in the first phrase may shift to the place of the secondary stress to avoid two stressed syllables next to each other. For instance, **ˌduty-ˈfree** has the main stress on **ˈfree**, but in the phrase **ˌduty-free ˈshops** the stress on **free** is missing.

**@** *symbol* (*written*) **at 1** the symbol used in email addresses: *jsmith@oup.com* **2** used to show a rate or price for sth, esp. on a bill: *5 boxes @ $12 per box*

**10 000-foot view** /ˌten ˈθaʊznd ˈfʊt ˈvjuː/ *n.* [C] (*infml.*) a broad general view of a problem

**2+2=5** /ˈtuː plʌs ˈtuː iːkwəlz ˈfaɪv/ *phr.* **two plus two equals five** a phrase used to express the idea that when two organizations work or join together, more can be achieved than if they work separately

**24/7** /ˌtwenti fɔː ˈsevən; *AmE* fɔːr/ *adv.*, *adj.* twenty-four hours a day, seven days a week (= 'all the time'): *The web store is open 24/7.*

**24-hour** /ˌtwenti fɔːr ˈaʊə(r)/ *adj.* **1** used to describe sth that is open or available all day and night: *a 24-hour store* **2** used to describe sth that relates to one day or happens only on one day: *a 24-hour strike*

**24-hour society** /ˌtwenti fɔːr aʊə səˈsaɪəti; *AmE* aʊər/ *n.* [U; sing.] the fact that people can now work, play, shop, etc. all day and all night

**2G** /ˌtuː ˈdʒiː/ = SECOND-GENERATION (2)

**360-degree feedback** /ˌθriː ˌsɪksti dɪˌgriː ˈfiːdbæk/ (*also* **ˌ360-degree apˈpraisal**, **ˌfull-circle ˈfeedback**) *n.* [U] (*HR*) information about sb's work from all the types of people they work with, including their manager, the people they manage, customers, etc.; a judgement of the value of their work based on this

**3G** /ˌθriː ˈdʒiː/ = THIRD-GENERATION (1)

**401(k)** /ˌfɔː(r) əʊ ˈwʌn (ˈkeɪ); *AmE* oʊ/ *n.* [C] (*pl.* **401(k)s** *or* **401(k)'s**) in the US, a way of saving money for your retirement, in which part of your wage is paid into an investment fund, to which employers may add a similar amount. Tax is only charged when you take money out of the fund: *a 401(k) plan*

**the 4 Ps** (*also* **four Ps**) /ˌfɔː ˈpiːz; *AmE* ˌfɔːr/ *n.* [pl.] (*Market.*) **product**, **price**, **promotions** and **place**, which together form the MARKETING MIX

**the 80/20 rule** /ˌeɪti ˈtwenti ruːl/ (*also* **the ˌ80/ˈ20 ˌprinciple**) *n.* [sing.] a theory that 80% of results come from 20% of effort or causes SYN PARETO'S PRINCIPLE

# Aa

**A1** /ˌeɪ ˈwʌn/ *adj.* **1** (*Finan.*) used to describe a company that is considered to be able to pay its debts and to be safe to lend money to: *The company is **rated** A1.* **2** used to describe sb/sth in the best possible condition

**AAA** /ˌtrɪpl ˈeɪ/ = TRIPLE-A

**ˌAA ˈrating** /ˌeɪ ˈeɪ/ = AVERAGE AUDIENCE RATING

**abˌbreviated acˈcounts** *n.* [pl.] (*BrE*) (*Account.*) a financial record with less detail than normal, which small companies can produce for official records

**ABC1** /ˌeɪ biː siː ˈwʌn/ *n.* [U] (*BrE*) (*Market.*) the top three social and economic groups in a society, considered as possible customers: *41% of ABC1 women aged 15–24 read a women's magazine.* → C2DE

**ˈA/ˈB/ˈC share** (*also* **class ˈA/ˈB/ˈC share**) *n.* [C, usu. pl.] (*Finan.*) in the UK, different types of shares that give the owners different rights

★ **ability** /əˈbɪləti/ *n.* (*pl.* **-ties**) **1** [sing.] the fact that sb is able to do sth: *the ability to work in a team* **2** [C,U] a level of skill or intelligence: *to prove your abilities*

**aˌbility-to-ˈpay ˌprinciple** *n.* [sing.] (*Econ.*) a theory that people who earn more money should pay more tax, so that there are higher rates of tax on higher incomes

★ **abolish** /əˈbɒlɪʃ; *AmE* əˈbɑːl-/ *v.* [T] to officially end a law, a system or an institution: *The tax has been abolished.* ▸ **abolition** /ˌæbəˈlɪʃn/ *n.* [U]

**aˌbove the ˈfold** *adv.*, *adj.* (*IT*) in the top part of a web page that you see first on the screen: *above-the-fold ads* → BELOW THE FOLD

**aˌbove-the-ˈline** *adj.* **1** (*Account.*) relating to the normal business costs and income that form a company's total profit: *Raw materials are recorded as above-the-line costs.* **2** (*Market.*) relating to advertising that uses the MASS MEDIA: *above-the-line promotion* ▸ **aˌbove-the-ˈline** *adv.*: *Property costs will be **taken** above-the-line.* → BELOW-THE-LINE

**ABS** /ˌeɪ biː ˈes/ *abbr* (*Finan.*) asset-backed securities; asset-backed securitization: *the ABS market*

**absence** /ˈæbsəns/ *n.* [U,C] when sb is not at work or at a meeting when they should be; the occasion or period of time when sb is away: *her repeated absences **from** work* ◇ *The decision was made **in my absence** (= while I was not there).*

**absentee** /ˌæbsənˈtiː/ *n.* [C] (*HR*) a person who is not at work when they should be: *a low* ***absentee rate***

**absenteeism** /ˌæbsənˈtiːɪzəm/ *n.* [U] (*HR*) staying away from work, esp. often and without good reasons: *Absenteeism costs the industry millions of dollars a year.*

**ˌabsolute adˈvantage** *n.* [C, usu. sing.] (*Econ.*) the ability to make a product more cheaply than other countries can

**ˌabsolute ˈauction** *n.* [C] (*AmE*) (*Comm.*) an **auction** in which there is no fixed price that must be reached, so that an item is simply sold to the person who offers the most money

**absorb** /əbˈsɔːb; -ˈzɔːb; *AmE* əbˈsɔːrb; -ˈzɔːrb/ *v.* [T] **1** (*often pass.*) to take a smaller business into a larger one; to take unemployed workers from other businesses into a company: *Several clothing chains were absorbed* ***into*** *the group.* **2** to be able to deal with high costs, losses or changes without showing any bad effects: *We absorb higher costs rather than pass them on to our customers.* **3** (about a market) to accept and be able to sell a product: *It took the market three years to absorb the increase in hotel rooms.* **4** to use up a large supply of sth, esp. money or time ▸ **abˈsorption** /-pʃn/ *n.* [U]: *The mergers included the absorption of two small banks.*

**abˈsorption ˌcosting** *n.* [U] (*Account.*) a way of calculating the cost of a product by including all costs involved in producing it and running the business

**abstract** /ˈæbstrækt/ *n.* [C] a short piece of writing containing the main ideas in a talk, a report, etc. SYN SUMMARY

**a/c** = ACCOUNT

**ACAS** /ˈeɪkæs/ *abbr* **Advisory Conciliation and Arbitration Service** in the UK, an organization that helps employers and employees settle disagreements

**accelerate** /əkˈseləreɪt/ *v.* **1** [T,I] to happen or to make sth happen faster or earlier than expected: *Technological change is accelerating.* OPP DECELERATE **2** [I] (about the economy) to increase in activity so that demand for goods increases OPP DECELERATE **3** (*Finan.*) [T] to demand that a debt is paid back more quickly than first agreed, because regular payments have not been made: *to accelerate a loan* ▸ **acˌceleˈration** /-ˈreɪʃn/ *n.* [sing; U]: *a sharp acceleration* ***in*** *the rate of growth*

**acˌcelerated ˈcost recovery ˌsystem** *n.* [U] (*abbr* **ACRS**) (*Account.*) in the US, a way of calculating the value of assets in a company's financial records, where the value of an asset is reduced over a period of time fixed by the tax rules

**acˌcelerated depreciˈation** *n.* [U] (*Account.*) a way of calculating the value of an asset in a company's accounts by reducing its value over a shorter period of time than usual or by larger amounts than usual in the first few years, as a form of TAX RELIEF

**acˌcelerated ˈpayment** *n.* [C,U] (*Finan.*) a payment that sb makes to pay back a debt or a loan more quickly than was first agreed, often because they have not made regular payments

**accelerator** /əkˈseləreɪtə(r)/ *n.* [C] a company that helps new companies get started by giving them office space, marketing services, etc. in exchange for payment

★**accept** /əkˈsept/ *v.* [T] **1** to be willing or able to receive payment in a particular form: *All major credit cards are accepted.* **2** (*Law*) to agree to take goods or services from a seller, which means that the buyer must then pay for them OPP REJECT **3** (*Market.*) to be willing to buy a product, a technology or a service: *Our products are* ***well/widely accepted*** *in the international market.* **4** (*Law*) to agree to what is stated in a contract: *to accept the terms of an agreement* **5** (*Insur.*) to agree to provide payments if sb loses sth or has a serious accident, etc. **6** (*Finan.*) to agree to pay the amount of money stated on a BILL OF EXCHANGE by signing it

★**acceptance** /əkˈseptəns/ *n.* **1** (*Finan.*) [C] the agreement of people who hold shares in a company to the offer of a TAKEOVER by another company: *They had acceptances from 60% of the shareholders.* **2** (*Law*) [U] the act of agreeing to accept sth that is offered: *Once acceptance has taken place, the buyer cannot reject the goods.* **3** [U] the willingness of people to buy or use a product, technology or service: *The product has* ***gained*** *acceptance worldwide.* ◇ *consumer/customer/market/public* ~ ◇ *brand/product* ~ **4** (*Insur.*) [U] the act of an insurance company agreeing to provide payments if sb loses sth or has a serious accident: *Acceptance into the plan is not guaranteed.*

**5** (*Finan.*) [U,C] the act of signing a BILL OF EXCHANGE to say that you promise to pay the amount of money mentioned on it; the words written; the document that has been signed

**ac'ceptance ˌbonus** *n.* [C] (*AmE*) (*HR*) an amount of money that is paid to an employee who agrees to do a difficult task

**ac'ceptance ˌsampling** *n.* [U] (*Product.*) testing a small number of a total amount of items in order to decide whether the quality of the whole amount is good enough to accept or not

**acceptor** (*AmE also* **accepter**) /ək'septə(r)/ *n.* [C] (*Finan.*) the person or bank that signs a BILL OF EXCHANGE and promises to pay it

★**access** /'ækses/ *n., v.*
• *n.* [U] **~ (to sth) 1** the chance or right to use or have sth: *Do you have access to the Internet?* ◇ *increased access to the American market*
⊕ *to **gain/get** ~* ◆ *to **give/offer/provide** ~*
**2** the right to remove some of the money that you have in an account **3** permission, esp. legal or official, to see sth or sb: *Someone gained unauthorized access to the files.* ◇ *to deny (sb)/get/have ~* **4** a way of entering or reaching a place, esp. for DISABLED people
• *v.* [T] **1** to find information on a computer: *to access an email account* **2** to remove some of the money that you have in an account: *to access an account* **3** to be able to obtain, reach or use sth: *How can we access the capital we need?*

**accessible** /ək'sesəbl/ *adj.* **~ (to sb) 1** able to be reached, used or seen: *information accessible to everyone* **2** (about a person) easy to talk to: *Is your manager accessible?* **3** (about a place) able to be reached or entered **4** easy to understand or use ▸ **acˌcessi'bility** /-'bɪləti/ *n.* [U]

**accessory** /ək'sesəri/ *n.* [C, usu. pl.] (*pl.* **-ries**) **1** an extra piece of equipment that you can add to sth and is useful or attractive but not essential: *computer accessories* **2** a thing that you can wear or carry, for example a belt or a bag: *fashion accessories* **3** small items sold to be used for a particular purpose or in a particular place: *office accessories*

**'accident inˌsurance** *n.* [U] a type of insurance in which money is paid for injury or death caused by an accident

**accommodation** /əˌkɒmə'deɪʃn; *AmE* əˌkɑːm-/ *n.* **1** [U] (*BrE*) (*AmE* **aˌccommo'dations** [pl.]) a place to live, work or stay in **2** (*fml.*) [U; C, usu. sing.] an agreement or arrangement between people or groups with different opinions: *to **arrive at/reach** an ~ **with** sb* **3** (*Finan.*) [sing.] (*esp. AmE*) money that is lent for a short time before a formal arrangement is made

★**account** /ə'kaʊnt/ *n., v.*
• *n.* [C] **1** (*abbr* **a/c**) an arrangement that sb has with a bank or BUILDING SOCIETY to keep money there: *to open a business account* ◇ *an ~ **with/at** Barclays*
⊕ *to **close/have/hold** an ~* ◆ *to **pay/put sth into** an ~* ◆ *to **take sth out of/withdraw sth from** an ~* ◆ *to **credit/debit** an ~*
**2** (*Comm.*) (*BrE also* **'credit acˌcount**) (*AmE also* **'charge acˌcount**) an arrangement with a shop/store or business to pay bills for goods or services at a later time, for example in regular amounts every month: *Please charge it to my account.*
⊕ *to **close/have/hold/open** an ~ (with sb)* ◆ *to **settle** an ~*
**3** (*Account.*) a statement of money paid, received or owed over a period of time: *an itemized account* ◇ *to **keep an account of** expenses* **4** (*Market.*) a regular customer who does a lot of business with a company, esp. a company working in advertising, marketing or PUBLIC RELATIONS: *to chase/land/lose/pitch for/win an ~* **5** (*IT*) an arrangement that sb has with a company that allows them to use the Internet or to receive, store and send emails
⊕ *to **get/have/set up/sign up for** an ~* ◆ *to **access/log onto** your ~*
IDM **on ac'count 1** to be paid for later: *Can I buy it on account?* **2** as part of the full amount you must pay
• *v.* PHR V **ac'count for sth 1** to form or be the source of a particular amount: *Sales to Europe accounted for 80% of our total sales last year.* **2** to give an explanation of sth; to be the explanation or cause of sth: *We can't account for the sudden fall in the share price.* **3** (*Account.*) to record an amount in a company's financial records in a particular way: *The capital gain has been accounted for in the P&L account.*

★**accountable** /ə'kaʊntəbl/ *adj.* [not usu. before n.] expected to explain your decisions or actions; responsible: *making companies more accountable to shareholders* ▸ **acˌcounta'bility** /-'bɪləti/ *n.* [U]

★**accountancy** /ə'kaʊntənsi/ *n.* [U] (*esp. BrE*) **1** the work or profession of an accountant: *an accountancy firm ◇ the ~ industry/profession* **2** the training you need in order to become an accountant: *a professional qualification in accountancy* SYN ACCOUNTING

★**accountant** /əˈkaʊntənt/ *n.* [C] a person whose job is to keep or check the financial records of a person or an organization and give financial advice: *a firm of accountants*

**acˈcount books** = BOOKS (1)

**acˈcount eˌxecutive** *n.* [C] an employee of a company, esp. in advertising, who is responsible for dealing with one of the company's regular customers

★**accounting** /əˈkaʊntɪŋ/ *n.* [U] **1** (*esp. AmE*) the work or profession of an accountant: *an accounting firm ◇ the ~ industry/profession* SYN ACCOUNTANCY **2** the work of keeping and checking the financial records of a person or an organization: *~ methods/practices/procedures ◇ ~ errors/irregularities* **3** (*esp. AmE*) the training you need in order to become an accountant: *to study accounting* SYN ACCOUNTANCY

**the acˈcounting ˌcycle** *n.* [sing.] (*Account.*) the series of steps used to follow what has happened in a business in a particular period and to report the financial effect

**the acˈcounting eˌquation** (*also* **the ˈbalance-sheet eˌquation**) *n.* [sing.] (*Account.*) the basic principle used by accountants to make the totals of the amounts in both parts of a BALANCE SHEET equal each other. This is 'assets = liabilities + capital'.

**acˈcounting ˌperiod** (*also* **ˈtrading ˌperiod**) *n.* [C] (*Account.*) the regular period of time over which a business prepares a set of financial records; the time between two BALANCE SHEETS

**acˈcounting ˌprinciple** *n.* [C, usu. pl.] (*Account.*) one of a group of rules or ideas that an accountant must follow when preparing a company's financial records, so that the records are an accurate and true description of the company's financial status

**acˈcounting ˈrate of reˈturn** *n.* [C] (*pl.* - **rates** -) (*abbr* **ARR**) (*Account.*) a percentage calculated by taking the amount of profit you expect to get from a particular investment each year and dividing it by the amount you have invested in it

**acˈcounting ˌratio** = FINANCIAL RATIO

**acˈcounting ˌstandard** (*also* **acˈcounting ˌrule**) *n.* [C] (*Account.*) a law that describes the way in which amounts must be recorded in a company's financial records

**acˈcounting ˌsystem** *n.* **1** [C] a particular way of keeping and preparing reports of a company's financial records; a computer system used to do this **2** [sing.] the practice and methods of keeping and checking financial records for businesses

**acˌcounting ˈyear** (*BrE*) (*AmE* **ˌnatural ˈbusiness year**) *n.* [C] (*Account.*) the period of twelve months over which a business prepares a set of financial records → FINANCIAL YEAR

**acˈcount ˌmanager** *n.* [C] an employee of a company who is responsible for one or more of the company's regular customers

**acˌcount paˈyee** *n.* [sing.] (*abbr* **a/c payee**) words written across a cheque to mean that it must only be paid into the bank account of the person or company named on the cheque

★**accounts** /əˈkaʊnts/ *n.* **1** (*Account.*) [pl.] a set of records for a business over a period, showing all the money received and paid out and how much profit has been made: *a set of accounts ◇ to file accounts* (= send them to the tax authorities) SYN BOOKS, BOOKS OF ACCOUNT
**●** *to audit/do/keep (the) ~* **♦** *annual/monthly/quarterly ~*
**2** [U with sing./pl. v.] the department in a company where money spent and owed is recorded: *She works in accounts.*

**acˌcounts ˈpayable** *n.* [pl.; U] (*Account.*) the amounts of money that a business owes to its suppliers or to people who have made loans, shown as a LIABILITY on its BALANCE SHEET; the department of a business that deals with this

**acˌcounts reˈceivable** *n.* [pl.; U] (*also* **ˈbook debt** [C,U]) (*Account.*) the amounts of money that are owed to a business by its customers, shown as an asset on its BALANCE SHEET; the department of a business that deals with this

**acˈcount terms** *n.* [pl.] (*Comm.*) the arrangement made between a seller and a buyer that states that the buyer does not have to pay immediately but must pay in an agreed time and in the agreed way

**accreditation** /əˌkredɪˈteɪʃn/ *n.* [U,C] the act of officially recognizing that sb/sth has achieved a required standard; the act of being recognized in this way

**accredited** /əˈkredɪtɪd/ *adj.* officially recognized, esp. as being of a required standard: *accredited training programmes*

**accretion** /əˈkriːʃn/ *n.* [C,U] (*Account.*) an increase or growth in the amount or value of sth: *a 13% accretion* **in** *the value of shares*
▸ **accretive** /-tɪv/ *adj.* [not usu. before n.]

**accrual** /əˈkruːəl/ *n.* (*Account.*) **1** [C,U] a gradual increase in an amount of money: *the accrual of interest* **2** (*also* **acˌcrued exˈpense**, **acˌcrued liaˈbility**) [C] an estimated amount of money that a business owes for goods or services that have been supplied to it but for which no request for payment has been received, recorded in the accounts at the end of the accounting period

**acˈcrual acˌcounting** (*also* **acˈcruals acˌcounting**) *n.* [U] (*Account.*) a system of keeping accounts where amounts of money are written down at the time when sth is bought or sold, and before the money has been paid or received → CASH ACCOUNTING

**acˈcrual ˌbasis** = ACCRUALS BASIS

**acˈcrual ˌmethod** = ACCRUALS BASIS

**acˈcruals acˌcounting** = ACCRUAL ACCOUNTING

**acˈcruals ˌbasis** (*BrE*) (*also* **acˈcrual ˌbasis**, *AmE, BrE*) (*AmE also* **acˈcrual ˌmethod**) *n.* [sing.] (*Account.*) the rule of accounting that ACCRUAL ACCOUNTING is based on: *accruals basis accounts* → CASH BASIS

**accrue** /əˈkruː/ *v.* (*Account.*) **1** [I] to increase over a period of time: *Interest accrues from the first of the month.* **2** [T] to allow an amount of money or debts to grow over a period of time: *The firm had accrued debts of over $10 m.* SYN ACCUMULATE **3** [I] (about a payment or a benefit) to be received by sb over a period of time: *economic benefits accruing* **to** *the country* **from** *tourism*

**acˌcrued ˈbenefits** *n.* [pl.] the money that is owed to an employee as a pension

**acˌcrued depreciˈation** *n.* [U,C] (*Account.*) the amount by which an asset has reduced in value at a particular point in time



**acˌcrued exˈpense** = ACCRUAL (2)

**acˌcrued ˈincome** *n.* [U] (*Account.*) income that a business earns during an accounting period but which it does not receive before the period ends

**acˌcrued ˈinterest** *n.* [U] (*Account.*) interest earned in a particular period of time that has not yet been received

**acˌcrued liaˈbility** = ACCRUAL (2)

★**accumulate** /əˈkjuːmjəleɪt/ *v.* **1** [I] to gradually increase over a period of time: *Interest charges have begun to accumulate.* **2** [T] to gradually get more of something over a period of time: *My savings are accumulating interest.* SYN ACCRUE
▸ **acˌcumuˈlation** /-ˈleɪʃn/ *n.* [U,C]

**acˌcumulated depreciˈation** *n.* [sing.] (*Account.*) (in a company's accounts) the total amount taken off the value of machinery, a vehicle, etc. up to a particular time because it is old or less useful

**acˌcumulated ˈdividend** *n.* [C, usu. pl.] (*Account.*) part of a company's profit owed but not yet paid to shareholders

**acˌcumulated ˈprofit** *n.* [C, usu. sing.] (*Account.*) (in a company's accounts) the profit that a company has kept for itself and not paid to shareholders

**acˌcumuˈlation ˌunit** *n.* [C] (*Finan.*) an amount invested in an INVESTMENT TRUST that does not pay regular DIVIDENDS, but adds the amount earned to the original investment

★**achieve** /əˈtʃiːv/ *v.* [T] to succeed in reaching a particular goal, status or standard, esp. by making an effort: *to ~ a goal/an objective/a target*
▸ **achievable** /-vəbl/ *adj.* **achiever** *n.* [C]: *our top achievers*

**achievement** /əˈtʃiːvmənt/ *n.* **1** [C] a thing that sb has done successfully, esp. using their own effort and skill **2** [U] the act or process of achieving sth

**aˈchievement motiˌvation** *n.* [U] (*HR*) a desire to be successful or to reach a very high standard

**ˈacid-test ˌratio** (*also* **ˈcurrent ˌratio**, **ˈliquid ˌratio**, **ˈquick ˌratio**) *n.* [C] (*Account.*) a way of measuring how much cash a company has available by comparing the total amount of money that it has in cash and is owed by customers with the total amount of money that it owes

**acknowledge** /ək'nɒlɪdʒ; *AmE* ək'nɑːl-/ *v.* [T] to tell sb that you have received sth that they sent to you: *All applications will be acknowledged.*

**acknowledgement** (*also* **acknowledgment**) /ək'nɒlɪdʒmənt; *AmE* ək'nɑːl-/ *n.* [C,U] a letter saying that sth has been received: *a letter of acknowledgement*

**a/c payee** = ACCOUNT PAYEE

★ **acquire** /ə'kwaɪə(r)/ *v.* [T] **1** (about a company) to buy a company or part of a company's business; to buy shares in a company: *Last year the company acquired its smaller rival for $6.9 bn.* **2** to obtain the legal right to use sth or perform an activity: *We **acquired the rights** to market the new tractors.* **3** to gain sth that is valuable to you or important for your business: *acquiring new skills*

**acquirer** /ə'kwaɪərə(r)/ *n.* [C] a company that wants to buy and take control of another company

★ **acquisition** /ˌækwɪ'zɪʃn/ *n.* **1** [C] a company that has been bought by another company: *the recent decline in **mergers and acquisitions***

⊕ ***to complete/make** an ~ • a **planned/potential/proposed** ~ • a **large/major/strategic** ~*

**2** [U] the activity of buying another company: *seeking new acquisition targets* (= companies to buy) ◇ *an ~ programme/strategy* **3** [U] the act of getting sth: *the acquisition of new skills*

**ˌacquiˈsition cost** *n.* [C] **1** (*Account.*) the total cost of buying an asset, including the price and any transport costs, fees, etc. **2** (*Market.*) (*also* **ˌcustomer acquiˈsition cost**) the total cost of getting a new customer

**acronym** /'ækrənɪm/ *n.* [C] a word formed from the first letters of several words, usu. said as a single word

**aˌcross the ˈboard** *adj., adv.* involving everyone or everything in a company or an industry: *a 10 per cent pay cut across the board*

**ACRS** /ˌeɪ siː ɑːr 'es/ = ACCELERATED COST RECOVERY SYSTEM

★ **act** /ækt/ *n., v.*

• *n.* [C] **1** (*usually* **Act**) a law that has been made by a parliament: *the Data Protection Act* ◇ *to amend/pass/repeal an ~* **2** (*Law*) something that sb does that is harmful to sb else: *to commit a criminal/an illegal ~*

**IDM** **be/get ˌin on the ˈact** (*esp. BrE*) (*AmE usu.* **get ˌinto the ˈact**) (*infml.*) to be/become involved in an activity that sb else has started, esp. to get some benefit for yourself **get your ˈact together** (*infml.*) to behave in a more effective or responsible way → idiom at CLEAN *v.*

• *v.* [I] to do sth for a particular purpose or to deal with a particular situation: *We have acted in the shareholders' best interests.* **PHR V** **ˈact as sth** to perform a particular function; to do a particular job, esp. one that needs special skills: *to act as a consultant for a company* **ˈact for sb/sth; ˌact on beˈhalf of sb/sth 1** to deal with sb's/sth's affairs for them **2** (*Law*) to represent sb/sth in a court **ˈact on sth** (*also* **ˈact upon sth**, *esp. fml.*) to do sth as a result of advice, information, etc. that you have received: *The board failed to act on the takeover offer.*

**acting** /'æktɪŋ/ *adj.* doing an important job that is usu. done by sb else : *the acting chief executive*

★ **action** /'ækʃn/ *n., v.*

• *n.* **1** [U,C] something that you do to deal with a problem or a difficult situation: *We need to **take** urgent action to control costs.* ◇ *a 15-point **plan of action*** **2** (*Law*) [C,U] a legal process to stop a person or company from doing sth, to make sb pay for a mistake or to settle a disagreement: *The buyer could **bring** an action **for** damages **against** the seller.* **3** [U] the important things that happen over a particular period of time, for example, changes in the price of shares

**IDM** **a piece/slice of the ˈaction** (*infml.*) a share or role in an interesting or exciting activity; a share in the profits: *Investors rushed to get a piece of the action.*

• *v.* [T] to take appropriate steps to make sure that sth is done or dealt with: *Your request will be actioned.*

**actionable** /'ækʃənəbl/ *adj.* **1** (*esp. AmE*) if an idea is **actionable**, it is practical and can actually be done **2** (*Law*) giving you a good reason to bring a claim against sb in a court

**ˈaction group** *n.* [C] a group formed to work for change, especially political or social

**ˈaction ˌitem** = ACTION POINT

**ˈaction ˌlearning** *n.* [U] (*HR*) a method of training in which small groups of people come together to help each other learn from real problems from the work situation

**'action-ˌoriented** *adj.* **1** (about a person or an organization) very active; likely to do sth in response to a situation rather than just think and plan **2** that involves particular actions; that helps you in a practical way to achieve sth: *action-oriented training*

**'action plan** *n.* [C] a description of a set of things you need to do in order to achieve an aim or to solve a problem

**'action point** (*also* **'action ˌitem**, *esp. in AmE*) *n.* [C] a job or task that is mentioned at a meeting and noted down to be done or dealt with by a particular person later

★ **active** /'æktɪv/ *adj.* **1** making a determined effort and not leaving sth to happen by itself: *playing an active* ***role*** *on the board* **2** (about a company) doing a particular type of business; operating in a particular place: *The company is active in 60 countries.* **3** operating or working; being used: *active customer accounts* **4** doing sth frequently; having a lot of activity: *The company has been active recently, with several new acquisitions.* **5** (*Finan.*) if shares, bonds, etc. or a market is **active**, there is a lot of buying and selling **6** (*Finan.*) used to describe a way of investing in which shares, bonds, etc. are bought and sold according to changes in value: *active fund management* **7** (*IT*) being used at a particular time: *an active window*

**ˌactive 'partner** (*also* **ˌworking 'partner**) *n.* [C] a member of a PARTNERSHIP who is involved in running the business → SLEEPING PARTNER

★ **activity** /æk'tɪvəti/ *n.* (*pl.* **-ties**) **1** [U] a situation in which sth is happening or a lot of things are being done: *Manufacturing activity fell.* **2** [C, usu. pl.] the things done by an organization or a person, esp. in order to make money: *the company's commercial activities*

**ac'tivity ˌsampling** = WORK SAMPLING

**ˌact of 'bankruptcy** *n.* [C] (*Law*) something that you do that shows you are BANKRUPT

**actual** /'æktʃuəl/ *adj.* real; that happened, as opposed to what was expected to happen: *Total actual sales have gone up by 8.9 per cent.*

**ˌactual 'damages** = COMPENSATORY DAMAGES

**actuals** /'æktʃuəlz/ *n.* [pl.] (*Account.*) real costs, sales, etc. that have happened, rather than ones that were estimated or expected: *Compare the targets with the actuals.*

**actuary** /'æktʃuəri; *AmE* -eri/ *n.* [C] (*pl.* **-ries**) a person whose job involves calculating insurance risks and payments for insurance companies and PENSION FUNDS by studying how frequently accidents, fires, deaths, etc. happen ▸ **actuarial** /ˌæktʃu'eəriəl; *AmE* -'eriəl/ *adj.*

**acumen** /'ækjəmən; *AmE* ə'kju:mən/ *n.* [U] the ability to judge things quickly and clearly: *business/financial ~*

★ **ad** /æd/ *n.* (*infml.*) **1** [C] an advertisement: *newspaper/TV/online ~s* ◇ *to place/post/put an ~ (in/on sth)* ◇ *to run an ad* **2** [U] advertising: *an ~ agency/campaign* ◇ *Our ad budget was cut.*

**'ad ˌagency** = ADVERTISING AGENCY

★ **adapt** /ə'dæpt/ *v.* **1** [T] to change sth to make it suitable for a new use or situation: *cars specially adapted* ***for*** *the US market* SYN MODIFY **2** [T,I] to change your behaviour to deal more successfully with a new situation: *to adapt* ***to*** *change* SYN ADJUST ▸ **aˌdapta'bility** /-tə'bɪləti/ *n.* [U] **a'daptable** /-təbl/ *adj.*

**add** /æd/ *v.* [T] **1 ~ A to B | ~ A and B (together)** to put numbers or amounts together to get a total OPP SUBTRACT **2 ~ sth (to sth)** to put sth/sb together with sth/sb else so as to increase the size, number or amount: *Increased sales will add $1 m a year to turnover.* **3 ~ sth (to sth)** (used about shares, bonds, etc.) to increase in value by a particular amount; to make sth do this: *Nokia shares added 2.2%.* ▸ **addition** /ə'dɪʃn/ *n.* [U,C]: *the latest addition to our range* PHR V **ˌadd sth 'on** to include or attach sth extra: *Add on a few dollars for delivery.* **ˌadd 'up (to sth)** to increase by small amounts until there is a large total: *The cost of calls soon adds up.* **ˌadd (sth) 'up** to calculate the total of two or more numbers or amounts; to make a total number or amount: *The figures were added up wrongly.* ◇ *The figures don't add up* (= make a sensible total). **ˌadd 'up to sth** to make a particular total or amount

**ˌadded 'value** *n.* [U] **1** an improvement or an extra feature that is added to a product or service to make it more useful and attractive to buyers: *E-commerce will work only if it can offer users added value.* ◇

*added-value services* **2** (*Econ.*) the amount by which the value of a product increases at each stage of the production process, not including the cost of the basic materials SYN VALUE ADDED

**addendum** /ə'dendəm/ *n.* [C] (*pl.* **-nda** /-ndə/) (*fml.*) a section of extra information that is added to sth such as a letter or a report

**'add-on** *n.* [C] **1** a piece of equipment or a program that can be added to a computer system to improve its performance: *~ devices/hardware/memory/software* **2** an extra part or service that can be joined to a product, system or service to improve it, esp. sth extra that can be sold to a customer: *People pay extra for add-ons* ***to*** *basic insurance cover.*

**ˌadd-on 'interest** *n.* [U] interest that is added to the original amount of money that sb has borrowed when they pay it back

★ **address** /ə'dres; *AmE* 'ædres/ *n.* [C] **1** a set of words, letters, symbols and/or numbers that tells you where you can find a business, etc. on the Internet, where you can send an email, etc: *a website/an email ~* **2** (*IT*) the number that states where a piece of information is stored in a computer memory

**addressee** /ˌædre'siː/ *n.* [C] a person or an organization that a letter is addressed to

**ad hoc** /ˌæd 'hɒk; *AmE* 'hɑːk/ *adj.*, *adv.* not planned in advance: *The meetings will be held* ***on an ad hoc basis*** (= when they are necessary).

**adhocracy** /ˌæd'hɒkrəsi/ *n.* [U] (*HR*) a form of management in which groups of people deal with specific projects and urgent problems, rather than with planning for the future of the business as a whole

★ **adjourn** /ə'dʒɜːn; *AmE* ə'dʒɜːrn/ *v.* [T,I] to stop a meeting or an official process for a period of time, esp. in a court: *The meeting adjourned* ***for*** *lunch.* ▸ **ad'journment** *n.* [C,U]

**adjudicate** /ə'dʒuːdɪkeɪt/ *v.* [T,I] (*Law*) **~ (on/upon/in) sth | ~ between A and B** to make an official decision about who is right in a disagreement between two groups: *to adjudicate (on) disputes*
▸ **aˌdjudi'cation** /-'keɪʃn/ *n.* [U]
**a'djudicator** *n.* [C]

**adjunct** /'ædʒʌŋkt/ *n.* [C] (*fml.*) a thing that is added or attached to sth larger or more important: *Our website is an adjunct* ***to*** *our stores.*

★ **adjust** /ə'dʒʌst/ *v.* [T] to change sth slightly to make it more suitable or more accurate: *We must adjust our prices to meet demand.*

**adjustable** /ə'dʒʌstəbl/ *adj.* that can be changed slightly, esp. to become better or more suitable: *an adjustable-rate mortgage*

**adˌjustable 'peg** *n.* [C] (*Econ.*) a way of controlling the EXCHANGE RATE by fixing the value of currencies in relation to another currency, such as the dollar, but changing it from time to time if necessary

**adjusted** /ə'dʒʌstɪd/ *adj.* changed slightly in a particular way or for a particular purpose: *an ~ operating profit/loss*

**a'djusted 'gross 'income** *n.* [U] (*abbr* **AGI**) (*Account.*) in the US, your total income after you have taken away particular costs, used when the amount of tax you have to pay is calculated

**adjuster** (*also* **adjustor**, *esp. in AmE*) /ə'dʒʌstə(r)/ = LOSS ADJUSTER

★ **adjustment** /ə'dʒʌstmənt/ *n.* [C,U] **1** a small change made to sth to correct or improve it: *We* ***made*** *a few adjustments* ***to*** *the design.* ◇ *Wages have fallen by 10% after adjustment* ***for*** *inflation.* ◇ *a major/minor/small ~* **2** a process of changing to meet a new situation: *the company's successful adjustment* ***to*** *the new markets* **3** (*Insur.*) the agreement reached between an insurance company and sb making a claim about how much money they will receive **4** (*Insur.*) the amount of money paid to sb making a claim

**ad'justment acˌcount** = CONTROL ACCOUNT

**ad'justment ˌfactor** *n.* [C] (*Tech.*) a figure that is used to correct the result of a calculation

**adland** /'ædlænd/ *n.* [U] (*infml.*) the advertising industry

**adman** /'ædmæn/ *n.* [C] (*pl.* **-men** /-men/) (*infml.*) a person who works in advertising

**admin** /'ædmɪn/ *n.* [U] (*BrE*) (*infml.*) administration: *She works in admin.* ◇ *admin staff*

★ **administer** /əd'mɪnɪstə(r)/ *v.* [T] **1** (*also* **administrate**) (*often pass.*) to manage and organize the affairs of a company, an organization or a country: *The pension funds are administered by commercial banks.* SYN MANAGE **2** to organize the way that sth is done: *The questionnaire was administered by trained interviewers.* **3** (*fml.*) to make sure that sth is done fairly and in the correct way: *to administer justice*

★ **administration** /ədˌmɪnɪˈstreɪʃn/ *n.* **1** (*BrE also* **ˈadmin**, *infml.*) [U] the activities that are done in order to plan, organize and run a business, etc: *day-to-day administration* ◇ *administration costs* **2** [U] the process or act of organizing the way that sth is done: *the administration of the new tax* **3** [C] the people who plan, organize and run a business, etc. **4** (*Law*) [U] the management of the financial affairs of a business that cannot pay its debts by an independent person: *The company may* ***go into administration.*** **5** (*often* **Administration** [C]) the government of a country, esp. the US

**adminiˈstration ˌorder** *n.* [C] (*Law*) in the UK, an order made by a court for sb to take over the management of a business that cannot pay its debts

★ **administrative** /ədˈmɪnɪstrətɪv; *AmE* -streɪtɪv/ *adj.* connected with organizing the work of a business, etc: *administrative staff* ◇ *There was an administrative error.*

○ ~ *charges/costs/expenses* ♦ ~ *duties/procedures/tasks/work*

**adˌministrative ˈleave** *n.* [U,C] (*AmE*) (*HR*) a time that you are allowed to be away from work with pay for special reasons, such as if you are needed to be on a JURY, or when there is an urgent problem

**adˌministrative ˈmanagement** *n.* [U] (*HR*) the traditional view of management that is concerned with how a business should be organized and what a good manager should do

★ **administrator** /ədˈmɪnɪstreɪtə(r)/ *n.* [C] **1** a person whose job is to manage and organize the public or business affairs of a company or an institution **2** (*Finan.*) a person chosen, often by a court, to manage the financial affairs of a business that does not have enough money to pay its debts: *to appoint/call in an* ~

**adˌmission of liaˈbility** *n.* [C] (*Law*) a statement or an act admitting legal responsibility for sth

**admit** /ədˈmɪt/ *v.* (-**tt**-) **1** [T,I] to say that you have done sth wrong or illegal: *He admitted theft.* **2** (*Law*) [T] **~ liability (for sth)** to say that you are legally responsible for sth **3** [T] **~ sb (to sth)** to allow sb to enter a place or an organization

**adopt** /əˈdɒpt; *AmE* əˈdɑːpt/ *v.* [T] **1** to accept and use a particular idea, system or proposal, esp. a new one: *to adopt modern methods* **2** (*Market.*) to buy and use a product or service as the normal or official one: *to persuade households to adopt digital TV*



**adopter** /əˈdɒptə(r); *AmE* əˈdɑːptər/ *n.* [C, usu. sing.] (*Market.*) a company or a person who accepts and uses a product, service or system as the normal or official one

**adoption** /əˈdɒpʃn; *AmE* əˈdɑːpʃn/ *n.* **1** [U] the act of accepting and using a particular idea, system or proposal, esp. a new one: *the adoption of the euro* **2** (*Market.*) [U,C] the wide use of a new product or service; the product or service that is used: *the market adoption of a product* ◇ *a high customer adoption rate*

**aˈdoption curve** *n.* [C] (*Market.*) a GRAPH showing the rate at which people buy a piece of new technology for the first time

**ADR** /ˌeɪ diː ˈɑː(r)/ = AMERICAN DEPOSITARY RECEIPT, ALTERNATIVE DISPUTE RESOLUTION

**ADSL** /ˌeɪ diː es ˈel/ *abbr* (*IT*) **asymmetric digital subscriber line** technology that allows large amounts of data to be carried over an ordinary phone line in such a way that data travels faster to the customer than from the customer: *high-speed ADSL Internet access*

**adultescent** /ˌædʌlˈtesnt/ *n.* [C] (*infml.*) an adult who is no longer young, but who dresses and behaves like a young person

**ad valorem** /ˌæd vəˈlɔːrem/ *adj., adv.* (*Econ.*) (about a tax) calculated as a percentage of the value of the goods: *VAT is an ad valorem tax.*

**advance** /ədˈvɑːns; *AmE* ədˈvæns/ *n., v., adj.*

• *n.* **1** [C, usu. sing.] money paid for work before it has been done; money paid earlier than expected: *She asked for an advance* ***on*** *her wages.* **2** [C] an increase in the price or value of sth: *advances* ***in*** *share prices* **3** [C,U] progress or a development in technology or a particular area of knowledge: *advances* ***in*** *the processing power of chips* **IDM in adˈvance (of sth)** before the time that is expected; before sth happens: *Rent is due one month in advance.* → IN ARREARS

• *v.* **1** [T] **~ (sb) sth | ~ sth (to sb)** to give sb money before the time it would usually be paid: *We can advance you the money.* **2** [I] if knowledge or technology **advances**, it develops and improves **3** [I] (about

prices, costs, profits, etc.) to increase **4** [T] to change the time or date of an event so that it takes place earlier: *The date of the meeting has been advanced by one week.* SYN BRING STH FORWARD OPP POSTPONE **5** [T] to help sth to succeed: *advancing your career*
• *adj.* done or given before sth happens: *an advance payment*

**ad,vance 'copy** *n.* [C] (*Product.*) a book, a magazine, etc. sent to sb to look at before it is published

**advancement** /əd'vɑːnsmənt; *AmE* -'væns-/ *n.* **1** [U] progress in a job or position: *opportunities for advancement* **2** [U,C] the process of helping sth to make progress or succeed; the progress that is made: *the ~ of knowledge/technology*

**ad,vance 'order** *n.* [C] (*Comm.*) an order for a product which is made before the product is available for sale

**advancer** /əd'vɑːnsə(r); *AmE* əd'vænsər/ *n.* [C, usu. pl.] (*Stock Ex.*) (used in newspapers) a share whose value has risen SYN GAINER OPP DECLINER

**adverse** /'ædvɜːs; əd'vɜːs; *AmE* -vɜːrs/ *adj.* negative; not likely to produce a good result: *adverse market conditions*

**,adverse 'balance** *n.* [C] (*BrE*) (*Account.*) an amount of debt shown in an account SYN UNFAVOURABLE BALANCE

**,adverse 'trade ,balance** (*also* **'adverse 'balance of 'trade**) *n.* [sing.] (*Econ.*) a situation when a country spends more on imports than it earns from exports SYN UNFAVOURABLE TRADE BALANCE

**advert** /'ædvɜːt; *AmE* -vɜːrt/ *n.* [C] (*BrE*) (*infml.*) an advertisement: *TV adverts* ◇ *an advert **for** jeans* ◇ *We placed a full-page advert in Vogue.*

★ **advertise** /'ædvətaɪz; *AmE* -vərt-/ *v.* **1** [T,I] to tell the public about a product or a service in order to encourage people to buy or use it: *to ~ a product/service* ◇ *The new service has been **heavily** advertised on TV.* **2** [I] to tell people about a job that is available: *to advertise **for** a new sales manager*
▸ **'advertiser** *n.* [C]

★ **advertisement** /əd'vɜːtɪsmənt; *AmE* ,ædvər'taɪz-/ *n.* [C] **1** a notice, picture or short film telling people about a company, product or service: *cigarette advertisements* ◇ *advertisements **for** cigarettes* ◇ *a full-page/half-page ~* ◇ *The advertisement appeared on TV last night.*
→ AD, ADVERT
⊙ ***online/print/television** ~s* • *to **place/run/take out** an ~*
**2** a notice telling people about a job that is available: *an advertisement **for** a job* ◇ *a job advertisement*
⊙ *to **place/put/take out** an ~ (in a newspaper)* • *to **answer/reply to/respond to** an ~*

★ **advertising** /'ædvətaɪzɪŋ; *AmE* -vərt-/ *n.* [U] **1** the act of making a company, product or service known to the public; the notices, pictures and short films that a company uses to tell people about itself and its products: *How much did we spend on advertising last year?* ◇ *a huge advertising budget* ◇ ***recruitment advertising*** (= for people to fill jobs)
⊙ ***Internet/point-of-sale/press/television** ~* • *an ~ **campaign*** • *~ **revenue(s)/sales***
**2** the industry of advertising things to people on television, in newspapers and magazines, etc: *people who work in advertising*
⊙ *the ~ **business/industry/sector*** • *an ~ **company/executive/group***

**'advertising ,agency** (*also* **'ad ,agency**, *infml.*) *n.* [C] a company that plans and designs advertisements for other companies

**'advertising mix** *n.* [U] (*Market.*) the different methods that a business uses to advertise a product

**advertorial** /,ædvə'tɔːriəl; *AmE* -vərt-/ *n.* [C,U] (*Market.*) an advertisement in a newspaper or magazine that is like a written article and seems to be giving facts rather than advertising a product

★ **advice** /əd'vaɪs/ *n.* **1** [U] an opinion or a suggestion about what sb should do in a particular situation: *a piece of advice*
⊙ ***career/financial/legal** ~* • *to **give/provide/offer** ~* • *to **follow/seek/take** sb's ~*
**2** (*Account.*) [C] a formal notice about some financial business: *a remittance advice* → idiom at TAKE

**ad'vice note** *n.* [C] (*BrE*) (*Comm.*) a document that is sent to a customer to tell them that goods they have ordered have been sent or are ready to send

**'ad view** = IMPRESSION

★ **advise** /əd'vaɪz/ *v.* **1** [T,I] to tell sb what you think they should do: *We advise our customers **against** sending cash.* **2** [T,I] to give sb help and information on a subject that you know a lot about: *We employ an expert to advise (us) **on** new technology.* **3** (*fml.*)

[T] to officially tell sb sth; to inform sb: *Please advise us of any changes in your personal details.* ▸ **ad'viser** (*also* **-sor**, *esp. in AmE*) *n.* [C]: *the CBI's chief economic adviser*

**ad'vising bank** *n.* [C] (*Finan.*) a bank in the country of an exporter that informs the exporter about a DOCUMENTARY CREDIT and receives documents on behalf of the buyer's bank

**advisory** /əd'vaɪzəri/ *adj.* giving professional advice; not having the power to make decisions: *the firm's advisory board* ◇ *to act **in an advisory capacity***

**ad'visory ˌservice** *n.* [C] part of an organization that gives expert information on a particular subject

**AEI** /ˌeɪ iː 'aɪ/ = AVERAGE EARNINGS INDEX

**AER** /ˌeɪ iː 'ɑː(r)/ *abbr* (*Finan.*) **annual equivalent rate** a rate of interest on investments and money you save that shows how much you would receive in one year if each interest payment was added to the deposit before the next payment was calculated → APR

**aeronautics** /ˌeərə'nɔːtɪks; *AmE* ˌerə-/ *n.* [U] the science or practice of building and flying aircraft ▸ **aero'nautic** *adj.* **aeronautical** /-'nɔːtɪkl/ *adj.*: *an aeronautical engineer*

**aerospace** /'eərəuspeɪs; *AmE* 'eroʊ-/ *n.* [U] (*often used as an adj.*) the industry of building aircraft and the vehicles and equipment to be sent into space

**affiliate** *n.*, *v.*

• ***n.*** /ə'fɪliət/ [C] a company, etc. that is connected with or controlled by another larger one: *Our organization has 32 overseas affiliates.*

• ***v.*** /ə'fɪlieɪt/ [T,I] (*usu. pass.*)
**1** (about an organization) to be connected to a larger one: *The union is affiliated **to** the TUC.* **2** (about a person) to have a close professional connection with an organization: *a consultant affiliated **with** McKinsey & Co.* ▸ **afˌfili'ation** /-'eɪʃn/ *n.* [U,C]

**afˌfiliated 'company** *n.* [C] a company that is closely connected to or controlled by another larger company or organization SYN SUBSIDIARY

**afˌfiliate 'marketing** *n.* [U] (*E-comm.*) the use of other websites to advertise and market the products and services of your website. The other websites receive a payment for this.

**af'finity card** *n.* [C] a credit card that has the name of a particular charity (in the UK) or organization (in the US) that receives an amount of money from the card company every time you use it

**afˌfirmative 'action** *n.* [U] (*AmE*) a practice or policy intended to make sure that everyone has the same chances of education or employment and to correct the fact that people from some groups are often treated unfairly because of their race or sex SYN POSITIVE DISCRIMINATION (*BrE*)

**affluent** /'æfluənt/ *adj.* having a lot of money and a good standard of living SYN PROSPEROUS ▸ **'affluence** *n.* [U]

★ **afford** /ə'fɔːd; *AmE* ə'fɔːrd/ *v.* [T] (*not used in the pass.*) HELP usu. used with **can, could** or **be able to**, esp. in questions or negative sentences. **1** to have enough money to be able to buy sth: *Buy the most powerful system you can afford.* ◇ *We can't afford the lawyer's fee.* **2** (*usu. used in negative sentences*) if you can't **afford sth/to do sth** you are not able to do sth or let sth happen because it would have a bad result for you: *We can't afford any more delays.*

★ **affordable** /ə'fɔːdəbl; *AmE* ə'fɔːrd-/ *adj.* that people can afford; that does not cost a lot of money: *We offer high quality at an extremely affordable price.* ▸ **afˌforda'bility** /-'bɪləti/ *n.* [U]

**AFL-CIO** /ˌeɪ ef 'el ˌsiː aɪ 'əʊ; *AmE* 'oʊ/ *abbr* **American Federation of Labor and Congress of Industrial Organizations** in the US, an organization that represents a large number of labor unions

**afloat** /ə'fləʊt; *AmE* ə'floʊt/ *adj.* (about a business, an economy, etc.) having enough money to pay debts; able to survive: *The company is trying to raise £15 m to **stay afloat**.*

**'after-hours** *adj.* happening after a business or financial market has officially closed for the day: *~ calls/prices/trading* ▸ **ˌafter 'hours** *adv.*: *We have voicemail after hours.*

**aftermarket** /'ɑːftəmɑːkɪt; *AmE* 'æftərmɑːrkɪt/ *n.* [C, usu. sing.]
**1** (*Market.*) (*esp. AmE*) the opportunities to sell other things that a customer needs after buying a particular product, such as new parts and extra pieces of equipment: *aftermarket sales and services*
**2** (*Stock Ex.*) the time when new shares that have just been made

available are bought and sold: *stock trading in the aftermarket*

**'after-sales** *adj.* (*BrE*) providing help to a customer after they have bought a product: *~ service/support*

**ˌafter 'sight** *adv.* (*abbr* **A/S, a/s**) (*Finan.*) written on a BILL OF EXCHANGE to show that the bill should be paid within a particular period after it has been given to the person who has to pay it

**ˌafter-'tax** *adj.* (*Account.*) after the tax has been paid or taken away: *an ~ charge/loss/profit*

**AG** /ˌeɪ 'dʒiː/ *abbr* used in the names of some companies in German-speaking countries: *Volkswagen AG*

**'age discrimiˌnation** *n.* [U] unfair treatment of people considered too old SYN AGEISM

**'age group** *n.* [C] people of a similar age or within a particular range of ages: *consumers in the 20–24 age group*

**ageism** (*AmE usu.* **agism**) /'eɪdʒɪzəm/ *n.* [U] unfair treatment of people considered too old SYN AGE DISCRIMINATION ▶ **'ageist** *adj.*: *ageist attitudes* **'ageist** *n.* [C]

★**agency** /'eɪdʒənsi/ *n.* (*pl.* **-cies**) **1** (*Comm.*) [C] a business that provides a particular service, esp. to other businesses: *an ad/a marketing ~ ◇ agency workers* (= employees provided by an employment agency) **2** (*often* **Agency** [C]) a government department that provides a particular service; an international organization that provides a service to several countries **3** (*Law*) [U] the situation that exists where sb (the **agent**) agrees to sth or does sth as the representative of sb else (the **principal**)

**'agency ˌbroker** *n.* [C] (*AmE*) (*Prop.; Stock Ex.*) a person or an organization that buys or sells shares or property for sb else

**'agency ˌlabour** *n.* [U] (*esp. AmE*) (*HR*) workers in a company who have been employed through an EMPLOYMENT AGENCY, usu. for temporary work

★**agenda** /ə'dʒendə/ *n.* [C] **1** a list of topics to be discussed at a meeting: *the next item* ***on the agenda*** **2** the things that sb thinks are important and wants to achieve; a plan of action: *In our company, quality is* ***high on the agenda.***

★**agent** /'eɪdʒənt/ *n.* [C] **1** a person or company paid by another to do business for them, esp. in discussing a contract, buying or selling, or finding work in entertainment or publishing: *You can hire an agent to negotiate on your behalf.* → PRINCIPAL **2** a person who sells a service or product for one or more companies: *an independent insurance agent ◇ We have 31 overseas agents and distributors.*

**'agent bank** *n.* [C] (*Finan.*) **1** (*also* **'lead bank**) a bank that organizes a loan for a person or company and represents the group of banks who lend the money **2** a bank in a foreign country that an investor has an account with to be able to make cash payments in a foreign currency

**ˌagent of 'change** = CHANGE AGENT

**'age ˌprofile** *n.* [C, usu. sing.] (*HR; Market.*) a description of the number of people of different ages who buy a particular product or who work in an organization

**aggregate** *n., adj., v.*

• ***n.*** /'ægrɪgət/ [C, usu. sing.] the total number or amount made up of smaller amounts that are collected together: *She has now purchased* ***an aggregate of*** *16% of the company's shares.* IDM **in (the) 'aggregate** (*fml.*) added together as a total or single amount

• ***adj.*** /'ægrɪgət/ (*Tech.*) made up of several amounts that are added together to form a total number: *~ figures/profits*

• ***v.*** /'ægrɪgeɪt/ [T] (*Tech.*) to combine different items or amounts into a single group or total: *This website aggregates thousands of sales and promotions.* ▶ **ˌaggre'gation** /-'geɪʃn/ *n.* [U,C]

**'aggregate ˌplanning** *n.* [U] a method of planning the best way to produce the right amount of goods at the right time and at the lowest cost, based on the total number of items that need to be produced and the total amount of equipment and number of workers available

★**aggressive** /ə'gresɪv/ *adj.* **1** (esp. about a company's policies) strong and determined to make sure that the company succeeds: *an aggressive advertising campaign ◇ aggressive price cuts* **2** (about a person or company) behaving in a firm and determined way in order to succeed: *an ~ seller/buyer* ▶ **ag'gressively** *adv.*: *The snacks are aggressively marketed.*

**agˌgressive 'growth fund** (*also* **per'formance fund**) *n.* [C] (*Finan.*) a type of investment fund that buys shares that are expected to increase in value very quickly but have a high risk, in the hope of making large profits

**AGI** /ˌeɪ dʒiː ˈaɪ/ = ADJUSTED GROSS INCOME

**agile** /ˈædʒaɪl; *AmE* ˈædʒl/ *adj.* (used esp. about new, small companies) able to adapt quickly to changing situations ▸ **aˈgility** /əˈdʒɪləti/ *n.* [U]

**ˈaging ˌschedule** *n.* [C, usu. sing.] (*esp. AmE*) (*Account.*) a list of amounts of money owed to a business, shown in the order of the dates they are due to be paid. The list is prepared every month to show how quickly money is being paid and what might not be paid.

**agio** /ˈædʒiəʊ; *AmE* ˈædʒioʊ/ *n.* [C, usu. sing.] (*pl.* **agios**) (*Finan.*) the charge that a bank makes for changing one form of money into another, for example changing coins into notes or changing one currency into another

**agism** = AGEISM

**AGM** /ˌeɪ dʒiː ˈem/ = ANNUAL GENERAL MEETING

**aˌgreed ˈbid** *n.* [C] the situation when most shareholders in a company agree to the offer that another company makes to buy it

**aˌgreed ˈvalue** *n.* [U] (*Insur.*) the amount that a vehicle, boat, etc. is worth that is agreed with the insurance company when the insurance is arranged. This amount will be paid if the item is destroyed or stolen: *an agreed-value policy*

★ **agreement** /əˈɡriːmənt/ *n.*
**1** [C] **~ (with sb)** | **~ (between A and B)** an arrangement, a promise or a contract that two people, groups or organizations have made together: *An agreement was finally reached* ***between*** *management* ***and*** *employees.*
⊙ *to conclude/make/sign an ~* ◆ *a* ***formal****/an* ***informal****/a* ***legal/verbal/written*** *~*
**2** [U; sing.] the state of having the same opinion; a state of understanding between people, organizations or countries: *Are we* ***in agreement*** *about the price?*
⊙ *to reach ~* ◆ *to* ***arrive at/come to*** *an ~* ◆ ***broad/general/total*** *~*

**aˌgreement of ˈsale** = CONTRACT OF PURCHASE

**agribusiness** /ˈæɡrɪbɪznəs/ *n.*
**1** [U] farming that uses modern technology to produce high profits
**2** [C] an organization that is involved in this

**ˌagricultural ˈbank** *n.* [C] (*Finan.*) a bank that helps farmers, esp. by lending money for longer periods than other banks



**ˌagricultural coˈoperative** *n.* [C] a business that sells food produced by small farmers

**agriculture** /ˈæɡrɪkʌltʃə(r)/ *n.* [U] the science or practice of farming ▸ **ˌagriˈcultural** /-ˈkʌltʃərəl/ *adj.*

**agrochemical** /ˌæɡrəʊˈkemɪkl; *AmE* ˌæɡroʊ-/ *n.* [C] a chemical used in farming, such as one for killing insects (a **pesticide**) or for helping crops grow (a **fertilizer**) ▸ **ˌagroˈchemical** *adj.*

**ˈagro-ˌindustry** *n.* [U] **1** the industry of farming **2** industry connected with farming ▸ **ˌagroinˈdustrial** *adj.*

**agronomy** /əˈɡrɒnəmi; *AmE* əˈɡrɑːn-/ *n.* [U] the science and study of crop production and the best ways of using the soil ▸ **aˈgronomist** *n.* [C]

**ahead** /əˈhed/ *adv.* **1** higher or greater than a previous level: *Sales are 5.6% ahead.* **2** further advanced: *Work hard to* ***keep*** *ahead.*

**aˈhead of** *prep.* **1** at an earlier time than sth; before an event: *The project was finished* ***ahead of schedule.***
**2** further advanced than sb/sth: *We work hard to* ***stay*** *ahead of the competition.* IDM **to stay/be ahead of the ˈgame** to stay/be the most successful in an industry or activity

**AI** /ˌeɪ ˈaɪ/ = ARTIFICIAL INTELLIGENCE

**aid** /eɪd/ *n.*, *v.*
• ***n.*** [U] **1** money, food, etc. sent to help countries or people in difficult situations: *foreign aid* **2** help given to sb: *financial aid* ◇ *The government* ***came to the aid of*** *the airline.*
• ***v.*** [T,I] to help sb/sth to do sth: *The increase in profits was aided by strong sales of trucks.* IDM **ˌaid and aˈbet** (*Law*) to help sb to do sth illegal or wrong: *She was accused of aiding and abetting fraud.*

**AIDA** /ˌeɪ aɪ diː ˈeɪ/ *abbr* (*Market.*) **awareness/attention, interest, desire, action** a description used by advertisers to try to explain how people make decisions about buying products and services

**ailing** /ˈeɪlɪŋ/ *adj.* (about a business, etc.) having financial problems and getting weaker

**AIM** /eɪm/ = ALTERNATIVE INVESTMENT MARKET

★ **aim** /eɪm/ *n.*, *v.*
• ***n.*** [C] the purpose of doing sth; sth that you are trying to achieve: *Our main aim is to increase sales in Asia.* ◇ *the company's* ***aims and objectives***

**○** *a key/long-term/strategic* ~ • *the primary/principal* ~ • *to achieve/fulfil/meet an* ~

• *v.* **1** [I] to try or plan to achieve sth: *We are aiming* **at/for** *2 000 new customers.* ◇ *They aim* **to** *increase sales by 20%.* **2** [T] **be aimed at** to have sth as an aim: *The proposals are aimed at reducing debt.* **3** [T] **~ sth at sb** (*usu. pass.*) to produce sth that meets the needs of a particular group of customers or tries to influence them: *a marketing campaign aimed at teenagers* SYN TARGET

**airfare** /ˈeəfeə(r); *AmE* ˈerfer/ *n.* [C] the money you pay to travel by plane: *airlines offering cheap/low ~s*

**airfreight** /ˈeəfreɪt; *AmE* ˈerf-/ *n.* [U] goods that are carried on a plane; the system of carrying goods in this way

**airline** /ˈeəlaɪn; *AmE* ˈerl-/ *n.* [C] a company that provides regular flights to take passengers and goods to different places

**○** ***domestic/international/national*** *~s* • ***commercial/private/state-owned*** *~s* • *a* ***charter/scheduled*** *~* • *the ~* ***business/industry***

**airmail** /ˈeəmeɪl; *AmE* ˈerm-/ *n.* [U] the system of sending letters and packages by air: *Send it (by) airmail.*

**airtime** /ˈeətaɪm; *AmE* ˈert-/ *n.* [U] **1** the amount of time that is given to a particular subject, or to an advertisement, on radio or television **2** the amount of time that a mobile phone/cellphone is used in a particular period for calls that you usu. pay for: *This deal gives you 180 minutes free airtime a month.*

**airway** /ˈeəweɪ; *AmE* ˈerweɪ/ *n.* [C] (often used in names of airlines) a route regularly used by planes: *British Airways*

**aisle** /aɪl/ *n.* [C] **1** a passage between rows of shelves in a supermarket; the shelves on either side of the passage: *Coffee and tea are in the next aisle.* **2** a passage between rows of seats in a plane, train, theatre, etc: *an aisle seat* (= on a plane)

**alienation** /ˌeɪliəˈneɪʃn/ *n.* [U] (*HR*) a feeling that some employees have that their work is not important and they are not a valuable part of their company

**align** /əˈlaɪn/ *v.* [T] to change sth slightly so that it is in the correct relationship to sth else: *Domestic prices have been aligned* **with** *those in world markets.* ▸ **aˈlignment** *n.* [U,C]: *The text and the graphics are slightly* **out of alignment.** PHRV **align yourself with sb/sth** to publicly support an organization, a set of opinions or a person

**A-list** /ˈeɪ lɪst/ *n.* [C] the most successful and popular people or companies, etc: *the magazine's A-list of high-return investments*

**ˌall-ˈcash** *adj.* (*Finan.*) (used about an offer to buy a company) consisting only of money

**allege** /əˈledʒ/ *v.* [T] (*often pass.*) to say that sb has done sth wrong or illegal, but without giving proof ▸ **allegation** /ˌæləˈɡeɪʃn/ *n.* [C]: *serious allegations of corruption*

**allfinanz** /ˌɔːlˈfaɪnæns; ˌɔːlfəˈnæns/ *n.* [sing.] (*BrE*) (*Finan.*; *Insur.*) the combination of banking and insurance services offered by many major banks SYN BANCASSURANCE

**ˌall-ˈhands** *adj.* that involves all the people who work in a company: *an all-hands meeting*

★ **alliance** /əˈlaɪəns/ *n.* [C] **1** an agreement between countries, companies, etc. to work together in order to achieve sth that they all want: *The two companies formed an alliance to improve distribution networks.*

**○** *to* ***enter into/form/make*** *an ~*

**2** a group of countries, companies, etc. who work together in order to achieve sth that they all want: *There are eight members of the alliance.*

**ˌall-ˈin** *adj.* (*BrE*) including everything, esp. all the costs: *an* ***all-in*** *price of €800* ▸ **ˌall ˈin** *adv.*

**ˌall-inˈclusive** *adj.* including everything: *an all-inclusive package*

**ˌall-in-ˈone** *adj.* (*BrE*) able to do the work of two or more things that are usu. separate: *an all-in-one printer and fax machine* ▸ **ˌall-in-ˈone** *n.* [C]: *printers and scanners, and all-in-ones that combine the two*

**ˌall-ˈloss** = ALL-RISK

**ˌall-ˈnighter** *n.* [C] (*infml.*) a period of work that lasts for a whole night: *The staff had to* **pull** *all-nighters to finish the job on time.*

★ **allocate** /ˈæləkeɪt/ *v.* [T] **~ sth (to sb/sth) | ~ (sb/sth) sth | ~ sth (for sth) 1** to decide officially that sth will be used for a particular purpose; to give sth officially to a particular person or thing: *We will allocate more capital to our wholesale business.* ◇ *All new staff have now been allocated jobs.* **2** (*Account.*) to decide which department, product, etc. (**cost centre**) a particular cost relates to ▸ **ˌalloˈcation** /-ˈkeɪʃn/ *n.* [C,U]: *We have spent our entire allocation for the year.*

**allot** /ə'lɒt; *AmE* ə'lɑːt/ *v.* [T] (**-tt-**) **~ sth (to sb/sth) | ~ (sb/sth) sth** to give time, money, tasks, etc. to sb/sth as a share of what is available: *How much money has been allotted to us/have we been allotted?*

**allotment** /ə'lɒtmənt; *AmE* ə'lɑːt-/ *n.* [C,U] **1** an amount of sth that sb is given or allowed to have; the process of giving sth to sb: *a monthly allotment of free minutes on the phone plan* **2** (*Stock Ex.*) a method of giving new company shares to people who apply for them; the number of shares given to each person

**ˌall-out 'strike** *n.* [C] (*HR*) a strike in which all employees of a company or all members of a union stop work

★ **allow** /ə'laʊ/ *v.* [T] **1** to make sth possible; to make it possible for sb to do sth: *The software allows comparison of sales in different regions.* **2** to give enough time for a particular purpose: *Allow 28 days **for** delivery.* **3** (*Comm.*) to take an amount of money off the price of sth, for example in exchange for another item: *How much will you allow me **for** my old PC?* **4** (*Account.*) to take an amount off an amount of money before tax is calculated: *to allow an expense* **5** to accept sth; to agree that sth is true or correct: *The court allowed the claim for compensation.*

**PHR V** **al'low for sb/sth** to include sb/sth when calculating sth: *All these factors must be allowed for.*

★ **allowance** /ə'laʊəns/ *n.* [C] **1** an amount of money that is paid to sb regularly or on particular occasions by their employer or by the state, to help them pay for travel, food, somewhere to live, etc.
⊕ *a **car/clothing**/an **entertainment**/a **housing/travel** ~ • to **give** sb/**pay** an ~ • to **be entitled to/claim** an ~*
**2** (*Account.*) (*esp. BrE*) an amount of money that you can take away from your income when calculating the amount of tax you have to pay **3** (*Account.*) an amount of money that a business can take away from its profit when calculating the amount of tax it must pay **4** a possible future expense or change in circumstances that a person or a company pays or plans for now: *an allowance for inflation* ◇ *to **make** proper **allowance** for marketing costs*

**ˌall-'risk** (*also* **ˌall-'risks**, **ˌall-'loss**) *adj.* (*Insur.*) that pays for all types of loss or damage, except in the circumstances mentioned: *to take out all-risks insurance*

**ˌall-'share** (*esp. BrE*) (*AmE usu.* **ˌall-'stock**) *adj.* (*Finan.*) used to describe the situation where a company buys another company by giving some of its own shares to the members of the other company, rather than paying money

**ˌAll-'Share ˌindex** (*also* **ˌAll-'Share**, *less freq.*) (*both esp. BrE*) (*AmE usu.* **ˌAll-'Stock ˌindex**) *n.* [C] an average of changes in share prices of most companies on a stock exchange, used to measure how a market is performing

**ˌall-'stock** = ALL-SHARE

**ˌAll-'Stock ˌindex** (*also* **ˌAll 'Stock**) = ALL-SHARE INDEX

**ˌall-'time** *adj.* the best or worst that has ever been recorded: *an ~ high/low/peak/record*

**alpha** /'ælfə/ = ALPHA TEST *n*

**alphanumeric** /ˌælfənjuː'merɪk; *AmE* -nuː'mer-/ (*also* **-numerical** /-njuː'merɪkl; *AmE* -nuː'mer-/) *adj.* having both letters and numbers: *an alphanumeric code*

**'alpha test** (*also* **'alpha**) *n.* [C,U] (*IT*; *Market.*) the first stage of testing a new product, esp. computer software, which is done by the manufacturer under controlled conditions: *The software is currently under alpha test.* ▶ **'alpha-test** *v.* [T] **'alpha-ˌtesting** (*also* **'alpha**) *n.* [U]

**Alt** /ɔːlt/ = ALT KEY

**alternate** /'ɔːltənət; *AmE* -tərn-/ *n.* [C] (*AmE*) a person who is chosen to do sb else's job when that person is ill/sick or away

**alˌternative dis'pute resoˌlution** *n.* [U] (*esp. AmE*) (*abbr* **ADR**) (*Law*) the name used to describe various methods of ending a legal disagreement without using a court, such as ARBITRATION

**alˌternative in'vestment** *n.* [C,U] ways of investing large amounts of money that are different from the traditional method of investing only in shares and bonds

**Alˌternative In'vestment ˌMarket** *n.* [sing.] (*abbr* **AIM**) a stock market at the London Stock Exchange that is designed for smaller or newer companies

**'Alt key** *n.* [C, usu. sing.] (*also* **Alt** [U]) a button on a computer keyboard that you press with other buttons for particular commands or symbols

**ˌalways-'on** *adj.* (*IT*) (about a computer system or service) giving continuous access to the Internet
→ DIAL-UP

**amalgamate** /ə'mælgəmeɪt/ [T,I] **~ (sth) (with sth) | ~ sth into sth** if two or more organizations **amalgamate** or are **amalgamated**, they join together to form one large organization ▶ **a'malgamated** *adj.*: *the Amalgamated Engineering Union* **a,malga'mation** /-'meɪʃn/ *n.* [U,C]

**amass** /ə'mæs/ *v.* [T] to collect a large amount of sth, esp. money or debt

**ambiguity** /,æmbɪ'gju:əti/ *n.* (*pl.* **-ties**) **1** (*Law*) [U,C] (about a legal document) the state of having more than one possible meaning; words or phrases that can be understood in more than one way: *ambiguities in the terms of the contract* **2** [U] the state of not being certain about the best way to do sth or to deal with sth

**ambition** /æm'bɪʃn/ *n.* **1** [C, usu. pl.] sth that you want to achieve: *He has ambitions for his group to become one of the world's top retailers.* **2** [C,U] the desire to be successful, powerful, etc. in your job: *lack of ambition*

**ambitious** /æm'bɪʃəs/ *adj.* **1** impressive but difficult to achieve because a lot of work or effort is needed: *an ambitious plan* **2** determined to be successful in your career

**amend** /ə'mend/ *v.* [T] to make a small change to sth such as a law or legal document, esp. to make it better or more correct: *The pension plan should be amended to allow early retirement.* ▶ **a'mendment** *n.* [C,U]: *to make amendments to sth*

**amenity** /ə'mi:nəti; *AmE* ə'menəti/ *n.* [C, usu. pl.] (*pl.* **-ties**) a pleasant or useful feature of sth, esp. a place, hotel, etc.

**A'merican De'positary Re'ceipt** *n.* [C] (*abbr* **ADR**) (*Stock Ex.*) a certificate issued by a US bank that represents a number of shares in a foreign company and is bought and sold on stock exchanges in the US

**A,merican 'Eagle** = EAGLE

**AMEX** /'æmeks/ *n.* [sing.] (*also* **Amex**) **American Stock Exchange** the second largest stock exchange in the US after the New York Stock Exchange. It is based in New York and deals in the shares of new and smaller companies and many foreign organizations.

**amortize, -ise** /ə'mɔ:taɪz; *AmE* 'æmərtaɪz/ *v.* [T] **1** (*Account.*) to reduce the cost of an asset in a company's accounts over a period of time, esp. an INTANGIBLE ASSET: *Goodwill was amortized against profits every quarter for up to 20 years.* **2** (*Finan.*) to pay back a debt by making small regular payments over a period of time
▶ **amortizable, -isable** /-zəbl/ *adj.*: *the amortizable assets* ◇ *an amortizable loan* **amorti'zation, -i'sation** /-taɪ'zeɪʃn; *AmE* -tə'z-/ *n.* [U,C]: *goodwill amortization*

**a,mortizing 'loan** *n.* [C] (*Account.*) a loan which is paid back in small regular payments

★**amount** /ə'maʊnt/ *n., v.*
• *n.* [C,U] **1** a quantity of money: *You will receive a bill for the full amount.*
○ *to pay/receive/refund an ~* ♦ *the full/right/total ~* ♦ *large/small ~*
**2** (*esp. with uncountable nouns*) a quantity of sth: *We want to double the amount of business we do in London.*
• *v.* PHR V **a'mount to sth** to add up to sth; to be equal to or the same as sth: *Total payments amounted to $13 m.* ◇ *Their actions amount to a breach of contract.*

**a'mount falling 'due after/ within one 'year** *n.* [C, usu. pl.] (*Account.*) in a company's financial records, the money which it will not/will have to pay back within the next year

**a,mounts 'differ** *phr.* (*Account., written*) words written on a cheque to show that the amount written on it in words is different from the amount written in figures SYN WORDS AND FIGURES DIFFER

**analogue** (*esp. BrE*) (*AmE usu.* **analog**) /'ænəlɒg; *AmE* -lɔ:g; -lɑ:g/ *adj.* using a continuously changing range of physical quantities to measure or store data: *a cellphone that works on both analog and digital phone systems* → DIGITAL

★**analyse** (*AmE* **analyze**) /'ænəlaɪz/ *v.* [T] to examine the nature or structure of sth, esp. by separating it into its parts, in order to understand or explain it: *gathering and analysing data* ▶ **'analyser** (*AmE* **analyzer**) *n.* [C]

★**analysis** /ə'næləsɪs/ *n.* [C,U] (*pl.* **-ses** /-si:z/) the detailed study or examination of sth, in order to find answers to particular questions; the results of the study: *a detailed analysis of each customer's buying habits*
○ *(an) in-depth/(a) thorough ~* ♦ *business/economic/industry/market ~* ♦ *to carry out/do/undertake (an) ~*

★**analyst** /'ænəlɪst/ *n.* [C] a person whose job involves examining facts, systems, companies, markets, etc. in order to give an opinion on them: *an industry/investment/a market ~*

**analytical** /ˌænəˈlɪtɪkl/ (*also* **analytic** /ˌænəˈlɪtɪk/) *adj.* using a logical method in order to understand or find out about sth: *analytical skills* ▸ **anaˈlytically** /-kli/ *adv.*

**ˈanalyze** = ANALYSE

**ˈanchor ˌtenant** *n.* [C] (*Prop.*) a very important TENANT in a building or on a piece of land, esp. one that will attract others

**ancillary** /ænˈsɪləri; *AmE* ˈænsəleri/ *adj.* **1** providing necessary support to the main work or activities of an organization: *~ equipment/services/staff/workers* **2** in addition to sth else but not as important: *ancillary rights under the law* ▸ **anˈcillary** *n.* [C] (*pl.* **-ries**)

**ˌand ˈCompany** (*also* **and Co, & Co**, *written*) *phr.* used with the name of a company that is owned by more than one person: *Levi Strauss & Co*

**ˌangel inˈvestor** (*BrE also* **ˈbusiness ˌangel**) *n.* [C] (*Finan., infml.*) a private person who invests their own money in a project, esp. a new business ▸ **ˌangel inˈvestment** *n.* [U,C]

**annex** (*BrE also* **annexe**) /ˈæneks/ *n.* [C] a section attached to the end of a document or report

★**annual** /ˈænjuəl/ *adj.* **1** happening or done once a year: *an annual bonus of 70% of basic pay* **2** relating to a period of one year: *an annual leave entitlement of 20 days* ▸ **ˈannually** /-əli/ *adv.*

**ˌannual ˌgeneral ˈmeeting** (*abbr* **AGM**) (*BrE*) (*AmE* **ˌannual ˈmeeting**) *n.* [C] **1** an important meeting of the shareholders or members of a company, held once a year, to present the accounts and discuss important topics **2** a meeting of the members of any organization, held once a year

**ˌannual ˈhours ˌcontract** *n.* [C] (*HR*) a contract in which employees agree to work for a particular number of hours per year rather than per week or per month, in exchange for an annual salary

**annualized, -ised** /ˈænjuəlaɪzd/ *adj.* (*Account.*) (about rates of interest, INFLATION, etc.) calculated for the period of a year, using figures for a shorter period

**ˌannual ˈmeeting** (*also* **ˈannual ˈmeeting of ˈstockholders, ˈannual ˈstockholders' ˈmeeting**) = ANNUAL GENERAL MEETING

**ˌannual reˈport** (*also* **reˈport**) *n.* [C] (*Account.*) a financial report that a company must by law present each year to its shareholders

**ˌannual reˈturn** *n.* [C] (*Law*) in the UK, a formal statement that a company must make each year for government records, giving details of the company, its directors, its shares and its assets: *to **make/file** an ~*

**ˈannual ˈstockholders' ˈmeeting** = ANNUAL MEETING

**annuitant** /əˈnjuːɪtənt; *AmE* -ˈnuː-/ *n.* [C] (*Insur.*) a person who receives an ANNUITY

**annuity** /əˈnjuːəti; *AmE* -ˈnuː-/ *n.* [C] (*pl.* **-ties**) (*Finan.*) **1** an amount of money paid to sb every year, usu. for the rest of their life **2** a type of investment that you can buy from an insurance company, usu. with one large amount of money, that pays an amount each year **3** a payment made from this type of investment

**annul** /əˈnʌl/ *v.* [T] (**-ll-**) (*Law*) to state officially that sth is no longer legally valid: *The contract was annulled.* ▸ **anˈnulment** *n.* [C,U]

**ANSI** /ˈænsi/ *abbr* **American National Standards Institute** an organization in the US that sets standards of quality and safety for manufactured items: *Our sunglasses pass the ANSI Standard Z80.3-1996.*

**ˌAnsoff ˈmatrix** /ˈænzɒf; *AmE* -zɔːf/ *n.* [C] (*Market.*) a way of analysing the possible strategies that a company could use to increase its business

**ˈanswering maˌchine** (*BrE also* **ˈanswerphone**) *n.* [C] a machine which you connect to your telephone to answer your calls and record any message left by the person calling

**ˈanswering ˌservice** *n.* [C] **1** a business that receives telephone calls for people or organizations and records messages for them to listen to **2** (*esp. BrE*) a service that provides recorded information when you telephone or allows you to record a message: *For timetable information please call the 24-hour answering service.*

**answerphone** /ˈɑːnsəfəʊn; *AmE* ˈaensərfoʊn/ = ANSWERING MACHINE

**ante** /ˈænti/ *n.* [sing.] **IDM raise/up the ˈante** to increase the level of sth, esp. sums of money or competition between businesses: *Quickbuy upped the ante in the battle for customers by slashing 5% off its prices.*

**ˌanticipatory ˈbreach** *n.* [C] (*Law*) the breaking of a contract in advance by sb who says they will not be able to do what the contract says they must do

**ˌanti-comˈpetitive** *adj.* (*Econ.*) not allowing other companies to compete in a fair way

**ˌanti-ˈdumping** *adj.* (*Econ.*) aimed at protecting the economy of a country by preventing other countries from selling goods there at prices that are unfairly low

**ˌanti-inˈflation** *adj.* aimed at lowering INFLATION or preventing it from rising: *anti-inflation policies*

**ˌanti-ˈspam** *adj.* (*IT*) aimed at preventing the sending of advertising emails that people do not want

**ˌanti-ˈtakeover** *adj.* aimed at preventing a company from taking over another one that does not want it or agree to it

**antitrust** /ˌæntiˈtrʌst/ *adj.* (*Econ.*) aimed at preventing groups of companies from working together illegally to reduce competition, control prices, etc.

**ˌantiˈvirus** /ˌæntiˈvaɪrəs/ *adj.* (*IT*) that prevents and removes computer viruses: *antivirus software*

**ˌany ˌother ˈbusiness** *phr.* (*abbr* **AOB**) a part of a meeting when subjects not mentioned on the AGENDA can be discussed

**APACS** /ˈeɪpæks/ *n.* [sing.] **Association for Payment Clearing Services** an organization in the UK for banks and other institutions that provide payment services, such as for cheques and credit cards

**Apex** (*also* **APEX**) /ˈeɪpeks / *n.* [U] a system of cheap tickets for train or air travel if you buy your ticket a particular number of days before you travel: *~ fares/tickets*

**apology** /əˈpɒlədʒi; *AmE* əˈpɑːl-/ *n.* [C, usu. pl.] (*pl.* **-gies**) information that you cannot go to a meeting or must leave early: *to **present/send** your apologies*

**app** /æp/ *n.* [C] (*IT, infml.*) **application** (= a computer program designed to do a particular job)

**apparel** /əˈpærəl/ *n.* [U] (*esp. AmE*) clothing, when it is being sold in shops/stores: *sports apparel*

**apˌparent ˈdamage** *n.* [U] (*Transpt.*) damage to goods that is noticed and reported when they are delivered or unloaded

**appeal** /əˈpiːl/ *n., v.*

• ***n.* 1** [C,U] a formal request to a court or to sb in authority to change a judgement or a decision made in a lower court: *She won an appeal **against** her dismissal.* **2** [U] a quality that makes a product attractive or interesting: *The car had mass appeal and was cheap to run.* ◇ *improving a product's appeal* ◇ *popular/universal/wide/youth ~*

• ***v.* 1** [T,I] to make a formal request to a court or to sb in authority to change a judgement or a decision: *The company said it would appeal (against) the decision.* **2** [I] to attract or interest sb: *This design appeals **strongly to** the Japanese consumer.*

**apˈpeal board** = APPEALS BOARD

**apˈpeal bond** *n.* [C] (*Law*) an amount of money that a person who appeals may have to leave with the court, which they will lose if the appeal fails

**apˈpeals board** (*also* **apˈpeal board**) *n.* [C] a group of officials who are appointed to listen to and judge cases where there is a dispute about an official decision that has been made

**appellant** /əˈpelənt/ *n.* [C] (*Law*) a person who appeals to a court to change a judgement or a decision made in a lower court

**appellate** /əˈpelət/ *adj.* (*Law*) concerned with appeals to change a judgement or decision made by a court or by sb in authority: *an **appellate court***

**append** /əˈpend/ *v.* [T] **~ sth (to sth)** to add sth to the end of a document: *text appended to an email*

**appendix** /əˈpendɪks/ *n.* [C] (*pl.* **-dices** /-dɪsiːz/) a section giving extra information at the end of a report, a book, etc.

**appliance** /əˈplaɪəns/ *n.* [C] an electrical machine that is designed to do a particular thing in the home, such as preparing food, cleaning, etc.

**applicant** /ˈæplɪkənt/ *n.* [C] a person who applies for sth, esp. a job, shares, etc.

★**application** /ˌæplɪˈkeɪʃn/ *n.*

**1** [C,U] a formal written request for sth, such as a job or permission to do sth: *applications **for** a post* ◇ *a planning application*

⊙ *to **make/send in/submit** an ~* ◆ *to **grant/reject/turn down** an ~* ◆ *to **consider/examine/process** an ~*

**2** [C] = APPLICATION FORM **3** [U,C] the practical use of sth, esp. a theory, discovery, etc: *The new invention would have wide application in industry.* **4** [U] the act of making a rule, etc. operate or become active: *strict application of the law* **5** (*IT*) (*also* **appliˈcation ˌprogram**) (*also* **app**, *infml.*) [C] a program designed to do a particular job; a piece of software: *to run an application*

**appli,cation for 'listing** (*also* **appli,cation for quo'tation**) *n.* [C] (*Stock Ex.*) a request by a company to be listed on a stock exchange

**appli'cation form** (*also* **,appli'cation**) *n.* [C] a document with spaces for writing in personal information, used for making a formal request for sth: *to **complete/fill in/fill out/send off** an ~*

**appli,cation for quo'tation** = APPLICATION FOR LISTING

**appli,cation for 'shares** = SHARE APPLICATION

**appli'cation ,letter** = LETTER OF APPLICATION

**appli'cation ,program** = APPLICATION (5)

**appli,cation 'software** *n.* [U] (*IT*) a program designed to do a particular job: *business/ERP ~*

★**apply** /ə'plaɪ/ *v.* (-lies, -lying, -lied, -lied) **1** [I] **~ (to sb/sth) (for sth)** to make a formal written request for sth: *She applied for the post of sales rep.* **2** [T] **~ sth (to sth)** to use sth or make sth work in a particular situation: *The new technology has been applied to farming.* **3** [T,I] (*not in the continuous tenses*) **~ (sth) (to sb/sth)** to concern or have an effect on sb/sth: *Special conditions apply to people under 21.*

★**appoint** /ə'pɔɪnt/ *v.* [T] **1 ~ sb (to/as sth)** to choose sb for a job or a position of responsibility: *He has recently been appointed **to** the board.* **2** (*fml.*) to arrange or decide on a time or place for doing sth: *I arrived ten minutes before **the appointed time**.*

**appointee** /ə,pɔɪn'tiː/ *n.* [C] (*HR*) a person who has been chosen for a job or a position of responsibility

★**appointment** /ə'pɔɪntmənt/ *n.* **1** [C] **~ (with sb)** a formal arrangement to meet or visit sb at a particular time, esp. for a reason connected with work: *I made an appointment to see the Manager.* ◇ *Visits can be arranged **by appointment**.*

⊙ *to **arrange/book/fix/have** an ~*
◆ *to **keep/miss** an ~*

**2** (*HR*) [C,U] **~ (as/to sth)** the act of choosing a person for a job or a position of responsibility: *Following her appointment to the post ...* **3** (*HR*) [C] a job or a position of responsibility: *a more senior appointment*

**ap'pointment ,letter** = LETTER OF APPOINTMENT

**ap'pointment(s) book** = DIARY (1)

**apportion** /ə'pɔːʃn; *AmE* ə'pɔːrʃn/ *v.* [T] **~ sth (among/between/to sb)** to divide sth among people; to give a share of sth to sb

**apportionment** /ə'pɔːʃnmənt; *AmE* ə'pɔːrʃn-/ *n.* [U,C] **1** the sharing of sth among people: the amount that each person gets when sth is shared: *the apportionment of risks between employer and contractor* **2** (*Account.*) (*also* **'cost ap,portionment**) the division of a cost between accounts in as fair a way as possible; the amount put in each account **3** (*Law*) **~ of blame/liability** a method of dividing payment between people involved in an accident, or their insurance companies, according to how responsible each person was for the accident; the amount that each has to pay

★**appraisal** /ə'preɪzl/ *n.* [C,U] **1** (*HR*) (*also* **per'formance ap,praisal, per'formance as,sessment, per'formance evalu,ation, per'formance re,view**) a meeting between an employee and their manager to discuss the quality of the employee's work and to plan future tasks **2** a judgement of the value, performance or nature of sb/sth: *an appraisal of the facilities*

★**appraise** /ə'preɪz/ *v.* [T] **1** (*HR*) to make a formal judgement about the value of a person's work, usu. after a discussion with them **2** (*fml.*) to consider or examine sb/sth and decide how much it is worth: *the company's appraised value*

**appraisee** /ə,preɪ'ziː/ *n.* [C] (*HR*) an employee whose work is **appraised** by their manager

**appraiser** /ə'preɪzə(r)/ *n.* [C] **1** (*AmE*) a person whose job is to estimate the value of sth **2** (*HR*) a manager who **appraises** an employee's work

**appreciate** /ə'priːʃieɪt/ *v.* [I] to increase in value over a period of time: *The currency has appreciated by 10% against the dollar.* OPP DEPRECIATE

**appreciation** /ə,priːʃi'eɪʃn/ *n.* [U; sing.] (*Econ.*) **~ (in sth)** increase in value over a period of time: *share price appreciation* OPP DEPRECIATION

**apprentice** /ə'prentɪs/ *n.* [C] (*HR*) a young person who works for an employer for a fixed period of time in order to learn the particular

skills needed in their job
▸ **ap'prenticeship** /-tɪsʃɪp/ *n.* [C,U]

**appropriate** /ə'prəʊprieɪt; *AmE* ə'proʊ-/ *v.* [T] **1** (*Finan.*) **~ sth (for sth)** to keep or save money for a particular purpose **2** to take sth for your own use, esp. illegally or without permission: *appropriating company funds*

**appropriation** /ə,prəʊpri'eɪʃn; *AmE* ə,proʊ-/ *n.* **1** (*Finan.*) [U] the act of keeping or saving money for a particular purpose: *the appropriation of funds* **2** (*Finan.*) [C] an amount of money to be used for a particular purpose, esp. by a government or company **3** [U; sing.] the act of taking sth that belongs to sb else: *appropriation of property*

**ap,propri'ation ac,count** *n.* [C] (*Account.*) a financial account that shows how the profits of a business, esp. a PARTNERSHIP, have been shared between its owners

**approval** /ə'pru:vl/ *n.* **1** [U,C] official agreement to or permission for sth, esp. a plan or request **2** (*Comm.*) [U] if you buy goods **on approval**, you can use them for a time without paying, until you decide if you want to buy them or not

★**approve** /ə'pru:v/ *v.* **1** [T] to officially agree to or give permission for sth, esp. a plan or request **2** [T] (*often pass.*) to say that sth is good enough to be used, or is correct: *The accounts were formally approved by the board.* **3** [I] **~ (of sth)** to think that sb/sth is good or acceptable; to have a positive opinion of sb/sth

**ap,proved ac'count** *n.* [C] (*Account.*) **1** [usu. pl.] a financial account that has been officially accepted by a company **2** a CREDIT ACCOUNT held by a customer who is known to be reliable

**ap,proved con'tractor** *n.* [C] a company or person that is officially recognized as doing good, reliable work for other companies

**ap,proved 'vendor** = PREFERRED VENDOR

**approx** *abbr* (*written*) approximate; approximately

★**approximate** *adj., v.*
• *adj.* /ə'prɒksɪmət; *AmE* ə'prɑ:k-/ almost correct or accurate, but not completely so; not exact: *The cost given is only approximate.* ◇ *an approximate number*
▸ **ap'proximately** *adv.*
• *v.* /ə'prɒksɪmeɪt; *AmE* ə'prɑ:k-/ **1** [T,I] **~ (to) sth** to be similar or close to sth in amount, nature, quality, etc: *The total cost will approximate 15 m dollars.* **2** [T] to calculate or estimate sth fairly accurately

**approximation** /ə,prɒksɪ'meɪʃn; *AmE* ə,prɑ:k-/ *n.* [C] **1** an estimate of a number or an amount that is almost correct, but not exact **2 ~ (of/to sth)** a thing that is similar to sth else, but is not exactly the same

**APR** /,eɪ pi: 'ɑ:(r)/ *abbr* (*Finan.*) **annual percentage rate** the total amount of money that is charged in one year for borrowing money compared with the amount of money borrowed, used when interest is normally paid more often than once a year; the amount received from money invested: *The bank offers an APR of 21% on its credit card.*

**aptitude** /'æptɪtju:d; *AmE* -tu:d/ *n.* [U,C] **~ (for sth)** natural ability or skill at doing sth: *She showed a natural aptitude for the work.* ◇ *Candidates were given* **aptitude tests**.

**arbiter** /'ɑ:bɪtə(r); *AmE* 'ɑ:rb-/ *n.* [C] a person who settles a dispute or who has the power to decide what will be done or accepted

**arbitrage** /'ɑ:bɪtrɑ:ʒ; -trɪdʒ; *AmE* 'ɑ:rbətrɑ:ʒ/ *n.* [U] (*Finan.*) the practice of buying sth (for example shares or foreign money) in one place and selling it immediately in another place where the price is higher ▸ **'arbitrage** *v.* [I]

**arbitrageur** /,ɑ:bɪtrɑ:'ʒɜ:(r); *AmE* ,ɑ:rbə-/ (*also* **arbitrager** /'ɑ:bɪtrɑ:dʒə(r); *AmE* 'ɑ:rbətrɑ:ʒər/) *n.* [C] (*Finan.*) a person whose job is ARBITRAGE

★**arbitrate** /'ɑ:bɪtreɪt; *AmE* 'ɑ:rb-/ *v.* [T,I] (*Law*) **~ (in/on sth)** to officially settle an argument or a disagreement between two people or groups. This is done by sb who is not involved rather than by a court: *to arbitrate in a dispute* ◇ *arbitrating between workers and management* ▸ **,arbi'tration** /-'treɪʃn/ *n.* [U]: *to go to arbitration* ◇ *an arbitration board/hearing/panel/system* **'arbitrator** *n.* [C]

**arcade** /ɑ:'keɪd; *AmE* ɑ:r'k-/ *n.* [C] (*BrE*) a large building with a number of shops/stores in it

**architect** /'ɑ:kɪtekt; *AmE* 'ɑ:rk-/ *n.* [C] **1** a person whose job is designing buildings, etc. **2** a person who is responsible for planning or creating an idea, an event or a situation: *the chief architects of the reform*

**architecture** /'ɑ:kɪtektʃə(r); *AmE* 'ɑ:rk-/ *n.* [U] **1** the art and study of designing buildings **2** the design or style of a building or buildings **3** (*IT*) the design or structure of a computing system and the way the different parts work together: *a client-server architecture* **4** the structure of an organization and the way the different parts and different people affect each other: *the social architecture of a company* ▸ ˌ**archi'tectural** /-tʃərəl/ *adj.*

**archive** /'ɑːkaɪv; *AmE* 'ɑːrk-/ *n., v.*
• *n.* **1** [C, usu. pl.] a collection of historical records kept by an organization; the place where these records are stored **2** (*IT*) [C] a part of a computer system, a tape or disk where data that is not often needed is stored **3** (*IT*) [C] a set of files and information that people can look at on the Internet
• *v.* [T] **1** to put or store a document or other material in an **archive**: *archived documents* **2** (*IT*) to move data that is not often needed to a tape, disk or another part of a computer system to store it: *archived emails*

★**area** /'eəriə; *AmE* 'eriə/ *n.* [C] **1** a part of a town, a country or the world: *an industrial area* ◇ *the area manager* **2** part of a room, building or particular space that is used for a special purpose: *the reception area* **3** a particular subject or activity, or an aspect of it: *our core business areas*

ˌ**area 'franchise** = MASTER FRANCHISE

**arena** /ə'riːnə/ *n.* [C] **1** a particular market or an area of business: *a highly* ***competitive*** *arena* **2** an area of activity that concerns the public, esp. one where there is a lot of opposition between different groups or countries: *the political arena*

ˌ**arithmetic 'mean** = MEAN *n.*

**arm** /ɑːm; *AmE* ɑːrm/ *n.* [C] a part of a large organization which is responsible for one area of its business: *our research arm*

ˌ**arm's-'length** *adj.* between companies or people that do not have close contact or any financial connections: *an arm's-length transaction*

**ARR** /ˌeɪ ɑːr 'ɑː(r)/ = ACCOUNTING RATE OF RETURN

★**arrange** /ə'reɪndʒ/ *v.* [T] **~ sth (with sb)** | **~ for sb to do sth** | **~ to do sth** to organize sth; to make plans for sth to happen: *I must arrange a meeting for next week.* ◇ *The company has arranged a $3.5 bn loan facility with its bankers.*

★**arrangement** /ə'reɪndʒmənt/ *n.* **1** [C, usu. pl.] plans or preparations for sth that will happen in the future: *travel arrangements* **2** [C,U] a way of doing or organizing things, esp. one formally agreed by two people or organizations, etc: *trading arrangements* ◇ *You can cash cheques here* ***by prior arrangement***. **3** [C] a formal relationship between two companies, etc. that provides some benefit to them both: *a new distribution arrangement with sb* **4** (*Finan.*) [C, usu. sing.] a formal agreement made between sb who owes money but cannot pay it all back and the person or organization they owe money to, so that only part of the money will be paid **5** [U] the act of arranging sth: *arrangement fees*

**array** /ə'reɪ/ *n.* [C] a group or collection of products, often one that is large or impressive: *a vast array of goods* SYN RANGE

**arrears** /ə'rɪəz; *AmE* ə'rɪrz/ *n.* [pl.] money that sb/sth owes that they should have paid earlier: *rent/tax ~*
IDM **be in arrears (with sth)**; **fall/get into arrears (with sth)** to be late in paying money that you owe: *Wages are more than two months in arrears.* **in arrears** after the time that work is done, items supplied, etc: *Suppliers are paid in arrears.* OPP IN ADVANCE

**arrival** /ə'raɪvl/ *n.* **1** [U,C] the act of coming or being brought to a place: *We record the date and time of arrival of all deliveries.* **2** [C] a person or a thing that comes to a place: *new arrivals* **3** [U] the time when sb starts a new job: *Since her arrival as chief executive ...* **4** [U] the time when sth new starts, esp. a new product or technology coming into the market: *the arrival of colour-screen mobile phones*

**article** /'ɑːtɪkl; *AmE* 'ɑːrt-/ *n.* [C] **1** a piece of writing in a newspaper or magazine **2** (*Law*) a section of a law, an agreement or other legal document that deals with a particular point

ˌ**articles of associ'ation** *n.* [pl.] (*usually* **Articles of Association**) (*BrE*) (*Law*) one of the legal documents that is created when a company is formed. It contains rules about how the company must be managed, what rights shareholders have, what the directors can do and what formal meetings must be held SYN BY-LAW (*AmE*)

ˌ**articles of incorpo'ration** *n.* [pl.] (*usually* **Articles of Incorporation**) (*AmE*) (*Law*) one of the legal documents that is created when a company is formed. It states the name and address of the company, its purpose and the amount of money it can raise by selling shares. SYN MEMORANDUM OF ASSOCIATION

**ˌartificial inˈtelligence** *n.* [U] (*abbr* **AI**) (*IT*) **1** the study of how to make computers function in an intelligent way like humans **2** technology that allows a computer to do something in an intelligent way

**ˌartificial ˈperson** = LEGAL PERSON

**A/S** (*also* **a/s**) = AFTER SIGHT

**as** /əz/ *or, in the strong form,* /æz/ *prep., adv., conj.* IDM **ˈas at ... /ˈas of ...** (*Account.*) used to show the exact date on which sth is correct or to which sth relates: *All prices are correct as at 1 July 2004.* **ˈas from ... /ˈas of ...** (*fml.*) used to show the time or date from which sth starts: *Our fax number is changing as from May 12.* **ˌas ˈis** (*BrE also* **ˌas ˈseen**) (*Comm.*) used to mean that sth is being sold in its present condition and that the person selling it does not make any promises about its quality: *All used equipment is sold as is.* → idiom at PER

**asap** (*also* **ASAP**, *esp. in AmE*) /ˌeɪ es eɪ ˈpiː; *AmE also* ˈeɪsæp/ *abbr* as soon as possible

**ASCII** /ˈæski/ *abbr* (*IT*) **American Standard Code for Information Interchange** a system that allows data to be moved between computers that use different programs: *an ASCII file*

**ˌAsian ˈtiger** *n.* [C] a term used esp. in newspapers for any South-East Asian country whose economy is growing very fast

**ask** /ɑːsk; *AmE* æsk/ *v.* [T] to say the price that you want for sth that you are selling: *He's asking €5 000 for the car.* IDM **ˌask sb to ˈleave** (*often pass.*) to dismiss sb from their job PHR V **ˌask sb ˈback** to ask sb to attend a further job interview

**ˈasking price** *n.* [C] **1** (*Comm.*) the price that sb/sth wants to sell sth for: *an asking price of $110 a share* **2** (*Stock Ex.*) (*also* **ˈasked price**, **ˈask price**, *less freq.*) = OFFER PRICE (2)

**aspiˈrational brand** *n.* [C] (*Market.*) a brand which people admire because they believe it is high quality and will give them a higher social position if they use it

★**assemble** /əˈsembl/ *v.* **1** [T,I] to bring people or things together as a group; to come together as a group: *to assemble a new management team* **2** [T] to fit together all the separate parts of a product: *The car is assembled in the UK.* **3** (*Finan.*) [T] if a financial institution **assembles** a loan, it gets a group of banks, etc. to provide money

★**assembly** /əˈsembli/ *n.* (*pl.* **-lies**) **1** [U] the process of fitting together the parts of a product: *car assembly* ◇ *an assembly plant* **2** [C] a large group of people who come together for a particular purpose

★**asˈsembly line** (*also* **proˈduction line**) *n.* [C] a line of workers and machines in a factory that fit the parts of a product together in a fixed order: *working* **on** *an assembly line* ◇ *An engine* **rolls off** *the assembly line every 72 seconds.* ◇ ~ *methods/problems/robots/workers*

**asˈsembly point** *n.* [C] a place where people must meet if there is an emergency

**asˈsembly ˌworker** *n.* [C] a person who works in a factory producing goods

**assent** /əˈsent/ *v.* [I] (*fml.*) **~ (to sth)** to agree to a request, an idea or a suggestion ▶ **asˈsent** *n.* [U]

**assertive** /əˈsɜːtɪv; *AmE* əˈsɜːrtɪv/ *adj.* expressing opinions and desires in a strong confident way so that people notice you or do what you want: *an assertive management style* ▶ **asˈsertiveness** *n.* [U]: *assertiveness training*

★**assess** /əˈses/ *v.* [T] **1** to judge sb/sth or form an opinion about sb/sth after looking carefully at all the information: *assessing candidates' strengths and weaknesses* SYN EVALUATE **2** to calculate the amount or value of sth: *Damage was assessed at €10 000.* **3** (*Account.*; *Law*) (*often pass.*) **~ sb/sth for sth** | **~ sb/sth on/upon sb/sth** to decide how much money sb/sth must pay as a tax or a fine: *The company tax is assessed on last year's activities.*

**asˌsessed ˈvalue** *n.* [U,C] (*Account.*) esp. in the US, the value of land and buildings used to calculate how much tax must be paid

★**assessment** /əˈsesmənt/ *n.* **1** [C,U] an opinion or a judgement about sb/sth made after all the information has been looked at carefully: *a detailed/thorough ~ of the risks* ◇ *to give/make an ~* **2** (*Account.*) [C,U] an amount of money, esp. tax, that has been calculated and must be paid; the process of calculating this amount: *to appeal against an income tax assessment* **3** [C] a calculation of the amount or value of sth: *an assessment of the damage* ◇ *to carry out/*

*make an* ~ **4** (*HR*) [C,U] the process of testing sb's knowledge and abilities, how well a system works, etc: *continuous assessment* ◇ *to carry out/do/use* ~

**as'sessment ˌcentre** *n.* [C] (*HR*) an event or place where people applying for a job are given a number of tests and interviews to find out what their strengths and weaknesses are

**assessor** /ə'sesə(r)/ *n.* [C] **1** an expert in sth who looks at all the information and judges how good sb/sth is **2** (*Prop.*) a person who decides the amount of tax you have to pay for the buildings and land that you own **3** (*Insur.*) a person whose job is to help you make a claim against an insurance company: *a claims assessor* SYN LOSS ASSESSOR **4** (*Law*) an expert in a particular subject who is asked by a court or other official group to give advice

★ **asset** /'æset/ *n.* [C, usu. pl.] a thing of value that a person or a company owns, such as money or property or the right to receive payment of a debt: *The group has total assets of €1.2 bn.* ◇ *The vehicle is recorded as an asset in the company accounts.* → LIABILITY
○ *to* ***have/hold/own/possess*** *~s* ◆ *to* ***acquire/buy/dispose of/increase/reduce/sell*** *~s* ◆ *to* ***record/show sth as*** *an ~* ◆ *to* ***freeze/release/unfreeze*** *~s*

**'asset acˌcount** *n.* [C] (*Account.*) a part of a company's financial records that shows the value of assets that the company owns

**ˌasset appreci'ation** = CAPITAL APPRECIATION

**'asset-ˌbacked** *adj.* (*Finan.*) used to describe a type of investment that a financial institution sells to investors. The company buys debts, such as car loans, and then sells investors the right to receive payments that the people who owe the money make: ~ *bonds/issue/debt*

**'asset ˌbacking** = ASSET VALUE PER SHARE

**'asset base** *n.* [C] (*Account.*; *Finan.*) the total value of the assets that a company has

**'asset ˌcoverage** *n.* [U] (*Account.*) a measure of how easily a company can pay its debts, calculated by dividing the total value of its assets by its debts

**'asset deˌflation** *n.* [U] (*Econ.*) a fall in the value of assets, for example property, compared to the rate of economic growth

**'asset inˌflation** *n.* [U] (*Econ.*) a rise in the value of assets, for example property, compared to the rate of economic growth

**'asset ˌmanagement** *n.* [U] (*Finan.*) **1** the act of managing a company's financial assets in order to get the highest amount of profit from them: *an asset management firm* **2** a service offered by banks and some other financial institutions that gives advice to customers on investments ▸ **'asset ˌmanager** *n.* [C]

**'asset mix** = INVESTMENT MIX

**'asset-ˌstripping** *n.* [U] (*Finan.*) the practice of buying a company which is in financial difficulties at a low price and then selling everything it owns in order to make a profit, without thinking about the future of the company ▸ **'asset-ˌstripper** *n.* [C]

**ˌassets under 'management** *n.* [U] (*abbr* **AUM**) (*Account.*) the total value of the shares, cash, etc. that an investment company manages for its customers

**ˌasset 'turnover** *n.* [U,C] (*also* **ˌasset 'turnover ˌratio** [C, usu. sing.]) (*Account.*) the total amount of goods or services sold by a company compared to the value of its assets, used as a measure of how efficiently the company uses its assets: *A typical grocery store has an asset turnover of 2.5 to 3.*

**'asset ˌvalue** *n.* [C,U] (*Account.*) the value of a company calculated by adding together the value of all its assets ▸ **'asset valuˌation** *n.* [U]

**'asset 'value per 'share** (*also* **'asset ˌbacking**) *n.* [U] (*Account.*) the total value of the assets that a company has, divided by the number of shares issued

★ **assign** /ə'saɪn/ *v.* [T] **1 ~ sth (to sb)** | **~ (sb) sth** to give money, equipment, staff, etc. to sth/sb for a particular purpose: *We have assigned 20% of our budget to the project.* **2 ~ sth to sb** | **~ sb sth** to give sb a particular job to do **3 ~ sb (to sth)** (*often pass.*) to send sb to work for a particular person or in a particular place: *I've been assigned to your team.* **4 ~ sth to sth** to say that sth has a particular value or function: *You need to assign priority levels to different tasks.* **5** (*Law*) **~ sth to sb** to officially arrange for your property or legal rights to belong to sb else

★ **assignment** /ə'saɪnmənt/ *n.* **1** [C] a piece of work that sb is given to do, usu. as part of their job: *to complete/finish/work on an* ~ **2** [U] the act of giving sb a particular task or sending them to work somewhere:

*He has requested assignment to other duties.* **3** (*Law*) [U,C] the act of officially arranging for your property or legal rights to belong to sb else

**as'signment clause** *n.* [C] (*Law*) a part of an insurance agreement or a contract that allows sb to pass their rights to sb else

**as'signment work** *n.* [U] (*AmE*) (*HR*) work done by people who do not have a permanent contract with a company SYN CONTINGENT WORK ▸ **as'signment ˌworker** *n.* [C]

★**assistant** /ə'sɪstənt/ *n., adj.* (*abbr* **asst**)

• *n.* [C] **1** a person who is below a senior person and helps them in their work: *the assistant to the marketing director* **2** (*BrE*) a person whose job is to serve customers in a shop/store → SALES CLERK

• *adj.* (*often used in titles*) having a rank below a senior person and helping them in their work, often doing the senior person's work when they are not there: *the Assistant Director*

**asˌsisted 'area** *n.* [C] in the UK, a region that receives financial support from the government in order to encourage new industries

**assistive** /ə'sɪstɪv/ *adj.* providing help for people whose physical condition makes it difficult for them to use computers and other equipment: *assistive aids*

**assn.** (*also* **Assn.**) *abbr* (*esp. AmE*) a short way of writing **association**

**Assoc.** *abbr* (*pl.* **Assoc.** *or* **Assocs.**) (*written*) **1** (in titles) Association **2** (in names of companies, etc.) Associate(s): *L. Horton and Assocs.*

★**associate** /ə'səʊʃiət; -siət; *AmE* ə'soʊ-/ *n., adj.*

• *n.* [C] **1** a person that you work with or do business with; a business partner: *business associates* **2 Associates** used in the name of an organization to show there are a number of professional partners: *Carver & Associates* **3** a member of an organization who does not have all the rights of ordinary members: *Some MBA students are summer associates at the company.*

• *adj.* **1** (often in titles) having a similar job as sb else but of a lower rank: *New Zealand's associate finance minister* **2** used to describe a member of an organization who does not have all the rights of ordinary members

**asˌsociate 'company** (*also* **asˌsociated 'company**) *n.* [C] a company of which more than 20% but less than 51% of the shares are held by another company

**Associated** /ə'səʊʃieɪtɪd; -sieɪt-; *AmE* ə'soʊ-/ *adj.* used in the name of a business company that is made up of a number of smaller companies: *Associated Newspapers*

**asˌsociated 'company** = ASSOCIATE COMPANY

★**association** /əˌsəʊʃi'eɪʃn; -si'eɪ-; *AmE* əˌsoʊ-/ *n.* **1** [C with sing./pl.verb] (*abbr* **Assoc.**) a group of people or organizations who have joined together for a particular purpose: *a business/consumer/employers'/professional/staff* ~ **2** [C,U] the act of joining or working with another person, company or group: *a long association with the firm*

**asst** (*also* **Asst**) *abbr* a short way of writing **assistant**: *asst managers*

**asˌsumed 'debt** *n.* [C,U] (*also* **asˌsumed lia'bilities** [pl.]) (*Account.*) the debts that a company has that another company agrees to be responsible for paying when it buys the first company

**assurance** /ə'ʃɔːrəns; -'ʃʊər-; *AmE* ə'ʃʊr-/ *n.* [U] (*BrE*) (*Insur.*) a type of insurance in which an amount of money is always paid out, for example when sb dies or after a fixed period of time

**assure** /ə'ʃɔː(r); -'ʃʊə(r); *AmE* ə'ʃʊr/ *v.* [T] (*BrE*) (*Insur.*) (*usu. pass.*) to insure sb/sth, so that money will be paid out, for example when sb dies or after a fixed period of time

**assured** /ə'ʃɔːd; -'ʃʊəd; *AmE* -'ʃʊrd/ *adj.* **1** certain to happen or to be available: ~ *income/market/profit/supply* **2** (*Insur.*) **the assured** *n.* [C] (*pl.* **the assured**) (*BrE*) the person who is insured in a contract with an insurance company

**assurer** /ə'ʃɔːrə(r); ə'ʃʊər-; *AmE* ə'ʃʊr-/ *n.* [C] (*BrE*) (*Insur.*) a person or company that provides people with ASSURANCE

**ˌat 'best** *adv.* (*Stock Ex.*) **sell/buy sth ~** to sell or buy shares at the best possible price

**ˌat 'call** *adv.* (*Finan.*) used to describe money that has been lent but must be paid back immediately if the lender asks for it back: *The sum will be lent at call.*

**ˌat-'home** *adj.* **1** used to describe people who work at home or parents who do not work outside their home: *at-home employees* **2** happening in the home rather than outside: *at-home training*

**ATM** /ˌeɪ tiː ˈem/ *n.* [C] **automated teller machine** a machine in or outside a bank, etc., from which you can get money from your bank account using a special plastic card: *to withdraw money from an ATM* SYN CASH MACHINE

**ˌat-risk ˈpay** (*also* **ˌat-risk comˈpenˈsation**, *less freq.*) *n.* [U] (*also* **ˌat-risk ˈsalary** [C]) (*HR*) a percentage of the pay of some employees that is linked to how well they are doing or how successful their company is. It can go up or down.

**at ˈsight** *adv.* (*Finan.*) written on a BILL OF EXCHANGE to show that the bill should be paid immediately

★**attach** /əˈtætʃ/ *v.* **1** [T] to fasten or join one thing to another: *an alarm attached* **to** *a laptop* **2** (*IT*) [T,I] to connect computer equipment together: *a PC attached to the network* SYN CONNECT **3** (*IT*) [T] to send a document to sb by email: *I attach the full conference timetable.* **4** [T,I] to be connected with sb/sth; to connect sth to sth: *She will be attached to this department for two months.*

★**attachment** /əˈtætʃmənt/ *n.* **1** (*IT*) [C] a document that you send to sb using email **2** (*Law*) [U] an order by a court for money or property to be taken from sb who owes money in order to pay their debt: *an* ***attachment of earnings*** *order* **3** [C,U] the act of joining one thing to another; a thing that joins one thing to another: (*fig.*) *the attachment of new conditions to the contract* **4** [C] an object or a device that you can fix onto a machine to make it do a particular job **5** (*HR*) [C,U] a short period of time when sb is connected to a particular company, department, etc: *Students spend two months* ***on attachment to*** *a company.*

★**attend** /əˈtend/ *v.* [T,I] to go to an event: *The meeting was attended by 90% of shareholders.* PHR V **atˈtend to sb/sth** to deal with sb/sth; to take care of sb/sth: *I have urgent business to attend to.*

**attendance** /əˈtendəns/ *n.* **1** [U,C] the act of being present at a place or an event: *Attendance at the talk is voluntary.* ◇ *He has a poor attendance record.* **2** [C,U] the number of people present at an organized event: *falling attendances at conferences*

**atˈtendance ˌbonus** *n.* [C] (*HR*) extra pay that some companies give their workers for coming to work regularly

**attendee** /əˌtenˈdiː/ *n.* [C] a person who is present at an organized event

★**attention** /əˈtenʃn/ *n.* [U] (*written*) (*also* **atˈtention of**) written on a business letter to show who it is intended for: ***for the attention of*** *Emma Walton* → FAO

**attest** /əˈtest/ *v.* **1** (*Law*) [T] to state that you believe that sth is true or genuine, for example in a court: *to ~ a will/signature* **2** (*fml.*) [T,I] **~ (to) sth** to show, prove or give evidence that sth is true: *users who will attest to the effectiveness of the products* ▸ **attestation** /ˌætesˈteɪʃn/ *n.* [C,U] **attestor** /əˈtestə(r)/ *n.* [C]

**atˌtested ˈcopy** = CERTIFIED COPY

**ˈattitude reˌsearch** *n.* [U] (*Market.*) an investigation into how people think and feel about an organization or its products

**attn** *abbr* a short way of writing **attention** on a business letter to show who it is intended for: *Fax 7028674 (attn Tony Kale)*

**attorney** /əˈtɜːniː; *AmE* əˈtɜːrni/ *n.* [C] (*Law*) **1** (*esp. AmE*) a lawyer, esp. one who can act for sb in a court **2** a person who is given the power to act on behalf of another in business or legal matters

**atˌtorney-at-ˈlaw** *n.* [C] (*pl.* **attorneys-at-law**) (*AmE*) (*Law*) a lawyer who is qualified to represent sb in a court

★**attract** /əˈtrækt/ *v.* [T] **1** to make sb/sth go somewhere or become involved in sth: *to* ***attract and keep*** *good staff* ◇ *What attracted you* **to** *IT?* **2** to make sb interested in a product or a business and want to spend money on it: *to attract new customers* **3** (*written*) (*BrE*) to be linked with sth, such as a particular rate of interest or tax, or a punishment: *Larger loans may attract a lower interest rate.*

**attributable** /əˈtrɪbjətəbl/ *adj.* caused or explained by the thing mentioned: *Our success is attributable* **to** *our marketing.*

**atˌtributable ˈprofit** *n.* [U,C] (*Account.*) (in a company's accounts) part of the profit from a long contract, for example for building work, that is related to the amount of work completed at the date of the accounts

**attribute** *n.*, *v.*
• *n.* [C] /ˈætrɪbjuːt/ **1** a quality that sb has: *the essential attributes for the job* **2** a feature of a product that a

customer thinks is important when deciding whether or not to buy it: *Quality may be the most important attribute.*

• ***v.*** /ə'trɪbju:t/ [T] (*often pass.*) to say or believe that sth is the result of a particular thing: *The sales boom is attributed **to** low unemployment.*

**attrition** /ə'trɪʃn/ *n.* [U] **1** (*HR*) the process of reducing the number of people employed by an organization by not replacing people who leave their jobs: *We will lose 150 jobs through attrition and retirement.* SYN NATURAL WASTAGE **2** (*Market.*) the loss of customers, esp. when they start buying another company's products: *a low rate of customer attrition*

**at 'warehouse** *adj., adv.* (*Trade*) used to describe goods that can be delivered immediately, with the buyer paying a price for delivery that includes loading the goods onto road or rail transport

★**auction** /'ɔ:kʃn; 'ɒk-; *AmE* 'ɔ:k-/ *n., v.* (*Comm.*)

• ***n.*** [C,U] a public event at which things are sold to the person who offers the most money for them: *be sold **at auction***

• ***v.*** [T] to sell sth at an **auction**

PHR V **ˌauction sth 'off** to sell sth at an **auction**, esp. sth that is no longer needed or wanted

**auctioneer** /ˌɔ:kʃə'nɪə(r); ˌɒk-; *AmE* ˌɔ:kʃə'nɪr/ *n.* [C] a person whose job is to direct an AUCTION and sell the goods

**audience** /'ɔ:diəns/ *n.* [C] a number of people or a particular group who watch, read or listen to the same thing: *TV advertising reaches mass audiences.* ◇ *The drama had a 29% **audience share**.*

⊕ *a **large/small/wide** ~* • *a **female/male/young** ~* • *sth **has/is aimed at/reaches/targets** an ~*

**ˌaudience 'flow** *n.* [C, usu. sing., U] (*Market.*) **1** the change in the number of people watching a television station before, during and after a particular programme **2** the number of people who continue to watch the same television station after a particular programme has finished

**ˌaudience re'search** *n.* [U] (*Market.*) research that is carried out on people who watch television or listen to the radio, in order to find out how popular particular shows, etc. are and the kind of people who watch or listen to them

**ˌaudio 'conferencing** *n.* [U] a system that allows people in different places to discuss sth at the same time by telephone; the activity of doing this ▸ **ˌaudio 'conference** *n.* [C] → TELECONFERENCING, VIDEOCONFERENCING

**ˌaudio-'visual** (*AmE* **audiovisual**) *adj.* (*abbr* **AV**) using both sound and pictures

★**audit** /'ɔ:dɪt/ *n., v.*

• ***n.*** [C,U] **1** (*Account.*) an official examination of business and financial records to see that they are true and correct: *an annual/year-end ~* ◇ *a tax audit*

⊕ *an **external/independent** ~* • *to **carry out/complete/conduct** an ~* • *an ~ **committee/firm/group/team***

**2** an official examination of the quality or standard of sth: *an audit of our software*

⊕ *to **carry out/complete/conduct/do** an ~*

• ***v.*** [T] **1** (*Account.*) to officially examine the financial accounts of a company: *We have just had our accounts audited.* → UNAUDITED **2** to officially examine the quality or standard of sth

**'audit ˌfailure** *n.* [C,U] (*Account.*) the situation when an **audit** does not find a problem that exists in a business's financial accounts

★**auditor** /'ɔ:dɪtə(r)/ *n.* [C] a person who officially examines the business and financial records of a company to see that they are true and correct

⊕ *an **external/independent/internal/outside** ~* • ***company** ~*

**'audit reˌport** *n.* [C] (*Account.*) a report written by an **auditor** for the members of a company after examining a company's financial records: *a **clean/qualified** ~*

**'audit trail** *n.* [C] **1** (*Account.*) a series of documents and records that shows the history of a company's financial records and can be checked by AUDITORS **2** (*IT*) a record kept by a computer of a series of events

**augˌmented 'product** *n.* [C, usu. sing.] (*Market.*) a product that has extra features or services that make it more attractive than the typical product of its kind; the extra features and services that are provided

**AUM** /ˌeɪ ju: 'em/ = ASSETS UNDER MANAGEMENT

**austerity** /ɒ'sterəti; ɔ:'ster-; *AmE* ɔ:'ster-/ *n.* [U,C] (*pl.* **-ties**) a situation when people do not have much money to spend because there are bad economic conditions

**authenticate** /ɔːˈθentɪkeɪt/ *v.* [T] to prove that sth is genuine or true ▸ **auˌthentiˈcation** /-ˈkeɪʃn/ *n.* [U]

**authenticity** /ˌɔːθenˈtɪsəti/ *n.* [U] the quality of being real and genuine

**authoring** /ˈɔːθərɪŋ/ *n.* [U] (*IT*) creating MULTIMEDIA computer products with special software, without using programming language: *~ packages/software/tools*

★**authority** /ɔːˈθɒrəti; *AmE* əˈθɔːr-; əˈθɑːr-/ *n.* (*pl.* **-ties**) **1** [U] the official power to give orders to people, make decisions, etc: *in a position of authority* ◇ *Only the manager has the authority to sign cheques.* **2** [U] official permission to do sth: *He signed cheques without the authority of his manager.* **3** [U] the power to influence people because they respect your knowledge or official position: *She speaks with authority on the subject.* **4** [C, usu. pl.] the people or an organization with the power to make decisions or with a particular area of responsibility in a country or region: *health authorities* **5** [C] a person with special knowledge: *She's an authority on trade law.*

★**authorization**, **-isation** /ˌɔːθəraɪˈzeɪʃn; *AmE* ˌɔːθərəˈz-/ *n.* **1** [U,C] official permission or power to do sth; the act of giving permission: *He acted without authorization.* ⊕ *to give/grant/refuse (sb) ~* ♦ *to ask for/get/have/need/obtain ~* **2** [C] a document that gives sb official permission to do sth

**authoriˈzation code** *n.* [C] a secret set of numbers or letters that allows sb to do sth such as use a website, accept payment with a bank card, etc.

★**authorize**, **-ise** /ˈɔːθəraɪz/ *v.* [T] to give official permission for sth, or for sb to do sth: *to authorize payments* ◇ *authorized dealers*

**ˌauthorized ˈcapital** (*BrE also* **ˌauthorized ˈshare ˌcapital**) *n.* [U] (*Finan.*) the maximum amount of money that a company is allowed to raise by selling shares

**ˌauthorized ˈshares** *n.* [pl.] (*also* **ˌauthorized ˈstock** [U]) (*Finan.*) the maximum number of shares that a company can issue

**auto** /ˈɔːtəʊ; *AmE* ˈɔːtoʊ/ *n.* [C] (*pl.* **autos**) (*AmE*) a car: *the auto industry* ◇ *~ dealers/manufacturers* ◇ *auto sales*

**autocratic** /ˌɔːtəˈkrætɪk/ *adj.* expecting to be obeyed and not caring about the feelings and opinions of others

**automaker** /ˈɔːtəʊmeɪkə(r); *AmE* ˈɔːtoʊ-/ *n.* [C] (*AmE*) a company that makes cars

★**automate** /ˈɔːtəmeɪt/ *v.* [T] (*usu. pass.*) to use machines and computers instead of people to do a job or task: *The factory is* ***fully automated.*** ◇ *an automated production line* SYN MECHANIZE ▸ **ˌautoˈmation** /-ˈmeɪʃn/ *n.* [U]

**automatic** /ˌɔːtəˈmætɪk/ *adj.* **1** (about a machine, device, etc.) having controls that work without needing sb to operate them: *automatic doors* **2** always happening as a result of a particular action or situation: *an automatic fine for late payment* ▸ **ˌautoˈmatically** /-kli/ *adv.*

**automobile** /ˈɔːtəməbiːl/ *n.* [C] (*esp. AmE*) a car: *the automobile industry* ◇ *automobile manufacturers*

**automotive** /ˌɔːtəˈməʊtɪv; *AmE* -ˈmoʊ-/ *adj.* (*usu. written*) connected with motor vehicles: *the automotive industry*

**ˌautomotive engiˈneer** *n.* [C] a person whose job is to design, develop and test cars and other motor vehicles

**ˈauto parts** (*also* **autoparts** /ˈɔːtəʊpɑːts; *AmE* ˈɔːtoʊpɑːrts/) *n.* [pl.] the pieces used to make cars

**AV** /ˌeɪ ˈviː/ = AUDIO-VISUAL

**av** *abbr* (*written*) average

**available** /əˈveɪləbl/ *adj.* **1** (about things) that you can get, buy or use: *The new service will be available to customers next month.* ◇ *freely/generally/readily/widely ~* **2** (about a person) free to see or talk to ▸ **aˌvailaˈbility** *n.* [U]: *This offer is* ***subject to availability.***

★**average** /ˈævərɪdʒ/ *adj., n., v.*
• *adj.* **1** calculated by adding several amounts together and dividing the total by the number of amounts: *Average earnings are around €35 000 per annum.* **2** typical or normal: *Forty hours is a fairly average working week.*
• *n.* [C,U] **1** the result of adding several amounts together and dividing the total by the number of amounts: *Prices have risen by* ***an average of*** *about 5%.* **2** a level which is usual: *Employees' pay is above average for the industry.* **3** (*Insur.*) = PARTIAL LOSS
• *v.* **1** [T] (*not used in the pass.*) to be equal to a particular amount as an average: *Economic growth is expected to average 2% next year.* **2** [T,I] to calculate the average of sth

**PHR V** ˌ**average 'out** to result in an average or equal amount over a period of time or after several occasions ˌ**average sth 'out (at sth)** to calculate the average of sth ˌ**average 'out at sth** to have a particular amount as the average over a period of time: *Sales growth has averaged out at 20% over the last three years.*

**'average adˌjuster** *n.* [C] (*Insur.*) a person whose job is to calculate how much the insurance companies should pay when a ship or its cargo has been lost or damaged, esp. when the payment is shared between several companies

**ˌaverage 'audience ˌrating** *n.* [C] (*abbr* **AA rating**) (*Market.*) esp. in the US, the percentage of homes that were watching or listening to a particular programme during an average minute

**ˌaverage 'earnings** *n.* [pl.] (*Econ.*) in a particular economy, the total amount of money that people earn for work divided by the number of people who are working

**ˌaverage 'earnings ˌindex** *n.* [sing.] (*abbr* **AEI**) (*Econ.*) an official measurement in the UK that shows the increase in the average amount of money earned by a worker in a year, sometimes within a particular industry: *the average earnings index for the services sector*

**ˌaverage 'revenue** *n.* [C] (*Account.*) the total money received from the sale of goods divided by the number of items sold

**ˌaverage 'stock** *n.* [U] (*Account.*) a method of calculating the average value of goods held during a particular period by adding the total value of goods held at the beginning and at the end and dividing by two

**aviation** /ˌeɪvi'eɪʃn/ *n.* [U] the designing, building and flying of aircraft

**⊙** *the ~ **industry/sector** • **civil/commercial** ~*

**avionics** /ˌeɪvi'ɒnɪks; *AmE* -'ɑːn-/ *n.* **1** [U] the science of electronics when used in designing and making aircraft **2** [pl.] the electronic devices in an aircraft, etc.

**avoidance** /ə'vɔɪdəns/ *n.* [U] not doing sth; preventing sth from existing or happening: *the avoidance of tax* ◇ *risk avoidance*

★ **award** /ə'wɔːd; *AmE* ə'wɔːrd/ *n.*, *v.*

• ***n.*** [C] **1** (*HR*) a decision about an increase in the amount of money sb earns: *a pay award* **2** (*HR*) in some countries, a written document that gives details of the conditions of employment in a company or an industry that are stated in law **3** (*HR*) = AWARD WAGE **4** (*Law*) the amount of money that a court decides should be given to sb who has won a case; the decision to give this money **5** (often in names) a prize

• ***v.*** [T] **~ sth (to sb)** | **~ (sb) sth** to make an official decision to give sth to sb as a payment, prize, etc: *They were awarded the contract.*

**a'ward wage** (*also* **a'ward**) *n.* [C] (*HR*) in some countries, the amount of money that an employer must pay by law for a particular kind of work

**a'ward-ˌwinning** *adj.* having won a prize: *~ books/designs*

**awareness** /ə'weənəs; *AmE* ə'wer-/ *n.* [U; sing.] knowing sth; knowing that sth exists and is important: *raising awareness of the brand*

**⊙** ***high/low/growing** ~ • to **build/heighten** ~*

**axe** (*AmE also* **ax**) /æks/ *n.*, *v.* (*infml.*)

• ***n.*** [sing.] **the axe** used esp. in newspapers to describe strong measures that are taken to reduce costs, such as removing workers from their jobs, closing parts of a company, etc: *workers **facing the axe***

• ***v.*** [T] to take strong measures to reduce costs, such as removing workers from their jobs, closing parts of a company, etc: *Some services are to be axed this year.*

**axis** /'æksɪs/ *n.* [C] (*pl.* **axes** /'æksiːz/) a fixed line against which the positions of points are measured, esp. points on a graph: *the horizontal/vertical ~*

# Bb

**B2B** (*also* **b2b**, **B-to-B**) /ˌbiː tə 'biː/ *adj.* (*E-comm.*) **business-to-business** used to describe the buying, selling and exchanging over the Internet of products, services or information between companies

**ˌB2'B exˌchange** *n.* [C] (*abbr* **B2X**, **B2BX**) (*E-comm.*) a network or website on the Internet that allows businesses to buy and sell goods and services directly between each other

**B2C** (*also* **b2c**, **B-to-C**) /ˌbiː tə 'siː/ *adj.* (*E-comm.*) **business-to-consumer/customer** used to describe the selling of products, services or information to consumers over the Internet: *B2C e-commerce*

**B2E** (*also* **b2e**, **B-to-E**) /ˌbiː tu ˈiː/ *adj.* **1** (*IT*) **business-to-employee** used about a website that all employees of a company use to enter the Internet, and which brings together all the information they need to do their job whether in the office or away from it **2** (*HR*) **business-to-employee** used to describe ways in which some companies try to help employees feel happy in their job and to develop their skills and education, so that the company will attract and keep good staff **3** (*E-comm.*) **business-to-employer** used to describe the selling over the Internet of products or services that help companies provide sth for employees or find new employees

**B2X** /ˌbiː tu ˈeks/ = B2B EXCHANGE

**ˈbaby boom** *n.* [C] a time when the population of a country increases rapidly, esp. used to refer to a time in the UK and the US between 1948 and 1964 ▶ **ˈbaby ˌboomer** *n.* [C]

**back** /bæk/ *adj., adv., v.*

• ***adj.*** **1** owed for a time in the past: *The company owed $2 m dollars in back taxes.* **2** of or from a past time: *back issues of a magazine* IDM **on the back ˈburner** (*infml.*) (about an idea, a plan, etc.) left for the present time, to be done or considered later OPP ON THE FRONT BURNER **take a back ˈseat (to sth) 1** to be given less importance than sth else: *Safety has taken a back seat to the need to cut costs.* **2** to let other people play a more active and important role in a particular situation than you do → idiom at QUEUE *n.*

• ***adv.*** in return or reply: *Could you call back later, please?* ◇ *Can I get back to you on that?* IDM **(go/get) back to ˈbasics** to think about the simple or most important ideas within a subject or an activity instead of new ideas or complicated details → idiom at CLAW

• ***v.*** [T] to give support or help to sb/sth: *Leading businesses have backed plans to reduce VAT.* PHR V **ˌback ˈout (of sth)** to decide that you are no longer going to take part in sth that has been agreed: *back out of a deal* **ˌback sth ˈup 1** (*IT*) to prepare a second copy of a file, program, etc. that can be used if the main one fails or needs extra support → BACKUP **2** to provide support for sb/sth

**backbone** /ˈbækbəʊn; *AmE* -boʊn/ *n.* [C] **1** the most important part of a system, an organization, etc. **2** (*IT*) the system of connections that carries information long distances over the Internet: *the* ***Internet backbone***

**ˌback ˈcatalogue** (*also* **ˈcatalogue**) *n.* [C, usu. sing.] the designs, films/movies or music that a company has produced or bought in the past and that it can still produce. A **back catalogue** can be sold to make money.

**backdate** /ˌbækˈdeɪt/ *v.* [T] **1** to write an earlier date on a cheque or other document than the date at the time of writing **2** (*BrE*) (*usu. pass.*) to make sth, esp. a payment, take effect from an earlier date: *a backdated pay rise* OPP POST-DATE

**ˈback end** *n., adj.*

• ***n.*** [C] **1** the part of a business that does not meet and deal directly with customers **2** the end of a project, a process, an investment, a period of time, etc: *extra payments on the back end of a loan* **3** (*IT*) the part of a computer system that processes data

• ***adj.*** **1** connected with the end of a project, a process, an investment, a period of time, etc: *back-end charges* **2** (*IT*) used to describe a program or part of a computer system that is not seen or used by the user, esp. in e-commerce: *a back-end database*

**ˌback-end ˈload** (*esp. AmE*) (*BrE usu.* **ˈexit charge**) *n.* [C] (*Finan.*) the fee an investor pays when they sell their shares in an investment fund, which is taken from the final payment they receive ▶ **ˌback-end ˈloaded** *adj.*

**ˌback-end ˈloading** *n.* [U] (*Finan.; Insur.*) an arrangement in which higher amounts are paid at the end of a financial agreement, such as a loan, than at the beginning

**backer** /ˈbækə(r)/ *n.* [C] (*Finan.*) a person or company that gives support to sth/sb, esp. financial support: *corporate/key/financial ~s*

**background** /ˈbækgraʊnd/ *n.* [C] **1** the details of a person's experience, education, family, etc: *a retail background* **2** the circumstances or past events which help explain why sth is how it is: *background information on the company* **3** (*IT*) the part of a computer where a program can continue to operate while the user is working with another program: *programs running* ***in the background***

**backhander** /ˈbækhændə(r)/ *n.* [C] a secret and illegal payment made to sb in exchange for a favour: *taking backhanders from suppliers* SYN BRIBE

**backhaul** /ˈbækhɔːl/ *n.* [C] (*Transpt.*) the return journey of a vehicle that transports goods after it has delivered its load

**backing** /ˈbækɪŋ/ *n.* [U] help; support: *The merger deal has **the full backing** of the board.*
⊙ *to **get/receive/win*** ~ ◆ ***financial/legal/political*** ~

**backload** /ˈbækləʊd; *AmE* -loʊd/ *v., n.*
• *v.* [T,I] **1** (*Finan.*) to arrange for higher amounts to be paid at the end of a financial agreement than at the beginning: *a backloaded insurance policy* **2** (*Transpt.*) to arrange for a vehicle to carry a load on its return journey after delivering sth
▸ **ˈbackloading** *n.* [U]
• *n.* [C] (*Transpt.*) a load that a vehicle carries on its return journey after delivering sth

**backlog** /ˈbæklɒg; *AmE* -lɔːg; -lɑːg/ *n.* [C] a quantity of work that should have been done already, but has not yet been done: *A huge backlog of work had built up.*
⊙ *a* ~ ***develops/grows*** ◆ *to **clear/reduce** a* ~ ◆ *a **large/mounting*** ~

**ˌback ˈoffice** *n.* [C] the part of a company which does not deal directly with the public: *He runs our back office.* ◇ *back-office jobs*

**ˈback ˌorder** *n.* [C] (*Comm.; Product.*) an order for goods that have not yet been produced or supplied: *We **fill** back orders as soon as the goods are available.*
▸ **ˌback ˈorder** *v.* [T,I]

**ˌback ˈroom** *n.* [C] a place where secret, administrative or other important work is done: *deals made in back rooms* ◇ *back-room staff*

**ˈback shift** (*BrE*) (*AmE* **ˈswing shift**) *n.* [C,U] (*HR*) a period of work from the middle of the afternoon until late at night, between the day and the night periods; the group of people who work during this period: *to work (the) back shift*

**backslash** /ˈbækslæʃ/ *n.* [C] a symbol (\) used in computer commands

**backspace** /ˈbækspeɪs/ *n., v.*
• *n.* [C] the key on a computer keyboard which you press to move back towards the beginning of the line of text and which removes the last letter that you typed
• *v.* [I] to use the **backspace** key on a keyboard

**ˌback-to-back ˈloan** (*also* **ˌparallel ˈloan**) *n.* [C] (*Finan.*) an arrangement where companies in different countries lend money to each other at the same time in different currencies, in order to avoid high interest rates or restrictions on changing currency

**backup** /ˈbækʌp/ *n.* [C] **1** (*IT*) a copy of a file, program, etc. that can be used if the original is lost or damaged **2** extra help, ideas, equipment, etc. that you can use if the first fails: *a **backup plan***

**backwardation** /ˌbækwəˈdeɪʃn; *AmE* -wərˈdeɪʃn/ *n.* [U] (*also* **inˌverted ˈmarket** [sing.]) (*Finan.*) a situation where prices for goods that will be delivered in the future are lower than prices for goods that will be delivered immediately: *a state of backwardation on the coffee futures market*

**ˌbackward inteˈgration** *n.* [U] (*Econ.*) a situation where a company buys a company which supplies it or begins to do the same work as that company

**BACS** /bæks/ *abbr* **Bankers' Automated Clearing System** a company owned by the UK banks that uses an electronic system to make payments between accounts in member banks, often used by companies to pay employees

**ˌbad ˈdebt** *n.* [C,U] (*Account.*) a debt that will not be paid: *They have **written off** $500 m of bad debts.*

**ˌbad ˈdebt reˌcovery** *n.* [U] **1** (*Law*) legal action to force sb to pay a debt which should have been paid already **2** (*Account.*) payment of a debt which seemed unlikely to be paid

**ˌbad ˈfaith** *n.* [C,U] an intention to deceive sb: *The garage owner had **acted in** bad faith.* → GOOD FAITH

**ˌbad ˈloan** *n.* [C] (*Finan.*) a loan that is not being paid back as arranged and may never be

**bail** /beɪl/ *v.* (*Law*) **PHR V** **ˌbail ˈout (of sth)** (*BrE also* **bale out (of sth)**) (*also* **bail**, *esp. in AmE infml.*) to stop doing or taking part in sth because it is difficult or unpleasant **ˌbail sb/sth ˈout (of sth)** (*BrE also* **bale sb/sth out (of sth)**) to rescue sb/sth from a difficult situation: *The government bailed the company out of financial difficulty.*

**bailiff** /ˈbeɪlɪf/ *n.* [C] (*Law*) **1** (*BrE*) a law officer whose job is to take the possessions and property of people who cannot pay their debts **2** (*AmE*) an official who keeps order in a court, watches prisoners, etc.

**bailout** /ˈbeɪlaʊt/ *n.* [C] an act of giving money to a company, a foreign country, etc. that has very serious financial problems: *a government bailout*

**ˌbait-and-ˈswitch** *n.* [C,U] (*Market.*) a selling method where advertisements for products with low prices are used to attract customers, who are then persuaded to buy something more expensive in the range: *bait-and-switch tactics* **NOTE** This method can be illegal.

★ **balance** /ˈbæləns/ *n., v.*
• ***n.*** **1** [C, usu. sing.] the difference in a bank account between the total amount of money coming in and the total amount going out at a particular time: *Check your account balance online.* **2** (*Account.*) [C, usu. sing.] in a company's financial records, the difference between the total DEBITS and total CREDITS in a particular account: *The balance on the profit and loss account at 31st March was $75 738.* **3** [C, usu. sing.] the amount of money still owed after sb has paid part of the total **4** [C] an amount of money that sb owes to the bank, etc. at a particular time, because they have bought things using a credit card: *I try to pay off my monthly credit-card balance in full.* **5** [U] what remains of sth after part of it has been used or taken: *The balance of your order will be supplied when we have new stock.* **6** [U; sing.] a situation in which different things exist in equal, correct or good amounts: *a balance* ***between*** *work* ***and*** *relaxation* **IDM** **on ˈbalance** after considering all the information: *On balance, we have had a good year.* → idioms at REDRESS *V.*, STRIKE *V.*
• ***v.*** **1** (*Account.*) [T] **~ sth (off)** in a company's financial records, to compare the total DEBITS and the total CREDITS in an account and calculate the amount needed to make them equal: *All the accounts should have been balanced (off) correctly.* **2** (*Account.*) [I] if an account **balances**, the DEBIT and CREDIT sides are equal **3** [T] to spend only the money that is available; to make the money available equal to the amount of money spent: *to balance your* ***budget*** **4** [T,I] **~ (sth) (out)** to be equal in value, amount, etc. to sth else that has the opposite effect: *The advantages and disadvantages seem to balance out.* **5** [T] **~ A against B** to compare the importance of two contrasting things

**ˌbalance brought ˈdown** (*abbr* **balance b/d**) (*also* **ˌbalance brought ˈforward** *abbr* **balance b/f, balance b/fwd**) *n.* [C] (*Account.*) the amount that you use to start an account for a new period, which is equal to the BALANCE at the end of the previous period

**ˌbalance carried ˈdown** (*abbr* **balance c/d**) (*also* **ˌbalance carried ˈforward** *abbr* **balance c/f, balance c/fwd**) *n.* [C] (*Account.*) the BALANCE at the end of one accounting period that will then become the BALANCE BROUGHT DOWN for the beginning of the next period

**ˌbalanced ˈbudget** *n.* [C, usu. sing.] (*Econ.*) a plan by a government to spend the same amount of money as it receives in a particular year

**ˌbalanced ˈfund** (*also* **ˌbalanced ˈmutual fund**) (*both esp. AmE*) *n.* [C] (*Finan.*) a type of fund that invests its customers' money in a way that makes a good profit but does not involve a lot of risk, by investing in both shares and bonds

**ˌbalanced ˈscorecard** *n.* [C, usu. sing.] a method of measuring how well a company's plans are helping it to achieve its aims by looking at a variety of areas of activity including finance, how efficient it is, and relations with customers

**ˌbalance of ˈpayments** *n.* [sing.] (*Econ.*) the difference between the amount of money one country pays to other countries, esp. for imports, and the amount it receives, esp. from exports; the official record of this over a particular period: *a ~ surplus/deficit*

**ˌbalance of ˈtrade** (*also* **ˈtrade ˌbalance, ˌvisible ˈbalance**) *n.* [C, usu. sing.] (*Econ.*) the difference in value between imports and exports of goods over a particular period: *a balance-of-trade* ***deficit*** **NOTE** The **balance of trade** is an important part of a country's BALANCE OF PAYMENTS.

★ **ˈbalance sheet** *n.* [C] (*Account.*) a written statement that shows the financial state of a company at a particular time. It lists the company's assets and all money owed
○ *a* ***healthy/strong*** *~* ♦ *to* ***improve/strengthen*** *your ~*

**the ˈbalance-sheet eˌquation** = THE ACCOUNTING EQUATION

**bale** /beɪl/ *n., v.*
• ***n.*** [C] a large amount of a light material pressed together and tied up: *~ of hay/cotton/wool*
• ***v.*** [T] to make sth into **bales**
**PHRV** **ˌbale ˈout (of sth)**; **ˌbale sb/sth ˈout (of sth)** = BAIL OUT (OF STH), BAIL SB/STH OUT (OF STH)

**balloon** /bəˈluːn/ *n.* [C] (*Finan.*) used to describe a type of loan where the final payment is much larger than the rest

**ballot** /ˈbælət/ *n., v.*

• *n.* **1** [U,C] the system of voting in writing and usu. in secret; an occasion on which a vote is held: *The union cannot call a strike unless it holds a ballot of members.* **2** (*also* **ˈballot ˌpaper**) [C] the piece of paper or card on which sb marks who or what they are voting for: *to* ***cast*** *your ballot (in favour of sth)* **3** (*Finan.*) [U,C] a fair way of choosing who to sell shares, bonds, etc. to in situations where there are not enough for everyone who wants them

• *v.* **1** [T] to ask sb to vote in writing and secretly about sth **2** [I] to vote secretly about sth

**ˈballpark** /ˈbɔːlpɑːk; *AmE* -pɑːrk/ *n.* IDM **in the (right) ˈballpark** (*infml.*) (used about a price, an amount, etc.) approximately right or acceptable: *If you said five million you'd be in the right ballpark.* **in the wrong/same ˈballpark** (*infml.*) (used about a price, an amount, etc.) wrong or almost the same: *The offers were all in the same ballpark.* **a ˈballpark figure/estimate/price** (*infml.*) a number, an amount, etc. that is approximately correct

**the ˌBaltic Exˈchange** *n.* [sing.] (*Trade*) an organization in London that arranges agreements for the transport of raw materials between countries, esp. by ship

★ **ban** /bæn/ *v., n.*

• *v.* [T] (**-nn-**) **1** to officially say that sth is not allowed, often by law **2** (*usu. pass.*) to officially say that sb is not allowed to do sth or go somewhere: *She was banned* ***from*** *holding public office.*

• *n.* [C] an official rule that says that sth is not allowed: *a ban* ***on*** *overtime* ◇ *to impose/lift a ~*

**bancassurance** /ˈbæŋkəʃɔːrəns; -ʃʊər-; *AmE* -əʃʊr-/ *n.* [U] (*BrE*) (*Finan.*; *Insur.*) the combination of banking and insurance services offered by many major banks SYN ALLFINANZ ▸ **ˈbancassurer** *n.* [C]

**bandwidth** /ˈbændwɪdθ; -wɪtθ/ *n.* [U,C] (*IT*) a measurement of the amount of information that a particular computer network or Internet connection can send in a particular time: (*fig.*) *He doesn't have enough* ***personal bandwidth*** (= time; mental ability) *to manage the project.*

**the Bank** /bæŋk/ *n.* [sing.] the Bank of England

★ **bank** /bæŋk/ *n., v.*

• *n.* [C] **1** an organization that provides various financial services to people and businesses, for example keeping or lending money; a local office or a particular **bank**

◉ ***a domestic/foreign/an international ~*** • ***a big/high-street/major/small ~***

**2** *often* **Bank, the Bank of ...** = CENTRAL BANK **3** an amount or a number of sth collected together; a place where sth is stored ready for use: *a bank of information* ◇ *a computer's memory bank*

• *v.* **1** [T] to put money into a bank account: *to bank a cheque* **2** [I] **~ (with/at ...)** to have an account with a particular bank

**bankable** /ˈbæŋkəbl/ *adj.* **1** (*infml.*) likely to make money for sb/sth: *The company's name is its most* ***bankable asset.*** **2** (*Finan.*) acceptable to a bank: *~ documents/checks*

★ **ˈbank acˌcount** (*also* **ˈbanking acˌcount**) *n.* [C] an arrangement that you have with a bank that allows you to keep your money there, to pay in or take out money, etc.

**ˈbank adˌvance** *n.* [C] money which a bank lends to a customer

**ˈbank asˌsistant** *n.* [C] (*esp. AmE*) a person who works in a bank but is not a manager

**ˈbank ˌbalance** *n.* [C] the amount of money that sb has in their bank account at a particular time

**ˈbank bill** *n.* [C] **1** (*Finan.*; *Trade*) (*BrE*) (*also* **ˌbanker's acˈceptance**, *BrE, AmE*) a type of BILL OF EXCHANGE that is signed by a bank, which means that it agrees to pay the amount stated on the **bill 2** (*AmE*) = BANKNOTE

**ˌbank ˈborrowing** *n.* **1** [U] the act of taking money from a bank and agreeing to pay it back over a period of time; the amount of money that sb borrows in this way **2 bank borrowings** [pl.] the amount of money that is borrowed from banks

**ˈbank card** (*also* **ˈbanker's card**) *n.* [C] a plastic card provided by your bank that you can use to pay for sth or to get money from your account out of a machine

**ˌbank-certified ˈcheque** *n.* [C] a cheque that a bank has officially said can be used, as the person who has written the cheque has enough money in their account to pay the amount on the cheque

**ˈbank charge** *n.* [C, usu. pl.] the amount that a customer pays their bank for the services it provides: *to*

*incur* bank charges (= do sth so that you have to pay them)

**ˈbank cheque** (*BrE also* **ˈbanker's** -) *n.* [C] a cheque signed by your bank that you buy and use to pay sb who will not accept an ordinary cheque SYN BANK DRAFT

**ˈbank clerk** *n.* [C] a person who works in a bank, receiving and paying out money, helping customers, keeping records of accounts, etc.

**ˈbank ˌcredit** *n.* [U,C] (*Finan.*) money that a bank makes available either as a loan or an OVERDRAFT; money that banks in general lend: *a ~ agreement/facility ◇ periods when bank credit is restricted*

**ˈbank debt** *n.* [U] money that a company, an organization, etc. owes to a bank

**ˈbank deˌposit** *n.* [C] **1** an amount of money that you leave in a bank **2** (*Econ.*) **bank deposits** [pl.] the total amount of money that has been paid into one bank or all banks in a particular place

**ˈbank draft** *n.* [C] **1** (*BrE also* **ˈbanker's draft**) a cheque signed by your bank that you buy and use to pay sb who will not accept an ordinary cheque SYN BANK CHEQUE, DRAFT **2** (*AmE*) = DIRECT DEBIT

★ **banker** /ˈbæŋkə(r)/ *n.* [C] **1** a person who owns a bank or who has an important job in a bank: *a merchant/senior ~* **2** an organization that lends money or provides the services of a bank: *a central/merchant/private/senior ~*

**ˌbanker's acˈceptance** = BANK BILL (1)

**ˈbanker's bank** *n.* [C] (*Finan.*) a bank that provides financial services to other banks

**ˈbanker's card** = CHEQUE CARD, BANK CARD

**ˈbanker's cheque** = BANK CHEQUE

**ˈbanker's draft** = BANK DRAFT (1)

**ˈbanker's hours** *n.* [pl.] (*infml.*) short working hours, often with a long lunch break

**ˌbanker's ˈorder** = STANDING ORDER

**ˈbanker's ˌreference** = BANK REFERENCE

**ˈbank faˌcility** *n.* [C] (*Finan.*) **1** [usu. sing.] an arrangement with a bank to borrow a particular amount of money **2** a bank

**the ˈBank for Interˈnational ˈSettlements** *n.* [sing.] (*abbr* **BIS**) an international organization in Switzerland that encourages central banks from different countries to work together and provides them with financial services

**ˌbank giro ˈcredit** *n.* [C] a method of payment, usu. used for paying bills, etc., in which a printed form is used to tell a bank to put a particular amount of money into a particular account at that branch; the form that is used

**ˌbank guaranˈtee** *n.* [C] (*Finan.*) a promise by a bank to pay money owed by a customer who cannot pay a debt or who fails to provide an agreed service to sb

**ˌbank ˈholiday** *n.* [C] (*BrE*) a public holiday, for example New Year's Day, when banks, businesses, government offices, etc. are officially closed

**ˌbank identifiˈcation ˌnumber** = SORT CODE

★ **banking** /ˈbæŋkɪŋ/ *n.* [U] **1** the business activity of banks: *a career in banking*

**⊙** ***business/corporate/personal ~*** **•** *the ~* ***industry/sector*** **•** *~* ***facilities/hours/services***

**2** the activity of using the services that a bank offers: *online banking ◇ electronic/telephone ~*

**ˈbanking acˌcount** = BANK ACCOUNT

**ˈbanking ˌsystem** *n.* [C] all the institutions that provide banking services in a country or region, and the way that they work together

**ˈbank ˌinterest** *n.* [U] the interest that a bank charges a customer for borrowing money

**ˌbank ˈlending** *n.* [U] (*Econ.*) the amount of money lent to people by banks within a country over a period of time

**ˌbank ˈmandate** *n.* [C] a written instruction that sb gives to a bank, for example to start a new account or make regular payments from their account

**banknote** /ˈbæŋknəʊt; *AmE* -noʊt/ (*AmE also* **ˈbank bill**) *n.* [C] a piece of paper money SYN NOTE

**the ˌBank of ˈEngland** (*also* **the Bank**) *n.* [sing.] (*abbr* **B/E, B of E**) the central bank of the UK

**ˌbank of ˈissue** *n.* [C] a bank that has the legal right to make its own notes and coins

**ˌbank ˈoverdraft** = OVERDRAFT

**ˈbank rate** *n.* [C] (*Finan.*) another name for BASE RATE

**ˌbank reconciliˈation** (*also* **ˌbank reconciliˈation ˌstatement**) *n.* [C,U] (*Account.*) a regular check that a company makes to make sure that its own financial records agree with the bank's record of its BANK BALANCE, for example by considering payments that have been made but not yet recorded by the bank; a document that explains the differences

**'bank ˌreference** (*also* **'banker's ˌreference**) *n.* [C] a statement that a bank can be asked to give about whether a customer is likely to be able to pay back a loan

**ˌbank re'serves** *n.* [pl.] (*Econ.*) the amount of money that banks must keep in the central bank, equal to a percentage of the money paid into their accounts (**deposits**)

**bankroll** /'bæŋkrəʊl; *AmE* -roʊl/ *v., n.*
• *v.* [T] (*esp. AmE*) (*infml.*) to support sb or a project financially: *investors who bankroll start-ups*
▸ **'bankroller** *n.* [C]
• *n.* [C] **1** (*esp. AmE*) a supply of money **2** a roll of paper money

**'bank run** *n.* [C] (*Econ.*) a time when too many people want to take their money out of the banks at the same time, so the banks cannot pay them all

★ **bankrupt** /'bæŋkrʌpt/ *adj., v., n.*
• *adj.* **1** without enough money to pay what you owe, esp. when this has been officially decided by a court: *a bankrupt software company* ◇ *to go/be declared ~* SYN INSOLVENT **2** (*fml.*) [not usu. before n.] not having something that has value: *a government bankrupt **of** new ideas*
• *v.* [T] to make sb **bankrupt**
• *n.* [C] (*Law*) a person who has been judged by a court to be unable to pay their debts

★ **bankruptcy** /'bæŋkrʌptsi; -rʌpsi/ *n.* [U,C] (*pl.* **-cies**) (*Law*) the state of being BANKRUPT: *The company has filed for bankruptcy.* ◇ *further bankruptcies among small farmers*
⊕ *to **be on the brink of/be on the verge of/face** ~* ♦ *to **declare/seek** ~* ♦ *to **avert/avoid/stave off** ~* ♦ *a ~ **court/judge***

**'bankruptcy-law proˌtection** = BANKRUPTCY PROTECTION

**'bankruptcy ˌnotice** *n.* [C] (*Law*) an official letter that tells a person or company who owes money that if they do not pay it within a particular number of days, they will be made BANKRUPT

**'bankruptcy ˌorder** *n.* [C] (*Law*) an order by a court that makes a person or company officially BANKRUPT, and allows their property to be taken and used to pay their debts

**'bankruptcy peˌtition** *n.* [C] (*Law*) a request made to a court by sb who is owed money to make the person or company that owes them money BANKRUPT: *to file/issue/present/serve a ~*

**'bankruptcy proˌceedings** *n.* [pl.] (*Law*) the legal process of asking the court to make a person or company BANKRUPT

**'bankruptcy proˌtection** (*also* **'bankruptcy-law proˌtection**) *n.* [U] (*Law*) laws that limit the amount that a person or company has to pay when they are made BANKRUPT: *to file for/seek ~* ◇ *to emerge from bankruptcy protection*

**'bank ˌstatement** (*also* **'statement**) *n.* [C] a printed record of all the money paid into and out of a customer's bank account within a particular period

**'bank ˌteller** (*also* **'teller**) *n.* [C] a person whose job is to receive and pay out money in a bank

**'bank ˌtransfer** *n.* [C] the sending of money from an account in one bank to an account in any branch of the same bank or another: *to arrange/make a ~* ◇ *to pay by bank transfer*

**'banner ad** (*also* **banner** /'bænə(r)/) (*also* **'banner adˌvertisement**, *fml.*) *n.* [C] (*Market.*) an advertisement in the form of a box with a design or symbol in that is spread across a web page, usu. at the top ▸ **'banner ˌadvertising** *n.* [U]

**the Bar** /bɑː(r)/ *n.* [sing.] (*Law*) (*often* **the bar**) **1** (*BrE*) the profession of a BARRISTER: *to be **called to the bar*** (= to be allowed to work as a qualified barrister) **2** (*AmE*) the profession of any kind of lawyer; lawyers as a group

**bar** /bɑː(r)/ *n., v.*
• *n.* **1** (*IT*) [C] a narrow box at the top of a computer screen that contains words or pictures of the common things that a computer can do for you to choose: *a task bar* **2** [sing.] **a ~ (to sth)** a thing that stops sb from doing sth: *a two-year bar on selling the company*
• *v.* [T] (**-rr-**) **~ sb (from sth)** to not allow or to prevent sb from doing sth

**'bar chart** (*AmE also* **'bar graph**) *n.* [C] a diagram which uses bands of different heights and equal widths to show different amounts, so that they can be compared easily

★ **'bar code** *n.* [C] a pattern of thick and thin lines printed on things that you buy in a shop/store. It con-

tains information that a computer can read: *to read/scan a* ~ SYN UPC
▸ 'bar ˌcoding *n.* [U]

★ **bargain** /ˈbɑːɡən; *AmE* ˈbɑːrɡən/ *n., v.*

• ***n.*** [C] **1** something that is bought or sold at a lower price than usual: *I **picked up** some bargains in the sale.* **2** an agreement between two or more people or groups to do sth: *I'll **make** a bargain **with you**.* **3** (*Comm.*) an agreement, often spoken, between two or more people to exchange sth for a particular price: *Buyer and seller **strike** a bargain.* **4** (*Stock Ex.*) a single act of buying or selling on the London Stock Exchange: *The average daily volume was 180 684 bargains.*
→ idiom at HARD *adj.*

• ***v.*** [I] **~ (with sb) (about/over/for sth)** to discuss prices, pay or conditions with sb in order to reach an agreement that suits everyone: *to bargain for wages*

**ˌbargain ˈbasement** *n.* [C] a part of a large shop/store, usu. on the floor below street level, where goods are sold at lower prices than usual

**ˈbargain ˌhunter** *n.* [C] a person looking for goods being sold at a lower price than usual ▸ **'bargain ˌhunting** *n.* [U]

**bargaining** /ˈbɑːɡənɪŋ; *AmE* ˈbɑːrg-/ *n.* [U] discussion of prices, pay, or conditions to try to reach an agreement that suits everyone: *pay/wage* ~ ◇ *a weak **bargaining position*** ◇ ***hard bargaining** on both sides*

**ˈbargaining ˌagent** *n.* [C] (*HR*) in the US, a union that a particular group of workers choose to belong to and that represents them in discussions about wages, etc.

**ˈbargaining ˌcounter** (*BrE*) (*also* **ˈbargaining chip**, *AmE, BrE*) *n.* [C] a fact or thing that you can use to get an advantage for yourself when you are trying to reach an agreement with sb

**ˈbargaining ˌpower** *n.* [U] the amount of control a person or group has when trying to reach an agreement with another group in a business or political situation

**ˈbargaining ˌunit** *n.* [C] (*HR*) in the US, a group of workers who are recognized as a separate part of a union in discussions about wages, etc.

**ˈbar graph** = BAR CHART

**barometer** /bəˈrɒmɪtə(r); *AmE* -ˈrɑːm-/ *n.* [C] sth that shows the changes happening in an economic, a social or a political situation

**baron** /ˈbærən/ *n.* [C] a person who owns or controls a large part of a particular industry: *a media/newspaper/oil/press* ~

★ **barrel** /ˈbærəl/ *n.* [C] **1** a large round container, usu. made of wood or metal, with flat ends and curved sides; the amount that such a container holds **2** a unit of measurement in the oil industry equal to between 120 and 159 litres: *Oil prices rose to $60 a barrel.* **3** a unit of measurement used in the beer-making industry equal to about 164 litres

★ **barrier** /ˈbæriə(r)/ *n.* [C] **1** a problem, rule or situation that prevents sb from doing sth, or that makes sth impossible: *barriers **against** imports* ◇ *barriers **to** promotion* **2** something that exists between one thing or person and another and keeps them separate

**ˌbarrier to ˈentry** (*pl.* **barriers** -) (*also* **ˈentry ˌbarrier**) *n.* [C] (*Econ.*) sth that makes it difficult for a company to start competing in a particular kind of business, for example high cost or advanced technology

**ˌbarrier to ˈexit** (*pl.* **barriers** -) (*also* **ˈexit ˌbarrier**) *n.* [C] **1** (*Econ.*) something that makes it difficult for a company to leave an area of business, for example government rules or the cost of stopping employing staff **2** something that makes it difficult for a customer to stop using a particular brand of goods or for sb to change their job, etc.

**barrister** /ˈbærɪstə(r)/ *n.* [C] (*Law*) a lawyer in the UK who has the right to argue cases in the higher courts

**barter** /ˈbɑːtə(r); *AmE* ˈbɑːrt-/ *v.* [T,I] (*Comm.; Econ.*) to exchange goods, services, etc. for others without using money ▸ **'barter** *n.* [U]

★ **base** /beɪs/ *n., v.*

• ***n.*** [C] **1** the main place where a business operates from **2** the people, activity, etc. from which sb/sth gets most of their support, income, power, etc: *an economy with a solid **manufacturing** base* **3** a situation, an idea, a fact, etc. from which sth is developed: *A new company must have a strong financial base.* → idiom at TOUCH *v.*

• ***v.*** [T] to use a particular city, town, etc. as the main place where you do business: *They based the new company in Belgrade.* PHR V **'base sth on/upon sth** to use a fact, a situation, an idea, etc. as the point from which sth can be developed

★**based** /beɪst/ *adj.* **1** if one thing is based on another, it uses it or is developed from it: *a broadly based technology company* (= one with a wide range of products) **2** working or doing business in or from a particular place: *a Prague-based company* ◇ *web-based training* **3 -based** (*used in compounds*) having sth as an important feature or part: *oil-based paint*

ˈ**base pay** = BASIC PAY

ˈ**base price** = BASIC PRICE

ˈ**base rate** *n.* [C] (*Finan.*) the lowest rate of interest at which the central bank lends money to other banks and financial institutions, used by banks, etc. to calculate how much interest they will charge to customers that they lend money to. SYN BANK RATE, PRIME RATE (*AmE*)

ˈ**base ˌsalary** = BASIC SALARY

ˈ**base wage** = BASIC WAGE

ˌ**basic ˈindustry** *n.* [C,U] **1** (*Econ.*) an industry that produces goods and services to be sold outside the region where they are produced **2** (*Manufact.*) an industry that supplies materials to other industries

ˌ**basic ˈpay** (*esp. BrE*) (*AmE usu.* ˈ**base pay**) *n.* [U] (*HR*) the normal amount that sb is paid, usu. every week, without extra payments

ˌ**basic ˈprice** (*AmE also* ˈ**base price**) *n.* [C] (*Comm.*) the lowest price of a product without charges for extra features, tax, etc.

ˈ**basic rate** *n.* [C] (*BrE*) (*Account.*) **~ (of tax/income tax)** the normal level of income tax, that most people or companies pay

ˌ**basic ˈsalary/ˈwage** (*esp. BrE*) (*AmE usu.* ˈ**base ˌsalary/wage**) *n.* [C] (*HR*) the normal amount that sb is paid, without any extra payments

★**basis** /ˈbeɪsɪs/ *n.* (*pl.* **bases** /-siːz/) **1** [sing.] the reason why people take a particular action: *They employed him* ***on the basis of*** *his experience.* **2** [sing.] the way things are done, organized or arranged: *She was employed* ***on a*** *temporary basis.* **3** [C, usu. sing., U] the important facts, ideas or events that support sth and that it can develop from **4** [sing.] the number that is used to calculate sth from: *On a three-year accounting basis, losses were €1.5 bn for the year.* → idiom at CONTINGENCY

ˈ**basis point** *n.* [C] (*Finan.*) one hundredth of one per cent. This is often used to express the interest rate on bonds.

ˈ**basket case** *n.* [C, usu. sing.] (*AmE*) (*infml.*) (used esp. in newspapers) a country or an organization whose economic or financial situation is very bad

ˌ**basket of ˈcurrencies** *n.* [C, usu. sing.] (*Econ.*) a fixed group of different currencies which some countries use to set a value for their own currency; the value that is calculated for this group

★**batch** /bætʃ/ *n., v.*

• *n.* [C] a number of things or tasks that are dealt with as a group: *a batch of bills* ◇ *We deliver the goods* ***in batches.*** ◇ *products with the same* ***batch number***

• *v.* [T] to put things into groups in order to deal with them: *The program will batch and sort orders.*

ˈ**batch ˌcosting** *n.* [U] (*Account.*) a way of expressing the cost of a product based on the cost of producing a group

ˈ**batch ˌprocessing** *n.* [U] (*IT*) a way of getting a computer to do a long series of jobs all at the same time automatically

ˈ**batch proˌduction** *n.* [U] (*Product.*) a way of manufacturing a product by making small or large groups of the items rather than producing them continuously

**battery** /ˈbætri; -təri/ *n.* [C] (*pl.* **-ries**) **1** a device that is placed inside a car engine, clock, radio, etc. and that produces the electricity that makes it work: *~-powered/-operated* **2** a large number of things of the same type: *a battery of tests* → idiom at RECHARGE

**battle** /ˈbætl/ *n., v.*

• *n.* **1** [C] **~ (between A and B) | ~ (with sb) (for/over sth)** a competition, an argument or a struggle between people or groups of people trying to win power or control
○ ***a bitter/fierce/hard-fought/long-running ~*** • ***a bid/boardroom/legal/takeover ~***
**2** [C, usu. sing.] a determined effort that sb makes to solve a difficult problem or succeed in a difficult situation: *a tough/an uphill ~* ◇ *Many firms are* ***facing*** *a battle for survival.*
IDM **do ˈbattle (with sb) (for/over sth)** to argue or be in competition with sb

• *v.* [T,I] **~ (with/against sb/sth) (for/over sth)** to try very hard to achieve sth difficult or to deal with sth unpleasant or dangerous: *battling for market share*

**battleground** /ˈbætlɡraʊnd/ *n.* [C] a subject or thing that people are arguing about or competing for

**BBA** /ˌbiː ˌbiː ˈeɪ/ *abbr* **1** (*AmE*) Bachelor of Business Administration, a university degree **2** British Banker's Association

**bcc** *abbr (IT, written)* **blind carbon copy** a copy of an email message sent to sb without showing their name, so that the main person that the email is addressed to does not know that the message has also been sent to the other person

**BDI** /ˌbiː diː ˈaɪ/ *abbr (AmE) (Market.)* **ˌbrand deˈvelopment ˌindex** a measure of how well a particular type of product sells in a particular area compared to the whole country

**B/E** = BILL OF EXCHANGE, BANK OF ENGLAND

**beachhead** /ˈbiːtʃhed/ *n.* [C, usu. sing.] a strong position that a company has gained in a new field or place

**ˈbean ˌcounter** *n.* [C] *(infml.)* a humorous word for an accountant

★ **bear** /beə(r); *AmE* ber/ *n.* [C] *(Finan.; Stock Ex.)* **1** a person who sells shares, a particular currency, etc., hoping to buy them back later at a lower price because they think prices are going to fall rather than rise **2** = BEAR MARKET → BULL

**bearer** /ˈbeərə(r); *AmE* ˈberər/ *n.* [C] *(Finan.)* **1** a person who presents a document, such as a cheque or a share, bond, etc., for payment **2** used to describe a document, such as a cheque or a share, bond, etc. which can be presented for payment by anyone, not only by a named person: *bearer bonds*

**bearish** /ˈbeərɪʃ; *AmE* ˈber-/ *adj.* *(Finan.; Stock Ex.)* showing or expecting a fall in the prices of shares, etc. OPP BULLISH

**ˈbear ˌmarket** *(also* **bear***)* *n.* [C] *(Finan.; Stock Ex.)* a period during which people are selling shares, etc. because they expect the prices to fall OPP BULL MARKET

**ˈbear poˌsition** *n.* [C] *(Finan.; Stock Ex.)* a situation in which an investor sells shares, etc. that he/she has borrowed but does not own yet, hoping to be able to buy them at a cheaper price later and return them to the owner SYN SHORT POSITION

**ˈbear raid** *n.* [C] *(Finan.; Stock Ex.)* an attempt by a dealer to make the price of a share, etc. go down by selling it in large numbers

**ˈbear run** *n.* [C] *(Finan.; Stock Ex.)* a situation where the value of shares, etc. is falling

**beat** /biːt/ *v.* [T] **(beat, beaten** /ˈbiːtn/**)** **1** to defeat sb/sth: *a strategy to beat the competition* **2** to do or be better than sth: *Nobody beats our prices!* IDM **beat sb at their own ˈgame** to do better than sb in an activity in which they think they are strong PHR V **ˌbeat sb/sth ˈdown (to sth)** to persuade sb to reduce the price at which they are selling sth: *I beat down the price to $6 000.* **ˌbeat ˈoff sb/sth**; **ˌbeat it, them, etc. ˈoff** to force sb/sth away: *They have beaten off competition from two large energy groups.*

**ˈbeauty paˌrade** *(BrE also* **ˈbeauty ˌcontest***)* *n.* [C] *(infml.)* an occasion when several competing companies or people try to persuade sb to use their services

**beef** /biːf/ *v.* PHR V **ˌbeef ˈup sth (with sth)**; **ˌbeef it, them, etc. ˈup** to make sth bigger, better, more interesting, etc: *We need to beef up our customer care.*

**beˈginning ˌinventory** = OPENING STOCK

**beˌginning of ˈyear** *n.* [sing.] *(abbr* **BOY***)* *(Account.)* the start of the FINANCIAL YEAR

**behemoth** /bɪˈhiːmɒθ; ˈbiːhɪmɒθ; *AmE* -mɔːθ/ *n.* [C] a very big and powerful organization

**ˈBeige Book** *n.* [sing.] *(Econ.)* in the US, one of the regular reports on the state of the economy in the regions of the US, published by the central bank

**beleaguered** /bɪˈliːgəd; *AmE* -gərd/ *adj.* **1** experiencing great financial problems: *beleaguered banks* **2** experiencing a lot of criticism and difficulties: *the beleaguered chairman*

**the bell** /bel/ *n.* [sing.] *(Stock Ex.)* the sound used to signal when business starts and ends at a stock exchange IDM **aˈlarm/ˈwarning bells** used in expressions to mean that people are starting to feel worried about sth: *These results should set alarm bells ringing.*

**ˈbell curve** *n.* [C] a line on a graph, shaped like a bell, that shows the normal way that measurements are spread when there are a large number of cases chosen without any particular method

**ˌbells and ˈwhistles** *n.* [pl.] *(infml.)* (used esp. about computers, cameras, etc.) extra features that are not really necessary but make a product more attractive to buyers

**bellwether** /ˈbelweðə(r)/ *n.* [C, usu. sing.] **1** sth that helps you to see what will happen in the future: *The company is a bellwether of global industrial trends.* **2** *(Stock Ex.)* esp. in the US, a share, bond, etc. whose changes in price are a good guide to what will happen to the prices of other shares, bonds, etc: *Technology bellwether Sony rose 7.2%.*

**belly** /ˈbeli/ *n.* IDM **go belly ˈup** (*infml.*) if a project or a business **goes belly up**, it fails

**beˌlow the ˈfold** *adv., adj.* (*IT*) in the middle and bottom part of a web page that you cannot see on the screen until you move down in the text: *below-the-fold advertising* → ABOVE THE FOLD

**beˌlow-the-ˈline** *adj.* **1** (*Account.*) relating to unusual costs or income after a company's total profit has been calculated that show its final profit **2** (*Market.*) relating to advertising activities that do not involve the MASS MEDIA, such as direct mail or exhibitions
▸ **beˌlow-the-ˈline** *adv.*: *What costs were taken below-the-line?* → ABOVE-THE-LINE

**ˈbelt-ˌtightening** *n.* [U] the act of spending less money because there is less available: *a period of corporate belt-tightening* → TIGHTEN YOUR BELT at TIGHTEN

★ **benchmark** /ˈbentʃmɑːk; *AmE* -mɑːrk/ *n., v.*
• *n.* [C] **1** a standard, usu. of quality or performance, that other things can be compared to: *Revenue per available room is the key benchmark in the hotels sector.* **2** (*Finan.*) (*also* **ˈbenchmark ˌindex**) a set of share prices that are used to judge the performance of other shares **3** (*IT*) a set of computer programs that can be used to measure what a computer can do and how fast it can do it
• *v.* [T] to find the best performance or process and use this as a standard to improve performance or processes in a company: *Many companies benchmarked Motorola.*
▸ **ˈbenchmarking** *n.* [U]

**ˌbeneficial ˈowner** *n.* [C] (*Law*) the owner of an investment, a property, etc. who has the right to benefit from it, for example, by receiving the profits made from it. This person may not be the legal owner and sb else may keep or look after the investment, etc. for them
▸ **ˌbeneficial ˈownership** *n.* [U]

**beneficiary** /ˌbenɪˈfɪʃəri; *AmE* -ˈfɪʃieri/ *n.* [C] (*pl.* **-ries**) **1** a person who gains an advantage as a result of sth: *the main beneficiaries of the cuts in income tax* **2** (*Law*) a person who receives money or property when sb dies **3** (*Law*) the person that a TRUST keeps and looks after property or money for → TRUSTEE **4** (*Finan.*) a person or company that receives a payment of money: *the beneficiary of a cheque*

★ **benefit** /ˈbenɪfɪt/ *n., v.*
• *n.* **1** [C,U] a helpful and useful effect that sth has: *Internet shopping has real benefits for both the consumer and the environment.*
⊙ *a* ***potential/tangible*** ~ • *an* ***immediate****/a* ***long-term/short-term*** ~ • ***economic/financial/tax*** *~s* • *to* ***derive/get/receive*** *a* ~
**2** [U,C] money that is paid to people who are unemployed, ill/sick, etc., by the government or through a system of insurance: (*BrE*) *to claim unemployment benefit* ◇ (*AmE*) *claiming jobless benefits*
⊙ ***disability/pension/retirement*** ~ • *to* ***apply for/get/qualify for*** ~
**3** (*HR*) [C, usu. pl.] the advantages that you get from your company in addition to the money you earn: *The company offers a competitive* ***benefits package.***
• *v.* (-t- *or* -tt-) **1** [I] to be in a better position because of sth: *Small businesses have benefitted* ***from*** *the new law.* **2** [T] to have a helpful or useful effect on sb/sth: *The new tax laws will benefit people on low wages.*

**ˌbenefit-ˈcost aˌnalysis** = COST-BENEFIT ANALYSIS

**ˈbenefit ˌdollar** *n.* [C] (*HR*) in the US, a unit of tax-free money that a company gives to its employees in addition to their pay so that they can buy a range of benefits such as medical care

**ˌbenefit in ˈkind** *n.* [C, usu. pl.] (*pl.* **benefits** -) (*Account.*) in the UK, a benefit, such as a car, that a person receives from their company as well as their pay, and for which they have to pay tax

**ˈbenefit ˌprinciple** *n.* [sing.] (*Econ.*) a theory that states that the people who benefit more from a government product or service should pay more tax for it than those who benefit less

**ˈbenefits coˌordinator** *n.* [C] (*HR*) a person whose job is to develop and manage the system of benefits that a company offers its employees

**bespoke** /bɪˈspəʊk; *AmE* bɪˈspoʊk/ *adj.* (*esp. BrE*) **1** designed and made for a particular customer: *~ software/solutions* SYN CUSTOM-MADE, TAILOR-MADE **2** making products or providing services according to the needs of an individual customer: *a bespoke ad agency*

**ˌbest-beˈfore date** (*BrE*) (*AmE* **ˌbest-if-ˈused-by date**) *n.* [C] the date by which you are advised to use some types of food and drink, printed on the container or package. Food will be safe after this, but the quality may not be so good

**ˌbest ˈbuy** *n.* [C] a product that has been tested and compared with others of the same type and has been found to be the best product and most worth the money you pay for it

**ˌbest ˈefforts** *n.* [pl.] **1** (*Law, written*) (*BrE also* **ˌbest enˈdeavours**) (*AmE* **-endeavors**) (often used in contracts) all the possible actions that you can take in order to achieve sth: *The software is supported on a best-efforts basis.* **2** (*Finan.*) in the US, if a financial institution (such as an INVESTMENT BANK) uses a **best-efforts** method to sell the shares in a new company, they agree to sell as many shares as they can, but do not promise they will sell them all

**ˌbest-if-ˈused-by date** = BEST-BEFORE DATE

**ˌbest in ˈclass** *adj.* (often used about a company, product or service) the best or most successful of its kind: *best-in-class software*

**ˌbest ˈpractice** *n.* [U,C] the best way of doing a particular task or activity, often recorded by companies in formal documents: *a **code of best practice** for training providers*

**ˌbest ˈprice** *n.* [C] the lowest price that a buyer can buy sth for; the highest price a seller can sell sth for

**ˌbest-ˈseller** (*also* **bestseller**) *n.* [C] a product, esp. a book, that is bought by large numbers of people ▸ **ˌbest-ˈselling** *adj.*

**bet** /bet/ *n., v.*

• *n.* [C] **1** an act of risking money on an investment: *The company is **making** a big bet **on** e-commerce.* **2 a good/safe/sure/fair ~** an investment that is likely to be successful; sth that is likely to happen or be suitable → idiom at HEDGE *V.*

• *v.* [T,I] (**betting, bet, bet**) to risk money on an investment, esp. because you think sth is likely to happen: *Investors have been betting that an economic recovery will come in the second half of the year.*

**beta** /ˈbiːtə; *AmE* ˈbeɪtə/ *n.* [C, usu. sing.] **1** (*IT; Market.*) (*often used as an adj.*) a new product, esp. software, that is in the second or final stage of testing, in which a few customers try it before the public buy or use it: *a beta version of the software* **2** (*Stock Ex.*) (*often used as an adj.*) = BETA COEFFICIENT **3** (*IT, infml.*) = BETA TEST

**ˈbeta coefˌficient** (*also* **ˈbeta**) *n.* [C] (*Stock Ex.*) a measurement of how much the price of a share has changed in a particular period of time, compared with the average change in the price of all shares in the market. A share with a high **beta coefficient** is likely to rise or fall more than the average

**ˈbeta test** (*also* **ˈbeta**, *infml.*) *n.* [C] (*IT; Market.*) the second or final test of a product, esp. a new piece of software, by a few customers before the final version is sold to or used by the public ▸ **ˈbeta-test** *v.* [T] **ˈbeta ˌtesting** (*also* **ˈbeta**, *infml.*) *n.* [U]

**ˌbetter-than-exˈpected** *adj.* (of sales, profits, results, etc.) higher than had been predicted

**beverage** /ˈbevərɪdʒ/ *n.* [C] (*fml.*) any drink that is produced and sold to people

**b/f** (*also* **b/fwd**) = BROUGHT FORWARD

**BFOQ** /ˈbiː ef əʊ ˈkjuː; *AmE* oʊ/ = BONA FIDE OCCUPATIONAL QUALIFICATION

**bi-** /baɪ/ *comb. form* (*in ns and adjs*) two; twice; double: *bilingual* ◇ *bimonthly* **NOTE** **Bi-** with a period of time can mean either 'happening twice' in that period of time, or 'happening once in every two' periods.

**biannual** /baɪˈænjuəl/ *adj.* happening twice a year: *a biannual meeting*

**bias** /ˈbaɪəs/ *n., v.*

• *n.* [U; C, usu. sing.] **1 ~ (against/for/towards/in favour of sb/sth)** if sb/sth has a **bias**, they are likely to prefer or dislike one thing, person or group rather than another, in an unfair way: *Some institutions still have a strong bias against women.* ◇ *to avoid/show (a) ~* ◇ *(an) age/(a) racial ~* **2** if sb/sth has a **bias** towards sth, they usu. choose that course of action rather than another because they believe it is better: *This bank has a bias **towards** lower interest rates.* ◇ *to have/show a ~* **3** (*Finan.*) the way that prices tend to either increase or decrease: *The market bias is positive* (= prices are rising). ◇ *a negative/neutral ~* ◇ *a downward/an upward ~* **4** (*Market.*) mistakes in the results of market research tests or interviews, caused by problems with the number or type of people questioned, the type of questions asked, the attitude of the person doing the research, etc.

• *v.* [T] (**biasing, biased** *or* **biassing, biassed**) **1 ~ sb/sth (towards/against/in favour of sb/sth)** to influence sb's opinions or decisions in an unfair way **2** (*Market.*) to produce market research results that are not accurate: *The size of the sample may bias the results.*

★ **bid** /bɪd/ *n., v.*

• *n.* [C] **1** (*Comm.; Finan.*) an offer to buy sth, esp. a company or its shares; the price that is offered: *a $150 m cash bid **for** the company* ◇ *the **bid battle** for Safeway*

⊕ *to **accept/launch/make/reject** a ~* • *to **increase/raise** a ~* • *a **failed/rival/successful** ~*

**2** (*Comm.*) an offer to do work or provide a service for a particular price, in competition with other companies

⊕ *to **make/put in/submit/win** a ~*

**3** [usu. sing.] **~ (to do sth)** (used esp. in newspapers) an attempt to do sth or to get sth

• *v.* [T,I] (**bidding, bid, bid**)

**1** (*Comm.; Finan.*) to offer to pay a particular price for sth, esp. a company or its shares: *How much did they bid?* **2** (*Comm.*) to offer to do work or provide a service for a particular price, in competition with other companies: *bidding **for/on** the contract*

SYN TENDER ▶ **'bidder** *n.* [C]: *sold to the highest bidder* **'bidding** *n.* [U]

PHR V **ˌbid sth 'up/'down** to pay or offer more/less money for sth than it is worth at the time, with the result that the price increases/decreases

**ˌbid and 'asked** (*also* **ˌbid and 'ask**, *esp. in AmE*) *adj.* (*Stock Ex.*) used to describe the price a dealer will pay when buying particular shares, bonds, etc. and accept when selling them: *Prices are quoted as bid and asked.*

**'bid/'ask spread** = BID-OFFER SPREAD

**'bid bond** *n.* [C] (*Law*) an amount of money that a company that wins a contract agrees to pay if it does not do the work

**ˌbid-'offer spread** (*also* **bid/offer spread**) (*also* **ˌbid/'ask spread, spread**) *n.* [C] (*Stock Ex.*) the difference between the price a dealer will pay when buying particular shares, bonds, etc. and accept when selling

**'bid price** *n.* [C] (*Stock Ex.*) the amount that a dealer will pay when buying particular shares, bonds, etc.

**'bid ˌrigging** *n.* [U] (*Comm.*)

**1** when two or more businesses who are competing to do work or provide services for a company, etc. secretly work together to gain an advantage for themselves and deceive the company buying the work or services. This is an illegal practice. **2** when two or more people agree not to bid against each other at an AUCTION in order to keep the price of the item low. This is illegal.

**biennial** /baɪ'eniəl/ *adj.* happening once every two years

**BIFFEX** /'bɪfeks/ *abbr* **the Baltic International Freight Futures Exchange** a market in London where people buy and sell contracts relating to the cost of transporting particular amounts of raw materials on specific dates in the future

**big** /bɪɡ/ *adj., adv.*

• *adj.* IDM **a ˌbig 'cheese** (*infml.*) a humorous way of referring to an important and powerful person in an organization **the big enchi'lada** (*AmE*) (*infml.*) a humorous way of referring to the most important and powerful person, department, etc. in an organization **a big 'gun** (*infml.*) a person in a particular organization or area who has a lot of influence or power: *They're bringing in the big guns.* **a big 'noise/'shot** (*infml.*) an important person. **the big 'three, 'four, etc.** the three, four, etc. most important countries, companies, etc.

• *adv.* → idioms at HIT *v.*, MAKE *v.*

**ˌBig 'Bang** *n.* [sing.] (*Stock Ex.*) the major changes that were made to the London Stock Exchange in 1986 in order to improve it: (*fig.*) *a **big bang approach** to introducing new computer systems* (=done suddenly and all at the same time)

**the ˌBig 'Board** *n.* [sing.] an informal name for the New York Stock Exchange

**ˌbig 'bucks** *n.* [pl.] (*AmE*) (*infml.*) a large amount of money: *She'll be earning big bucks soon!*

**ˌbig 'business** *n.* [U] **1** large companies which have a lot of power and influence, considered as a group: *links between politics and big business* **2** something that has become important because people are willing to spend a lot of money on it: *Health is now big business.*

**ˌbig 'hitter** = HEAVY HITTER

**the 'big league** *n.* [C, usu. sing.] the most important companies, people, etc. in a particular field

**ˌbig 'name** *n.* [C] a famous company, person, product, etc. in a particular field: *one of the biggest names in sports retailing* ◇ *We want to attract a big-name CEO.*

**ˌBig ˈSteel** *n.* [U] (*infml.*) a group name for the most important steel companies, esp. in the US

**ˌbig-ˈticket** *adj.* (*esp. AmE*) (*infml.*) costing a lot of money: *big-ticket items such as homes and cars*

**ˈbig-time** *adj.* (*infml.*) **1** successful and important: *a big-time lawyer* **2** big: *The company has taken on some big-time risks.*

**bilateral** /ˌbaɪˈlætərəl/ *adj.* involving two groups of people or two countries: *~ agreements/trade* ▸ **bilaterally** /-ˈlætrəli/ *adv.*

**biˌlateral ˈcontract** *n.* [C] (*Law*) an agreement in which both parties agree to do sth for the other

**biˌlateral moˈnopoly** *n.* [C] (*Econ.*) a situation in which a particular service or particular goods are only supplied by one organization and there is only one customer, so the price must be agreed between the two

★ **bill** /bɪl/ *n.*, *v.*
• ***n.*** [C] **1** a piece of paper that shows how much you owe sb for goods and services; the amount of money that you owe
⊙ *a **high/huge/large** ~* ◆ *a **monthly/quarterly/weekly** ~* ◆ ***outstanding/unpaid** ~s* ◆ *to **face/get/send (out)** a ~* ◆ *to **pay/settle** a ~*
**2** (*esp. BrE*) (*AmE usu.* **check**) a piece of paper that shows how much you have to pay for food and drinks that you have had in a restaurant; the amount that you must pay: *Can I have the bill, please?*
⊙ *a **big/huge/large** ~* ◆ *to **ask for/pay/settle** the ~*
**3** (*esp. AmE*) = NOTE (1) **4** (*Finan.*; *Trade*) (*BrE*) = BILL OF EXCHANGE → idioms at CLEAN *adj.*, FOOT *v.*
• ***v.*** [T] **1** to send sb a bill for sth: *You will be billed monthly **for** the service.* **2 ~ sth as sth** to advertise or describe sb/sth in a particular way

**billboard** /ˈbɪlbɔːd; *AmE* -bɔːrd/ *n.*, *v.*
• ***n.*** [C] a large board on the outside of a building or at the side of the road, used for putting advertisements on SYN HOARDING
• ***v.*** [T] (*often pass.*) **1** to advertise sth on a **billboard 2** (*esp. AmE*) to advertise sth: *the most billboarded game of the year*

**ˈbill ˌbroker** (*BrE also* **ˈdiscount ˌbroker**) *n.* [C] (*Finan.*) a person or business that buys BILLS OF EXCHANGE and sells them to banks or keeps them until they are paid

**billing** /ˈbɪlɪŋ/ *n.* **1** (*Account.*) [U] the act of preparing and sending bills to customers: *a billing clerk* ◇ *billing software* **2** (*Account.*) **billings** [pl.] the total amount of business that a company does in a particular period of time, esp. in advertising or insurance: *The company is worth $125 m **in** billings.* **3** [U] the way sb/sth is advertised or described: *the game's billing **as** the hottest on the market*

**ˈbilling ˌcycle** *n.* [C] (*Account.*) the period of time between the bills that a company sends to a customer: *a monthly/quarterly ~*

**ˌbill of ˈentry** *n.* [C] (*Trade*) a list giving details of goods being brought into or taken out of a country: *to file/prepare/present/submit a ~*

**ˌbill of exˈchange** *n.* [C] (*abbr* **B/E**) (*BrE also* **bill**) (*Finan.*; *Trade*) a written order for a person or an organization to pay a particular amount of money to sb/sth when asked or at a particular time, used esp. in international trade: *to accept/discount/draw/make out/sign a ~*

**ˌbill of ˈlading** *n.* [C] (*abbr* **BOL**, **B/L**, **b/l**) (*Trade*) a list giving details of the goods that a ship, etc. is carrying. It shows that the company transporting the goods has received them and allows the buyer to collect them: *a **clean** bill of lading* (= the goods were received in good condition)

**ˌbill of maˈterials** (*also* **ˌbill of maˈterial**) *n.* [C] (*abbr* **BOM**) **1** (*Manufact.*) a list giving details of the materials and parts that are needed for a particular project **2** (*Prop.*) = BILL OF QUANTITIES

**ˌbill of ˈquantities** (*also* **ˌbill of ˈquantity**) (*abbr* **BOQ**, **BQ**) (*also* **ˌbill of maˈterials**) *n.* [C] (*Prop.*) a list giving details of the materials that are needed for a particular building project, with the prices and the cost of doing the work

**ˌbill of ˈsale** *n.* [C] (*abbr* **BS**) (*Law*) a legal document showing that sb has sold an item and that the buyer is the new owner

**ˈbill rate** = DISCOUNT RATE (1)

**ˌbills ˈpayable** *n.* [U; pl.] (*Account.*) part of the financial records of a company that shows the BILLS OF EXCHANGE that the company has not yet paid

**ˌbills reˈceivable** *n.* [U; pl.] (*Account.*) part of the financial records of a company that shows the BILLS OF EXCHANGE that the company will receive money for

**BIN** /bɪn/ = BANK IDENTIFICATION NUMBER

**binary** /'baɪnəri/ *adj.* **1** (*IT*) using only 0 and 1 as a system of numbers **2** (*Tech.*) based on only two numbers; consisting of two parts: *binary codes* ▶ **'binary** *n.* [U]

**bind** /baɪnd/ *v.* [T] (**bound, bound** /baʊnd/) (*Law*) (*usu. pass.*) to force sb to do sth by a legal agreement, a law or an official decision

**binder** /'baɪndə(r)/ *n.* [C] **1** a hard cover for holding loose sheets of paper together: *a ring binder* **2** (*Law*) (*AmE*) an agreement that you sign, which, with a first payment, gives you the right to buy a property for a limited period of time **3** (*Insur.*) (*AmE*) an agreement that an insurance company will provide insurance until a permanent document is provided

**binding** /'baɪndɪŋ/ *adj.* that must be obeyed because it is accepted in law: *The decision is binding* **on** *both parties.* ◇ *a binding agreement*

**biodegradable** /ˌbaɪəʊdɪ'greɪdəbl; *AmE* ˌbaɪoʊ-/ *adj.* (*Tech.*) (about a product or material) that will change back into harmless natural substances and so will not damage the environment when it is thrown away

**biomass** /'baɪəʊmæs; *AmE* 'baɪoʊ-/ *n.* [U] animal and plant material, for example agricultural waste, that is used as fuel in order to produce heat, electricity, etc.

**biometrics** /ˌbaɪəʊ'metrɪks; *AmE* ˌbaɪoʊ-/ *n.* [U] (*IT*) the use of measurements of human features or characteristics, such as fingers, eyes or voices, in order to identify people ▶ ˌ**bio'metric** *adj.*: *biometric passwords* ˌ**bio'metric** *n.* [C]: *The system uses a biometric.*

**biopharma** /ˌbaɪəʊ'fɑːmə; *AmE* ˌbaɪoʊ'fɑːrmə/ *adj.*, *n.* (*infml.*)
• ***adj.*** biopharmaceutical: *biopharma companies*
• ***n.*** [U] biopharmaceutics: *global trends in biopharma*

**biopharmaceutical** /ˌbaɪəʊfɑːmə'suːtɪkl; -'sjuː-; *AmE* ˌbaɪoʊfɑːrmə'suː-/ *adj.*, *n.*
• ***adj.*** connected with the making and selling of drugs and medicines that are produced using living cells: *a biopharmaceutical company*
• ***n.*** [C, usu. pl.] a drug or medicine that is produced using living cells

**biopharmaceutics** /ˌbaɪəʊfɑːmə'suːtɪks; -'sjuː-; *AmE* ˌbaɪoʊfɑːrmə'suː-/ *n.* [U] the study and development of the production of drugs and medicine using living cells

**biotech** /'baɪəʊtek; *AmE* 'baɪoʊtek/ *adj.*, *n.* (*infml.*)
• ***adj.*** relating to BIOTECHNOLOGY: *a ~ company/group*
• ***n.*** **1** [U] biotechnology: *investing in biotech* **2** [C] a BIOTECHNOLOGY company: *profitable biotechs*

**biotechnology** /ˌbaɪəʊtek'nɒlədʒi; *AmE* ˌbaɪoʊtek'nɑːl-/ *n.* **1** [U,C] the use of living cells in industrial and scientific processes: *companies in the biotechnology sector* **2** [U] (*AmE*) = ERGONOMICS (1) ▶ ˌ**bioˌtechno'logical** /-nə'lɒdʒɪkl; *AmE* -nə'lɑːdʒ-/ *adj.*

**BIS** /ˌbiː aɪ 'es/ = BANK FOR INTERNATIONAL SETTLEMENTS

**bit** /bɪt/ *n.* [C] (*IT*) the smallest unit of information that is stored in a computer's memory → BYTE

**biz** /bɪz/ *n.* [sing.] (*infml.*) a business, esp. one related to entertainment or fashion; a company: *the music biz*

**B/L** (*also* **b/l**) = BILL OF LADING

**black** /blæk/ *n.*, *adj.*
• ***n.*** IDM **be, remain, etc. in the 'black; move into, return to, etc. the 'black 1** to be making a profit; to start to make a profit **2** (*Stock Ex.*) if markets or shares are in **the black**, they are higher in value than they were previously OPP BE, REMAIN, ETC. IN THE RED, MOVE INTO, RETURN TO, ETC. THE RED
• ***adj.*** used to describe days on which sth terrible occurs, esp. days when there is a sudden large decrease in the prices of shares: *the disaster of Black Wednesday in 1992*

**the ˌblack e'conomy** (*BrE*) (*AmE* ˌ**underground e'conomy**) *n.* [sing.] (*Econ.*) business activity or work that is done without the knowledge of the government or officials so that people can avoid paying tax on the money they earn

ˌ**black 'hole** *n.* [C, usu. sing.] something that costs you a lot of money or effort but does not provide any real benefit

ˌ**black 'knight** *n.* [C] (*Finan.*) a company that tries to buy another company that does not want to be bought or offers too low a price

**blackleg** /'blækleg/ *n.* [C] (*BrE*) (*infml.*) an offensive way of referring to a worker who refuses to join a strike or who works instead of sb on strike SYN SCAB

**blacklist** /'blæklɪst/ *n.* [C] a list of the people, companies, products or countries that an organization or a government cannot trust and tries to avoid ▸ **'blacklist** *v.* [T] (*often pass.*)

**ˌblack 'market** *n.* [C, usu. sing.] an illegal form of trade in which goods that are difficult to get or foreign money are bought and sold: *Dollars are being sold* **on** *the black market.* ▸ **ˌblack marke'teer** *n.* [C] **ˌblack marke'teering** *n.* [U]

**ˌblank 'cheque** *n.* **1** [C] a cheque that is signed but which does not have the amount of money to be paid written on it: (*fig.*) *The board has been given a blank cheque to buy new assets.* SYN OPEN CHEQUE **2** [sing.] permission or authority to do anything that you think is necessary in order to achieve a particular result

**blanket** /'blæŋkɪt/ *adj.* **1** that includes or affects all possible cases, situations or people: *a blanket ban on tobacco advertising* **2** (*Insur.*) (used about insurance contracts) that pays for damage to different items or for injury to different people, but has only one total sum insured: *blanket cover for machinery*

**bleed** /bliːd/ *v.* (**bled, bled** /bled/) **1** [T,I] (*esp. in the continuous tenses*) (about a company) to lose a large amount of sth, esp. money or jobs: *The business is bleeding cash at the rate of $1 m a day.* **2** [T] to take away a large amount of sb's money or resources: *The banking system has been bled* **of** *resources by the government this year.* IDM **bleed sb 'dry/'white** to take away all sb's money

**ˌblind 'test** *n.* [C] **1** = BLIND TRIAL **2** (*Market.*) a way of deciding which product out of a number of competing products is the best or most popular, or how a new product compares with others. People are asked to try the different products and to say which one/ones they prefer, but they are not told the names of the products.

**ˌblind 'trial** (*also* **ˌblind 'test**) *n.* [C] a type of research that is done to see the effects of a new product, esp. a new medicine. Two groups of people believe that they are testing the product but one group is given a substance that does not contain any of it in order to compare the results with the group who are testing the real product.

**'blister pack** (*also* **'bubble pack**) *n.* [C] (*both esp. BrE*) a packet in which small goods such as pills are sold, with each individual item in its own separate cover on a piece of card

**'blister ˌpackaging** (*esp. BrE*) (*also* **'bubble ˌpackaging**, *AmE, BrE*) *n.* [U] materials used to protect small goods such as pills in their own separate covers on a piece of card; the process of wrapping goods in this way

**bloated** /'bləʊtɪd; *AmE* 'bloʊ-/ *adj.* **1** too big and costing or using too much money: *the company's bloated workforce* **2** (*IT, infml.*) (about software, etc.) not efficient and needing too much computer memory: *bloated applications*

**bloatware** /'bləʊtweə(r); *AmE* -wer/ (*also* **'fatware**) *n.* [U] (*IT, infml.*) software that needs too much computer memory and does not work efficiently

**bloc** /blɒk; *AmE* blɑːk/ *n.* [C] **1** a group of countries that work closely together because they have similar political or financial interests: *a trade/trading ~* **2** (*Econ.*) = CURRENCY BLOC

**block** /blɒk; *AmE* blɑːk/ *n., v.*

• *n.* [C] **1** a quantity of sth or an amount of sth that is considered as a single unit, esp. a large quantity or amount: *a block of seats* **2** (*Finan.*) a very large number of shares or bonds: *a large block of shares*

IDM **be/go on the 'block** to be sold, esp. by AUCTION: *The group's assets are on the block.*

• *v.* [T] (*Finan.*) to stop sb from being able to remove money from their bank account: *a blocked account* → FREEZE

**blockade** /blɒ'keɪd; *AmE* blɑː'k-/ *n., v.*

• *n.* [C] **1** an organized action to stop people or goods from leaving or entering a particular place, often as a form of protest: *to impose/lift a ~* **2** a barrier that stops people or vehicles entering or leaving a place

• *v.* [T] to physically stop people or goods from leaving or entering a particular place, often as a protest

**blockbuster** /'blɒkbʌstə(r); *AmE* 'blɑːk-/ *n.* [C] (*Market.*) something that has great financial success, esp. a book, film/movie or medicine: *a single blockbuster product* ▸ **'blockbusting** *adj.*

**'block ˌdiagram** *n.* [C] a drawing that shows how the different parts of a machine, a system or a process are linked. The parts are shown as squares, etc. with labels.

**'blocking miˌnority** (*also* **'blocking stake**) *n.* [C] a large number of shares in a company that give their owner the power to stop other companies from buying or controlling the company

**ˌblock inˈsurance** *n.* [U] (*BrE*) a type of insurance that a company or an organization buys for all its employees or members

**ˌblock reˈlease** *n.* [U] (*HR*) in the UK, a way of studying or receiving training at a college, etc. while you are working in a job, that involves attending regular short courses

**ˌblock ˈvote** *n.* [C] in the UK, a voting system in which each person who votes represents the members of their organization; the votes themselves: *union leaders with hundreds of thousands of block votes*

**bloodletting** /ˈblʌdletɪŋ/ *n.* [U] (*usu. used in newspapers*) **1** a situation where a company removes lots of employees from their jobs because of serious financial problems **2** a situation where the prices of shares on the stock exchange decrease by a large amount

**blow** /bləʊ; *AmE* bloʊ/ *v.* (**blew** /bluː/ **blown** /bləʊn; *AmE* bloʊn/)
**IDM** **blow the ˈwhistle (on sb/sth)** (*infml.*) to try to stop sth wrong or illegal that sb is doing by telling sb in authority about it → WHISTLE-BLOWER

**blowout** /ˈbləʊaʊt; *AmE* ˈbloʊ-/ *n.*, *adj.* (*esp. AmE*) (*infml.*)
• ***n.*** [C, usu. sing.] **1** a period of great economic difficulty; a sudden decrease in value: *a stock-market blowout* **2** (*Stock Ex.*) a situation when new shares that are being offered are all sold very quickly and the price is high **3** a sudden large increase
• ***adj.*** very successful and making a large profit; very large: *a blowout end-of-year sale*

**ˈBlue Book** *n.* [sing.] (*Econ.*) a report on the economic state of the UK that is published every year

**ˌblue ˈchip** *n.* [C, usu. pl.] (*Stock Ex., infml.*) the shares of the best-known companies on the stock market, which are considered to be a safe investment: *US blue chips*
▸ **ˈblue-chip** *adj.*: *blue-chip stocks*

**ˌblue-ˈcollar** *adj.* connected with workers who do physical work in industry: *~ jobs/workers*

**blueprint** /ˈbluːprɪnt/ *n.* [C] **1** a plan that shows what can be achieved and how it can be achieved: *The system may become a blueprint for the rest of the country.* ◇ *to draft/draw up/provide a ~* **2** a print of a plan for a building or a machine, with white lines on a blue background: *plans and blueprints*

**ˈblue-sky** *adj.* (*infml.*) used to describe new and different ways of thinking about and solving problems, although the ideas produced may not yet be possible or practical

**Bluetooth™** /ˈbluːtuːθ/ *n.* [U] a technology that allows data to be transferred between mobile phones/cellphones, mobile computers and other devices over short distances without the use of wires

★ **board** /bɔːd; *AmE* bɔːrd/ *n.*, *v.*
• ***n.*** **1** [C with sing./pl. v.] a BOARD OF DIRECTORS: *The board is/are unhappy about falling sales.* ◇ *members of the board*
⊕ *to* ***be on/have a seat on/join/sit on*** *the ~* • *to* ***appoint/elect*** *sb to the ~* • *to* ***dismiss/remove*** *sb from the ~*
**2** [C] used in the name of some organizations: *the Welsh Tourist Board*
**IDM** **be above ˈboard** (esp. about a business arrangement) to be legal and honest **be, come, stay, etc. on ˈboard; bring, have, keep, etc. sb on ˈboard** to be, become, stay, keep, etc. sb, involved in sth: *It's good to have you on board* (= working with us). → idiom at TAKE *v.*

**ˌboard of diˈrectors** *n.* [C with sing./pl. v.] the group of people chosen by shareholders to control a company, decide its policies and appoint senior officers

**boardroom** /ˈbɔːdruːm; -rʊm; *AmE* ˈbɔːrd-/ *n.* [C] a room in which the meetings of the BOARD of a company are held: *a boardroom battle* (= a disagreement between directors) *over the future of the company*

**Bobo** /ˈbəʊbəʊ; *AmE* ˈboʊboʊ/ *n.* [C] (*pl.* **bobos**) a young professional who has lots of money and probably works in an Internet company, but who has ideas and attitudes that are different from what is usu. considered normal

**ˈbody ˌcopy** *n.* [U] the main section of text in an article, an advertisement, a web page, etc.

**ˌbody ˈcorporate** *n.* [C] (*pl.* **bodies -**) (*Law*) a group of people, for example an association or a business, that is treated as having its own legal status

**ˈbody ˌlanguage** *n.* [U] the process of communicating what you are feeling or thinking by the way you place and move your body

**ˈbody shop** *n.* [C] (*Manufact.*) **1** the part of a car factory where the main bodies of the cars are made **2** a place where repairs are made to the main bodies of cars

**the ˌB of ˈE** (*also* **ˌBoˈE**) *abbr* (*written*) the Bank of England

**BOGOF** /ˈbɒɡɒf; *AmE* ˈbɔːɡɔːf; -ɑːf/ *abbr* (*Market., usu. written*) **buy one get one free** used in a shop/store to tell customers that they can buy two of a particular item and only pay for one

**ˈboilerplate** /ˈbɔɪləpleɪt; *AmE* -lər-/ *n.* [U] (*esp. AmE*) a standard piece of writing or computer code that can be copied and used in different situations: *This boilerplate wording is used in most employment contracts.*

**BOL** /ˌbiː əʊ ˈel; *AmE* oʊ/ = BILL OF LADING

**ˈbolt-on** *adj.* something that can be easily added to a machine, a website, a company, etc. to enable it to do sth new: *They have added bolt-on e-commerce software to their website.*

**BOM** /ˌbiː əʊ ˈem; *AmE* oʊ/ = BILL OF MATERIALS

**ˈbona ˈfide occuˈpational qualifiˈcation** *n.* [C,U] (*abbr* **BFOQ**) (*HR; Law*) in the US, a reason that employers can give for employing a worker only from a particular group of people if they can prove that other people would not be able to do the job

**bona fides** /ˌbəʊnə ˈfaɪdiːz; *AmE* ˌboʊnə/ *n.* [U] (*Law*) evidence showing that sb is what they claim to be or that what they say is true: *Check the candidate's bona fides.* SYN GOOD FAITH ▶ **ˌbona ˈfide** *adj.*: *a bona fide* (= genuine) *deal*

★ **bond** /bɒnd; *AmE* bɑːnd/ *n.* [C]
**1** (*Finan.*) an agreement by a government or an organization to pay back the money an investor has lent plus a fixed amount of interest on a particular date; a document containing this agreement: *Government bonds* ◇ *the bond market*
● *to* ***buy/hold/invest in/issue/redeem/sell/trade*** *~s* ♦ ***high-yield/long-term/twenty-year*** *~s* ♦ *a ~* ***broker/investor/trader***
**2** (*Law*) (*esp. AmE*) an amount of money that sb pays in case they fail to do what they have agreed to do → BAIL **3** (*Law*) a legal written agreement or promise: *to make/sign a ~* **4** (*Insur.*) a word used for some kinds of insurance policy that protect companies from loss IDM **in ˈbond** (*Trade*) (about imported goods) being held until the buyer pays any necessary import taxes and other charges

**bonded** /ˈbɒndɪd; *AmE* ˈbɑːn-/ *adj.* **1** (*Trade*) (about imported goods) held until the buyer pays any necessary import taxes **2** (*Insur.*) (*BrE*) (about a travel company) having insurance that protects the customer in case anything goes wrong: *an ABTA bonded travel agent* **3** (*Insur.*) (*AmE*) (esp. about a person or company providing a service) having a type of insurance that promises the customer that the job will be done and will be done well

**ˌbonded ˈwarehouse** (*also* **ˌCustoms ˈwarehouse**, *less freq.*) *n.* [C] (*Trade*) a building where imported goods are stored until import taxes are paid on them

**ˈbond fund** *n.* [C] (*Finan.*) a fund where the money is invested in government or company bonds. It pays regular, fixed interest and has a low risk.

**bondholder** /ˈbɒndhəʊldə(r); *AmE* ˈbɑːndhoʊldər/ *n.* [C] (*Finan.*) a person who has bought government or company bonds

**ˈbond ˌrating** *n.* [U,C] (*Finan.*) a system of giving a grade to a bond according to how good and safe an investment it is considered to be; the grade that is given: *A triple-A bond rating guarantees a safe investment.*

★ **bonus** /ˈbəʊnəs; *AmE* ˈboʊ-/ *n.* [C] (*pl.* **-es**) **1** an extra amount of money that is added to a payment, esp. to sb's wages as a reward: *Productivity bonuses are paid to staff meeting agreed targets.*
● *to* ***earn/get*** *a ~* ♦ ***performance/productivity*** *bonuses* ♦ *an* ***annual/end-of year*** *~* ♦ *a* ***loyalty/signing*** *~*
**2** (*Finan.*) a payment in money or shares that a company makes to its shareholders: *The company will issue one bonus share for every share held.* ◇ *~ dividends/shares* **3** (*Insur.*) (*also* **ˌcapital ˈbonus**) a share of its profits that a LIFE INSURANCE company pays to its customers

**ˈbonus ˌissue** *n.* [C] (*esp. BrE*) (*Finan.*) a situation in which a company uses its RESERVES to create new shares, which are then given free to the shareholders in proportion to the number of shares that they already own SYN CAPITALIZATION ISSUE, SCRIP ISSUE

★ **book** /bʊk/ *n., v.*
• ***n.*** [C] (*Comm.; Finan.*) a list of clients and/or investments that a person or a company looks after → BOOKS IDM **by the ˈbook** following rules and instructions in a very strict way: *We do things by the book here.*
• ***v.*** [T] (*Account.*) to record or show sth in a company's accounts: *Last*

*year the company booked a $150 m gain.*

**bookbuilding** /ˈbʊkbɪldɪŋ/ *n.* [U] (*Stock Ex.*) a way of deciding the price of new shares by first asking important investors how many they would be willing to buy and at what price

**ˈbook debt** = ACCOUNTS RECEIVABLE

**ˈbook depreciˌation** *n.* [U] (*Account.*) how much value an asset loses each year, as written in a company's financial records

**ˈbook ˌentry** *n.* [U,C] (*Finan.*) a record kept on a computer system of the names of people who have bought a bond, share, etc.

**ˈbook ˌequity** *n.* [U] (*Account.*) the value of a company as shown in its financial records, which is its assets minus its LIABILITIES SYN BOOK VALUE

**ˈbook gain** = BOOK PROFIT

★**bookkeeping** /ˈbʊkkiːpɪŋ/ *n.* [U] the work of keeping an accurate record of the accounts of a business: *~ entries/errors*
▸ **ˈbookkeeper** *n.* [C]

**ˈbook of ˈfinal ˈentry** *n.* [C, usu. pl.] (*Account.*) an account book or computer record which contains a summary of all a business's financial records for a period of time

**ˈbook of ˈprime ˈentry** *n.* [C, usu. pl.] (*also* **ˈbook of ˈfirst ˈentry**, **ˈbook of oˈriginal ˈentry**) (*Account.*) an account book or computer record in which a company's financial TRANSACTIONS are first recorded

**ˈbook ˌprofit** (*also* **ˈbook gain**) *n.* [C,U] (*Account.*) a profit that has been made but not taken as real money yet, for example shares that have risen in value but have not yet been sold SYN PAPER PROFIT

**ˈbook ˌrunner** = MANAGING UNDERWRITER

**books** /bʊks/ *n.* [pl.] **1** (*Account.*) (*also* **acˈcount books**) the written record of the financial affairs of a business: *to audit/balance/do/keep the ~* SYN ACCOUNTS **2** a record of the customers, orders and stock that a company has: *There are no other large orders* **on the books**.
IDM **ˌcook the ˈbooks** (*infml.*) to put false information in a company's accounts **(be) on sb's ˈbooks** (*HR*) (to be) on an organization's list, for example the list of people who work for a company: *The firm has 10 000 staff on its books.*

**ˌbooks of acˈcount** *n.* [pl.] (*Account.*) the written financial records of a business SYN ACCOUNTS

**ˈbook ˌtransfer** *n.* [C] (*Finan.*) a record kept on a computer system of a change in the ownership of shares, bonds, etc. without using certificates

**ˈbook ˌvalue** *n.* [U; C, usu. sing.] (*abbr* **BV**) (*Account.*) **1** (*also* **ˌwritten-down ˈvalue**) the value that a business gives to an asset in its financial records, which is the original cost of the asset minus DEPRECIATION: *The old photocopier is still useful, although its book value is almost nothing.* **2** the value of a company as shown in its financial records, which is its assets minus its LIABILITIES SYN BOOK EQUITY, SHAREHOLDER EQUITY

★**boom** /buːm/ *n.*, *v.* (*Econ.*)
• ***n.*** [C] a sudden increase in trade and economic activity; a period of wealth and success: *a boom* **in** *sales* ◇ *a ~ period/year (for trade, exports, etc.)* OPP SLUMP IDM **ˌboom and ˈbust** a feature of an economic system or an industry where a period of success and wealth is followed by a period of difficulty, then by another period of success, and so on in a repeated pattern: *IT is an industry prone to boom and bust.* ◇ *a boom-and-bust cycle*
• ***v.*** [I] (about a business or an economy) to have a period of rapid growth; to become bigger, more successful, etc: *Business is booming!*
▸ **ˈbooming** *adj.*: *booming exports*

**boomlet** /ˈbuːmlət/ *n.* [C] (*Econ.*) a short period of sudden trade and economic activity and growth

★**boost** /buːst/ *v.*, *n.*
• ***v.*** [T] **1** to increase sth in strength, number or value: *We've boosted earnings by 18%.* **2** to take actions that will make an economy stronger and encourage business activity: *Low interest rates are boosting the economy.*
• ***n.*** [C, usu. sing.] **1** something that helps to increase or improve sth else: *Low interest rates should give a major boost to home sales.*
⊕ *to* ***get/receive*** *a ~ (from sth)* ◆ *a* ***big/much-needed/welcome*** *~*
**2** an increase: *a boost in exports*
⊕ *to* ***announce/enjoy/experience*** *a ~* ◆ *a* ***big/dramatic*** *~*

**boot** /buːt/ *v.* **1** [T] **~ sth (up)** to start a computer or a piece of software and wait for it to become ready to use: *to boot up your Web browser* **2** [I] (about a computer or a piece of software) to prepare itself for use: *waiting for the machine to boot up*

**bootable** /bu:təbl/ *adj.* (*IT*) (about a computer disk) that contains the basic software that is necessary to start a computer

**bootleg** /'bu:tleg/ *adj., v., n.*
• ***adj.*** made and sold illegally: *bootleg software*
• ***v.*** [T] (**-gg-**) to make and sell an illegal copy of sth ▶ **'bootlegger** *n.* [C] **'bootlegging** *n.* [U]
• ***n.*** [C] a copy of a music recording, film/movie, book or piece of software that is made and sold illegally

**bootstrapping** /'bu:tstræpɪŋ/ *n.* [U] the act of building a business with little outside investment, but with a lot of imagination and effort

**BOQ** /ˌbi: əʊ 'kju:; *AmE* oʊ/ = BILL OF QUANTITIES

★ **borrow** /'bɒrəʊ; *AmE* 'bɑ:roʊ; 'bɔ:r-/ *v.* [T,I] to take money from a person, a bank, etc. and agree to pay it back within a particular period of time, usu. with an amount of interest added: *The group has borrowed €4 bn* ***from*** *banks.* ◇ *to borrow heavily* ◇ *borrowing* ***at*** *a low rate of interest*
**PHR V** **ˌborrow (sth) a'gainst sth** to borrow money by using sth valuable as COLLATERAL: *People are borrowing against their homes.*

★ **borrower** /'bɒrəʊə(r); *AmE* 'bɑ:roʊ-; 'bɔ:r-/ *n.* [C] a person or company that borrows money, esp. from a bank: *We offer the same rates of interest to new and existing borrowers.* **OPP** LENDER

★ **borrowing** /'bɒrəʊɪŋ; *AmE* 'bɑ:roʊɪŋ; 'bɔ:r-/ *n.* **1** [U] the money that a company, person or government borrows; the act of borrowing money: *household borrowing* (= money borrowed by families) ◇ *lower borrowing costs* **OPP** LENDING
◐ ***consumer/corporate*** ~ • ***foreign/government/public-sector*** ~ • ~ ***facilities/requirement(s)*** • *to* ***curb/cut/increase*** ~
**2 borrowings** [pl.] the amount of money that a company has borrowed: *The firm has total borrowings of €7.5 bn.*
◐ *to* ***cut/increase/repay*** ~ • ***bank/long-term/short-term*** ~

★ **boss** /bɒs; *AmE* bɔ:s/ *n.* [C] **1** a person who is in charge of other people at work and tells them what to do: *I like* ***being my own boss*** (= working for myself and making my own decisions). **2** (*infml.*) (often used in newspapers) the person in charge of a company

**the ˌBoston 'Matrix** /'bɒstən; *AmE* 'bɔ:s-/ (*also* **ˌgrowth-share 'matrix**) *n.* [C, usu. sing.] (*Market.*) a way of analysing how successful a range of a company's products or services are by looking at the percentage of sales it has in the market and how fast the sales are growing → CASH COW, DOG, PROBLEM CHILD, STAR

**bot** /bɒt; *AmE* bɑ:t/ *n.* [C] (*IT, infml.*) a piece of software that a computer uses for ordinary or very long tasks, esp. searching for particular information on the Internet

**bottleneck** /'bɒtlnek; *AmE* 'bɑ:tl-/ *n.* [C] sth that slows down development or progress, particularly in business or industry: *eliminating bottlenecks in the manufacturing process*
◐ *a* ***major/potential/severe*** ~ • *to* ***cause/create*** *a* ~ • *to* ***clear/eliminate/remove*** *a* ~

**bottler** /'bɒtlə(r); *AmE* 'bɑ:tlər/ *n.* [C] (*Manufact.*) a company that puts drinks into small containers such as bottles and cans, to sell ▶ **'bottling** *n.* [U]: *bottling plants*

**bottom** /'bɒtəm; *AmE* 'bɑ:təm/ *n., adj., v.*
• ***n.*** **1** [sing.] the lowest or worst level of sth: *He started* ***at*** *the bottom in the company.* ◇ *The decline in demand has now* ***hit bottom.*** **2** [C] the lowest part of sth: ***at*** *the bottom* ***of*** *the screen* **IDM** **the ˌbottom drops/falls 'out of sth** people stop buying or using the products of a particular industry **from the ˌbottom 'up** relying on the ideas and support of the people who have lower positions in an organization **OPP** FROM THE TOP DOWN → idiom at TOUCH
• ***adj.*** in the lowest, last or furthest place or position: *the bottom left-hand corner of the screen* ◇ *the bottom end of the market* (= people who cannot afford to spend much)
• ***v.*** [I] **~ (out)** to stop getting lower or worse ▶ **'bottoming, ˌbottoming 'out** *n.* [U; sing.]

**'bottom ˌfishing** *n.* [U] (*esp. AmE*) (*Stock Ex., infml.*) the activity of buying shares or businesses when the prices are unusually low and are not likely to fall much further ▶ **'bottom ˌfisher** *n.* [C]

★ **ˌbottom 'line** *n.* [C, usu. sing.] **1** (*Account.*) the amount of money that is a profit or a loss after everything has been calculated: *The bottom line for 2005 was a pre-tax profit of €60 m.* ◇ *a bottom-line loss/profit* ◇ *to affect/have an impact on/improve the* ~ **2 the bottom line** the most important thing that you have to consider or accept; the essential point: *The bottom line is that we have to make a decision today.* **3** the lowest price that sb will accept: *Two thousand—and that's my bottom line!*

**ˌbottom-ˈup** *adj.* **1** from or involving the people who have lower positions in an organization or their ideas: *a bottom-up approach to management* **2** starting from the beginning of a process: *bottom-up analysis* OPP TOP-DOWN

**ˌbought ˈdeal** *n.* [C] (*Stock Ex.*) a way of selling new shares or bonds that involves selling all of them to one bank, BROKER, etc., that then sells them to other investors

**ˈbought ˌledger** = PURCHASE LEDGER

**bounce** /baʊns/ *v., n.*
• *v.* **1** (*infml.*) [T,I] if a cheque **bounces**, or a bank **bounces** it, the bank refuses to pay it because there is not enough money in the account **2** [T,I] to increase suddenly in value or level: *The shares bounced 2.7 % to €55.* **3** [I] **~ around/up and down** to repeatedly increase and decrease in value or level **4** [T,I] if an email **bounces** or the system **bounces** it, it returns to the person who sent it because it cannot be delivered.
PHR V **ˌbounce ˈback (from sth)** to increase or become successful again after a period of difficulty
• *n.* [C] a rapid increase: *She predicts a 21% bounce in the FTSE next year.*

**bound** /baʊnd/ *adj.* (*Law*) having a legal duty to do sth: *You are **legally bound** to accept sterling.*

**bourse** /bʊəs; *AmE* bʊrs/ *n.* [C] (*Stock Ex.*) used esp. in newspapers to refer to the stock exchanges of particular countries, esp. France and other countries in Europe

**boutique** /buːˈtiːk/ *n., adj.*
• *n.* [C] **1** a small shop, often with a particular style, selling, for example, fashionable clothes: *a baby/designer/fashion ~* **2** (*Finan.*) = INVESTMENT BOUTIQUE
• *adj.* small and offering a particular or special service: *a ~ hotel/investment bank*

**ˈbox file** *n.* [C] a container for letters, and other documents in the shape of a box

**ˈbox ˌnumber** (*also* **box**) *n.* [C] (*abbr* **Box no**) a number used as an address to which letters can be sent

**BOY** /ˌbiː əʊ ˈwaɪ; *AmE* oʊ/ = BEGINNING OF YEAR

**boycott** /ˈbɔɪkɒt; *AmE* -kɑːt/ *v.* [T] to refuse to buy, use or take part in sth as a way of protesting: *Motorists may boycott the gas stations in protest at price rises.* ▸ **ˈboycott** *n.* [C]: *a trade boycott of British goods*

**bpd** /ˌbiː piː ˈdiː/ *abbr* **barrels per day** a way of measuring how much oil a country or a region produces

**BPO** /ˌbiː piː ˈəʊ; *AmE* ˈoʊ/ = BUSINESS PROCESS OUTSOURCING

**BPR** /ˌbiː piː ˈɑː(r)/ = BUSINESS PROCESS RE-ENGINEERING

**BQ** /ˌbiː ˈkjuː/ = BILL OF QUANTITIES

**bracket** /ˈbrækɪt/ *n.* [C] **1 age, price, income, etc. ~** ages, prices, etc. within a particular range: *people in the lower income bracket* **2** = TAX BRACKET

**ˈbracket creep** *n.* [U] (*esp. AmE*) (*Econ.*) a situation in which the small pay increases that you receive because INFLATION has risen result in you paying higher amounts of tax

**BRAD** /bræd/ = BRITISH RATE AND DATA

**brainchild** /ˈbreɪntʃaɪld/ *n.* [sing.] **the ~ of sb** the idea or invention of a particular person or group of people

**ˈbrain drain** *n.* [sing.] (*infml.*) the movement of highly skilled people from one country, area or industry to another, where they can earn more money or work in better conditions

★ **brainstorming** /ˈbreɪnstɔːmɪŋ; *AmE* -stɔːrm-/ *n.* [U] a way of solving problems or creating ideas in which a group of people think about sth and then discuss all the suggestions
▸ **ˈbrainstorm** *v.* [T,I]

**ˈbrains trust** *n.* [C] (*BrE*) (*AmE* **ˈbrain trust**) a group of experts that provide new ideas and advice to an organization or a government
→ THINK TANK

★ **branch** /brɑːntʃ; *AmE* bræntʃ/ *n., v.*
• *n.* [C] **1** a local office or shop/store belonging to a large organization or company, esp. a bank: *The bank has 170 branches in Brazil.* ◇ *our New York branch* ◇ *assistant branch manager*
⊙ *to **close/set up/open** a ~* • *a **central/high street/local/overseas/regional** ~* • *a ~ **network/office***
**2** a part of a government or other large organization that deals with one particular aspect of its work SYN DEPARTMENT
• *v.* PHR V **ˌbranch ˈout (into sth)** to start to do a new business activity: *We branched out into sports goods.*

★ **brand** /brænd/ *n., v.*
• *n.* **1** [C] a type of product or group of products sold using a particular name, often the name of the company that produces them; the name given to the products: *People tend to go on buying the same brand of break-*

*fast cereal.* ◇ *The company has strong core brands.*

⊙ *a* ***world-class/favourite/leading/major/top*** *~* ◆ ***big/global/popular/well-known*** *~s* ◆ *to* ***build/create/develop/establish*** *a ~*

**2** [C, usu. sing.] a particular type or kind of sth: *the company's particular brand of project management*

• **v.** [T] (*Market.*) (*often pass.*) to give a particular name, design, etc. to a type of product or group of products that you sell: *The phone is branded with the name of the service provider.*

**'brand ˌadvertising** *n.* [U] (*Market.*) advertising that aims to make people aware of and loyal to a particular brand of goods

**ˌbrand associ'ation** *n.* [U,C] (*Market.*) what people think of when they see or hear the name of a particular product: *Safety is Volvo's brand association.* ◇ *positive/strong ~*

**ˌbrand a'wareness** *n.* [U] (*Market.*) to what extent people know about and recognize a particular product

**'brand-ˌconscious** *adj.* (*Market.*) **1** (about people) aware of the most fashionable or famous products and wanting to buy them **2** (about companies) particularly concerned about what people think about the name and image of the company and its products

**branded** /'brændɪd/ *adj.* (about a product) having a label or name that shows it is made by a particular company, usu. a well-known one: *~ drugs/goods*

**ˌbrand 'equity** *n.* [U] (*Market.*) the financial value of a particular brand to the company that sells the product, based on how good people think it is, etc.

⊙ *to* ***build/increase/measure/track*** *~* ◆ ***high/positive/strong*** *~*

**'brand exˌtension** *n.* (*Market.*) **1** [U] using a successful brand name to sell new types of products: *The phone company's strategy includes brand extension into IT products.* **2** [C] a new product that is sold using an existing brand name

**ˌbrand 'image** *n.* [C,U] what people think or feel about a particular product, company name or symbol, etc: *a poor/strong ~*

★ **branding** /'brændɪŋ/ *n.* [U] (*Market.*) the use of a particular name, symbol and design for a company's products so that people will recognize them: *corporate branding*

**'brand ˌlabel** = BRAND NAME

**ˌbrand 'leader** *n.* [C] (*Market.*) the brand of product that has the largest number of sales among products of the same type: *'Lego' is the brand leader* **in** *construction toys.*

▸ **ˌbrand 'leadership** *n.* [U]

**ˌbrand 'loyalty** *n.* [U,C] (*Market.*) the support that people give to a particular brand of product by continuing to buy it rather than changing to other brands: *to build/develop ~* ◇ *powerful/strong ~*

**ˌbrand 'management** *n.* [U] (*Market.*) the way that a company controls how a particular type of product or group of products is advertised and sold to customers

**ˌbrand 'manager** *n.* [C] (*Market.*) a person at a company who is in charge of developing and selling a particular group of products

★ **'brand name** (*also* **'brand ˌlabel**) *n.* [C] the name given to a type of product or group of products by the company that produces or sells them, so that people will recognize them: *The company has a strong brand name.* ◇ *selling brand-name jeans at low prices*

⊙ *to* ***develop/protect/retain*** *a ~* ◆ *an* ***established****/a* ***leading/strong/well-known*** *~*

**ˌbrand perso'nality** *n.* [C] (*Market.*) the attractive and special human qualities that a company wants a product or group of products to suggest to people: *Our task was to create a new brand personality that was younger, livelier and healthier.* ◇ *a distinctive/strong/unique ~*

**ˌbrand recog'nition** *n.* [U] (*Market.*) the extent to which people recognize and value a particular brand: *to build/create/have/lack ~* ◇ *instant/powerful/strong ~*

**ˌbrand 'share** *n.* [U,C] (*Market.*) the amount that a company sells of a particular brand of product compared with other companies: *We expect our brand share to be about 60% by 2008.* ◇ *high/low ~* ◇ *to build/increase/lose ~*

**'brand ˌstretching** *n.* [U] (*Market.*) (often disapproving) using a successful brand name to sell new types of products

**'brand ˌswitching** *n.* [U] (*Market.*) when a customer buys a different brand of a product from the one they usu. buy, or often buys different products: *to encourage/prevent ~*

**brass** /brɑːs; *AmE* bræs/ = TOP BRASS

★ **breach** /briːtʃ/ *n.*, *v.*

• **n.** [C,U] (*Law*) a situation when sb does not do sth that is required by an

agreement, etc. or by law, or does sth that is not allowed: *We are suing the company for breach of contract.*
→ idiom at STEP *v.*
⊙ *(a) **clear/serious** ~ of sth* ♦ *(a) ~ of **agreement/copyright/promise*** ♦ *sth **amounts to/constitutes** a ~*
• *v.* [T] **1** (*Law*) to fail to do what is required by an agreement, a promise or a law: *breaching competition rules* **2** (about a figure) to become higher than a particular amount or level: *The index has breached the 2 000 mark.*

**ˌbreach of ˈconfidence** *n.* [U,C] (*Law*) the act of giving people information that you should keep secret

**ˌbreach of ˈtrust** *n.* [C,U] (*Law*) a failure to take good care of sth that you have been trusted to look after, such as sb else's money or secret information

**ˌbread and ˈbutter** *n.* [U] (*infml.*) a person or company's main source of income: *the bread-and-butter business of the company*

**breadwinner** /ˈbredwɪnə(r)/ *n.* [C] a person who supports their family with the money they earn

★ **break** /breɪk/ *v., n.*
• *v.* (**broke** /brəʊk; *AmE* broʊk/ **broken** /ˈbrəʊkən; *AmE* ˈbroʊkən/) [T] **1** to do sth that is against the law; to not do what you have agreed or promised to do: *They have broken the contract.* **2** to end a dispute or difficult situation, often by using strong action: *break the strike* **3** to reach a higher level or standard than has been done before: *We have broken $100 m in sales.* **4** (*esp. AmE*) to exchange a piece of paper money for coins: *Can you break a twenty-dollar bill?* IDM **break ˈeven** (*Finan.*) if a company or a piece of business **breaks even**, it earns just enough money to pay for its costs **ˌbreak ˈground** (*esp. AmE*) (*Prop.*) when you **break ground** on a new building or the building **breaks ground**, you start building it **ˌbreak new ˈground** to make a new discovery or do sth that has not been done before **ˌmake or ˈbreak sb/sth** to be the thing that makes sb/sth either a success or a failure: *a make-or-break issue* PHRV **ˌbreak aˈbove/beˈlow sth** to become slightly higher or lower than a particular figure or level **ˌbreak ˈdown 1** (about a machine or a vehicle) to stop working because of a fault **2** to fail: *The partnership between the firms is breaking down.* **ˌbreak (sth) ˈdown** to separate into parts that are easier to analyse; to divide sth into parts: *Each task is broken down into step-by-step procedures.* **ˌbreak ˈinto sth 1** to start to operate in a particular area of business: *We're trying to break into the Japanese market.* **2** to reach a particular level of success: *The company should soon break into profit.* **ˌbreak sth ˈoff** to end sth suddenly: *The company has broken off merger talks.* **ˌbreak ˈthrough sth** to succeed in going beyond a particular level or in dealing with a difficult problem: *Their income has broken through the $10 m barrier.* **ˌbreak (sth) ˈup (into sth)** to be divided into smaller parts; to divide sth in this way: *The company will be broken up or sold.*
• *n.* [C] **1** a short period of time when you stop what you are doing and rest, eat, etc: *a coffee/lunch/tea ~* ◇ *to have/take a ~* **2** a short holiday/vacation; a short time when an activity stops before it starts again: *The markets resumed trading after a three day break.* **3** a pause for advertisements in the middle of a television or radio programme: *a commercial break* **4** (*AmE*) a reduction in an amount that you have to pay: *a price break* ◇ *to get/be given a ~* **5** (*AmE*) a TAX BREAK

**ˈbreak clause** *n.* [C] (*Law*) esp. in the UK, a part of an agreement or LEASE that allows you to end it early

**breakdown** /ˈbreɪkdaʊn/ *n.* [C] **1** the failure or end of sth: *the breakdown of the talks* **2** (*AmE also* **ˈbreakout**) [usu. sing.] a list of the details of sth: *a breakdown of the costs*

**ˌbreak-ˈeven** *n.* [U] (*also* **ˌbreak-ˈeven point** [C,U]) (*Finan.*) a time when a company or a piece of business earns just enough money to pay for its costs; the state of not making a profit or a loss: *to **reach** break-even*

**ˌbreak-ˈeven aˌnalysis** *n.* [U,C] (*Finan.*) a way of finding out or studying when a new business or product will start earning enough money to pay for its costs

**ˌbreak-ˈeven chart** *n.* [C] (*Finan.*) a diagram that shows how the profits and costs of a company will increase or decrease according to how much business it does, and when the business or product will reach BREAK-EVEN

**ˌbreak-ˈeven point** = BREAK-EVEN

**ˈbreak fee** *n.* [C] (*Law*) **1** (*also* **ˈbreak-up fee**) esp. in the US, an amount of money that a company must pay if it breaks an agreement to be sold to another company **2** (*AmE*) money you must pay if you end a legal agreement before the agreed time

**ˈbreaking point** *n.* [U,C] (*usu. U in BrE and C in AmE*) the time when problems become so great that a person, an organization or a system can no longer deal with them: *The economy is close to breaking point.*

**breakout** /ˈbreɪkaʊt/ *n., adj.*
• ***n.*** [C] (*AmE*) **1** [usu. sing.] = BREAKDOWN (2) **2** an increase or decrease that is bigger than normal: *We expect a big breakout in new orders next year.* **3** a meeting of a smaller group of people away from the main meeting
• ***adj.*** **1** that is very successful and brings fame to sb/sth: *a breakout product* **2** (*AmE*) that takes place separately from a main meeting and involves a smaller group of people: *breakout sessions*

**breakthrough** /ˈbreɪkθruː/ *n.* [C] an important discovery or development: *a major breakthrough in chip design*
⊙ *to* ***achieve/make*** *a ~* • *a* ***big/significant/technological*** *~*

**ˈbreak-up** (*AmE* **breakup**) *n.* [C] the separation of a large company or group of companies into smaller parts: *the break-up of China Telecom*

**ˈbreak-up fee** = BREAK FEE (1)

**ˈbreak-up ˌvalue** (*BrE*) *n.* [C] (*Account.*) an estimate of the value a company would have if it was sold in separate parts rather than as a single active company

**bribe** /braɪb/ *n.* [C] money, etc. that you give or offer to sb to persuade them to help you, esp. by doing sth dishonest: *to accept/offer/pay/take a ~* ▶ **bribe** *v.* [T]: *He bribed them to stay with a pay rise.* **bribery** /ˈbraɪbəri/ *n.* [U]

**ˌbricks and ˈmortar** *n.* [U] buildings, esp. when you are thinking of them in connection with how much they cost to build or how much they are worth: *bricks-and-mortar businesses* (= with buildings that customers go to) ◇ (*AmE*) *brick-and-mortar businesses* → idiom at CLICK

**bridging** /ˈbrɪdʒɪŋ/ (*BrE*) (*AmE* **bridge**) *adj.* (*Finan.*) used about money that you borrow for a short time until you can arrange a longer loan: *~ finance/loans*

★**brief** /briːf/ *n., v.*
• ***n.*** [C] **1** the instructions that a person is given explaining what their job is: *a* ***design*** *brief for a new product* ◇ *to give sb/prepare/write a ~* **2** (*Law*) (*BrE*) a legal case that is given to a lawyer to argue in court; a piece of work for a BARRISTER: *to accept/prepare a ~* **3** (*Law*) (*AmE*) a written summary of the facts supporting one side of a legal case, that will be presented to a court: *to file/submit a ~*
• ***v.*** [T] **1** to give sb information about sth or instructions to do a particular job: *The director has been briefed* ***on*** *what questions to expect.* **2** (*Law*) (*BrE*) to give a lawyer, esp. a BARRISTER, the main facts of a legal case so that it can be argued in a court

**briefcase** /ˈbriːfkeɪs/ *n.* [C] a flat case used for carrying papers

**briefing** /ˈbriːfɪŋ/ *n.* **1** [C] a meeting in which people are given instructions or information: *a daily/press ~* **2** [C,U] the detailed instructions or information that are given at such a meeting: *briefing papers*

**bring** /brɪŋ/ *v.* (**brought, brought** /brɔːt/) IDM **bring sth into ˈforce** to cause a law, rule, etc. to start being used PHRV **ˈbring sb/sth before sb** (*fml.*) to present sb/sth for discussion or judgement: *The case will be brought before the bankruptcy judge today.* **ˌbring sth ˈdown** to reduce sth: *We need to look at ways of bringing down costs.* **ˌbring sth ˈforward 1** to move sth to an earlier date or time: *The meeting was brought forward by two days.* **2** to suggest sth for discussion: *to bring forward new proposals* **3** (*Account.*) to move a total sum from the bottom of one page or column of numbers to the top of the next **ˌbring sb ˈin** to ask sb to do a particular job or to be involved in sth, esp. to help or advise: *He brought in a team of consultants to sort out the problems.* **ˌbring sth ˈin 1** to make a new product or service available to people for the first time: *We plan to bring in a new range of vans next year.* SYN INTRODUCE **2** to introduce a new law, rule, etc: *bringing in limits on overtime* SYN INTRODUCE **3** to attract sb/sth to a place of business: *Our website should bring in a lot of new business.* **4** (*Law*) to give a decision in a court: *The jury brought in a verdict of guilty.* **ˌbring ˈin sth**; **ˌbring sb ˈin sth** to make or earn a particular amount of money: *The campaign brought in over €6 m in sales.* **ˌbring sth ˈout** to produce sth; to publish sth **ˌbring sth ˈup 1** to mention a subject or start to talk about it SYN RAISE **2** to make sth appear on a computer screen

**brisk** /brɪsk/ *adj.* (**-er, -est**) quick; busy, with a lot of activity: *We are* *doing brisk business in umbrellas today.*

**'British 'Rate and 'Data** *n.* [sing.] (*abbr* **BRAD**) (*Market.*) in the UK, a book published every month that contains information about all the newspapers, magazines and other media that have advertising

**BRM** /ˌbiː ɑːr ˈem/ *abbr* (*AmE*) business reply mail

**broadband** /ˈbrɔːdbænd/ *n.* [U] (*IT*) a system that can send large amounts of electronic data at a very fast speed ▸ **'broadband** *adj.*

**ˌbroad 'banding** *n.* [U] (*HR*) a way of dividing the jobs and ranges of pay in a company into only a small number of levels with a big difference between the lowest and highest pay in each level

**ˌbroad-'based** (*also* **ˌbroadly-'based**) *adj.* based on a wide variety of people, things or ideas; not limited

**'broad ˌmoney** *n.* [U] (*Econ.*) a term used in the measurement of a country's MONEY SUPPLY, that includes more than just notes and coins and the money that people have in ordinary bank accounts → M0, M1, ETC., NARROW MONEY

★ **brochure** /ˈbrəʊʃə(r); *AmE* broʊˈʃʊr/ *n.* [C] (*Market.*) a small magazine or book that contains pictures and information about sth or advertises sth

⊙ ***a marketing/product ~*** ♦ ***to produce/publish/write a ~***

**broke** /brəʊk; *AmE* broʊk/ *adj.* (*infml.*) having no money: *They've gone broke.*

**ˌbroken-'line graph** *n.* [C] a graph that shows data as points joined by lines

★ **broker** /ˈbrəʊkə(r); *AmE* ˈbroʊ-/ *n., v.*

• ***n.*** [C] **1** (*Comm.*) a person or company that buys and sells things, for example shares, bonds, etc., for other people: *a firm of insurance brokers.* ◇ *a money/mortgage ~* **2** (*Stock Ex.*) = STOCKBROKER

• ***v.*** [T] to arrange the details of an agreement: *to broker a deal with sb*

**brokerage** /ˈbrəʊkərɪdʒ; *AmE* ˈbroʊ-/ *n.* (*Comm.*) **1** [U] the business of being a BROKER; the work a BROKER does: *~ services/fees* ◇ *a ~ firm/house* **2** [C] a company whose business is buying and selling things, for example, shares, bonds, etc., for other people **3** [C,U] an amount of money charged by a BROKER for the work done

**ˌbroker-'dealer** (*also* **broker/dealer**) *n.* [C] (*Stock Ex.*) a person or company that sells shares, bonds, etc. for other people and themselves

**broking** /ˈbrəʊkɪŋ; *AmE* ˈbroʊ-/ *n.* [U] (*BrE*) the business or service of buying and selling things, for example shares, bonds, etc., for other people

**Bros** (*also* **Bros.**, *esp. in AmE*) *abbr* (*written*) (used in the names of companies) brothers: *Moss Bros*

**ˌbrought 'forward** (*abbr* **b/f**, **b/fwd**) (*also* **ˌbrought 'down** *abbr* **b/d**) *adv., adj.* (*Account.*) used to describe an amount copied from a previous period or page of accounts: *Enter the amount brought forward.*

**brownfield** /ˈbraʊnfiːld/ *adj., n.* (*Prop.*)

• ***adj.*** used to describe an area of land in a city that was used by industry or for offices in the past and that may now be cleared for new building: *a brownfield site* ◇ *~ development/land*

• ***n.*** [C] **1** (*esp. AmE*) (*BrE usu.* **'brownfield site**) an area of land in a city that was used by industry or for offices in the past and that may now be cleared for new building **2** an area of land that was used by industry and that could be used for new development, but may be affected by dangerous substances

**'brown goods** *n.* [pl.] (*Comm.*) small electrical items such as televisions, radios, and music equipment

**browse** /braʊz/ *v.* [T,I] **1** (*IT*) to look for information on a computer, esp. on the Internet **2** to look at a lot of things in a shop/store rather than one particular thing ▸ **browse** *n.* [sing.]: *to have a browse*

**browser** /ˈbraʊzə(r)/ *n.* [C] **1** (*IT*) a program that lets you look at or read documents on the Internet: *a Web ~* **2** a person who looks at things in a shop/store but may not intend to buy anything

**BRS** /ˌbiː ɑːr ˈes/ = BUSINESS REPLY SERVICE

**BS** /ˌbiː ˈes/ *abbr* **1 British Standard** a number given to a particular standard of quality set by the British Standards Institution: *BS 5750* **2** (*Law*) (*BrE*) = BILL OF SALE

**'B-school** *n.* [C] (usu. used in newspapers) a business school

**'B share** (*also* **class 'B share**) → A/B/C SHARE

**BSI** /ˌbiː es ˈaɪ/ *abbr* **British Standards Institution** an organization in the UK that sets and tests quality and safety standards for industry, esp.

for building, engineering, chemical, TEXTILE and electrical products

**ˌB-to-ˈB** = B2B

**ˌB-to-ˈC** = B2C

**ˌB-to-ˈE** = B2E

**BTW** *abbr* used in informal writing for 'by the way', to introduce sth that is not directly related to what you have been talking about

**bubble** /ˈbʌbl/ *n.* [C, usu. sing.] (*Econ.*) a situation that cannot last in which prices rise very quickly and many people make a lot of money: *They went out of business when the Internet bubble* ***burst***.

**ˈbubble eˌconomy** *n.* [C] (*Econ.*) a temporary situation when businesses grow very fast, the prices of shares, etc. rise and employment increases

**ˈbubble wrap** (*AmE also* **Bubble Wrap™**) (*also* **ˈbubble pack**, **ˈbubble ˌpackaging**) *n.* [U] plastic material containing small bubbles of air, used to protect goods that are easily damaged

**buck** /bʌk/ *n., v.*
• ***n.*** **1** (*infml.*) [C] (*esp. AmE*) a US or an Australian dollar: *They cost ten bucks.* **2 the buck** [sing.] used in some expressions to refer to the responsibility or blame for sth: ***to pass the buck*** (= not accept responsibility for sth) **IDM bang for your/the ˈbuck** (*AmE*) (*infml.*) value for the money that you spend: *You get more bang for your buck with a desktop than with a laptop.* **make a (quick, fast, etc.) ˈbuck** (*infml.*) to make a lot of money quickly and easily
• ***v.*** [T] to resist or oppose sth: *Most share prices fell, but one or two bucked* ***the trend*** *with a small rise.*

**ˈbucket shop** *n.* [C] (*infml.*) **1** (*Stock Ex.*) a company that buys and sells shares without having a licence and often deals in a dishonest way **2** (*BrE*) a company that only provides very cheap air tickets for travellers

★ **budget** /ˈbʌdʒɪt/ *n., v., adj.*
• ***n.*** **1** (*Account.*) [C,U] a plan for a particular period of time of the income and spending of all or part of a company, etc: *Each department sets its own budget.* ◇ *Sales have exceeded budget expectations this year.*
➊ *an* ***annual****/a* ***draft*** ~ • *to* ***approve/draw up/present*** *a* ~ • ***below/on/over/under/within*** ~
**2** (*Econ.*) (*BrE also* **Budget**) [C] the official statement made by a government of the country's income from taxes, etc. and how it will be spent: *this year's Budget*
➊ *the* ***annual/federal/government*** ~ • *a* ***balanced*** ~ • *a* ***tax-cutting/tough*** ~ • *a* ~ ***deficit/surplus***
**3** [C,U] an amount of money that a person or company can spend on particular activities, equipment, etc: *He was given a budget of $1 bn to buy assets.* ◇ *How much is left in the advertising budget?* ◇ *They* ***went over budget*** (= spent too much).
➊ *a* ***generous/small/tight*** ~ • *to* ***have/keep to*** *a* ~ • *to* ***be/come in below/over/under/within*** ~ • *to* ***cut/trim*** *a* ~
• ***v.*** **1** (*Account.*) [T,I] **~ (sth) (for sth)** | **~ sth (at sth)** to plan to spend an amount of money for a particular purpose: *I budgeted for two new members of staff.* **2** [I] to be careful about the amount of money you spend: *If we budget carefully we'll be able to afford the trip.* ▶ **ˈbudgeting** *n.* [U]
• ***adj.*** low in price; selling things that are low in price: *a ~ airline/flight/hotel*

**ˈbudget acˌcount** *n.* [C] (*BrE*) (*Account.*) a type of account, usu. at a bank, that you put fixed regular amounts of money into in order to be able to pay large bills when they are due; an arrangement with a shop/store or company to pay your bills in fixed regular amounts

**budgetary** /ˈbʌdʒɪtəri; *AmE* -teri/ *adj.* (*Account.*; *Econ.*) connected with a budget

**ˌbudgetary acˈcounting** *n.* [U] (*Account.*) a type of accounting that records how a budget is spent and how much of it is left

**ˌbudgetary conˈtrol** *n.* [U] (*Account.*) the process by which an organization plans how much money can be spent on each one of its activities or costs during the next accounting period and then continuously compares the actual amounts with the planned amounts to see if any changes are necessary

**ˈbuffer stock** *n.* [U,C] **1** (*Comm.*; *Product.*) an extra quantity of goods that is kept in case it is needed **2** (*Econ.*) an amount of a product or raw material, owned, for example, by a government, that is stored or sold in order to keep the supply and price of the product level

**bug** /bʌg/ *n.* [C] (*IT*) a problem in a computer system or program: *a* ***bug fix*** (= a program that will remove the problem)

★ **build** /bɪld/ *v., n.*
• ***v.*** (**built, built** /bɪlt/) **1** [T,I] to make sth, esp. a building, by putting

parts together: *a suitable site to build on ◇ The cars are built in Detroit.* **2** [T] to create or develop sth: *building a new career ◇ to build a website* **3** (*IT*) [T] to write a set of instructions for a computer PHRV **ˌbuild sth ˈin**; **ˌbuild sth ˈinto sth** (*often pass.*) to make sth a permanent part of a system, plan, etc: *a PC with a CD-writer built in* **ˈbuild on sth** to use sth as a basis for further progress: *to build on your success* **ˌbuild ˈup (to sth)** to become greater, more powerful or larger in number: *All the pressure built up.* **ˌbuild sth ˈup** to create or develop sth: *She built up a successful business.*

• *n.* **1** [C] the way that sth such as a vehicle is made **2** [C] an increase in the size, amount or degree of sth over a period of time: *a large build in product stocks* SYN BUILD-UP **3** (*IT*) [C] the process of developing a computer program; the program that is being developed: *We do the builds at night.* **4** (*Manufact.*) [U,C] the process of building sth; sth that is built: *We have enough cash for the build.*

**builder** /ˈbɪldə(r)/ *n.* [C] **1** a person or company whose job is to build or repair houses or other buildings **2** (*usu. used in compounds*) a person or thing that builds, creates or develops sth: *a shipbuilder ◇ a good team builder*

**building** /ˈbɪldɪŋ/ *n.* **1** [C] a structure with a roof and walls: *office buildings* **2** [U] the process or work of building: *a building firm ◇ building materials*

**ˌbuilding and ˈloan associˌation** = SAVINGS AND LOAN ASSOCIATION

**ˈbuilding blocks** *n.* [pl.] parts that are joined together in order to make a large thing: *Chips are the building blocks of computers.*

**ˈbuilding reguˌlation** *n.* [C, usu. pl.] in the UK, an official rule that must be followed when building: *to comply with/meet ~s*

**ˈbuilding soˌciety** *n.* [C] (*BrE*) (*Finan.*) in the UK, an organization like a bank that lends money to people who want to buy a home, where you can also save money

**ˌbuild-to-ˈorder** *adj.* (*Manufact.*) made for a particular customer, who chooses what parts, functions, etc. the product will have: *build-to-order computer systems*

**ˌbuild-to-ˈstock** *adj.* (*Manufact.*) made with the same parts, functions, etc. for all customers

**ˈbuild-up** *n.* **1** [sing; U] an increase in the amount of sth over a period of time: *a build-up of household debt* **2** [C, usu. sing.] the time before an important event, when people are preparing for it: *the build-up **to** the conference*

**built** /bɪlt/ *comb. form* (*used after advs and in compound adjs*) made in the particular way or place mentioned: *American-built cars*

**ˌbuilt-ˈin** (*also* **ˌin-ˈbuilt**, *less freq.*) *adj.* included as part of sth: *a phone with a tiny built-in camera*

**ˌbuilt to ˈflip** *adj.* used to describe companies that people create just to make money quickly by selling them soon after they start: *built-to-flip Internet businesses*

**ˌbuilt to ˈlast** *adj.* created or manufactured so that it will last for a long time

**ˈbulge-ˌbracket** (*also* **bulge bracket**) *adj.* (used about INVESTMENT BANKS) largest and most successful

**bulk** /bʌlk/ *n., adj.*

• *n.* [C,U] **1 the ~ (of sth)** the main part of sth; most of sth: *What accounts for the bulk of group profits?* **2** (used about goods such as grain, oil or milk) loose; not packed: *grain transported **in bulk***

IDM **buy/order/sell (sth) in ˈbulk** to buy/order/sell sth in large amounts, usu. at a reduced price

• *adj.* (*Comm.*) in large amounts: *bulk orders of over 100 copies*

**ˌbulk ˈcargo** *n.* [C,U] (*Transpt.*) a large amount of goods carried in a ship loose and not packed in bags or boxes

**ˌbulk ˈcarrier** *n.* [C] (*Transpt.*) a company or a large ship that carries large amounts of goods loose and not packed in bags or boxes

**ˌbulk ˈcash** *n.* [U] a large amount of money in the form of coins and notes/bills

**ˌbulk ˈdiscount** *n.* [C,U] (*Comm.*) a reduction in the price of goods when you buy a large amount SYN VOLUME DISCOUNT

**ˈbulk goods** *n.* [pl.] **1** (*Transpt.*) items that are transported in large amounts and not packed in bags or boxes: *Coal and grain are bulk goods.* **2** large items, for example furniture

**ˈbulk mail** *n.* [U] (*esp. AmE*) advertisements, etc. sent to large numbers of people by post or email

**ˌbulk ˈshipping** *n.* [U] (*Transpt.*) the activity of moving large amounts of goods such as grain or coal, usu. loose and not packed, in a large ship ▸ **ˌbulk ˈshipment** *n.* [C]

★ **bull** /bʊl/ *n.* [C] (*Finan.*; *Stock Ex.*) **1** a person who buys shares, a particular currency, etc., hoping to sell them soon afterwards at a higher price because they think prices are going to rise rather than fall **2** = BULL MARKET → BEAR

**'bullet** /'bʊlɪt/ = BULLET POINT

**bulletin** /'bʊlətɪn/ *n.* [C] **1** a printed report that gives news about an organization or a group **2** a short news report

**'bulletin board** *n.* [C] (*IT*) a place in a computer system where any user can write or read messages

**'bullet point** (*also* **'bullet**) *n.* [C] a black circle, square, etc. at the beginning of each item in a printed list; an item marked in this way

**bullion** /'bʊliən/ *n.* [U] gold or silver in large amounts or in the form of bars

**bullish** /'bʊlɪʃ/ *adj.* **1** (*Finan.*; *Stock Ex.*) connected with, causing or expecting an increase in the price of shares, etc: *a bullish market* OPP BEARISH **2** confident about the future: *a bullish forecast*

**'bull ˌmarket** (*also* **bull**) *n.* [C] (*Finan.*; *Stock Ex.*) a long period during which the prices of shares, etc. are rising and people are buying them OPP BEAR MARKET

**'bull poˌsition** *n.* [C] (*Finan.*; *Stock Ex.*) a situation in which a dealer has bought shares, etc. and plans to sell them later at a higher price SYN LONG POSITION

**'bull run** *n.* [C] (*Finan.*; *Stock Ex.*) a situation where the value of shares, etc. is rising

**'bull ˌsession** *n.* [C] (*AmE*) (*infml.*) an informal discussion

**bumper** /'bʌmpə(r)/ *adj.* (*infml.*) unusually large; producing an unusually large amount: *bumper sales* ◇ *a ~ crop/season*

**bumpy** /'bʌmpi/ *adj.* (**-pier**, **-piest**) IDM **to have/give sb a bumpy 'ride** to have/give sb a difficult time: *The shares have had a bumpy ride* (= have gone up and down in price several times).

**bundle** /'bʌndl/ *n.*, *v.*
• ***n.*** **1** [C] a number of things that belong or are sold together **2 a bundle** [sing.] (*infml.*) a lot of money: *An MBA can* ***cost*** *a bundle.*
• ***v.*** [T] **~ sth (with sth)** to supply a product, service or piece of extra equipment with another at no extra cost OPP UNBUNDLE

**buoy** /bɔɪ; *AmE also* 'buːi/ *v.* [T] (*usu. pass.*) to keep prices or figures at a high or satisfactory level: *Shares rose, buoyed* ***up*** *by strong sales.*

**buoyant** /'bɔɪənt/ *adj.* (about prices, business activity, etc.) tending to increase or stay at a high level, usu. showing financial success: *~ prices/sales* ◇ *a ~ economy/market*
▸ **'buoyancy** /-ənsi/ *n.* [U]

**burden** /'bɜːdn; *AmE* 'bɜːrdn/ *n.*, *v.*
• ***n.*** [C] **1** a duty, responsibility, etc. that causes difficulty or hard work: *Consumers will bear the burden of the price rises.* **2** the fact of having to pay an amount of money; the amount of money that you owe: *the burden of debt* ◇ *a debt/tax ~* SYN LOAD
• ***v.*** [T] (*often pass.*) to give sb a duty, responsibility, etc. that causes difficulty or hard work: *burdened* ***with*** *huge debts*

**ˌburden of 'proof** *n.* [sing.] (*Law*) the task or responsibility of proving that sth is true

**bureau** /'bjʊərəʊ; *AmE* 'bjʊroʊ/ *n.* [C] (*pl.* **bureaux** *or* **bureaus** /-rəʊz; *AmE* -roʊz/) **1** an office or organization that provides information on a particular subject: *an employment bureau* **2** in the US and other countries, a government department or part of one

**bureaucracy** /bjʊə'rɒkrəsi; *AmE* bjʊ'rɑːk-/ *n.* [U] the system of official rules and ways of doing things that an organization or a government has, esp. when these seem to be too complicated SYN RED TAPE

**bureaucrat** /'bjʊərəkræt; *AmE* 'bjʊr-/ *n.* [C] an official working in an organization or a government department, esp. one who follows the rules too strictly ▸ **ˌbureau'cratic** /-'krætɪk/ *adj.* **ˌbureau'cratically** /-kli/ *adv.*

**bureau de change** /ˌbjʊərəʊ də 'ʃɑːnʒ; *AmE* ˌbjʊroʊ/ *n.* [C] (*pl.* **bureaux** - /ˌbjʊərəʊ; *AmE* ˌbjʊroʊ/) an office at a hotel, in an airport, etc., where you can exchange one currency for another

**burgeon** /'bɜːdʒən; *AmE* 'bɜːrdʒən/ *v.* [I] to begin to grow or develop rapidly: *The leisure industry has burgeoned.* ▸ **'burgeoning** *adj.*: *burgeoning demand*

**burn** /bɜːn; *AmE* bɜːrn/ *v.*, *n.*
• ***v.*** (**burnt**, **burnt** /bɜːnt; *AmE* bɜːrnt/) *or* (**burned**, **burned** /bɜːnd; *AmE* bɜːrnd/) **1** (*infml.*) [T,I] to spend a lot of money in a careless way: *The firm was burning* ***(through)*** *cash at a rate of $2 m a day.* **2** (*IT*, *infml.*) [T] to put information onto a computer

disk: *to burn a CD* **3** (*infml.*) [T] **be/get burned** to cause sb to lose money because they do sth without realizing the possible bad results: *We were badly burnt by the rise in fuel tax.* IDM **get your 'fingers burnt**; **burn your 'fingers** to lose money as a result of doing sth without realizing the possible bad results → idiom at CRASH *v.* PHR V **,burn (sth) 'out** to stop working or make sth stop working because it gets too hot or is used too much **,burn (yourself/sb) 'out** to become extremely tired or ill/sick by working too hard over a period of time

• ***n.*** [U,C] (*infml.*) the process of a company spending money: *cash burn* ◊ *a* ***burn rate*** *of $7m a month*

**burnout** /'bɜːnaʊt; *AmE* 'bɜːrnaʊt/ *n.* **1** [U,C] the state of being extremely tired or ill/sick because you have worked too hard: *preventing burnout* **2** [C] (*esp. AmE*) a person who is suffering from **burnout**

★**business** /'bɪznəs/ *n.* **1** [U] the activity of making, buying, selling or supplying goods or services for money: *She works in the computer business.* ◊ *She set up in business as a translator.* ◊ *to* ***do business with*** *sb*
**o** *to* ***go into*** *~* ◆ *~* ***activities/dealings/interests*** ◆ *a ~* ***consultant/executive/guru/leader*** ◆ *a ~* ***deal/transaction*** ◆ *a ~* ***contact/partner*** ◆ *a ~* ***proposition/venture***
**2** [U] work that is part of your job: *He's away* ***on business.*** **3** [U] the amount of work done by a company, etc.; the rate or quality of this work: *Business was bad.* ◊ *Her job was to drum up* (= increase) *business.*
**o** *~ is* ***booming/brisk/slow*** ◆ *to* ***grow/increase*** *~* ◆ *to* ***attract/generate/win*** *new ~*
**4** [C] a commercial organization such as a company, shop/store or factory: *a catering business* ◊ *business premises*
**o** *to* ***have/manage/run/set up/start*** *a ~* ◆ *to* ***build up/grow*** *a ~*
**5** [U] important matters that need to be dealt with or discussed: *the main business of the meeting* **6** [U] the fact of being a customer: *Thank you for your business.* SYN CUSTOM **7** [U] something that concerns a particular person or organization: *She* ***made it her business*** *to help new employees.* IDM **business as 'usual** things will continue as normal in spite of difficulties **,business is 'business** a way of saying that financial and commercial matters are the important things to consider and you should not be influenced by friendship, etc. **get down to 'business** to start dealing with the matter or work that needs to be dealt with **go/put sb out of 'business** to stop or to make sb stop operating as a business because there is no more money or work **in 'business 1** to be operating as a business **2** to have everything that you need in order to be able to start sth immediately: *All we need is a van and we'll be in business.* → idioms at LAND OFFICE, ORDER *n.*

**,business admini'stration** *n.* [U] the study or practice of planning, organizing and running a business

**'business ,agent** *n.* [C] **1** a person whose job is to represent another person in business matters: *our business agent in China* **2** (*HR*) in the US, a member of a union who represents all the members from one company

**'business ,analyst** = COMPUTER ANALYST

**'business ,angel** = ANGEL INVESTOR

★**'business card** (*also* **card**) *n.* [C] a small card printed with sb's name and the details of their job and company: *to exchange/swap ~s*

**'business case** *n.* [C] (*Finan.*) a document that presents the reasons that show why a product, project, etc. would be successful and make money: *to build a business case for sth*

**'business ,centre** *n.* [C] a place that people can pay to use for work, meetings, etc. away from their place of work

**'business class** *n.* [U] the part of a plane, etc. where passengers have a high level of comfort and service, designed for people travelling on business ▸ **'business class** *adv.*: *to fly business class*

**'business ,college** *n.* [C] a college where students can learn basic business skills, such as accounting, managing an office, etc.

**'business combi,nation** *n.* [U,C] **~ (with sb)** the act of joining or working with another company after a TAKEOVER or MERGER

**,business conti'nuity** *n.* [U] the process of making sure that the important parts of a business continue working if there is a disaster: *~ planning/management/services*

**'business ,cycle** *n.* [C] (*Econ.*) the usual pattern of a country's economy over a period of time, with periods of success and difficulty happening regularly one after another SYN ECONOMIC CYCLE, TRADE CYCLE

**ˈbusiness day** *n.* [C] a day when stock exchanges and banks are open

**ˈbusiness debt** (*also* **ˈtrade debt**) *n.* [U,C] (*Account.*) money that one company owes to others

**ˈbusiness ˌentity** *n.* [C] a business of a particular type, for example a PARTNERSHIP, a LIMITED COMPANY, etc.

**ˌbusiness ˈentity ˌconcept** *n.* [C] (*Account.*) the idea that a business is separate from the people who own it, so that the financial records only show the activities of the business, not the owners

**ˈbusiness game** (*also* **ˈmanagement game**) *n.* [C] (*HR*) a way of training people, esp. managers, in business skills that asks teams to deal with situations that could exist in reality

**ˈbusiness hours** *n.* [pl.] the times of day when a shop/store, an office, a bank, etc. is open: *Business hours are between 9 a.m. and 5 p.m.*

**ˌbusiness interˈruption** *n.* [U] (*Insur.*) a situation where a company loses money when it has to stop work because of a disaster

**businesslike** /ˈbɪznəslaɪk/ *adj.* (about a person) working in an efficient and organized way: *She has a brisk and businesslike manner.*

**ˈbusiness lunch** *n.* [C] a meeting with lunch to talk about business or to entertain customers

★ **businessman** /ˈbɪznəsmæn; -mən/, **businesswoman** /ˈbɪznəswʊmən/ *n.* [C] (*pl.* **-men** /-men; -mən/**-women** /-wɪmɪn/) **1** a person who works in business, esp. at a high level: *a leading/prominent/successful/wealthy* ~ **2** a person who is skilful in business and financial matters: *an astute/a good/shrewd/tough* ~ **NOTE** **Business people** is used to talk about a group of men and women, or to avoid having to say 'businessmen' or 'businesswomen'. **Business person/people** is also used in more formal language.

**ˈbusiness mix** *n.* [C] the types of product and/or customer that form a company's business

**ˈbusiness park** *n.* [C] an area of land, usu. outside a town or city, that is designed for offices and small factories

**ˈbusiness plan** *n.* [C] (*Finan.*) a written document that states what a company aims to do to sell its products, develop new products, etc. within a particular period, and how it will get the money it needs: *to draw up/develop/write a* ~

**ˌbusiness ˈprocess** *n.* [C] the systems, the way things are organized and the order in which things are done in a company to produce a product or service

**ˈbusiness ˈprocess outˈsourcing** *n.* [U] (*abbr* **BPO**) the practice of giving the responsibility for running a particular system or a service to people outside the company

**ˈbusiness ˈprocess ˌreengiˈneering** (*also* **ˈbusiness ˈprocess ˌredeˈsign**) *n.* [U] (*abbr* **BPR**) a method of improving a business and its value to customers by organizing its systems and the way things are done in a new and different way, esp. in order to make full use of computer systems: *to apply/implement/introduce* ~

**ˌbusiness reˈply ˌservice** *n.* [C] (*BrE*) (*abbr* **BRS**) (*AmE* **ˌbusiness reˈply mail** [U] (*abbr* **BRM**) a service that allows a company to supply cards or envelopes with its address on that people can use for replying without paying the POSTAGE. The company only pays for the ones sent back.

**ˈbusiness school** *n.* [C,U] a college, or part of a college or university, that teaches BUSINESS STUDIES

**ˈbusiness sense** *n.* **1** [U] action that may help to make a business make money, be efficient, etc: *It makes good business sense to keep employees happy.* **2** [sing; U] a good understanding and judgement of business: *He has a **sharp** business sense.*

**ˈbusiness ˌstrategy** *n.* [C] a plan for what a business wants to achieve and how they will do it that joins together all the different parts of the business

**ˈbusiness ˌstudies** *n.* [pl.] the study of subjects connected with money and managing a business

**ˌbusiness ˈsystems ˌanalyst** = SYSTEMS ANALYST

**ˈbusiness trip** *n.* [C] a journey to a place and back again in order to do business: *He's gone on a business trip to Greece.*

**ˈbusiness trust** *n.* [C] (*Finan.*) (in the US) an association that manages investments, property, etc. for businesses and people involved in them

★ **bust** /bʌst/ *adj., n., v.*
• ***adj.*** (*infml.*) (about a business or a person) failed because of a lack of money: *The company has **gone bust**.*
• ***n.* 1** (*Econ., infml.*) [C, usu. sing., U] a time when a period of economic

success ends suddenly: *the dot-com bust* **2** (*infml.*) [C] (*esp. AmE*) a person or thing that fails: *The plan was a bust.* → idiom at BOOM *n.*

• *v.* [T] (*infml.*) to make sth fail; to break sth: *The tax cuts could bust the budget.*

**busy** /ˈbɪzi/ *adj.* (**busier**, **busiest**) **1** having a lot of work to do; not free to do sth else because you are working on sth **2** spending a lot of time on sth **3** full of people, activity, vehicles, etc: *one of Europe's busiest airports* **4** full of work and activity: *Summer is our busiest season.*

**button** /ˈbʌtn/ *n.* [C] **1** a small part of a machine that you press to make it work: *You can get the figures* ***at the touch of a button.*** **2** (*IT*) a small place on a computer screen that you click on to make it work **3** (*Market.*) = BUTTON AD

**ˈbutton ad** (*also* **ˈbutton adˌvertisement**, **ˈbutton**) *n.* [C] (*Market.*) an advertisement in the form of a small square or circle on a web page

**ˈbuttoned-down** (*also* **ˈbutton-down**) *adj.* (*both esp. AmE*) used to describe a traditional approach to business: *a conventional, buttoned-down executive*

★ **buy** /baɪ/ *v.*, *n.*

• *v.* [T,I] (**bought**, **bought** /bɔːt/) **~ sth (for sb)** | **~ sb sth 1** to obtain sth by paying money for it: *They bought the company for $3 bn.* ◊ *If you need a new car, now is a good time to buy.* **2** (about money) to be enough to pay for sth: *In 2001, €1 would buy you $1.65.* → idiom at BULK *n.* **PHR V** **ˌbuy sth ˈin 1** (*BrE*) if a company **buys sth in**, it buys it from another company **2** to buy shares or bonds in a company, esp. for the first time **ˌbuy ˈinto sth 1** to buy shares in a company, esp. in order to gain some control over it **2** to invest in something: *It's a good time to buy into the stock.* **3** to believe that an idea is good or that a plan will be successful **ˌbuy sb ˈout** to pay money for someone to be freed from a contract **ˌbuy sb/sth ˈout** to buy sb's share in a company, usu. in order to get total control of it for yourself **ˌbuy sth ˈup** to buy all or as much as possible of sth, esp. because it is cheap

• *n.* **1** [C] sth that is bought or that is for sale: ***a good buy*** (= sth that is worth the money you pay for it) **2** (*Stock Ex.*) [U; sing.] = BUY RATING **3** (*Stock Ex.*) [C] = BUY ORDER

**ˈbuy-back** (*also* **buyback**) *n.* [U,C] **1** (*Comm.*) an act of buying sth from the person that you sold it to **2** (*Finan.*) a situation where a company buys its shares back from the people who own them, in order to reduce the number of its shares available, to reduce its debt, etc: *a 15% share buy-back* ◊ *buy-back contracts* SYN BUY-IN **3** (*Finan.*) a situation when a government reduces its country's debt to foreign banks by buying some of it back: *a debt buy-back plan* SYN REPURCHASE

★ **buyer** /ˈbaɪə(r)/ *n.* [C] **1** a person or company that buys sth, esp. something valuable like a business or a home: *a potential/prospective ~* ◊ *car/computer/home ~s* **2** the person or company that buys sth, rather than the person who sells it: *brokers who link* ***buyers and sellers*** **3** (*Comm.*) a person in a company who chooses the goods, equipment or materials that the company buys: *a buyer for a department store* **IDM** **buyer beˈware** (*also* **let the buyer beˈware**) (*Law*) used to say that when you are buying something it is your responsibility to check that there is nothing wrong with what you are buying → CAVEAT EMPTOR

**ˌbuyer concenˈtration** *n.* [C,U] (*Econ.*) the extent to which a large percentage of an industry's products are bought by only a small number of buyers: *The* ***lower*** *the buyer concentration* (= the more buyers there are) *the better it is for your industry.* ◊ *high/low ~*

**ˈbuyer ˌpower** *n.* [U] (*Econ.*) the amount that buyers are able to influence price

**ˈbuyer risk** (*also* **ˈbuyer's risk**) *n.* [U] (*Comm.*) the risk that sb takes when buying sth, for example that the goods will not be supplied or will be of poor quality

**ˌbuyer's ˈmarket** *n.* [C, usu. sing.] a situation where the price of a particular item is low and people have a choice, because there are more people selling the item than people who want to buy it OPP SELLER'S MARKET

**ˌbuyer's ˈrisk** *n.* [U] **1** (*Trade*) if goods are sent **at buyer's risk**, the buyer has to insure the goods during transport **2** (*Comm.*) = BUYER RISK

**ˌbuyer's ˈsurplus** = CONSUMER SURPLUS

**ˈbuy-in** *n.* **1** (*Finan.*) [C] a situation where a group of people from outside a company buy more than 50% of its shares because they want to take over the management **2** [U] support for an idea from other people **3** (*Finan.*) [C] a situation where a company buys its shares back from the people who own them SYN BUY-BACK

★ **buying** /ˈbaɪɪŋ/ *n.* [U] **1** the activity of getting sth by paying money for it: *online buying* ◇ *the buying habits of customers* **2** the activity of choosing the goods, equipment or materials that a company or shop/store buys: *I do my own buying for my store.*

**ˈbuying ˌagent** *n.* [C] (*Trade*) a person or company whose job is to find and buy sth for sb else

**ˈbuying ˌcentre** *n.* [C] **1** the group of people who make decisions about buying things for a company SYN DECISION-MAKING UNIT **2** (*Comm.*) (*often with another n.*) a place where a lot of a particular product can be bought: *a diamond buying centre*

**ˈbuying deˌcision** *n.* [C] the process involved in deciding to buy a particular product

**ˈbuying ˌorder** = BUY ORDER

**ˈbuying ˌpower** *n.* [U] **1** the amount of money that a person or business has available for buying goods and services **2** the amount of goods and services that a currency can buy at a particular time: *the dollar's buying power* SYN PURCHASING POWER

**ˈbuying price** *n.* [C, usu. sing.] **1** (*Comm.*) the price at which you can buy sth **2** (*Finan.*) the price at which an investor or a dealer will or can buy particular shares, bonds, etc. SYN PURCHASE PRICE

**ˈbuying ˌsignals** *n.* [pl.] words, movements or actions that show that sb is ready to buy sth

**ˈbuy limit ˌorder** *n.* [C] (*Stock Ex.*) an instruction to a BROKER to buy a number of shares, bonds, etc. at a particular price or lower: *to execute/place a ~*

**ˈbuy ˌorder** (*also* **buy**, **ˈbuying ˌorder**) *n.* [C] (*Stock Ex.*) an instruction to a BROKER to buy a particular number of shares, bonds, etc: *to execute/place a ~*

**buyout** /ˈbaɪaʊt/ *n.* [C] (*Finan.*) a situation in which a person or group gains control of a company or part of it by buying all or most of its shares
**⊙** ***to accept/fund/lead/reject** a ~* ◆ *a ~ **bid/deal/offer***

**ˈbuy ˌrating** *n.* [C] (*also* **buy** [U; sing.]) (*Stock Ex.*) a statement made by a bank, a dealer, etc. that a particular company's shares are worth buying: *to have/put a ~ on sth*

**ˈbuy ˌsignal** *n.* [C] (*Stock Ex.*) a situation where the pattern of recent movements in a share price indicates that it is a good time to buy shares: *to generate/give a ~*

**ˈbuzz group** *n.* [C] (*Market.*) one of the small groups of people that a large group can be divided into in order to discuss a particular subject

**ˈbuzz ˌmarketing** *n.* [U] (*Market.*) a form of marketing where a company creates interest in a new product by persuading interested users or websites to pass on the message about it to others SYN VIRAL MARKETING

**buzzword** /ˈbʌzwɜːd; *AmE* -wɜːrd/ (*also* **ˈbuzz-phrase**) *n.* [C] a word or phrase, esp. one connected with a particular subject, that has become fashionable and popular and is used a lot in newspapers

**BV** /ˌbiː ˈviː/ = BOOK VALUE

**ˈby-law** *n.* [C] (*Law*) **1** (*AmE also* **bylaw**) (*BrE also* **bye-law**) an official rule made by an organization for its members **2** (*usually* **Bylaws** [pl.]) (*AmE*) one of the legal documents created when a company is formed. It contains rules about how the company must be managed, what rights shareholders have, what the directors can do and what formal meetings must be held. SYN ARTICLES OF ASSOCIATION **3** (*esp. BrE*) a law that is made by a local authority only for that area

**ˈby-ˌproduct** (*also* **byproduct**) *n.* [C] **1** a substance produced during the process of making or destroying sth else **2** sth that happens, often unexpectedly, as the result of sth else

**byte** /baɪt/ *n.* [C] (*IT*) a unit of information stored in a computer, equal to 8 BITS. A computer's memory is measured in **bytes**.

# Cc

**C2C** (*also* **c2c**, **C-to-C**) /ˌsiː tə ˈsiː/ *adj.* (*E-comm.*) **consumer-to-consumer** used to describe the buying, selling and exchanging over the Internet of products, services or information between individuals: *C2C commerce*

**C2DE** /siː ˌtuː diː ˈiː/ *n.* [U] (*BrE*) (*Market.*) the lower three social and economic groups in a society, used to refer to these groups as possible customers for particular products → ABC1

**cable** /ˈkeɪbl/ *n.* **1** [C,U] a set of wires, covered in plastic or rubber, that carries electricity, telephone signals, etc. **2** (*IT*) [U] = CABLE TELEVISION **3** (*IT*) [U] a way of connecting a computer to the Internet using a **cable**: *fast cable connections*

**ˈcable ˌcompany** *n.* [C] a company that provides services such as television, the Internet, etc. by using underground cables

**ˌcable ˈtelevision** (*also* **ˈcable**) (*AmE also* **comˌmunity anˈtenna ˌtelevision**) *n.* [U] a service that uses a system of wires to broadcast television programmes

**ˌcable ˈtransfer** = WIRE TRANSFER

**CAC 40** /ˌkæk ˈfɔːti; ˌsiː eɪ siː -; *AmE* -ˈfɔːrti/ *n.* [sing.] a measurement of how well the Paris stock exchange is performing, calculated using the share prices of the 40 largest companies on the stock exchange

**cache** /kæʃ/ *n.* [C] (*IT*) a part of a computer's memory that stores copies of data so that the data can be found very quickly ▸ **cache** *v.* [T]: *cached data*

**CAD** *abbr* **1** /kæd/ (*IT*) computer-aided design; computer-assisted design **2** /ˌsiː eɪ ˈdiː/ (*Trade*) cash against documents

**CAE** /ˌsiː eɪ ˈiː/ *abbr* (*Manufact.*) computer-aided engineering; computer-assisted engineering

**C & F** *abbr* (*Trade, written*) carriage and freight

**cafeteria** /ˌkæfəˈtɪəriə; *AmE* -ˈtɪr-/ *n.* [C] a restaurant, esp. one for staff or workers, where people choose and collect their meals and carry them to their tables

**cafeˈteria plan** *n.* [C] (*also* **cafeˈteria ˌbenefits** [pl.]) (*HR*) a system that allows employees to choose the benefits, such as health insurance, etc. that they receive in addition to their pay, up to a particular amount of money

★**calculate** /ˈkælkjuleɪt/ *v.* [T] **1** to use numbers to find out a total number, amount, distance, etc: *calculating the interest on a loan* **2** to guess sth or form an opinion by using all the information available: *We calculated that the advantages would be greater than the disadvantages.*

**calculator** /ˈkælkjuleɪtə(r)/ *n.* [C] **1** a small electronic device for **calculating** with numbers **2** (*IT*) a piece of software used for **calculating** difficult things, such as income tax

**calendar** /ˈkælɪndə(r)/ *n.* [C] **1** a page or series of pages showing the days, weeks and months of a particular year, esp. one that you hang on a wall **2** (*AmE*) a record of what you have to do each day; the book or computer system where you keep this SYN DIARY, APPOINTMENT BOOK **3** [usu. sing.] a list of important events or dates during the year: *the busiest day in the City's calendar* **4 calendar 2006, 2007, etc.** (*AmE*) = CALENDAR YEAR

**ˌcalendar ˈmonth** *n.* [C] **1** one of the 12 months of the year **2** a period of time from a particular date in one month to the same date in the next one

**ˌcalendar ˈyear** (*AmE also* **calendar 2006, 2007, etc.**) *n.* [C] the period of time from 1 January to 31 December in the same year

★**call** /kɔːl/ *v., n.*

• *v.* **1** [I] (*esp. BrE*) **~ (on sb/in)** to make a short visit to a person or place: *When did the sales rep call?* **2** [T] to order sth to happen; to announce that sth will happen: *to ~ a meeting/strike* **3** [T] to predict sth: *to call the bottom of the market* (= predict that the prices of shares, etc. will begin to rise) **4** [T] (*often pass.*) to order sb to come to a place: *be called for interview* **5** (*Finan.*) [T] **~ sth (back/in)** to demand that sb immediately pays back the money they owe: *The bank has called the €460 m loan.* **6** (*Finan.*) [T] **~ a bond | ~ in a bond** to pay back the money that was borrowed with a bond **7** (*Law*) [T] to require sb to give evidence to a court or to government officials: *to call a witness* IDM **call in the reˈceivers** to appoint an independent person to manage the financial affairs of a business because it is unable to pay its debts **call sb/sth to ˈorder** to ask people in a meeting to be quiet so that the meeting can start or continue **ˌcall the ˈshots/ˈtune** (*infml.*) to be the person who controls a situation → idiom at PLAY *n.* PHR V **ˈcall for sth**; **ˈcall for sb to do sth** to publicly ask for sth to happen; to need sth: *The business plan calls for further cost reductions.* **ˌcall ˈin** to telephone the place where you work: *Several people have called in sick today.* **ˌcall sb ˈin** to ask for the services of sb: *We called in consultants.* **ˌcall sth ˈin** (*Comm.*) to order or ask for the return of sth SYN RECALL **ˌcall sth ˈoff** to cancel sth; to decide that sth will not happen **ˈcall on/upon sb 1** to ask or demand that sb do sth: *You might be called on to assist.* **2** to formally invite or ask sb to speak: *I now call upon the chairman to address the meeting.* **ˌcall sth ˈup** to use sth that is stored or kept available: *I called up his address on the computer.*

• *n.* **1** [C] a short visit to sb's house: *making calls* ◇ *to* ***pay a call on*** *a client* **2** [C] a request, an order or a demand for sth: *calls* ***for*** *a cut in interest rates* **3** [sing.] **a ~ on sth | no ~ for sth** the demand for sth; no demand for sth: *There isn't a lot of call for small specialist stores these days.* **4** [C] a decision; an act of predicting sth: *It's your call!* ◇ *Traders have made some bad calls recently.* **5** (*Finan.*) [C] = CALL OPTION **6** (*Finan.*) [C] a situation in which a company asks shareholders to pay part of the money that they owe for their shares IDM **at/on ˈcall** if your money is **at/on call** with a bank, you can have it when you like, but you must warn the bank first

**callable** /ˈkɔːləbl/ *adj.* (*Finan.*) if a bond or a similar investment is **callable**, the company or government that sold it can buy it back early at an agreed price OPP NON-CALLABLE

**ˈcall acˌcount** (*also* **ˌcall deˈposit acˌcount**) *n.* [C] (*BrE*) a type of bank account used for investing money that pays a higher rate of interest than a normal bank account. You can have your money when you like, but you may have to warn the bank first.

**callback** /ˈkɔːlbæk/ *n.* **1** (*HR*) [C] (*esp. AmE*) an occasion when sb is asked to return somewhere, esp. for a second interview for a job; a second interview **2** [C] a telephone call to sb who has just called you or to sb you have called earlier **3** [C] an occasion when people are asked to return goods that they have bought, usu. because they are not safe **4** [C] (*AmE*) an occasion when sb is asked to go back to work, esp. to deal with a sudden serious or dangerous situation **5** (*IT*) (*also* **ˈdial-back**) [U] a process in which sb LOGS ON to a company computer system which then calls their computer back, used for security or to reduce telephone costs

**ˈcallback pay** = CALL-IN PAY

**ˈcall ˌcentre** *n.* [C] an office in which a large number of people work using telephones, for example doing market research, or taking orders and answering questions for a large organization

**ˌcall deˈposit acˌcount** (*also* **ˈcall deˌposit**) = CALL ACCOUNT

**ˌcalled-up ˈcapital** (*also* **ˌcalled-up ˈshare ˌcapital**) *n.* [U] (*BrE*) (*Finan.*) the amount of money that a company has asked shareholders to pay for their shares at a particular time, when the full payment is made over a period of time

**caller** /ˈkɔːlə(r)/ *n.* [C] a person who is making a telephone call

**ˌcaller disˈplay** (*BrE*) (*AmE* **ˌcaller IˈD**) *n.* [U] a system that uses a device on your telephone to identify and display the telephone number of the person calling

**ˈcall ˌfeature** = CALL PROVISION (1)

**ˌcall ˈforwarding** *n.* [U] the ability of a telephone system to transfer a call to another telephone automatically

**ˈcalling card** *n.* [C] (*esp. AmE*) **1** a card that you buy in order to make telephone calls from public telephones, etc. It allows you to make calls up to the amount that you have paid **2** a card that you use to make telephone calls from public telephones, etc. that you pay for later with your home telephone bill

**ˈcall-in pay** (*also* **ˈcallback pay, reˈporting pay**) *n.* [U] (*all AmE*) (*HR*) an amount of money paid to workers who are asked to go to work outside their usual hours, even if there is no work for them

**ˈcall ˌmoney** *n.* [U] (*Finan.*) money that a bank invests for short periods of time and can get back whenever it demands

**ˈcall ˌoption** (*also* **call**) *n.* [C] (*Finan.*) a right to buy sth, such as a number of shares in a company or a quantity of raw materials, at a particular price within a fixed period or on a particular date → PUT OPTION

**ˈcall proˌvision** *n.* [C] (*Finan.*) **1** (*also* **ˈcall ˌfeature**) a section in a bond contract that allows the seller to buy the bond back early **2** part of an arrangement for a loan that allows the bank to demand full payment early if payments have not been made, or if a business has not achieved the results it expected

**ˈcall ˌrouting** *n.* [U] (*IT*) **1** the process by which a customer is connected to a particular place or person through a single central number **2** the ability to transfer calls from one telephone to another

**ˈcall ˌwaiting** *n.* [U] the ability of a telephone system to keep a person calling you waiting while you deal with another telephone call

**CAM** /kæm/ *abbr* [U] (*IT; Manufact.*) computer-aided manufacturing; computer-assisted manufacturing

★**campaign** /kæm'peɪn/ *n., v.*
• *n.* [C] a series of planned activities to persuade people to buy or to do something: *They launched a campaign **to** block the merger.* ◇ *We spent $15m on an advertising campaign.*
⭘ *to **build/fund** a ~* ◆ *an **advertising/a cost-cutting** ~* ◆ *a ~ **designed to do sth/aimed at sb/sth***
• *v.* [I] **~ for/against sth** to lead or take part in a series of planned activities designed to persuade sb to do sth: *campaigning for better pay*

**campus** /'kæmpəs/ *n.* [C,U] **1** the area of land where the main buildings of a college or university are: *She lives **on campus**.* **2** (*AmE*) an area of land where a company has many buildings

**can** /kæn/ *v.* [T] (**-nn-**) **1** (*esp. AmE*) to preserve food by putting it in a metal container (a **can**) **2** (*infml.*) (*AmE*) to dismiss sb from their job

★**cancel** /'kænsl/ *v.* (**-ll-**, *AmE* **-l-**) **1** [T] to decide that sth that has been planned or arranged will not happen: *The meeting has been cancelled.* **2** (*Law*) [T,I] to say that you no longer want to continue with an agreement, esp. one that has been legally arranged: *to cancel debts* (= say that they no longer need to be paid) **3** [T] to mark a ticket, a cheque or an official document in order to show that it has been used or that it must not be used: *a cancelled cheque* **4** [T] = STOP *v.* (1) **5** [T] to stop an instruction to a machine, esp. a computer
▸ **cancellation** (*AmE also* **cancelation**) /ˌkænsə'leɪʃn/ *n.* [U,C]: *order cancellations* ◇ *a cancellation charge* ◇ *the cancellation of the contract*

★**candidate** /'kændɪdət; -deɪt/ *n.* [C] a person who is applying for a job: *candidates **for** the post*
⭘ *to **interview/screen** a ~* ◆ *to **choose/hire/reject** a ~* ◆ *a **good/** a **successful/** an **unsuccessful** ~*

**'can-do** *adj.* willing to try new things and expecting that they will be successful: *a can-do attitude*

**cannibalize, -ise** /'kænɪbəlaɪz/ *v.* [T] **1** (*Market.*) (about a company) to reduce the sales of one of its products by introducing a similar new product **2** (*Manufact.*) to use the parts of a machine or a vehicle to repair or build another
▸ **ˌcannibali'zation, -i'sation** /-laɪ'zeɪʃn; *AmE* -lə'z-/ *n.* [U]

**canteen** /kæn'tiːn/ *n.* [C] (*esp. BrE*) a place where food and drink are served in a factory, an office, etc: *an office/a staff ~*

**canvass** /'kænvəs/ *v.* **1** (*Market.*) [T] to ask people about sth in order to find out what they think: *canvassing the views of young people* **2** [T,I] to try and get support from a group of people: *canvassing **support** for the merger* **3** [T] to discuss an idea thoroughly: *The proposal is being canvassed.* ▸ **'canvass** *n.* [C]: *to carry out a canvass* **'canvassing** *n.* [U]

**cap** /kæp/ *n., v.*
• *n.* **1** [C] an upper limit on an amount of money that can be spent, borrowed or charged: *to impose/put/set a ~ on sth* **2** (*Stock Ex., infml.*) [U; sing.] capitalization: *The company has a **market cap** of $30 m.*
• *v.* [T] (**-pp-**) (*often pass.*) to put a top limit on sth, for example, the amount of money that can be spent, lent, charged, etc: *to cap prices*

**capability** /ˌkeɪpə'bɪləti/ *n.* [C,U] (*pl.* **-ties**) the ability or qualities necessary to do sth: *The task is well **within her capabilities**.*

★**capacity** /kə'pæsəti/ *n.* (*pl.* **-ties**) **1** [U; C, usu. sing.] the number of things or people or the amount of sth that a container or space can hold: *a fuel tank with a capacity of 50 litres* **2** (*Manufact.*) [U; sing.] the quantity of goods that a factory, machine, etc. can produce; the number of people that a company can provide a service to: *The factory is working **at** full capacity.* ◇ *spare/total ~* ◇ *manufacturing/production ~* ◇ *to cut/expand/increase ~* **3** [C, usu. sing., U] the ability to understand or to do sth: *a capacity **for** hard work* **4** [C, usu. sing.] the official position or function that sb has: *He works for the bank in an advisory capacity.*

**ˌcap and 'collar** *n.* [sing.] (*Finan.*) an upper and a lower limit between which an interest rate or a share price is fixed for a period of time ▸ **ˌcap and 'collar** *v.* [T]

**capex** *abbr* (*Account.*) a short way of writing **capital expenditure**

★**capital** /'kæpɪtl/ *n.* **1** (*Account.; Finan.*) [U] the total value of the assets that a person or company owns, minus debts: *Our capital is all tied up in property* (= it can not easily be turned into money).
⭘ *to **free up/release/unlock** ~*
**2** (*Finan.*) [U; sing.] an amount of money that is invested in or is used to start a business: *They help start-up companies to raise capital.*

◆ *to attract/borrow ~ • to put up/provide ~ • initial/start-up ~ • foreign/private ~*
**3** (*Finan.*) [U] money that is lent or borrowed on which interest is paid: *Investors want a good return on their capital.*
◆ *to borrow/invest/lend ~ • foreign/private ~*
**4** (*Econ.*) [U] something of value that an organization has, such as machinery or money, that can be used to produce wealth: *Raw materials, labour and capital are used to produce finished goods.*

**'capital ac,count** *n.* [C]
**1** (*Econ.*) a record of the money coming into and going out of a country in the form of investments and loans: *the capital account **surplus***
**2** (*Account.*) a record of how much owners, shareholders or partners have invested in a company
**3** (*Account.*) a record of how much a company is worth at a particular time, minus its debts **4** (*Account.*) a record of the money that a company spends on assets

**'capital accumu,lation** (*also* **'capital for,mation**) *n.* [U] (*Econ.*) the process of getting more and more land, buildings, machinery, etc. that can be used to increase wealth; the process of getting more and more money to save or to invest in these

**,capital 'adequacy** *n.* [U] (*Finan.*) the fact of a bank, a BROKER, etc. having enough to cover possible losses and to pay debts

**,capital 'adequacy ,ratio** (*abbr* **CAR**) (*also* **'capital ,ratio**) *n.* [C] (*Account.*) the amount of money, or shares, bonds, etc. that can easily be changed into money, that a bank has, expressed as a percentage of the money it has lent and therefore risks losing

**,capital al'lowance** (*also* **in,vestment al'lowance**) *n.* [C] (*Account.*) an amount of money invested in a new building, machine, etc. that a company can take away from profits before calculating its tax

**,capital appreci'ation** (*also* **,capital 'growth, ,asset appreci'ation**) *n.* [U] (*Econ.*) an increase in the value of the assets that a company or person owns

**,capital 'asset** (*also* **,fixed 'asset**) *n.* [C, usu. pl.] (*Account.*) an item of value that a company owns and keeps, such as buildings, machinery, vehicles or shares in other companies

**,capital 'bonus** = BONUS (3)

**,capital 'budget** *n.* [C] (*Finan.*) the plan that a company or an organization makes for buying buildings, machinery, equipment, etc. over a period of time

**,capital con'sumption** *n.* [U] (*Econ.*) the loss or decrease in value over a particular period of money, buildings, machines, equipment, etc. used to produce goods and services in a country SYN DEPRECIATION

**,capital em'ployed** *n.* [U] (*Account.*) the amount of money invested in a business by its shareholders, equal to the total value of assets minus the total value of LIABILITIES

**,capital e'quipment** *n.* [U] the machinery, equipment, buildings, etc. that a company uses to produce goods or services

**,capital exp'enditure** *n.* [U] (*also* **,capital ex'pense** [C,U]) (*abbr* **capex**) (*Account.*) money that is spent on valuable items such as buildings, machines or vehicles, which are used for longer than the accounting period in which they are bought SYN CAPITAL OUTLAY

**'capital flight** *n.* [U] (*Econ.*) the sudden movement of money out of a country where it is invested to another, in order to reduce risk or to increase profit

**'capital flow** (*also* **'capital ,movement**) *n.* [C,U] (*Econ.*) the movement of money for investment from one country to another

**'capital for,mation** = CAPITAL ACCUMULATION

**,capital 'gain** *n.* [C,U] (*Account.*) a profit that is made from the sale of property or an investment: *to generate/make/realize a ~*

**,capital 'gains tax** *n.* [C,U] (*abbr* **CGT**) a tax that a person or company must pay when they have made a profit above a particular level on the sale of some types of assets

**'capital ,gearing** = GEARING

**'capital goods** (*also* **in'vestment goods**) *n.* [pl.] (*Econ.*) items such as machines, equipment or buildings that are used to produce goods or services: *to invest in/purchase ~*

**,capital 'growth** = CAPITAL APPRECIATION

**,capital 'growth share** = CAPITAL SHARE

**,capital-in'tensive** *adj.* used to describe an industry or a company in which the cost of raw materials, equipment, machinery, etc. is much higher than the cost of workers → LABOUR-INTENSIVE

**,capital in'vestment** *n.* [U,C] (*Finan.*) the act of spending money on machines, equipment, etc. for producing goods or services; money that is spent in this way

○ *big/heavy/high/major/small* ~ • *a* ~ *plan/programme*

**capitalism** /ˈkæpɪtəlɪzəm/ *n.* [U] an economic system in which a country's businesses and industry are controlled and run for profit by private owners rather than by the government

**capitalist** /ˈkæpɪtəlɪst/ *n., adj.*

• *n.* [C] **1** a person who supports CAPITALISM **2** a person who controls a lot of wealth and uses it to produce more wealth

• *adj.* (*also* **capitalistic** /ˌkæpɪtəˈlɪstɪk/ *less freq.*) based on the principles of CAPITALISM: *a* ~ *economy/ society*

**capitalization**, **-isation** /ˌkæpɪtəlaɪˈzeɪʃn; *AmE* -ləˈz-/ *n.* [U; sing.] **1** (*Finan.*) the act of starting to function as a company; the act of providing a company, etc. with the money it needs to function: *The paper planned to go straight to capitalization as a commercial company.* **2** (*Finan.*) = CAPITAL STRUCTURE **3** (*Stock Ex.*) (*abbr* **cap**) = MARKET CAPITALIZATION

**ˌcapitaliˈzation ˌissue** *n.* [C] (*esp. BrE*) (*Finan.*) when a company uses its spare profits to create new shares, which are then given free to the shareholders in proportion to the number of shares that they already own SYN BONUS ISSUE, SCRIP ISSUE

**ˌcapitaliˌzation of reˈserves** *n.* [C] (*Finan.*) a situation in which a company uses the spare profits that it has saved to create new shares

**ˌcapitaliˈzation ˌrate** *n.* [C] (*abbr* **ˈcap rate**) (*Account.*) a rate of interest that is used to help estimate the present value of an investment that will provide an income over a long period of time, such as a business or a property

★ **capitalize**, **-ise** /ˈkæpɪtəlaɪz/ *v.* **1** (*Finan.*; *Stock Ex.*) [T,I] (*often pass.*) to get enough money to start to function as a company; to provide a company with the money it needs to function: *The firm is being capitalized at about €3.5 bn.* **2** (*Account.*) [T] to record money spent on machines, equipment, buildings, etc. as an asset in a company's financial records

▸ **ˈcapitalized**, **-ised** *adj.*: *a highly/ thinly capitalized industry*

PHRV **ˈcapitalize on/upon sth** to gain an advantage for yourself from a situation: *How can we capitalize on our successes?*

**ˌcapital ˈlevy** = CAPITAL TAX

**ˌcapital ˈloss** *n.* [C,U] (*Account.*) a loss that is made when an asset is sold → CAPITAL GAIN

**ˈcapital ˌmarket** *n.* [C] (*Finan.*) the group of markets and stock exchanges where companies and governments sell shares, bonds, etc. in order to obtain the money they need

○ *to* ***borrow/raise*** *(money)* ***in/on*** *the* ~ • *to* ***invest in/on*** *the* ~

**ˈcapital ˌmovement** = CAPITAL FLOW

**ˌcapital ˈoutlay** *n.* [C] (*Finan.*) money that is spent to buy valuable items that will be kept, such as buildings, machines or vehicles SYN CAPITAL EXPENDITURE

**ˌcapital ˈproject** *n.* [C] (*Finan.*) a large project that involves building or improving factories, buildings, roads, etc.

**ˈcapital ˌratio** = CAPITAL ADEQUACY RATIO

**ˌcapital ˈrationing** *n.* [U] (*Finan.*) the policy of a company limiting the amount of money it uses to finance new projects and only investing in the ones most worth doing

**ˌcapital reˈdemption reˌserve** *n.* [C] (*Account.*) a supply of money that a company must keep and not give to shareholders when it buys back its own shares

**ˌcapital reˈquirement** *n.* [C] (*Finan.*) an amount of CAPITAL that a company is legally required to have; the rule that sets this amount

**ˌcapital reˈserve** *n.* [C, usu. pl.] (*Account.*) **1** (*also* **ˌundisˌtributable reˈserve**, **ˌnon-disˌtributable reˈserve**, *both esp. BrE*) profits, such as the increased value of a building, etc., that a company keeps as part of its CAPITAL and which cannot be paid to shareholders **2** a supply of money that a company or an organization keeps for an expected future cost, such as repairing property or buying new equipment

**ˈcapital ˌshare** (*also* **ˌcapital ˈgrowth share**) *n.* [C] (*esp. BrE*) (*Finan.*) a type of share in an INVESTMENT TRUST. The holders gain from any increase in value but do not receive regular payments from the company's profits.

**ˌcapital ˈstock** *n.* [U,C] **1** (*Econ.*) the total value of the buildings, equipment and materials that a company owns and uses to produce goods or services **2** (*Finan.*) (*AmE*) all the shares a company can make available; the value of those shares SYN SHARE CAPITAL, STOCK

**ˌcapital ˈstructure** (*also* **fiˌnancial ˈstructure, ˌcapitaliˈzation**) *n.* [C,U] (*Finan.*) the way in which a company obtains money for its business activities: *The company has a complex share and loan capital structure.*

**ˌcapital ˈsum** *n.* [C] (*Finan.*) a single payment that you receive, for example from an insurance policy, a gift or an investment

**ˈcapital tax** (*also* **ˌcapital ˈlevy**) *n.* [C] (*Econ.*) a tax based on the value of the assets owned by a person or a company ▸ **ˌcapital taxˈation** *n.* [U]

**ˌcapital ˈturnover** *n.* [C, usu. sing.] (*Account.*) the value of a company's sales for a year in relation to the total amount of money invested in it, used as a measure of how well it uses its assets to create sales

**ˌcapital ˈvalue** *n.* [C, usu. sing., U] (*Account.*) the total worth of a company's assets, as recorded in its financial accounts

**ˈcapped-rate** *adj.* (*BrE*) (*Finan.*) a **capped-rate** loan has a rate of interest that can change but will not increase above the level set

**ˈcap rate** = CAPITALIZATION RATE

**ˌcaptain of ˈindustry** *n.* [C] (used in newspapers, etc.) a person who manages a large company

**captive** /ˈkæptɪv/ *adj.* **1** not free to leave a particular place or to choose what you want do to: *As the only supplier they have a captive market* (= people have to buy from them). ◇ *a ~ audience/customer* **2** (*Market.*) only able to sell the products of a particular company: *a ~ agent/dealer*

**capture** /ˈkæptʃə(r)/ *v.* [T] **1** to succeed in making people buy your products or services rather than those of other companies: *We have captured 25% of the US market for refrigerators.* **2** (*IT*) to put sth into a computer in a form it can use: *to capture data*

**CAR** /ˌsiː eɪ ˈɑː(r)/ = CAPITAL ADEQUACY RATIO

**carbon** /ˈkɑːbən; *AmE* ˈkɑːrb-/ *n.* [U] **1** a chemical substance found in all living things, and also diamonds, coal, petrol, etc. **2** used to refer to gases, such as CARBON DIOXIDE, that are produced from burning fuels and can harm the planet if produced in large amounts: *carbon emissions* ◇ *a carbon tax*

**ˌcarbon ˈcopy** *n.* [C] **1** a copy of a document, letter, etc. made with CARBON PAPER **2** (*IT*) (*abbr* **cc**) a copy of an email message

**ˈcarbon ˌcredit** *n.* [C, usu. pl.] a right to send out a measured amount of harmful gases such as CARBON DIOXIDE into the air

**ˌcarbon diˈoxide** *n.* [U] (*abbr* **$CO_2$**) a gas that is produced by burning CARBON and which can harm the planet if it is produced in large amounts

**ˌcarbon-ˈneutral** *adj.* used to describe an activity where other action is taken to cancel the amount of CARBON gases produced by the activity

**ˈcarbon ˌpaper** *n.* [U] thin paper with a dark substance on one side, that is used between two sheets of paper for making copies of written or typed documents

★ **card** /kɑːd; *AmE* kɑːrd/ *n.* [C] **1** a small piece of plastic, esp. one given by a bank or a shop/store, used for buying things, obtaining money or using a telephone or computer system: *I put the meal on* (= paid for it with) *my card.* ◇ *card fraud*
⊕ *to* ***buy sth with/pay by/pay with/use*** *a ~* ◆ *to* ***insert/remove/swipe*** *a ~* ◆ *to* ***apply for/issue/withdraw*** *a ~*
**2** = BUSINESS CARD **3** a small piece of stiff paper or plastic with information on it, esp. information about sb's identity: *a membership card* **4** (*IT*) a small device containing an electronic CIRCUIT that is part of a computer or added to it, enabling it to perform particular functions: *installing a memory card*

**ˈcard ˌcatalog** = CARD INDEX

**cardholder** /ˈkɑːdhəʊldə(r); *AmE* ˈkɑːrdhoʊl-/ *n.* [C] a person who has a credit card from a bank, etc.

**ˈcard ˌindex** (*also* **ˈindex**) (*both esp. BrE*) (*AmE usu.* **ˈcard ˌcatalog**) *n.* [C] a box of cards with information about an item on each one, arranged in alphabetical order

**care** /keə(r); *AmE* ker/ *n.* [U]
IDM **ˈcare of sb** (*AmE also* **in ˈcare of sb**) (*abbr* **c/o**) used when writing to sb at another person's address: *Write to him care of his lawyer.* ◇ *S R Brown c/o Ms D Philips*

★ **career** /kəˈrɪə(r); *AmE* kəˈrɪr/ *n.* [C] the series of jobs that a person has in a particular area of work, usu. involving more responsibility as time passes: *When did she begin her career as an engineer?* ◇ *limited career prospects*
⊕ *to* ***build/pursue/take up*** *a ~ (in sth)* ◆ *to* ***change/give up*** *your ~* ◆ *~* ***goals/opportunities***

**caˈreer adˌvice** = CAREERS ADVICE

**ca'reer break** *n.* [C] a period of time when you do not do your usual job, for example because you have children to care for or want to study: *women returning to employment after a career break* ◇ *to be on/take a ~*

**ca'reer ˌcounsellor** (*also* **ca'reers -**) *n.* [C] (*HR*) **1** (*esp. AmE*) a person whose job is to give students advice and information about jobs and careers SYN CAREERS OFFICER **2** a person whose job is to give people advice and information about how to change or develop their career ▸ **ca'reer ˌcounselling** (*also* **ca'reers -**) *n.* [U]

**ca'reer fair** = CAREERS FAIR

**ca'reer ˌguidance** = CAREERS ADVICE

**ca'reer ˌladder** *n.* [C, usu. sing.] a series of jobs from junior to senior level in an organization or a profession, with increasing responsibility: ***climbing** the career ladder*

**ca'reer move** *n.* [C] the act of changing your job for one that you think is better and will bring the chance of more responsibility

**ca'reer path** *n.* [C, usu. sing.] a planned series of jobs in one or more professions: *to decide on/follow/have/map out a ~*

**ca'reers adˌvice** (*also* **ca'reers ˌguidance**) (*both BrE*) (*AmE* **ca'reer adˌvice/ˌguidance**) *n.* [U] (*HR*) advice about what career to choose or how to develop your career

**ca'reers adˌviser** = CAREERS OFFICER

**ca'reers ˌcounsellor** = CAREER COUNSELLOR

**ca'reers fair** (*AmE* **ca'reer -**) = JOB FAIR

**ca'reers ˌguidance** = CAREERS ADVICE

**ca'reers ˌofficer** (*also* **ca'reers adˌviser**) *n.* [C] (*both BrE*) (*HR*) a person whose job is to give students advice and information about jobs and careers SYN CAREER COUNSELLOR

**ca'reer ˌstructure** *n.* [C, usu. sing., U] (*HR*) the planned way in which people move to higher levels of responsibility in a particular company or profession: *The profession has no clear career structure.*
⊕ *to **build/develop/establish** a ~*

**ca'reer ˌwoman** *n.* [C] a woman who has a career or whose career is more important to her than getting married and having children

**careline** /'keəlaɪn; *AmE* 'kerl-/ *n.* [C] (*Market.*) a telephone service you can call to get help, advice or information on a company's products

**caretaker** /'keəteɪkə(r); *AmE* 'kert-/ (*BrE*) (*AmE* **cus'todian**, **'janitor**) *n.* [C] a person whose job is to take care of a building such as a school, offices or a block of flats/an apartment building

**cargo** /'kɑːɡəʊ; *AmE* 'kɑːrɡoʊ/ *n.* [C,U] (*pl.* **cargoes** *or* **cargos**) (*Transpt.*) the goods carried in a ship, plane or lorry/truck: *a cargo of sugar*
⊕ *to **carry/deliver/load/unload** (a) ~* ◆ *a ~ **plane/ship*** ◆ *~ **traffic/volumes***

**'cargo ˌhandling** *n.* [U] (*Transpt.*) the process of moving goods onto and off ships, aircraft and lorries/trucks

**carmaker** /'kɑːmeɪkə(r); *AmE* 'kɑːrm-/ *n.* [C] (*AmE*) a company that makes cars

**carnet** /'kɑːneɪ; *AmE* 'kɑːrneɪ/ *n.* [C] (*Trade*) a document that allows you to take goods into a country temporarily for your work without paying taxes on them

**'carpet-bomb** *v.* [T,I] (*Market.*) to send an advertisement to a very large number of people, esp. by email or to their computer screen: *They carpet-bombed the public with commercials.* ▸ **'carpet-ˌbombing** *n.* [U]

**'car pool** *n.* [C] **1** (*BrE*) (*also* **'motor pool**, *AmE, BrE*) a group of cars owned by a company, that its staff can use **2 carpool** a group of car owners who take turns to drive everyone in the group to work, so that only one car is used at a time ▸ **'car pool** (*also* **carpool**) /'kɑːpuːl; *AmE* 'kɑːrp-/ *v.* [I]: *When they work together they can carpool.*

**carr. fwd.** *abbr* (*Trade*) a short way of writing **carriage forward**

**carriage** /'kærɪdʒ/ *n.* [U] (*BrE*) (*Trade*; *Transpt.*) the act or cost of transporting goods from one place to another: *We charge €15 for **carriage and insurance**.* SYN HANDLING

**ˌcarriage and 'freight** = COST AND FREIGHT

**'carriage and in'surance 'paid to** *phr.* (*abbr* **CIP**) (*Trade*) the seller pays for the transport and insurance of goods to the place mentioned: *CIP Athens* → INCOTERM

**ˌcarriage 'forward** *phr.* (*BrE*) (*abbr* **carr. fwd.**) (*Trade*) the buyer pays for the transport of goods

**ˌcarriage 'paid to** *phr.* (*abbr* **CPT**) (*Trade*) the seller pays for the transport of goods to the place mentioned → INCOTERM

**ˌcarried ˈforward** *adj.* (*abbr* **c/f**, **c/fwd**) (*also* **ˌcarried ˈdown**) (*Account.*) used to describe an amount at the end of one accounting period or page of accounts that will be copied at the start of the next

**ˌcarried ˈover** *adj.* (*abbr* **c/o**) (*Account.*) used to describe an amount at the end of a page in an account that will be moved to the start of the next page

★ **carrier** /ˈkæriə(r)/ *n.* [C] **1** a company that carries goods or passengers from one place to another, esp. by air: *a budget/low-cost/no-frills* ~ **2** (*IT*) a company that provides access to a communications network

**ˌcarrier's ˈrisk** *n.* [U,C] (*Trade*) if goods are sent **at carrier's risk**, the transport company has to insure the goods during transport

**carryback** /ˈkæribæk/ *n.* [U,C] (*Account.*) a system which allows you to treat the current year's profit or loss as if it happened in an earlier year; the amount of money that you use in this way

**carryforward** /ˌkæriˈfɔːwəd; *AmE* -ˈfɔːrwərd/ *n.* [U,C] (*Account.*) a system which allows you to treat the current year's profit or loss as if it happened in a later year; the amount of money that you use in this way

**ˈcarrying charge** *n.* [C] **1** (*Account.*) (*also* **ˈcarrying cost**, **ˈholding cost**) the cost to a business of storing goods or holding assets rather than using them to earn income **2** (*Comm.*) (*esp. AmE*) money that you pay as interest and charges when you buy sth on credit

**ˈcarry-ˌover** (*also* **carryover**) *n.* **1** [C] something that is transferred from the previous period, situation, owner, etc. to the present one: *The slow trading was a carry-over from the big losses of last week.* **2** (*Account.*) [U] the amount that is moved to the next part of the accounts or the next accounting period

**cartel** /kɑːˈtel; *AmE* kɑːrˈtel/ (*also* **ˈprice ring**) *n.* [C with sing./pl. v.] (*Econ.*) a group of separate companies that agree to increase profits by fixing prices and not competing with each other
● *to form/join/take part in a* ~ ♦ *an illegal/a price-fixing* ~

**carton** /ˈkɑːtn; *AmE* ˈkɑːrtn/ *n.* [C] **1** a light cardboard or plastic box or pot for holding goods, esp. food or liquid; the contents: *a milk carton* ◊ *a carton of milk* **2** (*esp. AmE*) a box in which goods are packed, often in smaller containers

**case** /keɪs/ *n.* [C] **1** (*Law*) a question to be decided in court: *to bring a case against sb* **2** [usu. sing.] a set of facts or arguments that support one side in a court, discussion, etc: *You have a good case for compensation.* **3** a container or covering used to protect or store things; a container with its contents or the amount that it contains: *a packing case* (= a large wooden box for packing things in)

**ˈcase ˌstudy** *n.* [C] a detailed account of the development of a person, a group of people or a situation over a period of time, esp. for teaching or training: *The results are based on case studies of 27 companies.*

★ **cash** /kæʃ/ *n., v.*
• *n.* [U] **1** money in the form of coins or notes/bills: *to pay (in) cash* ◊ *to have/hold/withdraw* ~ **2** money generally, esp. if it is immediately available: *businesses generating* (= producing) *cash* ◊ *to be short of/raise/run out of* ~ IDM **cash ˈdown** (*BrE*) (*also* **ˌcash up ˈfront**, *AmE, BrE*) (*Comm.*) with immediate payment of cash: *We paid $100 cash down.* **ˌcash in ˈhand 1** (*infml.*) if you pay for sth **cash in hand**, you pay in cash, esp. so that the person being paid can avoid paying tax **2** (*AmE also* **ˌcash on ˈhand**) (*Account.*) money that you have and can use immediately **ˌcash up ˈfront** = CASH DOWN
• *v.* [T] to exchange a cheque, share, bond, etc. for money: *to cash a cheque* PHRV **ˌcash ˈin (on sth)** to gain an advantage for yourself from a situation: *Sports retailers are cashing in on the interest generated by the World Cup.* **ˌcash sth ˈin** to exchange sth, such as an insurance policy, for money before the date on which it would normally end **ˌcash (sth) ˈout** (*AmE*) to sell an asset or an investment in order to make a profit: *He sold the company and cashed out.* **ˌcash ˈup** (*BrE*) (*AmE* **ˌcash ˈout**) to add up the amount of money that has been received in a shop/store, etc., esp. at the end of the day

**cashable** /ˈkæʃəbl/ *adj.* that can be changed into cash

**ˈcash acˌcount** *n.* [C] **1** (*Account.*) a financial account where a record is kept of money spent and received in cash **2** (*esp. AmE*) = CURRENT ACCOUNT (1) **3** (*Stock Ex.*) an account with a BROKER where a customer buying shares, bonds, etc. has to pay immediately in cash

**'cash ac,counting** *n.* [U] (*Account.*) a system of keeping accounts where amounts of money are written down at the time when they are paid or received → ACCRUAL ACCOUNTING

**,cash against 'documents** *phr.* (*abbr* **CAD**) (*Trade*) a way of paying for imports where the buyer must first pay for the goods at the bank or agent to which the SHIPPING DOCUMENTS have been sent, and can then collect the goods

**,cash and 'carry** *n.* [C,U] (*Comm.*) a large WHOLESALE shop/store that sells goods in large quantities at low prices to customers from other businesses who pay in cash and take the goods away; the system of buying and selling in this way

**,cash at 'bank** *n.* [U] (*Account., usu. written*) used in financial records to show the total amount of money that a company has in the bank

**cashback** /'kæʃbæk/ *n.* [U] (*Comm.*) **1** (*also* **cash-back**) cash given to customers who buy a product or service, as a way of persuading people to buy it **2** (*BrE*) money from your bank account that you can get when you pay for sth in a shop using a DEBIT CARD

**'cash ,basis** *n.* [sing.] (*Account.*) the principle that CASH ACCOUNTING is based on

**,cash before de'livery** *phr.* (*abbr* **CBD**) (*Trade*) an arrangement where a buyer must pay for goods before they are sent

**'cash book** *n.* [C] (*Account.*) a record of money spent and received

**'cash box** (*AmE* **cashbox**) *n.* [C] a strong box with a lock in which cash is kept

**'cash ,budget** *n.* [C] (*Account.*) an estimate of how much money will be paid and received over a particular period of time

**'cash call** *n.* [C] (*Finan.*) a request by a company to its shareholders for more money

**'cash card** *n.* [C] (*esp. BrE*) a plastic card used to get money from a CASH MACHINE

**'cash con,version** *n.* [U] (*Account.*) the process by which a business changes the raw materials that it buys into money received from the sale of the finished goods: *the cash conversion cycle* (= the number of days that this process takes)

**'cash cow** *n.* [C] (*infml.*) **1** (*Finan.*) the part of a business or a product that always makes a profit and that provides money for the rest of the business **2** (*Market.*) in the BOSTON MATRIX, a product that has a large market share in a market that is growing very little

**'cash deal** = CASH SETTLEMENT

**,cash-de'posit ,ratio** = CASH RATIO (1)

**,cash 'discount** *n.* [C] (*Comm.*) a price reduction that is given if a buyer pays immediately or in cash

**'cash dis,penser** = CASH MACHINE

**,cash e'quivalent** *n.* [C] (*Account.*) **1** an asset or investment that can easily be sold or changed into money **2** an amount of money that is estimated to be equal to the value of sth: *the cash equivalent of employee benefits*

★ **'cash flow** *n.* [C,U] (*Account.*) the movement of money into and out of a business as goods are bought and sold; the difference between the amount of money a business receives and the amount it pays during a particular period of time

○ *a* ***good/healthy/negative/positive/strong/weak*** *~* ◆ *to* ***generate/improve*** *~* ◆ *a cash-flow* ***crisis/problem***

**'cash gene,ration** *n.* [U] (*Finan.*) the process of a company making extra money that can be invested after costs have been paid

**cashier** /kæ'ʃɪə(r); *AmE* -'ʃɪr/ *n.* [C] **1** a person whose job is to receive and pay out money in a bank, shop/store, etc. **2** (*Account.*) a person in a company who is responsible for paying out and receiving money and for keeping records of this

**ca,shier's 'cheque** *n.* [C] a cheque written by a bank against its own bank account

**'cash ,issue** *n.* [C] (*Finan.*) new shares that a company offers to existing shareholders in order to raise extra money

**cashless** /'kæʃləs/ *adj.* that works without using cash; done without using cash: *cashless transactions*

**'cash ma,chine** (*BrE also* **'cash dis,penser**, **'Cashpoint™**) *n.* [C] a machine in or outside a bank, etc., from which you can get money from your bank account using a special plastic card SYN ATM: *to withdraw money from/use a ~*

**'cash ,management** (*also* **'treasury ,management**) *n.* [U] (*Account.*) the activity of controlling the money that comes in and goes out of a company in order to maintain a good CASH FLOW

**'cash ˌmarket** = SPOT MARKET

**'cash pile** (*also* **'cash ˌmountain**) *n.* [C, usu. sing.] a large amount of money that a company has available for investment

**Cashpoint™** /'kæʃpɔɪnt/ = CASH MACHINE

**'cash poˌsition** *n.* [C, usu. sing.] (*Account.*) the amount of money that a company has immediately available: *We have reduced our debt levels and have a strong cash position.*

**'cash price** *n.* [C] **1** (*Comm.*) the price that a seller will accept if payment is made immediately **2** (*Finan.*) = SPOT PRICE **3** (*Finan.*) the price that a company will pay in cash to shareholders when it buys another company

**'cash ˌratio** *n.* [C] (*Account.*) **1** (*also* **ˌcash-de'posit ˌratio**) the relationship between the amount of money a bank holds in cash and the total amount it holds in deposits and investments SYN RESERVE REQUIREMENT **2** the relationship between the amount of money that a company holds in cash, in the bank, etc. and its LIABILITIES SYN LIQUIDITY RATIO

**ˌcash ratio de'posits** *n.* [pl.] (*abbr* **CRD**) (*Econ.*) the amount of money that banks must keep in the country's central bank

**'cash ˌregister** (*AmE also* **'register**) *n.* [C] a machine used in shops/stores, restaurants, etc. that has a drawer for keeping money in, and that shows and records the amount of money received for each thing that is sold SYN TILL

**ˌcash 'rich** *adj.* (*Account.*) (esp. about a company) having a lot of money available immediately

**'cash sale** *n.* [C] (*Comm.*) a sale where payment is made immediately

**'cash ˌsettlement** (*also* **'cash deal**) *n.* [C] (*Finan.*) an act of buying or selling shares, FUTURES, etc. where they are exchanged immediately for cash

**'cash shell** = SHELL COMPANY

**'cash-starved** *adj.* without enough money, usu. because another organization, such as the government, has failed to provide it: *cash-starved public services*

**'cash-strapped** *adj.* not having enough money

**ˌcasting 'vote** *n.* [C, usu. sing.] the vote given by the person in charge of an official meeting to decide sth when there are an equal number of votes on each side: *to give/have/use a ~*

★**casual** /'kæʒuəl/ *adj.*, *n.*
• ***adj.* 1** (*HR*) (about work or workers) not done regularly, or not doing sth regularly, but only when needed: *casual work* ◇ *employed **on a casual basis*** SYN TEMPORARY **2** not formal: *casual clothes* ▸ **'casually** *adv.*
• ***n.* 1** (*HR*) [C] a **casual** worker SYN TEMP **2 casuals** [pl.] informal clothes or shoes

**'casualty inˌsurance** *n.* [U] a type of insurance in which money is paid for injury or death or damage to property caused by a company's product or by the lack of care of the company's employees

★**catalogue** (*AmE usu.* **catalog**) /'kætəlɒg; *AmE* -lɔːg; -lɑːg/ *n.*, *v.*
• ***n.*** [C] **1** (*Market.*) a complete list of items that a company sells, often with pictures of the items and prices ✪ *a **home shopping/mail-order** ~* ♦ *a ~ **business/retailer*** ♦ *~ **shopping*** **2** [usu. sing.] = BACK CATALOGUE **3** (*IT*) a website that has lists of other sites in groups according to their type or subject, with links
• ***v.*** [T] to arrange a list of things in order in a **catalogue**; to record sth in a **catalogue**

**catch** /kætʃ/ *v.* (**caught, caught** /kɔːt/) IDM **have/be caught with your 'hand/'fingers in the till** used to describe a situation when sb is stealing money from their employer PHR V **ˌcatch 'on 1** (used about a product or an idea) to become popular with people: *The idea never really caught on.* **2** (*infml.*) **~ (to sth)** to understand or realize sth **ˌcatch 'up (with sb/sth)** (*BrE also* **ˌcatch sb/sth 'up**) to reach the same level or standard as sb/sth that was bigger, better or more advanced

**'catchment ˌarea** *n.* [C] (*BrE*) the area from which a business gets its customers

**catchphrase** /'kætʃfreɪz/ *n.* [C] a popular phrase that is connected with the person, company, advertisement, etc. that used it and made it famous

**'catch-up** *n.* [U] the process of trying to reach sb who is more advanced or better → idiom at PLAY *v.*

**catchy** /'kætʃi/ *adj.* (about words or music used to advertise sth) easy to remember

**categorize, -ise** /'kætəgəraɪz/ *v.* [T] to put people or things into groups according to what type they are SYN PIGEONHOLE

**category** /'kætəgəri; *AmE* -gɔːri/ *n.* [C] (*pl.* **-ries**) a group of people or products with particular features in common: *Our customers* ***fall into*** *two broad categories.*

**ˌcategory ˈkiller** *n.* [C] (*Market.*) a big company that sells a large collection of a particular type of BRANDED goods, such as toys or books, at low prices and puts smaller companies out of business

**ˌcategory ˈleader** *n.* [C] (*Market.*) the company that sells the most of a particular type of product

**ˈcategory ˌmanagement** *n.* [U] (*abbr* **CM**) (*Market.*) the process of manufacturers and businesses who sell to the public working together using data about what customers want in order to increase the sales of types of products

**ˌcategory ˈmanager** (*also* **ˌproduct line ˈmanager**) *n.* [C] (*Market.*) a person at a company who is in charge of developing and selling a group of related products or a type of product

**cater** /ˈkeɪtə(r)/ *v.* [T,I] to provide the food and drinks for an organization or an event ▶ **ˈcaterer** *n.* [C] **ˈcatering** /-ərɪŋ/ *n.* [U]
**PHR V** **ˈcater for/to sb/sth** to provide the things that a particular type of person or situation needs or wants

**CATV** /ˌsiː eɪ tiː ˈviː/ = COMMUNITY ANTENNA TELEVISION

**ˌcause and efˈfect ˌdiagram** = FISHBONE DIAGRAM

**caveat emptor** /ˌkæviæt ˈemptɔː(r)/ *phr.* (*Law*) used to say that when you are buying something it is your responsibility to check that there is nothing wrong with what you are buying → idiom at BUYER

**CBA** /ˌsiː biː ˈeɪ/ = COST-BENEFIT ANALYSIS

**CBD** /ˌsiː biː ˈdiː/ = CASH BEFORE DELIVERY, CENTRAL BUSINESS DISTRICT

**CBT** /ˌsiː biː ˈtiː/ = COMPUTER-BASED TRAINING

**CBU** /ˌsiː biː ˈjuː/ = COMPLETELY BUILT-UP

**cc** = CARBON COPY (2)

**CCTV** /ˌsiː siː tiː ˈviː/ = CLOSED-CIRCUIT TELEVISION

**CD** /ˌsiː ˈdiː/ *n.* [C] **1** a small disc on which sound or information is recorded **2** (*Finan.*) = CERTIFICATE OF DEPOSIT

**c/d** *abbr* (*Account., written*) carried down

**CD-ROM** /ˌsiː diː ˈrɒm; *AmE* ˈrɑːm/ *n.* [C,U] a plastic disc on which large amounts of information, sound and pictures can be stored, for use on a computer

**ceiling** /ˈsiːlɪŋ/ *n.* [C] the greatest amount of sth that is allowed; the top limit: *They have put a 10% ceiling on wage increases.* OPP FLOOR
⊙ *to* ***impose/lift/set*** *a ~ (on sth)* ♦ *to* ***exceed/hit/reach*** *a ~*

★ **cellphone** (*also* **cell phone**) /ˈselfəʊn; *AmE* -foʊn/ (*also* **ˌcellular ˈphone**) (*also* **cell**, *infml.*) *n.* [C] (*all esp. AmE*) a telephone that does not have wires and works by radio, that you can carry with you and use anywhere SYN MOBILE PHONE

**cellular** /ˈseljələ(r)/ *adj.* (often used in the names of companies) connected with a telephone system that works by radio instead of wires
⊙ *a ~* ***carrier/operator/provider*** ♦ *a ~* ***network/system***

**ˌcellular ˈphone** = CELLPHONE

**center** = CENTRE

**-centered** = -CENTRED

**ˌcentral ˈbank** (*also* **ˌnational ˈbank, reˈserve bank**) *n.* [C] the institution that controls the supply of money in a country and provides financial services to the government and other banks

**ˌcentral ˈbusiness ˌdistrict** *n.* [C] (*esp. AmE*) (*abbr* **CBD**) the part of a town or city where most of the offices are

**ˌcentral ˈcounterparty** *n.* [C] (*Finan.*) an organization that transfers and pays for investments on behalf of buyers and sellers so that they avoid dealing with each other directly and reduce risk

★ **centralize**, **-ise** /ˈsentrəlaɪz/ *v.* [T] to control the different parts of sth or operate sth from one particular place; to give control of sth to one group of people: *Most banks have centralized their telephone services.* OPP DECENTRALIZE

★ **centralized**, **-ised** /ˈsentrəlaɪzd/ *adj.* that controls the different parts of sth or operates sth from one particular place: *a centralized computer system*

**ˌcentral ˈprocessing ˌunit** (*abbr* **CPU**) (*also* **ˌcentral ˈprocessor**) *n.* [C] (*IT*) the part of a computer that controls all the other parts of the system SYN PROCESSOR

**centre** (*AmE* **center**) /ˈsentə(r)/ *n.* [C] **1** a building or place used for a particular purpose or activity: *a research centre* **2** a place where a lot of business activity takes place: *a com-*

*mercial/financial/an industrial* ~ **3** (*esp. BrE*) (*AmE usu.* ˈ**downtown** [U,C]) the main part of a town or city where there are a lot of shops/stores and offices

**-centred** (*AmE* **-centered**) /ˈsentəd; *AmE* -ərd/ *comb. form* (*in adjs*) having the person mentioned as the centre of attention: *a client-centred organization*

**ˌcentre of ˈexcellence** *n.* [C] a place where a particular kind of work is done extremely well

**CEO** /ˌsiː iː ˈəʊ; *AmE* ˈoʊ/ *abbr* chief executive officer

★ **certificate** *n., v.*

• ***n.*** /səˈtɪfɪkət; *AmE* sərˈt-/ [C] an official document that can be used to prove sth, for example, that facts are true, that you own sth or have a particular qualification

⊙ *to* ***get/issue*** *a* ~ ♦ *a* ***bond/share/ stock*** ~ ♦ *a* ***birth/death/marriage*** ~ ♦ *a* ~ *of* ***attendance/membership/ ownership***

• ***v.*** /səˈtɪfɪkeɪt; *AmE* sərˈt-/ [T] (*BrE*) (*usu. pass.*) to give a person, a course, etc. an official document to show that a particular standard has been reached

**certificated** /səˈtɪfɪkeɪtɪd; *AmE* sərˈt-/ *adj.* (*BrE*) (*HR*) having the certificate which shows that the necessary training for a particular job has been done or a particular standard has been reached: *a certificated notary* ◇ *a* ~ *vessel/aircraft*

**cerˌtificate of aˈnalysis** *n.* [C] (*Manufact.*) a certificate provided by a company that produces chemicals or raw materials, to show what the products contain and that they have a particular quality

**cerˌtificate of deˈposit** (*abbr* **CD**) (*also* **deˈposit cerˌtificate**) *n.* [C] (*Finan.*) a type of investment offered by banks and other financial institutions in which money is lent to the bank, etc. for a fixed period of time with a fixed rate of interest

**cerˌtificate of eˈxistence** *n.* [C] **1** (*Law*) (*AmE*) a document provided by a government office that an organization can show to people to prove that it legally exists **2** (*Insur.*) (*BrE*) an official document that proves that sb is still alive and can claim a pension

**cerˌtificate of inˌcorpoˈration** *n.* [C] (*Law*) **1** an official document that states that a company has officially been created **2** (*AmE*) in some states in the US, a name for ARTICLES OF INCORPORATION

**cerˌtificate of inˈsurance** (*also* **inˈsurance cerˌtificate**) *n.* [C] (*Insur.*) a document that you get from an insurance company that proves you have insurance and gives the details

**cerˌtificate of ˈoccupancy** *n.* [C] (*Law; Prop.*) esp. in the US, a document that proves that a building has been carefully checked and is suitable for the kind of business that will use it

**cerˌtificate of ˈorigin** *n.* [C] (*Trade*) an official document that states where sth was produced and who produced it, used esp. for importing goods into a country

**certification** /ˌsɜːtɪfɪˈkeɪʃn; *AmE* ˌsɜːrt-/ *n.* [U] the process of checking whether sb/sth has reached a particular standard and giving them an official document to show this; the qualification given: *to carry out certification of fire safety equipment*

⊙ *to* ***award/grant*** ~ ♦ *to* ***achieve/ gain*** ~ ♦ *a* ~ ***authority/body***

**ˌcertified ˈcheque** *n.* [C] a cheque that a bank promises to pay by writing 'Good for payment' on it

**ˌcertified ˈcopy** (*also* **atˌtested ˈcopy**) *n.* [C] (*Law*) a copy of a document that has been signed by a legal official who has examined it and believes it to be genuine

**ˌcertified ˈmail** = RECORDED DELIVERY

**ˈcertified ˈmanagement acˈcountant** *n.* [C] (*abbr* **CMA**) (*Account.*) in the US, a person who has received a qualification from the Institute of Management Accountants and so has training and experience in managing the finances of companies

**ˈcertified ˈpublic acˈcountant** *n.* [C] (*abbr* **CPA**) (*Account.*) in the US, a person who is qualified to work as a professional accountant in a particular state

★ **certify** /ˈsɜːtɪfaɪ; *AmE* ˈsɜːrt-/ *v.* [T] (**-fies**, **-fying**, **-fied**, **-fied**) (*usu. pass.*) **1** to give sth an official document proving that it has reached a particular standard of quality: *All our products are certified 100% organic.* **2** to give sb an official document proving that they are qualified to do a particular job: *She's certified to work on jet engines.* **3** to state officially, esp. in writing, that sth is true: *The accounts were certified (as) correct.*

**c/f** *abbr* (*Account., written*) carried forward

**CFO** /ˌsiː ef ˈəʊ; *AmE* ˈoʊ/ *abbr* chief financial officer

**CFR** /ˌsiː ef ˈɑː(r)/ = COST AND FREIGHT

**CGT** /ˌsiː dʒiː ˈtiː/ = CAPITAL GAINS TAX

**chaebol** /ˈtʃeɪbɒl; *AmE* ˈkaɪbɑːl; -bɔːl/ *n.* [C] (*pl.* **chaebol** *or* **chaebols**) a very large group of companies in South Korea that is involved in many kinds of business

★ **chain** /tʃeɪn/ *n.* [C] **1** a group of shops/stores, hotels, etc. owned by the same company: *a fast-food/grocery/hotel/retail/supermarket ~* **2** a series of things or people that are connected: *a* ***chain of command*** (= a system by which instructions are passed down from one person to another)

**ˌchain of distriˈbution** = DISTRIBUTION CHAIN

**ˈchain store** *n.* [C] a shop/store that is one of a series of similar shops/stores in many different towns and cities owned by the same company SYN MULTIPLE

★ **chair** /tʃeə(r); *AmE* tʃer/ *n.*, *v.*
• *n.* **1** (*usually* **the chair** [sing.]) the position of being in charge of a meeting or committee; the person who holds this position: *She* ***takes the chair*** *at meetings.* **2** [C] the person in charge of a company: *She's vice chair of the group.*
• *v.* [T,I] to act as the CHAIRMAN of a meeting, discussion, etc.

★ **chairman** /ˈtʃeəmən; *AmE* ˈtʃer-/ *n.* [C] (*pl.* **-men** /-mən/) **1** (*also* **ˌchairman of the ˈboard**) the person who leads a company's BOARD OF DIRECTORS: *She was the founder, chairman and CEO of the company.* ◇ *non-executive chairman*
⊙ *to serve as ~* ◆ *to resign/retire/step down as ~*
**2** the head of an official committee or organization: *the acting chairman of the BMA*
⊙ *to serve as ~* ◆ *to resign/retire/step down as ~*
**3** the person in charge of a meeting, who tells people when they can speak, etc. NOTE **Chairperson/chairpeople** is used to avoid having to say 'chairman' or 'chairwoman' and is also used in more formal language.

★ **chairwoman** /ˈtʃeəwʊmən; *AmE* ˈtʃer-/ *n.* [C] (*pl.* **-women** /-wɪmɪn/) a woman in charge of a meeting, a committee, an organization or a company's BOARD OF DIRECTORS

★ **challenge** /ˈtʃælәndʒ/ *n.*, *v.*
• *n.* [C] **1** a new or difficult task that tests sb/sth's ability and skill: *We are facing some real challenges.*
⊙ *a major/tough ~* ◆ *a competitive/management ~* ◆ *to be/pose a ~* ◆ *to accept/take on/meet a ~*
**2** an act of testing the authority or the strength of sb/sth: *The group is facing a* ***legal*** *challenge from its shareholders.* ◇ *to launch/mount a ~ (to sb/sth)*
• *v.* [T] **1** to question whether sth is right, legal, etc: *challenging his authority* **2** to compete with sb/sth for the highest position **3** to test sb's ability and skills, esp. in an interesting way: *The job doesn't really challenge her.*

**ˌChamber of ˈCommerce** (*also* **chamber of commerce**) *n.* [C] (*abbr* **C. of C.**) **1** (*BrE*) a group of business people in a particular town or area who work together to help their trade and provide information and training in business **2** a national organization that encourages trade between its own country and foreign companies: *the US Chamber of Commerce in Japan*

**ˌchampion of ˈchange** *n.* [C] **1** somebody who is enthusiastic about change in a company, etc. and tries to get others to support it **2** a person who is chosen to lead a CHANGE PROGRAMME SYN CHANGE AGENT

**ˌChancellor of the Exˈchequer** (*also* **chancellor** /ˈtʃɑːnsələ(r); *AmE* ˈtʃæns-/) *n.* [C] in the UK, the government minister responsible for financial affairs

★ **change** /tʃeɪndʒ/ *v.*, *n.*
• *v.* [T] **1** to exchange money into the money of another country: *to change dollars* ***into*** *yen* **2** to exchange money for the same amount in different coins or notes: *Can you change a £20 note?* **3** (*BrE*) to exchange sth that you have bought for sth else, esp. because there is sth wrong with it; to give a customer a new item because there is sth wrong with the one they have bought: *Of course we'll change it for a smaller size for you.*
IDM **change ˈhands** (*also* **exˌchange ˈhands**) to pass to a different owner: *The company has changed hands several times.*
• *n.* **1** [C,U] the act or result of sth becoming different: *a change* ***in*** *interest rates* ◇ *to resist change* **2** [C] the process of replacing sth/sb with sth/sb new or different; a thing that is used to replace sth: *a* ***change of address*** ◇ *management changes* **3** [U] the money that you get back if you pay

more than the amount sth costs **4** coins rather than paper money

**ˈchange ˌagent** (*also* **ˌagent of ˈchange**, *less freq.*) *n.* [C] a person who organizes and looks after change in a company, for example changes in the way the company operates SYN CHAMPION OF CHANGE

**ˈchange conˌtrol** *n.* [U] (*IT*; *Product.*) the process of controlling the changes that are made to a system, design or plan

**ˈchange ˌmanagement** *n.* [U] (*HR*) the process of organizing the way in which a new method of working is introduced into a business
▸ **ˈchange ˌmanager** *n.* [C]

**changeover** /ˈtʃeɪndʒəʊvə(r); *AmE* -oʊvər/ *n.* [C] a change from one system or method of working to another: *the changeover from a manual to a computerized system*

**ˈchange ˌprogramme** *n.* [C] a project to change the way sth operates, esp. a company: *The change programme includes 13 store openings.*

**channel** /ˈtʃænl/ *n., v.*
• *n.* [C] **1** a television station: *The programme was* **on** *Channel 4.* **2** a method or system that people use to get information or to communicate: *Complaints should be made* **through** *the proper channels.* **3** (*Market.*) (*also* **ˈsales ˌchannel**) a way in which a company makes its products available to customers
• *v.* [T] (-ll-, *AmE usu.* -l-) to direct money or effort towards a particular purpose; to do this using a particular route: *channelling income* **into** *R&D*

**ˌchannel of distriˈbution** = DISTRIBUTION CHANNEL

**CHAPS** /tʃæps/ *abbr* **Clearing House Automated Payment System** in the UK, a computer system that is used when a customer of one bank needs to pay a large amount of money to a customer of another bank: *The payments are made through CHAPS.*

**chapter** /ˈtʃæptə(r)/ *n.* [C] **1** (*Law*) a separate section of a written law or contract, usu. with a number and title **2** (*esp. AmE*) a local branch of a society, club, etc.

**ˌChapter ˈ11** *n.* [U] (*Law*) in the US, a section of the law dealing with BANKRUPTCY that allows companies to stop paying their debts in the normal way while they try to find a solution to their financial problems: *The company has* **filed for** (= applied for) *Chapter 11 bankruptcy protection.*

**ˌChapter ˈ7** *n.* [U] (*Law*) in the US, a section of the law dealing with BANKRUPTCY that allows a court to take assets belonging to a company or a person which are then sold to pay their debts: *The firm has* **filed for** (= applied for) *Chapter 7 bankruptcy.*

★ **charge** /tʃɑːdʒ; *AmE* tʃɑːrdʒ/ *n., v.*
• *n.* **1** [C,U] the amount of money that sb asks for goods or services; the money that you pay regularly for a service: *bank/interest/phone ~s* ◇ *a charge of $50* ◇ *a $50 charge* ◇ *There's no charge for the service.*
⊙ *to* ***impose/levy/make/waive*** *a ~ (for sth)* • *a* ***fixed*** *~*
**2** (*Account.*) [C] a large cost that a company has to pay, which affects its financial results: (*BrE*) *take* (= pay) *a one-off charge* ◇ (*AmE*) *a one-time charge*
⊙ *an* ***exceptional****/a* ***special*** *~*
**3** (*Law*) [C,U] a formal claim that sb has committed a crime or done sth wrong
⊙ *to* ***bring/file/lay/press*** *~s (against sb)* • *to* ***admit/deny*** *a ~/the ~s*
**4** [U] responsibility for a group of people, a job or a task: *When did he* **take charge** *as CEO?* ◇ *Who's* **in charge** *here?*
• *v.* **1** [T,I] **~ (sb) (for sth)** | **~ (sb) sth (for sth)** to require payment for goods or services: *They charge clients a monthly fee of $25.* **2** [T] to record the cost of sth as an amount that sb has to pay: *The amount will be charged* **to** *your account.* **3** (*Account.*) [T] to record that a cost belongs to a particular financial account: *The interest is charged* **to** *the P&L account.* SYN DEBIT **4** (*Law*) [T] **~ sb (with sth)** to accuse sb formally of committing a crime or doing sth wrong → INDICT **5** (*fml.*) [T] (*usu. pass.*) to give sb a job or task: *They were charged with developing new software.*

**chargeable** /ˈtʃɑːdʒəbl; *AmE* ˈtʃɑːrdʒ-/ *adj.* (*Account.*) **1** (used about an amount of money) that must be paid by sb: *Expenses will be chargeable* **to** *the company.* **2** (used about income or other money that you earn) that you must pay tax on

**ˌchargeable ˈasset** *n.* [C] (*BrE*) (*Account.*) an asset on which tax must be paid if it is sold

**ˈcharge acˌcount** = ACCOUNT *n.* (2)

**ˈcharge card** *n.* [C] **1** (*Comm.*) a small plastic card provided by a shop/store which you use to buy goods there, paying for them later **2** (*BrE*) a small plastic card with a special number on it that you can use to make calls from public phones, etc. which you pay for later with your home telephone bill

ˌ**charge on ˈassets** *n.* [C] (*Law*) the legal right to have some of a company's assets if the company fails to pay a debt

**charitable** /ˈtʃærətəbl/ *adj.* connected with a charity or charities: *a ~ foundation/trust*

**charity** /ˈtʃærəti/ *n.* (*pl.* **-ties**) **1** [C] an organization for helping people in need **2** [U] the aim of giving money, food, help, etc. to people who are in need: *raising money for charity*

★ **chart** /tʃɑːt; *AmE* tʃɑːrt/ *n., v.*
• ***n.*** [C] **1** a page or sheet of information in the form of diagrams, lists of figures, etc.
○ *to **draw/make/produce** a ~ • the ~ **depicts/shows** sth*
**2** (*esp. AmE*) = GRAPH
• ***v.*** [T] **1** to record or follow the progress or development of sb/sth: *to chart how a product is selling* **2** to plan a course of action

★ **charter** /ˈtʃɑːtə(r); *AmE* ˈtʃɑːrtər/ *n., v.*
• ***n.*** [C] **1** (*HR*) a formal written statement of the principles and aims of an organization **2** (*Law*) (*also* ˌ**corporate ˈcharter**) (*both AmE*) in some US states, the name used for the ARTICLES OF INCORPORATION **3** a written statement describing the rights that a particular group of people should have **4** (*Transpt.*) the system of hiring/renting a plane, boat, etc. for use by a group of people; a vehicle used in this way: *a **charter flight*** (= where a travel company buys all the seats and sells them to its customers)
• ***v.*** [T] (*Transpt.*) to hire/rent a plane, boat, etc. for your own use

★ **chartered** /ˈtʃɑːtəd; *AmE* ˈtʃɑːrtərd/ *adj.* **1** (*BrE*) qualified according to the rules of a particular professional organization: *a ~ surveyor/engineer* **2** (*AmE*) that has a CHARTER allowing it to operate: *a newly chartered bank* **3** (about an aircraft, a ship or a boat) hired for a particular purpose

ˌ**chartered acˈcountant** *n.* [C] (*Account.*) in the UK, a fully trained and qualified accountant who is a member of one of the Institutes of Chartered Accountants

ˈ**chartered ˈcertified acˈcountant** *n.* [C] (*Account.*) in the UK, a person who is a member of the Association of Chartered Certified Accountants (ACCA). They can do all types of accounting work and can become AUDITORS.

ˈ**chartered ˈlife ˈunderwriter** *n.* [C] (*abbr* **CLU**) (*Insur.*) in the US, a person who is fully qualified to sell and give advice on LIFE INSURANCE

**charterer** /ˈtʃɑːtərə(r); *AmE* ˈtʃɑːrt-/ *n.* [C] (*Transpt.*) a company or person that hires/rents or hires out a ship, an aircraft, etc.

ˌ**charter ˈmember** = FOUNDER MEMBER

ˈ**charter ˌparty** *n.* [C] (*Transpt.*) a contract in which the owner of a ship allows another company to use the ship to transport goods

**chartist** /ˈtʃɑːtɪst; *AmE* ˈtʃɑːrt-/ = TECHNICAL ANALYST

**cheap** /tʃiːp/ *adj., adv.*
• ***adj.*** (**-er**, **-est**) **1** costing little money or less money than you expected: *a source of cheap labour* **2** charging low prices: *a cheap supermarket* **3** low in price and quality: *cheap jewellery* ▶ ˈ**cheapness** *n.* [U]
IDM **on the ˈcheap** (*infml.*) spending less money than you usu. need to spend to do sth: *They tried to get the items on the cheap.*
• ***adv.*** (**-er**, *no superlative*) (*infml.*) for a low price: *You may get it cheaper on the Internet.* IDM **be ˌgoing ˈcheap** to be offered for sale at a lower price than usual **sth does not come ˈcheap** something is expensive: *Facilities like this don't come cheap.*

**cheaply** /ˈtʃiːpli/ *adv.* without spending or costing much money: *He hoped to buy the shares back more cheaply later.*

ˌ**cheap ˈmoney** *n.* [U] (*Econ.*) money that can be borrowed at a low rate of interest SYN EASY MONEY

**cheat** /tʃiːt/ *v., n.*
• ***v.*** **1** [T] to trick or deceive sb **2** [I] to act in a dishonest way in order to gain an advantage: *cheating on production quotas* PHR V ˈ**cheat sb (ˈout) of sth** to prevent sb from having sth, esp. in a way that is not honest or fair: *He cheated clients out of millions of dollars.*
• ***n.*** [C] (*esp. BrE*) **1** (*also* ˈ**cheater**, *esp. AmE*) a person who cheats: *tax cheats* **2** something that seems unfair or dishonest, for example a way of doing sth with less effort than it usu. needs: *By using a simple cheat, they avoid paying for phone calls.*

★ **check** /tʃek/ *n., v.*
• ***n.*** [C] **1** (*AmE*) = CHEQUE **2** an act of making sure that sth is safe, correct or in good condition by examining it: *Our machines are given regular checks.* ◇ *to **keep a check on** sth*
○ *a **regular/routine/security** ~ • to **do/run** a ~ (on sth)*

**3** something that slows down the progress of sth else or stops it from getting worse: *to* ***keep a check on*** *inflation* ◇ *to act as/serve as a ~ on sth* **4** (*esp. AmE*) = BILL *n.* (2) **5** (*AmE*) = TICK *n.* (1) **IDM hold/keep sth in 'check** to keep sth under control so that it does not spread or get worse: *keeping prices in check*

• ***v.* 1** [T,I] to examine sth to see if it is correct, safe or satisfactory, or to see if it contains sth: *Check the program* ***for*** *errors.* **2** [T,I] to find out if sth is correct or true or if sth is how you think it is: *Check what time he's coming.* **3** [T] to control sth; to stop sth from increasing or getting worse: *to check the growth of public spending* **4** [T] (*AmE*) to leave bags or cases with an official so that they can be put on a plane or train: *You must check your luggage at the desk.* **5** [T] (*AmE*) = TICK *v.* **PHR V ˌcheck 'in (at ...)**; **ˌcheck 'into ...** to tell an official at a hotel, etc. that you have arrived **ˌcheck sth 'in** (*BrE*) to leave bags or cases with an official to be put on a plane or train **ˌcheck sb/sth 'off** (*AmE*) = TICK SB/STH OFF **'check on sb/sth** to look to see how sb/sth is: *to check on an order* **ˌcheck 'out** (*esp. AmE*) if facts, etc. **check out**, they can be shown to be correct or true **ˌcheck 'out (of ...)** to pay your bill and leave a hotel, etc. **ˌcheck sth 'out 1** to find out if sth is correct, true or acceptable: *They check out all new employees.* **2** (*infml.*) to look at or examine sth that seems interesting or attractive: *Check out the prices at our new store!* **ˌcheck 'over/'through sth** to examine sth carefully to make sure it is correct or acceptable **ˌcheck 'up on sth** to find out if sth is true or correct: *I need to check up on a few facts.*

**'checkbook** = CHEQUEBOOK

**checkbox** /'tʃekbɒks; *AmE* -bɑːks/ (*BrE also* **'tickbox**) *n.* [C] (*IT*) a small square on a computer screen that you click on with the mouse to choose whether a particular function is switched on or off

**'check card** = DEBIT CARD

**checker** /'tʃekə(r)/ *n.* [C] **1** (*AmE*) a person who works at the CHECKOUT in a supermarket **2** (*IT*) (*used in compounds*) a computer program that you use to check sth, for example the spelling and grammar of sth you have written: *a grammar/spelling/virus ~*

**'check-in** *n.* **1** [C,U] the place where you go when you arrive at an airport, to show your ticket, etc. **2** [U] the act of showing your ticket, etc. when you arrive at an airport: *your check-in time*

**'checking acˌcount** = CURRENT ACCOUNT (1)

**'check mark** = TICK *n.* (1)

**checkoff** /'tʃekɒf/ *n.* [U] (*AmE*) (*HR*) in the US, money that an employee agrees can be taken from their wages to pay for being a member of a particular union

**checkout** /'tʃekaʊt/ *n.* **1** [C] the place where you pay for the things that you are buying in a supermarket: *to pay at the checkout* ◇ (*AmE*) *the* ***checkout counter*** **SYN** TILL (*BrE*)
○ *a ~* ***assistant/operator*** • *~* ***staff*** • *~* ***delays/lines/queues***
**2** [U] the time when you leave a hotel at the end of your stay

**chemical** /'kemɪkl/ *adj., n.*
• ***adj.* 1** connected with chemistry: *the chemical industry* ◇ *Eastman Chemical Co.* **2** produced by or using processes which involve changes to atoms, etc: *~ processes/reactions* ▸ **'chemically** /-kli/ *adv.*
• ***n.*** [C] a substance obtained by or used in a chemical process: *toxic chemicals* ◇ *a US chemicals group*

**ˌchemical engi'neering** *n.* [U] the study of the design and use of machines in industrial chemical processes ▸ **ˌchemical engi'neer** *n.* [C]

★ **cheque** (*AmE* **check**) /tʃek/ *n.* [C] (*Finan.*) a printed form that you can write on and sign as a way of paying for sth instead of using money: *a cheque* ***for*** *£100* ◇ *Will you* ***take*** *a cheque* (= can I pay by cheque)? ◇ *Cheques should* ***be made payable to...*** ◇ *He drew a large cheque on his company's account.*
○ *to* ***make out/sign/write (sb)*** *a ~* • *to* ***cash/deposit/pay in*** *a ~* • *to* ***clear/honour*** *a ~* • *to* ***bounce/cancel/stop*** *a ~*

**chequebook** (*AmE* **checkbook**) /'tʃekbʊk/ *n.* [C] a book of printed cheques

**'cheque card** (*also* **ˌcheque guaran'tee card**, **'banker's card**) *n.* [C] (*all esp. BrE*) a plastic card that you must show when you pay by cheque to prove that the bank where you have your account will pay the amount on the cheque

**'cheque run** *n.* [C] the process of using a computer to record payments to be made and print cheques

**'cherry-pick** *v.* [T,I] to choose the best things or people from a group and leave those which are not so good: *cherry-picking the most profit-*

*able services* ▸ **'cherry ˌpicker** *n.* [C] **'cherry-ˌpicking** *n.* [U]

**chief** /tʃiːf/ *adj., n.*
• ***adj.*** **1** most important; main: *Who is their chief competitor?* **2** highest in rank: *chief technology officer*
• ***n.*** [C] a person with a high rank or the highest rank in a company or an organization: *industry chiefs*

★ **ˌchief eˈxecutive ˌofficer** (*also* **ˌchief eˈxecutive**, *esp. in BrE*) *n.* [C] (*abbr* **CEO**) the person in a company who has the most power and authority and is responsible for managing its daily affairs under the authority of the BOARD OF DIRECTORS
NOTE The **chief executive officer** is usu. a member of a board of directors. In the US the CEO is often also the chairman of the board.

**ˌchief fiˈnancial ˌofficer** (*also* **ˌchief ˈfinance ˌofficer**) *n.* [C] (*abbr* **CFO**) the person in charge of the financial department of a company, often a member of the board of directors

**ˌchief inforˈmation ˌofficer** *n.* [C] (*abbr* **CIO**) **1** the person in an organization who is responsible for the computer systems and technology **2** the person in an organization who gives information about it to the public

**ˌchief ˈoperating ˌofficer** (*also* **ˌchief opeˈrations ˌofficer**) *n.* [C] (*abbr* **COO**) a person who is employed to manage the daily affairs of a company, usu. under the authority of a CEO

**childcare** (*AmE* **child care**) /ˈtʃaɪldkeə(r); *AmE* -ker/ *n.* [U] the job of taking care of children, esp. while their parents are at work

**childrenswear** /ˈtʃɪldrənzweə(r); *AmE* -wer/ *n.* [U] (used esp. in shops/stores) clothes for children

**ˌChinese ˈwall** (*also* **ˈfirewall**) *n.* [C, usu. sing.] **1** something that makes it difficult or impossible to do sth, esp. for people to communicate with each other: *a Chinese wall between shareholders and the board* ◇ *to create/raise a ~* **2** (*Stock Ex.*) a set of strict rules that prevent one department of a stock exchange business passing secret information to another that could result in the information being used illegally to gain money

**chip** /tʃɪp/ = MICROCHIP

**ˈchip card** *n.* [C] a small plastic card, for example a credit card, on which a large amount of information is stored in electronic form SYN SMART CARD

**chipmaking** /ˈtʃɪpmeɪkɪŋ/ *n.* [U] the business or process of making MICROCHIPS ▸ **ˈchipmaker** *n.* [C]

**CHIPS** /tʃɪps/ *abbr* **Clearing House Interbank Payments System** in the US, a computer system that is used for making large payments between banks

**choice** /tʃɔɪs/ *n., adj.*
• ***n.*** [sing; U] the number or range of things that you can choose from: *a good choice of products*
○ *an* ***extensive/a great/huge/large/wide*** *~* • *a* ***limited/restricted*** *~*
IDM **of ˈchoice (for sb/sth)** (*used after a n.*) that is chosen by a particular group of people or for a particular purpose: *It's the software of choice for business use.* **of your ˈchoice** (*used after a n.*) that you have chosen
• ***adj.*** (esp. about food) of very good quality: *choice farm-fresh produce*

**churn** /tʃɜːn; *AmE* tʃɜːrn/ *n., v.*
• ***n.*** [U] **1** (*Market.*) the situation when customers stop using a particular make of goods or services or change to another: *customer churn* **2** (*HR*) the situation of employees leaving a company and being replaced by other people: *management churn* **3** (*HR*) the situation when a company moves workers or equipment from one job or place to another
• ***v.*** **1** (*Market.*) [T,I] (used about customers) to stop using a particular make of goods or services or change to another: *customers who have churned* **2** (*HR*) [T] to move employees to another job or place: *Tasks change and staff are churned.*
PHR V **ˌchurn sth ˈout** (*infml.*) to produce sth quickly and in large amounts: *The plant churns out over a million vehicles a year.*

**ˈchurn rate** *n.* [C] **1** (*Market.*) the number of customers who stop using a particular make of goods or services or change to another **2** (*HR*) the number of people who leave jobs in an organization and are replaced by others

**CIF** /ˌsiː aɪ ˈef/ = COST, INSURANCE AND FREIGHT

**CIM** /ˌsiː aɪ ˈem/ = COMPUTER-INTEGRATED MANUFACTURING, RAIL CONSIGNMENT NOTE

**CIO** /ˌsiː aɪ ˈəʊ; *AmE* ˈoʊ/ *abbr* chief information officer

**CIP** *abbr* (*Trade, written*) carriage and insurance paid to ...

**circuit** /ˈsɜːkɪt; *AmE* ˈsɜːrkɪt/ *n.* [C] the complete path of wires and equipment along which an electric current flows

**'circuit-ˌbreaker** (*also* **circuit breaker**) *n.* **1** (*Tech.*) a device that can automatically stop an electric current if it becomes dangerous **2** (*Stock Ex.*) a rule that automatically stops or slows trading on a stock exchange when prices rise and fall too quickly or too far

**circular** /'sɜ:kjələ(r); *AmE* 'sɜ:rk-/ *n.* [C] a printed letter, notice or advertisement that is sent to a large number of people at the same time ▸ **'circular** *adj.*

**circulate** /'sɜ:kjəleɪt; *AmE* 'sɜ:rk-/ *v.* [T,I] if an idea, information, a document, etc. **circulates** or if you **circulate it**, it is passed from one person to another

**ˌcirculating 'asset** = CURRENT ASSET

**ˌcirculating 'capital** = WORKING CAPITAL

**circulation** /ˌsɜ:kjə'leɪʃn; *AmE* ˌsɜ:rk-/ *n.* **1** [U] the passing or spreading of sth from one person or place to another: *the ~ of information/ideas* **2** [U] the use of coins and notes as money: *the amount of forged money* ***in circulation*** **3** [C, usu. sing.] the usual number of copies of a newspaper or magazine that are sold each day, week, etc.

**the City** /'sɪti/ *n.* [sing.] Britain's financial and business centre, in the oldest part of London: *a City stockbroker* ◇ *What is the City's reaction to the news?*

**civil** /'sɪvl/ *adj.* **1** (*Law*) involving commercial issues and legal matters between individuals, companies, etc. and not criminal law: *~ law/damages* **2** connected with the state rather than with the armed forces or with religion: *civil aircraft*

**ˌcivil engi'neer** *n.* [C] a person whose job involves designing, building and repairing roads, bridges, etc. ▸ **ˌcivil engi'neering** *n.* [U]

**the ˌcivil 'service** *n.* [sing.] the government departments in a country, (except the armed forces), and the people who work for them ▸ **ˌcivil 'servant** *n.* [C]

**CKD** /ˌsi: keɪ 'di:/ = COMPLETELY KNOCKED-DOWN

★ **claim** /kleɪm/ *n.*, *v.*

• ***n.*** [C] **1** (*Insur.*) (*also* **in'surance claim**) a request that you make to an insurance company for an amount of money to be paid for loss or damage for which you are insured: *I made a claim on my insurance policy.*

⊙ *to* ***put in/submit*** *a ~* ♦ *to* ***pay/refuse/settle*** *a ~*

**2** a request for money that you believe you have a legal right to from the government, an official organization or a company: *claims* ***for*** *expenses*

⊙ ***disability/unemployment*** *~s* ♦ *to* ***file/make/submit*** *a ~* ♦ *to* ***pay/refuse*** *a ~*

**3** (*Law*) a demand for sth that you make by starting a court case: *a claim* ***for*** *unfair dismissal* (= from a job)

⊙ *to* ***bring/file/make*** *a ~* ♦ *to* ***allow/uphold*** *a ~* ♦ *to* ***dismiss/reject/strike out*** *a ~*

**4 ~ (to sth)** a legal right that sb believes they have to sth, esp. property, land, etc. **5** (*Market.*) a statement about the nature or quality of a product, that may not be true: *to* ***make*** *claims about a product*

• ***v.*** [T,I] **1** to ask for sth from sb/sth, esp. money, because you think it is your legal right to have it: *Both companies have claimed rights to the trademark.* ◇ *to claim on your insurance for sth* **2** to say that a product has a particular nature or quality although this may not be true

**'claim adˌjuster** = CLAIMS ADJUSTER

**claimant** /'kleɪmənt/ *n.* [C] **1** a person who is receiving money from the state because they are unemployed, etc: *benefit claimants* **2** (*Insur.*) a person or company that claims an amount of money from an insurance company **3** (*Law*) (*BrE*) a person or company that starts a court case against sb/sth SYN PLAINTIFF → DEFENDANT **4** (*Law*) a person who believes they have a legal right to sth, esp. property

**'claim form** *n.* [C] **1** a form that you complete in order to claim money from an insurance company or the government **2** (*Law*) in England and Wales, an official document that you complete in order to start a court case

**'claims adˌjuster** (*also* **'claim adˌjuster**, **'claims asˌsessor**) *n.* [C] (*all esp. AmE*) (*Insur.*) a person who investigates an insurance claim on behalf of an insurance company and decides how much the company should pay SYN LOSS ADJUSTER

**'claims asˌsessor** = LOSS ASSESSOR, CLAIMS ADJUSTER

**class** /klɑ:s; *AmE* klæs/ *n.* **1** [C with sing./pl. v.] one of the groups of people in a society that are thought of as being at the same social or economic level: *the professional classes* **2** [C] a group of things that have similar characteristics or qualities:

*The painkiller is part of a new class of drugs.* **3** [C] each of several different levels of comfort that are available to travellers in a plane, etc.

**ˌclass ˈA/ˈB/ˈC share** = A/B/C SHARE

**ˌclass ˈaction** *n.* [C] (*esp. AmE*) (*Law*) a type of court case in which one person or a small group of people make a claim on behalf of a larger group of people who have the same legal problem

**ˌclassifiˈcation soˌciety** (*AmE also* **ˌclassifiˈcation auˌthority**) *n.* [C] (*Insur.*) an official organization that checks whether a ship meets particular standards of design, safety, etc. and provides a certificate as proof of this

**classified** /ˈklæsɪfaɪd/ *adj., n.*
• ***adj.*** **1** containing or connected with CLASSIFIED ADVERTISEMENTS: *the New York Times classified section* **2** with information arranged in groups according to subjects: *a classified catalogue*
• ***n.*** [pl.] **classifieds** the part of a newspaper, magazine, etc. or an Internet site that contains CLASSIFIED ADVERTISEMENTS

**ˌclassified adˈvertisement** (*also* **ˌclassified ˈad**, *infml.*) (*BrE also* **ˈsmall ad**) *n.* [C, usu. pl.] a small advertisement, in a group with other similar ones, that you put in a newspaper or magazine or on an Internet site, if you want to buy or sell sth, employ sb, etc.

**ˌclassified diˈrectory** *n.* [C] a list of the names, addresses and telephone numbers of businesses in a particular area, arranged in groups according to the type of business

**classify** /ˈklæsɪfaɪ/ *v.* [T] (**-fies**, **-fying**, **-fied**, **-fied**) to put sb/sth into a group with other people or things of a similar type: *The report classifies companies* ***according to*** *income.*

★ **clause** /klɔːz/ *n.* [C] a sentence or group of sentences in a contract or legal document that has a number and deals with a particular topic, item or condition
⊙ *to* ***include/insert*** *a ~* • *to* ***delete/remove*** *a ~* • *a ~* ***provides for/states*** *sth* • *a ~* ***excludes/limits*** *sth*

**claw** /klɔː/ *v.* IDM **claw your way ˈback**; **claw your way into/out of/to sth** to gradually achieve sth by using a lot of determination and effort: *The group is clawing its way out of financial crisis.* PHR V **ˌclaw sth ˈback 1** (*also* **ˌclaw ˈback (from sth)**) to get back sth that has been lost by using a lot of effort: *The company is clawing back its share of the market.* **2** (*Finan.*) (about a government) to get money back from people who have received a benefit, usu. by taxing them **3** (*Finan.*) (*BrE*) (about a company) to offer existing shareholders the right to buy a proportion of the shares that have already been offered to new investors ▸ **clawback** /ˈklɔːbæk/ *n.* [C,U] (*Finan.*)

**clean** /kliːn/ *adj., v.*
• ***adj.*** (**-er**, **-est**) **1** free from harmful or unpleasant substances: *~ air/water* **2** not showing or having any record of doing sth dishonest or against the law: *a clean driver's license* **3** (*Finan.*) financially strong; having little or no debt: *a clean* ***balance sheet.*** IDM **a clean bill of ˈhealth** a report that says sth is reliable, safe or in good condition: *The auditors gave us a clean bill of health.*
• ***v.*** IDM **clean ˈhouse** to make an organization, etc. more honest and efficient, for example by removing people or things that are not necessary or not wanted **ˌclean up your ˈact** (*infml.*) to start behaving in a moral or responsible way
PHR V **ˌclean sb ˈout** (*infml.*) to use all of sb/sth's money: *Paying the fine cleaned me out.* **ˌclean sth ˈout** if you **clean out** a bank account, you remove all the money from it **ˌclean sth ˈup 1** to remove crime and immoral behaviour from a place or an activity **2** (*Finan.*) to make sth financially stronger; to reduce the amount of debt **3** to remove harmful substances from a river, piece of land, building, etc.

**ˈclean-up** (*AmE usu.* **cleanup**) *n.* [C, usu. sing.] **1** the process of removing POLLUTION **2** (*Finan.*) the act of making a company, an industry, etc. financially stronger, esp. by reducing the amount of debt

**clear** /klɪə(r); *AmE* klɪr/ *v.* **1** [T] to give or get official approval for sth to be done: *I'll have to* ***clear it with*** *the manager before I can refund your money.* **2** [T] to prove that sb is innocent: *She has been cleared* ***of*** *all charges.* **3** (*Comm.*) [T] **~ (out) sth** to sell all the goods that you have available **4** [T] to remove sth that is not wanted from a place: (*fig.*) *clearing bad debts from the company's books* **5** [T,I] when a cheque that you pay into your bank account **clears**, or a bank **clears** it, the money is available for you to use **6** (*Finan.*) [T] to calculate the total amount of money and the numbers of shares, etc. that investors have agreed to exchange on a particular date, in order to arrange the transfer of the money, shares, etc. between them: *authorized to clear* ***trades*** **7** (*Trade*) [T] to give official permission for goods to leave or enter a place: *to clear goods through customs* **8** [T] to gain or earn an amount of money as profit: *She cleared €2 000 on the deal.* **9** (*Finan.*) [T] if you **clear** a debt or a loan, you pay all the money back **10** [T] to decide officially, after finding out information about sb, that they can be given special work or allowed to see secret papers: *She hasn't been cleared by security.* IDM **clear your 'desk 1** (*also* **clear out your 'desk**) to remove everything from your desk at work because you are leaving your job **2** to finish the work that you need to do

**clearance** /ˈklɪərəns; *AmE* ˈklɪr-/ *n.* **1** [U,C] official permission given to sb before they can work somewhere, have particular information, or do sth they want to do: *to be given/get/require* ~ **2** (*Transpt.*) [U] official permission for a person, a vehicle or goods to enter or leave an airport or a country: *customs clearance ◇ to be given/get/require* ~ **3** [U,C] the process of a cheque being paid by a bank **4** (*Comm.*) [C] = CLEARANCE SALE

**'clearance sale** (*also* **'clearance**) *n.* [C] (*Comm.*) an occasion when a shop/store sells goods cheaply to make space for new goods

**clearing** /ˈklɪərɪŋ; *AmE* ˈklɪrɪŋ/ *n.* [U] (*Finan.*) the activity of exchanging payments that customers of different banks make to each other: *the cheque clearing* ***system***

**'clearing bank** *n.* [C] (*BrE*) (*Finan.*) **1** a bank that is a member of a CLEARING HOUSE **2** one of the major banks that people use

**'clearing house** *n.* [C] **1** (*Finan.*) an organization that exchanges payments between customers of different banks **2** (*Finan.*) an organization that manages the exchange of FUTURES, currencies, etc. between buyers and sellers

**clerical** /ˈklerɪkl/ *adj.* connected with office work, esp. the regular tasks and activities

◆ ~ ***assistants/officers/staff*** ◆ ~ ***jobs/work***

**clerk** /klɑːk; *AmE* klɜːrk/ *n.* [C] **1** a person whose job is to keep the records or accounts in an office, shop/store etc: *an office/invoice/a ticket/wages* ~ **2** (*AmE*) = SALES ASSISTANT **3** (*also* **'desk clerk**) (*both AmE*) a person whose job is dealing with people arriving at or leaving a hotel SYN RECEPTIONIST **4** an official in charge of the records of a council, court, etc: *the Clerk of the Court*

**click** /klɪk/ *v., n.*

• ***v.*** [T,I] to press one of the buttons on a computer mouse: *I clicked* ***on*** *the link to the website.*

• ***n.*** [C] the act of pressing a button on a computer mouse IDM **ˌclicks and 'mortar** (*also* **ˌclicks and 'bricks**) (*E-comm.*) that uses the Internet as well as physical shops/stores, etc. to sell products: *a clicks-and-mortar business*

**clickstream** /ˈklɪkstriːm/ *n.* [C] (*IT; Market.*) a record of a person's activities when spending time on the Internet, including the websites they visit, how long they spend on each one, emails they send or receive, etc: *Marketing companies find it useful to analyse clickstream data.*

**'click-through** *n.* [C,U] (*IT; Market.*) an occasion when sb visits a particular website because they clicked on an advertisement on another web page; the extent to which this happens: *improving click-through ◇ a click-through rate of between 1.5% and 9%*

★**client** /ˈklaɪənt/ *n.* [C] **1** a person who uses the services or advice of a professional person or organization

◆ *a big/an* ***important*** ~ ◆ *a* ***corporate/private*** ~ ◆ ***potential/prospective*** ~*s* ◆ *to* ***act for/advise/represent/serve*** *a* ~

**2** a person who buys goods or services in a shop/store: *A good hairdresser never lacks clients.* **3** (*IT*) a computer that is linked to a SERVER

**'client base** *n.* [C, usu. sing.] the group of regular customers that a business has: *to broaden/expand/increase a* ~

**clientele** /ˌkliːənˈtel; *AmE* ˌklaɪənˈtel/ *n.* [sing. with sing./pl. verb] all the customers or clients of a shop/store, an organization, etc.

◆ *an* ***exclusive****/a* ***regular/young*** ~ ◆ *to* ***attract/build up*** *a* ~

**'client-ˌserver** *adj.* (*IT*) used to describe a computer system in which a powerful central computer provides data to a number of smaller computers connected in a network

**clinch** /klɪntʃ/ *v.* [T] to succeed in getting or achieving sth: *to clinch a deal*

**ˌclinical 'trial** (*also* **ˌclinical 'study**) *n.* [C] a test of a new medicine/drug carried out on a small number of people, in order to see whether the drug is effective and safe to sell to the public

**'clip art** *n.* [U] (*IT*) pictures and symbols that are stored in computer programs or on websites for computer users to copy and add to their own documents

**clipboard** /ˈklɪpbɔːd; *AmE* -bɔːrd/ *n.* [C] **1** a small board with a part that holds papers at the top, used for writing while standing or moving around **2** (*IT*) a place where information from a computer file is stored for a short time until it is added to another file

**CLM** /ˌsiː el ˈem/ *abbr* (*infml.*) **career-limiting move** something you do that has a bad effect on your career, for example making mistakes or being rude to your boss

**clock** /klɒk; *AmE* klɑːk/ *v.* PHR V **ˌclock 'in/'on** (*BrE*) (*AmE* **ˌpunch 'in**) to record the time at which you arrive at work, esp. by putting a card into a machine **ˌclock 'out/'off** (*BrE*) (*AmE* **ˌpunch 'out**) to record the time at which you leave work, esp. by putting a card into a machine **ˌclock 'up sth** (*infml.*) to reach a large amount or number: *clocking up record profits*

**'clock speed** *n.* [C] (*IT*) the speed of a computer's CENTRAL PROCESSING UNIT, used as a measure of how fast the computer operates

**clone** /kləʊn; *AmE* kloʊn/ *n.* [C] **1** (*IT*) a computer designed to work in exactly the same way as another more expensive one made by a different company **2** (disapproving) used to say that sth/sb seems to be an exact copy of sth or sb else: *He's just a clone of the boss.*

★ **close** /kləʊz; *AmE* kloʊz/ *v.*, *n.* • *v.* **1** [T,I] (about a shop/store, business, etc.) to finish business for the day; to not be open for people to use: *What time do the banks close?* **2** [T,I] if a company, shop/store, etc. **closes**, or if you **close** it, it stops operating as a business: *Four factories may close.* **3** [T] to end an activity or event: *to close an account* **4** [T,I] to stop a computer program that has been running; to stop operating: *to close a window* **5** [I] if shares, currencies, etc. **close** at a particular price, they are worth that amount when people stop trading them at the beginning of the day: *a closing price of €19 a share* SYN FINISH **6** [T,I] to agree to sth after having discussed it for a period of time; to be agreed: *to close a deal* **7** [T,I] if a meeting **closes** or sb closes it, it ends **8** [T] to make it impossible for goods, people, etc. to come through: *to close borders* **9** (*Stock Ex.*) [T] **~ (out/off) sth** to sell all the shares in a particular collection, or to buy back shares you have borrowed and sold, in order to return the shares, resulting in a final profit or loss: *Many investors closed out their* ***positions*** *ahead of the New Year.* → OPEN PHR V **ˌclose (sth) 'down** if a company, shop/store, etc. **closes down**, or if you **close it down**, it stops operating as a business OPP OPEN (STH) UP **ˌclose sth 'out** (*AmE*) to sell goods very cheaply in order to get rid of them quickly • ***n.*** [C, usu. sing.] the end of the day of trading, esp. on a stock exchange; the price of a share, bond, etc. at this time: *a flat/low/weak ~ ◊ a firm/high/strong ~* SYN FINISH OPP OPEN

**ˌclose-circuit 'television** = CLOSED-CIRCUIT TELEVISION

**closed** /kləʊzd; *AmE* kloʊzd/ *adj.* **1** shut, used esp. about a shop/store or public building **2** limited to a particular group of people; not open to everyone: *a closed meeting* IDM **behind closed 'doors** with only particular people being allowed to attend or know what is happening; in private: *The merger was discussed behind closed doors.*

**ˌclosed-circuit 'television** (*also* **ˌclose-circuit 'television**, *less freq.*) *n.* [U] (*abbr* **CCTV**) a television system that works within a limited area, for example a public building, to protect it from crime

**ˌclosed-'door** *adj.* used to describe work, a meeting, etc. that takes place privately

**ˌclosed-'door ˌpolicy** *n.* [C] **1** (*Trade*) the practice of making it difficult for foreign companies to do business in your country in order to protect your own industry **2** the practice of keeping things secret and not allowing the media, etc. to know anything about them

**ˌclosed-'end** *adj.* (*Finan.*) **1** (used about a contract or a loan) that must finish or be paid back at a fixed time in the future **2** (*AmE*) used to describe a type of investment company that can only issue a fixed number of shares OPP OPEN-ENDED

**ˌclosed 'market** *n.* [C] (*Econ.*) a market in which foreign companies are not allowed to sell their goods or services

**'close-down** *n.* [C] (*BrE*) when a company, shop/store, etc. stops operating, usu. permanently: *planned close-downs of plants*

**ˌclosed ˈshop** (*AmE also* **ˈunion shop**) *n.* [C] (*HR*) a factory, business, etc. in which employees must all be members of a particular union: *to abolish/operate a ~*

**ˌclosely held ˈcompany** (*BrE*) (*AmE* **ˌclosely-held corpoˈration**) *n.* [C] a public company where up to five people own more than half the shares

**closeout** /ˈkləʊzaʊt; *AmE* ˈkloʊz-/ *n.* [C] (*AmE*) (*Comm.*) an occasion when all the goods in a shop/store that is going to stop operating are sold cheaply to get rid of them quickly SYN CLOSING-DOWN SALE

★ **closing** /ˈkləʊzɪŋ; *AmE* ˈkloʊzɪŋ/ *n., adj.*

• *n.* **1** [U,C] the act of shutting sth such as a factory permanently: *jobs lost through plant closings* **2** [U,C] the act of finishing business for the day, esp. on a stock market: *the share price at Friday's closing* **3** [U] the state of being closed: *the regular New Year closing* **4** [U] the final stage in a sale, the arranging of a loan, etc. when all the details have been agreed: *a sale progressing from cold call to closing* OPP OPENING

• *adj.* coming at the end of sth: *the closing stages* OPP OPENING

**ˌclosing ˈbalance** *n.* [C, usu. sing.] (*Account.*) the **balance** shown in an account at the end of an accounting period

**ˈclosing date** *n.* [C] the last date by which sth must be done, such as applying for a job

**ˌclosing-ˈdown sale** *n.* [C] (*BrE*) (*Comm.*) an occasion when all the goods in a shop/store that is going to stop operating are sold cheaply in order to get rid of them quickly SYN CLOSEOUT

**ˌclosing ˈentry** *n.* [C] (*Account.*) a final amount that is written in an account at the end of an accounting period, before moving the BALANCE to the account for the next period

**ˌclosing ˈstock** *n.* [U] (*Account.*) the amount of goods that a shop/store has available for sale at the end of a particular period of time; the value of these goods

**ˈclosing time** *n.* [C,U] the time when a pub, shop/store, bar, etc. ends business for the day and people have to leave

**closure** /ˈkləʊʒə(r); *AmE* ˈkloʊ-/ *n.* [C,U] the situation when a factory, school, hospital, etc. shuts permanently

⊙ ***branch/plant/store*** *~(s)* ♦ *to* ***avoid/face/force/lead to/prevent*** *~(s)*

**clothing** /ˈkləʊðɪŋ; *AmE* ˈkloʊðɪŋ/ *n.* [U] clothes, esp. a particular type of clothes: *a retailer of men's clothing* ◇ *protective clothing*

⊙ *an* ***article/item*** *of ~* ♦ *a ~* ***factory/store*** ♦ *the ~* ***industry/trade***

**CLU** /ˌsiː el ˈjuː/ = CHARTERED LIFE UNDERWRITER

**ˈcluster aˌnalysis** *n.* [U,C] (*Market.*) a way of analysing large amounts of data to find groups of people, things, etc. that are similar to each other in some way

**CLV** /ˌsiː el ˈviː/ *abbr* (*Market.*) customer lifetime value

**CM** /ˌsiː ˈem/ = CATEGORY MANAGEMENT

**CMA** /ˌsiː em ˈeɪ/ = CERTIFIED MANAGEMENT ACCOUNTANT

**CMR** /ˌsiː em ˈɑː(r)/ = ROAD CONSIGNMENT NOTE

**Co.** /kəʊ; *AmE* koʊ/ *abbr* (*usu. written*) (often in names) company: *the Consett Iron Co.* ◇ *Pitt, Briggs and Co.*

**co-** /kəʊ; *AmE* koʊ/ *prefix* (*used in ns, adjs, advs and vs*) together with: *co-director* ◇ *coexist*

**c/o** = CARRIED OVER, CARE OF SB at CARE

**coach** /kəʊtʃ; *AmE* koʊtʃ/ *n., v.*

• *n.* [C] **1** (*HR*) a person who trains sb to do sth or gives lessons or advice: *a business/career/team ~* **2** (*BrE*) a comfortable bus for carrying passengers over long distances **3** (*AmE*) the cheapest seats in a plane: *coach fares* ◇ *to fly coach*

• *v.* [T,I] (*HR*) to give sb training, lessons or advice: *She coached me* **on** *giving presentations.*

▸ **ˈcoaching** *n.* [U]

**coalface** /ˈkəʊlfeɪs; *AmE* ˈkoʊl-/ (*also* **face**) *n.* [C] the place deep inside a mine where the coal is cut out of the rock IDM **at the ˈcoalface** (*BrE*) where the real work is done

**coalition** /ˌkəʊəˈlɪʃn; *AmE* ˌkoʊə-/ *n.* **1** [C with sing./pl. v.] a group formed by people from several different groups agreeing to work together for a particular purpose: *to build/create/form/join/lead a ~* **2** [U] the act of two or more groups joining together: *their coalition with an American airline*

**COBOL** (*also* **Cobol**) /ˈkəʊbɒl; *AmE* ˈkoʊbɑːl; -bɔːl/ *n.* [U] (*IT*) **Common Business Oriented Language** a computer language designed to write programs for use in business

**COD** /ˌsiː əʊ ˈdiː; *AmE* oʊ/ *abbr* (*Trade*) **ˌcash on deˈlivery** *or in*

*AmE* **col,lect on de'livery** payment for goods will be made when the goods are delivered: *to pay COD*

★ **code** /kəʊd; *AmE* koʊd/ *n.* **1** [C,U] *(often used in compounds)* a system of words, letters, numbers or symbols that represent information about sth: *a code number ◇ an access/error/a log-in ~ ◇ a product/security ~* **2** [C] a set of standards that members of a particular profession, or people who do a particular activity, agree to follow or are recommended to follow: *a code of practice ◇ a voluntary* **code** *of conduct*
**○** *to* ***approve/draw up*** *a ~ of practice, etc.* ♦ *to* ***break/comply with/follow/observe*** *a ~ of practice, etc.*
**3** *(IT)* [U] a system of computer programming instructions: *to* ***write*** *code* **4** [C] = DIALLING CODE

**coder** /'kəʊdə(r); *AmE* 'koʊdər/ *n.* [C] *(IT)* a person whose job is writing computer code

**'code-,sharing** *n.* [U] an arrangement between airlines that allows them to carry each other's passengers and use their own set of letters and numbers for flights provided by another airline

**,co-determi'nation** *n.* [U] *(HR)* a system where workers as well as managers are involved in making decisions in a company, esp. when workers have representatives on boards of management

**C. of C.** = CHAMBER OF COMMERCE

**coffers** /'kɒfəz; *AmE* 'kɔːfərz; 'kɑːfərz/ *n.* [pl.] (usu. in newspapers) a way of referring to the money that a government, an organization, etc. has available to spend: *government coffers*

**,cognitive 'dissonance** *n.* [U] *(Market.)* a feeling of worry and disappointment that people often feel after they have bought sth, for example if they feel that it is not as good as they expected

**COGS** = COST OF GOODS SOLD

**coin** /kɔɪn/ *n., v.*
• *n.* **1** [C] a small flat piece of metal used as money: *a euro coin* **2** [U] money made of metal: *notes and coin*
• *v.* [T] to make coins out of metal
**IDM** **be 'coining it (in); be 'coining money** *(both BrE)* *(infml.)* to earn a lot of money quickly or easily

**coinage** /'kɔɪnɪdʒ/ *n.* [U] *(Econ.)* the coins or the system of money used in a particular country

**col.** *abbr* *(written)* column

**COLA** /'kəʊlə; *AmE* 'koʊlə/ = COST-OF-LIVING ADJUSTMENT, COST-OF-LIVING ALLOWANCE

**,cold-'calling** *n.* [U] *(Market.)* the practice of telephoning or visiting sb you do not know in order to sell them sth ▶ **,cold-'call** *v.* [T,I]: *I cold-called 500 companies.* **,cold 'call** *n.* [C] **,cold-'caller** *n.* [C]

**,cold-'canvassing** *n.* [U] *(Market.)* the practice of asking sb that you do not know if they are interested in sth, for example employing you or buying a product

**,cold 'cash** = HARD CASH

★ **collaborate** /kə'læbəreɪt/ *v.* [I] **~ (with sb) (on/in sth)** to work together with sb to do sth

★ **collaboration** /kə,læbə'reɪʃn/ *n.* **1** [U,C] **~ (with sb) (on sth) | ~ (between A and B)** the act of working with another person or group to do sth: *close collaboration between schools and industry* **2** [C] a piece of work produced by two or more people or groups working together

**collaborative** /kə'læbərətɪv; *AmE* -reɪtɪv/ *adj.* involving, or done by, several people or groups working together: *~ projects/research*

**col,laborative 'working** *n.* [U] *(HR)* a method of working in which people in different places or organizations work together using email, VIDEOCONFERENCING, etc.

★ **collapse** /kə'læps/ *v.* [I] **1** to fail suddenly or completely: *Investors lost their money when the company collapsed.* **2** to decrease suddenly in amount or value: *The share price has collapsed.* ▶ **col'lapse** *n.* [C,U]: *the collapse of two big companies ◇ share price collapses*

**collateral** /kə'lætərəl/ *n.* [U] **1** *(Finan.)* property or sth valuable that you promise to give sb if you cannot pay back money that you borrow **2** *(Market.)* *(AmE)* = COLLATERAL MATERIAL

**collateralize, -ise** /kə'lætərəlaɪz/ *v.* [T] *(Finan.)* *(usu. pass.)* to provide COLLATERAL for a loan, bonds, etc: *The loan is collateralized by the company's plant.*

**col,lateral ma'terial** *n.* [U] *(also* **col,lateral ma'terials** [pl.]) *(also* **col'lateral** [U]) *(all AmE)* *(Market.)* printed information about a product, service or company that is usu. sent or given directly to individual customers

★ **colleague** /'kɒliːg; *AmE* 'kɑː-/ *n.* [C] a person who works at the same place as you, esp. in a profession or a business: *a colleague of mine from the* *office* ◇ *an email from one of my colleagues*

★ **collect** /kəˈlekt/ *v.* **1** [T] to obtain money that is owed; to be paid: *The dealer collects a small fee for every trade.* ◇ *to ~ debts/rent/taxes* **2** [T] to bring things together from different people or places: *to ~ data/evidence* **3** (*Finan.*) [T] (about a bank) to receive a cheque and arrange for the money to be paid from the bank account of the person or company who wrote it: *the* ***collecting bank*** **4** (*infml.*) [I] to get sb/sth to pay back the money that they owe: *to collect on debts* ▸ **collection** /kəˈlekʃn/ *n.* [U,C]: *debt/rent/tax ~* ◇ *data collection* ◇ *a collection of resources*

**colˈlection ˌagency** (*also* **comˌmercial colˈlection ˌagency**) *n.* [C] (*Finan.*) a business whose work is to obtain payment of money owed to a company or an organization for a long time

**collective** /kəˈlektɪv/ *adj.*, *n.*
• ***adj.*** done or shared by all members of a group of people; involving a whole group of society
⊕ *a ~ effort/decision* ◆ *~ action/ownership/responsibility*
▸ **colˈlectively** *adv.*
• ***n.*** [C] a group of people who own a business or a farm and run it together; the business that they run: *an independent collective*

**colˌlective aˈgreement** *n.* [C,U] (*HR*) a signed agreement made between two groups of people, esp. an agreement made by a union and an employer about the pay and working conditions of the union members; the process of making the agreement

**colˌlective ˈbargaining** *n.* [U] (*HR*) discussions between a union and an employer about the pay and working conditions of the union members: *~ agreements/rules*

**colˌlective reˈdundancy** *n.* [U,C] (*HR*) the situation when a number of workers have to leave their jobs within a short period of time because there is no more work available for them

**collector** /kəˈlektə(r)/ *n.* [C] a person who obtains money that is owed: *debt/rent/tax ~*

**ˈcolour-code** (*AmE* **color-**) *n.* [C] a system of marking things with different colours so that you can easily identify them ▸ **ˈcolour-ˌcoded** *adj.*

**column** /ˈkɒləm; *AmE* ˈkɑːləm/ *n.* [C] **1** (*abbr* **col.**) one of the vertical sections into which the printed page of a book, newspaper, etc. is divided **2** a part of a newspaper or magazine which appears regularly and deals with a particular subject or is written by a particular writer: *the financial columns* **3** a series of numbers or words arranged one under the other: *a column of figures*

**ˌcolumn ˈinch** *n.* [C] (*Market.*) the amount of text or pictures that fits into 2.5 centimetres (one **inch**) of a column in a newspaper, magazine, etc., used esp. to measure the length of advertisements

**ˌco-ˈmanager** *n.* [C] (*Finan.*) a bank or other financial institution that works with the LEAD MANAGER in order to help a company sell new shares, bonds, etc.

★ **combine** *v.*, *n.*
• ***v.*** /kəmˈbaɪn/ **1** [T,I] to join two or more things or groups together to form a single one; to come together to form a single thing or group: *plans to combine the two firms* **2** [T] to have two or more different features or characteristics; to put two or more different things, features or qualities together: *The device combines a computer and mobile phone.*
▸ **combination** /ˌkɒmbɪˈneɪʃn; *AmE* ˌkɑːm-/ *n.* [C,U]: *a combination of skills* ◇ *working* ***in combination with*** *another firm* **comˈbined** *adj.*: *combined sales of £30 m*
→ idiom at FORCE *n.*
• ***n.*** /ˈkɒmbaɪn; *AmE* ˈkɑːm-/ [C] a group of people or organizations acting together in business

**comˌbined ˈratio** *n.* [C] (*Insur.*) a way of measuring how successful an insurance company's business is by comparing the amount of money the company receives from its customers with the amount it pays out in claims and expenses

**come** /kʌm/ *v.* [I] (**came** /keɪm/ **come**) **NOTE** Most idioms containing **come** are at the entries for the nouns, verbs or adjectives in the idioms. **IDM** **come under ˈfire** to be criticized strongly: *The directors have come under fire from shareholders.* **PHR V** **ˌcome ˈdown** to become lower in value or amount: *Our costs have come down.* **ˌcome ˈin** (about money) to be earned or received regularly: *There's no money coming in.* **ˌcome ˈin (at/below, etc. sth)** to be calculated as a final amount: *Revenues came in below estimates.* **ˌcome ˈin (on sth)** to become involved in sth: *Do you want to come in on the deal?* **ˌcome ˈoff** (*infml.*) to be successful; to happen: *The deal didn't come off.* **ˌcome ˈoff (sth)** (*not in the pass.*) (about prices, etc.) to start to change, esp. to start to decrease after increasing for a period of time: *The shares have just come off an all-time high.* ˌ**come 'off sth** (*not in the pass.*) to start to recover from sth: *coming off a recession* ˌ**come 'out at/to sth** (*not in the pass.*) to add up to a particular cost or sum: *The total bill comes out at €500.* ˌ**come 'out of sth** (*not in the pass.*) to reach the end of a difficult period: *coming out of recession* ˌ**come 'out with sth** (*not in the pass.*) to create sth and make it available: *They have come out with a new type of phone.* ˌ**come 'through (with sth)** to successfully do or provide sth that people expect or that you have promised: *The bank came through with the money.* '**come to sth** (*not in the pass.*) **1** to add up to sth: *Annual sales come to €70 m.* **2** to reach a particular state or situation: *The contract came to an end in March.* ˌ**come 'up for sth** (*not in the pass.*) to reach the time when a decision must be made about the future of sb/sth: *The contract is coming up for renewal.* ˌ**come 'up with sth** (*not in the pass.*) to find or produce an answer, an amount of money, etc: *How soon can you come up with the money?*

**COMEX** /'kɒmeks; *AmE* 'kɑːm-/ (*also* '**COMEX diˌvision**) *n.* [sing.] the part of the New York Mercantile Exchange that deals with metals such as gold and silver → NYMEX

'**comfort ˌletter** *n.* [C] (*Finan.*) **1** = LETTER OF COMFORT **2** a statement made by an AUDITOR when a company is planning to sell new shares, to say that they have found no problems in the company's financial records

'**comfort zone** *n.* [C] **1** a situation in which sb feels safe, relaxed and confident **2** if a person is **in the comfort zone**, he/she does not work very hard and so does not produce the best possible results

**command** /kə'mɑːnd; *AmE* kə'mænd/ *n.* [C] (*IT*) an instruction given to a computer

**comˌmand and con'trol** *n.* [U] a way of managing a company or country in which a single leader or small group makes all the decisions and gives people detailed instructions on what to do

**comˌmand e'conomy** (*also* **conˌtrolled e'conomy**) *n.* [C] (*Econ.*) a type of economic system in which a government controls its country's industries and decides what goods should be produced SYN PLANNED ECONOMY OPP MARKET ECONOMY

'**comment card** *n.* [C] (*Market.*) a small piece of stiff paper on which customers answer questions to give their opinions about a company's products or services

★ **commerce** /'kɒmɜːs; *AmE* 'kɑːmɜːrs/ *n.* [U] the business of buying and selling things; trade: *leaders of industry and commerce*

★ **commercial** /kə'mɜːʃl; *AmE* kə'mɜːrʃl/ *adj., n.*

• ***adj.*** **1** connected with the buying and selling of goods and services: *the commercial heart of the city* ◊ *Tesco's commercial director* **2** connected with businesses or the process of carrying out business: *industrial and commercial premises* ◊ *commercial insurance companies* **3** making or intended to make a profit: *The new product was not a* ***commercial success*** (= it did not make much money). **4** (about television or radio) paid for by the money charged for broadcasting advertisements: *a ~ radio station/TV channel*

▸ **com'mercially** /-ʃəli/ *adv.*: *commercially produced*

• ***n.*** **1** [C] an advertisement on television or on the radio **2** (*Stock Ex.*) **commercials** [pl.] shares in companies that buy and sell goods to individual customers

**comˌmercial 'agency** *n.* [C,U] **1** (*Prop.*) a business whose work is to buy and sell property, such as office buildings, for businesses to use **2** (*Finan.*) (*BrE*) a business whose work is to collect information about the financial position of a person or a business, esp. whether they would be able to pay back any money that they borrow SYN CREDIT REFERENCE AGENCY **3** (*Comm.*) a business that provides a service to other businesses and intends to make a profit

**comˌmercial 'agent** *n.* [C] **1** (*Trade*) an independent person who works on behalf of a company to find business for it, esp. abroad **2** (*Prop.*) a person or a business whose work is to buy and sell property, such as office buildings, for businesses to use

**comˌmercial 'art** *n.* [U] the activity of designing advertisements, the materials used to pack products, etc. ▸ **comˌmercial 'artist** *n.* [C]

**comˌmercial 'bank** *n.* [C] a bank with branches in many different places, providing a range of services for people and businesses: *big*

commercial banks, such as Barclays
▸ **com,mercial 'banking** *n.* [U]

**com'mercial bill** = TRADE BILL

**com,mercial col'lection ,agency** = COLLECTION AGENCY

**com,mercial corres'pondence** *n.* [U] business letters, emails, and other documents, esp. as a subject of study

**Com,mercial 'Counsellor** *n.* [C] (*Trade*) a government official who works in a foreign country and helps to develop trade between that country and their home country

**commercialize, -ise** /kə'mɜːʃəlaɪz; *AmE* -'mɜːrʃl-/ *v.* [T] **1** to develop a product into sth that can be produced and sold widely: *to commercialize vaccines for cancer* **2** to produce sth to try to make as much profit as possible: *Sport has become very commercialized.*
▸ **com,merciali'zation, -i'sation** /-ʃəlaɪ'zeɪʃn; *AmE* -ʃlə'z-/ *n.* [U]

**com,mercial 'law** *n.* [U] (*Law*) the collection of laws that deal with all aspects of business and trade, including contracts, buying, selling, storing and transporting goods, etc. SYN MERCANTILE LAW

**com,mercial 'loan** *n.* [C] (*Finan.*) a loan made to a business

**com,mercial 'manager** *n.* [C] the person who is in charge of the part of a company that deals with selling goods or services

**com,mercial mo'nopoly** *n.* [C] (*Econ.*) a situation where one buyer or supplier can fix the price of a product, a service, etc.

**com,mercial 'paper** *n.* [U] (*Finan.*) a method that a large company, bank, etc. can use to borrow money from investors, usu. for a period of less than a year. The lender cannot take the assets of the company if the loan is not repaid: *to default on/issue ~*

**com'mercial ,sector** *n.* [sing.] (*Econ.*) the part of a country's economy that consists of businesses that are not involved in manufacturing or transport, for example, hotels, offices, shops/stores and other businesses that offer services, and government organizations, health and education institutions, etc.

**com,mercial 'set** *n.* [C] (*Trade*) the documents that are required when exporting goods, usu. including a BILL OF EXCHANGE, a BILL OF LADING, an INVOICE and an insurance certificate



**com,mercial 'treaty** = TRADE AGREEMENT

**commingle** /kə'mɪŋgl/ *v.* [T,I] to mix different things together: *commingled fibres* ◇ *commingling data*
▸ **com'mingling** *n.* [U]: *the commingling of funds*

★ **commission** /kə'mɪʃn/ *n.*, *v.*
• *n.* **1** (*Comm.*) [U,C] an amount of money paid to sb for selling goods or services and which usu. increases with the quantity they sell: *to work on commission* (= be paid according to how much you sell) ◇ *to earn/get/pay (a) ~* **2** [U,C] an amount of money charged by a bank, for example, for providing a particular service: *commission rates* ◇ *to charge/pay a ~* **3** (*often* **Commission** [C]) a group of people who are officially asked to find out about a problem and suggest some actions in a report: *a commission of enquiry* ◇ *to appoint/set up a ~* **4** (*often* **Commission** [C]) an official organization with a particular purpose that manages sth or makes sure that the law is obeyed: *the Equal Opportunities Commission* ◇ *to appoint/set up a ~* **5** [C] a formal request to an artist, a writer, etc. to produce a piece of work: *to accept/be given/get/receive a ~* IDM **in/out of com'mission** available/not available to be used
• *v.* [T] to officially ask sb to write, make or create sth or to do a task for you: *The survey was commissioned by local stores.*

**com'mission ,agent** *n.* [C] (*Trade*) a person or company that sells goods for sb in another country and is paid a percentage of the value of the goods

**com'mission ,broker** *n.* [C] (*Stock Ex.*) a person who buys and sells shares, bonds, etc. for other people and is paid a percentage of their value SYN BROKER

**commissioner** /kə'mɪʃənə(r)/ *n.* [C] the person in charge of, or a member of, a COMMISSION

**commitment** /kə'mɪtmənt/ *n.* **1** [C,U] a promise to do sth or to behave in a particular way: *our commitment to providing quality at low prices*
⊕ *a clear/firm/strong ~* ♦ *a continuing/long-term ~* ♦ *to give/make a ~*
**2** [C,U] **~ (of sb/sth) (to sth/sb)** the willingness to give time, money, effort, etc. in order to achieve sth; complete loyalty to one organization, person, etc: *Developing a new product*

*requires a major commitment of time and money.*
○ *to **demand/lack/need** ~ ◆ **person-al/total** ~*
**3** [C] a thing that you have promised or agreed to do: *I have a prior commitment and am unable to attend.* ◇ *meeting financial commitments*
○ ***business/contractual/family*** ~
◆ *to **honour/meet** a ~*

**com'mitment fee** *n.* [C] (*Finan.*) a charge made by a bank for keeping a loan available for a customer to use later

**com'mitment ˌletter** *n.* [C] (*Finan.*) a document formally offering to lend money to sb

**committed** /kəˈmɪtɪd/ *adj.* willing to work hard and give your time and energy to sth; believing strongly in sth: *a highly committed workforce*

★ **committee** /kəˈmɪti/ *n.* [C with sing./pl. v.] a group of people who are chosen, usu. by a larger group, to make decisions or to deal with a particular subject: *a ~ member/a member of the ~* ◇ *a committee meeting*
○ *to **create/form/set up** a ~ ◆ to **be/serve/sit** on a ~ ◆ to **be appointed to/be elected to/chair** a ~*

**com'modities ˌmarket** = COMMODITY MARKET

★ **commodity** /kəˈmɒdəti; *AmE* -ˈmɑːd-/ *n.* [C] (*pl.* **-ties**) **1** (*Finan.*) a product or a raw material, such as grain, coffee, cotton or metals, that can be bought and sold in large quantities, esp. between countries
○ *to **deal/invest/trade** in commodities ◆ ~ **exports/prices/trading***
**2** a thing that is useful or has a useful quality: *Time is a precious commodity.*

**com'modity exˌchange** *n.* [C] (*Finan.*) an organization, a system or a place for business or trade in **commodities**

**comˌmodity 'futures** *n.* [pl.] (*Finan.*) **commodities** that are bought at an agreed price to be delivered at a date in the future

**com'modity ˌmarket** (*also* **com'modities ˌmarket**) *n.* [C] (*Finan.*) business or trade in **commodities**; a place where this is done

**com'modity ˌproduct** *n.* [C] (*Market.*) a product that looks the same, functions in the same way, etc., whoever produces it: *Car tyres are no longer a commodity product.*

**commonality** /ˌkɒməˈnæləti; *AmE* ˌkɑːm-/ *n.* [U,C] (*pl.* **-ties**) the state of sharing features or qualities; a feature or quality that is shared: *commonality between systems*

**ˌcommon 'carrier** (*also* **ˌpublic 'carrier**) *n.* [C] **1** (*IT*) a company that provides TELECOMMUNICATIONS services to the public **2** (*Law*; *Transpt.*) a company that transports people or goods for the general public

**ˌcommon 'law** *n.* [U] (*Law*) (in England, the US, Australia and some other countries) a system of laws that have been developed from customs and from decisions made by judges, not created by Parliament → CIVIL (1)

**ˌcommon 'market** *n.* [C, usu. sing.] (*Econ.*) **1** a group of countries that have agreed on low taxes on goods traded between them, and higher fixed taxes on goods imported from countries outside the group **2 Common Market** a former name of the European Union

**ˌcommon 'ownership** (*also* **ˌownership in 'common**) *n.* [U] (*Law*) **1** the fact of sth, such as a piece of land, a building or a company, being owned equally by more than one person or group: *land in common ownership* **2** the fact of one or more companies being owned by the same person or group

**ˌcommon 'pricing** = PRICE-FIXING

**ˌcommon 'share** = ORDINARY SHARE

**ˌcommon 'stock** (*BrE also* **ˌordinary 'stock**, *less freq.*) *n.* [C,U] (*Finan.*) shares in a company that give the owner the right to a DIVIDEND and the right to vote at meetings of shareholders

★ **communication** /kəˌmjuːnɪˈkeɪʃn/ *n.* **1** [U] the activity or process of expressing ideas and feelings or of giving people information: *Effective communication is the key to good sales.* **2** [U] (*often* **communications** [pl.]) methods of sending information, esp. telephones, radio, computers, etc.
○ *~(s) **equipment/technology** ◆ the ~ **industry/sector***
**3 communications** [pl.] the road, rail, aircraft, sea, etc. systems that allow goods and passengers to be transported from one place to another: *a ~ infrastructure/network/system* **4** (*fml.*) [C] a message, letter or telephone call: *Further to our recent email communication …*

**communicator** /kəˈmjuːnɪkeɪtə(r)/ *n.* [C] a person who is able to describe their ideas and feelings clearly to others: *a good/poor/skilled ~*

**communism** /ˈkɒmjənɪzəm; *AmE* ˈkɑːmjə-/ *n.* [U] a political movement that believes in an economic system in which the state controls the means of producing everything on behalf of the people. It aims to create a society in which everyone is treated equally. ▶ **ˈcommunist** *n., adj.*

**comˌmunity anˈtenna ˌtelevision** = CABLE TELEVISION

**commutation** /ˌkɒmjuˈteɪʃn; *AmE* ˌkɑːm-/ *n.* [C,U] **1** (*Insur.*) the right to exchange a series of future payments for one large sum that you receive now: *full commutation of pension benefits* **2** (*AmE*) the act of travelling regularly by bus, train, car, etc. between your place of work and your home

**commute** /kəˈmjuːt/ *v., n.*

• ***v.* 1** [I] to travel regularly by bus, train, car, etc. between your place of work and your home: *commuting* ***from*** *Oxford* ***to*** *London* **2** (*Law*) [T] to replace one punishment with another that is less severe: *death sentences commuted* ***to*** *life imprisonment* ▶ **comˈmuter** *n.* [C]

• ***n.*** [C] the journey that a person makes when they **commute**: *your daily commute*

**comp** /kɒmp; *AmE* kɑːmp/ *n., adj., v.* (*AmE*)

• ***n.* 1** (*infml.*) [U] compensation **2** (*infml.*) [C] something that you give or receive free of charge

• ***adj.*** (*infml.*) free of charge: *You will receive ten comp tickets.* SYN COMPLIMENTARY

• ***v.*** [T] (*infml.*) to give sb sth free of charge: *The manager comped us the meal.*

**ˌCompanies ˈHouse** *n.* [sing.] (*Law*) in the UK, the government organization that by law holds the names of all companies in the UK and the details of their directors, shareholders and accounts

**ˌcompanies ˈregister** (*also* **ˌregister of ˈcompanies**) *n.* [C] (*Law*) an official list of the companies that have been created in a country, with information about directors, shareholders, etc.

**ˌCompanies ˈRegistry** (*also* **ˌRegistry of ˈCompanies**) *n.* [C, usu. sing.] (*Law*) in the UK and some other countries, the official organization that keeps records of the companies that are created in the country and to which companies must send information. It also makes sure that laws relating to companies are obeyed

★**company** /ˈkʌmpəni/ *n.* [C] (*pl.* **-nies**) a business organization selling goods or services, esp. one that has been officially created in a particular country and is owned by shareholders: *The company was founded in 1995.* ◇ *She's been working for the same company for 15 years.* ◇ *The company* ***is listed*** *on the Stock Exchange.*

⊙ *a* ***big/medium-sized/small*** *~* ◆ *to* ***create/establish/set up/start (up)*** *a ~* ◆ *to* ***manage/operate/own/run*** *a ~* ◆ *to* ***join/leave*** *a ~* ◆ *to* ***acquire/buy/sell/take over*** *a ~* ◆ *to* ***dissolve/liquidate*** *a ~* ◆ *a ~* ***expands/fails/grows*** ◆ *a ~* ***goes bankrupt/goes out of business/goes under***

IDM **take a company ˈpublic; a company goes ˈpublic** if you take a company **public** or a company **goes public**, it becomes part of a stock exchange and its shares can be bought and sold by the public → idiom at PART *v.*

**ˌcompany ˈcar** *n.* [C] a car that a company provides for an employee

**ˌcompany diˈrector** = DIRECTOR (1)

**ˌcompany ˈdoctor** *n.* [C] **1** a specialist who is employed to manage a company during a period of financial difficulty **2** (*HR*) a medical doctor employed by a company to look after its employees

**ˈcompany ˈlimited by guarˈantee** *n.* [C] (*pl.* **companies -**) (*Law*) a type of company that does not sell shares to obtain funds, but is supported by a group of people who each promise to pay its debts up to a particular amount if it fails

**ˈcompany ˈlimited by ˈshares** *n.* [C] (*pl.* **companies -**) (*Law*) a type of company in which each shareholder pays debts up to the amount of the shares they have bought if it fails. Most companies in the UK are of this type.

**ˌcompany ˈmeeting** *n.* [C] **1** (*Law*) a meeting of the shareholders and directors of a company **2** a meeting of some or all of the employees of a company

**ˌcompany ˈofficer** (*AmE also* **ˌcorporate ˈofficer**) *n.* [C] (*Law*) a person who has an official position in a company and represents the company in its activities

**ˌcompany ˈpresident** = PRESIDENT (1)

**ˌcompany ˈsecretary** (*BrE*) (*also* **ˈsecretary**, *AmE, BrE*) (*AmE also* **ˌcorporate ˈsecretary**) *n.* [C] (*Law*) a person in a company, usu. chosen by the directors, who has various legal duties, such as looking after the company's official documents and arranging company meetings

**ˌcompany 'union** *n.* [C] (*HR*) an organization that a company forms for its employees to represent them when dealing with the managers. **Company unions** are not independent organizations like normal unions.

**ˌcomparable-store 'sales** (*also* **comps**, *infml.*) = SAME-STORE SALES

**ˌcomparable 'worth** *n.* [U] (*AmE*) (*HR*) the principle that men and women doing jobs that have the same value to their employer should get the same wage; the right of an employee to receive a wage that relates to the value of their work

**comˌparative ad'vantage** *n.* [C,U] (*Econ.*) the ability of a country to make a particular product or supply a particular service better and more cheaply than others

**comˌparative 'advertising** *n.* [U] (*Market.*) advertising that claims that the product being advertised is better or cheaper than a competitor's product

**comˌpassionate 'leave** *n.* [U] (*HR*) time that you are allowed to be away from work with pay because sb in your family is suddenly ill/sick or has died, or for other personal reasons

**compatibility** /kəmˌpætə'bɪləti/ *n.* [U] **~ (with sb/sth)** | **~ (between A and B)** the ability of machines, esp. computers, and computer programs to be used together

**compatible** /kəm'pætəbl/ *adj.*, *n.*
• ***adj.*** **~ (with sth)** (about equipment, esp. computers or programs) able to be used together; standard: *compatible software* ◇ *WAP compatible web pages* OPP INCOMPATIBLE
• ***n.*** [C] (*IT*) a computer designed to work in exactly the same way as another type or make and use the same software: *an IBM compatible*

★**compensate** /'kɒmpənseɪt; *AmE* 'kɑːm-/ *v.* **1** [T] to pay sb money because they have suffered some damage, loss, injury, etc: *be compensated **for** your injuries* **2** (*AmE*) [T] to pay sb for work that they have done: *They are compensated at a daily rate.* **3** [I] **~ (for sth)** to provide sth good to balance or reduce the bad effects of damage, loss, etc.

**ˌcompensating 'balance** *n.* [C] (*esp. AmE*) (*Finan.*) the amount of money a bank requires a customer to keep in an account in order to receive the bank's services free or to receive a loan

★**compensation** /ˌkɒmpən'seɪʃn; *AmE* ˌkɑːm-/ *n.* [U,C] **1** something, esp. money, that sb gives you because they have hurt you, or damaged sth that you own; the act of giving this to sb: *compensation **for** injuries* ◇ *She received $10 000 **in** compensation.*
◐ *to **award/give/pay** ~* • *to **accept/get** ~* • *to **be eligible for/be entitled to/claim/demand** ~*
**2** (*AmE*) the money or other benefits that an employee receives for the work that they do: *rising employee compensation* ◇ *to get/give/pay ~*

**compen'sation ˌpackage** *n.* [C] **1** a set of things, including money, that is given to sb because they have been hurt in some way, for example when sb loses their job **2** (*HR*) (*AmE*) everything that an employee receives from their employer including pay, benefits and other rewards

**compenˌsatory 'damages** (*also* **ˌactual 'damages**) (*both AmE*) *n.* [pl.] (*Law*) an amount of money that a court orders sb to pay you to help pay for the injury they have caused you or the damage to your property, not to punish them

★**compete** /kəm'piːt/ *v.* [I] to try to be more successful or better than sb else who is trying to do the same as you: *Several companies are competing **for** the contract.* ◇ *We can't compete **with** them on price.* ◇ *competing companies/products*

**competence** /'kɒmpɪtəns; *AmE* 'kɑːm-/ *n.* **1** (*also* **'competency**, *less freq.*) [U,C] the ability to do sth well: *a high level of competence **in** English* ◇ *professional/technical ~* **2** (*fml.*) (*also* **'competency**, *less freq.*) [C] a skill that you need in a particular job or for a particular task: *management competences* **3** [C] the power that a court, an organization or a person has to deal with sth

**'competence ˌprofiling** = COMPETENCY PROFILING

**competency** /'kɒmpɪtənsi; *AmE* 'kɑːm-/ (*pl.* **-cies**) = COMPETENCE (1,2)

**'competency-based** *adj.* (*HR*) that involves looking at the skills that an employee has or needs: *competency-based training*

**'competency ˌprofiling** (*also* **'competence ˌprofiling**) *n.* [U] (*HR*) a method of discovering the skills, knowledge and behaviour necessary for a particular task, job or career

▸ 'competency ˌprofile (*also* 'competence ˌprofile) *n.* [C]

**competent** /'kɒmpɪtənt; *AmE* 'kɑːm-/ *adj.* **1** (about a person) having enough skill or knowledge to do sth well or to the necessary standard: *a competent worker* **2** (about a piece of work) done well or to the necessary standard: *a very competent report* OPP INCOMPETENT
▸ **'competently** *adv.*

★**competition** /ˌkɒmpə'tɪʃn; *AmE* ˌkɑːm-/ *n.* **1** [U] a situation in which people or organizations compete with each other for sth that not everyone can have: *We are* ***in competition with*** *four other companies* ***for*** *the contract.* ◇ *growing competition from foreign firms* ◇ *fair/fierce/stiff/tough/unfair* ~ **2 the competition** [sing. with sing./pl. verb] the people who are competing against sb: *a strategy to beat the competition* ◇ *to keep ahead of/out-think the* ~

**compe'tition law** *n.* [U] (*Law*) the branch of law that deals with fair competition between companies and the control of MONOPOLIES

★**competitive** /kəm'petətɪv/ *adj.* **1** used to describe a situation in which people or organizations compete against each other: *a highly competitive market* **2** as good as or better than others: *a wide range of goods at competitive prices* **3** (about a person) trying hard to be better than others OPP UNCOMPETITIVE
▸ **com'petitively** *adv.*: *competitively priced goods* **com'petitiveness** (*also* **comˌpeti'tivity** /-'tɪvəti/ *less freq.*) *n.* [U]: *improving the competitiveness of British industry*

**comˌpetitive ad'vantage** *n.* [C,U] (*also* **comˌpetitive 'edge** [sing; U]) a situation where a company is in a position to be more successful than its competitors; something that helps a company be in this position

● *to* ***create/gain/have*** *(a)* ~ ◆ *a* ***key/significant/sustainable*** ~

**comˌpetitive a'nalysis** (*also* **comˌpetitor a'nalysis, comˌpetitor 'profiling**, *less freq.*) *n.* [C,U] (*Market.*) a detailed study of a company's competitors that looks for areas where the company has or could gain an advantage

**comˌpetitive 'balance** *n.* [C,U] (*Econ.*) a situation where none of the companies competing in a market has a very great or an unfair advantage

**comˌpetitive 'edge** = COMPETITIVE ADVANTAGE

**comˌpetitive in'telligence** (*also* **comˌpetitor in'telligence**, *less freq.*) *n.* [U] (*Market.*) the ability to get and use information about competitors; the information obtained

**comˌpetitive 'strategy** (*also* **comˌpetitor 'strategy**, *less freq.*) *n.* [C,U] a plan that is intended to gain an advantage for a company over its competitors; the process of making such a plan

★**competitor** /kəm'petɪtə(r)/ *n.* [C] a business, person, product, etc. that competes against others: *We need to win market share from our competitors.* SYN RIVAL

● *our* ***biggest/largest/main/major/nearest*** ~ ◆ *a* ***fierce/strong/tough*** ~

**comˌpetitor a'nalysis** = COMPETITIVE ANALYSIS

**comˌpetitor in'telligence** = COMPETITIVE INTELLIGENCE

**comˌpetitor 'profiling** = COMPETITIVE ANALYSIS

**comˌpetitor 'strategy** = COMPETITIVE STRATEGY

**compile** /kəm'paɪl/ *v.* [T] **1** to produce a list, report, book, etc. by bringing together different items, articles, data, etc: *statistics compiled by the Treasury* **2** (*IT*) to translate instructions from a computer language into a form that can be read directly by the computer ▸ **compilation** /ˌkɒmpɪ'leɪʃn; *AmE* ˌkɑːm-/ *n.* [C,U]

**compiler** /kəm'paɪlə(r)/ *n.* [C] **1** a person who **compiles** sth: *the compilers of the report* **2** (*IT*) a program that translates instructions from one computer language into another for a computer to understand

**complainant** /kəm'pleɪnənt/ *n.* [C] (*Law*) a person who makes a complaint, usu. to the police, that somebody has harmed them or committed a crime

★**complaint** /kəm'pleɪnt/ *n.* **1** [C] a reason for not being satisfied; a statement that sb makes saying that they are not satisfied: *I'd like to make a complaint.* ◇ *to* **lodge** *an official complaint*

● *to* ***have/receive*** *a* ~ ◆ ***common/customer*** ~*s* ◆ *to* ***deal with/handle/investigate/respond to*** *a* ~

**2** [U] the act of complaining: *a letter of complaint* **3** (*Law*) [C] a statement that gives the reasons why sb is bringing a case or making a claim in a court **4** (*Law*) [C] a formal statement that sb has committed a crime

**com'plaints ˌmanagement** *n.* [U] the system of analysing and responding to customers' complaints

**complementary** /ˌkɒmplɪ'mentri; *AmE* ˌkɑːm-/ *adj.* two things or people that are **complementary** are different but together form a useful or attractive combination of skills, qualities or physical features: *a team of people with complementary skills*

**ˌcomplementary 'goods** *n.* [pl.] (*Market.*) goods that are sold separately but that are used together, for example cars and petrol/gasoline

**comˌpletely built-'up** *adj.* (*abbr* **CBU**) (*Manufact.*) (about a machine, etc. that is made from parts) that has been manufactured and put together: *the import of completely built-up cars*

**comˌpletely knocked-'down** *adj.* (*abbr* **CKD**) (*Manufact.*) (about a machine, etc. that is made from parts) that has been manufactured but not put together

★ **completion** /kəm'pliːʃn/ *n.* [U,C] (*BrE*) (*Prop.*) the formal act of completing the sale of property: *You receive the keys on completion.*

**com'pletion date** *n.* [C] **1** the date on which a project, esp. a building project, is expected to be finished **2** (*BrE*) the date on which the ownership of something, esp. a piece of property, is legally transferred from one person to another

**compliance** /kəm'plaɪəns/ *n.* [U] (*usu. written*) the practice of obeying rules or requests made by people in authority: *All our products are **in compliance with** safety laws.*
OPP NON-COMPLIANCE

**com'pliance ˌofficer** *n.* [C] a person working in a financial organization whose job is to make sure that the company is obeying the laws and rules that apply to it

**compliant** /kəm'plaɪənt/ *adj.* **1** in agreement with the rules: *compliant **with** the law* **2** (*Tech.*) (about technical equipment, software, systems, etc.) that can be used with a particular system or set of rules: *fully Internet compliant*

**complimentary** /ˌkɒmplɪ'mentri; *AmE* ˌkɑːm-/ *adj.* **1** given free of charge **2** expressing admiration, praise, etc.

**compliˌmentary 'close** (*also* **compliˌmentary 'closing**) *n.* [sing.] (*AmE*) the word or words that you write at the end of a business letter just before you sign your name, for example 'sincerely' or 'regards'

**'compliments slip** (*also* **'compliment slip**) *n.* [C] (*both BrE*) a small piece of paper printed with the name of a company, that is sent out with information, goods, etc.

★ **comply** /kəm'plaɪ/ *v.* [I] (**-lies**, **-lying**, **-lied**, **-lied**) to obey a rule, an order, etc: *Three employees refused to comply **with** the new regulations.*

★ **component** /kəm'pəʊnənt; *AmE* -'poʊ-/ *n.* [C] one of several parts of which sth is made: *the components of a machine*
○ *computer/vehicle ~s* ◆ *a ~s **manufacturer*** ◆ *an **essential**/a **key**/an **important** ~ (of sth)*
▸ **com'ponent** *adj.*: *to break sth down into its component **parts***

**composite** /'kɒmpəzɪt; *AmE* kəm'pɑːzət/ *adj.* made of different parts or materials: *composite materials*

**composition** /ˌkɒmpə'zɪʃn; *AmE* ˌkɑːm-/ *n.* **1** [U] the different parts that sth is made of; the way the parts are organized: *the composition of the new board* **2** (*Manufact.*) [U] an artificial material made of several different substances, often used instead of a natural material: *composition floors* **3** (*Law*) [C, usu. sing.] a legal agreement by which a person who is owed money by sb who cannot pay it all agrees to accept a percentage of the money; the agreed percentage to be paid: *The defendant had **made a composition with** the creditors.*

**compound** *adj., n., v.*
• *adj.* /'kɒmpaʊnd; *AmE* 'kɑːm-/ **1** (*Account.*) that pays or charges interest on an amount of money that includes any interest already earned or charged **2** (*Tech.*) formed of two or more parts: *a compound lens*
• *n.* /'kɒmpaʊnd; *AmE* 'kɑːm-/ [C] a thing consisting of two or more separate things combined together: *a compound of skills*
• *v.* /kəm'paʊnd/ [T] (*Account.*) to keep adding interest, profit, etc. to an amount of money as it is earned, so that the amount used as a basis for calculations keeps growing: *compounded earnings on investments*

**comˌpounded 'rate** = COMPOUND RATE

**ˌcompound 'entry** *n.* [C] (*Account.*) an item in an account book that involves more than one amount of money to be recorded

**ˌcompound 'growth rate** *n.* [sing.] (*Account.*) a rate at which an economy, a company, an investment, etc. must grow in each of a number of years in order to reach a particular size

**ˌcompound ˈinterest** *n.* [U] (*Account.*) interest that is calculated on an amount of money to which all previous interest that has not yet been paid has been added → SIMPLE INTEREST

**ˌcompound ˈrate** (*also* **comˌpounded ˈrate**) *n.* [C] (*Account.*) the percentage of interest on an amount of money which includes interest that has already been added

**comprehensive** /ˌkɒmprɪˈhensɪv; *AmE* ˌkɑːm-/ *adj.* (*Insur.*) that pays for all types of loss or damage, except in the circumstances mentioned: *comprehensive insurance*

**compress** /kəmˈpres/ *v.* [T] (*IT*) to make computer files, etc. smaller so that they use less space on a disk, etc. SYN ZIP OPP DECOMPRESS
▸ **compression** /kəmˈpreʃn/ *n.* [U]

**comprise** /kəmˈpraɪz/ *v.* [T] (*not used in the continuous tenses*) **1** (*also* **be comˈprised of**) to have sb/sth as parts or members; to consist of sb/sth: *The Internet comprises more than 4 bn IP addresses.* **2** to be the parts or members that form sth: *Overseas sales comprise 52% of our total sales.* SYN MAKE STH UP

★ **compromise** /ˈkɒmprəmaɪz; *AmE* ˈkɑːm-/ *n.*, *v.*

• *n.* **1** [C,U] an agreement made between two people or groups in which each side gives up some of the things they want so that both sides are happy; the process of reaching this agreement: *The company has reached a compromise with its creditors.*

⊙ *to* ***arrive at/come to/make*** *a* ~ ♦ *a* ~ ***deal/plan/proposal***

**2** [C] a solution to a problem where two or more things cannot exist together as they are, in which each thing is changed slightly so that they can exist together: *the best compromise* ***between*** *price and quality*

• *v.* **1** [I] to give up some of your demands in a dispute with sb, in order to reach an agreement: *We won't compromise.* **2** [T] to allow the standard of sth to become lower: *They have not compromised the car's performance.* **3** [T] **~ sb/sth/yourself** to put sb/sth/yourself in danger or at risk: *to compromise your career*

**comps** /kɒmps; *AmE* kɑːmps/ = COMPARABLE-STORE SALES

**ˈcomp time** *n.* [U] (*AmE*) (*HR*) extra time away from work that employees can have if they have worked extra hours SYN TIME OFF IN LIEU



**comptroller** /kənˈtrəʊlə(r); kəmp-; *AmE* -ˈtroʊ-/ = CONTROLLER (2)

**compulsory** /kəmˈpʌlsəri/ *adj.* that must be done because of a law or a rule SYN OBLIGATORY

**comˌpulsory acquiˈsition** = COMPULSORY PURCHASE

**comˌpulsory liquiˈdation** (*also* **ˌforced liquiˈdation**) *n.* [U,C] (*Law*) a situation where a company is forced to stop doing business so that it can pay its debts SYN INVOLUNTARY LIQUIDATION OPP VOLUNTARY LIQUIDATION

**comˌpulsory ˈpurchase** (*also* **comˌpulsory acquiˈsition**) *n.* [U,C] (*BrE*) (*Law*) a situation in which sb has the legal right to force sb to sell sth, for example when the government needs to buy land in order to build a road: *a* ***compulsory purchase order*** *on the land*

★ **computer** /kəmˈpjuːtə(r)/ *n.* [C] an electronic machine that can store, organize and find information, do calculations and control other machines: *The data is all held on (the) computer.* ◇ *My computer has crashed* (= stopped working). ◇ *The computers are down* (= not working).

⊙ *to* ***boot up/log onto/reboot/restart/start up*** *a* ~ ♦ *to* ***log off/shut down*** *a* ~ ♦ ~ ***applications/files/hardware/programs/software*** ♦ *a* ~ ***network/system***

**comˌputer-ˈaided** (*also* **comˌputer-asˈsisted**) *adj.* that uses a computer to do most of the work: ~ *design/learning/manufacture*

**comˈputer ˌanalyst** (*also* **ˈbusiness ˌanalyst**) *n.* [C] a person whose job is to analyse the needs of a business company or an organization and then design processes for working efficiently using computer programs SYN SYSTEMS ANALYST
▸ **comˈputer aˌnalysis** (*also* **ˈbusiness aˌnalysis**) *n.* [U]

**comˌputer-asˈsisted** = COMPUTER-AIDED

**computerate** /kəmˈpjuːtərət/ = COMPUTER-LITERATE

**comˌputer-based ˈtraining** *n.* [U] (*abbr* **CBT**) training that uses computers as the main means of teaching

**comˌputer-ˈgenerated** *adj.* produced by a computer after data or instructions are put into it: *a computer-generated image*

**com,puter 'graphics** (*also* **'graphics**) *n.* [pl.] pictures that are made using a computer

**com,puter-integrated manu'facturing** *n.* [U] (*abbr* **CIM**) the use of computers to link and control all the stages of the design and manufacturing processes in a company

★ **computerize, -ise** /kəm'pju:təraɪz/ *v.* [T] **1** to use computers to run sth: *a computerized factory/system* **2** to store information on a computer: *computerized databases/information* ▸ **com,puteri'zation, -isation** /-raɪ'zeɪʃn; *AmE* -rə'z-/ *n.* [U]: *the computerization of stores*

**com'puter ,language** (*also* **'programming ,language**) *n.* [C,U] a set of words, symbols and rules that is used to write computer programs

**com,puter-'literate** (*also* **com'puterate**) *adj.* able to use computers well ▸ **com,puter 'literacy** *n.* [U]

**com'puter ,program** = PROGRAM *noun* (1)

**com,puter 'programmer** = PROGRAMMER

**com,puter 'programming** = PROGRAMMING (1)

**com,puter 'science** *n.* [U] the study of computers and how they can be used

**computing** /kəm'pju:tɪŋ/ *n.* [U] the fact of using computers; the use or development of computers of the type mentioned: *to work in computing* ◇ *It's better to have more computing power than a bigger monitor.*
⊙ *~ devices/services/skills/systems* ♦ *handheld/mobile/personal ~*

**con** /kɒn; *AmE* kɑ:n/ *n., v.* (*infml.*)
• *n.* (*BrE also* **'confidence trick**, *fml.*) [C, usu. sing.] (*infml.*) a trick; an act of cheating sb: *The so-called bargain was just a big con!* ◇ (*BrE*) *a con trick* ◇ (*AmE*) *a con game*
• *v.* [T] (-nn-) **~ sb (into doing sth/out of sth)** to trick sb, esp. in order to get money from them or persuade them to do sth for you: *I was conned into buying a useless car.*

**concentration** /,kɒnsn'treɪʃn; *AmE* ,kɑ:n-/ *n.* **1** [C] a lot of sth in one place: *This area has a high* ***concentration of industry.*** **2** [U] the act of bringing things together, or of coming together, to form a group: *concentration of investments in a single company's shares* **3** [U] the ability to direct all your effort and attention on one thing, without thinking of other things: *The job demands total concentration.* **4** [U] the process of people directing effort and attention on a particular thing: *their concentration* ***on*** *developing new markets*

**concept** /'kɒnsept; *AmE* 'kɑ:n-/ *n.* [C] **1** an idea for a new product or to help sell a product: *a new concept in corporate hospitality* ◇ *early concept testing of products* **2** an idea or principle that is connected with sth: *key business concepts*

**concern** /kən'sɜ:n; *AmE* -'sɜ:rn/ *n., v.*
• *n.* [C] a business: *a big publishing concern*
• *v.* (*often pass.*) to affect sb; to involve sb: *The matter doesn't concern us.* ◇ *The closure of the firm was upsetting to* ***all concerned*** *(= everyone involved).* **IDM** **To whom it may concern ...** (*written*) used, for example, at the beginning of a public notice or a job reference, when you do not know the name of the person you are writing to

★ **concession** /kən'seʃn/ *n.*
**1** [C,U] something that you allow or do, or allow sb to have, in order to end an argument or to make a situation less difficult: *They made concessions to avoid a strike.* ◇ *to* ***demand/seek/win/offer*** *~s* **2** [C, usu. pl.] (*BrE*) a reduction in an amount of money that has to be paid for sth; a ticket that is sold at a reduced price to a particular group of people: *tax concessions* ◇ *to* ***get/give/offer*** *~s*
**3** (*Comm.*) [C] (*esp. AmE*) the right to sell sth in a particular place; the place where you sell it, sometimes part of a larger building or store: *They run a burger concession at the stadium.* **4** (*Comm.*) [C] a right to trade or operate that is given to a company or a person, esp. by a government: *mining concessions* ◇ *to* ***award/grant*** *a ~*

**concessionaire** /kən,seʃə'neə(r); *AmE* -'ner/ (*also* **concessioner** /kən'seʃənə(r)/) *n.* [C] (*Comm.*) a company or a person that has been given a **concession** to trade or operate in a particular place

**concierge** /,kɒnsi'eəʒ; *AmE* ,kɑ:nsi'erʒ/ *n.* [C] a person who is employed, for example by a hotel, to provide services to a person or a group, such as booking accommodation and travel, shopping, finding out information, etc.

**conciliation** /kən,sɪli'eɪʃn/ *n.* [U] a process of helping two sides in a dispute to find a way to meet and discuss the problem and reach an agreement

**con,current engi'neering** (*also* **simul,taneous engi'neering**) *n.* [U] (*Product.*) a systematic method of developing new products in which people involved in designing, manufacturing, selling and using the products work together from the beginning

★ **condition** /kən'dɪʃn/ *n.* **1 conditions** [pl.] the circumstances or situation in which people live, work or do things: *creating better working conditions* ◇ *difficult market conditions* ◇ *to improve* ***pay and conditions*** **2** [C] a rule or decision that you must agree to, sometimes forming part of a contract or an official agreement: *The offer is* ***subject to*** *certain conditions.* ◇ *the* ***terms and conditions*** *of employment* ◇ *strict/tough ~s* **3** [C] a situation that must exist in order for sth else to happen: *a necessary condition* ***for*** *economic growth* → idiom at MINT *n.*

**conditional** /kən'dɪʃənl/ *adj.* that only happens if sth else is done or happens first: *Payment is ~* ***upon/on*** *delivery of the goods.*
▸ **con'ditionally** /-ʃənəli/ *adv.*

**con,ditional 'sale** *n.* [C] (*Comm.*) a type of sale where there is a contract with particular conditions, usu. that the buyer can pay in INSTALMENTS but will not legally own the goods until full payment has been made

**con,ditional 'takeover bid** *n.* [C] (*Finan.*) an offer to buy a company's shares at a particular price if particular conditions are met, for example that the buyer can buy enough shares to have control of the company

**con,ditions of 'sale** *n.* [pl.] (*Comm.*) details concerning how goods will be sold, which the seller decides and the buyer must accept, for example how the goods will be paid for and delivered

★ **conduct** *v., n.*
• *v.* /kən'dʌkt/ [T] **1** to organize and/or do a particular activity: *conducting interviews with customers* **2 ~ yourself** to behave in a particular way
• *n.* /'kɒndʌkt; *AmE* 'kɑːn-/ [U] **1** the way in which a business or an activity is organized and managed: *the conduct of the firm's affairs* **2** a person's behaviour in a particular place or situation: *professional conduct*

**confederation** /kən,fedə'reɪʃn/ *n.* [C] an organization consisting of countries, businesses, etc. that have joined together to help each other

**confer** /kən'fɜː(r)/ *v.* [I] (-rr-) **~ (with sb)** to discuss sth with sb, esp. in order to exchange opinions or get advice

★ **conference** /'kɒnfərəns; *AmE* 'kɑːn-/ *n.* [C] **1** a large official meeting, usu. lasting for a few days, at which people with the same work or interests come together to discuss their views SYN CONVENTION
⊕ *to* ***attend/go to*** *a ~* ◆ *to* ***hold/organize*** *a ~* ◆ *to* ***speak at/address*** *a ~* ◆ *a ~* ***centre/suite*** ◆ *a ~* ***attendee/delegate/participant***
**2** a meeting at which a small number of people have formal discussions: *She is* ***in conference with*** *her lawyers.*

**'conference call** *n.* [C] a telephone call in which three or more people take part

**conferencing** /'kɒnfərənsɪŋ; *AmE* 'kɑːn-/ *n.* [U] (*IT*) the act of taking part in discussions with other people by using telephones, video equipment, computers, etc.

★ **confidence** /'kɒnfɪdəns; *AmE* 'kɑːn-/ *n.* [U] **1** the feeling that you can trust, believe in and be sure about the abilities or good qualities of sb/sth: *We have complete confidence* ***in*** *our products.*
⊕ *to* ***express/lose*** *~ in sth* ◆ *to* ***build (up)/destroy/restore*** *~*
**2** a feeling that things will get better: *Business confidence has fallen sharply.* SYN SENTIMENT
⊕ ***investor/public*** *~* ◆ *~* ***declines/grows/returns***
**3** a feeling of trust that sb will keep information private: *He told me about the project* ***in confidence.***

**'confidence trick** (*AmE* **'confidence game**) = CON *n.*

★ **confidential** /,kɒnfɪ'denʃl; *AmE* ,kɑːn-/ *adj.* meant to be kept secret: *This information is strictly confidential.*
⊕ ***highly*** *~* ◆ ***to be/be kept/remain*** *~*

★ **confidentiality** /,kɒnfɪ,denʃi'æləti; *AmE* ,kɑːn-/ *n.* [U] the need to keep particular information secret: *My employment contract has a confidentiality* ***clause.***

**configure** /kən'fɪgə(r); *AmE* -'fɪgjər/ *v.* [T] (*IT; Tech.*) to organize or arrange sth, esp. computer equipment, for a particular task
▸ **con,figu'ration** /-'reɪʃn/ *n.* [C,U]

★ **confirm** /kən'fɜːm; *AmE* -'fɜːrm/ *v.* [T] **1** to say or show that sth is definitely true or correct: *The date of the meeting has not yet been confirmed.* **2** (*HR*) to make a position more definite or official: *Her position has been confirmed.* ▸ **confirmation** /,kɒnfə'meɪʃn; *AmE* ,kɑːnfər'm-/ *n.* [C,U]:

*email confirmation of the order* ◇ *to receive order/shipping ~*

★**conflict** *n., v.*
• ***n.*** /ˈkɒnflɪkt; *AmE* ˈkɑːn-/ [C,U] **1** **~ (with sb) (over sth)** | **~ (between A and B)** a situation in which people, groups or countries are involved in a serious disagreement or argument: *a conflict* ***between*** *two members of the team* ◇ *They were* ***in*** *conflict* ***over*** *the future of the firm.* ◇ ***conflict resolution*** (= settling disagreements). **2** a situation in which there are opposing ideas, opinions, feelings or wishes and it may be difficult to choose: *a conflict* ***between*** *long working hours and family life*
IDM **conflict of ˈinterest(s)** a situation in which there are two jobs, aims, roles, etc. and it is not possible for both of them to be treated equally and fairly at the same time **conflict of ˈlaw(s)** (*Law*) a situation in which a court must decide which country's laws apply to a dispute
• ***v.*** /kənˈflɪkt/ [I] **A and B ~** | **A ~s with B** if two ideas, beliefs, stories, etc. **conflict**, it is not possible for them to exist together or for them both to be true: *conflicting advice*

**conform** /kənˈfɔːm; *AmE* -ˈfɔːrm/ *v.* [I] **~ to/with sth** to obey a rule or a law: *This building does not conform* ***with*** *fire regulations.*

**confrontation** /ˌkɒnfrʌnˈteɪʃn; *AmE* ˌkɑːnfrən-/ *n.* [U,C] **~ (with sb)** | **~ (between A and B)** a situation in which there is an angry disagreement between people or groups who have different opinions

**confrontational** /ˌkɒnfrʌnˈteɪʃənl; *AmE* ˌkɑːnfrən-/ *adj.* that involves or causes conflict: *a confrontational style of leadership*

**conglomerate** /kənˈglɒmərət; *AmE* -ˈglɑːm-/ *n.* [C] a large organization formed by joining together a group of companies often with different business activities
➊ *a* ***financial****/an* ***industrial****/a* ***media*** *~* ♦ *to* ***build (up)/create/form*** *a ~*

**congress** /ˈkɒŋgres; *AmE* ˈkɑːŋgrəs/ *n.* [C with sing./pl. v.] a large formal meeting or series of meetings: *an international congress of trades unions*

**ˈcon man** *n.* [C] (*infml.*) a man who tricks other people into giving him money, etc.

★**connect** /kəˈnekt/ *v.* **1** [T,I] **~ (sth) (up) (to/with sth)** to join together two or more things; to be joined together: *I can connect to the office computer via a modem.* **2** (*IT*) [T,I] to link or be linked to the Internet: *connecting people* ***to*** *the Internet* **3** [T] to join telephone lines so that people can speak to each other: *I'm trying to connect you.* SYN PUT SB THROUGH **4** [I] (used about a bus, plane, train, etc.) to arrive at a particular time, so that passengers can change to another bus, train, plane, etc: *a connecting flight* → DISCONNECT IDM **connect the ˈdots** (*also* **join the ˈdots**, *esp. in BrE*) to find or show the relationships between different things: *Connect the dots for your audience—relate the training to real situations.*

★**connection** (*BrE also* **connexion**, *less freq.*) /kəˈnekʃn/ *n.* [C] **1** (*IT*) a link to the Internet, telephone system, etc: *a high-speed Internet connection* ◇ *There is a €150* ***connection fee*** (= when you start receiving the service) **2** [usu. pl.] a person or an organization that you know and that can help or advise you in your social or professional life: *She has good business connections.* **3** a bus, train, plane, etc. that leaves soon after another arrives: *Our plane was so late that we missed our connection.* **4** [usu. pl.] a means of travelling to another place: *There are good connections between the conference centre and the city.* IDM **in conˈnection with sb/sth** (*written*) about or concerning: *I am writing in connection with your application.*

**connectivity** /ˌkɒnekˈtɪvəti; kəˌnekˈtɪvəti; *AmE* ˌkɑːn-/ *n.* [U] (*IT*) the ability to be connected to the Internet or another computer: *Internet connectivity*

**conˌnect-the-ˈdots** *adj.* **1** that brings together facts and information from different places and shows the relationships between them: *a connect-the-dots article* **2** easy to do or understand: *connect-the-dots instructions*

**connexion** = CONNECTION

**conscientious** /ˌkɒnʃiˈenʃəs; *AmE* ˌkɑːn-/ *adj.* taking care to do things carefully and correctly: *conscientious work* ▸ **ˌconsciˈentiously** *adv.* **ˌconsciˈentiousness** *n.* [U]

**consensual** /kənˈsenʃuəl/ *adj.* (*fml.*) that involves getting everyone's agreement: *a consensual approach to management*

★**consensus** /kənˈsensəs/ *n.* [sing; U] **1** agreement among a group of people: *to reach a consensus* ***on*** *sth* ◇ *to achieve/build (a) ~* **2** (*Finan.*) the general view among experts of how well a company, an industry or an economy will perform: *a ~ estimate/forecast*

**conse,quential 'loss** (*also* **,indirect 'loss**) *n.* [U,C] (*Law*) money that a business loses as an indirect result of being harmed by sb, for example a loss of profits because a factory was damaged

**conservatism** /kən'sɜːvətɪzəm; *AmE* -'sɜːrv-/ *n.* [U] **1** the tendency to avoid unnecessary risks: *the conservatism of investors* **2** (*Account.*) (*esp. AmE*) = PRUDENCE (1)

**conservative** /kən'sɜːvətɪv; *AmE* -'sɜːrv-/ *adj.* **1** not taking or involving unnecessary risk: *a conservative approach to investment* **2** lower than what is probably the real amount or number: *conservative forecasts*

**conservator** /kən'sɜːvətə(r); 'kɒnsəveɪtə(r); *AmE* kən'sɜːrvətər/ *n.* [C] (*AmE*) (*Law*) a person chosen by a court to look after sb or their finances, because they are too old, ill/sick, etc. to do so themselves

**consignee** /,kɒnsaɪ'niː; *AmE* ,kɑːn-/ *n.* [C] (*Transpt.*) a person or an organization that goods are sent to → CONSIGNOR

**consignment** /kən'saɪnmənt/ *n.* **1** (*Transpt.*) [C] a quantity of goods that are sent or delivered somewhere SYN SHIPMENT **2** (*Comm.*) [C,U] goods that you deliver to sb, for them to sell on your behalf or return if they cannot sell them: *The goods are offered* ***on consignment***.

**con'signment note** *n.* [C] (*Transpt.*) a document that gives details of goods sent or delivered somewhere and is sent with them

**con'signment store** *n.* [C] esp. in the US, a type of shop/store where you can take items to be sold on your behalf or returned to you if not sold

**consignor** /kən'saɪnə(r)/ *n.* [C] **1** (*Comm.*) a person who delivers an item to sb for them to sell on their behalf **2** (*Transpt.*) a person or an organization that sends goods to sb/sth SYN SENDER → CONSIGNEE

**con'sistency ,concept** *n.* [sing.] (*Account.*) one of the principles used in accounting that says that similar items should be treated in the same way within each accounting period and from one period to the next, and that the organization's rules for accounting should always be followed

**consolidate** /kən'sɒlɪdeɪt; *AmE* -'sɑːl-/ *v.* **1** [T,I] to join things, esp. businesses, together into one; to be joined into one: *consolidated companies* ◇ *consolidating your debts* (= replacing smaller debts with one big debt) **2** (*Account.*) [T] to combine the financial results of a group of companies into one set of figures: *a set of consolidated accounts* **3** [T,I] to make a position of power or success stronger so that it is more likely to continue: *The merger will consolidate the group's position in the market.* **4** (*Transpt.*) [T] to combine separate items into one load to transport them ▸ **con,soli'dation** /-'deɪʃn/ *n.* [U,C]: *2 500 jobs were lost as part of the consolidation.* ◇ *the consolidation of skills* → GROUPAGE

**consolidator** /kən'sɒlɪdeɪtə(r); *AmE* -'sɑːl-/ *n.* [C] **1** (*Econ.*) a company that takes control of several others in the same industry to form a single business **2** (*Comm.*) a travel company that buys travel tickets, rents hotel rooms, etc. in large numbers and offers them to the public or TRAVEL AGENCIES at low prices: *consolidator airfares* **3** (*Transpt.*) a transport company that receives goods from different suppliers and packs them so that they can be transported together

**Consols** /'kɒnsɒlz; kən'sɒlz; *AmE* 'kɑːnsɑːlz; kən'sɑːlz/ *n.* [pl.] (*Finan.*) in the UK, government bonds that have a low fixed interest rate but do not have a fixed date for when the loan will be paid back

**consortium** /kən'sɔːtiəm; *AmE* -'sɔːrt-/ *n.* [C] (*pl.* **-tiums** *or* **-tia** /-tiə/) (*Finan.*) a group of companies, banks, etc. working together on a particular project: *a consortium of banks* ◇ *to form/join/lead a ~*

**constitute** /'kɒnstɪtjuːt; *AmE* 'kɑːnstətuːt/ *v.* **1** [T] (*usu. pass.*) to form a group legally or officially: *a properly constituted company* **2** (*linking v.*) (*not used in the continuous tenses*) to be the parts that together form sth: *In the UK, women constitute 30% of managers.* SYN MAKE STH UP **3** (*fml., usu. written*) (*linking v.*) (*not used in the continuous tenses*) to be considered to be sth: *Does this constitute a criminal offence?*

★**constitution** /,kɒnstɪ'tjuːʃn; *AmE* ,kɑːnstə'tuːʃn/ *n.* [C] the basic law or rules of a country or an organization: *to adopt/amend/draft/violate a ~* ▸ **,consti'tutional** /-ʃənl/ *adj.*

**construct** /kən'strʌkt/ *v.* [T] **1 ~ sth (from/out of/of sth)** (*often pass.*) to build or make sth large, such as a road, building or machine: *The frame is constructed from steel.* ◇ *a newly constructed hotel* **2** to create sth by putting different things or parts together: *construct a homepage*

★**construction** /kən'strʌkʃn/ *n.* **1** [U] the process or method of building or making sth large, esp. roads, buildings, bridges, etc: *Construction of the new offices has been completed.* ◇ *This web page is* **under** *construction.*
⊙ ***plant/road*** ~ • *a* ~ ***site/yard/worker*** • ~ ***costs/materials***
**2** [U] the business of building roads, buildings, etc.
⊙ *the* ~ ***industry/sector*** • *a* ~ ***business/company/firm/group***
**3** [U] the process or method of creating sth by putting different things or parts together: *the ~ of agreements*
**4** [U,C] the way that sth has been built or made: *walls of solid construction* **5** (*fml.*) [C] sth that has been built or made: *huge constructions*

**con,structive dis'missal** *n.* [U; C, usu. sing.] (*BrE*) (*HR*) the situation when an employer makes an employee's working conditions so difficult or unpleasant that they have to leave their job

**consul** /'kɒnsl; *AmE* 'kɑːnsl/ *n.* [C] a government official working in a foreign city who helps people from his/her own country who are living or visiting there and encourages trade between the two countries
▸ **consular** /'kɒnsjələ(r); *AmE* 'kɑːnsələr/ *adj.*

★**consultancy** /kən'sʌltənsi/ *n.* (*pl.* **-cies**) **1** [C] a company that gives expert advice on a particular subject
⊙ *a* ***design/management/marketing/recruitment*** ~ • *a* ~ ***business/company/firm/group***
**2** [U] expert advice that an independent company or person is paid to provide on a particular subject: *~ fees/work*

★**consultant** /kən'sʌltənt/ *n.* [C] a person who knows a lot about a particular subject and is paid to give advice about it to other people: *a firm of business consultants*
⊙ *a* ***career/design/financial/marketing*** ~ • *an* ***independent/outside*** ~ • *to* ***bring in/call in/hire/use*** *a* ~

★**consultation** /,kɒnsl'teɪʃn; *AmE* ,kɑːn-/ *n.* **1** [U] the act of discussing sth with sb or with a group of people before a decision is made: *The plant was closed* **without** *any consultation* **with** *workers.*
⊙ ***after/in*** ~ *(with sb)* • ***close/full*** ~ • ***public/wide*** ~ • *a* ~ ***document/paper/period/process***
**2** [C] a formal meeting to discuss sth: *to have/hold ~s* **3** [C] a meeting with an expert to get advice: *A 30-minute consultation will cost €60.*
⊙ *to* ***book/have*** *a* ~ *(with sb)* • *to* ***conduct/do*** *~s*

★**consulting** /kən'sʌltɪŋ/ *n.* [U] (often in the names of companies) the activity and business of providing expert advice, esp. about how a business can be improved: *She works in consulting.* ◇ *Delta Consulting*
⊙ *a* ~ ***business/company/firm/group/practice*** • *the* ~ ***business/industry*** • ~ ***services/work***

**consume** /kən'sjuːm; *AmE* -'suːm/ *v.* **1** [T,I] to buy goods and services to use yourself: *the consuming public* **2** [T] to use sth such as fuel, energy, time or money

★**consumer** /kən'sjuːmə(r); *AmE* -'suː-/ *n.* [C] **1** a person who buys goods or services for their own use: *Interest rate cuts have persuaded consumers to spend more.* ◇ *a* **consumer** *boom*
⊙ ***average/individual*** *~s* • ***domestic/foreign*** *~s* • ~ ***attitudes/choice/habits/needs*** • ~ ***spending/trends***
**2** a person, group, country, etc. that uses sth such as fuel or energy: *the world's largest consumer of natural resources*
⊙ ***commercial/industrial*** *~s (of sth)* • ***electricity/energy*** *~s*

**con,sumer 'advertising** *n.* [U] (*Market.*) advertising that is aimed at individual people and families, not businesses

**con,sumer a'wareness** *n.* [U] (*Market.*) how far buyers know that a product or service exists: *to build consumer awareness of a brand*

**con'sumer ,banking** = RETAIL BANKING

**con'sumer base** = CUSTOMER BASE

**con,sumer be'haviour** (*AmE* **-behavior**) *n.* [U] (*Market.*) the way in which individuals or families decide what product or service to buy and where and how to buy it

**con,sumer 'borrowing** *n.* [U] (*Econ.*) the amount of money that people have borrowed, for example by using credit cards, in order to buy things SYN CONSUMER DEBT

**con'sumer brand** *n.* [C] (*Market.*) a **brand** that members of the public buy regularly

**con,sumer 'confidence** *n.* [U] **1** (*Econ.*) (*also* **con,sumer 'sentiment**, *esp. in AmE*) a measure of how willing people are to spend money, because they feel that the economy will get better or worse: *falling consumer confidence* **2** the fact that people trust and are willing to buy particular products: *consumer confidence* **in** *the food industry*

**con,sumer co'operative** (*also* **con,sumers' co'operative, ,retail co'operative**) *n.* [C] (*Finan.*) a business that is formed, owned and controlled by a group of customers, who share the profits

**con,sumer 'credit** (*also* **,personal 'credit**) *n.* [U] (*Econ.*; *Finan.*) loans made by banks and shops/stores to customers, that allow them to buy sth now and pay for it later

**con,sumer 'credit in,surance** = CREDIT INSURANCE (2)

**con,sumer 'debt** *n.* [U] (*Econ.*) the money that people owe to shops/stores or banks for the things they have bought but not yet paid for SYN CONSUMER BORROWING

**con,sumer de'mand** *n.* [U,C] the desire or need of customers for particular goods or services: *strong ~ for housing*

**con,sumer 'durables** (*BrE*) (*AmE* **'durable goods**) (*also* **'durables**, *BrE, AmE*) *n.* [pl.] (*Econ.*; *Market.*) goods such as cars, televisions, computers, furniture, etc. that last for a long time after you have bought them OPP CONSUMER NON-DURABLES

**con,sumer elec'tronics** *n.* [pl.] electronic goods, such as radios, televisions and music systems, that are bought and used by members of the public

**con,sumer 'finance** *n.* [U] (*Finan.*) the business of lending money to customers so that they can buy goods and pay for them later: *a ~ company/unit*

**con'sumer goods** (*also* **con'sumer ,products**) *n.* [pl.] (*Econ.*; *Market.*) goods such as food, clothing, etc. bought and used by individual customers SYN CONSUMPTION GOODS

**con'sumer group** *n.* [C] **1** an organization that protects the rights of people who buy particular products or services SYN CONSUMER WATCHDOG **2** (*Market.*) one of a number of groups that individual buyers belong to and that influence their behaviour, such as a family group, or work group

**consumerism** /kən'sju:mərɪzəm; *AmE* -'su:-/ *n.* [U] **1** (*Market.*) the activity of protecting the interests of customers or of influencing the way manufacturers make and sell goods **2** (*Econ.*) the buying and using of goods and services; the belief that it is good for a society or a person to buy and use a large quantity of goods and services: *We are living in an age of mass consumerism.* ▸ **con'sumerist** *adj.*: *a consumerist society* **con'sumerist** *n.* [C]

**con'sumer ,market** *n.* [sing.] **1** the buying and selling of goods for individual and personal use **2** the buying and selling of a particular product or service: *the consumer market for leisure goods*

**con'sumer 'market re'search** = CONSUMER RESEARCH

**con,sumer non-'durables** (*also* **,non-'durables, ,non-'durable goods, dis'posables**) *n.* [pl.] (*Econ.*; *Market.*) goods such as food, newspapers, etc. that only last for a short time and need to be replaced often OPP CONSUMER DURABLES

**con'sumer ,panel** (*also* **'customer ,panel**, *esp. in BrE*) *n.* [C] (*Market.*) a carefully chosen group of customers used by an organization to give their opinions or advice on particular products, services, etc.

**con,sumer 'preference** *n.* [U; sing.] (*Market.*) the desire buyers have for one product or feature rather than another: *a shift in consumer preference*

**con'sumer price** *n.* [C, usu. pl.] (*Econ.*) the price that the public pays for ordinary goods and services

**con,sumer 'price ,index** *n.* [sing.] (*abbr* **CPI**) (*Econ.*) in the US and some other countries, a list of the prices of some ordinary goods and services which shows how much these prices change each month, used to measure the rate of INFLATION SYN COST-OF-LIVING INDEX, RETAIL PRICE INDEX

**con,sumer price in'flation** *n.* [U] (*Econ.*) a rise in the prices that people pay for ordinary goods and services over a period of time; the rate at which this happens

**con'sumer ,products** = CONSUMER GOODS

**con,sumer 'profile** = CUSTOMER PROFILE (1)

**con,sumer pro'motion** *n.* [U,C] (*Market.*) activities done in order to encourage people to try or to buy a product or service

**con͵sumer pro'tection** *n.* [U] (*Law*) the act of using laws to protect customers from dishonest businesses, products that are not safe or are too expensive, etc.

**con͵sumer re'search** (*also* **con'sumer 'market re'search**) (*also* **͵customer re'search**, *less freq.*) *n.* [U] (*Market.*) a study of the needs and opinions of customers, esp. in connection with a particular product or service

**con͵sumer re'sistance** (*also* **͵customer re'sistance**, *less freq.*) *n.* [U] (*Market.*) when people are unwilling to buy a particular product or service, or dislike an aspect of it: *overcoming consumer resistance to shopping online*

**con͵sumers' co'operative** = CONSUMER COOPERATIVE

**con͵sumer 'sentiment** = CONSUMER CONFIDENCE

**con͵sumer so'ciety** *n.* [C] (*Econ.*) a society in which the buying and selling of goods and services is the most important social and economic activity

**con͵sumer 'surplus** (*also* **͵buyer's 'surplus**, *less freq.*) *n.* [C] (*Econ.*) the difference between the highest amount that a buyer is willing to pay for sth and the lower price that he/she in fact pays

**con͵sumer 'watchdog** *n.* [C] (*infml.*) an independent organization that checks that companies are not doing anything illegal and protects the rights of individual customers SYN CONSUMER GROUP

★ **consumption** /kən'sʌmpʃn/ *n.* [U] the act of using goods, services, energy, food or materials; the amount used: *the consumption of soft drinks* ◇ *a country with high fuel consumption*
⊙ ***average/low/total*** *~* • ***household/mass/personal*** *~* • ***domestic/home/local*** *~* • *to* ***increase/reduce*** *~* • *~* ***falls/rises***

**con'sumption ex͵penditure** *n.* [U; pl.] (*Econ.*) the amount of money that is spent on the goods and services that people use during a particular period of time

**con'sumption goods** *n.* [pl.] (*Econ.*) goods that are designed to be used by individual customers, for example clothes, food, cars, etc. SYN CONSUMER GOODS

**con'sumption tax** *n.* [C,U] (*Econ.*) a tax that is added to the price of goods and services

★ **contact** /'kɒntækt; *AmE* 'kɑːn-/ *n., v.*
• ***n.*** **1** [U] the act of communicating with sb, esp. regularly: *They* ***put us in contact with*** *an investment banker.* ◇ *My contact details are on my business card.*
⊙ *to* ***get into/make*** *~ with sb* • *a ~* ***address/name/number***
**2** [C] a person that you know, esp. sb who can be helpful to you in your work: *a network of contacts*
⊙ *to* ***have/make*** *~s* • *a* ***business/personal/useful*** *~*
→ idiom at POINT *n.*
• ***v.*** [T] to communicate with sb, for example by telephone or letter: *Contact me* ***on/at*** *this number...*

**'contact ͵centre** *n.* [C] an office in which a large number of people work using telephones and email for communicating with customers

**container** /kən'teɪnə(r)/ *n.* [C] **1** a box, bottle, etc. in which sth can be stored or transported: *drinks in plastic containers* **2** (*Transpt.*) a large metal box used for transporting goods by sea, road or rail: ***container traffic*** (= the number of containers transported) ◇ *a ~ port/ship/truck* ◇ *to load/unload ~s*
▸ **con͵taineri'zation, -isation** /-aɪ'zeɪʃn; *AmE* -rə'z-/ *n.* [U] **con'tainerized, -ised** /-raɪzd/ *adj.*: *containerized cargo*

**contango** /kən'tæŋɡəʊ; *AmE* -ɡoʊ/ *n.* [U] (*Finan.*) a situation where the price of a COMMODITY that will be delivered in the future is higher than its price if it were delivered immediately: *Gold is generally* ***in*** *contango.*

★ **content** /'kɒntent; *AmE* 'kɑːn-/ *n.* **1 contents** [pl.] the things that are contained in sth: *the contents of the building* **2** [U; pl.] the ideas in sth or the subject that sth deals with: *the contents of the letter* **3** [U] the information or other material contained on a website, a CD-ROM, etc. **4** [sing.] (*after another n.*) the amount of a substance that is contained in sth else: *iron with a high carbon content* **5** (*Manufact.*) [U] the parts that make up a product: *100% local content* (= all the parts made within the country)

**contingency** /kən'tɪndʒənsi/ *n.* [C] (*pl.* **-cies**) an event that you hope will not happen, but for which you plan in case it does IDM **on a con'tingency basis** if you provide services to sb/sth on **a contingency basis**, you are only paid if your services help them to achieve their aim

**con'tingency ac͵count** = CONTINGENCY FUND

**con'tingency fee** (*AmE also* **con'tingent fee**) *n.* [C] (*Law*) an arrangement by which a client pays a lawyer only if the lawyer wins money for the client in court

**con'tingency fund** (*also* **con'tingency ac,count, con'tingency re,serve**) *n.* [C] (*Account.*) money that sb keeps to pay for a possible future expense or loss

**con,tingency lia'bility** = CONTINGENT LIABILITY

**con'tingency plan** *n.* [C] a plan a business makes that will be followed if a particular disaster or other event happens: *contingency plans* **for** *possible breakdowns* ▶ **con'tingency ,planning** *n.* [U]

**con'tingency re,serve** = CONTINGENCY FUND

**contingent** /kən'tɪndʒənt/ *adj.* (*fml.*) that will only take place if a particular event happens: *Bonuses are ~* **on/upon** *good results.*

**con'tingent fee** = CONTINGENCY FEE

**con,tingent lia'bility** (*also* **con,tingency lia'bility**) *n.* [C] (*Account.*) a debt shown in a company's financial records that does not exist now but may exist in the future if a particular event happens

**con'tingent work** *n.* [U] (*HR*) work done by people who do not have a permanent contract with a company SYN ASSIGNMENT WORK ▶ **con'tingent ,worker** *n.* [C]

**con,tinuous 'audit** *n.* [U,C] **1** (*Account.*) a system of keeping a constant check on a company's financial records at all times rather than checking them once a year **2** (*HR*) a system of keeping a constant check on how well part of a business or a system works

**con,tinuous em'ployment** *n.* [U] (*HR*) the fact of working for a company for a period of time with no breaks

**con,tinuous im'provement** *n.* [U] the process of continuing to improve a company, its products or services by making frequent small changes to deal with problems rather than fewer large changes

**con,tinuous 'inventory** (*also* **per,petual 'inventory**) *n.* [U,C] (*Account.*) a system of keeping a constant check on the type and quantity of products that a business has to sell

**con,tinuous pro'duction** (*also* **con,tinuous 'processing**) = FLOW PRODUCTION

**'contra ac,count** /'kɒntrə; *AmE* 'kɑːntrə/ *n.* [C] (*Account.*) a financial account that forms a pair with another account. When money goes out of one of the accounts, it goes into the other.

**contraband** /'kɒntrəbænd; *AmE* 'kɑːn-/ *n.* [U] goods taken into or out of a country illegally: *contraband goods* ◇ *to smuggle contraband*

★ **contract** *n., v.*

• *n.* /'kɒntrækt; *AmE* 'kɑːn-/ [C] **1** an official written agreement: *a contract* **for** *the supply of vehicles* ◇ *the contract* **between** *buyer and seller* ◇ *I was* **on** *a three-year contract.* ◇ ***Under the terms of the contract*** *the job should be finished tomorrow.* ◇ ***breach of contract*** (= not keeping to a contract)

○ *to* ***draw up/enter into/make/sign*** *a ~* ♦ *to* ***bid for/get/tender for*** *a ~* ♦ *a* ***casual/fixed-term/permanent*** *~*

**2** (*Finan.*) an agreement to buy or sell a fixed quantity of sth at a fixed price by a fixed date in the future: *The March cocoa contract closed $46 lower.*

• *v.* /kən'trækt/ **1** [T,I] to become less or smaller; to make sth less or smaller: *a contracting market* **2** [T] to make a legal agreement with sb for them to work for you or provide you with a service: *We have been contracted* **to** *build the plant.* **3** [I] to make a legal agreement to work for sb or to provide them with a service: *She has contracted to work 20 hours a week.*

PHR V **con,tract 'in (to sth)** (*BrE*) to formally agree that you will take part in sth **con,tract 'out (of sth)** (*BrE*) to formally agree that you will not take part in sth: *to contract out of a pension plan* **con,tract sth 'out (to sb)** to arrange for work to be done by another company or by sb outside your company: *Cleaning has been contracted out.*

**'contract bond** (*also* **per'formance bond**) *n.* [C] (*Law*) a guarantee provided by a bank or an insurance company that a customer who has a contract to supply sth or do some work for sb will complete the work or a sum of money will be paid

**,contract 'labour** *n.* [U] (*HR*) workers who are employed by a business, often through another organization, for a fixed period of time, for example in order to work on a particular project

**'contract note** *n.* [C] (*Stock Ex.*) a document that gives details of the shares, bonds, etc. that a BROKER has bought or sold for a customer

**ˌcontract of emˈployment** (*also* **ˌcontract of ˈservice**) *n.* [C] (*HR*) a formal agreement made between an employer and an employee, giving details of pay, holidays, hours of work, etc: *Under her contract of employment, she is entitled to three months' pay in lieu of notice.*

**ˌcontract of inˈsurance** = INSURANCE POLICY

**ˌcontract of ˈpurchase** (*also* **ˈpurchase aˌgreement**) *n.* [C] (*Law*) a document that gives details of the conditions under which sth is sold

**ˌcontract of ˈservice** = CONTRACT OF EMPLOYMENT

★ **contractor** /kənˈtræktə(r); *AmE* ˈkɑːntræktər/ *n.* [C] a person or company that has a contract to do work or provide goods or services for another company: *to use outside contractors ◇ a building/haulage ~*

**contractual** /kənˈtræktʃuəl/ *adj.* (*Law*) connected with the conditions of a legal written agreement; agreed in a contract

⊙ *a ~ **commitment/duty/obligation/relationship/responsibility** ◆ a ~ **agreement/requirement/right***

**ˈcontract ˌworker** *n.* [C] (*HR*) a person who works for a company for a fixed period of time, for example on a particular project, but is not an employee

**ˈcontra ˌentry** /ˈkɒntrə; *AmE* ˈkɑːntrə/ *n.* [C] (*Account.*) an amount recorded in a financial account that forms a pair with another amount. Both have the same value but one is a CREDIT and the other a DEBIT.

**conˌtributing ˈshares** = PARTLY PAID SHARES

**contribution** /ˌkɒntrɪˈbjuːʃn; *AmE* ˌkɑːn-/ *n.* **1** (*HR*) [C, usu. pl.] an amount of money that sb or their employer pays for benefits such as health insurance, a pension, etc. **2** [C] an amount of money given to a person or an organization to help pay for sth: *a small contribution **to** health care* **3** (*Account.*) [C, usu. sing., U] the amount of money that an individual product or service pays towards a company's FIXED COSTS, based on its sales and VARIABLE COSTS **4** (*Insur.*) [C,U] a share of a payment made for an item that is lost or damaged when it is insured with two or more companies; the act of sharing payments between insurance companies

**contributor** /kənˈtrɪbjətə(r)/ *n.* [C] **1** (*HR*) sb who makes regular payments to pay for benefits such as health insurance or a pension **2** sb/sth that gives money to help pay for sth, or provides support for a project

**contributory** /kənˈtrɪbjətəri; *AmE* -tɔːri/ *adj.* **1** helping to cause sth: *The bad weather was a contributory **factor** in the fall in sales.* **2** involving payments from the people who will benefit: *a ~ **pension plan/scheme*** OPP NON-CONTRIBUTORY

★ **control** /kənˈtrəʊl; *AmE* -ˈtroʊl/ *n., v.*

• ***n.*** **1** [U] the power to make decisions about how an organization, an area, a country, etc. is run: *to lose control **of** a company ◇ have more control **over** sth ◇ be **under** public control*

⊙ *to **acquire/assume/gain/get/take** ~ of sth ◆ to **give up/hand over/keep/relinquish** ~ of sth*

**2** [U] the ability to make sb/sth do what you want: *We have no control **over** the situation. ◇ to keep/lose ~ of/over sb/sth* **3** (*Finan.*) [U] the fact of owning sth such as shares: *the control of shares* (= who owns the shares) **4** [U,C] the act or method of restricting, limiting or managing sth: *poor cost control ◇ tough controls **on** steel imports*

⊙ ***strict/stringent/tight** ~s ◆ to **impose/relax/remove/tighten** ~s*

**5** [C, usu. pl.] the switches and buttons, etc. that you use to operate a machine or a vehicle **6** (*Tech.*) [C] a person, thing, group or test that you use as a standard of comparison when doing an experiment, in order to check your results: *a **control group*** **7** [U] (*also* **conˈtrol key** [sing.]) (*abbr* **Ctrl**) a button on a computer keyboard that you press with other buttons when you want to perform particular operations

IDM **be in conˈtrol (of sth)** to direct or manage an organization, an area or a situation **be/get/run out of conˈtrol** to be or become impossible to manage or to control: *Costs have got out of control.* **under conˈtrol** being dealt with successfully: *The situation's under control. ◇ keeping inflation under control*

• ***v.*** (-ll-) [T] **1** to have power over a person, company, country, etc. so that you decide what they must do or how it is run: *One oil company controls 60% of the petrol stations.* **2** (*Finan.*) to own sth such as shares: *The family still controls half the shares.* **3** to limit sth or make it happen in a particular way: *laws to control drug prices* **4** to stop sth from getting worse: *ways of controlling inflation* **5** to make sth, such as a machine or system, work in the way that you want it to: *The temperature is controlled by sensors.*

**con'trol ac,count** (*also* **ad'justment ac,count**) *n.* [C] (*Account.*) an account that is kept in addition to official accounts, in order to check that the official accounts are accurate

**con'trol key** = CONTROL *n.* (7)

**con,trolled e'conomy** = COMMAND ECONOMY

**controller** /kən'trəʊlə(r); *AmE* -'troʊ-/ *n.* [C] **1** a person who manages or directs sth, esp. a large organization or part of one: *She's controller of their US operations.* **2** (*also* **comp'troller**, *esp. in AmE*) a person who is in charge of the finances of a business or government department: *a financial controller*

**con,trolling 'interest** *n.* [C, usu. sing.] (*Finan.*) when sb/sth owns enough shares in a company to be able to make decisions about what the company should do; a number of shares that are bought in order to achieve this: *They have a 51% controlling interest* **in** *the new company.*

**con,trolling 'shareholder** (*esp. BrE*) (*AmE usu.* **con,trolling 'stockholder**) *n.* [C] (*Finan.*) a person or company that owns enough shares in a company to be able to make decisions about what its activities and policies should be

**convene** /kən'viːn/ *v.* (*fml.*) **1** [T] to arrange for people to come together for a formal meeting: *A special meeting has been convened.* **2** [I] to come together for a formal meeting: *The committee will convene at 9.*

**convenience** /kən'viːniəns/ *n.*
**IDM** **at sb's con'venience** (*fml.*) at a time or a place which is suitable for sb: *Can you telephone me at your convenience?*

**con'venience food** *n.* [C,U] food that is sold as a prepared meal or product, that you can cook or use very quickly and easily

**con'venience store** *n.* [C] (*esp. AmE*) a small shop/store that sells food, newspapers, etc. and often stays open all or most of the day and night

**convention** /kən'venʃn/ *n.* [C] a large meeting of the members of a profession, an organization, etc. **SYN** CONFERENCE
⊙ *to* ***hold/organize*** *a ~* ◆ *to* ***attend/go to*** *a ~* ◆ *a ~* ***centre/delegate***

**conversion** /kən'vɜːʃn; *AmE* -'vɜːrʒn; -ʃn/ *n.* [U,C] **1** the act or process of changing sth from one form, use or system to another: *the conversion of the business* **into** *a public company* ◇ *the conversion of dollars* **to** *pesos* **2** (*Finan.*) the act of exchanging special bonds or shares for ordinary shares in a company: *the conversion of preference shares* **into** *ordinary shares*

**con'version cost** *n.* [C, usu. sing.] **1** (*Account.*) the cost of the work, the wages and other regular expenses involved in producing finished goods from raw material or in changing material from one stage of production to the next **2** (*Market.*) the relationship between the cost of advertising products on the Internet and the number of items sold

★ **convert** /kən'vɜːt; *AmE* -'vɜːrt/ *v.* **1** [T,I] to change or make sth change from one form, purpose, system, etc. to another: *The software converts files* **from** *Macintosh format* **to** *Windows.* ◇ *a converted warehouse* **2** (*Finan.*) [T] to change an amount of one type of money, investment, unit, etc. into another type

**convertibility** /kən,vɜːtə'bɪləti; *AmE* -,vɜːrt-/ *n.* [U] (*Econ.*) the fact that the money of a particular country can easily be changed into the money of another country

**convertible** /kən'vɜːtəbl; *AmE* -'vɜːrt-/ *adj., n.* (*Finan.*)
• ***adj.*** (about bonds or shares) that can be exchanged for another type of investment in a company, usu. ordinary shares: *convertible bonds*
• ***n.*** [C] (*also* **con,vertible se'curity**) a special type of bond or share that can be exchanged for another investment in the company that sold it, usu. ordinary shares

**con,vertible 'currency** *n.* [C,U] (*Econ.*; *Finan.*) money of one country that can easily be changed into the money of another country, esp. into a strong currency such as the dollar or the euro

**con,vertible 'note** *n.* [C] (*Finan.*) a loan made to a company that has a fixed rate of interest and can either be paid back in cash or changed into ordinary shares

**con,vertible se'curity** = CONVERTIBLE *n.*

**conveyancer** /kən'veɪənsə(r)/ *n.* [C] (*Law*) a person, esp. a lawyer, who is an expert in **conveyancing**

**conveyancing** /kən'veɪənsɪŋ/ *n.* [U] (*Law*) the work done in legally moving property from one owner to another; the branch of law that is concerned with this: *We did our own conveyancing.*

**con'veyor belt** (*also* **conveyor** /kən'veɪə(r)/) *n.* [C] a continuous moving band for transporting goods from one part of a building to another, for example products in a factory or suitcases in an airport: *As the bottles move* ***along*** *the conveyor belt, tubes drop the right medicine into the right bottle.*

**COO** /ˌsiː əʊ 'əʊ; *AmE* oʊ 'oʊ/ *abbr* chief operating officer

**cookie** /'kʊki/ *n.* [C] (*IT*) a computer file that an Internet site sends to your computer, which is used to store information about how you use the site

**ˌcooling-'off ˌperiod** *n.* [C] **1** a period of time during which two sides in a dispute try to reach an agreement before taking further action, for example going on strike **2** (*Law*) a period of time after sb has agreed to buy sth, such as an insurance plan, during which they can change their mind

**'co-op** *n.* [C] (*infml.*) a COOPERATIVE shop/store, business or farm: *agricultural co-ops*

**cooperative** (*also* **co-operative**) /kəʊ'ɒpərətɪv; *AmE* koʊ'ɑːp-/ *n., adj.*

• ***n.*** (*BrE also* **ˌworkers' co'operative**) [C] a business or other organization that is owned and run by the people involved, who work together and share the profits: *The factory is now a workers' cooperative.*

• ***adj.*** owned and run by the people involved, with the profits shared by them: *a ~ association/society* ◇ *a ~ bank/farm/store*

**coˌoperative 'marketing** *n.* [U] (*Market.*) when two or more businesses work together to advertise and sell each other's products

★ **coordinate** (*also* **co-ordinate**) /kəʊ'ɔːdɪneɪt; *AmE* koʊ'ɔːrd-/ *v.* [T] to organize the different parts of an activity and the people involved in it so that it works well: *It is her job to coordinate the work of the teams.* ◇ *a coordinating committee*

▸ **coˌordi'nation** (*also* **co-ordination**) /-'neɪʃn/ *n.* [U]: *greater coordination between departments*

**co'ordinator** (*also* **co-ordinator**) *n.* [C]: *a project coordinator*

**copier** /'kɒpiə(r); *AmE* 'kɑːp-/ = PHOTOCOPIER

★ **copy** /'kɒpi; *AmE* 'kɑːpi/ *n., v.*

• ***n.*** (*pl.* **-pies**) **1** [C] one of a number of books, newspapers, pieces of software, etc. that have been produced and are the same: *a copy of 'The Financial Times'* **2** [C] a document or computer file that is the same as an original from which it is made: *Please make two copies of the letter.* SYN DUPLICATE **3** [C] a product that is made to be the same as or very similar to another product, esp. when this is done illegally: *a bootleg copy of a CD* **4** (*Market.*) [U] written material that is to be printed or used in an advertisement: *This will make great copy for the ad.*

• ***v.*** [T] (**copies, copying, copied, copied**) **1** to make another document, computer file, etc. that is the same as the original: *illegally copied software* **2** to do sth or try to do sth the same as sb/sth else: *to copy good ideas* PHR V **ˌcopy sb 'in (on sth)** to make sure that sb receives a copy of a letter, an electronic message, etc. that you are sending to sb else: *Please copy me in on all correspondence.*

**copycat** /'kɒpikæt; *AmE* 'kɑːp-/ *adj.* that copies sb else's successful idea, design, etc: *a ~ claim/drug/product*

▸ **'copycat** *n.* [C]: *copycats of the drug*

★ **copyright** /'kɒpiraɪt; *AmE* 'kɑːp-/ *n., adj., v.*

• ***n.*** [C,U] the right to be the only person who may publish, broadcast, make copies of, etc. an original piece of work, such as a book, film/movie or computer program and give other people permission to use it or any part of it: *The publisher has the copyright* ***on*** *all his books.* ◇ *This software is protected by copyright.*

⊙ *to* ***hold/own*** *~ in/on sth* ♦ *a* ***breach of****/an* ***infringement of*** *~* ♦ *the ~* ***holder/owner*** ♦ *be* ***in/out of*** *~*

• ***adj.*** protected by **copyright**; not allowed to be copied without permission: *a copyright work*

• ***v.*** [T] to have the **copyright** for sth: *copyrighted material*

**'copy ˌtesting** *n.* [U] (*Market.*) the process of testing an advertisement with a small group of people to see how effective it is before it is used publicly ▸ **'copy test** *v.* [T,I] **'copy test** *n.* [C]

**copywriter** /'kɒpiraɪtə(r); *AmE* 'kɑːp-/ *n.* [C] a person whose job is to write the words (**copy**) to be used in advertisements

**cordless** /'kɔːdləs; *AmE* 'kɔːrd-/ *adj.* not connected to a power supply or another device by wires: *a ~ drill/mouse*

★ **core** /kɔː(r)/ *n., adj.*
• ***n.*** [C, usu. sing.] the centre of sth; the most important or essential part of sth: *The customer is **at the core** of our business.*
• ***adj.*** most important, main or essential; making the most profit: *our core brands* OPP NON-CORE
○ *a ~ business/division/market* • *~ activities/skills* • *~ customers/workers* • *~ brands/markets/products*

ˌ**core ˈarea** *n.* [C] **1** the main part of a particular activity where most of the work or business is done; the place where most work or business is done: *three core business areas* **2** (*HR*) one of the essential parts of a particular job: *the five core areas*

ˌ**core ˈcapital** *n.* [U] (*Finan.*) the main part of a bank's funds that comes from the money that shareholders have invested in it and spare profits that it has kept SYN TIER I CAPITAL

ˌ**core ˈcompetency** (*also* ˌ**core ˈcompetence**) *n.* [C] **1** an important ability or strength that a company has that makes it successful and gives it an advantage over its competitors: *Manufacturing was their core competency.* **2** (*HR*) an important skill that is essential for a particular job: *five core competencies for executives*

ˌ**core deˈposits** *n.* [pl.] (*Finan.*) the part of a bank's funds that comes from customers who generally leave money in their bank accounts

ˌ**core ˈearnings** *n.* [pl.] (*Account.*) the profit that a company makes from its main business activities: *a 95% increase in core earnings*

ˌ**core inˈflation** *n.* [U] (*Econ.*) the rate at which the prices of goods and services rise over a period of time, measured without considering prices that change a lot, such as the cost of energy and some foods

ˌ**core ˈvalues** *n.* [pl.] **1** the ideas and beliefs of an organization that managers and employees share and practise in their work **2** the ideas and beliefs that a person has that influence what they do and help them make important decisions

ˈ**corner shop** (*BrE*) (*also* ˈ**corner store**, *BrE, AmE*) *n.* [C] a small shop/store that sells food, newspapers, cigarettes, etc., esp. one near people's houses

★ **Corp.** *abbr* (*esp. AmE*) (*written*) corporation: *Sony Corp.*

★ **corporate** /ˈkɔːpərət; *AmE* ˈkɔːrp-/ *adj., n.*
• ***adj.*** **1** connected with a company or a group, or with business in general: *His corporate clients include 3M and Nabisco.* ◇ *corporate profits* ◇ *cutbacks in corporate travel* **2** (*often* **Corporate**) **~ America, Britain, etc.** used esp. in newspapers to talk about the people and organizations that control a country's business **3** involving or shared by all members of a group: *Our success was a corporate effort.*
• ***n.*** [C] **1** a company, esp. a large one **2** (*Finan.*) = CORPORATE BOND

ˌ**corporate ˈadvertising** *n.* [U] (*Market.*) advertising that tells the public about a company, rather than the products that it sells, and tries to create a good image

ˌ**corporate ˈbond** (*also* ˈ**corporate**) *n.* [C] (*Finan.*) a bond that is issued by a company

ˌ**corporate ˈcharter** = CHARTER *n.* (2)

ˌ**corporate communiˈcation** (*also* ˌ**organizational communiˈcation**) *n.* [U; C, usu. pl.] (*HR; Market.*) the things a company does to share information with employees or customers and the public, in order to keep a good relationship with them and give a clear idea of what it is
→ PUBLIC RELATIONS

ˌ**corporate ˈculture** (*also* ˌ**organizational ˈculture**) *n.* [U,C] the ideas, beliefs and values of a particular organization

ˌ**corporate ˈdebt** *n.* [U] (*Econ.*) money that companies borrow from investors, banks, etc.; investments that involve lending money to companies

ˌ**corporate ˈfinance** *n.* [U] the activity of helping companies to get the money they need to run and develop their businesses ► ˌ**corporate fiˈnancier** *n.* [C]: *senior corporate financiers*

ˌ**corporate ˈgovernance** *n.* [U] the way in which directors and managers control a company and make decisions, esp. ones that have an important effect on shareholders

ˌ**corporate hospiˈtality** *n.* [U] (*Market.*) when companies entertain customers, business partners, their staff, etc. for example at a big sports event, in order to help develop good business relationships

ˌ**corporate iˈdentity** *n.* [C, usu. sing., U] (*Market.*) the features, qualities or personality of a company that make it different from others, often expressed in its name, in symbols, in its advertisements, etc: *to build/create/develop a ~*

**ˌcorporate ˈimage** *n.* [C, usu. sing., U] (*Market.*) what people think or feel about a particular company; the way that a company presents itself to the public: *a positive/good ~*

**ˌcorporate ˈincome tax** = CORPORATION TAX

**ˌcorporate ˈladder** *n.* [C, usu. sing.] a series of jobs from junior to senior level by which you can make progress in a company: ***climbing*** *the corporate ladder*

**ˌcorporate ˈmarketing** *n.* [U] the activity of planning and controlling a company's marketing, to make sure that it uses the same styles, messages, etc. and creates a particular image for the whole company

**ˌcorporate ˈofficer** = COMPANY OFFICER

**ˌcorporate ˈraider** *n.* [C] (*Finan.*) a person or company that regularly buys large numbers of shares in other companies against the companies' wishes, either to control them or to sell the shares again for a large profit

**ˌcorporate reˈnewal** *n.* [U,C] the act of making changes to a company in order to make it more successful; the process of becoming more successful in this way

**ˌcorporate responsiˈbility** *n.* [U] the fact of companies being concerned about social, political or environmental issues

**ˌcorporate ˈsecretary** = COMPANY SECRETARY

**ˈcorporate ˌsector** *n.* [C, usu. sing.] the part of a country's economy that is made up of the public and private companies

**ˈcorporate ˈsocial responsiˈbility** *n.* [U,C] (*abbr* **CSR**) the process of running a business in a way that helps people in society to improve their quality of life

**ˌcorporate ˈstrategy** *n.* [U,C] the things a company plans to do in order to become more successful; the activity of planning these actions: *Our corporate strategy is to increase the size of both of our core businesses.*

**ˌcorporate ˈstructure** *n.* [C,U] the way in which the different parts of a company or group of companies are connected with each other and managed

**ˌcorporate ˈveil** *n.* [sing.] (*Law*) the principle that a company's shareholders or employees are not personally responsible for its debts

**ˌcorporate ˈventuring** *n.* [U] (*Finan.*) the activity of a larger company investing in a smaller business in order to develop new products, markets, etc. and get a share of the profits ▶ **ˌcorporate ˈventure** *n.* [C]

★ **corporation** /ˌkɔːpəˈreɪʃn; *AmE* ˌkɔːrp-/ *n.* [C] **1** a large company or group of companies
⊕ ***a big/giant/large/major ~*** ♦ ***a global/multinational ~***
**2** (*Law*) (*abbr* **Corp.**) a business organization that has been officially created and is owned by shareholders: *the IBM Corporation*
⊕ *to* ***create/form/set up*** *a ~* ♦ *to* ***dissolve/liquidate*** *a ~*
**3** a large organization created by the government to provide a particular service to the public: *the British Broadcasting Corporation*

**ˌcorpoˈration tax** (*BrE*) (*AmE* **ˌcorporate ˈincome tax**) *n.* [U,C] (*abbr* **CT**) (*Account.*) a tax that companies pay on their profits

**correction** /kəˈrekʃn/ *n.* [C,U] **1** a change in prices, esp. a sudden temporary fall after they have been too high: *Share prices could rise until next week, but after that there should be a correction.* **2** a change that makes a calculation more accurate than it was before: *corrections made to the annual accounts*

**correspondence** /ˌkɒrəˈspɒndəns; *AmE* ˌkɔːrəˈspɑːn-; ˌkɑː-/ *n.* **1** [U,C] the activity of writing letters: *We have been* ***in correspondence with*** *the bank about the matter.* **2** [U] the letters a person sends and receives: *email correspondence*

**correˈspondence course** *n.* [C] a course of study that you do at home, using books and exercises sent to you by post/mail

**correspondent** /ˌkɒrəˈspɒndənt; *AmE* ˌkɔːrəˈspɑːn-; ˌkɑː-/ *n.* [C] **1** sb who reports news from a particular country or on a particular subject for a newspaper or a television or radio station **2** sb who writes letters to sb else **3** (*Finan.*) = CORRESPONDENT BANK

**ˌcorrespondent ˈbank** (*also* **ˌcorresˈpondent**) *n.* [C] (*Finan.*) a bank that provides services for a bank in another place, esp. one in another country ▶ **ˌcorrespondent ˈbanking** *n.* [U]

**corresponding** /ˌkɒrəˈspɒndɪŋ; *AmE* ˌkɔːrəˈspɑːn-; ˌkɑː-/ *adj.* matching or connected with sth that you have just mentioned: *Profits fell 10% in the corresponding period last year.* ▶ **ˌcorresˈpondingly** *adv.*

**corrupt** /kəˈrʌpt/ *adj., v.*
• ***adj.*** **1** (about people) willing to use their power to do dishonest or illegal

things in return for money or to get an advantage **2** (about behaviour) dishonest or immoral **3** (*IT*) containing changes or faults, and no longer in the original state: *corrupt files*
• *v.* **1** to make sb/sth start behaving in a dishonest or immoral way **2** (*IT*) to cause mistakes to appear in a computer file, etc. so that the information is no longer correct: *a corrupted disk*

**corruption** /kəˈrʌpʃn/ *n.* [U]
**1** dishonest or illegal behaviour, esp. of people in authority: *allegations of **bribery and corruption*** **2** (*IT*) damage to or loss of data caused by a computer, a disk, etc. not working correctly: *data corruption*

**$CO_2$** /ˌsiː əʊ ˈtuː; *AmE* oʊ/ = CARBON DIOXIDE

**cosmeceutical** /ˌkɒzməˈsuːtɪkl; -ˈsjuː-; *AmE* ˌkɑːzməˈsuː-/ *n.* [C, usu. pl.] a substance put on the face or body to improve the appearance (a **cosmetic**) that also has the qualities of a medicine/drug
▸ **ˌcosmeˈceutical** *adj.*: *the cosmeceutical industry*

★**cost** /kɒst; *AmE* kɔːst/ *n., v.*
• *n.* **1** [C,U] the amount of money that you need in order to buy, make or do sth: *The airport was built **at a cost of** $5.3 bn.* ◇ *the high cost of fuel*
◐ *an **average**/a **low** ~* • *the **estimated/full/gross/net/total** ~(s)* • *to **absorb/incur/meet/pay** the ~(s) (of sth)* • *to **cut/raise** the ~(s) (of sth)* • *to **calculate/weigh up** the ~(s) (of sth)*
**2 costs** [pl.] the amount of money that a business needs to spend regularly: *We are working to cut costs by 30%.* ◇ *high labour costs*
◐ *to **reduce/slash** ~* • *to **contain/control/pay** ~* • *to **keep** ~ **down/under control*** • ***falling/low/rising** ~* • ***labour/production** ~*
**3** (*Account.*) [C] a large amount of money that a company has to pay, which affects its financial results: *Profits fell by 7% **before exceptional costs**.* **4** [U] the amount of money that is paid to produce sth; the price that sb pays for goods they are going to sell: *The group has offered to provide the drugs to developing nations **at cost**.* SYN COST PRICE **5** (*Law*) **costs** (*also* **ˈcourt costs**) [pl.] the amount of money that sb is ordered or agrees to pay for lawyers, etc. in a legal case
• *v.* [T] (**cost, cost**) **1 ~ (sb) sth** if something **costs** a particular amount of money, you have to pay that amount in order to buy, make or do it: *The hotel costs €90 a night.* ◇ *The delays cost small businesses over €1 bn.* **2 ~ (sb) sth** to make sb/sth lose sth: *The reforms could cost thousands of jobs.* **3** (*Account.*) (**costed, costed**) **~ sth (out)** (*often pass.*) to calculate how much money is needed to make or do sth: *Calls are costed per unit.* IDM **cost a ˈbomb** (*BrE*) (*infml.*) to be very expensive: *An MBA can cost a bomb.* **cost the ˈearth; cost (sb) a (small) ˈfortune** (*infml.*) to be very expensive: *Office space in London costs a small fortune.*

**ˈcost acˌcounting** *n.* [U] (*Account.*) the process of calculating and recording the detailed costs of producing goods or providing services in order to help managers control and plan a company's work
▸ **ˈcost acˌcountant** *n.* [C]

**ˌcost and ˈfreight** (*abbr* **CFR, C&F**) (*also* **ˌcarriage and ˈfreight**, *less freq.*) *phr.* (*Trade*) the seller pays for the goods to be transported by ship to the port mentioned, but the buyer is responsible for insuring them on the ship: *Our prices are CFR Hamburg.* → INCOTERM

**ˈcost apˌportionment** = APPORTIONMENT (2)

**ˈcost base** *n.* [C, usu. sing.] (*Account.*) all the things that a business pays for in order to produce and sell its products: *The firm tried to reduce its cost base by cutting jobs.* ◇ *a high/low ~*

**ˈcost ˌbenefit** *n.* [U,C] (*Econ.*) the relationship between the cost of doing sth and the profit or advantages that result from it: *a cost-benefit approach to decisions*

**ˌcost-ˈbenefit aˌnalysis** (*abbr* **CBA**) (*also* **ˌbenefit-ˈcost aˌnalysis**) *n.* [C,U] (*Econ.*) the activity of comparing the cost of doing sth with the profit or advantages that result from it, in order to see if it is worth doing

**ˈcost centre** *n.* [C] (*Account.*) a part of a business that a company uses as a unit for accounting so that all the costs related to it can be calculated: *Manufacturing and distribution is our largest cost centre.* ◇ *to allocate/charge sth to a ~*

**ˈcost-ˌconscious** *adj.* careful not to spend more money than necessary

**ˈcost conˌtainment** *n.* [U] (*Account.*) the process by which a company controls and limits how much money it spends

**ˈcost conˌtrol** *n.* [U,C] (*Account.*) the process of making sure that the different parts of a company do not spend too much money; a particular method used to achieve this: *poor/tight ~(s)*

**'cost-ˌcutting** *n.* [U] (*often used like an adj.*) a reduction in the amount of money a company spends: *a ~ exercise/measure/plan* ▶ **'cost cut** *n.* [C]: *$20 m of cost cuts*

**ˌcost-ef'fective** *adj.* giving the best possible profit or benefits for the money spent: *a cost-effective way to distribute products* ▶ **ˌcost-ef'fectiveness** *n.* [U]

**ˌcost-ef'ficiency** *n.* **1** [U] COST-EFFECTIVENESS **2** [C] a way of saving or wasting less money in a business: *key areas where cost-efficiencies can be achieved*

**ˌcost-ef'ficient** *adj.* COST-EFFECTIVE

**ˌcost in'flation** (*also* **ˌcost-'push inˌflation**) *n.* [U] (*Econ.*) when a cost such as wages or raw materials increases and businesses increase their prices to keep their profits

**costing** /'kɒstɪŋ; *AmE* 'kɔːst-/ *n.* [C,U] (*Account.*) an estimate of how much money will be needed for sth: *You'd better do some costings.* ◇ *accurate costing of the work* ◇ *to prepare/produce a ~*

**'cost, in'surance and 'freight** *phr.* (*abbr* **CIF**) (*Trade*) the seller pays for the goods to be transported by ship to the port mentioned, and pays for basic insurance of the goods on the ship: *CIF Singapore* → INCOTERM

**'cost ˌleader** (*also* **'low-cost ˌleader**) *n.* [C] (*Market.*) a company that can make a particular product at a lower cost than its competitors

**ˌcost of goods 'sold** (*abbr* **COGS**) (*also* **ˌcost of 'sales**) *n.* [U] (*Account.*) the total amount of money that a business spends on obtaining and producing the goods that it sells in a particular accounting period, for example the cost of raw materials, workers, etc.

**the ˌcost of 'living** *n.* [sing.] the amount of money that people need to pay for ordinary goods and services, such as food, clothing and somewhere to live: *a high/low ~* ◇ *an increase/a rise/fall in the ~*

**ˌcost-of-'living adˌjustment** *n.* [C] (*abbr* **COLA**) (*Econ.*; *HR*) an increase that is made once a year to a wage, pension, etc. because the **cost of living** has increased

**ˌcost-of-'living alˌlowance** *n.* [C, usu. sing.] (*abbr* **COLA**) (*Econ.*; *HR*) extra money that an organization pays to its employees as part of their wages, because the **cost of living** has increased

**ˌcost-of-'living ˌindex** *n.* [C, usu. sing.] (*Econ.*) a list of the prices of some ordinary goods and services which shows how much these prices change in a particular period of time SYN CONSUMER PRICE INDEX, RETAIL PRICE INDEX

**ˌcost of re'placement** = REPLACEMENT COST

**ˌcost of 'sales** = COST OF GOODS SOLD

**ˌcost 'overrun** *n.* [C,U] a situation in which a manufacturer, building company, etc. spends more money on a project than planned; the extra amount spent: *huge cost overruns* **on** *building the factory*

**ˌcost per 'click** *n.* [U] (*abbr* **CPC**) (*Market.*) the amount an advertiser pays to the owner of a website each time a visitor to the site clicks on their advertisement

**ˌcost per im'pression** *n.* [U] (*abbr* **CPI**) (*Market.*) the cost of an advertisement divided by the number of times it is seen

**ˌcost per 'thousand** *n.* [U] (*abbr* **CPM**) (*Market.*) **1** the cost of showing an advertisement to a thousand people using a particular form of advertising, such as television or newspapers **2** the amount an advertiser pays to the owner of a website for every thousand people who see or click on their advertisement

**ˌcost-'plus** *adj.* used to describe a way of deciding on a price for sth that involves adding a fixed extra amount to the costs for profit or to cover an unexpected increase in costs: *The work will be charged* ***on a cost-plus basis.***

**'cost price** *n.* [C] the money paid to produce sth; the price that sb pays for goods they are going to sell: *the manufacturer's cost price* ◇ *selling items at* ***below*** *cost price* SYN COST

**ˌcost-'push inˌflation** = COST INFLATION

**'cost ˌsaving** *n.* [C, usu. pl.] (*often used like an adj.*) an amount of money that a business manages not to spend, for example by becoming smaller or more efficient: *achieving annual cost savings of $45 m.* ◇ *cost-saving measures*

◐ *to* ***make*** *~s* ♦ ***potential/substantial*** *~s* ♦ *cost-saving* ***targets***

**'cost ˌstructure** *n.* [C, usu. sing.] (*Account.*) the relationship between the different types of costs that a company has, which make up its total costs

◐ *a* ***high/low*** *~* ♦ *to* ***change/improve/manage*** *your ~*

**ˌcottage ˈindustry** *n.* [C] a small business in which the work is done by people in their homes

**cough** /kɒf; *AmE* kɔːf/ *v.*
**PHR V** **ˌcough (sth) ˈup** (*infml.*) to give sth, esp. money, unwillingly: *It's time to cough up some of the money you owe us.*

**council** /ˈkaʊnsl/ *n.* [C] **1** (used esp. in names) a group of people, esp. politicians or officials, that are chosen to give advice, make rules, do research, provide money, etc: *the Council for Economic Planning* **2** a group of people who are elected to govern an area such as a city or county: *the Boston City Council*

**counsel** /ˈkaʊnsl/ *n.* [U,C] (*pl.* **counsel**) (*Law*) **1** a lawyer or group of lawyers representing sb in a court case: *the ~ for the defence/prosecution ◇ defence/prosecuting ~* **2** (*AmE*) a person or group providing legal advice to an organization

**counselling** (*AmE* **counseling**) /ˈkaʊnsəlɪŋ/ *n.* [U] professional advice given to sb about a problem

**counsellor** (*AmE usu.* **counselor**) /ˈkaʊnsələ(r)/ *n.* [C] **1** a person whose job is to give advice: *a debt/stress ~ ◇ to be referrred to/see/talk to a ~* **2** (*Law*) (*AmE*) a lawyer

**counter** /ˈkaʊntə(r)/ *n.* [C] a long flat surface in a shop/store, bank, etc. where customers are served: *the information counter ◇ the assistant* ***behind*** *the counter* **IDM** **under the ˈcounter** goods that are bought or sold **under the counter** are sold secretly and sometimes illegally

**counterbid** (*also* **counter-bid**) /ˈkaʊntəbɪd; *AmE* -tərb-/ (*also* **ˈcounter-offer**) *n.* [C] (*Comm.*; *Finan.*) an offer to buy sth, esp. a company, that is higher than an offer made by sb else

**ˈcounterclaim** /ˈkaʊntəkleɪm; *AmE* -tərk-/ *n.* [C] (*Law*) a legal claim that a DEFENDANT makes against the CLAIMANT/PLAINTIFF
▸ **ˈcounterclaim** *v.* [T,I]

**counterfeit** /ˈkaʊntəfɪt; *AmE* -tərf-/ *adj., v.*
• ***adj.*** (esp. about money and goods for sale) made to look exactly like the real thing, in order to trick people ▸ **ˈcounterfeit** *n.* [C]: *trademark counterfeits*
• ***v.*** [T] to make an exact copy of sth in order to trick people into thinking that it is the real thing
▸ **ˈcounterfeiting** *n.* [U] **ˈcounterfeiter** *n.* [C]

**counterfoil** /ˈkaʊntəfɔɪl; *AmE* -tərf-/ *n.* [C] (*esp. BrE*) the part of a cheque, ticket, etc. that you keep as a record when you give the other part to sb else: *to fill in/keep/tear off the ~* SYN STUB

**ˌcounter-inˈflationary** *adj.* (*Econ.*) that reduces or tries to reduce **inflation**

**ˈcounter-ˌoffer** *n.* [C] **1** (*Comm.*; *Finan.*) = COUNTERBID **2** (*Law*) new conditions suggested for an agreement or a contract because the ones already suggested cannot be accepted **3** (*HR*) when a company offers better pay and conditions to an employee who has been offered a job in another company to try to keep him/her

**counterpart** /ˈkaʊntəpɑːt; *AmE* -tərpɑːrt/ *n.* [C] sb/sth with a similar position or function in a different country or organization

**counterparty** /ˈkaʊntəpɑːti; *AmE* -tərpɑːrti/ *n.* [C] (*pl.* **-ties**) (*Finan.*) one of the people or organizations involved in a contract or some financial business

**counterproductive** /ˌkaʊntəprəˈdʌktɪv; *AmE* -tərp-/ *adj.* [not usu. before n.] having the opposite effect to the one that was intended: *It's counterproductive to put too much pressure on your staff.*

**countersign** /ˈkaʊntəsaɪn; *AmE* -tərs-/ *v.* [T,I] to sign a document that has already been signed, usu. by another person, to show that it is valid

**countertrade** /ˈkaʊntətreɪd; *AmE* -tərt-/ *n.* [U] (*Econ.*) international trade that involves exchanging goods or services for goods or services, rather than for money
▸ **ˈcountertrader** *n.* [C] **ˈcountertrading** *n.* [U]

**ˌcountervailing ˈduty** *n.* [C] (*BrE*) (*Econ.*) an extra tax that must be paid on particular imports that can be produced very cheaply in the country they come from, in order to protect local producers

**ˌcountry ˈrisk** (*also* **ˌsovereign ˈrisk**) *n.* [U,C] (*Econ.*) the possibility that political events, financial problems, etc. in a country will decrease the value of investments in that country or make the government, etc. unable to pay its debts

**coupon** /ˈkuːpɒn; *AmE* -pɑːn; ˈkjuː-/ *n.* [C] **1** (*Market.*) a small piece of printed paper which you can use to buy goods at a lower price or to get sth free; a printed form that you fill in to order goods, etc: *money-off coupons ◇ Fill in and return the coupon below for your free T-shirt.* **2** (*Finan.*) the rate of interest that is paid to sb who invests in a bond: *The new bonds carry a 7% coupon.*

★**courier** /ˈkʊriə(r)/ *n., v.* (*esp. BrE*)
• ***n.*** [C] **1** a person or company whose job is to take packages or important papers somewhere: *We sent the documents* **by courier**. **2** a person who is employed by a travel company to give advice and help to a group of tourists
• ***v.*** [T] to send sth somewhere by courier

**course** /kɔːs; *AmE* kɔːrs/ *n.* [C] a complete series of lessons or talks on a particular subject: *All new employees attend a training course on company policy.*
⊕ *to* ***run/teach*** *a ~* ♦ *to* ***do/go on/take*** *a ~* ♦ *a* ***full-time****/an* ***intensive****/a* ***part-time/short-time*** *~*

**courseware** /ˈkɔːsweə(r); *AmE* ˈkɔːrswer/ *n.* [U] (*IT*) computer software that is designed to teach people about a particular subject or train them in a particular activity

★**court** /kɔːt; *AmE* kɔːrt/ *n.* **1** [U,C] the group of people, led by a judge, a group of judges or another official, who listen to legal cases and make decisions on them: *We would have to* **go to court** *to stop the merger.*
⊕ *a ~* ***hears/orders/rules*** *sth* ♦ *a ~* ***decision/ruling*** ♦ *a ~* ***action/case/hearing***
**2** [C,U] the place where legal cases are listened to and decided SYN LAW COURT **3** [C] the group of people, led by a judge or another official, who deal with a particular type of legal case or with cases from a particular area; the place where this happens
⊕ *a* ***bankruptcy/divorce*** *~* ♦ *a* ***county/federal/state*** *~*
IDM **rule/throw sth out of ˈcourt** to say that sth is completely wrong or not worth considering, esp. in a court: *The charges were thrown out of court.*

**ˈcourt costs** = COST *n.* (5)

**courtesy** /ˈkɜːtəsi; *AmE* ˈkɜːrt-/ *n., adj.*
• ***n.*** [U] polite and pleasant behaviour that shows respect for people: *I was treated with great courtesy.*
IDM **(by) courtesy of sb/sth**
**1** (*usu. written*) with the official permission of sb/sth and as a favour
**2** given as a prize or provided free by a person or an organization, often as a way of advertising: *Win a trip to Milan, courtesy of Fiat.*
• ***adj.*** provided free, at no cost to the person using it: *a courtesy car*

**ˈcourtesy call** *n.* [C] a telephone call from a bank or company that you are a customer of, to see if you are satisfied with their service

**ˌcourt of ˈlaw** (*BrE also* **ˈlaw court**) *n.* [C] (*fml.*) the group of people, led by a judge or another official, who deal with legal cases; the place where cases are listened to and decided

**ˌcourt ˈorder** *n.* [C,U] (*Law*) a decision by a court about a legal case; the official document in which the decision is written: *We sought a court order to stop them using our trademark.*
⊕ *to* ***apply for/obtain*** *a ~* ♦ *to* ***grant/issue*** *a ~* ♦ *to* ***comply with/defy*** *a ~*

**courtroom** /ˈkɔːtruːm; -rʊm; *AmE* ˈkɔːrt-/ *n.* [C] a room in which trials or other legal cases are held

**covenant** /ˈkʌvənənt/ *n., v.*
• ***n.*** **1** (*Law*) [C,U] a promise that is part of a formal written contract to take particular actions or avoid particular situations: *The lease contains a covenant given by the tenant to maintain the property.* ◇ *to breach/enforce a ~* **2** (*Finan.*) [C] a written promise to take particular actions or avoid particular situations made by sb borrowing money, so that the lender knows that the loan will be paid back: *a bank/banking/loan ~* ◇ *to breach/negotiate a ~*
• ***v.*** [I] (*Law*) to promise sth in a formal written contract: *They covenanted to repay the loan over two years.*

★**cover** /ˈkʌvə(r)/ *v., n.*
• ***v.*** **1** [T] to include sth; to deal with sth: *Do the rules cover this?* **2** [T] to provide a service to people or businesses in a particular area or market: *a distribution network covering 70 countries* **3** [T] to be or provide enough money for sth: *The show barely* **covered its costs**. **4** (*Insur.*) [T] to protect sb/sth against loss, injury, damage, etc. by insurance: *The policy covers you* **against** *personal injury.* **5** [I] to do sb's work or duties while they are away: *Who's covering for Joan while she's on leave?* **6** (*Finan.*; *Stock Ex.*) [T] to buy the shares, currency, etc. that you have already agreed to sell to sb, esp. so that you will not lose money if the price rises: *to cover a* **short position** **7** [T] **~ yourself (against sth)** to take action to protect yourself against being blamed for sth
• ***n.*** **1** [C] the outside of a book or a magazine **2** (*Insur.*) (*AmE* **ˈcoverage**) [U] **~ (for sth)** protection that an insurance company provides by promising to pay you money if a par-

ticular event happens SYN INSURANCE COVER

○ *to arrange/get/take out ~ • additional/extended/standard ~ • accident/fire/health/life/medical ~*

**3** (*Finan.*) [U] (*BrE*) an amount of money that is large enough to meet a debt, loss, expense, etc. **4** (*HR*) [U] when sb does another person's job when they are away or when there are not enough staff: *organizing cover for absent staff* IDM **under separate 'cover** if sth is sent **under separate cover**, it is sent in another envelope or package

**coverage** /ˈkʌvərɪdʒ/ *n.* [U] **1** (*Insur.*) (*AmE*) = COVER *n.* (2) **2** (*Comm.*) the area where a particular service is provided: *Mobile-phone coverage is limited to the big cities.* **3** (*Market.*) the percentage of a possible audience for an advertisement, etc. who see it at least once **4** (*Account.*) = INTEREST COVER

**coveralls** /ˈkʌvərɔːlz/ = OVERALL *n.* (2)

**ˌcovered ˈcall** (*also* **ˌcovered ˈcall ˌoption**, **ˌcovered ˈoption**) *n.* [C] (*Finan.*) a type of investment in which sb has the right to buy shares, bonds, etc. for a fixed price on or before a particular date from a seller who owns those shares, bonds, etc. and has them ready

**ˌcovering ˈletter** (*BrE*) (*AmE* **ˈcover ˌletter**) *n.* [C] a letter that you send with a document, package, etc. that gives more information about it

**ˈcover note** *n.* [C] (*BrE*) (*Insur.*) a document that an insurance company provides until it sends the full insurance policy, so that you can prove you have bought insurance

**ˈcowboy** /ˈkaʊbɔɪ/ *n.* [C] (*BrE*) (*infml.*) a dishonest person in business, esp. sb who produces work of bad quality or charges too much

**ˈco-ˌworker** (*AmE* **coworker**) *n.* [C] a person that sb works with, doing the same kind of job

**CPA** /ˌsiː piː ˈeɪ/ = CERTIFIED PUBLIC ACCOUNTANT, CRITICAL PATH ANALYSIS

**CPC** /ˌsiː piː ˈsiː/ = COST PER CLICK

**CPI** /ˌsiː piː ˈaɪ/ = CONSUMER PRICE INDEX, COST PER IMPRESSION

**CPM** /ˌsiː piː ˈem/ = COST PER THOUSAND, CRITICAL PATH METHOD

**CPT** *abbr* (*Trade, written*) carriage paid to: *CPT Osaka*

**CPU** /ˌsiː piː ˈjuː/ = CENTRAL PROCESSING UNIT

**Cr** (*also* **cr**) *abbr* (*Account.*) a short way of writing **credit** in accounts

**craftsmanship** /ˈkrɑːftsmənʃɪp; *AmE* ˈkræf-/ *n.* [U] **1** the skill used by sb to make sth of high quality with their hands **2** the quality of design and work shown by sth that has been made by hand: *the superb craftsmanship of the car's interior*

**crane** /kreɪn/ *n.* [C] a tall machine with a long arm, used to lift and move building materials and other heavy objects

★**crash** /kræʃ/ *n.*, *v.*

• *n.* [C] **1** a sudden serious fall in the price or value of sth; the occasion when a business, etc. fails: *a crash **in** share prices ◇ the dot-com crash* **2** (*IT*) a sudden failure of a computer or software

• *v.* **1** [I] to lose value or fail suddenly and quickly: *Share prices crashed **to** an all-time low yesterday. ◇ The business crashed with huge debts.* **2** (*IT*) [T,I] (about a computer or software) to suddenly stop or be stopped from working because there is a fault: *The system keeps crashing.* IDM **ˌcrash and ˈburn** (*infml.*) to fail in a dramatic way

**crate** /kreɪt/ *n.* [C] a large wooden, metal or plastic box in which goods are carried or stored; the amount of sth it contains: *a crate of bananas*

**ˌcrawling ˈpeg** (*also* **ˌsliding ˈpeg**) *n.* [C] (*Econ.*) a way of controlling the EXCHANGE RATE by changing it by small amounts at regular intervals

**CRD** /ˌsiː ɑː ˈdiː; *AmE* ɑːr/ = CASH RATIO DEPOSITS

★**creative** /kriˈeɪtɪv/ *adj.*, *n.*

• *adj.* **1** involving the use of skill and imagination to make or do new things: *a creative solution to the problem ◇ creative financing* **2** having the skill and imagination to make or do new things: *creative people*

▸ **creˈatively** *adv.* **ˌcreaˈtivity** /-ˈtɪvəti/ *n.* [U]

• *n.* [C] (*Market., infml.*) **1** sb in an advertising agency who designs advertisements: *ad agency creatives* **2** an advertisement, esp. on the Internet

**creˌative acˈcounting** (*also* **creˌative acˈcountancy**) *n.* [U] (*Account., infml.*) recording a company's financial activities in a way that hides the true situation

**creˌative diˈrector** *n.* [C] (*Market.*) a person in a company or an advertising agency who is responsible for planning and managing the imaginative work of advertising and selling products

**crèche** (*also* **creche**) /kreʃ/ *n.* [C] (*BrE*) a place where babies and small children are looked after while their parents are working, studying, etc: *workplace creches*

**credentials** /krəˈdenʃlz/ *n.* [pl.] the qualities, training or experience that make you suitable to do sth: *She doesn't* ***have*** *the right credentials for the job.* ◇ *impeccable/strong ~*

★**credit** /ˈkredɪt/ *n., v.*
• ***n.*** **1** (*Comm.*) [U] an arrangement that you make with a bank, shop/ store, etc., to be able to buy things now and pay for them later: *I bought it* ***on*** *credit.*
⊙ *to* ***get/have/use*** *~* ♦ *to* ***give/offer*** *~* ♦ *to* ***deny/refuse*** *~* ♦ *a ~* ***agreement/ limit*** ♦ *~* ***facilities/terms***
**2** (*Finan.*) [U] money that financial institutions lend to businesses, governments and people: *Will the bank extend additional credit to the firm?*
⊙ *to* ***have access to/get*** *~* ♦ *to* ***provide*** *~* ♦ ***domestic/international*** *~*
**3** [U] the fact that there is money in a bank account: *Your account is* ***in*** *credit.* **4** [C] an amount that is paid into a bank account; a record of this: *a credit of €100* OPP DEBIT
**5** (*Account.*) [C] (*abbr* **Cr**, **cr**) an amount written in a company's financial account to show an increase in money that the company owes or a decrease in the value of its assets: *the* ***credit side*** *of an account* OPP DEBIT
**6** [C,U] a reduction in an amount of money you have to pay; a payment that you have a right to receive
**7** (*Account.*) [C,U] an amount of money that is paid back or owed to you, because you paid too much; a record of the amount: *a credit of €60*
**8** [U] the status of being trusted to pay back money to sb who lends it: *Her credit isn't good anywhere now.*
• ***v.*** [T] **1** to put an amount of money into a bank account: *The funds will be credited* ***to*** *your account today.* ◇ *Your account has been credited* ***with*** *$50 000.* **2** (*Account.*) to write an amount in a company's financial account to show an increase in the money the company owes or a decrease in the value of its assets: *The cash was credited* ***to*** *the sales account.* OPP DEBIT

**ˈcredit acˌcount** = ACCOUNT *n.* (2)

**ˈcredit adˌvice** *n.* [C] a message from a bank to a customer, telling them that a payment has been made into their bank account

**ˈcredit ˌagency** = CREDIT RATING AGENCY

**ˈcredit aˌnalysis** *n.* [U,C] (*Finan.*) the activity and business of calculating the risks of lending money to particular companies or governments
▸ **ˈcredit ˌanalyst** *n.* [C]

**ˈcredit apˌpraisal** *n.* [U,C] (*Finan.*) an examination of how much money a person or a company can afford to borrow; an opinion about their ability to pay their debts: *The firm has a 'fair' credit appraisal.*

**ˈcredit ˌbalance** *n.* [C] **1** the amount of money that is left in a bank account at a particular time OPP DEBIT BALANCE **2** (*Account.*) in a company's financial records, the amount by which the total CREDITS are greater than the total DEBITS in a particular account

**ˈcredit ˌbureau** = CREDIT REFERENCE AGENCY

★**ˈcredit card** *n.* [C] a small plastic card that you can use to buy goods and services and pay for them later: *I'll* ***put it on*** *(= use) my credit card.* ◇ *We accept all major credit cards.*
→ DEBIT CARD
⊙ *to* ***pay by/use*** *a ~* ♦ *to* ***take*** *~s* ♦ *a credit-card* ***payment/transaction*** ♦ *a credit-card* ***bill/statement***

**ˈcredit check** *n.* [C] an act of checking how well sb has paid their debts in the past, to see if they are reliable: *We* ***run*** *credit checks on all loan applicants.*
▸ **ˈcredit ˌchecking** *n.* [U]

**ˈcredit ˌcompany** *n.* [C] **1** a company that lends money for people or companies to buy things **2** a company that provides credit cards to people

**ˈcredit conˌtrol** *n.* [C,U]
**1** (*Account.*) the way that a business manages the money it is owed, for example checking whether its customers can pay, making sure that payments are made on time, etc.
**2** (*Finan.*) the way that a bank controls the money it lends, for example checking who it lends money to and how much it can safely lend them: *to tighten credit controls.* **3** (*Econ.*) the actions of a government to limit the amount of money that people or companies can borrow or spend using credit

**ˈcredit coˌoperative** (*also* **ˌsavings and ˈcredit coˌoperative**) *n.* [C] (*Finan.*) in some countries, a group of people, esp. from a particular profession, who create a fund of money from which they can borrow at low rates of interest

**ˈcredit creˌation** *n.* [U] (*Econ.*) the fact of banks making more money available for borrowers, so increasing the MONEY SUPPLY

**'credit ex,posure** *n.* [U] (*Finan.*) money that an organization has lent to sb and so risks losing if it is not paid back SYN DEBT EXPOSURE

**'credit fa,cility** *n.* [C] (*Finan.*) an arrangement that a business has with a bank, company, etc. to be able to borrow money up to an agreed limit for a particular period of time SYN CREDIT LINE

**'credit ,history** *n.* [C, usu. sing.] a record of the loans and credit that sb has received and whether they have paid back the amounts that they owe in the right way
○ *a **good/bad/poor** ~ ◆ **little/no** ~ ◆ to **build/have** a ~*

**'credit in,surance** *n.* [U,C] **1** insurance that a company buys to protect themselves against financial losses if customers do not pay their bills **2** (*also* **con,sumer 'credit in,surance**) insurance that sb buys that will make payments on a loan, credit card, etc. if they cannot make them, for example because they become ill/sick and cannot work

**'credit ,limit** (*also* **,credit line**) *n.* [C, usu. sing.] the highest amount of money that a customer is allowed to owe, for example to a bank or on a credit card: *She has a credit limit of $6 500 on her Visa card.* ◇ *to be at/exceed a ~*

**'credit line** *n.* [C] **1** (*Finan.*) (*also* **,line of 'credit**) an amount of credit that a bank, company, etc. makes available to a person or a company for a particular period SYN CREDIT FACILITY
○ *to **have/open/set up** a ~ ◆ to **cut off/provide** a ~ ◆ to **draw (down) on/pay down/use** a ~*
**2** = CREDIT LIMIT

**'credit loss** *n.* [C,U] (*Account.*) money that a business loses because its customers have not paid the money they owe

**'credit ,market** *n.* [C] (*Econ.*) the business of financial institutions lending money to people, companies or governments

**'credit note** *n.* [C] (*BrE*) (*Comm.*) a document that a shop/store gives you when you have returned sth, that allows you to have goods of the same value in exchange

★ **creditor** /ˈkredɪtə(r)/ *n.* **1** [C] a person, company, country, etc. that sb/sth owes money to: *The property will be sold to pay off their creditors.* **2** (*Account.*) **creditors** [pl.] (*BrE*) the amounts that a business owes to its suppliers or to people who have made loans, shown as LIABILITIES on its BALANCE SHEET: *creditors falling due within one year* (= debts that must be paid within a year) SYN ACCOUNTS PAYABLE

**'creditor ,nation** *n.* [C] (*Econ.*) a country that has invested more in other countries than other countries have invested in it

**,creditors' com'mittee** *n.* [C] (*Law*) a group of people representing the **creditors** of a BANKRUPT company or person, that help decide how the debts will be paid back

**'creditors' ,ledger** *n.* [C] (*Account.*) in a company's financial records, the group of accounts in which amounts owed to suppliers are recorded SYN PURCHASE LEDGER

**'credit ,policy** *n.* [U,C] **1** (*Econ.*) the decisions that a government makes about how easy or expensive it will be for people and businesses to borrow money **2** (*Finan.*) the decisions a business has made about the way it will lend money or give credit; a document that describes these decisions

**'credit ,quality** *n.* [U] (*Finan.*) **1** how likely or unlikely it is that people or businesses will pay back money they borrow: *a decline in consumer credit quality* **2** how likely or unlikely it is that a company issuing a bond will be able to make regular payments of interest and repay the value of the bond: *stocks with good credit quality*

**'credit ,rating** (*also* **'rating**) *n.* [C,U] (*Finan.*) a measurement of the ability of a company, person or government to pay their debts; the process of estimating this: *The company's credit rating has been downgraded to 'junk' status.* SYN DEBT RATING

**'credit ,rating ,agency** (*also* **'credit ,ratings ,agency, 'credit ,agency**) *n.* [C] (*Finan.*) an organization that provides scores for how likely companies, people or governments are to pay their debts SYN RATING AGENCY

**'credit ,rationing** *n.* [U] (*Econ.*) when lenders limit the amount of money available for borrowers or the rate of interest is very high

**,credit 'reference ,agency** (*BrE*) (*also* **'credit ,bureau**, *esp. in AmE*) *n.* [C] (*Finan.*) an organization that keeps information about whether people have paid their debts and provides this information to banks or companies

**'credit re,pair** *n.* [U] (*Finan.*) the activity of helping a person or a company to improve their CREDIT RATING, so that they will be able to borrow money or get credit

**'credit re,port** *n.* [C] (*Finan.*) a document giving information about a borrower's financial position and how they have paid back loans in the past ▸ **'credit re,porting** *n.* [U]

**'credit re,search** *n.* [U] (*Finan.*) studying the financial state of particular companies and their ability to pay their debts

**'credit risk** *n.* (*Finan.*) **1** [U,C] how likely it is that sb/sth will be able to pay their debts **2** [C] a particular person or company who is likely not to be able to pay their debts

**'credit sale** *n.* **1** (*Comm.; Law*) [C,U] an act of selling sth where the price will only be paid in the future but the buyer becomes the owner as soon as the goods are received **2** (*Account.*) **credit sales** [pl.] the amount of money that a business receives in an accounting period for goods or services sold in this way

**'credit score** (*also* **'credit ,scoring**) *n.* [C] (*Finan.*) a number that is a measurement of a person's ability to pay their debts

**'credit ,scoring** *n.* (*Finan.*) **1** [U] the activity of calculating a **credit score** for sb before deciding whether or not to give them a loan or credit **2** [C] = CREDIT SCORE

**'credit so,ciety** *n.* [C] (*Finan.*) a group of people, esp. from a particular profession, who create a fund of money from which they can borrow at low rates of interest SYN CREDIT UNION

**'credit squeeze** *n.* [C, usu. sing.] (*Econ.*) a period of time during which it becomes difficult and expensive to borrow money; actions taken by a government to achieve this

**'credit ,standing** (*also* **'credit ,status**) *n.* [sing.] the reputation that a person or an organization has for paying their debts: *a low/satisfactory ~* SYN CREDITWORTHINESS

**'credit terms** *n.* [pl.] (*Comm.*) the conditions on which a business is prepared to give credit to sb, such as the time limit for paying the debt, the amount that can be spent, etc: *Our standard credit terms are full payment within 30 days.*
✪ *easy/favourable ~* ♦ *to agree/grant/negotiate/offer ~*

**'credit ,transfer** *n.* [U,C] (*BrE*) the process of sending money from one person's bank account to another's: *Your salary will be paid* **by** *automated credit transfer.*

**'credit ,union** *n.* [C] (*Finan.*) an organization whose members create a fund of money from which they can borrow at low rates of interest

**creditworthy** /'kredɪtwɜːði; *AmE* -wɜːrði/ *adj.* safe to lend money to ▸ **'creditworthiness** *n.* [U]

**creep** /kriːp/ *v., n.*
• ***v.*** [I] to change very slowly or by a small amount, esp. to increase or rise: *Unemployment has crept back to 9%.* ▸ **'creeping** *adj.*: *~ control/inflation*
• ***n.*** [U] slow, steady movement, esp. an increase: *the gradual creep of inflation*

**crime** /kraɪm/ *n.* **1** [C] an illegal act that can be punished by law
✪ *to carry out/commit a ~* ♦ *to accuse sb of/charge sb with a ~*
**2** [U] illegal activities
✪ *petty/serious ~* ♦ *computer/corporate/white-collar ~*

**criminal** /'krɪmɪnl/ *adj., n.*
• ***adj.*** **1** connected with or involving crime: *a criminal offence* **2** connected to the laws and institutions that deal with crime: *the criminal justice system* ◇ *a ~inquiry/investigation*
• ***n.*** [C] a person who commits a crime

**,criminal 'law** *n.* [U] (*Law*) law that deals with crimes, rather than with commercial issues and the relationships between individuals, companies, etc. → CIVIL (1) ▸ **,criminal 'lawyer** *n.* [C]

**crisis** /'kraɪsɪs/ *n.* [C,U] (*pl.* **crises** /-siːz/) a time of great danger or difficulty when problems must be solved or important decisions must be made: *The country's economic crisis has deepened.* ◇ *The business is still in crisis.*
✪ *a major/serious ~* ♦ *a ~ arises/is over/worsens* ♦ *to face/avert/resolve a ~* ♦ *sth causes/creates/triggers a ~*

**'crisis-hit** *adj.* experiencing a **crisis**, esp. a financial one: *a ~ company/industry*

**'crisis ,management** *n.* [U] actions taken by an organization to deal with a very difficult or unexpected situation

**criterion** /kraɪ'tɪəriən; *AmE* -'tɪr-/ *n.* [C] (*pl.* **-ria** /-riə/) a standard that you use when you make a decision or form an opinion about sb/sth: *What criteria do you use* **for** *hiring staff?* ◇ *to meet/satisfy/set criteria*

**,critical 'incident** *n.* [C] (*HR*) an example of the way a person doing a job behaves that has a good or bad effect: *identifying the critical incidents that distinguish satisfactory workers from unsatisfactory workers*

**,critical 'incident ,method** (*also* **,critical 'incidents ,method**) *n.*

[C] (*HR*) a way of deciding what abilities are needed to do a particular job and discovering how well sb is doing it, by looking at real examples of the way people have behaved in the job that have had good or bad effects

**ˌcritical ˈmass** *n.* [U,C; sing.] the number of customers, amount of resources, etc. needed to allow a business, an industry, etc. to make a profit and continue without outside help: *We need five or six stores to achieve critical mass.*

**ˌcritical ˈpath** *n.* [sing.] (*Econ.; Product.*) the series of tasks in a project that must be completed on time for the project to finish on time

**ˌcritical ˈpath aˌnalysis** (*abbr* **CPA**) (*also* **ˌcritical ˈpath ˌmethod** *abbr* **CPM**) (*also* **ˈnetwork aˌnalysis**) *n.* [U,C] (*Econ.; Product.*) a way of planning a project and calculating how long it will last by examining which order of tasks will have the fewest delays and complete the project in the fastest and cheapest way

**ˌcritical sucˈcess ˌfactor** *n.* [C, usu. pl.] one of the areas of a business that are most important for it to be successful: *Customer service is a critical success factor for any retailer.*

**CRM** /ˌsiː ɑːr ˈem/ = CUSTOMER RELATIONSHIP MANAGEMENT

**ˌcrony ˈcapitalism** *n.* [U] (*infml.*) a system in some CAPITALIST countries in which business contracts, bank loans, etc. are given to the family and friends of the government and business leaders

**crop** /krɒp; *AmE* krɑːp/ *n.* [C] **1** a plant that is grown in large quantities, esp. as food **2** the amount of grain, fruit, etc. that is grown in one season: *a fall in this year's coffee crop*

**cross** /krɒs; *AmE* krɔːs/ *v.* [T] (*BrE*) if you **cross** a cheque, you draw two lines across it to show that it must be paid into sb's bank account and not exchanged for cash: *a crossed cheque*

**ˌcross-ˈborder** *adj.* that takes place between people or businesses in different countries, esp. ones that are next to or near each other: ~ *trade/trading*

**ˌcross-eˈxamine** *v.* [T,I] to question sb carefully and in a lot of detail about answers that they have already given, esp. a witness for the other side in a court case ▸ **ˌcross-examiˈnation** *n.* [U,C]

**ˌcross-ˈfunctional** *adj.* (*HR*) that involves people, departments, etc. with different jobs or skills working together: *cross-functional* **teams**

**ˌcross guaranˈtee** *n.* [C] (*Finan.*) a promise made by members of a particular group of companies to pay back the debts of a company in the group if it fails to do so, in order to help the company borrow money ▸ **ˌcross-guaranˈtee** *v.* [T]

**ˈcross-ˌholding** (*also* **ˌcross-ˈshareholding**) *n.* [C] (*esp. BrE*) (*Finan.*) a situation in which two companies or groups own some of each other's shares; the shares that each company or group owns

**ˌcross-ˈmedia** *adj.* involving or using different types of media such as television, radio, etc: *cross-media publishing*

**ˌcross-media ˈownership** (*also* **ˌcross-ˈownership**) *n.* [U] (*esp. BrE*) (*Econ.*) when a single organization controlling several different kinds of media company such as newspapers, television stations, etc.

**ˌcross-ˈmerchandising** *n.* [U] (*Market.*) the activity of displaying related products together in a shop/store to encourage customers to buy several items instead of just one: *the cross-merchandising of swimwear* **with** *sunglasses* ▸ **ˌcross-ˈmerchandise** *v.* [T,I]

**ˌcross-ˈownership** = CROSS-MEDIA OWNERSHIP

**ˌcross-ˈplatform** *adj.* (*IT*) that can be used with or involves different types of computer systems: *cross-platform compatibility*

**ˌcross-proˈmotion** *n.* [C,U] (*Market.*) **1** a set of advertisements or other activities that are designed to help two companies sell their products or services together **2** a situation where a company advertises one of its products, such as a newspaper or a book, in another ▸ **ˌcross-proˈmotional** *adj.* **ˌcross-proˈmote** *v.* [T,I]

**ˈcross-rate** *n.* [C] (*Finan.*) an EXCHANGE RATE for two currencies calculated by comparing the value of each currency to a third (esp. the US dollar): *the cross-rate* **between** *the yen and the krone*

**ˌcross-ˈselling** *n.* [U] (*Market.*) the activity of selling other products or services that your company or another company provides at the same time as a customer is buying one product or service ▸ **ˌcross-ˈsell** *v.* [T]

**ˌcross-ˈshareholding** = CROSS-HOLDING

**ˌcrowded ˈmarket** *n.* [C] a situation where there are a lot of companies all trying to sell similar products

**ˌcrown ˈjewel** *n.* [C] the most valuable part of sth, esp. of a business or an industry

**crude** /kruːd/ *adj., n.*
• ***adj.* 1** (about oil and other natural substances) in its natural state, before it has been treated with chemicals: *the refining of crude oil*
**2** (**cruder, crudest**) simple and not very accurate but giving a general idea: *a ~ estimate/measure (of sth)*
• ***n.*** (*also* **ˌcrude ˈoil**) [U] oil in its natural state, before it has been treated with chemicals: *a rise in crude prices*

**crunch** /krʌntʃ/ *n., v.*
• ***n.*** [C, usu. sing.] a situation in which there is suddenly not enough of sth, esp. money: *The company is facing a severe cash crunch.*
• ***v.*** [T] (*IT*) to deal with large amounts of data very quickly
→ NUMBER CRUNCHER

**ˈC share** (*also* **class ˈC share**)
→ A/B/C SHARE

**CSR** /ˌsiː es ˈɑː(r)/ = CORPORATE SOCIAL RESPONSIBILITY

**ˈC-suite** *n.* [C, usu. sing.] (*often* **the C-suite**) the most important managers in a company: *C-suite executives*

**CT** /ˌsiː ˈtiː/ = CORPORATION TAX

**ˌC-to-ˈC** = C2C

**Ctrl** = CONTROL *n.* (7)

**cu.** *abbr* a short way of writing **cubic**: *a volume of 15 cu. m* (= 15 cubic metres)

**ˈcube farm** *n.* [C] (*infml.*) an office that is divided into CUBICLES

**cubic** /ˈkjuːbɪk/ *adj.* (*abbr* **cu.**) used to show that a measurement is the volume of sth, that is the height multiplied by the length and the width: *The plant processes 7 million cubic metres of gas a day.*

**cubicle** /ˈkjuːbɪkl/ *n.* [C] (*esp. AmE*) a small office that is made by separating off part of a larger room

**culture** /ˈkʌltʃə(r)/ *n.* [C,U] the ways in which people in an organization relate to each other and deal with their work: *Team meetings are part of the company's culture.*

**cum** /kʌm/ *prep.* (*Finan.*) used to show that the buyer of a share, bond, etc. is getting the right to claim the thing mentioned: *The shares will trade cum bonus until 1 March 2008.* ◇ *buying shares cum dividend/cum div.* OPP EX

**cume** /kjuːm/ = CUMULATIVE AUDIENCE

**cumulative** /ˈkjuːmjələtɪv; *AmE* -leɪtɪv/ *adj.* (about a figure) that includes all the amounts that have been added previously: *We predict that cumulative sales will exceed 2 million units by 2009.*

**ˌcumulative ˈaudience** (*also* **cume**, *infml.*) *n.* [C, usu. sing.] (*Market.*) the number of different people who watch a particular television channel, hear a radio programme, etc. over one or more periods of time

**ˌcumulative ˈdividend** *n.* [C] (*Finan.*) the regular payment that is made to sb who owns a CUMULATIVE PREFERENCE SHARE

**ˌcumulative ˈpreference share** *n.* [C] (*BrE*) (*AmE* **ˌcumulative preferred ˈstock** [U]) (*Finan.*) a type of share that a company issues that gives its owner the right to receive regular payments from the company. If the company cannot afford to make a payment on time, it has to pay the amount later when it can afford to.

**curb** /kɜːb; *AmE* kɜːrb/ *v.* [T] to control or limit sth, esp. sth bad: *raising interest rates to curb inflation* ▶ **curb** *n.* [C]: *curbs in imports*

**ˈcurb ˌmarket** = KERB MARKET

★ **currency** /ˈkʌrənsi; *AmE* ˈkɜːr-/ *n.* (*pl.* **-cies**) **1** [C,U] the system of money that a country uses; the value of the country's money: *Brazil's currency* ◇ *trading in foreign currencies*
● *common/local/national ~* • *a stable/strong/volatile/weak ~* • *to buy/change/exchange/sell ~* • *to devalue/depreciate/prop up a ~* • *a ~ dealer/speculator/trader*
**2** [U] the period of time during which sth is valid or is used: *Did the injury occur during the currency of the insurance?*

**ˈcurrency acˌcount** (*also* **ˌforeign ˈcurrency acˌcount**) *n.* [C] (*Finan.*) a type of CURRENT ACCOUNT for businesses that is available in a wide range of foreign currencies

**ˈcurrency bloc** (*also* **bloc**) *n.* [C] (*Econ.*) a group of countries that use the same type of money: *the euro currency bloc*

**ˈcurrency board** *n.* [C] (*Econ.*) in some countries, a government institution that controls the value of the country's money, for example, by deciding its EXCHANGE RATE

**ˈcurrency efˌfect** *n.* [C, usu. pl.] (*Account.*) the way that changes in the value of currency can change a financial result: *Sales were up 5%—or 1% excluding currency effects.*

**'currency ex,posure** (*also* **,foreign 'currency ex,posure**) *n.* [U,C] (*Finan.*) the amount of an investment that is in a foreign currency and could be affected by changes in the value of the currency; the state of being at risk in this way: *The company* ***manages*** *its currency exposure by keeping dollar reserves.* SYN CURRENCY RISK

**'currency hedge** *n.* [C] (*Finan.*) a way of trying to protect investments from problems caused by changes in the value of foreign currency; an investment that reduces this risk

**'currency ,market** *n.* [C] (*Finan.*) a market in which traders buy and sell currencies: *The euro weakened against the dollar* ***on*** *the currency markets.* SYN FOREIGN EXCHANGE MARKET

**'currency note** *n.* [C, usu. pl.] money of a particular system in the form of BANKNOTES

**'currency pair** *n.* [C] (*Finan.*) the relation in value between two particular currencies

**'currency rate** *n.* [C] the relation in value between one currency and another: *the currency rate* ***between*** *the yen and the pound* SYN EXCHANGE RATE

**'currency re,serves** = FOREIGN CURRENCY RESERVES

**'currency risk** (*also* **,foreign 'currency risk**) *n.* [U,C, usu. pl.] (*Finan.*) the possibility that an investment that is in a foreign currency could lose value because of changes in the value of the currency; the state of being at risk in this way: *The group* ***is exposed to*** *currency risk from its international business.* ◇ *to* ***hedge (against)*** (= protect against) *currency risk* SYN CURRENCY EXPOSURE

**current** /'kʌrənt; *AmE* 'kɜːr-/ *adj.* happening now; of the present time: *your current employer* ◇ *the current year*

**'current ac,count** *n.* [C] **1** (*BrE*) (*AmE* **'checking ac,count**) (*also* **'cash ac,count**, *AmE, BrE*) a bank account that you use to receive payments and pay bills, for example by cheque or BANK TRANSFER **2** (*Econ.*) (*also* **ex,ternal ac'count**) a record of the money coming into and going out of a country as a result of imports and exports of goods and services, income from investments, etc.

**,current 'asset** (*also* **,circulating 'asset**) *n.* [C, usu. pl.] (*Account.*) an asset that a company holds for a short period of time, including cash or sth that can easily provide cash, such as products to be sold; the value of these assets

**,current 'cost** *n.* [C] (*Account.*) the present value of sth, calculated by increasing its original cost to include a sum for INFLATION, or by considering the cost of buying or producing the same item today

**,current ,lia'bility** *n.* [C, usu. pl.] (*also* **,short-term lia'bilities** [pl.]) (*Account.*) a debt that must be paid within a year; the value of these debts in a company's financial records: *Total current liabilities were $149 m.*

**,current 'prices** *n.* [pl.] (*Account.; Econ.*) **1** the prices that are being paid today for similar things: ***At*** *current prices, the company is worth around €23 bn.* **2** the original amount increased to include a sum for INFLATION: *The 1992 strike cost the industry almost $10 bn* ***in*** *current prices.*

**'current ,ratio** = ACID-TEST RATIO

**,current 'yield** *n.* [C, usu. sing.] (*Finan.*) the amount of interest paid on an investment that compares the annual interest payment to the current price of the investment: *The current yield* ***on*** *the bond is 5.2%.*

**curriculum vitae** /kə,rɪkjələm 'viːtaɪ/ = CV

**cursor** /'kɜːsə(r); *AmE* 'kɜːrs-/ *n.* [C] a small mark on a computer screen that can be moved and that shows the place, for example, where text will appear when typing

**curtail** /kɜː'teɪl; *AmE* kɜːr't-/ *v.* [T] (*fml.*) to limit or reduce sth: *Union powers have been curtailed.*
▸ **cur'tailment** *n.* [U]

**curve** /kɜːv; *AmE* kɜːrv/ *n.* **1** [C] a line on a graph that shows the relationship between two things: *a steep sales curve* ◇ *a flat/shallow ~* ◇ *to plot a ~ (on a graph)* **2 the curve** [sing.] the general level of skill, knowledge, etc. that exists in a particular industry or area of activity: *We invest in research to stay* ***ahead of*** *the curve.*

**cushion** /'kʊʃn/ *v., n.*
• *v.* [T] to reduce the unpleasant effects of sth: *The south was cushioned* ***from*** *the effects of the recession.*
• *n.* [C] something that protects you against sth unpleasant that might happen: *a* ***cash*** *cushion*

**custodial** /kʌ'stəʊdiəl; *AmE* -'stoʊ-/ *adj.* **1** that involves spending time in prison: *a* ***custodial sentence***

**2** (*Finan.*) relating to the work of a CUSTODIAN (2): *custodial fees*

**cu'stodial ac,count** *n.* [C] (*Finan.*) in the US, a collection of money, property or shares, etc. that sb manages on behalf of a child; the account in which these items are recorded

**custodian** /kʌ'stəʊdiən; *AmE* -'stoʊ-/ *n.* [C] **1** a person who is responsible for taking care of or protecting sth: *the museum's custodians* **2** (*Finan.*) a financial institution that looks after shares, bonds, etc. and their certificates on behalf of investors: *a custodian bank* **3** (*Law*) (*AmE*) in the US, a person or company that is given the responsibility of looking after property or money on behalf of a child **4** (*AmE*) = CARETAKER

**custody** /'kʌstədi/ *n.* [U] **1** the legal right or duty to take care of or keep sb/sth; the act of taking care of sth/sb: *The records are* ***in the custody of*** *the National Archives.* **2** (*Finan.*) the activity of keeping shares, bonds, etc. and their certificates on behalf of investors: *The bank holds millions of pounds' worth of assets* ***in custody*** *for pension funds.*

**custom** /'kʌstəm/ *n., adj.*
• ***n.*** **1** [U] (*esp. BrE*) the fact of being a customer: *They have cut their prices to* ***attract*** *custom.* SYN BUSINESS **2** [C,U] an accepted way of behaving or of doing sth in a particular company or industry: *a* ***trade*** *custom*
• ***adj.*** (*esp. AmE*) = CUSTOM-BUILT, CUSTOM-MADE

**,custom-'built** (*also* **'custom**, *esp. in AmE*) *adj.* built according to a special design, usu. for a particular person or company: *custom-built computers*

★ **customer** /'kʌstəmə(r)/ *n.* [C] a person or an organization that buys a product or service from a shop/store or a business: *We have around 7 million customers worldwide.* ◇ *one of the store's biggest customers*
○ *to* ***attract/find/get/keep/lose*** *~s* • *a* ***good/loyal/regular*** *~* • *an* ***awkward/a demanding/difficult*** *~* • ***existing/new/potential*** *~s* • *~* ***feedback/preferences***

**,customer acqui'sition** *n.* [U] (*Market.*) the activity of getting new customers for a business: *poor customer acquisition rates*

**,customer acqui'sition cost** = ACQUISITION COST (2)

**'customer base** (*also* **con'sumer base**, *less freq.*) *n.* [C, usu. sing.] all the people who buy or use a particular product or service: *We must appeal to a wider customer base.*

**,customer 'capital** *n.* [U] (*Econ.*; *HR*) the value of a company's relationship with its customers and the businesses that it sells goods or services to

**,customer 'care** = CUSTOMER SERVICE

**,customer-'centric** *adj.* organized around the needs of customers

**,customer-'focused** *adj.* giving all your attention and effort to the needs of customers ▸ **,customer 'focus** *n.* [U; C, usu. sing.]

**'customer 'lifetime 'value** = LIFETIME VALUE

**,customer 'loyalty** *n.* [U] the fact that a customer prefers to use a particular shop/store, etc. or continues to buy a particular type of product: *to develop/strengthen ~*

**,customer 'management** *n.* [U] a system of collecting and analysing information about customers in order to provide them with the products or services they need

**'customer ,panel** = CONSUMER PANEL

**,customer 'profile** *n.* [C] (*Market.*) **1** (*also* **con,sumer 'profile**) a detailed description of the type of person who buys a particular product or service, uses a particular store, etc. **2** a detailed description of a particular customer

**,customer re'lations** *n.* (*Market.*) **1** [pl.] the way in which a company deals with its customers: *a customer relations manager* ◇ *excellent/good ~* **2** [U with sing./pl. v.; pl.] the department of a company responsible for dealing with customers

**,customer re'lationship** *n.* [C] (*often* **the customer relationship**) the way in which a company and its customers behave towards each other: *managing the customer relationship*

**,customer re'lationship ,management, ,customer re'lationship ,marketing** (*abbr* **CRM**) (*also* **re'lationship ,management**) *n.* [U] (*IT*; *Market.*) a system in which a business aims to develop a good relationship with customers, for example by keeping information about their needs, in order to sell as many goods or services as possible and keep customers satisfied; software that helps businesses do this: *CRM solutions/software*
▸ **,customer re'lationship ,manager** (*also* **re'lationship ,manager**) *n.* [C]

**ˌcustomer reˈsearch** = CONSUMER RESEARCH

**ˌcustomer reˈsistance** = CONSUMER RESISTANCE

**ˌcustomer ˌsatisˈfaction** *n.* [U] the extent to which customers are happy with a particular product or service: *Our staff work as a team to achieve customer satisfaction.*

**o** *to create/increase/measure ~* ◆ *a ~ index/rating*

★ **ˌcustomer ˈservice** (*also* **ˌcustomer ˈcare** [U]) *n.* **1** [U,C] the way in which a company treats its customers and answers their questions, complaints, etc: *How you handle complaints is an important part of customer service.* ◇ *changes in the way some customer services are delivered*

**o** ***excellent/good/poor ~*** ◆ ***to deliver/improve/provide ~*** ◆ ***a ~ centre/department/manager***

**2** **ˌcustomer ˈservices** [U with sing./pl. v.; pl.] the department in a company that deals with customers' questions, complaints, etc: *Customer Services has/have improved its/their efficiency.*

**customize, -ise** /ˈkʌstəmaɪz/ *v.* [T] to make or change sth to meet the needs of the customer or user: *We customize our training courses.* ▸ **ˈcustomized, -ised** *adj.*: *customized software* **ˌcustomiˈzation, -iˈsation** *n.* [U] /-aɪˈzeɪʃn; *AmE* -məˈz-/

**ˌcustom-ˈmade** (*also* **ˈcustom**) *adj.* (*both esp. AmE*) designed and made for a particular person: *custom-made shoes* SYN BESPOKE

★ **customs** /ˈkʌstəmz/ *n.* [pl.] **1** (*usually* **Customs**) the government department that gives permission for goods to be imported and charges taxes on them; the officials at an airport, etc. that work for this department: *The Customs have seized large quantities of cigarettes.* ◇ *obtaining **customs clearance** for the goods* (= permission to import them) HELP AmE uses a singular verb with **customs** in this meaning. **2** the place at an airport, etc. where your bags are checked as you come into a country: *to **go through** customs* **3** (*Trade*) = CUSTOMS DUTY

**ˈcustoms ˌagent** = CUSTOMS OFFICER, CUSTOMS BROKER

**ˌCustoms and ˈExcise** → HM REVENUE AND CUSTOMS

**ˈcustoms bond** *n.* [C,U] (*esp. AmE*) (*Trade*) a type of insurance that an importer must buy, which promises that all taxes on goods that they import will be paid and all the rules obeyed

**ˈcustoms ˌbroker** (*also* **ˈcustoms ˌagent**) *n.* [C] (*Trade*) a person or company that is paid to arrange for goods to be brought into a country on behalf of an importer

**ˈcustoms declaˌration** *n.* [C] (*Trade*) an official description of the goods that you want to send to another country or bring into a country

**ˈcustoms ˌduty** *n.* [C, usu. pl., U] (*also* **ˈcustoms** [pl.]) (*Trade*) taxes that must be paid when goods are imported: *the customs duties **on** foreign cars*

**ˈcustoms ˌentry** *n.* [C,U] (*Trade*) an official record that must be made of goods brought into or taken out of a country; the process of bringing goods into or taking goods out of a country in the official way

**ˈcustoms ˌofficer** (*also* **ˈcustoms ofˌficial**) (*also* **ˈcustoms ˌagent**, *esp. in AmE*) *n.* [C] a government official that works at an airport, etc., whose job involves checking for illegally imported goods

**ˈcustoms ˌunion** *n.* [C] (*Econ.*) a group of countries that have agreed not to charge taxes on goods they trade with each other, and to charge the same taxes on goods imported from other countries

**ˌCustoms ˈwarehouse** = BONDED WAREHOUSE

**cut** /kʌt/ *v., n.*
• *v.* [T] (**cutting, cut, cut**) **1** to reduce sth, esp. by a large amount: *The airline is to cut 2 500 more jobs.* ◇ *His salary has been cut **by** 10%.* **2** to remove text or images from one place on a computer screen, in order to put them somewhere else: *You can **cut and paste** between the programs.*
IDM **cut a ˈdeal (with sb); cut (sb) a ˈdeal** (*infml.*) to make an arrangement with sb **a cut and ˈpaste job** (*infml.*) a document that sb has created quickly by taking ideas or sections of text from other documents
PHR V **ˌcut ˈback (on sth); ˌcut sth ˈback** to reduce sth: *If we don't sell more we'll have to cut back production.* **ˌcut ˈdown (on sth); ˌcut sth ˈdown (to sth)** to reduce the size, amount or number of sth: *She wants to cut her travel load down to two days a week.* **ˌcut sb ˈin (on sth)** (*infml.*) to give sb a share of the profit in a business or an activity **ˌcut ˈoff sb/sth** (*often pass.*) to stop the supply of sth to sb/sth: *The bank may cut off their credit.*
• *n.* [C] **1** a reduction in the amount or number of sb/sth: *making a cut **in** interest rates* ◇ *The carmaker has an-*

*nounced a further 1 000 job cuts.* ◇ *We all had to **take** a 20% cut **in** pay.*
**⊙** ***interest-rate/tax** ~s* ◆ ***budget/ cost/spending** ~s* ◆ ***pay/wage** ~s* ◆ *a **big/deep/dramatic** ~*
**2** (*infml.*) [usu. sing.] a share in a profit or money: *The agency takes a cut of our revenues.*

**cutback** /ˈkʌtbæk/ *n.* [C, usu. pl.] a reduction in sth: *cutbacks **in** production* ◇ *staff cutbacks*

**ˈcut-off** *adj.*, *n.*
• ***adj.*** forming a limit at which sth must stop: *When is the cut-off **date**?*
• ***n.*** [C, usu. sing.] a point or limit when you stop sth: *Mortgage lending should have an upper limit cut-off.*

**ˈcut-off score** *n.* [C] (*HR*) the number of points on a test below which sb will not be considered for employment

**cutover** /ˈkʌtəʊvə(r); *AmE* -oʊ-/ *n.* [C] a time when an organization stops using one system, esp. a computer system, and immediately starts using a new one: *The cutover is planned for 31 May.*

**ˌcut-ˈprice** (*esp. BrE*) (*AmE usu.* **ˈcut-rate**) *adj.* **1** sold at a reduced price: *~ deals/fares/goods* **2** selling goods or services at a reduced price: *a ~ airline/store*

**ˈcut-throat** *adj.* (about an activity) in which people compete with each other in aggressive and unfair ways: *rival companies engaged in cut-throat competition*

**ˌcutting ˈedge** *n.* [sing.] **1 the ~ (of sth)** the newest, most advanced stage in the development of sth: *They are **at** the cutting edge of scientific research.* ◇ *cutting-edge designs* SYN LEADING EDGE **2** a quality or feature that gives sb/sth an advantage

★ **CV** /ˌsiː ˈviː/ *abbr* **curriculum vitae** a written record of your education and employment that you send when you are applying for a job SYN RÉSUMÉ (*AmE*)

**c.w.o.** (*also* **CWO**) /ˌsiː ˌdʌbljuː ˈəʊ; *AmE* ˈoʊ/ *abbr* (*Trade*) **cash with order** payment for goods will be made when the goods are ordered: *Our normal terms are c.w.o.*

**cwt.** *abbr* (*pl.* **cwt.**) a short way of writing **hundredweight**

**cyber-** /ˈsaɪbə(r)/ *comb. form* (*in ns and adjs*) connected with electronic communication networks, esp. the Internet: *a cybercafe* ◇ *cybersales*

**ˈcyber mall** (*also* **ˌelectronic ˈmall**) *n.* [C] (*E-comm.*) a website that is shared by two or more businesses

**cyberspace** /ˈsaɪbəspeɪs; *AmE* -bərs-/ *n.* [U] the imaginary place where electronic messages, Internet pages, etc. exist while they are being sent between computers

**cybersquatting** /ˈsaɪbəskwɒtɪŋ; *AmE* ˈsaɪbərskwɑːtɪŋ/ *n.* [U] the illegal activity of buying and officially recording an address on the Internet that is the name of an existing company or a well-known person, with the intention of selling it to the owner to make a profit
▸ **ˈcybersquatter** *n.* [C]

★ **cycle** /ˈsaɪkl/ *n.* [C] **1** a regular pattern of events: *a vicious* (= very bad) *cycle of reduced spending, lower production and unemployment* ◇ *Fashions tend to go **in** cycles.* **2** a pattern that an economy, an industry, a market, etc. tends to follow, with periods of success and periods of difficulty happening regularly one after another: *the **boom-and-bust** cycles of the IT industry* **3** a single period of success, failure, etc. that forms part of a regular series: *a **growth** cycle* **4** a regular period of time during which sb/sth completes a particular activity: *the product-development cycle*

**ˈcycle time** *n.* [U,C] (*Product.*) the time between starting and completing a production process

**cyclical** /ˈsaɪklɪkl; ˈsɪk-/ *adj.*, *n.*
• ***adj.*** (*Econ.*; *Finan.*) **1** that follows a regular pattern of success and failure, increase and decrease, etc: *the cyclical demand for steel products* **2** easily affected by the success or failure of the general economy: *cyclical unemployment*
**⊙** *~ **shares/stocks*** ◆ *a ~ **company/ industry***
• ***n.*** [C, usu. pl.] (*Finan.*) an investment whose value is easily affected by the success or failure of the general economy

# Dd

**D/A** = DOCUMENTS AGAINST ACCEPTANCE, DEPOSIT ACCOUNT

**DA** /ˌdiː ˈeɪ/ = DISTRICT ATTORNEY

**DAF** /ˌdiː eɪ ˈef/ = DELIVERED AT FRONTIER

**the ˈDaily Ofˈficial ˈList** *n.* [sing.] (*Stock Ex.*) a detailed record that gives information about the shares that are traded on a stock exchange on a particular day, esp. the London Stock Exchange

★ **damage** /ˈdæmɪdʒ/ *n.*, *v.*
• ***n.*** **1** [U] physical harm caused to sth which makes it less valuable or for which sb can claim money from

an insurance company: *The cost of the damage is estimated at $30 m.*
⊕ *to* ***cause/do*** *~ (to sb/sth)* ♦ *to* ***suffer/repair*** *~* ♦ ***irreparable/permanent/serious*** *~* ♦ ***accidental/environmental/structural*** *~* ♦ ***fire/flood*** *~*
**2** [U] harmful effects on sb/sth: *damage* ***to*** *a person's reputation*
⊕ *to* ***cause/do*** *~ (to sb/sth)* ♦ ***inflict*** *~ (on sb/sth)* ♦ *to* ***suffer/repair*** *~* ♦ ***irreparable/serious*** *~* ♦ ***financial/political*** *~*
**3** (*Law*) **damages** [pl.] money that a court orders a person, company, etc. to pay to sb, because they have caused them harm, injury or loss: *He was ordered to* ***pay*** *damages of €50 000.*
⊕ *to* ***be awarded/receive/recover/win*** *~* ♦ *to* ***claim/sue for*** *~*
• *v.* [T] to harm or spoil sb/sth: *The fire badly damaged the offices.*

**'damage limi,tation** (*also* **'damage con,trol**, *esp. in AmE*) *n.* [U] the process of trying to limit the amount of harm caused by a particular event or situation

**'danger ,money** (*BrE*) (*AmE* **'hazard pay**) *n.* [U] (*HR*) extra money paid to sb who works in a dangerous situation

★ **data** /'deɪtə; *BrE also* 'dɑːtə; *AmE also* 'dætə/ *n.* **1** [U; pl.] (*used as a pl. n. in technical English, when the sing. is* **datum**) facts or information, esp. when examined and used to find out things or to make decisions: *This data was collected from 73 countries.*
⊕ *to* ***analyse/interpret*** *~* ♦ *the* ***analysis/interpretation*** *of ~* ♦ *~* ***indicate(s)/show(s)/suggest(s)*** *sth*
**2** (*IT*) [U] information that is stored by a computer: *Enter the data into the computer.*
⊕ *to* ***access/process/retrieve/store*** *~* ♦ *~* ***management/processing/retrieval/storage***

**databank** (*also* **data bank**, *esp. in AmE*) /'deɪtəbæŋk; *AmE also* 'dætə-/ *n.* [C] (*IT*) a large amount of data on a particular subject that is stored in a computer

★ **database** /'deɪtəbeɪs; *AmE also* 'dætə-/ *n.* [C] (*IT*) an organized set of data that is stored in a computer and can be looked at and used in various ways: *We have more than 10 000 CVs* ***on*** *our database.*
⊕ *to* ***build/set up*** *a ~* ♦ *to* ***maintain/manage/update*** *a ~* ♦ *a* ***customer*** *~*

**'data ,capture** *n.* [U] (*IT*) the process of putting information into a computer system

**'data ,centre** *n.* [C] **1** an organization that collects scientific information about a particular subject; the place or system where the data is stored **2** (*IT*) a safe place at which a number of computers that store or process data are kept

**'data ,entry** *n.* [U] (*IT*) the work of putting information into a computer, for example from paper documents: *data entry clerks*

**'data ,mining** *n.* [U] (*IT*; *Market.*) using software to look at large amounts of information that has been collected on a computer and find new patterns, etc.

**,data pro'tection** *n.* [U] (*Law*) legal restrictions that keep information stored on computers private and that control who can read it or use it

**,data 'warehouse** *n.* [C] (*IT*) a collection of business information, for example about costs and profits, that a company keeps on a computer system, so that it can be analysed and used to make decisions ▸ **,data 'warehousing** *n.* [U]

**date** /deɪt/ *n.*, *v.*
• *n.* **1** [C] a particular day of the month given in numbers and words: *We need to fix/set a date* ***for*** *the next meeting.* **2** [sing.] a time in the past or future that is not a particular day: *The work will be carried out* ***at a future date.*** IDM **to 'date** up to the present time: *The new plant is their largest to date.*
• *v.* [T] to write or print the date on sth: *Thank you for your letter dated 24th March.* → UNDATED

**'datebook** /'deɪtbʊk/ = DIARY (1)

**,dated se'curity** *n.* [C, usu. pl.] (*Finan.*) an investment, such as a bond, that has a fixed MATURITY → UNDATED

**'date stamp** *n.* [C] **1** a date that is printed on sth, esp. an envelope or a food product **2** a device for printing the date on a document ▸ **'date-stamp** *v.* [T] **'date-,stamping** *n.* [U]

**datum** /'deɪtəm/ *n.* [C] (*pl.* **data**) (*Tech.*) a fact or piece of information

**'daughter ,company** *n.* [C] a company that is owned completely or partly by another company (a **parent company**) SYN SUBSIDIARY

**,dawn 'raid** *n.* [C] (*esp. BrE*) (*Stock Ex.*) a situation when a company suddenly and unexpectedly buys a large number of shares in another company at the beginning of a day's business on the stock exchange

**the DAX** (*also* **Dax**) /dæks/ *n.* [sing.] **Deutsche Aktienindex** a SHARE INDEX of shares in 30 of the most important companies on the Frankfurt stock market

**daybook** /'deɪbʊk/ *n.* [C] (*Account.*) a record of the sales made and the goods bought by a business each day: *a purchase/sales ~*

**ˌday 'off** *n.* [C] (*pl.* **days -**) a day on which you do not have to work: *She took a few days off.*
⊙ *to* ***ask for/have*** *a ~* ◆ ***be due for/be owed*** *a ~*

**'day ˌorder** *n.* [C] (*Stock Ex.*) an order to buy or sell shares, bonds, etc. that is only valid on the day it is made

**ˌday re'lease** *n.* [U] (*BrE*) (*HR*) a system of allowing an employee days away from work in order to study at a college: *She goes to college* ***on*** *day release.* ◇ *a day-release course*

**ˌday-to-'day** *adj.* involving the usual events or tasks of each day: *the day-to-day running of the business*

**'day ˌtrading** *n.* [U] (*Stock Ex.*) the process of buying and selling shares very quickly using the Internet in order to take advantage of small price changes and so make small quick profits ▸ **'day ˌtrader** *n.* [C] **'day-trade** *v.* [T,I]

**dba** *abbr* (*esp. AmE*) a short way of writing **doing business as** in the name of a business, esp. one owned by a SOLE PROPRIETOR: *Kim Winton, dba Winton Tractors*

**DBR** /ˌdiː biː 'ɑː(r)/ = DRUM-BUFFER-ROPE

**DC** /ˌdiː 'siː/ = DOCUMENTARY CREDIT

**DCF** /ˌdiː siː 'ef/ = DISCOUNTED CASH FLOW

**DDI** /ˌdiː diː 'aɪ/ *abbr* **Direct Dial Inwards** (*BrE*) (*AmE* **DID Direct Inward Dialing**) a system where an office building, a hotel, etc. can have a large range of telephone numbers sharing one or a small number of direct lines. Calls go directly to an EXTENSION.

**DDP** /ˌdiː diː 'piː/ = DELIVERED DUTY PAID

**DDU** /ˌdiː diː 'juː/ = DELIVERED DUTY UNPAID

**deadbeat** /'dedbiːt/ *n.* [C] (*AmE*) (*infml.*) a person or company that tries to avoid paying money that they owe

**ˌdead cat 'bounce** *n.* [sing.] (*Stock Ex.*) a temporary and small upward movement in share prices after a large fall, often before they start to fall again

**ˌdead-'end** *adj.* in which no more progress or development is possible: *a ~ job/project*

★**deadline** /'dedlaɪn/ *n.* [C] a time or date by which sth must be done or completed: *The deadline* ***for*** *applications is next Friday.* ◇ *You must be able to* ***work to*** *deadlines.*
⊙ *to* ***extend/impose/set*** *a ~* ◆ *to* ***hit/make/meet/miss*** *a ~* ◆ ***strict/tight*** *~s* ◆ *a ~* ***approaches/looms/passes***

**ˌdead 'load** → DEADWEIGHT (1)

**deadlock** /'dedlɒk; *AmE* -lɑːk/ *n.* [sing; U] a complete failure to reach agreement or settle a dispute: *The two sides met to try to break* (= end) *the deadlock* ***on/over*** *the pay deal.* ◇ *to end in/reach (a) ~*
▸ **deadlocked** /'dedlɒkt; *AmE* -lɑːkt/ *adj.*: *deadlocked talks*

**'dead ˌseason** *n.* [sing.] the time of year when the level of demand is at its lowest point

**'dead time** *n.* [U,C] (*Product.*) time that is not being used

**deadweight** (*also* **dead weight**, *esp. in AmE*) /ˌded'weɪt/ *n.* [C,U]
**1** (*Tech.*) (*abbr* **dwt**) (*also* **ˌdead 'load**) the weight of a structure or a vehicle that has no load or is empty **2** (*Transpt.*) (*abbr* **dwt**) a measure of the total goods, fuel, passengers, etc. that a ship can carry: *~ capacity/tonnage* **3** (*Econ.*) (*used as an adj.*) a financial cost or loss that is the result of money, materials, etc. not being shared out in an efficient way, for example because of the tax system: *high deadweight* ***costs***

**ˌdead 'wood** (*AmE also* **'deadwood**) *n.* [U] useless or unnecessary people or things in an organization: *clearing out the dead wood from the department*

★**deal** /diːl/ *n.*, *v.*
• *n.* (*Comm.*) **1** [C] a formal business agreement, esp. an agreement to buy or sell goods or provide a service: *The two companies signed a deal worth $1.7 bn.* ◇ *We* ***did a deal*** *with the management.* ◇ *a good pay deal*
⊙ *to* ***make/reach*** *a ~* ◆ *to* ***clinch/close/conclude/strike*** *a ~* ◆ *to* ***block/reject*** *a ~* ◆ *a ~* ***falls through/goes ahead/goes through***
**2** a reduction in the price of a product, usu. for a short period of time only: *The airline is offering great deals on flights this month.* → idioms at CUT *v.*, DONE
• *v.* (**dealt, dealt** /delt/) IDM **deal sb/sth a (serious, severe, etc.) 'blow; deal a (serious, severe, etc.) 'blow to sb/sth** to be very harmful to sb/sth: *The oil spill dealt a severe blow to the fishing industry.*

**PHR V** '**deal in sth** (*Comm.; Finan.*) to buy or sell a particular product; to trade: *The company deals in computer software.* '**deal with sb** to talk or behave in an appropriate way according to who you are talking to, managing, etc: *You need to be good at dealing with the public.* '**deal with sb/sth** to do business regularly with a person, a company or an organization: *I usually deal with the sales manager.* '**deal with sth 1** to take action to solve a problem, carry out a task, etc., esp. as part of your job: *Your order was dealt with yesterday.* **2** to be concerned with a particular subject: *This report deals with three issues.*

★**dealer** /'di:lə(r)/ *n.* [C] **1** (*Comm.*) a person or shop/store whose business is buying and selling a particular product: *a car dealer* **2** (*Finan.; Stock Ex.*) (*BrE*) (*AmE* '**trader**) a person who buys and sells shares, bonds, currencies, etc. without using a BROKER or an agent: *Wall Street dealers* **3** (*Finan.; Stock Ex.*) a bank employee who buys and sells shares, bonds, etc. or foreign currency on behalf of the bank

**dealership** /'di:ləʃɪp; *AmE* -lərʃ-/ *n.* [C] (*Comm.*) a business that sells products, esp. cars, for a particular company; the position of being a dealer: *an auto/a Mercedes ~*

**dealing** /'di:lɪŋ/ *n.* **1 dealings** [pl.] business activities between people or organizations: *the group's financial dealings* **2** (*Finan.; Stock Ex.*) [C,U] (*esp. BrE*) buying and selling shares, foreign currencies, etc: *Dealings* ***in*** *the shares have been suspended.* **3** [U] a way of doing business with sb: *fair/honest ~ ◇ dodgy/shady ~*

'**dealing floor** = TRADING FLOOR

**dealmaker** (*also* **deal maker**) /'di:lmeɪkə(r)/ *n.* [C] a person who is skilled at making financial deals or taking part in NEGOTIATIONS ▸ '**dealmaking** (*also* **deal making**) *n.* [U]

**dear** /dɪə(r); *AmE* dɪr/ *adj., adv.*
• ***adj.* 1** (**-er, -est**) costing a lot of money or more money than you expected: *The company was hit by dearer oil prices.* → EXPENSIVE **2 Dear** used at the beginning of a letter before the name or title of the person you are writing to: *Dear Ms Lim*
• ***adv.*** at a high price: *to buy cheap and sell dear*

ˌ**dear** '**money** *n.* [U] (*Econ.*) a situation when money is difficult to borrow and can only be borrowed at a high rate of interest: *a dear money policy* SYN TIGHT MONEY

'**death** ˌ**benefit** *n.* [C,U] (*Insur.*) money that is paid to the family of an insured person who dies

'**death** ˌ**duty** = INHERITANCE TAX (1)

'**death tax** = ESTATE TAX, INHERITANCE TAX (2)

**deb** (*also* **deb.**) *abbr* **1** (*Account.*) (*also* **Deb**) a short way of writing **debit 2** (*Finan.*) a short way of writing **debenture**

**debenture** /dɪ'bentʃə(r)/ (*abbr* **deb**) (*AmE also* **de'benture bond**) *n.* [C, usu. pl.] (*Finan.*) a loan for a long period of time on which a company promises to pay a fixed rate of interest; the official document given to the lender: *a debenture holder*

**de'benture stock** *n.* [C,U] (*Finan.*) a type of share in a company that pays fixed amounts at fixed times

★**debit** /'debɪt/ *n., v.*
• ***n.* 1** [C] an amount that is taken from a bank account; a record of this: *a debit of €100* OPP CREDIT **2** [U] the fact that there is no money in a bank account: *Your account is €200* ***in*** *debit.* → OVERDRAWN **3** (*Account.*) [C] (*abbr* **Deb, deb**) an amount that is written in a company's accounts to show a decrease in money that the company owes or an increase in the value of its assets: *on the* ***debit side*** *of an account* OPP CREDIT
• ***v.*** [T] **1** to take an amount of money from an account, esp. a bank account: *Premiums will be debited monthly* ***from*** *your account.* **2** (*Account.*) to write an amount in a company's financial account to show a decrease in the money the company owes or an increase in the value of its assets NOTE You **debit** a traditional T-account by writing amounts on the left side. OPP CREDIT

'**debit ac**ˌ**count** *n.* [C] (*Comm.*) an arrangement with a bank, shop/store or business to pay for the cost of goods or services using money that you already have or have paid

'**debit** ˌ**balance** *n.* [C] **1** the amount by which the money paid out of a bank account is greater than the amount paid into it at a particular time OPP CREDIT BALANCE **2** (*Account.*) in a company's financial records, the amount by which the total DEBITS are greater than the total CREDITS in a particular account

'**debit card** (*AmE* '**check card**) *n.* [C] a plastic card that can be used to take money directly out of your bank account when you pay for goods and services

**'debit note** (*BrE*) (*AmE* **'debit re,ceipt**) *n.* [C] (*Comm.*) **1** a note sent to a customer showing that they owe money: *to **raise** a debit note* **2** a note sent by a customer to a supplier showing the amount that will be taken away from the total bill, for example because goods supplied were not correct

**debriefing** /ˌdiːˈbriːfɪŋ/ *n.* [C,U] a meeting where sb gives a report about a task that they have just completed

★**debt** /det/ *n.* **1** [C] an amount of money that a person, company, country, etc. owes: *The group has debts **of** $3 bn.*

✪ *a **crippling/huge** ~* ◆ *to **amass/incur/run up** ~s* ◆ *to **clear/pay back/pay off/repay/settle** a ~* ◆ *to **default on** a ~*

**2** [U] the situation of owing money, esp. when you cannot pay: *The business is heavily in debt.*

✪ *to **get into/run into** ~* ◆ *to **get out of/stay out of** ~*

**3** (*Finan.*) [U,C] CAPITAL that a company or government borrows, on which interest is paid: *Sales proceeds would be used to pay down debt* (= reduce the amount of debt that is owed). ◇ *the burden of **servicing** a debt* (= *paying interest on it*)

✪ *to **cancel/default on/write off** a ~* ◆ *to **refinance/reschedule/restructure** a company's ~* ◆ ***long-term/short-term** ~*

**'debt adˌjustment** *n.* [U,C] **1** the process in which sb who owes money agrees to make regular payments to a person or business, who arranges with the businesses who are owed money how the debt will be paid **2** (*Law*) a legal process that a person who is BANKRUPT can use to reduce the amount of their debts and the period of time over which they must be paid ▸ **'debt adˌjuster** *n.* [C] **'debt adˌjusting** *n.* [U]

**'debt ˌcapital** *n.* [U] (*Finan.*) CAPITAL that a company gets by borrowing from banks, investors, etc: *The firm has access to about $1.65 bn of debt capital.* ◇ *the debt capital markets* SYN LOAN CAPITAL

**'debt colˌlection** *n.* [U] the activity of obtaining money from people who owe money for goods or services they have received, often by going to their homes to get it ▸ **'debt colˌlector** *n.* [C]

**ˌdebt consoli'dation** *n.* [U,C] the act of borrowing a larger amount of money from one lender in order to pay back several smaller debts to other lenders ▸ **ˌdebt con'solidator** *n.* [C]

**debt-'equity ˌratio** (*also* **debt/equity ratio**) (*also* **ˌdebt-to-'equity ˌratio**) *n.* [C] (*Account.*) a measure of how much debt (= loans, bonds, etc.) a company uses in order to finance its activities, compared to money invested by shareholders SYN GEARING

**debt-'equity swap** (*also* **debt/equity swap**) (*also* **ˌdebt-for-'equity swap**, **'debt swap**) *n.* [C] (*Finan.*) an arrangement in which a lender reduces the amount of a company's debt, in exchange for receiving shares in the company

**'debt exˌposure** *n.* [U] (*Finan.*) money that an organization has lent to sb and so risks losing if it is not paid back SYN CREDIT EXPOSURE

**'debt ˌfinance** *n.* [U] (*Finan.*) money that a company borrows from banks, investors, etc. in order to finance its activities; the business of providing this money ▸ **'debt-ˌfinanced** *adj.*: *a debt-financed acquisition* **'debt ˌfinancing** *n.* [U,C]

**ˌdebt-for-'equity swap** = DEBT-EQUITY SWAP

**'debt-ˌladen** *adj.* (used esp. in newspapers) having a lot of debt; badly affected by debt

**'debt ˌleverage** *n.* [U] (*esp. AmE*) (*Finan.*) **1** the relationship between the amount of money that a company owes (**debt**) and the value of its shares (**equity**) **2** using borrowed money to buy an investment or to add to the amount invested, in order to try to increase possible profits from the investment

★**debtor** /ˈdetə(r)/ *n.* **1** [C] a person, a country or an organization that owes money: *It is too easy for debtors to default on their loans.* **2** (*Account.*) **debtors** [pl.] (*BrE*) the amounts of money that are owed to a company, recorded as assets on its BALANCE SHEET SYN ACCOUNTS RECEIVABLE → CREDITOR

**ˌdebtor-in-pos'session ˌfinancing** *n.* [U] (*abbr* **DIP Financing**) (*Finan.*) in the US, a type of loan that a company can get while it is officially BANKRUPT

**'debt ˌoverhang** *n.* [C, usu. sing., U] (*Econ.*) a situation in which the debts that a government, an organization or a person has are larger than they can pay back in the agreed time

**'debt ˌpayment** *n.* [C] an amount of money that a government or an organization must pay back to a lender

**'debt ˌrating** *n.* [C] (*Finan.*) a measurement of the ability of a government or an organization to pay its debts and interest on them; the process of estimating this: *The company's debt rating has been downgraded to 'junk' status.* SYN CREDIT RATING

**'debt ˌratio** *n.* [U] (*AmE*) (*Account.*) a figure that is equal to a company's total debts divided by its total assets, used as a measure of a company's ability to pay back its loans and other debts

**'debt reˌstructuring** (*also* **'debt reˌscheduling**) *n.* [U] (*Finan.*) the act of finding a new way for an organization or a government to pay back money that they have borrowed and are having difficulty paying back

**'debt reˌtirement** *n.* [U] (*Finan.*) the fact of a debt being paid back completely: *early debt retirement*

**'debt-ˌridden** *adj.* (used esp. in newspapers) having a lot of debt; badly affected by debt

**'debt ˌservice** (*also* **'debt ˌservicing**) *n.* [U] (*Finan.*) the act of making regular payments to a lender; the payments that are made

**'debt service ˌratio** *n.* [C] (*abbr* **DSR**) **1** (*Econ.*) the amount of money that a government needs to pay to foreign lenders every year, compared to the amount of money received from exporting goods and services **2** (*Finan.*) the amount of money that a company or a person needs to pay to lenders, compared to the amount of particular types of income

**'debt swap** *n.* [C] (*Finan.*) **1** = DEBT-EQUITY SWAP **2** an arrangement between a government and a foreign lender. The lender agrees to reduce the amount of the government's debt in exchange for the government spending money on developing the country

**ˌdebt-to-'equity ˌratio** = DEBT-EQUITY RATIO

**debug** /ˌdiːˈbʌɡ/ *v.* [T] (**-gg-**) (*IT*) to look for and remove the faults in computer software or equipment

**debut** (*also* **début**) /ˈdeɪbjuː; ˈdebjuː; *AmE* deɪˈbjuː/ *n.* [C] the first time that sb/sth appears in public; the first time that sth is available to buy: *The new car* **makes** *its debut in the UK this weekend.* ▶ **'debut** *v.* [T,I]: *The shares debuted at €15.25.*

**deceased** /dɪˈsiːst/ *adj.* **1** dead **2 the deceased** *n.* [C] (*pl.* **the deceased**) a person who has died, esp. recently

**decelerate** /ˌdiːˈseləreɪt/ *v.* **1** [T,I] to happen or make sth happen more slowly: *Growth has decelerated rapidly.* **2** (*Econ.*) [I] (about the economy) to decrease in activity so that demand for goods decreases OPP ACCELERATE ▶ **ˌdeceleˈration** /-ˈreɪʃn/ *n.* [C,U]: *a sharp deceleration* ***in*** *consumer spending*

★**decentralize, -ise** /ˌdiːˈsentrəlaɪz/ *v.* [T,I] to give some of the power of a central organization to smaller organizations in different areas or countries; to divide the responsibilities of running an organization between many different people, departments, etc. OPP CENTRALIZE ▶ **deˌcentraliˈzation, -iˈsation** /-laɪˈzeɪʃn; *AmE* -ləˈz-/ *n.* [U; sing.] **ˌdeˈcentralized, -ised** *adj.*: *a decentralized recruitment process*

**deˈcision-ˌmaking** *n.* [U] the process of deciding about sth important, esp. in a group of people or in an organization: *corporate/management ~ ◇ consensus (-based) ~* ▶ **deˈcision-ˌmaker** *n.* [C]: ***key*** *decision-makers*

**deˈcision-making ˌunit** *n.* [C] (*abbr* **DMU**) (*Market.*) the group of people in an organization who help to make a decision about whether to buy sth SYN BUYING CENTRE

**deˌcision supˈport ˌsystem** *n.* [C] (*abbr* **DSS**) (*IT*) a computer program that analyses business data so that users can make decisions more easily

**deˈcision tree** *n.* [C] a diagram that is used to help decide the best action to take in a particular situation. Possible actions and their results are represented as 'branches', using lines, boxes and circles

**declaration** /ˌdekləˈreɪʃn/ *n.* [C,U] **1** an official or formal statement, esp. about the plans of an organization; the act of making such a statement: *to issue/make/sign a ~* **2** (*Law*) an official statement by a court about the legal rights or status of sb/sth: *to grant/make/seek a ~* **3** an official written statement giving information or stating that sth is true: *a declaration of income ◇ to complete/submit a ~*

★**declare** /dɪˈkleə(r); *AmE* dɪˈkler/ *v.* [T] **1** to say sth officially or publicly: *The company was declared insolv-*

ent (= by a court). ◇ (*AmE*) *The company has **declared bankruptcy**.* **2 ~ a dividend (of ...)** to announce that a share of a company's profits will be paid to shareholders **3** to tell the tax authorities how much money you have earned, etc: *declare a loss of ...* **4** to tell customs officers that you are carrying goods on which you should pay tax: *Nothing to declare.*

IDM **declare an 'interest (in sth)** to tell people that you have a connection with sth that could affect the decisions you make, because you may benefit in some way

★**decline** /dɪ'klaɪn/ *n., v.*

• ***n.*** [C, usu. sing., U] a process or period of becoming weaker, smaller or less good: *a sharp decline **in** exports* ◇ *The currency is **in decline**.*

⊙ *a **dramatic/rapid/steep** ~* ♦ *a **gradual/slight/slow/steady** ~* ♦ *to **halt/reverse/stop/suffer** a ~*

• ***v.*** [I] to become weaker, smaller or less good: *The number of tourists has declined by 10%.* ◇ *declining sales*

⊙ *to ~ **dramatically/sharply/steeply*** ♦ *to ~ **gradually/slowly/steadily***

**decliner** /dɪ'klaɪnə(r)/ (*also* **de,clining 'stock**) *n.* [C, usu. pl.] (*Stock Ex.*) (used in newspapers) a company whose shares have decreased in value in a particular period SYN FALLER OPP ADVANCER

**de,clining 'balance ,method** = REDUCING BALANCE METHOD

**de,clining 'stock** (*also* **de,clining 'share**) = DECLINER

**decompress** /,di:kəm'pres/ *v.* [T] (*IT*) to return computer files, etc. to their original size after they have been COMPRESSED SYN UNZIP OPP COMPRESS

**decontrol** /,di:kən'trəʊl; *AmE* -'troʊl/ *v.* [T] (-ll-) (*esp. AmE*) (*Econ.*) (*often pass.*) to remove official rules or controls from sth, esp. prices ▶ **,decon'trol** *n.* [U]

**decouple** /,di:'kʌpl/ *v.* [T,I] to break the connection between two activities or systems: *decoupling pay from productivity*

**decoy** /'di:kɔɪ/ = SEED *n.* (2)

**decrease** *v., n.*

• ***v.*** /dɪ'kri:s/ [T,I] to become or make sth become smaller in size, number, etc: *Profits decreased **by** 9.4%.* ◇ *decreasing costs*

⊙ *to ~ **dramatically/sharply*** ♦ *to ~ **gradually/slightly/steadily*** ♦ *to ~ in **number/size/value***

▶ **de'creased** *adj.*: *decreased productivity*

• ***n.*** /'di:kri:s/ [C,U] the process of reducing sth; the amount that sth is reduced by: *a slight decrease **in** consumer spending* ◇ *a decrease of nearly 6% in the number of visitors* OPP INCREASE

⊙ *a **large/marked/sharp** ~* ♦ *a **price/revenue/sales/tax** ~*

**decree** /dɪ'kri:/ *n., v.*

• ***n.* 1** (*Law*) [C] a decision that is made in a court: *to grant a decree* **2** [C,U] an official order from a ruler or a government that becomes the law: *a presidential decree*

• ***v.*** [T] (**-creeing, -creed, -creed**) to decide, judge or order sth officially: *to decree a state of emergency*

**decrypt** /di:'krɪpt/ *v.* [T] (*IT*) to change text or a message that is written in code into a form that can be understood by anyone OPP ENCRYPT ▶ **decryption** /-'krɪpʃn/ *n.* [U,C]

**dedicated** /'dedɪkeɪtɪd/ *adj.* designed to do only one particular type of work; used for one particular purpose only: *Use a dedicated server for the software.*

★**deduct** /dɪ'dʌkt/ *v.* [T,I] (*often pass.*) to take away money, a number, etc. from a total amount: *Income tax is deducted **at source**.* ▶ **deduction** /-'dʌkʃn/ *n.* [C,U]: *The deductions **from** your salary are **made** directly by your employer.*

**deductible** /dɪ'dʌktəbl/ *adj., n.*

• ***adj.*** (*Account.*) that can be taken away from an amount on which you must pay tax: *Costs are deductible **from** profits.* ▶ **de,ducti'bility** *n.* [U]

• ***n.*** [C] (*AmE*) (*Insur.*) a fixed charge that you must pay before an insurance company will pay the costs of sth: *a $600 deductible* SYN EXCESS

**deed** /di:d/ *n.* [C] a type of written agreement that is made and signed in a formal way. **Deeds** are required, for example, when a house is sold.

**,deed of ar'rangement** *n.* [C] (*Law*) in the UK, a formal written agreement between a failing company and the people it owes money to, in which it agrees to pay its debts in a particular way

**,deed of 'partnership** *n.* [C] (*Law*) a legal agreement to form a PARTNERSHIP that gives the details of the arrangement

**,deed of 'transfer** = TRANSFER DEED

**,deed of 'trust** = TRUST DEED

**deep** /di:p/ *adj., adv.* (**-er, -est**)

• ***adj.*** extreme or serious: *The market is in a deeper recession than expected.*

◇ *to make deep cuts in costs*
IDM ˌ**deep 'pockets** if sb/sth has deep pockets, they have a lot of money available to spend on sth
**jump/be thrown in at the 'deep end** (*infml.*) to start or be made to start a new and difficult activity that you are not prepared for
• **adv.** to an extreme or serious degree: *The company is being dragged deeper and deeper into debt.*

**ˌdeep-'discount** *adj.* (*Comm.; Market.*) very much reduced in price; selling at a very low price: *deep-discount brands*

**deepen** /ˈdiːpən/ *v.* [T,I] to become worse; to make sth worse: *a deepening economic crisis*

**de facto** /ˌdeɪ ˈfæktəʊ; ˌdiː; *AmE* -toʊ/ *adj., adv.* (*Law or fml.*) (about an authority, a system, etc.) that exists because of the circumstances, rather than because it was created officially: *For a while he was the de facto plant manager.*

**defamation** /ˌdefəˈmeɪʃn/ *n.* [U] (*Law or fml.*) the act of causing harm to sb by saying or writing bad or false things about them: *He will* **sue** *the newspaper* **for** *defamation.*
▸ **defame** /dɪˈfeɪm/ *v.* [T]

★**default** /dɪˈfɔːlt; ˈdiːfɔːlt/ *n., v.*
• **n. 1** (*Law*) [U,C] failure to do sth that is required by an agreement or by law, esp. paying a debt: *a default* **on** *foreign debt* ◇ *loan defaults* **2** (*IT*) [U,C] what happens or appears if you do not make any other choice or change: *your default browser* IDM **by de'fault** if something happens **by default**, it happens because nothing has been done to make things happen differently or because sb has not done what they should have done
• **v.** [I] **1** (*Law*) **~ (on sth)** to fail to do sth that you are legally required to do, esp. by not paying a debt: *to default on a loan repayment.* **2** (*IT*) to happen when you do not make any other choice or change: *The browsers default* **to** *the internal home page.*
▸ **de'faulter** *n.* [C]: *loan defaulters*

**deˌfault 'judgement** (*also* **judgement by/in de'fault**) *n.* [C] (*Law*) a decision that a court makes against sb/sth because they do not defend a claim that is brought against them

**defect** *n., v.*
• **n.** /ˈdiːfekt; dɪˈfekt/ [C] a fault in sth or in the way it has been made which means that it is not perfect: *defects* **in** *the design*
✪ *an* **important***/a* **major/minor/serious/slight** *~* ◆ *a* **design/mechanical/safety/structural** *~*
• **v.** /dɪˈfekt/ [I] **~ (from sb/sth) (to sb/sth) 1** to stop using a particular supplier, product, etc. and use a competing one: *Customers are defecting to rival firms.* **2** to leave an employer, political party, etc. to join another that is considered to be a competitor or enemy ▸ **defection** /-ˈfekʃn/ *n.* [U,C] **de'fector** *n.* [C]

**defective** /dɪˈfektɪv/ *adj.* having a fault or faults; not perfect or complete: *~ equipment/products/workmanship*

**defence** (*AmE* **defense**) /dɪˈfens/ *n.* **1** (*Law*) [C] (in a legal case) the reasons that sb/sth gives for not being guilty of a crime or of doing sth wrong; the act of presenting this argument in a court **2** (*Law*) **the defence** [sing. with sing./pl. verb] the lawyer or lawyers whose job is to prove in a court that sb/sth did not commit a crime or do sth wrong **3** [C] (*in compounds*) a particular method by which a company tries to avoid a TAKEOVER: *preparing a bid defence*

**de'fence ˌdocument** *n.* [C] (*BrE only*) a document that is written by a company to its shareholders, explaining why they should reject an offer to buy the company

★**defend** /dɪˈfend/ *v.* **1** [T,I] to protect sb/sth against an attack or harm: *defending market share* **2** [T] to say or write sth in support of sb/sth that has been criticized: *They have defended their decision to close the plant.* **3** (*Law*) [T] to resist a legal claim that is brought against you **4** (*Law*) [T] to act as a lawyer for sb who has been charged with a crime

**defendant** /dɪˈfendənt/ *n.* [C] (*Law*) the person in a court who is being SUED by another person or who is accused of committing a crime

**defense** = DEFENCE

**defensive** /dɪˈfensɪv/ *adj., n.*
• **adj. 1** (*Finan.*) (about an investment) safe in times of economic difficulty, because the price or value is not easily affected by circumstances: *defensive sectors, such as health care and food* **2** that tries to protect sb/sth from attack or harm: *The job cuts were a defensive move against decreasing sales.*
• **n.** [C, usu. pl.] (*Finan.*) an investment that is not easily affected by times of economic difficulty

**defer** /dɪˈfɜː(r)/ *v.* [T] (**-rr-**) to delay sth until a later time: *to defer a deci-*

*sion for six months* ◇ *a deferred payment* ▸ **de'ferment** (*also* **deferral** /dɪ'fɜːrəl/) *n.* [C,U]

**de,ferred 'credit** *n.* [C] (*also* **de,ferred 'income** [U]) (*Account.*) an amount written in a company's financial records which represents money received that has not yet been earned, for example for goods or services that will be provided during a later accounting period. These amounts are shown as LIABILITIES.

**de,ferred ,lia'bility** *n.* [C] (*Account.*) an amount written in a company's financial records which represents money that the company will pay back during a future accounting period

**de,ferred 'share** *n.* [C] (*Finan.*) a type of share for which a company can delay the payment of a DIVIDEND

**de,ferred tax'ation** *n.* [U] (*also* **de,ferred 'tax** [U,C]) (*Account.*) a sum kept to pay tax on profits made during a particular accounting period which only needs to be paid during a later period

**deficiency** /dɪ'fɪʃnsi/ *n.* [C] (*pl.* **-cies**) **1** the amount by which sth, esp. income, is less than it should be: *a budget deficiency of $96 bn* SYN DEFICIT **2** (*Account.*) (*AmE*) a situation in which sb owes more tax than they have shown on their tax forms; the amount they owe

**de'ficiency ,judgment** *n.* [C] (*AmE*) (*Law*) a court decision that forces sb to finish paying a debt for which they did not give enough SECURITY

**de'ficiency ,notice** = NOTICE OF DEFICIENCY

★**deficit** /'defɪsɪt/ *n.* [C] **1** (*Account.*; *Econ.*) the amount by which money that a government or business spends or owes is greater than money received in a particular period: *to run a budget deficit of 3.75%* ◇ *The trade balance is* **in deficit**.

⊙ *a high/large/low/small* ~ ◆ *to have/run/show a* ~ *(of sth)* ◆ *to make up/reduce a* ~ ◆ *to finance/fund a* ~

**2** [usu. sing.] the amount by which sth, esp. an amount of money, is too small or smaller than sth else: *a $47 m deficit* **in** *the pension fund*

**'deficit ,financing** *n.* [U] (*Econ.*) the practice of a government borrowing money in order to pay for things not paid for by the money received from taxes

**'deficit ,spending** *n.* [U] (*Econ.*) money that a government spends which it needs to borrow, because it does not receive enough tax, etc.

**de,fined 'benefit** *n.* [C] a fixed amount of money that will be paid by a PENSION PLAN

**de,fined contri'bution** *n.* [C] fixed payments that are made to a PENSION PLAN where the amount that will be paid out can change

**deflate** *v.* [T,I] **1** (*Econ.*) /,diː'fleɪt/ to reduce the amount of money being used in a country so that prices fall or stay steady: *raising interest rates to deflate the economy* **2** /,diː'fleɪt; dɪ'fleɪt/ to become or make sth less valuable, expensive or active: *a badly deflated share price*

★**deflation** /,diː'fleɪʃn/ *n.* [U] **1** (*Econ.*) a reduction in the amount of money in a country's economy so that prices fall or remain the same: *measures to combat deflation* **2** a situation in which prices continuously become lower: *the deflation of raw materials prices* ▸ **,de'flationary** /-ʃənri; *AmE* -neri/ *adj.*: *deflationary policies*

**deflator** /,diː'fleɪtə(r)/ *n.* [C] (*Econ.*) a figure that is used to reduce the current price of sth, so that it can be compared fairly with a price in the past: *a price deflator*

**defraud** /dɪ'frɔːd/ *v.* [T,I] to get money illegally from a person or an organization by tricking them: *They defrauded the company* **of** *$600 m.*

**defray** /dɪ'freɪ/ *v.* [T] (*fml.*) to provide money to pay or help pay for the cost of sth: *to* ~ *costs/expenses*

**defunct** /dɪ'fʌŋkt/ *adj.* no longer existing or being used: *a now defunct airline*

**degrade** /dɪ'greɪd/ *v.* [T,I] (*Tech.*) to become or to make sth become worse, esp. in quality

**de jure** /,deɪ 'dʒʊəri; ,diː; *AmE* 'dʒʊri/ *adj.*, *adv.* (*Law*) according to the law; official: *The group will now take de jure control of the company.*

**Del** *abbr* (*written*) delete; delete key

**delayering** /,diː'leɪərɪŋ; *AmE* -'leər-/ *n.* [U] (*HR*) the act of reducing the number of levels of staff in a company, esp. by removing a level of managers from their jobs: *the delayering of middle management* ▸ **,de'layer** *v.* [T,I]

**,del 'credere ,agent** /,del 'kreɪdəri:/ *n.* [C] (*Trade*) a person or company that sells goods for another and who agrees to pay for them if the customers fail to do so, receiving an extra COMMISSION for this risk

★ **delegate** *n., v.*
• ***n.*** /ˈdelɪɡət/ [C] a person who is chosen to speak and take decisions for a group of people, esp. at a meeting
• ***v.*** /ˈdelɪɡeɪt/ [T,I] **~ (sth) (to sb)** to give part of your work, power or authority to sb or a group of people, usu. in a lower position than you: *Some managers find it hard to delegate.* ◇ *to ~ responsibility/tasks*

**delegation** /ˌdelɪˈɡeɪʃn/ *n.* **1** [C] a group of people who represent the views of an organization, a country, etc: *They are sending a delegation of business people to the talks.* **2** [U] the process of giving sb work or responsibilities that would usu. be yours

**delete** /dɪˈliːt/ *v., n.*
• ***v.*** [T] **1** to remove sth that has been written or printed, or stored on a computer **2** to stop making or selling a particular product, esp. a CD, video, etc: *The recording has been deleted in the UK.* ▶ **deletion** /-ˈliːʃn/ *n.* [C,U]: *a monthly list of additions and deletions to our products*
• ***n.*** [U] (*also* **deˈlete key** [C]) (*abbr* **Del**) a button on a computer keyboard that you press to remove text or images

**deleveraging** /ˌdiːˈliːvərɪdʒɪŋ; *AmE* ˈlev-/ *n.* [U] (*Finan.*) a method of changing how a company funds its activities in which it reduces the amount of money that it borrows
▶ **ˌdeˈleverage** *v.* [T,I]

**delinquency** /dɪˈlɪŋkwənsi/ *n.* [C] (*pl.* **-cies**) (*esp. AmE*) (*Account.*) an act of failing to pay money that you owe to a bank or business: *credit-card delinquencies*
▶ **deˈlinquent** /-kwənt/ *adj.*: *customers with delinquent accounts*

**delist** /ˌdiːˈlɪst/ *v.* [T,I] (*Stock Ex.*) to remove a company from the official list of a stock exchange so that its shares are no longer traded there
▶ **ˌdeˈlisting** *n.* [U,C]

★ **deliver** /dɪˈlɪvə(r)/ *v.* **1** [T,I] **~ (sth) (to sb/sth)** to take goods, letters, etc. to the person or people they have been sent to: *We deliver within 48 hours.* **2** [T,I] to make and supply sth that has been requested by a customer: *We aim to deliver* ***on time*** *and* ***on budget.*** **3** [T] to provide a service: *They deliver exceptional customer service.* **4** [T,I] to produce, provide or achieve sth that people expect or that will benefit sb/sth: *to deliver strong results* ◇ *We are delivering* ***on*** *our targets.* **5** [T] to give a speech, talk, etc. or make an official statement: *The company has delivered a profit warning.* → idiom at GOODS

★ **deliverable** /dɪˈlɪvərəbl/ *n., adj.*
• ***n.*** [C, usu. pl.] (*Comm.; Product.*) a piece of work that must be completed, esp. as part of a long project: *to agree on dates for all deliverables*
• ***adj.*** [not usu. before n.] that can be achieved, provided or delivered: *Is the proposal deliverable?* ◇ *The futures contract becomes deliverable on January 31.*

**deˌlivered at ˈfrontier** *phr.* (*abbr* **DAF**) (*Trade*) (*usu. used as an adj. or adv.*) the seller delivers the goods to the border of the country mentioned. The buyer collects the goods and is responsible for bringing them into their country in the official way. → INCOTERM

**deˈlivered ˈduty ˈpaid** *phr.* (*abbr* **DDP**) (*Trade*) (*usu. used as an adj. or adv.*) the seller delivers the goods to the place mentioned, in the buyer's country, and pays for any IMPORT DUTIES → INCOTERM

**deˈlivered ˈduty unˈpaid** *phr.* (*abbr* **DDU**) (*Trade*) (*usu. used as an adj. or adv.*) the seller delivers the goods to the place mentioned, in the buyer's country. The buyer arranges for the goods to be brought into the country in the official way, and pays for any IMPORT DUTIES.
→ INCOTERM

**deˌlivered ex ˈquay** *phr.* (*abbr* **DEQ**) (*Trade*) (*usu. used as an adj. or adv.*) the seller delivers the goods by ship to the port in the buyer's country that is mentioned. The buyer collects the goods from the port and is responsible for bringing them into the country in the official way.
→ INCOTERM

**deˌlivered ex ˈship** *phr.* (*abbr* **DES**) (*Trade*) (*usu. used as an adj. or adv.*) the seller delivers the goods by ship to the port in the buyer's country that is mentioned. The buyer collects the goods from the ship and is responsible for bringing them into the country in the official way.
→ INCOTERM

**deˈlivered price** *n.* [C] (*Comm.*) a price that includes all the costs for packing and transporting the goods as far as the place where they are going

★ **delivery** /dɪˈlɪvəri/ *n.* (*pl.* **-ries**) **1** [U,C] the act of taking goods, letters, etc. to the people they have been sent to: *next-day delivery* ◇ *Please pay for the goods* ***on delivery.***

◇ *We do our deliveries in the morning.* ◇ *The airline will* **take delivery of** (= receive) *11 new planes in 2008.*
◆ *express/overnight/same-day* ~ ◆ *a* ~ *business/van*
**2** [C] a load of goods that is received: *The store receives one delivery of books a week.* **3** [U] the act of supplying sth or providing a service to sb/sth: *a new training delivery system* **4** (*Law*) [U,C] the act of sb receiving or getting control of sth they have bought: *Delivery will take place at the seller's place of business.*

**de'livery date** *n.* [C] **1** (*Product.*) the date on which a manufacturer or supplier agrees to deliver goods or raw materials that have been bought: *We need a firm delivery date.* **2** (*Product.*) the date on which a new product will be available and ready for use: *There's a six-month delivery date on the new system.* **3** (*Finan.*) the date on which an investment, such as a FUTURES CONTRACT, must be finally completed

**de'livery note** (*esp. BrE*) (*AmE usu.* **de'livery re,ceipt**) *n.* [C] (*Transpt.*) a form that you sign when goods are delivered

**de'livery ,order** *n.* [C] (*abbr* **DO**) (*Trade*) a written document that a seller of goods gives to a buyer, to allow them to collect the goods from the place where they are being stored

**de'livery re,ceipt** = DELIVERY NOTE

**'Delphi tech,nique** (*also* **'Delphi ,method**) /ˈdelfi; *AmE* ˈdelfaɪ/ *n.* [C, usu. sing.] a method of getting a group of experts to agree about sth, but without them discussing it. The experts write down their opinions in response to a set of questions and then in response to the results based on the opinions of all the experts. A group leader decides when the written opinions show that the experts have reached an agreement.

★**demand** /dɪˈmɑːnd; *AmE* dɪˈmænd/ *n., v.*
• *n.* **1** [U,C] the desire or need of customers for goods or services which they want to buy or use: *Demand* **for** *new cars has fallen.* ◇ *a sharp fall in car demand* ◇ *The plant has increased production to meet demand.*
◆ ~ *grows/rises* ◆ *to* **keep up with/satisfy** ~ ◆ *to* **boost/create/reduce/stimulate** ~ ◆ ~ **outstrips/exceeds** *supply*
**2** [C] a very firm request for sth; sth that sb needs or asks for: *Management has rejected the union's demand for a 40% pay rise.* ◇ *to* **accept/agree to/meet** *a* ~ **3** [C] a written request to pay money that is owed: *a demand for extra tax* ◇ *to* **get/ignore/issue/receive** *a* ~ IDM **on de'mand 1** as soon as requested: *The loan is repayable on demand.* **2** (*usu. used with a n.*) when you want it: *on-demand computing*
• *v.* [T] to ask for sth firmly: *They are demanding €1.6 m in compensation.*

**de'mand curve** *n.* [C, usu. sing.] (*usually* **the demand curve**) (*Econ.*) a line on a graph that shows the relationship between the price of a product or service and the quantity of it that people buy

**de'mand de,posit** = SIGHT DEPOSIT

**de'mand draft** = DEMAND NOTE (1)

**de'mand in,flation** (*also* **de,mand-'pull in,flation**) *n.* [U] (*Econ.*) an increase in prices due to the fact that the demand for goods and services rises quicker than the amount that can be supplied

**de'mand note** *n.* [C] (*Finan.*) **1** (*also* **de'mand draft**) (*both esp. AmE*) a document in which sb agrees to pay an amount of money to sb else whenever they ask for it **2** a written demand for a debt to be paid: *an income tax demand note*

**de'mand price** *n.* [C, usu. sing.] (*Econ.*) the price that customers are willing to pay when a particular amount of a product or service is available

**de,mand-'pull in,flation** = DEMAND INFLATION

**de'mand side** *n.* [sing.] (*usually* **the demand side**) (*Econ.*) the part of an economy that relates to the buying or using of goods and services, rather than their production ▸ **de'mand-side** *adj.*: *the demand-side effects of a change in income tax rates*

**demarcation** /ˌdiːmɑːˈkeɪʃn; *AmE* -mɑːrˈk-/ *n.* [U] (*BrE*) (*HR*) when a company can give particular types of jobs only to members of particular unions

**,demar'cation dis,pute** *n.* [C] (*BrE*) (*HR*) a disagreement between different unions about who should do particular jobs in a company

**dematerialized, -ised** /ˌdiːməˈtɪəriəlaɪzd; *AmE* -ˈtɪr-/ *adj.* (*Stock Ex.*) used to describe shares, bonds, etc. that only exist in electronic records

**demerge** /ˌdiːˈmɜːdʒ; *AmE* -ˈmɜːrdʒ/ *v.* [T,I] **~ (sth) (from sth)** to make a new company out of part of a larger business; to split from a larger business and become a separate company ▶ **ˌdeˈmerger** *n.* [C]

★**demo** /ˈdeməʊ; *AmE* -moʊ/ *n.*, *v.*

• ***n.*** [C] (*pl.* **demos**) (*infml.*) **1** a demonstration **2** (*infml.*) = DEMONSTRATION VERSION

• ***v.*** [T] (**demos, demoing, demoed, demoed**) (*Market.*) to show or be shown the features of a piece of equipment or software: *Click here to demo the software.*

**democracy** /dɪˈmɒkrəsi; *AmE* -ˈmɑːk-/ *n.* [U] fair and equal treatment of everyone in an organization, etc., and their right to take part in making decisions: *promoting democracy in the workplace* ▶ **democratic** /ˌdeməˈkrætɪk/ *adj.*: *a democratic company* **democratically** /-kli/ *adv.*

**demographic** /ˌdeməˈɡræfɪk/ *n.*, *adj.*

• ***n.*** **1 demographics** [pl.] the basic features of the members of a group of people, such as how old, rich, etc. they are, how many males and females there are, etc: *analysing customer demographics* **2** (*Market.*) [sing.] a group of customers who are of a similar age, sex, etc: *the 15 to 24-year-old male demographic*

• ***adj.*** **1** connected with the features of a population, esp. as these change over a period of time: *demographic changes* **2** (*Market.*) connected with a particular group of people who are of a similar age, sex, etc: *demographic groups* ▶ **ˌdemoˈgraphically** /-kli/ *adv.*: *a demographically representative audience*

**ˌdemographic ˈprofile** *n.* [C] (*Market.*) a description of the age, sex, income, etc. of people in a particular group

**demography** /dɪˈmɒɡrəfi; *AmE* -ˈmɑːɡ-/ *n.* [U] **1** the changing number of births, deaths, diseases, etc. in a community over a period of time; the scientific study of these changes **2** the basic features of a particular population

**ˈdemo ˌmodel** = DEMONSTRATION MODEL

**demonetize**, **-ise** /ˌdiːˈmʌnɪtaɪz/ *v.* [T] to decide officially that particular notes, coins, etc. can no longer be used as money: *demonetized notes* ▶ **deˌmonetiˈzation**, **-iˈsation** /-taɪˈzeɪʃn; *AmE* -təˈz-/ *n.* [U]

★**demonstrate** /ˈdemənstreɪt/ *v.* [T] to show and explain how sth works or how to do sth: *I demonstrated the features of the new videophone.* ◇ *demonstrating how to use a product*

★**demonstration** /ˌdemənˈstreɪʃn/ *n.* [C,U] (*abbr* **demo**) (*Market.*) an act of showing or explaining a product or service, esp. a new one

⊙ *to give/provide a* ~ ♦ *a product/sales* ~ ♦ *(an) in-store/a practical* ~

**ˌdemonˈstration efˌfect** *n.* [C, usu. sing.] (*Econ.*) the way that people, businesses, etc. are likely to copy the actions of others that they see are successful or to use sth that they can see is useful; an influence on sb to copy or avoid sth

**ˌdemonˈstration ˌmodel** (*also* **ˈdemo ˌmodel**, *infml.*) *n.* [C] one example of a product that is used to show to possible customers

**ˌdemonˈstration ˌversion** (*also* **ˈdemo ˌversion**, **ˈdemo**, *infml.*) *n.* [C] (*IT*) a form of a computer program that you can try before deciding whether you want to buy the complete program

★**demote** /ˌdiːˈməʊt; *AmE* -ˈmoʊt/ *v.* [T] (*often pass.*) **1** (*HR*) **~ sb (from sth) (to sth)** to move sb to a lower position in an organization, often as a punishment **2** (*Finan.*) **~ sth (from sth) (to sth)** to move a company to a lower position within a particular system, such as a stock exchange index OPP PROMOTE ▶ **demotion** /ˌdiːˈməʊʃn; *AmE* -ˈmoʊ-/ *n.* [U,C]

**demotivate** /ˌdiːˈməʊtɪveɪt; *AmE* -ˈmoʊ-/ *v.* [T] (*HR*) (*often pass.*) to make sb not want to work or study OPP MOTIVATE ▶ **ˌdeˈmotivated** *adj.* **ˌdeˈmotivating** *adj.* **ˌdeˌmotiˈvation** /-ˈveɪʃn/ *n.* [U]: *the problems of staff demotivation* **ˌdemotiˈvational** *adj.* **ˌdeˈmotivator** *n.* [C]: *Continually correcting someone can be a big demotivator.*

**ˈdemo ˌversion** = DEMONSTRATION VERSION

**demutualize**, **-ise** /ˌdiːˈmjuːtʃuəlaɪz/ *v.* [T,I] (*Finan.*) to change a MUTUAL organization into a company with shareholders; to be changed in this way ▶ **ˌdeˌmutualiˈzation**, **-iˈsation** /-laɪˈzeɪʃn; *AmE* -ləˈz-/ *n.* [U,C]

**denationalize**, **-ise** /ˌdiːˈnæʃnəlaɪz/ *v.* [T] (*Econ.*) to sell a company or an industry so that it is no longer owned by the government SYN PRIVATIZE OPP NATIONALIZE ▶ **ˌdeˌnationaliˈzation**, **-iˈsation** /-laɪˈzeɪʃn; *AmE* -ləˈz-/ *n.* [U]

**denominate** /dɪˈnɒmɪneɪt; *AmE* -ˈnɑːm-/ *v.* [T] (*usu. pass.*) to measure or state the value of sth using a particular currency: *loans denominated in dollars*

**denominated** /dɪˈnɒmɪneɪtɪd; *AmE* -ˈnɑːm-/ *comb. form* (*used in adjs*) expressed in the unit of money mentioned: *euro-denominated bonds* (= that pay interest, etc. in euros)

**denomination** /dɪˌnɒmɪˈneɪʃn; *AmE* -ˌnɑːm-/ *n.* [C] the value stated on a note, coin, stamp, etc: *banknotes in denominations of 10, 20 and 50 ◇ a high/large/low/small ~*

★**department** /dɪˈpɑːtmənt; *AmE* -ˈpɑːrt-/ *n.* [C] a section of a large organization, store or government: *the company's legal department ◇ the home furnishings/sports ~ ◇ to* ***head (up)/manage/run*** *a ~ ◇ ~ heads/staff* ▸ **departmental** /ˌdiːpɑːtˈmentl; *AmE* -pɑːrt-/ *adj.*: *a ~ budget/manager/meeting* IDM **be sb's department** (*spoken*) to be sth that sb is responsible for or knows a lot about: *That's not my department—ask James.*

**the Deˈpartment of ˈTrade and ˈIndustry** *n.* [sing.] (*abbr* **DTI**) the name in some countries for the government department that supports the development of businesses and helps them trade with foreign companies

**deˈpartment store** *n.* [C] a large shop/store that is divided into several parts, each part selling a different type of goods

**departure** /dɪˈpɑːtʃə(r); *AmE* -ˈpɑːrtʃər/ *n.* **1** [C,U] the act of leaving a job; an example of this: *her departure* ***from*** *the company*

⊕ *an* ***abrupt/a sudden*** *~ ◆ a* ***forced/voluntary*** *~ ◆* ***management/staff*** *~s*

**2** [U,C] the act of leaving a place; a plane, train, etc. leaving a place at a particular time → idiom at POINT *n.*

**deplete** /dɪˈpliːt/ *v.* [T] (*usu. pass.*) to reduce sth by a large amount so that there is not enough left: *Stocks are severely depleted.* ▸ **depletion** /-ˈpliːʃn/ *n.* [U]: *stock depletion*

★**deposit** /dɪˈpɒzɪt; *AmE* -ˈpɑːz-/ *n., v.*

• *n.* **1** [C] an amount of money that is paid into a bank or SAVINGS ACCOUNT: *Deposits can be made at any branch.* OPP WITHDRAWAL

**2** (*Econ.*) **deposits** [pl.] the total amount of money that has been paid into bank accounts in a particular area or country: *deposits of more than $22 bn.* **3** (*Comm.*) [C, usu. sing.] an amount of money given as the first part of a larger payment, esp. to prevent the goods being sold to sb else: *You pay a $250 deposit now and the balance within 30 days.* SYN DOWN PAYMENT

⊕ *to* ***put down*** *a ~ ◆ to* ***forfeit/lose*** *a ~ ◆ a* ***refundable/returnable/non-refundable*** *~*

**4** (*Prop.*) [C, usu. sing.] an amount of money paid by sb when they rent sth and that is returned to them if they do not lose or damage it: *Tenants need to pay a deposit of one month's rent.*

⊕ *to* ***leave*** *a ~ ◆ to* ***forfeit/lose/repay/return*** *a ~*

• *v.* [T] **1** to put money into a bank or SAVINGS ACCOUNT OPP WITHDRAW **2** to put documents, money or sth valuable into a bank or other safe place: *Accounts are deposited with Companies House.*

**deˈposit acˌcount** (*abbr* **D/A**) (*BrE also* **ˈnotice acˌcount**) (*AmE also* **ˈtime acˌcount**) *n.* [C] a type of account at a bank or BUILDING SOCIETY that pays interest on money left in it. You have to warn the bank a few days before you want to take the money out.

**depositary** /dɪˈpɒzɪtri; *AmE* dɪˈpɑːzəteri/ *n.* [C] (*pl.* **-ries**) **1** (*also* **depository**) a person or company with whom money or documents can be left **2** = DEPOSITORY (1)

**deˈposit cerˌtificate** = CERTIFICATE OF DEPOSIT

**deˈposit inˌsurance** *n.* [U] (*Econ.*) insurance payments made by banks to a central organization so that people with money in accounts at a bank will be paid if the bank goes BANKRUPT

**deposition** /ˌdepəˈzɪʃn/ *n.* [C] (*Law*) a formal statement, taken from sb and used in a court

**deˈposit liaˌbilities** *n.* [pl.] (*Finan.*) money that is paid into a bank, thought of as money that the bank owes and will have to pay back at some time

**depositor** /dɪˈpɒzɪtə(r); *AmE* -ˈpɑːz-/ *n.* [C] a person or an organization that puts money in a bank account

**depository** /dɪˈpɒzɪtri; *AmE* dɪˈpɑːzətɔːri/ *n.* [C] (*pl.* **-ries**) **1** (*also* **depositary**) a place where things, esp. money or documents, can be stored or kept safely: *The documents are stored in a public UK depository.* **2** = DEPOSITARY (1)

**de'pository insti,tution** *n.* [C] a DEPOSIT-TAKING financial institution

**de'posit slip** (*also* **de'posit re,ceipt**) *n.* [C] (*both esp. AmE*) a printed form on which you record the amount of money, the date, etc. when you put money into your bank account SYN PAYING-IN SLIP (*BrE*)

**de'posit-,taking** *adj.* (about a financial institution) which accepts deposits, for which it pays interest or provides services

**depot** /'depəʊ; *AmE* 'di:poʊ/ *n.* [C] **1** (*Comm.*) a place where large amounts of goods or equipment are stored, esp. before being sent somewhere else: *a distribution/storage ~* **2** (*Transpt.*) (*BrE*) a place where vehicles such as buses are kept and repaired **3** (*Transpt.*) (*AmE*) a small station where trains or buses stop

**depreciable** /dɪ'pri:ʃəbl/ *adj.* (*Account.*) able to be DEPRECIATED over a period of time: *depreciable assets with a fixed useful life*

**de,preciable 'life** *n.* [C] (*Account.*) the period of time over which an asset is DEPRECIATED

**depreciate** /dɪ'pri:ʃieɪt/ *v.* **1** (*Econ.*) [T,I] (about a currency) to decrease in value, compared to the currencies of other countries: *Sterling may depreciate **against** the US dollar.* OPP APPRECIATE **2** (*Account.*) [T] to gradually reduce the value of machinery, a vehicle or other asset over a particular period of time, as stated in a company's accounts **3** [I] to decrease in value over a period of time: *New cars start to depreciate as soon as they are on the road.*

**de,preciated 'cost** *n.* [C, usu. sing.] (*Account.*) the cost of an asset with the amount that is being claimed against tax for DEPRECIATION taken away

★**depreciation** /dɪ,pri:ʃi'eɪʃn/ *n.* **1** (*Econ.*) [U; sing.] a fall in the value of a country's currency, compared to the currencies of other countries: *a **sharp** depreciation in the euro* OPP APPRECIATION **2** (*Account.*) [U] a gradual reduction in the value of machinery, a vehicle or other asset over a particular period of time, as stated in a company's accounts: *the calculation of depreciation on business furniture and equipment* **3** [U] a gradual reduction in the value of sth over a period of time

**de,preci'ation ac,count** *n.* [C] (*Account.*) a financial record in which the amount of **depreciation** on an asset is recorded

**de,preci'ation ,method** *n.* [C] (*Account.*) any of the methods used to calculate the **depreciation** of an asset over the time it is expected to be in use

**de,preci'ation rate** (*also* **,rate of depreci'ation**, *less freq.*) *n.* [C] (*Account.*) the rate at which a company's asset is calculated as reducing in value each year in the accounts

★**depress** /dɪ'pres/ *v.* [T] **1** to make an economy or market less active: *The recession has depressed the housing market.* **2** to reduce the value of prices, wages, sales, etc: *Profits were depressed by reorganization costs.*

**depressed** /dɪ'prest/ *adj.* **1** without enough economic activity or employment: *The manufacturing sector remains firmly depressed.* **2** having a lower amount or level than usual: *Car sales remain depressed.*

**de,pressed 'market** *n.* [C] a market where there is not much demand for the products and services being offered for sale: *the depressed market for IT stocks*

★**depression** /dɪ'preʃn/ *n.* **1** (*Econ.*) [C,U] a long period when there is little economic activity, many businesses fail and many people are poor or without jobs: *Is the country sliding into depression?*
⊙ *(a) **full-scale/severe** ~* ◆ *a ~ **deepens/ends***
**2 the Depression** (*also* **the ,Great De'pression**) [sing.] the period from 1929 to 1934 when large numbers of people in the US and Europe were unemployed and poor because there was little economic activity **3** [sing.] the lowering or reducing of sth: *the depression of energy prices*

**Dept** (*also* **dept**) (*both BrE*) (*AmE* **Dept., dept.**) *abbr* (*written*) department

**'depth ,interview** *n.* [C] (*Market.*) an interview in which sb is asked detailed questions to find out their opinions about a product
▸ **'depth ,interviewing** *n.* [U]

**deputize, -ise** /'depjutaɪz/ *v.* [I] **~ (for sb)** to do sth that sb in a higher position than you would usu. do SYN STAND IN

**deputy** /'depjuti/ *n.* [C] (*pl.* **-ties**) a person who is immediately below the head of an organization, a department, etc. in rank and who is officially in charge when that person is not there: *a ~ chairman/chief executive/governor/manager*

**DEQ** /ˌdiː iː ˈkjuː/ = DELIVERED EX QUAY

**derail** /dɪˈreɪl/ *v.* [T] to prevent a plan, an agreement, etc. from continuing or succeeding

**deregulate** /ˌdiːˈregjuleɪt/ *v.* [T] (*usu. pass.*) to remove government rules and controls from an industry, a business activity, etc. OPP REGULATE ▶ **ˌdeˈregulated** *adj.*: *a deregulated, competitive industry* **ˌdeˌreguˈlation** *n.* [U]: *electricity deregulation* **ˌdeˈregulatory** /-ˈregjələtəri; *AmE* -tɔːri/ *adj.*

**derivative** /dɪˈrɪvətɪv/ (*also* **deˌrivative ˈinstrument, deˌrivative ˈproduct**) *n.* [C, usu. pl.] (*Finan.*) a financial investment such as an OPTION or a FUTURE whose price depends on the value of the shares, bonds, raw materials, etc. that it relates to: *trading in energy derivatives* ◇ *the ~s market* ◇ *energy/equity/gold/property ~s*

**deˌrivative ˈproduct** *n.* [C] **1** (*Finan.*) = DERIVATIVE **2** (*Market.*) a new product based on changes made to some of the features of an existing product to improve it or make it suitable for different customers

**deˌrived deˈmand** *n.* [U,C] (*Econ.*) the idea that the demand for sth, such as a natural material used to produce sth, depends on the demand for the final goods produced

**derrick** /ˈderɪk/ *n.* [C] **1** a tall machine used for moving or lifting heavy weights, esp. on a ship **2** a tall structure over an oil well for holding a drill (= machine that makes the hole in the ground)

**DES** /ˌdiː iː ˈes/ *abbr* **1** (*IT*) **data encryption standard** a popular method for protecting business information **2** (*Trade*) = DELIVERED EX SHIP

★**design** /dɪˈzaɪn/ *n., v.*

• ***n.*** **1** [C,U] the general arrangement of the different parts of sth that is made, such as a building, machine etc.; a drawing or plan that shows how to make it: *The building suffers from poor design.* ◇ *The architects can refine their designs on screen.*

◉ *to **create/produce** a ~* ◆ *to **change/modify** the ~ (of sth)* ◆ *(a) **bad/good/new/unique** ~* ◆ *a ~ **feature/flaw***

**2** [U] the art or process of deciding how sth will look, work, etc: *the design and development of new products* ◇ *the design process* ◇ *a ~ agency/firm/studio*

• ***v.*** [T] **1** to decide how sth will look, work, etc: *a contract to design and build two new ships* ◇ *a well-designed desk* **2** to think of and plan a system, a way of doing sth, etc: *designing a solution to meet customers' needs* **3** (*usu. pass.*) to make, plan or intend sth for a particular purpose or use: *a strategy designed **to** cut costs*

**designate** *v., adj.*

• ***v.*** /ˈdezɪgneɪt/ [T] (*usu. pass.*) **1 ~ sth (as/for sth)** to say officially that sth has a particular name or purpose: *Park in the designated areas only.* **2 ~ sb (as sth/to do sth)** to choose or name sb for a particular job or position: *Who has she designated **as** her successor?*

• ***adj.*** /ˈdezɪgneɪt; -nət/ [after n.] chosen to do a job but not yet having officially started it: *the chief executive designate*

**designation** /ˌdezɪgˈneɪʃn/ *n.* **1** [U] the action of choosing sb/sth for a particular purpose, or of giving them or it a particular status: *They met the criteria for designation as a 'certified organic grower'.* **2** [C] a name, title or description

★**designer** /dɪˈzaɪnə(r)/ *n., adj.*

• ***n.*** [C] a person whose job is to decide how things will look or work and to make drawings or plans showing this; a business that makes designs for a particular type of product: *a fashion/games ~* ◇ *a clothing designer and manufacturer*

• ***adj.*** made by a famous **designer**; expensive and having a famous brand name: *designer brands*

**deˌsigner ˈlabel** *n.* [C] a famous company that makes expensive clothes, bags, belts, etc. and puts a label with its name on them; the clothing, etc. that such a company makes: *high-profile designer labels such as Prada* ◇ *designer-label jeans*

**deˈsign proˌtection** *n.* [U] (*esp. BrE*) (*AmE usu.* **deˈsign ˌpatent** [C]) (*Law*) the way that the law protects how sth looks, so that it cannot be copied or used by anyone else

**desk** /desk/ *n.* [C] **1** a piece of furniture like a table that you sit at to work, use your computer, etc: *All staff have to be at their desks* (= working) *by nine o'clock.* **2** the part of an organization where a particular type of work is done: *our dealing desks* **3** a place where you can get information or be served at an airport, a hotel, etc: *the person behind the reception desk* → idiom at CLEAR

**ˈdesk clerk** = CLERK (3)

**deskill** /ˌdiːˈskɪl/ *v.* [T] (*HR*) **1** to change the form of a job so that sb needs less special knowledge and training to do it: *Much office work has become deskilled.* **2** (*often pass.*) to reduce the skills that a worker has, or that workers in general have, by giving them less skilled work to do ▸ **ˌde'skilled** *adj.*: *a deskilled labour force in restaurants and hotels* **ˌde'skilling** *n.* [U]

**'desk job** *n.* [C] a job that involves working for long periods of time at a desk

**'desk jockey** *n.* [C] (*infml.*) a person whose job involves spending a long time sitting at a desk

**'desk rage** *n.* [U] a situation in an office when sb who works there becomes very angry or violent

**'desk reˌsearch** *n.* [U] (*Market.*) a form of MARKET RESEARCH that is done using data that already exists and is easy to collect, such as company records or published research results

**desktop** /'desktɒp; *AmE* -tɑːp/ *n.* [C] **1** the top of a desk: *a ~ machine/PC* **2** = DESKTOP COMPUTER **3** (*IT*) a screen on a computer which shows the ICONS of the programs and files that can be used

**ˌdesktop com'puter** (*also* **'desktop**) *n.* [C] a computer with a keyboard, screen and main processing unit, that fits on a desk

**ˌdesktop 'publishing** *n.* [U] (*abbr* **DTP**) the use of a small computer and a printer to produce a small book, a magazine or other printed material ▸ **ˌdesktop 'publisher** *n.* [C]

**despatch** = DISPATCH

**destination** /ˌdestɪ'neɪʃn/ *n.* [C] **1** (*abbr* **destn**) a place where sb/sth is going or being sent: *The goods have arrived at the port of destination.*
⊙ *to reach a ~* ◆ *an* ***attractive****/a* ***favourite/popular*** *~* ◆ *a* ***holiday/ tourist*** *~* ◆ *the* ***final/ultimate*** *~* ◆ *a* ***business****/an* ***investment*** *~*
**2** a place that an airline flies passengers to
⊙ *to* ***fly to/serve*** *a ~* ◆ *a* ***long-haul/ short-haul*** *~* ◆ *a* ***domestic/foreign/ overseas*** *~*

**ˌdesti'nation site** *n.* [C] (*IT*) **1** a website that people often visit as it has a strong image in their minds because of the information and features they can find there SYN PORTAL **2** a website that sb visits by clicking on a BANNER AD or other link

**ˌdesti'nation store** *n.* [C] a store that has a strong image in customers' minds because of the variety or quality of goods, the prices, etc. and is the place they choose to go



**destn** *abbr* a short way of writing destination

**destock** /ˌdiː'stɒk; *AmE* -'stɑːk/ *v.* [T,I] (*Comm.*) to reduce the amount of goods that are kept available for customers to buy; to reduce the amount of materials that are kept available for making new products, etc: *A number of products are being destocked.* ▸ **ˌde'stocking** *n.* [U]

**detailer** /'diːteɪlə(r); *AmE also* dɪ'teɪlər/ *n.* [C] (*esp. AmE*) **1** (*Market.*) a person whose job is to visit shops/ stores and inform them about a company's products and make sure the products are displayed well **2** a person whose job is to clean a car thoroughly and carefully to protect it and keep it in good condition

**deteriorate** /dɪ'tɪəriəreɪt; *AmE* -'tɪr-/ *v.* [I] to become worse: *Economic conditions have deteriorated rapidly.* ◇ *to ~ dramatically/sharply/ significantly* ▸ **deˌterio'ration** /-'reɪʃn/ *n.* [U,C]: *a sharp deterioration in the group's financial position*

**determination** /dɪˌtɜːmɪ'neɪʃn; *AmE* -ˌtɜːrm-/ *n.* **1** [U] the quality that makes you continue trying to do sth even when this is difficult: *We need people with drive and determination.* **2** (*fml.*) [C,U] an official decision or judgement; the process of deciding sth officially

**devalue** /ˌdiː'væljuː/ *v.* **1** (*Econ.*) [T,I] to reduce the value of the money of one country when it is exchanged for the money of another; to become a less valuable currency compared to another: *to devalue the peso* ***against*** *the US dollar* ◇ *The country was forced to devalue.* OPP REVALUE **2** [T] to make sth seem less important or valuable than it should be: *The skill of selling has become devalued.* ▸ **ˌdeˌvalu'ation** /-'eɪʃn/ *n.* [C,U]: *a currency devaluation*

★**develop** /dɪ'veləp/ *v.* **1** [T,I] to gradually grow or become bigger, more advanced, stronger, etc.; to make sth do this: *It developed* ***from*** *a small family firm* ***into*** *a multinational.* **2** [T] to think of or produce a new idea, product, etc. and make it successful: *They develop and market new software.* **3** [T,I] to start to have a skill, an ability, a quality, etc. that becomes better and stronger; to become better and stronger: *developing new skills* **4** (*Prop.*) [T] to build new houses, factories, etc. on an area of land, esp. land that was not being used effectively before: *The site is being developed as an airport.* **5** [T] to start using an area of land, a mine, etc. as a source of natural materials

**developed** /dɪˈveləpt/ *adj.* **1** (used about a country, society, etc.) having many industries and an advanced economic system: *less developed countries* **2** in an advanced state: *people with highly developed business skills*

★ **developer** /dɪˈveləpə(r)/ *n.* [C] **1** (*Prop.*) a person or company that buys land or buildings in order to build new houses, shops/stores, etc., or to improve the old ones, and make a profit: *a property/real-estate ~* **2** a person or a company that designs and creates new products: *a product/website ~*

**developing** /dɪˈveləpɪŋ/ *adj.* (used about a country, society, etc.) poor, and trying to make its industry and economic system more advanced: *the developing world*

★ **development** /dɪˈveləpmənt/ *n.* **1** [U] the gradual growth of sth so that it becomes more advanced, stronger, etc: *key stages in the company's development* **2** [U,C] the process of producing or creating sth new or more advanced; a new or advanced product: *The software is still **in/under** ~* (= being designed).

**○** ***product/website ~ • a ~ department/team • to finance/lead/oversee the ~ (of sth)***

**3** (*HR*) [U] the process of getting new skills or knowledge, esp. so that you can do a job more effectively: *career/personal/professional/staff ~* **4** (*Prop.*) [U,C] the process and business of building new houses, offices, etc. in order to make a profit; a piece of land with new buildings on it: *(a) commercial/real-estate/residential ~ ◇ ~ land* **5** [U] the process of preparing an area of land, a mine, etc. to be a source of natural materials

**deˈvelopment ˌarea** *n.* [C] in the UK, an area where new industries are encouraged in order to create jobs

**deˈvelopment bank** *n.* [C] (often used in names) a bank that gives loans to help improve or protect the economy of a country or an area

**deˈvelopment corpoˌration** *n.* [C] (often used in names) an organization created by a government or a group of organizations or people in order to provide money for starting new businesses, developing local economies, etc.

**deˈvelopment ecoˌnomics** *n.* [U] (*Econ.*) the branch of economics that is concerned with the economic problems of less developed countries and how they can grow and change

**deˈvelopment grant** *n.* [C] an amount of money that a government or public organization gives for a project that will improve the economy of a particular area

**deviation** /ˌdiːviˈeɪʃn/ *n.* [C,U] **1** a difference from what is normal, expected or required: *The loss is a 20% deviation **from** our targets.* **2** (*Tech.*) the amount by which a single measurement is different from the average

**device** /dɪˈvaɪs/ *n.* [C] **1** an object or a piece of equipment that has been designed to do a particular job **2** a method of doing sth that produces a particular result or effect: *a good marketing device*

**devolve** /dɪˈvɒlv; *AmE* -ˈvɑːlv/ *v.* [T,I] **~ (sth) (from sb/sth) (to sb/sth)** if a duty, responsibility, power, etc. **devolves** or sb **devolves** it, it passes to a more local group or to sb who has less authority: *Decision-making will devolve to a local level.* ▶ **deˈvolved** *adj.* **PHR V** **deˌvolve sth ˈinto sth** to divide sth into smaller parts: *The group was devolved into dozens of smaller businesses.*

**diagnostic** /ˌdaɪəɡˈnɒstɪk; *AmE* -ˈnɑːs-/ *adj., n.* (*Tech.*)

• ***adj.*** connected with identifying sth, such as an illness or a problem with a computer system: *~ software/tests/tools*

• ***n.*** [C] **1** a device or system that is used to identify a problem, an illness or a problem with a piece of equipment or software: *A computer will run diagnostics on your car.* **2** a message on a computer screen giving information about a fault

**diagram** /ˈdaɪəɡræm/ *n.* [C] a simple drawing using lines to explain where sth is, how sth works, etc: *a diagram of the wiring system ◇ to draw a diagram* ▶ **ˌdiagramˈmatic** /-ɡrəˈmætɪk/ *adj.*: *The process is shown in diagrammatic form.* **ˌdiagramˈmatically** /-kli/ *adv.*

**dial** /ˈdaɪəl/ *v.* [T,I] (**-ll-**, *AmE* **-l-**) to use a telephone, for example by pushing buttons: *Dial 0032 for Belgium. ◇ phones with voice dialling* **PHR V** **ˌdial ˈin (to sth)**; **ˌdial ˈinto sth**; **ˌdial sb/sth ˈin** (*also* **ˌdial (sth) ˈup**) (*IT*) to make a temporary connection between your computer and the Internet or another computer system using a telephone line and a MODEM

**'dial-back** = CALLBACK (5)

**'dial-in** = DIAL-UP

**'dialling code** (*BrE*) (*also* **code**, *AmE, BrE*) *n.* [C] the numbers for a particular area or city, that you use when you are making a telephone call from outside the local area

**'dialog box** (*BrE also* **dialogue** -) *n.* [C] (*IT*) a box that appears on a computer screen asking the user to choose what they want to do next

⊙ *a ~ appears/opens/pops up* ♦ *to bring up/close/open a ~*

**'dial-up** (*also* **'dial-in**) *adj.* (*IT*) (about a computer system or service) temporarily connected to another system or to the Internet by a telephone line: *a ~ connection/service* ▸ **'dial-up** (*also* **'dial-in**) *n.* [U]: *Their broadband service is up to 25 times faster than dial-up.*

**diary** /'daɪəri/ *n.* [C] (*pl.* **-ries**) **1** (*esp. BrE*) (*AmE usu.* **'datebook**) (*also* **ap'pointment(s) book**, *BrE, AmE*) a book with spaces for each day of the year in which you write down things you have to do; an electronic device or program that you use in the same way

⊙ *to put sth/write sth in a ~* ♦ *a desk/an electronic ~*

**2** a book in which you can write down the events that occur each day: *to keep a diary of a project*

**Dictaphone™** /'dɪktəfəʊn; *AmE* -foʊn/ *n.* [C] a small machine used to record what you want to say in a letter, report, etc., so that sb can listen later and type it

**dictate** *v., n.*

• *v.* /dɪk'teɪt; *AmE* 'dɪkteɪt/ **1** [T,I] to say words for sb else to write down or type: *to dictate a letter* **2** [T,I] to decide sth or tell sb what to do, esp. in a way that seems unfair: *Carmakers can dictate how and where their cars are sold.* **3** [T] to control or influence sth: *The price is dictated by market forces.*

• *n.* /'dɪkteɪt/ [C, usu. pl.] an order, a rule, etc. that you must obey

**dic'tating ma,chine** = DICTATION MACHINE

**dictation** /dɪk'teɪʃn/ *n.* [U,C] the act of speaking or recording a letter, report, etc. so that it can be written down or typed; the words that are spoken: *to* ***take***~ (= write/type words that are being spoken)

**dic'tation ma,chine** (*esp. BrE*) (*AmE usu.* **dic'tating ma,chine**) *n.* [C] a machine, esp. an electronic one, used for DICTATING

**DID** /,di: aɪ 'di:/ = DDI

**differential** /,dɪfə'renʃl/ *n., adj.*

• *n.* [C] a difference in the amount, value or size of sth, esp. the difference in rates of pay for people doing different work in the same industry or profession: *the differential* ***between*** *men's and women's pay* ◇ *a differential* ***in*** *prices*

⊙ *to* ***create/narrow/widen*** *a ~* ♦ ***income/pay*** *~s* ♦ ***interest rate*** *~s*

• *adj.* not equal; that treats different people or things differently: *differential pay levels for similar skills* ◇ *differential pricing* (= supplying the same product to different markets at different prices)

**differentiate** /,dɪfə'renʃieɪt/ *v.* **1** (*Market.*) [T] to make your product or service seem different from other similar products or services, for example to attract a particular group of customers: *We differentiate ourselves* ***from*** *our rivals by our standard of customer service.* **2** [T] to be the particular thing that shows that things or people are not the same: *What differentiates us* ***from*** *our competitors?* **3** [T,I] **~ (between) A and B | ~ A (from B)** to recognize or show that two things are not the same: *to differentiate between high- and low-risk borrowers*

**,differentiated 'product** *n.* [C] (*Market.*) a product that is similar to other products but is different in design, quality or the way it is presented or advertised, for example to attract a particular group of customers: *a differentiated product for low-price markets*

**differentiation** /,dɪfə,renʃi'eɪʃn/ *n.* [U] (*Market.*) the process of making your product or service seem different from other similar products or services that it is competing with: *price/product ~*

**digerati** /,dɪdʒə'rɑ:ti/ *n.* [pl.] (*infml.*) (often used in newspapers) people who are considered to be, or who think they are, experts or important in the area of computers and the Internet

**digit** /'dɪdʒɪt/ *n.* [C] **1** any of the ten numbers from 0 to 9: *a seven-digit telephone number* **2** used with a number or an adjective to describe an amount of money or the amount by which a number has increased or decreased: ***double-digit*** *rises* (= 10% or more) *in sales*

★ **digital** /'dɪdʒɪtl/ *adj., n.*

• *adj.* **1** that uses a series of numbers in order to store, send or deal with

information: *converting from analogue to digital technology* ◇ *a ~ camera/TV* **2** that relies on computer technology or the Internet: *The company has several digital brands* (= products sold on the Internet). ◇ *~ publishing* ▸ **'digitally** /-təli/ *adv.*
**IDM the ˌdigital di'vide** the difference between communities that have computer equipment and can use the Internet and those that do not
• ***n.*** [U] digital television

**ˌdigital 'cash** = E-CASH

**ˌdigital 'currency** = E-CURRENCY

**ˌdigital 'money** = E-MONEY

**ˌdigital 'rights ˌmanagement** = DRM

**ˌdigital 'signature** (*also* **ˌelectronic 'signature**) *n.* [C] (*IT*) a unique number that is added to a computer file in order to show who has created it, sent it, etc.

**ˌdigital 'wallet** *n.* [C] (*E-comm.*) software that can store details of your name, bank account, address, etc. and provide them automatically whenever you make a payment on the Internet

**diligence** /'dɪlɪdʒəns/ *n.* [U] careful and thorough work or effort

**dilute** /daɪ'lu:t; *BrE also* -'lju:t/ *v.* [T] **1** to make sth less valuable or effective: *We won't dilute our brand image with cheaper models.* **2** (*Finan.*) to make shares less valuable by issuing more of them without increasing assets; to reduce the percentage of a company's shares that sb owns by doing this: *The share issue will dilute the value of existing shares.*
▸ **di'lutive** *adj.*: *the dilutive effect of the new share issue* **di'lution** /-'lu:ʃn; *BrE also* -'lju:ʃn/ *n.* [sing; U]: *brand/trademark ~*

**diluted** /daɪ'lu:tɪd; *BrE also* -'lju:tɪd/ *adj.* (*Account.*) used about a figure that is based on the number of shares that a company has issued plus the shares that it may need to issue in the future, for example because it has sold CONVERTIBLE bonds

**dime** /daɪm/ *n.* [C] a coin of the US and Canada worth ten cents

**dimension** /daɪ'menʃn; dɪ-/ *n.* [C] **1** a measurement in space, for example the height, width or length of sth: *computer design tools that work in three dimensions* **2** (*Market.*) an important aspect of a product or service: *The 24-hour help desk adds a new dimension to the product.*

**-dimensional** /daɪ'menʃənl; dɪ-/ *comb. form* (*used in adjs*) having the number of **dimensions** mentioned: *three-dimensional models*

**diˌminishing 'balance ˌmethod** = REDUCING BALANCE METHOD

**diˌminishing re'turns** *n.* [pl.] (*Econ.*) a situation where you gain less and less benefit or profit from sth, even though you spend more time or money on it

**dip** /dɪp/ *v.*, *n.*
• ***v.*** [I] (-pp-) **~ (from sth) (to/below sth)** to go down in value or level, esp. by a small amount or for a short period of time: *Sales have started to dip.* **IDM dip into your 'pocket** (*infml.*) to spend some of your money on sth **dip a 'toe in/into sth; dip a 'toe in/into the water** to start doing sth very carefully to see if it will be successful or not: *to dip a toe in risky markets* **PHR V ˌdip 'into sth** to take an amount from money that has been saved: *to dip into emergency funds*
• ***n.*** [C] a decrease in the amount or success of sth, usu. for only a short period: *The survey shows a slight dip in consumer confidence.*

**'DIP ˌFinancing** /dɪp/ = DEBTOR-IN-POSSESSION FINANCING

**direct** /də'rekt; dɪ-; daɪ-/ *adj.*, *v.*, *adv.*
• ***adj.*** **1** happening or done without involving other people or actions in between: *direct access to the central computer system* **2** happening as an immediate result of sth, without the influence of sth else: *a direct connection between performance and pay*
• ***v.*** [T] **1 ~ sth to/towards sb/sth | ~ sth at/against sb/sth** to aim sth in a particular direction or at a particular person: *We are directing our efforts towards expanding the business.* **2** to control or be in charge of sb/sth: *to direct a project* **3** to send a letter, etc. to a particular place or person: *Enquiries should be directed to the Customer Services department.*
• ***adv.*** without involving other people or businesses: *selling direct to consumers*

**diˌrect 'action** *n.* [U,C] (*HR*) the use of strikes, protests, etc. in order to achieve a political or social aim

**diˌrect 'advertising** *n.* [U] (*Market.*) advertising that uses normal methods, such as magazine or television advertisements

**diˌrect com'petitor** *n.* [C] a business or product that is competing for the same group of customers as your business or product: *We have*

*no direct competitor in the UK.*
▶ **di,rect compe'tition** *n.* [U]

**di,rect 'cost** *n.* [C, usu. pl.] (*Account.*) the cost of raw materials and workers involved in making a particular product or providing a particular service: *The project manager's salary is a direct cost.* SYN PRIME COST

**di,rect 'costing** = VARIABLE COSTING

**di,rect 'debit** (*AmE also* **'bank draft**) *n.* [U,C] esp. in the UK, an instruction to your bank to allow sb else to take an amount of money from your account on a particular date, esp. to pay bills: *to pay by direct debit* ◇ *to set up/cancel a ~*

**di,rect de'posit** *n.* [U,C] the system of paying sb's wages, etc. straight into their bank account

**di,rect 'dialling** *n.* [U] the ability to make telephone calls without needing to be connected by the OPERATOR OR A RECEPTIONIST
▶ **di,rect-'dial** *adj.*: *a direct-dial number*

**di,rect 'export** *n.* [C, usu. pl., U] (*Econ.*; *Trade*) goods that are sold directly to customers in another country; this method of selling goods ▶ **di,rect ex'porting** *n.* [U]

**di,rect 'import** *n.* [C, usu. pl., U] (*Econ.*; *Trade*) goods that are bought directly from producers in another country; this method of buying goods ▶ **di,rect im'porting** *n.* [U]

**di,rect in'vestment** = FOREIGN DIRECT INVESTMENT

**directive** /də'rektɪv; dɪ-; daɪ-/ *n.* [C] an official instruction: *The EU has issued a new set of directives* **on** *data protection.*

**di,rect 'labour** *n.* [U]
**1** (*Account.*) the people who work to produce a particular product or supply a particular service; the money spent on their wages: *direct labour* **costs** **2** (*HR*) people who are employed directly by a company or an organization to build or produce sth

**di,rect 'mail** *n.* [U] (*Market.*) advertisements that are sent in the post/mail, usu. to people who might be interested in buying the products or services: *We plan to use direct mail to promote our new magazine.* ◇ *~ advertising/marketing/selling*
▶ **di,rect 'mailing** *n.* [U,C]: *a good response to the direct mailing*

**di,rect 'marketing** *n.* [U] (*Market.*) the business of selling products or services directly to customers by contacting them by mail or telephone, by visiting their homes or through online computer shopping ▶ **di,rect 'marketer** *n.* [C]

**di,rect ma'terials** *n.* [pl.] (*Account.*) the basic things that a business uses in order to produce a particular product or provide a particular service; money that is spent on these: *Direct materials* **costs** *for each unit were €4.30.*

★**director** /də'rektə(r); dɪ-; daɪ-/ *n.* [C] **1** (*also* **,company di'rector**) one of a group of people who are chosen by shareholders to run a company and decide its policies: *The bank has cut the number of directors on its board.* ◇ *to resign/step down as ~* ◇ *an acting/an assistant/a deputy ~*
**2** a person who is in charge of a particular activity or department in a company, an organization, etc: *She became director of finance at the company.* ◇ *a finance/marketing/research/sales ~*

**directorate** /də'rektərət; dɪ-; daɪ-/ *n.* [C] **1** a section of a government department in charge of one particular activity: *the EU's Competition Directorate* **2** the group of directors who run a company

**di,rector 'general** (*AmE also* **director-general**) *n.* [C] (*pl.* **directors -**) the head of a large organization, esp. a public one

**directorship** /də'rektəʃɪp; dɪ-; daɪ-; *AmE* -tərʃ-/ *n.* [C] the position of a company director; the period during which this is held
⊙ *to* ***hold/resign/take up*** *a ~* ◆ *an* ***executive/a non-executive*** *~*

**di,rector's 'interest** *n.* [C, usu. pl.] (*Law*) the fact that a company director benefits in a personal way from a contract, deal, etc. with the company

**di,rectors' re'port** *n.* [C] a report that a company's directors must write for shareholders every year, giving a summary of the company's activities, details about the DIVIDEND, and the names of the directors and what they earned

**directory** /də'rektəri; dɪ-; daɪ-/ *n.* [C] (*pl.* **-ries**) **1** a book or series of Internet pages containing lists of information, usu. in alphabetical order, for example people's telephone numbers or the names and addresses of businesses in a particular area
⊙ *a* ***business/telephone/trade*** *~* ◆ *to* ***be listed in*** *a ~* ◆ *to* ***consult/look sb/sth up in/search*** *a ~*
**2** (*IT*) a file containing a group of other files or programs in a computer

● *to create/delete a ~* ◆ *to copy sth from/into/to a ~* ◆ *a current/default/root ~*

**di,rectory en'quiries** (*BrE*) (*AmE* **di'rectory as,sistance, ,infor'mation**) *n.* [U with sing./pl. v.] a telephone service that you can use to find out a person's telephone number

**di,rect 'overhead** *n.* [C] (*Account.*) a share of **overheads** that are considered to be part of the cost of producing a particular product or supplying a service

**di,rect par,tici'pation** *n.* [U] (*HR*) a system in which managers in an organization provide opportunities for individual employees to take part in decision-making

**di,rect re'port** *n.* [C] a person who has a position directly below someone else in an organization: *meetings with my direct reports*

**di,rect res'ponse ,advertising** (*also* **di,rect res'ponse ,marketing**) *n.* [U] (*Market.*) advertising that asks people to reply to the company in some way in order to buy a product, for example by making a telephone call or sending an email ▸ **di,rect res'ponse ad** *n.* [C]: *online ~s*

**di,rect 'sale** *n.* (*Market.*) **1** [C, usu. pl., U] (*also* **di,rect 'selling** [U]) the practice of selling goods or services directly to customers, rather than through a system of suppliers or shops/stores: *Direct sales rose by nearly 11%.* **2** [C] an item sold in this way: *The car was a direct sale from the factory.*

**di,rect 'tax** *n.* [C,U] (*Econ.*) tax which is collected directly from the person or company who pays it, for example income tax ▸ **di,rect tax'ation** *n.* [U]

**di,rect-to-con'sumer** *adj.* (*abbr* **DTC**) (*Market.*) aimed at or involving members of the public directly: *a ~ product/sale*

**dirty** /'dɜːti; *AmE* 'dɜːrti/ *adj.* (**-tier, -tiest**) **1** unpleasant or dishonest: *dirty fighting in the boardroom* **2** causing POLLUTION; containing substances that may be harmful: *dirty fuels, such as coal and oil* OPP CLEAN IDM **(do sb's) 'dirty work (to do)** the unpleasant or dishonest jobs that sb else does not want to do **,quick and 'dirty** (*infml.*) **quick and dirty** methods or systems provide fast, simple solutions to problems but may not last or be effective for a long time

**,dirty 'money** *n.* [U] money that sb gains from dishonest or illegal activities

**disability** /,dɪsə'bɪləti/ *n.* (*pl.* **-ties**) **1** [C] a physical or mental condition that means that you cannot use a part of your body completely or easily or carry out some normal day-to-day activities: *making computers easier to use for people with disabilities* **2** [U] the state of not being able to use a part of your body completely or easily or carry out some normal day-to-day activities: *He qualifies for help on the grounds of disability.* **3** [U,C] the state of not being able to work because of an injury or an illness; the injury or illness itself: *insuring against unemployment and disability* **4** [U] (*AmE*) money that is paid to sb who cannot work because of an injury, illness, etc: *a monthly disability check*

**disabled** /dɪs'eɪbld/ *adj.* **1** unable to use a part of your body completely or easily because of a physical condition, illness, injury, etc: *employing disabled workers* **2 the disabled** *n.* [pl.] people who are **disabled**

**disallow** /,dɪsə'laʊ/ *v.* [T] to officially refuse to accept sth or give permission for sth: *Their claim for a tax deduction was disallowed.*

**di'saster ,management** *n.* [U] the actions that a business takes before, during and after a disaster such as a flood a fire, etc. to reduce the effects on the business

**di'saster re,covery** *n.* [U] (*abbr* **DR**) (*IT*) (*often used as an adj.*) the process of making sure that the computer systems of a business operate again as quickly as possible after a disaster such as a flood, a fire, etc., and that as little data as possible is lost: *~ services/software/systems*

**disburse** /dɪs'bɜːs; *AmE* -'bɜːrs/ *v.* [T] to pay money to sb from a large amount that has been collected for a purpose: *The funds were disbursed in two instalments.*

**disbursement** /dɪs'bɜːsmənt; *AmE* -'bɜːrs-/ *n.* **1** [U,C] money that is paid to sb/sth from a large fund; the act of paying it: *the disbursement of funds* **2** (*Account.*) [C] a payment that a professional person makes on behalf of a customer while performing services for them, such as a payment of court fees by a lawyer

**disc** (*also* **disk**, *esp. in AmE*) /dɪsk/ *n.* [C] **1** a thin flat circular device that is used for storing information: *a blank disc* **2** (*BrE*) a computer disk

**discharge** /dɪs'tʃɑːdʒ; *AmE* -'tʃɑːrdʒ/ *v.* [T] **1** (*usu. pass.*) to give sb official permission to leave a place or job; to make sb leave a job: *She was discharged **from** the police force for bad conduct.* **2** (*fml.*) to do everything that is necessary to perform and complete a particular duty or task: *to ~ your duties/obligations/responsibilities* ◇ *to ~ a debt/liability* (= to finish paying back money you owe) **3** (*fml.*) to free sb from a particular duty or responsibility: *The judge discharged the jury **from** reaching a decision.* **4** (*Law*) to officially allow a BANKRUPT person to stop paying back their debts and do business again ▶ **'discharge** *n.* [U,C]: *the ~ of debts/liabilities/duties* ◇ *the port of discharge* (= where goods or passengers come off a ship) ◇ *the discharge of chemicals into rivers*

**disciplinary** /'dɪsəplɪnəri; ˌdɪsə'plɪnəri; *AmE* 'dɪsəpləneri/ *adj.* (*HR*) connected with punishing people who break the rules of an organization or society, esp. employees or professional people: *Disciplinary measures were taken but no one was fired.*

**O** *~ **proceedings** • a ~ **committee/tribunal***

**ˌdisciplinary 'action** *n.* [U,C] (*HR*) ways in which an employer or an authority can punish sb who does not meet the required standards of the organization or who breaks the rules: *The firm will **take** disciplinary action **against** staff who violate* (= break) *safety rules.*

**ˌdisciplinary 'hearing** *n.* [C] (*HR*) a meeting like a court trial, at which senior people decide if an employee or a member of the organization has broken the rules and, if so, how they should be punished

**ˌdisciplinary pro'cedure** *n.* [C, usu. pl.] (*HR*) the formal process that an employer or authority must follow if sb has broken the rules of the organization; action that is taken against sb according to this process

**disclaimer** /dɪs'kleɪmə(r)/ *n.* [C] (*Law*) a statement in which sb says that they are not connected with or responsible for sth, or that they do not have any knowledge of it: *to issue/make/publish/use a ~*

★ **disclose** /dɪs'kləʊz; *AmE* -'kloʊz/ *v.* [T] to tell sb sth; to make sth known publicly: *They refused to disclose details of the takeover **to** the press.*

★ **disclosure** /dɪs'kləʊʒə(r); *AmE* -'kloʊ-/ *n.* [C,U] **1** the act of making sth known or public; the facts that are made known: *the disclosure of confidential information* **2** information that a company is required to make public about its financial position, important events, etc.; the act of doing this: *Privately owned companies make only limited financial disclosures.* OPP NON-DISCLOSURE

**disconnect** /ˌdɪskə'nekt/ *v.*, *n.*
• *v.* **1** [T,I] to separate two things that were joined together: *Disconnect the modem **from** the computer.* **2** (*IT*) [T,I] to end a connection to the Internet: *I keep getting disconnected.* **3** [T] (*usu. pass.*) to break the contact between two people who are talking on the telephone OPP CONNECT
▶ **ˌdiscon'nection** *n.* [U,C]
• *n.* [C] a situation where there is no connection between sb/sth: *There can be a disconnect between boardrooms and IT departments.*

**discontinue** /ˌdɪskən'tɪnjuː/ *v.* [T] to stop doing sth, esp. making a particular product: *They have discontinued their adult line of clothing.*

★ **discount** *n.*, *v.*
• *n.* /'dɪskaʊnt/ **1** (*Comm.*) [C,U] an amount of money that is taken off the usual cost of sth: *We give a 15% discount **on** large orders.* ◇ *They were forced to sell their old stock **at a discount**.*

**O** *a **big/deep/heavy** ~ • ~ **airlines/fares/prices/tickets** • a ~ **chain/warehouse***

**2** (*Finan.*) [C, usu. sing.] if a share, etc. is bought or sold at a **discount**, its price is lower than sth, such as its earlier price or its PAR VALUE
• *v.* /dɪs'kaʊnt; *AmE also* 'dɪskaʊnt/ **1** (*Comm.*) [T,I] to take an amount of money off the usual cost of sth; to sell sth at a **discount**: *The airline has discounted its fares by 20%.* ◇ *aggressive price discounting* **2** (*Finan.*) [T] (*often pass.*) (about a price) to include the effect of what investors expect to happen: *Analysts believe the share price already discounts lower profits next year.* **3** (*Finan.*) [T] to buy or sell a BILL OF EXCHANGE before its payment date for less than the amount that will be paid on it in the future ▶ **dis'countable** /-əbl/ *adj.*

**'discount ˌbroker** *n.* [C] **1** (*Stock Ex.*) a type of BROKER that charges low fees but does not provide extra services, such as advice **2** (*Finan.*) (*BrE*) = BILL BROKER ▶ **'discount ˌbrokerage** *n.* [C]

**disˌcounted 'cash flow** *n.* [U; C, usu. sing.] (*abbr* **DCF**) (*Account.*) a method of comparing how much profit investments will make by calculating what the future income would be worth now

**discounter** /ˈdɪskaʊntə(r)/ *n.* [C] (*Comm.*) **1** a shop/store that sells things very cheaply, often in large quantities or from a limited range of goods **2** a business that offers its products at very low prices

**ˈdiscount house** *n.* [C] **1** (*Finan.*) a financial institution that buys and sells BILLS OF EXCHANGE before their payment date for less than the value shown on them **2** (*Comm.*) (*AmE*) = DISCOUNT STORE

**discounting** /ˈdɪskaʊntɪŋ/ *n.* [U] **1** (*Comm.*) taking an amount of money off the usual cost of sth
**○** *aggressive/heavy/widespread ~*
**◆** *fare/price ~*
**2** (*Finan.*) = INVOICE DISCOUNTING **3** (*Finan.*) the act of buying a BILL OF EXCHANGE for less than the amount that will be paid on it in the future

**ˈdiscount loan** *n.* [C] (*Finan.*) an amount of money that sb borrows from which the interest and other charges have been taken away before they receive the money

**ˈdiscount ˌmarket** *n.* [C, usu. sing.] **1** (*Finan.*) the part of the financial market that deals in the buying and selling of BILLS OF EXCHANGE **2** (*Comm.*) the part of a market in which goods or services are sold at low prices

**ˈdiscount rate** *n.* [C] **1** (*Finan.*) (*also* **ˈbill rate**) the amount the price of a BILL OF EXCHANGE is reduced by when it is bought before it reaches its payment date **2** (*Finan.*) in the US and other countries, the rate of interest at which banks can borrow money from the Federal Reserve Bank **3** (*Account.*) a rate of interest used to calculate how much an amount of money that will be paid or received in the future is worth now

**ˈdiscount store** (*AmE also* **ˈdiscount house**) *n.* [C] a shop that sells goods at prices that are much lower than normal

**ˈdiscount ˌwindow** *n.* [C] (*Finan.*) in the US, a time when banks are able to borrow money from the central bank at low rates of interest

**discrepancy** /dɪsˈkrepənsi/ *n.* [C,U] (*pl.* **-cies**) a difference between two or more numbers or amounts that should be the same: *Why is there a discrepancy* ***between*** *these two figures?* ◇ *accounting/price discrepancies*

**discretion** /dɪˈskreʃn/ *n.* [U] the freedom or power to decide what should be done in a particular situation: *Firms have a lot of discretion about the wage rates they set.* **IDM** **at sb's disˈcretion** according to what sb decides or wishes to do: *Bonuses are paid at the manager's discretion.*

**discretionary** /dɪˈskreʃənəri; *AmE* -neri/ *adj.* **1** decided according to the judgement of a person in authority about what is necessary in each particular situation, rather than being decided by a set of rules: *a ~ award/bonus/payment* **2** (*Finan.*) relating to investment funds placed with a BROKER or manager who is free to make decisions about how to invest them on the investor's behalf: *a ~ account/portfolio*

**disˌcretionary ˈincome** *n.* [U] (*Econ.*) the income sb is left with to spend or save as they want after taxes, etc. and necessary living expenses have been taken away from it

**disˈcretionary ˌorder** *n.* [C] (*Stock Ex.*) a piece of financial business in which the BROKER can decide when to buy or sell in order to get the best price for the investor

**disˌcretionary ˈspending** *n.* [U] **1** (*Econ.*) the amount of money that consumers spend on things they want rather than on things they need **2** (*Account.*) the amount of money that a company spends that can easily be controlled

**disˈcretionary trust** *n.* [C] (*Law*) a TRUST in which the person managing it is able to decide what kind of investments to make or how the money should be shared out

**discriminate** /dɪˈskrɪmɪneɪt/ *v.* **1** (*Law*) [I] **~ (against sb/in favour of sb)** to treat one person or group differently from another in an unfair way: *It is illegal to discriminate on grounds of race, sex or religion.* **2** [T,I] to recognize that there is a difference between people or things; to show a difference between people or things: *These regulations do not discriminate a large company* ***from*** *a small one.* ▶ **disˈcriminatory** /-nətəri; *AmE* -nətɔːri/ *adj.*: *~ laws/measures/practices/rules*

**disˌcriminating ˈduty** (*also* **disˌcriminating ˈtariff**) *n.* [C,U] (*Trade*) a tax charged on imported goods which varies depending on the country the goods come from

**discrimination** /dɪˌskrɪmɪˈneɪʃn/ *n.* [U] (*Law*) the practice of treating a person, a particular group of people or a particular class of things differently from another in an unfair way: *discrimination **on the** grounds of age ◇ gender/race/racial/sex/sexual ~*

**dis'criminatory tax** *n.* **1** (*Econ.*) [C,U] a tax that is charged only on a particular group of producers or goods, for example producers from other countries, so that other groups can compete more easily **2** [C] a particular tax that some people think is unfair as it does not affect everyone equally ▸ **dis,criminatory ta'xation** *n.* [U]

**diseconomy** /ˌdɪsɪˈkɒnəmi; *AmE* -ˈkɑːn-/ *n.* [C, usu. pl., U] (*pl.* **-mies**) (*Econ.*) a financial or economic disadvantage such as increases in cost; sth that produces an increase in cost

**ˌdiseconomy of 'scale** *n.* [C, usu. pl., U] (*Econ.*) an economic disadvantage, such as an increase in the average cost of producing goods, that may happen when an organization becomes larger

**disequilibrium** /ˌdɪsˌiːkwɪˈlɪbriəm; ˌdɪsˌek-/ *n.* [U] (*Econ.*) a loss or lack of balance in a situation, esp. in relation to supply, demand and prices: *A surplus or a shortage indicates market disequilibrium.*

**dishoarding** /dɪsˈhɔːdɪŋ; *AmE* -ˈhɔːrd-/ *n.* [U] (*Econ.*) spending or investing money rather than keeping or saving it, esp. the selling of gold by investors

**dishonour** (*AmE* **dishonor**) /dɪsˈɒnə(r); *AmE* -ˈɑːn-/ *v.* [T] **1** (used about a bank) to refuse to pay a cheque, usu. because there is not enough money in the account SYN BOUNCE **2** (*Finan.*) to fail to accept a BILL OF EXCHANGE or fail to pay it after accepting it **3** to fail to keep an agreement or promise you have made

**disincentive** /ˌdɪsɪnˈsentɪv/ *n.* [C] something that makes sb less willing to do sth: *removing financial disincentives **for** people to work after the age of 55* OPP INCENTIVE

**disinflation** /ˌdɪsɪnˈfleɪʃn/ *n.* [U] (*Econ.*) a gradual reduction in the rate of INFLATION in a country's economy, without increasing unemployment, for example by raising interest rates, restricting consumers' spending, introducing price controls, etc. ▸ **ˌdisin'flationary** /-ʃənri; *AmE* -neri/ *adj.*

**disintegration** /dɪsˌɪntɪˈɡreɪʃn/ *n.* [U] the breaking up of a company or group

**disintermediation** /ˌdɪsɪntəˌmiːdiˈeɪʃn; *AmE* -tərˌm-/ *n.* [U] (*Econ.*) **1** a reduction in the use of banks, etc. to arrange business between borrowers and lenders, or between buyers and sellers of investments, etc. **2** a reduction in the use of a person or an organization to arrange business between producers and customers

**disinvest** /ˌdɪsɪnˈvest/ *v.* [I] (*Econ.*) to stop investing money in a company, an industry or a country; to reduce the amount of money invested ▸ **ˌdisin'vestment** *n.* [U,C]

**disk** /dɪsk/ *n.* [C] **1** (*esp. AmE*) = DISC **2** (*also* **magˌnetic 'disk**) a flat piece of metal or plastic used for storing information on a computer: *I'm running out of disk space.*

**'disk drive** *n.* [C] (*IT*) a device in a computer that passes data between a disk and the memory of the computer or from one disk or computer to another

**diskette** /dɪsˈket/ = FLOPPY DISK

**dislocation** /ˌdɪsləˈkeɪʃn; *AmE* -loʊ-/ *n.* [U,C] (*Econ.*) the state of no longer being in the usual place or continuing in the usual way; the process of making this happen: *a period of economic dislocation ◇ the dismissal and dislocation of workers*

★ **dismiss** /dɪsˈmɪs/ *v.* [T] **1** (*HR*) **~ sb (from sth)** to officially remove an employee from their job: *He was dismissed **for** breach of contract.* **2** (*Law*) to say that a trial or legal case should not continue, usu. because there is not enough evidence: *The case was dismissed.*

★ **dismissal** /dɪsˈmɪsl/ *n.* [U,C] **1** (*HR*) the act of removing an employee from their job; an example of this: *Six employees face dismissal.* **2** (*Law*) the act of not allowing a trial or legal case to continue, usu. because there is not enough evidence: *the dismissal of the appeal*

**dispatch** (*also* **despatch**, *esp. in BrE*) /dɪˈspætʃ/ *v.* [T] **1** to send sb somewhere, esp. for a special purpose: *A courier was dispatched to collect the documents.* **2** (*Comm.*) to send a letter, parcel/package or message somewhere: *Goods are dispatched within 24 hours.* ▸ **dis'patch** (*also* **despatch**, *esp. in BrE*) *n.* [U]: *The goods are ready for dispatch.*

**dispatcher** /dɪˈspætʃə(r)/ *n.* [C] **1** (*Transpt.*) (*esp. AmE*) a person whose job is to control a group of vehicles such as lorries/trucks or taxis and send them to where they are needed **2** (*Transpt.*) a person whose job is to see that planes, trains or buses leave on time **3** (*Comm.*) a person or a company that has sent goods to customers

**dis'patch note** *n.* [C] (*Comm.*) a document that is sent to a customer giving details of the items that have been sent

**dis'patch ˌrider** *n.* [C] (*BrE*) a person who delivers urgent business documents using a motorcycle

**dispense** /dɪˈspens/ *v.* **1** [T] to provide sth or give it out to people: *The machine dispenses a range of drinks and snacks.* **2** [T,I] to prepare medicine and give it to people, as a job PHRV **di'spense with sb/sth** to stop using sb/sth because you no longer need them or it: *Debit cards dispense with the need for cash.*

**dispenser** /dɪˈspensə(r)/ *n.* [C] **1** (*usu. with another n.*) a machine or container holding money, drinks, etc., that you can obtain quickly, for example by pulling a handle or pressing buttons: *a drinks/tape ~* **2** sb who prepares medicine and gives it to people, as a job **3** a person or thing that provides sth

**display** /dɪˈspleɪ/ *n., v.*
• ***n.*** **1** [C] an arrangement of goods for people to look at or buy, often in a shop/store: *an attractive display of merchandise* ◇ *window displays* **2** (*IT*) [C] a computer screen or other piece of equipment that shows information: *a ~ panel/screen* ◇ *a 15 inch LCD display* **3** (*IT*) [U] the words, pictures, etc. shown on a computer screen; the way in which these appear on the screen: *There are some display problems with this model.* IDM **on di'splay** put in a place where people can see it: *All the goods on display are in the sale.*
• ***v.*** [T] **1** to arrange sth in a place where people can see it easily, esp. sth that is for sale: *new ways to display our products* ◇ *Their merchandise is attractively displayed in the window.* **2** (*IT*) to show information on a computer screen

**di'splay ad** (*also* **di'splay ˌadvert**, **di'splay adˌvertisement**) *n.* [C] (*Market.*) an advertisement that is designed in a way that will attract people's attention ▶ **di'splay ˌadvertising** *n.* [U]

**di'splay alˌlowance** *n.* [C] (*Market.*) a fee that a manufacturer pays to a shop/store to put their goods in a place where people will easily see them

**di'splay bin** = DUMP BIN

**di'splay case** (*also* **di'splay ˌcabinet**) *n.* [C] a special container, made all or partly of glass, used for showing items in a shop/store

**di'splay ˌmedium** *n.* [C] **1** (*Market.*) a thing, such as a POSTER, sign, card, etc., that attracts people's attention to goods on sale **2** a way of showing information to people: *The Web is mainly a display medium.*

**di'splay pack** *n.* [C] (*Market.*) a box designed to show goods on sale and attract people's attention

**disposable** /dɪˈspəʊzəbl; *AmE* -ˈspoʊ-/ *adj., n.*
• ***adj.*** **1** (about goods, etc.) produced cheaply and intended to be thrown away after use: *a ~ camera/razor/bottle* SYN THROWAWAY **2** available for use: *~ assets/capital/resources*
• ***n.*** **disposables** [pl.] (*Econ.*; *Market.*) = CONSUMER NON-DURABLES

**diˌsposable 'income** (*also* **exˌpendable 'income**, *esp. in AmE*) *n.* [U,C] (*Econ.*) **1** income left after taxes, etc. have been taken away from it and that you are free to spend or save **2** in a particular country, the total amount of money that people have to spend or save, after taxes, etc. have been paid

★**disposal** /dɪˈspəʊzl; *AmE* -ˈspoʊ-/ *n.* **1** [C,U] the sale of part of a business, property, etc: *the disposal of the company's chemical services division* **2** [U] the act of getting rid of sth that you do not want or cannot keep: *waste disposal* IDM **at sb's dis'posal** available for sb to use: *They have larger resources at their disposal.*

**dispose** /dɪˈspəʊz; *AmE* dɪˈspoʊz/ *v.* PHRV **di'spose of sth** **1** to sell part of a business, property, etc: *He is disposing of his stake in the company.* **2** to get rid of sth that you do not want or cannot keep: *Chrome is difficult to dispose of safely.*

**dispute** *n., v.*
• ***n.*** /dɪˈspjuːt; ˈdɪspjuːt/ [C,U] an argument or a disagreement between two people, groups or countries; discussion about a subject where there is disagreement: *The union is **in dispute with** management over job cuts.* ⊙ *to **have/resolve/settle** a ~* ◆ ***industrial/labour/pay** ~s*
• ***v.*** /dɪˈspjuːt/ [T] to question whether sth is true and valid: *These figures have been disputed.*

**di'spute proˌcedure** = DISPUTES PROCEDURE

**di'spute resoˌlution** *n.* [U] (*Law*) the process of settling disputes, for example by using a court or an ARBITRATOR

**di'sputes pro,cedure** (*also* **di'spute proc,edure**) *n.* [C] (*Law*) an official process that is followed in order to settle a dispute, esp. one involving members of an organization

**disqualify** /dɪs'kwɒlɪfaɪ; *AmE* -'kwɑ:l-/ *v.* [T] (**-fies**, **-fying**, **-fied**, **-fied**) to prevent sb from doing sth because they have broken a rule or are not suitable: *She has been disqualified* ***from*** *practising as a lawyer.* ▸ **dis,qualifi'cation** /-fɪ'keɪʃn/ *n.* [C,U]

**dis,ruptive tech'nology** *n.* [C,U] (*Tech.*) any new technology that completely changes the way people and businesses work

**dissaving** /dɪs'seɪvɪŋ/ *n.* (*Econ.*) **1** [U,C] the act of spending more money than you earn during a particular period of time: *Borrowing money from a bank is a form of dissaving.* **2 dissavings** [pl.] the amount by which the money spent is more than the money earned ▸ **dis'save** *v.* [T,I]

**dissolve** /dɪ'zɒlv; *AmE* -'zɑ:lv/ *v.* [T,I] to officially end a contract or business relationship; to come to an end: *The partnership dissolved in 2004.* ▸ **dissolution** /,dɪsə'lu:ʃn/ *n.* [U; C, usu. sing.]

**'distance ,learning** (*also* **,open 'learning**) *n.* [U] a system of education or training in which people study at home, at the place where they work, etc. with the help of special Internet sites and/or television and radio programmes, and send or email work to their teachers: *an MBA by distance learning*

**distress** /dɪ'stres/ *n.* [U] (*Law*) when the goods of a person or a company are legally taken in order to pay money that they owe: *a distress sale*

**distressed** /dɪs'trest/ *adj.* (*esp. AmE*) **1** (*Law*) used to describe property or goods that have been legally taken from sb who cannot pay money that they owe, and are offered for sale cheaply: *distressed assets* **2** used to describe goods that have been damaged or used

**dis,tributable 'profit** *n.* [C, usu. pl., U] (*Account.*) the profit from normal business activities that a company has left at the end of an accounting period, which it can pay to shareholders as DIVIDENDS

**dis,tributable re'serve** *n.* [C, usu. pl.] (*Account.*) a fund of money that a company keeps which it can use to make payments to shareholders; the money in this fund

★ **distribute** /dɪ'strɪbju:t; *AmE* 'dɪstrɪbju:t/ *v.* **1** (*Market.*) [T,I] to make a product available to customers, for example, by supplying it to shops/stores and businesses: *Who distributes our products in the UK?* ◇ *We distribute worldwide.* **2** [T] to share money, goods or property between a group of people; to give things to a large number of people: *The company distributes most of its profits* ***to*** *investors as dividends.*

**dis,tributed 'profit** *n.* [C, usu. pl.] (*Account.*) the amount of the profits that a company has left at the end of an accounting period and has paid to shareholders

★ **distribution** /,dɪstrɪ'bju:ʃn/ *n.* **1** (*Market.*) [U] the activity of making a product available to customers, for example by supplying it to shops/stores; the system of transporting and delivering a product to shops/stores or customers: *marketing, sales and distribution* ◇ *high distribution costs*

⊙ *to* ***control/handle/organize*** ~ • ***broad/limited/local/wide*** ~ • *a* ~ ***network/operation/system*** • *a* ~ ***facility/warehouse***

**2** [U,C] the act of sharing money, goods or property between a group of people or giving people things; the money or goods that people receive: *the distribution of leaflets* ◇ *a cash distribution*

**,distri'bution ,centre** *n.* [C] a large WAREHOUSE that receives goods from factories and suppliers and sends them to shops/stores or customers

**,distri'bution chain** (*also* **,chain of distri'bution**, *less freq.*) *n.* [C] (*Market.*) the series of businesses that deal with a product between the time when it is produced and when customers receive it: *pushing products* ***through*** *the distribution chain*

**,distri'bution ,channel** (*also* **,channel of distri'bution**, *less freq.*) *n.* [C] (*Market.*) the way that products are made available to customers

★ **distributor** /dɪ'strɪbjətə(r)/ *n.* [C] a person or business that supplies goods produced by other companies to shops/stores or directly to the public: *the largest software distributor*

⊙ *an* ***authorized/exclusive/a sole*** ~ • *a* ***foreign/local*** ~

▸ **dis'tributorship** *n.* [C]: *We have an exclusive distributorship for the range.*

**ˌdistrict atˈtorney** *n.* [C] (*abbr* **DA**) in the US, a government lawyer in a particular area or state who decides whether to accuse sb of a crime and start a court case against them

**div** /dɪv/ *abbr* **1 Div.** a short way of writing **division** (= a part of a large company) **2** (*Finan.*) a short way of writing or saying **dividend**

**dive** /daɪv/ *v., n.*
• ***v.*** [I] (**dived**, **dived**, *AmE also* **dove** /dəʊv; *AmE* doʊv/**dived**) (about a price, figure, etc.) to fall suddenly: *Sales have dived* **by** *28%.*
• ***n.*** [C, usu. sing.] a sudden drop in a price, figure, etc: *a dive in the company's share price* → idiom at TAKE *V.*

**diverge** /daɪˈvɜːdʒ; *AmE* -ˈvɜːrdʒ/ *v.* [I] **1** if two things **diverge**, or one thing **diverges** from another, they become different and the difference between them increases: *The country's interest rates have diverged further* **from** *those in Europe.* **2** (about opinions, decisions, etc.) to be different: *Opinions diverge greatly on this issue.* **3** to be or become different from what is expected, planned, etc: *to diverge from the norm*
▸ **diˈvergence** /-dʒəns/ *n.* [C,U]: *a continuing divergence* **between** *the prices of goods and services* **diˈvergent** /-dʒənt/ *adj.*: *divergent views*

**diversify** /daɪˈvɜːsɪfaɪ; *AmE* -ˈvɜːrs-/ *v.* [T,I] (**-fies**, **-fying**, **-fied**, **-fied**) (about a business, an investor, etc.) to develop a wider range of products, markets, investments, etc. in order to be more successful or reduce risk: *The company has grown and diversified.* ▸ **diˌversifiˈcation** /-fɪˈkeɪʃn/ *n.* [U,C] **diˈversified** *adj.*: *a diversified business mix*

**diversion** /daɪˈvɜːʃn; *AmE* -ˈvɜːrʒn/ *n.* [C,U] **1 ~ (from sth) (into/to sth)** the act of changing what sth is used for or of using sth for a different purpose from what was intended **2** (*Econ.*; *Market.*) (*also* **ˌproduct diˈversion**) the situation when goods supplied to be sold in a particular area or place are sold in a different one more cheaply than when they are bought from an official local supplier: *the diversion of cheap drugs intended for poor countries to rich countries*

**diversity** /daɪˈvɜːsəti; *AmE* -ˈvɜːrs-/ *n.* [U; C, usu. sing.] a range of many people or things, esp. different skills and qualities: *valuing and managing diversity in an organization*

**divert** /daɪˈvɜːt; *AmE* -ˈvɜːrt/ *v.* [T] **1 ~ sb/sth (from sth) (into/to sth)** to use money, materials, etc. for a different purpose from their original one: *diverting resources away from research and development* **2** (*Econ.*; *Market.*) to sell goods outside the area or place where they were intended to be sold: *There are things you can do to avoid having your products diverted.* **3** (*Transpt.*) to change the place that a load of goods is going to or the way it is being sent: *divert the shipment from motor to air transportation* ▸ **diˈverter** *n.* [C]

**divest** /daɪˈvest/ *v.* [T] (*fml.*) to sell part of a business or assets; to get rid of sth you own: *The company is not planning to divest its auto-parts business.* ◇ *to ~ assets/brands*
▸ **diˈvestment** *n.* [C,U] **diˈvestiture** /-ˈvestɪtʃə(r)/ *n.* [C,U]: *mergers, acquisitions and divestitures*

**divi** /ˈdɪvi/ *n.* [C] (*pl.* **divis**) (*BrE*) (*Finan.*) an informal word for DIVIDEND SYN DIVVY

★**dividend** /ˈdɪvɪdend/ (*abbr* **div**) (*also* **ˈshare ˌdividend**) *n.* [C] (*Finan.*) an amount of the profits that a company pays to shareholders: *The company will pay a dividend of 10 cents a share.* → idioms at PAY *V.*, PASS *V.*
**o** *to* ***declare/receive*** *a ~* • *to* ***pass/scrap/suspend*** *a ~* • *a ~* ***forecast/payment/payout***

**ˈdividend cheque** (*BrE also* **ˈdividend ˌwarrant**) *n.* [C] (*Finan.*) a cheque that a shareholder receives as payment of a **dividend**, that also gives details of the tax paid

**ˈdividend ˌcover** *n.* [sing; U] (*Account.*) the number of times a company's profits would pay the dividend

**ˌdividend reinˈvestment plan** *n.* [C] (*abbr* **DRIP**) (*Finan.*) in the US, an investment plan that some companies offer in which shareholders can buy more shares in the company instead of receiving regular cash **dividends**

**ˈdividend ˌwarrant** = DIVIDEND CHEQUE

**ˌdividend ˈyield** *n.* [C,U] (*Finan.*) the **dividend** that a company pays on each share, compared to the current price of the share: *a dividend yield of over 5%*

★**division** /dɪˈvɪʒn/ *n.* [C] (*abbr* **div**) a large and important unit or section of an organization that has responsibility for a particular market or area of activity: *the finance/research/sales ~* ◇ *the chemicals/truck ~* ▸ **diˈvisional** /-ʒənl/ *adj.*: *a divisional head*

**di͵vision of ˈlabour** *n.* [U,C] **1** (*HR*) the way in which different people do different tasks in a process in order to make the best use of time and money and produce as many goods as possible **2** a way of arranging a society, an organization or a group so that each type of work is done by a particular group of people

**divvy** /ˈdɪvi/ *v., n.*
• *v.* (**divvies, divvying, divvied, divvied**) PHR V **͵divvy sth ˈup** (*infml.*) to divide sth, esp. sth valuable, into two or more parts: *The profits have been divvied up to shareholders.*
• *n.* [C] (*pl.* **divvies**) (*BrE*) (*Finan.*) an informal word for DIVIDEND SYN DIVI

**DIY** /͵diː aɪ ˈwaɪ/ *abbr* (*esp. BrE*) **do-it-yourself** (*used as an uncountable n.*) the activity of making, repairing or decorating things in the home yourself: *DIY stores* SYN HOME REPAIR ▸ **͵DIˈY'er** *n.* [C]

**DJIA™** /͵diː dʒeɪ aɪ ˈeɪ/ = DOW JONES INDUSTRIAL AVERAGE

**DLC** /͵diː el ˈsiː/ *abbr* **1** (*Trade*) documentary letter of credit → DOCUMENTARY CREDIT **2** (*Stock Ex.*) = DUAL-LISTED COMPANY

**DMU** /͵diː em ˈjuː/ = DECISION-MAKING UNIT

**DO** /͵diː ˈəʊ; *AmE* ˈoʊ/ = DELIVERY ORDER

**doable** /ˈduːəbl/ *adj.* that is possible and likely to be achieved: *The price increase seems doable.*

**dock** /dɒk; *AmE* dɑːk/ *n., v.*
• *n.* **1** [C] a part of a port where ships are repaired or where goods are put onto or taken off them: *dock workers* ◇ *The ship is* **in dock**. **2 docks** [pl.] a group of **docks** in a port and the buildings around them, used for repairing ships, storing goods, etc: *He works at the docks.* **3** [C] (*AmE*) a raised platform for loading vehicles or trains **4** [C] the part of a court where the person accused of a crime stands or sits during a trial IDM **be in the ˈdock (over sth)** (esp. in newspapers) to be heavily criticized for sth; to be asked questions that are difficult to deal with
• *v.* **1** [T,I] if a ship **docks** or you **dock** a ship, it sails into a harbour and stays there **2** [T] to take away part of sb's wages, etc: *They have docked the strikers' wages.* **3** (*IT*) [T] to connect a computer to a DOCKING STATION: *I docked my laptop and started work.*

**docker** /ˈdɒkə(r); *AmE* ˈdɑːk-/ *n.* [C] (*BrE*) sb whose job is moving goods on and off ships SYN STEVEDORE (*AmE*)

**docket** /ˈdɒkɪt; *AmE* ˈdɑːk-/ *n.* [C] **1** a document or label that shows what is in a package, which jobs have been done, etc: *a delivery docket* **2** (*AmE*) a list of items to be discussed or things to be done

**ˈdocking ͵station** *n.* [C] (*IT*) a device to which a LAPTOP computer can be connected so that it can be used like a DESKTOP computer

**dockyard** /ˈdɒkjɑːd; *AmE* ˈdɑːkjɑːrd/ *n.* [C] an area with DOCKS and equipment for building and repairing ships

**ˈdoctor's cer͵tificate** = MEDICAL CERTIFICATE

★**document** *n., v.*
• *n.* /ˈdɒkjumənt; *AmE* ˈdɑːk-/ [C] **1** an official paper or book that gives information about sth, or that can be used as evidence or proof of sth: *a consultation document* **on** *pay* ◇ *tickets and travel documents*
➊ *a* ***formal/legal/an official*** *~* ◆ *a* ***discussion/policy*** *~* ◆ *to* ***draft/draw up*** *a ~* ◆ *a ~* ***outlines/states*** *sth*
**2** a computer file that contains text that has a name that identifies it
➊ *to* ***create/edit/save*** *a ~* ◆ *to* ***close/download/open/print (out)*** *a ~*
• *v.* /ˈdɒkjument; *AmE* ˈdɑːk-/ [T] to record the details of sth in writing: *The problem is well documented.*

**͵documentary colˈlection** *n.* [C,U] (*Trade*) a way of arranging payment for exports, esp. by ship, in which the seller gives the documents that are needed to collect the goods to the buyer's bank, which keeps them until it receives payment for the goods

**͵documentary ˈcredit** *n.* [U,C] (*abbr* **DC**) (*also* **ˈdocumentary ˈletter of ˈcredit** [C] (*abbr* **DLC**) (*Trade*) a LETTER OF CREDIT in which a bank promises to pay an exporter for goods when documents are provided that prove the goods have been sent

**documentation** /͵dɒkjumenˈteɪʃn; *AmE* ͵dɑːk-/ *n.* [U] **1** the documents that are required for sth, or that give evidence or proof of sth **2** the act of recording sth in a document; the state of being recorded: *the documentation of accounting decisions* **3** the documents that describe how sth works or how to operate it: *technical documentation*

**͵document of ˈtitle** *n.* [C] (*Law; Trade*) a document, such as a BILL OF LADING, that allows sb to claim the goods that are described in it

**ˌdocuments aˌgainst acˈceptance** *phr.* (*abbr* **D/A**) (*Trade*) a way of paying for imports where the buyer signs a document (**bill of exchange**) promising to pay for the goods within a particular time before the bank gives them the documents needed to collect the goods

**ˌdocuments aˌgainst ˈpayment** *phr.* (*abbr* **D/P**) (*Trade*) a way of paying for imports in which the buyer pays for the goods when the bank gives them the documents needed to collect the goods

**ˈdocument ˌsharing** *n.* [U] (*IT*) the ability that some computer systems have that allows people in different places to look at/work on the same document at the same time

**dodge** /dɒdʒ; *AmE* dɑːdʒ/ *v.* [T] to avoid doing sth, esp. in a dishonest way: *to dodge paying taxes* ▸ **dodge** *n.* [C]: *a tax dodge* **ˈdodger** *n.* [C]: *tax dodgers*

**dodgy** /ˈdɒdʒi; *AmE* ˈdɑːdʒi/ *adj.* (**dodgier, dodgiest**) (*BrE*) (*infml.*) seeming or likely to be dishonest: *dodgy accounting*

**dog** /dɒg; *AmE* dɔːg/ *n.* [C] **1** (*Market.*) in the BOSTON MATRIX, a product that has a small market share in a market that is growing very little **2** (*infml.*) used to describe sth that is very bad or a failure, esp. an investment that always does badly: *I'd bought a dog fund!* IDM **(a case of) ˌdog eat ˈdog** a situation in business, etc. where there is a lot of competition and people are willing to harm each other in order to succeed: *It's a dog-eat-dog world.* **eat your own ˈdog food** (*IT, infml.*) when a company tests or uses its own software products in the organization **that dog won't ˈhunt** (*AmE*) (*infml.*) used to say that an idea will not work

**dogsbody** /ˈdɒgzbɒdi; *AmE* ˈdɔːgzbɑːdi/ *n.* [C] (*pl.* **-dies**) (*BrE*) (*infml.*) a person who does all the boring jobs that nobody else wants to do, and is treated as being less important

**ˌdo-it-yourˈself** = DIY

**dol.** *abbr* a short way of writing **dollar** or **dollars**

**doldrums** /ˈdɒldrəmz; *AmE* ˈdoʊl-/ *n.* [pl.] a lack of activity or improvement: *The media sector remains* **in the doldrums**.

**dole** /dəʊl; *AmE* doʊl/ *n.* [sing.] (*usu.* **the dole**) (*BrE*) (*infml.*) money paid by the state to unemployed people: *How many people are* **on the dole**? SYN WELFARE (*AmE*)

**ˈdole queue** (*BrE*) (*AmE* **ˌunemˈployment line**) *n.* [C] used esp. in newspapers to describe the group of unemployed people in a society: *the country's lengthening dole queues*

**dollar** /ˈdɒlə(r); *AmE* ˈdɑːl-/ *n., adj.*
• *n.* **1** [C] (*abbr* **dol., $**) the unit of money in the US, Canada, Australia and several other countries: *All prices are quoted* **in** *dollars.* ◇ *a million dollar investment* **2 the dollar** [sing.] the value of the US dollar compared with the value of the money of other countries: *The dollar closed two cents down.* **3** [C] dollars spent on a particular activity or that come from a particular source: *competing for investment dollars* **4** [C] a BANKNOTE or coin worth one dollar: *a dollar bill*
• *adj.* having a price or value that is measured in US dollars: *~ assets/ bonds*

**the ˈdollar ˌarea** *n.* [sing.] (*Econ.*) the area of the world where the US dollar is used as the main currency or where the currency is linked to the dollar

**ˌdollar-cost ˈaveraging** *n.* [U] (*Finan.*) in the US, a method of investing money that involves investing a fixed amount regularly in particular shares, whatever their price

**dollarization, -isation** /ˌdɒləraɪˈzeɪʃn; *AmE* ˌdɑːlərəˈz-/ *n.* [U,C] (*Econ.*) **1** the process of a country or group of countries starting to use the US dollar in addition to or instead of their own currency **2** the process of linking the value of a country's currency with the value of the US dollar ▸ **ˈdollarize, -ise** *v.* [T,I]: *a dollarized economy*

**domain** /dəˈmeɪn; dəʊ-; *AmE* doʊ-/ *n.* [C] **1** (*IT*) a set of Internet addresses that end with the same group of letters: *.com is the most popular domain on the Internet.* ◇ *a* **domain name** (= an individual Internet address) **2** an area of knowledge or activity, esp. one that sb is responsible for: *I'm afraid that's outside my domain.*

★**domestic** /dəˈmestɪk/ *adj.* **1** of or inside a particular country; not foreign or international: *domestic sales of vehicles* ◇ *foreign and domestic investment* SYN INTERNAL **2** used in the home; connected with the home or family: *domestic appliances* ▸ **doˈmestically** /-kli/ *adv.*

**dominant** /ˈdɒmɪnənt; *AmE* ˈdɑːm-/ *adj.* more important or powerful than other things: *a domin-*

*ant market position* ◇ *dominant players in the industry* ▸ **'dominance** /-əns/ *n.* [U]: *market dominance*

★ **dominate** /'dɒmɪneɪt; *AmE* 'dɑːm-/ *v.* **1** [T,I] to control or have a lot of influence over sth: *The market was dominated by Nokia.* **2** [T] to be the most important or noticeable feature of sth: *an economy dominated by oil* ▸ **ˌdomi'nation** /-'neɪʃn/ *n.* [U]

**'domino efˌfect** *n.* [C, usu. sing.] a situation in which one event causes a series of similar events to happen one after the other: *Employers fear the strike could cause a domino effect* (= that there will be many other strikes as a result).

**donate** /dəʊ'neɪt; *AmE* 'doʊneɪt/ *v.* [T,I] **~ sth (to sb/sth)** to give money, equipment, etc. to sb/sth to help them: *The school's PCs were donated by IBM.* ▸ **do'nation** /-'neɪʃn/ *n.* [C,U]: *to make a donation to sb/sth*

**done** /dʌn/ *adj.* **IDM** **a ˌdone 'deal** (*esp. AmE*) a plan, an agreement or a project that has been completely arranged and agreed

**ˌdoor to 'door** *adv.* **1** (*Market.*) visiting all the homes or offices in an area, esp. to try to sell sth: *They sell household goods door to door.* **2** if sth is delivered **door to door**, it is brought directly from the factory or supplier to the customer ▸ **ˌdoor-to-'door** *adj.*: *a ~ salesman/delivery*

**dormant** /'dɔːmənt; *AmE* 'dɔːrm-/ *adj.* **1** not active or growing now but able to become active or to grow in the future: *a dormant company* ◇ *to become/lie/remain ~* **2** (about a bank account) that has not been used for a long time: *a dormant account* ◇ *to become/lie/remain ~*

**DOS** /dɒs; *AmE* dɑːs/ *abbr* (*IT*) **disk operating system** a set of programs that control the way a computer works and runs other programs

**dossier** /'dɒsieɪ; *AmE* 'dɔːs-; 'dɑːs-/ *n.* [C] **~ (on sb/sth)** a collection of documents that contain information about a person, an event or a subject: *to compile/keep/prepare/publish a ~* SYN FILE

**dot** /dɒt; *AmE* dɑːt/ *n.* [C] a small symbol (.) that is used to separate different parts of an email or Internet address: *Please email us at enquiry@oup.com.* **NOTE** This email address would be said as 'enquiry at o u p **dot** com'. **IDM** **on the 'dot** (*infml.*) exactly on time or at the exact time mentioned: *The meeting will start at 12 on the dot.* → idiom at CONNECT

**dotcom** (*also* **dot-com, dot.com**) /ˌdɒt'kɒm; *AmE* ˌdɑːt'kɑːm/ *n.* [C] a company that sells goods and services on the Internet, esp. one whose address ends '.com': *The weaker dotcoms have collapsed.* ◇ *the ~ boom/bubble/crash*

**ˌdot 'matrix ˌprinter** *n.* [C] (*IT*) a machine that prints letters, numbers, etc. formed from very small dots

**ˌdouble 'bind** *n.* [C, usu. sing.] a situation in which it is difficult to choose what to do because whatever you choose will have negative results

**ˌdouble-'blind** (*also* **ˌdouble-'blinded**) *adj.* used to describe a type of research that tests the effects of a new product, esp. a new medicine. Neither the testers nor the people trying the product know who has received the real thing and who has received a substance that does not contain any of it: *a ~ trial/study*

**ˌdouble-'check** *v.* [T,I] to check sth for a second time or with great care: *I'll double-check the figures.* ▸ **ˌdouble-'check** *n.* [C]

**ˌdouble-'click** *v.* [T,I] to press one of the buttons on a computer mouse twice quickly in order to open a file, program, etc: *Just double-click on the icon to open the file.* ▸ **ˌdouble-'click** *n.* [C]

**ˌdouble-declining 'balance ˌmethod** *n.* [sing.] (*Account.*) a way of reducing the value of an asset in a company's financial records in which the amount taken from the asset's value decreases each year. The value of the asset is reduced at a fixed rate each year, calculated as the difference between the original value of the asset and its final value, divided by a particular number of years and multiplied by two.

**ˌdouble 'digits** = DOUBLE FIGURES

**ˌdouble 'dip** *n.* [C] a situation where there is a second decrease in prices, etc. after a short period of improvement: *a double-dip recession*

**ˌdouble-'dip** *v.* [I] (-pp-) (*esp. AmE*) (*infml.*) to obtain two incomes, pensions, etc. in an illegal or unfair way; to be paid twice for sth ▸ **ˌdouble-'dipper** *n.* [C] **ˌdouble-'dipping** *n.* [U]

**ˌdouble-entry 'bookkeeping** *n.* [U] (*Account.*) the usual way of keeping a company's financial records, in which each amount spent, received, etc. is recorded with a credit in one account and a DEBIT in another

**ˌdouble ˈfigures** (*esp. BrE*) (*AmE usu.* **ˌdouble ˈdigits**) *n.* [pl.] used to describe a number that is not less than 10 and not more than 99: *Inflation is in double figures.* ▸ **ˌdouble-ˈfigure** (*esp. BrE*) (*AmE usu.* **ˌdouble-ˈdigit**) *adj.*: *a double-figure pay rise*

**ˌdouble inˈdemnity** *n.* [U,C] (*AmE*) (*Insur.*) an arrangement in which an insurance company will pay twice the normal amount in particular circumstances, for example if the person who is insured is injured or dies in an accident: *a double-indemnity clause/policy*

**ˌdouble inˈsurance** *n.* [U,C] (*Insur.*) a situation in which sb has bought insurance to protect themselves against sth from more than one company

**ˌdouble taˈxation** *n.* [U] (*Account.*) **1** a situation in which sb must pay tax on the same income, etc. to two different governments **2** a situation in which the authorities charge tax twice on the same income

**ˌdouble ˈtime** *n.* [U] (*HR*) twice sb's normal pay, that they earn for working at times which are not normal working hours: *We are paid double time for public holidays.*

**ˌdoubtful ˈdebt** *n.* [C] (*Account.*) a debt that is not likely to be paid

**dough** /dəʊ; *AmE* doʊ/ *n.* [U] (*slang*) money: *They made a pile of dough on the deal.*

**ˌDow ˈJones™** /ˌdaʊ ˈdʒəʊnz; *AmE* ˈdʒoʊnz/ *n.* **1** (*usu.* **the Dow Jones™**) (*also* **the Dow™**) [sing.] used to refer to the Dow Jones Industrial Average **2** [U] a company in the US that publishes measures of the share prices of important companies: *Dow Jones Averages™*

**the ˈDow ˈJones Inˈdustrial ˈAverage** (*abbr* **DJIA™**) *n.* [sing.] a measure of the share prices of the 30 most important companies that are traded on the New York Stock Exchange

**ˈDow ˈJones inˈdustrials** *n.* [pl.] (*Stock Ex.*) the 30 companies whose share prices make up the Dow Jones Industrial Average; the Dow Jones Industrial Average

**down** /daʊn/ *adv., v., adj.*

• *adv.* **1** at a lower level or rate: *Output went down by 20%.* **2** having lost the amount of money mentioned: *At the end of the day we were $200 down.* **3** if you pay an amount of money down, you pay that to start with, and the rest later: *You can buy this car with no money down.* IDM **be down to sth** to have only a little money left: *I'm down to my last dollar.* → idiom at CASH *n.*

• *v.* IDM **ˌdown ˈtools** (*BrE*) to stop work; to go on strike

• *adj.* if a computer or a computer system is **down**, it is not working

**downbeat** /ˈdaʊnbiːt/ *adj.* not feeling much hope about the future: *The group remained downbeat* ***about*** *next year.* OPP UPBEAT

**downgrade** /ˌdaʊnˈɡreɪd/ *v.* [T] **1** (*Econ.*; *Finan.*) to give sth a lower grade, value or status: *They have downgraded the group's credit rating.* **2** (*HR*) to give sb a less important job; to make a job less important: *They plan to downgrade three managers.* ▸ **ˈdowngrade** *n.* [C]: *a credit-rating downgrade* **ˌdownˈgrading** *n.* [U,C]

★**download** /ˌdaʊnˈləʊd; *AmE* -ˈloʊd/ *v.* [T,I] (*IT*) to move data to a smaller computer system from a larger one; to be moved in this way: *data downloaded from the Internet* OPP UPLOAD ▸ **download** /ˈdaʊnləʊd; *AmE* -loʊd/ *n.* [U,C]: *a popular download* **ˌdownˈloadable** /-əbl/ *adj.*: *downloadable software*

**downmarket** /ˌdaʊnˈmɑːkɪt; *AmE* -ˈmɑːrk-/ (*AmE also* **ˈdownscale**) *adj.* **1** designed for or used by large numbers of customers who have less money; cheap and of poor quality: *a downmarket fashion chain* ◇ *a ~ brand/hotel/store* **2** used to describe people who have less money and cannot afford expensive products and services: *downmarket customers* ▸ **ˌdownˈmarket** (*AmE also* **ˌdownˈscale**) *adv.*: *to move downmarket* OPP UPMARKET

**ˌdown ˈpayment** *n.* [C] (*Comm.*) an amount of money that is given as the first part of a larger payment when you buy sth over a period of time or invest in sth: *a down payment* ***on*** *a car* SYN DEPOSIT

**downscale** /ˈdaʊnskeɪl; ˌdaʊnˈskeɪl/ *v., adj.* (*AmE*)

• *v.* [T] to reduce the size or extent of sth: *We had to downscale the programme due to lack of funds.*

• *adj.* = DOWNMARKET

**downshift** /ˈdaʊnʃɪft/ *v.* [T,I] **1** to change to a job where you may earn less but which puts less pressure on you: *He downshifted to spend more time with his family.* **2** to reduce sth; to become or make sth less active or important: *The union has downshifted its demands.* ▸ **ˈdownshift** *n.* [C,U]: *a career downshift* **ˈdownshifter** *n.* [C] **ˈdownshifting** *n.* [U]

**downside** /'daʊnsaɪd/ *n.* **1** (*Econ.*; *Finan.*) [sing; U] the possibility that sth will decrease in price or value: *There is little downside to the oil price at the moment.* **2** [C] the disadvantages or less positive aspects of sth: *The major downside* **to** *the new model is that it uses more fuel.* OPP UPSIDE

**downsize** /'daʊnsaɪz/ *v.* [T,I] **1** (*HR*) to reduce the number of people who work in a company, business, etc. in order to cut costs: *Their smaller offices are being downsized.* **2** (*esp. AmE*) to make sth smaller; to produce sth in a smaller size: *downsized cars* ▶ **'downsizing** *n.* [U,C]

**downstream** /ˌdaʊn'stri:m/ *adj.* (*Econ.*; *Product.*) at a late stage in an industrial or commercial process: *downstream activities, such as refining* ◇ *~ assets/operations* OPP UPSTREAM ▶ **ˌdown'stream** *adv.*: *Many manufacturers are moving downstream into retailing.*

**downswing** /'daʊnswɪŋ/ = DOWNTURN OPP UPSWING

**downtick** /'daʊntɪk/ (*also* **'minus tick**) *n.* [C, usu. sing.] (*both AmE*) (*Econ.*; *Finan.*) a small decrease in the level or value of sth, esp. in the price of shares: *a ~* **in** *unemployment/the economy* OPP UPTICK

**'downtime** /'daʊntaɪm/ *n.* [U] **1** (*IT*) the period of time when a machine, esp. a computer, is not working and cannot be used: *The downtime resulted in lost production.* **2** (*Product.*) a period of time when a factory is not working, for example because a machine needs to be repaired or there is not enough demand for goods: *scheduled downtime* **3** (*esp. AmE*) the time when sb stops working and is able to relax: *Everyone needs a little downtime.*

**downtown** /ˌdaʊn'taʊn/ *adv.* (*esp. AmE*) in or towards the centre of a city, esp. its main business area: *to go/work ~* ▶ **'downtown** *adj.*: *a downtown hotel* **'downtown** *n.* [U,C] = CENTRE *n.* (3)

**downtrend** /'daʊntrend/ *n.* [sing.] (*esp. AmE*) a situation in which business activity or performance decreases over a period of time: *a global downtrend* **in** *the car market* OPP UPTREND

★**downturn** /'daʊntɜ:n; *AmE* -tɜ:rn/ (*also* **'downswing**) *n.* [C, usu. sing.] a time when an economy, industry, etc. is weaker than normal; a fall in the amount of business that is done: *a sharp downturn* **in** *sales* SYN TURNDOWN OPP UPTURN

● *a dramatic/severe/steep ~* ◆ *a business/global/market ~* ◆ *an economic/industry ~*

**dowry** /'daʊri/ *n.* [C] (*pl.* **-ries**) (*fig.*) (esp. in newspapers) an extra amount of money that a company offers to encourage another company to agree to a TAKEOVER

**D/P** = DOCUMENTS AGAINST PAYMENT

**dpi** /ˌdi: pi: 'aɪ/ *abbr* (*IT*) **dots per inch** a measure of how clear the images produced by a printer, SCANNER, etc. are: *a 600 dpi laser printer*

**DPS** /ˌdi: pi: 'es/ *abbr* (*Finan., usu. written*) **dividend per share** the amount of profits that a company pays to each shareholder: *a $2 DPS*

**DR** /ˌdi: 'ɑ:(r)/ = DISASTER RECOVERY, OVERDRAWN

★**draft** /drɑ:ft; *AmE* dræft/ *n., v.*
• *n.* [C] **1** a rough written version of a document that is not yet in its final form: *the first draft of the report* ◇ *a ~ agreement/letter*
● *to* **draw up/prepare** *a ~* ◆ *an* **early**/*the* **final/latest** *~*
**2** (*Finan.*) a written order to a bank to pay money to sb: *Please pay by draft or cheque.* ◇ *a draft* **on** *a bank in New York.* SYN BANK DRAFT
• *v.* [T] (*also* **draught**, *esp. in BrE*) to write the first rough version of a document: *to draft a contract*
▶ **'drafter** (*also* **draughter**, *esp. in BrE*) *n.* [C]: *legal drafters*
PHR V **ˌdraft sb 'in**; **ˌdraft sb 'into sth** to choose sb or a group of people and send them somewhere for a special task: *He was drafted in to try to save the group.*

**drag** /dræg/ *v., n.*
• *v.* (**-gg-**) **1** [T] to move some text, an ICON, etc. across the screen of a computer using the mouse: *drag and drop* **2** [T,I] (*used with an adv. or a prep.*) to make an economy, a market, etc. decrease in size or grow more slowly; to bring sth to a lower level: *Low consumer demand is dragging the economy down.* **3** [T] (*used with an adv. or a prep.*) to use a lot of effort to make sb/sth go in a particular direction: *discounts to drag shoppers in*
• *n.* [C, usu. sing.] something that causes an economy, a market, etc. to decrease in size or value or to grow more slowly: *Rising oil prices are a drag* **on** *growth.*

**drain** /dreɪn/ *n., v.*
• *n.* [sing.] **1** a thing that uses a lot of the time, money, etc. that could be used for sth else: *The training pro-*

*gramme was a huge drain* ***on*** *resources.* **2** a process by which people with important skills, etc. leave in order to work somewhere else: *a drain of top talent from the company* → idiom at MONEY
• *v.* **1** [T] to make sth/sb poorer, weaker, etc. by gradually using up their money, supplies, strength, etc: *Going into new markets has drained our resources.* ◇ *She's physically drained.* **2** [I] (about money, supplies, strength, etc.) to gradually disappear: *The cash was draining* ***away.***

**draught** = DRAFT *V.*

**draw** /drɔː/ *v., n.*
• *v.* [T] (**drew** /druː/ **drawn** /drɔːn/) **1** (*Finan.*) **~ sth out (of sth)** | **~ sth from sth** to take money from a bank account: *to ~ $500 from/out of an account* SYN WITHDRAW **2** (*Finan.*) (*often pass.*) to write out a cheque or BILL OF EXCHANGE: *The cheque was drawn* ***on*** *his personal account.* **3** to receive a regular income or a pension: *He draws a €40 000 salary.* **4** (*Finan.*) = DRAW STH DOWN (FROM STH), DRAW DOWN ON STH
PHRV ˌ**draw (sth) 'down** (*esp. AmE*) to reduce a supply of sth that has been created over a period of time; to be reduced: *events that can draw down savings* ˌ**draw sth 'down (from sth)**; ˌ**draw 'down on sth** (*esp. AmE*) (*BrE usu.* **draw**) (*Finan.*) to take money from a fund that a bank, etc. has made available: *They can draw down on the loan at any time.* '**draw sth from sth** to get sth from a particular source: *The country draws most of its revenue from exports.* '**draw on/upon sth** to start using a supply of sth that has been created over a period of time: *drawing on oil reserves* ˌ**draw sth 'out** (*Finan.*) = DRAW (1) ˌ**draw sth 'up** to make or write sth that needs careful thought or planning: *to ~ a plan/list/contract*
• *n.* [C] **1** a person, a thing or an event that attracts a lot of people: *The new store is a big draw.* **2** (*esp. AmE*) = DRAWDOWN (1)

**drawback** /'drɔːbæk/ *n.* **1** [C] a disadvantage or problem that makes sth a less attractive idea: *The main drawback* ***to*** *the plan is the cost.* **2** (*Trade*) [U,C] (*AmE*) = DUTY DRAWBACK

**drawdown** /'drɔːdaʊn/ *n.* [C,U] **1** (*also* **draw**, *esp. in AmE*) the act of reducing a supply of sth that has been created over a period of time; the amount used: *a drawdown on oil stocks* **2** (*Finan.*) the act of using money that is available to you; the amount used : *a drawdown of cash from the company's reserves*

**drawee** /ˌdrɔː'iː/ *n.* [C] (*Finan.*) **1** (*also* ˌ**drawee 'bank**) the bank of the person or organization that has written a cheque, which is therefore asked to pay the amount written on it to the person named **2** the bank or company that agrees to pay the amount written on a BILL OF EXCHANGE

**drawer** /'drɔːə(r)/ *n.* [C] (*Finan.*) a person who writes a cheque or BILL OF EXCHANGE that asks for a payment to be made to sb

'**drawing acˌcount** *n.* [C] (*AmE*) **1** (*Account.*) an account in which the money that the owners of a company take for their personal use is recorded **2** a company account that its SALESPEOPLE can use when they are spending money doing their job

**drayage** /'dreɪɪdʒ/ *n.* [U] (*AmE*) (*Transpt.*) the process of moving goods a short distance by lorry/truck; the charge made for this

**dress** /dres/ *n., v.*
• *n.* [U] clothes for men or women: *a policy of casual dress in the office*
• *v.* PHRV ˌ**dress 'down** to wear clothes that are more informal than those you usu. wear: *Staff are allowed to dress down on Fridays.* ◇ *dress-down Friday*

'**dress code** *n.* [C] a set of rules that an organization has about what people must or must not wear

**drift** /drɪft/ *v.* [I] (*usu. used with an adv. or a prep.*) (about a share price, figure, etc.) to change slowly, esp. to a lower level and in a way that does not seem to be controlled: *The Nikkei average drifted lower yesterday.*
▸ **drift** *n.* [sing; U]: *a downward drift in inflation*

**drill** /drɪl/ *v.* [T,I] to make a deep hole in the ground using a machine, in order to look for valuable natural substances, esp. oil or gas: *drilling for oil* ▸ '**drilling** *n.* [U] PHRV ˌ**drill 'down** (*IT*) to go to deeper and deeper levels of an organized set of data on a computer or a website in order to find more and more detail: *View orders by customer and date and then drill down to view order details.*

**DRIP** /drɪp; ˌdiː ɑːr aɪ 'piː/ = DIVIDEND REINVESTMENT PLAN

'**drip ˌadvertising** *n.* [U] (*Market.*) a continuous small amount of advertising for a product over a long period of time

'**drip ˌmarketing** *n.* [U] (*Market.*) the activity of trying to sell products to customers by contacting them often over a period of time

**drive** /draɪv/ *v., n.*

• *v.* [T] (**drove** /drəʊv; *AmE* droʊv/ **driven** /ˈdrɪvn/) **1** (*often pass.*) to cause sth; to be the main influence on sth: *Our products are driven by customers' needs.* **2 ~ sth (forward)** to make sth grow stronger, develop or progress: *Profits rose, driven by strong sales in Asia.* **3** (*with an adv. or a prep.*) to force a price, figure, etc. to go up or down or move to a particular level: *We must drive down costs.* **4** to force sb to act in a particular way: *You're driving yourself too hard* (= making yourself work too much). **IDM be in the ˈdriving seat** (*also* **be in the ˈdriver's seat**) to be the person in control of a situation → idioms at GROUND *n.*, HARD *adj.* **PHR V ˌdrive sb/sth ˈout (of sth)** to make sb/sth disappear or stop doing sth: *The supermarkets are driving small shopkeepers out of business.*

• *n.* [C] **1** an organized effort by a group of people to achieve sth: *a drive **for** greater efficiency ◇ a cost-cutting/recruitment ~* **2** (*IT*) the part of a computer that reads and stores information on disks or tapes

**ˈdrive-in** *n.* [C] a place where you can buy food or other goods, watch films/movies, etc. without leaving your car

★**-driven** /ˈdrɪvn/ *comb. form* (*in adjs*) **1** influenced or caused by a particular thing or person: *a customer-driven approach to marketing ◇ a results-driven sales team* **2** (about machines, computer systems, etc.) operated, moved or controlled by a particular thing: *a petrol-driven engine ◇ menu-driven software*

**driver** /ˈdraɪvə(r)/ *n.* [C] **1** a person who drives a vehicle: *a cab/truck ~* **2** an important influence on sth, esp. sth that makes it grow, develop or progress: *Technology is a key business driver.* **3** (*IT*) software that controls the sending of data between a computer and a piece of equipment that is attached to it such as a printer **IDM be in the ˈdriver's seat** = BE IN THE DRIVING SEAT at DRIVE *v.*

**ˈdrive-through** (*AmE also* **-thru**, *infml.*) *n.* [C] (*esp. AmE*) a restaurant, bank, etc. where you can be served without leaving your car

**ˈdrive time** *n.* [U] (*Market.*) a time during the day when many people are driving their cars, for example to or from work, and listening to the radio, considered to be a good time to advertise on the radio

**ˈdrive-up** *n.* [C] (*esp. AmE*) a place at a bank, restaurant, etc. where you can be served in your car

**ˈdriving force** *n.* [C] a person or an event with a very strong influence on sth and that causes a big change: *Who was the driving force **behind** the company's growth?*

**DRM** /ˌdiː ɑːr ˈem/ *abbr* (*E-comm.*) **digital rights management** actions and devices designed to prevent people from illegally copying software or other electronic material from the Internet: *The songs are DRM protected.*

**drop** /drɒp; *AmE* drɑːp/ *v., n.*

• *v.* (**-pp-**) **1** [T,I] to become or make sth weaker, lower or less: *The price of the shares dropped sharply. ◇ He had to drop his price by $300.* **2** [T] to not continue with sth; to stop using sb/sth: *They have dropped their plans to build a new factory.* **3** [T] to lose money: *I dropped $3 000 in salary when I changed jobs.* **4** [T] to place text, a file, etc. in a particular place on a computer screen by using the mouse button: *Drag the file and drop it in the folder.* **IDM ˌdrop the ˈball (on sth)** (*AmE*) (*infml.*) to be responsible for sth going wrong or for doing sth badly; to stop taking responsibility for sth: *Who dropped the ball on this project?* → idiom at BOTTOM **PHR V ˌdrop aˈway** = DROP OFF **ˌdrop ˈback (to sth)** to return to a lower level or amount: *The price of gold dropped back to $378 an ounce.* **ˌdrop ˈoff** (*BrE*) (*also* **ˌdrop aˈway**, *AmE, BrE*) to decrease in level or amount, esp. after being high for a long time: *Consumer spending has dropped off sharply.* **ˌdrop ˈout (of sth)** to no longer take part in or be part of sth: *to drop out of the deal*

• *n.* [C, usu. sing.] a fall or reduction in the amount, level or number of sth: *a 15% drop in profits ◇ a dramatic/sharp/slight ~*

**ˈdrop box** *n.* [C] (*esp. AmE*) a box in which you can safely leave sth for sb to collect later, such as a payment, the keys of a car, etc.

**ˌdrop-ˈdead date** *n.* [C] (*AmE*) (*infml.*) a final date by which sth must be done, esp. one fixed in a contract

**ˈdrop-down** (*also* **ˈpull-down**) *adj.* (*IT*) used to describe a list of choices that appears on a computer screen below the place where you click: *a drop-down menu*

**ˈdrop-off** *n.* **1** [C, usu. sing., U] a decrease in the level or amount of sth, esp. after being high for a long time: *a sharp drop-off **in** sales* **2** [C]

the act of delivering sth/sb to a particular place; the place where sb/sth is delivered or the thing or person delivered: *the number of drop-offs that our drivers have to make*

**'drop ˌshipment** *n.* (*Comm.*; *Transpt.*) **1** [U] = DROP SHIPPING **2** [C] an amount of goods advertised and sold by a business but delivered directly from the producer to the customer: *an additional charge for each drop shipment*

**'drop ˌshipping** (*also* **'drop ˌshipment**, *less freq.*) *n.* [U] (*Comm.*; *Transpt.*) an arrangement in which a business advertises and sells goods, but they are delivered directly from the producer to the customer: *We offer drop shipping at an extra charge.* ▶ **'drop-ship** *v.* [T,I] (**-pp-**)

**drug** /drʌg/ *n.* [C] **1** a substance used as a medicine or used in a medicine: *a* ***blockbuster*** *drug* (= one that sells very well) ◇ *a drug company* **2** an illegal substance that people use to give them pleasant or exciting feelings

**drugmaker** (*also* **drug maker**) /'drʌgmeɪkə(r)/ *n.* [C] a company that manufactures medicines

**drugstore** /'drʌgstɔː(r)/ *n.* [C] (*AmE*) a shop/store that sells medicines and also other types of goods, for example substances for the face and body (**cosmetics**)

**drum** /drʌm/ *n.*, *v.*
• *n.* [C] a tall metal or plastic container with round ends that is used for oil or chemicals: *an oil drum* ◇ *a 50-gallon drum*
• *v.* (-mm-) **PHR V** **ˌdrum sth 'up** to try hard to get support or business: *to ~ up business*

**ˌdrum-'buffer-rope** *adj.* (*abbr* **DBR**) (*Product.*) using a method of planning a production process which makes sure that there is always an efficient flow of work by considering possible problems and delays: *~ production/scheduling*

**dry** /draɪ/ *v.* (**dries, drying, dried, dried**) **PHR V** **ˌdry 'up** if a supply of sth **dries up**, there is gradually less of it until there is none left: *Orders have dried up.*

**ˌdry 'cargo** *n.* [U] (*Transpt.*) goods that are not liquid that are transported on ships, esp. goods that are transported in large quantities, such as coal, wood, metals, etc: *We handle containerized and dry cargo.*

**'dry goods** *n.* [pl.] **1** (*Trade*) (*also* **'dry comˌmodities**) goods such as coffee, sugar, cloth, etc. that are not liquid and must be kept in dry conditions **2** (*Comm.*) (*AmE*) goods such as cloth and things made out of cloth, materials for sewing, etc.

**'dry lease** *n.* [U,C] an arrangement that allows a company to use another company's aircraft, but not people to fly them, for a period of time

**'dry spell** *n.* [C] (*Stock Ex.*) a time when there is little buying or selling or business activity

**DSL** /ˌdiː es 'el/ *abbr* (*IT*) **digital subscriber line** a telephone line which can carry data for television, video and Internet access, at high speed

**DSR** /ˌdiː es 'ɑː(r)/ = DEBT SERVICE RATIO

**DSS** /ˌdiː es 'es/ = DECISION SUPPORT SYSTEM

**DTC** /ˌdiː tiː 'siː/ = DIRECT-TO-CONSUMER

**DTI** /ˌdiː tiː 'aɪ/ = DEPARTMENT OF TRADE AND INDUSTRY

**DTP** /ˌdiː tiː 'piː/ = DESKTOP PUBLISHING

**dual** /'djuːəl; *AmE* 'duːəl/ *adj.* having two parts or aspects: *the dual role of chairman and CEO*

**ˌdual ca'reer** *n.* [C, usu. pl., U] **1** the situation when a husband and wife or other couple both have careers **2** the situation when one person has two careers

**ˌdual 'currency** *n.* [C,U] (*Econ.*) when two valid currencies are used for accounts, trading, etc.

**ˌdual e'conomy** *n.* [C] (*Econ.*) an economy that has two clearly different parts

**ˌdual-listed 'company** *n.* [C] (*abbr* **DLC**) (*Stock Ex.*) a business that is made of two companies whose shares are traded on stock exchanges in different countries

**ˌdual 'listing** *n.* [C] (*Stock Ex.*) a situation in which a company sells its shares on two different stock exchanges; the shares that are sold in this way ▶ **ˌdual-'listed** *adj.*: *dual-listed stocks*

**ˌdual 'pricing** *n.* [U] **1** (*Econ.*) the act of selling the same goods or services for different prices in different markets **2** (*Finan.*) when there is one price for people who are selling sth, such as shares, and a different, higher one for people who are buying **3** (*Comm.*) when prices are given in two different currencies

**ˌdual-'purpose** *adj.* that can be used for two different purposes: *a dual-purpose vehicle* (= for carrying passengers or goods)

**ˌdual ˈsourcing** *n.* [U] (*Product.*) when a company, esp. a manufacturer, buys its supplies of a particular product from two different suppliers ▸ **ˌdual-ˈsource** *v.* [T,I]

**due** /djuː; *AmE* duː/ *adj.* **1** [not usu. before n.] (about a payment or debt) that must be paid immediately or at the time mentioned: *Payment is due on 1 October.* ◇ *a payment, etc. becomes/comes/falls* ~ **2** ~ **(to do sth)** | ~ **(for sth)** arranged or expected: *We are due to meet on Tuesday.* **3** ~ **(for sth)** owed or deserving sth: *I'm still due 15 days' leave.* IDM **in ˌdue ˈform** (*Law*) in the legally correct way

**ˈdue bill** *n.* [C] (*AmE*) a document that shows what sb owes SYN IOU

**ˈdue date** *n.* [C, usu. sing.] the date on or by which sth, esp. an amount of money, is owed or expected

**ˌdue ˈdiligence** *n.* **1** [U] the process of taking great care in doing sth or deciding sth, esp. in buying or selling sth: *We try to exercise due diligence in selecting employees.* **2** (*Law*) [U,C] a process in which sb examines the financial records, documents, etc. of a business in order to decide whether they want to buy it and how much money to offer: *The deal is subject to due diligence.* ◇ *to conduct/do/undertake* ~ ◇ *a* ~ *exercise/procedure*

**dues** /djuːz; *AmE* duːz/ *n.* [pl.] **1** money that you pay regularly to belong to an organization, esp. a union **2** (*Comm.*; *Product.*) orders accepted for goods that cannot be supplied immediately **3** (*Transpt.*) money that the owner of a ship pays for using a port

**dump** /dʌmp/ *v.* [T] **1** to get rid of sth you do not want, esp. in a place which is not suitable: *Too much toxic waste is being dumped at sea.* **2** to sell sth that is not worth keeping, esp. in large quantities and at low prices: *Worried investors dumped 8 million shares at just 40¢ each.* **3** (*Econ.*) to sell your goods in another country at very low prices, with the result that local companies cannot compete fairly ▸ **ˈdumping** *n.* [U]: *a dumping ground for cheap goods*

**ˈdump bin** (*BrE*) (*also* **disˈplay bin**, *AmE*, *BrE*) *n.* [C] (*Market.*) a container like a box in a shop/store for displaying goods, esp. goods whose prices have been reduced

**ˈDUNS™ ˌnumber** /dʌnz/ *abbr* **Data Universal Numbering System number** a unique number given to a business by D&B™, (= an organization that supplies financial information about companies), used to identify an individual business

**duopoly** /djuːˈɒpəli; *AmE* duːˈɑː-/ *n.* [C] (*pl.* **-lies**) (*Econ.*) a situation in which an industry is controlled by two companies; the two companies themselves

★**duplicate** *v.*, *adj.*, *n.*
• *v.* /ˈdjuːplɪkeɪt; *AmE* ˈduː-/ [T] **1** (*often pass.*) to make an exact copy of sth: *a duplicated form/letter* **2** to do sth again, esp. when it is unnecessary: *The two departments are duplicating each other's efforts.*
▸ **ˌdupliˈcation** /-ˈkeɪʃn/ *n.* [U,C]
• *adj.* /ˈdjuːplɪkət; *AmE* ˈduː-/ exactly like sth else; made as a copy of sth else: *a duplicate invoice*
• *n.* /ˈdjuːplɪkət; *AmE* ˈduː-/ [C] one of two or more things that are the same in every detail: *Is this a duplicate or the original?* SYN COPY IDM **in ˈduplicate** (about documents, etc.) as two copies that are exactly the same in every detail: *The form must be completed in duplicate.*

**durable** /ˈdjʊərəbl; *AmE* ˈdʊr-/ *adj.* likely to last for a long time without breaking or getting weaker: ~ *plastics/fabrics* OPP NON-DURABLE
▸ **ˌduraˈbility** /-ˈbɪləti/ *n.* [U]

**ˈdurable goods** (*also* **ˈhard goods**) = CONSUMER DURABLES

**durables** /ˈdjʊərəblz; *AmE* ˈdʊr-/ = CONSUMER DURABLES

**duress** /djuˈres; *AmE* du-/ *n.* [U] (*Law*) threats or force that are used to make sb do sth: *She claims the payment was made* **under** *duress.*

**ˌDutch ˈauction** *n.* [C] **1** (*Comm.*) a type of **auction** in which the price of the item being sold is gradually reduced until sb offers to buy it **2** (*Comm.*; *Finan.*) (*also* **ˌuniform ˈprice ˌauction**) a way of selling a number of similar items in which people offer to buy a particular number at a particular price. The seller accepts as many of the highest offers as are needed to sell all the items and the selling price is set at the price of the lowest successful offer: *The company is selling $1.5 m of bills in a Dutch auction.*

**dutiable** /ˈdjuːtiəbl; *AmE* ˈduː-/ *adj.* (*Trade*) (about goods brought into a country) on which tax must be paid: ~ *goods/imports*

★**duty** /ˈdjuːti; *AmE* ˈduːti/ *n.* (*pl.* **duties**) **1** (*Econ.*; *Trade*) [C,U] a tax that you pay on things that you buy, esp. those that you bring into a country: *They have put higher duties on steel imports.* **2** [U] the work that is your job: *I'm on night duty this week.* **3 duties** [pl.] tasks that are part of your job: *Your duties will include setting up a new computer system.*

**'duty diffe,rential** *n.* [C] (*Econ.*) **1** a difference in the rate of tax charged on two similar types of imported goods or materials **2** a difference in the rate of tax that one country charges on particular imported goods compared to another country

**,duty 'drawback** (*AmE also* **'drawback**) *n.* [U,C] (*Trade*) all or part of a tax paid on imported goods that is paid back when the goods are exported again or used to make new goods for export

**,duty-'free** *adj., n.*

• ***adj.*** (*Trade*) used to describe goods that can be brought or sent into a country without paying tax on them: *duty-free exports to the US* ▸ **,duty-'free** *adv.*: *selling goods into the US market duty-free*

• ***n.*** (*pl.* **duty-frees**) (*infml.*) **1** [U; pl.] (*BrE*) goods that can be brought into a country without paying tax on them: *We bought our duty-frees at the airport.* **2** (*also* **,duty-'free shop**) [C] a shop/store in an airport or on a ship, etc. that sells goods such as cigarettes, alcohol, jewellery, etc. without tax on them

**,duty-'paid** *adj.* (*Trade*) used to describe goods being imported on which taxes have been paid

**'dwell time** *n.* [U,C] **1** (*Market.*) the amount of time that people spend at a shop/store, website, etc. or looking at sth such as a piece of advertising **2** (*Product.*) the amount of time that sth spends in a particular stage of a process

**dwindle** /'dwɪndl/ *v.* [I] to become gradually less or smaller: *dwindling audiences/profits*

**dwt** *abbr* (*Transpt.*) a short way of writing **deadweight** or **deadweight tonnes/tonnage**

**dynamic** /daɪ'næmɪk/ *adj., n.*

• ***adj.*** **1** always changing or adapting to new circumstances and making progress: *a dynamic market* OPP STATIC **2** having a lot of energy and a strong personality: *a dynamic boss*

• ***n.*** **1 dynamics** [pl.] the way in which people or things behave and react to each other in a particular situation: *market dynamics* **2** [sing.] a force that produces change, action or effects: *a changing dynamic in the telecoms industry*

# Ee

★ **e-** /iː/ *comb. form* (*used to form ns and vs*) **1** connected with the use of electronic communication, esp. the Internet, for sending information, doing business, etc: *e-banking* ◇ *e-marketing* ◇ *e-sales* **2** stored in electronic form on a disk, MICROCHIP, etc: *e-money*

**ea.** *abbr* (*written*) each (used esp. when giving prices): *T-shirts €20 ea.*

**Eagle** /'iːgl/ (*also* **A,merican 'Eagle**) *n.* [C] in the US, a coin made from gold, silver or PLATINUM that you can buy as an investment

**EAI** /,iː eɪ 'aɪ/ = ENTERPRISE APPLICATION INTEGRATION

**E&OE** *abbr* (*Comm.*) **errors and omissions excepted** written in a document, for example a list of prices, to show that the writer is not responsible for any mistakes it contains, nor for leaving out any information: *All prices are correct as of today's date, E&OE.*

**EAP** /,iː eɪ 'piː/ = EMPLOYEE ASSISTANCE PROGRAMME, EMPLOYMENT ASSISTANCE PROGRAMME

**EAR** /,iː eɪ 'ɑː(r)/ *abbr* (*Finan.*) **effective annual rate** the amount of interest paid in one year for borrowing money compared with the amount borrowed, used when interest is normally paid more often than once a year; the amount of interest received from money invested: *Interest is charged at an EAR of 10%.*

**early** /'ɜːli; *AmE* 'ɜːrli/ *adj.* IDM **at your earliest con'venience** (*written*) as soon as possible

**,early a'dopter** *n.* [C] (*Market.*) a person or an organization that starts using a new product, esp. a piece of technology, as soon as it is available

**,early ma'jority** *n.* [sing.] **1** (*Market.*) the group of customers who will start to use a new product once some people have tried it and shown it is successful, but before many other people use it **2** (*HR*) the people in an organization who start to use a new method, process or system after some people in the organization have tested it, but before many others

**,early re'tirement** *n.* [U] (*HR*) the act of stopping work before the usual age: *She took early retirement for health reasons.*

**'early-stage** *adj.* used to describe sth that is being developed or that began not very long before: *small, early-stage companies*

**ˌearly-stage ˈfinancing** *n.* [U] (*Finan.*) the first stages of investment in a young company

**earmark** /ˈɪəmɑːk; *AmE* ˈɪrmɑːrk/ *v.* [T] (*usu. pass.*) to decide that sth will be used for a particular purpose; to state that sth will happen to sb/sth in the future: *They earmarked €8 m of their budget for new stores.*

★ **earn** /ɜːn; *AmE* ɜːrn/ *v.* **1** [T,I] to get money for work that you do: *She earns about €40 000 in pay and bonuses.* ◇ *I only have to pay back the loan when I start earning.*
⊕ *to ~ a* ***fee****/an* ***income****/a* ***salary/wage*** ◆ *to ~ a* ***bonus/raise/rise***
**2** [T] to obtain money from business activities: *In the last quarter the company earned $1.16 bn, or 47 cents a share.*
⊕ *to ~ an* ***income****/a* ***profit/return*** ◆ *to ~* ***income/money/profits/revenue(s)***
**3** [T] to get money as a profit or interest on money that you invest, lend, etc: *How much interest do you earn* ***on*** *your savings?* ◇ *to ~ a dividend/return* **4** [T] to get a benefit because you buy sth from a particular shop/store, etc. or use a particular credit card: *Shoppers will be able to earn points on all credit-card purchases.* **IDM** **ˌearn your/its ˈkeep** to be worth the amount of time or money that is being spent

**ˌearned ˈincome** *n.* [U] (*Account.*) money you receive from the work you do, not from investments, etc. **OPP** UNEARNED INCOME

**earner** /ˈɜːnə(r); *AmE* ˈɜːrn-/ *n.* [C] **1** a person who earns money for a job that they do: *a high/low ~* ◇ *income/salary/wage ~s* **2** an activity or a business that makes a profit: *Tourism is our biggest foreign currency earner.* ◇ *a dollar/an export ~*

**ˈearnest ˌmoney** *n.* [U] (*also* **earnest** /ˈɜːnɪst; *AmE* ˈɜːrn-/ [C]) (*both esp. AmE*) (*Comm.*) an amount of money that you pay to show sb that you are serious about doing business with them, esp. when you are buying a home

**ˈearning ˌpower** *n.* [U] the ability of sb to earn money from work; the ability of sth to make a profit: *the earning power of an investment*

★ **earnings** /ˈɜːnɪŋz; *AmE* ˈɜːrn-/ *n.* [pl.] **1** the money that you earn for the work that you do; the money that people earn in a particular industry or during a particular time: *She* ***has*** *earnings of $60 000 per year.* ◇ *compensation for loss of earnings*
⊕ *high/low ~* ◆ *annual/weekly ~* ◆ *gross/net/pre-tax/taxable ~*
**2** the profit that a country, a company, an industry or an investment makes: *Germany's earnings* ***from*** *exports* ◇ *our 2009 earnings forecast*
⊕ *annual/full-year/quarterly ~* ◆ *expected/strong ~* ◆ *to* ***boost/grow/have/report*** *~*

**ˈearnings before ˈinterest and ˈtax(es)** = EBIT

**ˈearnings before ˈinterest, ˈtax(es), depreciˈation and amortiˈzation** = EBITDA

**ˈearnings diffeˌrential** *n.* [C] (*Econ.*) the amount of money that one group of people in society generally earn compared to another group: *the male-female earnings differential*

**ˌearnings per ˈshare** *n.* [pl.] (*abbr* **EPS**) (*Account.*) the amount of profit that a company has made during a particular period, divided by the number of ORDINARY SHARES that people own **HELP** This phrase can also be used as a sing. noun: *an earnings per share of 121 cents.*

**ˈearnings-reˌlated** *adj.* (*BrE*) (about payments, etc.) connected to the amount of money that you earn and changing as that amount does: *an earnings-related pension scheme*

**ˈearnings reˌport** *n.* [C] (*AmE*) (*Account.*) a record that a company publishes of its income and expenses for a particular period that shows if it has made a profit **SYN** PROFIT AND LOSS ACCOUNT

**ˈearnings ˌstatement** = STATEMENT OF EARNINGS

**ˈearnings yield** *n.* [C] (*Account.*) a financial measure that compares the amount of profit that a company has available to pay on each share with the current share price

**ˈearn-out** *n.* [C] (*Finan.*) an extra payment that is made to the seller of a company, in addition to the original price, if the company's income goes above a fixed level after the company has been sold but before the new owner has control

**ease** /iːz/ *v.* [T,I] **1** to become or to make sth less unpleasant, severe, etc: *They imported fuel to ease the shortage.* **2** to become or make sth lower in value or level: *Share prices eased back today.* **3** if a central bank eases, or **eases** interest rates, the rates become slightly lower
▸ **easing** /ˈiːzɪŋ/ *n.* [U,C]: *an easing of the tax rules* **PHRV** **ˌease ˈoff (sth)** to start to become lower in value or level: *Consumer spending*

*may be easing off.* ˌ**ease 'up** to do sth in a more reasonable and less extreme way: *You should ease up a bit* (= not work so hard).

**easy** /ˈiːzi/ *adj.* (**-sier**, **-siest**)
IDM **be, close, finish, etc. 'easier** (*Stock Ex.*) to be, close, etc. slightly lower in price or level: *The index was 0.4% easier.* **(be, live) on 'easy street** (*AmE*) (to be) enjoying a comfortable way of life with plenty of money

ˌ**easy 'monetary ˌpolicy** (*also* ˌ**easy 'money ˌpolicy**) *n.* [C,U] (*Econ.*) a policy of making it cheap and easy for people to borrow money, so that they will invest more money in business activities and help the economy to grow

ˌ**easy 'money** *n.* [U] **1** money that you get without having to work very hard for it **2** (*Econ.*) money that can be borrowed at a low rate of interest SYN CHEAP MONEY

ˌ**easy 'terms** *n.* [pl.] (*esp. BrE*) (*Comm.*; *Finan.*) a way of borrowing money to pay for sth at a low rate of interest and paying it back in small amounts: *loans **on** easy terms*

**EBIT** (*also* **ebit**) /ˈebɪt/ *abbr* (*Account.*) **earnings before interest and tax(es)** (*used as a sing. or an uncountable n.*) the amount of profit a company makes during a particular period, without taking away the tax it owes or the interest it has paid to its lenders: *an EBIT of €151 m*

**EBITDA** (*also* **ebitda**) /ˈebɪtdə/ *abbr* (*Account.*) **earnings before interest, tax(es), depreciation and amortization** (*used as a sing. or an uncountable n.*) the amount of profit a company makes during a particular period, without taking away the tax it owes, the interest it has paid to its lenders, or the amount by which its assets have become less valuable: *EBITDA is expected to reach €2 bn this year.* ◇ *the debt to EBITDA ratio*

**'e-ˌbusiness** (*also* ˌ**electronic 'business**, *less freq.*) *n.* [U,C] any business activity that is done using the Internet, such as selling goods and services or linking parts of a business together; a company that uses the Internet in this way

**EC** /ˌiː ˈsiː/ = EUROPEAN COMMISSION

**'e-cash** (*also* ˌ**electronic 'cash**, *less freq.*) (*also* ˌ**digital 'cash**) *n.* [U] **1** (*E-comm.*) a system for paying for goods or services on the Internet. You store a small amount of money in electronic form which is used whenever you need to pay for sth. **2** a way of paying for small items without cash. You store money in electronic form on a plastic card which you use in a similar way to a BANK CARD

**ECB** /ˌiː siː ˈbiː/ = EUROPEAN CENTRAL BANK

**echelon** /ˈeʃəlɒn; *AmE* -lɑːn/ *n.* [C, usu. pl.] a rank or position of authority in an organization or a society; the people who have that rank or position: *people in the top echelons of organizations*

**ECN** /ˌiː siː ˈen/ *abbr* (*Stock Ex.*) **electronic communications network** (*used as a countable n.*) an electronic system that allows people to buy and sell shares privately at any time without using a BROKER

★ **'e-ˌcommerce** (*also* ˌ**electronic 'commerce**, *less freq.*) (*also* **'Internet ˌcommerce**) *n.* [U] the business of buying and selling things using the Internet
○ *to **be involved in/move into** ~* • *an ~ **business/company*** • *~ **software/solutions***

**econometrics** /ɪˌkɒnəˈmetrɪks; *AmE* ɪˌkɑːn-/ *n.* [U] (*Econ.*) the branch of economics that uses mathematical methods to understand how economies operate
▶ ˌ**econo'metric** *adj.* **eˌcono-me'trician** /-məˈtrɪʃn/ *n.* [C]

★ **economic** /ˌiːkəˈnɒmɪk; ˌekə-; *AmE* -ˈnɑːm-/ *adj.* **1** connected with the trade, industry and development of wealth of a country, an area or a society: *social, economic and political issues* ◇ *a global economic downturn*
○ *~ **activity/development/growth/weakness*** • *an ~ **boom/recovery*** • *an ~ **slowdown/slump*** • *the ~ **climate/environment/outlook***
**2** (about a process, a business or an activity) producing enough profit to continue: *The company will have to cut staff to remain economic.* SYN PROFITABLE OPP UNECONOMIC
**3** that costs less money or uses less time, materials or effort: *an economic use of resources* SYN ECONOMICAL OPP UNECONOMIC

ˌ**economic 'agent** *n.* [C] (*Econ.*) any person or organization that influences an economy by making or spending money

★ **economical** /ˌiːkəˈnɒmɪkl; ˌekə-; *AmE* -ˈnɑːm-/ *adj.* **1** providing good value, profit or service in relation to the amount of time or money spent; not wasting time or money: *It is not economical to sell these items in small quantities.* OPP UNECONOMIC-

AL **2** using no more of sth than necessary: *an economical use of space*

★ **economically** /ˌiːkəˈnɒmɪkli; ˌekə-; *AmE* -ˈnɑːm-/ *adv.* **1** in a way that is connected with the trade, industry and development of wealth of a country, an area or a society: *The country is facing a crisis, both economically and socially.* **2** in a way that provides good value, profit or service in relation to the amount of time or money spent: *Is the project **economically viable**?* **3** in a way that uses no more of sth than is necessary: *using space economically*

**ˌeconomic ˈcycle** *n.* [C, usu. sing.] (*Econ.*) the usual pattern of a country's economy over a period of time, with periods of success (**growth**) and periods of difficulty (**recession**) happening regularly one after another SYN BUSINESS CYCLE

**ˌeconomic ˈindicator** *n.* [C, usu. pl.] (*Econ.*) a figure, such as the level of employment or prices, that is seen as a measure of the success of an economy

**ˌeconomic ˈlife** *n.* [C, usu. sing.] (*Account.*) the period of time that you can use an asset such as a machine or vehicle before it is worth buying a new one to replace it SYN USEFUL LIFE

**ˌeconomic ˈorder ˌquantity** *n.* [C,U] (*abbr* **EOQ**) (*Account.*; *Product.*) the best amount of sth to order that is enough for what you need and keeps all the costs involved, such as the cost of storing items, as low as possible

★ **economics** /ˌiːkəˈnɒmɪks; ˌekə-; *AmE* -ˈnɑːm-/ *n.* **1** [U] the study of the production, DISTRIBUTION and use of goods and services; the study of how a society organizes its money, trade and industry: *a degree in politics and economics* ◇ *Keynesian/Marxist/market* ~ **2** [pl.; U] the financial aspects of a business, a project, etc., esp. the relationship between money spent and the benefits or profit produced: *The economics of the project are very encouraging.*

**ˌeconomic ˈvalue** *n.* [U,C] (*Account.*) the value of sth, such as a business, a product or an asset, that is based on the future income it will produce

★ **economist** /ɪˈkɒnəmɪst; *AmE* ɪˈkɑːn-/ *n.* [C] a person who studies or writes about economics; a person whose job involves studying particular economies and predicting their future progress

**economize**, **-ise** /ɪˈkɒnəmaɪz; *AmE* ɪˈkɑːn-/ *v.* [I] to use less money, time, etc. than you normally use: *We need to economize **on** electricity costs.*

★ **economy** /ɪˈkɒnəmi; *AmE* ɪˈkɑːn-/ *n.* (*pl.* **-mies**) **1** (*often* **the economy** [C]) the relationship between production, trade and the supply of money in a particular country or region: *The economy is in recession.* ◇ *The US is moving from a manufacturing economy to a service one.* ➊ *to **control/manage/run** the* ~ ◆ *to **boost/strengthen/weaken** the* ~ ◆ *a **strong/weak*** ~ ◆ *the* ~ ***grows/recovers*** ◆ *the* ~ ***slows/weakens*** **2** [C] a country, when you are thinking about its economic system: *China is one of the world's fastest-growing economies.* **3** [U,C] the use of the time, money, etc. that is available in a way that avoids waste: *economy of effort in the handling of loads* **4** [C, usu. pl.] a reduction in the amount of money that you spend: *We made substantial economies.* **5** [U] (*used as an adj.*) offering good value for the money that you spend: *a regular pack of 30 tablets or an economy pack of 60* **6** [U] = ECONOMY CLASS

**eˈconomy class** (*also* **eˈconomy**) *n.* [U] the cheapest class of air travel; the part of a plane where people with the cheapest tickets sit ▸ **eˈconomy class** *adv.*: *to fly economy class*

**eˈconomy drive** *n.* [C, usu. sing.] an organized effort to reduce costs and avoid wasting money

**eˌconomy of ˈscale** (*also* **ˈscale eˌconomy**, *less freq.*) *n.* [C, usu. pl., U] (*Econ.*) the fact that as the amount of goods or services produced increases, the cost decreases: *To **achieve** economies of scale, many retailers have merged.*

**eˈconomy-size** (*also* **eˈconomy-sized**) *adj.* used to describe sth you buy that offers a larger quantity than usual, esp. when it is the best value for money of the sizes available: *an economy-size bottle of shampoo*

**ecotourism** /ˌiːkəʊˈtʊərɪzəm; -ˈtɔːr-; *AmE* ˌiːkoʊˈtʊr-/ *n.* [U] organized holidays/vacations to places that not many people have the chance to see, designed so that the tourists damage the environment as little as possible, esp. when some of the money they pay is used to protect the local environment and animals ▸ **ˌecoˈtourist** *n.* [C]

**ECR** /ˌiː siː ˈɑː(r)/ = EFFICIENT CONSUMER RESPONSE

**ˈe-ˌcurrency** (*also* **ˌelectronic ˈcurrency**, *less freq.*) (*also* **ˌdigital**

'currency) *n.* [C,U] (*E-comm.*) one of the electronic forms of money that you can buy from particular companies on the Internet and use for making and receiving payments on the Internet

**edge** /edʒ/ *n., v.*
• *n.* [sing.] **1** a slight advantage over sb/sth: *They have the edge in design.*
○ *to* ***gain/keep/lose*** *an ~ (on/over sb/sth)* • *sth* ***gives*** *you an ~*
**2** (*usually* **the edge**) the point at which sth, esp. sth bad, may begin to happen: *The country is on the edge of financial collapse.* IDM **be on 'edge; put sb/sth on 'edge** to be nervous or uncertain: *The increasing oil price has* ***put*** *markets on edge.*
• *v.* [I] (*with an adv. or a prep.*) (esp. in newspapers) to increase or decrease slightly in value or level: *The share price edged up 1%.*

**EDI** /ˌiː diː 'aɪ/ = ELECTRONIC DATA INTERCHANGE

**EDR** /ˌiː diː 'ɑː(r)/ = EUROPEAN DEPOSITARY RECEIPT

**edutainment** /ˌedju'teɪnmənt/ *n.* [U,C] products such as computer software, books and television programmes that both educate and entertain; the activity of using a form of entertainment in order to teach sb sth ▸ **ˌedu'tain** *v.* [T,I]

**EEA** /ˌiː iː 'eɪ/ = EUROPEAN ECONOMIC AREA

**'e-eˌnabled** *adj.* using the Internet to do business, to communicate with other people, companies, etc: *an ~ business/company*

**EEO** /ˌiː iː 'əʊ; *AmE* 'oʊ/ *abbr* (*HR*) equal employment opportunity

**EEOC** /ˌiː iː əʊ 'siː; *AmE* oʊ/ = EQUAL EMPLOYMENT OPPORTUNITIES COMMISSION

★**effect** /ɪ'fekt/ *n., v.*
• *n.* **1** [C,U] a change that sb/sth causes in sb/sth else; a result: *The fall in tourism is having an adverse effect* ***on*** *business.* ◇ *Excluding the effect of exchange rates, profits grew 9.7%.*
○ *a* ***big/dramatic*** *~* • ***little/no*** *~* • *a* ***negative/positive*** *~* • *to* ***feel/suffer*** *the ~s (of sth)* • *to* ***offset/reverse*** *the ~s (of sth)*
**2 effects** [pl.] (*fml., written*) your personal possessions: *The insurance policy covers all personal effects.*
IDM **bring/put sth into ef'fect** to cause sth to come into use: *The recommendations will soon be put into effect.* **come into ef'fect** (*also* **take ef'fect**) to come into use; to begin to apply: *New controls come into effect soon.* **in ef'fect** (about a law or rule) in use: *These laws are in effect in twenty states.* **take ef'fect** = COME INTO EFFECT **to the effect that ...; to this/that ef'fect** (*fml.*) used in formal or legal documents to say that what has been written has a particular meaning, purpose or result **with immediate ef'fect; with effect from ...** starting now; starting from ...: *She has resigned with immediate effect.*
• *v.* [T] (*fml.*) to make sth happen: *You may* ***effect payment*** *for your order in several currencies.*

★**effective** /ɪ'fektɪv/ *adj.* **1** producing the result that is wanted or intended; producing a successful result: *The ad was simple but highly effective.* **2** (about laws, contracts, etc.) officially starting to apply: *The law becomes effective on 1 March.* **3** in reality, although not officially intended: *The bank has effective control of the company.* ▸ **ef'fectiveness** *n.* [U]

**efˌfective 'age** *n.* [C,U] (*Account.*) the age of an asset plus or minus a number of years depending on how bad or good its condition is judged to be

**ef'fective date** *n.* [C] (*usually* **the effective date** [sing.]) (*Law*) **1** the date on which a law or rule comes into use: *The effective date of the court order has been delayed for two weeks.* **2** a date chosen in a legal contract for when sth will happen or when sth must be done

**efˌfective 'tax rate** *n.* [C] (*abbr* **ETR**) (*Account.*) the total amount of tax that a business pays in a particular period of time divided by its total profit

★**efficiency** /ɪ'fɪʃnsi/ *n.* **1** [U] the ability to do sth well with no waste of time or money: *improvements in efficiency at the factory*
○ *to* ***achieve/boost/increase/maximize*** *~* • *~* ***gains/savings*** • *an ~* ***drive/programme***
**2 efficiencies** [pl.] ways of wasting less time and money or of saving time and money: *Where can efficiencies be made?* **3** (*Tech.*) [U] the relationship between the amount of energy that goes into a machine or an engine, and the amount that it produces: *The generator runs at 70% efficiency.*

★**efficient** /ɪ'fɪʃnt/ *adj.* doing sth well and thoroughly with no waste of time, money or energy: *an ~ organization/manager/service* ◇ *a fuel-efficient car* OPP INEFFICIENT
▸ **e'fficiently** /-ntli/ *adv.*: *an efficiently run company*

**ef'ficient con'sumer res'ponse** *n.* [U; sing.] (*abbr* **ECR**) (*Market.*; *Product.*) (used esp. in the food industry) a process in which manufacturers, suppliers and RETAILERS work together to reduce costs and give the public a better, faster service

**ef,ficient 'market** *n.* [C] (*Econ.*) a market in which the prices of shares, bonds, etc. are set by buyers and sellers who know all the current information that affects their value, with the result that prices are always accurate

**EFT** /eft; ,i: ef 'ti:/ *abbr* (*Finan.*) **,electronic 'fund(s) ,transfer** a system for making payments to and from bank accounts using computers; a payment that is made in this way: *Payment must be made by EFT.* ◇ *an EFT payment*

**EFTPOS** /'eftpɒs; *AmE* -pɑ:s/ *abbr* (*Comm.*) **electronic funds transfer at point of sale** a system used in shops/stores to allow people to pay for goods or services using a bank card or credit card. The money is paid directly from the customer's account by a computer link.

**egalitarian** /i,gælɪ'teəriən; *AmE* -'ter-/ *adj.* based on, or holding, the belief that everyone is equal and should have the same rights and opportunities: *~ companies/workplaces*

**EGM** /,i: dʒi: 'em/ = EXTRAORDINARY GENERAL MEETING

**'e-goods** *n.* [pl.] (*E-comm.*) products that you can buy on the Internet and transfer to your computer, such as software or electronic books

**EHO** /,i: eɪtʃ 'əʊ; *AmE* 'oʊ/ = ENVIRONMENTAL HEALTH OFFICER

**EI** /,i: 'aɪ/ = EMPLOYEE INVOLVEMENT

**EIS** /,i: aɪ 'es/ *abbr* **1 environmental impact statement** in the US, a written document that describes the good and bad effects on the environment of proposed projects, based on a scientific study **2** (*IT*) = EXECUTIVE INFORMATION SYSTEM

**'e-lance** *adj.* used to describe a way of earning money by using the Internet to sell your work or services to different organizations anywhere in the world: *e-lance workers* ▸ **'e-lance** *v.* [I] **'e-lancer** *n.* [C]

**elastic** /ɪ'læstɪk/ *adj.* (*Econ.*) used to describe the situation when a small change in one thing, such as the price of a product or service, or a change in people's incomes, results in a larger change in another thing, such as the amount that people want to buy: *Demand for oil is not very elastic.* OPP INELASTIC

**elas,ticity of 'demand** (*also* **'price elas'ticity of de'mand**) *n.* [C, usu. sing., U] (*Econ.*) the extent to which people want to buy more or less of a product or service when its price changes

**'e-,learning** *n.* [U] the process of learning sth using the Internet or an INTRANET

★ **elect** /ɪ'lekt/ *v.* [T] **~ sb (to sth) | ~ sb (as) sth** (*often pass.*) to choose sb to do a particular job by voting for them: *elected directors/representatives* ◇ *He has been elected to the committee.*

**election** /ɪ'lekʃn/ *n.* **1** [U,C] the process of choosing a person or a group of people for a position by voting: *the election of directors to the board* ◇ *to call/have/hold an ~* ◇ *to lose/win an ~* **2** [U] the fact of being chosen for a position by **election**: *Her election was a surprise.*

**e,lectrical engi'neering** *n.* [U] the design and building of machines and systems that use or produce electricity; the study of this ▸ **e,lectrical engi'neer** *n.* [C]

**electrician** /ɪ,lek'trɪʃn/ *n.* [C] a person whose job is to connect, repair, etc. electrical equipment

**electronic** /ɪ,lek'trɒnɪk; *AmE* -'trɑ:nɪk/ *adj.* HELP You will find most words formed with **electronic** at the form **e-**. **1** (about a device) having many small parts, such as MICROCHIPS, that control and direct a small electric current: *a manufacturer of ~ components/parts* **2** (about information) stored in electronic form on a disk, computer or MICROCHIP: *an electronic form of cash* **3** using an electronic system of communication, esp. the Internet, in order to exchange information, do business, etc: *electronic banking*

**,electronic 'cottage** *n.* [C] (*HR*; *IT*) a home, usu. in the country, where sb has the necessary computer and telephone equipment to work there instead of travelling to an office in a town or city

**,electronic 'data ,interchange** *n.* [U] (*abbr* **EDI**) (*IT*) the activity of exchanging standard business documents, such as order forms and INVOICES, electronically rather than on paper

**,electronic 'mail** = EMAIL *n.* (1)

**,electronic 'mall** = CYBER MALL

**ˌelectronic ˈpurse** *n.* [C] a small amount of money that is stored in electronic form, for example on a SMART CARD, and can be used to pay for sth instead of cash

★**electronics** /ɪˌlekˈtrɒnɪks; *AmE* -ˈtrɑːn-/ *n.* **1** [U] the branch of science and technology that studies electronic currents in electronic equipment **2** [U] the use of electronic technology, esp. in developing new equipment: *the ~ industry/sector* **3** [pl.] the electronic CIRCUITS and COMPONENTS (= parts) used in electronic equipment: *a fault in the electronics* **4** [pl.] electronic goods, such as CD players, televisions, etc: *strong demand for clothing and electronics*

**ˌelectronic ˈsignature** = DIGITAL SIGNATURE

**elephant** /ˈelɪfənt/ *n.* [C] (*infml.*) a way of referring to a company that is very large and employs a lot of people, but creates few new jobs

**ˈelevator pitch** *n.* [C] a very short, clear summary of a business idea or company for possible investors, that should last only the few minutes that a ride in an **elevator** would take

★**eligible** /ˈelɪdʒəbl/ *adj.* having the right to have sth or do sth, because you have the right qualifications, are the right age, etc: *Are you eligible* ***for*** *the new tax credit?* ◇ *All shareholders are eligible* ***to*** *vote.* OPP INELIGIBLE
▸ **ˌeligiˈbility** /-ˈbɪləti/ *n.* [U]

★**email** (*also* **e-mail**) /ˈiːmeɪl/ *n.*, *v.*
• *n.* **1** (*also* **ˌelectronic ˈmail**, *fml.*) [U] a way of sending messages and data to other people by means of computers connected together in a network: *You can contact us* ***by*** *email.*
✪ *to **have/use** ~* ♦ *an ~ **program/service/system***
**2** [C,U] a message sent by email: *We will send you an email confirming your order.*
✪ *to **fire off/forward/send** an ~ (to sb)* ♦ *to **get/receive** an ~ (from sb)* ♦ *to **check/delete/read** ~s*
• *v.* [T,I] **~ sth (to sb)** | **~ (sb) (sth)** to send a message to sb by email: *I'll email the documents to her.* ◇ *I'll email her the documents.*

**ˈemail acˌcount** *n.* [C] an arrangement with a company that allows you to receive, store and send emails

**EMAS** /ˈiːmæs/ *abbr* **Eco-Management and Audit Scheme** in the EU, a system that organizations can join if they want to reduce the harmful effects of what they do on the environment

**embargo** /ɪmˈbɑːɡəʊ; *AmE* ɪmˈbɑːrɡoʊ/ *n.* [C] (*pl.* **-goes**) (*Econ.*) an official order that prevents trade with another country: *The government has put an embargo* ***on*** *oil exports.*
✪ *to **enforce/impose** an ~ (on sth)* ♦ *to **end/lift** an ~* ♦ *an **oil**/a **trade** ~*
▸ **emˈbargo** *v.* [T] (**-goes**, **-going**, **-goed**, **-goed**): *All grain sales were embargoed.*

**embattled** /ɪmˈbætld/ *adj.* (used esp. in newspapers) surrounded by problems and difficulties: *the embattled chief executive*

**embed** (*also* **imbed**) /ɪmˈbed/ *v.* [T] (**-dd-**) (*IT*) (*usu. pass.*) **1** to fix electronic parts or a computer system inside a product so that it can perform a special function: *a washing machine with an embedded computer* **2** to include text, a piece of computer code or a computer program as part of a file, an Internet page, an email, etc: *an email with an embedded hyperlink*

**embezzle** /ɪmˈbezl/ *v.* [T,I] to steal money that you are responsible for or that belongs to your employer
▸ **emˈbezzlement** *n.* [U] **embezzler** /-ˈbezlə(r)/ *n.* [C]

**emerge** /iˈmɜːdʒ; *AmE* iˈmɜːrdʒ/ *v.* [I] **1** to appear or become known; to start to gain influence, power or wealth: *Amazon has emerged as a leader in e-commerce.* ◇ *emerging markets* **2** (about facts, ideas, etc.) to become known **3** to return to a normal state after a period of difficulty: *to emerge* ***from*** *bankruptcy*
▸ **eˈmergence** /-dʒəns/ *n.* [U]: *the emergence of new technologies*

**emergency** /iˈmɜːdʒənsi; *AmE* iˈmɜːrdʒ-/ *n.* [C,U] (*pl.* **-cies**) a sudden serious event or situation which needs immediate action: *an emergency board meeting*

**emission** /iˈmɪʃn/ *n.* **1** [C, usu. pl.] harmful gas, etc. that is sent out into the air: *~s from vehicles/power stations* **2** [U] the production or sending out of harmful gas, etc: *low emission cars*

**eˈmission ˌcredit** (*also* **eˈmissions ˌcredit**, **polˈlution ˌcredit**) *n.* [C, usu. pl.] a right to send out a measured amount of harmful gases into the air

**eˈmissions ˌtrading** *n.* [U] the activity of buying and selling EMISSION CREDITS

**eˈmission ˌunit** *n.* [C, usu. pl.] a right to send out a measured amount of harmful gases such as CARBON DIOXIDE into the air: *The Kyoto Protocol permits trading of emission units between countries.*

**emolument** /ɪˈmɒljumənt; *AmE* ɪˈmɑːl-/ *n.* [C, usu. pl.] (*Account., fml.*) the total amount of money that sb gets for the job they do or the position they hold, including any extra benefits that they receive

**ˈe-ˌmoney** (*also* **ˌelectronic ˈmoney, ˌdigital ˈmoney**) *n.* [U] money stored in electronic form, for example on a SMART CARD or in the memory of a computer, that can be used to make electronic payments

**emoticon** /ɪˈməʊtɪkɒn; *AmE* ɪˈmoʊtɪkɑːn/ *n.* [C] a short set of keyboard symbols that represents the expression on sb's face, used in email, etc. to show your feelings. For example, :-) means a smiling face.

**eˌmotional ˈcapital** *n.* [sing; U] (*HR*) the feelings, beliefs and values of a company's employees that make good relationships possible and help a business to be successful

**eˌmotional inˈtelligence** *n.* [U] (*HR*) the ability of a person to understand, control and use their feelings and to understand the feelings of others

**empire** /ˈempaɪə(r)/ *n.* [C] a group of commercial organizations controlled by one person or company

⊙ *to* ***build (up)/expand/run*** *an ~* ♦ *a* ***business/media/retail*** *~*

★**employ** /ɪmˈplɔɪ/ *v., n.*

• *v.* [T] **1** to give sb a job to do for payment: *How many people does the company employ?* ◇ *He is employed* ***as*** *a systems analyst.* **2** (*fml.*) to use sth such as a skill, method, etc. for a particular purpose: *the accounting practices employed by large companies*

• *n.* IDM **in sb's emˈploy; in the emˈploy of sb** (*fml.*) working for sb; employed by sb: *How long has she been in your employ?*

**employable** /ɪmˈplɔɪəbl/ *adj.* having the skills and qualifications that will make sb want to employ you

▸ **emˌployaˈbility** /-ˈbɪləti/ *n.* [U]

**employed** /ɪmˈplɔɪd/ *adj.* **1** having a job: *~ people/adults/workers* ◇ *a fully employed economy* SYN WORKING **2 the employed** *n.* [pl.] people who are **employed**: *Factory-floor workers account for 50% of the employed.*

★**employee** /ɪmˈplɔɪiː/ *n.* [C] a person who is paid to work for sb: *The firm has over 500 employees.*

⊙ ***full-time/part-time*** *~s* ♦ ***key/junior/senior*** *~s* ♦ *to* ***hire/recruit/retain*** *~s* ♦ *to* ***dismiss/fire/lay off*** *~s* ♦ *~* ***benefits/rights***

**emˌployee asˈsistance ˌprogramme** (*also* **emˌployment asˈsistance ˌprogramme**) *n.* [C] (*abbr* **EAP**) (*HR*) a service that employers offer that helps employees with problems that may affect the way they do their job

**emˌployee ˈbuyout** *n.* [C] (*Finan.*) a situation in which the employees gain control of a company, or a particular part of it, by buying most of its shares

**emˌployee inˈvolvement** *n.* [U] (*abbr* **EI**) (*HR*) ways of making employees feel that they are an important part of a company so that they will work better, esp. by allowing them to take part in making decisions on things that affect them

**emˌployee ˈleasing** *n.* [U] (*HR*) **1** an arrangement in which workers are supplied to work in a company for a short time **2** an arrangement in which a business that has special skill in employing people takes over responsibility for some or all of the employees of a company and pays them, arranges their benefits, etc.

**emˌployee ˈownership** *n.* [U] (*HR*) the situation when workers own some or all of the shares in their company

**emˌployee partiˈcipation** (*also* **ˌworker partiˈcipation**) *n.* [U] (*HR*) a system where employees take part in making decisions

**emˌployee reˈferral ˌprogramme** *n.* [C] (*HR*) esp. in the US, a policy of encouraging employees to suggest people that they know for a job, usu. by offering money

**emˌployee reˈlations** *n.* [pl.] (*abbr* **ER**) (*HR*) ways in which managers exchange information and ideas with their employees, involve them in making decisions and encourage them to want to work well; the department of a company responsible for this

**emˌployee self ˈservice** *n.* [U] (*abbr* **ESS**) (*HR*) a system in which employees can use the Internet to do administrative tasks connected with their pay, benefits, etc. that used to be done by managers or office staff

**em͵ployee 'share ͵owner-ship plan** (*BrE*) (*AmE* **em͵ployee 'stock ͵ownership plan**) *n.* [C] (*abbr* **ESOP**) (*Finan.*; *HR*) a system in which a company gives its employees shares, or allows them to buy shares, so that they receive part of the profit SYN SHARE INCENTIVE PLAN

**em͵ployee 'stock ͵option** *n.* [C] (*abbr* **ESO**) (*Finan.*; *HR*) the right given to some employees in a company to buy shares in the company at a fixed price

**em͵ployee 'stock ͵owner-ship plan** = EMPLOYEE SHARE OWNERSHIP PLAN

★ **employer** /ɪm'plɔɪə(r)/ *n.* [C] a person or company that pays people to work for them: *one of the largest employers in the area* ◇ *How long have you been working for your current employer?*
⊕ ***a big/major/small*** *~* ◆ ***a private sector/public sector*** *~* ◆ ***a former/potential/previous/prospective*** *~*

**em͵ployer of 'record** *n.* [C] (*AmE*) (*HR*; *Law*) the person or company who is legally responsible for employees' pay, taxes, benefits, etc.

★ **employment** /ɪm'plɔɪmənt/ *n.* **1** [U,C] work, esp. when it is done to earn money; the state of being employed: *to be in paid employment* ◇ *conditions/terms of ~*
⊕ ***full-time/part-time/seasonal/temporary*** *~* ◆ *to* ***find/get/have/take up*** *~* ◆ *an ~* ***contract***
**2** [U] the situation in which people have work: *full employment* (= when nobody is unemployed) ◇ *school-leavers entering the employment market* OPP UNEMPLOYMENT
⊕ ***falling/high/low*** *~* ◆ *to* ***boost/create/cut*** *~* ◆ *~* ***data/figures***
**3** [U] the act of employing sb: *Expansion will mean the employment of sixty extra workers.*

**em'ployment ͵agency** (*BrE also* **'staff ͵agency**) *n.* [C] (*HR*) a business that helps people to find work and employers to find workers

**em͵ployment as'sistance ͵programme** = EMPLOYEE ASSISTANCE PROGRAMME

**em'ployment costs** *n.* [pl.] the amount of money that a business spends on employing people, including wages, payments for health insurance, pensions, etc.

**em͵ployment 'equity** *n.* [U] the policy of giving everyone the same chances of employment, esp. by helping groups that are often treated unfairly because of their race, sex, etc.

**em'ployment law** *n.* [U] the collection of laws that deal with all aspects of employment and the rights of people who are employed SYN LABOUR LAW

**em'ployment pro͵tection** (*also* **'job pro͵tection**) *n.* [U] (*HR*) a group of laws that protect the rights of workers in a company, including pay, time away from work, etc.; the rights that are protected

**em͵ployment re'lations** *n.* [pl.] (*HR*) the rights of employees, employers, unemployed and SELF-EMPLOYED people and the relations between individuals, organizations and the government; the laws that deal with this: *the 1999 Employment Relations Act*

**em͵ployment re'lationship** *n.* [sing.] (*Law*) the situation that exists when an employer pays an employee for work or services, usu. with written conditions

**em͵ployment se'curity** (*also* **se͵curity of em'ployment**) *n.* [U] a situation where a job is likely to last for a long time and you will keep the job if you do what you are expected to SYN JOB SECURITY

**em'ployment tax** *n.* [U,C] (*AmE*) (*Account.*) the amount of money that you pay to the government according to how much you earn, which is taken out of your pay by your employer

**em͵ployment tri'bunal** (*also* **in͵dustrial tri'bunal**, *old-fash.*) *n.* [C] (*HR*) in the UK, a type of court that can deal with disagreements between employees and employers

**emporium** /em'pɔːriəm/ *n.* [C] (*pl.* **-riums** *or* **-ria** /-riə/) **1** a shop/store where you can buy a wide variety of a particular type of goods: *a fashion emporium* **2** (*old-fash.*) a large shop/store

**empower** /ɪm'paʊə(r)/ *v.* [T] (*often pass.*) **1** to give sb the ability and confidence to control the situation they are in: *The Internet empowers consumers to shop efficiently.*
**2** (*fml.*) to give sb the power or authority to do sth: *Congress has empowered a committee to investigate the claims.* SYN AUTHORIZE

**empowerment** /ɪm'paʊəmənt; *AmE* -'paʊər-/ *n.* [U] (*HR*) when managers give employees more responsibility to control their own work, make their own decisions, etc.

ˌ**empty ˈnester** /ˌempti ˈnestə(r)/ *n.* [C, usu. pl.] a parent whose children have grown up and left home

**EMS** /ˌiː em ˈes/ *n., abbr*
• *n.* **1** [U] **enhanced message service** a system for sending pictures, music and long written messages from one mobile phone/cellphone to another **2** [C] a message sent by **EMS**
• *abbr* = ENVIRONMENTAL MANAGEMENT SYSTEM

**EMU** /ˈiːmjuː; ˌiː em ˈjuː/ *abbr* **European Monetary Union** an arrangement by which countries in Europe use similar economic policies and a single currency (the **euro**); the group of countries who use the euro: *~ entry/membership*

**-enabled** /ɪˈneɪbld/ *comb. form* (*used in compound adjs*) that can be used with a particular system or technology, esp. the Internet: *Your browser is not Java-enabled.*

**enabling** /ɪˈneɪblɪŋ/ *adj.* giving sb/sth new powers or abilities to do particular things: *We are developing an* ***enabling technology*** *for wireless Internet.*

**enc.** = ENCL.

**encash** /ɪnˈkæʃ/ *v.* [T] (*BrE*) (*fml.*) **1** (*Finan.; Insur.*) to exchange an investment for money: *You will receive a lump sum when the policy is encashed.* SYN CASH STH IN at CASH **2** (*Finan.*) to exchange a cheque, etc. for money: *a charge for encashing foreign cheques* SYN CASH
▸ **enˈcashment** *n.* [U,C]

**encl.** (*also* **enc.**) *abbr* a short way of writing **enclosed** or **enclosure** on business letters: *draft agenda encl.*

**enclose** /ɪnˈkləʊz; *AmE* ɪnˈkloʊz/ *v.* [T] to put sth in the same envelope, parcel/package, etc. as sth else: (*fml.*) *Please* ***find enclosed*** *a cheque for €300.*

**enclosure** /ɪnˈkləʊʒə(r); *AmE* -ˈkloʊ-/ *n.* [C] something that is placed in an envelope with a letter

**encrypt** /ɪnˈkrɪpt/ *v.* [T] (*IT*) to put information into a special code, esp. in order to prevent people from looking at it without permission: *encrypted data* OPP DECRYPT ▸ **encryption** /-ˈkrɪpʃn/ *n.* [U,C]

**end** /end/ *n., v.*
• *n.* **1** [sing.] the final part of a period of time, an event or an activity: *They plan to cut 2 500 jobs by the end of the year.* ◇ *an end-of-season sale* **2** [C] a point or level that is the highest or lowest in a particular range: *We are aiming at the premium* (= very expensive) *end of the market.* **3** [sing.] a situation in which sth does not exist any more: *Her contract* ***comes to an end*** *in June.* **4** [C, usu. sing.] a part of an activity with which sb is concerned, esp. in business: *the marketing end of the business* **5** [C, usu. sing.] either of two places connected by a telephone call, journey, etc.
IDM **make (both) ends ˈmeet** to earn just enough money to be able to buy the things you need, pay what you owe, etc. → idioms at DEEP *adj.*, SHARP
• *v.* [T,I] to finish; to make sth finish: *The meeting ended early.* ◇ *a loss for the year ending 31 August*

ˌ**end conˈsumer** *n.* [C] a member of the public who buys and uses a product

ˌ**end-of-ˈyear** *adj.* relating to the end of December; relating to the end of a FINANCIAL YEAR: *the company's end-of-year results*

**endorse** (*AmE also* **indorse**) /ɪnˈdɔːs; *AmE* ɪnˈdɔːrs/ *v.* [T] **1** to say publicly that you support a person, statement or course of action: *I strongly endorse the directors' plans.* **2** (*Market.*) to say in an advertisement that you use and like a particular product or service so that other people will want to buy or use it: *We used a celebrity to endorse our restaurant.* **3** (*Finan.*) to sign the back of a cheque or BILL OF EXCHANGE so that it can be paid to sb else; to sign the back of a cheque in order to receive cash from the bank: *to endorse a cheque* **4** (*Insur.*) to add conditions to a standard insurance policy so that it applies to particular circumstances ▸ **enˈdorsement** (*AmE also* **indorsement**) *n.* [C,U]: ***celebrity*** *endorsement* ◇ *a policy endorsement* **enˈdorser** (*AmE also* **indorser**) *n.* [C]: *a celebrity endorser*

**endowment** /ɪnˈdaʊmənt/ *n.* **1** [C,U] money that is given to a school, a college or another institution to provide it with an income; the act of giving this money: *The university has a $10.5 bn endowment fund.* **2** (*Finan.; Insur.*) [C] a type of investment that you can buy from an insurance company in which you make regular payments over a period of time, or until you die, after which the company pays out an amount of money: ***25-year endowment policies***

**enˈdowment ˌmortgage** *n.* [C] (*BrE*) a type of **mortgage** in which money is regularly paid into an **endowment**. At the end of a particular period of time this money is then used to pay back the money that was borrowed.

**ˌend ˈproduct** *n.* [C] sth produced by a particular activity or process: *This report is the end product of two years of market research.*

**ˌend-to-ˈend** *adj.* (*IT*) connected with all the stages of a process or an activity: *end-to-end testing of the system*

**ˌend-ˈuser** (*AmE also* **end user**) *n.* [C] a person who actually uses a product rather than one who makes or sells it SYN ULTIMATE CONSUMER

**energy** /ˈenədʒi; *AmE* -ərdʒi/ *n.* [U] a source of power, such as fuel, used for driving machines, providing heat, etc: *energy-saving equipment* ○ *nuclear/solar/wind ~* ◆ *an ~ company/supplier*

★**enforce** /ɪnˈfɔːs; *AmE* ɪnˈfɔːrs/ *v.* [T] **1** to make sure that people obey a particular law or rule: *The rules were strictly enforced.* **2** to make sth happen or force sb to do sth: *enforced redundancies* ▸ **enˈforceable** /-əbl/ *adj.*: *legally enforceable contracts* **enˈforcement** *n.* [U]

**engage** /ɪnˈɡeɪdʒ/ *v.* [T] (*fml.*) **~ sb (as sth/to do sth)** to employ sb to do a particular job: *He is currently engaged as a consultant.*

**engagement** /ɪnˈɡeɪdʒmənt/ *n.* **1** [C] an arrangement to do sth at a particular time, esp. sth official or sth connected with your job: *I had to refuse because of a* ***prior*** *engagement.* ◇ *an ~ book/diary* **2** (*HR*) [U,C] an arrangement to employ sb: *the* ***terms of engagement***

**enˈgagement ˌletter** = LETTER OF ENGAGEMENT

**engine** /ˈendʒɪn/ *n.* [C] **1** the part of a vehicle that produces power to make the vehicle move: *a diesel/petrol ~* **2** a thing that makes sth happen or has a very strong influence: *China will become the* ***engine of growth*** *for Asia.* **3** (*IT*) the part of a computer program designed to keep performing a particular task: *charges processed through the payment engine*

★**engineer** /ˌendʒɪˈnɪə(r); *AmE* -ˈnɪr/ *n., v.*

• *n.* [C] **1** a person whose job involves designing and building engines, machines, roads, bridges, etc. **2** a person who is trained to repair machines and electrical equipment: *a telephone engineer* **3** a person whose job is to control and repair engines, esp. on a ship or an aircraft: *a flight engineer*

• *v.* [T] **1** to design and build sth: *The car is beautifully engineered.* **2** to arrange for sth to happen or take place, esp. when this is done secretly in order to give yourself an advantage: *to engineer a merger*

★**engineering** /ˌendʒɪˈnɪərɪŋ; *AmE* -ˈnɪr-/ *n.* [U] the activity of applying scientific knowledge to the design, building and control of machines, roads, bridges, electrical equipment, etc: *an impressive piece of engineering* ◇ *an ~ company/firm*

**enhance** /ɪnˈhɑːns; *AmE* -ˈhæns/ *v.* [T] to improve the good quality, value or status of sb/sth: *enhancing the reputation of the company* ◇ *The acquisition has enhanced earnings.* ▸ **enˈhanced** *adj.*: *enhanced productivity* **enˈhancement** *n.* [U,C]: *software enhancements*

**enquire** (*also* **inquire**, *esp. in AmE*) /ɪnˈkwaɪə(r)/ *v.* [I] to ask sb for some information: *Several people called to enquire* ***about*** *the service.* ▸ **enˈquirer** (*also* **inquirer**, *esp. in AmE*) *n.* [C] PHR V **enˈquire into sth** to find out more information about sth

★**enquiry** (*also* **inquiry**, *esp. in AmE*) /ɪnˈkwaɪəri; *AmE usu.* ˈɪnkwəri/ *n.* (*pl.* **-ries**) **1** [C] **~ (from sb) (about sb/sth)** a request for information about sb/sth; a question about sb/sth: *a telephone enquiry* ◇ *I'll have to* ***make*** *a few* ***enquiries*** (= try to find out about it). ◇ *to answer/deal with/handle an ~* **2** [C] an official process to find out the cause of sth or to find out information about sth: *an internal enquiry into the accident* ◇ *to conduct/hold/launch an ~* **3** [U] the act of asking questions or collecting information about sb/sth: *scientific enquiry* **4 enquiries** [pl.] (*BrE*) a place where you can get information: *Ask about your bag at enquiries.* **5** (*IT; Product.*) [C,U] the act of finding information, for example about orders, costs or stock, that is stored in electronic form: *using SAP for a basic stock enquiry*

**enter** /ˈentə(r)/ *v.* [T] **1** to begin taking part in an activity or a situation, esp. to start competing in a particular kind of business: *As more manufacturers enter* ***the market****, price falls sharply.* **2** (*not pass.*) (about people or products) to arrive in a country or region: *tariffs on steel entering the US market* **3** to begin or reach a particular period of time in a process: *The strike is entering its seventh month.* **4** (*not pass.*) to start working in a profession or career: *the number of young people entering the workforce*

**5 ~ sth (in/into/on sth)** to put information into a set of accounts, a list, a computer file, etc: *Enter your username and password.* IDM **enter/join the 'fray** to join in a situation in which people or companies are competing with each other for sth **enter 'service** to start to be used for the first time: *The new aircraft will be ready to enter service in 2009.* → idiom at FORCE *n.* PHR V **'enter into sth (with sb)** to begin sth or become involved in sth, esp. an official discussion or agreement: *Management has agreed to enter into discussions with the unions.*

★ **enterprise** /'entəpraɪz; *AmE* -tərp-/ *n.* **1** [C] a company or business: *a thriving fast-food enterprise* ◇ *a loss-making enterprise*
○ *a* ***family/multinational/state-owned*** *~* ◆ *a* ***large/medium-sized/small*** *~* ◆ *to* ***invest in/manage/run*** *an ~* ◆ *an ~* ***grows/fails/succeeds***
**2** [C] a business project or activity, esp. one that is difficult or involves taking risks: *a joint enterprise between French and Japanese companies* SYN VENTURE
○ *a* ***business/commercial*** *~* ◆ *an* ***ambitious****/a* ***difficult****/an* ***exciting*** *~* ◆ *to* ***start/undertake*** *an ~* ◆ *an ~* ***fails/succeeds***
**3** [U] the activity of starting and developing businesses: *grants to encourage enterprise in the region* **4** [U] the ability to think of new projects and make them successful, esp. by taking risks: *She has shown great enterprise.*

**'enterprise appli,cation** *n.* [C] (*IT*) software that is designed to help an organization manage an important part of the business, such as the payment of staff and supplies of goods, and is used by many different parts of the organization

**,enterprise appli,cation inte'gration** *n.* [U] (*abbr* **EAI**) (*IT*) a central service that links other pieces of software within an organization so that information can easily be shared

**,enterprise 'bargaining** = WORKPLACE BARGAINING

**'enterprise ,centre** *n.* [C] an office where people who want to start or develop a small business can get information, advice and help

**,enterprise re'source ,planning** *n.* [U] (*abbr* **ERP**) (*Product.*) a software system that links together all the aspects of a company's activities, such as finance, manufacturing, HR and DISTRIBUTION, designed to help the business manage and control its work most efficiently

**'enterprise zone** *n.* [C] (*Econ.*) an area of a country which the government helps by encouraging companies to open new offices and factories there, usu. by offering them financial benefits

**enterprising** /'entəpraɪzɪŋ; *AmE* -tərp-/ *adj.* able to think of new projects or new ways of doing things and make them successful

**entertainment** /,entə'teɪnmənt; *AmE* -tər't-/ *n.* [U] **1** (*HR*) the act of taking a company's customers out for meals, drinks, etc.; the money spent on this: *corporate entertainment* ◇ *an entertainment budget* **2** the business of making films/movies, television programmes, records, etc. to entertain people: *the entertainment industry*

**entitle** /ɪn'taɪtl/ *v.* [T] (*usu. pass.*) to give sb the right to do or to have sth: *If you are over 65 years of age you are entitled to a reduction.*

**entitlement** /ɪn'taɪtlmənt/ *n.* **1** [U] the official right to have or do sth: *This may affect your entitlement to the full pension.* **2** [C] something that you have an official right to; the amount that you have the right to receive: *Staff must use their full holiday entitlement.* **3** [C] (*AmE*) a government system that provides financial support to a particular group of people: *a reform of entitlements*

**entity** /'entəti/ *n.* [C] (*pl.* **-ties**) (*Account.*; *Law*) a business that exists as a separate unit and has its own legal identity: *giant corporate entities* ◇ *an independent entity*

**entrant** /'entrənt/ *n.* [C] **~ (to sth)** **1** (*Market.*) a company that starts to sell goods or services in a particular market: *new entrants in the market* ◇ *a late entrant to the industry* **2** a person who has recently joined a profession, university, etc.

**entrepôt** /'ɒntrəpəʊ; *AmE* 'ɑːntrəpoʊ/ *n.* [C] (*Trade*) a port or other trading centre where goods are brought for import and export and are stored before being sent somewhere else

★ **entrepreneur** /,ɒntrəprə'nɜː(r); *AmE* ,ɑːn-/ *n.* [C] a person who makes money by starting or running businesses, esp. when this involves taking financial risks: *a dotcom/fashion/an Internet ~*
▸ **,entrepre'neurial** /-'nɜːriəl/ *adj.*: *entrepreneurial skills* **,entrepre'neurialism** /-'nɜːriəlɪzm/ *n.* [U]

**ˌentrepreˈneurship** /-ˈnɜːʃɪp; *AmE* -ˈnɜːr-/ *n.* [U]

**entry** /ˈentri/ *n.* (*pl.* **-ries**) **1** [U] the right or opportunity to take part in sth or become a member of an organization, a profession or a group: *They opposed early entry* **into** *the euro.* ◇ *We have 30 graduate entry positions.* ◇ *to gain/negotiate ~ (to sth)* **2** (*Market.*) [U] when a company starts competing in a particular kind of business: *Shell's entry* **into** *Japan's retail gas market* ◇ *to gain/plan ~ (into sth)* **3** (*Account.*; *IT*) [C] an item, for example a piece of information, that is written or printed in a set of accounts, a computer file, a diary, etc: *an accounting entry* ◇ *to check/make/write an ~* **4** (*IT*) [U] the act of putting information into a computer: *The manual entry of some information led to errors.* ◇ *to do/handle/speed up ~* **5** [U] the right of people or goods to enter a place; the act of entering a place: *an entry visa* ◇ *new entry points for goods* ◇ *to be denied/be granted/be refused ~*

**ˈentry ˌbarrier** = BARRIER TO ENTRY

**ˈentry ˌlevel** (*also* **entry-level**, *esp. in AmE*) *n.* [C,U] **1** (*HR*) (*esp. AmE*) the lowest level of job in a particular profession, company, etc: *recruiting at the entry level* **2** the most basic of a group of similar products, suitable for new users who may later move on to a more advanced product ▸ **ˈentry-ˌlevel** *adj.*: *an entry-level job* ◇ *an entry-level computer*

**envelope** /ˈenvələʊp; ˈɒn-; *AmE* ˈenvəloʊp; ˈɑːn-/ *n.* [C] **1** a flat paper container used for sending letters in: *an airmail/a padded/prepaid ~* **2** a flat container made of plastic for keeping papers in → idiom at PUSH *v.*

**environment** /ɪnˈvaɪrənmənt/ *n.* **1** [C,U] the conditions that affect the behaviour and development of sb/sth; the physical conditions that sb/sth exists in: *a pleasant working environment* ◇ *the changing business environment* **2 the environment** [sing.] the natural world in which people, animals and plants live: *to protect the environment* **3** (*IT*) [C] the complete structure within which a user, computer or program operates: *a desktop development environment* ▸ **enˌvironˈmental** /-ˈmentl/ *adj.*: *environmental damage* **enˌvironˈmentally** /-ˈmentəli/ *adv.*

**enˌvironmental aˈnalysis** = ENVIRONMENTAL SCANNING

**enˌvironmental ˈhealth** *n.* [U] the activity of making sure that people are not damaged by the conditions in which they live or work: *the environmental health department*

**enˌvironmental ˈhealth ˌofficer** *n.* [C] (*abbr* **EHO**) sb responsible for making sure that people are not damaged by the conditions in which they live or work

**enˌvironmental ˈimpact** *n.* [C, usu. sing., U] the effect that sth such as a new development, a business activity, etc. has on the environment: *the environmental impact of tourism*

**environmentalist** /ɪnˌvaɪrənˈmentəlɪst/ *n.* [C] a person who is concerned about the natural environment and wants to improve and protect it
▸ **enˌvironˈmentalism** *n.* [U]

**enˌvironmentally-ˈfriendly** (*also* **enˌvironment-ˈfriendly**) *adj.* (about products) not harming the environment: *~ cars/energy/fuel/packaging*

**enˌvironmental ˈmanagement ˌsystem** *n.* [U] (*abbr* **EMS**) the way in which a business plans to manage and control its activities in order to protect and preserve natural resources such as clean air and water, the countryside, etc.

**enˌvironmental ˈmarketing** = GREEN MARKETING

**enˌvironmental ˈscanning** *n.* [U] (*also* **enˌvironmental aˈnalysis** [U,C]) the process of obtaining and using information about current events, developments, changes, etc. that may affect an organization, so that the managers of the organization can plan its future

**enˌvironment-ˈfriendly** = ENVIRONMENTALLY-FRIENDLY

**EOC** /ˌiː əʊ ˈsiː; *AmE* oʊ/ = EQUAL OPPORTUNITIES COMMISSION

**EoI** /ˌiː əʊ ˈaɪ; *AmE* oʊ/ = EXPRESSION OF INTEREST

**EOQ** /ˌiː əʊ ˈkjuː; *AmE* oʊ/ = ECONOMIC ORDER QUANTITY

**EPOS** /ˈiːpɒs; *AmE* -pɑːs/ *abbr* (*Comm.*) **electronic point of sale** the electronic machines and computer systems used in shops/stores to record information about the goods sold

**ˌe-proˈcurement** *n.* [U] (*Product.*) the process of businesses obtaining supplies of goods or services using the Internet

**EPS** (*AmE usu.* **eps**) /ˌiː piː ˈes/ = EARNINGS PER SHARE

**EQ** /ˌiː ˈkjuː/ *abbr* (*HR*) **emotional quotient** (*used as a countable n.*) a measurement of a person's EMOTIONAL INTELLIGENCE, sometimes calculated from the results of special tests: *to have a high/low ~*

**equal** /ˈiːkwəl/ *adj.*, *v.*
• ***adj.*** **1** the same in size, quantity, value, etc. as sth else: *a commission equal **to** 5% of the selling price* ◇ *We have an equal number of men and women here.* **2** having the same rights or being treated the same as other people: *an equal partner in the business* **IDM** **on ˌequal ˈterms (with sb)** having the same advantages and disadvantages as sb else: *competing on equal terms*
• ***v.*** [T] (-ll-, *AmE* -l-) to be the same in size, quantity, value, etc. as sth else: *Profits equalled last year's.*

**ˌEqual Emˈployment Opporˌtunities Comˌmission** *n.* [sing.] (*abbr* **EEOC**) (*HR*) the organization in the US that tries to make sure that everyone has the same chances of employment, and is treated the same way at work, without differences of race, colour, religion or sex being considered

**ˌequal emˈployment opporˌtunity** = EQUAL OPPORTUNITY

**equality** /iˈkwɒləti; *AmE* iˈkwɑː-/ *n.* [U] the fact of being equal in rights, status, advantages, etc: *equality of opportunity* ◇ *promoting equality in the workplace*
⊕ *economic/gender/social ~* ♦ *to achieve/demand/promote ~*

**ˌEqual Opporˈtunities Comˌmission** *n.* [sing.] (*abbr* **EOC**) the organization in the UK that tries to make sure that women have the same chances of employment and the same pay as men, and that men and women are treated fairly at work

**ˌequal opporˈtunity** (*also* **ˌequal emˈployment opporˌtunity**) *n.* [U;C, usu. pl.] (*HR*) the idea that everyone should have the same chances of employment, without differences such as race, religion, sex or age being considered: *We are an equal opportunity employer.*

**ˌequal ˈpay** *n.* [U] (*HR*) the idea that men and women should receive the same pay for the same work

**equation** /ɪˈkweɪʒn/ *n.* [C] a statement showing that two amounts or values are equal

★ **equilibrium** /ˌiːkwɪˈlɪbriəm; ˌek-/ (*also* **ˌmarket equiˈlibrium**) *n.* [U; sing.] (*Econ.*) a situation in which the amount of particular goods or services that people want to buy (**demand**) at a particular price equals the amount that businesses want to supply (**supply**): *The steel market is **reaching** an equilibrium.* ◇ *The market is **in** equilibrium.*

**equiˈlibrium price** *n.* [C] (*Econ.*) the price at which the amount of a particular product or service being supplied equals the amount demanded

**equiˈlibrium ˌquantity** *n.* [C] (*Econ.*) the amount of a particular product or service being bought or sold at the EQUILIBRIUM PRICE

**equip** /ɪˈkwɪp/ *v.* [T] (-pp-) (*often pass.*) to supply sb/sth with what is needed for a particular purpose or task: *to build and equip a manufacturing plant* ◇ *a **fully** equipped office*

★ **equipment** /ɪˈkwɪpmənt/ *n.* [U] the machines, tools, etc. that are needed for a particular purpose or activity: *They supply equipment for the food industry.* ◇ *computer equipment* ◇ *a **piece of** equipment*
⊕ *to **install/use** ~* ♦ ***business/industrial/office/telecoms** ~*

★ **equity** /ˈekwəti/ *n.* **1** (*Finan.*) [U] the money for business activities (**capital**) that a company obtains by selling shares rather than from loans: *The company has raised €7 m of fresh equity.* ◇ *holding equity **in** a company*
⊕ *to **issue** ~* ♦ *an ~ **stake** (in sth)* ♦ *~ **holdings/investments*** ♦ *~ **markets/prices/values*** ♦ *an ~ **investor/trader***
**2** (*Finan.*; *Stock Ex.*) **equities** [pl.] shares in companies, esp. ORDINARY SHARES; the business of trading shares: *Investing in equities carries a fairly high risk.* ◇ *the equities market*
⊕ *to **buy/hold** equities* ♦ *to **invest in/sell/trade** equities*
**3** (*also* **ˈhome ˌequity** [U]) the value of a property after all debts have been paid: *to have/take out/use ~*

**ˈequity acˌcounting** *n.* [U] (*also* **ˈequity ˌmethod** [sing.]) (*Account.*) the practice of recording in your company's financial records the share of profits that you could claim from another company because you own part of it

**ˈequity ˌfinance** *n.* [U] (*Finan.*) money that a company gets by selling shares in order to finance its activities; the business of helping companies get money in this way: *to raise equity finance* ◇ *the bank's equity finance division* ▸ **ˈequity-ˌfinanced** *adj.*: *The firm is entirely equity-financed.* **ˈequity ˌfinancing** *n.* [U,C]

**ˈequity fund** *n.* [C] (*Finan.*) an investment company that invests the money that people pay into it in shares: *an equity fund manager*

**ˈequity ˌgearing** = GEARING

**ˈequity ˌkicker** *n.* [C] (*Finan.*) **1** a right to buy shares, often at a lower price than usual, that a company gives to sb as extra payment for receiving a loan **2** (*esp. AmE*) a share of the profits from a property that you promise to sb who lends you money to buy it

**the ˈequity ˌmethod** = EQUITY ACCOUNTING

**ˈequity share** *n.* [C] (*Finan.*) a share in a company that gives its owner the right to receive payments from profits and vote in company meetings; a number of these that sb owns: *issuing equity shares*

**ER** /ˌiː ˈɑː(r)/ = EMPLOYEE RELATIONS

**ˈe-reˌcruitment** *n.* [U] (*HR*) the practice of using the Internet to find new people to join a company

**ergonomic** /ˌɜːɡəˈnɒmɪk; *AmE* ˌɜːrɡəˈnɑːm-/ *adj.* designed to be used or operated in a safe, comfortable and efficient way: *an ~ chair/keyboard* ▸ **ˌergoˈnomically** /-ɪkli/ *adv.*

**ergonomics** /ˌɜːɡəˈnɒmɪks; *AmE* ˌɜːrɡəˈnɑːm-/ *n.* **1** (*AmE also* **ˌbiotechˈnology**) [U] the study of how offices, equipment, furniture, etc. can be made more comfortable, safe and efficient for working people to use **2** [pl.] the aspects of the design of sth that make it comfortable, safe and efficient to use: *the ergonomics of the workstation*
▸ **ergonomist** /ɜːˈɡɒnəmɪst; *AmE* ɜːrˈɡɑːn-/ *n.* [C]

**ERISA** /eˈrɪsə/ *abbr* **Employee Retirement Income Security Act** in the US, a law that protects the rights of people who take part in employee benefit and pension plans

**ERM** /ˌiː ɑːr ˈem/ = EXCHANGE RATE MECHANISM (1)

**erode** /ɪˈrəʊd; *AmE* ɪˈroʊd/ *v.* [T,I] (*often pass.*) to gradually destroy sth or make it weaker over a period of time; to be destroyed or made weaker in this way: *Unemployment is eroding consumer confidence.* ▸ **erosion** /ɪˈrəʊʒn; *AmE* ɪˈroʊʒn/ *n.* [U]: *brand/price erosion*

**ERP** /ˌiː ɑː ˈpiː; *AmE* ɑːr/ = ENTERPRISE RESOURCE PLANNING

**error** /ˈerə(r)/ *n.* [C,U] a mistake, esp. one that causes problems or affects the result of sth: *errors* ***in*** *the accounts* ◇ *The payment was made* ***in error*** (= by mistake).
⊙ *to correct/find/make an ~* ♦ *an accounting/a clerical ~* ♦ *a computer/factual/pricing ~* ♦ *a fatal/serious/small ~*

**ˈerror corˌrection** *n.* [U] (*IT*) a process by which a computer automatically corrects mistakes in data

**ˈerror ˌmessage** *n.* [C] (*IT*) a message that appears on a computer screen which tells you that you have done sth wrong or that the program cannot do what you want it to do

**Esc** = ESCAPE

**escalate** /ˈeskəleɪt/ *v.* **1** [T,I] to become or to make sth greater, more serious, etc: *The action could escalate the price war.* ◇ *escalating costs* **2** [T] to increase a price, charge, etc. in order to pay for a rise in the cost of materials, wages, etc: *Our fees are escalated* ***at*** *3% a year.*
▸ **ˌescaˈlation** /-ˈleɪʃn/ *n.* [C,U]

**ˈescalator clause** (*also* **escalator** /ˈeskəleɪtə(r)/, **escaˈlation clause**) *n.* [C] (*all esp. AmE*) a condition in a contract that allows wages, prices, etc. to increase or decrease in particular circumstances, for example when costs rise or fall: *The pension includes an escalator clause that raises payments in line with inflation.*

**escape** /ɪˈskeɪp/ *n.* [U] (*also* **esˈcape key** [C]) (*abbr* **Esc**) (*IT*) a button on a computer keyboard that you press to stop a particular operation or leave a program

**eˈscape clause** *n.* [C] a condition in a contract that allows you to break part of the contract in particular circumstances

**esˈcape key** = ESCAPE

**escrow** /ˈeskrəʊ; *AmE* ˈeskroʊ/ *n.* [U,C] (*IT; Law*) an arrangement in which sth valuable, such as a document, an amount of money, etc. is held by an independent person or organization until a particular condition has been met, when it is transferred to the person or organization who has a right to claim it; a document or valuable item held in this way: *The shares will be held* ***in escrow*** *pending completion of the sale.* ◇ *an escrow account* ▸ **ˈescrow** *v.* [T]

**ESO** /ˌiː es ˈəʊ; *AmE* ˈoʊ/ = EMPLOYEE STOCK OPTION

**ESOP** /ˈiːsɒp; *AmE* ˈiːsɑːp/ = EMPLOYEE SHARE OWNERSHIP PLAN, EMPLOYEE STOCK OWNERSHIP PLAN

**espionage** /ˈespiənɑːʒ/ *n.* [U] the activity of finding out secret information about a country or an organization for another one: ***industrial*** *espionage*

**ESS** /ˌiː es ˈes/ = EMPLOYEE SELF SERVICE

**est.** *abbr* **1** a short way of writing **established** to show when a company was formed: *Grove's Tea Merchants, est. 1982* **2** a short way of writing **estimated** to show that a figure is not exact: *Est. total cost: $47 m*

**establish** /ɪˈstæblɪʃ/ *v.* [T] **1** to start or create an organization, a system, etc. that is meant to last for a long time: *The treaty established a free trade zone across Europe.* **2 ~ sb/sth/yourself (in sth) (as sth)** to become successful, esp. in a new business: *It has quickly established itself as one of the top companies.*

**establishment** /ɪˈstæblɪʃmənt/ *n.* **1** [C] an organization, a large institution, a hotel or a restaurant: *a fast-food establishment* ◇ *a survey of business establishments* **2** (*usu.* **the establishment**) [sing. with sing./pl. verb] the people in a society or a profession who have influence and power and who usu. do not support change: *the banking establishment* **3** [U] the act of starting or creating sth that is meant to last for a long time: *the establishment of a pension scheme*

**estate** /ɪˈsteɪt/ *n.* **1** [C] (*BrE*) an area of land with a lot of houses, office buildings or factories of the same type on it: *There are several office buildings empty on the estate.* **2** (*Law*) [C,U] all the money and property that a person owns, esp. everything left when they die: *Her estate was left to her daughter.*

**eˈstate ˌagent** (*BrE*) (*also* **ˈreal estate ˌagent**, *AmE, BrE*) (*AmE also* **ˈRealtor™**) *n.* [C] a person or business that sells or rents houses, buildings and land for the owners, usu. in return for a fee that is a percentage of the price of the property ▸ **esˈtate ˌagency** (*BrE*) (*also* **ˈreal estate ˌagency**, *AmE, BrE*) *n.* [C]: *an estate agency chain*

**eˈstate tax** (*also* **ˈdeath tax**, *infml.*) *n.* [C,U] in the US, tax that must be paid on the value of the money and property of sb who has died

★ **estimate** *n., v.*
• *n.* /ˈestɪmət/ [C] **1** a judgement that you make without having the exact details or figures about the size, amount, cost, etc. of sth: *a rough estimate* ◇ *Earnings are in line with our estimates.*
⊙ *a **final**/an **initial**/a **preliminary** ~* ♦ *a **best** ~* ♦ *to **revise** an ~*
**2** (*Comm.*) a statement of how much a piece of work will probably cost: *We got estimates from three firms and accepted the lowest.*
⊙ *to **give (sb)**/**prepare**/**submit** an ~* ♦ *to **accept**/**ask for** an ~*
→ idiom at BALLPARK
• *v.* /ˈestɪmeɪt/ [T] (*often pass.*) to form an idea of the cost, size, value etc. of sth, but without calculating it exactly: *Sales are estimated **at** £6 bn.* ◇ *a contract estimated **to be** worth €100 m* ▸ **ˌestiˈmation** /-ˈmeɪʃn/ *n.* [C]: *Estimations of our total sales are around 50 million.*

**estimator** /ˈestɪmeɪtə(r)/ *n.* [C] a person whose job involves calculating the cost, price or value of sth

**ˈe-ˌtailer** *n.* [C] (*E-comm.*) a business that sells goods to the public on the Internet ▸ **ˈe-ˌtailing** *n.* [U]

**Ethernet** /ˈiːθənet; *AmE* -θərn-/ *n.* [sing.] (*IT*) a system for connecting a number of computer systems to form a network

**ethic** /ˈeθɪk/ *n.* **1 ethics** [pl.] moral principles that control or influence a person's behaviour: *professional/business/corporate ~* **2** [sing.] a system of moral principles or rules of behaviour: *a strong work ethic*

**ethical** /ˈeθɪkl/ *adj.* **1** morally correct or acceptable: *an ethical investment fund* (= that invests in companies, etc. considered morally acceptable) **2** connected with beliefs and principles about what is right and wrong: *an ethical problem* ▸ **ˈethically** /-kli/ *adv.*

**ˌethnic ˈmonitoring** *n.* [U] (*HR*) the activity of collecting and analysing information about the race of all the employees in a company to check that all races are present in a fair way

**ethos** /ˈiːθɒs; *AmE* ˈiːθɑːs/ *n.* [sing.] the moral ideas and attitudes that belong to a particular group, organization or society: *the company ethos*

**ˈe-ˌticket** (*also* **ˌelectronic ˈticket**) *n.* [C] **1** a series of numbers, letters or symbols that you receive instead of a paper ticket when you pay on the Internet or by telephone for a service, esp. to travel on a plane. It is recorded on the computer of the business that provides the service. **2** a ticket, for example, one to travel on a train or bus, which is stored electronically on a small plastic card ▸ **ˈe-ˌticketing** (*also* **ˌelectronic ˈticketing**) *n.* [U]

**etiquette** /ˈetɪket; *AmE* -kət/ *n.* [U] the rules of polite and correct behaviour: *business etiquette*

**ETR** /ˌiː tiː ˈɑː(r)/ = EFFECTIVE TAX RATE

**EU** /ˌiː ˈjuː/ = EUROPEAN UNION

**Euribor** /ˈjʊəribɔː(r); *AmE* ˈjʊribɔːr/ *abbr* (*Finan.*) **Euro Interbank Offered Rate** the average rate of interest that the largest European banks charge each other for borrowing an amount of euros for a particular period of time

**Euro** /ˈjʊərəʊ; *AmE* ˈjʊroʊ/ *adj.* (*infml.*) **1** (used esp. in newspapers) connected with Europe or the EU: *~ laws/leaders* **2** (*Finan.*) used to describe a currency or an investment that is traded in the EUROMARKETS: *Euro commercial paper*

**euro** /ˈjʊərəʊ; *AmE* ˈjʊroʊ/ *n.* (*pl.* **euros**) **1** [C] the unit of money of some countries of the EU; **€**: *The price is given in dollars or euros.* **2** (*often* **the euro** [sing.]) the system of using the **euro** as a national currency: *Will Denmark join the euro?*

**Euro-** /ˈjʊərəʊ; *AmE* ˈjʊroʊ/ *comb. form* **1** (*used to form ns and adjs*) connected with Europe or the EU: *a Euro-MP* **2** (*Finan.*) used with the name of a currency or an investment to indicate that it is traded in the EUROMARKETS: *Euro-Yen*

**ˈeuro ˌarea** = EUROZONE

**Eurobond** /ˈjʊərəʊbɒnd; *AmE* ˈjʊroʊbɑːnd/ (*also* **ˈglobal bond**) *n.* [C] (*Finan.*) a type of bond in a particular currency that governments and large organizations sell to international investors outside the country that uses that currency: *a five-year dollar-denominated eurobond*

**Eurocurrency** /ˈjʊərəʊkʌrənsi; *AmE* ˈjʊroʊkɜːr-/ *n.* [C,U] (*pl.* **-cies**) (*Finan.*) a form of money that is held or bought and sold outside its home country

**Eurodollar** /ˈjʊərəʊdɒlə(r); *AmE* ˈjʊroʊdɑːl-/ *n.* [C] (*Finan.*) a US dollar that is held in a bank account or borrowed by an organization outside the US

**Euroland** (*also* **euroland**) /ˈjʊərəʊlænd; *AmE* ˈjʊroʊ-/ *n.* [U] (*infml.*) (used esp. in newspapers) the countries in the EU that use the euro as a unit of money

**Euromarket** /ˈjʊərəʊmɑːkɪt; [C] *AmE* ˈjʊroʊmɑːrk-/ *n.* (*Finan.*) **1** [C] an international market in which banks and large organizations buy and sell EUROBONDS, EUROCURRENCIES, etc. **2** [sing.] the EU considered as a single financial or commercial market

**the ˈEuropean ˈCentral ˈBank** *n.* [sing.] (*abbr* **ECB**) a central bank for the countries in Europe who use the euro as their currency

**the ˌEuropean Comˈmission** *n.* [sing.] (*abbr* **EC**) a group of officials, led by a president, who run the EU and apply its laws. Its members are chosen by the governments of the countries in the EU

**ˈEuropean Deˈpositary Reˈceipt** *n.* [C] (*abbr* **EDR**) (*Stock Ex.*) a certificate issued by a European bank that represents a number of shares in a foreign company and is bought and sold on stock exchanges in Europe

**the ˈEuropean ˈEconomic ˈArea** *n.* [sing.] (*abbr* **EEA**) an agreement between many countries in Europe. People living in one of these countries can work in any of the others, and goods, money, etc. can be moved between the countries without having to pay taxes.

**ˈEuropean ˈMonetary ˈUnion** = EMU

**the ˌEuropean ˈUnion** *n.* [sing.] (*abbr* **EU**) an economic and political organization that many European countries belong to

**Eurostocks** /ˈjʊərəʊstɒks; *AmE* ˈjʊroʊstɑːks/ *n.* [pl.] (used esp. in newspapers) shares that are traded on European stock exchanges

**Eurozone** (*also* **eurozone**) /ˈjʊərəʊzəʊn; *AmE* ˈjʊroʊzoʊn/ (*also* **ˈeuro ˌarea**) *n.* [sing.] the countries in the EU that use the euro

**evade** /ɪˈveɪd/ *v.* [T] to find a way of not doing sth, esp. sth that legally or morally you should do: *evading taxes* ▸ **evasion** /ɪˈveɪʒn/ *n.* [C,U]: *fare evasion on public transport*

★ **evaluate** /ɪˈvæljueɪt/ *v.* [T] to study all the available information about sb/sth and then form an opinion about them/it: *We use tests to evaluate job candidates.* SYN ASSESS ▸ **eˈvaluative** /-juətɪv/ *adj.*

**evaluation** /ɪˌvæljuˈeɪʃn/ *n.* **1** [U] the process of studying all the available information about sb/sth and forming an opinion about them/it **2** [C] a spoken or written opinion about the quality, value, importance, etc. of sb/sth: *an annual performance evaluation*

**eˈvent ˌmanagement** *n.* [U] **1** (*Market.*) the activity of organizing events such as concerts, sports competitions, parties, etc. for companies as part of their marketing activities **2** (*Product.*) = SUPPLY CHAIN EVENT MANAGEMENT

**e'vent ˌmarketing** *n.* [U] **1** the activity of showing and advertising products or services to people in public places or at special events such as TRADE SHOWS **2** the activity of advertising and attracting people to a special event

**evidence** /'evɪdəns/ *n.* [U] the information that is used in a court to try to prove sth: *They found no evidence of wrongdoing.*

⊙ *to give/produce ~ ♦ to* ***consider/examine/hear/study*** *~ ♦ to* ***admit/allow/exclude*** *~*

**evolve** /i'vɒlv; *AmE* i'vɑːlv/ *v.* [T,I] to develop gradually, esp. from a simple to a more complicated form: *They have evolved* ***into*** *a major manufacturer.*

**EVP** /ˌiː viː 'piː/ = EXECUTIVE VICE-PRESIDENT

**ex** /eks/ *prep.* **1** (*BrE*) not including sth: *The price is €2 000 ex VAT.* **2** (*Trade*) used to show that a price or contract includes the cost of delivering goods to the place mentioned: *All prices are ex dock New York.* **3** (*Trade*) used to show that a price or contract does not include transport from the place mentioned: *ex factory* **4** (*Finan.*) used to show that the buyer of a share, bond, etc. will not receive the right to claim the thing mentioned: *As of 11 May, the shares will be traded ex bonus.* ◇ *ex-dividend (xd)* OPP CUM

★**exceed** /ɪk'siːd/ *v.* [T] **1** to be greater than a particular number or amount: *Sales are expected to exceed €250 m.* **2** to do more than the law or an order, etc. allows you to do: *exceeding your overdraft limit*

**excellence** /'eksələns/ *n.* [U] the quality of being extremely good: *an award for excellence* ***in*** *design* ◇ *to achieve manufacturing excellence*

**exception** /ɪk'sepʃn/ *n.* [C] **1** (*Insur.*) in an insurance policy, particular risks that you are not protected for **2** (*IT*) the fact that a computer cannot process an instruction in the normal way: *a daily exception report of sales that cannot be processed*

**exceptional** /ɪk'sepʃənl/ *adj.*, *n.*

• ***adj.*** **1** unusually good: *2006 was an exceptional year for us.* **2** very unusual: *exceptional* ***circumstances*** **3** (*Account.*) used to describe an amount of money in a company's financial records that is connected with normal business activities but is much larger than usual and will have an important effect on profits: *an exceptional* ***charge/item***

• ***n.*** [C] (*usu.* **exceptionals** [pl.]) (*Account.*) an **exceptional** item in a company's accounts

★**excess** *n.*, *adj.*

• ***n.*** /ɪk'ses/ **1** [sing; U] more than is necessary or acceptable: *an excess of diamonds in the marketplace* ◇ *Growth may be* ***in excess of*** (= more than) *5%.* **2** [C,U] an amount by which sth is larger than sth else: *We cover costs up to €800 and then you pay the excess.* **3** (*Insur.*) [C,U] the part of an insurance claim that you must pay while the insurance company pays the rest

• ***adj.*** /'ekses/ in addition to an amount that is necessary or that can be used: *trying to reduce excess stock*

**ˌexcess ca'pacity** *n.* [U] (*Econ.*; *Product.*) the ability to produce or supply more of a product or service than is needed; the extra quantity that could be produced or supplied

**ˌexcess de'mand** *n.* [U] (*Econ.*) a situation in which more of a product or service is wanted by buyers at a particular price than the industry can supply

**ˌexcess sup'ply** *n.* [U,C] (*Econ.*) a situation in which more of a product or service is supplied by an industry than buyers want at the price; the extra goods or services available

★**exchange** /ɪks'tʃeɪndʒ/ *n.*, *v.*

• ***n.*** **1** [C,U] an act of giving sth to sb or doing sth for sb and receiving sth in return: *an exchange of emails* ◇ *We agreed to a pay cut* ***in exchange for*** *shares in the company.* **2** (*Comm.*; *Finan.*) [C] an organized system that allows traders to buy and sell currencies, investments, goods, etc.; a place where this takes place: *trading* ***on*** *the Euronext exchange* ◇ *an electronic trading exchange for wood products* **3** [U] the process of changing an amount of one currency for an equal value of another **4** [C] an arrangement when two people or groups from different countries visit each other's homes or do each other's jobs for a short time

• ***v.*** [T] **1** to give sth to sb and receive sth else from them: *We exchanged business cards.* **2** to change an amount of one currency for another: *to exchange dollars for pesos* **3** if you **exchange** sth you have bought, or a shop/store **exchanges** it, you return it and get sth different or better **4** (*Law*) (*BrE*) **~ contracts (on sth)** to sign a contract with the person that you are buying a building or piece of land from IDM **exˌchange** 'hands = CHANGE HANDS at CHANGE *v.*

**exchangeable** /ɪks'tʃeɪndʒəbl/ *adj.* **1** that can be exchanged: *These vouchers are not exchangeable **for** cash.* **2** (*Finan.*) (about bonds) that can be exchanged for shares in another company at a particular time in the future

**ex'change con,trol** *n.* [C, usu. pl., U] (*Econ.*) a set of rules that a government uses to limit the amount of local currency that people can sell or the price at which they can sell it

**ex'change e,conomy** *n.* [C] (*Econ.*) an economy in which people trade goods with each other or buy goods using money

**ex'change ,market** = FOREIGN EXCHANGE MARKET

**ex,change of 'shares** (*BrE*) (*AmE* **ex,change of 'stock**) *n.* [C,U] (*Finan.*) when a company buys or joins with another company by using some of its shares to pay for shares in the other company: *The merger will be financed by an exchange of shares.*

**ex'change rate** (*also* **,rate of ex'change**) *n.* [C] the relation in value between one currency and another: *The current exchange rate is 50 rupees to the euro.* ◇ *The euro has a high exchange rate **against** the yen.* SYN CURRENCY RATE
● *a strong/weak ~* ◆ *a favourable ~* ◆ *the ~ drops/falls/rises*

**ex'change rate ex,posure** *n.* [U,C] (*Finan.*) the fact that a business may lose money in the future by needing to change one currency for another less valuable one: *Our high percentage of foreign sales means we face significant exchange rate exposure.*

**ex'change rate ,mechanism** *n.* (*Econ.*) **1 Exchange Rate Mechanism** (*abbr* **ERM**) [sing.] a way of linking the currencies of some EU countries and controlling their EXCHANGE RATES, before the euro was introduced in 1999 **2** [C] any system in which the values of different currencies are linked

**excise** /'eksaɪz/ *n.* [U] a tax on particular goods and services that are sold within a country, such as alcohol and cigarettes: *to freeze the excise **on** fuel* ◇ *~ duty/tax*

**excl.** *abbr* (*written*) excluding: *Price: $15 each (excl. GST)*

★ **exclude** /ɪk'sklu:d/ *v.* [T] **1** to deliberately not include sth: *The price of the trip excludes insurance.* OPP INCLUDE **2** to prevent sb/sth from entering a place or taking part in sth: *The public were excluded **from** the board meeting.*

**excluding** /ɪk'sklu:dɪŋ/ *prep.* not including: *Lunch costs $25 per person, excluding drinks.*

★ **exclusion** /ɪk'sklu:ʒn/ *n.* **1** [U] the act of preventing sb/sth from entering a place or taking part in sth: *The company faces exclusion **from** the FTSE 100.* **2** (*Law*) [C] a particular person, thing or situation that a contract, law, tax, etc. does not apply to: *Check the list of exclusions in the insurance policy.*

**exclusive** /ɪk'sklu:sɪv/ *adj.* **1** only given to one particular person, group or organization; not involving others: *The CEO has exclusive use of a company car.* ◇ *These products are exclusive **to** our company* (= no one else sells them). **2** being the only official one/ones: *the exclusive distributor of the products* **3** of a high quality and very expensive so not bought by many people: *an exclusive hotel* **4 ~ of sb/sth** not including sb/sth: *The price is exclusive of VAT.*

**exclusivity** /,eksklu:'sɪvəti/ *n.* [U] **1** the right to be the only person or organization to do sth: *Agents are given exclusivity to trade in certain areas.* ◇ *an ~ agreement/clause/contract/deal* **2** (*also* **exclusiveness** /ɪk'sklu:sɪvnəs/) the fact that people see a product or service as being of high quality and very expensive and therefore only for a few people: *a designer whose clothes have not lost their exclusivity*

**excuse** /ɪk'skju:s/ = SICK NOTE

**,ex-di'rectory** *adj.* (*BrE*) (about a person or telephone number) not listed in the public telephone book, at the request of the owner of the telephone SYN UNLISTED

**exec** /ɪg'zek/ *n.* [C] (*infml.*) an executive in a business: *high salaries paid to top execs*

**execute** /'eksɪkju:t/ *v.* **1** [T] to do a piece of work, put a plan into action, etc: *to ~ an order/a plan/strategy* ◇ *All trades* (= in shares, etc.) *are executed through a broker.* **2** [I] to achieve a particular business goal; to be successful as a business: *our managers' ability to execute* **3** (*IT*) [T] to make a computer perform an action: *~ a command/an instruction/a query* SYN RUN ▶ **,exe'cution** /-'kju:ʃn/ *n.* [U]: *The idea was good, but the execution was poor.* ◇ *an online execution service for futures*

PHR V 'execute on sth to complete a task or perform an activity

**exe'cution risk** *n.* [U,C] the risk that a new business, project, etc. will fail because it is not managed or carried out in the right way: *the execution risks associated with expanding into a new region*

★ **executive** /ɪg'zekjətɪv/ *n., adj.*
• *n.* **1** [C] a person who has an important job as a manager of a company or an organization: *Several top executives have left the company.*
○ *high-ranking/key/senior ~s • company/corporate/industry ~s • an advertising/a marketing/sales ~*
**2** [C with sing./pl. v.] a group of people who run a company or an organization: *the union's executive*
• *adj.* **1** connected with managing a business or an organization, and with making plans and decisions: *the executive management team*
○ *~ decisions/positions • ~ bonuses/pay/perks*
**2** having the power to put important laws and decisions into effect; connected with this: *He sits on the board but has no executive power.* **3** for the use of sb who is important; expensive and of good quality: *an ~jet/lounge/suite*

**e,xecutive as'sistant** *n.* [C] a person whose job is to help a senior manager or **executive** in a company by organizing their affairs, dealing with letters, etc. SYN EXECUTIVE SECRETARY

**e,xecutive 'chairman** *n.* [C] a person who is the most senior member of the BOARD of a large company and is also involved in running it

**e,xecutive di'rector** *n.* [C] a member of the BOARD that controls a company who is also employed as a senior manager of the company

**e,xecutive infor'mation ,system** *n.* [C] (*abbr* **EIS**) (*IT*) computer software that contains all the data and information that senior managers need to make decisions

**e'xecutive search** *n.* [C,U] (*HR*) the process of finding sb who is suitable for a very senior job in a company by looking at people working in other companies who have the right skills and experience

**e,xecutive 'secretary** *n.* [C]
**1** a person who works as secretary for a senior manager or an **executive** in a company SYN EXECUTIVE ASSISTANT, PA **2** the leader of some types of public or government organizations; a senior official in some businesses

**e,xecutive 'summary** (*also* **,management 'summary**, *less freq.*) *n.* [C] a short statement that gives the important facts, conclusions and suggestions of a report, usu. printed at the beginning

**e,xecutive ,vice-'president** *n.* [C] (*esp. AmE*) (*abbr* **EVP**) an important person who is in charge of a particular part of a business and who works closely with the CHIEF EXECUTIVE OFFICER

**e,xemplary 'damages** = PUNITIVE DAMAGES

★ **exempt** /ɪg'zempt/ *adj., v.*
• *adj.* **1** if sb/sth is **exempt** from sth, they are not affected by it, do not have to do it, pay it, etc: *Payments into a pension fund are exempt from tax.* **2** (*with ns*) not having to do, pay, etc. the thing mentioned: *to lose your **tax-exempt** status*
• *v.* [T] **~ sb/sth (from sth)** to decide officially that a rule or law, esp. one concerning payment of tax, will not apply to particular people or things: *They may exempt some products from the import tax.*

★ **exemption** /ɪg'zempʃn/ *n.*
**1** [U,C] official permission not to do sth or pay sth that you would normally have to do or pay: *You may qualify for exemption **from** some examinations.* ◇ *The law has a small-business exemption* (= it does not apply to small businesses). ◇ *to claim/grant (an) ~* **2** [C] an amount of income, profit, etc. on which you do not have to pay tax; a product or service on which tax is not charged: *a $4 000 personal exemption on income tax* ◇ *to claim/grant (an) ~*

**exercise** /'eksəsaɪz; *AmE* -sərs-/ *n., v.*
• *n.* **1** [C] an activity or series of activities that is designed to achieve a particular result: *a training/rebranding exercise* ◇ *to carry out/conduct/undertake an ... ~* **2** [U] the use of power or a right to make sth happen: *the exercise of choice by consumers* ◇ *to encourage/limit the ~ of sth* **3** (*Finan.*) [U] **~ of an option** an act of using an OPTION, esp. to buy or sell shares in a company: *revenues from the exercise of share options*
• *v.* [T] **1** to use your power or rights in order to achieve sth: *exercising tight control over costs* ◇ *to exercise a veto* **2** (*Finan.*) if you **exercise** an OPTION you use it, esp. in order to buy or sell shares in a company

**'exercise price** (*also* **'strike price, 'striking price**) *n.* [C] (*Finan.*) the price at which sb/sth can buy or sell shares in a company for which they own OPTIONS

**ˌex ˈfactory** = EX WORKS

**ˌex ˈgratia** /ˌeks ˈgreɪʃə/ *adj.* (*written*) given or done as a gift or favour, not because there is a legal duty to do it: *ex gratia payments* ▸ **ˌex ˈgratia** *adv.*

**exhaust** /ɪgˈzɔːst/ *v.* [T] to use all of sth so that there is none left: *The trust had exhausted its funds.*

**exhibit** /ɪgˈzɪbɪt/ *v.*, *n.*

• *v.* [T,I] to show sth in a public place for people to enjoy or to give them information: *They will be exhibiting new designs at the trade fairs this spring.*

• *n.* [C] **1** (*esp. AmE*) = EXHIBITION **2** an object or a collection of objects put in a public place for people to see

**exhibition** /ˌeksɪˈbɪʃn/ (*esp. BrE*) (*AmE usu.* **exˈhibit**) *n.* [C] a collection of things, for example products produced by different companies, that are shown to the public; an event at which these things are shown: *an exhibition of books* ◇ *The hotel has space for exhibitions.*

⊙ *to* ***have/hold*** *an* ~ ♦ *to* ***organize/set up*** *an* ~ ♦ *an* ~ ***centre/hall/stand***

**exhibitor** /ɪgˈzɪbɪtə(r)/ *n.* [C] an organization that shows their products or services at an exhibition

**Eximbank** /ˈeksɪmbæŋk/ = EXPORT-IMPORT BANK

**exit** /ˈeksɪt; ˈegzɪt/ *n.*, *v.*

• *n.* [C] **1** a way out of a public building or vehicle: *a fire exit* **2** an act of leaving, esp. when sb leaves a job, or an investor leaves a market: *the group's exit* ***from*** *the insurance business* ◇ *to find/look for/make an* ~ *(from sth)* **3** a way of ending an agreement, a contract, a loan, etc.; an act of doing so: *We must have an exit from the contract.* ◇ *an* ~ *charge/penalty*

• *v.* **1** [T,I] to go out; to leave a building, vehicle, etc: *We exited via the fire escape.* **2** [T] to leave a job; to stop being involved in sth, such as a type of business or an investment: *senior executives exiting the company* **3** (*IT*) [T] to finish using a computer program or a part of it

**ˈexit ˌbarrier** = BARRIER TO EXIT

**ˈexit charge** = BACK-END LOAD

**ˈexit ˌinterview** *n.* [C] (*HR*) a meeting between an employer and an employee who is leaving the company to find out why they are leaving

**ˌex ofˈficio** /ˌeks əˈfɪʃiəʊ; *AmE* -ʃioʊ/ *adj.*, *adv.* (*fml.*) included or allowed because of your job, position or rank: *an ex officio member of the committee*

**exorbitant** /ɪgˈzɔːbɪtənt; *AmE* -ˈzɔːrb-/ *adj.* (about a price) much too high: ~ *prices/fees/costs*

▸ **eˈxorbitantly** *adv.*: *exorbitantly high rates*

★ **expand** /ɪkˈspænd/ *v.* [T,I] **1** to become, or to make sth, greater in size, number or value: *The company recently expanded its board from 11 to 15 members.* ◇ *an expanding range of products* **2** if a business **expands** or **is expanded**, new branches are opened, it makes more money, etc: *Our business has expanded rapidly, from 16 to 30 stores in a year.*

▸ **expansion** /-ˈspænʃn/ *n.* [U,C]: *a period of rapid economic expansion* ◇ *plans for a major expansion of our retail business*

**expatriate** /ˌeksˈpætriət; *AmE* -ˈpeɪt-/ (*also* **expat** /ˌeksˈpæt/ *infml.*) *n.* [C] a person living in a country that is not their own ▸ **ˌexˈpatriate** (*also* **ˌexˈpat**, *infml.*) *adj.*: *expatriate workers*

**exˈpectancy ˌtheory** *n.* [sing.] (*HR*) the idea that employees will want to work hard if they feel that they will be successful and that there are likely to be good results for them that they think are important

**ˌexpectation of ˈlife** = LIFE EXPECTANCY (1)

**expedite** /ˈekspədaɪt/ *v.* [T] (*fml.*) to make a process happen more quickly: *expedited delivery*

**expendable** /ɪkˈspendəbl/ *adj.* **1** that you believe you can get rid of without causing yourself or your business harm: ~ *assets/staff* **2 expendable** supplies are items that have little value and are used in such a way that they cannot be used again or there is little or none left afterwards **3** made to be used for a limited period of time and then replaced: *expendable items such as car tyres and batteries* ▸ **exˈpendable** *n.* [C]

**exˌpendable ˈincome** = DISPOSABLE INCOME

★ **expenditure** /ɪkˈspendɪtʃə(r)/ *n.* [U,C] (*Account.*; *Econ.*) the act of spending or using money; an amount of money that sb/sth spends during a particular period of time: *a reduction in government/corporate* ~ ◇ *expenditure* ***on*** *advertising* ◇ *a total expenditure of $27 bn*

⊙ ***heavy/high/low/major*** ~ ♦ *to* ***cut (back)/limit*** ~ ♦ *to* ***increase/raise*** ~

**exˈpenditure tax** *n.* [C,U] (*Econ.*) a tax that is based on the amount of money that people spend rather than on their income

★ **expense** /ɪk'spens/ *n.*
**1** (*Account.*) [C,U] money that a business spends on supplies, workers, services, etc. in order to operate: *Labour is the airline industry's biggest expense.* ◇ *marketing/sales ~s* ◇ *pension/relocation ~s*
○ *to* ***bear/incur*** *an ~* ♦ *to* ***cover/meet*** *an ~* ♦ *to* ***deduct sth/treat sth/write sth off*** *as an ~* ♦ *to* ***control/cut/reduce/trim*** *~s* ♦ ***big/high/large/low/unexpected*** *~s*
**2 expenses** [pl.] money that you spend while doing a job that your employer or the person you are working for will pay back to you later: *We will cover your travel expenses.* ◇ (*BrE*) *to take a client out for a meal* ***on expenses*** ◇ *an* ***all-expenses-paid*** *trip*
○ ***basic/out-of-pocket*** *~* ♦ *to* ***incur*** *~* ♦ *to* ***cover/pay/refund/reimburse*** *sb's ~* ♦ *to* ***claim (back)/recover*** *your ~*
**3** [U] the money that you spend on sth: *The factory was rebuilt* ***at*** *considerable expense.* IDM **at sb's expense** paid for by sb/sth: *We were taken for a meal at the company's expense.*

**ex'pense ac,count** *n.* [C] an arrangement by which money spent by sb while they are at work is later paid back to them by their employer; a record of money spent in this way

**ex'penses claim** (*BrE*) (*AmE* **ex'pense re,port**) *n.* [C] a list of amounts that you spend while you are working that your employer will pay back

★ **expensive** /ɪk'spensɪv/ *adj.* costing a lot of money: *~ equipment/tools* ◇ *expensive hotels* ◇ *The new model is less expensive* ***to*** *produce.* OPP INEXPENSIVE
○ *to* ***look/prove/sound*** *~* ♦ ***extremely/prohibitively/relatively*** *~*
▸ **ex'pensively** *adv.*: *expensively priced*

**experience** /ɪk'spɪəriəns; *AmE* -'spɪr-/ *n.* **1** [U] the knowledge and skill that you have gained through doing sth for a period of time; the process of gaining this: *Do you have any previous experience of this type of work?* ◇ *You need a degree and at least 2 years' business experience.*
○ ***practical/relevant/valuable*** *~* ♦ ***considerable/little*** *~* ♦ ***financial/industry/management*** *~* ♦ *to* ***have/gain/lack*** *~*
**2** [C] an event or activity that affects you in some way: *We have to provide a better customer experience.* ◇ *a negative/positive ~* **3** [U] the things that have happened to you that influence the way you think and behave: *direct/first-hand/past/personal ~*

**ex'perience curve** (*also* **'learning curve**) *n.* [C, usu. sing.] the rate at which the cost of producing sth falls as the number produced increases, as a result of the knowledge and skill that a company and its workers gain

**experienced** /ɪk'spɪəriənst; *AmE* -'spɪr-/ *adj.* having knowledge or skill in a particular job or activity: *an experienced management team* ◇ *Are you experienced* ***in*** *marketing?*

★ **expert** /'ekspɜːt; *AmE* -pɜːrt/ *n.*, *adj.*
• ***n.*** [C] a person with special knowledge, skill or training in sth: *a legal/financial/tax ~* ◇ *a leading ~* ***on/in*** *tax law*
• ***adj.*** done with, having or involving great knowledge or skill: *to seek ~ advice/help* ◇ *be expert* ***at*** *running corporate events*

**expertise** /,ekspɜː'tiːz; *AmE* -pɜːr't-/ *n.* [U] expert knowledge or skill in a particular subject, activity or job: *We have the expertise to help you run your business.*
○ ***great/little*** *~* ♦ ***business/financial/technical*** *~* ♦ *to* ***gain/lack*** *~*

**,expert 'system** *n.* [C] (*IT*) a computer system that can provide information and expert advice on a particular subject. The program asks users a series of questions about their problem and gives them advice based on its store of knowledge.

**expiration** /,ekspə'reɪʃn/ = EXPIRY

**,expi'ration date** = EXPIRY DATE

★ **expire** /ɪk'spaɪə(r)/ *v.* [I] **1** (about a document, an agreement, a right to buy or sell shares, etc.) to be no longer valid because the period of time for which it could be used has ended: *Our lease on the property expires next month.* SYN RUN OUT **2** (about a period of time, esp. one during which sb holds a position of authority) to end: *The chairman's three-year term is due to expire in March.*

**expiry** /ɪk'spaɪəri/ (*pl.* **-ries**) (*esp. BrE*) (*AmE usu.* **,expi'ration**) *n.* [U,C] **1** an ending of the period of time when an official document can be used, or when an agreement or contract is valid: *The licence can be renewed on expiry.* ◇ *patent expiries* **2** (*Finan.*) the end of the period of time when an OPTION can be used or a FUTURES CONTRACT is valid

**exˈpiry date** (*esp. BrE*) (*AmE usu.* **ˌexpiˈration date**) *n.* [C] **1** the date after which an official document, agreement, etc. is no longer valid: *What is the expiry date on your credit card?* **2** (*Finan.*) the final or only day on which you can use your right to buy or sell particular shares, bonds, etc. **3** the date, printed on a container or package, by which an item of food, a medicine, etc. should be eaten or a product should be used. The items must not be sold after this date.

**exploit** /ɪkˈsplɔɪt/ *v.* [T] **1** to treat sb unfairly by making them work and not giving them much in return **2** to use sth as an opportunity to gain an advantage for yourself: *He exploited his father's name to get a job.* **3** to develop or make the best use of sth for business or industry: ***fully** exploiting the brand's potential*
▸ **exploitation** /ˌeksplɔɪˈteɪʃn/ *n.* [U]

**expo** /ˈekspəʊ; *AmE* -poʊ/ *n.* [C] **1** (*Trade*) **Expo** a large international event at which representatives from different countries show the products, machinery, buildings, etc. that their countries are producing **2** (*Market.*) a public event at which one company or many different companies producing related products show and sell their new products and services SYN TRADE SHOW

★ **export** *n., v.*

• *n.* /ˈekspɔːt; *AmE* ˈekspɔːrt/ **1** [C, usu. pl.] a product or service that is sold and sent or supplied to another country: *Copper is Chile's biggest export.* ◇ *Demand for Asian exports has grown.* **2 exports** [pl.] the amount or value of goods and services that are sold and sent or supplied to other countries over a period of time: *oil/steel/wheat ~* ◇ *Exports account for around 40 per cent of the country's GDP.* **3** [U] the selling and sending of goods or services to another country: *goods **for export*** ◇ *~ earnings/revenue* OPP IMPORT

• *v.* /ɪkˈspɔːt; *AmE* ɪkˈspɔːrt/ **1** [T,I] to sell and send goods or services to another country: *90% of the engines are exported to Europe.* ◇ *an exporting country* **2** [T] to introduce an idea or activity to another country or area: *The retailer has exported its marketing expertise to the US.* **3** (*IT*) [T] to change data into a form that allows it to be used with a different type of software: *Can you export it as an ASCII file?* OPP IMPORT
▸ **exˌportaˈbility** /-əˈbɪləti/ *n.* [U]
**exˈportable** /-əbl/ *adj.* **ˌexporˈtation** /-ˈteɪʃn/ *n.* [U,C]

**ˈexport ˌcredit** *n.* [U,C] (*Trade*) an arrangement by which an importer can buy foreign goods or services now and pay for them later

**ˌexport ˈcredit guaranˌtee** *n.* [C] (*Trade*) a promise, often by a government, to pay for goods that are exported if the importer does not pay

★ **exporter** /ekˈspɔːtə(r); *AmE* ekˈspɔːrt-/ *n.* [C] **1** a business, country or person that sells goods or services to another country: *A stronger yen hurts Japanese exporters because it makes their goods more expensive abroad.* ◇ *Ecuador is the world's largest banana exporter.* **2** a country whose people or businesses invest in companies, funds, etc. in other countries: *The country was a supplier of cheap goods but is now an exporter of capital.* → IMPORTER

**ˈexport ˌfactoring** *n.* [U] (*Trade*) a financial arrangement in which a bank takes responsibility for collecting payments for goods that an exporter sends abroad, so that the exporter can borrow money from the bank before customers pay their debts

**ˌExport-ˈImport Bank** (*also* **ˈEximbank**) *n.* [C] (*Trade*) in some countries, a bank that is created by the government to provide loans, etc. so that foreign companies and governments can buy goods and services that are exported by local businesses

**exposed** /ɪkˈspəʊzd; *AmE* ɪkˈspoʊzd/ *adj.* (*Finan.*) **~ (to sth)** likely to experience financial losses: *The decision to invest only in shares left a number of investors exposed.*

**exposition** /ˌekspəˈzɪʃn/ *n.* [C] (*Market., fml.*) a public event at which many different companies producing related products show and sell their new products and services SYN TRADE SHOW

★ **exposure** /ɪkˈspəʊʒə(r); *AmE* -ˈspoʊ-/ *n.* [U,C] **1** (*Finan.*) the fact that a business, an investor, etc. risks losing money, for example if customers do not pay their bills, or if investments fail; the amount that could be lost: *exposure **to** bad debt*
◐ *to **have** (an) ~* ◆ *to **avoid/increase/limit** ~* ◆ ***heavy/high** ~*
**2** (*Finan.*) the opportunity to invest money in sth: *It's hard to **gain** exposure **to** property with small amounts of money.* **3** (*Market.*) opportunities for people to see advertisements and information about a company or its products on television, in the newspapers, on the Internet, etc: *gaining*

*media exposure for your products* ◇ *to have/increase* ~

**express** /ɪk'spres/ *v., adj., adv., n.*
• *v.* [T] **1** to describe an amount, a quantity, etc. using a particular unit of measurement: *Costs are expressed as a percentage of sales.* ◇ *Expressed in dollars, sales increased by 23%.*
**2** to send sth by **express** post/mail
• *adj.* **1** travelling very fast; sent or delivered very quickly: *express mail* ◇ *an **express delivery** service* **2** (about a piece of business, etc.) that can be done very quickly: *express clearance through customs* **3** (*Law*) (about a part of a contract) that is stated or put in writing and agreed: *an express term of the contract*
• *adv.* using a special fast service: *to send sth express*
• *n.* **1** [C] a fast train or bus that does not stop at many places **2** [U] a service for sending or transporting things quickly: *The books were sent **by** express.*

**ex,pression of 'interest** *n.* [C] (*abbr* **EoI**) (*Comm.*) a formal statement in which a company or person says that they would be interested in doing sth, such as making an offer to supply sth or do a piece of work, buying shares, joining sth, etc: *They have received 23 expressions of interest from developers interested in building the stadium.*
○ *to make/submit an* ~ ◆ *to set a deadline for/invite ~s of interest*

**ex'press lane** *n.* [C] (*AmE*) a place in a shop/store where particular customers can go to avoid waiting for a long time

**,ex-'rights** *adv., adj.* (*Finan.*) (about a share) that is sold without giving the buyer the right to buy any new shares that the company may offer

**,ex 'stock** *adv., adj.* (*Comm.; Product.*) used to describe goods that can be delivered immediately as the seller has a supply of them available

**ext.** *abbr* (*written*) extension (used with a telephone number)

★ **extend** /ɪk'stend/ *v.* **1** [T,I] to make sth last longer: *to ~ a contract/lease* ◇ *extended trading hours* **2** [T] to make a business, a law, etc. cover more areas or operate in more places: *extending our operations into Asia* **3** [T] to offer or give sth to sb: *to extend credit to sb* **4** (*Market.*) [T] if a business **extends** a brand, it uses a successful brand name to sell new products

**ex,tended 'credit** *n.* [U] an arrangement by which you can spend as much money as you wish using your credit card, if you do not spend more than the limit you are allowed and if you pay back a particular amount every month

**ex,tended 'warranty** (*also* **ex,tended guaran'tee**, *less freq.*) *n.* [C] a type of insurance that shops/stores sell to customers that increases the period of time during which a product will be repaired or replaced if it breaks

★ **extension** /ɪk'stenʃn/ *n.* **1** [C,U] the act of making sth longer, larger, more complicated, etc.; the thing that is added to do this: *the extension of the subway* ◇ *We see the website as an extension **of** our telephone service.* **2** [C] an extra period of time allowed for sth: *a 14-month extension **to** the loan facility* **3** [C] a new part that is added to a building **4** [C] (*abbr* **ext.**) one of many telephone lines that are connected to a SWITCHBOARD in a large building, each with its own number: *Ext. 1125* **5** (*IT*) [C] the set of letters that are placed after a dot at the end of the name of a file and that show what type of file it is

**ex'tension ,strategy** *n.* [C] (*Market.*) a plan for reaching new customers for an existing product by making small changes to it, finding new uses for it, etc.

**external** /ɪk'stɜːnl; *AmE* ɪk'stɜːrnl/ *adj.* **1** coming from outside an organization: *an external auditor* ◇ *external candidates for a job* **2** used to describe the situation when a company increases in size by buying or joining with other companies: *external growth* **3** connected with foreign countries: *external trade* **4** (*IT*) not built into the main computer or device but must be connected to it
OPP INTERNAL

**ex,ternal ac'count** = CURRENT ACCOUNT (2)

**ex,ternal com'petitiveness** *n.* [U] **1** (*Econ.*) the ability to sell goods and services to foreign customers at an attractive (= good) price **2** (*HR*) = EXTERNAL EQUITY

**ex,ternal 'debt** *n.* [U] (*Econ.*) money that the government and organizations in a particular country owe to lenders in other countries
SYN FOREIGN DEBT

**ex,ternal 'equity** (*also* **ex,ternal com'petitiveness**) *n.* [U] (*HR*) a situation in which the basic pay that employees in an organization receive is similar to the pay for the same type of work in other organizations: *achieving external equity in pay*

**ex,ternal 'labour ,market** *n.* [C] (*HR*) the people who are available for work in the area outside an organization that an employer is likely to get new workers from

**ex,ternal ,lia'bility** *n.* [C, usu. pl., U] **1** (*Account.*) the money that an organization owes that is not owed to its shareholders **2** (*Econ.*) the money that a country owes to foreign lenders

**extinguish** /ɪk'stɪŋgwɪʃ/ *v.* [T] to stop sth from continuing or developing: *to ~ a debt/liability/right*

**extort** /ɪk'stɔːt; *AmE* ɪk'stɔːrt/ *v.* [T] **~ sth (from sb)** to make sb give you sth, esp. money, by threatening them ▸ **extortion** /-'stɔːʃn; *AmE* -'stɔːrʃn/ *n.* [U,C]

**extra** /'ekstrə/ *adj., n., adv.*

• ***adj.*** more than is usual, expected, or than exists already: *to borrow an extra $500 m*

• ***n.*** [C] **1** a thing that is added to sth that is not usual, standard or necessary and that costs more: *The CD player is an optional extra.* **2** (*Finan.*) = EXTRA DIVIDEND

• ***adv.*** **1** in addition; more than is usual, expected or exists already: *to charge/cost/pay ~* **2** (*used with an adj. or adv.*) more than usu: *an extra-large T-shirt*

**extract** *v., n.*

• ***v.*** /ɪk'strækt/ [T] **~ sth (from sth/sb) 1** to remove or obtain a substance from sth, for example by using an industrial or a chemical process: *The gas is extracted from coal.* **2** to get money, information, etc., esp. from sb who is unwilling to give it **3** to find information in a computer file, a document, etc. to use for a particular purpose: *The program extracts email addresses from websites.*

• ***n.*** /'ekstrækt/ [C] a substance that has been obtained from sth else using a particular process: *natural plant extracts*

**extractor** /ɪk'stræktə(r)/ *n.* [C] **1** (*also* **ex'tractor fan**) a device that removes hot air, unpleasant smells, etc. from a room **2** a device or machine that removes sth from sth else **3** (*IT*) software that finds and collects particular information from a computer file, web page, etc.

**,extra 'dividend** (*also* **'extra**) = SPECIAL DIVIDEND

**extranet** /'ekstrənet/ *n.* [C] (*IT*) a type of INTRANET which a company's customers and suppliers can link to using the Internet in order to obtain or provide information

**extraordinary** /ɪk'strɔːdnri; *AmE* ɪk'strɔːrdəneri/ *adj.* **1** not normal or ordinary; greater or better than usual: *These bonds pay an extraordinary rate of interest.* **2** (*Account.*) (about a cost) that is unusual for a company to pay and does not relate to its normal business activities **3** arranged for a special purpose in addition to what normally happens: *an extraordinary meeting*

**ex'traordinary 'general 'meeting** *n.* [C] (*BrE*) (*abbr* **EGM**) a meeting of the shareholders or members of a company that is held to discuss an urgent issue

**extravagant** /ɪk'strævəgənt/ *adj.* spending or costing too much money: *an extravagant pay package*

**,ex 'works** (*abbr* **EXW**) (*also* **,ex 'factory, ,ex 'warehouse**) *adv., adj.* (*BrE*) (*Trade*) goods are delivered to the buyer at the factory or the place where they are made or stored, and the buyer pays for transporting and insuring the goods from there: *Prices start at £9 000 ex works.* ◇ *ex-factory prices* → INCOTERM

**eyeballs** /'aɪbɔːlz/ *n.* [pl.] (*Market., infml.*) people who watch a particular television channel or visit a particular website: *The more eyeballs you can claim, the more you can charge advertisers.* **IDM** **(be) up to your eyeballs (in sth)** to have a lot of sth to deal with: *They're up to their eyeballs in work.*

**e-zine** /'iːziːn/ *n.* [C] a magazine published in electronic form on the Internet or sent by email

# Ff

**F2F** (*also* **f2f, F-to-F**) /,ef tuː 'ef/ *adj.* (*infml.*) **face-to-face** used to describe a situation where people meet together in order to discuss sth: *an F2F meeting*

**FA** /,ef 'eɪ/ = FUNCTIONAL ACKNOWLEDGEMENT

**the FAA** /,ef eɪ 'eɪ/ = FEDERAL AVIATION ADMINISTRATION

**fab** /fæb/ *n.* [C] (*Manufact.*) a factory where MICROCHIPS are made ▸ **fab** *v.* [T] (**-bb-**): *The chips are fabbed by IBM.*

**fabricate** /'fæbrɪkeɪt/ *v.* [T] (*Manufact.*) (*often pass.*) to build or make equipment, structures, etc., esp. by putting together different parts or materials: *The firm fabricates metals.*

▸ ˌfabriˈcation /-ˈkeɪʃn/ *n.* [U]
ˈ**fabricator** *n.* [C]: *a steel/metal* ~

**face** /feɪs/ = COALFACE

ˈ**face aˌmount** *n.* [C,U] (*esp. AmE*) **1** (*Insur.*) the amount of money stated in an insurance policy to be paid if the person who is insured dies or the contract ends **2** (*Finan.*) = FACE VALUE

**facelift** /ˈfeɪslɪft/ *n.* [C, usu. sing.] changes made to a building, product, service, etc. to make it more attractive to customers

ˈ**face time** *n.* [U] (*HR, infml.*) **1** time that you spend talking to sb in the same room rather than talking to them on the telephone, etc: *getting more face time with clients* **2** the time that sb spends at work, esp. beyond their normal working hours: *a strong face time culture*

ˌ**face-to-ˈface** *adj., n.*
• ***adj.*** involving people in the same room or place: *a ~ meeting/interview*
▸ ˌ**face-to-ˈface** *adv.*: *The discussions will take place face-to-face.*
• ***n.*** [C] (*pl.* **face-to-faces**) (*infml.*) a face-to-face meeting: *to have a face-to-face with the boss*

ˌ**face ˈvalue** (*also* ˈ**face aˌmount**, *esp. in AmE*) *n.* [C,U] (*Finan.*) the value that is shown on a coin, a note, a financial document, etc.

**facia** = FASCIA

★**facilitate** /fəˈsɪlɪteɪt/ *v.* [T] **1** to make an action or a process possible or easier: *a website that facilitates online payments* **2** to help people work together or reach an agreement
▸ **faˌciliˈtation** /-ˈteɪʃn/ *n.* [U; sing.]
**faˈcilitator** *n.* [C]: *They trained 40 people as facilitators.*

**faˈcilities ˌmanagement** *n.* [U] the activity of looking after or operating a building, factory, equipment, etc., often on behalf of another organization

★**facility** /fəˈsɪləti/ *n.* (*pl.* **-ties**)
**1** [C] a factory or a set of buildings where particular goods are produced or particular work is done: *an oil storage facility*
⊙ *a* ***distribution/manufacturing*** *~* • *to* ***build/close/open*** *a ~*
**2 facilities** [pl.] buildings, services, equipment, etc. that are provided for a particular purpose
⊙ ***conference/sports*** *~* • *to* ***improve/provide/use*** *~*
**3** (*Finan.*) [C] an arrangement that a person, a business, etc. has with a bank or a company to be able to borrow money during a particular period of time up to an agreed amount: *to draw down on* (= borrow money using) *a facility*
⊙ *to* ***arrange/have*** *a ~* • *a bank, etc.* ***extends/provides/withdraws*** *a ~* • *a ~* ***ends/matures*** • *to* ***have access to/use*** *a ~*
**4** [C] **~ (for sth/for doing sth)** a special feature of a machine, piece of software, etc. that makes it possible to do sth extra

**facsimile** /fækˈsɪməli/ = FAX

**factor** /ˈfæktə(r)/ *n., v.*
• ***n.*** **1** [C] one of several things that cause or influence sth: *Training is a big factor* ***in*** *the success of a company.* ◇ *a critical/deciding ~* **2** [sing.] **the ... ~** a quality or feature that has an important influence on whether sb/sth is popular, successful, etc: *He has the 'cool' factor.* **3** [C] the amount by which sth increases or decreases: *The real wage of the average worker has increased by* ***a factor of*** *ten* (= by ten times) *in the last 70 years.*
**4** (*Finan.*) [C] a business that buys the right to collect payments that are owed to a manufacturer: *a debt/invoice ~* **5** (*Comm.*) [C] a person or business that acts as an agent in particular trades, usu. receiving COMMISSION. They hold the goods and sell them in their own name.
→ idiom at FEEL-GOOD
• ***v.*** [T] (*Finan.*) to sell the right to collect payments from customers to a bank, company, etc: *to factor an invoice* PHR V ˌ**factor sth ˈin/ˈout**; ˌ**factor sth ˈinto/ˈout of sth** (*Tech.*) to include/not include a particular fact or situation when you are calculating sth or when you are thinking about or planning sth

ˈ**factor cost** *n.* [C,U] (*Econ.*) the cost of producing goods and services based on the cost of what is needed to produce it, such as labour, land and CAPITAL

**factoring** /ˈfæktərɪŋ/ *n.* [U] (*Finan.*) a financial arrangement in which a FACTOR buys the right to collect payments owed to a manufacturer. The **factor** pays the debts and then collects the money, receiving a percentage of the money owed for doing this: *debt/invoice ~* ◇ *a ~ company/agent*

ˌ**factor of proˈduction** *n.* [C] (*Econ.*) any person or thing that is involved in producing goods or providing services: *Land, labour and capital are the main factors of production.* SYN INPUT

★**factory** /ˈfæktri; -təri/ *n.* [C] (*pl.* **-ries**) a building or group of buildings where goods are made: *a car factory* ◇ *to work* ***in*** *a factory* ◇ *fac-*

*tory workers* ◇ *a fall in factory output* ◇ *to build/close/open a ~*

**ˈfactory cost** *n.* [C, usu. sing.] (*Account.*) the cost of manufacturing a product, including labour and raw materials

**ˌfactory ˈfloor** *n.* [sing.] (*often* **the ~**) the part of a factory where the goods are actually produced: *workers on the factory floor*

**ˌfactory ˈgate** *n.* [C] (*Econ.*) the entrance to a factory, used to describe the time when a finished product leaves a factory: *a fall in* ***factory-gate prices*** (= the basic prices paid to the manufacturer before transport or any profits have been added)

**ˈfactory ˌoutlet** = FACTORY SHOP

**ˈfactory price** *n.* [C, usu. pl.] the price at which a manufacturer sells goods, used esp. in advertising to show that a shop/store is selling sth at a very low price

**ˈfactory shop** (*BrE*) (*AmE* **ˈfactory store**) (*also* **ˈfactory ˌoutlet**, *AmE, BrE*) *n.* [C] a shop/store in which goods, esp. goods that are slightly damaged or not needed, are sold directly by the company that produces them at a cheaper price than normal

**ˈfact sheet** *n.* [C] (*esp. BrE*) a piece of paper or a small book giving information about a product or service

**fail** /feɪl/ *v., n.*

• ***v.*** **1** [I] to not be successful in achieving sth: *Their marketing strategy failed to increase sales.* **2** [I] to not do sth: *She failed to keep the appointment.* **3** [I] (about a business) to be unable to continue: *Statistics show that 80% of businesses fail within the first five years.* ◇ *a failing company* **4** [I] (about a machine or system) to stop working **5** [T] to not pass a test or an exam; to decide that sb/sth has not passed a test or an exam: *190 units failed inspection last month.* OPP PASS

• ***n.*** [C] the result of a test or an exam when sb/sth is not successful

IDM **without ˈfail 1** when you tell sb to do sth **without fail**, you are telling them that they must do it: *I want you here by two o'clock without fail.* **2** always: *She attends board meetings without fail.*

**failed** /feɪld/ *adj.* **1** not successful: *a failed attempt to merge the companies* **2** (about a business) that has stopped operating: *a failed airline*

**ˈfail-safe** *adj.* (about machinery or equipment) designed to stop working if sth goes wrong: *a fail-safe device*

**failure** /ˈfeɪljə(r)/ *n.* **1** [U] lack of success in doing or achieving sth: *the failure of the company's marketing strategy* **2** [C] sb/sth that is not successful: *He was a failure as a manager.* **3** [U,C] an act of not doing sth, esp. sth that you are expected to do: *Failure to comply with the regulations will result in prosecution.* **4** [C,U] a situation in which a business has to close because it is not successful: *Business failures dropped by 6% last year.* ◇ *a high failure rate* **5** [U,C] (about a machine or system) the state of not working correctly or as expected; an occasion when this happens: *a systems failure*

★**fair** /feə(r); *AmE* fer/ *adj., adv., n.*

• ***adj.*** (**-er, -est**) **1** acceptable and appropriate in a particular situation: *a ~ deal/price* **2** treating everyone equally and according to the rules or law: *a fairer tax system* OPP UNFAIR

IDM **(give sb/get) a fair ˈhearing** (to allow sb) the opportunity to give their opinion of sth before deciding if they have done sth wrong **(give sb/get) a fair ˈshake** (*AmE*) (*infml.*) (to give sb/get) fair treatment that gives you the same chance as sb else

• ***adv.*** according to the rules; in a way that is considered to be acceptable: *He claims they didn't* ***play fair*** *in winning the contract* (= they did sth dishonest).

• ***n.*** [C] an event at which people, businesses, etc. show and sell their goods: *a technology/agricultural ~*

**ˈfair ˈaverage ˈquality** *n.* [U] (*abbr* **FAQ**) (*Trade*) used to describe goods, esp. crops, sold on the understanding that the quality will be the same as the average quality of goods produced in the same country in the same period, or the average quality of several samples

**ˌfair ˈdealing** *n.* [U] (*Law*) **1** ways of doing business that are honest and fair to your customers and the people you do business with **2** (*esp. BrE*) (*AmE usu.* **ˌfair ˈuse**) conditions under which you can use or copy an original piece of work, such as part of a book, a song, etc.

**ˈfair ˈmarket ˈvalue** = FAIR VALUE

**ˌfair ˈtrade** *n.* [U] **1** trade which supports producers in developing countries by paying fair prices and making sure that workers have good working conditions and fair pay **2** trade that is fair to customers

**ˌfair ˈtrading** *n.* [U] **1** buying and selling activities that are honest and fair to businesses, producers, sellers and customers **2** (*Econ.*) a system of international trade where the countries involved agree not to put taxes on particular items they import from each other

**ˌfair ˈuse** = FAIR DEALING (2)

**ˌfair ˈvalue** (*also* **ˈfair ˈmarket ˈvalue**) *n.* [C,U] **1** a price paid for an item that is fair to both the buyer and the seller **2** (*Account.*) a way of valuing the assets of a business based on the price at which they could be sold

**ˌfair ˈwage** *n.* [C] (*HR*) an amount of money paid to a worker that is equal to the work done: *fair wages for coffee farmers*

**faithfully** /ˈfeɪθfəli/ *adv.* IDM **Yours faithfully** (*BrE*) (*written*) used at the end of a formal letter before you sign your name, when you have addressed sb as 'Dear Sir/Dear Madam', etc. and not by their name

**fake** /feɪk/ *adj., n., v.*
• *adj.* **1** not genuine; appearing to be sth it is not: *fake designer clothing* **2** made to look like sth else: *a jacket in fake fur*
• *n.* [C] a product, work of art, piece of jewellery, etc. that is not genuine but has been made to look as if it is
• *v.* [T] to make sth false appear to be genuine, esp. in order to deceive sb: *to fake sb's signature*

**fall** /fɔːl/ *v., n.*
• *v.* [I] (**fell** /fel/ **fallen** /ˈfɔːlən/) **1** to decrease in amount, value or level: *Orders have continued to fall.* ◇ *Their profits fell (by) 30 per cent.* ◇ *falling prices* **2** to pass into a particular state; to begin to be sth: *The first interest payment **falls due*** (= must be paid) *in January.* IDM **fall foul of sb/sth** to be guilty of not obeying sb/sth: *They fell foul of the new accounting rules.* **ˌfall on your ˈsword** to take responsibility for sth bad that has happened, esp. by leaving your job **fall ˈshort of sth** to fail to reach the standard that you expected or need: *We're going to fall short of our sales targets.* → idioms at ARREARS, PREY *n.* PHRV **ˌfall aˈpart 1** to be in very bad condition so that parts break off: *The machines are falling apart.* **2** to have so many problems that it is no longer possible to exist or function: *The merger plans fell apart.* **ˌfall aˈway** to become gradually fewer or smaller; to disappear: *The market for their products fell away to almost nothing.* **ˌfall ˈback** to decrease in value or amount: *Share prices fell back after brisk early trading.* **ˌfall beˈhind (sb/sth)** to fail to keep level with sb/sth: *The project has fallen behind schedule.* **ˌfall beˈhind with sth** to not pay or do sth at the right time: *to fall behind with loan repayments* **ˌfall ˈoff** to decrease in quantity or level: *Sales may fall off in the new year.* **ˌfall ˈout of sth** to no longer be part of a particular group or have a particular status: *The group is in danger of falling out of the FTSE 100.* **ˌfall ˈthrough** to not be completed, or not happen: *The deal has fallen through.*
• *n.* [C] a decrease in size, number, rate or level: *a 5% fall **in** profits* ◇ *a dramatic/sharp/slight/steep ~*
→ idiom at RIDE *v.*

**fallback** /ˈfɔːlbæk/ *n.* [C] **1** a plan or course of action that is ready to be used in an emergency if other things fail: *We need a fallback **position** if they don't accept our offer.* **2** a reduction or decrease in sth: *a fallback in energy prices* SYN FALL

**ˌfallen ˈangel** *n.* [C] (*Finan., infml.*) a company whose bonds were once a good investment but have now dropped in value

**faller** /ˈfɔːlə(r)/ *n.* [C] (*Stock Ex.*) (used in newspapers) a company whose shares have decreased in value SYN DECLINER OPP GAINER

**ˌfalling ˈmarket** *n.* [C] **1** a market in which most investments are decreasing in value **2** a situation in which the demand for a particular type of product is decreasing

**ˈfall-off** (*AmE* **falloff**) (*BrE also* **ˌfalling-ˈoff**) *n.* [sing.] a reduction in the amount, level or quality of sth: *a recent fall-off **in** demand*

**fallout** /ˈfɔːlaʊt/ *n.* [U] the bad results of a situation or an action: *The banks were hit by the fallout from the economic crisis.*

**false** /fɔːls/ *adj.* **1** wrong; not correct or true: *false information* ◇ *false marketing claims* **2** not genuine, but made to look real to deceive people: *a false passport* **3** wrong, because it is based on sth that is not true or correct: *Buying a cheap computer is a **false economy*** (= will not actually save you money). ▶ **ˈfalsely** *adv.*: *to be falsely accused of sth* IDM **by/under/on false preˈtences** (*AmE* **- pretenses**) by claiming that sth is true which is not, esp. in order to gain some advantage for yourself: *obtaining money by false pretences*

**ˌfalse acˈcounting** *n.* [U] the crime of reporting information about a company's financial state that is not true, so that people believe it has less debt, more profit, etc. than it really has

**ˌfalse ˈbottom** *n.* [C] (*Econ.*) if a market in which share prices are falling has a **false bottom**, it seems as if prices have reached their lowest level because they begin to rise, but then they fall even lower

**falsify** /ˈfɔːlsɪfaɪ/ *v.* [T] (**-fies**, **-fying**, **-fied**, **-fied**) to change a written record or information so that it is no longer true: *to ~ data/records/accounts* ▶ **ˌfalsifiˈcation** /-ˈkeɪʃn/ *n.* [U,C]: *the deliberate falsification of the company's records*

**falter** /ˈfɔːltə(r)/ *v.* [I] to become weaker or less effective; to stop increasing or improving: *The business faltered and collapsed.* ▶ **ˈfaltering** *adj.*: *the country's faltering economy*

**ˈfamily brand** *n.* [C] (*Market.*) a name that a company uses to sell a range of different products ▶ **ˈfamily ˌbranding** *n.* [U]: *a strong family branding*

**ˌfamily-ˈfriendly** *adj.* (*HR*) suitable for workers who have children: *~ policies/working hours*

**ˌfamily ˈlife ˌcycle** *n.* [C, usu. sing.] (*Market.*) the different stages of family life that depend on the age of the parents and children, and how many children are living at home

**Fannie Mae™** /ˌfæni ˈmeɪ/ *n.* (*Finan., infml.*) **1** [sing.] (*abbr* **FNMA**) in the US, the Federal National Mortgage Association, a private company supported by the government that supplies money for MORTGAGES **2** [C, usu. pl.] the bonds issued by **Fannie Mae**: *to invest in Fanny Maes*

**fao** /ˌef eɪ ˈəʊ; *AmE* ˈoʊ/ *abbr* (*BrE*) for the attention of; written on a business letter or document to say who should deal with it

**FAQ** /ˌef eɪ ˈkjuː/ *abbr*, *n.*
• ***abbr*** **1** (*IT, usu. written*) (*also* /fæk/ *esp. in AmE*) frequently asked questions: *The site has a list of FAQs on the new tax law.* **2** (*Trade*) = FAIR AVERAGE QUALITY
• ***n.*** [C, usu. pl.] (*pl.* **FAQs**) (*IT*) an Internet page on which there are answers to questions that people often ask about the site or a special topic: *an ~ page/section*

**fare** /feə(r); *AmE* fer/ *n.* **1** [C,U] the money that you pay to travel by bus, plane, taxi, etc: *Children over 16 pay full fare.* ◇ *a 7% fare increase* **2** [C] a passenger in a taxi: *to pick up a fare*

**farm** /fɑːm; *AmE* fɑːrm/ *v.*
PHR V **ˌfarm sth ˈout to sb** (*BrE*) to send out work for other people to do

**ˌfarmer's ˈmarket** (*also* **farmers'** -) *n.* [C] a market where farmers sell their fruit and vegetables

**FAS** /ˌef eɪ ˈes/ = FREE ALONGSIDE SHIP

**FASB** /ˈfæsbi/ = FINANCIAL ACCOUNTING STANDARDS BOARD

**fascia** (*BrE also* **facia**) /ˈfeɪʃə/ *n.* [C] (*BrE*) **1** a board above the entrance of a shop/store, with the name of the shop/store on it; the name of a shop/store **2** the hard cover on a mobile phone/cellphone

**fashion** /ˈfæʃn/ *n.* **1** [U,C] a popular style of clothes, hair, etc. at a particular time or place: *Black is always in fashion.* ◇ *shoes and fashion accessories* **2** [U] the business of making or selling clothes, shoes, etc., esp. in new and different styles: *a career in the fashion industry* ◇ *a ~ designer/show*

**ˈfashion goods** *n.* [pl.] (*Comm.*) items such as clothes, shoes, etc. that manufacturers need to change often as styles change

**ˌfast-ˈchanging** *adj.* changing quickly: *fast-changing consumer demands*

**ˌfast ˈfood** *n.* [U] hot food that is served very quickly in special restaurants, and often taken away to be eaten in the street: *the world's largest fast-food chain*

**ˌfast-ˈforward** *v.*, *adj.*
• ***v.*** [T,I] (*infml.*) to grow or progress quickly; to make sth do this: *We will fast-forward the product and bring it to the market by 2008.*
• ***adj.*** (*infml.*) growing or progressing very quickly: *a ~ company/marketplace*

**ˌfast-ˈgrowing** *adj.* getting bigger quickly: *a ~ business/market segment*

**ˈfast lane** *n.* [sing.] **1** a very busy life, where a lot is happening, that often also has a lot of stress and worry: *life in the fast lane* **2** (*HR*) = FAST TRACK

**ˌfast-ˈmoving** *adj.* **1** growing, developing or changing quickly: *fast-moving technology companies* **2** selling quickly: *fast-moving goods*

**ˌfast-ˈpaced** *adj.* developing or changing quickly: *a fast-paced marketplace*

**ˈfast track** (*also* **ˈfast lane**) *n.* [sing.] (*HR*) a plan or path that brings success in your career and more important jobs more quickly than normal: *He's on a fast track to higher management.* ◇ *a fast-track career* ▶ **ˈfast-track** *v.* [T]: *to be fast-tracked into positions of greater responsibility* **ˈfast-ˌtracking** *n.* [U]

**ˈfat cat** *n.* [C] (*infml.*) a person who earns, or who has, a lot of money: *corporate/industry ~s*

**fatware** /'fætweə(r); *AmE* -wer/ = BLOATWARE

**fault** /fɔːlt/ *n.* [C] something that is wrong or not perfect with sth; something that is wrong with a machine or system that stops it from working correctly: *a technical fault* ◇ *faults in design*

**'fault ˌtolerance** *n.* [U] (*IT*) the ability of a computer or a network to continue to work even when there is an unexpected problem with the HARDWARE or software
▸ **'fault-ˌtolerant** *adj.*

**faulty** /'fɔːlti/ *adj.* **1** not perfect; not working or made correctly: ~ *goods/workmanship* **2** (about a way of thinking) wrong or containing mistakes, often resulting in bad decisions: *faulty analysis*

**favourable** (*AmE* **favorable**) /'feɪvərəbl/ *adj.* **1** good for sth/sb and making it/them likely to be successful or have an advantage: *favourable economic conditions* **2** fairly good and not too expensive: *The company can buy supplies* ***on favourable terms.***

★**fax** /fæks/ *n., v.*
• *n.* (*also* **fac'simile**, *fml.*) **1** (*also* **'fax maˌchine**) [C] a machine that sends and receives documents in an electronic form along telephone wires and then prints them **2** [U] a system for sending documents using a **fax** machine: *Can you send it to me by fax?* **3** [C] a letter or message sent by **fax**: *I can send faxes from my computer.*
• *v.* [T,I] to send sb a document, message, etc. by **fax**

**faxback** /'fæksbæk/ *n.* [U,C] a system in which sb can automatically receive information by **fax** from a website, or, when they ask, from a fax machine or a telephone

**'fax maˌchine** = FAX *n.* (1)

**FCA** /ˌef siː 'eɪ/ = FREE CARRIER

**FCL** /ˌef siː 'el/ = FULL CONTAINER LOAD

**FCM** /ˌef siː 'em/ = FUTURES COMMISSION MERCHANT

**fco** /ˌef siː 'əʊ; *AmE* 'oʊ/ = FRANCO

**FDI** /ˌef diː 'aɪ/ = FOREIGN DIRECT INVESTMENT

**ˌfeasi'bility ˌstudy** (*also* **ˌfeasi'bility reˌport**, *less freq.*) *n.* [C] an examination of every detail of a new project, such as the costs, benefits and risks, in order to decide if it is possible and likely to be achieved; the document that is produced

**feasible** /'fiːzəbl/ *adj.* that is possible and likely to be achieved: *It is not feasible to complete the project in under 3 months.* ▸ **ˌfeasi'bility** /-'bɪləti/ *n.* [U]: *a feasibility study*

**ˌfeather-'bedding** (*AmE* **featherbedding**) *n.* [U] (*HR*) the activity of limiting the production of goods or of using too many workers, in order to save or create jobs, esp. because of a contract with a union

★**feature** /'fiːtʃə(r)/ *n., v.*
• *n.* [C] **1** something important, interesting or typical of a thing or place: *Ease of use is a key feature of all their products.*
➊ ***a distinguishing/major/standard/striking/unique*** ~ ◆ ***a handy/an interesting/a useful*** ~ ◆ ***design/safety/security*** ~*s*
**2** (in newspapers, on television, etc.) a special article or programme about sth/sb: *a special feature* ***on*** *Japan*
• *v.* **1** [T] to include a particular thing or person as a special **feature**: *The latest models of notebook computers feature a 30 cm screen.* **2** [I] to be included as an important part of sth: *The plant does not feature* ***in*** *the company's plans for the future.* SYN FIGURE

**the Fed** /fed/ = FEDERAL RESERVE BOARD, FEDERAL RESERVE BANK, FEDERAL RESERVE SYSTEM

**federal** /'fedərəl/ *adj.* **1** having a system of government in which the individual states of a country have control over their own affairs, but are controlled by a central government for national decisions, etc: *a federal republic* **2** within a **federal** system, esp. the US, connected with national government rather than the local government of an individual state: *state and federal income taxes* ◇ *a federal court* ▸ **'federally** *adv.*

**the ˌFederal Avi'ation Adminiˌstration** *n.* [sing. with sing./pl. verb] (*abbr* **FAA**) the department of the US government that is responsible for non-military air travel

**ˌFederal 'funds** (*also* **'fed funds**) *n.* [pl.] money that is put into FEDERAL RESERVE BANKS by other banks that can be used for short, temporary loans to banks that need it. The rate of interest charged on such loans is an important sign of what the economy is doing

**the ˌFederal Re'serve** = FEDERAL RESERVE SYSTEM

**the 'Federal Re'serve 'Bank** (*also* **the Fed**, *infml.*) *n.* [C] (*abbr* **FRB**) one of the 12 banks that form the central bank of the US

**the ˌFederal Re'serve Board** (*also* **the 'Federal Re'serve 'Board**

of 'Governors) (*also* **the Fed**, *infml.*) *n.* [sing. with sing./pl. verb] (*abbr* **FRB**) a group of seven people who are named by the US President and elected politicians (the **Senate**) to manage the Federal Reserve System

**the ˌFederal Re'serve ˌSystem** (*also* **the ˌFederal Re'serve**) (*also* **the Fed**, *infml.*) *n.* [sing.] (*abbr* **FRS**) the banking system in the US that lends money to banks and the government and issues notes and coins

**ˌFederal 'Trade Comˌmission** *n.* [sing. with sing./pl. verb] (*abbr* **FTC**) in the US, an independent government organization that makes sure that business is done in a legal and fair way and protects the rights of consumers, etc.

**federated** /'fedəreɪtɪd/ *adj.* (about states, organizations, etc.) united under a central government or organization but keeping some local control

**federation** /ˌfedə'reɪʃn/ *n.* [C] a group of companies, unions, clubs, etc. that have joined together to form an organization

★**fee** /fiː/ *n.* [C] **1** (*Comm.*) an amount of money that you pay for professional advice or services: *legal fees* ◇ *Does the bank charge a fee* ***for*** *setting up the account?*

○ *to* ***collect/earn/pay*** *a ~* ♦ *a* ***fat/high/huge/low/nominal*** *~* ♦ *an* ***annual/hourly****/a* ***monthly*** *~* ♦ *a* ***fixed/flat/one-off****/an* ***upfront*** *~* ♦ ***consultancy/transaction*** *~s*

**2** an amount of money that you pay to join an organization or to do sth: *a membership fee*

○ ***access/entry/registration*** *~s* ♦ *to* ***charge/collect/pay*** *a ~*

**'fee-based** *adj.* (*Comm.*) (about a service) that you have to pay a fee to use: *a fee-based information service*

**feed** /fiːd/ *v.*, *n.*

• *v.* **(fed, fed** /fed/**)** [T] **1 ~ A (with B)** | **~ B into A** to supply sth to sb/sth: *The electricity line is fed with power through an underground cable.* **2 ~ A (with B)** | **~ B into/through A** to put or push sth into or through a machine: *Feed the sheets into the printer one at a time.* **PHR V** **ˌfeed 'back (into sth)** to have an influence on the development of sth; to help to improve sth: *The goodwill feeds back into increased store sales.* **ˌfeed sth 'back (into sth)** to return sth, esp. money, to an organization, etc. so that it can be used to help improve it: *Our profits are fed back into the company.* **ˌfeed sth 'back (to sb)** to give sb information, advice or opinions about sth such as how good a product or sb's work is, esp. so that it can be improved: *The results of our research will be fed back to the teams.* **'feed into sth**; **ˌfeed 'through into sth** (about information, an opinion, etc.) to affect sth; to help to form or develop sth: *The report's findings will feed into company policy.* **ˌfeed 'through (to sb/sth)** to reach sb/sth after going through a process or system: *It will take time for the higher rates to feed through to investors.*

• *n.* **1** [C] a pipe, device, etc. which supplies a machine with sth: *The printer has an automatic paper feed.* **2** [U,C] material supplied to a machine: *a feed pipe* **3** [U] (*AmE*) television programmes that are sent from a central station to other stations in a network; the system of sending out these programmes

★**feedback** /'fiːdbæk/ *n.* [U] **1** (*HR*) advice or information that is given to an employee about how good their work is so that they can improve

○ ***constructive/immediate/negative/positive/useful*** *~* ♦ *to* ***get/give/offer/provide/receive*** *~*

**2** (*Market.*) information that is given by users to a business about how useful a product or service is so that it can be improved

○ ***consumer/customer/investor*** *~* ♦ ***good/immediate/negative/positive/useful*** *~* ♦ *to* ***get/give/offer/provide/receive/solicit*** *~*

**'feeding ˌfrenzy** *n.* [C] (*infml.*) a situation in which a lot of people compete with each other to buy or get sth for themselves

**feedstock** /'fiːdstɒk; *AmE* -stɑːk/ *n.* [C,U] (*Manufact.*) a raw material used in the process of manufacturing a product, or as fuel for a machine

**'feel-good** (*also* **feelgood**) *adj.* making you feel happy and pleased about life: *The social events organized for staff are important for their feel-good effect.* **IDM** **the/a 'feel-good factor** (*BrE*) a feeling of confidence in the future that is shared by many people

**feminization, -isation** /ˌfemɪnaɪ'zeɪʃn; *AmE* -nə'z-/ *n.* [U] (*HR*) the fact that more women than before are involved in an activity: *the feminization of management*

**FEU** /ˌef iː 'juː/ *n.* [C] (*Transpt.*) **forty-foot equivalent unit** a standard container for transporting goods, that is approximately twelve metres long

**ff.** *abbr (written)* following pages

**FHLMC** /ˌef eɪtʃ el em 'siː/ = FREDDIE MAC

**fiber optics**, **fiber-optic** = FIBRE OPTICS

**fibre** (*AmE* **fiber**) /'faɪbə(r)/ *n.* **1** [C,U] a material that is made from a mass of natural or artificial threads: *nylon and other man-made fibres* **2** [C] one of the many thin threads that form natural materials, such as wood and cotton: *cotton fibres*

**ˌfibre 'optics** *n.* [U] (*IT*) the use of thin **fibres** of glass, etc. for sending information in the form of light signals ▸ **ˌfibre-'optic** *adj.*: *fibre-optic cables*

**fickle** /'fɪkl/ *adj.* **1** changing often and suddenly: *the notoriously fickle fashion sportswear market* **2** (about a person) often changing their mind so you cannot rely on them: *~ consumers/investors* ▸ **'fickleness** *n.* [U]: *the fickleness of financial markets*

**fiddle** /'fɪdl/ *v.* [T] (*infml.*) to change the details or figures of sth in order to try to get money dishonestly, or gain an advantage: *to fiddle the accounts* ▸ **'fiddle** *n.* [C]: *an insurance/a tax ~*

**fi'delity bond** *n.* [C] (*also* **fi'delity inˌsurance** [U]) (*Insur.*) protection that a company can have to pay for losses caused by an employee doing sth dishonest or making a mistake

**fiduciary** /fɪ'djuːʃəri; -'duːʃ-; *AmE also* fɪ'duːʃieri/ *adj.*, *n.* (*Law*)
• ***adj.*** used to describe the relationship based on trust between the people who manage money or property for sb, and the person/people they manage it for: *The company's directors were accused of breaching their **fiduciary duty** to the shareholders.*
• ***n.*** [C] (*pl.* **-ries**) a person or an organization that is responsible for managing money or property for another person or group of people SYN TRUSTEE

**field** /fiːld/ *n.* **1** [sing. with sing./pl. verb] all the people or products competing in a particular area of business: *They **lead** the field in home entertainment systems.* **2** [C] a particular subject or activity that sb works in or is interested in: *What field of business are you in?* **3** [sing.] (*often used as an adj.*) used to describe work or study that is done outside the office, factory or LABORATORY and the people who do this work: *our agents **in the field*** ◊ *field research* **4** (*IT*) [C] a space for a separate item of data: *Create separate fields for first name, surname and address.*

**'field sales** *n.* [U; pl.] (*Market.*) the business of selling things outside a company's offices; the people who do this work: *jobs in field sales* ◊ *an experienced field sales force* ◊ *the field sales manager*

**'field-test** *v.* [T] to test sth, such as a product or a piece of equipment, in the place where it will be used ▸ **'field test** *n.* [C]

**FIFO** /'faɪfəʊ; *AmE* -foʊ/ = FIRST IN, FIRST OUT

**ˌfifty-'fifty** *adj.*, *adv.* (*infml.*) divided equally between two people, groups or possibilities: *Our bid has a fifty-fifty chance of success.* ◊ *Let's split the money fifty-fifty.*

**fig.** *abbr* (*written*) a figure: *See fig. 34.*

★**figure** /'fɪgə(r); *AmE* 'fɪgjər/ *n.*, *v.*
• ***n.*** [C] **1** a number representing a particular amount, esp. one given in official information: *The latest figures show that prices are still rising.* ◊ *Profits are well below last year's figure of $58 m.*
⊕ *a **high/low** ~* ◆ *an **average/exact**/a **rough** ~* ◆ ***final/interim** ~s* ◆ ***current/official** ~s*
**2** a symbol representing one of the numbers between 0 and 9: *a six-figure salary* (= over 100 000 dollars, euros, etc.) **3** a person of the type mentioned: *a leading figure in the industry*
⊕ *an **important**/a **key/senior** ~* ◆ ***government/industry/public** ~s*
**4** (*abbr* **fig.**) a picture, diagram, etc. in a book, referred to by a number
IDM **put a 'figure on sth** to say the exact price or number of sth → idiom at BALLPARK
• ***v.*** **1** [T] (*AmE*) to calculate an amount or the cost of sth: *We've figured the cost of moving offices at about $10 000.* **2** [I] **~ (as sth) (in/among sth)** to be part of a process, situation, etc. esp. an important part: *The factory doesn't figure in their future plans.* SYN FEATURE
PHR V **ˌfigure sth 'out 1** to calculate an amount or the cost of sth: *Have you figured out the cost?* **2** to find the answer to sth; to solve sth: *We have to figure out how to improve cash flow.* **3** to plan or think of sth: *I can't figure out what to do next.* SYN WORK STH OUT

★**file** /faɪl/ *n., v.*

• ***n.*** [C] **1** (*IT*) a collection of information stored together in a computer, under a particular name

⊕ *to* ***access/copy/create/delete/save*** *a ~* ◆ *a* ***computer/data/text*** *~*

**2** a box or folded piece of card for keeping loose papers together and in order: *Put that letter in the file marked 'Urgent'.* **3** a **file** and the information it contains, for example about a particular person or subject: *Your application will be kept* ***on file.***

⊕ *to* ***have/keep/maintain*** *a ~ (on sb/sth)* ◆ *to* ***consult/have access to/read/refer to*** *a ~*

• ***v.*** **1** [T] to put and keep documents, etc. in a particular place and in a particular order so that you can find them easily: *The forms should be filed alphabetically.* **2** [T,I] to present sth so that it can be officially recorded and dealt with: *to file* ***for*** *bankruptcy* ◇ *to ~ a claim/a lawsuit* ◇ *The company filed its accounts last week.*

**'file ˌcabinet** = FILING CABINET

**'file clerk** = FILING CLERK

**'file ˌmanager** *n.* [C] (*IT*) a computer program that is used to organize, arrange and find files and DIRECTORIES

**'file ˌserver** = SERVER

**filing** /'faɪlɪŋ/ *n.* **1** [U] the act of putting documents, letters, etc. into a file: *to do the filing* ◇ *a filing system* **2** [U] the act of presenting sth so that it can be officially recorded and dealt with: *penalties for late filing of accounts* **3** [C] (*esp. AmE*) an act of presenting documents to a court or government department; a document that is presented in this way: *bankruptcy/regulatory/tax ~s*

**'filing ˌcabinet** (*AmE also* **'file ˌcabinet**) *n.* [C] a piece of office furniture with deep drawers for storing files

**'filing clerk** (*BrE*) (*AmE* **'file clerk**) *n.* [C] a person whose job is to file letters, etc. and do general office tasks

**fill** /fɪl/ *v.* [T] **1** to appoint sb to a job: *The post has been filled.* **2** to do a job, have a role or position, etc: *He fills the post satisfactorily* (= performs his duties well). **3** to make or sell sth that is not yet available: *to fill a gap in the market* **4** to provide sth that will stop people from continuing to want or need sth: *filling customers' needs* **5** if a company **fills** an order, it gives the customer the goods they have asked for **6** if sb **fills** a SHORTFALL, they provide sth so that there will be as much as is needed or expected **IDM** **fill your 'pockets** to make or take a lot of money for yourself **fill sb's 'shoes/'boots** to do sb's job in a satisfactory way when they leave or are not there **PHRV** **ˌfill 'in (for sb/as sth)** to do sb's job for a short time while they are not there **ˌfill sth 'in** (*also* **ˌfill sth 'out**) to complete a form, etc. by writing information on it **ˌfill sb 'in (on sth)** to tell sb about sth that has happened: *Can you fill me in on what happened in the meeting?* **ˌfill sth 'out** = FILL STH IN **ˌfill (sth) 'up (with sth)** to become, or to make sth, completely full: *Our order books are filling up.*

**ˌfill or 'kill ˌorder** (*also* **ˌfill or 'kill**, *less freq.*) *n.* [C] (*abbr* **FOK**) (*Stock Ex.*) an instruction to a BROKER to buy or sell a particular number of shares at a particular price immediately or else not at all: *The trade was carried out on a fill or kill basis.* ◇ *to submit an FOK*

**Filofax™** /'faɪləʊfæks; *AmE* -loʊ-/ *n.* [C] a small book with pages that can be added or removed easily, for writing notes, addresses, etc. in

**filter** /'fɪltə(r)/ *v.* **1** (*IT*) [T] (about a computer program) to process data according to particular rules before displaying it or sending it somewhere in order to stop particular figures, text, etc. from being seen: *The program filters web pages for unsuitable contents.* **2** [I] (*used with an adv. or a prep.*) to have an effect on sth, esp. in small amounts over a period of time: *The economic recovery is beginning to filter through to the job market.* ▸ **'filter** *n.* [C]: *We use a web filter to block access to certain websites.* **'filtering** *n.* [U]: *an email filtering program* **PHRV** **ˌfilter sth 'out** to remove sth that you do not want using a special device or system: *The system filters out junk emails.*

**fin.** *abbr* (*written*) **1** financial **2** finance

★**final** /'faɪnl/ *adj., n.*

• ***adj.*** **1** at the end of a series of events, actions, statements, etc: *the final quarter of the year* ◇ *a ~ report/draft/payment* **2** being the result of a particular process: *the final product* **3** that cannot be argued with or changed: *our best final offer*

▸ **'finally** /-əli/ *adv.*

• ***n.*** **finals** [pl.] (*Account., infml.*) a company's **final results**: *Finals are expected this week.*

**ˌfinal ac'counts** *n.* [pl.] (*Account.*) the set of accounts that a business produces at the end of the FINANCIAL YEAR

**ˌfinal deˈmand** *n.* **1** (*Econ.*) [U] the extent to which people and businesses are buying goods and services; a measure of this: *An increase in final demand leads to an increase in production.* **2** (*Account.*) (*also* **ˌfinal reˈminder**) [C] (*both BrE*) the last request for payment of a bill or a debt before court action is taken

**ˌfinal ˈdividend** *n.* [C] (*Finan.*) a **dividend** paid at the end of the FINANCIAL YEAR that must be approved by the shareholders at the AGM

★**finalize, -ise** /ˈfaɪnəlaɪz/ *v.* [T] to complete the last part of a plan, a project, an agreement, etc: *We have finalized the deal.* ▸ **ˌfinaliˈzation, -iˈsation** /-laɪˈzeɪʃn; *AmE* -ləˈz-/ *n.* [U]: *the finalization of details*

**ˌfinal reˈminder** = FINAL DEMAND (2)

**ˌfinal salary ˈpension scheme** *n.* [C] (*HR*) esp. in the UK, an arrangement in which employees receive a pension when they retire based on how long they have worked for the company and the amount of money they were earning when they stopped

★**finance** /ˈfaɪnæns; faɪˈnæns; fəˈnæns/ *n.*, *v.*

• ***n.*** **1** [U] money that sb/sth borrows from a bank, receives from investors, etc. in order to run a business, complete an activity or buy sth: *The project will only go ahead if they can raise the necessary finance.* ◇ *international sources of finance*

⊕ *to* ***apply for/get/obtain/raise/secure*** ~ • *to* ***arrange/provide*** ~ *(for sth)* • ***long-term/short-term*** ~ • *a* ~ ***business/group***

**2** [U] the activity of managing money, esp. by a commercial organization or a government: *the company's new finance chief* ◇ *She works in the finance department.*

⊕ *a* ~ ***chief/director*** • *a* ~ ***committee/department/team*** • ***company/corporate/personal/public*** ~*s*

**3 finances** [pl.] the money available to a person, an organization or a country; the way this money is managed: *Buying new premises put a strain on our finances.*

⊕ *to* ***sort out/handle/manage*** *your* ~ • ***company/corporate/government/household/public*** ~ • ***healthy/sound/strong*** ~ • ***deteriorating/shaky/weak*** ~ • *sth* ***boosts/strengthens*** *your* ~

• ***v.*** [T] to provide or obtain money for a project, or for a business or government to operate: *The deal was largely financed by/with/through a share issue.* SYN FUND

**ˈfinance charge** *n.* [C] the amount you must pay when you arrange a loan; the amount of interest you pay on the money you borrow

**ˈfinance ˌcompany** (*also* **ˈfinance house**, *esp. in BrE*) *n.* [C] a company that lends money to people or businesses so that they can buy expensive items, such as vehicles, pieces of equipment, etc. and pay the money back over a period of time

**ˈfinance house** *n.* [C] (*esp. BrE*) **1** = FINANCE COMPANY **2** (*Finan.*) a company that arranges loans, investors, etc. for business projects

**ˈfinance lease** *n.* [C] an arrangement in which a financial institution buys a vehicle, piece of machinery, etc. and lets a business use it for an agreed period of time in exchange for regular payments

★**financial** /faɪˈnænʃl; fəˈnæn-/ *adj.*, *n.*

• ***adj.*** **1** connected with money and finance: *a* ~ *transaction/arrangement* ◇ *a* ~ *adviser/consultant* ◇ *The firm has run into financial difficulties.* **2** interested in making a profit; intended to make a profit: *Our stake in the company is a financial investment.* ▸ **fiˈnancially** /-ʃəli/ *adv.*: *a financially viable project*

• ***n.*** **1** (*Stock Ex.*) [C, usu. pl.] a company that provides **financial** services whose shares are traded on a stock exchange, for example, a bank: *Financials recorded strong gains today.* **2** (*Account.*) **financials** [pl.] (*infml.*) a company's **financial results**

**fiˌnancial acˈcounting** *n.* [U] (*Account.*) the branch of accounting concerned with preparing accurate records of the activities and state of a business, rather than with looking at the profit and costs of different parts of the business

**Fiˈnancial Acˈcounting ˈStandards Board** *n.* [sing.] (*abbr* **FASB**) in the US, the organization that decides on **accounting standards**

**fiˌnancial acˈcounts** *n.* [pl.] (*Account.*) the written records of an organization's assets, debts, profits, etc.; a summary of these that is prepared for shareholders, lenders, etc. and describes the financial activity during a particular period of time: *to prepare a set of financial accounts*

**fiˌnancial ˈanalyst** *n.* [C] a person whose job involves studying the financial state of particular com-

panies and advising people whether to buy or sell those shares
▸ **fiˌnancial a'nalysis** *n.* [U,C]

**fiˌnancial 'asset** *n.* [C] (*Account.*) an asset that is not physically useful but has a financial value, for example money or an investment

**fiˌnancial engi'neering** *n.* [U] (*Finan.*) (often disapproving) the practice of changing the way a company borrows money, owns assets, pays debts, etc., esp. in order to make its profits seem greater

**fiˌnancial 'indicator** *n.* [C] a figure that is seen as a measure of the success of a company, an economy, a market, etc.

**fiˌnancial insti'tution** *n.* [C] an organization such as a bank that offers financial services, such as accepting deposits, making loans or investing customers' money

**fiˌnancial 'instrument** *n.* [C] (*Finan.*) any investment that has a cash value and can be bought and sold in an organized system, such as shares, bonds, FUTURES, etc: *banks trading in all types of financial instruments* SYN INSTRUMENT

**fiˌnancial inter'mediary** *n.* [C] (*Finan.*) a financial organization such as a bank that holds money from lenders in order to make loans to borrowers

**fiˌnancial 'market** (*also* **'market**) *n.* [C] (*Finan.*) the activity of buying and selling shares, bonds, currencies, etc.; the organized structure for doing this or the place where it happens: *Brazil's financial markets* ◇ *shares traded on the financial market*

**fiˌnancial 'ratio** (*also* **ac'counting ˌratio**) *n.* [C] (*Account.*) the result of comparing two figures that describe a company's financial state, for example its share price and the amount of profit each shareholder can claim, used by managers or investors to decide how well a company is performing

**fiˌnancial re'porting** *n.* [U] (*Account.*) the act of giving investors and authorities regular financial information about a company's profits, debts, assets, etc: ~ *rules/standards*

**fiˌnancial re'sults** = RESULTS (1)

**fiˌnancial 'services** *n.* [pl.] (*Finan.*) the business of dealing with money for people or providing advice about money and investments: *the* ~ *industry/market/sector*

**the Fiˌnancial 'Services Auˌthority** *n.* [sing.] (*abbr* **FSA**) in the UK, the public organization that controls companies that provide financial services, for example insurance companies and banks

★**fiˌnancial 'statement** *n.* [C, usu. pl.] (*Account.*) a document that a company must prepare regularly, showing its financial performance during a particular period of time. It usu. includes the PROFIT AND LOSS ACCOUNT, the BALANCE SHEET and other information: *audited financial statements*
⊙ *to* ***issue/publish*** *~s* ◆ *to* ***file/submit*** *~s* ◆ *to* ***certify/sign (off on)*** *~s* ◆ ***annual/quarterly/year-end*** *~s*

**fiˌnancial 'structure** = CAPITAL STRUCTURE

**fiˌnancial 'supermarket** *n.* [C] (used in newspapers) a bank or company that provides many kinds of financial services, such as loans, insurance policies, investments, etc.

**fiˌnancial 'year** (*BrE*) (*also* **ˌfiscal 'year**, *AmE, BrE*) *n.* [C] (*abbr* **FY**) (*Account.*) a period of twelve months that a company chooses as the time over which it will complete a full set of financial records: *the 2007/2008* ~ (= for example, from 1 April 2007 to 31 March 2008)

**financier** /faɪ'nænsiə(r); fə-; *AmE* ˌfɪnən'sɪr/ *n.* [C] (*Finan.*) a person who is an expert in financial matters and who lends money to businesses or manages large amounts of money for a business

★**financing** /'faɪnænsɪŋ; faɪ'nænsɪŋ; fə'nænsɪŋ/ *n.* [U] (*Finan.*) money that is made available to sb/sth in order to buy sth or run a business or activity; the process of obtaining this money or making it available: *financing* ***for*** *the project*
⊙ *to* ***get/raise/secure*** ~ ◆ *to* ***arrange/offer/provide*** ~ ◆ ***long-term/short-term*** ~ ◆ ***bank/bond/debt/equity*** ~ ◆ *a* ~ ***arrangement/deal/facility/package*** ◆ *a* ~ ***plan/strategy*** ◆ ~ ***charges/costs***

**find** /faɪnd/ *v.* (**found, found** /faʊnd/) **1** [T] to have sth available so that you can use it: *How are we going to find €1 m for the new equipment?* **2** (*Law*) [T,I] to make a particular decision in a court: *The jury found him guilty of fraud.* ◇ *to* ~ *against/for/in favour of sb*

**finding** /'faɪndɪŋ/ *n.* **1** [C, usu. pl.] information that is discovered as the result of research into sth: *What were the main findings from the survey?*
⊙ *to* ***present/publish/report*** *~s* ◆ ***initial/preliminary*** *~s*

**2** (*Law*) [C] a decision made by a court, etc. concerning a dispute
⊙ to ***make/reach*** *a ~* ◆ *a ~* ***against/ in favour of*** *sb/sth*

**fine** /faɪn/ *n., v.*
• ***n.*** [C] an amount of money that must be paid as punishment for breaking a law or rule: *The firm has been ordered to pay a fine of $7.5 m* ***for*** *misleading customers.*
⊙ *to* ***impose/levy*** *a ~* ◆ *to* ***avoid/be liable to/face*** *a ~* ◆ *a* ***heavy/hefty/ large****/an* ***unlimited*** *~*
• ***v.*** [T] to make sb pay money as an official punishment: *The five banks were fined $100 000 for fixing prices.*

**the 'fine print** = SMALL PRINT

**ˌfine-'tune** *v.* [T] to make very small changes to sth so that it is as good as it can possibly be ▸ **ˌfine-'tuning** *n.* [U]

**finish** /'fɪnɪʃ/ *v., n.*
• ***v.*** [T,I] to be at a particular price or level at the end of a period of trading on a stock exchange: *The Nikkei stock average finished 2% higher yesterday.* SYN CLOSE
• ***n.* 1** [sing.] the end of a period of trading on a stock exchange; the level of share prices, etc. at this time: *At London's finish, the Dow Jones was down 0.8 per cent.* SYN CLOSE **2** [C] the final details that are added to sth to make it complete: *The packaging gives the product a stylish finish.*

**finished** /'fɪnɪʃt/ *adj.* (about a product) that has been put together from different parts or materials and is fully completed: *transforming raw materials into finished products*

**ˌfinite ca'pacity ˌscheduling** *n.* [U] (*Product.*) the process, using computer software, that organizes tasks in a production process so that the best and most efficient way of producing what is needed at the right time is achieved using the available resources

★**fire** /'faɪə(r)/ *v.* [T] (*HR*) to force sb to leave their job: *'You're fired!'* ◇ *She got fired for always being late.* ◇ ***hiring and firing*** *staff* SYN SACK
PHR V **ˌfire sth 'off 1** to write or say sth to sb very quickly, often when you are angry: *He fired off a letter of complaint.* **2** if you **fire off** an email, you send it **ˌfire sth 'up** (*infml.*) to start a machine, piece of equipment, etc: *I'll fire up my laptop.*

**'fire cerˌtificate** *n.* [C] a legal document that shows that a building meets the official standards for keeping workers safe in case of fire and gives details of safety measures, ways of escape, etc.

**firefighting** /'faɪəfaɪtɪŋ; *AmE* 'faɪərf-/ *n.* [U] the activity of dealing with problems in a company or an organization as they happen: *Most of the CEOs were focused on daily firefighting rather than strategy.*

**'fire inˌsurance** *n.* [U] insurance that pays for goods, vehicles, etc. that are damaged by fire

**'fire ˌmarshal** = FIRE SAFETY OFFICER

**firepower** /'faɪəpaʊə(r); *AmE* 'faɪərp-/ *n.* [U] the amount of money, power or influence that an organization has available: *The company has enormous financial firepower.*

**'fire safety ˌofficer** (*also* **'fire ˌmarshal**) *n.* [C] an employee in an organization responsible for keeping places of work and workers safe in case of fire

**'fire sale** *n.* [C] **1** an occasion when a company sells goods cheaply because they have been damaged in a fire **2** a situation in which a company sells its machinery, parts of its business, etc. cheaply because it needs money quickly

**firewall** /'faɪəwɔːl; *AmE* 'faɪərw-/ *n.* [C, usu. sing.] **1** (*IT*) a part of a computer system that is designed to prevent people from getting at information without authority but still allows them to receive information that is sent to them: *~ programs/software* ◇ *to build/install a ~* **2** (*Stock Ex.*) = CHINESE WALL

**'firing line** *n.* IDM **be in the 'firing line** (*BrE*) (*AmE* **be on the 'firing line**) to be in a position where people can criticize or blame you: *The employment secretary found himself in the firing line over recent job cuts.* → idiom at LINE *n.*

★**firm** /fɜːm; *AmE* fɜːrm/ *n., adj., v.*
• ***n.*** [C] a business or company, esp. one that provides a professional service: *an accounting/engineering/investment ~* ◇ *a law firm* ◇ *a firm of management consultants*
⊙ *to* ***create/found/set up/start (up)*** *a ~* ◆ *to* ***manage/run*** *a ~* ◆ *to* ***close (down)/shut (down)*** *a ~*
• ***adj.* 1** (*not used in the form* **firmer**, **firmest**) that cannot be changed after it has been decided or agreed: *The airline has placed firm orders for 10 new planes.*
⊙ *a ~* ***date/offer*** ◆ *a ~* ***agreement/ commitment/decision/promise***
**2** (**-er**, **-est**) at a good or high price or level; steady: *The pound remained firm* ***against*** (= compared to) *the dollar.* OPP SOFT

• *v.* [I] (about shares, prices, etc.) to become steady or rise steadily: *Philips' shares firmed 5.8 per cent to €18.19.* ▸ **'firmness** *n.* [U]

**PHR V** **ˌfirm 'up** to become stronger or more stable: *Prices are firming up.* **ˌfirm 'up sth** to make sth stronger, more stable or fixed: *The details still have to be firmed up.*

**firmware** /ˈfɜːmweə(r); *AmE* ˈfɜːrmwer/ *n.* [U] (*IT*) a type of software that is stored in such a way that it cannot be changed or lost

**ˌfirst 'class** *n.* [U] **1** the best and most expensive seats or accommodation on a train, ship, etc. **2** in the UK, the class of mail that is delivered most quickly: *first-class stamps* **3** in the US, the class of mail used for letters and cards ▸ **ˌfirst 'class** *adv.*: *to travel first class* ◇ *Orders within the UK are sent first class.*

**ˌfirst 'cost** = PRIME COST

**ˌfirst-geneˈration** *adj.* used to describe the first type of a machine to be developed: *first-generation PCs*

**ˌfirst 'half** *n.* [C, usu. sing.] **1** (*Account.*) (*also* **ˌfiscal first 'half**, *esp. in AmE*) the first six months of a company's FINANCIAL YEAR: *a good first half* ◇ *first-half profits* **2** the period of six months between 1 January and 30 June

**ˌfirst 'in, ˌfirst 'out** *phr.* **1** (*Product.*) (*abbr* **FIFO**) a method of STOCK CONTROL in which the first goods or raw materials bought or produced are the first ones used or sold **2** (*Account.*) (*abbr* **FIFO**) a method of valuing supplies of goods or units of raw materials based on the idea that the first goods bought or produced are the first ones used or sold. The value of goods left at the end of the year is based on the most recent prices. **3** (*HR*) used, for example in a situation when people are losing their jobs, to say that the first people to be employed will be the first to go **4** (*IT*) used to describe a system where data received first is the first to be processed

**ˌfirst-line 'manager** *n.* [C] (*HR*) the lowest level of manager in an organization

**ˌfirst 'mover** *n.* [C] (*Market.*) a business that is the first to offer a new product or service or to use a new technology

**ˌfirst order of 'business** *n.* [C] the most important task that sb must deal with

**ˌfirst re'fusal** = RIGHT OF FIRST REFUSAL

**ˌfirst-round 'financing** *n.* [U] (*Finan.*) the first investment in a young company made by investors not closely connected with the company or its managers, to help the company develop manufacturing, marketing and selling

**ˌfirst 'section** *n.* [sing.] the part of the Tokyo Stock Exchange on which the shares of the largest and most successful companies are traded

**ˌfirst 'tier** *n.* [C] the first or top level of sth: *first-tier companies* (= the biggest, most important companies)

**ˌfirst-tier sup'plier** *n.* [C] (*Product.*) a company responsible for delivering raw materials or goods directly to the customer's factory

**ˌfirst-'time** *adj.* doing or experiencing sth for the first time: *a computer program designed for first-time users*

★ **fiscal** /ˈfɪskl/ *adj., n.*

• *adj.* **1** (*Econ.*) connected with government or public money, esp. taxes: *fiscal reforms* ◇ *~ austerity/prudence* ◇ *a ~ deficit/surplus* **2** (*Finan.*) (*esp. AmE*) connected with financial matters: *More companies are facing a fiscal crisis.* **3** (*Account.*) (*esp. AmE*) connected with the period of twelve months over which a government or a company prepares a full set of financial records, or part of this period: *the fiscal third quarter* ▸ **'fiscally** /-əli/ *adv.*

• *n.* [C] **fiscal 2007, 2008, etc.** (*AmE*) (*Account.*) = FISCAL YEAR

**ˌfiscal 'drag** *n.* [U] (*Econ.*) a situation in which a government takes an increasing proportion of people's wages in income tax because it does not increase the levels of income at which tax is charged at the same rate as INFLATION

**ˌfiscal first 'half** = FIRST HALF (1)

**ˌfiscal 'policy** *n.* [C,U] (*Econ.*) the way in which a government charges taxes or spends money in order to manage the economy: *loose ~* (= low taxes and/or high government spending)

**ˌfiscal second 'half** = SECOND HALF

**ˌfiscal 'year** (*abbr* **FY**) (*AmE also* **fiscal 2007, 2008, etc.**) *n.* [C] **1** (*Account.*) (*esp. AmE*) = FINANCIAL YEAR **2** (*Econ.*) the period of twelve months over which a government prepares a full set of financial records

**NOTE** In the UK, the **fiscal year** runs from 6 April of one year to 5 April of the next. In the US it runs from 1 October to 30 September.

**'fishbone ˌdiagram** (*also* **ˌcause and ef'fect ˌdiagram,**

ˌIshi'kawa ˌdiagram) *n.* [C] a diagram that is used to analyse the different causes of a particular effect or problem

**fishery** /ˈfɪʃəri/ *n.* (*pl.* **-ries**) **1** [C] a part of the sea or a river where fish are caught in large quantities: *a herring/tuna* ~ **2** [C] = FISH FARM **3** [U; pl.] the business or industry of catching fish: *EU fishery ministers*

**'fish farm** (*also* **'fishery**) *n.* [C] a place where fish are bred as a business

**fit** /fɪt/ *v., n., adj.*
• ***v.*** (**fitting, fitted, fitted**) (*AmE usu.* **fitting, fit, fit** *except in the pass.*) **1** [T] (*often pass.*) to put or fix sth somewhere: *Several features are fitted as standard on these cars.* **2** [T,I] (*used with an adv. or a prep.*) to put or join sth in the right place: *The parts don't fit together properly.* **3** [T,I] (*not used in the continuous tenses*) to agree with, match or be suitable for sth: *software that fits your company's needs* ◇ *This doesn't fit with our plans.* **4** [T] (*esp. BrE*) **~ sb (for sth/to do sth)** to make sb/sth suitable for a particular job: *His experience fitted him perfectly **for** the job.* → idiom at SIZE *n.* **PHR V** **ˌfit sb/sth 'in; ˌfit sb/sth 'in/'into sth** to find time to see sb or to do sth: *I'll try and fit you in after lunch.* **ˌfit 'in (with sb/sth) 1** to work in an easy and natural way with sb/sth: *She fits in well here.* **2** to agree with, match or be suitable for sth: *The offer didn't fit in with our main business.* **ˌfit sb/sth 'out/'up (with sth)** to supply sb/sth with all the equipment, clothes, etc. that they need: *the cost of fitting out the store*
• ***n.*** [C, usu. sing., U] **~ (for/with sth)** the way in which things or people match each other or are suitable for each other: *She is a good fit **for** the job.* ◇ *We need to work out the best fit **between** the staff needed and the people available.* **IDM** **by/in ˌfits and 'starts** frequently starting and stopping again; not continuously: *Economic recovery is proceeding in fits and starts.*
• ***adj.*** (**fitter, fittest**) healthy and strong: *a **leaner and fitter** industry* (= employing fewer people and with lower costs)

**fitness** /ˈfɪtnəs/ *n.* [U] **1** the state of being physically healthy and strong: *the health and ~ sector/industry* ◇ (*fig.*) *financial fitness* **2** the state of being suitable or good enough for sth: *There were doubts about her fitness for the position.*

**fitter** /ˈfɪtə(r)/ *n.* [C] **1** a person whose job is to put together or repair equipment: *a pipe/gas* ~ **2** a person whose job is to cut and fit clothes or carpets, etc: *carpet fitters*

**ˌfive 'nines** *n.* [U] (*IT*) 99.999 per cent, the percentage of the time that some computer systems are expected to work properly: *a server with five nines availability*

★ **fix** /fɪks/ *v., n.*
• ***v.*** **1** [T] to decide on a date, a time, an amount, etc. for sth: *Has the date of the next meeting been fixed?* **SYN** SET **2** [T] **~ sth (up)** to arrange or organize sth: *I'll fix up a meeting with the supplier.* **3** [T] to repair or correct sth: *We're trying to fix the problem.* **4** (*Econ.*) [T] **~ prices** to decide with other businesses that you will sell particular goods or services at the same prices and not compete with each other. This is illegal in many countries **5** (*Finan.*) [T,I] (*usu. pass.*) to decide on the official price of sth, esp. gold, at a particular time of the day, based on supply and demand
▸ **'fixing** *n.* [C]: *Gold was $341.50 an ounce at London's afternoon fixing.*
• ***n.*** [C] **1** (*infml.*) a solution to a problem, esp. an easy or temporary one: *There is no **quick fix** for the steel industry.* **2** (*IT*) a small computer program that is used to repair a problem with a larger piece of software: *a bug fix* **3** (*Finan.*) the official price of sth, esp. gold, at a particular time of the day, based on supply and demand; the process of deciding this price: *Gold's lowest fix this week was below $354 per ounce.*

**fixed** /fɪkst/ *adj.* staying the same; not changing or able to be changed: *fixed prices* ◇ *a fixed rate of interest*

**ˌfixed 'asset** = CAPITAL ASSET

**ˌfixed 'capital** *n.* [U] (*Account.*) money that a company has invested in its buildings, machinery, etc.

**ˌfixed 'cost** (*also* **ˌfixed ex'pense**) *n.* [C, usu. pl.] (*Account.*) an amount of money used to run a business that remains the same whatever quantity of goods is produced: *Rent is a fixed cost.*

**ˌfixed 'currency** *n.* [C] (*Econ.*) a currency whose value is fixed compared to sth else, esp. units of another currency

**ˌfixed de'posit** *n.* [C,U] an arrangement where you leave an amount of money in a bank account for a particular period of time in order to get a better rate of interest

**ˌfixed ex'pense** = FIXED COST

**ˌfixed 'income** *n.* [C,U] (*Finan.*) **1** money that sb receives from an investment or a pension that does not change or increase: *retired people living on fixed incomes* **2** investments that offer an income that does not change over a period of time: *fixed-income trading*

**ˌfixed-interest seˈcurity** *n.* [C, usu. pl.] (*Finan.*) an investment that pays you agreed regular amounts of income that do not change

**ˌfixed inˈvestment** *n.* [U,C] (*Econ.*) money that a business invests in machinery, buildings, vehicles, etc. that will be used over a long period of time

**ˌfixed ˈline** (*also* **ˈlandline**) *n.* [C] a series of wires carried on poles or under the ground that joins a home, an office, etc. to a telephone network: *calls to fixed-line phones*

**ˌfixed ˈnetwork** *n.* [C] (*IT*) a series of wires and devices that permanently joins together telephones, computers, etc. in different places

**ˌfixed ˈparity** *n.* [C,U] (*Econ.*) a fixed price at which a unit of a currency can be bought; a system in which there is a fixed relationship between the value of two currencies: *The currency has fixed parity against the euro.*

**ˌfixed-ˈprice** *adj.* a **fixed-price** contract, deal, etc. is one in which a particular fee is agreed which does not change even if there is an increase in costs

**ˈfixed-rate** *adj.* charging or paying a particular fixed rate of interest, etc: *~ bonds/mortgages*

**ˌfixed ˈtax** (*BrE also* **ˌflat ˈtax**, **proˌportional ˈtax**) *n.* [C, usu. sing.] (*Account.*; *Econ.*) a system in which tax is paid at the same rate, however much you earn or spend

**ˌfixed ˈtelephone** *n.* [C] a telephone that is permanently attached to a network using wires

**ˌfixed ˈterm** *n.* [C] (*Comm.*) an agreed or limited period of time: *employees taken on for a fixed term* ◇ *fixed-term contracts*

**ˌfixed ˈwireless** *n.* [U] (*IT*) a system or device that does not use wires to connect to other telephones, computers, etc. and is situated in one place, such as a home or an office

**flag** /flæg/ *v., n.*

• *v.* (-gg-) **1** [I] to become tired, weaker or less enthusiastic: *flagging sales/demand/confidence* **2** [T] to put a special mark next to information, an email, etc. that you think is important **3** [T] **~ (up) sth** to announce or draw attention to sth: *We have flagged up various problems with the deal.*

• *n.* [C] a special mark that you put next to information, an email, etc. that you think is important

**flagship** /ˈflægʃɪp/ *n.* [C, usu. sing.] **1** the most important product, service, building, etc. that an organization owns or produces: *a ~ brand/product/store* **2** the most important company in an industry or economy: *They were once the flagship of the chocolate industry.*

**flame** /fleɪm/ *n., v.*

• *n.* [C] a rude, offensive or unacceptable message sent by email

• *v.* [T] to send sb a **flame**; to criticize sb in a **flame**

**ˈflame mail** *n.* [C,U] rude, offensive or unacceptable messages sent by email; a message of this type

**flash** /flæʃ/ *n.* **1** (*Market.*) [C] a band of colour or writing across a book, pack, etc. **2** (*IT*) **Flash™** [U] a program which creates moving images for websites

**ˈflash drive** (*also* **ˈflash ˌmemory drive**, **ˌflash memory ˈpen drive**) *n.* [C] (*IT*) a small device that you can connect to a computer and use to store data and move it from one computer to another

**flat** /flæt/ *adj.* (**flatter**, **flattest**) **1** not very successful because very little is being sold: *flat sales* **2** (about prices, numbers, etc.) increasing only a small amount; not increasing or falling: *Shares were flat at €53.* **3** (*not used in the forms* **flatter**, **flattest**) (about a payment) fixed; without any extra payments or charges: *to charge a flat fee* **4** (*HR*) used to describe an organization where there are few levels between the top and the bottom: *a flat organizational structure*

**ˌflatbed ˈscanner** (*also* **flatbed** /ˈflætbed/) *n.* [C] (*IT*) a SCANNER on which the picture or document can be laid flat for copying

**ˌflat-ˈpanel** = FLAT-SCREEN

**ˌflat ˈrate** *n.* [C, usu. sing.] a price for sth that is fixed at a particular amount and does not change; an amount paid or charged that is the same for everyone

**ˌflat-ˈscreen** (*also* **ˌflat-ˈpanel**) *adj.* (*both esp. BrE*) (esp. about televisions or computer screens) not curved and usu. in a thin case: *a flat-screen monitor*

**ˌflat ˈtax** = FIXED TAX

**flatten** /ˈflætn/ *v.* [T,I] **1** if a price or number **flattens** or sb/sth **flattens** it, it stops increasing or continues to increase at a slower rate: *Sales of its* *portable computers have flattened.* **2** (*HR*) if sb/sth **flattens** an organization or it **flattens**, the number of levels between the top and the bottom are reduced PHR V ˌ**flatten** ˈ**out/**ˈ**off** to stay at a steady level of development or progress after a period of sharp rises or falls: *Oil prices are now flattening out.* SYN LEVEL OFF/OUT

**flaw** /flɔː/ *n.* [C] a mistake in sth that means that it is not correct or does not work correctly: *The plan has fundamental* (= very serious) *flaws.* ◇ *design/security/structural ~s*

**flawed** /flɔːd/ *adj.* having a **flaw**: *flawed products* ◇ *deeply/fatally/fundamentally/seriously ~*

**fledgling** (*also* **fledgeling**) /ˈfledʒlɪŋ/ *n.* [C] (*usu. used before another n.*) a person, an organization or a system that is new and without experience: *a ~ business/company/start-up* ◇ *protecting fledgling industries*

**fleece** /fliːs/ *v.* [T] (*infml.*) to take a lot of money from sb by charging them too much

**fleet** /fliːt/ *n.* [C] **1** a group of planes, vehicles, ships, etc. travelling together or owned by the same organization: *the company's new fleet of vans* **2** (*used before another n.*) a **fleet** customer, business, etc. is one that uses the same supplier, insurance company, etc. for all its vehicles **3** a group of ships fishing together: *a fishing/whaling ~*

ˈ**fleet** ˌ**management** *n.* [U] the activity of looking after, repairing, etc. a **fleet** of vehicles on behalf of a company: *We offer fleet management for companies with both big and small fleets.* ◇ *a ~ company/service* ▶ ˈ**fleet** ˌ**manager** *n.* [C]

ˈ**Fleet Street** *n.* [U] a street in central London where many national newspapers used to have their offices (now used to mean British newspapers and journalists in general)

**flexecutive** /flekˈsekjətɪv/ *n.* [C] a manager whose hours or place of work can change easily because of new technology; a professional worker who has many skills and can change jobs or tasks easily

★**flexible** /ˈfleksəbl/ *adj.* able to change or be changed to suit new conditions or situations: *Our plans need to be flexible.* ◇ *a flexible approach to clients' requirements* OPP INFLEXIBLE ▶ ˌ**flexiˈbility** /-ˈbɪləti/ *n.* [U] ˈ**flexibly** *adv.*: *to work flexibly*

ˌ**flexible** ˈ**benefits** *n.* [pl.] (*HR*) benefits, such as health insurance, use of a car, etc. that employees receive in addition to their pay and can choose themselves

ˌ**flexible** ˈ**hours** (*also* ˌ**flexible** ˈ**working hours**) *n.* [pl.] (*HR*) a system in which an employee can choose what time he or she will start or finish work each day

ˌ**flexible** ˈ**working** (*also* ˌ**flexible** ˈ**work**) *n.* [U] (*HR*) a way of organizing work in a company that is different from the traditional way and may not have fixed times or places of work

ˌ**flexible** ˈ**working hours** = FLEXIBLE HOURS

**flexing** /ˈfleksɪŋ/ *n.* [U] (*HR*) changing the hours that employees work to suit the changing needs of the company: *the ~ of working days/hours* ▶ **flex** /fleks/ *v.* [T]: *Buyers can flex their start time.*

**flexitime** /ˈfleksitaɪm/ (*esp. BrE*) (*AmE usu.* **flextime** /ˈflekstaɪm/) *n.* [U] (*HR*) a system in which employees work a particular number of hours each week or month but can choose when they start and finish work each day: *She works flexitime.*

**flier** = FLYER

**flight** /flaɪt/ *n.* **1** [C] a journey made by air, esp. in a plane; a plane making a particular journey: *Did you have a good flight?* ◇ *They operate 78 daily flights between the UK and US.* ◇ *I'd like to catch an earlier flight.* **2** (*Econ.*; *Finan.*) [U; sing.] a situation in which people quickly move their money from one country to another or from one type of investment to another in order to avoid risk or to improve profits: *There has been a flight of capital away from the stock market*.

ˈ**flight** ˌ**capital** *n.* [U] (*Econ.*) money that people move out of a country to avoid taxes or because they believe there is too much financial risk there

**flighting** /ˈflaɪtɪŋ/ *n.* [U] (*Market.*) a pattern of advertising a product during a period of time in which there is more advertising at some times and less or none at others

ˈ**flip chart** *n.* [C] large sheets of paper fixed at the top to a stand so that they can be turned over, used for presenting information at a talk or meeting

★**float** /fləʊt; *AmE* floʊt/ *v.*, *n.*
• *v.* **1** (*Stock Ex.*) [T,I] to sell a company's shares on a stock exchange for the first time: *The business was floated on the stock market in 1992.* ◇ *The*

*shares floated* **at** *$14.50.* **2** (*Econ.*) [T,I] if a government **floats** its currency or allows it to **float**, it removes controls on the price so that its value is decided by what people are willing to pay for it: *a floating currency/regime/system* **3** [T] to suggest an idea or a plan for other people to consider: *The idea of a merger has been floated.* PHR V **ˌfloat 'off/'out sth** (*Stock Ex.*) (*often pass.*) to form a new company from part of a business and sell its shares on a stock exchange

• ***n.*** **1** (*Stock Ex.*) [C,U] = FLOTATION **2** (*Econ.*) [C, usu. sing.] a situation where a government stops controlling the price of its currency and allows it to be bought and sold freely: *The currency fell by 40% against the dollar on the first day of the float.* **3** [C] (*esp. BrE*) an amount of money consisting of coins and notes of low value that is given to sb before they start selling things so that they can give customers CHANGE **4** (*Finan.*) [C, usu. sing.] the number of a company's shares that are owned by the public and are available to be bought and sold

**floatation** = FLOTATION

**floater** /'fləʊtə(r); *AmE* 'floʊ-/ *n.* [C] (*AmE*) **1** (*Finan., infml.*) = FLOATING-RATE NOTE **2** (*Insur.*) insurance you can buy that pays for items that are lost, damaged, etc. wherever they are: *a personal articles floater* **3** a person who is employed to do a variety of jobs as needed: *a floater secretary*

**floating** /'fləʊtɪŋ; *AmE* 'floʊt-/ *adj.* not fixed permanently at a particular level or value: *fixed and floating prices*

**ˌfloating ex'change rate** (*also* **'floating rate**) *n.* [C] (*Econ.*) an **exchange rate** for a currency that is not controlled by the government but changes as the demand for the currency changes

**ˌfloating popu'lation** *n.* [C] used to describe people who frequently move from one place to another

**'floating rate** *n.* [C] **1** (*Finan.*) a percentage of interest that you pay or receive that changes because it is linked to the cost of borrowing money in a market: *Most mortgages sold in the UK have floating rates.* **2** (*Econ.*) = FLOATING EXCHANGE RATE

**ˌfloating-rate 'note** (*abbr* **FRN**) (*also* **'floater**, *infml.*) *n.* [C] (*Finan.*) a type of bond that pays interest at a rate which can vary, for example when the rate at which banks lend money to each other changes

**flog** /flɒg; *AmE* flɑːg; flɔːg/ *v.* [T] (**-gg-**) (*infml.*) to sell sth to sb: *The airline plans to flog the tickets over the Internet.* PHR V **ˌflog sth 'off** **1** to sell all or part of an industry, a company, etc., often at a low price in order to get rid of it **2** to sell things cheaply because you want to get rid of them or because you need the money

★ **flood** /flʌd/ *n., v.*

• ***n.*** [C] a very large number or amount of sth that appears at the same time: *There has been a flood of cheap imports into the market.*

• ***v.*** **1** [I] **~ in/into/out of sth** to arrive or go somewhere in large numbers or amounts: *Investment has flooded into the country.* **2** [T] (*usu. pass.*) to send sth somewhere in large numbers: *We've been flooded with complaints.* **3** [T] to become or to make sth become available somewhere in large numbers or amounts: *Cheap imported goods are* ***flooding the market.***

**floor** /flɔː(r)/ *n.* **1** [C, usu. sing.] the area in a factory, shop/store, stock exchange, etc. where things are made, displayed or traded: *trading on the floor of the Stock Exchange* ◇ *77 000 sq m of floor space* **2** [C, usu. sing.] a level below which it is difficult for a price, number, etc. to fall: *The market could lose 500 points before reaching a floor.* OPP CEILING **3 the floor** [sing.] the group of people who attend a formal talk or discussion: *questions from the floor* IDM **get/be given/have the 'floor** to get/be given/have the right to speak during a formal discussion → idiom at HOLD *v.*

**'floor ˌbroker** *n.* [C] (*Stock Ex.*) a person who is employed to buy and sell shares, OPTIONS, etc. on behalf of others on an EXCHANGE

**'floor ˌlimit** *n.* [C] (*Comm.*) the value of goods or services that you can buy with a bank or credit card without the shop/store having to get permission from the bank, etc. to accept the payment

**'floor ˌmanager** *n.* [C] (*AmE*) (*Comm.*) a person who works in a large store and who is in charge of one floor or department

**'floor ˌtrader** *n.* [C] (*Stock Ex.*) an individual investor who is allowed to buy and sell shares, OPTIONS, etc. on an EXCHANGE

**flop** /flɒp; *AmE* flɑːp/ *v.* [I] (-pp-) to be a complete failure: *The business flopped.* ▶ **flop** *n.* [C]: *a costly flop*

**floppy** /ˈflɒpi; *AmE* ˈflɑːpi/ (*pl.* -pies) = FLOPPY DISK

**ˌfloppy ˈdisk** (*also* **disˈkette**, **ˈfloppy**) *n.* [C] (*IT*) a flat disk inside a plastic cover, that is used to store data in the form that a computer can read, and that can be removed from the computer

**flotation** (*also* **floatation**) /fləʊˈteɪʃn; *AmE* floʊ-/ (*also* **float**) (*both esp. BrE*) *n.* [C,U] (*Stock Ex.*) the act of selling shares in a company on a stock exchange for the first time: *plans for flotation on the stock exchange* ◇ *a stock-market flotation* SYN IPO

**flounder** /ˈflaʊndə(r)/ *v.* [I] (*often used in newspapers*) to have a lot of problems and to be in danger of failing completely: *The drop in business travel left the airline floundering.*

**flourish** /ˈflʌrɪʃ; *AmE* ˈflɜːrɪʃ/ *v.* [I] to develop quickly and be successful or common: *a flourishing business* SYN THRIVE

★**flow** /fləʊ; *AmE* floʊ/ *n., v.*

• *n.* [C, usu. sing., U] the continuous movement of sth from one person, place or thing to another; the thing that moves: *a constant flow of investment into the region* ◇ *the flow of work through the factory*

⊕ *a* ***continuous/free/steady*** *~ of sth* • *to* ***control/improve/increase/manage/speed (up)*** *the ~* • *to* ***disrupt/prevent/reduce/reverse/stop*** *the ~*

• *v.* [I] **1** (*usu. used with an adv. or a prep.*) to move or pass continuously from one place or person to another, esp. in large numbers or amounts: *Capital is flowing back into the country.* ◇ *We try to keep information flowing between departments.* ◇ *to ~ easily/freely/smoothly* **2** to be available easily and in large amounts: *Once demand improves, profits will start to flow.* PHR V **ˈflow from sth** (*fml.*) to come or result from sth: *These changes flowed from the reorganization of the company.* **ˌflow ˈthrough to sth** to reach sb/sth or have an effect on them/it: *When will the drop in manufacturing costs flow through to consumers?*

**ˈflow chart** (*also* **flowchart**) (*also* **ˈflow ˌdiagram**, **ˈflowsheet**) *n.* [C] a diagram that shows the connections between the different stages of a process or parts of a system

**ˌflow of ˈfunds** *n.* [C, usu. sing.] (*Econ.*) the way in which money moves from one country to another or between different parts of the economy, for example by people giving and receiving loans

**ˈflow proˌduction** (*also* **conˌtinuous proˈduction**) *n.* [U] (*Product.*) a way of manufacturing a product in large quantities in which each unit moves continuously through the stages of production one after the other

**flowsheet** /ˈfləʊʃiːt; *AmE* ˈfloʊ-/ = FLOW CHART

★**fluctuate** /ˈflʌktʃueɪt/ *v.* [I] to change frequently in size, amount, level, etc., esp. from one extreme to another: *The price of cocoa can fluctuate wildly on world markets.* ◇ *fluctuating prices* ▶ **ˌfluctuˈation** /-ˈeɪʃn/ *n.* [C,U]: *wild* ***fluctuations in*** *sales from week to week*

**flush** /flʌʃ/ *adj.* (*infml.*) having a lot of money, usu. for a short time: *companies ~* ***with*** *cash/funds/money*

**fly** /flaɪ/ *v.* (**flies, flying, flew** /fluː/, **flown** /fləʊn; *AmE* floʊn/) **1** [T] to transport goods or passengers in a plane: *The replacement parts had to be flown in specially.* **2** (*AmE*) [I] to be successful: *It remains to be seen whether his project will fly.*
→ idiom at SHELF

**flyback** /ˈflaɪbæk/ *n.* [C] (*AmE*) (*HR*) a very thorough job interview that sb, esp. a student, has in an employer's office, usu. after a first general interview with the employer: *a flyback interview* SYN CALLBACK

**ˈfly-by-night** *adj.* (about a person or business) dishonest and only interested in making money quickly: *fly-by-night operators looking for easy money* ▶ **ˈfly-by-night** *n.* [C]

**flyer** (*also* **flier**) /ˈflaɪə(r)/ *n.* [C] (*Market.*) a small sheet of paper that advertises a product or an event, copies of which are given to a large number of people: *We put out a flyer promoting our product range.*
IDM **take a ˈflyer (on sb/sth)** (*esp. AmE*) (*infml.*) to risk your money, reputation, etc. on sb/sth that you are not sure of: *risk taking a flyer on something new*

**FMCG** /ˌef em siː ˈdʒiː/ *abbr* (*Market.*) **fast-moving consumer goods** goods that sell quickly because people use them in large quantities every day, esp. food and drinks

**FNMA** /ˌef en em ˈeɪ/ = FANNIE MAE

**FOB** /ˌef əʊ ˈbiː; *AmE* oʊ/ = FREE ON BOARD

★**focus** /ˈfəʊkəs; *AmE* ˈfoʊ-/ *v., n.*

• *v.* [T,I] (-s- *or* -ss-) to give attention, effort, etc. to one particular subject, situation or person rather than another: *They need to focus more* **on** *marketing.* ◇ *Resources are focussed on our big brands.*

• ***n.*** **1** [C, usu. sing., U] the thing or person that is most important to a business or a group of people; the act of paying special attention to a particular aim or activity: *The focus will remain* **on** *improving sales.* ◇ *a* **customer focus** (= concentrating on treating customers well) ◇ *to have/lack (a) ~* ◇ *to change/shift your ~* **2** [U] the quality of being able to give all your attention to a particular aim or activity and not spend time and energy on other things

**focused** (*also* **focussed**) /ˈfəʊkəst; *AmE* ˈfoʊ-/ *adj.* with very clear aims; with your attention directed to sth or to what you want to do: *a focused approach to marketing*

**ˈfocus group** *n.* [C] **1** (*Market.*) a small group of people, specially chosen to represent different social classes, etc., who are asked to discuss and give their opinions about a particular subject. This information is used in MARKET RESEARCH: *to conduct/do/hold/run/use a ~* **2** (*HR*) a small group of employees who are asked to discuss and give their opinions about aspects of company policy such as management or changes

**ˈfocus list** *n.* [C] (*Stock Ex.*) a list of companies whose shares are worth buying or selling, according to a particular bank, etc: *a focus list of poor performers*

**focussed** = FOCUSED

**FOK** /ˌef əʊ ˈkeɪ; *AmE* oʊ/ = FILL OR KILL ORDER

**fold** /fəʊld; *AmE* foʊld/ *v.* [T,I] (about a business) to close because it is not successful: *The company will fold unless it gets more financing.*

**PHR V** **ˌfold sth ˈinto sth** to make a smaller business, service, etc. part of a larger one; to join different businesses, services, etc. together: *The company is being folded into GM's European operations.*

★ **folder** /ˈfəʊldə(r); *AmE* ˈfoʊld-/ *n.* [C] **1** a cardboard or plastic cover for holding loose papers, etc: *a folder of invoices* **2** (*IT*) (in some computer systems) a way of organizing and storing computer files: *You can organize your emails into folders.* ◇ *to* **create/delete/name/rename** *a ~* ◇ *to* **close/open** *a ~*

**ˈfold-out** (*AmE* **foldout**) *adj.* used to describe a page in a book, magazine, etc. that is designed to be opened out to make a larger page

▸ **ˈfold-out** (*AmE* **foldout**) *n.* [C]

**follower** /ˈfɒləʊə(r); *AmE* ˈfɑːloʊ-/ *n.* [C] **1** a company that only produces new products, uses new technologies, etc. once others have tried to do so; a company that enters a market after others: *Their company is a follower rather than an innovator.* ◇ *a market follower* **2** a person who is very interested in a particular activity and is aware of all the recent news about it: *Followers of the company think that will have good results.*
→ LEADER

**ˌfollow-ˈthrough** *n.* [U] the actions that sb takes in order to complete a plan: *The project could fail without proper follow-through.*

**ˈfollow-up** *n.* [C,U] **~ (to sth)** an action or a thing that continues sth that has already started or comes after sth similar that was done earlier: *a ~ call/letter/meeting/report*

**food** /fuːd/ *n.* **1** [U] things that people eat: *the food industry* ◇ *imports of food products* **2** [C,U] a particular type of food: *packaged/frozen/chilled ~* ◇ *Iberia Foods*
→ idiom at DOG

**ˈfood ˌservice** *n.* [U] the business of making, transporting and serving food, for example in schools, stores, airports or companies

**foodstuff** /ˈfuːdstʌf/ *n.* [C, usu. pl.] (*Econ.*) any substance that is used as food: *There is no sales tax on basic foodstuffs.*

**foot** /fʊt/ *n., v.*

• ***n.*** [C] (*pl.* **feet** /fiːt/ *or* **foot**) a unit for measuring length equal to 12 inches or 30.48 centimetres **IDM** **be run/rushed off your ˈfeet** to be extremely busy; to have too many things to do **get your ˈfeet wet** (*esp. AmE*) (*infml.*) to start doing sth new: *getting your feet wet in e-commerce* **get/have a/your ˌfoot in the ˈdoor** to manage to enter an organization, a field of business, etc. that could bring you success: *to get a foot in the door of the telecoms industry* **on your ˈfeet** in a normal state again after a period of trouble or difficulty: *The business should soon be back on its feet.*

• ***v.*** **IDM** **foot the ˈbill** (*infml.*) to be responsible for paying the cost of sth

**footer** /ˈfʊtə(r)/ *n.* [C] a line or block of text that is automatically added to the bottom of every page that is printed from a computer
→ HEADER

**footfall** /ˈfʊtfɔːl/ (*esp. BrE*) (*AmE usu.* **ˈfoot ˌtraffic**) *n.* [U,C] (*Market.*) the number of people that visit a particular shop/store, shopping centre, etc. over a period of time: *The centre has an average weekly footfall of 600 000 visitors.*

**foothold** /ˈfʊthəʊld; *AmE* -hoʊld/ *n.* [C, usu. sing.] a strong position in a business, profession, etc. from which sb can make progress and achieve success: *The deal will give us a foothold in the US market.* ◇ *to establish/gain/have/obtain/secure a ~*

**footing** /ˈfʊtɪŋ/ *n.* **1** [sing; U] the state of being strong and steady: *The loan has put the company back on a sound financial footing.* **2** [sing.] the position or status of sb/sth in relation to others; the relationship between two or more people or groups: *We are competing on an equal footing with foreign firms.*

**footprint** /ˈfʊtprɪnt/ *n.* [C] **1** the amount of space on a desk that a computer or other piece of equipment fills **2** (*IT*) the area on the earth in which a signal from a communications SATELLITE can be received

**Footsie** /ˈfʊtsi/ = FTSE 100 INDEX

**ˈfoot ˌtraffic** *n.* [U] **1** (*Market.*) (*esp. AmE*) = FOOTFALL **2** the movement of people from one place to another

**footwear** /ˈfʊtweə(r); *AmE* -wer/ *n.* [U] (used esp. in shops/stores) things that people wear on their feet, esp. shoes or boots: *the ~ market/industry*

**foray** /ˈfɒreɪ; *AmE* ˈfɔː-; ˈfɑː-/ *n.* [C] (often used in newspapers) an attempt to become involved in a different business activity or market: *We have made our first foray into Brazil.*

**force** /fɔːs; *AmE* fɔːrs/ *n.* **1** [C] a person or thing that has a lot of power or influence: *The company is a major force in the cellphone industry.* **2** [U] the authority of sth: *These guidelines do not have* ***the force of law.*** **3** (*HR*) [C with sing./pl. v.] a group of people who have been organized for a particular purpose IDM **come/enter into ˈforce** (about a law, rule, etc.) to start being used: *New rules come into force next year.* **in ˈforce** (about a law, rule, etc.) being used or applied **join/combine ˈforces (with sb)** to work together in order to achieve a shared aim → idiom at BRING

**ˌforced liquiˈdation** = COMPULSORY LIQUIDATION

**ˌforced ˈselling** *n.* [U] (*Finan.*) a situation in which an investment fund must sell particular shares, bonds, etc. in order to follow its own rules, for example, rules about the quality of investments it can keep ▸ **ˌforced ˈseller** *n.* [C]

**ˌforce field aˈnalysis** *n.* [C,U] (*HR*) a way of making change more acceptable in an organization by analysing the positive and negative aspects and working to increase the positive and decrease the negative

**force majeure** /ˌfɔːs mæˈʒɜː(r); *AmE* ˌfɔːrs/ *n.* [U] (*Law*) unexpected circumstances, such as war, that can be used as an excuse when they prevent sb from doing sth that is written in a contract: *a force majeure clause* (= in a written contract)

★**forecast** /ˈfɔːkɑːst; *AmE* ˈfɔːrkæst/ *n.*, *v.*

• ***n.*** [C] a statement about what will happen in the future, based on information that is available now: *It is difficult to give an accurate forecast of sales.*

⊙ *an* ***economic/a financial*** *~* ◆ *an* ***earnings/inflation/a growth/profit/sales*** *~* ◆ *to* ***make/provide*** *a ~*

• ***v.*** [T] (**forecast, forecast** *or* **forecasted, forecasted**) to say what you think will happen in the future based on information that you have now: *Experts are forecasting a recovery in the economy.* ◇ *Sales were lower than forecast.* SYN PREDICT

▸ **ˈforecasting** *n.* [U]: *forecasting models/techniques*

**forecaster** /ˈfɔːkɑːstə(r); *AmE* ˈfɔːrkæstər/ *n.* [C] a person or an organization that studies an economy, industry, etc. and says what they think will happen to it in the future: *an economic/a financial ~*

**foreclose** /fɔːˈkləʊz; *AmE* fɔːrˈkloʊz/ *v.* [T,I] (*Finan.*) (esp. about a bank) to take control of sb's property because they have not paid back money that they have borrowed: *to ~* ***on*** *a mortgage/property*

▸ **foreˈclosure** /-ˈkləʊʒə(r); *AmE* -ˈkloʊ-/ *n.* [U,C]: *Mortgage foreclosures reached their highest level in April.*

**forefront** /ˈfɔːfrʌnt; *AmE* ˈfɔːrf-/ *n.* [sing.] **at/in/to the ~ (of sth)** in or into an important or leading position in a particular group or activity: *The group was at the forefront of new drug development.*

★**foreign** /ˈfɒrən; *AmE* ˈfɔːrən; ˈfɑːrən/ *adj.* **1** in or from a country that is not your own: *earning foreign currency from exporting goods* **2** dealing with or involving other countries: *~ policy/trade*

**ˌforeign ˈbond** *n.* [C] (*Finan.*) a bond that investors in a particular country can buy in their own currency but which is issued by a foreign company

**ˌforeign ˈcurrency acˌcount** = CURRENCY ACCOUNT

**ˌforeign ˈcurrency exˌposure** = CURRENCY EXPOSURE

**ˌforeign ˈcurrency reˌserves** (*also* **ˈcurrency reˌserves**) *n.* [pl.] (*Econ.*) supplies of foreign money, and LIQUID assets such as gold, that a government keeps to buy its own currency when it needs to protect its value compared to other currencies SYN FOREIGN EXCHANGE RESERVES

**ˌforeign ˈcurrency risk** = CURRENCY RISK

**ˌforeign ˈdebt** *n.* [C,U] (*Econ.*; *Finan.*) money that the government and organizations in a particular country owe to lenders in other countries SYN EXTERNAL DEBT

**ˈforeign diˈrect inˈvestment** (*abbr* **FDI**) (*also* **diˌrect inˈvestment**) *n.* [U; C, usu. sing.] (*Econ.*) money that people or companies of one country invest in another by buying property, building factories, buying businesses, etc.

★ **ˌforeign exˈchange** *n.* (*Econ.*; *Finan.*) **1** [U] (*abbr* **forex**) the system of exchanging the money of one country for that of another **2** [U] money that is obtained using this system: *a ~ trader/dealer* **3** [C] a place where money of different countries is exchanged: *The pound fell on the foreign exchanges yesterday.*

**ˌforeign exˈchange ˌmarket** (*also* **exˈchange ˌmarket**, *less freq.*) *n.* [C] (*Finan.*) the system in which organizations, governments and investors buy and sell currencies; anywhere that this happens SYN CURRENCY MARKET

**ˌforeign exˈchange reˌserves** (*also* **ˌforeign reˈserves**, **ˌinternational reˈserves**) *n.* [pl.] (*Econ.*) supplies of foreign money and LIQUID assets such as gold, which a government keeps to buy its own currency when it needs to protect its value compared to other currencies SYN FOREIGN CURRENCY RESERVES

**ˌforeign ˈtrade zone** *n.* [C] (*abbr* **FTZ**) (*AmE*) (*Trade*) an area in the US where you can receive, work with and store imported goods without paying taxes on them

**foreman** /ˈfɔːmən; *AmE* ˈfɔːrmən/, **forewoman** /ˈfɔːwʊmən; *AmE* ˈfɔːrw-/ *n.* [C] (*pl.* **-men** /-mən/ **-women** /-wɪmɪn/) **1** a worker who is in charge of a group of other factory or building workers **2** a person who acts as the leader of a JURY in a court

**foˌrensic acˈcounting** /fəˈrensɪk; -ˈrenzɪk/ *n.* [U] (*Account.*) the activity of investigating financial records in order to find evidence of illegal payments, stolen money, etc. ▸ **ˌforensic acˈcountant** *n.* [C]

**forestry** /ˈfɒrɪstri; *AmE* ˈfɔːr-; ˈfɑːr-/ *n.* [U] the science or industry of planting and taking care of trees and forests: *a forestry company*

**forex** (*also* **Forex**) /ˈfɒreks; *AmE* ˈfɔːr-; ˈfɑːr-/ (*also* **FX**) *abbr* (*Finan.*) a short way of saying or writing **foreign exchange**: *trading in the forex market*

**forfeit** /ˈfɔːfɪt; *AmE* ˈfɔːrfət/ *v.* [T] to lose sth or have sth taken away from you because you have done sth wrong: *If you cancel your flight you will forfeit your deposit.*
▸ **forfeiture** /-fɪtʃə(r); *AmE* -fətʃər/ *n.* [U,C]: *the forfeiture of property*

**forge** /fɔːdʒ; *AmE* fɔːrdʒ/ *v.* **1** [T] to put a lot of effort into making sth successful or strong so that it will last: *We want to forge closer links with our suppliers.* **2** [T] to make an illegal copy of sth in order to deceive people: *a forged signature* **3** [I] (*with adv. or prep.*) to move forward or make progress very quickly: *Sales have forged* ***ahead*** *(by) 7%.* ◇ *Sterling forged* ***higher*** *against the dollar.*

**forgery** /ˈfɔːdʒəri; *AmE* ˈfɔːrdʒ-/ *n.* (*pl.* **-ries**) **1** [U] the crime of copying money, documents, etc. in order to deceive people **2** [C] something, for example a document, piece of paper money, etc., that has been copied in order to deceive people

**forgive** /fəˈɡɪv; *AmE* fərˈɡɪv/ *v.* [T] (**forgave** /-ˈɡeɪv/ **forgiven** /-ˈɡɪvn/) (*fml.*) (about a bank, company, etc.) to say that sb does not need to pay back money that they have borrowed: *forgiving developing countries' debt* ▸ **forˈgiveness** /-nəs/ *n.* [U]: *debt forgiveness*

**fork** /fɔːk; *AmE* fɔːrk/ *v.* PHRV **ˌfork ˈout (for sth)**; **ˌfork ˈout sth (for/on sth)** (*AmE also* **ˌfork ˈover sth (for sth)**) (*infml.*) to spend a lot of money on sth, esp. unwillingly: *Will consumers fork out for such an expensive service?* SYN SHELL (STH) OUT

**forklift** /ˈfɔːklɪft; *AmE* ˈfɔːrk-/ (*also* **ˌforklift ˈtruck**) *n.* [C] a vehicle with special equipment on the front for moving and lifting heavy objects

★**form** /fɔːm; *AmE* fɔːrm/ *n.*, *v.*

• ***n.*** [C] an official paper or electronic document containing questions and spaces for answers or information: *to complete/fill in/fill out/sign a* ~ ◊ *to file/return/submit a* ~
→ idiom at DUE

• ***v.*** [T,I] to start a group of people, such as an organization, a committee, etc.; to come together in a group of this kind: *a newly formed company* ◊ *The partnership formed in 1996.*

★**formal** /ˈfɔːml; *AmE* ˈfɔːrml/ *adj.* **1** (about a style of dress, speech, writing, behaviour, etc.) very correct and suitable for official or important occasions: *You should use a formal style of writing in the report.* **2** official; following an agreed or official way of doing things: *formal legal processes* **3** (*Econ.*) used to describe the part of an economy that involves businesses which are officially established or recognized and employment in these businesses: *the formal sector* ▸ **ˈformally** /-məli/ *adv.*

**formality** /fɔːˈmæləti; *AmE* fɔːrˈm-/ *n.* (*pl.* **-ties**) **1** [C, usu. pl.] a thing that you must do as a formal or an official part of a legal process, a social situation, etc: *It takes a month to complete the legal formalities of the sale.* **2** [C, usu. sing.] a thing that you must do as part of an official process, but which has little meaning and will not affect what happens: *He already knows he has the job so the interview is a mere formality.* **3** [U] correct and formal behaviour

**formalize**, **-ise** /ˈfɔːməlaɪz; *AmE* ˈfɔːrm-/ *v.* [T] **1** to give sth a fixed structure or form by introducing rules: *Entry to jobs at all levels has become more formalized.* **2** to make an arrangement, a plan, etc. legal or official: *They have now formalized the investigation.* ▸ **ˌformaliˈzation**, **-iˈsation** /-laɪˈzeɪʃn; *AmE* -ləˈz-/ *n.* [U]

**format** /ˈfɔːmæt; *AmE* ˈfɔːrmæt/ *n.*, *v.*

• ***n.*** [C] **1** the arrangement, plan, design, etc. that is chosen for sth: *a convenience store format* **2** the way in which information is stored on a computer, disk, tape, etc: *Convert the document into HTML format.* **3** (*Market.*) the shape and size of a book, magazine, etc: *The magazine is being relaunched in a new format.*

• ***v.*** [T] (-tt-) **1** to arrange text or numbers in a particular way on a page or a screen: *Format the document in two columns.* **2** (*IT*) to prepare a computer disk so that data can be recorded on it SYN INITIALIZE

**formatting** /ˈfɔːmætɪŋ; *AmE* ˈfɔːrm-/ *n.* [U,C] the way in which you arrange text and numbers on the screen in an electronic document, a SPREADSHEET, etc.

**ˈform ˌletter** *n.* [C] a letter with standard content that can be sent to a large number of people, esp. one produced in large numbers using a computer program

**formula** /ˈfɔːmjələ; *AmE* ˈfɔːrm-/ *n.* [C] (*pl.* **formulas** *or, especially in scientific use,* **formulae** /ˈfɔːmjəliː; *AmE* ˈfɔːrm-/) **1** (*Tech.*) a series of letters, numbers or symbols that represent a rule or law: *mathematical formulas* **2** a particular method of doing or achieving sth: *There's no simple formula **for** success.*

**ˈformula inˌvesting** *n.* [U] (*Finan.*) a way of investing money by following a particular set of rules

★**formulate** /ˈfɔːmjuleɪt; *AmE* ˈfɔːrm-/ *v.* [T] to create or prepare sth carefully, giving particular attention to the details: *to ~ a plan/policy/strategy*
▸ **ˌformuˈlation** /-ˈleɪʃn/ *n.* [U,C]

**ˌfor-ˈprofit** *adj.* used to describe a company or an organization that is run with the aim of making a profit

**fortune** /ˈfɔːtʃuːn; *AmE* ˈfɔːrtʃ-/ *n.* **1** [C] a large amount of money: *She made a fortune in real estate.* ◊ *to amass/build/lose/spend a* ~ **2** [C, usu. pl., U] the good and bad things that happen to a person, business, country, etc: *the changing fortunes of the film industry* ◊ *to restore/revive sb's/sth's ~s* → idiom at COST *v.*

**ˌFortune ˈ500** *n.* [sing.] a list published every year of the 500 US companies with the largest income

★**forum** /ˈfɔːrəm/ *n.* [C] a place where people can exchange opinions and ideas on a particular issue; a meeting organized for this purpose: *an electronic discussion forum*

★**forward** /ˈfɔːwəd; *AmE* ˈfɔːrwərd/ *adv.*, *adj.*, *v.*

• ***adv.*** **1** towards a good result: *technologies that will drive the industry forward* **2** in or concerning the future: ***Looking forward,*** *we expect sales to increase significantly.* **3** (*Comm.*; *Finan.*) if sth is sold or bought **forward**, the seller agrees to provide it for a fixed price at a particular time in the future, when they have produced or obtained it
IDM **ˌgoing ˈforward** in the future: *The competition will be less intense going forward.*

• *adj.* **1** relating to the future: *forward economic growth* **2** (*Comm.*) relating to sth that will be provided or delivered in the future: *the forward market for crude oil*
• *v.* [T] **1** to send or pass goods, information, an email, etc. to sb: *The message is automatically forwarded to your email account.* SYN SEND STH ON **2** to send a letter, etc. received at the address a person used to live or work at to their new address SYN SEND STH ON

**ˈforward ˌcontract** *n.* [C] (*Finan.*) an agreement to supply sth for a fixed price at a particular time in the future, when it has been produced or obtained, esp. an amount of a COMMODITY or a currency

**ˌforward ˈcover** *n.* [U,C] (*Finan.*) a right to buy or sell an amount of currency for a fixed price at a particular time in the future. Businesses buy **forward cover** to protect against changes in the value of currencies they will need in the future.

**forwarder** /ˈfɔːwədə(r); *AmE* ˈfɔːrwərdər/ = FREIGHT FORWARDER

**ˌforward exˈchange rate** *n.* [C] (*Finan.*) the price agreed for buying an amount of currency at a particular time in the future

**forwarding** /ˈfɔːwədɪŋ; *AmE* ˈfɔːrwərd-/ *n.* [U] (*Trade*; *Transpt.*) the process of arranging for goods to be transported and/or exported on behalf of others

**ˈforwarding adˌdress** *n.* [C] a new address to which letters should be sent from an old address that sb has moved away from

**ˈforwarding ˌagent** *n.* [C] (*Trade*; *Transpt.*) a company that is paid to arrange for goods to be transported and often exported on behalf of others SYN FREIGHT FORWARDER

**ˌforward inteˈgration** *n.* [U] (*Econ.*) a situation where a company buys a business that it normally supplies goods or services to, or starts doing the same work as that business

**ˈforward-ˌlooking** *adj.* planning for the future; willing to consider modern ideas and methods: *a forward-looking company*

**ˈforward price** *n.* [C] (*Finan.*) the price agreed for goods, currencies, etc. which will be delivered at a particular time in the future

**ˈforward sale** *n.* [C] (*Finan.*) a type of sale where sb agrees to supply sth for a fixed price at a particular time in the future, when they have produced or received it

**ˈforward ˌselling** *n.* [U] (*Finan.*) the practice of agreeing to supply sth for a fixed price at a particular time in the future, when it has been produced or obtained

**ˈforward slash** *n.* [C] the symbol (/) used in computer commands and in Internet addresses to separate the different parts

★**found** /faʊnd/ *v.* [T] to start sth, such as an organization or an institution, esp. by providing money: *Fiat was founded in 1899.* ◇ *a founding member of the firm*

★**foundation** /faʊnˈdeɪʃn/ *n.* **1** [C] an organization that is established to provide money for a particular purpose, for example charity, or that does research on a particular subject **2** [U] the act of starting a new institution or organization

★**founder** /ˈfaʊndə(r)/ *n.*, *v.*
• *n.* [C] a person who starts an organization, a company, etc: *He is the group's founder and chief executive.*
• *v.* [I] (about a plan, business, etc.) to fail because of a particular problem or difficulty: *Negotiations foundered* **on** *the issue of pay.*

**ˌfounder ˈmember** (*BrE*) (*AmE* **ˌcharter ˈmember**) *n.* [C] one of the first members of an organization, etc., esp. one who helped start it

**foundry** /ˈfaʊndri/ *n.* [C] (*pl.* **-ries**) **1** a factory where metal or glass is melted and made into different shapes or objects **2** a factory where MICROCHIPS are made

**ˌfour-colour ˈprocess** *n.* [C] a system used in printing in which the colours blue, red, yellow and black are combined to create a wide range of colours

**ˈfour-pack** *n.* [C] a set of four things wrapped and sold together

**fraction** /ˈfrækʃn/ *n.* [C] a small part or amount of sth: *The shares are now worth only a fraction of their original value.*

**fractional** /ˈfrækʃənl/ *adj.* **1** (*fml.*) very small; not important: *a fractional decline in earnings* **2** forming or connected with a part of sth larger: *They sold most of the business but kept the fractional part that was profitable.* ▶ **ˈfractionally** /-nəli/ *adv.*: *Sales are fractionally higher.*

**ˌfractional ˈownership** *n.* [U] (*Finan.*; *Law*) a situation where different people or companies buy and share an asset; the right that they each have to use, keep, etc. the asset ▶ **ˌfractional ˈowner** *n.* [C]

**ˈframework aˌgreement** *n.* [C] a formal arrangement between two or more groups, companies, countries, etc. to behave in a particular way or do particular things. It also suggests future actions or discussions.

★**franchise** /ˈfræntʃaɪz/ *n., v.*
• ***n.*** **1** (*Comm.*) [C,U] a right that sb buys from a company that allows them to do particular business activities, such as selling the company's goods and services in a particular area; formal permission given by a government to sb who wants to operate a public service as a business: *They won the franchise to operate outlets in the UK.* ◇ *to operate a business* ***under franchise***
⊙ *to* ***buy/have/hold/lose/own*** *a ~* • *to* ***give sb/grant sb/sell*** *a ~* • *a* ***catering/fast food/rail/television*** *~* • *a ~* ***business/company/operation*** • *a ~* ***agreement/holder/owner***
**2** (*Comm.*) [C] a business or service run under **franchise**: *a burger franchise* **3** (*Market.*) [C] the successful products or services produced by one company; the people that buy them: *We needed to widen the brand's franchise.* **4** (*Market.*) [C] the right to sell a particular film/movie, television show, computer program, etc. and use the name to market other products; the group of products that have the name: *They own the Tomb Raider franchise.*
• ***v.*** [T] (*Comm.*) (*usu. pass.*) to give or sell a **franchise** to sb: *The group has 9 000 franchised restaurants.*
▸ **ˈfranchising** *n.* [U]

**franchisee** /ˌfræntʃaɪˈziː/ *n.* [C] (*Comm.*) a person or company that has been given a **franchise**

**franchiser** (*also* **franchisor**) /ˈfræntʃaɪzə(r)/ *n.* [C] (*Comm.*) a company or an organization that gives sb a **franchise**

**franco** /ˈfræŋkəʊ; *AmE* -oʊ/ *adv.* (*abbr* **fco**) (*Trade*) used to say that goods will be delivered to a particular place without any charge for transport: *The goods will be delivered franco to your warehouse.*

**frank** /fræŋk/ *v.* [T] (*often pass.*) to stamp a mark on an envelope, etc. to show that the cost of posting it has been paid or does not need to be paid: *a franked envelope*

★**fraud** /frɔːd/ *n.* [U,C] the crime of deceiving sb to get money or things illegally: *a $12 m accounting fraud* ◇ *She was accused of committing fraud* ***against*** *her clients.* ◇ *bank/corporate/credit-card/financial ~*

**fraudulent** /ˈfrɔːdjələnt; *AmE* -dʒə-/ *adj.* intended to deceive sb, usu. in order to make money illegally: *He had made several fraudulent insurance claims.* ▸ **ˈfraudulently** /-tli/ *adv.*

**FRB** /ˌef ɑː ˈbiː; *AmE* ɑːr/ = FEDERAL RESERVE BANK, FEDERAL RESERVE BOARD

**Freddie Mac™** /ˌfredi ˈmæk/ *n.* (*Finan.*) **1** [sing.] (*abbr* **FHLMC**) in the US, the Federal Home Loan Mortgage Corporation, a private company supported by the government that supplies money for MORTGAGES **2** [C, usu. pl.] the bonds issued by **Freddie Mac**

★**free** /friː/ *adj., v., adv.*
• ***adj.*** (**freer** /ˈfriːə(r)/ **freest** /ˈfriːɪst/) **1** costing nothing: *free samples of products* **2** able to move or be exchanged between people without restrictions: *free movement of capital within the EU* **3** not containing or affected by sth harmful or unpleasant: *Our products are free* ***from*** *harmful chemicals.* **4** **-free** (*in adjs*) without the thing mentioned; not affected by the thing mentioned: *a risk-free investment* **5** available to be used: *free hard-disk space* **6** (about a person or a time) without particular plans or arrangements: *Keep Monday morning free.* **IDM** **there's no such ˌthing as a free ˈlunch** used to say that it is not possible to get sth for nothing
• ***v.*** [T] **~ sb/sth (up)** to make sb/sth available for a particular purpose: *Selling these assets will free up capital to invest.*
• ***adv.*** without payment: *Children under five travel free.*

**ˌfree ˈagent** *n.* [C] (*Comm.*) a person who is independent and works for several different companies
▸ **ˌfree ˈagency** *n.* [U]

**ˈfree aˈlongside ˈship** *phr.* (*abbr* **FAS**) (*Trade*) the seller delivers the goods to a ship at a particular port and gets official permission for them to be exported. The buyer is responsible for having the goods loaded onto the ship and transported: *We deliver FAS Tokyo.*
→ INCOTERM

**freebie** /ˈfriːbi/ *n.* [C] (*infml.*) something that is given to sb without payment, usu. by a company: *They always put some freebies in with the orders.*

**ˌfree ˈcarrier** *phr.* (*abbr* **FCA**) (*Trade*) the seller gets official permission for the goods to be exported and delivers them to the person or company who will transport them on behalf of the buyer: *Our delivery terms are FCA Stockholm airport.*
→ INCOTERM

**ˌfree ˈcash flow** *n.* [U,C] (*Account.*) income that a business has left at the end of an accounting period after paying for its supplies, workers, etc. and any assets that it has bought: *The group needs to generate free cash flow in order to repay debt.*

**ˌfree collective ˈbargaining** *n.* [U] (*BrE*) (*HR*) formal talks between unions and employers, about pay and working conditions, that are not limited by the law or government

**ˌfree compeˈtition** *n.* [U] (*Econ.*) a system in which prices, incomes, etc. are controlled by supply and demand and businesses compete freely with each other

**ˌfreedom of associˈation** *n.* [U] (*Law*) the right to join or form an organization, esp. a union

**ˌfree ˈenterprise** *n.* [U] an economic system in which private businesses compete with each other without much government control

**ˌfree ˈfall** *n.* [U] a sudden drop in the value of sth that cannot be stopped: *The share price* ***went into*** *free fall after the firm announced poor year-end results.*

**ˌfree-ˈfloating** *adj.* able to move freely; not controlled by anything: *a free-floating exchange rate*

**Freefone™** = FREEPHONE

**ˈfree-for-all** *n.* [sing.] a situation in which there are no rules or controls and everyone acts for their own advantage: *a price-cutting free-for-all*

**freehold** /ˈfriːhəʊld; *AmE* -hoʊld/ *n.* [C,U] (*esp. BrE*) (*Law*; *Prop.*) the fact of owning a building or piece of land for a period of time that is not limited: *Private tenants in flats have the right to buy the freehold from their landlord.* ▸ **ˈfreehold** *adj., adv.* **ˈfreeholder** *n.* [C]

**ˈfree ˌissue** = SCRIP ISSUE

**freelance** /ˈfriːlɑːns; *AmE* -læns/ *adj., n., v.*
• ***adj.*** used to describe a way of earning money by selling your work or services to several different organizations rather than being employed by one particular one: *a ~ writer/journalist/executive* ◇ *~ work/income* ▸ **ˈfreelance** *adv.*
• ***n.*** (*also* **ˈfreelancer**) [C] a person who works **freelance**
• ***v.*** [I] to earn money by selling your work to several different companies: *He freelances* ***for*** *three newspapers.*

★ **ˌfree ˈmarket** *n.* [C] (*Econ.*) an economic system in which the price of goods and services is affected by supply and demand rather than controlled by a government

**ˌfree-market eˈconomy** = MARKET ECONOMY

**ˌfree markeˈteer** *n.* [C] a person who believes that countries should have FREE MARKETS ▸ **ˌfree markeˈteering** *n.* [U]

**ˌfree on ˈboard** *phr.* (*abbr* **FOB**) (*Trade*) the seller delivers the goods to a ship at a particular port and gets official permission for them to be exported. The buyer is responsible for the goods once they are put on the ship: *All our prices are FOB Rotterdam.* → INCOTERM

**Freephone** (*also* **Freefone™**) /ˈfriːfəʊn; *AmE* -foʊn/ *n.* [U] in the UK, a system in which the cost of a telephone call is paid for by the organization being called, rather than by the person making the call

**ˌfree ˈport** *n.* [C] (*Trade*) a port at which tax is not paid on goods that have been brought there temporarily before being sent to a different country

**Freepost** /ˈfriːpəʊst; *AmE* -poʊst/ *n.* [U] in the UK, a system in which the cost of sending a letter is paid for by the organization receiving it, rather than by the person sending it

**ˌfree ˈrider** *n.* [C] a person or an organization that accepts a benefit or service that other people pay for or have worked to get ▸ **ˌfree ˈride** *n.* [C, usu. sing.] **ˈfreeride** *v.* [I]

**freesheet** /ˈfriːʃiːt/ *n.* [C] (*BrE*) a free newspaper, esp. one that is delivered to all the homes in a particular area and is paid for by advertising: *Metro, the London freesheet*

**ˌfree-standing ˈinsert** *n.* [C] (*abbr* **FSI**) (*Market.*) a printed advertisement of one or more pages that is put inside a newspaper or magazine, but is not attached to it

**ˌfree ˈtelevision** = FREE TV

**ˌfree-to-ˈair** *adj.* (about television programmes) that you do not have to pay to watch ▸ **ˌfree-to-ˈair** *adv.*

**ˌfree ˈtrade** *n.* [U] (*Econ.*) a system of international trade in which there are no restrictions or taxes on imports and exports: *a free-trade agreement/zone*

**ˌfree ˈtrial** *n.* [C] (*Market.*) the chance to use a product or service for a short period without paying anything before you decide whether to buy it or not

**ˌfree ˈTV** (*also* **ˌfree ˈtelevision**) *n.* [U] a system of television broadcasting in which you do not pay to watch programmes

**freeware** /ˈfriːweə(r); *AmE* -wer/ *n.* [U] (*IT*) software that is offered free for anyone to use

★**freeze** /friːz/ *v.* (**froze** /frəʊz; *AmE* froʊz/**frozen** /ˈfrəʊzn; *AmE* ˈfroʊzn/) **1** [T] to hold costs, wages, prices, etc. at a fixed level for a period of time: *Salaries have been frozen for the current year.* SYN PEG **2** [T] to prevent money, a bank account, etc. from being used, esp. by getting a court order: *The company's assets have been frozen.* **3** [I] when a computer screen **freezes**, you cannot move any of the images, etc. on it, because there is a problem with the system ▸ **freeze** *n.* [C]: *a pay/recruitment ~* ◇ *a freeze on exports* PHR V ˌ**freeze sb ˈout (of sth)** to deliberately try to prevent other businesses from competing in a particular market, for example by selling goods very cheaply

ˈ**free zone** *n.* [C] (*AmE*) (*Trade*) an area in a country where goods can be imported and stored without paying taxes on them

★**freight** /freɪt/ *n.*, *v.* (*Transpt.*)

• *n.* [U] **1** goods that are transported by ships, planes, trains or lorries/trucks; the system of transporting goods in this way: *shifting freight off the roads and onto rail* ◇ *Freight was organized by our distributor.*

⊕ *a ~ **depot/terminal/yard*** • *to **carry/haul/transport** ~* • *a ~ **carrier/hauler/operator***

**2** the amount charged to transport a load of goods by ship, plane, train or lorry/truck: *to pay the freight*

• *v.* [T] to send or carry goods by air, sea or train: *The goods were freighted by air.* ▸ ˈ**freighting** *n.* [U]

**freightage** /ˈfreɪtɪdʒ/ *n.* [U] (*Transpt.*) the amount charged to transport a load of goods by ship, plane, train or lorry/truck

ˌ**freight colˈlect** (*also* ˌ**freight ˈforward**, *esp. in BrE*) *phr.* (*Trade*) the person or company receiving the goods pays the delivery costs when they receive the goods from the transport company: *All shipments are freight collect.*

**freighter** /ˈfreɪtə(r)/ *n.* [C] a large ship or plane that carries goods

ˌ**freight ˈforward** = FREIGHT COLLECT

ˈ**freight ˌforwarder** (*also* ˈ**forwarder**) *n.* [C] (*Trade*; *Transpt.*) a company that is paid to arrange for goods to be transported and often exported on behalf of others SYN FORWARDING AGENT ▸ ˈ**freight ˌforwarding** *n.* [U]

ˌ**freight ˌpreˈpaid** *phr.* (*esp. AmE*) (*Trade*) the person or company sending the goods pays for the delivery costs before giving them to the transport company

ˈ**frequency ˌdiscount** *n.* [C] (*Market.*) a reduced price offered to advertisers who publish an advertisement a particular number of times during a particular period of time

ˌ**frequent ˈflyer** *n.* [C] a person who uses a particular airline a lot, esp. sb who belongs to a club which allows them to receive free flights or special advantages from the airline

ˌ**frictional unemˈployment** (*also* ˌ**search unemˈployment**) *n.* [U] (*Econ.*) the number of people who are not doing paid employment because they are moving between jobs and have not yet found another one, although there are jobs available

**friendly** /ˈfrendli/ *adj.* (**-lier**, **-liest**) **1** (*often in compound adjs*) helpful and easy to use; that helps sb/sth or does not harm them/it **2** (*Finan.*) (about an attempt to buy or gain control of a company) that the directors of the company to be bought want and are willing to accept or consider: *a ~ acquisition/bid/offer/takeover*

**frills** /frɪlz/ *n.* [pl.] things that are not necessary but are added to make sth more attractive or interesting: *cheap flights with no frills*

**fringe** /frɪndʒ/ *n.* [C] the outer or less important part of an area or a group: *offices on the fringe of the City*

ˈ**fringe ˌbenefit** *n.* [C, usu. pl.] (*HR*) extra things that an employer gives you as well as your wages

**FRN** /ˌef ɑːr ˈen/ = FLOATING-RATE NOTE

**front** /frʌnt/ *n.*, *adj.*, *v.*

• *n.* **1** [sing.] behaviour that is not genuine, done to hide your true feelings or opinions: *to **present a united front*** (= show that you have the same views and demands) **2** [C, usu. sing.] a person or an organization used to hide an illegal or secret activity **3** [C] the front side of a building: *a shop/store ~* IDM ˌ**front of ˈmind** (*also* ˌ**top of ˈmind**) (*Market.*) if a brand or product is **front of mind**, it is one that people are very aware of and will name first when thinking about a particular type of product (ˌ**out**) ˌ**in ˈfront** leading a particular industry ˌ**up ˈfront** (*infml.*) as payment in advance: *They wanted three* *months' rent up front.* → idioms at CASH, LEAD *v.*, QUEUE *n.*

• *adj.* IDM **on the front 'burner** (*esp. AmE*) (*infml.*) (about an issue, a plan, etc.) being given a lot of attention because it is considered important OPP ON THE BACK BURNER

• *v.* [T] to lead or represent a company, an organization, etc., esp. in a particular activity or project: *He fronts a multinational.*

**frontage** /ˈfrʌntɪdʒ/ *n.* [C,U] (*Prop.*) the front of a building such as a shop/store, esp. when this faces a road or river

**'frontage road** = SERVICE ROAD

**ˌfront 'desk** *n.* [C, usu. sing.] the place where visitors go to introduce themselves or get information when they enter a hotel or an office building

**'front end** *n.*, *adj.*

• *n.* [C] **1** the part of a business that meets and deals with customers: *The website serves as the front end of the supply chain.* **2** the beginning of a project, a process, an investment, a period of time, etc: *You pay a fee at the front end of the loan.* **3** (*IT*) the part of a computer program that a user sees and uses to operate other parts of the program or system: *a graphical front end*

• *adj.* **1** connected with the beginning of a project, a process, an investment, a period of time, etc: *The policy has a front-end fee.* **2** (*IT*) that allows the user to operate other parts of a computer program or system

**ˌfront-end 'load** *n.* [C] (*Finan.*) the fee an investor pays when they buy shares in an investment fund, an insurance policy, etc., which is included in the first payment ▸ **ˌfront-end 'loaded** *adj.*

**ˌfront-end 'loading** *n.* [U] (*Finan.*) the practice of a fund, bank, etc. taking most of its fees and expenses from payments that are made at the beginning of the period of an investment, a loan, etc.; the fees and expenses taken in this way

**ˌfront 'line** (*also* **frontline**) *n.* [C] (*usually* **the ~**) **1** the area of greatest activity, where you can have an important effect on sth: *The company is in the front line of the telecoms industry.* **2** the group of employees in a company who deal directly with customers or who physically produce sth; the work that they do

**'front-line** (*also* **frontline**) *adj.* (*HR*) **1** used to describe an employee who deals directly with customers or physically makes a product: *Front-line staff should know all the products on sale.* **2** used to describe a manager who deals directly with a group of workers

**ˌfront-'load** *v.* [T] (*Finan.*) (*usu. pass.*) to charge or pay for sth at or near the beginning: *the front-loaded costs of acquiring a new business* ▸ **ˌfront-'loading** *n.* [U]

**ˌfront 'office** *n.* [sing.] (*esp. AmE*) the part of a business concerned with managing things or dealing with the public

**ˌfront of 'house** *n.* [U] the part of a hotel, restaurant or other business that involves dealing directly with customers: *a front-of-house manager/worker*

**ˌfront 'runner** *n.* [C] a person or an organization that seems most likely to win a race or competition

**frozen** /ˈfrəʊzn; *AmE* ˈfroʊzn/ *adj.* **1** (about food) kept at a very low temperature in order to preserve it: *~ desserts/meals/vegetables* **2** (about money, assets, etc.) not available to be used or sold because of an official rule or order: *People's savings remain frozen in bank accounts.*

**FRS** /ˌef ɑːr ˈes/ = FEDERAL RESERVE SYSTEM

**frugal** /ˈfruːgl/ *adj.* using only as much money or food as is necessary: *frugal shoppers* OPP EXTRAVAGANT ▸ **frugality** /fruˈgæləti/ *n.* [U] **'frugally** /-gəli/ *adv.*

**FSA** /ˌef es ˈeɪ/ = FINANCIAL SERVICES AUTHORITY

**FSI** /ˌef es ˈaɪ/ = FREE-STANDING INSERT

**FT** /ˌef ˈtiː/ *abbr* **1** in the UK, Financial Times **2** (*written*) = FULL-TIME

**FTA** /ˌef tiː ˈeɪ/ *abbr* (*Econ.*) a FREE TRADE agreement

**FTC** /ˌef tiː ˈsiː/ = FEDERAL TRADE COMMISSION

**FTSE™** /ˈfʊtsi/ *n.* [sing.] **1** a company that publishes INDICES for particular markets: *The main FTSE indices enjoyed strong gains.* **2** an average of the share prices of particular companies traded on the London Stock Exchange, usu. the 100 largest companies: *On Friday, the FTSE closed down 11 points at 3 567.*

**ˌFTSE '100 ˌIndex** (*also* **ˌFTSE '100**) /ˌfʊtsi wʌn ˈhʌndrəd/ (*also* **'Footsie**, *infml.*) *n.* [sing.] an average of the share prices of the 100 largest companies traded on the London Stock Exchange: *The FTSE 100 Index fell 11 points to 3567.*

**FTZ** /ˌef tiː ˈzed; *AmE* ˈziː/ = FOREIGN TRADE ZONE

**fuel** /ˈfjuːəl/ *n., v.*
• ***n.*** [U,C] any material that produces heat or power, usu. when it is burnt: *fossil/nuclear ~*
• ***v.*** [T] (**-ll-**) ( (*AmE* **-l-**) **1** to supply sth with material that can be burnt to produce heat or power: *oil-fuelled power stations* **2** to increase sth; to make sth stronger: *Higher salaries helped to fuel inflation.*

★ **fulfil** (*AmE* **fulfill**) /fʊlˈfɪl/ *v.* [T] (**-filling, -filled, -filled**) **1** to do or have what is required or necessary: *to ~ the terms/conditions of an agreement* ◇ *to ~ a duty/an obligation* **2** to do or achieve what was hoped for or expected: *helping employees to fulfil their potential* ◇ *to ~ an ambition/a dream* **3** to have a particular role or purpose: *The 'touch screen' fulfils the function of a keyboard.* **4** (*Comm.*) if a business **fulfils** an order, they supply the full amount of sth that has been asked for **5** if a job **fulfils** you or you **fulfil** yourself, you feel happy and satisfied with what you are doing or what you have done
▸ **fulˈfilment** (*AmE* **fulfillment**) *n.* [U]: *The offer is subject to the fulfilment of certain conditions.* ◇ *order fulfilment* ◇ *personal fulfilment*

**fulfilled** /fʊlˈfɪld/ *adj.* feeling happy and satisfied that you are doing sth useful with your life

**fulfilling** /fʊlˈfɪlɪŋ/ *adj.* causing sb to feel satisfied and useful: *I'm finding the work much more fulfilling now.*

**fulˈfilment house** *n.* [C] (*Comm.*) an organization paid to deal with mail, requests for information or orders for another company

**ˌfull-circle ˈfeedback** = 360-DEGREE FEEDBACK

**ˌFull Conˈtainer Load** *n.* [C] (*abbr* **FCL**) (*Transpt.*) an amount of goods being transported for sb that fills one whole container

**ˌfull ˈcosting** *n.* [U] (*Account.*) a way of calculating the cost of a product by including all costs involved in producing it and running the business, such as raw materials, rent, electricity or wages SYN ABSORPTION COSTING

**ˌfull-ˈpage** *adj.* filling a complete page of a newspaper or magazine: *a full-page ad*

**ˌfull-ˈservice** *adj.* providing a complete range of services for customers: *a ~ bank/brokerage*

**ˌfull -ˈsize** (*also* **ˌfull-ˈsized**) *adj.* not made smaller; of the usual size: *full-size trucks*

**ˌfull-ˈtime** *adj., adv.* (*abbr* **FT**) for all the hours of a week during which people normally work: *a full-time employee* ◇ *a full-time job*
▸ **ˌfull-ˈtimer** *n.* [C]

**ˌfull-ˈyear** *adj.* (*Account.*) relating to a complete FINANCIAL YEAR: *~ results/profits/forecasts*

★ **function** /ˈfʌŋkʃn/ *n., v.*
• ***n.*** **1** [C,U] a special activity or purpose of a person or thing: *to fulfil/perform a useful ~* **2** [C] the part of a company that is responsible for a particular area: *Our key business functions are not all in one place.* **3** (*IT*) [C] a part of a program, etc. that carries out a basic operation: *the function keys* **4** [C] a social event or official ceremony: *The staff are allowed two social functions a year.* **5** [sing.] **a ~ of sth** if one thing is a **function of** another, its value depends on the varying values of the other thing: (*fig.*) *Salary is a function of age and experience.*
• ***v.*** [I] to work in the correct way: *The fire alarm system is now functioning again.* SYN OPERATE
PHR V **ˈfunction as sb/sth** to perform the action or the job of the thing or person mentioned: *The sofa also functions as a bed.*

**functional** /ˈfʌŋkʃənl/ *adj.* **1** having a special purpose: *Any project can be broken down into different functional roles.* **2** (*HR*) connected with a particular area of activity or skill, esp. within a business: *The main functional areas of a business are finance, production, personnel and marketing.* **3** practical and useful, often with little or no decoration: *The design is simple and functional.* **4** working; able to do the job for which it is intended: *The system is only 80% functional.*
▸ **ˈfunctionally** /-nəli/ *adv.*

**ˌfunctional ackˈnowledgement** *n.* [C] (*abbr* **FA**) (*E-comm.*) an electronic message sent to sb to say that their electronic order, INVOICE, etc. has been received

**ˌfunctional flexiˈbility** *n.* [U] (*HR*) the policy of training workers so that they have more skills and abilities and can do a greater variety of tasks

★ **functionality** /ˌfʌŋkʃəˈnæləti/ *n.* (*pl.* **-ties**) **1** (*IT*) [U,C] the range of functions that a computer or other electronic system can perform: *a phone with email functionality* **2** [U] the quality in sth of being very suitable for the purpose it was designed for

**ˌfunctional organiˈzation** *n.* [C] (*HR*) an organization where employees are put into different departments depending on the type of work that they do

★**fund** /fʌnd/ *n., v.* (*Finan.*)
• ***n.*** **1** [C] an amount of money that is saved or collected for a particular purpose, esp. for investing in companies, projects, etc.; an organization that controls this money: *We set up a fund for technological research.* ◇ *a $7.5 bn* ***investment*** *fund* **2 funds** [pl.] money that sb/sth has available to spend: *limited funds for research* ◇ *to borrow/obtain/raise/secure ~* ◇ *private/public finds*
• ***v.*** [T] **~ sth (by/with/from sth)** (*often pass.*) to provide money for sth: *a government-funded programme*
▸ **ˈfunder** *n.* [C]: *the only funders of the business*

**fundamentals** /ˌfʌndəˈmentlz/ *n.* [pl.] (*Econ.*) the important aspects of an economy, an industry or a business, which lead to its success or failure over a long period of time; measures of these

★**funding** /ˈfʌndɪŋ/ *n.* [U] money for a particular purpose; the act of providing money for such a purpose: *cuts in government funding for research* ◇ *finding alternative sources of funding* ◇ ***private/public/state*** *~* ◇ *a ~* ***crisis/deficit/gap/problem/shortfall***

**ˈfund ˌmanagement** *n.* [U] (*Finan.*) the act of managing an amount of money which is used to buy and sell shares, bonds, etc. on behalf of investors to make as much profit as possible SYN INVESTMENT MANAGEMENT
▸ **ˈfund ˌmanager** *n.* [C]

**ˌfund of ˈfunds** *n.* [C] (*Finan.*) a type of investment fund, esp. a UNIT TRUST, that invests money in a range of other investment funds

**ˈfund-ˌraising** *n.* **1** (*Finan.*) [C,U] the act or activity of obtaining money from investors, lenders, etc: *a ~ exercise/plan* **2** [U] the activity of collecting money for a charity, etc.

**fungible** /ˈfʌndʒəbl/ *adj., n.*
• ***adj.*** (*Finan.; Law*) that can be replaced or exchanged with sth of the same kind without changing the quality, characteristics or value: *Oil is a fungible commodity: if one producer stops supplying you, you can simply go to another.* ◇ *These bonds are fungible with those already listed.*
• ***n.*** [C, usu. pl.] **1** (*Finan.; Law*) shares, bonds, etc. that can replace or be exchanged with others without losing their value **2** (*Comm.; Law*) goods that are valued and sold by their number or weight: *Grain and flour are typical fungibles.*

**ˈfunny ˌmoney** *n.* [U] **1** money with little or no value, such as money that has been printed illegally or is in an unusual currency **2** an unusual type of shares, bonds, etc. that a company issues, whose value often moves up and down rapidly

**furnish** /ˈfɜːnɪʃ; *AmE* ˈfɜːrnɪʃ/ *v.* [T] **1** to put furniture in an office, a room, etc: *furnished accommodation* (= with furniture) **2** (*fml.*) **~ sb/sth with sth | ~ sth** to supply or provide sb/sth with sth; to supply sth to sb: *Please furnish us with the correct information.*

**ˈfurther to** *prep.* (*fml.*) used in letters, emails, etc. to refer to a previous letter, email, conversation, etc: *Further to our conversation of last Friday, I would like to book the conference centre for 26 June.*

**future** /ˈfjuːtʃə(r)/ *n.* [C, usu. pl.] (*also* **ˈfutures ˌcontract** [C]) (*Finan.*) a contract to buy or sell a particular amount of sth, such as a raw material, currency or shares, at a particular time in the future and for a particular price
⊕ ***coffee/gold/oil/energy*** *~s* ♦ ***bond/commodity/stock*** *~s* ♦ *to* ***buy/sell/trade (in)*** *~s* ♦ *~s* ***expire/trade*** ♦ *a ~s* ***broker/trader***
→ idiom at HITCH *v.*

**ˌfutures comˈmission ˌmerchant** *n.* [C] (*abbr* **FCM**) (*Finan.*) a person or an organization that tries to get or accepts orders from people who want to buy or sell **futures**

**ˈfutures ˌcontract** = FUTURE

**ˈfutures exˌchange** *n.* [C] (*Finan.*) a market at a particular place where **futures** are traded

**ˈfutures ˌmarket** *n.* [C] (*Finan.*) the buying and selling of **futures**; a particular place where this type of trading occurs: *The price of cocoa has shot up on the futures market.*

**fwd** (*AmE* **fwd.**) *abbr* a short way of writing **forward**

**FX** /ˌefˈeks/ = FOREX

**FY** = FINANCIAL YEAR, FISCAL YEAR

**FYI** *abbr* (*infml.*) a short way of writing **for your information**: *FYI, I have attached our programme for next year.*

# Gg

**G** /dʒiː/ *abbr* (*infml.*) a short way of saying or writing **grand** (= one thousand dollars, etc.)

**the G10** /ˌdʒiː ˈten/ *abbr* **Group of Ten** the eleven nations whose central banks meet and work together to support the international finance and currency system and who lend money to the IMF

**the G7** /ˌdʒiː ˈsevn/ *abbr* **Group of Seven** the seven leading industrial nations whose finance officers meet regularly to discuss economic and financial matters

**the G8** /ˌdʒiː ˈeɪt/ *abbr* **Group of Eight** the eight leading industrial nations that meet regularly to discuss political and economic issues

**G&A(E)** /ˌdʒiː ənd ˈeɪ (ˈiː)/ *abbr* **general and administrative (expenses)** (*Account.*) used to describe the general costs of running a business, such as those of employing accountants or lawyers, rather than those connected with a particular product or service

**GAAP** /ɡɑːp/ = GENERALLY ACCEPTED ACCOUNTING PRINCIPLES

**gadget** /ˈɡædʒɪt/ *n.* [C] a small tool or device that does sth useful: *electronic gadgets*

**ˈgag clause** = GAGGING CLAUSE

**gage** = GAUGE

**ˈgagging clause** (*BrE*) (*AmE* **ˈgag clause**) *n.* [C] (*HR*) a part of a contract of employment that prevents an employee from giving information about the company to journalists, politicians, union officers, etc.

**ˈgagging ˌorder** (*BrE*) (*AmE* **ˈgag ˌorder**) *n.* [C] (*Law*) an order made by a court, a government, etc. that prevents sth being discussed in public or reported by journalists

★ **gain** /ɡeɪn/ *v., n.*

• ***v.*** **1** [T] to gradually get more of sth: *I have gained a lot of experience in the job.* **2** [T,I] (about a currency, share price, etc.) to increase in value: *The shares gained 5 per cent to $14.70.* OPP LOSE → idiom at GROUND *n.*

• ***n.*** **1** [C] an increase or an improvement in the amount, value or level of sth: *The company reported a 16% gain* ***in*** *market share.* ◇ *Media shares enjoyed strong gains this week.* OPP LOSS **2** [C] an advantage, benefit or profit that is achieved from doing sth: *The potential gains of doing business online are great, but so are the challenges.* **3** [U] financial profit, esp. when this benefits only yourself: *They sold the company purely* ***for*** *short-term gain.*

**gainer** /ˈɡeɪnə(r)/ *n.* [C] **1** (used in newspapers) shares, a currency, an investment, etc. that increases in value over a period of time: *the FTSE 100 gainers* SYN WINNER OPP LOSER **2** a person, an organization, etc. that benefits from sth

**gainsharing** (*also* **gain sharing**) /ˈɡeɪnʃeərɪŋ; *AmE* -ʃer-/ *n.* [U] (*HR*) a system in which employees receive part of the increased profit that has been made by improvements in the rate, the amount or the cost of producing goods that they have helped to make

**galleria** /ˌɡæləˈriːə/ *n.* [C] a collection of small shops/stores under a single roof

**galloping** /ˈɡæləpɪŋ/ *adj.* increasing or growing rapidly: *galloping* ***inflation***

**Gallup poll™** /ˈɡæləp pəʊl; *AmE* poʊl/ *n.* [C] a way of finding out public opinion by asking a typical group of people questions

**gamble** /ˈɡæmbl/ *v., n.*

• ***v.*** [T,I] **1** to take a risk with sth, hoping that you will be successful: *We gambled* ***that*** *consumers would pay more for an online service.* **2** to risk money on a card game, horse race, etc: *He gambled all his money* ***on*** *the race.* ▸ **ˈgambler** /-blə(r)/ *n.* [C]
PHR V **ˌgamble sth aˈway** to lose sth such as money, possessions, etc. by gambling

• ***n.*** [sing.] an action that you take when you know there is a risk but when you hope that the result will be a success: *They* ***took*** *a gamble* ***on*** *the yen going up in value.*

**game** /ɡeɪm/ *n.* [C] (*infml.*) a type of activity or business: *How long have you been in this game?* IDM **the only, best, biggest, etc. game in ˈtown** (*esp. AmE*) the only, best, biggest, etc. thing or person that is available or worth dealing with: *At that time, bonds were the only game in town.* **raise/lift/up your ˈgame** to improve the way that you perform an activity or do business → idioms at AHEAD OF, BEAT, RULE *n.*

**ˈgame plan** *n.* [C] a plan for success in the future: *to* ***develop*** *a game plan for the business*

**ˈgame ˌtheory** *n.* [U] an economic theory in which situations where people, businesses, etc. compete with each other are analysed as a type of game, with each person, business, etc. choosing the best action from a limited set of actions, based on what the others are likely to do

**gaming** /'geɪmɪŋ/ *n.* [U] **1** the business of taking bets from people or providing games, activities, etc. that allow people to bet money: *regulation of the gaming industry* **2** playing computer games: *online gaming*

**'Gantt chart** /'gænt/ *n.* [C] a chart used for managing the tasks involved in a project that shows when each stage should start and end and compares the amount of work done with the amount planned

★**gap** /gæp/ *n.* [C] **1** a difference that separates two people, groups or things: *The gap* **between** *men's and women's pay has narrowed.*
⊙ *to* ***bridge/close/narrow*** *a ~* ◆ *a* ***big/growing/small/wide/widening*** *~*
**2** a space where sth is missing: *We need to fill the gaps in our top management.* ◇ *a €1.5 bn financing gap*
⊙ *to* ***bridge/close/fill/plug*** *a ~* ◆ *a* ***big/major/significant*** *~*
**3** an area of business in which few or no companies operate but where profits could be made: *We saw a* ***gap in the market*** *for low-cost pensions.*
⊙ *to* ***fill/identify/leave/see*** *a ~*

**'gap a,nalysis** *n.* [C,U] (*Market.*) a comparison between the products, skills, etc. that are available and what is needed, used to decide what products, skills, etc. to develop

**garbage** /'gɑːbɪdʒ; *AmE* 'gɑːrb-/ *n.*
**IDM** **garbage ,in, garbage 'out** (*abbr* **GIGO**) (*IT*) used to express the idea that if wrong or poor quality data is put into a computer, wrong or poor quality data will come out of it

**'gardening leave** (*also* **'garden leave**) *n.* [U] (*both BrE*) (*HR*) a period when an employee, esp. a senior person, who is going to leave a company is not allowed to work but is sent home on full pay, so that they will not be able to compete with the company or pass important information to a competitor

**garnish** /'gɑːnɪʃ; *AmE* 'gɑːrnɪʃ/ (*also* **,garni'shee**) *v.* [T] (*Law*) to take away part of sb's income or money and pay it to a person or an organization that they owe money to: *He's had his wages garnished.*
▸ **'garnishment** *n.* [U,C]: *wage garnishments*

**garnishee** /,gɑːnɪ'ʃiː; *AmE* ,gɑːrn-/ *n.*, *v.* (*Law*)
• *n.* [C] a company, bank, etc. that is ordered by a court to keep or to GARNISH sb's income or money
• *v.* [T] (**-shees**, **-sheeing**, **-sheed**) **1** to make sb a **garnishee** **2** = GARNISH

**gas** /gæs/ *n.* (*pl.* **gases** *or* **gasses** *less frequent*) **1** [C,U] any substance like air that is neither a solid nor a liquid: *CFC gases* **2** [U] a particular type of **gas** or mixture of **gases** used as fuel for heating, cooking, etc: *a gas-fired power station*

**gatekeeper** /'geɪtkiːpə(r)/ *n.* [C] a person in an organization who controls access to information, goods or services, or to the people in the organization who make the important decisions: *He told me you've got to get past the gatekeeper to the decision-maker before you can make a sale.*

**gateway** /'geɪtweɪ/ *n.* **1** [C, usu. sing.] a place through which you can go to reach another larger place: *The port is an important ~* ***to/into*** *southern Africa.* **2** [C, usu. sing.] a means of getting or achieving sth: *A good education is the gateway* **to** *success.* **3** (*IT*) [C] a device that is used to connect two computer networks together, esp. a connection to the Internet

**gauge** (*AmE also* **gage**) /geɪdʒ/ *n.*, *v.*
• *n.* **1** [C, usu. sing.] a fact or an event that can be used to estimate or judge sth: *The retail sector is closely watched as a key gauge of consumer spending.* **2** [C] a system that is used to calculate or measure the level, size, etc. of sth: *the consumer price index, the main US inflation gauge* **3** [C] (*often in compounds*) an instrument for measuring the amount or level of sth: *a fuel/petrol/temperature ~*
• *v.* [T] **1** to estimate or measure the level, size, etc. of sth: *We rely on previous sales figures to gauge demand.* **2** to make a judgement about sb/sth: *It's too early to gauge* **whether** *the scheme was a success.* **3** (*Tech.*) to measure sth accurately using a special instrument

**gazelle** /gə'zel/ *n.* [C] (*infml.*) a way of referring to a company that is growing very quickly

**gazette** /gə'zet/ *n.* [C] **1** a newspaper or magazine published by an organization, a government, etc. containing official notices and information **2 Gazette** used in the titles of some newspapers

**gazump** /gə'zʌmp/ *v.* [T] (*BrE*) (*Prop.*) (*usu. pass.*) when sb who has made an offer to pay a particular price for sth, and who has had this offer accepted, is **gazumped**, their offer is no longer accepted by the seller, because sb else has made a higher offer ▶ **ga'zumping** *n.* [U]

**GB** (*also* **Gb**) = GIGABYTE

★**GDP** /ˌdʒiː diː ˈpiː/ *abbr* (*Econ.*) **gross domestic product** the total value of all the goods and services produced by a country in one year: *Tourism contributes about 5% of GDP.* ◇ *GDP grew by 0.5 per cent in the fourth quarter.*

**gear** /ɡɪə(r); *AmE* ɡɪr/ *v., n.*

• *v.* [T] **~ sth for/to/towards sth** (*usu. pass.*) to make, change or prepare sth so that it is suitable for a particular purpose or for particular people: *The magazine is geared* **towards** *women over 35.* PHR V **'gear sth/yourself for sth** to make sth/yourself ready for sth: *The company is gearing itself for future success.* **'gear sth/yourself to sth** to depend on sth; to be connected with sth: *Salary adjustments are geared to the cost of living.* **ˌgear (sb/sth) 'up (for/to sth)** to prepare yourself/sb/sth to do sth: *The country is gearing up for elections.*

• *n.* **1** [U] (*infml.*) a piece of equipment or a system: *computer gear* **2** [U] equipment or clothing used for a particular purpose: *sports/protective ~* **3** (*infml.*) [U,C] the speed at which sth takes place; the effort involved in doing sth: (*BrE*) *Sales growth has moved into* **top gear**. IDM **get, kick, swing, etc. into 'gear; get, kick, etc. sth into 'gear** to start working, or to start sth working, in an efficient way: *If you fill in the form, within 24 hours the service will kick into gear.*

**geared** /ɡɪəd; *AmE* ɡɪrd/ *adj.* (*BrE*) (*Finan.*) **1** (about a company or an organization) using borrowed money in order to operate, in addition to money from shareholders: *The firm is about 88% geared.* **2** (about an investment) using borrowed money: *a geared investment* → LEVERAGED

**gearing** /ˈɡɪərɪŋ; *AmE* ˈɡɪrɪŋ/ (*also* **'capital ˌgearing, 'equity ˌgearing**) (*all esp. BrE*) *n.* [U] (*Finan.*) the relationship between the amount of money that a company owes (**debt**) and the value of its shares (**equity**): *There is concern about the company's* ***high*** *gearing* (= it has borrowed a large amount compared to the value of its shares). SYN DEBT-EQUITY RATIO, LEVERAGE

**gender** /ˈdʒendə(r)/ *n.* [U] the fact of being male or female: *not to discriminate on the basis of gender*

**'gender ˌbias** *n.* [U; C, usu. sing.] (*HR*) the situation where men and women are not treated in the same way, often in a way that is unfair to women ▶ **'gender-ˌbiased** *adj.*: *a gender-biased profession*

**ˌgender 'pay gap** *n.* [sing.] (*HR*) the difference in the average amount of money that men and women earn

**general** /ˈdʒenrəl/ *adj.* **1** used in some job titles to indicate that the person is the head of the organization or business, or part of it: *She is the general director for human resources.* **2** not limited to one thing, aspect, subject, etc: *sales of general merchandise, including clothing, shoes and gifts*

**ˌgeneral con'tractor** *n.* [C] (*esp. AmE*) (*Prop.*) a person or company that takes responsibility for building sth, such as an office, a factory, etc. and hires other businesses to do the work

**ˌgeneral 'counsel** *n.* [U,C] (*esp. AmE*) (*Law*) an organization's senior lawyer, who usu. works as an employee of the organization

**ˌgeneral 'creditor** *n.* [C] (*esp. AmE*) (*Law*) a person, company, etc. that lends money to sb without an agreement that they will receive some of the borrower's assets if the borrower does not pay back the money

**ˌgeneral ex'penses** *n.* [pl.] (*Account.*) money that is spent on managing and organizing a business rather than on any one activity such as producing goods, selling services, etc: *administrative and general expenses*

**ˌgeneral in'surance** *n.* [U] insurance that you buy to protect any kind of property or goods ▶ **ˌgeneral in'surer** *n.* [C]

**generalist** /ˈdʒenrəlɪst/ *n.* [C] a person who has knowledge of several different subjects or activities; a business that is involved in a range of activities, investments, etc.

**ˌgeneral 'ledger** (*also* **ˌnominal 'ledger**) *n.* [C] (*Account.*) a set of financial accounts in which a company records all the amounts it pays, receives, etc.

**'Generally Ac'cepted Ac'counting ˌPrinciples** *n.* [pl.] (*abbr* **GAAP**) (*Account.*) in the US, a set of rules and principles that accountants must follow when keeping financial records and preparing financial reports

**ˌgeneral 'manager** *n.* [C] a person who is responsible for running a business, or part of it, on a daily basis: *assistant general manager for supply-chain planning*

**ˌgeneral ˈmeeting** *n.* [C] (*Law*) a meeting of the shareholders of a company, at which important decisions about the company are made

**ˌgeneral ˈoffer** *n.* [C] (*Finan.*) an offer to buy all the shares in a company

**ˌgeneral ˈpartner** *n.* [C] a member of a business PARTNERSHIP who shares its profits and can be made to pay all its debts if it fails

**ˌgeneral ˈpartnership** *n.* [C] (*esp. AmE*) a type of business **partnership** in which members share profits and any member can be made to pay all the debts if the business fails

**ˌgeneral ˈpractice** *n.* [U,C] (*esp. AmE*) (*Law*) the work of a lawyer who deals with all kinds of legal cases and who is not a specialist in one particular area of law; the place where a lawyer like this works

**ˌgeneral ˈretailer** *n.* [C] (*Comm.*) a shop/store, or a group of shops/stores, that sells a wide variety of goods

**ˌgeneral ˈstore** *n.* [C] (*BrE also* **ˌgeneral ˈstores** [pl.]) a shop/store that sells a wide variety of goods, esp. one in a small town or village

**ˌgeneral ˈstrike** *n.* [C] a period of time when most of the employees in a country stop working because of a disagreement over pay or conditions

**ˌgeneral ˈunion** *n.* [C] (*HR*) esp. in the UK, a union that organizes workers from different industries and jobs

★ **generate** /ˈdʒenəreɪt/ *v.* [T] **1** to produce or create sth: *to ~ cash/cost savings/income* **2** to produce energy, esp. electricity: *to ~ electricity/power* ◇ *a generating station*

**generation** /ˌdʒenəˈreɪʃn/ *n.* **1** [C, usu. sing.] a stage in the development of a product or system, usu. a technical one: *the latest generation of handheld computers* **2** [U] the production of sth: *methods of income generation* **3** [U] the production of energy, esp. electricity

**ˌGeneration ˈX** /ˈeks/ *n.* [U] the group of people who were born between the early 1960s and the middle of the 1970s, who are often thought to lack a sense of direction in life and not feel an important part of society ▶ **Generation Xer** /-ˈeksə(r)/ *n.* [C]

**generative** /ˈdʒenərətɪv/ *adj.* that can produce sth: *The company is strongly **cash generative**.*

**generator** /ˈdʒenəreɪtə(r)/ *n.* [C] **1** a machine or series of machines for producing electricity: *a nuclear/wind ~* **2** a person, company, product, etc. that produces or creates sth: *the role of small companies as generators of jobs* **3** (*BrE*) a company that produces and sells electricity

**generic** /dʒəˈnerɪk/ *adj.*, *n.*
• *adj.* **1** (about products, esp. drugs) produced as a standard type of product, that does not have a brand name or is not protected by a TRADEMARK: *generic copies of patented drugs* **2** typical of or connected with a whole group of things; not specific: *A name like 'service provider' is too generic to trademark.*
• *n.* (*also* **geˌneric ˈdrug**) [C] a drug that is sold with a name that is not protected by a TRADEMARK

**geˌnetically ˈmodified** = GM (1)

**geˌnetic discrimiˈnation** *n.* [U] unfair treatment of people because they are likely to develop a particular disease that their parents or other members of their family have: *genetic discrimination in health insurance*

**geˌnetic ˌengiˈneering** *n.* [U] the science of changing how a living creature or plant develops by changing the information in its cells

**geˌnetic modifiˈcation** = GM (1)

**ˌgentleman's aˈgreement** (*also* **ˌgentlemen's aˈgreement**) *n.* [C] an informal agreement between people who trust each other, which is not written down and does not have legal status

**get** /get/ *v.* [T] (**getting, got, got** /gɒt; *AmE* gɑːt/) (*not used in the pass.*) **HELP** In spoken AmE the past participle **gotten** is almost always used. **1** to receive sth: *She gets* (= earns) *€50 000 a year.* **2** to obtain sth: *He just got a new job.* **3** to obtain or receive an amount of money by selling sth: *We got a good price **for** the van.* **4** to buy sth regularly: *Which newspaper do you get?* → idiom at ARREARS **PHR V** **ˌget aˈhead (of sb)** to make progress (further than others have done): *She wants to get ahead in her career.* **ˌget ˈback to sb** to speak or write to sb again later, esp. in order to give a reply: *I'll find out the price and get back to you.* **ˌget beˈhind (with sth)** to fail to make enough progress or to produce sth at the right time: *She got* *behind with her loan repayments.* ˌ**get 'down to sth** to begin to do sth; to give serious attention to sth: *Let's **get down to business**.* ˌ**get 'into sth** to start a career in a particular profession: *How did you get into programming?* ˌ**get 'off (sth)** to leave work with permission: *What time do you get off (work) on Friday?* ˌ**get 'on to sb (about sth)** to contact sb by telephone, letter or email: *I'll get on to our accounts department about this.* ˌ**get 'out (of sth)** to stop being involved in sth; to escape a difficult situation: *to make a quick profit and then get out* (= of the market, deal, etc.) ˌ**get sth 'out** to produce or publish sth: *Can we get the new model out by the end of the year?* ˌ**get 'through sth** to manage to do or complete sth: *There's a lot to get through today.* ˌ**get (sth) 'through (sth)** to be, or to make sth, officially accepted: *to get the drug through the approval process*

**'get-out clause** *n.* [C, usu. sing.] (*BrE*) a way of avoiding sth, esp. a responsibility or duty: *a get-out clause in the contract*

**giant** /'dʒaɪənt/ *n., adj.*
• ***n.*** [C] a very large and powerful organization: *a banking/an oil/a retail/software ~*
• ***adj.*** very large; much larger or more important than similar things usu. are: *a giant poster ◇ giant banks*

**'giant-sized** (*also* **'giant-size**) *adj.* (*Comm.*) used to describe sth that you buy that is very large or the largest you can get: *a giant-size box of tissues*

**GIF™** (*also* **gif**) /gɪf/ *abbr* (*IT*) **Graphic Interchange Format** (*used as a countable n.*) a type of computer file that contains images and is used a lot on the Internet: *Send it as a GIF.*

**gift** /gɪft/ *n., v.*
• ***n.*** [C] **1** a thing, an amount of money, etc. that you give to sb: *We are not allowed to accept gifts from clients.* **2** (*Law*) property or money that is given to sb and recognized as a present in law: *She **made a gift of** her property to charity.* **3** (*infml.*) [usu. sing.] a thing that is very easy to do or cheap to buy: *At €17 a share, this stock is a gift.*
• ***v.*** [T] to give money or property to sb, esp. in order to help them financially

**'gift card** *n.* [C] **1** a small plastic card that is worth a particular amount of money and that can be used to buy goods in a particular shop/store up to that amount **2** a card with a picture on, used for sending sb a GIFT VOUCHER

**'gift cerˌtificate** = GIFT VOUCHER

**'gift ˌcoupon** = GIFT VOUCHER

**'gift pack** *n.* [C] a small attractive container with several products inside, usu. sold to be given to people as presents

**'gift tax** *n.* [U,C] tax that is charged on gifts made by people who are still alive that are worth more than a particular amount

**'gift ˌvoucher** (*also* **'gift ˌtoken**, **'gift ˌcoupon**) (*all esp. BrE*) (*AmE usu.* **'gift cerˌtificate**) *n.* [C] a piece of paper that is worth a particular amount of money and that can be exchanged for goods in a particular shop/store: *to **redeem** a gift voucher* (= to exchange it for goods)

**'gift wrap** *n.* [U] attractive coloured or patterned paper used for wrapping presents in ▸ **'gift-wrap** *v.* [T] (**-pp-**): *a gift-wrapping service*

**gig** /gɪg/ *n.* [C] **1** (*IT, infml.*) = GIGABYTE **2** (*infml.*) (*AmE*) a temporary job or task: *Time to get a new gig.*

**gigabyte** /'gɪgəbaɪt/ (*also* **gig**, *infml.*) *n.* [C] (*abbr* **GB**) (*IT*) a unit of computer memory, equal to $2^{30}$ (or about a billion) BYTES

**GIGO** /'gaɪgəʊ; *AmE* -goʊ/ = GARBAGE IN, GARBAGE OUT at GARBAGE

**gilt** /gɪlt/ *n.* [C, usu. pl.] (*Finan.*) bonds paying a fixed amount of interest sold by the British government to obtain funds: *to buy/issue/sell/trade (in) ~s*

**ˌgilt-'edged** *adj.* (*Finan.*) **1** (used esp. about investments) very safe **2** connected with GILTS

**gimmick** /'gɪmɪk/ *n.* [C] an unusual trick or unnecessary device that is intended to attract attention or to persuade people to buy sth ▸ **'gimmicky** *adj.*: *a gimmicky title*

**Ginnie Mae™** /ˌdʒmi 'meɪ/ *n.* (*AmE*) (*Finan.*) **1** [sing.] (*abbr* **GNMA**) **Government National Mortgage Association** a US government organization that is responsible for helping to provide MORTGAGES for people with low incomes **2** [C, usu. pl.] the bonds issued by **Ginnie Mae**

**giro** /'dʒaɪrəʊ; *AmE* -roʊ/ *n.* (*pl.* **giros**) [U,C] a system in which money can be moved from one bank or post office account to another by a central computer: *to pay by giro ◇ a ~ payment/transfer*

**GIS** /ˌdʒiː aɪ ˈes/ *abbr* (*IT*) **geographical information system** software and other tools that are used to collect and analyse information about the earth's surface, physical features, divisions, products, population, etc.

**gismo** = GIZMO

**giveaway** /ˈɡɪvəweɪ/ *n., adj.*
• *n.* [C] something that a company or an organization gives free, usu. with sth else that is for sale; an occasion when things are given in this way: *the airline's latest ticket giveaway*
• *adj.* (*infml.*) (about prices) very low: *giveaway prices on furniture*

**giveback** /ˈɡɪvbæk/ *n.* [C,U] (*AmE*) (*HR*) a situation in which employees agree to accept lower wages or fewer benefits than had been agreed, usu. in return for new benefits later

**gizmo** (*also* **gismo**) /ˈɡɪzməʊ; *AmE* -moʊ/ *n.* [C] (*pl.* **gizmos**) (*infml.*) a general word for a small piece of equipment, often one that does sth in a new and clever way: *a new electronic gizmo for storing telephone numbers*

**ˈglamour ˌstock** (*AmE* **glamor**-) *n.* [C] (*Stock Ex.*) a company whose shares become very popular with investors at a particular time

**ˌglass ˈceiling** *n.* [sing.] (*HR*) the imaginary barrier that stops women, or other groups, from getting the best jobs in a company, etc. although there are no official rules to prevent this: *the first woman to break through the glass ceiling in engineering*

**ˌglass ˈwall** *n.* [sing.] (*HR*) the imaginary barrier that stops women, or other groups, from being employed outside particular industries or jobs, although there are no official rules to prevent this: *Women at the radio station were confined to office jobs—the glass wall.*

**glitch** /ɡlɪtʃ/ *n.* [C] (*infml.*) a small problem or fault that stops sth working successfully: *technical glitches*

★**global** /ˈɡləʊbl; *AmE* ˈɡloʊbl/ *adj.* **1** covering or affecting the whole world: *global demand for oil* ◊ *to build a global brand* (= that will be sold everywhere) **2** considering or including all parts of sth: *a global email to all staff*
▸ **ˈglobally** /-bəli/ *adv.*

**ˈglobal bond** = EUROBOND

★**globalization, -isation** /ˌɡləʊbəlaɪˈzeɪʃn; *AmE* ˌɡloʊbələˈz-/ *n.* [U] **1** the process by which businesses and organizations grow and start to operate in countries all over the world, which has been made easier by new technology and political developments: *Globalization may not be a viable strategy for most US steelmakers.* **2** the fact that different cultures and economic systems around the world are becoming connected with and similar to each other because of the influence of large MULTINATIONAL companies and of improved communication: *the globalization of world markets*

★**globalize, -ise** /ˈɡləʊbəlaɪz; *AmE* ˈɡloʊ-/ *v.* [T,I] if something, for example a business, **globalizes** or is **globalized**, it operates all around the world: *If companies hope to grow, then their only choice is to globalize.*
▸ **ˈglobalized, -ised** *adj.*: *a globalized operation*

**ˌglobal ˈmarket** *n.* [C] the world population who might buy goods

**ˌglobal ˈmarketing** *n.* [U] presenting, advertising and selling a product all over the world

**ˌglobal ˈvillage** *n.* [sing.] the whole world, looked at as a single community that is connected by electronic communication systems

**globe** /ɡləʊb; *AmE* ɡloʊb/ *n.* [sing.] the world, esp. when considered as a commercial unit: *The bank operates across the globe.*

**globetrotting** /ˈɡləʊbtrɒtɪŋ; *AmE* ˈɡloʊbtrɑːtɪŋ/ *adj.* (*infml.*) travelling often to many different places around the world ▸ **ˈglobetrotter** *n.* [C] **ˈglobetrotting** *n.* [U]

**glocalization, -isation** /ˌɡləʊkəlaɪˈzeɪʃn; *AmE* ˌɡloʊkələˈz-/ *n.* [U] (*Market.*) a strategy where a company is operating all round the world but adapts its products or services and its manufacturing methods to make them suitable for local conditions

**gloom** /ɡluːm/ *n.* [U; sing.] a feeling that things will not get better; a situation without much hope: *Lower interest rates will lift the economic gloom.*

**gloomy** /ˈɡluːmi/ *adj.* (**-mier**, **-miest**) without much hope of success for the future: *The outlook is gloomy.*

**glut** /ɡlʌt/ *n., v.*
• *n.* [C, usu. sing.] a situation where there is a greater supply of sth than there is demand: *Prices fell because of a glut of steel on world markets.* SYN SURPLUS OPP SHORTAGE
• *v.* [T] (**-tt-**) (*usu. pass.*) to supply or provide sth, usu. a market, with too much of sth: *The market was glutted with small cars.* SYN SATURATE

**GM** /ˌdʒiː ˈem/ *abbr* **1** (*Tech.*) **genetically modified**, **genetic modification** (about food, animals, etc.) having had units in their cells deliberately changed to make them able to resist insects or disease; the process of doing this: ~ *crops/food* **2** (*Account.*) = GROSS MARGIN

**GmbH** /ˌdʒiː em biː ˈeɪtʃ/ *abbr* (*written*) used in the names of some companies in German-speaking countries: *Mertz Pharmaceuticals GmbH*

**GNMA** /ˌdʒiː en em ˈeɪ/ = GINNIE MAE (1)

**Gnomes of Zurich** /ˌnəʊmz əv ˈzjʊərɪk; ˈzʊərɪk; *AmE* ˌnoʊmz əv ˈzʊrɪk/ *n.* [pl.] Swiss BANKERS who control foreign money

**GNP** /ˌdʒiː en ˈpiː/ *abbr* (*Econ.*) **gross national product** the total value of all the goods and services produced by a country in a particular period including the income from investments in foreign countries: *Farming produces about 2–4% of GNP.*

**go** /ɡəʊ; *AmE* ɡoʊ/ *v., n.*

• *v.* [I] (**goes** /ɡəʊz; *AmE* ɡoʊz/**went** /went/**gone** /ɡɒn; *AmE* ɡɔːn; ɡɑːn/) **1** when money **goes**, it is spent or used for sth: *5% of the profits went on repairs.* ◇ *I don't know where the money goes!* **2** to be sold: *The firm went for €400 m.* **3** (about jobs, opportunities, etc.) to disappear or no longer exist: *If the merger happens, 250 jobs will go.* **4** (*infml.*) **be going** to be available: *There aren't any jobs going in this area.* **5** (about a machine, an economy, etc.) to work or function properly: *to get the economy going again* **6** to leave a place or an organization: *He has agreed to go* (= to leave his job). **7** (*usu. with an adj.*) to become different in a particular way: *to go bankrupt* IDM NOTE Most idioms containing **go** are at the entries for the nouns, verbs or adjectives in the idioms. **go all 'out for sth**; **go all out to 'do sth** to make a very great effort to get sth or do sth: *We continue to go all out to meet our targets.* **go 'plural** (*infml.*) to leave an important job that you do for all the hours of the working week and take several less important jobs for shorter hours **go through the 'roof** (about prices, etc.) to rise or increase very quickly PHR V **ˌgo 'after sb/sth** to try to get sb/sth: *We're both going after the same job.* **ˌgo a'head** to happen; to be done: *The project will go ahead as planned.* SYN PROCEED **ˌgo 'down 1** to become lower or smaller: *The price of oil is going down.* ◇ *Oil is going down in price.* **2** to stop working temporarily: *The system is going down in ten minutes.* **'go for sth 1** to try hard to get or achieve sth: *It sounds a great idea. Go for it!* **2** to choose sth; to be persuaded that sth is a good idea: *Shoppers are going for the cheap options.* **ˌgo 'forward (with sth)** to continue with a plan, project, etc: *Prices will rise if either of the deals goes forward.* **ˌgo 'in with sb** (*infml.*) to join sb in starting a business: *My brothers are opening a garage and they want me to go in with them.* **ˌgo 'into sth 1** to start working in a particular field or for a particular organization, esp. in order to have a career in it: *After college, she went into corporate law.* **2** to examine sth carefully: *to go into the costs* **3** (about money, time, effort, etc.) to be spent on sth or used to do sth: *A lot of money has gone into the project.* **ˌgo 'on to sth** to pass from one item to the next: *Let's go on to the next item on the agenda.* **ˌgo 'over sth** to examine or check sth carefully: *We went over the contract several times.* **ˌgo 'through** if a law, contract, etc. **goes through**, it is officially accepted or completed **ˌgo 'through sth 1** to look at or examine sth carefully, esp. in order to find sth: *She went through the company's accounts.* **2** to perform a series of actions; to follow a method or procedure: *New staff go through an orientation program.* **3** to experience or suffer sth: *We are going through an economic downturn.* **ˌgo 'through with sth** to do what is necessary to complete a course of action, esp. one that is difficult or unpleasant: *They decided not to go through with the merger.* **ˌgo 'under** (*infml.*) to become BANKRUPT **ˌgo 'up 1** to become higher or larger: *The price of cigarettes is going up.* ◇ *Cigarettes are going up in price.* **2** to be built: *New offices buildings are going up everywhere.* **'go with sth 1** to be included with or as part of sth: *A car goes with the job.* **2** to accept or choose sth, for example a plan or an offer: *You're offering $5 000? I think we can go with that.*

• *n.* [C] (*pl.* **goes** /ɡəʊz/) IDM **be a 'go** (*AmE*) (*infml.*) to be planned and possible or allowed: *We're still not sure if the project is a go.* **make a 'go of sth** (*infml.*) to be successful in sth: *We want to make a go of this business.*

**'go-aˌhead** *n., adj.*

• *n.* [sing.] permission for sb to start doing sth: *The project has finally* **got** *the go-ahead.* ◇ *We have been* **given** *the go-ahead for the development.*

• *adj.* willing to try new ideas, methods, etc. and therefore likely to succeed: *a go-ahead company*

★ **goal** /gəʊl; *AmE* goʊl/ *n.* [C] something that you hope to achieve: *Our goal is to increase market share this year.* SYN OBJECTIVE
○ *to* ***establish/set*** *a ~ •* ***to achieve/meet*** *a ~ • your* ***long-term/short-term/ultimate*** *~ • a* ***clear/main/primary*** *~ •* ***career/financial/profit*** *~s*

**ˈgoal-diˌrected** (*also* **ˈgoal-ˌoriented**) *adj.* **1** (about a person or a group) working hard because they want to achieve the tasks that have been set **2** (about a plan, an activity, etc.) that aims to achieve particular things: *goal-directed training*

**ˈgoal ˌsetting** *n.* [U] (*HR*) the process of deciding and agreeing on what you will try to achieve

**ˈgo-beˌtween** *n.* [C,U] a person or an organization that takes messages between one group and another: *to act as (a) go-between*

**godown** /ˈgəʊdaʊn; *AmE* ˈgoʊ-/ *n.* [C] a word used in India and some other countries to mean a WAREHOUSE

**gofer** (*also* **gopher**) /ˈgəʊfə(r); *AmE* ˈgoʊ-/ *n.* [C] (*infml.*) a person whose job is to do small boring tasks for other people in a company

**ˈgo-ˌgetter** *n.* [C] (*infml.*) a person who is determined to succeed, esp. in business

**ˈgo-go** *adj.* **1** (about an investment, shares, etc.) expected to make a lot of money quickly: *the go-go stock of the hi-tech boom* **2** used to describe a period of time when businesses are growing and people are making money fast: *the go-go 1990s*

**ˌgoing conˈcern** *n.* [C] **1** a business or an activity that is making a profit and is expected to continue: *He sold the cafe as a going concern.* **2** (*Account.*) a method of valuing an asset, a project or a business that assumes that the business will continue to operate for a long period of time: *the going concern concept*

**ˌgoing ˈrate** *n.* [C] **the going rate** (*Tech.*) the usual amount of money paid for goods or services at a particular time

**gold** /gəʊld; *AmE* goʊld/ *n.* [U] a chemical element. **Gold** is a yellow substance used for making coins, jewellery, etc. and kept by central banks as part of their FOREIGN EXCHANGE RESERVES: *safe investments like gold and bonds*
→ idiom at STRIKE *v.*

**ˌgolden fareˈwell** = GOLDEN GOODBYE

**ˌgolden ˈformula** *n.* [sing.] (*HR*) in the UK, a rule that says that strikes organized by unions are only legal if they are about matters that are connected with employment rather than about political matters, and that workers involved in legal strikes should not lose their jobs

**ˌgolden goodˈbye** (*also* **ˌgolden fareˈwell**) *n.* [C] (*HR*) a large amount of money given by a company to a senior employee when they are forced to leave their job before they want to

**ˌgolden ˈhandcuffs** *n.* [pl.] (*HR*) a large amount of money and other financial benefits that are given to sb to persuade them to continue working for a company rather than leaving to work for another company

**ˌgolden ˈhandshake** (*also* **ˈhandshake**) *n.* [C] (*HR*) a large amount of money given by a company to an employee when they retire or when they are forced to leave their job

**ˌgolden helˈlo** *n.* [C] (*HR*) a large amount of money or other financial benefits given by a company to some new employees in order to attract good people

**ˌgolden ˈparachute** *n.* [C] (*HR, infml.*) a part of a contract in which a company promises to give a large sum of money to a very senior employee if they have to leave their job, for example if the company is bought by another company; the money that is given

**ˌgolden ˈshare** *n.* [C] (*BrE*) a share in a company that gives the holder, usu. the government, the power to stop any changes to the company that they do not approve of

**ˈgold mine** *n.* [C] **1** a place where gold is dug out of the ground **2** a business or an activity that makes a large profit

**ˈgold reˌserve** *n.* [C, usu. pl.] an amount of gold kept by a country's central bank in order to support the supply of money

**ˈgold rush** *n.* [C, usu. sing.] a situation in which a new opportunity to make money appears and a lot of people try to take advantage of it: *the Internet gold rush*

**ˈgold ˌstandard** *n.* [sing.] (*usually* **the gold standard**) **1** (*Econ.*) an economic system in which the value of money is based on the value of gold: *Britain left the gold standard in 1931.* **2** something that is considered to be the best in a particular field and that other similar things are compared to: *This system is considered the* gold standard for 3-D computer games.

**Goliath** (*also* **goliath**) /ɡəˈlaɪəθ/ *n.* [C, usu. sing.] a person or company that is very large or powerful

**gondola** /ˈɡɒndələ; *AmE* ˈɡɑːn-; ɡɑːnˈdoʊlə/ *n.* [C] (*Comm.*) (*BrE*) a set of shelves in a shop/store or supermarket with goods on all sides

**ˈgone-aˌway** *n.* [C] (*Market.*) people on a company's MAILING LIST who no longer live at the address on the list; items that are sent to these people

**good** /ɡʊd/ *n.* [sing.] (*Econ.*) a thing that is made to be used or sold: *a graph of the demand for a good against income* → GOODS

**ˌgood ˈfaith** *n.* [U] the intention to be honest and helpful: *Customers buy our product* ***in good faith*** (= they trust us).

★ **goods** /ɡʊdz/ *n.* [pl.] **1** physical things that are produced to be sold, including things that are manufactured and raw materials: *agricultural/electrical/household ~* ◇ *buying* ***goods and services*** *on the Internet* ◇ *the time between invoicing and delivery of the goods*

○ ***cheap/low-priced/mass-produced ~*** ♦ ***branded/own-label ~*** ♦ *to* ***make/manufacture/produce ~*** ♦ *to* ***export/import/sell ~*** ♦ *to* ***deliver/supply/transport ~***

**2** (*BrE*) (*often used before a n.*) things (not people) transported by rail, road, ship, etc: *a ~ train/vehicle*

**IDM** **deliver/come up with the ˈgoods** (*infml.*) to do what you have promised to do or what people expect or want you to do

**ˌgood-till-ˈcancelled ˌorder** (*AmE* **good-til-canceled** -) *n.* [C] (*abbr* **GTC order**) (*Stock Ex.*) an order to a to buy or sell shares, FUTURES, etc. at a particular price that remains valid until it is completed or until it is cancelled by the investor

★ **goodwill** /ˌɡʊdˈwɪl/ *n.* [U] (*Account.*) assets that a company has that do not exist physically but are calculated as part of its value, such as a good relationship with its customers, its name, the knowledge and skill of its workers, etc: *Goodwill is the amount a buyer pays above a company's assets.*

○ *to* ***build (up)/keep/lose/value ~*** ♦ *to* ***amortize/write off ~*** ♦ ***~ accounting/amortization/impairment*** ♦ *a ~* ***charge/write-down/write-off***

**goodˈwill ˌpayment** *n.* [C] an amount of money that a company believes it should pay to sb even though they may not have a legal right to it, for example a payment to a customer who has experienced problems

**gopher** = GOFER

**ˌgo-ˈslow** (*BrE*) (*AmE* **ˈslowdown**) *n.* [C] (*HR*) a protest that workers make by doing their work more slowly than usual: *to be on/resort to/stage/start a ~*

**ˈgo-to** *adj.* (*infml.*) used to refer to the person, place, system, etc. that is the best person, place, etc. to go to if you need help, advice or information: *This is the go-to site for researching companies.*

**governance** /ˈɡʌvənəns; *AmE* -vərn-/ *n.* [U] the activity of controlling a company, an organization, or a country; the way in which this is done: *the group's governance structure* ◇ *poor governance*

**ˌgovernment-ˈbacked** *adj.* **1** (*Finan.*) used to describe credit, debt, loans, etc. that the government has promised to pay if the borrower is unable to do so: *~ bonds/insurance* **2** a plan, project, etc. that receives money and support from the government: *government-backed research*

**ˌgovernment ˈbond** *n.* [C] (*Finan.*) a bond that is sold by a government: *a 10-year government bond*

**ˌgovernment seˈcurity** *n.* [C, usu. pl.] (*also* **ˌgovernment ˈstock** [C,U]) (*Finan.*) a bond issued by a government in order to raise money

**governor** /ˈɡʌvənə(r); *AmE* -vərn-/ *n.* [C] **1** a person who is in charge of an institution such as the Central Bank: *the governor of the Bank of England* **2** a member of a group of people who are responsible for controlling an institution such as a school, hospital, etc: *a BBC governor*

**GPM** /ˌdʒiː piː ˈem/ = GROSS PROFIT MARGIN

**GPRS** /ˌdʒiː piː ɑːr ˈes/ *abbr* **General Packet Radio Service** a system that allows you to send and receive information such as emails using a mobile phone/cellphone

**gr** (*also* **gr.**) = GROSS (1,2)

**grace** /ɡreɪs/ *n.* [U] extra time that is given to sb to enable them to pay a bill, finish a piece of work, etc: *The banks have given him a month's grace to pay the amount.*

**grade** /ɡreɪd/ *n., v.*

• *n.* [C] **1** the quality of a particular product or material: *The materials used are of the highest grade.* **2** (*HR*) a level in a system of pay or employment in an organization: *salary* grades (= levels of pay) **3** (*Finan.*) a measurement of how good or safe sth such as an investment is: *non-investment grade* **IDM make the 'grade** to reach the necessary standard; to succeed: *About 10% of trainees fail to make the grade.*

• ***v.*** [T] (*often pass.*) to arrange people or things in groups according to their ability, quality, size, etc: *The containers are graded according to size.* ◇ *the highest-graded hotel in the area*

**grading** /'greɪdɪŋ/ *n.* [U,C] **1** the process of examining a product, a company, etc. and giving it a label to show its quality, size, etc: *gradings of companies' creditworthiness* **2** (*HR*) the process of giving a grade to an employee that shows how well they are doing their job; the grade that is given

**graduated** /'grædʒueɪtɪd/ *adj.* divided into groups or levels on a scale: *a graduated tax scale* (= the more you earn, the higher the rate of tax you pay)

**graft** /grɑːft; *AmE* græft/ *n., v.*

• ***n.*** [U] **1** (*esp. AmE*) the use of illegal or unfair methods, esp. giving or taking BRIBES, in order to gain advantage in business, etc.; money obtained in this way **2** (*BrE*) (*infml.*) hard work: *Their success was the result of* ***hard graft.***

• ***v.*** **1** [T] **~ sth (onto sth)** to make one idea, system, etc. become part of another one: *The new regulations were grafted onto the old.* **2** [I] (*BrE*) (*infml.*) to work hard: *She's been grafting all day.*

**grain** /greɪn/ *n.* [U] food crops such as corn and rice: *~ imports/exports*

**grandfather** /'grænfɑːðə(r)/ *v.* [T] (*AmE*) (*Law, infml.*) **~ sb/sth (in)** to give sb official permission not to do sth that is required by a new law, or to continue doing sth that is now illegal: *The new zoning law grandfathered in existing buildings.*

**'grandfather clause** (*also* **'grandfather pro,vision**) *n.* [C] (*also* **'grandfather rights** [pl.]) (*all AmE*) (*Law, infml.*) a part of a new law that allows those who already do the activity that is controlled or made illegal by the new law to continue to do so

**'grandfather rights** *n.* [pl.] (*AmE*) (*infml.*) **1** (*Law*) = GRANDFATHER CLAUSE **2** (*Transpt.*) the rights of airlines that have operated at an airport for a long time to keep the same times for landing or taking off that they have always had

**grant** /grɑːnt; *AmE* grænt/ *v., n.*

• ***v.*** [T] **1 ~ sth (to sb/sth)** | **~ (sb) sth** to agree to give sb what they ask for, esp. formal or legal permission to do sth: *The bank has granted the company a loan.* **2** (*Law*) to transfer the legal right to own particular property or a piece of land from one person to another ▸ **grantee** /grɑːn'tiː; *AmE* græn'tiː/ *n.* [C] **grantor** /grɑːn'tɔː(r); *AmE* græn't-/ *n.* [C]: *the grantor trust* ◇ *credit grantors*

• ***n.*** **1** [C] an amount of money that is given by the government or by another organization to be used for a particular purpose: *grants* ***to*** *develop new methods of crop production* **2** [U,C] the action of formally giving sb sth, or giving them legal permission to do sth

**the grapevine** /'greɪpvaɪn/ *n.* [C, usu. sing.] an informal way in which information and news is spread simply by people talking to each other: *I heard* ***on*** *the grapevine* (= by talking to other people) *that you're leaving.*

★**graph** /græf; *BrE also* grɑːf/ (*also* **chart**, *esp. in AmE*) *n.* [C] a planned drawing, usu. consisting of a line or lines, showing how two or more sets of numbers are related to each other: *to plot a graph of price against earnings* ◇ *to draw/plot a ~* ▸ **graph** *v.* [T]: *The results are graphed in Fig.2*

★**graphic** /'græfɪk/ *adj., n.*

• ***adj.*** **1** connected with diagrams or pictures used on a computer screen: *~ images/software* **2** shown in the form of a graph: *graphic information* **3** connected with drawings, printing and design, esp. in books, magazines, etc: *a graphic artist*

• ***n.*** [C] a diagram or picture, esp. one that appears on a computer screen or in a newspaper or book

**graphical** /'græfɪkl/ *adj.* **1** connected with art or computer **graphics**: *a graphical interface* **2** in the form of a diagram or **graph**: *a graphical presentation of results*

**,graphic de'sign** *n.* [U] the process of arranging text and pictures in a magazine, an advertisement, etc. in a clear and effective way; the result of this process: *poor graphic design* ▸ **,graphic de'signer** *n.* [C]

**graphics** /'græfɪks/ = COMPUTER GRAPHICS

**graphology** /græ'fɒlədʒi; *AmE* -'fɑːl-/ *n.* [U] (*HR*) the study of the way sb writes (their **handwriting**), sometimes used to find out more about a person who has applied for a job

**grass roots** (*also* **grassroots**) /,grɑːs'ruːts; *AmE* 'græsruːts/ *n.* [pl.]

the ordinary people in an organization or in society, rather than the leaders or people who usu. make the decisions: *Change begins at the grassroots of an organization.*
▸ **'grassroot** *adj.*: *people working at grassroot level*

**gratis** /'grætɪs; 'grɑːtɪs; 'greɪtɪs/ *adv.* done or given without having to be paid for: *She agreed to work gratis* (= for no money) *for the first few months.* ▸ **'gratis** *adj.*: *Gratis software can be downloaded.*

**gratuity** /grə'tjuːəti; *AmE* -'tuː-/ *n.* [C] (*pl.* **-ties**) **1** money that you give to sb who has provided a service for you SYN TIP **2** (*BrE*) money that is given to employees when they leave their job

**'graveyard ˌmarket** *n.* [C] (*Stock Ex.*) a BEAR MARKET in which owners of shares who have already lost a lot of money want to sell their shares but buyers do not want to buy until the market improves

**'graveyard shift** *n.* [C, usu. sing.] (*HR*) a period of time worked late at night or in the very early morning, esp. the hours between midnight and 8 a.m.; the people who work these hours: *working the graveyard shift at the plant*

**'gravy train** *n.* [sing.] (*infml.*) a way of getting a lot of money easily without much work: *Investors are trying to jump on the gravy train.*

**gray** = GREY

**the ˌGreat De'pression** = DEPRESSION (2)

**green** /griːn/ *adj.* (**-er**, **-est**) not harming the environment; concerned with the protection of the environment, often as a political principle: *~ energy/products*

**ˌgreen 'audit** *n.* [C] an official examination of the effect of a company or an industry on the environment

**greenback** /'griːnbæk/ *n.* [C, usu. sing.] (*AmE*) (*infml.*) an American dollar note or other note; the dollar when it is traded on currency markets: *The greenback rose to 124.6 yen.*

**ˌgreen 'belt** (*also* **Green Belt**) *n.* [U; C, usu. sing.] (*esp. BrE*) an area of open land around a city where new building is not usu. allowed

**ˌgreen 'card** (*also* **Green Card**) *n.* [C] a document that legally allows sb to live and work in a country that is not their own

**ˌgreen con'sumerism** *n.* [U] when customers choose to buy and use products that cause the least harm to the environment

**greenfield** /'griːnfiːld/ *adj.*, *n.* (*Prop.*)
• ***adj.*** used to describe an area of land that has not yet had buildings on it, but for which building development may be planned: *a ~ site/area*
• ***n.*** [C] (*esp. AmE*) (*BrE usu.* **ˌgreenfield 'site**) an area of land that has not yet had buildings on it, but for which building development may be planned

**ˌgreen 'light** *n.* [sing.] permission for a project, etc. to start or continue: *The company has given the plan the green light.* ▸ **'green-light** *v.* [T] (*esp. AmE*): *to green-light an idea*

**ˌgreen 'marketing** (*also* **enˌvironmental 'marketing**) *n.* [U] marketing that tries to present a product or company as not harmful to the environment

**grey** (*AmE* **gray**) /greɪ/ *adj.* **1** (*Econ.*) used to describe the situation when goods are not bought from an official supplier but are bought in another country and then imported to be sold at a lower price than the official price: *the **grey trade** in drugs through the Internet* **2** belonging to or aimed at the older section of the population: *the **gray dollar*** (= the money that older people can spend on goods)

**'grey goods** *n.* [pl.] (*Comm.*) computer equipment

**ˌgrey 'knight** *n.* [C] (*Finan.*) a third company or person that is a possible buyer for another company. They are 'grey' because it is not known if they will be good or bad for the company.

**ˌgrey 'market** *n.* [C, usu. sing.] **1** (*Stock Ex.*) the buying and selling of new shares before they are officially issued on the stock market
**2** (*Econ.*) the buying and selling of goods that have not been obtained from an official supplier, usu. at a lower price than the official price
NOTE The **grey market** is legal but secret; the **black market** is illegal.
**3** (*also* **ˌsilver 'market**) older people, when they are thought of as customers for goods; the goods that are produced for them or that they buy: *~ buyers/products*

**grid** /grɪd/ *n.* [C] **1** a system of cables, pipes, etc. for sending electricity, gas or water over a large area **2** (*IT*) a number of computers that are linked together using the Internet so that they can share power, data, etc. in order to work on difficult problems **3** a pattern of straight lines, usu. crossing each other to form squares

**grievance** /ˈgriːvəns/ *n.* [C,U] **1** (*HR*) a complaint that an employee or a union makes to an employer about sth at work that they feel is unfair: *a formal* ***grievance procedure*** (= a way of telling sb your complaints) **2** the feeling that you have been treated unfairly: *He had been* ***nursing*** *a grievance* ***against*** *the boss for months.*

**grind** /graɪnd/ *n., v.*
• ***n.*** [sing.] an activity, esp. work, that is tiring or boring and takes a lot of time: *the* ***daily*** *grind of work*
• ***v.*** (**ground, ground** /graʊnd/) **IDM grind to a ˈhalt; come to a grinding ˈhalt** to go slower gradually and then stop: *Production ground to a halt during the strike.*

**grocer** /ˈgrəʊsə(r); *AmE* ˈgroʊ-/ *n.* [C] **1** (*also* **grocer's** *pl.* **grocers**) a shop/store or company that sells food and some other things used in the home; a supermarket **2** a person who owns, manages or works in a grocer's

**grocery** /ˈgrəʊsəri; *AmE* ˈgroʊ-/ *n.* (*pl.* **-ries**) **1** (*esp. BrE*) (*AmE usu.* **ˈgrocery store**) [C] a shop/store that sells food and other things used in the home **HELP** In AmE 'grocery store' often means 'supermarket' **2 groceries** [pl.] food and other goods sold by a **grocer** or at a supermarket ▶ **ˈgrocery** *adj.*: *grocery chains*

★ **gross** /grəʊs; *AmE* groʊs/ *adj., adv., v., n.*
• ***adj.*** **1** (*Account.*) (*abbr* **gr**) (about an amount of money) being the total before tax or other costs are taken away: *a gross income of $55 000* ◇ *Gross revenues rose.* → NET **2** (*abbr* **gr**) (about a weight) including everything such as the container or wrapping as well as the contents: *goods vehicles with a maximum gross weight of less than 3 500 kg* **3** (*Law, fml.*) (about behaviour) very bad and unacceptable: *gross mismanagement*
• ***adv.*** in total, before tax or any other costs are taken away: *She earns $30 000 a year gross.* → NET
• ***v.*** [T] to earn a particular amount of money before tax and other costs are taken away: *The company may gross $20 m in 2009.* **PHRV ˌgross sth ˈup** (*Account.*) to calculate a total amount by adding the amount that is taken off in taxes, etc. to a NET amount
• ***n.*** [C] **1** (*pl.* **grosses**) (*esp. AmE*) a total amount of money earned by sb/sth, esp. a film/movie, before any costs are taken away **2** (*pl.* **gross**) (*abbr* **gr.**) a group of 144 things: *to sell sth by the gross*

**ˈgross doˈmestic ˈproduct** = GDP

**ˌgross inˈvestment** *n.* [U,C, usu. sing.] (*Account.*; *Econ.*) the total amount spent in a particular period on buying new equipment and structures, and repairing and replacing old ones

**ˌgross ˈloss** = TRADING LOSS

**ˌgross ˈmargin** (*abbr* **GM**) (*also* **ˌgross ˈprofit ˌmargin** *abbr* **GPM**) *n.* [C,U] (*Account.*) a percentage showing the relationship between a business's profits before OVERHEADS are taken away and the total amount of income from sales: *We need a gross margin of 25% to become profitable.*

**ˈgross ˈnational ˈproduct** (*also* **ˌnational ˈproduct**) = GNP

**ˌgross ˈprofit** = TRADING PROFIT

**ˌgross ˈprofit ˌmargin** = GROSS MARGIN

**ˌgross ˈrating point** *n.* [C] (*abbr* **GRP**) (*Market.*) a measurement of the number of people who see a particular TV programme or advertisement, used to show if it is good at reaching the group of people that a business wants to sell its products to. It is equal to the percentage of the possible audience who see it multiplied by the number of times it is shown: *An average GRP goal for a typical packaged product is 1 000 to 5 000 in a year.*

**ˌgross ˈsales** *n.* [pl.] (*Account.*) the total amount of money received from selling goods or services before taking away money for goods returned by customers, DISCOUNTS, etc.

**ˈgross-up** *n.* [C,U] (*Account.*) the act of calculating a total amount by adding the amount that is usu. taken off in taxes, etc. to a NET amount

**ground** /graʊnd/ *n., v.*
• ***n.*** [C, usu. pl.] a good or true reason for saying, doing or believing sth: *You have no grounds* ***for*** *complaint.* ◇ *He retired* ***on health grounds.***
**IDM drive/run/work sb/yourself into the ˈground** to work sb/yourself so hard that they/you become very tired and unable to work **gain/make up ˈground 1** to rise in value: *The yen has gained ground* ***against*** *the euro.* **2** to gradually become more powerful or successful in relation to a competitor: *The store is gaining ground* ***on*** *its main rival.* **get (sth) off the ˈground** to start or to make sth start happening successfully **give/lose ˈground (to sb/sth)** to

allow sb to have an advantage; to lose an advantage for yourself: *They lost a lot of ground to their rival.* **run/drive sth into the 'ground** to use sth so much that it is broken or damaged: *The country has been overtaxed and almost run into the ground.* → idioms at BREAK *v.*, HIT *v.*, LOSE *v.*
• *v.* [T] to prevent an aircraft from taking off: *Flights were grounded by the strikes.*

**'groundbreaking** /'graʊndbreɪkɪŋ/ *adj.* making new discoveries; using new methods: *a groundbreaking piece of research*
▸ **'groundbreaker** *n.* [C]: *These programs were groundbreakers in their time.*

**ˌground 'floor** *n.* IDM **be/get in on the ground 'floor** to become involved in a plan, project, etc. at the beginning and so gain an advantage over those who follow later

**grounding** /'graʊndɪŋ/ *n.* **1** [sing.] knowledge of, or training in, the basic parts of a subject: *The course will give you a good grounding in advertising.* **2** [U,C] the act of keeping a plane on the ground or a ship in a port

**'ground rules** *n.* [pl.] the basic rules on which sth is based

**groundwork** /'graʊndwɜːk; *AmE* -wɜːrk/ *n.* [U] work that is done as preparation for sth else: *They are **laying** the groundwork **for** a possible takeover bid.*

★**group** /gruːp/ *n.* [C with sing./pl. v.] **1** (*also* **ˌgroup of 'companies**) a number of companies owned by the same person or organization: *a media group* ◇ *the **group accounts*** (= showing the costs, profit, etc. for each part of the group) **2** a number of people or things in the same place or connected in some way: *A group of 10 banks will provide the new loan.*

**ˌgroup 'action** *n.* [C] (*Law*) a type of court case in which a large number of claims against the same person or organization, or resulting from the same event, are dealt with together

**groupage** /'gruːpɪdʒ/ (*BrE*) (*AmE* **conˌsoli'dation**) *n.* [U,C] (*Transpt.*) the action of putting items from different exporters together into one load in order to transport them; a load consisting of different items of this kind: *a ~ company/service/load* ◇ *to send a shipment groupage*

**ˌgroup in'centive** *n.* [C] (*BrE*) (*HR*) a reward given to a group or team of employees based on the group's achievements

**ˌgroup in'surance** *n.* [U] a single insurance contract that protects a group of people such as the employees a particular company

**ˌgroup of 'companies** = GROUP (1)

**groupthink** /'gruːpθɪŋk/ *n.* [U] (*esp. AmE*) a process in which bad decisions are made because the different members of a group do not express their individual opinions about a plan, proposal, etc. but only say what they think the rest of the group would agree with

**groupware** /'gruːpweə(r); *AmE* -wer/ *n.* [U] (*IT*) software that is designed to help a group of people on different computers to work together

**grow** /grəʊ; *AmE* groʊ/ *v.* (**grew** /gruː/**grown** /grəʊn; *AmE* groʊn/) **1** [I] to increase in size, number, strength or quality: *Profits grew **by** 5% last year.* ◇ *a growing business* ◇ *the fastest-growing sector of the industry* **2** [T] to increase the size, quality or number of sth: *We are trying to grow the business.*

★**growth** /grəʊθ; *AmE* groʊθ/ *n.* [U] **1** an increase in the size, amount or degree of sth: *Sales showed 0.3 per cent growth in the first quarter.* ◇ *rapid growth **in** consumer spending*
⊙ ***fast/slow/steady/strong ~*** • ***~ companies/industries/markets***
**2** (*Econ.*) an increase in economic activity: *Growth forecasts were cut for Japan and Europe.*
⊙ ***fast/high/strong/sustainable ~*** • ***low/slow/sluggish/weak ~***

**'growth fund** *n.* [C] (*Finan.*) a fund that invests in shares likely to increase in value quickly, rather than those paying large DIVIDENDS

**'growth share** = GROWTH STOCK

**ˌgrowth-share 'matrix** = BOSTON MATRIX

**'growth stock** *n.* [U,C] (*BrE also* **'growth share** [C, usu. pl.]) (*Stock Ex.*) shares in companies that grow more quickly than average companies and are likely to continue to grow fast because they invest in order to do so

**GRP** /ˌdʒiː ɑː 'piː; *AmE* ɑːr/ = GROSS RATING POINT

**gr. wt.** (*also* **GR. Wt.**) *abbr* a short way of writing **gross weight**

**GSM** /ˌdʒiː es 'em/ *abbr* **Global System for Mobiles** a system that allows you to use a mobile phone/cellphone in different countries

**GST** /ˌdʒiː es 'tiː/ *abbr* (*Account.*) **Goods and Services Tax** in Australia, Canada, New Zealand and some other countries, a general tax on the supply of almost all goods and services

**GTC order** /ˌdʒiː tiː ˈsiː/ = GOOD-TILL-CANCELLED ORDER

★**guarantee** /ˌɡærənˈtiː/ *n., v.* (*abbr* **guar.**)

• *n.* **1** [C,U] a written promise given by a company that sth you buy will be replaced or repaired without payment if it goes wrong within a particular period: *a 5-year guarantee* ***against*** *manufacturing faults* ◇ *The watch is still* ***under guarantee***. SYN WARRANTY **2** (*Finan.*; *Law*) (*also* **ˈguaranty**) [C,U] money or sth valuable that you give or promise to a bank, for example, to make sure that you will pay back money that you borrow: *to give/offer/provide (sth as) a ~* **3** (*Finan.*; *Law*) (*also* **ˈguaranty**) [C] an agreement to be legally responsible for sth, esp. for paying sb's debts if they cannot pay them: *loan guarantees* ◇ *to get/seek/give/provide a ~* **4** [C] a firm promise that you will do sth or that sth will happen: *They have given a guarantee that the business will not be sold.* ◇ *to ask for/get/give/offer/provide a ~*

• *v.* [T] **1** to promise to do sth; to promise that sth will happen: *We guarantee to deliver your goods within a week.* **2** to give a written promise to replace or repair a product free if it goes wrong: *The toaster is guaranteed for a year* ***against*** *faulty workmanship.* **3** (*Finan.*; *Law*) to agree to be legally responsible for sth or for doing sth such as paying back a loan: *to guarantee to pay somebody's debts*

**ˌguaranteed ˈwage** *n.* [sing.] (*also* **ˌguaranteed ˈwages** [pl.]) (*also* **ˌguaranteed ˈpay** [U]) (*HR*) the level of pay that employees are promised in their contract during a particular period of time, even if there is little or no work to do

**ˌguaranˈtee fund** *n.* [C] (*Finan.*) an amount of money that can be used to pay back a loan if the borrower is unable to do so, or to pay sb for a financial loss

**guarantor** /ˌɡærənˈtɔː(r)/ *n.* [C] **1** (*Finan.*; *Law*) (*AmE also* **ˈguaranty**) a person or an organization that agrees to pay back a loan or a debt, etc. if the person or company that borrowed the money is not able to do so: *a mortgage guarantor* **2** (*Law*) a person who agrees to be responsible for sb or sth: *You may need a guarantor in order to rent an apartment.*

**guaranty** /ˈɡærənti/ (*pl.* **-ties**) = GUARANTEE (2), GUARANTEE (3), GUARANTOR (1)

**guardian** /ˈɡɑːdiən; *AmE* ˈɡɑːrd-/ *n.* [C] **1** a person who is responsible for protecting sth: *Board members are the guardians of shareholders' interests.* **2** (*Law*) a person who is legally responsible for the care of another person

**guerˈrilla ˌmarketing** (*also* **guerilla -**) *n.* [U] a type of marketing that uses different and unusual methods to achieve the greatest effect for the smallest amount of money

▸ **guerˈrilla ˌmarketer** *n.* [C]

**guesstimate** (*also* **guestimate**) /ˈɡestɪmət/ *n.* [C] (*infml.*) an attempt to calculate sth that is based more on guessing than on real information

▸ **ˈguesstimate** /-meɪt/ *v.* [T,I]

**guest** /ɡest/ *n.* [C] **1** a person who is visiting a place, for example sb else's home, company or country, usu. after being invited to go there: *They are here as guests* ***of*** *our company.* ◇ *Is she on the guest list?* **2** a customer in a hotel or restaurant: *Guests should vacate their rooms by 10.30 a.m.*

**guestimate** = GUESSTIMATE

**ˈguest ˌworker** *n.* [C] a person who is allowed to come and work in a country which is not their own country for a period of time

**GUI** /ˌdʒiː juː ˈaɪ/ *abbr* (*IT*) **graphical user interface** a way of giving instructions to a computer using things that can be seen on the screen such as symbols, windows and MENUS

★**guidance** /ˈɡaɪdns/ *n.* [U] **1** help or advice: *Managers need to monitor progress and offer guidance.* **2** the act of managing or guiding sb/sth: *The fund was set up* ***under the guidance of*** *the finance director.* **3** written instructions which tell you what you may or must do when dealing with a particular thing: *guidance* ***on*** *employment rights* SYN GUIDELINE

**guide** /ɡaɪd/ *n., v.*

• *n.* [C] **1** something that indicates what may happen or what is happening: *Past performance is no guide* ***to*** *future returns.* **2** something that helps you to form an opinion or make a decision: *These figures are just a rough guide.* **3** a book or document which tells you about sth: *a restaurant/hotel/city ~* **4** = GUIDE PRICE

• *v.* [T] **1** to help sb/sth to move in a particular direction: *He guided the company to sales of more than $60 m.* **2** to explain to sb how to do sth, esp.

sth complicated or difficult: *I will guide you through the safety procedures.*

**guideline** /ˈɡaɪdlaɪn/ *n.* **1 guidelines** [pl.] written instructions which tell you what you may or must do when dealing with a particular thing: *Some companies have breached government guidelines* **on** *pollution.* SYN GUIDANCE

○ *to* ***draw up/give/issue/publish*** *~s* • *to* ***follow/stick to*** *~s* • ***clear/revised/strict*** *~s*

**2 guidelines** [pl.] advice: *basic guidelines to help you delegate effectively* **3** [C] something that helps you to form an opinion or make a decision: *The figure is just a guideline.*

**ˈguide price** (*also* **guide**, *less freq.*) *n.* [C] a price which is approximately the amount that you will have to pay for sth such as property or shares

**gun** /ɡʌn/ *v.*, *n.*

• *v.* PHRV **be ˈgunning for sth** to be trying very hard to achieve or get sth: *She's gunning for the top job.*

• *n.* → idiom at BIG *adj.*

**guru** /ˈɡʊruː/ *n.* [C] (*infml.*) an expert on a particular subject who shares his or her knowledge through books, articles, and training: *a management guru*

# Hh

**hack** /hæk/ *v.*, *n.*

• *v.* [T,I] **1** (*IT*) to use a computer to steal, change or look at data on sb else's computer system without permission: *He hacked* **into** *the bank's computer.* **2** (*often used with an adv. or a prep.*) to reduce jobs, costs, etc. in a very severe way: *They are planning to hack back bonuses.* ▸ **ˈhacker** *n.* [C] **ˈhacking** *n.* [U]

**haemorrhage** (*AmE* **hemorrhage**) /ˈhemərɪdʒ/ *n.*, *v.*

• *n.* [C, usu. sing.] a serious loss of people or money from a company or an organization: *The haemorrhage of senior staff has continued.*

• *v.* [T,I] if a company or an organization **haemorrhages** money, people or jobs, it loses a large amount: *We must stop the company haemorrhaging cash.* IDM **haemorrhage red ˈink** (often used in newspapers) to lose a large amount of money

**haggle** /ˈhæɡl/ *v.* [I] **~ (with sb) (over sth)** to argue with sb in order to reach an agreement, esp. about the price of sth ▸ **ˈhaggle** *n.* [C]

**the ˈHague Rules** /ˈheɪɡ/ *n.* [pl.] a set of international rules relating to the transport of goods by ship

**haircut** /ˈheəkʌt; *AmE* ˈherkʌt/ *n.* [sing.] **1** a reduction, esp. in an amount of money: *Many stocks* ***took a haircut*** (= lost value) *yesterday.* **2** (*Finan.*) an amount of money that dealers take off the price that they pay for shares, bonds, etc. or add to the price that they sell them for, which pays their fee ▸ **ˈhaircut** *v.* [T]

**ˌhalf a ˈdozen** = HALF-DOZEN

**ˌhalf ˈday** *n.* [C] a day on which people work only in the morning or in the afternoon: *Tuesday is her half day.*

**ˈhalf-day** *adj.* lasting for either the morning or the afternoon: *a half-day strike*

**ˌhalf-ˈdozen** (*also* **ˌhalf a ˈdozen**) *n.* [sing.] a set or group of six: *a half-dozen companies* ◇ *We have about half a dozen new products.*

**ˌhalf-ˈpage** *adj.* using or covering half a page: *a half-page advertisement*

**ˌhalf ˈpoint** *n.* [C] (*Finan.*) one of two equal divisions of a unit of measurement, esp. half of one per cent: *a half-point cut in interest rates*

**ˌhalf-ˈprice** *adj.* costing half the usual price: *a half-price ticket* ▸ **ˌhalf-ˈprice** *adv.* **ˌhalf ˈprice** *n.* [U]: *We have many items at half price or less.*

**ˌhalf-ˈyear** *adj.* relating to a period of six months: *~ losses/profits* ▸ **ˌhalf-ˈyear** *n.* [sing.]: *the half-year ending Feb 28th*

**ˌhalf-ˈyearly** *adj.* happening every six months; happening after the first six months of the year: *the half-yearly sales figures* ▸ **ˌhalf-ˈyearly** *adv.*: *Interest is paid half-yearly.*

**hallmark** /ˈhɔːlmɑːk; *AmE* -mɑːrk/ *n.* [C] **1** a feature or quality that is typical of sth: *Cooperation has been the hallmark* **of** *the project.* **2** in the UK, a mark put on a gold, silver or PLATINUM object, showing the quality of the metal and where and when the object was made ▸ **ˈhallmark** *v.* [T]

**ˈhall test** *n.* [C] (*Market.*) a form of MARKET RESEARCH in which a group of people are asked to come into a room and give their opinions about a product, an advertisement, etc.

**ˈhalo efˌfect** *n.* [sing.] the way that a good feeling or opinion about one thing, or about one aspect of a person, is likely to give you a good feeling about other things or about the whole person: *The new sports car* *has provided a halo effect for the whole brand.*

**hammer** /ˈhæmə(r)/ *n., v.*
• *n.* IDM **be/come/go under the ˈhammer** (*Comm.*) to be sold at an AUCTION
• *v.* [T] to reduce the amount or value of sth in a sudden or extreme way: *The cold weather hammered ice cream sales.* ▸ **ˈhammering** *n.* [C, usu. sing.]: *Shares have **taken** a hammering.* PHRV ˌ**hammer sth ˈdown** to reduce prices, costs, etc. by a large amount: *hammered-down prices* ˌ**hammer sth ˈout** to discuss a plan or a deal until all the details are agreed: *Final details have yet to be hammered out.*

**hand** /hænd/ *n., v.*
• *n.* **1** (*used in adjs and vs*) by a person rather than a machine: *hand-painted pottery* **2** [C] a person who does physical work, esp. on a farm or in a factory IDM **by ˈhand 1** by a person rather than a machine: *painted by hand* **2** if a letter is delivered **by hand**, it is delivered personally rather than sent by post/mail **get your ˈhands on sth/sb** to find or get sb/sth: *They want to get their hands on the company's assets.* **in ˈhand 1** if you have sth **in hand**, it is available to be used: *We have the money in hand to begin the work now.* **2** if you have a particular situation **in hand**, you are in control of it: *Don't worry about the trip—everything is in hand.* **3** the job or task **in hand** is the one that you are dealing with **in the hands of sb**; **in sb's ˈhands 1** owned or controlled by a particular person or group: *The airline will remain in UK hands.* **2** being dealt with by sb: *I'll leave that in your hands.* **on ˈhand 1** available: *Staff are on hand to help.* **2** (*AmE*) = TO HAND ˌ**out of your ˈhands** no longer your responsibility: *I'm afraid the matter is now out of my hands.* **put your ˌhand in your ˈpocket** (*BrE*) to provide the money for sth, usu. unwillingly **to ˈhand** (*BrE*) (*AmE* **on ˈhand**) available immediately; easy to reach: *Do you have the figures to hand?* → idioms at CASH *n.*, CATCH *v.*, CHANGE *v.*, EXCHANGE *v.*, HOLD *v.*, MONEY, SHOW
• *v.* PHRV ˌ**hand sth ˈdown (to sb) 1** to give or leave sth to a younger member of your family: *skills handed down from father to son* **2** (*Law*) (*esp. AmE*) to officially give a decision, statement, etc: *A judgement may be handed down soon.* ˌ**hand sth ˈin (to sb)** to give sth to sb in authority, esp. a piece of work, a plan, etc: *to hand in your **notice/resignation*** ˌ**hand sth ˈoff (to sb)** (*AmE*) to give sb else your responsibility for sth: *handing off the project to your successor* ˌ**hand sth ˈon (to sb)** to give or leave sth to sb else: *The company did not hand this benefit on to customers.* SYN PASS STH ON ˌ**hand sth ˈout (to sb)** to give a number of things to members of a group: *Copies of the report were handed out.* SYN DISTRIBUTE ˌ**hand (sth) ˈover (to sb)** to give sb else your position of power or the responsibility for sth: *She will hand over the job to Ms Pitt.*

**handbill** /ˈhændbɪl/ *n.* [C] a small printed advertisement that is given to people by hand

**handbook** /ˈhændbʊk/ *n.* [C] a book that contains information or instructions on a particular subject

**hand-held** *adj., n.*
• *adj.* ˌ**hand-ˈheld** small enough to be held in the hand while being used: *a hand-held camera*
• *n.* **ˈhand-held** [C] a small computer that can be used in the hand

★ **handle** /ˈhændl/ *v., n.*
• *v.* [T] **1** to deal with sth, esp. products, money or customers: *Banks are used to handling large amounts of cash.* ◇ *The UK's seven airports handle about 10 million passengers a month.* **2** to manage, organize or be responsible for sth: *Eddie handles marketing, sales and finance.* **3** (*Transpt.*) to store, pack or move goods: *We handle merchandise for several well-known firms.* **4** to touch, hold or move sth with your hands: *'Fragile. **Handle with care.**'* **5** to deal with a difficult situation or person: *The crisis was handled very badly.*
• *n.* IDM **get/have a ˈhandle on sth** (*infml.*) to get/have the information that you need in order to deal with sth: *online tools to help employees get a handle on their finances*

**handler** /ˈhændlə(r)/ *n.* [C] **1** a company that moves, stores or packs goods: *grain/freight ~s* **2** a person who carries or touches sth as part of their job: *food handlers*

**handling** /ˈhændlɪŋ/ *n.* [U]
**1** (*Transpt.*) the act or cost of storing, packing and moving goods: *a $2 charge for postage and handling* ◇ *the firm's handling division* SYN CARRIAGE (*BrE*) **2** (*Comm.*) the cost of dealing with an order, booking tickets, etc: *There is a small handling charge for advance bookings.* **3** the way that sb deals with a situation: *I was impressed by his handling **of** the recent buy-out.* **4** the act of touching,

carrying or moving sth: *products that can stand up to rough handling* **5** (*IT*) the activities of storing, moving, and processing data; the ability to do this **6** the process of dealing with sth: *the firm's cash handling operations*

**handmade** /ˌhændˈmeɪd/ *adj.* made by a person using their hands rather than by machines: *handmade shoes and bags*

**ˌhand-ˈoperated** *adj.* (about a machine) controlled by a person rather than working automatically

**handout** /ˈhændaʊt/ *n.* [C] **1** money that is given to a person or an organization by the government, etc., for example to encourage commercial activity **2** a document that is given out at a meeting or other event

**handover** /ˈhændəʊvə(r); *AmE* -oʊvər/ *n.* [C,U] an act of giving sth to sb else, for example control of an organization or a country; the period when this is done: *Everything is in place for a smooth handover.*

**ˌhand-ˈpicked** *adj.* **1** chosen very carefully, often by a particular person: *a hand-picked team* **2** picked by people rather than by machines: *hand-picked fruit* ▸ **ˌhand-ˈpick** *v.* [T]: *to hand-pick your team*

**ˈhands-free** *adj.* (about a telephone) able to be used without needing to be held in the hand: ~ *phones/headsets*

**handshake** /ˈhændʃeɪk/ *n.* [C] **1** an act of shaking sb's hand, used esp. to say hello or goodbye or when you have made an agreement: *Everything was agreed* **on** *a handshake.* **2 ~ deal/agreement** a deal which has been agreed in a conversation or an email, although there is not yet a formal written agreement **3** = GOLDEN HANDSHAKE **4** (*IT*) an instance of **handshaking**

**handshaking** /ˈhændʃeɪkɪŋ/ *n.* [U] (*IT*) the process or sound of your computer connecting with another computer, for example when you use the Internet

**ˌhands-ˈoff** *adj.* dealing with people or a situation by not becoming directly involved and by allowing people to do what they want

**ˌhands-ˈon** *adj.* **1** dealing with sth by becoming directly involved, rather than leaving other people to do it: *I'm a hands-on manager.* **2** doing something rather than just talking about it: *They both have hands-on* **experience** *of marketing.*

**ˈhang-out loan** *n.* [C] (*AmE*) (*Finan.*) the amount of money that you still have to pay at the end of the period of a loan

**the ˌHang ˈSeng ˌIndex** (*also* **the Hang Seng**) /ˌhæŋ ˈseŋ/ *n.* [sing.] a figure which shows the average price of shares on the Hong Kong stock exchange: *The Hang Seng Index was up 35.81 points.*

**ˌhappy ˈcamper** *n.* [C] (*infml.*) a customer, an employee, etc. who has no complaints

**harassment** /ˈhærəsmənt; həˈræsmənt/ *n.* [U] behaviour which is deliberately unpleasant or frightening, and which causes sb to feel upset
**o** *to* ***be subjected to/be subject to/suffer*** *~* • ***racial/sexual*** *~*
▸ **ˈharass** *v.* [T]: *She claimed she was harassed at work.*

**hard** /hɑːd; *AmE* hɑːrd/ *adj.*, *adv.*
• *adj.* (**-er**, **-est**) **1** definite; based on information that can be proved: ~ *facts/figures/numbers* **2** if the market is **hard**, or if prices are **hard**, prices remain high **IDM** **drive/strike a hard ˈbargain** to argue in an aggressive way to try to force sb to agree on the best possible price or arrangement
• *adv.* **IDM** **be hard ˈup for sth** to have too few or too little of sth: *We're hard up for good ideas.* → idiom at HIT *v.*

**ˌhard ˈasset** *n.* [C, usu. pl.] (*Finan.*) an investment in physical things such as gold, silver, coins and art

**hardball** /ˈhɑːdbɔːl; *AmE* ˈhɑːrd-/ *n.* [U] a way of behaving which shows that you are very determined to get what you want and will not let sb else gain an advantage: *BA is prepared to* **play hardball**. ◇ *a hardball negotiator*

**ˌhard ˈcash** (*BrE*) (*AmE* **ˌcold ˈcash**) *n.* [U] money, esp. in the form of coins and notes, that you can spend: *hard cash on the balance sheet*

**ˌhard-ˈcharging** *adj.* working very hard and being very determined to get what you want: *hard-charging executives*

**ˌhard-ˈcode** *v.* [T] (*IT*) to write data so that it cannot easily be changed

**ˌhard comˈmodity** *n.* [C, usu. pl.] (*Finan.*) a raw material such as metal, chemicals, oil, etc. that can be bought and sold to make a profit: *trading in hard commodities*

**ˌhard ˈcopy** *n.* [C,U] text, pictures, etc. on paper rather than in a computer file

**ˈhard-core** *adj.* **1** particularly active or enthusiastic: ~ *emailers/gamers* **2** involving people who are unlikely to change their opinions or behaviour: *the hard-core unemployed* (= who have had no work for a long time and are not very likely to find a job)

**'hard costs** *n.* [pl.] (*Account.*) money that is spent on physical equipment and materials

**,hard 'currency** *n.* [U,C] (*Econ.*) money which is easy to exchange for money from another country because it is not likely to lose its value

**,hard 'data** *n.* [U] information that can be measured or proved: *hard data in the form of tables and graphs*

**,hard 'disk** (*also* **'hard drive**) *n.* [C] (*IT*) the part inside a computer on which data and programs are stored: *Save it to the hard disk.*

**,hard-'earned** *adj.* that you get only after a lot of work and effort: *their hard-earned cash*

**harden** /'hɑːdn; *AmE* 'hɑːrdn/ *v.* [I] if prices **harden**, or if the market **hardens**, prices rise and stay high: *Gold hardened to around $347 an ounce.*

**'hard goods** = DURABLE GOODS

**hard hat** *n.* [C] **1** **,hard 'hat** a hat worn for safety in areas where building work is being done, or in factories **2** (*infml.*) **'hard hat** (*esp. AmE*) a worker in the building trade

**,hard HR'M** *n.* [U] (*HR*) an approach to managing people that regards them as assets that must be used for the benefit of the business

**,hard 'landing** *n.* [C, usu. sing.] (*Econ., infml.*) a situation when the economy, or part of it, experiences a rapid decrease in trade and activity after a long period when it has been growing

**,hard 'loan** *n.* [C] (*Finan.*) a loan to a person or country at a normal rate of interest and which must be paid back in HARD CURRENCY

**,hard 'sell** *n.* (*Market.*) **1** [sing; U] the process of trying very hard to persuade sb to buy sth, in a way that puts pressure on them: *Customers don't like the hard sell.* ◇ *hard-sell advertising* **2** [sing.] (*AmE*) a product that is not easy to sell: *The shares will be a hard sell in the current market.*

**,hard 'selling** *n.* [U] (*Market.*) the activity of trying very hard to persuade sb to buy sth, in a way that puts pressure on them ▸ **,hard-'selling** *adj.*: *hard-selling salespeople*

**hardship** /'hɑːdʃɪp; *AmE* 'hɑːrd-/ *n.* [sing; U] a situation that is difficult or unpleasant because you do not have enough money or are working in difficult conditions: *economic/financial* ~

**,hard 'up** *adj.* (*infml.*) not having enough money: ~ *companies/consumers* → idiom at HARD *adv.*

★ **hardware** /'hɑːdweə(r); *AmE* 'hɑːrdwer/ *n.* [U] **1** (*IT*) the machinery and electronic parts of a computer system: *computer hardware and software suppliers* **2** electronic or mechanical equipment: *suppliers of machinery, trucks and hardware*

**,hard-'wired** *adj.* (*IT*) being part of a computer system, rather than being provided by software ▸ **,hard-'wire** *v.* [T]

**,hard-'working** *adj.* putting a lot of effort into your work

**harmonization, -isation** /,hɑːmənaɪ'zeɪʃn; *AmE* ,hɑːrmənə'z-/ *n.* [U; sing.] **1** the activity of making systems, rules or standards the same in different areas, countries, parts of an organization, etc. **2** (*HR*) the process of giving all of your employees the same status or conditions, for example by removing the difference between workers and managers, or by making everyone wear the same uniform

**harmonize, -ise** /'hɑːmənaɪz; *AmE* 'hɑːrm-/ *v.* **1** [T,I] to successfully combine different ideas, systems or people; to combine successfully: *The leader's role is to harmonize such views.* **2** [T] to make systems, rules or standards the same in different parts of an organization or area: *the need to harmonize tax levels across the EU*

**harness** /'hɑːnɪs; *AmE* 'hɑːrnɪs/ *v.* [T] to use energy, skills or resources in order to achieve sth: *We must harness the skill and creativity of our workforce.*

**harvesting** /'hɑːvɪstɪŋ; *AmE* 'hɑːrv-/ *n.* [C,U] (*Market.*) the practice of no longer investing in a product but continuing to sell it, so that profits increase, before the product is removed from the market

**'hatchet man** *n.* [C] (*infml.*) a person in an organization who is responsible for telling people that they have lost their jobs or for making other changes which are not popular

**haul** /hɔːl/ *v., n.*

• *v.* [T] (*Transpt.*) to transport or move goods by road or rail: *a trucking business that hauls containers to and from the ports*

• *n.* [C] **1** (*Transpt.*) the distance covered in a particular journey: *The truck's last haul was less than 75 miles.* **2** a quantity of fish caught at one time

**haulage** /ˈhɔːlɪdʒ/ (*esp. BrE*) (*AmE usu.* ˈ**hauling**) *n.* [U] (*Transpt.*) the activity or business of transporting goods by road or rail; money charged for this: *the road haulage industry* ◇ *How much is haulage?*

**haulier** /ˈhɔːliə(r)/ (*BrE*) (*AmE* **hauler** /ˈhɔːlə(r)/) *n.* [C] (*Transpt.*) a company or person whose business is transporting goods by road or rail

**hauling** /ˈhɔːlɪŋ/ = HAULAGE

**the ˈHawthorne efˌfect** *n.* [sing.] (*HR*) the fact that people's behaviour changes if they believe they are being observed or studied

**the ˈHay ˌsystem** *n.* [sing.] (*HR*) a system for measuring the knowledge and skills that are needed or used in a particular job

**hazard** /ˈhæzəd; *AmE* -ərd/ *n.* [C] a thing that can be dangerous or cause damage: *This may* **pose** *a safety hazard.*

**ˌhazardous ˈsubstances** *n.* [pl.] types of solids, liquids or gases which may be present where people work and are dangerous to their health

**ˈhazard pay** = DANGER MONEY

★ **head** /hed/ *n., v.*
• ***n.*** [C,U] the person in charge of a group of people or an organization: *She's head of marketing.* ◇ *department heads* ◇ *the head buyer of women's wear* IDM **a/per ˈhead** for each person: *The meal was $50 a head.* **get your ˈhead around/round sth** to be able to understand sth: *We need to get our heads around this problem.* **have/get/keep your ˈhead down** to start/continue to work very hard: *Let's get our heads down and finish the project.* **have a ˈhead for sth** to be good at sth: *She has a good head for business.* **have/get/give sb a head ˈstart (in sth/on sb/over sb)** to have or give sb an advantage at the beginning of sth: *This course will give you a head start in your career.* **heads will ˈroll** (*infml.*) used to say that some people will be punished because of sth that has happened **keep your ˈhead above water** to deal with a difficult situation, esp. one in which you have financial problems, and just manage to survive: *The company is struggling to keep its head above water.* **over sb's ˈhead 1** too difficult or complicated for sb to understand: *The technical information was over my head.* **2** to a higher position of authority than sb: *She went over my head to ask for time off.* → idiom at TURN *v.*
• ***v.* 1** [T] to lead or be in charge of sth: *She heads a team of 50 sales staff.* SYN HEAD UP STH **2** [I] (*also* **be headed**, *esp. in AmE*) (*used with an adv. or a prep.*) to move in a particular direction: *Where is the economy heading?* ◇ *100 000 copies of the game are headed* **for** *the US.* **3** [T] (*usu. pass.*) to put a word or words at the top of a page or section of a book or an article as a title: *a section of the report headed 'Strengths and weaknesses'* IDM **head ˈnorth/ˈsouth** (*infml.*) (about share prices, currencies, etc.) to rise/fall in value PHRV **ˌhead ˈup sth** to lead or be in charge of sth: *They are searching for someone to head up the department.* SYN HEAD

**headcount** (*AmE usu.* **head count**) /ˈhedkaʊnt/ *n.* [C,U] an act of counting the number of people who are employed by an organization, are at an event, etc.; the number of people that have been counted in this way: *We will cut our headcount to about 45 000.*

**header** /ˈhedə(r)/ *n.* [C] a line or block of text that is automatically added to the top of every page that is printed from a computer → FOOTER

**headhunt** /ˈhedhʌnt/ *v.* [T] (*HR*) (*usu. pass.*) to find sb who has the right skills and experience for a senior job in a company or an organization and persuade them to leave their present job: *I was headhunted by a marketing agency.*
▸ **ˈheadhunter** *n.* [C] **ˈheadhunting** *n.* [U]: *a headhunting firm*

**heading** /ˈhedɪŋ/ *n.* [C] **1** a title printed at the top of a page or at the beginning of a section of a book, report, etc. **2** the subject of each section of a speech or piece of writing: *The company's aims can be grouped under three main headings.*

★ **headline** /ˈhedlaɪn/ *adj.* (*BrE*)
**1** (*Econ.*) used to describe a number, figure, rate, etc. that includes everything: *The unadjusted headline figure for unemployment is 4.2 million.*
**2** (*Finan.*) used to describe a figure that does not include profits or losses related to unusual events: *Headline pre-tax profits before goodwill rose 32% to $98 m.* → UNDERLYING

**ˌheadline ˈearnings** *n.* [pl.] (*BrE*) (*Finan.*) the profit that a company makes, not including profits or losses related to unusual events such as the sale of assets, etc: *They reported a sharp fall in headline earnings.*

**ˌheadline inˈflation** *n.* [U] (*also* **ˈheadline ˈrate of inˈflation** [C, usu.

sing.]) (*both BrE*) (*Econ.*) the rate at which the prices of goods and services rise over a period of time, including costs which are likely to change, such as food and fuel and, in the UK, the cost of MORTGAGES → UNDERLYING INFLATION

★ **ˌhead ˈoffice** (*abbr* **HO**) (*also* **ˌmain ˈoffice**) *n.* [C; U with sing./pl. v.] the main office of a company; the managers who work there: *Their head office is in New York.* ◇ *I don't know if head office know(s).*

**ˌhead-ˈon** *adj.* in which people compete or deal with sb/sth in a direct and determined way: *head-on competition with the supermarkets* ▸ **ˌhead-ˈon** *adv.*: *We must tackle the problem head-on.*

**headquartered** /ˌhedˈkwɔːtəd; *AmE* ˈhedkwɔːrtərd/ *adj.* having **headquarters** in the place mentioned: *The business will be headquartered in London.*

★ **headquarters** /ˌhedˈkwɔːtəz; *AmE* ˈhedkwɔːrtərz/ *n.* [U with sing./pl. v.; C] (*pl.* **headquarters**) (*abbr* **HQ**) the place from where an organization is controlled; the people who work there: *The company's ~ is/are in Cambridge.* ◇ *I'm now based **at** headquarters.*

**headset** /ˈhedset/ *n.* [C] equipment worn on the head, for example when using a telephone or computer

**ˌheads of aˈgreement** *n.* [C,U] (*pl.* **heads of agreement**) (*BrE*) (*Law*) a document that states the main points in a deal or an agreement that two organizations are discussing, before a full legal contract is written

**ˈheads-up** *n.* [C, usu. sing.] **1** a warning about sth: *Thanks for the heads-up about the complaints!* **2** a short report giving the most recent information, esp. about what is going to happen: *Let me give you a quick heads-up on the new design.*

**ˌhead-to-ˈhead** *adj.* in which two people or groups face each other directly in order to decide the result of a dispute: *a head-to-head battle between the low-fares airlines* ▸ **ˌhead-to-ˈhead** *adv.*: *The two banks will go head-to-head to win the deal.*

**headway** /ˈhedweɪ/ *n.* IDM **make ˈheadway** to rise in value: *The pound made headway **against** the euro.*

**health** /helθ/ *n.* [U] **1** how successful or strong sth is: *the company's financial health* **2** the work of providing medical services: *health benefits* **3** the condition of a person's body or mind: ***Health and beauty** sales were up 3.3%.* → idiom at CLEAN *adj.*

★ **ˌhealth and ˈsafety** *n.* [U] (*HR*) activities connected with recognizing risks and dangers to health in places of work and protecting employees from these risks: *improving health and safety standards for employees* ◇ *the head of Health and Safety*

**ˈhealth care** (*also* **healthcare**) *n.* [U] **1** the service of providing medical care: *employee health-care benefits* **2** medical products and services: *beauty and health-care products*

**ˈhealth inˌsurance** *n.* [U] a type of insurance in which a person receives money to pay for medical treatment if they are ill/sick or injured: *We offer private health insurance as part of your employment package.* SYN MEDICAL INSURANCE

**ˈhealth ˌwarning** *n.* [C] a notice on particular products, required by law, that warns people that using the items can damage their health: *Cigarette packets carry a health warning.*

**healthy** /ˈhelθi/ *adj.* (**-thier, -thiest**) large or successful, working well, etc: *a ~ economy/profit* ▸ **healthily** /ˈhelθɪli/ *adv.*

**hearing** /ˈhɪərɪŋ; *AmE* ˈhɪr-/ *n.* [C] an official meeting at which the facts about a crime, complaint, etc. are presented to the person or group who will have to decide what action to take → idiom at FAIR *adj.*

⊕ *to **attend/conduct/hold** a ~* • *a **committee/court/tribunal** ~* • *a **private/public** ~*

**heartland** /ˈhɑːtlænd; *AmE* ˈhɑːrt-/ *n.* [C] (*also* **heartlands** [pl.]) **1** an area where an activity or an organization is esp. successful, popular or important: *the industrial heartlands of Germany* **2** a place which is considered to be at the centre of a country or region: *a dairy company in America's heartland*

**heatseeker** /ˈhiːtsiːkə(r)/ *n.* [C] (*infml.*) a customer who always buys the newest version of a product as soon as it is available

**heavy** /ˈhevi/ *adj.* (**-vier, -viest**) **1** more or worse than usual in amount, degree, etc: *~ losses/trading* **2** (about machines, vehicles, etc.) large and powerful: *~ machinery/trucks* **3** (*BrE*) **~ on sth** using or having a lot of sth: *We're light on stocks and heavy on bonds.* **4** involving a lot of work or activity; very busy: *a heavy schedule* **5** needing a lot of physical strength: ***heavy lift-***

*ing* → LIGHT ▸ **heavily** /ˈhevɪli/ *adv.*: *a heavily loaded van*

**ˌheavy-ˈduty** *adj.* very strong and suitable for hard physical work or to be used all the time: *heavy-duty trucks* (= strong and large)

**ˌheavy engiˈneering** *n.* [U] businesses that design and produce large things such as ships, machinery and vehicles; the activities of these businesses

**ˌheavy ˈgoods ˌvehicle** = HGV

**ˈheavy half** *n.* [sing.] (*Market.*) the group of customers which are half or less than half of the total number, who buy more than half of the total goods sold

**ˌheavy ˈhaulage** *n.* [U] (*Transpt.*) the activity or business of transporting heavy goods or materials; the vehicles or systems used for this

**ˌheavy ˈhitter** (*also* **ˌbig ˈhitter**) *n.* [C] (*often used in newspapers*) **1** a person who has a lot of influence in business, politics or public life **2** a product or business which is very successful: *The business will focus on its heavy hitters.*

**ˌheavy ˈindustry** *n.* [U,C] businesses that use large amounts of raw materials and large machines to produce metal, coal, vehicles, etc. ▸ **ˌheavy inˈdustrial** *adj.*

**heavyweight** /ˈheviweɪt/ *n.* [C] **1** a successful or important person, company or thing, that has a lot of influence: *technology/software/oil ~s* ◇ *the appointment of several heavyweights to the Board* **2** a thing, material, etc. that weighs more than usual ▸ **ˈheavyweight** *adj.*: *heavyweight stocks*

**hedge** /hedʒ/ *v.* [T,I] (*Finan.*) to protect yourself against the risk of losing money in the future because of changes in the value of shares, currencies, raw materials, etc., for example by buying or selling FUTURES, OPTIONS, etc: *They want to hedge their exposure to interest-rate risk.* ▸ **hedge** *n.* [C]: *Real estate can be a hedge* ***against*** *inflation* (= property will rise in value more than the rate of inflation). **ˈhedging** *n.* [U]: *~ strategies/techniques* IDM **ˌhedge your ˈbets** to reduce the risk of losing or making a mistake by supporting more than one side in a competition, an argument, etc., or by having several choices available to you: *She hedged her bets by applying for several jobs.* PHR V **ˈhedge against sth** to do sth to protect yourself against problems, esp. against losing money: *hedging against a fall in the dollar*

**ˈhedge fund** *n.* [C] (*Finan.*) a type of UNREGULATED investment fund used by people or organizations with large amounts of money to invest and not open to the general public, that tries to gain maximum profit by using a variety of investment strategies, including some with very high risk

**hefty** /ˈhefti/ *adj.* (**-tier**, **-tiest**) large; in large quantities: *make a hefty profit*

**ˈhelicopter view** *n.* [C] (*infml.*) a broad general view or description of a problem SYN OVERVIEW

**helm** /helm/ *n.* IDM **at the ˈhelm (of sth)** in charge of an organization or a project: *With Mr Munro at the helm, the company has continued to grow.* **take the ˈhelm (of/at sth)** to take charge of an organization or a project

**ˈhelp desk** *n.* [C] a service, usu. in a company, that gives people information and help, esp. if they are having problems with a computer

**helpline** /ˈhelplaɪn/ *n.* [C] (*BrE*) a telephone service that provides advice and information about particular problems: *a 24-hour telephone helpline*

**hemorrhage** = HAEMORRHAGE

**heritage** /ˈherɪtɪdʒ/ *n.* [C, usu. sing.] the history, traditions and qualities that a country, society or company has had for many years and that are considered an important part of its character: *Aston Martin's prestigious brand heritage*

**ˈheritage ˌindustry** *n.* [C with sing./pl.verb] organizations that are involved in the history, traditions and culture of a place

**HFE** /ˌeɪtʃ ef ˈiː/ = HUMAN FACTORS ENGINEERING

**HGV** /ˌeɪtʃ dʒiː ˈviː/ *abbr* (*BrE*) **heavy goods vehicle** a large lorry/truck: *an HGV licence* ◇ *HGV drivers*

**ˌhidden unemˈployment** *n.* [U] (*Econ.*) people who have no work or very little work but who are not officially recorded as unemployed, for example people who are ill/sick or who are caring for sb ▸ **ˌhidden unemˈployed** *n.* [pl.]: *The number of hidden unemployed has risen.*

★**hierarchy** /ˈhaɪərɑːki; *AmE* -rɑːrki/ *n.* (*pl.* **-chies**) **1** [C,U] the different levels at which people or things are organized, depending on how much authority, responsibility or im-

portance they have: *the corporate hierarchy* ◇ *She's quite high up in the management hierarchy.* **2** [C with sing./pl. v.] the group of people in control of a large organization
▸ ˌ**hieˈrarchical** /-kɪkl/ *adj.*: *hierarchical organizations* ˌ**hieˈrarchically** /-kli/ *adv.*

ˌ**hierarchy of ˈneeds** = MASLOW'S HIERARCHY OF NEEDS

**high** /haɪ/ *adj., adv., n.*
• ***adj.*** (**-er**, **-est**) **1** greater or better than normal in quantity, size or degree: *high prices* ◇ *The job needs a high degree of accuracy.* **2** above other people or things in importance or status: *We place a high priority on employees' development.* **3** containing a lot of a particular substance: *foods which are high* ***in*** *fat* **4** above the usual or expected standard: *the highest quality of service* OPP LOW
→ idioms at PLAY *v.*, RIDE *v.*
• ***adv.*** (**-er**, **-est**) at or to a large cost, value or amount: *Prices will rise even higher.* ◇ *high-priced products* OPP LOW
• ***n.*** [C] the highest level or amount: *Unemployment hit record highs.* OPP LOW **IDM** **on ˈhigh** used in a humorous way to refer to the people in senior positions in an organization: *an order from on high*

ˌ**high aˈchiever** *n.* [C] a person who is very successful in their work or studies

ˌ**high-ˈconcept** *adj.* used to describe sth that has a very interesting, attractive and clear idea: *high-concept designer stores*

ˌ**high-ˈcost** (*also* ˌ**higher-ˈcost**) *adj.* involving high costs; expensive: *the higher-cost airports*

ˈ**high-end** *adj.* having the highest price, quality or importance: *a high-end product* ▸ ˈ**high-end** *n.* [sing.]

ˌ**higher-ˈcost** = HIGH-COST

ˌ**higher-ˈincome** = HIGH-INCOME (1)

ˌ**higher-ˈup** (*esp. AmE*) (*BrE usu.* ˌ**high-ˈup**) *n.* [C] (*infml.*) a person with a high position in a company or an organization: *We should improve the way higher-ups communicate with employees.*

ˌ**high ˈfinance** *n.* [U] business activities which involve very large amounts of money

ˌ**high-ˈflyer** *n.* [C] **1** a person who has the desire and the ability to be very successful in their job: *high-flyers in banking* **2** a company or an investment that is or has been very successful: *a stock market high-flyer*
▸ ˌ**high-ˈflying** *adj.*: *a high-flying career*

ˌ**high-ˈgrade** *adj.* **1** having a high level or quality: *~ workers/specialists* **2** (*Finan.*) not likely to lose money: *high-grade bonds*

ˌ**high-ˈgrowth** *adj.* growing quickly in value or importance; likely to do this: *high-growth stocks*

ˌ**high-ˈimpact** *adj.* making a strong impression; having a strong influence: *a high-impact ad campaign*

ˌ**high-ˈincome** *adj.* **1** (*also* ˌ**higher-ˈincome**) having or earning a lot of money: *higher-income earners/taxpayers* **2** earning a high level of interest: *high-income bonds*

ˌ**high-inˈvolvement ˌproduct** *n.* [C] (*Market.*) a product that customers are willing to spend a lot of time and effort looking for and buying

ˌ**high-ˈlevel** *adj.* **1** involving senior people: *high-level meetings* **2** (*IT*) (about a computer language) similar to an existing language such as English, making it fairly simple to use

**highlight** /ˈhaɪlaɪt/ *v., n.*
• ***v.*** [T] **1** to make sth very obvious so that people give it more attention: *The figures highlighted the need for reforms to the market.* **2** to emphasize parts of a text with colour, using a pen or a computer
• ***n.*** **highlights** [pl.] the most important information about sth; a document containing this information: *sales highlights*

**highly** /ˈhaɪli/ *adv.* **1** at or to a high standard, level or amount: *a highly paid job* **2** very: *a highly successful business*

ˌ**high-ˈmargin** *adj.* (*Account.*; *Market.*) providing a high profit: *sales of high-margin products*

ˌ**high net ˈworth** *adj.* having a large amount of money; involving a large amount of money: *~ customers/clients/investors*

ˌ**high-ˈpaid** *adj.* **1** earning a lot of money: *high-paid accountants and lawyers* **2 the high-paid** *n.* [pl.] people who are paid a lot of money

ˌ**high-perˈformance** *adj.* that can go very fast or do complicated things: *~ companies/computers*

ˌ**high-perˈforming** *adj.* working to a very high standard: *a ~ company/team*

ˌ**high-ˈpowered** *adj.* **1** (about people) having a lot of power and influence; full of energy: *high-powered executives* **2** (about a job) important; with a lot of responsibility **3** (*also* ˌ**high-ˈpower**) (about machines) very powerful

ˌ**high-ˈpressure** *adj.* **1** that involves aggressive ways of persuading sb to do sth or to buy sth: *high-pressure selling techniques* **2** that involves a lot of worry and anxiety: *a high-pressure job* SYN STRESSFUL

ˌ**high-ˈpriced** (*also* ˌ**high-ˈprice**) *adj.* expensive: *high-priced hotels*

ˌ**high-ˈprofile** *adj.* receiving a great deal of attention in the media; well-known: *high-profile companies*

ˌ**high-ˈquality** *adj.* of a high standard: *high-quality products*

ˌ**high-ˈranking** *adj.* senior; important: *the highest-ranking executives/positions*

ˌ**high-resoˈlution** (*also* **hi-res, high-res** /ˌhaɪ ˈrez/) *adj.* showing a lot of clear, sharp detail: ~ *cameras/photos*

ˈ**high-rise** *adj.* a **high-rise** building is very tall, with many levels ▸ ˈ**high-rise** *n.* [C]: *the city's high-rises*

ˈ**high road** *n.* [sing.] (*HR*) a method of gaining an advantage in business which involves developing workers' skills, paying them high wages, giving them good conditions, etc. and producing goods of high value: *a high-road company* → LOW ROAD

ˌ**high ˈroller** *n.* [C] (*AmE*) (*infml.*) **1** a person who gambles very large amounts of money, either on the stock exchange or in clubs where you play games for money (**casinos**): *City high rollers* **2** an important person who earns or spends a great deal of money ▸ ˌ**high-ˈrolling** *adj.*

**the** ˌ**high ˈseas** *n.* [pl.] (*fml.*) areas of the oceans that are not under the legal control of a particular country

ˌ**high ˈseason** *n.* [U; sing.] (*esp. BrE*) the time of year when a hotel or tourist area receives most visitors

ˌ**high-ˈspeed** *adj.* fast: *high-speed Internet access*

ˈ**high street** *n.* [C, usu. sing.] (*BrE*) the main road in a town, where the shops/stores, banks, etc. are: *high-street stores/retailers*

★ˌ**high-ˈtech** (*also* **hi-**) *adj., n.*
• ***adj.*** **1** using the most modern methods, machines or devices, esp. electronic ones: ~ *equipment/systems* **2** (about objects, designs, etc.) very modern in appearance; using modern materials **3** producing things that include very modern technologies
• ***n.*** [U] (*infml.*) = HIGH TECHNOLOGY

ˌ**high techˈnology** (*fml.*) (*also* ˌ**high-ˈtech**) *n.* [U] areas of business which provide or use very advanced computers and methods; the computers and methods involved: *people working in high technology* ◇ *high-tech stocks*

ˌ**high ˈtouch** *adj.* involving a lot of human contact or activity, rather than relying on machines ▸ ˌ**high ˈtouch** *n.* [U]: *The focus is on high touch rather than high tech.*

ˌ**high-ˈup** = HIGHER-UP

ˌ**high ˈvolume** *n.* [C,U] a large quantity of sth: *a high volume of calls* ◇ *high-volume production*

ˌ**high-ˈyield** (*also* ˌ**high-ˈyielding**) *adj.* (*Finan.*) used to describe investments that produce a high income but may have some risk: ~ *bonds/funds/debt* ▸ ˌ**high-ˈyielder** *n.* [C]

**hike** /haɪk/ *v.* [T,I] (*infml.*) **~ sth (up)** to increase prices, taxes, etc. suddenly or by a large amount: *They will not hike up prices.* ▸ **hike** *n.* [C] (*esp. AmE*): *a tax/rate/price* ~

★**hire** /ˈhaɪə(r)/ *v., n.*
• ***v.*** **1** (*HR*) [T,I] (*esp. AmE*) to give sb a job: *She was hired three years ago.* ◇ *He does the* ***hiring and firing.*** **2** [T] to employ sb for a short time to do a particular job: *to hire a lawyer* **3** [T] (*esp. BrE*) to pay money to borrow sth for a short time: *to ~ a car/DVD*
PHR V ˌ**hire sth ˈout** (*Comm.*) to let sb use sth for a short time, in return for payment: *The rooms are hired out for meetings.* ˌ**hire yourself ˈout (to sb)** to arrange to work for sb
• ***n.*** **1** (*Comm.*) [U] (*esp. BrE*) the act of paying to use sth for a short time: *The price includes the hire of the hall.* ◇ *a hire car* ◇ *a car hire firm* SYN RENTAL **2** (*HR*) [C] (*esp. AmE*) a person that a company has recently given a job to: *new hires* SYN RECRUIT

ˌ**hired ˈgun** *n.* [C] (*AmE*) (*infml.*) **1** an expert who is brought into a company to solve difficult legal or financial problems, for example during a TAKEOVER **2** a person who works for different companies as they are needed

ˌ**hire ˈpurchase** *n.* [U] (*abbr* **h.p.**) (*BrE*) (*also* **inˈstalment plan** [C] *AmE, BrE*) (*Comm.*) a way of paying for goods gradually over a long period. You have the goods immediately, but legally you do not own them until you have finished paying: *They bought it* ***on*** *hire purchase.*

**hirer** /ˈhaɪərə(r)/ *n.* [C] **1** (*esp. AmE*) a person who employs other people: *She's a skilled hirer.* **2** (*BrE*) a person who hires sth such as a tool or vehicle **3** (*Comm.*) (*BrE*) a person who buys sth by HIRE PURCHASE

**ˌhi-ˈres** = HIGH-RESOLUTION

**ˈhiring hall** *n.* [C] (*AmE*) (*HR*) an EMPLOYMENT AGENCY, managed by a union, which provides skilled workers as employers need them

**histogram** /ˈhɪstəgræm/ *n.* [C] a diagram which uses bands of different heights to show the rate at which sth happens and different widths to show a range, so that they can be compared → BAR CHART

**hisˌtorical ˈcost** = HISTORIC COST

**hisˌtorical ˈcost acˌcounting** = HISTORIC COST ACCOUNTING

**hisˌtorical ˈhigh** = HISTORIC HIGH

**hisˌtorical ˈlow** = HISTORIC LOW

**hisˌtoric ˈcost** (*also* **hisˌtorical ˈcost**) *n.* [U,C] (*Account.*) the original price or value of an item

**hisˌtoric ˈcost acˌcounting** (*also* **hisˌtorical ˈcost acˌcounting**) *n.* [U] (*Account.*) a method of accounting that uses the original price or value of items

**hisˌtoric ˈhigh** (*also* **hisˌtorical ˈhigh**) *n.* [C] a time when a value or an amount is higher than at any other time; this value or amount: *The dollar hit a historic high of 760 pesos.*

**hisˌtoric ˈlow** (*also* **hisˌtorical ˈlow**) *n.* [C] a time when a value or an amount is lower than at any other time; this value or amount: *Interest rates are* **at** *historic lows.*

**history** /ˈhɪstri/ *n.* [C] (*pl.* **-ries**) a record of the things that a person has done or that have happened to them: *your employment history*

★ **hit** /hɪt/ *v., n.*

• *v.* (**hitting, hit, hit**) **1** [T,I] to have a bad effect on sb/sth: *The industry has been hit by a series of strikes.* **2** [T] to reach a particular price or level, esp. one that is very high or low: *Unemployment has hit a 10-year high.* **3** (*infml.*) [T] to experience sth difficult; to stop making progress with sth: *We hit a problem installing the system.* **4** (*infml.*) [T] if a product **hits** the shelves, stores, etc. it becomes available and starts being sold **IDM** **be hit ˈhard (by sth); be hard ˈhit (by sth)** to be affected very badly by sth: *The area has been hard hit by a decline in manufacturing.* ◇ *the hard-hit steel industry* **hit (it) ˈbig** (*infml.*) to be very successful **hit the ˈbuffers** (*esp. BrE*) (*infml.*) if sth **hits the buffers** it suddenly stops happening or being successful: *Consumer spending has hit the buffers.* **ˌhit the ground ˈrunning** (*infml.*) to start doing sth and continue very quickly and successfully **hit a ˈwall** if a company, a person, a price, etc. **hits a wall**, they reach a point where they are unable to make any further progress **hit the ˈwall** if a company **hits the wall**, it starts to fail or fails completely **PHR V** **ˌhit sb ˈup (for sth); ˈhit sb for sth** (*AmE*) (*infml.*) to ask sb for money: *When starting the firm they hit up friends and family.*

• *n.* [C] **1** (*IT*) a result of a search on a computer, esp. on the Internet; a person who visits an Internet page: *The site had 20 000 hits on one day.* **2** a person or thing that is very popular: *The drink is a big hit* **with** *young consumers.* **3** something that has a bad effect on sb/sth: *the hit to taxpayers* **IDM** **take a ˈhit 1** to be damaged or badly affected by sth: *The airline industry took a hit last year.* **2** if a company's profits **take a hit**, they are reduced by the amount mentioned, esp. because the company has had to pay an unusual cost: *The company took a €170 m hit* **to** *its earnings.*

**hitch** /hɪtʃ/ *n., v.*

• *n.* [C] a problem or difficulty that causes a short delay: *The change has gone ahead without a hitch.* ◇ *a last-minute/legal/technical ~*

• *v.* **IDM** **hitch your ˈwagon/ˈfortunes/ˈfuture to sb/sth** (*esp. AmE*) to rely on a particular person or thing for your success: *The firm had hitched its fortunes to the US technology boom.* **PHR V** **ˌhitch ˈup (with sb/sth)** (*infml.*) (about two businesses) to join together

**ˌhi-ˈtech** = HIGH-TECH

**ˈhit list** *n.* [C] (*infml.*) a list of people, organizations, etc. against whom some action is being planned or is needed

**hive** /haɪv/ *v.* **PHR V** **ˌhive sth ˈoff (into/to sth)** (*esp. BrE*) (*often pass.*) to separate one part of a group from the rest; to sell part of a business: *The retail business is being hived off into a separate company.*

**ˈHM ˈRevenue and ˈCustoms** *n.* [U] (*abbr* **HMRC**) the government organization in the UK that is now responsible for collecting all taxes, including taxes on goods bought and sold or brought into the country, and for paying some benefits, protecting borders, etc.

**HNWI** /ˌeɪtʃ en ˌdʌblju: ˈaɪ/ *abbr* (*infml.*) **high net worth individual** a very rich person

**HO** /ˌeɪtʃ ˈəʊ; *AmE* ˈoʊ/ = HEAD OFFICE

**Ho.** = HOUSE (2)

**hoard** /hɔːd; *AmE* hɔːrd/ *v.* [T,I] to collect and keep large amounts of money, supplies, food, etc., esp. secretly: *The group hoards any spare cash rather than returning it to shareholders.* ▸ **hoard** *n.* [C]: *a huge hoard of investments* **ˈhoarder** *n.* [C]: *cash hoarders*

**hoarding** /ˈhɔːdɪŋ; *AmE* ˈhɔːrd-/ *n.* [C] (*BrE*) (*Market.*) a large board on the outside of a building or at the side of the road, used for putting advertisements on SYN BILLBOARD

★**hold** /həʊld; *AmE* hoʊld/ *v., n.*
• *v.* (**held, held** /held/) **1** [T] to have or own sth: *The government holds a 55% stake in the firm.* ◇ *a* ***privately/publicly held*** *company* **2** [T] to organize and have a meeting, a discussion, an event, etc: *The board will hold a meeting on Tuesday.* **3** [T] to have a particular job or position, esp. an important or official one: *Few women hold top jobs.* **4** [T] to have enough space for sth/sb; to contain sth/sb: *This barrel holds 25 litres.* **5** [T] to keep a price, cost, etc. at a particular level: *Interest rates were held at 4.0 per cent.* **6** [T,I] to remain the same: *How long can these prices hold?* **7** [T] to keep sth so that it can be used later: *records held on computer* **8** [T,I] ~ **(on)** to wait until you can speak to the person you have telephoned: *Mr Smith is busy right now. Can you hold?* **9** (*Law*) [T,I] to make a judgement about sb/sth in a court: *The judge held (that) she had been negligent.* IDM **be in a ˈholding pattern** to be in a situation where there is not much change or activity **hold sb's ˈhand** to give sb a lot of support and help (often disapproving) **ˌhold the ˈfloor** to speak during a formal discussion, esp. for a long time so that nobody else is able to say anything **ˌhold the ˈpurse strings** to be in control of how money is spent → idiom at CHECK *n.* PHR V **ˌhold sb/sth ˈback** to limit or slow down the progress of sb/sth: *High interest rates are holding back growth.* **ˌhold sth ˈdown 1** to keep sth at a low level: *holding down costs* **2** to keep a job for some time: *He can't hold down a job.* **ˌhold ˈonto/ˈon to sth/sb** to keep sth/sb that is valuable or that provides an advantage; to not give or sell sth to sb else: *You should hold on to your oil shares.* **ˌhold ˈout for sth** to cause a delay in reaching an agreement because you hope you will gain sth: *The union is holding out for a higher pay offer.* **ˌhold sth ˈover** (*usu. pass.*) to not deal with sth immediately; to leave sth to be dealt with later: *This matter will be held over until the next meeting.* **ˌhold ˈup** to remain strong; to work well: *Sales held up well.* **ˌhold sb/sth ˈup** to delay or block the movement or progress of sb/sth
• *n.* **1** [sing.] influence, power or control over sb/sth: *The management have a strong hold* ***over*** *the company.* ◇ *to gain/lose/maintain/tighten a ~ (on/over sth)* **2** (*Stock Ex.*) [U; sing.] = HOLD RATING **3** (*Transpt.*) [C] the part of a ship or plane where the goods being carried are stored IDM **on ˈhold 1** delayed until a later time or date: *The project has been* ***put*** *on hold due to lack of funding.* **2** (esp. about interest rates) remaining the same: *Interest rates on hold.* **3** if a person on the telephone is put **on hold**, they have to wait until the person that they want to talk to is free **take ˈhold** to start to have an effect; to become strong: *The new theory took hold in business schools.*

★**holder** /ˈhəʊldə(r); *AmE* ˈhoʊ-/ *n.* [C] a person who has or owns the thing mentioned: *a licence holder* ◇ *a ~ of bonds/shares* ◇ *an account holder* ◇ *previous holders of the post*

**ˌholder of ˈrecord** = SHAREHOLDER OF RECORD

★**holding** /ˈhəʊldɪŋ; *AmE* ˈhoʊ-/ *n.* (*Finan.*) **1** [C, usu. pl.] an amount of sth that a company, fund, etc. owns as an asset: *Central banks have increased their euro holdings.* **2** [C] a share of the ownership of a company; the number or value of the shares owned: *They have a 27% holding* ***in*** *the company.* ◇ *a majority/minority ~* SYN SHAREHOLDING **3 Holdings** [pl.] used esp. in the names of companies to show that the company is a HOLDING COMPANY

**ˈholding ˌcompany** *n.* [C] (*Finan.*) a company formed to buy shares in other companies which it then controls: *a holding company with three subsidiaries*

**ˈholding cost** = CARRYING CHARGE (1)

**ˈholding opeˌration** *n.* [C] a series of actions that are taken so that a particular situation stays the same or does not get any worse

**holdout** /ˈhəʊldaʊt; *AmE* ˈhoʊld-/ *n.* [C] (*esp. AmE*) a person who resists or delays accepting sth; an act of resisting sth: *The last holdouts were the engineers, who refused to accept pay cuts.*

**ˈhold ˌrating** *n.* [C] (*also* **hold** [U; sing.]) (*Stock Ex.*) a statement by a bank, a dealer, etc. that investors should keep a particular company's shares rather than buy or sell them

**ˈhold-up** *n.* [C] a situation in which sth is prevented from happening for a short time: *a hold-up in production*

**ˌhole in the ˈwall** *n.* [C] (*BrE*) (*infml.*) a CASH MACHINE

**holiday** /ˈhɒlədeɪ; *AmE* ˈhɑːl- *BrE also* -di/ *n.* **1** [U] (*also* **holidays** [pl.]) (*both BrE*) (*AmE* **vaˈcation**) a period of time when you are not at work: *He's away* ***on holiday*** *this week.* ◇ *20 days' paid holiday a year* **2** [C] (*BrE*) (*AmE* **vaˈcation**) a period of time spent travelling or resting away from home: *booking holidays on the Internet* **3** [C] a day when most people do not go to work or school, esp. because of a religious or national celebration **4 holidays** [pl.] (*AmE*) the time in December and early January that includes Christmas, Hanukkah and New Year **5** [C] (*BrE*) a period of time when you do not need to make a particular payment: *a contribution/payment ~*

**ˈholiday rep** = REPRESENTATIVE *n.* (3)

**holidays** = HOLIDAY (1,4)

**home** /həʊm; *AmE* hoʊm/ *adj.*, *adv.*
• ***adj.*** **1** connected with the place where sb lives: *your home address* ◇ *free home delivery* **2** connected with the place where a business or an organization is established: *our home state of North Carolina* **3** used or made at home: *a home computer* **4** (*esp. BrE*) connected with your own country or region rather than foreign countries or regions: *the home market* SYN DOMESTIC
• ***adv.*** IDM **bring home the ˈbacon** (*infml.*) to earn money for your company, your family, etc.; to be successful at sth **take/bring home sth** to earn the amount mentioned: *The directors took home an additional $5 m in bonuses.*

**ˌhome ˈbanking** *n.* [U] a system for controlling a bank account from your home, for example, giving instructions to the bank by telephone

**ˌhome ˈcountry** *n.* [C] the country where an organization that operates in many countries is based

**ˌhome enterˈtainment** *n.* [U] all the electronic equipment, movies/films, music recordings, etc. that people use in their homes for entertainment; the business of selling these things: *the home entertainment sector*

**ˈhome ˌequity** = EQUITY (3)

**ˌhome ˈequity loan** (*also* **home-equity**-) *n.* [C] a loan that you can get by using the value of your home after all debts have been paid as COLLATERAL

**ˌhome imˈprovement** *n.* [U; pl.] making changes to your home in order to make it better; the business of providing equipment, tools, supplies, etc. for this: *a ~ store/loan*

**ˌhome ˈloan** *n.* [C] a loan that you get from a bank or similar financial organization to buy a house, flat/apartment, etc.

**ˌhome ˈoffice** *n.* [C] a part of your home that you use regularly for business: *She works out of her home office in Chicago.*

**homeowner** /ˈhəʊməʊnə(r); *AmE* ˈhoʊmoʊ-/ *n.* [C] a person who owns their house or flat/apartment

★ **ˈhome page** *n.* [C] (*IT*) **1** the main page created by an organization, etc. on the Internet from which connections to other pages can be made **2** a page on the Internet that you choose to appear first on your screen whenever you make a connection to the Internet

**ˈhome ˌproduct** *n.* [C, usu. pl.] goods that are used in the home, such as items for the kitchen and bathroom, sheets, furniture, etc.

**ˌhome reˈpair** *n.* [U] the activity of repairing or decorating things in the home yourself SYN DIY

**ˌhome ˈshopping** *n.* [U] a way of choosing goods at home and buying them by ordering by telephone, email, or on the Internet and having them delivered to your home

**homeshoring** /ˈhəʊmʃɔːrɪŋ; *AmE* ˈhoʊm-/ *n.* [U] (*HR*, *infml.*) the act of moving part of your company's operations to smaller towns in your own country or to people working from their homes → OFFSHORE *v.*

**homeworker** /ˈhəʊmwɜːkə(r); *AmE* ˈhoʊmwɜːrk-/ *n.* [C] (*HR*) a person who works for a company at home ▸ **ˈhomeworking** *n.* [U]

**Hon** (*also* **Hon.**, *esp. in AmE*) *abbr* (*BrE*) a short way of writing **Honorary** in official titles of jobs: *Hon Treasurer*

**honcho** /ˈhɒntʃəʊ; *AmE* ˈhɑːntʃoʊ/ *n.* [C] (*pl.* **honchos**) (*esp. AmE*) (*infml.*) the person who is in charge: *the company's* ***head honcho***

**hone** /həʊn; *AmE* hoʊn/ *v.* [T] to develop and improve sth, esp. a skill, over a period of time: *She has honed* *her skills working for top accounting firms.*

**honor** = HONOUR

**honorarium** /ˌɒnəˈreəriəm; *AmE* ˌɑːnəˈrer-/ *n.* [C] (*pl.* **-raria** /-ˈreəriə; *AmE* -ˈrer-/) (*HR, fml.*) a payment made for sb's professional services

**honorary** /ˈɒnərəri; *AmE* ˈɑːnəreri/ *adj.* (*abbr* **Hon**) (about a position in an organization) not paid: *an honorary chairman*

**honour** (*AmE* **honor**) /ˈɒnə(r); *AmE* ˈɑːnər/ *v.* [T] **1** to do what you have agreed or promised to do: *The bank refused to honour the cheque* (= keep an agreement to pay it). ◇ *to ~ a commitment/contract/obligation* **2** to pay money that you owe: *They were unable to honour their debts.*

**hook** /hʊk/ *n., v.*

• *n.* [C] (*infml.*) something interesting, clever, strange, etc. that is used to attract people's attention: *The promotion is a hook to attract consumers.*
IDM **be on the ˈhook (for sth/to do sth)** (*AmE*) (*infml.*) to be legally responsible for paying sth or for doing sth: *Unless you report the theft of your credit card immediately you may be on the hook for $500.*

• *v.* [T] (*infml.*) to attract and keep sb's attention: *The show hooked around 2.4 million viewers.*
PHR V **ˌhook ˈin; ˌhook ˈinto sth; ˌhook sth ˈinto sth** (*IT*) to be connected or to connect sth to a computer or telephone system, etc: *Our customers can still hook in from America.* **ˌhook ˈup (with sb)** (*infml.*) to start working with sb: *She hooked up with a partner to start a children's clothing company.* **ˌhook (sth) ˈup (to sth)** to connect sb/sth to a piece of electronic equipment or to a power supply: *Is the modem hooked up to the phone line?* **ˌhook sb ˈup (with sb/sth)** (*infml.*) to arrange for sb to meet sb or to do sth: *I can hook you up with their chief buyer.*

**ˈhook-up** (*also* **hookup**) *n.* [C] a connection between two or more pieces of equipment, esp. electronic equipment: *a high-speed Internet hook-up*

**HOQ** /ˌeɪtʃ əʊ ˈkjuː; *AmE* oʊ/ = HOUSE OF QUALITY

**horizontal** /ˌhɒrɪˈzɒntl; *AmE* ˌhɔːrəˈzɑːntl; ˌhɑːr-/ *adj.* **1** (*HR*) having few levels of management or control between the top and the bottom: *a horizontal management structure* **2** (*HR*) having the same level in a group or an organization; involving people or jobs at the same level: *Her transfer was a horizontal move rather than a promotion.* SYN LATERAL **3** (about a line, etc.) flat and level; going across and parallel to the ground rather than going up and down: *the horizontal axis of the graph* → VERTICAL

**ˌhorizontal ˈequity** *n.* [U] (*Econ.*) the principle that people with the same characteristics should be treated in the same way, for example that people with a similar level of income should pay the same rate of tax

**horiˌzontal inteˈgration** (*also* **horiˌzontal exˈpansion, ˌlateral inteˈgration**) *n.* [U,C] (*Econ.*) a situation where different companies that are involved in the same stage of producing or selling sth join together

**ˌhorizontal ˈloading** *n.* [U] (*HR*) the fact of giving sb more tasks to do in their job, but no more responsibility

**ˌhorizontal ˈmerger** *n.* [C] (*Econ.*) a situation where a company joins with another company that produces similar goods or provides similar services

**ˌhorizontal segreˈgation** *n.* [U] (*HR*) used to describe the fact that there are more men than women in some kinds of jobs or industry, and more women than men in others

**ˈhorse-ˌtrading** *n.* [U] (often used in newspapers) the activity of discussing business with sb using clever or strong methods in order to reach an agreement that suits you

**hospitality** /ˌhɒspɪˈtæləti; *AmE* ˌhɑːs-/ *n.* [U] **1** food, drink or services that are provided by an organization for guests, customers, etc: *the hospitality industry* (= hotels, restaurants, etc.) **2** friendly and generous behaviour towards guests

**host** /həʊst; *AmE* hoʊst/ *n., v.*

• *n.* [C] **1** a country, a city or an organization that provides the space, services, etc. for a special event and may also arrange it: *The school is* ***playing host to*** *the conference this year.* **2** a country, a city or an area where an organization operates, esp. one based in another country or city: *The country is host* ***to*** *96 multinationals.* **3** (*IT*) a computer that provides information or services to other computers connected to it

• *v.* [T] **1** to act as a **host** for an event, an organization, etc: *to ~ a conference/an event/a meeting* **2** (*IT*) to store a website on a computer connected to the Internet, usu. in exchange for a fee: *a hosting service*

**ˌhost ˈcountry** *n.* [C] a country where an organization that is based in another country operates

**hostile** /ˈhɒstaɪl; *AmE* ˈhɑːstl; -taɪl/ (*also* **unˈfriendly**, *less freq.*) *adj.* (*Finan.*) (about an attempt to buy or gain control of a company) not wanted by the directors of the company that is to be bought: *They are trying to fight off a $1.2 bn hostile bid from a rival travel operator.*
○ *a ~ offer/takeover* ♦ *a ~ acquisition/approach/deal* ♦ *a ~ acquirer/bidder*
IDM **to go/turn ˈhostile** (*Finan.*) to try to force the sale of a company against the wishes of its directors, by offering to buy large enough quantities of shares from its shareholders

**ˌhot-ˈdesking** *n.* [U] (*HR*) the practice in an office of giving workers an available desk when they need one, rather than giving each worker their own desk ▸ **ˌhot-ˈdesk** *v.* [I]

**hotelier** /həʊˈteliə(r); -lieɪ; *AmE* hoʊˈteljər; ˌoʊtelˈjeɪ/ *n.* [C] a person who owns or manages a hotel

**hotelling** (*also* **hoteling**, *esp. in AmE*) /həʊˈtelɪŋ; *AmE* hoʊ-/ *n.* [U] (*esp. AmE*) (*HR*) a system in which employees who normally work outside the company offices, or employees of another company, can arrange to have office space when they need it ▸ **hotel** /həʊˈtel; *AmE* hoʊ-/ *v.* [T,I] (-ll-, *AmE* -l-)

**ˈhot key** *n.* [C] (*IT*) one key, or a group of two or three keys, on a computer keyboard that you can press to make a program perform a particular task quickly

**hotline** /ˈhɒtlaɪn; *AmE* ˈhɑːt-/ *n.* [C] a special telephone line that people can use in order to get information or to talk about sth

**hotlink** /ˈhɒtlɪŋk; *AmE* ˈhɑːt-/ *n.* [C] (*IT*) a place in an electronic document that you can click on to move from there to another place in the document or to another electronic document SYN HYPERLINK
▸ **ˈhotlink** *v.* [T]

**ˈhot ˌmoney** *n.* [U] **1** (*Finan.*) money that is moved quickly between countries in order to make profits from changes in interest rates or in the value of currencies **2** used to say what people who know a lot think will happen: *The hot money is on an outsider as the new CEO.*

**the ˈhot seat** *n.* [sing.] (*infml.*) a difficult or unpleasant position where you have to take responsibility for decisions and actions that people may not like: *He has resigned as CEO after four years* **in the hot seat.**

**hotshot** /ˈhɒtʃɒt; *AmE* ˈhɑːtʃɑːt/ *n.* [C] (*infml.*) a person who is extremely successful in their career
▸ **ˈhotshot** *adj.*: *a hotshot lawyer*

**ˈhot spot** (*also* **hotspot**) *n.* [C] (*IT*) **1** an area on a computer screen that you can click on to start an operation such as loading a file **2** a place in a hotel, restaurant, station, etc. that is fitted with a special device that enables you to connect a computer to the Internet without using wires: *a wireless/wi-fi ~*

**ˌhourly ˈrate** *n.* [C] the amount paid for each hour worked: *be paid an hourly rate*

**house** /haʊs/ *n.* (*pl.* **houses** /ˈhaʊzɪz/) **1** [C] (*with other ns*) a company involved in a particular kind of business; an institution of a particular kind: *a fashion/banking/publishing ~* ◇ *a house magazine* (= for the people who work in that company or business) **2 House** [sing.] (*BrE*) (*abbr* **Ho.**) used in the names of office buildings: *Their offices are in Chester House.* **3** [C] (*with other ns*) a restaurant: *a coffee house* → idiom at CLEAN *adj.*

**ˈhouse brand** (*also* **ˈhouse ˌlabel**) *n.* [C] (*both esp. AmE*) (*Comm.*; *Market.*) a product that a shop/store sells with its own name on: *Tesco's house brands* SYN OWN BRAND, PRIVATE BRAND, STORE BRAND

**household** /ˈhaʊshəʊld; *AmE* -hoʊld/ *n.*, *adj.*
• ***n.*** [C] all the people living together in a single house or flat/apartment, considered as a unit: *a survey of 5 000 households*
○ *high-income/low-income/middle-income ~s* ♦ *rural/urban ~s*
• ***adj.*** **1** connected with looking after a house or flat/apartment and the people living in it: *household debt* **2** designed for use in the home: *household goods, such as televisions and washing machines*

**householder** /ˈhaʊshəʊldə(r); *AmE* -hoʊld-/ *n.* [C] (*fml.*) a person who owns or rents the home that they live in; the person who is in charge of a **household**

**ˌhousehold ˈname** (*also* **ˌhousehold ˈword**) *n.* [C] a name or brand that has become very well known

**ˌhousehold ˈproduct** *n.* [C, usu. pl.] a small item that is used in the home, esp. for cleaning

**ˌhousehold ˈword** = HOUSEHOLD NAME

**housekeeping** /ˈhaʊskiːpɪŋ/ *n.* [U] **1** jobs that are done to enable an organization or a computer system to work well: *A spending review is simply good housekeeping.* **2** the work involved in taking care of a hotel, an office building, etc. esp. cleaning the rooms; the department that is responsible for this

**ˌHouse of ˈQuality** *n.* [C,U] (*abbr* **HOQ**) (*Product.*) a technique used when new products are being planned, that collects information from customers about what they want and need, information about competing products, and technical information

**houseware** /ˈhaʊsweə(r); *AmE* -wer/ *n.* [U] (*also* **ˈhousewares** [pl.]) (*esp. AmE*) small things that are used in the home, esp. kitchen equipment and electrical items

**housing** /ˈhaʊzɪŋ/ *n.* **1** [U] houses, flats/apartments, etc. that people live in, esp. when referring to their type, price or condition: *a boom/slowdown in the ~ market* **2** [U] the job of providing houses, flats/apartments, etc. for people to live in: *a ~ department/officer* **3** [C] a hard cover that protects part of a machine or a piece of equipment

**ˈhousing start** *n.* [C] (*Econ.*) a new home that has started to be built. These are used as an important sign of the state of the economy.

**ˈhow-to** *adj., n.*
- *adj.* used to describe a book, course, etc. that gives you detailed and practical advice: *a how-to guide to building a business plan*
- *n.* [C] (*pl.* **how-tos**) a piece of detailed and practical advice; a book, etc. containing this kind of advice: *the how-tos of web design*

**h.p.** (*also* **HP**) /ˌeɪtʃ ˈpiː/ = HIRE PURCHASE

**HQ** /ˌeɪtʃ ˈkjuː/ = HEADQUARTERS

**HR** /ˌeɪtʃ ˈɑː(r)/ = HUMAN RESOURCES (2)

**HRD** /ˌeɪtʃ ɑː ˈdiː; *AmE* ɑːr/ = HUMAN RESOURCE DEVELOPMENT

**HRIS** /ˌeɪtʃ ɑːr aɪ ˈes/ = HUMAN RESOURCE INFORMATION SYSTEM

**HRM** /ˌeɪtʃ ɑːr ˈem / = HUMAN RESOURCE MANAGEMENT

**HRP** /ˌeɪtʃ ɑː ˈpiː; *AmE* ɑːr/ = HUMAN RESOURCE PLANNING

★ **HTML** /ˌeɪtʃ tiː em ˈel / *abbr* (*IT*) **Hypertext Mark-up Language** a system used to mark text for WORLD WIDE WEB pages in order to obtain colours, style, pictures, etc: *an HTML document*

**HTTP** /ˌeɪtʃ tiː tiː ˈpiː/ *abbr* (*IT*) **Hypertext Transfer Protocol** the set of rules that control the way data is sent and received over the Internet

**hub** /hʌb/ *n.* [C, usu. sing.] **1** the central and most important part of a particular place or activity: *the commercial hub of the city* **2** (*IT; Transpt.*) in a system of transport or communication, a central place to which passengers, messages, etc. go before going on to another place: *a distribution/transportation/network ~*

**ˌhub-and-ˈspoke ˌsystem** *n.* [C] (*Transpt.*) a system of transport in which passengers or cargo go from local airports, stations, etc. to a central one (a **hub**), from where flights, etc. go to other places; any organization, system of communication, etc. with this structure

**ˌhuman ˈcapital** *n.* [U] (*Econ.; HR*) people, when considering the value of their skills, knowledge and experience to an organization or a country: *to invest in human capital* (= provide better education, training, etc.)

**ˌhuman ˈfactors engiˌneering** *n.* [U] (*abbr* **HFE**) the use of scientific knowledge in designing systems, equipment, tools, etc. for work so that people can use them in the safest and most effective way

**ˌhuman reˈlations** *n.* (*HR*) **1** [pl.] the way in which employees treat and deal with each other in an organization **2** [U] the study of how to improve this in order to make an organization more friendly or efficient

**ˌhuman reˈsource deˌvelopment** *n.* [U] (*abbr* **HRD**) (*HR*) the process of encouraging employees to gain new skills and knowledge through training, courses, etc.

**ˈhuman reˈsource inforˈmation ˌsystem** *n.* [C] (*abbr* **HRIS**) (*HR*) a computer system used to collect, store and provide information about employees that will be used in HUMAN RESOURCE MANAGEMENT

**ˌhuman reˈsource ˌmanagement** *n.* [U] (*abbr* **HRM**) (*HR*) the activities involved in choosing, training, and taking care of employees in an organization, esp. in helping them develop their skills and abilities in a way that will help the organization

**ˌhuman reˈsource ˌplanning** *n.* [U] (*abbr* **HRP**) (*HR*) the activity of deciding what skills, knowledge and abilities an organization needs and how these can be met by existing and new employees

★ **ˌhuman reˈsources** *n.* (*HR*) **1** [pl.] the people who work for a particular organization; their skills and abilities, seen as sth the organization can use: *investing in human resources* **2** [U with sing./pl. v.] (*abbr* **HR**) the department in a company that deals with employing and training people SYN PERSONNEL
▸ **ˌhuman reˈsource** *adj.*: *a ~ manager/policy*

**ˈhush ˌmoney** *n.* [U] money that is paid to sb so that they do not tell others about sth secret or dishonest

**hybrid** /ˈhaɪbrɪd/ *n.* [C] something that is the product of mixing two or more different things

**hygiene** /ˈhaɪdʒiːn/ *n.* [U] the practice of keeping yourself and your working areas clean in order to prevent illness and disease: *food hygiene* ◇ *hygiene standards*

**hype** /haɪp/ *n.* [U] advertisements and discussion on television, radio, etc. telling the public about a product, service, etc. and about how good or important it is: *marketing/media ~*
▸ **hype** *v.* [T] (*infml.*) **~ sth (up)**

**hyper-** /ˈhaɪpə(r)/ *prefix* (*used in adjs and ns*) more than normal; too much: *a period of hypergrowth*

**hypercompetition** /ˌhaɪpəˌkɒmpəˈtɪʃn; *AmE* ˌhaɪpərˌkɑːm-/ *n.* [U] (*Econ.*) a situation in which all the companies producing particular goods or services continue to compete with each other in order to try to make the way they produce them as cheap and efficient as possible
▸ **ˌhypercomˈpetitive** /-kəmˈpetətɪv/ *adj.*

**hyperinflation** /ˌhaɪpərɪnˈfleɪʃn/ *n.* [U] (*Econ.*) a situation in which prices and wages rise very fast, causing damage to a country's economy

**hyperlink** /ˈhaɪpəlɪŋk; *AmE* -pərl-/ *n.* [C] (*IT*) a place in an electronic document, for example an Internet page, that you can click on in order to show another document or a different part of the same document SYN HOTLINK ▸ **ˈhyperlink** *v.* [T]: *a hyperlinked set of web pages*

**hypermarket** /ˈhaɪpəmɑːkɪt; *AmE* -pərmɑːrk-/ *n.* [C] a very large shop/store, usu. outside a town, that sells a wide range of goods

**hypertext** /ˈhaɪpətekst; *AmE* -pərt-/ *n.* [U] (*IT*) text stored in a computer system that contains links that allow the user to move from one piece of text or document to another

# Ii

**I-ˈ9 form** /aɪ ˈnaɪn/ *n.* [C] (*HR*) an official document that an employer must have which shows that an employee has the right to work in the US

**IAS** /ˌaɪ eɪ ˈes/ = INTERNATIONAL ACCOUNTING STANDARDS

**IASB** /ˌaɪ eɪ es ˈbiː/ = INTERNATIONAL ACCOUNTING STANDARDS BOARD

**IATA** /aɪˈɑːtə/ *abbr* **International Air Transport Association** the organization that most of the world's airlines belong to, which helps them to operate efficiently and sets standards for how tickets are sold, the safety of aircraft, etc.

**IC** /ˌaɪ ˈsiː/ = INDEPENDENT CONTRACTOR

**ICAO** /ˌaɪ siː eɪ ˈəʊ; *AmE* ˈoʊ/ = INTERNATIONAL CIVIL AVIATION ORGANIZATION

**ICC** /ˌaɪ siː ˈsiː/ = INTERNATIONAL CHAMBER OF COMMERCE

**icon** /ˈaɪkɒn; *AmE* -kɑːn/ *n.* [C] **1** (*IT*) a small picture on a computer screen that represents a program or a file **2** a famous person, organization or thing that people admire and see as a symbol of a particular idea, style, way of doing things, etc: *Fiat became an icon of Italian industry.*
▸ **iˈconic** *adj.*: *The Body Shop achieved iconic status.*

**ICT** /ˌaɪ siː ˈtiː/ *abbr* (*BrE*) **information and communication technology/technologies** the use of computers, the Internet, video, and other technology in an organization to collect, store and send information; the computers and other equipment that are used for this

**ID** /ˌaɪ ˈdiː/ *n.*, *v.*
• *n.* [U,C] an official way of showing who you are, for example a document with your name, date of birth and often a photograph on it: *You must carry ID at all times.* ◇ *an ID card*
• *v.* [T] (**ID's, ID'ing, ID'd, ID'd**) (*infml.*) to ask sb to show an official document that shows who they are, how old they are, etc: *You can't get into the building without being ID'd.*

**IDD** /ˌaɪ diː ˈdiː/ *abbr* **International Direct Dialling** a system that allows you to telephone people in other countries without needing to be connected by the OPERATOR

**identification** /aɪˌdentɪfɪˈkeɪʃn/ *n.* **1** [U,C] the process of showing, proving or recognizing who or what sb/sth is: *Each part has a number for easy identification.* **2** [U] official papers or a document that can prove who you are

**identifier** /aɪˈdentɪfaɪə(r)/ *n.* [C] **1** a number, name, etc. that is used to identify a person or thing **2** (*IT*) a series of characters used to refer to a program or set of data within a program

**identify** /aɪˈdentɪfaɪ/ *v.* [T] (**-fies, -fying, -fied, -fied**) **1** to find or discover sb/sth: *We think we have identified a gap in the market.* **2** to recognize sb/sth and be able to say who or what they are: *How does the machine identify you?*

**iˈdentity theft** *n.* [U] using sb else's name to obtain credit cards or take money out of their account ▶ **iˈdentity thief** *n.* [C]

**idle** /ˈaɪdl/ *adj., v.*

• ***adj.*** **1** (about machines, factories, etc.) not being used: *Many of the factories lie idle in the summer.* **2** (about people) not working; without work: *Over ten per cent of the workforce is now idle.*

• ***v.*** [T] (*AmE*) to close a factory, etc. or stop providing work for the workers, esp. temporarily: *The strikes have idled nearly 4 000 workers.*

**ˈidle time** *n.* [U] (*IT*) the time that a machine, esp. a computer, is not being used although it is available

**IFA** /ˌaɪ ef ˈeɪ/ = INDEPENDENT FINANCIAL ADVISER

**IFRS** /ˌaɪ ef ɑːr ˈes/ = INTERNATIONAL FINANCIAL REPORTING STANDARDS

**IHT** /ˌaɪ eɪtʃ ˈtiː/ = INHERITANCE TAX

★**illegal** /ɪˈliːɡl/ *adj.* not allowed by the law: *It is illegal to use personal information for marketing purposes.* OPP LEGAL

○ *~ activities/payments/practices/trading* • *to declare/judge/make/rule sth ~*

▶ **ilˈlegally** /-ɡəli/ *adv.*: *illegally copied CDs*

**illegality** /ˌɪliˈɡæləti/ *n.* (*pl.* **-ties**) **1** [U] the state of being illegal: *There was no illegality in their actions.* **2** [C] an illegal act

**illicit** /ɪˈlɪsɪt/ *adj.* not allowed by the law: *the illicit trade in tobacco products* SYN ILLEGAL ▶ **ilˈlicitly** *adv.*

**illiquid** /ɪˈlɪkwɪd/ *adj.* (*Account.; Finan.*) **1** (about assets) that cannot easily be sold and changed into cash: *Property is a highly illiquid investment.* **2** (about a company, an investor, etc.) having little cash or few assets that can easily be changed into cash **3** an **illiquid** market is one where there is little buying and selling OPP LIQUID ▶ **ˌilliˈquidity** /-dəti/ *n.* [U]

**ILM** /ˌaɪ el ˈem/ = INTERNAL LABOUR MARKET

**ILO** /ˌaɪ el ˈəʊ; *AmE* ˈoʊ/ = INTERNATIONAL LABOUR ORGANIZATION

**IM** /ˌaɪ ˈem/ = INFORMATION MANAGEMENT, INSTANT MESSAGING

**image** /ˈɪmɪdʒ/ *n.* **1** [C,U] the impression that a person, an organization or a product, etc. gives to other people or to the public: *We are trying to convey an image of a reliable, safe brand.*

○ *to **build/create/present/project** an ~* • *to **change/improve/shed** an ~* • *sth **damages/tarnishes** sb's/sth's ~* • *a **positive/strong** ~* • *a **negative/poor** ~*

**2** [C] a picture of sb/sth seen through a camera or on a television or computer: *The camera produces sharp, high-resolution images.*

○ *to **display/scan/store** an ~* • *a **black-and-white/colour/digital** ~*

**ˈimage ˌadvertising** *n.* [U] (*Market.*) advertising that creates an attractive impression of a company or a product ▶ **ˈimage adˌvertisement** *n.* [C]

**ˈimage ˌmarketing** *n.* [U] (*Market.*) the activity of trying to sell products by creating an attractive image for a company or a product

**imaging** /ˈɪmɪdʒɪŋ/ *n.* [U] (*IT*) the use of computers and electronic equipment to obtain, store and display images of objects, documents, pictures, etc.

**imbalance** /ɪmˈbæləns/ *n.* [C,U] a situation in which two or more things are not the same size or are not treated the same, in a way that is unfair or that causes problems: *an ~ in/of supply and demand* ◇ *to redress* (= put right) *the imbalance **between** export and import figures*

**imbed** = EMBED

**IMC** /ˌaɪ em ˈsiː/ = INTEGRATED MARKETING COMMUNICATIONS

**IMF** /ˌaɪ em ˈef/ *abbr* **International Monetary Fund** an organization within the United Nations which encourages trade and economic development. It lends money to countries that are having economic problems and sometimes tells governments to change their economic policies.

**impairment** /ɪmˈpeəmənt; *AmE* -ˈperm-/ *n.* [U] (*Account.*) a situation where an asset becomes less valuable and a company must show this by reducing its value in the financial records: *a charge for goodwill impairment*

**impeach** /ɪmˈpiːtʃ/ *v.* [T] (about a court or other official body, esp. in the US) to charge an important person with a serious crime
▸ **imˈpeachment** *n.* [U,C]

**imperfect** /ɪmˈpɜːfɪkt; *AmE* -ˈpɜːrf-/ *adj.* containing mistakes or faults: *All our sale items are slightly imperfect.*

**impˌerfect compeˈtition** *n.* [U] (*Econ.*) a situation where there are a limited number of sellers, each with a lot of control over prices and little information about what the others are doing

**imperfection** /ˌɪmpəˈfekʃn; *AmE* -pərˈf-/ *n.* [C,U] a fault or weakness in sb/sth: *imperfections* **in** *the glass*

**imˌperfect ˈmarket** *n.* [C, usu. sing.] (*Econ.*) a situation where individual buyers and sellers can influence the price of goods, for example if there are only a few sellers, buyers do not have enough information about products and prices, or there are not enough goods of the same type produced

★**implement** /ˈɪmplɪment/ *v.* [T] **1** to make sth that has been officially decided start to happen or be used: *These changes will be implemented over a five-year period.*
○ *to ~* ***measures/reforms*** ♦ *to ~ a* ***decision/policy/strategy*** ♦ *to ~ sth* ***extensively/fully/successfully***
**2** (*IT*) to introduce or start to use a new system: *We have implemented the software across our distribution network.* ▸ **ˌimplemenˈtation** /-ˈteɪʃn/ *n.* [U,C]

**imˌplicit ˈknowledge** = TACIT KNOWLEDGE

**implied** /ɪmˈplaɪd/ *adj.* (*Law*) **1** an **implied** condition is one that becomes part of an agreement automatically because of the law and does need to be stated **2** (about a legal agreement) that is believed to exist because of people's behaviour rather than agreed in a formal way: *They argued that they had an implied licence to use the software.*
▸ **imˈpliedly** *adv.*

**implode** /ɪmˈpləʊd; *AmE* ɪmˈploʊd/ *v.* [I] (about an organization, a system, etc.) to fail suddenly and completely ▸ **implosion** /-ˈpləʊʒn; *AmE* -ˈploʊ-/ *n.* [C,U]

★**import** *n., v.*
• ***n.*** /ˈɪmpɔːt; *AmE* ˈɪmpɔːrt/ **1** [C, usu. pl.] a product or service that is brought into one country from another: *food imports from abroad*
**2 imports** [pl.] the amount or value of goods and services that are brought from one country into another over a period of time: *Exports fell while imports rose.* **3** [U] the act of buying a product or service from another country and bringing it into a country: *products approved for import* ◇ *an import licence* OPP EXPORT
• ***v.*** /ɪmˈpɔːt; *AmE* ɪmˈpɔːrt/ **1** [T,I] to bring a product or service into one country from another: *We have to import most of its raw materials.* ◇ *importing countries* **2** [T] to introduce an idea or activity from another country or area: *management ideas imported from the business world*
**3** (*IT*) [T] to move data into one computer file, program or system from another OPP EXPORT ▸ **imˈportable** /-təbl/ *adj.*: *importable goods*
**ˌimporˈtation** /-ˈteɪʃn/ *n.* [U,C]

**ˈimport ˌduty** *n.* [C,U] (*Trade*) a tax that is paid on particular goods or services that are brought into a country

★**importer** /ɪmˈpɔːtə(r); *AmE* -ˈpɔːrt-/ *n.* [C] **1** a business, country or person that buys and brings in goods or services from another country: *a London-based importer of Italian goods* ◇ *The country is a* ***net importer*** *of oil* (= it imports more than it exports). **2** a country whose government or businesses borrow money or receive investment from other countries → EXPORTER

**ˌimport-ˈexport** *adj.* (*Trade*)
**1** an **import-export** company, business, etc. is one that buys goods from foreign suppliers to sell to local companies, as well as supplying local goods to foreign buyers **2** connected with goods and services that are brought into or sent out of a country: *the import-export market*

**ˈimport ˌsurcharge** *n.* [C] (*Econ.*) an extra tax charged on goods being brought into a country in addition to the normal tax

**impose** /ɪmˈpəʊz; *AmE* ɪmˈpoʊz/ *v.* [T] to introduce a new law, rule, tax, etc.; to order that a rule, punishment, etc. be used: *A new tax was imposed **on** fuel.* ◇ *to impose fines*
▶ **imposition** /ˌɪmpəˈzɪʃn/ *n.* [U]

**impound** /ɪmˈpaʊnd/ *v.* [T] to officially take sth away from sb, so that they cannot use it: *Customs agents impounded the goods at the docks.*

**impression** /ɪmˈpreʃn/ (*also* **ˈad view**) *n.* [C] (*Market.*) **1** the number of times a web page or a BANNER AD is shown: *What is the cost per thousand impressions?* **2** the number of times that one person sees an advertisement

**imprest** /ˈɪmprest/ *n.* [C] (*Account.*) **1** a fund that is used by a business for making regular small payments: *an ~ account/fund* **2** an amount of money that is given in advance to sb for a particular purpose

**imprint** /ˈɪmprɪnt/ *n.* [C] **1** a brand name under which books are published **2** the name of the PUBLISHER of a book, usu. printed below the title on the first page

**improper** /ɪmˈprɒpə(r); *AmE* -ˈprɑːp-/ *adj.* dishonest; against the rules: *improper accounting practices*
▶ **imˈproperly** *adv.*

**impropriety** /ˌɪmprəˈpraɪəti/ *n.* [U,C] (*pl.* **-ties**) (*fml.*) behaviour or actions that are dishonest or not appropriate for a person in a position of responsibility: *allegations of financial impropriety*

**improve** /ɪmˈpruːv/ *v.* [T,I] to become better than before; to make sth/sb better than before: *Market conditions have improved considerably.* ▶ **imˈprovement** /-mənt/ *n.* [U,C]: *The economy is showing signs of improvement.* ◇ *making improvements to the design of a product*
PHR V **imˈprove on/upon sth** to achieve or produce sth that is of a better quality than sth else: *We've improved on last year's figures.*

**imprudent** /ɪmˈpruːdnt/ *adj.* (*fml.*) not wise or sensible: *imprudent purchases* OPP PRUDENT
▶ **imˈprudence** /-dns/ *n.* [U] **imˈprudently** *adv.*

**ˈimpulse buy** (*also* **ˈimpulse ˌpurchase**) *n.* [C] (*Market.*) a product that you see in a shop/store, etc. and suddenly decide to buy without planning to do so ▶ **ˈimpulse ˌbuyer** (*also* **ˈimpulse ˌpurchaser**) *n.* [C] **ˈimpulse ˌbuying** (*also* **ˈimpulse ˌpurchasing**) *n.* [U]

**in.** (*pl.* **in.** *or* **ins.**) = INCH

**inactive** /ɪnˈæktɪv/ *adj.* **1** not doing anything; not active: *~ customers/markets* **2** not in use; not working: *an inactive bank account*
▶ **ˌinacˈtivity** /-ˈtɪvəti/ *n.* [U]

**inadmissible** /ˌɪnədˈmɪsəbl/ *adj.* (*Law*) that cannot be allowed or accepted, esp. in court: *inadmissible evidence*

**ˈin-ˌbasket** = INBOX (2)

**inbound** /ˈɪnbaʊnd/ *adj.* going towards a place rather than leaving it: *~ flights/calls* OPP OUTBOUND

**ˌinbound ˈtelemarketing** *n.* [U] (*Market.*) selling goods or services by inviting people to telephone the company selling the product

★**inbox** /ˈɪnbɒks; *AmE* -bɑːks/ *n.* [C] **1** (*IT*) the place in a computer where email messages are shown when they arrive **2** (*also* **in-box**, *AmE also* **ˈin-ˌbasket**) = IN TRAY

**ˌin-ˈbuilt** = BUILT-IN

**Inc.** (*also* **inc**) /ɪŋk/ *abbr* used in the names of companies in the US as a short way of writing **Incorporated**: *Microsoft Inc.*

**inc.** = INCL.

**incaˈpacity ˌbenefit** *n.* [U,C] in the UK, money that the government pays to people who cannot work because they are ill, injured, etc.

★**incentive** /ɪnˈsentɪv/ *n.* [C,U] something that encourages people to do sth, esp. to work harder, spend more money, etc: *generous incentives **for** small businesses **to** invest in new equipment* ◇ *an incentive plan to retain key workers* SYN INDUCEMENT OPP DISINCENTIVE
⊙ ***big/powerful/real/strong** ~s* ♦ ***to create/offer/provide** ~s* ♦ *an ~ **package/payment/plan/system***

**inˈcentive ˌmarketing** *n.* [U] a way of selling more goods or services by offering rewards such as low prices, gifts, etc. to customers to persuade them to buy

**inˈcentivize, -ise** /ɪnˈsentɪvaɪz/ *v.* [T] to encourage sb to do sth, esp. to work harder or to buy sth, by offering them a reward for doing it: *We set up a system of bonuses to incentivize sales staff.*

**inch** /ɪntʃ/ *n.*, *v.*
• *n.* [C] (*abbr* **in.**) a unit for measuring length, equal to 2.54 centimetres: *a 14-inch monitor*
• *v.* [I] (*used with an adv. or a prep.*) to move slowly towards a particular level or position: *The euro inched higher against the yen.*

**incidental** /ˌɪnsɪˈdentl/ *adj., n.*
• ***adj.*** happening in connection with sth else, but not as important as it: *The delivery service is incidental* ***to*** *our main business.* ◇ ***incidental expenses*** (= small costs related to your main activity)
• ***n.*** [C, usu. pl.] something that happens in connection with sth else, but is less important: *incidentals such as tips and taxis*

**incl.** (*BrE also* **inc.**) *abbr* **1** a short way of writing **including** or **included**, esp. in advertisements: *€170 inc. all taxes* **2** a short way of writing **inclusive**: *9 to 16 June incl.*

★**include** /ɪnˈkluːd/ *v.* [T] **1** if one thing **includes** another, it has the second thing as one of its parts: *Does the price include tax?* **2 ~ sb/sth (as/in/on sth)** to make sb/sth part of sth: *We haven't included February's sales in these figures.* OPP EXCLUDE

**including** /ɪnˈkluːdɪŋ/ *prep.* (*abbr* **incl.**) having sth as part of a group or set: *a fare of €79, including taxes* OPP EXCLUDING

**inclusive** /ɪnˈkluːsɪv/ *adj.* **1** having the total cost, or the cost of the thing mentioned, contained in the price: *Prices are inclusive* ***of*** *all packaging and delivery.* OPP EXCLUSIVE **2** (*BrE*) (*abbr* **incl.**) including all the days, months, numbers, etc. mentioned: *1 to 14 July inclusive* **3** including a wide range of people, not only the people with power or authority

★**income** /ˈɪnkʌm; -kəm/ *n.* [C,U] the money that a person, a region, a country, etc. earns from work, from investing money, from business, etc: *people* ***on*** *high/low ~s* ◇ *Tourism is a major* ***source of income*** *for the area.*
● *an* ***annual****/a* ***monthly/quarterly/weekly*** *~* ◆ ***family/household/national/personal*** *~* ◆ ***gross/net*** *~* ◆ ***after-tax/pre-tax/post-tax/taxable*** *~* ◆ *to* ***earn/generate/have/provide/receive*** *(an) ~*

**ˌincome and exˈpenditure acˌcount** *n.* [C] (*Account.*) a financial account used by NON-PROFIT organizations such as charities, universities, etc. to record income and expenses; a report of the income and expenses for a particular period

**ˈincome bond** *n.* [C] (*Finan.*) **1** in the UK, a type of bond that pays the investor an amount of interest regularly, for example every month **2** in the US, a bond that pays interest at a rate which is related to the amount of money earned by the company selling it

**ˈincome efˌfect** *n.* [C] (*Econ.*) the way in which a change in the price of a product or service results in a change in the quantity demanded because the consumer is able to buy more or less with their money

**ˈincome elasˈticity of deˈmand** *n.* [C,U] (*Econ.*) the extent to which people buy more or less of a product or service when the amount of money that they earn changes

**ˈincome fund** *n.* [C] (*Finan.*) a type of fund that invests in shares, bonds, etc. that are safe and pay a regular income

**ˈincome group** *n.* [C] (*Econ.*) a group of people within the population who earn similar wages: *high/low/middle ~s*

**ˈincome inˌsurance** (*also* **ˌincome proˈtection inˌsurance**) *n.* [U,C] a type of insurance in which you receive money if you are unable to work, because you are ill/sick, etc.

**ˈincome share** *n.* [C, usu. pl.] (*also* **ˈincome stock** [U,C]) (*Finan.*) a share in a company that is likely to provide investors with high, regular DIVIDENDS

**ˈincome ˌstatement** *n.* [C] (*AmE*) (*Account.*) an official financial record that gives details of all a company's income and expenses for a particular period and shows if it has made a profit or a loss SYN PROFIT AND LOSS ACCOUNT

**ˈincome stock** = INCOME SHARE

**ˈincome stream** *n.* [C] (*Finan.*) **1** regular payments that sb receives from an investment or a property, esp. over a long period of time **2** the money that a business produces

**ˈincome tax** *n.* [U,C] the amount of money that you pay to the government according to how much you earn or receive from some other sources. In the US, businesses also pay income tax: *cuts in the rate of income tax* ◇ *the agency collecting federal income tax*
● ***corporate/personal*** *~* ◆ *to* ***avoid/evade/pay*** *~* ◆ *to* ***cut/increase/raise/reduce*** *~*

**incoming** /ˈɪnkʌmɪŋ/ *adj.* **1** recently elected or chosen: *the incoming chairman* **2** arriving somewhere, or being received: *~ mail/orders* OPP OUTGOING

**incomings** /ˈɪnkʌmɪŋz/ *n.* [pl.] (*BrE*) (*infml.*) income OPP OUTGOINGS

**ˌin-ˈcompany** = IN-HOUSE

**incompatible** /ˌɪnkəmˈpætəbl/ *adj., n.*

• ***adj.*** (about equipment, esp. computers or programs) not able to be used together; not standard: *New software is often incompatible* ***with*** *older computers.* OPP COMPATIBLE
▸ **ˌincomˌpatiˈbility** /-ˈbɪləti/ *n.* [U,C] (*pl.* **-ties**)
• ***n.*** [C, usu. pl.] something, such as a piece of equipment, a computer program, a drug, a chemical, etc. that cannot be used with something else

**incompetence** /ɪnˈkɒmpɪtəns; *AmE* -ˈkɑːm-/ *n.* [U] the lack of skill or ability to do a job as it should be done: *managerial/professional ~*

**incompetent** /ɪnˈkɒmpɪtənt; *AmE* -ˈkɑːm-/ *adj.* not having the skill or ability to do a job as it should be done: *~ managers/workers* OPP COMPETENT ▸ **inˈcompetent** *n.* [C] **inˈcompetently** *adv.*

★ **incorporate** /ɪnˈkɔːpəreɪt; *AmE* -ˈkɔːrp-/ *v.* (*often pass.*) **1** [T,I] to form a legal company or organization, for example by obtaining a certificate from the authorities: *The business was incorporated* ***as*** *a limited liability company.* ◇ *The firm incorporated in Delaware in 1997.* **2** [T] **~ sth (in/into/within sth)** to include sth as part of sth else: *Your suggestions have been incorporated into the plan.*

★ **incorporated** /ɪnˈkɔːpəreɪtɪd; *AmE* -ˈkɔːrp-/ *adj.* formed into an official company or organization with legal status: *an incorporated company* ◇ *Wal-Mart Stores Incorporated*

**incorporation** /ɪnˌkɔːpəˈreɪʃn; *AmE* -ˌkɔːrp-/ *n.* [U,C] an act of forming a legal company or organization: *Delaware is the most popular state in the US for incorporation.* ◇ *new incorporations*

**Incoterm** /ˈɪnkəʊtɜːm; ˈɪŋ-; *AmE* -koʊtɜːrm/ *n.* [C] (*Trade*) (used in contracts between exporters, importers, etc.) one of a list of standard phrases, usu. used as abbreviations, that show who is responsible for the delivery and insurance of goods being sent between countries

★ **increase** *v., n.*
• ***v.*** /ɪnˈkriːs/ [T,I] to become or to make sth greater in amount, number, value, etc: *The rate of inflation increased by 2%.* ◇ *Oil has increased in price.* ◇ *increasing unemployment* ◇ *We need to increase productivity.* OPP DECREASE
✪ *to ~* ***dramatically/sharply/significantly*** ♦ *to ~* ***gradually/slightly/steadily*** ♦ *to ~ in* ***number/size/value***
▸ **inˈcreased** *adj.*: *increased demand*
• ***n.*** /ˈɪŋkriːs/ [C,U] a rise in the amount, number or value of sth: *a 12% increase* ***in*** *costs* ◇ *a year-on-year increase* ◇ *Industrial activity is* ***on the increase.*** ◇ *The rate of increase has slowed.* OPP DECREASE
✪ *a* ***big/dramatic/sharp/significant*** *~* ♦ *a* ***pay/salary/wage*** *~* ♦ *a* ***cost/*** *(an* ***interest) rate/price/tax*** *~*

**increment** /ˈɪŋkrəmənt/ *n.* [C] **1** (*HR*) a regular increase in the amount of money that sb is paid for their job: *The pay system contains automatic annual increments in the early years.* **2** an increase in a number or an amount, esp. one in a series: *The bids rose in increments of $1000.*

**incremental** /ˌɪŋkrəˈmentl/ *adj.* **1** used to describe sth that happens gradually, a little at a time: *incremental improvements to existing products* **2** used to describe an increase in a number or amount: *We began production runs in incremental jumps, from 1000 to 10000 and on up.* **3** (*HR*) used to describe a system in which the amount of money that sb is paid for their job increases regularly: *the next point on the incremental scale* **4** (*Account.*) used to describe the total change in income, sales, costs, etc. that results from an extra activity, product, service, customer, employee, etc: *The incremental cost of delivering one more page of data is zero.* ▸ **ˌincreˈmentally** /-təli/ *adv.*

**incubator** /ˈɪŋkjubeɪtə(r)/ *n.* [C] a company that helps people to start businesses, esp. ones connected with modern technology or the Internet

**ˈincubator space** *n.* [C,U] offices, buildings, etc. that are provided free or at low cost to small, new businesses

**incumbent** /ɪnˈkʌmbənt/ *n., adj.*
• ***n.*** [C] **1** a person who has an official position **2** a company that has a large share of a particular market: *the Swedish telecoms incumbent*
• ***adj.*** **1** having an official position: *the incumbent chief executive* **2** having a large market share: *incumbent operators*

★ **incur** /ɪnˈkɜː(r)/ *v.* [T] (**-rr-**) **1** to do sth that means you lose or have to pay an amount of money: *You risk incurring bank charges if you exceed your overdraft limit.* ◇ *to ~ costs/debts/expenses/losses* **2** to do sth that means you have to deal with sth unpleasant: *At busy times, orders may incur delays.* ◇ *to ~ anger/risks*

**indebted** /ɪnˈdetɪd/ *adj.* (*fml.*) **~ (to sb/sth)** (about companies, governments, etc.) owing money to

other countries or organizations: *heavily indebted companies*
▸ **in'debtedness** *n.* [U]: *a rise in consumer indebtedness*

**indemnify** /ɪn'demnɪfaɪ/ *v.* [T] (**-fies**, **-fying**, **-fied**, **-fied**) (*Law*) to promise to pay sb an amount of money if they suffer any damage or loss: *The contract indemnifies them against loss of earnings.*
▸ **in,demnifi'cation** /-fɪ'keɪʃn/ *n.* [U,C]

**indemnity** /ɪn'demnəti/ *n.* [U,C] (*pl.* **-ties**) (*Law*) **1** protection against damage or loss, esp. in the form of a promise to pay for anything that happens; a payment that is made for damage or loss: *an ~ fund/policy* ◇ *They only paid a small indemnity for loss of the package.* **2** an agreement not to make sb legally responsible for sth: *indemnity from prosecution*

**indenture** /ɪn'dentʃə(r)/ *n.* [C] (*Finan.*) a legal document that states the conditions that apply to a particular bond

★ **independent** /,ɪndɪ'pendənt/ *adj.*, *n.*
• ***adj.*** **1** not part of a larger company or group of companies: *small independent retailers* **2** not connected with or controlled by sb/sth; not connected with each other: *a review by independent auditors* **3** done or given by sb who is not involved in a situation and so is able to judge it fairly: *an independent inquiry* **4** supported by private money rather than government money: *the independent sector*
▸ **,inde'pendently** *adv.*: *a small independently owned airline*
• ***n.*** [C] a business that is not connected with a larger company or group of companies

**inde,pendent con'tractor** *n.* [C] (*abbr* **IC**) a person or business that has a contract with a company to do particular work

**inde,pendent di'rector** = NON-EXECUTIVE DIRECTOR

**inde'pendent fi'nancial ad'viser** *n.* [C] (*abbr* **IFA**) (*BrE*) a person who gives advice about different companies' insurance policies, investments, etc. and helps people to buy them

★ **index** /'ɪndeks/ *n.*, *v.*
• ***n.*** [C] **1** (*Econ.*; *Finan.*) (*pl.* **indices** /'ɪndɪsiːz/ *or* **indexes**, *esp. in AmE*) a system that shows the level of prices, wages, etc. so that they can be compared with those of a previous day or time: *the cost-of-living index* ◇ *In the US, all three major indices fell today.* **2** (*pl.* **indices** /'ɪndɪsiːz/) a sign or measure that sth else can be judged by: *The number of new houses being built is a good index of a country's prosperity.* **3** (*pl.* **indexes**) (*esp. BrE*) = CARD INDEX
• ***v.*** [T] (*Econ.*; *Finan.*) (*usu. pass.*) to link wages, payments, etc. to the level of prices of particular items, so that they both increase at the same rate: *Salaries are indexed to the rate of inflation.* ▸ **,index'ation** /-'eɪʃn/ *n.* [U]

**'index card** *n.* [C] a small card used for recording information, kept with others in a box

**-indexed** /'ɪndekst/ *comb. form* (*Finan.*) (about investments) having a value or payments that are linked to the thing mentioned: *inflation-indexed securities*

**,indexed 'bond** *n.* [C] (*Finan.*) a bond whose value or interest payments vary according to changes in a particular index, esp. one that measures the general level of prices

**'index fund** = TRACKER FUND

**,index-'linked** *adj.* (*esp. BrE*) (*Econ.*; *Finan.*) if a bond, pension, wage, etc. is **index-linked**, its value or payments vary according to the rate of INFLATION ▸ **,index-'linking** *n.* [U]

**'index ,option** *n.* [C] (*Finan.*) a type of investment which involves buying the right to receive or pay an amount of money in the future that is based on the change in value of a particular SHARE INDEX

**indicative** /ɪn'dɪkətɪv/ *adj.*
**1** (*Finan.*) an **indicative** offer, price, etc. shows the amount you expect to pay, charge, etc., but is not decided definitely **2** showing or suggesting sth: *These results are not indicative of future sales trends.*

★ **indicator** /'ɪndɪkeɪtə(r)/ *n.* [C] a sign or figure that shows you what sth is like or how a situation is changing: *January sales are closely watched as an early indicator of consumer confidence.*
⊙ ***a good/an important/a key/reliable ~*** • ***~s point towards/show/signal/suggest/tell us*** *sth*

**indices** pl. of INDEX

**indict** /ɪn'daɪt/ *v.* [T] (*esp. AmE*) (*Law*) (*usu. pass.*) to officially charge sb with a serious crime

**indictment** /ɪn'daɪtmənt/ *n.* [C,U] (*Law*) **1** (used in connection with serious crimes) a formal document that accuses sb of committing a crime **2** in the US, a decision by a

JURY to accuse sb of committing a crime

**indie** /ˈɪndi/ *n.* [C] (*infml.*) a small independent company, esp. one producing films/movies, books, music CDs, etc.

**ˌindirect ˈadvertising** *n.* [U] (*Market.*) advertising that a company uses to make people aware of a product often without them realizing it, for example putting a name on clothing, paying for a sports event or a concert, or giving the product to people free

**ˌindirect ˈcost** *n.* [C, usu. pl.] (*Account.*) costs that are not directly connected with making a particular product or providing a particular service, for example training, heating, rent, etc. OPP DIRECT COST

**ˌindirect ˈexport** *n.* [C, usu. pl., U] (*Econ.*; *Trade*) **1** goods or services that are sold to another country through another company, sometimes in a different country, rather than sold directly to customers; this method of selling goods **2** parts, materials, etc. that are sent from one producer to another before being made into goods that are exported; this method of exporting goods ▸ **ˌindirect exˈporting** *n.* [U]

**ˌindirect ˈlabour** *n.* [U] **1** (*Account.*; *HR*) the people in a business who are not directly involved in producing goods or providing services, for example senior managers, secretaries, etc.; the money that is spent on these people **2** (*HR*) people who work for a company or an organization but are employed by an independent business that provides their services under a contract → DIRECT LABOUR

**ˌindirect ˈloss** = CONSEQUENTIAL LOSS

**ˌindirect ˈmaterials** *n.* [pl.] (*Account.*) things such as electricity, gas, etc. that are used when making a product but that do not form part of the finished product

**ˌindirect ˈoverhead** *n.* [C] (*Account.*) a share of the **overheads** that are not connected to a particular project but form part of the general cost of running a business

**ˌindirect particiˈpation** *n.* [U] (*HR*) the system of workers taking part in making important decisions through a representative

**ˌindirect ˈsale** *n.* (*Market.*) **1** [C, usu. pl., U] (*also* **ˌindirect ˈselling** [U]) the practice of using another company's shops/stores, salespeople, etc. in order to sell your product rather than selling it yourself; goods that are sold in this way **2** [C] an item sold in this way

**ˌindirect ˈtax** *n.* [C,U] (*Econ.*) tax which is collected from businesses on the goods and services that people buy from them: *indirect taxes such as VAT and duty on fuel* ▸ **ˌindirect taxˈation** *n.* [U]

**individual** /ˌɪndɪˈvɪdʒuəl/ *adj.*, *n.*
• *adj.* **1** connected with one person; designed for one person: *individual income tax* ◇ *individual investors* **2** considered separately rather than as part of a group: *Our products are designed for individual markets.*
• *n.* [C] a person considered separately rather than as part of a group: *assessing the individual's strengths and weaknesses*

**indorse** = ENDORSE

**inducement** /ɪnˈdjuːsmənt; *AmE* ɪnˈduːs-/ *n.* [C,U] **~ (to sb) (to do sth)** something that is given to sb to persuade them to do sth: *She was offered a large block of shares as an inducement to take the job.* SYN INCENTIVE

**induction** /ɪnˈdʌkʃn/ *n.* [U,C] (*HR*) the process of introducing sb to a new job, skill, organization, etc: *an ~ course/programme*

★**industrial** /ɪnˈdʌstriəl/ *adj.*, *n.*
• *adj.* **1** connected with industry: *an expansion in industrial activity* ◇ *~ development/production/output* **2** used by industries: *~ chemicals/equipment* **3** connected with businesses rather than individuals: *industrial advertising* (= advertising to businesses) **4** having many industries: *an industrial area* **5** (*HR*) connected with the work that you do: *an ~ accident/disease* SYN JOB-RELATED, WORK-RELATED
• *n.* **industrials** [pl.] (*Stock Ex.*) manufacturers whose shares are bought and sold on the stock exchange: *the industrials sector*

**inˌdustrial ˈaction** (*BrE*) (*AmE* **ˈjob ˌaction**) *n.* [U,C] (*HR*) action that workers take, esp. stopping work, to protest to their employers about sth
◐ *to call (for)/organize/take/threaten ~ (over sth)* ♦ *to* ***avert/avoid/call off*** *~*

**inˈdustrial and ˌorganiˈzational psyˈchology** *n.* [U] (*abbr* **I/O psychology**) (*esp. AmE*) (*HR*) the study of how people behave at work and what influences their attitudes and behaviour, in order to make organizations better places to work in and more successful

▸ **in͵dustrial and organi͵zational psy'chologist** *n.* [C] (*abbr* **I/O psychologist**)

**in'dustrial base** = MANUFACTURING BASE (1)

**in͵dustrial con'trol** *n.* [C] (*Manufact.*) an electronic or a mechanical device that is used to control machinery

**in͵dustrial de'sign** *n.* [U] the job or skill of designing the shape and appearance of manufactured products such as furniture, electronic equipment, etc. ▸ **in͵dustrial de'signer** *n.* [C]

**in͵dustrial dis'pute** *n.* [C] (*BrE*) (*HR*) **1** a disagreement between workers and employers about pay or conditions **2** a strike SYN LABOUR DISPUTE, TRADE DISPUTE

**in͵dustrial eco'nomics** *n.* [U] the branch of economics that studies how businesses operate and compete with each other within industries

**in͵dustrial engi'neering** *n.* [U] the branch of engineering that studies and designs the most efficient ways that organizations can use people, processes, technology, materials, information, etc. to make or process a product ▸ **in͵dustrial engi'neer** *n.* [C]

**in͵dustrial es'tate** (*BrE*) (*AmE* **in͵dustrial 'park**) (*BrE also* **'trading es͵tate**) *n.* [C] an area esp. for factories, on the edge of a town

**in'dustrial goods** (*also* **in'dustrial ͵products**) *n.* [pl.] (*Econ.*) machines, tools, parts, etc. that are produced for use in industry rather than by the public

**in͵dustrial 'hygiene** (*also* **͵occupational 'hygiene**) *n.* [U] (*HR*) the study and practice of protecting and improving the safety and health of people at work

**industrialist** /ɪn'dʌstriəlɪst/ *n.* [C] a person who owns or runs a large factory or industrial company: *a leading/wealthy ~*

★ **industrialize, -ise** /ɪn'dʌstriəlaɪz/ *v.* [T,I] if a country or an area is **industrialized** or if it **industrializes**, industries are developed there: *the world's largest industrialized nations* ▸ **in͵dustriali'zation, -i'sation** /-laɪ'zeɪʃn; *AmE* -lə'z-/ *n.* [U]

**in͵dustrial 'marketing** *n.* [U] the activity of selling goods and services to other businesses or organizations rather than the public → B2B

**in͵dustrial 'park** = INDUSTRIAL ESTATE

**in͵dustrial pro'duction** *n.* [U] **1** (*Econ.*) the total amount that factories, mines, gas and electricity industries, etc. in a country produce during a particular period: *the industrial production index for October* **2** (*Manufact.*) the process of making sth in large amounts in a factory: *the industrial production of iron*

**in'dustrial ͵products** = INDUSTRIAL GOODS

**in͵dustrial re'lations** *n.* [pl.] (*abbr* **IR**) (*HR*) relations between employers and employees in an organization or an industry, particularly through trade/labor unions: *an industrial relations breakdown* SYN LABOUR RELATIONS

**in'dustrial-strength** *adj.* (*often used in a humorous way*) very strong or powerful: *an industrial-strength cleaner* ◇ *industrial-strength coffee*

**in͵dustrial tri'bunal** = EMPLOYMENT TRIBUNAL

**industrious** /ɪn'dʌstriəs/ *adj.* working hard; busy: *an industrious labour force* SYN HARD-WORKING ▸ **in'dustriously** *adv.*

★ **industry** /'ɪndəstri/ *n.* (*pl.* **-tries**) **1** [U] the production of goods from raw materials, esp. in factories: *They raised import duties to protect local industry.* ◇ *He left college and went into industry.* **2** [C] the people and activities involved in producing a particular thing, or in providing a particular service: *the banking/car/steel ~* ◇ *We're in a growth industry.* ◇ *Sales fell **across** the industry.*
◆ *a* ***global/growing/growth/key/mature*** *~* ◆ ***domestic/global/local/traditional*** *industries* ◆ ***communications/manufacturing/service*** *industries* ◆ *to* ***create/dominate/lead*** *an ~* ◆ *to* ***regulate/restructure*** *an ~* ◆ *an* ***analyst/expert/observer***

**'industry associ͵ation** *n.* [C] an organization for companies in the same industry, that provides advice, information and other services for its members SYN TRADE ASSOCIATION

**͵industry 'leader** *n.* [C] **1** a company which is the most successful in its area of business **2** a successful and important business person

**industrywide** /͵ɪndəstri'waɪd/ *adj.* through all of an area of business: *the industrywide drop in advertising* ▸ **͵industry'wide** *adv.*: *Revenue fell 1.5% industrywide in November.*

★ **ine'fficiency** /͵ɪnɪ'fɪʃənsi/ *n.* [C,U] (*pl.* **-cies**) failure to use time, money, resources or people in the best way; an example of this: *operating inefficiencies*

★ **inefficient** /ˌɪnɪˈfɪʃnt/ *adj.* not using time, money, resources or people in the best way: *The industry remains highly inefficient.* OPP EFFICIENT

**inelastic** /ˌɪnɪˈlæstɪk/ *adj.* (*Econ.*) used to describe the situation when a change in one thing, such as the price of a product or service, or a change in people's incomes, results in only a small change in another thing, such as the amount that people want to buy: *Some products such as petrol/gas are* ***price-inelastic****—even when prices go up demand doesn't fall.* OPP ELASTIC

**ineligible** /ɪnˈelɪdʒəbl/ *adj.* **~ (for sth)** not having the right to do sth or have sth, because you do not have the necessary qualifications, are not the right age, etc. OPP ELIGIBLE ▸ **inˌeligiˈbility** /-ˈbɪləti/ *n.* [U]

**inertia** /ɪˈnɜːʃə; *AmE* -ɜːrʃə/ *n.* [U] lack of action or change; lack of desire to act or to change things: *inertia in consumer prices*

**inexpensive** /ˌɪnɪkˈspensɪv/ *adj.* not costing a lot of money: *simple, inexpensive software* SYN CHEAP OPP EXPENSIVE

**inflate** /ɪnˈfleɪt/ *v.* **1** [T] to deliberately make a number, an amount, etc. appear higher or be higher, often in a dishonest way: *He knowingly inflated sales figures.* **2** [T,I] to increase in price; to increase the price of sth: *Oil prices were inflated by the threat of war.*

**inflated** /ɪnˈfleɪtɪd/ *adj.* (esp. about prices) very high; much higher than normal or reasonable: *to pay highly inflated prices for designer clothes*

★ **inflation** /ɪnˈfleɪʃn/ *n.* [U] a rise in the general prices of goods and services in a particular country over a period of time, resulting in a fall in the value of money; the rate at which this happens: *Inflation rose again this year.* ◇ *an annual inflation rate of 3%* ● *~ falls* ◆ *falling/rising ~* ◆ *a decline/rise in ~* ◆ ***high/low/stable/zero ~*** ◆ ***galloping/rapid/runaway ~*** ◆ *to* ***bring down/control/reduce ~***

**inˈflation acˌcounting** *n.* [U] (*Account.*) a method of keeping a company's financial records which considers the general increase in prices, and values assets according to how much it would cost to buy them today

**inˈflation-adˌjusted** *adj.* (*Econ.*) (about prices, income, etc.) that takes into account a general increase in prices and a general decrease in the value of money: *inflation-adjusted interest rates*

**inflationary** /ɪnˈfleɪʃənri; *AmE* -neri/ *adj.* causing or connected with a general increase in prices and a general decrease in the value of money: *inflationary pay awards*

**inˈflection point** *n.* [C] a time of very noticeable change in a business or an industry; a time when sth important happens: *The software industry is at an inflection point.*

★ **inflexible** /ɪnˈfleksəbl/ *adj.* **1** that cannot change or be changed to suit new conditions or situations: *an ~ attitude/system* **2** (about a material) difficult or impossible to bend OPP FLEXIBLE ▸ **inˌflexiˈbility** /-ˈbɪləti/ *n.* [U]

**inflow** /ˈɪnfləʊ; *AmE* -floʊ/ *n.* [U,C] the movement of money or assets into a business or a country; the amount of money or assets coming in: *inflows of foreign funds into the region* OPP OUTFLOW

**influencer** /ˈɪnfluənsə(r)/ *n.* [C] (*Market.*) a person or a group that can directly affect the opinions and behaviour of those who make decisions

**influx** /ˈɪnflʌks/ *n.* [C, usu. sing.] a sudden arrival of many things or people at the same time: *the influx of jobs brought in by new investment*

**info** /ˈɪnfəʊ; *AmE* ˈɪnfoʊ/ *n.* **1** (*infml.*) [U] information: *I shall send info to all dept heads asap.* **2 info-** (*in ns*) connected with information: *an infosheet*

**infobahn** /ˈɪnfəʊbɑːn; *AmE* ˈɪnfoʊ-/ = INFORMATION SUPERHIGHWAY

**infomediary** /ˌɪnfəˈmiːdiəri/ *n.* [C] (*pl.* **-ries**) (*E-comm.*) a website that collects and provides information for businesses and their customers

**infomercial** /ˌɪnfəʊˈmɜːʃl; *AmE* ˌɪnfoʊˈmɜːrʃl/ (*also* ˌ**inforˈmercial**) *n.* [C] (*Market.*) a long advertisement on television or the Internet that tries to give a lot of information about a subject, so that it does not appear to be an advertisement

★ **inform** /ɪnˈfɔːm; *AmE* ɪnˈfɔːrm/ *v.* [T] **1 ~ sb (of/about sth)** to tell sb about sth, esp. in an official way: *I am pleased to inform you* ***that*** *you have been selected for interview.* ◇ *It's vital to keep staff informed.* **2** to influence sth; to be the basis for sth: *This* *belief has always informed the board's decisions.*

**the in͵formal e'conomy** = SHADOW ECONOMY

**informant** /ɪn'fɔːmənt; *AmE* -'fɔːrm-/ *n.* [C] (*Market.*) a person who answers questions in a survey or gives information about their attitudes, opinions, etc: *informant interviews*

★**information** /͵ɪnfə'meɪʃn; *AmE* ͵ɪnfər'm-/ *n.* **1** [U] facts or details about sth or sb: *For further information, call ... ◇ a piece of information ◇ an information desk*

⊕ *to* ***collect/obtain/receive*** ~ ◆ *to* ***give/pass on/provide*** ~ ◆ ***company/ financial*** ~

**2** (*AmE*) [U with sing./pl. v.] = DIRECTORY ENQUIRIES

▸ **͵infor'mational** /-'meɪʃənl/ *adj.*

IDM **for information 'only** written on documents that are sent to sb who needs to know the **information** in them but does not need to deal with them → FYI

**͵information 'architecture** *n.* [U] (*IT*) the process of designing the way websites are organized and used, in order to help users find and manage information successfully

**͵infor'mation ex͵change** *n.* [C,U] the act of giving and receiving information, esp. electronically; a system, an opportunity or a place for doing this

**͵infor'mation ͵management** *n.* [U] (*abbr* **IM**) the collection, control and use of data in an organization; a system for organizing and using data

**͵information re'trieval** *n.* [U] (*IT*) the process of finding particular data that is stored in a computer

**infor'mation ͵science** *n.* [U] the study of processes for storing and obtaining data electronically

**͵information super'highway** (*also* **͵super'highway, 'infobahn**) *n.* [C, usu. sing.] (*IT*) a large electronic network such as the Internet, used for sending information such as sound, pictures and video quickly

**͵information tech'nology** = IT (1)

**informercial** /͵ɪnfɔː'mɜːʃl; *AmE* ͵ɪnfɔːr'mɜːr-/ = INFOMERCIAL

**infraction** /ɪn'frækʃn/ *n.* [C,U] an act of breaking a rule or law: *minor infractions of company regulations*

★**infrastructure** /'ɪnfrəstrʌktʃə(r)/ *n.* [C,U] **1** (*Econ.*) the basic systems and services that are necessary for a country to run smoothly, for example buildings, transport, and water and power supplies **2** the systems or equipment that an organization needs in order to be able to operate efficiently: *IT infrastructure* ▸ **͵infra'structural** /-tʃərəl/ *adj.*

**infringe** /ɪn'frɪndʒ/ *v.* [T,I] to break a law or rule: *infringing copyright* ▸ **in'fringement** /-mənt/ *n.* [U,C]: *copyright infringement*

**infusion** /ɪn'fjuːʒn/ *n.* [C,U] ~ **(of sth) (into sth)** the act of adding sth to sth else in order to make it stronger or more successful: *a cash infusion into the business*

**in͵herent 'vice** *n.* [C] (*Insur.*) a natural tendency that particular goods, such as foods, have to become damaged or be destroyed, esp. when they are being transported

**inherit** /ɪn'herɪt/ *v.* **1** [T,I] to receive money, property, etc. from sb when they die: *She inherited the company* ***from*** *her father.* **2** [T] if you **inherit** a particular situation from sb, you are now responsible for dealing with it, esp. because you have replaced that person in their job: *He's inherited a very talented team.* ▸ **in'heritor** *n.* [C]

**inheritance** /ɪn'herɪtəns/ *n.* [C, usu. sing., U] the money, property, etc. that you receive from sb when they die; the fact of receiving sth when sb dies SYN LEGACY

**in'heritance tax** *n.* [C,U] (*abbr* **IHT**) **1** (*BrE also* **'death ͵duty**, *old-fash.*) in the UK, tax that is paid on the total value of the money and property of sb who has died **2** (*AmE also* **'death tax**, *infml.*) tax that you must pay on the value of the money or property that you receive from sb when they die

**͵in-'home** *adj.* happening in sb's home: *in-home selling*

**͵in-'house** (*also* **͵in-'company**) *adj.* existing or happening within a company or an organization: *an in-house magazine ◇ in-company training* ▸ **͵in-'house** *adv.*: *The software was developed in-house.*

**initialize, -ise** /ɪ'nɪʃəlaɪz/ *v.* [T] (*IT*) **1** to make a computer program or system ready for use **2** to prepare a computer disk so that data can be recorded on it SYN FORMAT ▸ **i͵nitiali'zation, -i'sation** /-laɪ'zeɪʃn; *AmE* -lə'z-/ *n.* [U]

**i͵nitial 'price** *n.* [C] **1** (*Finan.*) the price that a new share, bond, etc. is sold for SYN ISSUE PRICE

**2** the first or original price that sth is sold for

**i'nitial 'public 'offering** (*also* **i'nitial 'public 'offer**) = IPO

**i͵nitial 'yield** *n.* [C] (*Finan.*) **1** the amount of profit that an investment makes within the first financial period, that compares the income to the original cost **2** the amount of interest that a bond offers when it is first issued

**initiative** /ɪ'nɪʃətɪv/ *n.* **1** [C] a new plan for dealing with a problem or for achieving sth: *cost-cutting initiatives* **2 the initiative** [sing.] the power or opportunity to act and gain an advantage before other people do: *to take/seize/lose the* ~ **3** [U] the ability to decide and act on your own without waiting for sb to tell you what to do

**injunction** /ɪn'dʒʌŋkʃn/ *n.* [C] (*Law*) an official order given by a court which demands that sth must or must not be done: *They are seeking an injunction to prevent the sale of the product in the UK.*

⊙ *to **apply for/obtain** an* ~ ♦ *to **grant/issue/refuse/uphold** an* ~ ♦ *to **lift/withdraw** an* ~ ♦ *a **permanent/temporary*** ~

**injury** /'ɪndʒəri/ *n.* (*pl.* **-ries**) **1** [C,U] harm done to a person's body, for example in an accident: *insuring staff against injuries at work* **2** [U] harm done to a company, an industry, a person's career or reputation, etc.

**ink** /ɪŋk/ *v.* [T] (*infml.*) to sign a document, esp. a contract: *The group has just inked a $10 m deal.*

**PHR V** **͵ink sth/sb 'in** to decide on a definite date for an appointment, a meeting, etc. → PENCIL SB/STH IN at PENCIL

**the ͵Inland 'Revenue** → HM REVENUE AND CUSTOMS

**͵in-'line** *adj.* (*Finan.*; *Stock Ex.*) used to describe sth that is making as much profit as expected or the same amount as other similar things: *Retail sales were in-line.*

★**innovate** /'ɪnəveɪt/ *v.* [T,I] to introduce new things, ideas or ways of doing sth: *innovating new products* ◇ *We must innovate to ensure success.* ▸ **͵inno'vation** /-'veɪʃn/ *n.* [U,C]: *product innovation* ◇ *innovations in technology* **'innovator** *n.* [C]

**innovative** /'ɪnəveɪtɪv; *BrE also* 'ɪnəvətɪv/ (*also* **innovatory**, *less freq.* /͵ɪnə'veɪtəri; *AmE also* 'ɪnəvətɔːri/) *adj.* introducing or using new ideas, ways of doing sth, etc: *an innovative approach to training* ▸ **'innovatively** *adv.*

**inoperative** /ɪn'ɒpərətɪv; *AmE* ɪn-'ɑːp-/ *adj.* **1** (about a rule, system, etc.) not valid or able to be used **2** (about a machine) not working

**inorganic** /͵ɪnɔː'gænɪk; *AmE* ͵ɪnɔːr'g-/ *adj.* used to describe the situation when a company increases in size by buying or joining with other companies: ~ *development/growth*

**͵in-'pack** *adj.* (*Market.*) inside the container that goods are sold in: *in-pack promotions*

**͵in-'person** *adj.* involving a direct meeting with another person rather than communicating by letter, telephone, etc: *an in-person interview*

★**input** /'ɪnpʊt/ *n.*, *v.*

• *n.* **1** (*Econ.*) [U,C, usu. pl.] any person or thing that is involved in producing goods or providing services: *Women provide 25% of the labour input in farming.* SYN FACTOR OF PRODUCTION **2** [U,C] advice, ideas, knowledge, etc. that you give to a project, meeting, etc. in order to make it succeed; the act of doing this: *I'd appreciate your input **on** this.* ◇ *customer input* **3** (*IT*) [U] the act of putting information into a computer; the information that you put in: *data input* **4** [C] a place or means for electricity, data, etc. to enter a machine or system: *Is there an audio input on the PC?* → OUTPUT

• *v.* (**inputting, input, input**) *or* (**inputting, inputted, inputted**) [T] (*IT*) to put information into a computer: *to* ~ *text/data/figures* → OUTPUT

**͵input/'output** *adj.* **1** (*IT*) (*abbr* **I/O**) relating to information passing into and out of a computer, computer system, etc. or the devices that control this: *the basic input/output system of your computer* **2** (*Econ.*) used to describe a method of analysing the economy of an area that considers the relationships between different parts of the economy and how changes in the amount that one part produces affects what happens in others ▸ **͵input/'output** *n.* [U] (*IT*)

**'input tax** *n.* [C,U] (*Account.*) the tax that a company pays on goods and services that it buys

**inquire** = ENQUIRE

**inquiry** = ENQUIRY

**inroad** /'ɪnrəʊd; *AmE* -roʊd/ *n.* [C] something that is achieved, esp. by reducing the power or success of sth else: *their first major inroad **into** the US market*

**IDM make inroads (into/on sth)** if one thing **makes inroads into** another, it has an important effect on the second thing, esp. by reducing it, or influencing it: *Tax rises have made some inroads into the national debt.*

**insert** *v., n.*
• *v.* [T] /ɪn'sɜːt; *AmE* ɪn'sɜːrt/ **1 ~ sth (in/into/between sth)** to put sth into sth else or between two things: *leaflets inserted in the magazine* **2** to add sth to a piece of writing: *to insert a word* OPP DELETE ▸ **insertion** /-'sɜːʃn; *AmE* -'sɜːrʃn/ *n.* [U,C]: *full-page insertions*
• *n.* /'ɪnsɜːt; *AmE* 'ɪnsɜːrt/ (*also* **'inset**, *less freq.*) [C] an extra section added to a book, newspaper or magazine, esp. to advertise sth

**ˌin-'service** *adj.* (*HR*) **1** (about training, courses of study, etc.) done while sb is working in a job, in order to learn new skills **2** used to describe sb who is working or sth that is being used for a particular purpose: *in-service teachers*

**ˌin-service with'drawal** *n.* [U,C] when an employee leaves a company pension plan while they are still employed by the company

**inset** /'ɪnset/ = INSERT *n.*

**inside** /ˌɪn'saɪd/ *adj.* known or done by sb in a group or an organization: *an inside knowledge of the industry*

**ˌinside infor'mation** (*also* **inˌsider infor'mation**) *n.* [U] (*Finan.*) secret information known by people who work for an organization but not known by the public NOTE It is usu. illegal to make use of this information when buying or selling shares, bonds, etc.

**insider** /ɪn'saɪdə(r)/ *n.* [C] **1** a person who knows a lot about a group or an organization, because they are part of it **2** (*Finan.*) the directors, senior officers, lawyers, accountants, etc. of a company and anyone who owns more than ten per cent of the company's voting shares: ***corporate ~s*** ◇ *insider trade* (= buying and selling of the company's shares)

**inˌsider 'dealing** = INSIDER TRADING

**inˌsider infor'mation** = INSIDE INFORMATION

**inˌsider 'trading** (*also* **inˌsider 'dealing**) *n.* [U] (*Stock Ex.*) **1** the crime of buying or selling shares, bonds, etc. in a company with the help of secret information about it that is not available to the public **2** the buying and selling of a company's shares, bonds, etc. by directors or senior managers of the company

**ˌinside 'track** *n.* [sing.] (*esp. AmE*) a position in which you have an advantage over sb else or know about sth before other people do: *to get on the inside track for future career opportunities*

**ˌinside 'worker** *n.* [C] (*HR*) an employee who works in a company's offices, factory, etc.

★ **insolvency** /ɪn'sɒlvənsi; *AmE* -'sɑːl-/ *n.* [U,C] (*pl.* **-cies**) (*Account.*; *Law*) the state of not having enough money to pay what you owe: *The company is close to insolvency.* ◇ *a wave of corporate insolvencies* OPP SOLVENCY
➲ *to file for/go into* ~ • *to avoid/be rescued from/stave off* ~ • *an* ~ *expert/lawyer*

**inˌsolvency prac'titioner** *n.* [C] (*BrE*) in the UK, a person or company that is legally qualified to manage the affairs of a company that is INSOLVENT

★ **insolvent** /ɪn'sɒlvənt; *AmE* -'sɑːl-/ *adj.* (*Account.*; *Law*) not having enough money to pay what you owe: *The company has been declared insolvent.* ◇ *insolvent banks* OPP SOLVENT
➲ *to become* ~ • *to be/declare yourself* ~

**insourcing** /'ɪnsɔːsɪŋ; *AmE* -sɔːrs-/ *n.* [U] (*HR*) the process of producing goods or providing services within a company rather than buying them from outside ▸ **'insource** *v.* [T,I]: *We insource our training.*

**inspect** /ɪn'spekt/ *v.* [T] **1** to look closely at sth/sb, esp. to check that everything is as it should be **2** to officially visit a factory, restaurant, etc. in order to check that laws are being obeyed and that standards are acceptable ▸ **inspection** /-'spekʃn/ *n.* [U,C]: *to carry out/make an* ~ ◇ *to fail/pass an* ~

**inspector** /ɪn'spektə(r)/ *n.* [C] **1** a person whose job is to visit factories, restaurants, etc. to check that laws are being obeyed and that standards are acceptable: *factory inspectors* **2** (*AmE*) = SURVEYOR (2)

**inspectorate** /ɪn'spektərət/ *n.* [C with sing./pl. v.] (*esp. BrE*) an official group of INSPECTORS who work together on the same subject or at the same kind of institution

**inˌspector of 'taxes** (*also* **'tax inˌspector**) *n.* [C] in the UK, a person who is responsible for collecting INCOME TAX SYN TAXMAN

**inst.** *abbr* **1** (*old-fash.*) **instant**, used in business letters to mean 'of this month': *your letter of 14 inst.* **2** institute; institution

★ **install** /ɪnˈstɔːl/ *v.* [T] **1** (*IT*) to put a new program into a computer: *The new software was installed* ***on*** *850 desktops.* **2** to fix equipment onto sth or into position so that it can be used: *to install motion detectors* **3** to put sb in a new position of authority: *He was installed* ***as*** *CEO last May.*

**installation** /ˌɪnstəˈleɪʃn/ *n.* **1** [U,C] the act of fixing equipment or furniture in position so that it can be used: *free installation* ◇ *installation costs* **2** (*IT*) [U] the act of putting a new program into a computer: *the installation of the software* **3** [C] a piece of equipment or machinery that has been fixed in position so that it can be used: *a heating installation* **4** [C] a place where specialist equipment is kept and used: *a chemical/an oil* ~ **5** [U] the act of placing sb in a new position of authority: *the installation of a new CEO*

**inˈstalled base** *n.* [C, usu. sing.] (*IT*; *Market.*) the total number of a particular product, esp. computers, that have been sold and are still used by customers

**inˌstalled caˈpacity** *n.* [U; C, usu. sing.] (*Tech.*) the full amount of energy that a particular power station, machine, etc. could supply

**installer** /ɪnˈstɔːlə(r)/ *n.* [C] **1** (*IT*) a piece of software that helps you to put another larger piece onto your computer **2** a person or company that fixes equipment or furniture in position so that it can be used: *an installer of security systems*

★ **instalment** (*AmE usu.* **installment**) /ɪnˈstɔːlmənt/ *n.* [C] (*Comm.*) one of a number of payments that are made regularly over a period of time until sth has been paid for or an agreed amount has been paid: *We paid for it* ***by/in*** *instalments.* ◇ *to keep up/pay/repay (the) ~s*

**inˈstalment plan** = HIRE PURCHASE

**inˈstalment sale** *n.* [U,C] (*Comm.*) an arrangement in which the seller of goods, assets, etc. receives the money in regular payments over a fixed period of time

**ˌinstant ˈaccess acˌcount** *n.* [C] (*BrE*) a bank account that allows you to take money out at any time you like without paying a fee

**ˌinstant ˈmessaging** *n.* [U] (*abbr* **IM**) (*IT*) a system on the Internet that allows people to exchange written messages with each other quickly ▸ **ˌinstant ˈmessage** *n.* [C]

**institute** /ˈɪnstɪtjuːt; *AmE* -tuːt/ *n.*, *v.*

• *n.* [C] an organization that has a particular purpose, esp. one connected with education or a particular profession; the building used by this organization

• *v.* [T] to introduce a system, policy, etc. or start a process: *to institute changes* ◇ *to institute criminal proceedings against sb*

★ **institution** /ˌɪnstɪˈtjuːʃn; *AmE* -ˈtuːʃn/ *n.* **1** [C] a large important organization that has a particular purpose, for example a bank: *a banking/an investment* ~ **2** [C] a custom or system that has existed for a long time among a particular group of people **3** [U] the act of starting or introducing sth such as a system or a law: *the institution of new safety procedures* ▸ **instiˈtutional** /-ʃənl/ *adj.*: *~ clients/investors* **ˌinstiˈtutionally** /-ʃənəli/ *adv.*

**instiˌtutional ˈadvertising** *n.* [U] (*Market.*) advertising that tells the public about a company or a product in general (for example coffee), rather than about particular products. It usu. tries to create an attractive image and is used by large well-known companies.
▸ **instiˌtutional adˈvertisement** *n.* [C]

**ˌinstiˈtutional fund** *n.* [C] (*Finan.*) an investment fund only open to large financial organizations

**ˌin-ˈstore** *adj.* **1** within a large shop/store: *~ promotions* **2** belonging to a particular shop/store: *special discounts for shoppers who use in-store credit cards* ▸ **ˌin-ˈstore** *adv.*

★ **instruct** /ɪnˈstrʌkt/ *v.* [T] **1** to tell sb to do sth, esp. in a formal or an official way: *They were instructed* ***to*** *do jobs they weren't trained to do.* **2** to teach sb sth, esp. a practical skill: *instructing new employees* ***in/on*** *the use of the equipment* **3** (*Law*) (*esp. BrE*) to employ a lawyer to represent you in a legal situation and give them information or orders

★ **instruction** /ɪnˈstrʌkʃn/ *n.*, *adj.*
• *n.* **1 instructions** [pl.] detailed information on how to do or use sth: *step-by-step instructions* (= that tell you exactly what to do at each stage) ⊕ *to* ***follow/read*** *(the) ~s* ◆ ***clear/detailed*** *~s* ◆ ***assembly/operating*** *~s*
**2** [C, usu. pl.] something that sb tells you to do: *Have you given the payment instructions to the bank?*

◆ *to get/issue/receive ~s* ◆ *to carry out/ignore sb's ~s* ◆ *clear/strict ~s*
**3** (*IT*) [C] a piece of information that tells a computer to perform a particular operation: *to carry out/execute ~s*
• **adj.** giving detailed information on how to do or use sth: *an ~ book/manual*

**instructional** /ɪnˈstrʌkʃənl/ *adj.* that teaches people sth: *instructional videos*

**instrument** /ˈɪnstrəmənt/ *n.* [C] **1** (*Finan.*) any investment such as shares, bonds, OPTIONS, FUTURES, etc. bought and sold in an organized system: *fixed-income/low-risk ~s* SYN FINANCIAL INSTRUMENT **2** a tool or device used for a particular task, esp. for delicate or scientific work: *optical/precision ~* **3** a device used for measuring speed, distance, temperature, etc. in a vehicle or on a piece of machinery: *flight instruments* **4** (*Law*) a formal legal document: *an instrument of transfer* (= that shows that property has been passed to sb else)

**insufficient** /ˌɪnsəˈfɪʃnt/ *adj.* not large, strong or important enough for a particular purpose: *insufficient funds* ▸ **ˌinsufˈficiency** /-ʃənsi/ *n.* [U; sing.] **ˌinsufˈficiently** *adv.*

★ **insurable** /ɪnˈʃɔːrəbl; -ˈʃʊər-; *AmE* -ˈʃʊr-/ *adj.* able to be **insured**: *What risks are insurable?* OPP UNINSURABLE

★ **insurance** /ɪnˈʃɔːrəns; -ˈʃʊər-; *AmE* -ˈʃʊr-/ *n.* **1** [U,C] an arrangement with a company in which you pay them regular amounts of money or make a single payment and they agree to pay the costs, for example if you die or are ill/sick, or if you lose or damage sth: *car/travel/home ~* ◇ *Make sure you take out adequate insurance.* ◇ *to claim for a loss* **on** *insurance*
◆ *to arrange/have/renew (an) ~* ◆ *to buy/sell ~* ◆ *to provide/refuse ~* ◆ *~ covers/pays for sth* ◆ *~ payments/premiums*
**2** [U] (often used in the names of companies) the business of providing people with insurance: *She works* **in** *insurance.* ◇ *Cox Insurance* **3** [U] money paid to an insurance company; money paid by an insurance company: *After the accident he received €15 000 in insurance.* **4** (*Stock Ex.*) [pl.; U] used to refer to shares in insurance companies: *Insurances did well.*

**inˈsurance adˌjuster** *n.* [C] (*AmE*) an independent person or company that decides whether insurance claims are valid and how much should be paid SYN CLAIMS ADJUSTER, LOSS ADJUSTER (*BrE*)

**inˈsurance ˌagent** *n.* [C] a person or company whose job is to give advice about and sell insurance on behalf of one or more companies: *life insurance agents*

**inˈsurance ˌbroker** *n.* [C] an independent person or company that gives people advice about insurance and arranges it for them

**inˈsurance ˌcarrier** = INSURANCE COMPANY

**inˈsurance cerˌtificate** = CERTIFICATE OF INSURANCE

**inˈsurance claim** = CLAIM *n.* (1)

**inˈsurance ˌcompany** (*AmE also* **inˈsurance ˌcarrier**) *n.* [C] an organization whose business is providing insurance SYN INSURER

**inˈsurance ˌcover** (*also* **inˈsurance ˌcoverage**) *n.* [U] protection that an insurance company provides by promising to pay money if a particular event happens SYN COVER

**inˈsurance ˌpolicy** (*also* **ˌcontract of inˈsurance**) *n.* [C] a written agreement between a person or company and an insurance company
◆ *to take out/apply for/have an ~* ◆ *an accident/a life/travel ~*

**inˈsurance ˌrating** = RATING (5)

**inˈsurance risk** *n.* [C] the possibility of loss or damage that sth is insured against SYN RISK

**inˈsurance ˌunderwriter** *n.* [C] **1** (*Insur.*) a person whose job is to estimate the risks involved in a particular activity or in insuring a particular client and decide how much sb must pay for insurance **2** a company or person that agrees to accept all the risks involved in an insurance contract: *Lloyd's, the insurance underwriters.* SYN UNDERWRITER

★ **insure** /ɪnˈʃɔː(r); -ˈʃʊə(r); *AmE* -ˈʃʊr/ *v.* **1** [T,I] **~ (sth/sb/yourself) (for/against sth)** to make an arrangement with a company in which you pay them regular amounts of money or make a single payment and they agree to pay you money, for example if you die or are ill/sick, or if you lose or damage sth: *The painting is insured for $10 m.* ◇ *Are you adequately insured?* **2** [T] to sell insurance to sb for sth: *The company insures high-risk drivers.*

**insured** /ɪnˈʃɔːd; -ˈʃʊəd; *AmE* -ˈʃʊrd/ *adj.* **1** having insurance: *Her life was insured* ***for*** *$250 000.* ◇ *Are you insured to drive this car?* **2 the insured** *n.* [C] (*pl.* **the insured**) the person who has made an agreement with an insurance company and who receives money if they are ill/sick, if they lose or damage sth, etc.

★ **insurer** /ɪnˈʃɔːrə(r); -ˈʃʊər-; *AmE* -ˈʃʊr-/ *n.* [C] a company that provides insurance
SYN INSURANCE COMPANY

**intangible** /ɪnˈtændʒəbl/ *adj.*, *n.*
• *adj.* **1** that exists but is not physical: ~ *benefits/rewards* **2** that does not exist physically, but represents a cost or a benefit to a company: ~ *capital/expenses/liabilities* OPP TANGIBLE *adj.*
• *n.* **1** [C] a thing that exists but is not physical **2** (*Account.*; *Finan.*) [C, usu. pl.] = INTANGIBLE ASSET OPP TANGIBLE *n.*

**inˌtangible ˈasset** (*also* **inˈtangible**) *n.* [C, usu. pl.] (*Account.*; *Finan.*) something that a company has and that benefits it but does not exist physically, for example a brand or the company's reputation
OPP TANGIBLE ASSET

★ **integrate** /ˈɪntɪɡreɪt/ *v.* [T,I] **~ (A) (into/with B) | ~ A and B** to combine two or more things so that they work together; to combine with sth else in this way: *These programs will integrate* ***with*** *your existing software.* ◇ *integrating two businesses*

**integrated** /ˈɪntɪɡreɪtɪd/ *adj.* **1** in which several different parts are closely connected and work well together: *an integrated print and online recruitment strategy* **2** (about a company or business) that does everything connected with producing and selling its products **3** included as part of a product, not supplied separately: *phones with integrated cameras*

**ˌintegrated ˈmarketing** *n.* [U] the process of organizing all the different areas of marketing, for example PROMOTION, PACKAGING, DISTRIBUTION and price, so that they all work well together

**ˌintegrated ˌmarketing communiˈcations** *n.* [U; pl.] (*abbr* **IMC**) a way of managing a company's marketing so that all forms of information about products or the company are carefully linked

**ˌintegrated proˈducer** *n.* [C] (*Manufact.*) a company producing goods that owns more than one stage in the process

★ **integration** /ˌɪntɪˈɡreɪʃn/ *n.* [U] **1** a process of combining two or more organizations or systems so that they work together well: *The aim is to promote closer economic integration.* **2** (*Econ.*) a situation in which a company gains control of its competitors, customers or suppliers, so that there are fewer companies in a particular area: *increasing integration in the car industry*

**integrator** /ˈɪntɪɡreɪtə(r)/ *n.* [C] **1** (*IT*) (*also* **ˈsystems ˌintegrator**, **ˈsystem ˌintegrator**) a person or company that puts together computers and programs to make a complete system for a particular business **2** a person who is skilled at making the different parts of a business or different businesses work well together

**ˌintelˌlectual ˈassets** *n.* [pl.] (*HR*) the knowledge and skills of a company's employees that can be used to make the business more successful

**ˌintelˌlectual ˈcapital** *n.* [U] (*HR*) anything that is not physical that can be used to make a business more successful, for example relationships with customers, brands, ideas for new products, the knowledge and skills of employees, etc.

**ˌinteˌllectual ˈproperty** *n.* [U] (*Law*) an idea, a design, a piece of writing, etc. that belongs to a person or an organization and cannot be sold or copied without the owner's permission: *the need to protect intellectual property rights*

**inter-** /ˈɪntə(r)/ *prefix* (*used in vs, ns, adjs and advs*) between; from one to another: *interaction* ◇ *inter-company loans*

★ **interactive** /ˌɪntərˈæktɪv/ *adj.* **interactive** technology allows information to be passed continuously and in both directions between the user and the piece of technology, so the user can control what happens: ~ *media/software* ▶ **ˌinterˈactively** *adv.* **ˌinteracˈtivity** /-ˈtɪvəti/ *n.* [U]

**ˌinteractive ˈmarketing** *n.* [U] the use of a website to sell products in a way that allows the customer and the seller to influence what happens

**ˌinteractive ˈwhiteboard** *n.* [C] a piece of equipment using a computer linked to a large screen like a **whiteboard** that you can write on or use to control the computer by touching it or pointing at it with a pen

**interbank** /ˈɪntəbæŋk; *AmE* -terb-/ *adj.* happening between banks: *the interbank lending trade*

★ **interest** /ˈɪntrəst; -trest/ *n.* **1** [U] the extra money that you have to pay when you borrow money: *to pay interest* ***on*** *a loan* ◇ *The money was repaid* ***with*** *interest.*
**⊙** *to* ***charge*** *~* ◆ *~* ***charges/payments*** ◆ ***annual/monthly*** *~*
**2** [U] the extra money that you receive when you invest money: *That cash could be earning interest.*
**⊙** *to* ***pay*** *~* ◆ *~* ***payments*** ◆ ***annual/monthly*** *~*
**3** (*Finan.*) [C, usu. pl.] a share in a business or company and a legal right to a share of its profits: *She has business interests in France.*
**⊙** ***commercial/economic*** *~s* ◆ ***energy/oil*** *~s*
**4** [C,U] a connection with sth which affects your attitude to it, esp. because you may benefit from it in some way: *We* ***have an interest in*** *keeping our employees happy.* **5** [C, usu. pl.] a group of people who are in the same business or who share the same aims which they want to protect: *powerful farming interests*
**6** (*Law*) [C] a legal right to land or property: *Who has an interest in the land?* → idioms at CONFLICT *n.*, DECLARE

ˈ**interest-ˌbearing** *adj.* (*Finan.*) used to describe loans, etc. on which interest is paid

ˈ**interest ˌcover** *n.* [U] (*Account.*) a company's profit in relation to the amount of interest it has to pay on loans: *Interest cover is comfortable.*

ˌ**interested ˈparty** *n.* [C] a person or an organization in a position to gain from a situation or be affected by it, esp. one with a financial interest in a company

ˈ**interest exˌpense** *n.* [U,C; usu. pl.] (*Account.*) the amount that a company has to pay in interest on money it has borrowed

ˌ**interest-ˈfree** *adj.* used to describe loans on which the borrower does not have to pay **interest**

★ ˈ**interest rate** (*also* ˌ**rate of ˈinterest**) *n.* [C] the cost of borrowing money, usu. expressed as a percentage of the amount borrowed: *The Bank has cut interest rates by half a percentage point.* ◇ *an interest-rate cut*
**⊙** ***high/low*** *~s* ◆ *to* ***raise/reduce/slash*** *~s* ◆ *~s* ***fall/rise***

ˈ**interest-rate risk** *n.* [U] (*Finan.*) the risk that the value of an investment or an asset will fall if rates of interest change, for example that the value of a bond will fall as rates of interest rise

ˈ**interest-rate swap** *n.* [C] (*Finan.*) an agreement between two organizations that have borrowed money at different rates of interest, for example one at a fixed rate and the other at a rate that changes. In order to reduce INTEREST-RATE RISK, they agree to exchange regular payments based on the rates of interest at which they have borrowed.

★ **interface** /ˈɪntəfeɪs; *AmE* -tərf-/ *n.*, *v.*
• *n.* [C] **1** the point where two systems, subjects, etc. meet and affect each other: *the interface* ***between*** *big business and small communities*
**2** (*IT*) the way a computer program presents information to a user or receives information from a user → GUI **3** (*IT*) a connection between one device or system and another: *the interface* ***between*** *the computer and the printer*
• *v.* **1** [I] to come into contact with a person, product, system, etc. and to affect them or be affected by them in some way: *how users interface* ***with*** *the product* **2** (*IT*) [T,I] **~ (sth) (with sth)** | **~ A and B** to connect sth using an **interface**; to be connected in this way: *The system interfaces with many financial software packages.*

★ **interim** /ˈɪntərɪm/ *adj.*
**1** (*Account.*) **interim** results, figures, etc. are calculated before the final figures are known **2** intended to last for only a short time, until sth/sb more permanent is found: *The union agreed to an interim 4% pay offer.* ◇ *be under interim management*

ˌ**interim ˈdividend** *n.* [C] (*Finan.*) a **dividend** paid half way through the FINANCIAL YEAR

ˌ**interim inˈjunction** (*BrE*) (*AmE* **preˌliminary inˈjunction**) *n.* [C] (*Law*) an official order from a court that a person or company must not do sth until a dispute has been resolved

ˌ**interim ˈpayment** *n.* [C] **1** a payment that is made before full payment, or while the size of the full payment is being decided **2** (*Finan.*) an INTERIM DIVIDEND

**interims** /ˈɪntərɪmz/ *n.* [pl.] (*Account.*) results or figures that are calculated before the final figures are known

**intermediary** /ˌɪntəˈmiːdiəri; *AmE* ˌɪntərˈmiːdieri/ *n.* [C] (*pl.* **-ries**) a person or an organization that helps others who are unable or unwilling to deal with each other directly to reach an agreement: *The company acts as an intermediary* ***between*** *buyers and growers.* SYN

MIDDLEMAN ▸ ˌinter'mediary *adj.*: *an intermediary role*

**inter'mediate goods** *n.* [pl.] (*Manufact.*) partly finished goods that are used in the manufacture of other goods

**ˌintermediate tech'nology** *n.* [C,U] **1** technology that is suitable for use in developing countries, because it is cheap and simple and can use local materials **2** a technology that comes between early and later versions, and is less successful than either

**intermediation** /ˌɪntəˌmiːdiˈeɪʃn; *AmE* -tər'm-/ *n.* [U] (*Finan.*) an arrangement where a bank, etc. helps two people or groups to borrow and lend money, bearing all or part of the risk

**intern** (*also* **interne**) /ˈɪntɜːn; *AmE* ˈɪntɜːrn/ *n.* [C] (*AmE*) a student, or a person who has recently finished studying, who is getting practical experience in a job ▸ **'internship** /-ʃɪp/ *n.* [C]

**internal** /ɪnˈtɜːnl; *AmE* ɪnˈtɜːrnl/ *adj.* **1** involving or concerning only the people who are part of a particular organization: *internal emails* ◇ *internal recruitment* **2** used to describe the situation when a company develops its existing business rather than growing by buying other companies, etc: *internal growth* **3** connected with a country's own affairs: *~ trade/markets* SYN DOMESTIC OPP EXTERNAL
▸ **in'ternally** /-nəli/ *adv.*

**inˌternal 'audit** *n.* [C,U] (*Account.*) an examination that an organization does of its own activities, esp. to see if its own controls and systems are working properly
▸ **inˌternal 'auditor** *n.* [C]

**inˌternal con'sistency** = INTERNAL EQUITY

**inˌternal con'sultancy** *n.* [C,U] (*HR*) a situation where one department with special skills in an organization sells its services to other departments
▸ **intˌernal con'sultant** *n.* [C]

**inˌternal 'customer** *n.* [C] (*HR*) the idea that an employee working on one stage of a process is a customer of employees working on the stage before. This encourages employees to produce work of a good quality at each stage.

**inˌternal 'equity** (*also* **inˌternal con'sistency**) *n.* [U] (*HR*) a situation in which the pay that employees in an organization receive is related to the type of job they do in the organization

**inˌternal 'labour ˌmarket** *n.* [C] (*abbr* **ILM**) (*HR*) in an **internal labour market**, employers find people for senior positions from employees within the organization

**inˌternal 'market** *n.* [C, usu. sing.] (*Econ.*) **1** = SINGLE MARKET **2** a situation in which different departments in the same organization buy goods and services from each other

**in'ternal 'rate of re'turn** *n.* [C,U] (*abbr* **IRR**) (*Account.*) a way of comparing the value of different investments based on the income they will produce and the amount spent on them. A rate of interest is calculated for which the value of the income from each investment equals the amount spent on it.

**Inˌternal 'Revenue Code** *n.* [sing.] (*abbr* **IRC**) the tax laws of the US

**Inˌternal 'Revenue ˌService** *n.* [sing.] (*abbr* **IRS**) the branch of government in the US that is responsible for collecting most taxes, including INCOME TAX

**inˌternal 'search** *n.* [C,U] (*Market.*) the process by which consumers use information from their own experiences and memory when they make a decision about buying a product or service

★ **international** /ˌɪntəˈnæʃnəl; *AmE* -tər'n-/ *adj.* connected with or involving two or more countries: *~ trade/flights* ▸ **ˌinter'nationally** /-nəli/ *adv.*

**Interˌnational Ac'counting ˌStandards** *n.* [pl.] (*abbr* **IAS**) a set of rules for accounting, produced by the International Accounting Standards Board

**Interˌnational Ac'counting ˌStandards Board** *n.* [sing.] (*abbr* **IASB**) an independent organization that decides on rules for accounting that can be used all over the world

**Inter'national 'Chamber of 'Commerce** *n.* [sing.] (*abbr* **ICC**) an international association of business people based in Paris that aims to encourage, support and protect world business and trade

**Inter'national 'Civil Avi'ation Organiˌzation** *n.* [sing.] (*abbr* **ICAO**) an international organization that advises airlines and sets safety standards for air travel

**Inter'national Fi'nancial Re'porting ˌStandards** *n.* [pl.] (*abbr* **IFRS**) a set of rules for accounting, produced by the International Accounting Standards Board

**the ˌInternational 'Labour Organiˌzation** *n.* [sing.] (*abbr* **ILO**) an organization formed by the United Nations to improve working conditions in all parts of the world

**interˌnational 'labour ˌstandards** *n.* [pl.] a set of instructions for employment conditions produced by the International Labour Organization

**ˌinternational 'law** *n.* [U] the system of laws that are recognized by most states as controlling their relations with each other and their treatment of each other's citizens

**ˌinternational 'management** *n.* **1** [U; C with sing./pl. v.] the process of running a business that operates in several different countries; the people who do this **2** [U] the process of developing an organization's activities across national borders

**interˌnational 'monetary ˌsystem** *n.* [sing.] the system which controls the sale and exchange of different currencies

**ˌInternational 'Motor Inˌsurance Cerˌtificate** = GREEN CARD (2)

**ˌInternational Re'ply ˌCoupon** *n.* [C] (*abbr* **IRC**) a printed form that can be bought from a post office and sent with a letter to another country and is then exchanged for the cost of sending a reply by air from that country

**ˌinternational re'serves** = FOREIGN EXCHANGE RESERVES

**ˌInternational Se'curities Exˌchange** *n.* [sing.] (*abbr* **ISE**) in the US, a system that allows people to use a computer to trade OPTIONS

**interne** = INTERN

**Internesia** /ˌɪntə'niːziə; *AmE* ˌɪntər'n-/ *n.* [U] (*infml.*) an inability to remember on which website you saw a particular piece of information or to find it again

★ **Internet** /'ɪntənet; *AmE* -tərn-/ (*usually* **the Internet**) (*also* **the Net**, *infml.*) *n.* [sing.] (*IT*) an international computer network that connects other networks and computers all over the world

**ˌInternet 'cafe** *n.* [C] a place with computers where you can use the Internet and buy drinks and food

**'Internet ˌcommerce** (*also* **'Net ˌcommerce**, *less freq.*) = E-COMMERCE

**interoperable** /ˌɪntər'ɒpərəbl; *AmE* -'ɑːp-/ *adj.* (*IT*) (about computer systems or programs) able to exchange information or be used together ▸ **ˌinterˌopera'bility** /-'bɪləti/ *n.* [U]

**interpersonal** /ˌɪntə'pɜːsənl; *AmE* -tər'pɜːrs-/ *adj.* connected with relationships between people: *people with good interpersonal skills*

**interruption** /ˌɪntə'rʌpʃn/ *n.* [C,U] **1** the act of stopping sb from speaking or working **2** an event that temporarily stops an activity or a process; a time when an activity is stopped: *an ~ to/in the power supply*

**interstate** /'ɪntəsteɪt; *AmE* -tərs-/ *adj.* between states, esp. in the US: *interstate commerce*

**interventionism** /ˌɪntə'venʃənɪzəm; *AmE* -tər'v-/ *n.* [U] (*Econ.*) the policy or practice of a government influencing the economy of its own country ▸ **ˌinter'ventionist** *adj.*, *n.* [C]

**ˌinter'vention price** *n.* [C] (*Econ.*) the minimum price for a product, esp. an agricultural product, set by a government or an organization such as the EU. If the market price falls below this, the government, etc. pays the difference to the producer, or buys the product at the agreed price.

★ **interview** /'ɪntəvjuː; *AmE* -tərv-/ *n.* [C] **1** a formal meeting at which sb is asked questions to see if they are suitable for a particular job: *a job interview* ◇ *He has an interview for the manager's post.*
● *to* ***carry out/conduct/do/hold*** *an ~* • *to* ***attend/be called for/be invited for*** *an ~* • *an ~* ***board/panel***
**2** a way of finding out sb's opinion about products or services by asking them questions in a private meeting
● *a* ***face-to-face/telephone*** *~* • *to* ***carry out/conduct*** *an ~*
▸ **'interview** *v.* [T,I]: *We interviewed ten people* ***for*** *the job.* ◇ *He doesn't interview well* (= answer questions well). **'interviewing** *n.* [U]: *interviewing skills*

**interviewee** /ˌɪntəvjuː'iː; *AmE* -tərv-/ *n.* [C] the person who answers the questions in an interview

**interviewer** /'ɪntəvjuːə(r); *AmE* -tərv-/ *n.* [C] the person who asks the questions in an interview

**ˌin-the-ˈtrenches** *adj.* in-the-trenches employees and managers are directly involved in the most active part of the business

**intra-** /ˈɪntrə/ *prefix* (*used in adjs and advs*) inside; within: *intra-departmental*

**intraday** /ˈɪntrədeɪ/ *adj.* (*AmE*) (*Finan.*) happening within one day: *Shares dropped to an intraday low.*

★**intranet** /ˈɪntrənet/ *n.* [C, usu. sing.] (*IT*) a computer network that is private to a company or an organization but is connected to and uses the same software as the Internet: *You need a password to access the company intranet.*

**intrapreneur** /ˌɪntrəprəˈnɜː(r)/ *n.* [C] an employee in a large company who develops new products or services, starts SUBSIDIARY businesses, etc. for the company rather than leaving to form their own company ▸ **ˌintrapreˈneurial** /-ˈnɜːriəl/ *adj.* **ˌintrapreˈneurship** /-ʃɪp/ *n.* [U]

**ˈin tray** (*also* **ˈinbox**) *n.* [C] a container on your desk for letters and other documents that are waiting to be read or answered

**inˌtrinsic ˈvalue** *n.* [C,U] (*Finan.*) the real value that a company, an asset, etc. has, rather than the current value as shown by share prices or its market value

★**introduce** /ˌɪntrəˈdjuːs; *AmE* ˈduːs/ *v.* [T] **1** to make a new product or service available for the first time SYN BRING STH IN **2** to start to use a new system or a new method of doing sth: *We've introduced a computerized system for orders.* SYN BRING STH IN ▸ **ˌintroˈduction** /-ˈdʌkʃn/ *n.* [C,U]: *new product introductions* ◇ *the introduction of new methods* ◇ *Shall I do the introductions?*

**introductory** /ˌɪntrəˈdʌktəri/ *adj.* **1** offered for a short time only, when a product or service is first on sale or when a new customer buys it: *an ~ discount/offer/price* **2** intended as an introduction to sth: *~ paragraphs/remarks* ◇ *an ~ book/course*

**invalid** /ɪnˈvælɪd/ *adj.* **1** not legally or officially acceptable: *an invalid contract* **2** (*IT*) of a type that a computer cannot recognize: *The URL is invalid.* **3** not based on all the facts and therefore not correct: *an invalid argument* OPP VALID ▸ **invalidity** /ˌɪnvəˈlɪdəti/ *n.* [U]

**invalidate** /ɪnˈvælɪdeɪt/ *v.* [T] to make a document, contract, etc. no longer legally or officially valid SYN NULLIFY OPP VALIDATE ▸ **inˌvaliˈdation** /-ˈdeɪʃn/ *n.* [U]

**invaluable** /ɪnˈvæljuəbl/ *adj.* **~ (to/for sb/sth)** | **~ (in sth)** extremely useful: *This information is invaluable.* SYN VALUABLE

**invent** /ɪnˈvent/ *v.* [T] to design or produce a product or method that has not existed before ▸ **invention** /-ˈvenʃn/ *n.* [C,U]: *the invention of air conditioning* **inˈventor** *n.* [C]

★**inventory** /ˈɪnvəntri; *AmE* -tɔːri/ *n.*, *v.*

• *n.* **1** (*Comm.*; *Product.*) [C,U] (*esp. AmE*) the goods that a business has for sale at a particular time: *Crude oil inventories are running low.* SYN STOCK

⊙ *to* ***buy (in)/order/replenish*** *~* ◆ *to* ***carry/have/hold*** *~* ◆ *to* ***control/reduce/run down/sell off*** *~*

**2** (*Account.*; *Product.*) [U,C] (*esp. AmE*) all the goods owned by a business, including raw materials, parts, work not yet finished and finished products: *The company has no factories and no inventory.* SYN STOCK, STOCK-IN-TRADE

⊙ *to* ***build (up)/maintain/order/replenish/store*** *~* ◆ *to* ***control/reduce/run down/sell (off)*** *~*

**3** [C] a complete list of something, esp. of all the goods and property owned by sb/sth: *They made/took an ~ of all the goods in the store.*

• *v.* [T] (**-ries**, **-rying**, **-ried**, **-ried**) to make a complete list of sth: *The equipment was rarely inventoried.*

**ˈinventory conˌtrol** (*also* **ˈinventory ˌmanagement**) *n.* [U] (*esp. AmE*) (*Comm.*; *Product.*) the process of making sure that a suitable quantity of goods, materials or parts are stored and available at any time while keeping the costs of doing this as low as possible; the department in a company responsible for this SYN STOCK CONTROL ▸ **ˈinventory conˌtroller** (*also* **ˈinventory ˌmanager**) *n.* [C]

**ˈinventory count** *n.* [C] (*Account.*) an act of checking how many items a shop/store or business has available for sale SYN STOCK COUNT

**ˌinventory on ˈhand** *n.* [U] (*esp. AmE*) (*Account.*; *Comm.*) the materials, parts, finished products, etc. that a company holds ready to be used SYN STOCK IN HAND

**ˈinventory risk** *n.* [U] (*Comm.*; *Product.*) the risk that the goods and materials that a business has will fall in value, costing the business money

**ˌinventory-to-ˈsales ˌratio** *n.* [C] (*Econ.*) a measure of the demand for goods or of how well supplies are being managed, calculated by dividing the value of the supply of goods that a business or an industry has by the sales in a particular period

**ˌinventory ˈturnover** (*also* **ˌinventory ˈturn**) *n.* [C,U] (*also* **ˌinventory ˈturnover ˌratio** [C]) (*Account.*) the relationship between the value of goods that a business sells in a particular period and the average value of the goods it has available to sell: *They achieve 14 inventory turns a year.* SYN STOCK TURNOVER

**inverse** /ˌɪnˈvɜːs; *AmE* ˌɪnˈvɜːrs/ *adj.* opposite in amount or position to another thing: *There is an inverse **relationship** between shares and the dollar* (= the value of one goes up as the value of the other goes down). ▸ **inˈversely** *adv.* IDM **in inverse proˈportion to** if one thing is **in inverse proportion to** another, the more of one thing there is, the less there is of the other

**inˌverted ˈmarket** = BACKWARDATION

★**invest** /ɪnˈvest/ *v.* **1** [T,I] to buy property, shares, etc. in order to sell them again and make a profit: *We have invested €100 000 **in** the business.* ◇ *More individuals are investing.* **2** [T,I] (about a company, government, etc.) to spend money on sth in order to make it better or more successful: *investing **heavily** in public transport* **3** [T] to save money in a bank account, an insurance policy, etc. in order to receive interest ▸ **inˈvestable** (*also* **investible**, *less freq.*) /-təbl/ *adj.*

**inˌvested ˈcapital** *n.* [U] (*Account.*) the amount of money invested in a business by its owners or shareholders

★**investment** /ɪnˈvestmənt/ *n.* **1** [U] the action or process of using money in order to make a profit or earn interest, for example by buying shares, bonds, property, etc: *We need to attract foreign investment.* ◇ *an attractive investment opportunity* ◇ *domestic/private/public* ~ **2** [C] the amount of money that a person or business invests: *There is a minimum investment of $10 000.*

⊙ *an **initial**/a **maximum/one-off** ~* ◆ *to **make** an ~*

**3** [C] the thing that a person or business invests in: *The value of an investment can go down as well as up.*

⊙ *a **good/low-risk/safe** ~* ◆ *a **bad/high-risk/risky** ~* ◆ ***long-term/medium-term/short-term** ~s* ◆ *to **buy/have/hold/sell** ~s*

**4** [C,U] the act or process of buying materials, machines, etc. to make goods to sell: *The area must attract new industrial investment.*

⊙ ***business/corporate** ~* ◆ ***heavy** ~ (in sth)* ◆ ***infrastructure/technology** ~* ◆ *to **boost/stimulate** ~ (in sth)*

**inˌvestment alˈlowance** = CAPITAL ALLOWANCE

**inˈvestment bank** *n.* [C] (*esp. AmE*) (*Finan.*) a bank that provides finance for companies by buying their shares and selling them to the public. It also advises on TAKEOVERS and MERGERS and on ways of raising money ▸ **inˈvestment ˌbanker** *n.* [C] **inˈvestment ˌbanking** *n.* [U]

**inˈvestment bouˌtique** (*also* **bouˈtique**) *n.* [C] (*Finan.*) a small business that offers advice and help about a particular industry or area to people or organizations that want to invest money

**inˈvestment ˌcompany** (*also* **inˈvestment trust, inˈvestment trust ˌcompany**) *n.* [C] (*Finan.*) a company that invests its money in other companies' shares, bonds, etc. to make profits

**inˈvestment goods** = CAPITAL GOODS

**inˈvestment grade** *adj.* (*Finan.*) used to describe companies, bonds, etc. that are fairly safe to invest in because they have a low risk

**inˈvestment ˌmanagement** *n.* [U] (*Finan.*) the act of managing an amount of money which is used to buy and sell shares, bonds, etc. on behalf of investors in order to make as much profit as possible SYN FUND MANAGEMENT, MONEY MANAGEMENT ▸ **inˈvestment ˌmanager** *n.* [C]

**inˈvestment mix** (*also* **ˈasset mix**) *n.* [C, usu. sing., U] (*Finan.*) a combination of different investments that are put together to get the highest amount of profit

**inˈvestment trust** = INVESTMENT COMPANY

**inˈvestment trust ˌcompany** = INVESTMENT COMPANY

★**investor** /ɪnˈvestə(r)/ *n.* [C] a person or an organization that invests money in order to make a profit or receive interest

⊙ ***institutional/large/major** ~s* ◆ ***individual/private** ~s* ◆ ***foreign/international/overseas** ~s*

**inˈvestor group** *n.* [C] (*Finan.*) a group of investors acting together, esp. to take over a company

**in,vestor pro'tection** *n.* [U] systems and rules designed to make sure that financial institutions treat investors fairly and do not cheat them

**in,vestor re'lations** *n.* [U] (*abbr* **IR**) the process by which a company communicates with investors and possible investors, providing them with accurate information about the company and how successful it is likely to be in the future

**invisibles** /ɪnˈvɪzəblz/ *n.* [pl.] (*also* **in,visible 'trade** [U]) (*Econ.*) services such as banking, education, TOURISM, etc. that countries sell to and buy from each other

★**invite** /ɪnˈvaɪt/ *v.* [T] **1** (*fml.*) **~ sth | ~ sb to do sth | ~ sb (to/for sth)** to offer sb the opportunity to do sth: *Applications are invited from suitably qualified persons.*
⊕ ~ ***bids/offers/tenders*** ◆ ~ ***comments/questions***
**2** (*fml.*) **~ sb (to/for sth) | ~ sb to do sth** to ask sb formally to go somewhere: *to be invited for interview*

★**invoice** /ˈɪnvɔɪs/ *n.*, *v.* (*Account.*)
• ***n.*** [C] a list of goods that have been sold, work that has been done, etc. showing what you must pay
⊕ *to* ***generate/issue/raise/send/submit*** *an* ~ ◆ *to* ***pay/settle*** *an* ~
• ***v.*** [T] **~ sb (for sth) | ~ sth (to sb/sth)** to write or send a bill for work done or goods provided: *You will be invoiced at the end of the month.*
▸ **'invoicing** *n.* [U]

**'invoice ,discounting** (*also* **'discounting**) *n.* [U] (*Finan.*) a financial arrangement in which a bank or other business buys the right to receive payments owed to a company. The bank pays the debts immediately, receiving a percentage of the money owed for doing this, and then gets the money when the company has collected it. ▸ **'invoice ,discounter** *n.* [C]

**invoke** /ɪnˈvəʊk; *AmE* ɪnˈvoʊk/ *v.* [T] **1** to mention or use a law, rule, etc. as a reason for doing sth **2** (*IT*) to begin to run a program: *This command will invoke the HELP system.*

**involuntary** /ɪnˈvɒləntri; *AmE* ɪnˈvɑːlənteri/ *adj.* happening without the person concerned wanting it to: *involuntary unemployment*
OPP VOLUNTARY

**in,voluntary 'bankruptcy** *n.* [U,C] (*Law*) a situation in which a person's CREDITORS ask a court to officially declare that person BANKRUPT

**in,voluntary liqui'dation** *n.* [U,C] (*Law*) a situation where a company is forced to stop doing business so that it can pay its debts SYN COMPULSORY LIQUIDATION OPP VOLUNTARY LIQUIDATION

**,inward in'vestment** *n.* [U,C] (*Finan.*) investment in one country or area by another: *Inward investment into the UK plunged last year.*
▸ **,inward in'vestor** *n.* [C]
→ OUTWARD INVESTMENT

**I/O** = INPUT/OUTPUT (1)

**,I/'O psy,chology** = INDUSTRIAL AND ORGANIZATIONAL PSYCHOLOGY

**IOU** /ˌaɪ əʊ ˈjuː; *AmE* oʊ/ *n.* [C] (*infml.*) a written promise that you will pay sb the money that you owe them: *I wrote him an IOU for $200.*

**IPO** /ˌaɪ piː ˈəʊ; *AmE* ˈoʊ/ *abbr* (*Stock Ex.*) **initial public offering/offer** the act of selling shares in a company on a stock exchange for the first time: *The company had its IPO in September 2004.* ◇ *IPO shares*
SYN FLOTATION, PUBLIC ISSUE
⊕ *to* ***announce/launch/seek*** *an* ~ ◆ *to* ***complete/subscribe (to)*** *an* ~ ◆ *to* ***handle/manage*** *an* ~ ◆ *a* ***big/lucrative/successful*** ~ ◆ *a* ***partial*** ~

**IR** /ˌaɪ ˈɑː(r)/ = INDUSTRIAL RELATIONS, INLAND REVENUE, INVESTOR RELATIONS

**IRC** /ˌaɪ ɑː ˈsiː; *AmE* ɑːr/ = INTERNAL REVENUE CODE, INTERNATIONAL REPLY COUPON

**iron** /ˈaɪən; *AmE* ˈaɪərn/ *n.* [U] a hard metal that is used to make steel: *an iron and steel works*

**IRR** /ˌaɪ ɑːr ˈɑː(r) / = INTERNAL RATE OF RETURN

**irrecoverable** /ˌɪrɪˈkʌvərəbl/ *adj.* **irrecoverable** debts, losses, etc. will never be paid back
OPP RECOVERABLE

**irredeemable** /ˌɪrɪˈdiːməbl/ *adj.* (*Finan.*) used to describe bonds or other loans that pay interest but have no date when they must be paid back
▸ **,irre'deemables** *n.* [pl.]

**irregular** /ɪˈregjələ(r)/ *adj.* **1** not according to the usual rules or laws: *irregular trading* **2** not happening regularly: *irregular work*
OPP REGULAR ▸ **i,rregu'larity** /-ˈlærəti/ *n.* [C, usu. pl., U] (*pl.* **-ties**): *accounting irregularities*

**IRS** /ˌaɪ ɑːr ˈes/ = INTERNAL REVENUE SERVICE

**ISBN** /ˌaɪ es biː ˈen/ *abbr* **International Standard Book Number** a number that identifies an individual book, that you can use when ordering the book

**ISDN** /ˌaɪ es diː ˈen/ *abbr* (*IT*) **integrated services digital network** a system that uses telephone connections to send sound, images and data between computers at high speed

**ISE** /ˌaɪ es ˈiː/ = INTERNATIONAL SECURITIES EXCHANGE

**ˌIshiˈkawa ˌdiagram** /ˌɪʃɪˈkɑːwə/ = FISHBONE DIAGRAM

**ISIC** /ˌaɪ es aɪ ˈsiː/ *abbr* **International Standard Industrial Classification of all economic activities** an international list in which industries and services are given a code of letters and numbers to show which type of economic activity they are involved in, for reference and research purposes

**ˈisland disˌplay** *n.* [C] (*Market.*) a type of structure for displaying goods with shelves on all four sides

**ˈisland poˌsition** *n.* [C] (*Market.*) a place for an advertisement with no other advertisements near it

**ISO** /ˌaɪ es ˈəʊ; ˈaɪsəʊ; *AmE* ˈoʊ; ˈaɪsoʊ/ *abbr* **1 International Organization for Standardization** the organization that sets international quality and safety standards for industry and business **2** (*E-comm.*) **Independent Service Organization** a company that offers to deal with credit-card payments made on the Internet

**ˌISO ˈ14000** /ˌfɔːtiːn ˈθaʊznd; *AmE* ˌfɔːrtiːn -/ *n.* [sing.] (*Product.*) a set of standards to ensure that businesses do not use processes that harm the environment: *All facilities must reach the ISO 14001 standard.*

**ˌISO ˈ9000** /naɪn ˈθaʊznd/ *n.* [sing.] (*Product.*) a set of standards connected with the processes organizations use to ensure the quality of their products and services

**ISP** /ˌaɪ es ˈpiː/ *abbr* (*IT*) **Internet service provider** a company that provides you with an Internet connection and services such as email, etc.

**issuance** /ˈɪʃuəns; *BrE also* ˈɪsju-/ *n.* [C, usu. sing., U] **1** (*Finan.*) the act of issuing shares, bonds, etc.; the shares, bonds, etc. that are issued **2** the act of making sth available: *the issuance of audit reports* SYN ISSUE

★**issue** /ˈɪʃuː; *BrE also* ˈɪsjuː/ *n.*, *v.*
• *n.* [C] **1** (*Finan.*) the act of offering shares, bonds, etc. for sale: *a new share issue* SYN ISSUANCE **2** (*Finan.*) the number of shares that a company offers for sale at one time: *new corporate bond issues* **3** the act of producing coins and paper money and making them available to the public; the coins and paper money produced: *a new issue of banknotes*
• *v.* [T] **1** (*Finan.*) to offer shares, bonds, etc. for sale: *The group issued $105 m of bonds.* **2** to produce coins and paper money and make them available to the public: *to issue banknotes* **3** **~ sb with sth | ~ sth (to sb)** to give or supply sth to sb; to make sth available: *You will be issued with a temporary identity card.* **4** to announce sth formally or officially: *The group has issued a profits warning.*

**ˌissued ˈcapital** (*also* **subˌscribed ˈcapital**, *less freq.*) (*BrE also* **ˌissued ˈshare ˌcapital**) *n.* [U] (*Finan.*) the amount of money that a company has raised from the sale of its shares

**ˈissue price** (*also* **ˈissued price**, *less freq.*) *n.* [C] (*Finan.*) the price that a new share, bond, etc. is sold for SYN INITIAL PRICE

**issuer** /ˈɪʃuːə(r); *BrE also* ˈɪsjuːə(r)/ *n.* [C] **1** a person or an organization that supplies sth to sb: *credit card issuers* **2** (*Finan.*) a company or government that offers shares, bonds, etc. for sale

**ˈissues ˌmanagement** *n.* [U] the process of considering how a business's plans might cause problems for members of the public, the government, etc. in the future, and then making plans to deal with this if it happens

**ˈissuing bank** *n.* [C] (*Finan.*) **1** a bank or other financial institution that supplies sb with a credit card and is responsible for their account **2** a bank that supplies sth such as a cheque or a LETTER OF CREDIT

**ˈissuing house** *n.* [C] (*BrE*) (*Finan.*) a financial institution, esp. a MERCHANT BANK, that sells a company's shares to the public

★**IT** /ˌaɪ ˈtiː/ *n.* [U] **1 information technology** the study or use of electronic systems and equipment, esp. computers, for storing, sending and receiving information: *Mary works in IT.* ◇ *good IT skills* **2** a company that deals in computers, software, computer services, the Internet, etc: *IT stocks* **3** the department in a company or an organization that runs the computer systems

**item** /ˈaɪtəm/ *n.* [C] **1** a single article or object, esp. one that you buy: *The store reduced the prices of 1 000 items.* **2** (*Account.*) a single piece of information in a set of accounts: *Fuel formed one of the biggest items in the* *accounts.* **3** a single thing on a list, esp. on a list of things to be discussed at a meeting: *the next item on the agenda*

**itemize, -ise** /ˈaɪtəmaɪz/ *v.* **1** [T] to produce a detailed list of things: *itemized bills/receipts* **2** [T,I] (*esp. AmE*) to list separately on a tax form all the amounts that you can take away from your income before tax is calculated

**itinerant** /aɪˈtɪnərənt/ *adj.* travelling from place to place, esp. to find work: *itinerant workers*

# Jj

**janitor** /ˈdʒænɪtə(r)/ = CARETAKER

**jargon** /ˈdʒɑːɡən; *AmE* ˈdʒɑːrɡən/ *n.* [U] words or expressions used by a particular profession or group of people and difficult for others to understand: *computer/legal ~*

**Jasdaq** /ˈdʒæzdæk/ *n.* [sing.] a type of stock market in Japan that deals with the shares of young successful companies

**J-curve** /ˈdʒeɪ kɜːv; *AmE* - kɜːrv/ *n.* [C] (*Tech.*) any curve in the shape of the letter 'J', which shows sth first decrease slightly then rapidly increase to a much higher level

**JE** /ˌdʒeɪ ˈiː/ = JOB EVALUATION

**jettison** /ˈdʒetɪsn/ *v.* [T] **1** to get rid of sth/sb that you no longer need or want: *They had to jettison 217 staff.* **2** to reject an idea, a belief, plan, etc. that you no longer think is useful or likely to be successful

**Jiffy™** /ˈdʒɪfi/ *n.* [C] (*pl.* **Jiffies**) a thick soft envelope for sending things that might break or tear easily: *a Jiffy bag/mailer*

**jingle** /ˈdʒɪŋɡl/ *n.* [C] (*Market.*) a short song or tune that is easy to remember and is used in an advertisement on radio, television, etc.

**JIT** /ˌdʒeɪ aɪ ˈtiː/ = JUST-IN-TIME

**jitters** /ˈdʒɪtəz; *AmE* -tərz/ *n.* [pl.] (used in newspapers) feelings of being anxious about whether sth bad is about to happen: *investor jitters* ▶ **ˈjittery** *adj.*: *a jittery market*

★**job** /dʒɒb; *AmE* dʒɑːb/ *n.*, *v.*
• *n.* [C] **1** work for which you receive regular payment: *She applied for a job* **as** *director of marketing.* ◇ *The plan involves 10 000 job losses.*
⊕ *to* **look for** *a* ~ ♦ *to* **find/get/have/keep/take** *a* ~ ♦ *to* **leave/lose/quit** *a* ~ ♦ *to* **offer** *sb/***fill** *a* ~ ♦ *a* **full-time/part-time/steady** ~ ♦ *to* **create/cut/shed** ~*s* ♦ ~ **cuts** ♦ ~ **offers/openings/opportunities**
**2** a particular task or piece of work: *Fighting inflation is the bank's main job.* ◇ *They have done a couple of design jobs for us.* **3** a responsibility or duty: *It's not my job to lock up!* **4** (*IT*) an item of work which is processed by a computer as a single unit SYN TASK IDM **do a good, great, bad, etc. ˈjob (on sth); make a good, bad, etc. job of sth** to do sth well, badly, etc: *They did a very professional job.* **don't give up the ˈday job** used to tell sb in a humorous way that you do not think they are very good at sth they are doing that is not their real job **jobs for the ˈboys** (*BrE*) (*infml.*) used to criticize the fact that sb in power has given work to friends or relatives **more than your ˈjob's worth (to do sth)** (*BrE*) (*spoken*) not worth doing because it is against the rules or because it might cause you to lose your job **on the ˈjob** while doing a particular job: *on-the-job training* → idiom at WALK *v.*
• *v.* (-**bb**-) [I] to do work for different people that is not regular or permanent: *He jobbed* **as** *a truck driver.*
PHR V **job sth ˈout** (*esp. AmE*) to arrange for work to be done by another company: *Some of the work was jobbed out to other printers.* SYN CONTRACT STH OUT

**ˈjob ˌaction** = INDUSTRIAL ACTION

**ˈjob aˌnalysis** *n.* [C,U] (*HR*) a detailed study of a job and its relation to other jobs in the organization, esp. in order to see what skills it needs

**ˈjob bank** *n.* [C] (*AmE*) (*HR*) **1** a collection of job advertisements or details of people looking for work: *an online job bank* **2** an arrangement by which workers who lose their jobs continue to receive wages and sometimes training while waiting for a new job; the fund of money from which they are paid

**jobber** /ˈdʒɒbə(r); *AmE* ˈdʒɑːb-/ *n.* [C] **1** (*Stock Ex.*) in the UK in the past, a person who earned money on the stock exchange by buying shares, bonds, etc. from BROKERS and selling them to other BROKERS
**2** (*Comm.*) (*AmE*) a business that buys large amounts of particular goods and sells them to other businesses SYN WHOLESALER

**jobbing** /ˈdʒɒbɪŋ; *AmE* ˈdʒɑːb-/ *adj.* **1** (*BrE*) used to describe sb who does work for different people that is not regular or permanent: *a jobbing builder* **2** (*Comm.*; *Stock Ex.*) used to describe a company that buys and sells goods, shares, etc. as an agent

**jobcentre** /ˈdʒɒbsentə(r); *AmE* ˈdʒɑːb-/ *n.* [C] (*BrE*) a government office where jobs are advertised and people can get advice on finding work

**ˈjob ˌcosting** *n.* [U] (*Account.*) the practice of calculating a separate cost for each piece of work, project or order that is done by a business

**ˈjob creˌation** *n.* [U] (*Econ.*) the process of providing opportunities for paid work, esp. for people who are unemployed

**ˈjob desˌcription** *n.* [C] (*HR*) a written description of the exact work and responsibilities of a job, its position in the organization, the conditions of employment and the pay

**ˈjob deˌsign** *n.* [U,C] (*HR*) the process of putting together the tasks that need to be done in an organization to form jobs that individual people will do: *poor job design*

**ˈjob enˌrichment** *n.* [U] (*HR*) a way of increasing the variety of tasks that an employee does by giving them more difficult tasks to do or more responsibility

**ˈjob evaluˌation** *n.* [U,C] (*abbr* **JE**) (*HR*) a method of studying jobs and their relation to each other in an organization in order to give them a position on a scale and decide on the rate of pay for each level; an occasion when this is done

**ˈjob fair** (*BrE also* **caˈreers fair, reˈcruitment fair**) *n.* [C] (*HR*) an event where people looking for a job can meet companies looking for new employees

**ˈjob ˌfamily** *n.* [C] (*HR*) a group of jobs in a company that have similar activities and need similar skills but have different levels on a scale

**job for ˈlife** *n.* [C] (*pl.* **jobs -**) the idea that once you had a job with a company, you could keep it until you retired

**ˈjob ˌgrading** *n.* [U] (*HR*) a system of arranging similar jobs in an organization in order according to the type of tasks, amount of responsibility, etc. that they have; the rank that a particular job has: *a job grading structure based on skills and abilities*

**jobholder** (*also* **job holder**) /ˈdʒɒbhəʊldə(r); *AmE* ˈdʒɑːbhoʊldər/ *n.* [C] (*HR*) a person who has a particular job or a regular job

**ˈjob ˌhopping** *n.* [U] (*HR*) the practice of changing jobs very often ▸ **ˈjob ˌhopper** *n.* [C]

**ˈjob-ˌhunter** *n.* [C] a person who is trying to find a job ▸ **ˈjob-hunt** *v.* [I]: *I've been job-hunting for over a year.* **ˈjob-hunt** *n.* [C]: *to go on a job-hunt* **ˈjob-ˌhunting** *n.* [U]

**jobless** /ˈdʒɒbləs; *AmE* ˈdʒɑːb-/ *adj.* (*HR*) **1** unemployed; without a job: *The closure left 500 people jobless.* **2 the jobless** *n.* [pl.] people who are unemployed ▸ **ˈjoblessness** *n.* [U]

**ˈjob lock** *n.* [U,C] (*HR, infml.*) in the US, the situation where employees cannot leave their jobs because they are afraid they will lose their health benefits

**job ˈlot** *n.* [C] (*BrE*) (*Comm.*) a collection of different things that are sold together, usu. at a low price: *a job lot of car parts*

**ˈjob ˌmarket** = LABOUR MARKET

**ˈjob ˌorder** *n.* [C] **1** (*Product.*) an order for a particular piece of work, quantity of items, etc. for a particular customer **2** (*HR*) information that an employer provides to an EMPLOYMENT AGENCY when they are looking for sb for a particular job

**ˈjob proˌduction** *n.* [U] (*Product.*) a way of producing things in which products are made one at a time for individual customers

**job-protected ˈleave** *n.* [U] (*HR*) a longer period of time when you are officially allowed to be away from your work for a special reason and will not lose your job

**ˈjob proˌtection** = EMPLOYMENT PROTECTION

**ˈjob-reˌlated** *adj.* (*esp. AmE*) connected with the work that you do: *~ skills/activities/illness*

**ˈjob roˌtation** *n.* [U,C] (*HR*) the practice of regularly changing the job sb does so that they have a variety of tasks and become experienced in different areas

**ˈjob satisˌfaction** *n.* [U] the feeling of achievement and enjoyment that a worker gets from their job ○ ***high/low/poor ~*** ◆ ***to give/improve/obtain/provide ~***

**ˈjob seˌcurity** *n.* [U] a situation where a job is likely to last for a long time and you will keep the job if you do what you are expected to SYN EMPLOYMENT SECURITY ○ ***a high/low level of ~*** ◆ ***to have/provide ~***

**ˈjob ˌseeker** (*also* **jobseeker**) *n.* [C] often used in official language in the UK to describe a person without a job who is trying to find one: *claiming the job seeker's allowance* ▸ **ˈjob-ˌseeking** *n.* [U]

**'job-ˌsharing** (*also* **'work-ˌsharing**, *less freq.*) *n.* [U] (*HR*) an arrangement where two or more people do one job, dividing the hours between them ▶ **'job-share** *v.* [I] **'job-share** *n.* [C] **'job-sharer** *n.* [C]

**'job shop** *n.* [C] (*Manufact.*) a small factory that makes small quantities of goods, often designed for a particular customer

**'job specifiˌcation** *n.* [C] (*HR*) a written statement about a job that includes a JOB DESCRIPTION and the skills, experience and personal qualities that sb needs in order to do the job, used when an organization is looking for a new person for a job

**'job staˌbility** *n.* [U] (*HR*) **1** how long workers or groups of workers keep the same job **2** how long sb has kept the jobs they have had

★**join** /dʒɔɪn/ *v., n.*
• ***v.* 1** [T,I] to become a member of an organization, a company, etc: *She joined the company as a trainee three years ago.* **2** [T] to take part in sth that sb else is doing or to go somewhere with them: *to join a strike* **3** [T,I] **~ A to B | ~ A and B (together/ up)** to fix or connect two or more things together **4** [T,I] if you **join** a train, plane, etc. you get on it
→ idioms at ENTER, FORCE *n.*
**PHR V** **join 'up (with sb)**; **'join with sb/sth** to combine with sb else to do sth
• ***n.*** [C] a place where two things are fixed together: *You can hardly see the join.*

**ˌjoined-'up** *adj.* (often used in newspapers) intelligent and involving good communication between different parts so that they can work together effectively: *We need more joined-up **thinking** in our approach to the environment.*

**joint** /dʒɔɪnt/ *adj.* involving two or more people, organizations, etc. together: *The two firms will take joint control of the fund.* ▶ **'jointly** *adv.*: *a jointly owned company*

**ˌjoint ac'count** *n.* [C] a bank account that is used by two or more people such as a husband and wife

**ˌjoint consul'tation** *n.* [C,U] (*HR*) in the UK, a formal arrangement for managers and union representatives in an organization to meet to discuss matters that affect both sides before decisions are made

**ˌjoint-stock 'company** *n.* [C] a business organization that is owned by a group of people (shareholders) who provide its funds, appoint its managers and share its profits and debts

**ˌjoint 'venture** *n.* [C] a new business that is started by two or more companies, often in the form of an independent company whose shares they own; the product or service that the business sells or provides: *The two firms plan to launch a 50-50 joint venture* (= one which they each own half of).

**journal** /'dʒɜːnl; *AmE* 'dʒɜːrnl/ *n.* [C] **1** a newspaper or magazine that deals with a particular subject or profession: *a business/professional ~* **2** used in the title of some newspapers: *the Wall Street Journal* **3** (*Account.*) a written record that is used to move amounts from one financial account to another

**judge** /dʒʌdʒ/ *n., v.*
• ***n.*** [C] **1** a person who has authority to decide legal cases: *a High Court judge* **2** a person who decides who has won a competition
• ***v.* 1** [T,I] to form an opinion about sb/sth, based on the information you have: *Each project is judged **on** the profits it could generate.* **2** [T] to decide the result of a competition; to be the **judge** in a competition **3** [T] to decide whether sb/sth has committed a crime or is legally responsible for sth

**judgement** (*also* **judgment**, *esp. in AmE*) /'dʒʌdʒmənt/ *n.* **HELP** **Judgement** is the usual spelling in BrE, but **judgment** is used in legal situations and is the normal spelling in AmE. **1** [U] the ability to make sensible decisions after carefully considering the best thing to do: *good/poor/sound ~* **2** [C,U] an opinion that you form about sth after thinking about it carefully; the act of making this opinion known to others: *I would like to **reserve judgement** until I have seen the report.* **3** [C,U] a decision of a court or judge; the reasons for the decision

**ˌjudgement by/in de'fault** (*pl.* **judgements -**) = DEFAULT JUDGEMENT

**judiciary** /dʒu'dɪʃəri; *AmE* -ʃieri/ *n.* [C with sing./pl. v.] (*pl.* **-ries**) (*usu.* **the judiciary**) (*Law*) the judges of a country or a state, when they are considered as a group

**juggernaut** /'dʒʌgənɔːt; *AmE* -gərn-/ *n.* [C] **1** a very large lorry/ truck **2** a large and powerful force or institution that cannot be controlled: *a multimedia juggernaut*

**juggle** /'dʒʌgl/ *v.* [T,I] **1** to try to deal with two or more important jobs or activities at the same time:

*juggling work and home life* **2** to organize information, figures, the money you spend, etc. in the most useful or effective way

**jumbo** /ˈdʒʌmbəʊ; *AmE* -boʊ/ *n., adj.*
• ***n.*** [C] (*pl.* **jumbos**) (*also* ˌ**jumbo** ˈ**jet**) a very large plane
• ***adj.*** (*infml.*) very large; larger than usual: *a jumbo pack of cornflakes*

**jump** /dʒʌmp/ *v., n.*
• ***v.*** [I] (*usu. used with an adv. or a prep.*) (about a price, level, etc.) to rise suddenly by a large amount: *The yen jumped* **to** *its highest level against the dollar.* IDM **jump ˈship** to change the organization that you are loyal to, esp. the company you work for → idioms at DEEP *adj.*, SHIP *n.*
PHR V ˌ**jump ˈin**; ˌ**jump ˈinto sth** to become involved in sth: *They are keen to jump into the US market.*
• ***n.*** [C] a sudden increase in a price, cost, level, etc: *a 17% jump* **in** *insurance costs* IDM **get/have a ˈjump on sb** (*AmE*) (*infml.*) to get or have an advantage over sb, because you have acted quickly

ˈ**jump-start** *v.* [T] to put a lot of energy into starting a process or an activity or into making it start more quickly: *The Fed has cut interest rates to jump-start the economy.* ► ˈ**jump-start** *n.* [C]

**jumpy** /ˈdʒʌmpi/ *adj.* (**-pier**, **-piest**) (*infml.*) nervous and anxious: *Financial markets are extremely jumpy* (= prices may go up and down quickly).

★**junior** /ˈdʒuːniə(r)/ *adj., n.*
• ***adj.*** **1** having a lower rank in an organization or profession than others: *~ lawyers/bankers* ◇ *He is junior* **to** *me.* OPP SENIOR
○ *a ~* ***executive/manager*** ♦ *a ~* ***associate/partner*** ♦ *a ~* ***position/post***
**2** (*Finan.*) used to describe a debt that will only be paid after all other debts have been paid if the borrower has financial problems SYN SUBORDINATED
○ *~* ***bonds/debentures/debt*** ♦ *~* ***creditors/lenders***
• ***n.*** [C] a person with a lower level of job or status than others OPP SENIOR

**junk** /dʒʌŋk/ *n.* [U] **1** (*Finan.*) used to show that a company or government has a low CREDIT RATING or that there is a lot of risk involved in buying their bonds: *The company's long-term debt is now rated as junk.* **2** used to describe sth that is of little value: *There's so much junk in my office!*

ˈ**junk bond** *n.* [C] (*Finan.*) a type of bond that pays a high rate of interest because there is a lot of risk involved, often used if a company wants to raise money quickly in order to buy the shares of another company

ˈ**junk mail** *n.* [U] advertising material that is sent either by post or by email to people who have not asked for it

**jurisdiction** /ˌdʒʊərɪsˈdɪkʃn; *AmE* ˌdʒʊr-/ *n.* (*Law*) **1** [U,C] the authority that an official organization has to make legal decisions about sb/sth: *The commission has no jurisdiction over foreign companies.*
○ *to* ***exercise*** *~* ***over*** *sth* ♦ *to be/come/fall* ***outside/under/within*** *the ~ of sb/sth*
**2** [C] an area or a country in which a particular system of laws has authority: *The tax rules are different in each jurisdiction.*

**jurist** /ˈdʒʊərɪst; *AmE* ˈdʒʊr-/ *n.* [C] (*fml.*) a person who is an expert in law

**juˌristic ˈperson** = LEGAL PERSON

**juror** /ˈdʒʊərə(r); *AmE* ˈdʒʊr-/ *n.* [C] a member of a JURY

**jury** /ˈdʒʊəri; *AmE* ˈdʒʊri/ (*pl.* **-ries**) (*also* ˈ**panel**, ˈ**jury** ˌ**panel**, *both esp. AmE*) *n.* [C with sing./pl. v.] a group of members of the public who listen to the facts of a case in a court and decide who the winner is or whether sb is guilty of a crime: *The jury has/have returned a verdict of guilty.*
IDM **the jury is (still) ˈout on sth** used when you are saying that sth is still not certain: *The jury is out on whether the ad campaign will work.*

ˌ**just-in-ˈtime** *adj.* (*abbr* **JIT**) (*Product.*) used to describe a system, esp. one for manufacturing goods, where things are done, supplied, made, etc. only when they are needed: *Our suppliers deliver on a just-in-time basis.* ◇ *JIT delivery of products to customers* ► ˌ**just-in-ˈtime** *n.* [U] (*abbr* **JIT**): *The industry has adopted just-in-time.*

# Kk

**K** /keɪ/ *abbr* **1** (*infml.*) (*used esp. about an amount of money*) a thousand: *He earns nearly 100 K* (= 100 thousand pounds/dollars per year). **2** (*IT*) kilobyte(s) **3** (*IT*) kilobit(s): *a 56K modem*

**kaizen** /ˌkaɪˈzen/ *n.* [U] the practice of continuously improving the way a company operates

**kai'zen e,vent** *n.* [C] a series of activities, usu. over a number of days, in which a team of managers and workers decide how to improve a particular process within a company and then do so

**KAM** /,keɪ eɪ 'em/ = KEY ACCOUNT MANAGEMENT

**kanban** /'kænbæn/ *n.* (*Product.*) **1** (*also* **'kanban ,system**) [U,C] a system of manufacturing in which the production of parts and their movement around the factory is controlled using instructions, usu. written on cards, that are sent to the relevant group of workers whenever the parts are needed **2** [C] in this type of system, a card with information about the type and number of parts needed

**Kb** (*also* **KB**) *abbr* (*IT, written*) kilobyte(s): *a 512 Kb memory*

**Kbps** *abbr* (*IT*) a short way of writing **kilobits per second** (= a unit for measuring the speed at which data is sent or received, for example along a telephone line): *a 56 Kbps modem*

**KD** /,keɪ 'di:/ = KNOCK-DOWN (2)

**keen** /ki:n/ *adj.* (**-er**, **-est**) **1** (*esp. BrE*) if prices are **keen**, they are kept low to compete with other prices **2** involving people, businesses, etc. competing very hard with each other: *keen competition from rivals* ▸ **'keenly** *adv.*: *keenly priced items*

**keep** /ki:p/ *v.* (**kept**, **kept** /kept/) **1** [T,I] to stay in a particular condition, or at a particular level; to make sb/sth do this: *Competition is keeping down prices.* **2** [T] to continue to have sth: *The CEO is keeping his job.* **3** [T] to have a supply of sth: *We keep a large supply of popular items.* **4** [T] to write down sth as a record: *We* ***keep a record of*** *all phone conversations.* ◇ *to* ***keep the books*** (= the accounts) **5** [T] to do what you should do or what you have agreed to do: *She didn't keep the appointment.* **6** [I] (about food) to remain in good condition: *Milk won't keep more than a few days.* **7** [T] (*BrE*) to own and manage a shop/store or restaurant: *Her father kept a grocer's shop.* → SHOPKEEPER **NOTE** Idioms containing **keep** are at the entries for the nouns or adjectives in the idioms. **PHR V** **,keep sb 'on** to continue to employ sb: *If the company is sold, some of the staff will be kept on.* **,keep 'up (with sb/sth)** to move, make progress or increase at the same rate as sb/sth: *keeping up with demand* **,keep 'up with sth** to continue to pay or do sth regularly: *to keep up with payments*

**keiretsu** /keɪ'retsu:/ *n.* [C] (*pl.* **keiretsu**) in Japan, a group of companies that own large numbers of shares in each other, with the result that it is difficult for companies outside the group to gain control of any of them

**'kerb ,market** (*also* **kerb**) (*both BrE*) (*AmE* **curb** -) /kɜ:b; *AmE* kɜ:rb/ *n.* [C] (*Finan.*) trading of shares that takes place outside the official system of stock markets

★**key** /ki:/ *adj.*, *n.*, *v.*

• *adj.* most important; essential: *Japan is a key market for us.*

• *n.* **1** [C, usu. sing.] a thing that makes you able to achieve or understand sth: *The key* ***to*** *success is cutting costs.* **2** [C] any of the buttons that you press to operate a computer

• *v.* [T] **~ sth (in)** | **~ sth (into sth)** to put information into a computer using a keyboard **SYN** ENTER **PHR V** **'key sth to sth** (*usu. pass.*) to link sth closely to sth else: *Pricing is keyed to value.*

**,key ac'count** *n.* [C] one of the most important customers that a company has

**,key ac'count ,management** *n.* [U] (*abbr* **KAM**) the work of maintaining and developing a company's relationship with its most important customers ▸ **,key ac'count ,manager** *n.* [C]

**keyboard** /'ki:bɔ:d; *AmE* -bɔ:rd/ *n.*, *v.*

• *n.* [C] the set of keys for operating a computer, etc.

• *v.* [T] to type information into a computer ▸ **'keyboarder** *n.* [C] **'keyboarding** *n.* [U]

**keynote** /'ki:nəʊt; *AmE* -noʊt/ *n.* [C] a **keynote** speech, speaker, etc. is an important one that introduces a meeting or its subject ▸ **'keynoter** *n.* [C]

**keypad** /'ki:pæd/ *n.* [C] a small set of buttons with numbers, etc. on used to operate a telephone, television, etc.; the buttons on the right of a computer keyboard

**,key per'formance ,indicator** *n.* [C, usu. pl.] (*abbr* **KPI**) **1** a measure that shows if a company has reached the necessary standard in one of the factors that are essential for its success: *Our key performance indicators are price, quality and delivery.* **2** (*HR*) a measure that shows if a person, team or department has achieved a particular standard and is often connected with rates of pay

**ˌkey ˈprospect** *n.* [C] (*Market.*) a person, company, etc. that could become a customer

**ˈkey rate** *n.* [C] (*Finan.*) the rate of interest at which a central bank lends money to other banks, etc.

**keyword** /ˈkiːwɜːd; *AmE* -wɜːrd/ *n.* [C] (*IT*) a word or phrase that you type on a computer keyboard to give an instruction or to search for information about sth: *Type in the keyword 'hotels' and click on Search.*

**ˌkeyword ˈadvertising** *n.* [U] (*Market.*) a system of advertising on the Internet in which a business pays for an advertisement and a link to a website to be displayed when a user searches for particular words
▶ **ˌkeyword ˈad** (*also* **ˌkeyword adˈvertisement**) *n.* [C]

**kick** /kɪk/ *v.* **IDM kick the ˈtyres** (*AmE* - **tires**) (*esp. AmE*) (*infml.*) to test the quality of sth; to see if sth is suitable for you: *We now spend longer kicking the tyres before investing in start-ups.* → TYREKICKER
**PHR V ˌkick sth aˈbout/aˈround** (*infml.*) to discuss an idea, a plan, etc. in an informal way **ˌkick ˈback (sth)** (*AmE*) (*often pass.*) to pay money illegally to sb who has helped you do sth or gain an advantage

**kickback** /ˈkɪkbæk/ *n.* [C] *often* [pl.] money paid illegally to sb who has helped you do sth or gain an advantage: *to accept kickbacks*

**ˈkick-off** *n.* [sing.] the start of an activity: *a kick-off meeting*

**ˈkick-start** *v.* [T] to do sth to help a process or project start more quickly: *kick-starting the economy* ▶ **ˈkick-start** *n.* [C, usu. sing.]

**kidult** /ˈkɪdʌlt/ *n.*, *adj.* (*infml.*)
• ***n.*** [C] an adult who enjoys films/movies, books, games, television programmes, etc. that are intended for children and young people
• ***adj.*** intended for adults and children: *kidult movies*

**kill** /kɪl/ *v.* [T] to spoil or destroy sth; to stop or end sth: *Too many features can kill a product.* **PHR V ˌkill sth ˈoff** to stop or get rid of sth: *to kill off brands*

**ˈkiller app** (*also* - **ap**, *less freq.*) (*also* **ˈkiller appliˌcation**) *n.* [C]
**1** (*IT*, *infml.*) a computer program that is so popular that it encourages people to buy or use the computer system, etc. that it runs on: *Email is the killer app of the Internet.*
**2** (*Market.*) a special feature of a product that is presented as being essential or much better than competitors' products

**killing** /ˈkɪlɪŋ/ *n.* **IDM ˌmake a ˈkilling** (*infml.*) to make a lot of money quickly

**kilo-** /ˈkɪləʊ; *AmE* ˈkɪloʊ/ *comb. form* (*used in ns; often used in units of measurement*) one thousand: *kilogram* ◇ *kilometre*

**kilobit** /ˈkɪləbɪt/ *n.* [C] (*abbr* **K**) (*IT*) a unit for measuring computer memory or information, equal to 1 024 BITS

**kilobyte** /ˈkɪləbaɪt/ *n.* [C] (*abbr* **Kb**, **K**) (*IT*) a unit for measuring computer memory or information, equal to 1 024 BYTES

**kind** /kaɪnd/ *n.* **IDM in ˈkind** (about a payment) consisting of goods or services, not money

**king** /kɪŋ/ *n.* [C] a person, an organization or a thing that is thought to be the best or most successful of a particular type: *Nokia, king of the mobile phone industry* **IDM sb/sth is ˈking** the person or thing mentioned is the most important part of sth and should be considered carefully: *The customer is king.*

**ˈking-size** (*also* **ˈking-sized**) *adj.* very large; larger than normal

**kiosk** /ˈkiːɒsk; *AmE* -ɑːsk/ *n.* [C] **1** a small shop/store, open at the front, where newspapers, drinks, etc. are sold **2** a small machine consisting of a computer and screen, that is fixed in a particular place and that members of the public can use, for example to get information about sth

**kit** /kɪt/ *n.* **1** [C,U] a set of tools, equipment, materials, etc. that you use for a particular purpose: *a tool kit* ◇ *a* ***starter kit*** (= one to help you start using sth) **2** [C] a set of parts ready to be made into sth: *furniture in kit form*

**kite** /kaɪt/ *v.* [T] (*AmE*) (*infml.*) to use an illegal cheque to obtain money or credit dishonestly: *to kite checks*

**Kitemark™** /ˈkaɪtmɑːk; *AmE* -mɑːrk/ *n.* [C, usu. sing.] in the UK, an official mark that is put on products to show that they have been approved by the British Standards Institution because they are of good quality and safe to use

**kitty** /ˈkɪti/ *n.* [C] (*pl.* **kitties**) (*infml.*) an amount of money that a person, a group, an organization, etc. has available to spend

**KM** /ˌkeɪ ˈem/ = KNOWLEDGE MANAGEMENT

**knock** /nɒk; *AmE* nɑːk/ *v.*, *n.*
• *v.* [T] (*often used with an adv.*) to affect sb/sth badly: *The news knocked investor confidence.* IDM **knock on/at sb's/the 'door; knock on 'doors** (*infml.*) to talk to or visit sb because you want sth from them: *Investment bankers are knocking on our door* (= wanting to invest).
PHR V **ˌknock sb/sth 'back** (*usu. pass.*) **1** to have a bad effect on sb/sth; to prevent sb/sth from achieving sth or making progress: *The economy was knocked back by last year's recession.* **2** (*infml.*) (*esp. BrE*) to reject sb/sth: *Their takeover bid has been knocked back.* **ˌknock sb 'down (from sth) (to sth)** (*infml.*) to persuade sb to reduce the price of sth: *I managed to knock him down to $400.* **ˌknock sth 'down (from sth) (to sth)** (*infml.*) to reduce the price of sth **'knock sth from sth** to cause the value of sth to fall by the amount mentioned: *The weakness of the currency knocked $30 m from our profits.* **ˌknock 'off (sth)** (*infml.*) to stop doing sth, esp. work: *to knock off early* **ˌknock sth 'off sth** (*infml.*) to produce a product that is a cheap copy of sb else's design, often illegally **ˌknock sth 'off (sth)** to reduce the price, value, length, etc. of sth: *The news knocked 13% off the shares.*
• *n.* IDM **take a (hard, severe, etc.) 'knock** (*infml.*) to have an experience that makes sb/sth less confident or successful; to be harmed or damaged

**'knock-down** (*AmE also* **knockdown**) *adj.* **1** (*infml.*) (about prices, etc.) much lower than usual: *They sold the business at a knock-down price.* SYN ROCK-BOTTOM **2** (*AmE*) (*abbr* **KD**) used to describe furniture that can easily be put together and taken apart, and is sold in separate pieces

**'knocking ˌcopy** *n.* [U] (*BrE*) (*Market., infml.*) advertising that criticizes an opponent's product

**'knock-off** (*AmE also* **knockoff**) *n.* [C] a copy of a product, esp. an expensive product

**'knock-on** *adj.* (*esp. BrE*) causing other events to happen one after another in a series: *The rising oil price will **have** a knock-on **effect** on airfares.*

**'know-how** *n.* [U] knowledge of how to do sth and experience in doing it: *business/financial ~*

**knowledge** /'nɒlɪdʒ; *AmE* 'nɑːl-/ *n.* [U,C] the information, understanding and skills that people gain through education or experience: *a working* (= basic) *knowledge of French* ◇ *How long does it take to master the skills and knowledge to do the job?*

**'knowledge ˌasset** *n.* [C, usu. pl.] (*also* **'knowledge ˌcapital** [U]) a collection of information, for example in the form of data or documents, or a set of skills that an organization has and that helps it to succeed: *knowledge assets such as knowledge of markets, products and technologies*

**'knowledge base** *n.* [C] a collection of information or rules that can be used to perform tasks or solve problems, esp. one that forms part of a computer system: *a knowledge base of our customers*

**'knowledge-based** *adj.* **1** making particular use of information, ideas, or modern technology, esp. computer systems: *a knowledge-based economy* **2** (*IT*) (about a computer system) that uses a collection of information or rules to solve problems: *knowledge-based software*

**'knowledge ˌcapital** = KNOWLEDGE ASSET

**'knowledge eˌconomy** *n.* [C] (*Econ.*) an economy in which information and modern technology produces economic benefits

**'knowledge ˌmanagement** *n.* [U] (*abbr* **KM**) ways of organizing, keeping and sharing important information in a company, for example about customers, suppliers, etc. in order to make the company more successful: *~ software/systems*

**'knowledge ˌofficer** *n.* [C] a person who is responsible for how a company keeps important information and makes it available to staff

**'knowledge ˌworker** *n.* [C] a person whose job involves working with information rather than producing goods

**Kon'dratieff ˌcycle** (*also* **Kon'dratieff wave**) (*also* **Kondratiev**) /kɒn'drɑːtjef; *AmE* kɑːn-/ *n.* [C] (*Econ.*) a pattern in a country's economy that lasts 50–60 years in which a long period of economic success is followed by a long period of difficulty

**KPI** /ˌkeɪ piː 'aɪ/ = KEY PERFORMANCE INDICATOR

# Ll

**L** /el/ *abbr* (esp. for sizes of clothes) large

**lab** /læb/ = LABORATORY

★**label** /ˈleɪbl/ *n., v.*
• *n.* [C] **1** a piece of paper, etc. that is attached to sth and gives information about it: *price/address ~s* **2** a name that is used to sell a range of goods to the public, esp. food, clothes or music; the goods themselves: *She sells the foods* ***under*** *the label Zest.* ◇ *famous labels* **3** a company that produces and sells goods under a particular name
• *v.* [T] (**-ll-**, *AmE* **-l-**) (*often pass.*) to fix a label on sth or write information on sth: *We label each item* ***with*** *the contents and date.* ▸ **ˈlabelling** (*AmE* **labeling**) *n.* [U]: *new rules for food labelling*

**labor** = LABOUR

**ˈlabor aˌgreement** = LABOR CONTRACT

**laboratory** /ləˈbɒrətri; *AmE* ˈlæbrətɔːri/ *n.* [C] (*pl.* **-ries**) (*also* **lab**, *infml.*) (sometimes used in the pl. in the names of companies) a room or building used for scientific research, experiments, testing, etc: *Abbott Laboratories*

**ˈlabor ˌcontract** (*also* **ˈlabor aˌgreement**) *n.* [C] (*both AmE*) (*HR*) an agreement between a union and a company about the pay, benefits, etc. that workers will receive

**laborer** = LABOURER

**ˈlabor ˌunion** = TRADE UNION

★**labour** (*AmE* **labor**) /ˈleɪbə(r)/ *n., v.*
• *n.* [U] **1** work, esp. physical work: *The price includes labour and materials.* **2** the people who work or are available for work in a country or a company: *a shortage of skilled labour*
• *v.* [I] to try very hard to do sth difficult or to deal with a difficult problem: *The group is labouring* ***under*** *€5 bn of debt.*

**ˈlabour court** *n.* [C] a type of court that can deal with disagreements between employees and employers

**ˈlabour disˌpute** *n.* [C] (*HR*) **1** a disagreement between workers and employers about pay or conditions **2** a strike SYN INDUSTRIAL DISPUTE

**labourer** (*AmE* **laborer**) /ˈleɪbərə(r)/ *n.* [C] a person whose job involves hard physical work that is not skilled, esp. outdoors

**ˈlabour ˌfederation** *n.* [C] a union or a group of unions

**ˈlabour force** *n.* [C with sing./pl. v.] all the people who work for a company or country: *a skilled/an unskilled ~* SYN WORKFORCE

**ˌlabour-inˈtensive** *adj.* (about a type of work) needing a lot of people to do it; involving a lot of workers

**ˈlabour law** *n.* [U] the collection of laws that deal with all aspects of employment and the rights of people who are employed SYN EMPLOYMENT LAW

**ˈlabour ˌmarket** (*also* **ˈjob ˌmarket**) *n.* [C] the number of people available for work in relation to the number of jobs available: *young people about to enter the labour market*

**ˌlabour moˈbility** (*also* **moˌbility of ˈlabour**) *n.* [U] (*Econ.*; *HR*) the ability and willingness of workers to move from one place or job to another

**ˈlabour reˌlations** *n.* [pl.] (*HR*) relations between employers and employees SYN INDUSTRIAL RELATIONS

**ˈlabour-ˌsaving** *adj.* designed to reduce the amount of work or effort needed to do sth: *a ~ device/gadget*

**laden** /ˈleɪdn/ *adj.* **1** heavily loaded with sth: *a* ***fully/heavily~*** *truck* **2** having a lot of sth, esp. sth unpleasant: *The firm is laden* ***with*** *debts of $13 bn.* **3** **-laden** used to form adjs showing that sth has a lot of, or is loaded with, the thing mentioned: *a debt-laden firm*

**lading** /ˈleɪdɪŋ/ *n.* [U,C] (*Trade*) the act of loading a ship with goods; the cargo

**lag** /læg/ *v., n.*
• *v.* (**-gg-**) **1** [T,I] to grow, increase, develop, etc. more slowly than sb/sth else: *We're lagging* ***behind*** *our competitors.* **2** [I] to grow, increase, etc., more slowly than normal: *lagging sales*
• *n.* [C] = TIME LAG

**laggard** /ˈlægəd; *AmE* -gərd/ *n.* [C] **1** (used esp. in newspapers) a company, an economy, etc. that is slow to improve or grow compared to others **2** (*Market.*) a person or an organization that is among the last to start using a new product or service

**ˌlaid-ˈoff** *adj.* (*HR*) (used about workers) told to stop work for a short period or permanently because there is not enough work

**laissez-faire** (*also* **laisser-faire**, *less freq.*) /ˌleseɪ ˈfeə(r); *AmE* ˈfer/ *n.* [U] (*Econ.*) the policy of allowing businesses and the economy to develop without government control

**ˌlame ˈduck** *n.* [C] **1** sb/sth that is not very successful and needs help: *lame-duck industries* **2** an official whose period of office will soon end and who will not be elected again or kept in the same position: *a lame-duck chairman*

**LAN** /læn/ *abbr* (*IT*) **local area network** a number of computers and other devices, in the same building or in buildings next to each other, that are connected together so that equipment and information can be shared

**ˈland bank** *n.* **1** [U; C] an amount of land that a person or a company owns and is waiting to build on **2** (*Finan.*) (*often* **Land Bank** [C]) (often used in names) a bank that helps farmers or people who live in the countryside, esp. by lending money for longer periods than other banks

**landed** /ˈlændɪd/ *adj.* (*Trade*) including all taxes and transport costs connected with bringing goods into a country: *the ~ cost/price of oil*

**landfill** /ˈlændfɪl/ *n.* **1** [C,U] an area of land where large amounts of waste material are buried under the earth: *landfill sites* **2** [U] the process of burying waste material: *landfill taxes* **3** [U] waste material that will be buried

**landing** /ˈlændɪŋ/ *n.* [C] **1** the moment when an aircraft comes down to the ground after a journey OPP TAKE-OFF **2** (*Transpt.*) an act of taking goods off a ship or plane onto land; the amount of goods taken off: *good landings of fish*

**ˈlanding card** *n.* [C] a card recording personal details that some passengers must complete when they arrive in a country

**ˈlanding charge** (*also* **ˈlanding fee**, *less freq.*) *n.* [C, usu. pl.] (*Transpt.*) a fee charged for using an airport or a harbour

**ˈlanding page** *n.* [C] (*IT*) the first page of a website that sb sees

**landline** /ˈlændlaɪn/ = FIXED LINE

**landlord** /ˈlændlɔːd; *AmE* -lɔːrd/ *n.* [C] a person or company that rents a building or land to sb → TENANT

**landmark** /ˈlændmɑːk; *AmE* -mɑːrk/ *n.* [C] an event, achievement, etc. that is seen as very important, esp. one that is the first of its kind: *a ~ court case/decision*

**ˈland ˌoffice** *n.* [C, usu. sing.] in the US, a government office that keeps records of sales of public land
IDM **do (a) ˈland-office business** to do a lot of successful business

**the ˈLand ˌRegistry** *n.* [sing.] a government office that keeps records of who owns land in England and Wales

**language** /ˈlæŋɡwɪdʒ/ *n.* **1** [U] a particular style of speaking or writing: *scientific/technical ~* ◇ *the ~ of business/law* **2** (*IT*) [C,U] a system of symbols and rules that is used to operate a computer: *HTML.*
IDM **speak/talk the same ˈlanguage** to be able to communicate easily with another person because you share similar experience or knowledge

**languish** /ˈlæŋɡwɪʃ/ *v.* [I] (used esp. in newspapers) to become weaker or fail to make progress: *Our economy continues to languish.*

**lapse** /læps/ *v.*, *n.*
• *v.* [I] (about a contract, an offer, an agreement, etc.) to be no longer valid because the period of time that it lasts has come to an end or because payments have not been made: *The patent on the drug lapses in 2009.*
▸ **lapsed** *adj.*: *a lapsed subscription*
PHR V **ˈlapse into sth** to gradually pass into a worse or less active state
• *n.* [C] **1** a small mistake, esp. one that is caused by forgetting sth or by being careless: *a serious lapse* **in** *security* **2** a period of time between two things that happen: *a time lapse of 30 minutes*

★ **laptop** /ˈlæptɒp; *AmE* -tɑːp/ (*also* **ˌlaptop comˈputer**) *n.* [C] a small computer that can work without wires and be easily carried

**larceny** /ˈlɑːsəni; *AmE* ˈlɑːrs-/ *n.* [U,C] (*pl.* **-nies**) (*AmE or BrE old-fash.*) the crime of stealing property or money from sb; an occasion when this takes place

**ˈlarge cap** *n.* [C] (*Stock Ex.*) a company that has a high total value of shares on the stock exchange

**ˈlarge-scale** *adj.* (about an organization or activity) involving many people or things, esp. over a wide area: *~ job cuts/layoffs* OPP SMALL-SCALE

**ˈlarge-sized** (*also* **ˈlarge-size**) *adj.* large; important

**largesse** (*also* **largess**) /lɑːˈdʒes; *AmE* lɑːrˈdʒes/ *n.* [U] *often* (*fml.*) (used esp. in newspapers, in a humorous or disapproving way) the act or quality of being generous with money

**laser** /ˈleɪzə(r)/ *n.* [C] a device that produces a very strong line of controlled light that can be used as a tool: *a laser bar-code reader*

**ˈlaser gun** *n.* [C] a piece of equipment which uses a very strong line of controlled light to read BAR CODES

**ˈlaser ˌprinter** *n.* [C] (*IT*) a printer that produces good quality printed material using a **laser**

**ˌlast-ˈditch** *adj.* used esp. in newspapers to describe a final attempt to achieve sth, when there is not much hope of succeeding: *a ~ **attempt/effort** to avoid a strike*

**ˌlast ˈin, ˌfirst ˈout** *phr.* **1** (*Comm.*; *Product.*) (*abbr* **LIFO**) a method of STOCK CONTROL in which the last goods or raw materials bought or produced are the first used or sold **2** (*Account.*) (*abbr* **LIFO**) a method of valuing supplies of goods or units of raw materials based on the idea that the last goods bought or produced are the first used or sold. The value of goods left at the end of the year is based on the earliest price paid. **3** (*HR*) used when people are losing their jobs, to say that the last people to be employed will be the first to go **4** (*IT*) used to describe a system where data received last is the first to be processed

**ˌlate maˈjority** *n.* [sing.] **1** (*Market.*) the group of customers who will only start to use a new product after many other people **2** (*HR*) the people in an organization who will only start to use a new method, process or system after most people in the organization

**latent** /ˈleɪtnt/ *adj.* existing, but not yet very noticeable, active or well-developed: *a latent market* ◇ *a huge latent demand for e-books*

**ˌlatent ˈdefect** *n.* [C,U] (*Law*) a fault in a product that you notice only after you have bought it

**lateral** /ˈlætərəl/ *adj.* having the same level of status or authority; involving people or jobs at the same level: *a lateral career move* SYN HORIZONTAL ▸ **ˈlaterally** /-rəli/ *adv.*

**ˌlateral inteˈgration** = HORIZONTAL INTEGRATION

★ **launch** /lɔːntʃ/ *v.*, *n.*

• ***v.*** [T,I] **1** to start an activity, esp. an organized one: *He has launched a bid for the supermarket chain.* ◇ *The business launched last year with 15 employees.* **2** to start selling a product or service for the first time; to make sth available so that it can be bought and sold: *They are launching a new telephone service this year.*

PHR V **ˌlaunch ˈout** to do sth new in your career, esp. sth more exciting: *I launched out on my own.*

• ***n.*** [C,U] the action of **launching** sth; an event at which sth is launched: *the successful launch of euro notes and coins* ◇ *The launch date is in June.*

**launder** /ˈlɔːndə(r)/ *v.* [T] to move money that has been obtained illegally into foreign bank accounts or legal businesses so that it is difficult for people to know where the money came from: *$8 m had been laundered **through** the firm.* ▸ **ˈlaunderer** *n.* [C] **ˈlaundering** *n.* [U]

**ˈlaundry list** *n.* [C] a long list of people or things: *a ~ of problems*

★ **law** /lɔː/ *n.* **1** (*also* **the law**) [U] the whole system of rules that everyone in a country or society must obey: *Car insurance is required **by** law.* ◇ *What they did is not **against** the law.* ◇ *to **break/enforce/respect** the ~* **2** [U] *usually ...* **law** a particular branch of the law; the laws of a particular country or area: *company/contract ~* ◇ *international/federal/local ~* ◇ *The merger would be **in breach of** EU competition law.* ◇ *to **break/enforce/respect** ... ~* **3** [C] a rule that deals with a particular crime, agreement, etc: *Existing laws **on** store opening hours should be relaxed.* ◇ *to **enact/introduce/pass** a ~* ◇ *to **amend/change** a ~* ◇ *strict/tough ~s* **4** [U] the study of the law as a subject at university, etc.; the profession of being a lawyer: *Chris is studying law.* ◇ *to **go into/practise** ~* ◇ *a ~ firm/practice* **5** [C] the fact that sth always happens in the same way in an activity or in nature: *the law of supply and demand* SYN PRINCIPLE → idioms at CONFLICT *n.*, LETTER *n.*

**ˈlaw-aˌbiding** *adj.* obeying and respecting the law

**ˈlaw court** = COURT OF LAW

**lawful** /ˈlɔːfl/ *adj.* allowed or recognized by law; legal OPP UNLAWFUL ▸ **ˈlawfully** /-fəli/ *adv.* **ˈlawfulness** *n.* [U]

**ˈlaw of ˈone ˈprice** *n.* [sing.] (*Econ.*) the rule that without trade restrictions, transport costs, etc. the same goods would cost the same in all countries

**lawsuit** /ˈlɔːsuːt; *BrE also* -sjuːt/ (*also* **suit**) *n.* [C] a claim or complaint against sb that a person or an organization can make in court: *to bring/file/settle a ~*

★ **lawyer** /ˈlɔːjə(r)/ *n.* [C] a person who is trained and qualified to advise people about the law, to represent them in court, and to write legal documents: *to seek advice from a lawyer* ◇ *corporate lawyers* ◇ *a bankruptcy lawyer*

**lay** /leɪ/ *v.* [T] **1** to put something down: *to ~ a cable/pipe* **2** to present a proposal, some information, etc. to sb for them to think about and decide on: *Proposals will be laid before the committee.* **PHR V** ˌ**lay sth** ˈ**down** if you **lay down** a rule or a principle, you state officially that people must obey it or use it ˌ**lay sb** ˈ**off** (*HR*) to stop employing sb because there is not enough work for them to do: *About 1 000 workers at the factory will be laid off.* ˌ**lay (sth)** ˈ**out (for/on sth)** (*infml.*) to spend money on sth: *I don't want to have to lay out for a new phone again!*

**layaway** /ˈleɪəweɪ/ *n.* [U] (*AmE*) (*Comm.*) a system of buying goods in a store, where the customer pays a small amount of the price for an item and the store keeps the goods until the full price has been paid: *furniture bought on layaway*

**layer** /ˈleɪə(r); ˈleə(r); *AmE* ler/ *n., v.*
• *n.* [C] **1** a level or part within a system or set of ideas: *layers of management* **2** a quantity or thickness of sth that lies over a surface or between surfaces
• *v.* [T] to arrange sth in levels or layers: *a big layered company*

ˈ**lay-off** *n.* [C] (*pl.* **lay-offs**) **1** an act of making people unemployed because there is no more work for them to do; an example of this: *the temporary* **lay-off** *of 8 000 car workers* ◇ *There may be more lay-offs.* **2** a period of time when sb is not working or not doing sth that they normally do

**layout** /ˈleɪaʊt/ *n.* [C, usu. sing.] the way in which the parts of sth such as the page of a book, a building or a town are arranged

**lb** (*AmE* **lb.** *pl.* **lb** *or* **lbs**) = POUND (3)

**LBO** /ˌel biː ˈəʊ; *AmE* ˈoʊ/ *abbr* (*Finan.*) **leveraged buyout** when a person or an organization buys a company with a large amount of borrowed money, using the assets of the company as COLLATERAL in order to obtain the money

**l.c.** (*also* **L/C**) = LETTER OF CREDIT

**LCD** /ˌel siː ˈdiː/ *abbr* **liquid crystal display** a way of showing information in electronic equipment such as LAPTOPS, etc. An electric current is passed through a thin layer of liquid and images can be seen on a small screen: *an LCD monitor*

**LCL** /ˌel siː ˈel/ = LESS THAN CONTAINER LOAD

**LDC** /ˌel diː ˈsiː/ = LESS-DEVELOPED COUNTRY

★**lead** /liːd/ *v., n.*
• *v.* (**led, led** /led/) **1** [T,I] to be the best at sth; to be in first place: *We* **lead the field** *in magazine publishing.* **2** [T] to be in control of sth; to be the leader of sth: *Snell leads the marketing team.* **IDM** **lead from the** ˈ**front** to take an active part in what you are telling or persuading others to do **PHR V** ˈ**lead to sth** to have sth as a result: *These contacts may lead to future business.*
• *n.* **1** [sing.] the position ahead of everyone else in a competition or race; the amount that sb/sth is ahead: *to have/increase/lose/maintain a* ~ **2** (*usu. used as an adj.*) the most important person, product, etc: *the lead engineer on the project* **3** [sing.] an example or action for people to copy or follow: *They have* **taken the lead** *in attracting younger consumers.* **4** (*Market.*) [C] a piece of information that may help you find new customers: *to follow up/generate/have ~s* **5** (*Insur.*) [C] the group of Lloyd's UNDERWRITERS that accepts the most responsibility for an insurance policy

ˈ**lead bank** = AGENT BANK

★**leader** /ˈliːdə(r)/ *n.* [C] **1** a company, a thing, a person, etc. that is the best or in first place in a business, competition, etc: *a world leader* **in** *IT* **2** a person who leads a group of people, esp. the head of a country, an organization, etc: *business leaders*

★**leadership** /ˈliːdəʃɪp; *AmE* -dərʃ-/ *n.* **1** [U] the state or position of being a leader: *We worked under the leadership of Mike Potter.* **2** [U] the ability to be a leader; the qualities a good leader should have: *strong leadership* ◇ *~ qualities/skills* **3** [C with sing./pl.verb] a group of leaders of a particular organization, etc: *The leadership was/were not popular.*

**leading** /ˈliːdɪŋ/ *adj.* most important or most successful: *a leading provider of business information* ◇ *a leading player in the market*

ˌ**leading** ˈ**edge** *n.* [sing.] the most important and advanced position in an area of activity, esp. technology: *We operate* **at/on** *the ~ of technology.* **SYN** CUTTING EDGE

ˌ**leading** ˈ**indicator** *n.* [C] (*Econ.*) a measure of economic activity that changes before the economy begins to follow a particular pattern and helps to show what the economy will do

ˌ**lead** ˈ**manager** (*also* ˌ**lead** ˈ**underwriter**, ˌ**managing** ˈ**underwriter**) *n.* [C] (*Stock Ex.*) the main bank or financial organization responsible for organizing an INITIAL PUBLIC OFFERING, the sale of bonds, etc. ▸ ˌ**lead-ˈmanage** *v.* [T]: *to lead-manage the sale of a company*

**ˈlead time** *n.* [U,C] (*Product.*) the time between receiving an order and delivering the product or service to the customer: *She's brought the lead time down from ten days to three.*

**ˌlead ˈunderwriter** = LEAD MANAGER

**ˌlead ˈuser** *n.* [C] (*Market.*) a company, person, etc. that is the first to experience a particular need, and therefore adapts an existing product or service to meet this need or is the first to use a new service or product: *Lead users are a valuable source of new product ideas.*

**leaflet** /ˈliːflət/ *n.*, *v.*

• *n.* [C] a printed sheet of paper or a few printed pages that advertise or give information about sth

• *v.* [T,I] to give out **leaflets** to people

**ˈleaflet drop** *n.* [C] (*Market.*) a method of advertising by delivering **leaflets** to a large number of houses

**leakage** /ˈliːkɪdʒ/ *n.* **1** [C,U] an amount of liquid or gas escaping from a container that has a fault; an occasion when this happens: (*fig.*) *the continuing leakage of deposits from the banking system* **2** (*Comm.*) = SHRINKAGE (2)

**lean** /liːn/ *adj.* (**-er**, **-est**) **1** used to describe a method of production that aims to cut costs while keeping quality high by producing only the quantity of goods ordered and reducing the amount of time and space that the production process uses: *lean manufacturing* ◇ *leaner processes* **2** (about costs, quantities, etc.) very low; as low as possible: *Companies are trying to keep their workforces lean.* **3** (about organizations, etc.) strong and efficient, esp. because the number of employees has been reduced: *a leaner, fitter business* **4** used to describe a difficult period of time that does not produce much money, etc: *the leanest time of year for the tourist industry*
▸ **leanness** /ˈliːnnəs/ *n.* [U]

**leap** /liːp/ *v.* (**leapt**, **leapt** /lept/ *or* **leaped**, **leaped**) [T,I] to increase suddenly and by a large amount: *Shares leapt in value.* ▸ **leap** *n.* [C]

**leapfrog** /ˈliːpfrɒg; *AmE* -frɔːg; -frɑːg/ *v.* (**-gg-**) [T,I] to get to a higher position or rank by going past sb else or by missing out some stages: *We're looking at how to leapfrog the competition.*

**ˈlearning curve** *n.* [C, usu. sing.] **1** the rate at which you learn a new subject or skill; the process of learning from the mistakes you make: *a **steep** learning curve* (= there is a lot to learn in a short time) **2** = EXPERIENCE CURVE

★ **lease** /liːs/ *n.*, *v.* (*Law*; *Prop.*)

• *n.* [C] a legal agreement that allows you to use a building, a piece of equipment or some land for a period of time, usu. in return for rent: *The lease expires on 31 March.* ◇ *to take on/take out a ~*

• *v.* [T] **~ sth (from sb)** | **~ sth (out) (to sb)** | **~ sb sth** to use, or to let sb use sth, esp. property or equipment, in exchange for rent or a regular payment: *We lease all our vans.* ◇ *Some offices are leased out to tenants.*
▸ **ˈleasing** *n.* [U]: *car leasing*

**PHR V** ˌ**lease sth ˈback (to sb)** to sell property or an asset and continue to use it by paying rent to the new owner; to buy property or an asset and allow the seller to continue using it in exchange for rent

**leaseback** /ˈliːsbæk/ *n.* [U,C] (*Prop.*) the process of selling property or another valuable asset and continuing to use it by paying rent to the new owner; a legal agreement where this happens

**leasehold** /ˈliːshəʊld; *AmE* -hoʊld/ *n.* [C,U] (*Law*; *Prop.*) the right to use a building or a piece of land according to the arrangements in a LEASE → FREEHOLD ▸ **ˈleasehold** *adj.*, *adv.*: *leasehold properties* ◇ *to purchase land leasehold* **ˈleaseholder** *n.* [C]: *tenants and leaseholders* → FREEHOLDER

★ **leave** /liːv/ *n.* [U] **1** (*HR*) a period of time when you are allowed to be away from work for a holiday/vacation or for a special reason: *to take a month's paid/unpaid ~* ◇ *She is **on** leave this week.* ◇ *a basic annual leave entitlement of 20 days.* **HELP** In this meaning, **leave** is U in BrE but can be U or C in AmE.

● *to be **entitled to/get/have** ~* ♦ *to **apply for/be given/be granted** ~*

**2** official permission to do sth: *to be absent **without** leave*

● *to **ask/obtain/request** ~ (to do sth)* ♦ *to **give/grant/refuse** sb ~*

**ˌleave of ˈabsence** *n.* [U,C] (*HR*) permission to have time away from work for a particular period; the period of time you are allowed: *four months' leave of absence*

**-led** /led/ *comb. form* (*used to form adjs*) **1** having the thing mentioned as its main influence: *consumer-led product development* **2** organized or controlled by the person or organization mentioned: *manager-led discussions*

**ledger** /'ledʒə(r)/ *n.* [C] (*Account.*) a book or computer file in which a bank, a business, etc. records the money it has paid and received: *balancing a ledger*

**'ledger clerk** *n.* [C] a person whose job is to make and check entries in a company **ledger**

**leg** /leg/ *n.* IDM **have, gain, grow 'legs** (*infml.*) if you say that sth **has legs**, you mean that it will continue, or people will be interested in it, for a long time: *The rally (in share prices) still has legs.*

**legacy** /'legəsi/ *n., adj.*
• *n.* [C] (*pl.* **-cies**) **1** a situation that exists now because of events, actions, etc. that took place in the past: *The project failed, leaving us with a legacy of debt.* **2** money or property that is given to you by sb when they die SYN INHERITANCE
• *adj.* **1** (*IT*) used to describe a system, product, etc. that is no longer generally available, but that is still used: *legacy software* **2** used to describe something that took place in the past but still affects the present: *poor legacy decisions*

★ **legal** /'liːgl/ *adj.* **1** connected with the law: *to take/seek ~ advice ◇ the company's legal department* **2** allowed or required by law: *the legal rights of shareholders ◇ legal currency* OPP ILLEGAL ▸ **'legally** /-gəli/ *adv.*: *a legally binding contract*

**,legal 'action** *n.* [U] (*also* **,legal pro'ceedings** [pl.]) the act of using the legal system to settle a disagreement, etc: *He threatened to **take** legal action against the hospital.*

**,legal 'aid** *n.* [U] money that is given by the government or another organization to sb who needs help to pay for legal advice or a lawyer

**,legal ca'pacity** *n.* [U,C] (*Law*) the right or ability to make legal arrangements, to be legally responsible for sb/sth, etc.

**'legal costs** (*also* **'legal ex,penses**) *n.* [pl.] money that sb involved in a legal case must pay

**,legal 'entity** *n.* [C] (*Law*) an organization or a person that has the right to make contracts, use the legal system to settle disputes, and make other legal arrangements: *The company is a separate legal entity that can sue or be sued.*

**legalese** /,liːgə'liːz/ *n.* [U] (*infml.*) the sort of language used in legal



documents that is difficult to understand

**'legal ex,penses** = LEGAL COSTS

**,legal 'holiday** *n.* [C] in the US, a public holiday that is fixed by law

**,legal in'vestment** *n.* [C] (*Finan.*) in the US, a type of investment that is suitable for a person or an organization that is looking after money for sb else

**legality** /liː'gæləti/ *n.* (*pl.* **-ties**) **1** [U] the fact of being legal: *Shareholders challenged the legality of the merger.* **2** [C] the legal aspect of an action or a situation: *the legalities of the contracts* → ILLEGALITY

**legalize, -ise** /'liːgəlaɪz/ *v.* [T] to make sth legal ▸ **,legali'zation, -i'sation** /-laɪ'zeɪʃn; *AmE* ,-lə'z-/ *n.* [U]

**,legal 'list** *n.* [C] (*Finan.*) in the US, a list of LEGAL INVESTMENTS

**,legal mo'nopoly** *n.* [C] (*Econ.*) **1** a situation in which only one company has the legal right to provide a particular service or product in a particular area **2** a company that has this right

**'legal pad** *n.* [C] (*AmE*) a book of writing paper, which is usu. yellow and has lines for writing on

**,legal 'person** (*also* **,artificial 'person, ju,ristic 'person**) *n.* [C] (*pl.* **- persons**) (*Law*) an organization or company that has its own legal status and is treated in law as a person, separate from the people who run and own it

**,legal pro'ceedings** = LEGAL ACTION

**,legal re'serve** *n.* [C] (*Account.*) the smallest amount of money that a bank, an insurance company, etc., is legally required to keep in case it is needed in the future

**'legal ,system** *n.* [C] the institutions and laws that exist in a particular country to deal with legal cases

**,legal 'tender** *n.* [U] money that can legally be used to pay for things in a particular country

**legible** /'ledʒəbl/ *adj.* (about written or printed words) clear enough to read: *a legible signature* ▸ **,legi'bility** /-'bɪləti/ *n.* [U] **'legibly** /-bli/ *adv.*

★ **legislation** /,ledʒɪs'leɪʃn/ *n.* [U] **1** a law or a set of laws passed by a parliament: *to draft/draw up ~ ◇ to amend/introduce/pass ~* **2** the process of making and passing laws

**legit** /lɪˈdʒɪt/ *adj.* (*infml.*) legal, or acting according to the law or the rules: *The business seems legit.*

**legitimate** *adj., v.*
• ***adj.*** /lɪˈdʒɪtɪmət/ allowed and acceptable according to the law: *a perfectly legitimate business* SYN LEGAL ▸ **leˈgitimacy** /-məsi/ *n.* [U]: *I intend to challenge the legitimacy of his claim.* **leˈgitimately** *adv.*
• ***v.*** /lɪˈdʒɪtɪmeɪt/ [T] = LEGITIMIZE

**legitimize, -ise** /lɪˈdʒɪtəmaɪz/ (*also* **leˈgitimate**, *less freq.*) *v.* [T] **1** to make sth legal SYN LEGALIZE **2** to make sth that is wrong or unfair seem acceptable

**ˈleisure ˌindustry** *n.* [C] the people and activities involved in providing goods and services for things that people do in their free time: *the hotel and leisure industry*

**lemon** /ˈlemən/ *n.* [C] (*infml.*) a product, esp. a car, that is useless and does not work as it should; a poor investment

★ **lend** /lend/ *v.* (**lent, lent** /lent/) [T,I] **~ (sth) (to sb/sth)** | **~ sb sth** (about a bank or financial institution) to give money to sb on condition that they pay it back over a period of time and pay interest: *The bank refused to lend the money to us.* ◇ *They refused to lend us the money.* ◇ *Some banks have stopped lending to small businesses.* SYN LOAN → BORROW

★ **lender** /ˈlendə(r)/ *n.* [C] a person or an organization that lends money: *The company is in talks with its lenders.* OPP BORROWER

**ˈlender of ˈlast reˈsort** *n.* [C] (*Econ.*) the role of a country's central bank when it lends money in a time of difficulty to a bank that does not have enough to cover what its customers are taking out and cannot borrow money from anywhere else

★ **lending** /ˈlendɪŋ/ *n.* [U] the act of lending money; the amount of money that is lent: *Lending by banks rose last year.* ◇ *the consumer lending market* OPP BORROWING
○ ***commercial/mortgage/personal ~*** ◆ ***an increase/a rise in ~*** ◆ ***a decrease/downturn in ~*** ◆ ***a ~ bank/institution***

**ˈlending rate** *n.* [C] (*Finan.*) the rate of interest that you must pay when you borrow money from a bank or other financial organization

**less** /les/ *prep.* used before a particular amount that must be taken away from the amount just mentioned: *a monthly salary of €2 500 less tax and insurance* SYN MINUS → PLUS

**ˌless-developed ˈcountry** *n.* [C] (*abbr* **LDC**) (*Econ.*) a country that is poor and trying to make its industry and economic system more advanced

**lessee** /leˈsiː/ *n.* [C] (*Law*; *Prop.*) a person who has use of a building, an area of land, etc. on a LEASE

**lessor** /leˈsɔː(r)/ *n.* [C] (*Law*; *Prop.*) a person who gives sb the use of a building, an area of land, etc. on a LEASE

**ˈLess than Conˈtainer ˈLoad** *n.* [C] (*abbr* **LCL**) (*Transpt.*) an amount of goods being transported for sb that does not fill a whole container so will go with other goods

**let** /let/ *v., n.*
• ***v.*** [T] (**letting, let, let**) (*esp. BrE*) **~ sth (out) (to sb)** to allow sb to use rooms, a building, etc. in return for regular payments: *They let out the smaller offices at low rents.* ▸ **ˈletting** *n.* [U,C]: *an office letting agency*
IDM **let sb ˈgo** (*infml.*) to dismiss sb: *I'm going to have to let you go.*
• ***n.*** [C] (*BrE*) an act of renting a home, etc: *offices* ***on a short-term let***

**letter** /ˈletə(r)/ *n., adj.*
• ***n.*** [C] a message that is written down or printed on paper and usu. put in an envelope and sent to sb: *a letter of complaint* ◇ *Who is the letter addressed to?* IDM **the ˌletter of the ˈlaw** the exact words of a law or rule rather than its general meaning **to the ˈletter** exactly as sb/sth says: *I followed your instructions to the letter.*
• ***adj.*** (*AmE*) = LETTER-SIZE

**letterhead** /ˈletəhed; *AmE* ˈletər-/ *n.* [C] the name and address of a business that is printed at the top of the paper it uses for letters

**ˌletter of adˈvice** *n.* [C] (*Comm.*) a letter sent to sb giving them some information or telling them of sth the sender has done

**ˌletter of appliˈcation** (*also* **appliˈcation ˌletter**, *less freq.*) *n.* [C] (*HR*) a letter written by sb who is asking to be considered for a job

**ˌletter of apˈpointment** (*also* **apˈpointment ˌletter**, *less freq.*) *n.* [C] (*HR*) a letter from an employer offering sb a job and giving details of pay and conditions

**ˌletter of atˈtorney** = POWER OF ATTORNEY

**ˌletter of ˈcomfort** (*also* **ˈcomfort ˌletter**) *n.* [C] (*Finan.*) a letter that a company writes to a bank to support a SUBSIDIARY company that needs to borrow money

**ˌletter of ˈcredit** *n.* [C] (*abbr* **l.c.**, **L/C**) (*Finan.*; *Trade*) a letter that a bank prepares for a customer in which it agrees to pay sb an amount of money under particular circumstances, used esp. as a way of paying for imported goods

**ˌletter of enˈgagement** (*also* **enˈgagement ˌletter**) *n.* [C] (*HR*) a letter which states the conditions under which sb is employed to do work for a company

**ˌletter of inˈdemnity** *n.* [C] (*Law*) a letter from one person, company, etc. to another in which they agree to be responsible for particular damage, loss, etc. if it happens

**ˌletter of inˈtent** *n.* [C] (*Law, fml.*) a formal letter in which sb states what they intend to do about sth. It is not a promise or a legal contract but shows that they are serious about it.

**ˌletter of ˈlicence** *n.* [C] (*Law*) a letter in which sb who is owed money agrees to allow the person who owes the money more time in which to pay

**ˌletter of reˈgret** (*also* **reˈgret ˌletter**) *n.* [C] a letter that is sent to a person who has had an interview, a company that has tried to win a contract, etc., to tell them that they have not been successful

**lettershop** /ˈletəʃɒp; *AmE* ˈletərʃɑːp/ *n.* [C] (*Market.*) a company that organizes and sends letters or advertisements to large numbers of people for other companies

**ˈletter-size** (*also* **ˈletter**) *adj.* (*both AmE*) used to describe paper that is 8½ inches (215.9 mm) wide and 11 inches (279.4 mm) long

★ **level** /ˈlevl/ *n., adj., v.*
• ***n.*** **1** [C] the amount of sth that exists in a particular situation at a particular time: *a high/low ~ of risk* ◇ *production levels* ◇ *Profits were* ***at*** *the same level as the year before.* **2** [C,U] a particular standard or quality: *We offer the highest level of customer service.* ◇ *to achieve/reach an advanced/a basic ~* **3** [C,U] a position on a scale of quantity or value: *The euro has dropped to its lowest level since 2003.* **4** [U,C] a position or rank in an organization or a system: *a decision taken* ***at*** *board level* ◇ *a junior/senior ~*
• ***adj.*** having the same value or position as sth: *keeping wages level* ***with*** *inflation* → idiom at PLAYING FIELD
• ***v.*** [T] (-ll-, *AmE* -l-) to make sth equal or similar: *New technology has a levelling effect on industries.* PHR V **ˌlevel (sth) ˈdown** to make standards, amounts, etc. be of the same low or lower level; to become the same low or lower level as sth: *levelling down the salaries of executives* **ˌlevel ˈoff/ˈout** to stay at a steady level of development or progress after a period of sharp rises or falls: *Sales have levelled off after a period of rapid growth.* SYN FLATTEN OUT/OFF **ˌlevel sth ˈup** to make standards, amounts, etc. be of the same high or higher level

**lever** /ˈliːvə(r); *AmE* ˈlevər/ *n., v.*
• ***n.*** [C] **1** a handle used to operate a piece of machinery or a vehicle **2** an action or thing that is used to persuade sb to do sth
• ***v.*** [T] to move sth with a **lever**: (*fig.*) *to lever money from investors*

★ **leverage** /ˈliːvərɪdʒ; *AmE* ˈlev-/ *n., v.*
• ***n.*** [U] **1** the ability to influence sth: *Large stores use their size as leverage to lower suppliers' prices.* **2** (*Finan.*) (*esp. AmE*) the relationship between the amount of money that a company owes (**debt**) and the value of its shares (**equity**) SYN GEARING **3** (*Finan.*) (*esp. AmE*) using borrowed money to buy an investment or to add to the amount invested, in order to try to increase possible profits from the investment
• ***v.*** [T] **1** to get as much advantage or profit as possible from sth that you have: *leveraging the skills of your workforce* **2** (*Finan.*) to use borrowed money to buy an investment or to add to the amount invested, in order to try to increase possible profits from the investment: *a leveraged takeover bid* **3** to attract money or other advantages: *The design award leveraged large loans from several sources.* ▸ **ˈleveraging** *n.* [U]
PHR V **ˌleverage (sth) ˈup** **1** (*Finan.*) if a company or an investor **leverages up**, they borrow more money in order to try to increase profits **2** to increase or improve sth: *Our software will leverage up your efficiency.*

**leveraged** /ˈliːvərɪdʒd; *AmE* ˈlev-/ *adj.* (*Finan.*) **1** (about a company or an organization) having borrowed a large amount of money in relation to the value of the shares it has sold: *The business is highly leveraged.* **2** (about an investment) involving a large amount of borrowed money: *a highly-leveraged transaction*

**ˈlever arch file** *n.* [C] a type of file for holding papers in which metal rings that are opened and closed with a **lever** go through the edges of the pages and hold them

**levy** /ˈlevi/ *n., v.*
• ***n.*** [C] (*pl.* **-vies**) (*Finan.*) an extra amount of money that has to be paid, esp. as a tax to the government
⊙ *to* ***be exempt from/pay*** *a ~* ♦ *to* ***impose/put*** *a ~* ***on*** *sth* ♦ *to* ***abolish/end*** *a ~*
• ***v.*** [T] (**-vies**, **-vying**, **-vied**, **-vied**) to demand and collect a payment, tax, etc: *A tax is levied* ***on*** *the sale of shares.*

**LFL** /ˌel ef ˈel/ = LIKE-FOR-LIKE

★ **liability** /ˌlaɪəˈbɪləti/ *n.* (*pl.* **-ties**) **1** (*Account.*; *Finan.*) [C, usu. pl.] the amount of money that a company or person owes: *The company has liabilities of nearly €90 000.* SYN DEBT
⊙ *to* ***meet/reduce/take on*** *liabilities* ♦ ***future/long-term/short-term*** *liabilities* ♦ ***insurance/pension/tax*** *liabilities*
**2** (*Law*) [U] the state of being legally responsible for sth: *We cannot accept liability* ***for*** *goods damaged in the mail.*
⊙ *to* ***admit/deny*** *~* ♦ ***full/legal*** *~*

**liaˈbility inˌsurance** (*also* **liaˈbility ˌcover**) *n.* [U] insurance that a person or an organization buys to protect them against legal claims made by others

★ **liable** /ˈlaɪəbl/ *adj.* (*Law*) **1** legally responsible for paying the cost of sth: *Are we liable* ***for*** *damage our products do?* **2** likely to be punished by law for sth: *Offenders are liable* ***to*** *large fines.* **3** having to do sth by law: *The supply of services is liable* ***to*** *VAT.*

**liaise** /liˈeɪz/ *v.* [I] **1** (*esp. BrE*) to work closely with sb and exchange information with them **2** to act as a link between two or more people or groups: *to liaise* ***between*** *the staff and management*

**liberalize, -ise** /ˈlɪbrəlaɪz/ *v.* [T] to make the rules that apply to an activity, industry, etc. less strict; to make it easier for more people to take part: *plans to liberalize world trade* ▸ **ˌliberaliˈzation, -iˈsation** /-laɪˈzeɪʃn; *AmE* -ləˈz-/ *n.* [U]: *market liberalization*

**LIBOR** /ˈlaɪbɔː(r)/ = LONDON INTER-BANK OFFERED RATE

★ **licence** (*AmE* **license**) /ˈlaɪsns/ *n.* [C] (*Law*) an official document that shows that permission has been given to do, own or use sth: *a licence* ***for*** *the software* ◇ *a licence holder*
⊙ *to* ***have/get*** *a ~* ♦ *to* ***apply for/renew*** *a ~* ♦ *to* ***grant/issue/refuse/suspend/take away*** *a ~* ♦ *a ~* ***expires/runs out***

IDM **a licence to print ˈmoney** (*infml.*) used to describe a business which makes a lot of money with little effort **under ˈlicence** (about a product) made with the permission of a company or an organization

**ˈlicence aˌgreement** *n.* [C] (*Law*) a legal document with a piece of software that states it can be used and by how many people

**ˈlicence fee** (*also* **ˈlicensing fee**, *esp. in AmE*) *n.* [C] an amount of money paid to obtain a licence

★ **license** /ˈlaɪsns/ *v., n.*
• ***v.*** [T] (*Comm.*; *Law*) to give a person or an organization official permission to do, own, or use sth, often in exchange for a fee: *The drug has not yet been licensed in Europe.*
• ***n.*** [C] (*AmE*) (*Law*) = LICENCE

**licensed** /ˈlaɪsnst/ *adj.* (*Comm.*) **1 ~ (to do sth)** having official permission to do, make or use sth: *licensed dealers* **2** that you have official permission to make, own or use: *licensed products*

**licensee** /ˌlaɪsənˈsiː/ *n.* [C] (*Law*) a person or company who has been given official permission to do, make, own or use sth

**licenser** = LICENSOR

**ˈlicensing fee** = LICENCE FEE

**licensor** (*also* **licenser**) /ˈlaɪsənsə(r)/ *n.* [C] (*Law*) a person or an organization that gives a licence to sb: *the licensor of the software*

**lien** /ˈliːən; liːn/ *n.* [C] (*Law*) **~ (over/on/against sth)** a right to keep property belonging to sb else until they pay what they owe: *They hold a lien* ***on*** *the shares as security for the debt.* ◇ *to claim/exercise a ~* ▸ **lienee** /ˌliːəˈniː; ˌliːˈniː/ *n.* [C] **lienor** /ˈliːənɔː(r); ˈliːnɔː(r)/ *n.* [C]

**lieu** /luː; *BrE also* ljuː/ *n.* IDM **in lieu (of sth)** (*fml.*) instead (of sth): *She received six months' salary in lieu of notice.*

**ˈlife asˌsurance** = LIFE INSURANCE

**ˈlife-ˌbalance** *adj.* (*HR*) used to describe the relationship between your work and the rest of your life

**lifeboat** /ˈlaɪfbəʊt; *AmE* -boʊt/ *n.* [C] (*Finan.*) (used in newspapers) financial help given to a company that is in trouble: *a financial lifeboat from the banks*

**ˈlife ˌcycle** *n.* [C] the period during which a product, a project, or an organization exists; the developments and changes which occur during this period: *the natural life cycle of new businesses*

**ˈlife exˌpectancy** *n.* [U,C] **1** (*also* **ˌexpectation of ˈlife**) the number of years that a person is likely to live **2** the length of time that sth is likely to exist or continue for: *the short life expectancy of dotcoms* **3** the length of time that an asset is likely to be used for

**ˈlife fund** *n.* [C] money paid to insurance companies for LIFE INSURANCE and invested by them. Claims are paid from this.

**ˈlife inˌsurance** (*BrE also* **ˈlife asˌsurance**) *n.* [U] a type of insurance in which you make a single payment or regular payments so that you receive a sum of money when you are a particular age, or your family receive money when you die

**lifeline** /ˈlaɪflaɪn/ *n.* [C, usu. sing.] help given to a person or an organization that is in trouble; sth that sb/sth depends on: *The deal offers us a much-needed lifeline.*

**ˌlifelong ˈlearning** *n.* [U] (*HR*) the idea that employees need to keep developing their knowledge and skills throughout their working lives

**lifespan** /ˈlaɪfspæn/ *n.* [C] the length of time that sth will last, will be useful, or will be wanted: *The product has a 10-year lifespan.*

**lifestyle** /ˈlaɪfstaɪl/ *n.* [C,U] the way in which a person or group lives and works: *people with busy lifestyles* ○ *a comfortable/healthy/outdoor ~* • *~ brands/choices/magazines*

**ˈlife ˌtables** (*also* **morˈtality ˌtables**) *n.* [pl.] (*Insur.*) lists that show how many years people in particular groups are expected to live, used in calculating insurance risks

**ˌlifetime emˈployment** *n.* [U] (*HR*) when employees in an organization are promised a job until they retire

**ˌlifetime ˈvalue** (*abbr* **LTV**) (*also* **ˈcustomer ˈlifetime ˈvalue** *abbr* **CLV**) *n.* [U] (*Market.*) the total amount of profit that a company expects to make from each customer during the period of time that they buy the company's products

**ˌlife-work ˈbalance** (*also* **life/work**-) = WORK-LIFE BALANCE

**LIFFE** /laɪf/ *abbr* **London International Financial Futures and Options Exchange** a market for buying and selling FUTURES and OPTIONS

**LIFO** /ˈlaɪfəʊ; *AmE* -oʊ/ = LAST IN, FIRST OUT

**lift** /lɪft/ *v., n.*

• *v.* **1** [T] to make an amount or level of sth greater: *to lift consumer confidence* **2** [T,I] to become or to make sth become more valuable or successful: *efforts to lift the economy out of recession* **3** [T] to remove or end a restriction, policy or threat: *The ban was lifted.* **4** [T] to raise sth to a higher position or level: *lifting heavy objects* ▸ **ˈlifting** *n.* [U]: *a partial lifting of the ban* ◇ ***heavy lifting***

• *n.* [C, usu. sing.] an increase in sth; an improvement in sth: *a 3% lift in sales*

**light** /laɪt/ *adj.* (**-er**, **-est**) **1** not great in amount or degree: *light trading* **2** used to describe smaller vehicles, machines, etc. that are not of the most powerful type: *light vehicles* **3** (*BrE*) **~ on sth** not having a large amount or enough of sth: *The firm is very light on assets.* **3** not involving a lot of work or activity; not very busy: *a light schedule* **4** not needing a lot of physical strength: *After his accident he was moved to lighter work.* → HEAVY **IDM** **make light ˈwork of sth** to do sth quickly and with little effort

**ˌlight-ˈduty** *adj.* designed to carry or operate with normal or small loads: *small, light-duty trucks*

**ˌlight engiˈneering** *n.* [U] businesses that design and build machinery or equipment which is small or light; their activities

**ˌlight ˈindustry** *n.* [U,C] businesses that produce small or light goods, such as things used in the house, using small machines and factories ▸ **ˌlight inˈdustrial** *adj.*: *light industrial goods*

**ˌlightning ˈstrike** *n.* [C] (*BrE*) (*HR*) a strike by a group of workers that happens very suddenly

**ˈlight pen** *n.* [C] (*IT*) **1** a piece of equipment, shaped like a pen, that is sensitive to light and can be used to pass information to a computer when it touches the screen **2** a similar piece of equipment that is used for reading BAR CODES

**lightweight** /ˈlaɪtweɪt/ *adj.* **1** not heavy: *lightweight laptops* **2** not as powerful or successful as other people or things ▸ **ˈlightweight** *n.* [C]: *You're a lightweight.*

**ˌlike-for-ˈlike** *adj.* (*abbr* **LFL**) (*Account.*) used to describe figures that are adjusted to allow comparison with a similar period, excluding for example any new stores or businesses or any unusual activities: *Full-year like-for-like growth was 4.8%.* ▸ **ˌlike-for-ˈlike** *adv.*: *Sales fell 1.5% like-for-like.*

**ˌlike-for-ˈlikes** *n.* [pl.] (*Account., infml.*) figures that have been adjusted so that they can be compared with figures for a similar period, excluding for example any new stores or businesses or any unusual activities

**limit** /ˈlɪmɪt/ *n., v.*

• ***n.*** [C] the greatest or smallest amount of sth that is possible or allowed: *Some banks* **set** *a daily limit on cash withdrawals.* ◇ *to keep spending within limits*

• ***v.*** [T] **1** to stop sth from increasing beyond a particular amount or level: *The agreement limits the number of layoffs to 400.* **2 ~ yourself/sb (to sth)** to restrict or reduce the amount of sth that you/sb can have or use: *We are limited to two short breaks a day.* PHR V **ˈlimit sth to sb/sth** (*usu. pass.*) to make sth exist or happen only in a particular place or group: *The service will be limited to the US market.*

**limitation** /ˌlɪmɪˈteɪʃn/ *n.* [C] a rule, fact or condition that limits sth: *to impose limitations on imports* SYN CURB, RESTRAINT

**limiˌtation of liaˈbility** *n.* [U,C] (*Law*) the fact that sb's responsibility for sth such as damage, loss, etc., esp. their financial responsibility, is limited

**Limited** /ˈlɪmɪtɪd/ *adj.* used in the UK after the name of a LIMITED COMPANY: *LW Investments Limited* → LTD

**limited** /ˈlɪmɪtɪd/ *adj.* **1** restricted; only for a particular time, particular numbers, etc: *This offer is for a limited period only.* **2** not great in amount or extent; small: *a limited product range* ◇ *He has limited experience in this area.*

**ˌlimited ˈcompany** *n.* [C] in the UK, a company whose owners have responsibility for paying only a limited amount of the company's debt

**ˌlimited liaˈbility** *n.* [U] (*Law*) the legal position in which shareholders of a company are only responsible for the money they have given if the company cannot pay its debts

**ˌlimited ˈpartnership** *n.* [C] (*abbr* **LP**) a business owned by two or more people who are responsible only for the amount that they have invested in the business if it is unable to pay its debts

▸ **ˌlimited ˈpartner** *n.* [C]

**ˈlimit ˌorder** *n.* [C] (*Stock Ex.*) an order not to sell shares below a particular price, or not to buy shares above a particular price

**linchpin** (*also* **lynchpin**) /ˈlɪntʃpɪn/ *n.* [C, usu. sing.] the person or thing that an organization or a project depends on; the most important person or thing: *Consumers are the linchpin of the economy.*

★**line** /laɪn/ *n., v.*

• ***n.*** **1** [C] a type of product made or sold by the same company: *an exclusive line of children's clothing* SYN RANGE **2** [C] a system of making sth in a factory, in which the product moves from one worker to the next until it is finished: *A new car rolls off the line every 49 seconds.* **3** [C] a telephone connection; a particular telephone number: *Your bill includes line rental.* **4** [C, usu. sing.] a series of people in order of importance: *a line of command* ◇ *He is second* **in line** *to the CEO.* **5** [sing.] a type or area of business, activity or interest: *my line of work* **6** [C] (*AmE*) = QUEUE (1,2) **7** [C] a company that provides transport for people or goods: *a cruise line* **8** (*Finan.*) [C] a number or group of a particular share, bond, etc: *a line of 1.9 m shares* IDM **be, come, etc. on ˈline 1** to start to operate; to become available: *New power plants are coming on line.* **2** using or connected to a computer or the Internet; communicating with other people by computer: *All our offices are now on line.* **be in the line of ˈfire** to be in a position where people can criticize or blame you **bring sb/sth, come, get, fall, etc. into ˈline (with sb/sth)** to behave, or make sb/sth behave, in the same way as other people/things or with how they should behave: *to bring capacity into line with demand* **in ˈline** under control or at an appropriate or expected level: *getting expenses in line* **in ˈline (for sth)** likely to get sth: *She's in line for promotion.* **in ˈline with sth** similar to sth or so that one thing is closely connected with another: *Pay increases will be in line with inflation.* **(put sth) on the ˈline** (*infml.*) at risk: *The cutbacks have put jobs on the line.* → idioms at FIRING LINE, SIGN *v.*

• ***v.*** IDM **ˌline your (own)/sb's ˈpockets** to get richer or make sb richer, esp. by taking unfair advantage of a situation or by being dishonest PHR V **ˌline ˈup** to stand in a line or row; to form a QUEUE

**lineage** /ˈlaɪnɪdʒ/ *n.* [U] (*Market.*) the total amount of space used by an advertisement

**ˈline auˌthority** *n.* [U] (*HR*) the power that managers have to control and give orders to the people that they are responsible for, in order to achieve the things that their own managers expect

**'line chart** = LINE GRAPH

**'line exˌtension** *n.* [C,U] (*Market.*) a new product that is closely related to existing products and is sold using an existing brand name; the practice of marketing products in this way

**'line ˌfilling** *n.* [U] (*Market.*) the activity of adding new products to an existing range in order to make the range more complete

**'line graph** (*also* **'line chart**) *n.* [C] a type of graph which displays data by means of a series of points connected by a line

**'line ˌmanagement** *n.* (*BrE*) (*HR*) **1** [U] a system of organizing a company in which information and instructions are passed from each employee or manager to the person one rank above or below them **2** [U with sing./pl. v.] the managers in a company who are responsible for the main activities of the company, such as manufacturing, sales, etc.
▸ **'line manager** *n.* [C]

**line of 'credit** = CREDIT LINE

**line ˌstretching** (*also* **'product line ˌstretching**) *n.* [U] (*Market.*) the activity of adding new products to an existing range that are higher or lower in price, in order to attract a different group of customers

★**link** /lɪŋk/ *n., v.*
• *n.* [C] **1** a relationship between two or more people, countries or organizations: *to establish/maintain trade ~s **with** Asia* ◇ *strengthen links **between** the two companies* **2** a means of travelling or communicating between two places: *a high-speed rail link* ◇ *a video ~* **3** (*IT*) a place in an electronic document which connects one part of the document to another part or to a different one
• *v.* [T] (*often pass.*) **1 ~ A to/with B | ~ A and B (together)** to make a connection between people, places, or things: *The computers are linked in a network.* **2 ~ A to/with B** to say that there is a connection or relationship between two or more things or people: *He had been linked to the vacant post of CEO.* **3** (*Finan.*) if the value of an investment, a currency, or a payment **is linked** to something else, it changes in the same way that the other thing does: *The currency is linked to the US dollar.* **4** (*IT*) **~ A to/with B** to connect websites or parts of a web page so that a user can move to another website or part of a document by clicking PHR V **ˌlink 'up (with sb/sth)** to work with another person or organization to achieve sth

**'link-up** *n.* [C] a connection formed between two things, for example two companies or two broadcasting systems: *a live video link-up **with** the conference*

**the 'lion's share** *n.* [sing.] (*BrE*) the largest or best part of sth when it is divided: *They are grabbing the lion's share of the business.*

**liquid** /'lɪkwɪd/ *adj.* (*Account.*; *Finan.*) **1** (about assets) that can easily be sold and changed into cash **2** (about a company, an investor, etc.) having cash or assets that can easily be changed into cash: *one of the most liquid companies in the industry* **3** a **liquid** market is one in which there is a lot of buying and selling OPP ILLIQUID

★**liquidate** /'lɪkwɪdeɪt/ *v.* **1** (*Law*) [T,I] to sell a company's assets and pay its debts in order to close it: *The company has been ordered to liquidate.* SYN WIND UP **2** (*Account.*; *Finan.*) [T] to sell sth in order to get money or to avoid losing money: *to liquidate assets* SYN REALIZE **3** (*Account.*) [T] to pay a debt: *liquidating debts*

**ˌliquidated 'damages** *n.* [pl.] (*Law*) in a contract, a fixed amount of money that sb agrees to pay if they do not do what they have promised

★**liquidation** /ˌlɪkwɪ'deɪʃn/ *n.* [U] **1** (*Law*) the process of closing a company, selling its assets and paying its debts: *The firm has **gone into** liquidation.* SYN WINDING UP **2** (*Account.*; *Finan.*) the action of selling sth to get money or to avoid losing money: *liquidation of stocks*

**liquidator** /'lɪkwɪdeɪtə(r)/ *n.* [C] (*Law*) a person responsible for selling a company's assets and paying its debts, so that it can be closed: *to appoint/call in a ~*

**liquidity** /lɪ'kwɪdəti/ *n.* [U] (*Finan.*) **1** the state of owning cash or things of value that can easily be exchanged for cash in order to pay debts, etc: *Asset sales will improve the company's liquidity.* **2** the quality of being easy to exchange for cash: *the liquidity of an investment* **3** the amount of trading that takes place in a market

**li'quidity ˌpreference** *n.* [U] (*Econ.*) the way that people, esp. investors, prefer to have money or LIQUID assets

**li'quidity ˌratio** *n.* [C] (*Account.*) a way of measuring a company's ability to pay its debts by comparing the amount of money that it holds in cash or LIQUID assets and its LIABILITIES SYN CASH RATIO

**li'quidity risk** *n.* [C,U] (*Finan.*) the possibility that a person or company will not be able to pay the money they owe because they do not have enough cash or LIQUID assets

**'liquid ˌratio** = ACID-TEST RATIO

**list** /lɪst/ *n., v.*
• ***n.*** [C] a series of names, items, figures, etc., esp. when they are written or printed: *We'll send you a list of current prices.* ◇ *to compile/draw up/make a ~*
• ***v.* 1** [T] to provide a list of things in a particular order: *The directory lists more than 900 000 lawyers and law firms.* **2** (*Stock Ex.*) [T,I] to make shares in a company available for trading on a stock exchange: *The company has applied to list its shares on the NYSE.* **3** [T,I] (*AmE*) to advertise sth for sale at a particular price; to be advertised for sale at a particular price: *The new model lists for $28 105.*

**'list box** *n.* [C] (*IT*) a list of choices in a box on a computer screen

**listed** /'lɪstɪd/ *adj.* (*Stock Ex.*) **1** a listed company is one whose shares may be bought and sold on a stock exchange: *a London-listed bank* ◇ *a ~ business/company* **2** that may be bought and sold on a stock exchange: *~ securities/shares/stocks* SYN QUOTED

**listener** /'lɪsənə(r)/ *n.* [C] someone who listens to a particular radio programme or station

**listing** /'lɪstɪŋ/ *n.* [C] **1** (*Stock Ex.*) a place on the official list of companies whose shares can be bought and sold on a stock exchange: *a stock exchange listing* **2** a list, esp. an official or published list of people or things, often arranged in alphabetical order: *a listing of all airlines*

**listless** /'lɪstləs/ *adj.* developing or happening more slowly than usual: *listless retail sales*

**'list price** (*AmE also* **'sticker price**) *n.* [C] (*Comm.*) the advertised or published price for sth, esp. a car

**'list ˌrental** *n.* [U] (*Market.*) an arrangement in which the owner of a list of the names and addresses of possible customers allows it to be used on a temporary basis by another organization in exchange for a fee ▸ **'list ˌrenting** *n.* [U]

**lite** /laɪt/ *adj.* (often used in the names of food or drink) light; containing less fat or sugar than other similar food or drink

**literature** /'lɪtrətʃə(r); *AmE also* -tʃʊr/ *n.* [U] pieces of writing or printed information on a product, company, etc: *promotional/sales ~*

★ **litigate** /'lɪtɪgeɪt/ *v.* [T,I] (*Law*) to take a claim or disagreement to court ▸ **'litigant** /-gənt/ *n.* [C]: *large payouts to litigants* **ˌliti'gation** /-'geɪʃn/ *n.* [U]: *be in litigation over sth* **'litigator** *n.* [C] (*AmE*): *They called in a top litigator.*

**litigious** /lɪ'tɪdʒəs/ *adj.* (*fml.*) too ready to take disputes to a court of law ▸ **li'tigiousness** *n.* [U]

**livelihood** /'laɪvlihʊd/ *n.* [U; C, usu. sing.] a means of earning money in order to live

**livery** /'lɪvəri/ *n.* [C,U] (*pl.* **-ries**) (*BrE*) (*Market.*) the colours used by a particular company for its vehicles or products: *aircraft painted in the new BA livery*

**living** /'lɪvɪŋ/ *n.* **1** [C, usu. sing.] money to buy the things that you need in life: *What do you* ***do for a living?***
⊕ *to earn/make a ~* ♦ ***a good/decent/modest ~***
**2** [U] a way or style of life
⊕ ***daily/day-to-day/everyday ~***
♦ ***~ conditions/standards***

**ˌliving 'trust** *n.* [C] (*Law*) an arrangement which allows sb to transfer their assets to sb else while they are alive but keep control of them, used in order to avoid the legal process of dealing with a WILL when they die

**ˌliving 'wage** *n.* [sing.] a wage that is high enough for sb to buy the things they need in order to live

**LLC** /ˌel el 'si:/ *abbr* (*AmE*) (*usu. written*) limited liability company (used after the name of a company or business)

**Lloyd's** /lɔɪdz/ (*also* **ˌLloyd's of 'London**) *n.* [U] (*Insur.*) an organization consisting of groups of insurance UNDERWRITERS, providing insurance esp. for ships and large risks

**ˌLloyd's 'Register** (*also* **'Lloyd's 'Register of 'Shipping**) *n.* [sing.] (*abbr* **LR**) (*Transpt.*) a list of ships arranged in groups according to their size, with detailed information about them, published once a year; the organization that produces the list and sets the standards for the groups

**LME** /ˌel em 'i:/ *abbr* **London Metal Exchange** a market for trading metals that are bought at agreed prices but delivered and paid for at a later time

**load** /ləʊd; *AmE* loʊd/ *n.*, *v.*
• *n.* [C] **1** something that is being carried, esp. in large amounts: *heavy/large ~s ◇ to carry/deliver/pick up/transport a ~* **2** (*often with another noun*) the total amount of sth that sth can carry or contain: *a busload of tourists* **3** an amount of work that a person or machine has to do: *to lighten/reduce/share/spread the ~* **4** the fact of having to pay an amount of money, esp. a large amount; the amount of money that you owe: *a debt/tax ~* SYN BURDEN **5** (*Finan.*) a fee that is charged when an investor buys or sells shares in an investment fund, an insurance policy, etc: *The fund carries a 5.75% load.*
• *v.* **1** [T,I] **~ sth (into/onto sth)** to put goods into or onto sth: *He's finished loading.* OPP UNLOAD **2** [I] to receive a load: *The tankers were still loading.* OPP UNLOAD **3** [T,I] **~ (sth) (up)** to put data or a program into the memory of a computer
PHR V **ˌload (sth) ˈup (with sth)** to put a large amount of goods onto a vehicle **ˌload ˈup on sth** to get or buy a large amount of sth: *investors loading upon stocks*

**loader** /ˈləʊdə(r); *AmE* ˈloʊdər/ *n.* [C] **1** a person who puts goods into or onto sth: *dock loaders* **2** a lorry/truck of the type mentioned: *a seven tonne loader*

**ˈload ˌfactor** *n.* [C] (*Tech.; Transpt.*) the relationship between the actual amount of sth and the total possible amount: *the cargo/passenger load factor*

**ˈload fund** *n.* [C] (*Finan.*) a type of fund, esp. a UNIT TRUST, that charges a fee when investors buy or sell

**loading** /ˈləʊdɪŋ; *AmE* ˈloʊd-/ *n.* [C,U] **1** an extra amount added to the basic cost of sth such as insurance: *a 2% loading for using the card abroad* **2** (*HR*) esp. in Australia and New Zealand, extra money that sb is paid for their job because they have special skills or qualifications

**ˈload line** (*also* **ˈPlimsoll line, ˈPlimsoll mark**) *n.* [C] (*Transpt.*) a line on the side of a ship showing the highest point that the water can safely reach when the ship is loaded

**loan** /ləʊn; *AmE* loʊn/ *n.*, *v.*
• *n.* [C] money that an organization such as a bank lends and sb borrows: *Many people take out a loan to buy a car.* ◇ *The loans should be repaid within ten years.* → SERVICE *v.* (1,2)
✪ ***a high-interest/an interest-free/a low-interest ~ • a long-term/short-term ~ • corporate/personal ~s • to apply for/arrange a ~ • to give sb/make sb a ~ • to pay back/pay off a ~ • a ~ agreement/facility/repayment***
• *v.* [T] (*esp. AmE*) **~ sth (to sb)** | **~ (sb) sth** to lend sth to sb, esp. money: *The bank loaned the business $200 000.* SYN LEND

**ˈloan ˌcapital** *n.* [U] (*Finan.*) money used to start and run a business that comes from borrowing rather than selling shares SYN DEBT CAPITAL

**ˈloan loss** *n.* [C,U] (*Account.*) money that is lost by a bank because a borrower does not pay back a loan

**ˈloan note** *n.* [C] (*Finan.*) a written agreement to pay a sum of money that you owe

**ˈloan ˌservicing** *n.* [U] (*Finan.*) the process of collecting and managing the regular payments made to pay back a loan

**ˈloan shark** *n.* [C] (*infml.*) a person who lends money at very high rates of interest

**ˈloan stock** *n.* [C,U] (*Finan.*) investments in the form of loans to a company for a fixed period of time that receive a fixed rate of interest

**local** /ˈləʊkl; *AmE* ˈloʊkl/ *adj.*, *n.*
• *adj.* belonging to or connected with the particular place or area that you are talking about or with the place where you live: *Foreign oil companies began to compete in the local market.* ◇ *free local calls* (= phone calls to a place that is near)
▸ **ˈlocally** /-kəli/ *adv.*
• *n.* [C] **1** (*AmE*) a local branch of an organization, esp. a trade union **2** (*AmE*) a bus or train that stops at all the places on the route **3** (*Stock Ex., infml.*) a trader at a stock exchange who buys and sells shares, etc. for themselves rather than for other investors

**ˌlocal ˈcontent** *n.* [U] (*Manufact.*) the part of a manufactured product that is made or supplied within a particular country or area

**localize, -ise** /ˈləʊkəlaɪz; *AmE* ˈloʊ-/ *v.* [T] **1** (*Market.*) to adapt a product or service to make it more suitable for a particular region or country **2** if a company **localizes** its activities, they happen in particular areas rather than in a central area

**locate** /ləʊˈkeɪt; *AmE* ˈloʊkeɪt/ *v.* **1** [T] to put or build sth in a particular place: *They located their HQ in Brus-*

sels. **2** [I] (*esp. AmE*) (*used with an adv. or a prep.*) to start a business in a particular place: *businesses locating in rural areas* ▸ **lo'cated** *adj.*: *Our clients are located in several states.*

**location** /ləʊ'keɪʃn; *AmE* loʊ-/ *n.* **1** [C] a place where sth happens or exists; the position of sth: *Coffee shops need to be in high street locations.* **2** [U] the act of finding a place for sth or of placing sth somewhere: *Location of a suitable site may take some time.*

**lock** /lɒk; *AmE* lɑːk/ *v., n.*
• *v.* [T] **be locked in/into sth** to be involved in a discussion or an argument that continues for a long time: *They are locked in a legal dispute.* IDM **lock 'horns (with sb) (over sth)** to get involved in an argument or a dispute with sb PHR V ˌ**lock sth a'way** (*also* ˌ**lock sth 'up**) to put money into an investment that you cannot easily turn into cash: *locking up money in a long-term annuity* ˌ**lock 'into sth** (*Finan.*) to agree to pay or receive a fixed rate of interest for a fixed period of time: *We were able to lock into a good interest rate.* ˌ**lock sb/sth/yourself 'into sth** to involve sb, sth or yourself in a situation that cannot easily be changed: *to lock yourself into a lease agreement* ˌ**lock sb 'out (of sth)** **1** (*HR*) (about an employer) to refuse to allow workers into their place of work until they agree to particular conditions **2** to stop sb from doing a particular activity or becoming involved in sth: *those now locked out of the job market* ˌ**lock sth 'up** = LOCK STH AWAY
• *n.* IDM **get/have a 'lock on sth** (*esp. AmE*) to get or have complete control, possession or use of sth: *These dealers had a lock on a small section of the market.*

**lockbox** /'lɒkbɒks; *AmE* 'lɑːkbɑːks/ *n.* [C] (*AmE*) **1** a strong box with a lock that is used for keeping mail or valuable items safe **2** (*also* **'lockbox** ˌ**service**) a bank or other business that receives a fee for dealing with payments sent to a company by mail

**lockout** /'lɒkaʊt; *AmE* 'lɑːk-/ *n.* [C] (*HR*) a situation when an employer refuses to allow workers into their place of work until they agree to various conditions

**'lock-up** *n.* [C] **1** (*Finan.*) an agreement not to sell or exchange shares for a particular period of time: *The shares will be subject to a lock-up for 180 days.* **2** (*BrE*) a small shop/store that the owner does not live in; a small building for cars (a **garage**) that is usu. separate from other buildings and is rented to sb ▸ **'lock-up** *adj.*: *a ~ agreement* ◇ *a ~ garage*

**lodge** /lɒdʒ; *AmE* lɑːdʒ/ *v.* [T] **1 ~ sth (with sb) (against sb/sth)** to make a formal statement about sth to a public organization or authority: *to ~ an appeal/a complaint* SYN FILE **2** (*Law*) (*BrE*) to present sth so that it can be officially recorded and dealt with: *Copies of the audited results were lodged with the stock exchange.* SYN FILE **3 ~ sth with sb/in sth** to leave money or sth valuable in a safe place ▸ **'lodgement** *n.* [U]

**log** /lɒg; *AmE* lɔːg; lɑːg/ *v., n.*
• *v.* [T] (**-gg-**) **1** to put information in an official record or write a record of events: *All incoming calls are logged.* SYN RECORD **2** to do or get a large amount of sth: *They logged about $60 m in sales last year.* PHR V ˌ**log 'in/'on**; ˌ**log 'into/'onto sth** to perform the actions that allow you to begin using a computer system ˌ**log 'off/'out (of sth)** to perform the actions that allow you to finish using a computer system
• *n.* [C] **1** (*also* **'logbook**) a record of events during a particular period of time **2** (*HR*) in Australia, a set of demands for better pay or conditions, esp. claims made by a trade union to an INDUSTRIAL TRIBUNAL

**logbook** /'lɒgbʊk; *AmE* 'lɔːg-; 'lɑːg-/ *n.* [C] **1** = LOG *n.* (1) **2** (*Transpt.*) (*BrE*) a document that records official details about a vehicle, esp. a car, and its owner

**'log file** *n.* [C] (*IT*) a computer file that keeps a record of tasks performed by a computer

**logic** /'lɒdʒɪk; *AmE* 'lɑːdʒɪk/ *n.* **1** [U; sing.] sensible reasons for doing sth: *sound commercial logic* **2** (*IT*) [U] a system or set of principles used in preparing a computer to perform a particular task

**logistics** /lə'dʒɪstɪks/ *n.* [U with sing./pl. v.] **1** (*Product.*) the work of planning and organizing the supply of materials, goods and staff: *logistics and distribution* ◇ *A logistics firm organizes deliveries.* **2 ~ of sth** the practical organization that is needed to make a complicated plan successful: *the logistics of opening a new store* ▸ **lo'gistic** (*also* **lo'gistical** /-ɪkl/) *adj.*

**logjam** /'lɒgdʒæm; *AmE* 'lɔːg-; 'lɑːg-/ *n.* **1** [C, usu. sing.] a complete failure to make progress, reach agreement or settle sth **2** [C] a large amount of work that has not been done because there are too many things to do

★ **logo** /ˈləʊgəʊ; *AmE* ˈloʊgoʊ/ *n.* [C] (*pl.* **logos**) a printed design or symbol that a company or an organization uses as its special sign

**ˈLondon ˈInter-Bank ˈOffered Rate** *n.* [sing.] (*abbr* **LIBOR**) the rate of interest at which London banks lend money to each other

**long** /lɒŋ; *AmE* lɔːŋ/ *adj.* (*Finan.; Stock Ex.*) if somebody is **long on/in** shares, currencies, etc., they have bought them, intending to sell them later at a profit when their value rises OPP SHORT ▸ **long** *adv.*: *to go long on particular shares*
IDM **work/have long ˈhours/ˈdays** to work more hours in the day than usual → idiom at LONG RUN

**ˈlong bond** *n.* [C] (*Finan.*) **1** an investment in the form of an agreement to lend a sum of money for ten years or more to a company or government who will pay it back with interest **2** a thirty-year bond issued by the US Treasury

**ˌlong-ˈdated** *adj.* (*Finan.*) used to describe investments that will be paid back after a long period of time

**ˈlong-haul** *adj.* that involves transporting people or goods over long distances

**ˈlong poˌsition** *n.* [C] (*Finan.; Stock Ex.*) a situation in which a dealer or an investor has bought shares, currencies, etc. and holds them intending to sell them later at a profit as they expect their value to rise: *Speculative traders held long positions in the currency.* SYN BULL POSITION

**ˌlong-ˈrange** *adj.* made for a period of time that will last a long way into the future: *long-range planning*

**ˌlong ˈrun** (*also* **ˌlong ˈterm**) *n.* [sing.] (*Econ.*) a period of time long enough for a business or an industry to change everything that can be changed IDM **in/over the ˈlong run**; **in the ˈlong term** over a long period in the future: *Shares are a good investment in the long run.*

**ˈlong-run** = LONG-TERM *adj.* (1)

**longs** /lɒŋz; *AmE* lɔːŋz/ *n.* [pl.] (*Finan.*) **1** investments such as government bonds that will be paid back after a long period of time, for example 15 years **2** shares, bonds, currency, etc. that a dealer or an investor holds and is intending to sell later at a profit when the value rises

**ˌlong-ˈserving** *adj.* having had the same job or position or worked for the same employer for a long time: *long-serving members of staff*

**longshoreman** /ˈlɒŋʃɔːmən; *AmE* ˈlɔːŋʃɔːrmən/ (*pl.* **-men** /-mən/) = STEVEDORE

**ˌlong ˈterm** = LONG RUN *n.*

**ˈlong-term** *adj.* **1** (*also* **ˈlong-run**) that will continue or have an effect for a long period of time: *long-term unemployment* **2** (*Account.*) relating to a period of one year or longer: *long-term financing* **3** (*Finan.*) (about money) that is borrowed, lent or invested for a long period of time, usu. more than five years

**ˌlong-term liaˈbilities** *n.* [pl.] (*Account.*) debts that do not need to be paid until after a particular period of time, usu. 12 months SYN NON-CURRENT LIABILITIES

**ˌlong ˈton** *n.* [C] (*esp. BrE*) (*abbr* **lt.**) a unit for measuring weight, equal to 2 240 pounds or 1016.05 kilograms

**look** /lʊk/ *v.* IDM **be just ˈlooking** (*BrE*) used in a shop/store to say that you are not ready to buy sth: *'Can I help you?' 'I'm just looking, thank you.'* **be looking to do sth** (often used in newspapers) to be trying to find ways of doing sth; to be planning to do sth: *The firm is looking to sell its car insurance unit.* **look ˈgood** to show success or that sth good might happen: *This year's sales figures are looking good.*
PHR V **ˌlook ˈafter sth/sb** to be responsible for sth/sb: *She looks after export sales.* **ˌlook ˈinto sth** to examine sth **ˌlook ˈup** (*infml.*) to improve: *The economy is starting to look up.*

**loom** /luːm/ *v.* [I] to appear important or threatening and likely to happen soon: *There was a staffing crisis looming.*

**loop** /luːp/ *n.* [C] (*IT*) a set of instructions that is repeated again and again until a particular set of conditions is satisfied IDM **be in the ˈloop** (*infml.*) be part of a group of people who know what is happening and are dealing with important matters **be out of the ˈloop** (*infml.*) not be informed about important matters and so unable to help make decisions about them

**loophole** /ˈluːphəʊl; *AmE* -hoʊl/ *n.* [C] a small mistake in the way a law or contract has been written that allows people to legally avoid sth that the law or contract intended them to do: *to close/plug a legal/tax* ~

**ˌlo-ˈres** = LOW-RESOLUTION

**lorry** /ˈlɒri; *AmE* ˈlɔːri/ *n.* [C] (*pl.* **lorries**) (*BrE*) a large motor vehicle for carrying heavy loads by road
SYN TRUCK

**lose** /luːz/ *v.* (**lost**, **lost** /lɒst; *AmE* lɑːst; lɔːst/) **1** [T,I] **~ (sth) (on sth)** | **~ sb sth** to fail to keep money; to cause sb to fail to keep money: *The business is losing money.* ◇ *We lost* **on** *that deal.* **2** [T] **~ sth (to sb)** | **~ sb sth** to have sth taken away by sb; to fail to keep sth: *You may lose your deposit if you cancel.* **3** [T] (about a currency, share price, etc.) to fall to a lower level or price: *The FTSE 100 lost a quarter of its value last year.* OPP GAIN IDM **lose 'face** to be less respected or look stupid because of sth you have done **lose 'ground** to fall in value: *Tokyo shares lost ground on Wednesday.* **lose your 'shirt** (*infml.*) to lose everything you have
PHR V **ˌlose 'out (on sth)** to not get sth that you expected or wanted: *We lost out on an important contract.* **ˌlose 'out to sb/sth** to not get sth that you expected to get or used to get, because someone else has taken it: *They lost out to a rival group in the bidding war.*

**loser** /ˈluːzə(r)/ *n.* [C] **1** (*Stock Ex.*) (used esp. in newspapers) a company whose shares lose value in trading on a stock exchange: *the day's biggest loser* OPP GAINER **2** a person or company that loses or suffers in a particular situation: *The real losers are the taxpayers.* OPP WINNER

★**loss** /lɒs; *AmE* lɔːs/ *n.* **1** [C] money lost by a business or an organization: *The company has announced losses of $324 m.* ◇ *We are now operating* **at a** *loss.* OPP PROFIT
○ *to* ***make/post/record/report*** *a ~* • *to* ***face/suffer*** *a ~* • ***heavy/pre-tax/substantial*** *losses*
**2** [C,U] the state of no longer having sth or as much of sth; the process that leads to this: *the loss of 2 000 jobs* **3** [U] property that has been damaged or stolen and that an insurance company will pay you money to replace IDM **loss of 'face** a situation when sb is less respected or looks stupid because of sth they have done

**'loss aˌdjuster** (*also* **a'djuster**) *n.* [C] (*Insur.*) an independent person or company that decides whether insurance claims are valid and how much should be paid
SYN INSURANCE ADJUSTER (*AmE*), CLAIMS ADJUSTER (*AmE*)

**'loss asˌsessor** (*also* **'claims asˌsessor**) *n.* [C] (*both BrE*) (*Insur.*) a person who helps sb who has an insurance policy to make a claim
SYN ASSESSOR

**'loss-ˌleader** *n.* [C] (*Market.*) a product or service that is sold at a very low price in order to attract customers, who will then buy goods or services that produce more profit

**'loss-ˌmaking** (*also* **lossmaking**) *adj.* **1** a **loss-making** company, business, or part of a business does not make a profit **2** a **loss-making** period of time is a period in which a company does not make a profit
▸ **'loss-ˌmaker** *n.* [C]

**ˌloss of 'earnings** *n.* [U] a situation in which a person or company does not earn money that they expected to earn, as a result of illness, an accident, sb's actions, etc.

**ˌlost 'time** *n.* [U] working time that is lost, for example because workers are injured or because machines are broken

**lot** /lɒt; *AmE* lɑːt/ *n.* [C] **1** (*Comm.*) an item or a group of items that is sold at an AUCTION **2** (*Product.*) a quantity of goods that are produced or sold together: *The products bear the lot number L32891.* **3** an area of land used for a particular purpose: *a parking lot*

**low** /ləʊ; *AmE* loʊ/ *adj.*, *adv.*, *n.*
• ***adj.*** (**-er**, **-est**) **1** below the usual or average amount, level or value: *The brand offers high value at low prices.* ◇ *Inflation is at its lowest level for ten years.* **2** having a reduced amount or not enough of sth: *Many supermarkets are now low* **on** *staples such as bread.* **3** below the usual or expected standard: *goods of low quality* **4** below other people or things in importance or status: *Training was given a very low priority.* → HIGH
• ***adv.*** (**-er**, **-est**) at a level below what is usual or expected: *a low-powered PC*
• ***n.*** [C] a low level, point or figure: *The pound fell to a new low against the euro.* OPP HIGH

**lowball** /ˈləʊbɔːl; *AmE* ˈloʊ-/ *v.* [T] (*AmE*) (*infml.*) to deliberately make an estimate of the cost, value, etc. of sth that is too low: *He lowballed the cost of the project in order to obtain federal funding.* ▸ **lowball** *n.* [C] (*usu. used as an adj.*): *a lowball bid*

**ˌlow-'cost** (*also* **ˌlower-'cost**) *adj.* costing or charging less than others: *Europe's largest low-cost airline*

**ˌlow-cost 'leader** = COST LEADER

**'low-end** *adj.* low-end goods are among the cheapest available
▸ **'low-end** *n.* [sing.]

**lower** /ˈləʊə(r); *AmE* ˈloʊ-/ *v.* [T,I] to reduce sth, or to become less in value, quality, etc: *The Fed lowered interest rates again yesterday.* SYN CUT OPP RAISE

**ˌlower-ˈcost** = LOW-COST

**ˌlower-ˈincome** = LOW-INCOME (1)

**ˌlower-than-exˈpected** *adj.* **lower-than-expected** sales, profits, results etc. are smaller than had been predicted previously → BETTER-THAN-EXPECTED

**ˌlow-ˈfare** (*also* **ˌlow-ˈfares**, *less freq.*) *adj.* (about an airline) that sells very cheap tickets

**ˌlow-ˈgrade** *adj.* **1** of poor quality or status: *people in low-grade jobs* **2** (*Finan.*) **low-grade** investments carry a high risk of failing

**ˌlow-hanging ˈfruit** *n.* [U] a term used by some managers to refer to easy ways of increasing profits, cutting costs, etc: *A lot of the low-hanging fruit has been picked.*

**ˌlow-ˈimpact** *adj.* not having a strong influence or making many changes

**ˌlow-ˈincome** *adj.* **1** (*also* **ˌlower-ˈincome**) not having or earning much money: *financial services for lower-income customers* **2** earning a low level of interest

**ˌlow-inˈvolvement ˌproduct** *n.* [C] (*Market.*) a product that customers buy often and do not spend a lot of time and effort looking for and buying

**ˌlow-ˈlevel** *adj.* **1** involving people at a junior level: *a low-level job* **2** (*IT*) (about a computer language) similar to MACHINE CODE

**ˌlow-ˈmargin** *adj.* (*Account.*; *Market.*) **low-margin** products cost almost as much to produce as they can be sold for

**ˌlow-ˈpaid** *adj.* **1** earning very little money; providing very little money: *part-time or lower-paid jobs* **2 the low-paid** *n.* [pl.] people who are low-paid

**ˈlow-ˌpressure** *adj.* **1** (*Market.*) that involves encouraging people to do or to buy sth rather than using aggressive methods to persuade them: *low-pressure selling* **2** that involves little worry and anxiety

**ˌlow-ˈpriced** (*also* **ˌlow-ˈprice**) *adj.* not expensive; cheap: *~ brands/goods/fashion*

**ˌlow-ˈprofile** *adj.* receiving or involving very little attention in the media; not very well-known: *a low-profile company*

**ˌlow-ˈranking** *adj.* junior; not very important

**ˌlow-resoˈlution** (*also* **lo-res**, **low-res** /ˌləʊ ˈrez; *AmE* ˌloʊ/) *adj.* not showing a lot of clear detail: *a low-resolution scan*

**ˈlow road** *n.* [sing.] (*HR*) a method of trying to gain an advantage in business which involves paying workers low wages, giving them poor working conditions and producing goods of low value: *a low-road company*

**ˌlow ˈseason** *n.* [U; sing.] (*esp. BrE*) the time of year when a hotel or tourist area receives fewest visitors SYN OFF SEASON OPP HIGH SEASON ▸ **ˌlow-ˈseason** *adj.*: *low-season prices*

**ˌlow-ˈtech** *adj.* not involving the most modern technology or methods

**ˌlow ˈvolume** *n.* [C,U] a small quantity of sth: *low-volume trading*

**ˌlow-ˈyield** (*also* **ˌlow-ˈyielding**) *adj.* (*Finan.*) used to describe investments that do not produce a high income but also have a low level of risk

**loyal** /ˈlɔɪəl/ *adj.* **1** a **loyal** customer tends to buy the same products all the time, rather than trying different ones **2** a **loyal** employee works for the same company for a long time

**loyalty** /ˈlɔɪəlti/ *n.* [U] the quality of being faithful to a particular product, company, etc.

**ˈloyalty card** *n.* [C] (*Market.*) a card given to customers by a shop/store to encourage them to shop there regularly. Each time they buy sth they collect points which will allow them to have an amount of money taken off goods they buy in the future.

**LP** /ˌel ˈpiː/ = LIMITED PARTNERSHIP

**LR** /ˌel ˈɑː(r)/ = LLOYD'S REGISTER

**LSE** /ˌel es ˈiː/ *n.* [sing.] **London Stock Exchange plc** a market for buying and selling company shares, bonds, etc.

**lt.** = LONG TON

**Ltd** (*AmE* **Ltd.**) *abbr* (*written*) **limited**, used after the names of particular types of companies in some countries: *Oxford Cameras Ltd*

**LTV** /ˌel tiː ˈviː/ = LIFETIME VALUE

**lucrative** /ˈluːkrətɪv/ *adj.* producing a large amount of money; making a large profit: *The deal proved highly lucrative for the company.* ◐ *a ~ business/contract/market* ◆ *extremely/highly ~* ▸ **ˈlucratively** *adv.*

**Luddite** /ˈlʌdaɪt/ *n.* [C] (*BrE*) a word used in a disapproving way to describe sb who is opposed to new technology or working methods

**lull** /lʌl/ *n.* [C, usu. sing.] a quiet period between times of activity

**lumber** /ˈlʌmbə(r)/ = TIMBER (2)

**lump** /lʌmp/ *n.* [C] (*infml.*) = LUMP SUM IDM **take your ˈlumps** (*AmE*) (*infml.*) to accept bad things that happen to you without complaining

**ˌlump ˈsum** (*also* **ˌlump sum ˈpayment**) (*also* **lump**, *infml.*) *n.* [C] a single payment of money: *You can take up to 25% of your pension as a tax-free lump sum.*

**ˈlunch hour** *n.* [C] the time around the middle of the day when you stop work to eat lunch

**lure** /lʊə(r); ljʊə(r); *AmE* lʊr/ *v.*, *n.*
• ***v.*** [T] (*usu. used with an adv. or a prep.*) to persuade sb to go somewhere or do sth by promising them a reward or making it seem exciting: *lowering prices to lure customers into the stores*
• ***n.*** [C, usu. sing.] the attractive qualities of sth: *the lure of cheap credit*

**luxury** /ˈlʌkʃəri/ *adj.* expensive and of high quality; not essential: *~ goods/hotels* SYN PRESTIGE

**lynchpin** = LINCHPIN

# Mm

**M** /em/ *abbr* (esp. for sizes of clothes) medium

**m** (*also* **m.**) *abbr* **1** million(s): *€16 m* **2** male: *m or f* **3** married

**M0, M1, etc.** /ˌem ˈzɪərəʊ, ˌem ˈwʌn; *AmE* ˈzɪroʊ; ˈziː-/ *n.* [U] (*Econ.*) different ways of measuring the amount of money being used or that is available in an economy → MONEY SUPPLY

**M & A** /ˌem ənd ˈeɪ/ *abbr* a short way of writing **mergers and acquisitions**

★**machine** /məˈʃiːn/ *n.*, *v.*
• ***n.*** [C] **1** (*often used in compounds*) a piece of equipment with moving parts that is designed to do a particular job and uses electricity, gas, wind power, etc. in order to operate: *The stone is cut **by** machine.* ◇ *a machine operator*
○ *to **install/service** a ~* • *to **operate/run/use** a ~* • *a ~ **breaks down/runs/works***
**2** a particular machine, when you do not refer to it by its full name, esp. a computer: *desktop machines* **3** [usu. sing.] a group of people that control an organization or part of an organization: *the company's marketing machine*
• ***v.*** [T] (*Manufact.*) to make or shape sth with a machine: *This material can be cut and machined easily.*
▸ **maˈchining** *n.* [U]

**maˈchine code** (*also* **maˈchine ˌlanguage**) *n.* [U] (*IT*) the basic language that is used to write instructions that can be read directly by a computer, consisting only of numbers

**maˌchine-ˈmade** *adj.* made by a machine

**maˌchine-ˈreadable** *adj.* (*IT*) (about data) in a form that a computer can understand

★**machinery** /məˈʃiːnəri/ *n.* [U] machines as a group, esp. large ones: *investing in new machinery and equipment* ◇ *a piece of machinery*
○ ***agricultural/electrical/heavy/industrial** ~* • *to **install/maintain/service/set up** ~* • *to **control/operate/use** ~* • *a ~ **maker/manufacturer***

**maˈchine shop** *n.* [C] (*Manufact.*) a room or building in which there are machines for making things, esp. out of metal

**maˈchine tool** *n.* [C] (*Manufact.*) a tool for cutting or shaping metal, wood, etc., driven by a machine

**machinist** /məˈʃiːnɪst/ *n.* [C] (*Manufact.*) **1** a person whose job is operating a machine, esp. machines used for cutting and shaping things, or a sewing machine **2** a person whose job is to make or repair machines

**macro** /ˈmækrəʊ; *AmE* ˈmækroʊ/ *n.* [C] (*pl.* **macros**) (*IT*) a single instruction in a computer program that automatically causes a complete series of instructions to be put into effect, in order to perform a particular task

**macro-** /ˈmækrəʊ; *AmE* ˈmækroʊ/ *comb. form* (*used to form ns, adjs. and advs*) large; on a large scale OPP MICRO-

**macroeconomics** /ˌmækrəʊˌiːkəˈnɒmɪks; *AmE* -kroʊˌekəˈnɑːm-/ *n.* (*Econ.*) **1** [U] the study of large economic systems, such as those of whole countries or areas of the world **2** [pl.; U] the features or state of such a system
▸ **ˌmacroˌecoˈnomic** *adj.*
**ˌmacroeˈconomist** /-ɪˈkɒnəmɪst; *AmE* -ɪˈkɑːn-/ *n.* [C]

**macromarketing** /ˌmækrəʊˈmɑːkɪtɪŋ; *AmE* ˌmækroʊˈmɑːrk-/ *n.* [U] (*Market.*) the study of the system of producing and selling goods and services in a country or an economy, including the effects of cultural, political, social and economic conditions

**madam** /ˈmædəm/ *n.* [sing.] (*fml.*) used when speaking or writing to a woman in a formal or business situation: *Dear Madam* (= in a letter)

**made** /meɪd/ *adj., comb. form*
• ***adj.*** past tense, past participle of MAKE: *made in China*
• ***comb. form* -made** (*used in adjs*) made in the way, place, etc. mentioned: *well-made* ◇ *British-made steel*

**ˌmade to ˈmeasure** *adj.* **1** (esp. about clothes) made specially to fit a particular person, place, etc. **2** made to solve a particular problem: *a made-to-measure solution for your IT needs*

**ˌmade to ˈorder** *adj.* made or produced specially for a particular customer, in the way they want

**ˌMadison ˈAvenue** /ˈmædɪsən -/ *n.* [U] used to refer to the US advertising industry

**mag** /mæg/ *n.* [C] (*infml.*) a magazine: *teen mags*

**magalog** /ˈmægəlɒg; *AmE* -lɔːg; -lɑːg/ *n.* [C] (*Market.*) a CATALOGUE that looks like a magazine and has articles to read in it

**magazine** /ˌmægəˈziːn; *AmE* ˈmægəziːn/ *n.* [C] a type of large thin book with a paper cover that you can buy every week or month, containing articles, photographs, etc., often on a particular topic: *a women's/men's ~* ◇ *glossy fashion magazines*
⊙ *a copy/ an* ***issue*** *of a ~* ♦ *to* ***produce/publish/run*** *a ~* ♦ *to* ***buy/get/subscribe to*** *a ~*

**ˌmagic ˈbullet** *n.* [C, usu. sing.] (used esp. in newspapers) a fast, effective solution to a serious problem

**ˌmagic ˈcircle** *n.* [C, usu. sing.] (*BrE*) a small group of people or organizations that have a lot of influence and work together to help each other, but are not willing for other people to join them

**magistrate** /ˈmædʒɪstreɪt/ *n.* [C] an official who acts as a judge, usu. in the lowest courts of law

**magnate** /ˈmægneɪt/ *n.* [C] a person who is rich, powerful and successful in business

**magˌnetic ˈcard** *n.* [C] a plastic card with a line of black material containing information on it

**magˌnetic ˈdisk** = DISK (2)

**magˌnetic ˈmedia** *n.* [pl.; U] (*IT*) the different methods that are used to store information for computers, for example disks, etc.

**magˌnetic ˈstrip** (*also* **magˌnetic ˈstripe**) *n.* [C] a line of black material on a plastic card, containing information

★**mail** /meɪl/ *n., v.*
• ***n.*** [U] **1** the official system used for sending and delivering letters, packages, etc: *The cheque is* ***in the mail.*** ◇ *a mail distribution centre* SYN POST (*BrE*) **2** letters, packages, etc. that are sent and delivered: *We received the cheque* ***in the mail*** *today.* ◇ *an item/a piece of ~* ◇ ***bulk mail*** (= letters, etc. sent in large numbers by businesses) SYN POST (*BrE*) **3** messages that are sent or received on a computer: *Check regularly for new mail.*
• ***v.*** [T] **1 ~ sth (to sb/sth) | ~ (sb) sth** to send sth to sb by post/mail: *We'll mail you a brochure.* SYN POST **2** to put a letter, etc. into a public box to be sent: *Could you mail this letter for me?* SYN POST **2 ~ sb | ~ sth (to sb/sth) | ~ (sb) sth** to send a message to sb by email: *Mail your order to ...* PHR V **ˌmail sth ˈout** to send out a large number of letters, etc. at the same time SYN SEND STH OUT

**ˈmail bomb** *n.* [C] an extremely large number of email messages sent to sb ▸ **ˈmail-bomb** *v.* [T]

**mailbox** /ˈmeɪlbɒks; *AmE* -bɑːks/ *n.* [C] an area of a computer's memory where email messages for a particular user are stored

**mailer** /ˈmeɪlə(r)/ *n.* [C] (*AmE*) **1** (*AmE*) = MAILING (2) **2** an envelope, a box, etc. for sending small things by mail **3** a person or company that sends a letter, package, etc. **4** a program that sends email messages

**mailing** /ˈmeɪlɪŋ/ *n.* **1** [U] the act of sending items by mail: *the mailing of invoices* **2** (*AmE also* **ˈmailer**) [C] an item sent by mail, esp. an advertisement sent to a large number of people: *a mass mailing*

**ˈmailing list** *n.* [C] **1** a list of the names and addresses of people who are regularly sent information, advertising material, etc. by an organization **2** a list of names and email addresses kept on your computer so that you can send a message to a number of people at the same time

**ˈmail merge** *n.* [U,C] the process by which names and addresses are automatically added to a document on a computer, so that the same letter can be sent to many people
▸ **ˈmail-merge** *v.* [T]

**ˈmail ˌorder** *n.* [U] (*abbr* **MO**) a system of buying and selling goods through the mail: *We sell clothing* **by** *mail order.* ◇ *a mail-order catalogue* ▸ **ˈmail-order** *v.* [T]

**ˈmail-out** *n.* [C] (*Market.*) an act of sending an item of mail to a large number of people, esp. by email

**ˈmail room** = POST ROOM

**mailshot** /ˈmeɪlʃɒt; *AmE* -ʃɑːt/ *n.* [C] (*BrE*) (*Market.*) an act of sending advertising or information to a large number of people at the same time by mail; an item sent in this way

**mainframe** /ˈmeɪnfreɪm/ (*also* **ˌmainframe comˈputer**) *n.* [C] (*IT*) a large powerful computer, usu. the centre of a network and shared by many users

**ˌmain ˈmarket** *n.* [sing.] the part of the London Stock Exchange that deals with the shares of large valuable companies

**ˌmain ˈoffice** = HEAD OFFICE

**mainstream** /ˈmeɪnstriːm/ *n.* [sing.] **the mainstream** the main part of sth; the usual or normal way of doing or thinking about sth: *Sales has now come into the mainstream of business.* ▸ **ˈmainstream** *adj.*: *~ companies/banks*

**mainstreaming** /ˈmeɪnstriːmɪŋ/ *n.* [U] (*HR*) the practice of considering the effect of government and company policy on women as well as men, and on the equal rights of all workers

**ˈmain street** *n.* (*often* **Main Street**) **1** [C] the most important street in a small town in the US, where the shops/stores, banks, etc. are **2** [U] used to refer to small businesses in the US as a group

★ **maintain** /meɪnˈteɪn/ *v.* [T] **1** to make sth continue at the same level, standard, etc: *We will maintain prices at their current level for six months.* **2** to keep a building, a machine, etc. in good condition by checking or repairing it regularly **3** to keep records and add new information

★ **maintenance** /ˈmeɪntənəns/ *n.* [U] **1** the act of keeping sth in good condition by checking or repairing it regularly: *building/car ~* ◇ *The maintenance work is done by an outside contractor.* SYN UPKEEP
⊕ *to* **carry out** *~* ♦ **day-to-day/essential/routine** *~* ♦ *sth* **needs/requires** *~* ♦ *a ~* **contract** ♦ *~* **staff**
**2** the act of making a state or situation continue: *price maintenance*

**major** /ˈmeɪdʒə(r)/ *n.* [C, usu. pl.] a very large company in a particular industry: *oil majors BP and Shell*

★ **majority** /məˈdʒɒrəti; *AmE* -ˈdʒɔːr-; -ˈdʒɑːr-/ *n.* (*pl.* **-ties**) **1** [sing. with sing./pl. verb] the largest part of a group of people or things: *The majority was/were in favour of the proposal.* ◇ *Women are* **in a/the majority** *in this industry.* OPP MINORITY **2** [C] the number of votes by which one side in an election, a discussion, etc. wins: *a ~ vote/decision* **3** [sing.] (*usu. used as an adj.*) used to describe a group of shares that is more than half of the total number of shares in a company, or sb who owns this amount: *a majority shareholder* ◇ *The group is* **majority-owned** *by Anglo American.*
⊕ *a ~* **holding/investment/share/stake** ♦ *a ~* **investor/owner**

**maˌjority ˈinterest** *n.* [C, usu. sing., U] (*Finan.*) a number of shares owned by a particular person or organization that is greater than half of a company's total shares

★ **make** /meɪk/ *v.*, *n.*
• *v.* [T] (**made, made** /meɪd/) **1** to create or prepare sth by combining materials or putting parts together: *to ~ a chip/model* ◇ *bags made from recycled plastic* ◇ *What is the shirt made of?* **2** to earn or gain money: *She makes around €80 000 a year.* ◇ *to ~ a profit/loss* **3** to elect or choose sb as sth: *She made him her assistant.*
IDM NOTE Other idioms containing **make** are at the entries for the nouns, verbs or adjectives in the idioms. **make ˈgood** to become rich and successful **make sth ˈgood** to pay for, replace or repair sth that has been lost or damaged **make sth ˈgood; make ˈgood on sth** to do sth that you have promised to do, pay back money that you owe, etc. **ˈmake it; make it ˈbig** to be successful in your career or business
PHR V **ˌmake sth ˈout** to write out or complete a form or document: *He made out a cheque for €100.* **ˌmake sth ˈup 1** to form sth: *Older workers make up 18% of our staff.* → COMPRISE (2) **2** to put sth together from several different things **3** to complete a number or an amount required: *We need one more person to make up the team.* **4** to replace sth that has been lost: *Can I leave early today and make up the time tomorrow?* **5** to prepare sth: *Can you make up my bill please?*
• *n.* [C] the name or type of a machine, piece of equipment, etc. that is made by a particular company: *What make of car does she drive?* IDM **on**

the 'make (*infml.*) trying to get money or an advantage for yourself

**makegood** /'meɪkgʊd/ *n.* [C] (*Market.*) a free advertisement that a publishing company, TV station, etc. gives a company if they have made a mistake in the advertisement that the company paid for or if not as many people have seen it as they promised

**ˌmake-or-'buy** *adj.* (*Product.*) used to describe a decision a company must make about whether to make sth itself or pay another company to make it for them

**makeover** /'meɪkəʊvə(r); *AmE* -oʊ-/ *n.* [C,U] the process of changing the impression sth gives to others: *Some of the stores will be given a makeover.*

★ **maker** /'meɪkə(r)/ *n.* [C] a company that makes or produces sth; a person or a piece of equipment that makes sth: *an aircraft/a computer/ soft drinks ~* ◇ *If it doesn't work, send it back to the maker.* ◇ *an electric coffee-maker*

**ˌmake-to-'order** *n.* [U] (*abbr* **MTO**) (*Product.*) a system of manufacturing in which a product is only made when an order is received

**ˌmake-to-'stock** *n.* [U] (*abbr* **MTS**) (*Product.*) a system of manufacturing in which products are made and stored before orders are received

**'make-up** *n.* [sing.] the different things, people, etc. that combine to form sth; the way in which they combine: *The make-up of their board of directors needs to change.*

**'make-work** *n.* [U] (*AmE*) work that has little value but is given to people to keep them busy

**maladministration** /ˌmælədˌmɪnɪ'streɪʃn/ *n.* [U] the fact of managing a business, an organization, an official process, etc. in a bad or dishonest way

**malfunction** /ˌmæl'fʌŋkʃn/ *v.* [I] (about a machine) to fail to work correctly: *The bank's ATMs malfunctioned nationwide.* ▸ **ˌmal'function** *n.* [C,U]

**mall** /mɔːl; *BrE also* mæl/ = SHOPPING MALL

**malpractice** /ˌmæl'præktɪs/ *n.* [U,C] careless, wrong or illegal behaviour while in a professional job: *financial malpractices*

**man** /mæn/ *v.* [T] (**-nn-**) (*HR*) to work at a place or be in charge of a place or a machine; to supply people to work somewhere: *The telephones are manned 24 hours a day.*
▸ **'manning** *n.* [U]: *manning levels*



★ **manage** /'mænɪdʒ/ *v.* **1** [T,I] to control or be in charge of a business, an organization, a team of people, a project, etc: *to manage a company* ◇ *The firm manages $3 bn in investments.* **2** [T] to use time, money, etc. in a sensible way

**manageable** /'mænɪdʒəbl/ *adj.* possible to deal with or control

**ˌmanaged e'conomy** *n.* [C] (*Econ.*) a system in which the government owns large parts of industry and sets prices for goods and services

**ˌmanaged 'fund** *n.* [C] (*Finan.*) an amount of money that is given by an organization or many different investors to a company to invest for them, usu. in shares and bonds

**ˌmanaged 'hosting** *n.* [U] (*IT*) a system in which the company that you pay to store your website and put it on the Internet also provides technical help

★ **management** /'mænɪdʒmənt/ *n.* **1** [U] the act of running and controlling a business or similar organization: *a management training course* ◇ *day-to-day management of the company* ◇ *hotel management*
⊕ ***effective/good/strong ~ ◆ bad/poor ~ ◆ overall/routine ~ ◆ a ~ company/consultancy ◆ ~ practices/skills/styles/techniques***
**2** [C with sing./pl. v.; U] the people who run and control a business: *The management is/are closing the factory.* ◇ *The store is now* ***under new management.*** ◇ *employees and management*
⊕ ***junior/senior/top ~ ◆ a ~ decision/meeting/team ◆ a layer/level/tier of ~***
**3** [U; C with sing./pl. v.] the act of running a particular part of a company's activities; the people who do this: *sales management* ◇ *senior HR management* **4** [U] the process or skill of dealing with or controlling things or people: *poor management of people*

**'management acˌcounting** (*also* **mana'gerial acˌcounting**) *n.* [U] (*Account.*) the process of collecting, analysing and presenting financial information about a company for managers to use in order to make decisions about company organization, future strategy, etc.
▸ **'management acˌcountant** (*also* **mana'gerial acˌcountant**) *n.* [C]
**'management acˌcounts** *n.* [pl.]
→ FINANCIAL ACCOUNTING

**'management ˌaudit** *n.* [C] an examination of the way in which a company is organized and managed in order to identify areas that could be improved and to find any potential problems ▸ **'management ˌauditing** *n.* [U]

**'management board** *n.* [C with sing./pl.verb] a group of senior executives that are responsible for deciding on the way an organization is managed

**ˌmanagement 'buy-in** *n.* [C] (*abbr* **MBI**) (*Finan.*) a situation where a group of directors from outside a company buy more than 50% of its shares because they want to take over the management

**ˌmanagement 'buyout** *n.* [C] (*abbr* **MBO**) (*Finan.*) a situation in which the senior managers gain control of a company or a particular part of it by buying all or most of its shares

**ˌmanagement by ex'ception** *n.* [U] (*abbr* **MBE**) (*HR*) a style of management in which the senior managers give those below them as much authority to control a project as possible and only become involved if there is a problem

**ˌmanagement by ob'jectives** *n.* [U] (*abbr* **MBO**) (*HR*) a style of management in which aims and goals are set for the staff in order to direct their work and measure how well they do it

**ˌmanagement by 'walking a'round** (*BrE also* **'management by 'walking a'bout**) *n.* [U] (*abbr* **MBWA**) (*HR, infml.*) a style of management in which the manager regularly makes informal visits to different departments to talk to staff and check progress

**'management comˌmittee** *n.* [C with sing./pl. v.] **1** a group of people who are elected to be responsible for deciding on the way a VOLUNTARY organization, a club, etc. is managed **2** a group of people who are responsible for deciding on the way a particular part of an organization or a particular activity or problem is managed, with less power than the MANAGEMENT BOARD

**'management ˌcompany** *n.* [C] a company that manages sth, such as property or investments, for different people or businesses

**'management conˌsultant** *n.* [C] a person that a company pays to advise them on how to improve the management and control of their company and its activities, how to deal with a problem, etc.
▸ **'management conˌsulting** *n.* [U]

**'management game** = BUSINESS GAME

**ˌmanagement infor'mation ˌsystem** *n.* [C] (*abbr* **MIS**) a computer system that is designed for business use in order to supply information to managers from different departments of a company

**'management ˌscience** *n.* [U] (*abbr* **MS**) the study of the efficient and effective management of organizations, using ideas and techniques from mathematics, computing, science, etc. to understand how they work, to analyse problems and make decisions

**ˌmanagement 'summary** = EXECUTIVE SUMMARY

★ **manager** /'mænɪdʒə(r)/ *n.* [C] a person who is in charge of running a business, shop/store, department of an organization, project, etc: *She's the manager of the accounts department.* ◇ *regional sales managers*
▸ **'managership** *n.* [U,C]

**manageress** /ˌmænɪdʒə'res/ *n.* [C] (*BrE old-fash.*) a woman who is in charge of a small business, for example, a shop/store, restaurant or hotel

**managerial** /ˌmænə'dʒɪəriəl; *AmE* -'dʒɪr-/ *adj.* connected with the work of a manager: *managerial skills* ◇ *decisions taken at managerial level*

**mana'gerial acˌcounting** = MANAGEMENT ACCOUNTING

**ˌmanaging 'agent** *n.* [C] a person or company paid to manage a property, an investment, etc. for the owner

**ˌmanaging di'rector** *n.* [C] (*esp. BrE*) (*abbr* **MD**) the member of a company's BOARD OF DIRECTORS who is responsible for running the business on a daily basis → CHIEF EXECUTIVE OFFICER

**ˌmanaging 'underwriter** (*also* **'book ˌrunner**) = LEAD MANAGER

**mandate** *n., v.*

• ***n.*** /'mændeɪt/ [C] **1** (*fml.*) an official order and instruction given to sb to perform a particular task: *Her mandate is* **to** *help the company perform well.* **2** a document that gives a bank or sb else the power to deal with your account

• ***v.*** /'mændeɪt; ˌmæn'deɪt/ [T] (*fml.*) (*often pass.*) **1** to order sb to do sth, to behave or vote in a particular way; to order that sth should happen in a particular way: *The number of days' vacation is not mandated by law.* **2** to give sb, esp. a government or a committee, the authority to do sth

**mandatory** /ˈmændətəri; *AmE* -tɔːri *BrE also* mænˈdeɪtəri/ *adj.* if a particular action is **mandatory**, you must do it, usu. because it is required by law

**ˌmandatory conˈvertible ˈbond** *n.* [C] (*Finan.*) a type of bond that a company issues that must be changed into shares in the company by a particular date

**ˈman-hour** *n.* [C, usu. pl.] the amount of work done by one person in one hour: *Back injury is the main cause of* **lost** *man-hours.*

**manifest** /ˈmænɪfest/ *n.* [C] (*Transpt.*) a list of goods or passengers on a ship or an aircraft: *a cargo manifest*

★ **manipulate** /məˈnɪpjuleɪt/ *v.* [T] **1** to control or influence sb/sth, often in a dishonest way so that they do not realize it: *advertisers manipulating our attitudes* **2** to control or use sth in a skilful way: *to manipulate the levers of a machine* **3** to change or present information in a way that will deceive people: *manipulating financial records* ▸ **maˌnipuˈlation** /-ˈleɪʃn/ *n.* [U,C]: *data manipulation* **maˈnipulator** *n.* [C]

**manpower** /ˈmænpaʊə(r)/ *n.* [U] the number of workers needed or available to do a particular job: *trained/skilled* ~ ◇ *a manpower shortage* ◇ *manpower planning*

**mantra** /ˈmæntrə/ *n.* [C] a word, phrase or sentence that is often repeated and that expresses an idea or a belief: *The company's mantra is 'No Excuses'.*

**manual** /ˈmænjuəl/ *adj., n.*
• *adj.* **1** (used about work) involving using the hands or physical strength: *manual and non-manual workers* **2** operated or controlled by hand rather than automatically or using electricity, etc: *manual functions* ▸ **ˈmanually** /-əli/ *adv.*
• *n.* [C] a book that tells you how to do a task or how to operate sth, esp. one that comes with a machine, etc.

**ˌmanual ˈhandling** *n.* [U] any activity in which a person must use force to lift, carry, hold or move an object: *manual handling injuries*

**manufactory** /ˌmænjuˈfæktri; -təri/ *n.* [C] (*pl.* **-ries**) used in the names of some companies that manufacture goods

★ **manufacture** /ˌmænjuˈfæktʃə(r)/ *v., n.*
• *v.* [T,I] to make goods in large quantities from raw materials or parts, using machinery: *The plant manufactures 500 000 cars annually.*
• *n.* **1** [U] the process of producing goods in large quantities: *the manufacture of microchips* **2 manufactures** [pl.] goods that are manufactured: *a major importer of cotton manufactures*

★ **manufacturer** /ˌmænjuˈfæktʃərə(r)/ *n.* [C] a person or company that produces goods in large quantities from raw materials or parts: *an auto/computer/drugs/steel* ~ ◇ *Follow the manufacturer's instructions.*

**ˌmanuˈfacturer's brand** *n.* [C] (*Market.*) a brand owned by a manufacturer that has their name

★ **manufacturing** /ˌmænjuˈfæktʃərɪŋ/ *n.* [U] the business or industry of producing goods in large quantities in factories, using parts or raw materials: *jobs in manufacturing* ◇ *a manufacturing plant* ◇ *the manufacturing sector*

**ˌmanuˈfacturing base** *n.* [C] **1** (*Econ.*) (*also* **inˈdustrial base**) the part of the economy of a country or an area that is related to producing goods in large quantities in factories: *a strong/weak* ~ **2** a place where a company has one or more factories that produce goods in large quantities

**ˌmanufacturing inforˈmation ˌsystem** *n.* [C] (*abbr* **MIS**) (*Product.*) a computer system that is designed to supply information to managers to help them organize production in an efficient way

**map** /mæp/ *v.* [T] (**-pp-**) **1** to discover or give information about sth, esp. the way it is arranged or organized: *software to map and manipulate data* **2** to match or link one or more items or qualities with those in a different group or area: ***Skills mapping*** *is used to assign employees to specific tasks.* **PHR V** **ˈmap sth on/onto sth** to link data, a group of qualities, items, etc. with their source, cause, position on a scale, etc: *to map information onto a graph* **ˌmap sth ˈout** to plan or arrange sth in a careful, detailed way

★ **margin** /ˈmɑːdʒɪn; *AmE* ˈmɑːrdʒən/ *n., v.*
• *n.* **1** (*Account.*) [C,U] the difference between the cost of buying or producing sth and the price that it is sold for, calculated as a percentage of the selling price: *They make an 18% margin on each sale.* ◇ *high-margin products* SYN PROFIT MARGIN → MARKUP **2** [C] an extra amount of sth such as time, space, money, etc.

that you include in order to make sure that sth is successful: *a safety margin* **3** [C, usu. sing.] the amount by which one quantity is greater or smaller than another: *The strike was approved by a margin of 4 to 1.* ◇ *a narrow/wide ~* **4** (*Stock Ex.*) [C,U] money, shares, bonds, etc. that an investor must leave with a BROKER to cover any possible losses **5** [C] the empty space at the side of a written or printed page or web page **6** [C] the part that is not included in the main part of a group, an organization or a situation: *Oil producers at the margin were driven out of business.* **7** (*HR*) [C, usu. pl.] in Australia and New Zealand, an amount that is added to a basic wage, paid for special skill or responsibility **IDM on 'margin** (*Stock Ex.*) if an investor buys shares, FUTURES, etc. **on margin**, they borrow money from their BROKER to pay for them, using their account as a guarantee

• *v.* [T] (*Stock Ex.*) to buy, or allow sb to buy, shares, bonds, etc. with money borrowed using their account with the BROKER as a guarantee: *Some brokerages may not margin certain stocks.*

▸ **'marginable** /-əbl/ *adj.*

**'margin ac,count** *n.* [C] (*Stock Ex.*) an arrangement that an investor has with a BROKER in which the investor can borrow money for investments but must leave a particular amount of money, shares, etc. in their account

★ **marginal** /'mɑːdʒɪnl; *AmE* 'mɑːrdʒ-/ *adj.* **1** small and not having an important effect: *a marginal improvement in sales* **2** (*Econ.*) connected with a single change in the level of an activity **3** (*Econ.*) that can hardly make enough money to cover the costs of production: *marginal oil development* **4** not part of a main or an important group or system: *our marginal brands*

**,marginal 'cost** *n.* [C,U] (*Econ.*) the amount of extra money that a business must spend in order to increase its level of production or supply by one unit

**,marginal 'costing** (*also* **,marginal 'pricing**) *n.* [U] (*Account.*) a method of calculating the cost of a unit of a product that includes only the amount spent on producing it, such as the cost of materials or labour SYN VARIABLE COSTING

**marginally** /'mɑːdʒɪnəli; *AmE* 'mɑːrdʒ-/ *adv.* very slightly; not very much: *This figure is marginally above what we predicted.*

**,marginal produc'tivity** *n.* [U] (*Econ.*) the extra amount that can be produced as a result of adding one unit of sth used in production

**'marginal pro'pensity to con'sume** *n.* [sing.] (*abbr* **MPC**) (*Econ.*) the relationship between a change in the money people have to spend and the change in the amount they spend

**'marginal pro'pensity to im'port** *n.* [sing.] (*abbr* **MPM**) (*Econ.*) the relationship between a change in the total income of a country and the change in the amount that is spent on imported goods

**'marginal pro'pensity to 'save** *n.* [sing.] (*abbr* **MPS**) (*Econ.*) the relationship between a change in the money people have to spend and the change in the amount they save

**,marginal 'rate** (*also* **'marginal 'rate of 'tax, ,marginal 'tax rate**) *n.* [C] (*Account.*) a rate of tax that is paid on your next unit of income; the highest rate of tax that sb pays

**,marginal 'revenue** *n.* [U,C] (*Econ.*) the amount of extra money that a business can earn by increasing its level of production or supply by one unit

**,marginal 'tax rate** = MARGINAL RATE

**'margin call** *n.* [C] (*Stock Ex.*) a demand by a BROKER for an investor to add money, shares, etc. to their account because it has fallen below the amount allowed

**,margin of 'error** *n.* [C, usu. sing.] an amount that you allow when you calculate sth for the possibility that a number is not completely accurate

**,margin of 'safety** *n.* [C, usu. sing.] (*Account.*) the difference between the quantity of goods or services that a business must sell in order to BREAK EVEN and the total quantity it expects to sell

**marine** /mə'riːn/ *adj.* (often used in the names of companies) connected with ships or transporting goods by sea

**ma'rine in,surance** *n.* [U] insurance that pays for damage to ships or goods transported by ship

**,marital 'status** *n.* [U] (used esp. on official forms) the fact of whether you are single, married, etc.

**maritime** /'mærɪtaɪm/ *adj.* connected with the sea or ships, esp. in relation to trade

ˌ**maritime 'law** *n.* [U,C] the official rules that apply to ships and transporting goods or people by sea

**mark** /mɑːk; *AmE* mɑːrk/ *v., n.*

• *v.* [T] **1 ~ A (with B) | ~ B on A** to write or draw words, a symbol, line, etc. on sth in order to give information about it: *We mark each packet with a sell-by date.* **2** (*Stock Ex.*) **~ sth higher/lower** (*usu. pass.*) if shares are **marked higher/lower**, investors think they are worth more/less and so their value on the stock exchange increases/decreases **IDM** ˌ**mark 'time 1** to pass the time while you wait for sth more interesting **2** if prices **mark time**, they stay at the same level although they may change soon **PHR V** ˌ**mark sth 'down 1** (*Comm.*) to lower the price of sth: *marked-down items* **2** (*Stock Ex.*) if shares are **marked down**, their value on the stock exchange decreases ˌ**mark sth 'up 1** (*Comm.*) to raise the price of sth **2** (*Stock Ex.*) (*usu. pass.*) if shares are **marked up**, their value on the stock exchange increases **3** to mark or correct a text, etc., for example for printing

• *n.* **1** [C, usu. sing.] a level or point that sth reaches that is thought to be important: *Unemployment remains below the four million mark.* **2 Mark** [sing.] (followed by a number) a particular type or model of a machine or vehicle: *the Mark II engine*

**markdown** /ˈmɑːkdaʊn; *AmE* ˈmɑːrk-/ *n.* [C] **1** (*Comm.*) a reduction in the price of goods to encourage sales; an act of reducing prices: *a 20% markdown* **on** *many items* **2** (*Finan.*) an amount of money earned by a dealer when buying shares, bonds, etc., equal to the difference between the amount the dealer pays for the shares, bonds, etc. and the price at which they can sell them **3** (*Stock Ex.*) a reduction in the price of shares on the stock exchange OPP MARKUP

**marked** /mɑːkt; *AmE* mɑːrkt/ *adj.* easy to see: *a marked increase in profits* ▸ **'markedly** /-kɪdli/ *adv.*: *Sales have risen markedly.*

**marker** /ˈmɑːkə(r); *AmE* ˈmɑːrk-/ *n.* **1** [C, usu. sing.] a sign that sth exists or that shows what it is like: *Price is not always a good marker* **of** *quality.* **2** [C, usu. sing.] a standard for judging or deciding things: *The rate of inflation is used as a marker* **for** *pay deals.* **3** [C] (*also* **'marker pen**) a pen with a soft thick tip

★ **market** /ˈmɑːkɪt; *AmE* ˈmɑːrk-/ *n., v.*

• *n.* **1** [sing.] business or trade; the amount of trade in a particular type of goods, services, investments, etc: *the world market* **in** *coffee* ◇ *the advertising/insurance/telecoms* ~ ◇ *difficult market conditions*

○ *to* ***break into/enter*** *the* ~ ◆ *to* ***capture/dominate*** *the* ~ *(in sth)* ◆ *the* ***global/international/local*** ~ *(in sth)* ◆ *a* ***booming/strong*** ~ ◆ *a* ***competitive/tough*** ~ ◆ *a* ***depressed/weak*** ~ ◆ ~ ***prices/rates***

**2** [C] a particular area, country or section of the population that might buy goods or services: *They hope to break into the teenage market.*

○ *to* ***enter/find/penetrate*** *a* ~ ◆ *the* ***domestic/international/local*** ~ ◆ *a* ***developed/developing/mature*** ~ ◆ *a* ***key/large/main*** ~

**3** [C] a demand for a product; the number of people, businesses, etc. who buy it or want to buy it: *a slump in the global market for PCs*

○ *to* ***build/create*** *a* ~ ◆ *a* ***big/good/poor/small*** ~ *(for sth)* ◆ *a* ***growing/shrinking*** ~ ◆ *the* ***annual/domestic/world/worldwide*** ~ *for sth*

**4** (*Econ.*) [C] (*usually* **the market** [sing.]) an economic system in which the price of goods and services is affected by supply and demand rather than controlled by government: *Power supply cannot be left to the market.* ◇ *~-based/~-driven/~-led*

**5** (*Finan.*) [C] = FINANCIAL MARKET

**6** (*Stock Ex.*) [C] = STOCK MARKET

**7** [C] an occasion when people buy and sell goods; the open area or the building where they meet to do this: *We buy our vegetables* **at/in** *the market.* ◇ *Wednesday is market day.*

**8** [C] (*esp. AmE*) a shop/store, esp. one that sells food or one kind of goods: *a local mini-market* **IDM be first, quick, etc. to 'market** to be the first, be quick, etc. to get a product ready to sell **come to (the) 'market 1** (*Stock Ex.*) (about a company) to offer shares for sale on a stock exchange **2** to be ready to start selling a new product **corner the 'market (in/on sth)** to get control of the trade in a particular type of goods or services; to control the whole supply of sth **get, bring, etc. sth to 'market** to make a product ready to be sold **in the 'market for sth** interested in buying sth **make a 'market** (*Stock Ex.*) (about a dealer) to be ready, willing and able to buy and sell particular shares **on/onto the 'market** available for people to buy: *It's one of the best laptops on the market.* → idioms at PLAY *v.*, PRICE *v.*, SKIM

• *v.* [T] to advertise and offer a product for sale; to present sth in a particular way and make people want to buy it: *a drink marketed* **to** *18 to 24 year-olds* ◇ *The funds were marketed* **as** *low-risk.*

**marketable** /ˈmɑːkɪtəbl; *AmE* ˈmɑːrk-/ *adj.* **1** easy to sell; attractive to customers or employers: *~ goods/products* ◇ *marketable skills* **2** (*Finan.*) (about shares, bonds, etc.) that can be bought and sold by investors: *marketable securities* OPP NON-MARKETABLE

▸ **ˌmarketaˈbility** /-ˈbɪləti/ *n.* [U]

**ˌmarket ˈanalyst** *n.* [C] (*Finan.*) a person who collects and analyses information about a market, esp. a stock market

**ˈmarket ˌbasket** *n.* [C] (*Econ.*) a collection of different products that consumers buy regularly; the price paid for them. This is used to measure the COST OF LIVING.

**ˌmarket capitaliˈzation** (*also* **ˌmarket ˈcap**, **ˌcapitaliˈzation**) *n.* [U,C] (*Stock Ex.*) the total value of all a company's shares, calculated by multiplying the number of shares by their price on the stock exchange

**ˌmarket ˈclearing price** *n.* [C] (*Econ.*) the price at which the level of demand equals the level of supply

**ˌmarket concenˈtration** *n.* [U] (*Econ.*) the situation when a small number of companies control a large part of a market

**ˌmarket conˈtrol** *n.* [U] (*Econ.*) the ability of buyers or sellers to affect the price or quantity of goods or services

**ˌmarket eˈconomy** (*also* **ˌfree-market eˈconomy**) *n.* [C] (*Econ.*) a system in which businesses manage their own affairs and compete with each other and people can choose what they buy

**marketeer** /ˌmɑːkɪˈtɪə(r); *AmE* ˌmɑːrkəˈtɪr/ *n.* [C] **1** a person whose job involves getting people to buy things **2** a person who is in favour of a particular system of buying and selling

**ˌmarket equiˈlibrium** = EQUILIBRIUM

**marketer** /ˈmɑːkɪtə(r); *AmE* ˈmɑːrk-/ *n.* [C] **1** a specialist in marketing: *the company's chief marketer* **2** a business that sells goods or services to the public or that sells in a particular way: *a marketer of frozen foods*

**ˈmarket-ˌfacing** *adj.* used to describe a business that gives special attention to its customers and their needs

**ˌmarket ˈforces** *n.* [pl.] (*Econ.*) things that affect the price of a product or service or the quantity in which it is produced or sold, for example the amount of raw materials available or the number of customers

**ˌmarket ˌfragmenˈtation** *n.* [U] (*Econ.*) an increase in the number of different groups of customers for a product or service or different companies providing it

★ **marketing** /ˈmɑːkɪtɪŋ; *AmE* ˈmɑːrk-/ *n.* [U] the activity of presenting, advertising and selling a company's products in the best possible way: *She works in* **sales and marketing**. ◇ *The company invests heavily in the marketing of its brands.*

○ *aggressive/successful ~* • ***email/online/traditional ~*** • *a ~* ***campaign/strategy*** • *the ~* ***budget/spend*** • *a ~* ***director/manager***

**ˈmarketing board** *n.* [C with sing./pl. v.] an organization, usu. created by the government, that promotes and controls the sale of an agricultural product

**ˌmarketing communiˈcations** *n.* [U] (*Market.*) all the ways in which a company gives information about its products or services to customers or possible customers

**ˈmarketing ˌconcept** *n.* **1** (*Market.*) [C] an idea for a product and the way it should be sold and presented to the public **2** (*Econ.*) **the marketing concept** [sing.] the theory that a company should concentrate on finding out what kinds of product customers want and then produce them rather than produce sth and then try to persuade the customer to buy it

**ˈmarketing enˌvironment** *n.* [C] all the things that a company must consider when developing its marketing plans, such as people's incomes, the products of competitors, new technology, etc.

**ˈmarketing mix** *n.* [C, usu. sing.] (*Market.*) the main factors that influence a customer's decision to buy a particular product or service, which a business must consider when it is deciding how to advertise and sell its products → 4 Ps

**ˌmarketing myˈopia** *n.* [U] (*Market.*) the situation when a business focuses on its products rather than on the needs of customers and so may miss changes in the market

**ˈmarketing orienˌtation** = MARKET ORIENTATION

**ˌmarketing reˈsearch** = MARKET RESEARCH

**ˌmarketing reˈsource ˌmanagement** *n.* [U] (*abbr* **MRM**) (*Market.*) the use of computer software to organize, plan and improve a company's marketing

**ˈmarketing ˌservices** *n.* [pl.; U] (*Market.*) activities connected with market research, advertising products and services, etc.; the department of a company that deals with this

**ˌmarket inˈtelligence** *n.* [U] (*Market.*) the process of collecting and analysing information about a market that can help a company decide how to sell their goods

**ˌmarket ˈleader** *n.* [C] (*Market.*) **1** the company that sells the largest quantity of a particular kind of product: *the market leader* **in** *car insurance* **2** a product that is the most successful of its kind ▸ **ˌmarket ˈleadership** *n.* [U]: *to achieve/establish/win market leadership*

**ˈmarket-ˌmaker** (*also* **market maker**) *n.* [C] (*abbr* **MM**) (*Stock Ex.*) a company or person that deals in shares, bonds, etc. and agrees to buy and sell particular shares at specific prices

**ˈmarket map** *n.* [C] (*Market.*) a diagram that shows the positions of brands in terms of the most important brand characteristics

**ˈmarket ˌmechanism** = PRICE MECHANISM

**ˌmarket ˈniche** *n.* [C] (*Market.*) a group of customers that a company's products are esp. suitable for and which the company is seen as belonging to; a product, service or company that is different from or better than others in the same area: *to carve out/create/establish/spot a* ~

**ˈmarket ˌorder** *n.* [C] (*Stock Ex.*) an order to a dealer to buy or sell shares, bonds, etc. immediately at the current market price

**ˈmarket orienˌtation** (*also* **ˈmarketing orienˌtation**) *n.* [C, usu. sing., U] (*Market.*) the situation when a company focuses on what products customers need or want rather than on what they want to make

**ˌmarket parˈticipant** *n.* [C] (*Finan.*) a person or company that buys or sells shares, bonds, etc.

**ˌmarket peneˈtration** *n.* [U] (*Market.*) **1** the number of buyers who have bought a particular type of product, or a particular company's product, compared with the total number of possible buyers: *to gain/increase* ~ **2** the policy of trying to gain a larger share of an existing market, for example by changing the price of a product, rather than changing the product itself

**ˌmarket-peneˈtration ˌpricing** *n.* [U] (*Market.*) the policy of trying to get a share of a market for a new brand or product by first offering it at a low price

★ **marketplace** /ˈmɑːkɪtpleɪs; *AmE* ˈmɑːrk-/ *n.* **1 the marketplace** [sing.] the activity of competing with other companies to buy and sell goods, services, etc: *How can we compete successfully in the global marketplace?* **2** (*also* **ˌmarket ˈsquare**) [C] an open area in a town where a market is or was held

**ˌmarket ˈprice** (*also* **ˌmarket ˈvalue**) *n.* [C] the price that a product or service will currently sell for

**ˌmarket ˈrate** *n.* [sing.] the usual price or rate for sth at a particular time: *We charge interest below the market rate on loans.* SYN GOING RATE

★ **ˌmarket reˈsearch** (*also* **ˌmarketing reˈsearch**) *n.* [U] (*abbr* **MR**) the process of collecting and analysing information about markets, competitors, customers' opinions and problems connected with advertising and selling goods and services

⊙ *to carry out/do* ~ ◆ *a* ~ ***interview/questionnaire/survey*** ◆ *a* ~ ***company/firm***

▸ **ˌmarket reˈsearcher** *n.* [C]

**ˌmarket ˈrisk** = SYSTEMATIC RISK

**ˌmarket ˈsector** *n.* [C] a part of a market such as a particular industry or group of customers: *Key market sectors include IT, telecoms, finance and insurance.*

**ˌmarket ˈsegment** *n.* [C] (*Market.*) **1** a group of possible customers who are similar in income, age, habits, etc. **2** products produced for one particular group of customers

**ˌmarket ˌsegmenˈtation** *n.* [U,C] (*Market.*) the act of dividing possible customers into groups according to their age, income, sex, class, etc.; one of these parts

★ **ˌmarket ˈshare** *n.* [C,U] (*Market.*) the amount of sales of a particular type of product that a company has, compared with the total sales: *The company's US market share fell from 23.4% to 21.2%.*

⊙ *to* ***boost/build/grow/increase*** ~ ◆ *to* ***gain/grab/take/win*** ~ ◆ *to* ***lose/maintain*** ~

**ˌmarket-skimming ˈpricing** = SKIMMING (1)

**ˌmarket ˈsquare** = MARKETPLACE (2)

**ˌmarket ˈtest** *n.* [C] (*Market.*) when a product is made available in one or more areas to see if consumers like it and will buy it ▸ **ˈmarket-test** *v.* [T]: *market-tested products* **ˌmarket ˈtesting** *n.* [U]

**ˌmarket ˈvalue** *n.* [C,U] **1** = MARKET PRICE **2** (*Account.*) the value of an asset if it was sold at the current MARKET PRICE **3** (*Stock Ex.*) the total value of the shares of a particular company

**ˈmarket weight** (*also* **market-weight**) *adj.* (*Stock Ex.*) if a collection of shares, bonds, etc. is **market weight** in a particular industry, you have the same proportion of these shares in your collection as the index that you are following

**ˌmark-to-ˈmarket** *n.* [U] (*Finan.*) (*usu. used as an adj.*) the practice of valuing shares, bonds and other investments at their current price rather than an earlier price or the price that was paid for them: *mark-to-market accounting*

**markup** /ˈmɑːkʌp; *AmE* ˈmɑːrk-/ *n.* **1** (*Comm.*) [C, usu. sing.] an increase in the price of sth, usu. one that is the difference between the cost of producing or buying sth and the price it is sold at, calculated as a percentage of the cost **2** (*IT*) [U] the symbols on a computer document that tell the computer how to organize the text on the computer screen or on the page when printed; the process of adding these symbols: *hypertext markup language (HTML)*

**marque** /mɑːk; *AmE* mɑːrk/ *n.* [C] a well-known make of a product, esp. a car, that is expensive and fashionable: *the Porsche marque*

**mart** /mɑːt; *AmE* mɑːrt/ *n.* [C] (*esp. AmE*) a place where things are bought and sold: *a discount mart*

**ˈMaslow's ˈhierarchy of ˈneeds** /ˈmæzləʊz; *AmE* -loʊz/ (*also* **ˌhierarchy of ˈneeds**) *n.* [sing.] (*HR*) the theory, developed by Abraham Maslow, that people will feel satisfied and work best when they have everything that they require. These needs fall into several groups, which must be met in a particular order, starting with physical needs.

**mass** /mæs/ *adj.* affecting or involving a large number of people or things: *~ unemployment/advertising*

**ˌmass customiˈzation, -iˈsation** *n.* [U] the ability to produce a product in large quantities but also include small changes to meet the demands of different customers ▸ **ˌmass-ˈcustomize, -ise** *v.* [T]

**ˌmass ˈmarketing** *n.* [U] the activity of selling a product to as many people as possible, for example by advertising through newspapers, magazines, radio or television ▸ **ˌmass-ˈmarket** *v.* [T] **ˌmass-ˈmarket** *adj.*: *mass-market brands* **ˌmass ˈmarketer** *n.* [C]

**ˌmass ˈmedia** *n.* [pl.] (*usually* **the mass media** [U with sing./pl. v.]) all the sources of information that are able to reach large numbers of the public, such as TV, radio, newspapers, etc.

**ˌmass ˈmerchant** (*also* **ˌmass ˈmerchandiser**) *n.* [C] (*esp. AmE*) (*Comm.*) a business or shop/store that buys and sells a wide variety of products in very large amounts

**ˌmass-proˈduce** *v.* [T] to produce goods in large quantities, using machinery: *CDs are cheap and easy to mass-produce.* ▸ **ˌmass-proˈduced** *adj.*: *mass-produced goods* **ˌmass-proˈducer** *n.* [C] **ˌmass proˈduction** *n.* [U]

**ˌmaster ˈfranchise** (*also* **ˌarea ˈfranchise**) *n.* [C] (*Comm.*) a contract that gives one particular person or company the right to develop a business in a specific area or country for another company ▸ **ˌmaster franchiˈsee** (*also* **ˌarea franchiˈsee**) *n.* [C]

**masthead** /ˈmɑːsthed; *AmE* ˈmæst-/ *n.* [C] **1** the name of a newspaper at the top of the front page **2** (*IT*) a box or an area at the top of a web page that tells users what page they are on and may give the name of the company, etc.

**matching** /ˈmætʃɪŋ/ *n.* [U] (*Account.*) the process of relating amounts of money paid and received to the accounting period in which they occur

**material** /məˈtɪəriəl; *AmE* -ˈtɪr-/ *n.*, *adj.*

• ***n.*** [C,U] **1** a substance that things can be made from : *building materials* **2** things that are needed in order to do a particular activity: *cleaning/packaging ~s* **3** written information, ideas, etc. used for a particular purpose: *marketing/promotional ~*

• ***adj.*** **1** connected with physical objects, money, etc: *changes in material circumstances* OPP NON-MATERIAL **2** important: *The deal will have a ma-*

*terial impact on our results.*
▸ **ma'terially** /-riəli/ *adv.*

**materiality** /məˌtɪəri'æləti; *AmE* -ˌtɪr-/ *n.* [U] (*Law*) the quality of being important or needing to be considered: *the materiality of the evidence*

**maˌterial re'quirements ˌplanning** *n.* [U] (*abbr* **MRP**) (*Product.*) a process that uses computer programs to organize the correct amounts of materials or parts needed for particular levels of production and the correct time for ordering them

**ma'terials ˌbuyer** *n.* [C] (*Product.*) sb whose job is to choose suppliers and buy the equipment or materials a company needs to produce sth SYN PURCHASING OFFICER

**ma'terials ˌhandling** *n.* [U] (*Product.*) the process of loading, unloading and moving raw materials and goods in a factory, using machines

**ma'ternity leave** *n.* [U] (*HR*) a period of time when a woman is allowed to leave her job temporarily to have a baby

**ma'ternity pay** *n.* [U] (*HR*) money paid to a woman employee while she is not working before and after the birth of a baby

**matrix** /'meɪtrɪks/ *n.* [C] (*pl.* **matrices** /-trɪsiːz/) a way of organizing a company or a project in which people from different departments work together and so each employee has two or more managers in different departments

**ˌmatters a'rising** *n.* [pl.] used in a meeting to refer to sth connected with the last meeting that must be considered or dealt with: *Are there any matters arising?*

★ **mature** /mə'tʃʊə(r); -'tjʊə(r); *AmE* -'tʃʊr; -'tʊr/ *adj.*, *v.*
• ***adj.*** **1** (about an industry, a market or an economy) no longer growing very quickly and difficult for new companies to enter **2** well developed and well established: *a mature company* **3** (about a product, etc.) that has been produced, used, etc. for a long time and is now more difficult to sell or develop: *mature products near the end of their life cycles*
• ***v.*** [I] **1** (*Finan.*; *Insur.*) (about a bond, an insurance policy, etc.) to reach the date when it must be paid or paid back **2** (about an industry, a market, etc.) to stop growing as fast as before and become difficult for a new company to enter **3** to become more developed: *The problems will be solved as the software matures.* **4** (about a product, etc.) to become more difficult to sell or develop as it has been produced or used for a long time

★ **maturity** /mə'tʃʊərəti; -'tjʊər-; *AmE* -'tʃʊr-; -'tʊr-/ *n.* (*pl.* **-ties**)
**1** (*Finan.*; *Insur.*) [C,U] (*also* **re'demption date** [C]) the time when bonds, loans, insurance agreements, etc. must be repaid or paid; a bond, loan or an insurance agreement that has reached this time: *keeping securities until they* ***reach maturity*** ◇ *bonds with maturities of 20 years*
**2** [U] when an industry, an economy, a market, etc. is fully developed and no longer growing very quickly **3** [U] the time when a product has been sold for a long time and is well known, but its sales are not increasing

**maven** /'meɪvn/ *n.* [C] (*AmE*) (*infml.*) an expert in a particular subject: *Wall Street money mavens*

**maverick** /'mævərɪk/ *n.* [C] a person who does not behave or think like everyone else, but who has independent, unusual opinions
▸ **'maverick** *adj.*: *a maverick entrepreneur*

**max** /mæks/ *abbr*, *v.* (*infml.*)
• ***abbr*** **1** (*also* **max.**, *esp. in AmE*) maximum: *max temperature 18°C* **2** at the most: *It'll cost $50 max.* OPP MIN.
• ***v.*** PHR V **ˌmax (sth) 'out** (*AmE*) (*infml.*) to reach the limit at which nothing more is possible: *I've maxed out my credit card.*

★ **maximize**, **-ise** /'mæksɪmaɪz/ *v.* [T] **1** to increase sth as much as possible: *to ~ efficiency/profits* **2** to make the best use of sth: *to ~ opportunities/resources* **3** (*IT*) to make a window on a computer screen larger OPP MINIMIZE
▸ **ˌmaximi'zation**, **-i'sation** /-maɪ'zeɪʃn; *AmE* -mə'z-/ *n.* [U]

★ **maximum** /'mæksɪməm/ *adj.*, *n.* (*abbr* **max**)
• ***adj.*** as large, fast, etc. as is possible; the most that is possible or allowed: *the ~ price/quantity* OPP MINIMUM
• ***n.*** [C, usu. sing.] (*pl.* **-mums** *or* **-ma** /-mə/) the greatest amount, size, speed, etc. that is possible, recorded or allowed: *What is the absolute maximum you can afford to pay?* OPP MINIMUM

**MB** (*also* **Mb**) = MEGABYTE

**MBA** /ˌem biː 'eɪ/ *abbr* **Master of Business Administration** a university degree in subjects connected with managing businesses: *to do/have an ~*

**MBE** /ˌem biː ˈiː/ = MANAGEMENT BY EXCEPTION

**MBI** /ˌem biː ˈaɪ/ = MANAGEMENT BUY-IN

**MBO** /ˌem biː ˈəʊ; *AmE* ˈoʊ/ (*also* **MbO**) = MANAGEMENT BY OBJECTIVES, MANAGEMENT BUYOUT

**MBS** /ˌem biː ˈes/ = MORTGAGE-BACKED SECURITY

**MBTI™** /ˌem biː tiː ˈaɪ/ = MYERS-BRIGGS TYPE INDICATOR

**MBWA** /ˌem biː dʌbljuː ˈeɪ/ = MANAGEMENT BY WALKING AROUND

**Mbyte** /ˈembaɪt/ = MEGABYTE

**ˈm-ˌcommerce** *n.* [U] **mobile commerce** the buying and selling of products on the Internet by using mobile phones/cellphones and other WIRELESS technology

**MD** /ˌem ˈdiː/ = MANAGING DIRECTOR

**meagre** (*AmE* **meager**) /ˈmiːɡə(r)/ *adj.* small in quantity and poor in quality: *Sales rose by a meagre 0.1%.*

**mean** /miːn/ *adj., n.* (*Tech.*)
• ***adj.*** average: *products with a mean price of €3.44*
• ***n.*** [C, usu. sing.] (*also* ˌ**arithmetic ˈmean**) the average calculated by adding together all the numbers in a group, and dividing the total by the number of numbers

**means** /miːnz/ *n.* [pl.] the money that a person has: *living* ***beyond your means*** (= spending more than you can afford)

**ˈmeans test** *n.* [C] an official check of sb's wealth or income in order to decide if they are poor enough to receive money from the government, etc. for sth ▸ **ˈmeans-test** *v.* [T] **ˈmeans-ˌtested** *adj.*: *means-tested benefits* **ˈmeans-ˌtesting** *n.* [U]

**measurable** /ˈmeʒərəbl/ *adj.*
**1** that can be measured: *measurable goals* **2** large enough to be noticed or to have a clear and noticeable effect: *measurable improvements*
▸ **ˈmeasurably** /-əbli/ *adv.*

★**measure** /ˈmeʒə(r)/ *n., v.*
• ***n.*** **1** [C] a way of judging or measuring sth: *The consumer price index is a key measure of inflation at the retail level.* ◇ *a broad/good/reliable ~ of sth* SYN METRIC **2** [C,U] a unit used for stating the size, quantity or degree of sth; a system or scale of these units: *weights and measures* **3** [C] **~ (to do sth)** an official action that is done in order to achieve a particular aim: *Banks are introducing measures to make it easier for customers to change accounts.* ◇ *an economy measure* (= to save money)
⊙ ***austerity/cost-cutting*** *~s* • ***emergency/preventive/safety*** *~s* • ***drastic/necessary/tough*** *~s* • *to* ***adopt/take*** *~s (to do sth)*
• ***v.*** **1** [T] to judge the importance, value or effect of sth: *measuring staff performance* **2** [T] to find the size, quantity, etc. of sth in standard units: *measuring temperature* **3** [I] (*not used in the continuous tenses*) to be a particular size, length, amount, etc: *The room measures 4 m by 6 m.*
PHRV **ˈmeasure sb/sth against sb/sth** to compare sb/sth with sb/sth ˌ**measure ˈup (to sth/sb)** to be as good, successful, etc. as expected or needed: *The job didn't measure up to her expectations.*

**measurement** /ˈmeʒəmənt; *AmE* ˈmeʒərm-/ *n.* **1** [C] the size, length or amount of sth: *an inflation measurement* **2** [U] the act or process of finding the size, quantity or degree of sth

**mechanical** /məˈkænɪkl/ *adj.*
**1** connected with machines: *~ problems/defects* ◇ *mechanical work* **2** operated with power from an engine, a wheel, etc: *a ~ clock/device* ◇ *mechanical parts*
▸ **meˈchanically** /-ɪkli/ *adv.*

**meˌchanical engiˈneering** *n.* [U] the study of how machines are designed, built and repaired
▸ **meˌchanical engiˈneer** *n.* [C]

★**mechanism** /ˈmekənɪzəm/ *n.* [C] **1** a method or system for achieving sth: *What mechanisms are in place for dealing with complaints?*
⊙ *a* ***control/feedback/financial*** *~* • *to* ***have/put*** *a ~* ***in place*** • *to* ***create/set up*** *a ~*
**2** a set of moving parts in a machine that performs a task: *a safety mechanism*

★**mechanize**, **-ise** /ˈmekənaɪz/ *v.* [T] (*usu. pass.*) to change a process so that the work is done by machines rather than people: *a fully mechanized process* SYN AUTOMATE
▸ ˌ**mechaniˈzation**, **-ˈisation** /-naɪˈzeɪʃn; *AmE* -nəˈz-/ *n.* [U]

**med.** *abbr* (*written*) (esp. for sizes of clothes) medium

**media** /ˈmiːdiə/ *n.* **the media** [U with sing./pl. v.] the main ways that large numbers of people receive information and entertainment, that is television, radio, newspapers and the Internet: *advertising in the media* ◇ *The media was/were accused of influencing the decision.*

◘ *the international/local/national ~ ♦ the broadcast(ing)/electronic/ print ~ ♦ a ~ business/giant/group/ empire*

**'media ˌagency** *n.* [C] a business that plans and buys space or time for advertisements in newspapers, on TV, etc. on behalf of other businesses

**'media ˌbuying** *n.* [U] (*Market.*) the activity of buying space in newspapers, time during broadcasts, etc. for advertisements
▸ **'media ˌbuyer** *n.* [C]

**median** /'mi:diən/ *adj., n.* (*Tech.*)
• ***adj.*** having a value in the middle of a series of values: *The median age of the magazine's readership is 24.*
• ***n.*** [C] the middle value of a series of numbers arranged in order of size

**'media ˌplanning** *n.* [U] (*Market.*) the activity of deciding how, where and how much to advertise sth and how much money to spend ▸ **'media plan** *n.* [C] **'media ˌplanner** *n.* [C]

**mediate** /'mi:dieɪt/ *v.* **1** [T,I] to try to end a disagreement between two or more people or groups by talking to them and trying to find things that everyone can agree on: *to mediate **between** staff and management* ◇ *mediate **in** a dispute* **2** [T] to succeed in finding a solution to a disagreement between people or groups: *~ a settlement/solution* ▸ **ˌmedi'ation** /-'eɪʃn/ *n.* [U] **'mediator** *n.* [C]: *independent mediators*

**Medicaid** /'medɪkeɪd/ *n.* [U] in the US, the insurance system that provides medical care for poorer people

**'medical cerˌtificate** (*also* **'doctor's cerˌtificate**, *infml.*) *n.* [C] (*both BrE*) **1** a statement by a doctor that sb has been ill and unable to work **2** a statement by a doctor that sb is in good health and can do a particular job

**'medical inˌsurance** (*also* **'medical ˌcover**) *n.* [U] a type of insurance in which a person receives money to pay for medical treatment if they are ill/sick or injured SYN HEALTH INSURANCE

**Medicare** /'medɪkeə(r); *AmE* -ker/ *n.* [U] **1** in the US, the national insurance system that provides medical care for people over 65 **2** in Australia and Canada, the national medical care system for everyone that is paid for by taxes

**mediocre** /ˌmi:di'əʊkə(r); *AmE* -'oʊkər/ *adj.* not very good; of only average standard: *mediocre results*

**medium** /'mi:diəm/ *n.* [C] (*pl.* **media** /'mi:diə/ *or* **mediums**) **1** a way of communicating information, etc. to people: *the ~ of radio/television* ◇ *The ad campaign will run across all media.* HELP The plural in this meaning is usu. **media**.
◘ *an **effective**/a **powerful** ~ ♦ an **electronic/interactive** ~ ♦ an **outdoor**/a **print** ~*
**2** something that is used for a particular purpose: *Euros are used as a medium of exchange.*

**ˌmedium-'duty** *adj.* suitable for use in average, normal or slightly difficult conditions: *~ trucks*

**'medium-sized** (*also* **'medium-size**) *adj.* of average size; between small and large

**'medium-term** *adj.* **1** used to describe a period of time that is a few weeks, months or years into the future: *the medium-term outlook*
**2** (*Finan.*) used to describe sth such as a bond, contract, loan, etc. that lasts for a period of time in the middle between the shortest and the longest possible

★**meet** /mi:t/ *v., n.*
• ***v.*** (**met, met** /met/) **1** [T,I] to come together formally in order to discuss sth: *The committee meets twice a month.* ◇ *We have agreed to meet their lawyers.* **2** [T] to do or satisfy what is needed or what sb asks for: *meeting customers' needs* ◇ *to ~ targets/deadlines* **3** [T] to pay sth: *to meet costs*
IDM **meet sb half'way** to reach an agreement with sb by giving them part of what they want → idiom at END *n.* PHR V **'meet with sb** to have a meeting with sb
• ***n.*** [C] (*BrE*) (*infml.*) a meeting

★**meeting** /'mi:tɪŋ/ *n.* **1** [C] an occasion when people come together to discuss or decide sth: *a meeting **between** workers and management* ◇ *a meeting of shareholders* ◇ *She's in a meeting at the moment.*
◘ *to **arrange/call/have/hold/set up** a ~ ♦ to **cancel/put off/postpone** a ~ ♦ to **reschedule/schedule** a ~ ♦ to **take part in/attend** a ~ ♦ to **chair/ conduct/run** a ~ ♦ an **emergency**/a **special/team** ~*
**2 the meeting** [sing.] (*fml.*) the people at a meeting: *The meeting voted to accept the pay offer.*

**meg** /meg/ = MEGABYTE

**mega** /'megə/ *adj.* (*infml.*) very large or impressive: *mega deals*
▸ **mega** *adv.*: *They're mega rich.*

**mega-** /'megə-/ *comb. form* (*in ns*)
**1** very large or great: *a megastore*
**2** (*Tech.*) (in units of measurement) one million: *megawatts* **3** (*IT*) 1 048 576 (= $2^{20}$): *megabytes*

**megabucks** /ˈmegəbʌks/ *n.* [pl.] (*infml.*) a very large amount of money: *She earns megabucks.*

**megabyte** /ˈmegəbaɪt/ (*also* **meg**, *infml.*) *n.* [C] (*abbr* **MB**, **Mbyte**) (*IT*) a unit of computer memory, equal to $2^{20}$ (or 1 048 576) BYTES: *510MB of memory*

**meltdown** /ˈmeltdaʊn/ *n.* [U,C] a situation where sth fails or becomes weaker in a sudden and dramatic way: *economic meltdown*

★**member** /ˈmembə(r)/ *n.* [C] **1** a person, a country or an organization that has joined a particular group or team: *a full member of the EU* ◇ *eight new members of staff* OPP NON-MEMBER **2** a person or company that owns part of a business organization, for example by buying some of its shares: *The company auditors are appointed by the members* (= shareholders).

**membership** /ˈmembəʃɪp; *AmE* -bərʃ-/ *n.* **1** [U,C] (*BrE*) **~ (of sth)** (*AmE*) **~ (in sth)** the state of being a member of a group, an organization, etc: *to apply for membership of the association*

○ *to **qualify for/seek** ~ (of/in sth)* ◆ *to **grant/offer/refuse** (sb) ~* ◆ *a ~ **card/fee***

**2** [C with sing./pl. v.] the members of a group, an organization, etc: *The membership votes/vote on the proposal this week.* **3** [C,U] the number of members in a group, etc: *Union membership has fallen.*

★**memo** /ˈmeməʊ; *AmE* -moʊ/ *n.* [C] (*pl.* **memos**) an official note from one person to another or others in the same organization

○ *a **company**/an **internal**/a **staff** ~* ◆ *to **circulate/send/write** a ~*

**memorandum** /ˌmeməˈrændəm/ *n.* [C] (*pl.* **-da** /-də/ *or* **-dums**) **1** (*fml.*) a MEMO **2** (*Law*) a record of a legal agreement which has not yet been formally prepared and signed: *a memorandum to develop the product jointly* **3** a proposal or report on a particular subject for sb/sth

**memoˌrandum of associˈation** *n.* [C] (*BrE*) (*Law*) one of the legal documents that is created when a company is formed, that gives basic details about the company such as its name, address and the number and value of its shares SYN ARTICLES OF INCORPORATION

**memoˌrandum of underˈstanding** *n.* [C] (*abbr* **MOU**) (*Law*) a temporary written agreement between two companies, etc. that explains how they intend to do business with each other and what their relationship will be

**memory** /ˈmeməri/ *n.* (*pl.* **-ries**) (*IT*) **1** [C,U] the part of a computer where information is stored; the amount of space in a computer for storing information **2** [U,C] (*used with other ns*) a way in which information can be stored in a temporary or permanent form: *flash memory*

**menial** /ˈmiːniəl/ *adj.* used to describe work that is not skilled or important and is often boring or badly paid

**menswear** /ˈmenzweə(r); *AmE* -wer/ *n.* [U] (used esp. in shops/stores) clothes for men

**mentality** /menˈtæləti/ *n.* [C, usu. sing.] (*pl.* **-ties**) the particular attitude or way of thinking of a person or group SYN MINDSET

**mentee** /menˈtiː/ *n.* [C] (*HR*) a person who receives advice and help from sb with more experience over a period of time

**mentor** /ˈmentɔː(r)/ *n.* [C] (*HR*) an experienced person who advises and helps sb with less experience over a period of time ▸ **ˈmentor** *v.* [T] **ˈmentoring** *n.* [U]: *a mentoring programme*

**menu** /ˈmenjuː/ *n.* [C] (*IT*) a list of possible choices that are shown on a computer screen

**ˈmenu bar** *n.* [C] (*IT*) a horizontal bar at the top of a computer screen that contains PULL-DOWN **menus** such as 'File', 'Find' and 'Help'

**the Merc** /mɜːk; *AmE* mɜːrk/ *n.* [sing.] an informal way of referring to the **Chicago Mercantile Exchange**, a market for trading FUTURES that deals with financial and agricultural products

**mercantile** /ˈmɜːkəntaɪl; *AmE* ˈmɜːrk-; -tiːl/ *adj.* (*fml.*) connected with trade and commercial affairs

**ˌmercantile ˈlaw** *n.* [U] (*Law*) the collection of laws that deal with all aspects of business and trade, including contracts, buying, selling, storing and transporting goods, etc. SYN COMMERCIAL LAW

★**merchandise** *n.*, *v.*

• ***n.*** /ˈmɜːtʃəndaɪs; -daɪz; *AmE* ˈmɜːrtʃ-/ [U] **1** (*fml.*) goods that are bought or sold; goods for sale in a shop/store: *a range of non-food merchandise* ◇ *a general merchandise retailer* **2** things you can buy that are connected with or that advertise a particular event, film/movie, etc: *official Olympic merchandise*

• *v.* (*also* **merchandize**) /ˈmɜːtʃəndaɪz; *AmE* ˈmɜːrtʃ-/ [T] (*esp. AmE*) **1** to buy and sell products for profit: *a plan to merchandise Mexican food products in grocery stores* **2** to encourage the sale of goods, esp. by the way they are packaged and displayed in shops/stores: *well merchandised products* ▶ **ˈmerchandiser** *n.* [C] (*esp. AmE*)

**ˈmerchandise mix** *n.* [C, usu. sing.] (*esp. AmE*) (*Market.*) the types and quantities of goods that a shop/store chooses to sell

★ **merchandising** /ˈmɜːtʃəndaɪzɪŋ; *AmE* ˈmɜːrtʃ-/ *n.* [U] **1** (*esp. AmE*) the activity of selling or trying to sell goods by advertising or displaying them: *better merchandising and store design* **2** products connected with a popular film/movie, person or event; the process of selling these goods: *Batman merchandising*

**merchant** /ˈmɜːtʃənt; *AmE* ˈmɜːrtʃ-/ *n., adj.*

• *n.* [C] (*Comm.*) **1** a person or business that buys and sells goods in large quantities, esp. one who imports and exports goods: *a tea merchant* ◇ *builders' merchants* (= that sell supplies to the building trade) **2** (*esp. AmE*) a business or person that sells goods directly to the public SYN RETAILER **3** a shop/store, etc. that has an arrangement with a bank so that it can accept payments by credit card: *a merchant account*

• *adj.* connected with the transport of goods by sea: *~ ships/vessels*

**merchantable** /ˈmɜːtʃəntəbl; *AmE* ˈmɜːrtʃ-/ *adj.* (*Law*) in a good enough condition to be sold: *goods of merchantable quality*

**ˌmerchant ˈbank** *n.* [C] (*BrE*) a bank that deals with large businesses, for example providing finance for trade with foreign companies, helping with the sales of shares or bonds, etc.

▶ **ˌmerchant ˈbanker** *n.* [C] **ˌmerchant ˈbanking** *n.* [U]

**ˌmerchant ˈnavy** (*BrE*) (*AmE* **ˌmerchant maˈrine**) *n.* [C with sing./pl. v.] a country's commercial ships and the people who work on them

★ **merge** /mɜːdʒ; *AmE* mɜːrdʒ/ *v.* [T,I] **~ (sth) (with/into) sth | ~ A with B | ~ A and B (together)** (used esp. about business organizations) to combine, or make two or more organizations or parts combine: *The bank merged with Swiss Bank Corp. in 1999.* ◇ *The two departments are being merged.*

**ˈmerge/purge** (*also* **merge-purge**) *n.* [U,C] the process of combining lists of names, addresses, etc. and removing items from the combined list that appear more than once: *merge/purge software*

▶ **ˈmerge/purge** *v.* [T,I]

★ **merger** /ˈmɜːdʒə(r); *AmE* ˈmɜːrdʒ-/ *n.* [C] (*Finan.*) **~ (with sb/sth) | ~ (between A and B)** the act of joining two or more businesses or organizations into one: *a merger between the two banks* ◇ *mergers and acquisitions*

⊕ *to plan/propose/seek a ~* ♦ *to agree (to)/approve/block/oppose a ~* ♦ *~ negotiations/talks*

**merit** /ˈmerɪt/ *n.* [U] **1** (*fml.*) the quality of being good, deserving reward, etc: *I got the job* **on** *merit.* **2** (*HR*) used to describe increases in pay that relate to how well, hard, etc. people work: *a ~ award/bonus/increase* ◇ *~ pay*

**meritocracy** /ˌmerɪˈtɒkrəsi; *AmE* -ˈtɑːk-/ *n.* [C] (*pl.* **-cies**) an organization, an industry or a system where people get power or money on the basis of their ability

▶ **ˌmeritoˈcratic** /-təˈkrætɪk/ *adj.*

**message** /ˈmesɪdʒ/ *n., v.*

• *n.* [C] **1** a written or spoken piece of information, etc. that you send to sb or leave for sb when you cannot speak to them yourself: *He isn't here at the moment. Can I* **take** *a message?* ◇ *an email message* **2** (*Market.*) an important idea about a product, brand, etc. that a company tries to communicate in its advertising: *a marketing message* **3** (*IT*) a piece of information produced automatically by a computer program and shown on a computer screen **4** (*AmE*) a television advertisement: *We'll be back after the messages.*

• *v.* [T] to send a piece of information, a question, etc. to sb, esp. an email or a TEXT MESSAGE: *I messaged the results to my boss.* ▶ **ˈmessaging** *n.* [U]: *an electronic messaging system*

**ˈmessage board** *n.* [C] (*IT*) a place on a website where you can leave messages, information, etc. for other people to see

**messenger** /ˈmesɪndʒə(r)/ *n.* [C] **1** a person who gives a message to sb or who delivers messages, letters, etc. as a job: *a bike messenger* **2** (*IT*) a computer program that allows two or more people to communicate over the Internet using short written messages: *an instant messenger program*

**Messrs** (*AmE* **Messrs.**) /ˈmesəz; *AmE* -sərz/ *abbr* (*esp. BrE*) used as the plural of **Mr** before a list of names and before names of businesses: *Messrs L Jones and Co*

**meteoric** /ˌmiːtiˈɒrɪk; *AmE* -ˈɔːr-; -ˈɑːr-/ *adj.* achieving success very quickly: *the meteoric rise of the airline*

**meter** /ˈmiːtə(r)/ *n., v.*
• ***n.*** [C] **1** a device that measures and records the amount of electricity, gas, water, time, etc. that you have used, or the money you must pay **2 -meter** (*used to form ns*) a device for measuring the thing mentioned: *speedometer*
• ***v.*** [T] to measure sth (for example how much gas, electricity, etc. has been used) using a **meter**

★**method** /ˈmeθəd/ *n.* [C] a particular way of doing sth: *a new method* ***for*** *measuring unemployment* ◇ *your preferred method* ***of*** *payment* ◇ *cheaper production methods*
**o** *to* ***develop/use*** *a ~* ◆ ***traditional/unconventional*** *~s* ◆ ***effective/reliable*** *~s*

**ˌme-ˈtoo** *adj.* (*Market., infml.*) produced by a company in response to the success of a similar product sold by another company: *~ products/marketing*

**metric** /ˈmetrɪk/ *n., adj.*
• ***n.*** [C] a system for measuring sth, esp. how well a business is performing: *Earnings per customer is a key metric for our business.*
**o** ***business/financial/performance/quality*** *~s* ◆ *to* ***create/establish/track/use*** *~s*
• ***adj.*** based on the system of measurements that uses the metre, kilogram, etc. as basic units: *metric sizes*

**ˌmetric ˈton** (*also* **tonne**) *n.* [C] a unit for measuring weight, equal to 1 000 kilograms

**ˌmezzanine ˈdebt** /ˈmezəniːn; ˈmetsə-/ *n.* [U] (*Finan.*) money that a business obtains from investors through MEZZANINE FINANCE

**ˌmezzanine ˈfinance** (*also* **ˌmezzanine ˈfinancing**) /ˈmezəniːn; ˈmetsə-/ *n.* [U] (*Finan.*) a way of providing funds for a business that involves lending money with a high rate of interest and often with the right to obtain shares in the business in the future

**mfg.** *abbr* (*esp. AmE*) a short way of writing **manufacturing**, esp. in the names of companies

**mgmt.** *abbr* (*written*) management

**MICR** /ˌem aɪ siː ˈɑː(r); ˈmaɪkə(r)/ *abbr* **magnetic ink character recognition** a system in which words and numbers are printed on official documents such as cheques in special ink that can be read by an electronic device

**micro** /ˈmaɪkrəʊ; *AmE* -kroʊ/ (*pl.* **micros**) = MICROCOMPUTER

**micro-** /ˈmaɪkrəʊ; *AmE* -kroʊ/ *comb. form* **1** (*in ns, adjs and advs*) small; on a small scale: *a microchip* ◇ *micro-lending* OPP MACRO- **2** (*in ns*) used in units of measurement to mean one millionth: *a microlitre*

**microcap** /ˈmaɪkrəʊkæp; *AmE* -kroʊ-/ *n.* [C] (*esp. AmE*) (*Stock Ex.*) one of the smallest companies on the stock exchange, that have a very low total value of shares

**microchip** /ˈmaɪkrəʊtʃɪp; *AmE* -kroʊ-/ (*also* **chip**) *n.* [C] (*IT*) a very small piece of a material that is used inside a computer, etc. in order to carry a complicated electronic CIRCUIT: *A small microchip is embedded in the card.*

**microcomputer** /ˈmaɪkrəʊkɒmpjuːtə(r); *AmE* -kroʊ-/ (*also* **ˈmicro**) *n.* [C] (*IT*) a small computer that contains a MICROPROCESSOR

**microeconomics** /ˌmaɪkrəʊˌiːkəˈnɒmɪks; -ˌekə-; *AmE* ˌmaɪkroʊˌekəˈnɑːm-/ *n.* [U] (*Econ.*) the branch of **economics** that studies individual markets or the decisions and choices made by individual businesses, families, etc. about spending or earning money, for example the choice to charge a particular price for goods ▸ **ˌmicroˌecoˈnomic** *adj.*

**microelectronics** /ˌmaɪkrəʊɪˌlekˈtrɒnɪks; *AmE* -kroʊɪˌlekˈtrɑːn-/ *n.* [U] the design, production and use of very small electronic CIRCUITS ▸ **ˌmicroeˌlecˈtronic** *adj.*

**microengineering** /ˌmaɪkrəʊˌendʒɪˈnɪərɪŋ; *AmE* ˌmaɪkroʊˌendʒɪˈnɪrɪŋ/ *n.* [U] engineering on a very small scale, often involving MICROELECTRONICS

**micromanage** /ˈmaɪkrəʊmænɪdʒ; *AmE* -kroʊ-/ *v.* [T,I] (*esp. AmE*) to control every aspect and detail of a business, project, etc. ▸ **ˈmicromanagement** *n.* [U] **ˈmicromanager** *n.* [C]

**microprocessor** /ˌmaɪkrəʊˈprəʊsesə(r); *AmE* -kroʊˈproʊ-/ *n.* [C] (*IT*) a small unit of a computer that contains all the functions of the CENTRAL PROCESSING UNIT

**microsite** /ˈmaɪkrəʊsaɪt; *AmE* -kroʊ-/ *n.* [C] (*Market.*) a small extra website that a business creates for a particular purpose, esp. to advertise or sell a new product

**mid-** /mɪd/ *comb. form* (*used in ns and adjs*) in the middle of: *a mid-season sale*

**'mid cap** *n.* [C] (*Stock Ex.*) a company that has a medium total value of shares on the stock exchange

**ˌmiddle-'income** *adj.* earning an average amount of money

**middleman** /'mɪdlmæn/ *n.* [C] (*pl.* **-men** /-men/) **1** a person or company that buys goods or services from a supplier and sells them to sb else: *Buy direct and cut out the middleman.* **2** a person or an organization who helps to arrange things between people who are unable or unwilling to deal with each other directly SYN INTERMEDIARY

**ˌmiddle 'management** *n.* [U with sing./pl. v.] the people in charge of small groups of people and departments in a business organization but who are not involved in making important decisions affecting the whole organization
▸ **ˌmiddle 'manager** *n.* [C]

**ˌmiddle 'market** *n.* [sing.] (*usu.* **the ~**) the group of customers that are prepared to buy a product with an average price rather than the most or least expensive kind; trade in products with an average price

**ˌmiddle-'ranking** *adj.* having a responsible job or position, but not one of the most important: *middle-ranking executives*

**midmarket** (*also* **mid-market**) /ˌmɪd'mɑːkɪt; *AmE* -'mɑːrk-/ *adj.* (*Market.*) **1** designed for or used by the group of customers prepared to buy a product with an average price rather than the most or least expensive kind: *a ~ brand/hotel/retailer* **2** used to describe people who are prepared to buy products or services with average prices: *midmarket customers*

**ˌmid-'price** (*also* **ˌmid-'priced**) *adj.* (about a product for sale) not very expensive and not very cheap
▸ **ˌmid-'price** *n.* [U; sing.]

**ˌmid-'range** (*also* **midrange**) *adj.* **1** (about a product for sale) not the cheapest or most expensive, not the best or worst, not the largest or smallest, etc: *mid-range computers* **2** (about a number, a value, etc.) not the highest or lowest; in the middle
▸ **'mid-range** (*also* **midrange**) *n.* [U; sing.]

**midsession** (*also* **mid-session**) /ˌmɪd'seʃn/ *n.* [U; sing.] (*Stock Ex.*) the middle of a period of trading on the stock exchange, usu. around midday

**ˌmid-'sized** (*also* **ˌmid-'size**) (*both esp. AmE*) *adj.* of average size, neither large nor small: *a mid-sized company*

**midstream** /ˌmɪd'striːm/ *adj.* (*Econ.*; *Product.*) used to describe the middle stages in an industrial or commercial process: *a midstream energy company*

**migrate** /maɪ'greɪt; *AmE* 'maɪgreɪt/ *v.* **1** [I] (about a lot of people) to move from one town, country, etc. to go to live and work in another **2** [I] to move from one place to another: *Jobs have migrated abroad.* **3** (*Comm.*; *IT*) [T,I] to change, or cause sb/sth to change, from one service or technology to another: *Newspaper readers are migrating to the Internet.* ◇ *We are migrating customers to our new service.* **4** (*IT*) [T] to move programs or HARDWARE from one computer system to another ▸ **mi'gration** /-'greɪʃn/ *n.* [U,C] **migratory** /'maɪgrətri; maɪ'greɪtəri; *AmE* 'maɪgrətɔːri/ *adj.*

**milage** = MILEAGE

**mileage** (*also* **milage**) /'maɪlɪdʒ/ *n.* **1** [U; C, usu. sing.] the distance that a vehicle has travelled, measured in miles: *a huge weekly mileage* **2** [C,U] the number of miles that a vehicle can travel using a particular amount of fuel: *The new model gets good mileage.* **3** [U] (*infml.*) the amount of advantage or use that you can get from a particular event or situation: *There's still plenty of mileage in our older products.*

**milestone** /'maɪlstəʊn; *AmE* -stoʊn/ *n.* [C] **1** (*also* **milepost** /'maɪlpəʊst; *AmE* -poʊst/ (*esp. in AmE*)) a very important stage or event in the development of sth: *The appointment represents a milestone* **in** *her career.* ◇ *to pass/reach a ~* **2** a time in a project by which particular tasks should be completed: *Milestones and deliverables are defined in the project plan.* ◇ *to agree/set ~s*

**'milestone ˌpayment** *n.* [C] a payment for completing a particular stage of a business project

**'milk round** *n.* [C, usu. sing.] (*also* **the ~**) in the UK, a series of visits that large companies make each year to colleges and universities, to talk to students who are interested in working for them

**mill** /mɪl/ *n.*, *v.* (*Manufact.*)
• *n.* [C] (*often used with other ns*) a factory that produces a particular type of material: *paper mills*

• *v.* [T] to cut or shape metal in a special machine: *machine-milled steel*

**milli-** /ˈmɪli/ *comb. form* (*in ns; used in units of measurement*) one thousandth: *milligram* ◇ *millimetre*

**millionaire** /ˌmɪljəˈneə(r); *AmE* -ˈner/ *n.* [C] a person who has a million euros, dollars, etc. or more; a very rich person

**min.** *abbr* (*written*) minimum: *min. charge €25* OPP MAX.

**mindset** /ˈmaɪndset/ *n.* [C, usu. sing.] a set of attitudes or fixed ideas that sb has and that are often difficult to change: *the corporate mindset* SYN MENTALITY

**mindshare** /ˈmaɪndʃeə(r); *AmE* -ʃer/ *n.* [U] (*Market.*) how aware consumers are of a particular product or brand, compared with similar ones

**mine** /maɪn/ *n.* [C] a deep hole or holes under the ground where minerals such as coal, gold, etc. are dug ▸ **mine** *v.* [T,I] **ˈminer** *n.* [C] **ˈmining** *n.* [U]

**mini-** /ˈmɪni/ *comb. form* (*used in ns*) small: *minivan* ◇ *fears of a mini-recession*

**minicomputer** /ˈmɪnikəmpjuːtə(r)/ *n.* [C] (*IT*) a computer of medium size that is larger and faster than a personal computer

**minimal** /ˈmɪnɪməl/ *adj.* very small in size or amount; as small as possible: *The work was carried out at minimal cost.* ▸ **ˈminimally** *adv.*

**minimarket** /ˈmɪnimɑːkɪt; *AmE* -mɑːrk-/ *n.* [C] a small supermarket or food shop/store

★**minimize**, **-ise** /ˈmɪnɪmaɪz/ *v.* [T] **1** to reduce sth, esp. sth bad, to the lowest possible level: *minimizing costs/risk* **2** to make sth small, esp. on a computer screen: *Minimize any windows you have open.* OPP MAXIMIZE

★**minimum** /ˈmɪnɪməm/ *adj.*, *n.*
• *adj.* (*abbr* **min.**) the smallest possible or allowed; extremely small: *a minimum charge of 50¢* ▸ **ˈminimum** *adv.*: *You'll need $300 minimum for expenses.*
• *n.* [C, usu. sing.] (*pl.* **minima** /-mə/) (*abbr* **min.**) the smallest amount or level that is possible, allowed or required: *Job losses were **kept to a** minimum.* OPP MAXIMUM

**ˌminimum ˈwage** *n.* [sing.] the lowest wage that an employer is allowed to pay by law

**minor** /ˈmaɪnə(r)/ *n.* [C] a person who is under the age at which you legally become an adult and are responsible for your actions

★**minority** /maɪˈnɒrəti; *AmE* -ˈnɔːr-; -ˈnɑːr-/ *n.* (*pl.* **-ties**) **1** [sing. with sing./pl. verb] the smaller part of a group; less than half of the people or things in a large group: *Only a small ~ of these businesses makes/make decent profits.* ◇ *Women were still **in a/the ~**.* OPP MAJORITY
**2** [sing.] (*usu. used as an adj.*) used to describe a person or an organization that owns a smaller share of a business than the main owner; the share of the business that they own: *They hold a minority stake in the business.*
◆ *a ~ **investor/owner/partner/shareholder*** ◆ *a ~ **holding/investment/share***

**miˌnority ˈinterest** *n.* **1** (*Finan.*) [C] a number of shares owned by a particular person or organization that is less than the number owned by the CONTROLLING SHAREHOLDER **2** (*Account.*) [C,U] in the financial records of a HOLDING COMPANY, an amount of profit, income, etc. that belongs to a person or an organization that owns a part of a company that it controls

**mint** /mɪnt/ *n.*, *v.*
• *n.* **1** [C] a place where money is made **2 a mint** [sing.] (*infml.*) a large amount of money: *He made a mint selling used cars.* IDM **in mint conˈdition** new; in perfect condition
• *v.* [T] to make a coin from metal

**minted** /ˈmɪntɪd/ *adj.* **1** recently produced, created, etc: *a newly minted dot-com* **2** (*infml.*) very rich

**minus** /ˈmaɪnəs/ *prep.*, *adj.*, *n.*
• *prep.* **1** used when one number or amount is being taken away from another: *$100 minus $92.50 gives you $7.50.* SYN LESS **2** (*infml.*) without sth that was there before: *We're minus a van.* OPP PLUS → idiom at PLUS *prep.*
• *adj.* **1** used before a number to show that it is lower than zero: *Sales were minus $24 m in June.* **2** making sth seem negative and less attractive or good: *the car's minus points*
• *n.* [C] **1** (*infml.*) a negative quality; a disadvantage: *the pluses and minuses of changing the system*
**2** (*also* **ˈminus sign**) the symbol (−), used in mathematics OPP PLUS

**ˈminus tick** = DOWNTICK

★**minute** /ˈmɪnɪt/ *n.* **the minutes** [pl.] a summary or record of what is said or decided at a formal meeting:

*Our secretary takes (= writes) the minutes.*

◆ *to approve/read/sign the ~* ◆ *to circulate/write up the ~*

▸ **'minute** *v.* [T]: *Was this minuted?*

**'mirror site** (*also* **mirror** /'mɪrə(r)/) *n.* [C] (*IT*) a website which is a copy of another website but has a different address on the Internet so that more people can visit and use it

**MIS** /ˌem aɪ 'es/ = MANAGEMENT INFORMATION SYSTEM, MANUFACTURING INFORMATION SYSTEM

**misappropriate** /ˌmɪsə'prəʊprieɪt; *AmE* -'proʊ-/ *v.* [T] (*fml.*) to take sb else's money or property for yourself, esp. when they have trusted you to take care of it

▸ **ˌmisapˌpropri'ation** /-'eɪʃn/ *n.* [U]: *the misappropriation of company funds*

**misc.** *abbr* a short way of writing miscellaneous

**miscalculate** /ˌmɪs'kælkjuleɪt/ *v.* [T,I] to make a mistake in calculating or judging an amount, a situation, etc. ▸ **ˌmiscalcu'lation** /-'leɪʃn/ *n.* [C,U]: *to make a miscalculation*

**miscellaneous** /ˌmɪsə'leɪniəs/ *adj.* consisting of many different kinds of things that are not connected and do not easily form a group: *miscellaneous expenses*

**misconduct** /ˌmɪs'kɒndʌkt; *AmE* -'kɑːn-/ *n.* [U] (*fml.*) **1** behaviour that is unacceptable, esp. because it breaks the rules of a particular profession or job: *professional misconduct* **2** bad management of a company, etc: *misconduct of financial affairs*

**misdirect** /ˌmɪsdə'rekt; -daɪ'rekt/ *v.* [T] to send sb/sth in the wrong direction or to the wrong place: *Investors have been misdirected.* ◇ *misdirected mail*

▸ **ˌmisdi'rection** /-'rekʃn/ *n.* [U]

**'misery ˌindex** *n.* [C] (*Econ.*) a measure of the performance of an economy that considers the rate of unemployment and INFLATION

**mismanage** /ˌmɪs'mænɪdʒ/ *v.* [T] to deal with or manage sth badly

▸ **ˌmis'management** *n.* [U]: *financial mismanagement*

**misrepresent** /ˌmɪsˌreprɪ'zent/ *v.* [T] to give information about sb/sth that is not true or complete so that other people have the wrong impression about them/it

▸ **ˌmisˌrepresen'tation** /-'teɪʃn/ *n.* [C,U]

**ˌmis-'sell** *v.* [T] to sell sth to sb that is not suitable for their needs, for example by not giving them all the information they need ▸ **ˌmis-'sale** *n.* [C,U] **ˌmis-'selling** *n.* [U]

**mission** /'mɪʃn/ *n.* [C] **1** a particular purpose or aim that a company has: *We need to focus on our core mission and values.* **2** an important official job that a group of people is given, esp. when they are sent to another country; the group of people who do this job: *a fact-finding mission* **3** an important job that sb is given to do: *a tough mission*

**'mission creep** *n.* [U] the gradual addition of new work and duties to a project, or to the responsibilities of a group or department

**ˌmission-'critical** *adj.* essential for an organization to function successfully: *~ employees/projects*

**'mission ˌstatement** (*also* **ˌstatement of 'purpose**) *n.* [C] an official statement of the aims of a company or an organization: *to create/draft a ~*

**misstate** /ˌmɪs'steɪt/ *v.* [T] to write or say sth that is wrong or not accurate, esp. in order to deceive sb: *misstating or hiding expenses*

▸ **ˌmis'statement** *n.* [C,U]: *accounting misstatements*

**misuse** *n., v.*

• *n.* /ˌmɪs'juːs/ [U; C, usu. sing.] the act of using sth in a dishonest way or for the wrong purpose: *the misuse of company funds*

• *v.* /ˌmɪs'juːz/ [T] to use sth in the wrong way or for the wrong purpose: *misusing company funds*

**mitigate** /'mɪtɪgeɪt/ *v.* [T] to make sth less harmful, serious, dangerous, etc: *The bank uses several methods to mitigate risk.*

**mitigation** /ˌmɪtɪ'geɪʃn/ *n.* [U] a reduction in how unpleasant, serious or dangerous sth is: *risk mitigation*

**IDM in miti'gation** (*Law*) with the aim of making a crime seem less serious or easier to forgive: *In mitigation, I did correct the mistake quickly.*

**mix** /mɪks/ *n.* [C, usu. sing.] **1** a combination of different things or people: *The store sells a mix of frozen food and groceries.* **2** a situation, esp. a difficult one, that has different things or people in it

**ˌmixed e'conomy** *n.* [C] (*Econ.*) an economic system in a country in which some companies are owned by the state and some are private

**ˌmixed 'media** *n.* [U] (*Market.*) the use of different kinds of media for advertising, such as TV, radio, newspapers, etc: *a mixed-media campaign*

**ml** /mɪl/ *abbr* (*usu. written*) millilitre: *25ml water*

**MLM** /ˌem el ˈem/ = MULTILEVEL MARKETING

**MM** /ˌem ˈem/ = MARKET-MAKER

**mm** *abbr* (*written*) millimetre: *a 35mm camera*

**MMS** /ˌem em ˈes/ *n.* **Multimedia Messaging Service 1** [U] a system for sending pictures, sounds and short written messages from one mobile phone/cellphone to another: *to subscribe to MMS* **2** [C] a message sent by MMS

**mngmt** (*also* **mngmt.**) *abbr* (*written*) management

**mngr** (*also* **mngr.**) *abbr* (*written*) manager

**MO** = MAIL ORDER, MONEY ORDER

**mobile** /ˈməʊbaɪl; *AmE* ˈmoʊbl/ *adj., n.*

• ***adj.*** **1** that is not fixed in one place and can be moved easily and quickly: *mobile equipment* **2** able to change your social class, your job or the place where you live easily: *a highly mobile workforce*

• ***n.*** [C] (*BrE*) (*often in the names of companies*) a mobile phone

⊙ *a ~* ***business/maker/operator*** • *~* ***networks/sales***

★ **ˌmobile ˈphone** (*also* **ˈmobile**) *n.* [C] (*both BrE*) a telephone without wires that works by radio, and you can carry with you and use anywhere SYN CELLPHONE

**ˌmobile ˈworker** *n.* [C] (*HR*) an employee who does not have one fixed place of work but moves from place to place

▸ **ˌmobile ˈworking** *n.* [U]

**mobility** /məʊˈbɪləti; *AmE* moʊ-/ *n.* [U] **1** the ability to move easily from one place, social class or job to another **2** the ability to move, be moved or travel around easily: *a person with limited mobility*

**moˌbility of ˈlabour** = LABOUR MOBILITY

**ˈmock-up** *n.* [C] a model or copy of sth, often the same size as the original object, that is used for testing, or for showing people what the real thing will look like

**mode** /məʊd; *AmE* moʊd/ *n.* **1** [C] a particular way of doing sth; a particular type of sth: *a ~ of transport/payment* **2** [C,U] the way in which a piece of equipment is set to perform a particular task: *automatic mode* **3** (*Tech.*) [sing.] the value that appears most frequently in a series of numbers

★ **model** /ˈmɒdl; *AmE* ˈmɑːdl/ *n., v.*

• ***n.*** [C] **1** a particular design or type of product: *Prices are down on basic models.*

⊙ ***luxury/popular/standard*** *~s* • ***current/the latest/new/old/previous*** *~s* • *to* ***design/develop/make/produce*** *a ~*

**2** a simple description of a system, used for explaining how sth works or calculating what might happen, etc.

⊙ *an* ***economic****/a* ***financial*** *~* • *a* ***business/marketing*** *~*

**3** a copy of sth, usu. smaller than the original object: *a* ***working*** *model* **4** a particular system or way of doing sth that can be copied by other people

• ***v.*** [T] (-**ll**-, *AmE* -**l**-) to create a copy of an activity, a situation, etc. so that you can study it before dealing with the real thing

**modem** /ˈməʊdem; *AmE* ˈmoʊ-/ *n.* [C] (*IT*) a device that connects one computer system to another using a telephone line so that data can be sent

**moderate** *adj., v.*

• ***adj.*** /ˈmɒdərət; *AmE* ˈmɑːd-/ neither very good, large, etc. nor very bad, small, etc.; reasonable: *moderate growth* ▸ **ˈmoderately** *adv.*: *a moderately successful career*

• ***v.*** /ˈmɒdəreɪt; *AmE* ˈmɑːd-/ [T,I] to become or make sth become less extreme, severe, etc: *We've moderated our demands.*

**moderator** /ˈmɒdəreɪtə(r); *AmE* ˈmɑːd-/ *n.* [C] a person whose job is to help the two sides in a disagreement to reach an agreement

**modernize, -ise** /ˈmɒdənaɪz; *AmE* ˈmɑːdərn-/ *v.* [T,I] to make sth more modern by starting to use new equipment, ideas, etc: *modernizing factories* ▸ **ˌmoderniˈzation, -iˈsation** /-naɪˈzeɪʃn; *AmE* -nəˈz-/ *n.* [U]

**modest** /ˈmɒdɪst; *AmE* ˈmɑːd-/ *adj.* not very large, expensive, important, etc: *He only charges a modest fee.*

▸ **ˈmodestly** *adv.*

★ **modify** /ˈmɒdɪfaɪ; *AmE* ˈmɑːd-/ *v.* [T] (**-fies, -fying, -fied, -fied**) to change sth slightly, esp. in order to make it more suitable for a particular purpose: *The software is modified for specific customers.* SYN ADAPT

▸ **ˌmodifiˈcation** /-ˈkeɪʃn/ *n.* [C,U]: *slight modifications to the design*

**modular** /ˈmɒdjələ(r); *AmE* ˈmɑːdʒə-/ *adj.* **1** consisting of separate parts or units that can be joined together: *modular furniture* **2** (*Manufact.*) used to describe a system in which the parts or units of a car, machine, etc. are made separately by suppliers and then joined together by the manufacturer

**module** /ˈmɒdjuːl; *AmE* ˈmɑːdʒuːl/ *n.* [C] **1** (*IT*) a unit of a computer system or program that has a particular function: *software modules* **2** one of a set of separate parts or units that go together to make a machine, a piece of furniture, etc.

**mogul** /ˈməʊgl; *AmE* ˈmoʊgl/ *n.* [C] a very rich, important and powerful person: *a media mogul*

**ˌmom-and-ˈpop** *adj.* (*AmE*) used to describe a small local shop/store or business that is often owned by a family: *mom-and-pop stores*

**momentum** /məˈmentəm; *AmE* moʊˈm-/ *n.* [U] an energy or a force, particularly one that helps to increase or improve sth: *The economic recovery is gaining momentum.*

**monetarism** /ˈmʌnɪtərɪzəm/ *n.* [U] (*Econ.*) the theory and policy that considers the best way to manage an economy and keep INFLATION low is by controlling the amount of money and credit that is available ▸ **ˈmonetarist** *n.* [C] **ˈmonetarist** *adj.*

★ **monetary** /ˈmʌnɪtri; *AmE* -teri/ *adj.* **1** connected with money or currencies: *the monetary rewards of running a company* **2** (*Econ.*) connected with the amount of money and credit available within a particular country or economy and the way this is controlled: *monetary easing by the central bank* ◇ *~ expansion/tightening*

**ˈmonetary base** *n.* [C, usu. sing.] (*Econ.*) all the cash that is available within a particular economy including all the bills/notes and coins that are held by individuals and by banks

**ˌmonetary ˈpolicy** *n.* [C] (*Econ.*) the way in which a government or central bank controls the supply of money and credit in an economy → FISCAL POLICY

❶ *loose/tight ~* ◆ *to ease/loosen/tighten ~*

**ˈmonetary ˌsystem** *n.* [C] (*Econ.*) the system that controls the supply and exchange of money within a country or between different countries: *the European/international ~*

**ˈmonetary ˌunit** *n.* [C] (*Econ.*) the standard form of currency in a country SYN UNIT OF CURRENCY

★ **money** /ˈmʌni/ *n.* **1** [U] what you can use to buy and sell things and earn through your work, investments, sales, etc: *How much money is there in my account?* ◇ *If the item is faulty, you will get your money back.* ◇ *New systems can save you time and money.*

❶ *to earn/make/spend ~* ◆ *to* ***borrow/lend/owe/raise ~*** ◆ *to* ***pour/pump/put ~ into*** *sth*

**2** [U] coins or paper notes **3** [U] a person's wealth including their property: *He lost all his money.* **4** (*Law*) **moneys** (*or* **monies** [pl.]) sums of money: *a statement of all monies paid into your account* IDM **be, pour, throw, etc. money down the ˈdrain** to waste money **make ˈmoney** to earn a lot of money; to make a profit: *There's money to be made from tourism.* **make/lose money ˌhand over ˈfist** to make/lose money very fast and in large quantities **money ˈtalks** people who have a lot of money have more power and influence **time is ˈmoney** time is valuable, and should not be wasted → idioms at COIN *v.*, LICENCE, THROW

**ˌmoney at ˈcall** *n.* [U] (*Finan.*) money which must be paid as soon as the lender demands it

**ˈmoney at ˈcall and short ˈnotice** *n.* [U] (*Finan.*) money which must be paid either as soon as the lender demands it, or within 14 days

**ˌmoney-back guaranˈtee** *n.* [C] (*Comm.*) a promise to return customers' money if they are not satisfied with a product or service

**ˈmoney ˌbroker** *n.* [C] (*Finan.*) a person or an organization that arranges loans between banks, etc. for short periods of time

**ˈmoney ˌcentre bank** *n.* [C] (*Finan.*) in the US, a large bank that lends money to governments, large companies and other banks rather than to individual customers

**ˈmoney fund** = MONEY MARKET FUND

**ˈmoney-ˌgrubbing** (*also* **ˈmoney-ˌgrabbing**) *adj.* (*infml.*) trying to get a lot of money ▸ **ˈmoney-ˌgrubber** (*also* **ˈmoney-ˌgrabber**) *n.* [C]

**ˈmoney ˌlaundering** *n.* [U] the act of moving money that has been obtained illegally into foreign bank accounts or legal businesses so that it is difficult for people to know where the money came from ▸ **ˈmoney ˌlaunderer** *n.* [C]

**moneylender** /ˈmʌnilendə(r)/ *n.* [C] (*Finan.*) a person or an organization whose business is lending money, to be paid back with interest, but who are not part of the official banking system

**'money ˌloser** *n.* [C] a product, service, company, etc. that makes a loss rather than a profit
▸ **'money-ˌlosing** *adj.*: *a money-losing enterprise*

**moneymaker** /ˈmʌnimeɪkə(r)/ *n.* [C] **1** a product, service, company, etc. that makes a large profit **2** a person who is good at finding or creating opportunities to make money: *City moneymakers and investors*
▸ **'moneymaking** *adj.*: *a moneymaking service* **'moneymaking** *n.* [U]

**'money ˌmanagement** *n.* [U] (*Finan.*) **1** the activity of organizing the investments of a person, an organization or a financial institution so that they make as much profit as possible SYN INVESTMENT MANAGEMENT **2** the activity of organizing income, savings, payments, etc. for yourself or on behalf of sb else

**'money ˌmanager** *n.* [C] a person who manages investments on behalf of a company or an individual SYN INVESTMENT MANAGER

**'money ˌmarket** *n.* [C] (*Finan.*) **1** the activity of buying and selling short loans between banks and other financial institutions, for example in the form of CERTIFICATES OF DEPOSIT or TREASURY BILLS; the banks, etc. involved: *Cash was flowing out of the money market into the stock market.* **2** the buying and selling of foreign money: *The pound rose again on the money markets.*

**'money ˌmarket fund** (*also* **'money fund**) *n.* [C] (*Finan.*) a type of fund that buys investments with a low risk, such as CERTIFICATES OF DEPOSIT or TREASURY BILLS, rather than shares

**'money ˌorder** (*abbr* **MO**) (*also* **ˌpostal 'money ˌorder**) (*BrE also* **'postal ˌorder**) *n.* [C] an official document that you can buy at a bank or a post office and send to sb so that they can exchange it for money

**'money-ˌspinner** *n.* [C] (*BrE*) (*infml.*) a product, an idea, etc. that earns a lot of money
▸ **'money-ˌspinning** *adj.*

**'money suˌpply** (*also* **'money stock**) *n.* [sing; U] (*Econ.*) the total amount of money that exists in the economy of a country at a particular time: *measures to control the money supply* ◊ *to increase/reduce/restrict (the)* ~ → MO, MI, ETC.

**'money transˌmission** *n.* [U] (*Finan.*) the process of moving money and making payments from one individual or organization to another, done by banks, etc.

**'money ˌwages** *n.* [pl.] (*Econ.*) the amount of money sb is paid for the work they do, expressed as a figure without considering what it can buy → REAL WAGES

★ **monitor** /ˈmɒnɪtə(r); *AmE* ˈmɑːn-/ *n.*, *v.*
• *n.* [C] **1** a screen that shows information from a computer: *a 17-inch, flat-screen monitor* **2** a person whose job is to check that sth is done fairly and honestly
• *v.* [T] to watch and check a process over a period of time in order to see how it develops and make any necessary changes: *The situation is being closely monitored.*

★ **monopolize**, **-ise** /məˈnɒpəlaɪz; *AmE* məˈnɑːp-/ *v.* [T] (*Econ.*) to have or take control of all or almost all of sth such as a market or an industry so that others are prevented from sharing it: *companies trying to monopolize the market*
▸ **moˌnopoli'zation**, **-i'sation** /-laɪˈzeɪʃn; *AmE* -ləˈz-/ *n.* [U]

★ **monopoly** /məˈnɒpəli; *AmE* məˈnɑːp-/ *n.* [C] (*pl.* **-lies**) (*Econ.*) the complete control of trade in particular goods or the supply of a particular service; the type of goods or service that is controlled in this way: *They have a virtual monopoly* **in** *video games.* ◊ *Health care is a public/state* ~ (= owned and controlled by the government).
⊙ *to create/extend a* ~ • *to* ***break*** *(up)/end/lose a* ~
▸ **mo'nopolist** *n.* [C] **moˌnop-o'listic** *adj.*: *monopolistic corporations*

**monopsony** /məˈnɒpsəni; *AmE* məˈnɑːp-/ *n.* (*pl.* **-nies**) (*Econ.*) **1** [U] a situation where there is only one buyer in a particular market or where one buyer controls most of a market **2** [C] a person or an organization that is the only buyer or the main buyer in a particular market
▸ **mo'nopsonist** *n.* [C]

**ˌmonth-on-'month** *adj.*, *adv.* compared with the same date one month earlier: *Consumer spending showed a 6% month-on-month drop in January.* → YEAR ON YEAR at YEAR

**moonlight** /ˈmuːnlaɪt/ *v.* [I] (**-lighted**, **-lighted**) to have a second job that you do secretly, usu. without paying tax on the extra money that you earn: *moonlighting as a cab driver* ▸ **'moonlighter** *n.* [C]

**'moonlighting** *n.* [U]: *doing a bit of moonlighting*

**'Moore's law** *n.* [sing.] (*IT*) the theory that the possible power of computing doubles every 18 months

**morale** /mə'rɑːl; *AmE* -'ræl/ *n.* [U] the amount of confidence and enthusiasm, etc. that a person or a group has at a particular time: *ways of keeping employee morale high*

**,moral 'hazard** *n.* [U] the situation where people or organizations are more likely to take risks because they are protected against the results, for example by insurance

**,moral 'rights** *n.* [pl.] (*Law*) the rights of an author in relation to their work, for example the right for the work not to be changed in a way that damages the author's reputation

**moratorium** /,mɒrə'tɔːriəm; *AmE* ,mɔːr-/ *n.* [C] (*pl.* **-riums** *or* **-ria** /-riə/) **1** a temporary stopping of an activity, esp. by an official agreement: *a moratorium* **on** *all new projects* ◇ *to end/impose/lift a ~* **2** (*Law*) a period of time during which an organization does not have to pay a debt or tax

**moribund** /'mɒrɪbʌnd; *AmE* 'mɔːr-; 'mɑːr-/ *adj.* (*fml.*) no longer effective or active, and likely to fail or end soon: *moribund state industries*

**morph** /mɔːf; *AmE* mɔːrf/ *v.* [T,I] (*infml.*) **1** to change into sth different: *Our small company is morphing* **into** *a global business.* **2** (*IT*) to gradually change from one computer image into another
▸ **'morphing** *n.* [U]

**mor'tality ,tables** = LIFE TABLES

★ **mortgage** /'mɔːgɪdʒ; *AmE* 'mɔːrg-/ *n., v.*
• *n.* [C] (*also* **'property loan**) a legal agreement by which a bank or similar organization lends you money to buy a house, flat/apartment, etc. or land, and you pay the money back over a number of years; the sum of money that you borrow
⊙ *to* ***apply for/get/have/take out*** *a ~* ♦ *to* ***pay/pay off/repay*** *a ~* ♦ *~* ***payments/repayments*** ♦ *~* ***arrears***
• *v.* [T] to borrow money from a bank or similar organization, giving the bank the legal right to own your house or land if you do not pay back the money that you have borrowed: *to mortgage your property*

**,mortgage-backed se'curity** *n.* [C] (*abbr* **MBS**) (*Finan.*) a type of investment that represents a share in a group of **mortgages** and that receives income from the payments made by the borrowers

**'mortgage bond** *n.* [C] (*Finan.*) a safe type of investment which is protected by property or physical equipment that can be sold to pay the investor

**mortgagee** /,mɔːgɪ'dʒiː; *AmE* ,mɔːrg-/ *n.* [C] a person or an organization that lends money to people to buy property

**'mortgage ,finance** *n.* [U] money lent to people or organizations to buy property

**'mortgage ,lender** *n.* [C] an organization such as a bank that lends money to people and businesses to buy property

**'mortgage ,market** *n.* [C] (*Finan.*) **1** (*also* **,primary 'mortgage ,market**) the activity of lending money to people and organizations to buy property; the banks and financial institutions that do this **2** (*also* **,secondary 'mortgage ,market**) the activity of buying and selling existing mortgages

**'mortgage rate** *n.* [C] the rate of interest that banks and other lenders charge on loans that they give people to buy property

**mortgagor** /'mɔːgɪdʒɔː(r); *AmE* 'mɔːrg-/ *n.* [C] a person or company that borrows money to buy property

**mothball** /'mɒθbɔːl; *AmE* 'mɔːθ-/ *v.* [T] to stop using or developing a business or part of a business for a period of time: *They had to mothball several plants.*
▸ **'mothballing** *n.* [U]

**motherboard** /'mʌðəbɔːd; *AmE* 'mʌðərbɔːrd/ *n.* [C] (*IT*) the main board of a computer, containing all the sets of electrical connections that make up the computer's memory and power

**motion** /'məʊʃn; *AmE* 'moʊʃn/ *n.* [C] a formal proposal that is discussed and voted on at a meeting: *Shareholders tabled a motion* **to** *adjourn the meeting.*
⊙ *to* ***propose/put forward*** *a ~* ♦ *to* ***adopt/approve/carry/pass*** *a ~* ♦ *to* ***defeat/reject*** *a ~*

★ **motivate** /'məʊtɪveɪt; *AmE* 'moʊ-/ *v.* [T] to make sb want to do sth, esp. to work hard or try hard: *How can we motivate employees* **to** *become more productive?* OPP DEMOTIVATE ▸ **'motivated** *adj.*: *highly motivated staff* **,moti'vation** /-ɪ'veɪʃn/ *n.* [C,U]: *Size was the main motivation for the merger.*

ˌ**moti'vational** /-ˈveɪʃənl/ *adj.*: *motivational programs for employees*

ˌ**motivational re'search** *n.* [U] (*Market.*) research that tries to discover the reasons behind consumers' decisions about which brands or products to buy

**motivator** /ˈməʊtɪveɪtə(r); *AmE* ˈmoʊ-/ *n.* [C] **1** something such as money that encourages people to work or try hard **2** a person who is good at encouraging others to work or try hard

'**motor pool** = CAR POOL

**MOU** /ˌem əʊ ˈjuː; *AmE* oʊ/ = MEMORANDUM OF UNDERSTANDING

**mount** /maʊnt/ *v.* [I] to increase, often in a way that causes worry: *mounting debts* **PHRV** ˌ**mount 'up** to increase gradually in size and quantity: *Debts were mounting up.*

**mouse** /maʊs/ *n.* [C] (*pl.* **mouses** *or* **mice** /maɪs/) **1** a small device that you move and press with your hand in order to perform actions on a computer screen: *You can sign up just by a click of the mouse.* ◇ (*BrE*) *a mouse mat* ◇ (*AmE*) *a mouse pad* **2** a way of referring to a very small company that can create no new jobs

**move** /muːv/ *v., n.*

• *v.* **1** [I] to change the place where you live or work or where sth is situated: *The company is moving* **to** *Madrid.* → RELOCATE **2** [T] to make sb change from one job, department, etc. to another: *I'm being moved* **to** *the New York office.* **3** [I] (*with an adv. or a prep.*) to make progress in the way or direction mentioned: *Share prices moved ahead today.* ◇ *The project is moving on steadily.* **4** [T] to suggest sth formally so that it can be discussed and decided: *I move* **that** *a vote be taken.* **SYN** PUT STH FORWARD **5** [T,I] to be sold very quickly; to make sth be sold very quickly: *High street fashion is moving fast.* ◇ *Heavier advertising failed to move the goods.* ▸ '**movement** *n.* [C,U]: *laws to allow free movement of goods* ◇ *no movement in oil prices* **PHRV** ˌ**move 'on (to sth) 1** to progress or start sth new: *I've been here for five years—it's time to move on.* **2** to start discussing sth else: *Can we move on to the next item on the agenda?* ˌ**move 'over to sth** to change to doing or using sth different

• *n.* [C] **1** an action that you do or need to do to achieve sth: *Selling the smaller stores was a good move.* **2** a change in ideas, attitudes, or behaviour: *a move away from rail freight to road transport* **3** an act of changing the place where you live or work, or where sth is situated: *What's the date of your move?*

**mover** /ˈmuːvə(r)/ *n.* [C] **1** sth that changes its position, for example a company or currency that changes its position in a market: *the biggest upward mover in the index* **2** (*esp. AmE*) = REMOVER **IDM** ˌ**movers and 'shakers** people with power in an important organization: *the movers and shakers of the media world*

ˌ**moving 'average** *n.* [C] (*Tech.*) the average price or value of sth such as shares over a particular period up to the present, for example the past 30 days

**MPC** /ˌem piː ˈsiː/ = MARGINAL PROPENSITY TO CONSUME

**MPM** /ˌem piː ˈem/ = MARGINAL PROPENSITY TO IMPORT

**MPS** /ˌem piː ˈes/ = MARGINAL PROPENSITY TO SAVE

**MR** /ˌem ˈɑː(r)/ = MARKET RESEARCH

**MRM** /ˌem ɑːr ˈem/ = MARKETING RESOURCE MANAGEMENT

**MRP** /ˌem ɑː ˈpiː; *AmE* ɑːr/ = MATERIAL REQUIREMENTS PLANNING

**MS** /ˌem ˈes/ = MANAGEMENT SCIENCE

**MSRP** /ˌem es ɑː ˈpiː; *AmE* ɑːr/ *abbr* (*Comm.*) **manufacturer's suggested retail price** the price at which the maker of a product suggests that it should be sold to customers in shops/stores **SYN** RRP, SRP

**MTO** /ˌem tiː ˈəʊ; *AmE* ˈoʊ/ = MAKE-TO-ORDER

**MTS** /ˌem tiː ˈes/ = MAKE-TO-STOCK

**multi-** /ˈmʌlti/ *comb. form* (*used in ns and adjs*) more than one; many: *multicoloured packaging* ◇ *the multi-billion-dollar software industry*

**multidisciplinary** /ˌmʌltiˈdɪsəplɪnəri; ˌmʌltiˌdɪsəˈplɪnəri; *AmE* -ˈdɪsəpləneri/ *adj.* involving several different subjects of study or areas of activity: *a multidisciplinary team*

**multilateral** /ˌmʌltiˈlætərəl/ *adj.* in which three or more nations, companies, groups, etc. take part: *multilateral agreements*
▸ ˌ**multi'laterally** /-ˈlætrəli/ *adv.*

**multi'level ˌmarketing** (*abbr* **MLM**) (*also* '**network ˌmarketing**) *n.* [U] a system of selling a company's products directly to consumers, in which you sell to people you know and persuade them to help you sell as well. They then persuade others. You usu. get paid both for what you sell and for what the others sell.

**multimedia** /ˌmʌltiˈmiːdiə/ *adj.* **1** (*IT*) using sound, pictures and film in addition to text on a screen: *a multimedia presentation* **2** producing or selling several different types of media such as films/movies, books, or television programmes

**multinational** /ˌmʌltiˈnæʃnəl/ *adj., n.*

• ***adj.*** operating in or involving many countries: *~ corporations/companies*

• ***n.*** [C] a company that operates in several different countries, esp. a large and powerful company

**multipack** /ˈmʌltipæk/ *n.* [C] (*Market.*) a set of several items of the same type, sold together in one pack

**multiple** /ˈmʌltɪpl/ *n.* [C] **1** (*Stock Ex.*) a number expressing the current market price of a particular share divided by the EARNINGS PER SHARE of the company: *Technology shares are still trading at high multiples.* **2** (*Comm.*) (*also* **ˌmultiple ˈstore**) (*both BrE*) a shop/store that is one of a series of shops/stores owned by the same company: *It's hard for us to compete against the big multiples.* SYN CHAIN STORE

**multiple appliˈcations** *n.* [pl.] (*IT*) several different pieces of software running on a computer at the same time

**multiple-ˈchoice** *adj.* used to describe questions that show several possible answers from which you must choose one

**multiple ˈpricing** *n.* [U] (*Comm.*) **1** the practice of giving the same product a different price in different markets, in order to make the best profit **2** the practice of charging less for two or more units of an item bought together than the price of the units separately, in order to encourage people to buy more

**multiple ˈstore** = MULTIPLE (2)

**multiple taxˈation** *n.* [U] (*Account.*) a situation in which an amount of money is taxed more than once, for example by two different countries or authorities

**multiply** /ˈmʌltɪplaɪ/ *v.* (**-lies**, **-lying**, **-lied**, **-lied**) **1** [T] to add a number to itself a particular number of times: *This figure was calculated by multiplying the company's cash flow by 2.24.* **2** [T,I] to increase or make sth increase very much in number or amount: *The number of private shareholders has multiplied.*



**multiskilling** /ˌmʌltiˈskɪlɪŋ/ *n.* [U] (*HR*) the fact that a person is trained in several different jobs which require different skills

**multitask** /ˌmʌltiˈtɑːsk; *AmE* ˈmʌltitæsk/ *v.* [I] **1** (*IT*) to operate several programs at the same time **2** (of a person) to do several things at the same time

▸ **ˌmultiˈtasking** *n.* [U]

**ˌmulti-ˈunit** *adj.* (*Comm.*) consisting of or involving more than one shop/store or business unit: *the modern multi-unit business enterprise*

**ˌmulti-ˈuser** *adj.* **1** (*IT*) able to be used by more than one person at the same time: *All mainframes are multi-user systems, but most PCs are not.* **2** (*Comm.*) used by many different customers or organizations

**ˌmulti-ˈyear** *adj.* taking place over or including a period of several years: *a multi-year restructuring plan*

**muni** /ˈmjuːni/ (*pl.* **munis**) (*also* **ˈmuni bond**) = MUNICIPAL BOND

**municipal** /mjuːˈnɪsɪpl/ *adj., n.*

• ***adj.*** **1** connected with the local government of a town, city, or district: *municipal employees* **2** (*Finan.*) connected with MUNICIPAL BONDS

▸ **muˈnicipally** /-sɪpli/ *adv.*

• ***n.*** [C] (*Finan.*) = MUNICIPAL BOND: *trading in municipals*

**muˌnicipal ˈbond** (*also* **muˈnicipal**) (*also* **ˈmuni**, *infml.*) *n.* [C] (*Finan.*) a bond issued by a state or local government

**municipality** /mjuːˌnɪsɪˈpæləti/ *n.* [C] (*pl.* **-ties**) a town, city or district with its own local government; the group of officials who form the government

**ˌMurphy's ˈLaw** /ˌmɜːfiz ˈlɔː; *AmE* ˌmɜːrfiz/ *n.* [sing.] the humorous idea that if anything can possibly go wrong, it will go wrong

**mushroom** /ˈmʌʃrʊm; -ruːm/ *v.* [I] to rapidly grow or increase in number, esp. when this is a bad thing: *mushrooming costs*

**ˈmust-have** *adj.* used to say that sth is so good, interesting, useful, fashionable, etc. that people will want to own it: *Web access will soon become a standard, must-have feature for mobile phones.* ▸ **ˈmust-have** *n.* [C]: *What are the latest trendy must-haves?*

**mutual** /ˈmjuːtʃuəl/ *adj.* (*Finan.*) relating to a financial organization such as an insurance company that is a MUTUAL COMPANY: *a mutual life*

*insurer* ▶ **'mutual** *n.* [C]
**ˌmutu'ality** /-tʃu'æləti/ *n.* [U]

**'mutual ˌcompany** *n.* [C] (*Finan.*) a type of financial organization such as an insurance company which has no shareholders but is owned by its members, with profits shared among them

**'mutual fund** = UNIT TRUST

**ˌMyers-Briggs Type ˌIndicator™** /ˌmaɪəz 'brɪgz; *AmE* ˌmaɪərz/ *n.* [C, usu. sing.] (*abbr* **MBTI™**) (*HR*) a set of questions that people answer about themselves to find out their strengths and the type of person that they are

**ˌmystery 'shopper** *n.* [C] (*Market.*) a person whose job is to visit or telephone a shop/store or other business pretending to be a customer, in order to get information on the quality of the service, the buildings, special features, etc.
▶ **ˌmystery 'shopping** *n.* [U]

# Nn

**n/a** *abbr* (*written*) **1 not applicable** written on a form to show that you cannot answer a particular question because it does not affect you **2** (*Comm.*) **not available** written next to an item on a list, to show that the item is not available to buy

**NACE** /neɪs/ *abbr* **Nomenclature générale des Activités économiques dans les Communautés européennes** in the EU, a system in which industries and services are given a code to show which type of economic activity they are involved in, for reference and research

**nagware** /'nægweə(r); *AmE* -wer/ *n.* [U] (*IT*) software that repeatedly shows messages asking the user to do sth, such as pay to continue to use the product

**NAICS** /neɪks/ *abbr* **North American Industry Classification System** in the US, Canada and Mexico, a system in which industries and services are given a code to show which type of economic activity they are involved in, for reference and research

**nail** /neɪl/ *v.*, *n.*
• *v.* [T] (*AmE*) (*infml.*) to achieve sth or do sth successfully: *They've just nailed the deal.* **PHR V** **ˌnail sth 'down** to reach a definite agreement or decision on sth, usu. after a lot of discussion
• *n.* **IDM** **on the 'nail** (*BrE*) (*infml.*) without delay: *They always pay on the nail.*

**ˌnaked de'benture** *n.* [C] (*Finan.*) money that a company borrows that is not supported by particular assets that the company will lose if the loan is not repaid

**name** /neɪm/ *n.*, *v.*
• *n.* [C] **1** (*often with another n. or an adj. to form an adj.*) a very well-known person, company, product, etc: *one of the biggest names in the Italian fashion industry* ◇ *brand-name goods* **2** (*Insur.*) one of the investors in the insurance company Lloyd's who promise their own money to pay claims and share in the profits or losses
• *v.* **IDM** **ˌname and 'shame** (*BrE*) to publish the names of people or organizations who have done sth wrong or illegal

**'name-brand** *adj.* (*Comm.*; *Market.*) used to describe goods marked with the name of a well-known product or manufacturer

**ˌnarrow 'market** = THIN MARKET

**'narrow ˌmoney** *n.* [U] (*Econ.*) a term used to refer to the part of a country's MONEY SUPPLY that is money in its more limited sense, meaning only cash and things that can be easily turned into cash
**NOTE** This is known as **M1**.

**NASDAQ™** /'næzdæk/ *n.* [sing; U] an electronic system for buying and selling shares, esp. shares in particular companies that are not on an official stock exchange list, and giving price information about them: *The NASDAQ gained over 4.4 per cent.*

**NASDAQ-100™** /ˌnæzdæk wʌn 'hʌndrəd/ *n.* [sing.] a list of 100 shares traded on the **NASDAQ**, chosen to give a guide to share prices in general

**ˌnational ac'count** *n.* **1** (*Market.*) [C] an important customer, usu. a company, that does business with another company in many different parts of a country **2** (*Econ.*) [C, usu. pl.] the financial records of a country: *China's national accounts*

**ˌnational 'bank** *n.* [C] **1** = CENTRAL BANK **2** in the US, a COMMERCIAL BANK that is officially approved by the government and is a member of the FEDERAL RESERVE SYSTEM

**'national brand** *n.* [C] (*Market.*) a brand of product that is available in shops/stores in all areas of a country rather than one produced for a particular shop/store or area

**ˌnational ˈdebt** *n.* [C, usu. sing.] (*Econ.*) the total amount of money that the government of a country has borrowed and still owes

**ˌNational Inˈsurance** *n.* [U] (*abbr* **NI**) in the UK, a system of payments that have to be made by employers and employees to provide help for people who are ill/sick, old or unemployed

★ **nationalize**, **-ise** /ˈnæʃnəlaɪz/ *v.* [T] (*Econ.*) to put an industry or a company under the control of the government, which becomes its owner: *The Kofuku Bank was nationalized in 1998.* OPP PRIVATIZE ▸ **ˌnationaliˈzation, -iˈsation** /-laɪˈzeɪʃn; *AmE* -ləˈz-/ *n.* [U,C]: *the nationalization of the oil industry*

**ˌNational ˈMarket ˌSystem** *n.* [sing.] (*abbr* **NMS**) a computer trading system for some shares, bonds, etc. in the US

**ˌnational ˈproduct** = GROSS NATIONAL PRODUCT

**nationwide** /ˌneɪʃnˈwaɪd/ *adj.* happening or existing in all parts of a particular country: *a nationwide campaign* ▸ **ˌnationˈwide** *adv.*: *We have over 500 stores nationwide.*

**ˌnatural ˈbusiness year** = ACCOUNTING YEAR

**ˌnatural ˈgas** *n.* [U] gas that is found under the ground or the sea and that is used as a fuel

**ˌnatural reˈsource** *n.* [C, usu. pl.] a supply of sth that exists naturally in a country and can be used, esp. to create wealth: *Russia has abundant natural resources.*

**ˌnatural ˈwastage** (*also* **ˈwastage**) *n.* [U] (*both BrE*) (*HR*) the process of reducing the number of people who are employed by an organization by, for example, not replacing people who leave their jobs

**NAV** /ˌen eɪ ˈviː/ = NET ASSET VALUE

**navigate** /ˈnævɪgeɪt/ *v.* [T,I] (*IT*) to find your way around on the Internet or on a particular website: *Their website is very easy to navigate.* ▸ **ˌnaviˈgation** /-ˈgeɪʃn/ *n.* [U]

**ˌnaviˈgation bar** *n.* [C] (*IT*) an area along the top or one side of a web page where you can click on items from a list to go to other parts of the website

**NAVPS** /ˌen eɪ viː piː ˈes/ = NET ASSET VALUE PER SHARE

**NBV** /ˌen biː ˈviː/ = NET BOOK VALUE

**NDPB** /ˌen diː piː ˈbiː/ *n.* [C] **non-departmental public body** in the UK, an organization dealing with public matters, started and financed by the government, but working independently and with its own legal powers SYN QUANGO

**ˈnear-term** *adj.* lasting a short time; lasting only for a short period of time in the future: *The near-term economic outlook is good.* SYN SHORT-TERM OPP LONG-TERM

**necktie** /ˈnektaɪ/ = TIE *n.* (2)

**need** /niːd/ *n.* [C, usu. pl.] the things that sb requires in order to live in a comfortable way or achieve what they want: *Tailor your services to fit your customers' needs.*
⊕ *to* ***analyse/assess/determine/identify/understand*** *sb's ~s* ◆ *to* ***address/fit/meet/serve/suit*** *sb's ~s*

★ **negative** /ˈnegətɪv/ *adj., n.*
• ***adj.*** **1** less than zero: *a negative trade balance* **2** bad or harmful: *The crisis had a negative effect on trade.* **3** without enthusiasm or support: *The response to our plans has been very negative.* OPP POSITIVE ▸ **ˈnegatively** *adv.*
• ***n.*** [C] (*Tech.*) the result of a test or an experiment that shows that a substance or condition is not present OPP POSITIVE

**ˈnegative cerˈtificate of ˈorigin** *n.* [C] (*Trade*) a certificate that states that a product was not produced in a particular country that the buyer refuses to accept goods from

**ˌnegative ˈinventory** *n.* [U,C] (*Product.*) a situation when the number of items in the stock of a business appears to be less than zero, often as a result of a mistake in recording the movement of items

**ˌnegative ˈterritory** *n.* [U] often used in newspapers to describe a level that is below zero, or below the previous or expected level: *Share prices ended the day* **in** *negative territory.*

**negligence** /ˈneglɪdʒəns/ *n.* [U] (*Law*) the failure to give enough care or attention to sb/sth that you are responsible for: *to sue a company for negligence* ▸ **ˈnegligent** *adj.* **ˈnegligently** *adv.*

**negligible** /ˈneglɪdʒəbl/ *adj.* of very little importance or size and not worth considering: *negligible growth*

**negotiable** /nɪˈgəʊʃiəbl; *AmE* -ˈgoʊ-/ *adj.* **1** that you can discuss or change before you make an agreement or a decision: *The price was not negotiable.* **2** (*Finan.*) that you can exchange for money or give to another person in exchange for money:

*negotiable securities* OPP NON-NEGOTIABLE

★ **negotiate** /nɪˈgəʊʃieɪt; *AmE* -ˈgoʊ-/ *v.* **1** [I] to try to reach an agreement by formal discussion: *We negotiated **for** more pay.* **2** [T] to arrange sth or agree to sth by formal discussion: *negotiate better prices* **3** (*Finan.*) [T] to transfer sth such as a cheque or a bill to sb else in exchange for money: *The bill of exchange was negotiated several times.*

**negotiated** /nɪˈgəʊʃieɪtɪd; *AmE* -ˈgoʊ-/ *adj.* that is the result of discussions: *a ~ deal/fee/settlement/solution*

**the neˈgotiating ˌtable** *n.* [sing.] used in newspapers to describe formal discussions to try to reach an agreement

★ **negotiation** /nɪˌgəʊʃiˈeɪʃn; *AmE* -ˌgoʊʃi-/ *n.* **1** [C, usu. pl., U] formal discussions between people who are trying to reach an agreement: *the next **round of** wage negotiations* ◇ *The deal is still **under** negotiation.*
⊙ *to **begin/enter (into)/open/resume/start** ~s* ◆ *to **break off/complete** ~s*
**2** (*Finan.*) [U] the process of transferring sth such as a cheque or a bill to sb else, who then becomes the legal owner **3** (*Finan.*) [U] the process of changing a cheque into money

**negotiator** /nɪˈgəʊʃieɪtə(r); *AmE* -ˈgoʊʃi-/ *n.* [C] a person who is involved in formal discussions that aim to reach an agreement, esp. because it is their job

**nepotism** /ˈnepətɪzəm/ *n.* [U] giving advantages to your own family if you are in a position of power, esp. by giving them jobs

**ˈnest egg** *n.* [C, usu. sing.] (*infml.*) an amount of money that sb has saved for the future

★ **net** /net/ *n., adj., v.*
• *n.* **1 the Net** [sing.] = INTERNET **2** [C,U] (*AmE*) a **net** amount or weight: *The third quarter net was up 6%.*
• *adj.* (*BrE also* **nett**) **1** (*Account.*) a **net** amount of money is the amount that remains when nothing more is to be taken away: *net profits of £360 m* ◇ *The salary is €40 000 net of tax.*
⊙ *a ~ **loss/operating loss/operating profit*** ◆ *~ **earnings/income/proceeds/sales***
**2** final, after all the important facts have been included: *the **net result***
▸ **net** *adv.*: *Interest will be paid net* (= tax will already have been taken away). → GROSS
• *v.* [T] (-tt-) **1** to earn an amount of money as a profit after you have taken away some of it for tax, etc: *After paying all his debts, he netted $50 000.* **2** to manage to obtain sth: *The deal netted over €200 000.* → GROSS
PHR V **ˌnet sth ˈdown (to sth)**; **ˌnet ˈdown (to sth)** (*Finan.*) to take sth away from an amount until only the net amount is left **ˌnet ˈout at/to sth** (*Account.*) to produce an amount of money after some has been taken away for tax and other expenses

**net 10**, **net 30** *adv.* (*Account., written*) used on an INVOICE to show that it must be paid within 10 (or 30) days

**net 10 eom**, **net 30 eom** (*also* **net 10 prox**, **net 10th prox**, **net 30 prox**, **net 30th prox**) *adv.* (*Account., written*) used on an INVOICE to show that it must be paid on or before the 10th (or 30th) day of the next month: *Men's clothes are sold at net 30 eom.*

**ˌnet ˈassets** *n.* [pl.] (*Account.*) the value of a company's or person's total assets, minus their total LIABILITIES

**ˌnet ˈasset ˌvalue** *n.* [U; sing.] (*abbr* **NAV**) (*Account.*) **1** the value of a company's assets calculated by taking its total LIABILITIES away from its total assets **2** = NET ASSET VALUE PER SHARE

**ˈnet ˈasset ˌvalue per ˈshare** *n.* [U; sing.] (*abbr* **NAVPS**) (*Account.*) the value of a share in a company, calculated by taking its total LIABILITIES away from its total assets and dividing by the total number of shares

**ˌnet ˈbook ˌvalue** *n.* [U; sing.] (*abbr* **NBV**) (*Account.*) **1** the current value of an asset or a set of assets in a company's financial records, calculated by taking the DEPRECIATION away from its original cost **2** the current value of a company shown in its financial records, which is the difference between its total assets after DEPRECIATION and its total LIABILITIES

**ˌnet ˈborrowings** *n.* [pl.] (*Account.*) the total amount that a company has borrowed, minus the amount of cash or LIQUID assets it has

**Net-centric** /ˌnet-ˈsentrɪk/ *adj.* depending on or suited to the Internet: *Net-centric companies*

**ˈNet ˌcommerce** = INTERNET COMMERCE

**ˈnet ˈcurrent ˈassets** *n.* [pl.] (*Account.*) a company's CURRENT ASSETS minus CURRENT LIABILITIES

**ˌnet exˈporter** *n.* [C] (*Econ.*) a country that exports more than it imports

**ˌnet imˈporter** *n.* [C] (*Econ.*) a country that imports more than it exports

**netiquette** /ˈnetɪket/ *n.* [U] informal rules of behaviour for communicating with people over the Internet

**ˌnet ˈlending** *n.* [U] (*Account.*) the total amount of money that a bank lends in a particular period, minus amounts that have been paid back

**ˌnet ˈmargin** = OPERATING MARGIN

**ˈnet ˈpresent ˈvalue** *n.* [U,C] (*abbr* **NPV**) (*Account.*) the value of income from an investment calculated by taking the **present value** of money which will be received minus the **present value** of money which will be paid out

**ˌnet ˈprice** *n.* [C] the price that sb pays for goods or services after any reductions in price have been taken off and any tax has been added

**ˌnet ˈprofit** *n.* [C,U] (*Account.*) the money that you make in business or by selling things, after all costs, tax, interest, etc. have been taken off

**ˌnet ˈprofit ˌmargin** = OPERATING MARGIN

**ˈnet ˈrealizable ˈvalue** *n.* [C,U] (*abbr* **NRV**) (*Account.*) the amount of money that will be received for an asset when it is sold, minus the costs involved in selling it

**ˌnet ˈrevenue** *n.* [C,U] (*Account.*) the total amount of money received from sales of goods or services, minus the amount for goods returned by customers, etc.

**ˌnet ˈsales** *n.* [pl.] (*Account.*) the total value of goods and services sold, after an amount has been taken away for expenses such as transport, returned goods, reductions in price, etc.

**ˈNet ˌsurfer** *n.* [C] a person who spends a lot of time using the Internet

**nett** = NET *adj.*

**ˈnet ˈtangible ˈassets** *n.* [pl.] (*abbr* **NTA**) (*Account.*) the value of the physical assets that a company owns minus its CURRENT LIABILITIES

**ˌnet ˈton** = SHORT TON

★ **network** /ˈnetwɜːk; *AmE* -wɜːrk/ *n.*, *v.*

• *n.* [C] **1** a group of people, companies, etc. that exchange information or work together for a particular purpose: *a distribution network* **2** (*IT*) a number of computers and other devices that are connected together so that equipment and information can be shared

• *v.* **1** (*IT*) [T] to connect a number of computers and other devices together so that equipment and information can be shared **2** [I] to try to meet and talk to people who may be useful to you in your work: *Conferences are a good place to network.*

▸ **ˈnetworked** *adj.*: *networked companies* (= that use technology to form a single system) ◇ *networked computer systems*

**ˈnetwork aˌnalysis** *n.* [C,U] **1** (*Econ.*; *Product.*) = CRITICAL PATH ANALYSIS **2** (*IT*) the process of recording the movements of information to and from a computer network

**networker** /ˈnetwɜːkə(r); *AmE* -wɜːrk-/ *n.* [C] **1** a person who works for a company from home or from another office using a computer network **2** a person who tries to meet and talk to people in order to make business contacts

**networking** /ˈnetwɜːkɪŋ; *AmE* -wɜːrk-/ *n.* [U] **1** a system of meeting and talking to other people who may be useful or helpful to you in your work **2** (*IT*) a system of connecting a number of computers and other devices so that equipment and information can be shared: *wireless networking*

**ˈnetwork ˌmarketing** = MULTILEVEL MARKETING

**ˌnet ˈworth** *n.* [U,C] (*also* **ˌowners' ˈequity** [U]) (*Account.*) a measure of the current financial value of a company etc., calculated by taking CURRENT LIABILITIES away from the total assets

**net wt.** *abbr* a short way of writing net weight

**ˌnet ˈyield** *n.* [C,U] (*Account.*) the amount of profit an investment makes after taking off costs and taxes, expressed as a percentage of its price

**newbie** /ˈnjuːbi; *AmE* ˈnuːbi/ *n.* [C] (*infml.*) a person who has just begun to use a computer, a particular program or the Internet

**ˌnew ˈdeal** (*also* **New Deal**) *n.* [sing.] **1** policies introduced by a government or an organization to help a region, group of people, etc. return to normal after a difficult period **2 New Deal** the policies introduced in the US in the 1930s by President Roosevelt to help the economy return to normal

**the ˌNew Eˈconomy** (*also* **the new economy**) *n.* [sing.] used to describe the economy that developed in the late 20th century, with industries based on very new technology and the use of the Internet to do business

**ˌnew ˈissue** *n.* [C] (*Stock Ex.*) a number of shares that are made available for investors to buy for the first time: *the new issue market*

**ˈnewly inˈdustrialized ˈcountry** (*also* **ˈnewly inˈdustrializing ˈcountry**) *n.* [C] (*abbr* **NIC**) (*Econ.*) a country that did not have much industry previously, but where industries are now developing very fast

**ˌnewly issued ˈshare** = NEW SHARE

**ˌnewly issued ˈstock** = NEW STOCK

**ˌnew ˈmedia** *n.* [U] (*IT*) ways in which large numbers of people can receive information and entertainment through computers

**ˌnew ˈmoney** *n.* [U] **1** money that becomes available for use for the first time **2** wealth that has been gained recently; the people who have it

**ˌnew-ˈproduct** *adj.* used to describe activities related to developing and selling a new product: ~ *launches/teams*

**ˌnew-ˈproduct deˌvelopment** *n.* [U] (*abbr* **NPD**) (*Market.*) the process by which a company changes ideas into new or improved products or services

**ˈnews ˌconference** = PRESS CONFERENCE

**newsgroup** /ˈnjuːzgruːp; *AmE* ˈnuːz-/ *n.* [C] an area of the Internet, with its own address, where people discuss a particular topic; the people who belong to this group

**ˌnew ˈshare** (*also* **ˌnewly issued ˈshare**) *n.* [C, usu. pl.] (*Stock Ex.*) a share that a company makes available for investors to buy for the first time

**ˈnews reˌlease** = PRESS RELEASE

**ˌnew ˈstock** (*also* **ˌnewly issued ˈstock**) *n.* [U,C] (*Stock Ex.*) shares that a company makes available for investors to buy for the first time

**ˌnext-ˈday** *adj.* used to refer to a service that is provided on the day after you order it: *next-day delivery*

**ˌnext-geneˈration** *adj.* used to describe a product that has been developed and improved using the latest technology, and that is much more advanced than the versions available until now

**NGO** /ˌen dʒiː ˈəʊ; *AmE* ˈoʊ/ *abbr* **non-governmental/-government organization** an organization, such as a charity, that does not make a profit, is independent of government and business, and is formed for a particular purpose for the good of the public

**NI** = NATIONAL INSURANCE

**NIC** /ˌen aɪ ˈsiː/ = NEWLY INDUSTRIALIZED COUNTRY

★**niche** /niːʃ/ *n.* [C] (*Market.*) an opportunity to sell a particular type of product or service for which there is limited demand, but little or no competition: *They spotted a niche* **in** *the market.* ◇ *a small niche company*

**ˈniche ˌmarket** *n.* [C] (*Market.*) a market in which there is little or no competition for a particular type of product or service, for which there is limited demand: *The company has carved out a strong niche market for its software.* ▸ **ˈniche ˌmarketer** *n.* [C] **ˈniche ˌmarketing** *n.* [U]

**nicher** /ˈniːʃə(r)/ *n.* [C] (*Market.*) a niche company or product

**Nielsen™** /ˈniːlsən/ = NIELSEN RATING

**ˌNielsen/ˈNetRatings™** /ˌniːlsən ˈnetreɪtɪŋz/ *n.* [sing.] a company that measures and analyses Internet use and provides information and advice to companies so that they can develop strategies for using the Internet

**ˈNielsen™ ˌrating** /ˈniːlsən/ (*also* **ˈNielsen™**) *n.* [C] (*Market.*) in the US, a measure of how many people, and often what type of people, watch a particular programme on television. The information is used by companies who want to advertise their products to a suitable audience, and by television companies who set the price for advertising in and around particular programmes.

**ˈnight safe** (*BrE*) (*AmE* **ˈnight deˌpository**) *n.* [C] a box in the wall of a bank where companies, etc. can deposit money when the bank is closed

**NIH syndrome** /ˌen aɪ ˈeɪtʃ/ = NOT-INVENTED-HERE SYNDROME

**Nikkei™** /nɪˈkeɪ/ *n.* [sing.] (*usu.* **the Nikkei**) **1** used to refer to the **Nikkei Stock Average** or a **Nikkei Index**: *The Nikkei rose 19.25 points.* **2** a financial and business newspaper in Japan that publishes INDEXES of the share prices of important companies

**Nikˌkei ˈIndex** /nɪˈkeɪ/ *n.* [sing.] one of the measures of the share prices of the companies that are traded on the Tokyo Stock Exchange

**Nikˌkei ˈStock ˌAverage** /nɪˈkeɪ/ (*also* **Nikkei 225** /nɪˌkeɪ tuː tuː

'faɪv/) *n.* [sing.] a measure of the share prices of the 225 most important companies that are traded on the Tokyo Stock Exchange

**nil** /nɪl/ *n.* [U] nothing; zero: *Growth in sales last year was nil.*

**NMS** /ˌen em 'es/ = NATIONAL MARKET SYSTEM

**NMW** /ˌen em 'dʌblju:/ *abbr* **national minimum wage** in the UK, used to refer to the lowest wage that an employer is allowed to pay by law

**No.** (*also* **no.**) *abbr* (*pl.* **Nos, nos**) number: *invoice No. 5370*

**ˌno-'brainer** *n.* [C] (*infml.*) a question or problem that is so easy to answer or solve that it needs no thought ▸ **ˌno-'brainer** *adj.*

**no-'frills** *adj.* including only the basic features, without anything that is unnecessary, esp. things added to make sth more attractive or comfortable: *a no-frills airline*

**ˌno-'load fund** *n.* [C] (*Finan.*) a fund that does not charge investors a fee when they put their money into it or take it out

**noˌmadic 'worker** *n.* [C] a person who moves from place to place in order to get work

**nominal** /'nɒmɪnl; *AmE* 'nɑ:m-/ *adj.* **1** being sth in name only, and not in reality: *He was in nominal control of the business.* **2** (about a sum of money) very small and much less than the normal cost or change: *to pay a nominal rent* **3** used to describe a size or quantity that is stated on a product but may not be the exact size or quantity **4** (*Econ.*) used to describe a rate or other figure that refers to current prices or numbers, but has not been changed to consider the effects of INFLATION: *5% nominal GDP growth*
▸ **'nominally** /-nəli/ *adv.*

**ˌnominal 'capital** (*also* **ˌnominal 'share ˌcapital**) *n.* [U] (*Account.*) the value of all the shares issued by a company which is equal to the total number of shares multiplied by the price they were originally sold for

**ˌnominal 'damages** *n.* [pl.] (*Law*) a very small amount of money that is paid to sb by the person, company, etc. that has done sth wrong to them but has not caused them harm or financial loss

**ˌnominal 'ledger** = GENERAL LEDGER

**ˌnominal 'price** *n.* [C] **1** (*Account.*) the money value of a product, raw material, etc. without considering the effect of INFLATION



on this value **2** (*Finan.*) = PAR **3** a very small amount of money that is paid for sth, which is much less than the market price would be **4** (*Finan.*) (*also* **ˌnominal 'quotation**) the price estimated for a share, COMMODITY, etc. that has not yet been traded, and therefore has no market price

**ˌnominal 'share ˌcapital** = NOMINAL CAPITAL

**ˌnominal 'value** = PAR

**ˌnominal 'yield** *n.* [C,U] (*Finan.*) the rate of interest that is paid on the original value of a bond, without considering the effect of INFLATION

**nominate** /'nɒmɪneɪt; *AmE* 'nɑ:m-/ *v.* [T] **1** to formally suggest that sb/sth should be chosen for an important role, position, prize, etc. **2** to choose sb to do a particular job: *He has been nominated as the new CEO.* ▸ **ˌnomi'nation** /-'neɪʃn/ *n.* [C,U] **'nominator** *n.* [C]

**nominee** /ˌnɒmɪ'ni:; *AmE* ˌnɑ:m-/ *n.* [C] **1** a person who is suggested for a position, prize, etc. **2** a person, company, bank, etc. in whose name money is invested in a company or property, but who is not the real owner **3** (*Insur.*) a person who is named as the one to receive money if the insured person dies

**ˌnon-ac'ceptance** *n.* [U] the fact of not accepting sth

**ˌnon-'audit** *adj.* used to describe services other than AUDITING that a company pays an accountant to provide

**ˌnon-'callable** *adj.* (*Finan.*) used to describe a bond or other form of loan that the borrower may not pay back within the fixed time limit

**ˌnon-'cash** *adj.* not consisting of or involving money

**ˌnon-com'pliance** *n.* [U] (*usu. written*) **~ (with sth)** the fact of failing or refusing to obey a rule

**ˌnon-con'tributory** *adj.* that you do not have to pay part of: *a non-contributory pension plan*

**ˌnon-'core** *adj.* not the most important part of sth: *~ activities/operations*

**ˌnon-current lia'bilities** *n.* [pl.] (*Account.*) debts that do not need to be paid until after a particular period of time, usu. 12 months SYN LONG-TERM LIABILITIES

**ˌnon-de'livery** *n.* [U] the fact of sth not being delivered

**ˌnon-dis'closure** *n.* [U] (*Law*) the fact of keeping information secret: *non-disclosure of earnings*

**ˌnon-disˌtributable reˈserve** = CAPITAL RESERVE (1)

**ˌnon-ˈdurable** *adj.* that will not last for a long time: ~ *clothing*

**ˌnon-ˈdurable goods** = CONSUMER NON-DURABLES

**ˌnon-ˈdurables** = CONSUMER NON-DURABLES

**ˌnon-economic ˈdamages** *n.* [pl.] (*Law*) an amount of money that is paid to sb by the company, person, etc. who caused them harm or injury, even though they did not suffer financial loss

**ˌnon-eˈxecutive** *adj.* used to describe sb who is not employed by a company but takes part in meetings of the BOARD OF DIRECTORS and gives independent advice

**ˈnon-eˈxecutive diˈrector** (*also* **indeˌpendent diˈrector, ˌoutside diˈrector**) *n.* [C] a member of a company's BOARD OF DIRECTORS who is not employed by the company but takes part in meetings of the board and provides independent advice ▸ **ˈnon-eˈxecutive diˈrectorship** *n.* [C]

**ˌnon-ˈfarm** *adj.* not connected with or including farming: *the* ~ *economy*

**nonfeasance** /ˌnɒnˈfiːzəns; *AmE* ˌnɑːn-/ *n.* [U] (*Law*) not doing sth that you must do according to an agreement or a law

**ˌnon-ˈfood** *adj.* not being, or not connected with, food: *non-food products*

**ˌnon-inˈsurable** = UNINSURABLE (2)

**ˌnon-ˈlife** *adj.* (*Insur.*) used to describe insurance other than LIFE INSURANCE

**ˌnon-ˈmarketable** *adj.* (*Finan.*) (about shares, bonds, etc.) that cannot be bought and sold by investors

**ˌnon-maˈterial** *adj.* not consisting of physical objects or money: *Non-material capital includes knowledge and skills.*

**ˌnon-ˈmember** *n.* [C] a person, a country or an organization that has not joined a particular group

**ˌnon-neˈgotiable** *adj.* **1** fixed; that you cannot discuss or change before you make an agreement or a decision **2** (*Finan.*) that you cannot exchange for money or give to another person in exchange for money: *non-negotiable securities*

**ˌno-ˈnonsense** *adj.* simple and direct; only paying attention to important and necessary things: *a no-nonsense approach*

**ˌnon-ˈpayment** *n.* [U] failure to pay a debt, tax, rent, etc.

**ˌnon-perˈforming** *adj.* (*Finan.*) (about a loan) on which the borrower has not made a payment for a particular period of time

**ˌnon-proˈfessional** *adj.* **1** doing sth out of interest rather than as a paid job **2** (*HR*) having a job that does not need a high level of education or special training

**ˌnon-ˈprofit** (*AmE* **nonprofit**) (*AmE also* **ˌnot-for-ˈprofit**) (*BrE also* **ˌnon-ˈprofit-ˌmaking**) *adj.* (about an organization) that does not have the aim of making a profit

**ˌnon-reˈcourse** *adj.* (*Finan.*) used to describe a loan or debt where the lender only has the right to take back the asset that was bought with the loan if the money is not paid back, and cannot take any of the borrower's other assets

**ˌnon-reˈcurring** *adj.* (*Account.*) happening only once in a particular period rather than repeatedly: *non-recurring items such as redundancy costs*

**ˌnon-reˈfundable** *adj.* (*Comm.*) used to describe an amount of money that cannot be returned when you have paid it: *a non-refundable deposit*

**ˌnon-reˈnewable** *adj.* **1** that cannot be replaced after use: *non-renewable energy resources* **2** (*Law*) that cannot be continued or repeated for a further period after it has finished: *The contract is non-renewable.*

**ˌnon-ˈresident** *adj.*, *n.*
• ***adj.*** (about a person or company) not living or situated permanently in a particular country, esp. when this relates to tax
• ***n.*** [C] **1** a person who does not live permanently in a particular country or place **2** a person not staying at a particular hotel: *The restaurant is open to non-residents.*

**ˌnon-resiˈdential** *adj.* that is not used for people to live in

**ˌnon-ˈsmoking** (*also* **ˌno-ˈsmoking**) *adj.* (about a place) where you cannot smoke: *a non-smoking office* ▸ **ˌnon-ˈsmoking** (*also* **ˌno-ˈsmoking**) *n.* [U]

**ˌnon-ˈstandard** *adj.* **1** not the usual size, type, etc: *paper of a non-standard size* **2** (*HR*) connected with work that is not FULL-TIME and permanent

**ˌnon-systematic ˈrisk** = UNSYSTEMATIC RISK

**ˌnon-tariff ˈbarrier** *n.* [C] (*abbr* **NTB**) (*Econ.*) an official rule or policy, but not a tax, that a government uses to make it difficult for imports of particular goods to come into the country

**ˌnon-ˈtaxable** *adj.* (*Account.*) that you do not need to pay tax on: *non-taxable income*

**nontraditional** (*also* **non-traditional**) /ˌnɒntrəˈdɪʃənl; *AmE* ˌnɑːn-/ *adj.* (*HR*) different from the jobs or working arrangements that have usu. been expected in the past: *women in nontraditional occupations such as construction*

**ˌnon-ˈtransferable** *adj.* that cannot be given to or used by anyone else: *non-transferable tickets*

**ˌnon-ˈunion** (*also* **ˌnon-ˈunionized, -ised**, *less freq.*) *adj.* (*HR*) **1** not belonging to a trade/labor union: *~ labour/workers* **2** (about a business, company, etc.) not accepting trade/labor unions or employing union members

**ˌnon-verbal communiˈcation** *n.* [U] ways of making your thoughts and feelings known to other people that do not involve words or speech, for example by the position of your body

**ˌnon-ˈvoting** *adj.* (*Finan.*) used to describe shares that do not give their owners the right to vote at shareholders' meetings

**norm** /nɔːm; *AmE* nɔːrm/ *n.* **1** (*often* **the norm**) [C, usu. sing.] the usual or expected amount, number, situation, etc: *Spending on IT was about 4% below the norm this quarter.* ◇ *profits far above industry norms* **2** (*Tech.*) [C] a required or agreed standard, amount, maximum, etc: *bringing the system in line with international norms*

**nosedive** /ˈnəʊzdaɪv; *AmE* ˈnoʊz-/ *v.* [I] (about prices, costs, values, etc.) to fall suddenly and by a large amount: *The stock has nosedived from $20 to $2.* ▶ **ˈnosedive** *n.* [C, usu. sing.]

**ˌno-ˈshow** *n.* [C] **1** a customer who has reserved sth such as a restaurant table or plane seat but does not arrive to use it **2** an event that is expected to happen or arrive but does not

**ˌno-ˈsmoking** = NON-SMOKING

**ˌno-ˈstrike** *adj.* (*HR*) in which workers promise not to have a strike: *a no-strike deal*

**notary** /ˈnəʊtəri; *AmE* ˈnoʊ-/ *n.* [C] (*pl.* **-ries**) (*also* **ˌnotary ˈpublic** *pl.* **notaries public**) (*Law*) a person, esp. a lawyer, with official authority to watch a document being signed and make this document valid in law ▶ **ˌnoˈtarial** /-ˈteəriəl; *AmE* -ˈter-/ *adj.*

**notch** /nɒtʃ; *AmE* nɑːtʃ/ *n.*, *v.*
• ***n.*** [C] a level on a scale, often marking quality or achievement: *The bonds have been downgraded by one notch to AA.*
• ***v.*** [T] **~ sth (up)** (used in newspapers) to achieve sth: *The directors have notched up 50 years with the company between them.*

**note** /nəʊt; *AmE* noʊt/ *n.* [C] **1** (*esp. BrE*) (*AmE usu.* **bill**) a piece of paper money: *a €50 note* SYN BANKNOTE **2** (*Finan.*) a bond of a particular kind: *a 10-year note* **3** a short piece of writing to tell sb sth or help them remember sth **4** an official document that shows or proves sth: *a delivery note* **5** (*Finan.*) = PROMISSORY NOTE → idiom at STRIKE *v.*

**notebook** /ˈnəʊtbʊk; *AmE* ˈnoʊt-/ (*also* **ˌnotebook comˈputer**, **ˌnotebook PˈC**) *n.* [C] a very small computer that is easy to carry and use anywhere

**noteholder** /ˈnəʊthəʊldə(r); *AmE* ˈnoʊthoʊldər/ *n.* [C] (*AmE*) (*Finan.*) a person or an organization that owns bonds (**notes**) in a company

**ˈnote ˌissue** *n.* [C] (*Econ.*) a number of BANKNOTES that are made available at the same time; the value of these

**ˌnote ˈpayable** *n.* [C] (*Account.*) a note relating to an amount of money that a company must pay

**ˌnote reˈceivable** *n.* [C] (*Account.*) a note relating to an amount of money that a company is owed

**ˌnote to the acˈcounts** *n.* [C] (*pl.* **notes** -) (*Account.*) extra information given in a company's financial records to explain particular items

**ˌnot-for-ˈprofit** = NON-PROFIT

**notice** /ˈnəʊtɪs; *AmE* ˈnoʊ-/ *n.* **1** [C] written or printed news or information, usu. put in a public place: *legal notices* **2** [U] information or a warning given in advance of sth that is going to happen: *Prices may be altered without notice.* **3** (*HR*) [U,C] a formal letter or statement saying that you will or must leave your job at the end of a particular period of time: *She has **handed in** her notice.* ◇ *They **gave** him two weeks' notice.* ◇ *redundancy notices* **4** (*Prop.*) [U,C] a formal letter or statement saying that you will or must leave your home at the end of a particular period of time: ***notices of eviction***
IDM **put sb on ˈnotice** to give sb a formal warning about sth that is

going to happen or is likely to happen → idioms at SERVE, SHORT *adj.*

**ˈnotice acˌcount** = DEPOSIT ACCOUNT

**ˌnotice of deˈficiency** (*often* **Notice of Deficiency**) (*also* **deˈficiency ˌnotice**) *n.* [C] (*all AmE*) (*Account.*) an official document that shows that sb owes more tax than they have shown on their tax forms

**ˈnotice ˌperiod** *n.* [C] (*HR*) the period of time that there must be between sending or receiving a formal letter saying that you will or must leave your job and when this happens

★ **notify** /ˈnəʊtɪfaɪ; *AmE* ˈnoʊ-/ *v.* [T] (**-fies**, **-fying**, **-fied**, **-fied**) to formally or officially tell sb about sth, that sth is happening, etc: *You will be notified of any changes in the interest rate.* SYN INFORM ▸ **ˌnotifiˈcation** /-fɪˈkeɪʃn/ *n.* [C,U]

**ˌNot-Invented-ˈHere ˌsyndrome** *n.* [sing.] (*abbr* **NIH syndrome**) the way that companies or departments tend to reject or be suspicious of ideas, methods, systems, etc. that they have not developed themselves

**notional** /ˈnəʊʃənl; *AmE* ˈnoʊ-/ *adj.* used to describe a number or an amount that is estimated or guessed rather than real: *The shares are valued at a notional €7.50.*

**nought** /nɔːt/ *n.* [C,U] (*BrE*) the number 0 SYN ZERO

**novelty** /ˈnɒvlti; *AmE* ˈnɑːv-/ *n.* (*pl.* **-ties**) **1** [C, usu. pl.] a small cheap object that amuses or interests people, and is usu. produced and sold for only a short time **2** [C] a thing or person that is interesting because it is new or unusual

**ˈNOW acˌcount** /ˈnaʊ/ *n.* [C] **Negotiable Order of Withdrawal account** in the US, a type of bank account that pays interest

**no-ˌwin no-ˈfee** *phr.* (*Law*) if a lawyer or a company works on a **no-win no-fee** basis, they agree to be paid only if the case is won

**NPD** /ˌen piː ˈdiː/ = NEW-PRODUCT DEVELOPMENT

**NPV** /ˌen piː ˈviː/ = NET PRESENT VALUE

**NRV** /ˌen ɑː ˈviː; *AmE* ɑːr/ = NET REALIZABLE VALUE

**n.s.f.** (*also* **NSF**) /ˌen es ˈef/ *abbr* (*esp. AmE*) (*Finan., usu. written*) **non-sufficient/not sufficient funds** used when there is not enough money in a bank account to pay a cheque that has been written

**NTA** /ˌen tiː ˈeɪ/ = NET TANGIBLE ASSETS

**NTB** /ˌen tiː ˈbiː/ = NON-TARIFF BARRIER

**nudge** /nʌdʒ/ *v., n.*

• *v.* (*usu. used with an adv. or a prep.*) **1** [T,I] to reach a particular value or level; to make sth do this: *The news has nudged shares down a few cents.* **2** [I] to move slightly up or down: *The bonds nudged higher yesterday.*

• *n.* [C, usu. sing.] **1** a small action that encourages sth to happen: *The markets need a nudge.* **2** a small amount higher or lower

**ˌnull and ˈvoid** *adj.* (*Law*) having no legal force; not valid: *The contract was declared null and void.*

**nullify** /ˈnʌlɪfaɪ/ *v.* [T] (**-fies**, **-fying**, **-fied**, **-fied**) **1** (*Law*) to make sth such as an agreement or order lose its legal force SYN INVALIDATE, VOID **2** (*fml.*) to make sth lose its effect or power: *This tax will nullify efforts to revive the economy.*
▸ **ˌnullifiˈcation** /-fɪˈkeɪʃn/ *n.* [U]

**number** /ˈnʌmbə(r)/ *n., v.*

• *n.* **1** [C] (*abbr* **No.**) (*often with another n.*) a number used to identify sth or to communicate by telephone, etc: *My account number is 002345.* **2** [C] a quantity of people or things: *Passenger numbers have been falling.* ◇ *a declining/growing/large/small ~* HELP A plural verb is needed after **a/an (large, small, etc.) number of ….** **3** [C, usu. pl.] an amount, used esp. when talking about how a company or the economy is working: *The company posted worse-than-expected numbers.* SYN FIGURES IDM **make the/your ˈnumbers** to achieve the figures that have been predicted

• *v.* **1** (*linking v.*) to make a particular number when added together: *Our sales force numbers 8 000.* **2** [T] to give a number to sth as part of a series or list: *numbered receipts*

**ˈnumber ˌcruncher** *n.* [C] (*infml.*) **1** used to describe a person whose job involves dealing with numbers and doing large calculations; an accountant **2** a computer or a computer program that can do calculations with large amounts of data in a short time
▸ **ˈnumber ˌcrunching** *n.* [U]

**ˌnumbered acˈcount** *n.* [C] a bank account that is identified by a number only, so that the name of the person who holds the account remains secret

**ˌnumber 'one** *n.* [U] (*infml.*) the most important or best person or thing: *We're number one in fashion.*

**numerical** /nju:ˈmerɪkl; *AmE* nu:-/ (*also* **numeric** /nju:ˈmerɪk; *AmE* nu:-/ *less freq.*) *adj.* relating to numbers; expressed in numbers: *numerical data*

**nuˌmeric 'keypad** *n.* [C] a set of buttons on a computer keyboard that contain the numbers 0–9 and some symbols

**NVQ** /ˌen vi: ˈkju:/ *abbr* **National Vocational Qualification** a British qualification that shows you have reached a particular level in the work that you do: *an NVQ level 3 in catering*

**NYMEX** /ˈnaɪmeks/ *abbr* **1 New York Mercantile Exchange** a very important market where FUTURES and OPTIONS for physical goods such as oil, related products and metals are bought and sold **2** (*also* **'NYMEX diˌvision**) the part of the New York Mercantile Exchange that deals with oil, related products and some rare metals

**NYSE** /ˌen waɪ es ˈi:/ *abbr* **New York Stock Exchange** one of the world's biggest stock markets

# Oo

**O&M** /ˌəʊ ənd ˈem; *AmE* ˌoʊ/ = ORGANIZATION AND METHODS

**oath** /əʊθ; *AmE* oʊθ/ *n.* [C] (*pl.* **oaths** /əʊðz; *AmE* oʊðz/) a formal promise to do sth; a formal statement that sth is true: *to* **swear** *an oath* IDM **on/under 'oath** (*Law*) having promised to tell the truth in a court of law

**OB** /ˌəʊ ˈbi:; *AmE* ˌoʊ/ = ORGANIZATIONAL BEHAVIOUR

**o/b** *abbr* (*written*) **on or before** used before a date to show that it is the last possible date when sth can be done: *Payment o/b 15 April 2007.*

★**object** *n.*, *v.*
• ***n.*** /ˈɒbdʒɪkt; *AmE* ˈɑ:bdʒekt; -dʒɪkt/ [C] **1** a thing that can be seen and touched: *The factory produces vases and small decorative objects.* **2** an aim or a purpose: *Our object is to restore profitability.*
• ***v.*** /əbˈdʒekt/ [I] to say that you disagree with, disapprove of or oppose sth: *Many people objected* **to** *the new factory.* ◇ *Does anyone object?*
▸ **objection** /-ˈdʒekʃn/ *n.* [C]: *No objections were raised at the time.* **ob'jector** *n.* [C]

★**objective** /əbˈdʒektɪv/ *n.*, *adj.*
• ***n.*** [C] details of what you are trying to achieve and when: *You must set realistic* **aims and objectives** *for yourself.* ◇ *the company's long-term strategic objective* SYN GOAL
⊙ *the* **key/main/primary/principal** *~s* ♦ **learning/performance/strategic** *~s* ♦ *to* **deliver/establish** *~s* ♦ *to* **achieve/meet** *~s* ♦ *to* **fail to meet/fall short of** *(your) ~s*
• ***adj.*** not influenced by personal feelings or opinions; considering only facts: *an objective report*
▸ **ob'jectively** *adv.* **objectivity** /ˌɒbdʒekˈtɪvəti; *AmE* ˌɑ:b-/ *n.* [U]

**obˌjective justifi'cation** *n.* [U,C] (*HR*) in Europe, a legal reason that a company can use to show why it has to treat an employee in a different way from others

**'objects clause** *n.* [C] the part of a company's MEMORANDUM OF ASSOCIATION that states the aims and activities of the company

**obligate** /ˈɒblɪgeɪt; *AmE* ˈɑ:b-/ *v.* [T] (*esp. AmE*) **1** to make a person, company, etc. do sth, esp. for moral or legal reasons: *The contracts obligated customers to buy a certain quantity of goods.* **2** to state officially that a particular amount of money will be given for sth, for example to support a loan: *obligating corporate funds*

★**obligation** /ˌɒblɪˈgeɪʃn; *AmE* ˌɑ:b-/ *n.* **1** [C,U] a legal or moral duty to do sth: *The industry has an obligation* **to** *establish a pension scheme.* ◇ *We will send you an estimate for the work* **without** *obligation* (= you do not have to accept it). **2 obligations** [pl.] something that a person or an organization has to do, because of a promise, a law or rule, etc: *The bank must meet its financial obligations.*

**obligatory** /əˈblɪgətri; *AmE* -tɔ:ri/ *adj.* (*fml.*) that sb must do or have because of a law or rule: *The test is obligatory.* SYN COMPULSORY

★**oblige** /əˈblaɪdʒ/ *v.* **1** [T] (*usu. pass.*) to make a person, company, etc. do sth, because it is the law or their duty: *The distributor is not obliged to pay for the goods.* **2** [T,I] to help sb by doing what they ask or what they want: *We are* **happy to oblige**.

**OBM** /ˌəʊ bi: ˈem; *AmE* ˌoʊ/ = OPEN-BOOK MANAGEMENT

**o.b.o.** *abbr* (*esp. AmE*) (*written*) **or best offer** used in small advertisements to say that the person selling sth will accept a price that is slightly lower than the one they are asking: *For Sale: digital camera, $150 obo.*

**observer** /əbˈzɜːvə(r); *AmE* -ˈzɜːrv-/ *n.* [C] a person who watches and studies particular events, situations, etc. and is therefore considered to be an expert on them

**obsolescence** /ˌɒbsəˈlesns; *AmE* ˌɑːb-/ *n.* [U] (*fml.*) the state of becoming old-fashioned and no longer useful: ***planned/built-in*** ~ (= when things are designed not to last very long) ▸ **ˌobsoˈlescent** *adj.*

**obsolete** /ˈɒbsəliːt; *AmE* ˌɑːbsəˈliːt/ *adj.* no longer useful because sth new and better has been invented: *obsolete technology*

**occupancy** /ˈɒkjəpənsi; *AmE* ˈɑːk-/ *n.* [U] **1** (*Comm.*) the **occupancy** of a hotel, plane, etc. is the number of rooms, seats, etc. that are being used at any one time **2** (*fml.*) the fact of a building, room, piece of land, etc. being lived in or used: *The offices are ready for occupancy.*

**occupant** /ˈɒkjəpənt; *AmE* ˈɑːk-/ (*also* ˈ**occupier**) *n.* [C] a person or an organization that lives in, works in or uses a particular house, building or room

**occupation** /ˌɒkjuˈpeɪʃn; *AmE* ˌɑːk-/ *n.* **1** [C] a job or profession: *Please state your name, age and occupation below.* ◇ *to choose/follow/take up an* ~ **2** (*fml.*) [U] the act of living in or using a building, room, piece of land, etc.

**occupational** /ˌɒkjuˈpeɪʃənl; *AmE* ˌɑːk-/ *adj.* connected with a person's job or profession: *an* ~ *injury/pension* ▸ **occuˈpationally** *adv.*

**ˌoccupational ˈhazard** (*also* **ˌoccupational ˈrisk**) *n.* [C] a risk or danger connected with a particular job

**ˌoccupational ˈhygiene** = INDUSTRIAL HYGIENE

**ˌoccupational psyˈchology** *n.* [U] (*esp. BrE*) (*HR*) the study of how people behave at work and what influences their attitudes and behaviour ▸ **ˌoccupational psyˈchologist** *n.* [C]

**ˌoccupational ˈrisk** = OCCUPATIONAL HAZARD

**occupier** /ˈɒkjupaɪə(r); *AmE* ˈɑːk-/ = OCCUPANT

★ **occupy** /ˈɒkjupaɪ; *AmE* ˈɑːk-/ *v.* [T] (**-pies, -pying, -pied, -pied**) **1** (*fml.*) to live or work in a room, house or building: *He occupies an office on the 12th floor.* **2** to have an official job or position SYN HOLD

**OCR** /ˌəʊ siː ˈɑː(r); *AmE* ˌoʊ/ = OPTICAL CHARACTER RECOGNITION

**o/d** *abbr* (*Finan.*) a short way of writing **overdraft** or **overdrawn** → DR

**OECD** /ˌəʊ iː ˌsiː ˈdiː; *AmE* ˌoʊ/ *abbr* **Organization for Economic Cooperation and Development** an organization of thirty countries that produces economic information, helps governments decide the best economic policy and encourages trade

**OEIC** /ɔɪk/ *abbr* (*Finan.*) **open-ended/-end investment company** a company whose business is managing the money of its members by investing in a wide range of shares, bonds, etc. It sells or buys shares to meet the demand.

**OEM** /ˌəʊ iː ˈem; *AmE* ˌoʊ/ *abbr* **original equipment manufacturer** a company that buys equipment such as computers from a manufacturer in large quantities and then sells them under their own name. They may change the equipment first to make it suitable for a particular purpose or put different parts together to make a complete item.

**ˌoff-ˈbalance-sheet** *adj.* (*Account.*) used to refer to items that a company does not show on its BALANCE SHEET: *The company has revealed $2.3 bn in off-balance sheet debts.*

★ **offence** (*AmE* **offense**) /əˈfens/ *n.* [C] an act that is illegal or against the rules: *a disciplinary offence* ◇ *to commit an offence*

**offender** /əˈfendə(r)/ *n.* [C] **1** sb who commits a crime **2** sb/sth that does sth wrong: *When it comes to pollution, the chemical industry is the worst offender.*

**offending** /əˈfendɪŋ/ *adj.* **1** (*Law*) guilty of a crime **2** causing people to feel upset or angry: *The offending ads have been removed from the website.*

**offense** = OFFENCE

★ **offer** /ˈɒfə(r); *AmE* ˈɔːf-; ˈɑːf-/ *v., n.*

• *v.* [T] **1** ~ **sth (to sb) (for sth)** | ~ **sb sth** to say that you are willing to do sth for sb or give sth to sb: *They decided to offer her the job.* ◇ *He offered $4 000 for the car.* **2** to make sth available or to provide the opportunity for sth: *The hotel offers excellent facilities.*

• *n.* [C] **1** an act of saying that you are willing to do sth for sb or give sth to sb: *a firm job offer* ◇ *the offer of a 3% pay rise*

○ *to make/receive/withdraw an* ~
◆ *to accept/reject/turn down an* ~

**2** an amount of money that sb is willing to pay for sth: *an offer of $2 500 for the car* ◇ *The offer has been withdrawn.*
⊕ *to* ***make/receive*** *an ~* ◆ *to* ***accept/reject/turn down*** *an ~* ◆ *to* ***improve/increase/raise*** *an ~*
**3** a reduction in the normal price of sth, usu. for a short period of time
⊕ *a* ***bargain/free/****an* ***introductory*** *~*
**4** an act of saying that sth is available for sale: *The offer closes on March 12th.* **IDM on 'offer 1** that can be bought, used, etc. **2** (*esp. BrE*) on sale at a lower price than normal for a short period of time **under 'offer** (*BrE*) if a house or other building is **under offer**, sb has agreed to buy it at a particular price

**ˌoffer by pros'pectus** *n.* [C, usu. sing.] (*pl.* **offers** -) (*Stock Ex.*) an occasion when new shares are offered to the public with a written description of the aims, history and financial structure of the company

**'offer ˌdocument** *n.* [C] (*Finan.*) a document that a company sends to the shareholders of a business it wants to buy, giving details of the offer and why the shareholders should accept

**offering** /'ɒfərɪŋ; *AmE* 'ɔːf-; 'ɑːf-/ *n.* [C] **1** (*Comm.*) a product or service that a company offers for sale
**2** (*Stock Ex.*) an occasion when shares, bonds, etc. are offered for sale: *a share offering*

**'offering price** = OFFER PRICE (2)

**'offer price** *n.* [C] **1** (*Finan.*) the price that a buyer offers for shareholders' shares when taking over a company; the total price of all these shares **2** (*Stock Ex.*) (*also* **'offering price, 'asking price,** *less freq.*) the price at which a dealer offers shares, bonds, etc. for sale

**ˌoffer to 'purchase** = TAKEOVER BID

★ **office** /'ɒfɪs; *AmE* 'ɔːf-; 'ɑːf-/ *n.*
**1** [C] a room, set of rooms or building where people work, usu. sitting at desks: *We have offices in 19 countries.* ◇ *Are you going to the office today?*
⊕ *a* ***branch/local/****an* ***overseas*** *~* ◆ *to* ***close (down)/open/set up*** *an ~* ◆ *~* ***jobs/work*** ◆ *~* ***staff/workers***
**2** [C] a room in which a particular person works, usu. at a desk: *Some people have to share an office.* **3** [C] (*often used in compounds*) a room or building used for a particular purpose, esp. to provide information or a service: *the local tourist office* ◇ *a tax office* **4** [U,C] an important position of authority, esp. in government; the work and duties connected with this: *The present government took office in 2005.*

**'office block** (*BrE*) *n.* [C] a large building that contains offices, usu. belonging to more than one company: *high-rise office blocks*

**'office boy, 'office girl** *n.* [C] (*old-fash.*) a young person employed to do simple tasks in an office

**'office hours** *n.* [pl.] the time when people in offices are normally working

**ˌoffice 'junior** *n.* [C] (*old-fash.*) a person who has a low rank or status in an office

**'office lady** *n.* [C] (*abbr* **OL**) in Japan, a woman employed to work in an office

**ˌoffice ma'chinery** *n.* [U] equipment that is used in offices, such as telephones, computers, etc.

**'Office of 'Fair 'Trading** *n.* [sing.] (*abbr* **OFT**) the government organization in the UK that makes sure that businesses trade honestly and do not cheat people

**'office park** *n.* [C] (*AmE*) an area of land that is designed and developed for a number of office buildings, often with attractive grounds and other buildings such as restaurants, clubs, etc.

★ **officer** /'ɒfɪsə(r); *AmE* 'ɔːfɪsər; 'ɑːf-/ *n.* [C] **1** (often used in the titles of jobs) a person who has an important job in a company or an organization **2** a person who is in a position of authority: *customs officers*

**'office space** *n.* [U] one or more empty offices; a place that can be used for offices

★ **official** /ə'fɪʃl/ *adj., n.*
• ***adj.*** **1** agreed to, set, said, done, etc. by sb in authority, esp. a government: *Official figures show that business investment fell by 12%.*
**2** connected with a person's job, esp. an important one: *His official title is director of research.* **3** formal and attended by people in authority: *an official reception*
• ***n.*** [C] a person who is in a position of authority in an organization or a government: *union officials*

**ofˌficial re'ceiver** = RECEIVER (1)

**ofˌficial 'strike** *n.* [C] (*HR*) a strike that an accepted union organizes and approves of

**offline** (*also* **off-line**) /ˌɒf'laɪn; *AmE* ˌɑːf-ˌɔːf-/ *adj., adv.* (*IT*) not directly controlled by or connected to a computer or the Internet: *You can compose messages offline.* → ONLINE

**offload** /ˌɒfˈləʊd; *AmE* ˌɔːfˈloʊd; ˌɑːf-/ *v.* [T] to get rid of sth that you do not need by giving or selling it to sb else: *Someone was trying to offload 2 m shares.*

**ˌoff-ˈmarket** *adj.* involving the buying and selling of shares not through a stock market: *off-market transactions* ▸ **ˌoff-ˈmarket** *adv.*

**ˌoff-ˈpeak** *adj.* used to describe a time that is less popular or busy, and things that happen or are used during that time which are therefore cheaper: *travelling at off-peak times* ▸ **ˌoff-ˈpeak** *adv.*: *Calls cost 39 cents a minute off-peak.*

**ˌoff-ˈprice** *adj.* (*AmE*) **off-price** shops/stores sell goods more cheaply than others SYN CUT-PRICE ▸ **ˌoff-ˈprice** *adv.*

**ˈoff ˌseason** *n.* [sing.] the time of year that is less busy in business and travel SYN LOW SEASON ▸ **ˌoff-ˈseason** *adj.*: *off-season prices* **ˌoff-ˈseason** *adv.*

**offset** /ˈɒfset; *AmE* ˈɔːf-; ˈɑːf-/ *v.*, *n.*
• ***v.*** [T] (**offsetting**, **offset**, **offset**) to use one cost or payment in order to reduce or cancel the effect of another: *The sale had been offset against costs.*
• ***n.*** [C] **1** (*Account.*) a cost or payment that is used to reduce or cancel the effect of another: *corporation tax offsets* **2** (*Law*) the right that enables sb to reduce a debt that they owe to sb else because the other person also owes them money

**offshoot** /ˈɒfʃuːt; *AmE* ˈɔːf-; ˈɑːf-/ *n.* [C] a small organization, business, etc. that develops from a larger one

**offshore** /ˌɒfˈʃɔː(r); *AmE* ˌɔːf-; ˌɑːf-/ *adj.*, *v.*
• ***adj.*** **1** (*Finan.*) **offshore** accounts, investments, etc. are kept in countries that have less strict laws and lower taxes than most other countries: ~ *accounts/banks/companies/funds/investments* **2** happening or based in a different country: *an offshore supplier of software to US organizations* SYN FOREIGN, OVERSEAS **3** connected with oil and gas production that takes place in and under the sea ▸ **ˌoffˈshore** *adv.*
• ***v.*** [T,I] (*HR*) to move part of your company's operations to a foreign country, for example to reduce the cost of labour: *3.3 million jobs may be offshored in the next 15 years.*
▸ **ˌoffˈshoring** *n.* [U]

**ˌoff-ˈsite** *adj.*, *n.*
• ***adj.*** working or happening away from the main offices of a business: *an off-site meeting* ▸ **ˌoff-ˈsite** *adv.*
• ***n.*** [C] **ˈoff-site** an occasion when a company takes its employees away from the office, for example to discuss future strategy

**ˌoff-the-ˈbooks** *adj.* (*Account.*) not officially recorded, in order to avoid tax or deceive the authorities

**ˌoff-the-ˈjob** *adj.*, *adv.* (*HR*) that happens away from the employee's place of work: *off-the-job training*

**ˌoff-the-ˈpeg** (*BrE*) (*AmE* **ˌoff-the-ˈrack**) *adj.* of a standard type, design or size, rather than being made for a particular person or situation
▸ **ˌoff the ˈpeg** (*BrE*) (*AmE* **ˌoff the ˈrack**) *adv.*

**ˌoff-the-ˈshelf** *adj.* made to a standard design and available to buy and use immediately: *off-the-shelf software* ▸ **ˌoff the ˈshelf** *adv.*

**ˌoff-the-ˈshelf ˌcompany** = SHELF COMPANY

**OFT** /ˌəʊ ef ˈtiː; *AmE* ˌoʊ/ = OFFICE OF FAIR TRADING

**OHP** /ˌəʊ eɪtʃ ˈpiː; *AmE* ˌoʊ/ = OVERHEAD PROJECTOR

**OHT** /ˌəʊ eɪtʃ ˈtiː; *AmE* ˌoʊ/ = TRANSPARENCY (3)

**oil** /ɔɪl/ *n.*, *v.*
• ***n.*** [U] a thick liquid that is found in rock underground and is used as fuel and to make parts of machines move smoothly: *drilling for oil* ◇ *an oil well*
• ***v.*** [T] to put oil onto or into sth, for example a machine, in order to protect it or make it work smoothly
IDM **oil the ˈwheels** (*BrE*) (*AmE* **grease the ˈwheels**) to help sth to happen easily and without problems: *oiling the wheels of international finance*

**oilfield** /ˈɔɪlfiːld/ *n.* [C] an area where oil is found in the ground or under the sea

**oilman** /ˈɔɪlmæn/ *n.* [C] (*pl.* **-men** /-men/) **1** a man who owns an oil company: *a billionaire oilman* **2** a man who works in the oil business

**ˈoil rig** *n.* [C] a large structure with equipment for looking for oil under the sea or under the ground

**OL** /ˌəʊ ˈel; *AmE* ˌoʊ/ = ORGANIZATIONAL LEARNING, OFFICE LADY

**the ˌOld Eˈconomy** (*also* **the old economy**) *n.* [sing.] an economy based on traditional industries and businesses that lasted for a long time

**ˈold-line** *adj.* (*AmE*) **old-line** businesses have been established for a long time, have a good reputation and do things in a traditional way

**oligarchy** /ˈɒlɪɡɑːki; *AmE* ˈɑːləɡɑːr-/ *n.* [C] (*pl.* **-chies**) a small group of people who control a business, an organization, a country, etc. for a long time and are unwilling to let other people share power; the business, organization or country that they control ▸ ˈ**oligarch** *n.* [C]

**oligopoly** /ˌɒlɪˈɡɒpəli; *AmE* ˌɑːləˈɡɑːp-/ *n.* [C] (*pl.* **-lies**) (*Econ.*) the control of trade in particular goods or the supply of a particular service by a small group of companies; the type of goods or service that is controlled in this way; the companies that control the trade

**OM** /ˌəʊ ˈem; *AmE* ˌoʊ/ = ORGANIZATION AND METHODS

**ombudsman** /ˈɒmbʊdzmən; -mæn; *AmE* ˈɑːm-/ *n.* [C] (*pl.* **-men** /-mən/) a government official whose job is to examine and report on complaints made by members of the public about the government, companies, etc.

ˌ**one-of-a-ˈkind** *adj.* a **one-of-a-kind** product, service, company, etc. is the only one of its type that exists

ˌ**one-ˈoff** *adj., n.*

• ***adj.*** (*BrE*) (*AmE* ˈ**one-shot**) made or happening only once: *a ~ charge/payment* ◇ *~ gains/losses*

• ***n.*** [C, usu. sing.] a thing that is made or that happens only once and not regularly: *Their success is not just a one-off.*

ˌ**one-on-ˈone** = ONE-TO-ONE

ˈ**one-shot** = ONE-OFF *adj.*

ˌ**one-size-fits-ˈall** *adj.* suitable for a wide range of situations, people or circumstances

ˈ**one-stop** *adj.* (*BrE*) a **one-stop** shop/store or service offers a wide range of goods or services so that you only have to go to one place to buy or do everything you want

ˈ**one-time** (*AmE* **onetime**) *adj.* **1** happening only once: *a ~ cost/gain/loss* SYN ONE-OFF **2** former: *one-time competitors*

ˌ**one-to-ˈone** (*esp. BrE*) (*AmE usu.* ˌ**one-on-ˈone**) *adj.* between two people only: *a one-to-one meeting*

**on-lend** /ɒnˈlend; *AmE* ɑːn-; ɔːn-/ *v.* [T] (**on-lent, on-lent** /-lent/) to lend money that you have borrowed from sb to sb else ▸ ˈ**on-ˌlending** *n.* [U]

★ **online** (*also* **on-line**) /ˌɒnˈlaɪn; *AmE* ˌɑːn-; ˌɔːn-/ *adj.* (*IT*) (about a product or service) available on or done using the Internet or another computer network: *an ~ bank/retailer/database* ◇ *online sales* ▸ ˌ**onˈline** *adv.*: *do your banking online*

**o.n.o.** *abbr* (*esp. BrE*) (*written*) **or nearest offer** used in small advertisements to show that sth may be sold at a lower price than the price that has been asked: *PC for sale: €700 o.n.o.*

ˌ**on-ˈscreen** (*AmE also* **onscreen**) *adj.* **1** appearing on the screen of a computer, television or cinema: *an ~ logo/menu* **2** using a computer screen: *on-screen editing facilities* ▸ ˌ**on-ˈscreen** *adv.*

**onshore** /ˌɒnˈʃɔː(r); *AmE* ˌɑːn-; ˌɔːn-/ *adj.* **1** (*Finan.*) **onshore** accounts, investments, etc. are kept in countries that have strict laws and normal levels of taxes **2** happening or based within a particular country: *He is head of UK onshore business at the bank.* **3** relating to oil and gas production that takes place on land ▸ ˌ**onˈshore** *adv.*

ˌ**on-ˈsite** *adj.* **1** working, based, or happening at the main offices of a business: *~ training/visits* **2** (*IT*) on a website ▸ ˌ**on-ˈsite** *adv.*

ˌ**on-the-ˈjob** *adj., adv.* (*HR*) that takes place within an employee's place of work: *on-the-job experience* ◇ *Training is carried out on-the-job.*

**OOS** /ˌəʊ əʊ ˈes; *AmE* ˌoʊ oʊ/ *abbr* **occupational overuse syndrome** pain and swelling, esp. in the arms and hands, caused by performing the same movement many times in a job SYN RSI

**OPEC** /ˈəʊpek; *AmE* ˈoʊ-/ *n.* [sing.] **Organization for Petroleum Exporting Countries** an organization of countries that produce and sell oil, which controls the amount of oil produced in order to make sure that there is enough to meet needs, and to keep the price at a suitable level

★ **open** /ˈəʊpn; *AmE* ˈoʊpn/ *adj., v., n.*

• ***adj.*** **1** [not usu. before n.] if a shop/store, bank, business, etc. is **open**, it is ready for business and will admit customers or visitors OPP CLOSED **2** ~ **to sb** if a competition, building, etc. is **open** to particular people, those people can enter it **3** ~ **(to sb)** to be available and ready to use: *What options are open to us?* **4** ~ **to sth** (about a person) willing to listen to and think about new ideas **5** (*also* ˌ**open-ˈended**, ˌ**open-ˈend**, *both esp. in AmE*) (about a question) requiring sb to answer with an opinion rather than with 'yes' or 'no' IDM **have/keep an ˌopen ˈmind (about/on sth)** to be willing to listen to or accept new ideas or suggestions

• *v.* **1** [T,I] (about a shop/store, business, etc.) to start business for the day or for the first time: *What time do the banks open?* **2** [T] to start an activity or event: *to open a bank account* **3** [T,I] to start a computer program or file so that you can use it on the screen **4** [I] if shares, currencies, etc. **open** at a particular price, they are worth that amount when people start trading them at the beginning of the day **5** [T,I] if a meeting **opens** or sb **opens** it, it starts **6** [T] to make it possible for goods, people, etc. to come through: *The country has opened its borders to overseas business.* OPP CLOSE IDM **open 'doors for sb** to provide opportunities for sb to do sth and be successful: *A good CV/résumé will open doors for you.* **open the 'floodgates (to/for sth); the floodgates 'open (to/for sth)** to start a process that is very difficult to stop PHR V **ˌopen (sth) 'up 1** to become or make sth possible, available or able to be reached: *The new catalogue will open up the market for our products.* **2** to begin business for the day: *to open up the store* **3** to start a new business: *New banks are opening up here.* OPP CLOSE (STH) DOWN

• *n.* [sing.] the beginning of the day of trading, esp. on a stock exchange; the price of a share, currency, etc. at this time: *Stocks are set to rise at Friday's open.* ◊ *a flat/weak/strong ~* OPP CLOSE

**ˌopen ac'count** *n.* [C,U] (*Comm.*) an arrangement with a shop/store or business to pay for goods or services at a later time

**ˌopen-book 'management** *n.* [U] (*abbr* **OBM**) (*HR*) a method of managing a company where all employees are given financial and other information about the company in order to encourage them to work as efficiently as possible

**ˌopen 'border** *n.* [C, usu. pl.] (*Trade*) the fact of goods and people being able to pass freely between countries

**ˌopen 'cheque** *n.* [C] (*BrE*) **1** (*also* **ˌuncrossed 'cheque**) a cheque which can be exchanged for cash at the bank of the person who wrote it **2** a cheque that has been signed but on which the amount of money has not yet been filled in: (*fig.*) *We were given an open cheque* (= unlimited money) *to develop the product.* SYN BLANK CHEQUE

**ˌopen communi'cation** *n.* [U] a situation where employees and managers can freely exchange information and ideas

**ˌopen 'credit** = REVOLVING CREDIT

**ˌopen-'door ˌpolicy** *n.* [C] **1** (*HR*) used to describe a style of management in which employees are encouraged to bring any problems directly to their managers **2** (*Trade*) used to describe a situation in which imports or people can come into a country freely

**ˌopen-'ended** *adj.* **1** (*esp. BrE*) (*AmE usu.* **ˌopen-'end**) without any limits, aims or dates fixed in advance: *The contract is open-ended.* **2** (*Finan.*) (*also* **ˌopen-'end**, *esp. in AmE*) (about a loan) allowing extra amounts to be borrowed at a later time, under the same conditions as the original loan **3** (*Finan.*) (*usually* **ˌopen-'end**) used to describe a type of investment company that can issue and buy back shares at any time according to how many members it has, rather than having a fixed number of shares OPP CLOSED-END **4** (*esp. AmE*) = OPEN *adj.* (5)

★ **opening** /ˈəʊpnɪŋ; *AmE* ˈoʊ-/ *n.*, *adj.*

• *n.* **1** [U,C] the act of starting business for the first time: *the opening of our branch in Hong Kong* ◊ *new store openings* OPP CLOSING **2** [U,C] the act of starting business for the day, esp. on a stock market; the price of shares at this time: *a weak opening on Wall Street* OPP CLOSING **3** [U] the state of being open: *Late opening of stores is common in Britain now.* OPP CLOSING **4** [sing.] = OPENING UP (1) **5** [C] a job that is available: *There are openings in the sales department.* **6** [C] a good opportunity for sb: *This was the opening she needed.*

• *adj.* first; beginning: *the chairman's opening remarks* OPP CLOSING

**ˌopening 'balance** *n.* [C, usu. sing.] **1** (*Account.*) the **balance** that is shown in an account at the start of an accounting period **2** the amount of money that must be placed in a bank account when it is opened

**'opening hours** *n.* [pl.] the time during which a shop/store, bank, etc. is open for business

**'opening stock** (*BrE*) (*AmE* **be'ginning ˌinventory**) *n.* [U] (*Account.*) the amount of goods that a business holds at the start of a particular period of time; the value of these goods

**ˌopening 'up** *n.* [sing.] **1** (*also* **'opening**) the process of removing restrictions and making sth such as a market, jobs, land, etc. available to more people: *the opening up of new*

*opportunities for women in business* **2** the process of making sth ready for use: *the opening up of a new stretch of highway*

**ˌopen ˈlearning** = DISTANCE LEARNING

**ˌopen ˈmarket** *n.* [C] (*Econ.*) **1** a market where anyone can buy and sell **2** used to refer to the situation when a country's central bank buys and sells government bonds, etc. in financial markets in order to control interest rates and the MONEY SUPPLY

**ˌopen ˈoffer** *n.* [C] (*Finan.*) an offer that a company makes to its shareholders to buy new shares at a fixed price, usu. lower than the current market price

**ˌopen-ˈplan** *adj.* used to describe an office where people sit at desks in an open area rather than in individual rooms

**ˈopen poˌsition** *n.* [sing.] (*Stock Ex.*) a situation in which a dealer in shares, currencies, COMMODITIES, etc. is at risk if prices rise or fall

**ˌopen ˈshop** *n.* [C] (*HR*) a factory, business, etc. in which employees do not have to be members of a particular union → CLOSED SHOP

**ˌopen-ˈsource** *adj.* (*IT*) used to describe computer programs that anybody can adapt for their own uses as the original SOURCE CODE is freely available

**ˌopen ˈstandard** *n.* [C,U] (*IT*) (about computer equipment or software) a design that is available for everyone to use rather than one that belongs to a particular company

★ **operate** /ˈɒpəreɪt; *AmE* ˈɑːp-/ *v.* **1** [T] to use or control a machine or make it work: *You will be trained in how to operate this machinery.* **2** [I] (about machines, factories, etc.) to work in a particular way: *The refinery is only operating at 50% capacity.* SYN FUNCTION **3** [I] (about a business, service, etc.) to be used or working; to work in a particular way or from a particular place: *It has been operating* **as** *a commercial bank since 1993.* **4** [T] to manage or organize a system, service or business: *The airline operates flights to 25 countries.*

**operating** /ˈɒpəreɪtɪŋ; *AmE* ˈɑːp-/ *adj.* (*Account.*) connected with running a business and producing goods or services

◯ ~ ***assets/expenditure/expenses*** ◆ *an* ~ ***loss/profit*** ◆ ~ ***strategy***

**ˈoperating cost** *n.* [C, usu. pl., U] (*Account.*) **1** the costs involved in the activities of a business or part of a business, such as supplies, small equipment, training, etc. **2** the costs involved in using a machine, building, vehicle, etc., such as the cost of electricity and repairs

**ˈoperating ˌincome** *n.* [U] (*Account.*) the amount of money that a company makes from its normal business activities, calculated by taking OPERATING expenses away from GROSS PROFIT

**ˈoperating lease** *n.* [C] (*Finan.*) an arrangement by which a business pays to use a piece of equipment, a building, etc. for a period of time

**ˈoperating ˌmargin** (*also* **ˌoperating ˈprofit ˌmargin, ˌnet ˈprofit ˌmargin, ˌnet ˈmargin**) *n.* [C,U] (*Account.*) a measure of how efficiently a business is run and how successful its price levels are, calculated by dividing its OPERATING INCOME by its NET SALES: *Our operating margin is up 1% on last year.*

**ˌoperating ˈprofit ˌmargin** = OPERATING MARGIN

**ˈoperating ˌsystem** *n.* [C] (*abbr* **OS**) (*IT*) the main program on a computer, that controls how the computer works and allows other programs to run

★ **operation** /ˌɒpəˈreɪʃn; *AmE* ˌɑːp-/ *n.* **1** [C] a business involving many parts: *a multinational operation* **2** [C] the activity or work done in an area of business or industry: *manufacturing/retail ~s* **3 operations** [pl.; U] the main activities that a business does to make money, for example buying and selling goods or services, or manufacturing products: *funds to finance our operations* **4** [U,C] the process of working as a business: *We're in our fourth year of operation.* ◇ *to suspend operations* **5** [C,U] an act performed by a machine, esp. a computer **6** [U] the way that parts of a machine or a system work; the process of making sth work: *the smooth operation of the engine* **7** [C] an organized activity that involves several people doing different things: *a security operation* IDM **come into opeˈration** to start working; to start having an effect: *The new rules come into operation next week.* **in opeˈration** working, being used or having an effect **put sth into opeˈration** to make sth start working; to start using sth

**operational** /ˌɒpəˈreɪʃənl; *AmE* ˌɑːp-/ *adj.* **1** connected with the way in which a business, machine, system, etc. works: *operational procedures* **2** [not usu. before n.] being used or ready to be used: *Our customer support centre is now fully*

*operational.*
▸ ˌ**ope'rationally** /-nəli/ *adv.*

ˌ**operational re'search** = OPERATIONS RESEARCH

ˌ**operation 'process chart** *n.* [C] (*Product.*) a diagram that shows the stages of a manufacturing process, and gives information about the time, people and parts needed at each stage

ˌ**ope'rations ˌmanagement** *n.* [U] the process of managing the main activities that a business does to make money ▸ ˌ**ope'rations ˌmanager** *n.* [C]

ˌ**ope'rations ˌmanual** *n.* [C] (*HR*) a document that describes the systems and processes that a company or an organization uses to perform its activities

ˌ**operations re'search** (*also* ˌ**operational re'search**) *n.* [U] (*abbr* **OR**) the use of scientific methods and technology to improve the way a business performs its main activities

**operative** /'ɒpərətɪv; *AmE* 'ɑːp-/ *n., adj.*

• ***n.*** [C] a worker who performs a practical task for a company: *customer service/machine ~s*

• ***adj.*** ready to be used; in use: *Our online store is now **fully** operative.*

★ **operator** /'ɒpəreɪtə(r); *AmE* 'ɑːp-/ *n.* [C] **1** (*often used with another n.*) a person or company that runs a particular business: *a bus/train ~* **2** (*often used with another n.*) a person who operates equipment or machinery: *a computer/machine ~* **3** (*BrE also* **te'lephonist**) a person who works on the telephone SWITCHBOARD of a large company or organization

**o'pinion ˌleader** *n.* [C] (*Market.*) a person whose tastes and opinions are respected within a social group, and who therefore influences what people in that group buy

**o'pinion poll** = POLL

**OPM** /ˌəʊ piː 'em; *AmE* ˌoʊ/ *abbr* (*Account., infml.*) **other people's money** used to describe money that a business uses or invests which it has borrowed or which it owes

**opportunism** /ˌɒpə'tjuːnɪzem; *AmE* ˌɑːpər'tuː-/ *n.* [U] the practice of taking any opportunities that appear, without thinking about the future result of doing so ▸ **oppor'tunist** (*also* ˌ**opportu'nistic** /-'nɪstɪk/) *adj.* ˌ**oppor'tunist** *n.* [C] ˌ**opportu'nistically** /-kli/ *adv.*

★ **opportunity** /ˌɒpə'tjuːnəti; *AmE* ˌɑːpər'tuː-/ *n.* [C,U] (*pl.* **-ties**) a time when a particular situation makes it possible for you to do sth or achieve sth: *an opportunity **for** growth ◇ new business/market opportunities*

➊ *to **create/offer/open up/present/provide** opportunities • to **exploit/have/look for/see/seize/take** an ~ • an ~ **arises/exists** • **career/employment/job** opportunities • a **lost/missed** ~*

ˌ**oppor'tunity cost** *n.* [C,U] (*Econ.*) the value of sth that could be done, made, chosen, etc., that will be lost when a decision is made to do a particular thing

**opporˌtunity to 'see** *n.* [C, usu. pl.] (*abbr* **OTS**) (*Market.*) a measure of the number of times that possible customers might be expected to see a particular advertisement in a newspaper, on television, on a website, etc. during a particular period

ˌ**opposite 'number** *n.* [C] a person who does the same job as you in another organization

ˌ**optical 'character recogˌnition** *n.* [U] (*abbr* **OCR**) (*IT*) the process of using light to record printed information onto disks for use in a computer system

**optimal** /'ɒptɪməl; *AmE* 'ɑːp-/ *adj.* the best; the most likely to be successful

➊ *an ~ **level/performance/strategy/way** • ~ **conditions/effectiveness***

**optimism** /'ɒptɪmɪzəm; *AmE* 'ɑːp-/ *n.* [U] **~ (about/for/over sth)** a feeling that good things will happen and that sth will be successful; the tendency to have this feeling
OPP PESSIMISM

➊ ***business/consumer/investor** ~ • to **express/show** ~ • to **fuel/increase** ~*

▸ **'optimist** *n.* [C] ˌ**opti'mistic** /-'mɪstɪk/ *adj.* ˌ**opti'mistically** /-kli/ *adv.*

**optimize, -ise** /'ɒptɪmaɪz; *AmE* 'ɑːp-/ *v.* [T] to make sth as good as it can be; to use sth in the best possible way: *to optimize the use of resources*
▸ ˌ**optimi'zation, -i'sation** /-maɪ'zeɪʃn; *AmE* -mə'z-/ *n.* [U]

**optimum** /'ɒptɪməm; *AmE* 'ɑːp-/ *adj., n.*

• ***adj.*** the best; the number, size, etc. that will produce the best possible results: *What is the optimum team size?*

• ***n.*** [sing.] **the optimum** the best possible result, set of conditions, etc: *Conditions are close to the optimum.*

**'opt-in** *n.* [C] (*often used as an adj.*) **1** the act of choosing to be part of a system or an agreement **2** (*Market.*)

when the user of a company's website gives their email address so that they can be sent information about particular subjects, products or services

★ **option** /ˈɒpʃn; *AmE* ˈɑːp-/ *n.*
**1** [C,U] **~ (of doing sth/to do sth)** something that you can choose to have or do; the freedom to choose what you do: *I have the option of working four days a week.*
➊ *to* ***give sb/offer sb*** *an ~* ◆ *to* ***choose/take*** *an ~*
**2** (*Finan.*) [C] the right to buy or sell a fixed quantity of shares, currencies or COMMODITIES for a particular price within a particular period or on a particular date: *She has an option to buy 100 000 shares.* ◇ *When does the option expire?*
➊ *to* ***buy/exercise/sell/trade/write*** *an ~* ◆ *an ~s* ***contract*** ◆ *the ~s* ***exchange/market***
**3** (*Finan.*) [C] the right to buy sth or more of sth in the future: *We have an option* **on** *the land and will purchase it soon.*
➊ *to* ***exercise/take (up)*** *an ~*

**optional** /ˈɒpʃənl; *AmE* ˈɑːp-/ *adj.* that you can choose to do or have if you want to: *You must wear a tie, but jackets are optional.*

ˈ**opt-out** *n.* [C] (*often used as an adj.*) the act of choosing not to be involved in an agreement: *The contract contains an opt-out clause.*

**OR** /ˌəʊ ˈɑː(r); *AmE* ˌoʊ/ = OPERATIONS RESEARCH

**orchestrate** /ˈɔːkɪstreɪt; *AmE* ˈɔːrk-/ *v.* [T] to organize a complicated plan or event very carefully and sometimes secretly

★ **order** /ˈɔːdə(r); *AmE* ˈɔːrd-/ *n.*, *v.*
• ***n.*** **1** [C,U] a request to make, supply or send goods: *I would like to place an order* **for** *ten copies of this book.* ◇ *We have firm orders worth $9 m.* ◇ *The parts are still* **on order.**
➊ *to* ***put in*** *an ~* ◆ *to* ***have/fill/fulfil/meet/process*** *an ~* ◆ *to* ***cancel/get/lose/receive/win*** *an ~* ◆ *a* ***bulk/cash/large/small*** *~* ◆ *a* ***repeat*** *~*
**2** [C] goods made, supplied or sent in response to a particular order: *Your order will be dispatched today.*
**3** [C] an official instruction given by a court or similar authority
➊ *to* ***grant/issue/obtain/seek*** *an ~* ◆ *to* ***lift/remove*** *an ~* ◆ *to* ***appeal/comply with/execute/obey*** *an ~*
**4** [C] a formal written instruction for sb to be paid money or to do sth: *to cash an order* IDM **in 'order** (about an official document) that can be used because it is all correct and legal SYN VALID **in running/working 'order** (esp. about machines) working well **of/in the order of ...** (*BrE*) (*AmE* **on the order of ...**) (*fml.*) about sth; approximately sth: *She earns in the order of €50 000 a year.* **ˌorder of 'business** the arrangement of subjects for discussion at a meeting SYN AGENDA **ˌout of 'order 1** (about a machine etc.) not working correctly **2** not arranged correctly or neatly: *Some of the papers were out of order.* **3** (*fml.*) not allowed by the rules of a formal meeting or debate → idioms at BULK *n.*, CALL *v.*
• ***v.*** [T] **1 ~ (sb) sth | ~ sth (for sb)** to ask for goods to be made, supplied or sent; to ask for a service to be provided: *These boots can be ordered direct from the manufacturer.* ◇ *Shall I order you a cab?* ◇ *Shall I order a cab for you?* **2** to use your position of authority to tell sb to do sth or say that sth must happen: *The government has ordered an enquiry.* **3** to organize or arrange sth

ˈ**order book** *n.* [C] (*Comm.*; *Manufact.*) a record kept by a business of the products it has agreed to supply to its customers, often used to show how well the business is doing: *a full/strong ~*

ˈ**order form** *n.* [C] a document completed by customers when ordering goods

ˈ**order ˌgetter** (*also* **'order-ˌmaker**) *n.* [C] (*Market.*) a person whose job is to persuade new customers to place orders with a company and existing customers to buy more

ˈ**order ˌpicking** *n.* [U] (*Product.*) the process of taking the goods that a customer has ordered out of the place where they are stored

ˈ**order point** (*also* **re'order point**) *n.* [C] (*Comm.*; *Product.*) the time when an order is automatically made for more supplies of an item because the number has fallen below a particular level, considering future demand and the time it takes to deliver it

ˈ**order ˌprocessing** *n.* [U] (*Comm.*; *Product.*) **1** all the activities involved in dealing with customers' orders from receiving them to delivering the goods **2** the activity of checking and recording every stage of a customer's order as it is dealt with

ˈ**order ˌtaker** *n.* [C] (*Market.*) the role that a salesperson performs when they take orders from customers who already use or wish to use the company but do not persuade people to buy

**ordinary** /ˈɔːdnri; *AmE* ˈɔːrdneri/ (*pl.* **-ries**) = ORDINARY SHARE

**ˌordinary ˈcapital** *n.* [U] (*Finan.*) the amount of a company's CAPITAL that is held in ORDINARY SHARES

**ˌordinary ˈcreditor** *n.* [C] (*Finan.*) a company or person who will be paid money they are owed by a company that is BANKRUPT only after everybody else except people who hold ORDINARY SHARES

**ˌordinary ˈinterest** *n.* [U] (*Finan.*) interest calculated based on a year of 360 days instead of 365

**ˌordinary resoˈlution** *n.* [C] a formal statement that is accepted by a simple majority of shareholders present at a general meeting of a company

**ˌordinary ˈshare** (*also* **ˈordinary**) (*both BrE*) (*also* **ˌcommon ˈshare,** *esp. in BrE*) *n.* [C] (*Finan.*) a share in a company that gives the owner the right to a DIVIDEND according to how much profit the company has made, and usu. the right to vote at meetings of shareholders

**ˌordinary ˈstock** = COMMON STOCK

**organic** /ɔːˈɡænɪk; *AmE* ɔːrˈɡ-/ *adj.* **1** used to describe the situation when a company develops its existing business rather than growing by buying other companies, etc: *~ development/expansion/growth* **2** (about food, farming methods, etc.) produced or practised without using artificial chemicals: *~ milk/vegetables* ▸ **orˈganically** /-kli/ *adv.*

**organigram** (*also* **organogram**) /ɔːˈɡænəɡræm; *AmE* ɔːrˈɡæn-/ *n.* [C] a diagram that shows the structure of a company or an organization and the relationship between different jobs SYN ORGANIZATION CHART

★ **organization, -isation** /ˌɔːɡənaɪˈzeɪʃn; *AmE* ˌɔːrɡənəˈz-/ *n.* **1** [C] a group of people who form a business or other group together in order to achieve a particular aim: *a large international organization* ◇ *The World Trade Organization*

⊙ ***a business/commercial/profit-making ~*** ◆ ***a charitable/non-profit ~*** ◆ ***a high-performance/small ~*** ◆ ***to build/create/form/head/manage/run an ~*** ◆ ***to join/leave an ~***

**2** [U] the act of making arrangements or preparations for sth: *the organization of the conference* SYN PLANNING

⊙ ***careful/efficient/poor/smooth ~*** ◆ ***to lack/need/take ~***

**3** [U] the way in which the different parts of sth are arranged: *the organization of labour within the company* SYN STRUCTURE ▸ **ˌorganiˈzational, -iˈsational** /-naɪˈzeɪʃənl; *AmE* -nəˈz-/ *adj.*

**ˌorganizational beˈhaviour** (*AmE* - **behavior**) *n.* [U] (*abbr* **OB**) (*HR*) the study of the behaviour and attitudes of people within an organization and how they affect the way the organization works

**ˌorganizational communiˈcation** = CORPORATE COMMUNICATION

**ˌorganizational ˈculture** = CORPORATE CULTURE

**ˌorganizational ˈlearning** *n.* [U] (*abbr* **OL**) (*HR*) the process in which people and groups within an organization continuously gain knowledge and develop skills, with the result that the organization can change and improve

**ˌorganization and ˈmethods** *n.* [U with sing./pl. v.] (*abbr* **OM, O&M**) **1** an analysis of the way an organization works and is arranged, and how it could be made more efficient **2** the department in a company that does this

**ˌorganiˈzation chart** *n.* [C] a diagram that shows the structure of a company or an organization and the relationship between different jobs

**ˌorganiˈzation ˌtheory** *n.* [U] techniques for studying the structure, aims and strategies of organizations

★ **organize, -ise** /ˈɔːɡənaɪz; *AmE* ˈɔːrɡ-/ *v.* **1** [T] to arrange for sth to happen or to be provided: *to ~ workshops/meetings* **2** [T] to put or arrange things into a logical order or system: *Sales information is organized by area.* **3** [T,I] to form a union or a group of people with a shared aim: *the right of workers to organize themselves into unions*

**organized, -ised** /ˈɔːɡənaɪzd; *AmE* ˈɔːrɡ-/ *adj.* **1** arranged or planned in a particular way: *a well-organized event* **2** working well and in an efficient way: *an ~ person/company* **3** involving large numbers of people who work together to do sth in a way that is carefully planned: *an organized body of workers*

**ˌorganized ˈlabour** *n.* [U] employees who are members of a union

**organizer, -iser** /ˈɔːɡənaɪzə(r); *AmE* ˈɔːrɡ-/ *n.* [C] **1** a person who arranges for sth to happen or to be provided: *conference organizers* **2** (*IT*) a very small computer that keeps information about people, what you have arranged to do, etc: *an electronic organizer*

**'organizing ˌbusiness** *n.* [C] a company that offers products and services to help people arrange their offices, their homes or their work in a tidy and efficient way; all the companies involved in this

**organogram** = ORGANIGRAM

**-orientated** /'ɔːriənteɪtɪd/ = -ORIENTED

**orientation** /ˌɔːriən'teɪʃn/ *n.* **1** [U,C] the type of aims or interests that an organization or a person has; the act of directing your aims towards a particular thing: *The business school is international in orientation.* **2** (*HR*) [U] training or information that you are given before starting a new job, course, etc.

**-oriented** /'ɔːrientɪd/ (*BrE also* **-orientated**) *comb. form* (*used to form adjs*) having the aim mentioned: *market-oriented* ◇ *profit-oriented*

**origin** /'ɒrɪdʒɪn; *AmE* 'ɔːr-; 'ɑːr-/ *n.* [C,U] **1** (*also* **'origins** [pl.]) the point from which sth starts; the cause of sth: *What is the origin of the name 'Sony'?* **2** the place from which goods come: *We need to know the supplier, price and country of origin.*

**originate** /ə'rɪdʒɪneɪt/ *v.* **1** [I] to start in a particular way or place, or at a particular time: *The program tells you where your emails originated.* **2** [T] to create sth new: *to originate new business* **3** (*Finan.*) [T] to arrange a loan for sb, esp. a loan for buying a home ▸ **o'riginator** *n.* [C]: *a loan/mortgage originator*

**origination** /əˌrɪdʒɪ'neɪʃn/ *n.* [U] **1** (*Market.*) the process of finding or developing a new product or service to sell **2** (*Finan.*) the process of arranging a loan for a new customer: *mortgage origination* **3** the process of preparing images or text so that they can be printed

**OS** /ˌəʊ 'es; *AmE* ˌoʊ/ *abbr* **1** (*IT*) = OPERATING SYSTEM **2** (*Comm., written*) (*also* **O/S**) out of stock **3** (*Account.*) (*also* **O/S**) a short way to write **outstanding** in financial records **4** (*Comm., usu. written*) (about clothes) outsize

**oscillate** /'ɒsɪleɪt; *AmE* 'ɑːs-/ *v.* [I] **1** to keep moving from one position to another and back again: *The cylinder oscillates to mix the liquids.* **2** to keep changing from one level or value to another and back again: *The dollar has been oscillating between 107 and 110 yen.* SYN SWING ▸ **ˌoscil'lation** /-'leɪʃn/ *n.* [C]

**OTC** /ˌəʊ tiː 'siː; *AmE* ˌoʊ/ = OVER-THE-COUNTER

**OTE** *abbr* (*written*) (*HR*) **1** (*BrE*) **on-target earnings** used in advertisements to describe the pay that sb, esp. a SALESPERSON, should be able to earn, including any extra pay for the amount of goods they sell **2 ordinary time earnings** used esp. in Australia and New Zealand to describe the total pay that employees receive in a particular period of time, not including pay for working after the normal hours

**other** /'ʌðə(r)/ *adj.* (*Account.*) used in financial records to describe amounts of money that are small enough not to be listed separately in specific named groups: *other current assets*

**OTS** /ˌəʊ tiː 'es; *AmE* ˌoʊ/ = OPPORTUNITY TO SEE

**ounce** /aʊns/ *n.* [C] (*abbr* **oz**) a unit for measuring weight, equal to 28.35 grams

**oust** /aʊst/ *v.* [T] (used esp. in newspapers) to force sb out of a job or a position of power, esp. in order to take their place: *He was ousted as chairman.* ◇ (*fig.*) *The new product may oust the market leader from its position.* ▸ **'ousting** *n.* [U]

**ouster** /'aʊstə(r)/ *n.* [C, usu. sing.] (*AmE*) (often used in newspapers) the act of removing sb from a position of authority in order to put sb else in their place; the fact of being removed in this way: *shareholders seeking the CEO's ouster*

**outage** /'aʊtɪdʒ/ *n.* [C] (*AmE*) a period of time when the supply of electricity, etc. is not working: *a power outage*

**'out-ˌbasket** = OUT TRAY

**outbid** /ˌaʊt'bɪd/ *v.* [T] (**-bidding, -bid, -bid**) (*Comm.; Finan.*) to offer more money than sb else in order to buy sth, for example at an AUCTION: *We were outbid* **on** *the contract.*

**outbound** /'aʊtbaʊnd/ *adj.* travelling away from a place rather than arriving in it: *~ flights/calls* OPP INBOUND

**ˌoutbound 'telemarketing** *n.* [U] (*Market.*) selling goods or services by telephoning possible customers

**outbox** /ˈaʊtbɒks; *AmE* -bɑːks/ *n.* [C] **1** (*IT*) the place on a computer where new email messages that you write are stored before you send them **2** (*also* **out-box**) (*esp. AmE*) = OUT TRAY

★**outcome** /ˈaʊtkʌm/ *n.* [C] the result or effect of an action or event: *helping teams to achieve their desired business outcomes*

**outdated** /ˌaʊtˈdeɪtɪd/ *adj.* no longer useful because of being old-fashioned: *an outdated and inefficient system*

**ˌoutdoor ˈadvertising** (*also* **ˌout-of-home ˈadvertising**) *n.* [U] (*Market.*) methods of advertising that are used in the open air, for example BILLBOARDS, signs, advertisements on the outside of buildings, on vehicles, etc.

**outer** /ˈaʊtə(r)/ *n.* [C] (*Comm.*; *Transpt.*) a container in which goods already in boxes, bags, etc. are packed to be transported or displayed

**outfit** /ˈaʊtfɪt/ *n.*, *v.*
• ***n.*** **1** (*infml.*) [C with sing./pl.verb] a group of people working together as an organization, a business, a team, etc: *a market research outfit* **2** [C] a set of clothes that you wear, esp. for a particular occasion or purpose
• ***v.*** [T] (**-tt-**) (*esp. AmE*) (*often pass.*) to provide sb/sth with equipment or clothes for a special purpose SYN EQUIP ▸ **ˈoutfitting** *n.* [U]

**outflow** /ˈaʊtfləʊ; *AmE* -floʊ/ *n.* [C] **1** the movement of a large amount of money, people, etc. out of a country, an area, a company or an organization: *an outflow of cash from the group* **2** (*HR*) the way in which employees leave their jobs in an organization, for example, if they are dismissed, retire or stop work because there is no more work for them OPP INFLOW

**outgoing** /ˌaʊtˈgəʊɪŋ; *AmE* -ˈgoʊ-/ *adj.* **1** leaving the position of responsibility mentioned: *the outgoing chairman* **2** going away from a particular place rather than arriving in it: *outgoing calls* OPP INCOMING

**outgoings** /ˈaʊtgəʊɪŋz; *AmE* -goʊ-/ *n.* [pl.] (*BrE*) the amount of money that a business or person has to spend regularly, for example every month: *Many small businesses are struggling to meet their outgoings.* OPP INCOMINGS

**outlay** /ˈaʊtleɪ/ *n.* [C,U] (*Finan.*) the money that you have to spend in order to start a new project or to save yourself money or time later: *a huge outlay* **on** *advertising*

**outlet** /ˈaʊtlet/ *n.* [C] **1** a shop/store or an organization that sells goods made by a particular company or of a particular type: *a fast food/retail/sales* ~ **2** (*esp. AmE*) a shop/store that sells goods of a particular make at reduced prices **3** a way of making information or goods available to the public: *a media/an Internet* ~

**outline** /ˈaʊtlaɪn/ *v.*, *n.*
• ***v.*** [T] to give a description of the main facts or points involved in sth: *We outlined our proposals* **to** *the committee.*
• ***n.*** [C] a description of the main facts or points involved in sth: *an outline of our company's history* SYN OVERVIEW
⊙ *to* ***do/give/make/publish/write*** *an ~ (of sth)* ♦ *a* ***brief/broad/rough/simple*** ~ ♦ *an ~* ***agreement/plan/proposal***

★**outlook** /ˈaʊtlʊk/ *n.* [C] **1** the probable future for sb/sth; what is likely to happen: *The outlook* **for** *the financial industry is good.*
⊙ *a* ***bright****/an* ***improving/upbeat*** ~ ♦ *a* ***bleak/cautious/downbeat/gloomy****/an* ***uncertain*** ~ ♦ *a* ***corporate****/an* ***earnings/economic****/a* ***financial*** ~
**2** the way in which sb sees or judges sth: *his outlook* **on** *life*

**ˌout-of-ˈcourt** *adj.* (*Law*) agreed or decided without going to a court of law: *an out-of-court settlement*

**ˌout of ˈdate** *adj.* **1** old-fashioned or without the most recent information and therefore no longer useful: *out-of-date technology* **2** no longer valid

**ˌout-of-ˈfavour** (*AmE* **-favor**) *adj.* not popular: *out-of-favour stocks*

**ˌout-of-home ˈadvertising** = OUTDOOR ADVERTISING

**ˈout-of-ˈhouse** *adj.* working or happening outside a company: *an out-of-house designer* ▸ **ˌout-of-ˈhouse** *adv.* OPP IN-HOUSE

**ˌout-of-ˈpocket** *adj.* **1** used to describe costs that you pay directly yourself **2** (*Insur.*) (*AmE*) used to describe money that you pay for health care that is not covered by insurance

**ˌout-of-ˈtown** *adj.* **1** situated away from the centre of a town or city: *out-of-town superstores* **2** coming from or happening in a different place: *an out-of-town client*

**ˌout of ˈwork** *adj.*, *adv.* unemployed: *How long have you been out of work?* SYN UNEMPLOYED

**outpace** /ˌaʊt'peɪs/ *v.* [T] to go, improve, do sth, etc. faster than sb/sth: *Demand is outpacing production.* SYN OUTSTRIP

**outperform** /ˌaʊtpə'fɔːm; *AmE* -pər'fɔːrm/ *v.* **1** [T] to achieve better results than sb/sth **2** [T,I] (about shares, bonds, etc.) to provide more profit than the average shares, bonds, etc. of a similar type ▸ **outperformance** /-pə'fɔːməns; *AmE* -pər'fɔːrməns/ *n.* [U] ˌ**outper'former** *n.* [C]: *The stock is rated as a market outperformer.*

**outplacement** /'aʊtpleɪsmənt/ *n.* (*HR*) **1** [U,C] a service that a company offers to help people to find new jobs when the company can no longer employ them **2** [C, usu. pl.] a person that a company can no longer employ

★**output** /'aʊtpʊt/ *n., v.*

• *n.* [U,C] **1** the amount of sth that a person, a machine, an organization or an industry produces: *Manufacturing output has risen by 8%.*

**O** ***agricultural/economic/industrial ~ • global/national ~ • average/total ~ • high/low ~ • to boost/increase/lift/raise ~ • to cut/decrease/reduce ~ • falling/rising ~***

**2** (*IT*) the information, results, etc. produced by a computer: *data output* **3** (*Tech.*) the power, energy, etc. produced by a piece of equipment: *an output of 100 watts* **4** a place where energy, power, information, etc. leaves a system: *Connect the cable to the output.* → INPUT

• *v.* [T] (**-putting, -put, -put**) *or* (**-putting, -putted, -putted**) **1** (*IT*) to supply or produce information, etc: *Computers can now output data much more quickly.* **2** (*Manufact.*) to produce a quantity of goods: *outputting goods in huge runs* → INPUT

'**output tax** *n.* [C,U] (*BrE*) (*Account.*) the amount of tax that a company adds to the price of its goods or services

**outsell** /ˌaʊt'sel/ *v.* [T] (**-sold, -sold** /-'səʊld; *AmE* -'soʊld/) **1** (about a product) to be sold in larger quantities than sth else: *Laptops may outsell desktops.* **2** (about a company) to sell more products than another company

ˌ**outside di'rector** = NON-EXECUTIVE DIRECTOR

**outsider** /aʊt'saɪdə(r)/ *n.* [C] **1** a person who is not part of a particular organization or profession: *An outsider was brought in to assess efficiency.* **2** a person who is not accepted as a member of a society, group, etc.

ˌ**outside 'shareholder** *n.* [C] any shareholder in a company who is not the shareholder that owns more than half of the company's shares

ˌ**outside 'worker** *n.* [C] (*HR*) a person who works for a company but does not work in the offices, factory, etc. → INSIDE WORKER

**outsize** /'aʊtsaɪz/ (*also* **outsized** /'aʊtsaɪzd/) *adj.* **1** larger than the usual size: *These huge trucks deal with outsize cargo.* **2** designed for larger people: *outsize clothing*

★**outsourcing** /'aʊtsɔːsɪŋ; *AmE* -sɔːrs-/ *n.* [U] (*HR*) the process of arranging for sb outside a company to produce goods or provide services for that company: *the outsourcing of catering* ▸ '**outsource** *v.* [T,I]: *We outsource all our computing work.*

**outstanding** /aʊt'stændɪŋ/ *adj.* **1** (about payment, work, problems, etc.) not yet paid, done, solved, etc: *outstanding debts* ◇ *The payment was still outstanding after 28 days.* **2** extremely good; excellent: *outstanding performance*

ˌ**outstanding 'shares** (*also* ˌ**shares out'standing**) *n.* [pl.] (*also* ˌ**outstanding 'stock** [U]) (*Finan.*) the number of a company's shares that are currently owned by investors

**outstrip** /ˌaʊt'strɪp/ *v.* [T] (**-pp-**) **1** to become larger, more important, etc. than sb/sth: *Demand is outstripping supply.* SYN OVERTAKE **2** to be faster, better or more successful than a competitor

'**out tray** (*also* '**out-**ˌ**basket**, '**outbox**, *esp. in AmE*) *n.* [C] an open container in an office for letters or documents that are waiting to be sent out or passed to sb else

'**out-turn** (*also* **outturn**, *esp. in AmE*) *n.* [U; C, usu. sing.] (*Finan.*) **1** the amount of goods or money produced in a particular period of time SYN OUTPUT **2** (*BrE*) the amount of money spent by an organization in a particular period

**outvote** /ˌaʊt'vəʊt; *AmE* -'voʊt/ *v.* [T] (*usu. pass.*) to defeat sb/sth by winning a larger number of votes

ˌ**outward in'vestment** *n.* [U,C] (*Finan.*) investment by one country or area in another ▸ ˌ**outward in'vestor** *n.* [C]

**outwork** /'aʊtwɜːk; *AmE* -wɜːrk/ *n., v.* (*HR*)

• *n.* [U] (*BrE*) work that is done by people working outside the factory or office, for example at home ▸ '**outworker** *n.* [C]

• *v.* **1** [I] (*BrE*) to do **outwork** for a business **2** ˌ**out'work** [T] to work harder or faster than other people ▸ **'outworking** *n.* [U]

**overachieve** /ˌəʊvərə'tʃiːv; *AmE* ˌoʊ-/ *v.* [T,I] to do better than expected: *We overachieved our targets.* ▸ ˌ**overa'chievement** *n.* [U] ˌ**overa'chiever** *n.* [C]

**overage** /'əʊvərɪdʒ; *AmE* 'oʊ-/ *n.* [U,C] (*AmE*) an amount of goods, money, etc. that is more than is needed or expected: *an overage of funds* SYN OVERSUPPLY

**overall** *adj., adv., n.*
• *adj.* /ˌəʊvər'ɔːl; *AmE* ˌoʊ-/ including all the things or people that are involved in a particular situation; general: *the person with overall responsibility for the project*
• *adv.* /ˌəʊvər'ɔːl; *AmE* ˌoʊ-/ including everything or everyone; in total: *They will invest $1.6 m overall in new equipment.*
• *n.* /'əʊvərɔːl; *AmE* 'oʊ-/ [C] **1** (*BrE*) a loose coat worn over other clothes to protect them from dirt, etc. **2 overalls** (*BrE*) (*AmE* **'coveralls**) [pl.] a loose piece of clothing like a shirt and trousers/pants in one piece, made of heavy fabric and usu. worn over other clothing by workers doing dirty work

**overallotment** /ˌəʊvərə'lɒtmənt; *AmE* ˌoʊvərə'lɑːt-/ *n.* [U,C] (*Finan.*) a situation where people are allowed to order more shares, bonds, etc. than are available, as it is likely that some people will cancel their order ▸ ˌ**overal'lot** *v.* [T] (-tt-)

**overbanked** /ˌəʊvə'bæŋkt; *AmE* ˌəʊvər'b-/ *adj.* used to describe a financial system in which there are too many banks, which then cannot make much money

**overborrow** /ˌəʊvə'bɒrəʊ; *AmE* ˌoʊvər'bɑːroʊ/ *v.* [I] to borrow more money than you are able to pay back or pay interest on ▸ ˌ**over'borrowed** *adj.*: *overborrowed countries* ˌ**over'borrowing** *n.* [U,C]

**overbought** /ˌəʊvə'bɔːt; *AmE* ˌoʊvər'b-/ *adj.* (*Stock Ex.*) used to describe a situation when the value of shares, a currency, etc. has risen too high as too many people have been buying: *The stock market is currently overbought.* ◇ *overbought shares*

**overbuy** /ˌəʊvə'baɪ; *AmE* ˌoʊvər'b-/ *v.* [T,I] (**-bought, -bought** /-'bɔːt/) (*Comm.*) to buy too much of sth

**overcapacity** /ˌəʊvəkə'pæsəti; *AmE* ˌoʊvərkə-/ *n.* [U; sing.] (*Econ.*) a situation in which an industry or a factory cannot sell as much as it is designed to produce

**overcapitalized, -ised** /ˌəʊvə'kæpɪtəlaɪzd; *AmE* ˌoʊvər'k-/ *adj.* (*Finan.*) (about a business) having more money than is reasonable for its business needs or the amount of profit it is able to earn

★**overcharge** /ˌəʊvə'tʃɑːdʒ; *AmE* ˌoʊvər'tʃɑːrdʒ/ *v.* [T,I] to make sb pay too much for sth, often by mistake: *They have overcharged us* **for** *these parts.* ▸ **'overcharge** *n.* [C]: *The bills included overcharges or other errors.*

★**overdraft** /'əʊvədrɑːft; *AmE* 'oʊvərdræft/ (*also* ˌ**bank 'overdraft**) *n.* [C] (*Finan.*) the amount of money that you owe to a bank when you have spent more money than is in your bank account; an arrangement that allows you to do this: *We have a €20 m overdraft with the National Bank.* ◇ *an overdraft facility*
⊙ *to* ***apply for/arrange/extend*** *an* ~ • *to* ***pay off/run up*** *an* ~ • *an* ***agreed/authorized/unauthorized*** ~

★**overdraw** /ˌəʊvə'drɔː; *AmE* ˌoʊvər'drɔː/ *v.* [T] (**-drew** /-'druː/ **-drawn** /-'drɔːn/) (*esp. BrE*) (*Finan.*) to take more money out of your bank account than is in it: *We have overdrawn our account by €100 000.*

**overdrawn** /ˌəʊvə'drɔːn; *AmE* ˌoʊvər'd-/ *adj.* [not usu. before n.] (*abbr* **o/d, DR**) (*Finan.*) (about a company or person) having taken more money out of a bank account than was in it: *The firm is €5 m overdrawn.* ◇ *Your balance is €305 DR.*

**overdue** /ˌəʊvə'djuː; *AmE* ˌoʊvər'duː/ *adj.* not paid, done, returned, etc. by the required or expected time: *The payment is 90 days overdue.* ◇ *overdue payments*

**overestimate** /ˌəʊvər'estɪmeɪt; *AmE* ˌoʊ-/ *v.* [T] **1** to think or guess that the amount, cost or size of sth is larger than it really is: *The firm failed because it overestimated sales and underestimated costs.* **2** to think that sb is better, stronger, etc. than they really are: *Have we overestimated the competition?* ▸ **overestimate** /-'estɪmət/ *n.* [C] ˌ**overesti'mation** /-'meɪʃn/ *n.* [C,U]

**overextended** /ˌəʊvərɪk'stendɪd; *AmE* ˌoʊ-/ *adj.* [not usu. before n.] **1** (*Finan.*) spending or borrowing more money than you can manage without risking problems: *overextended borrowers* **2** involved in more work or activities than you can manage: *Many com-*

pany managers are severely overextended. ▸ ˌoverexˈtend *v.* [T]

**overfunded** /ˌəʊvəˈfʌndɪd; *AmE* ˌoʊvərˈf-/ *adj.* (*Finan.*) (about an organization, a project, etc.) having received more money than is necessary or than is allowed: *an ~ company/plan* ▸ ˌ**overˈfund** *v.* [T] ˌ**overˈfunding** *n.* [U]

**overgeared** /ˌəʊvəˈgɪəd; *AmE* ˌoʊvərˈgɪrd/ = OVER-LEVERAGED

**overhang** *n.*, *v.*

• ***n.*** /ˈəʊvəhæŋ; *AmE* ˈoʊvər-/ [C, usu. sing.] **1** (*Comm.*) (*esp. AmE*) the state of being extra to what is required; the things that are extra: *a stock overhang* ***in*** *childrenswear* **2** (*Stock Ex.*) a large number of shares that have not been sold or which are held by an important shareholder, and which, if they were offered for sale all at the same time, would make prices fall

• ***v.*** /ˌəʊvəˈhæŋ; *AmE* ˌoʊvərˈh-/ [T] (**-hung**, **-hung** /-ˈhʌŋ/) to have an influence and a negative effect on sth: *High oil prices continue to overhang the stock market.*

**overhaul** /ˈəʊvəhɔːl; *AmE* ˈoʊvər-/ *n.* [C] an examination of a system, machine, etc., including making changes to it or doing repairs: *The system is in need of a major overhaul.*

⊙ *a complete/radical ~* • *to* ***carry out/undergo*** *an ~*

▸ **overhaul** /ˌəʊvəˈhɔːl; *AmE* ˌoʊvərˈh-/ *v.* [T]

**overhead** /ˈəʊvəhed; *AmE* ˈoʊvərhed/ *n.*, *adj.*

• ***n.*** **1** (*Account.*) (*esp. AmE*) [U] = OVERHEADS **2** [C] a piece of transparent film with text, diagrams, etc. on, that is shown using an OVERHEAD PROJECTOR

• ***adj.*** (*Account.*) connected with the general costs of running a business or an organization, for example paying for rent or electricity: *overhead costs*

ˌ**overhead proˈjector** (*abbr* **OHP**) (*also* **proˈjector**) *n.* [C] a piece of equipment that sends an image onto a wall or screen so that many people can see it

★ **overheads** /ˈəʊvəhedz; *AmE* ˈoʊvər-/ *n.* [pl.] (*esp. BrE*) (*AmE usu.* **ˈoverhead** [U]) (*Account.*) regular costs that you have when you are running a business or an organization, such as rent, electricity, wages, etc: *We may need to close branches to reduce our overheads.* ◇ *high/low ~*

**overheat** /ˌəʊvəˈhiːt; *AmE* ˌoʊvər-/ *v.* [T,I] (about an economy or a market) to be too active, with high demand causing prices to rise; to make an economy or a market too active ▸ ˌ**overˈheating** *n.* [U]

**overhype** /ˌəʊvəˈhaɪp; *AmE* ˌoʊvər-/ *v.* [T] (*infml.*) to exaggerate the quality or the importance of sth: *overhyped Internet companies*

ˌ**over-inˈvestment** *n.* [U] (*Finan.*) the fact of more money being invested in sth than is needed: *Over-investment* ***in*** *steel production led to a fall in price.* ▸ ˌ**over-inˈvest** *v.* [I] ˌ**over-inˈvested** *adj.*

**overlay** /ˈəʊvəleɪ; *AmE* ˈoʊvərl-/ *n.* [C] **1** a transparent sheet with drawings, figures, etc. on it that can be placed on top of another sheet in order to change it **2** (*Market.*) extra data from another organization that is added to a company's MAILING LIST: *overlay data such as age, income or job*

ˌ**over-ˈleveraged** (*esp. AmE*) (*BrE usu.* ˌ**overˈgeared**) *adj.* (*Finan.*) if a company, etc. is **over-leveraged**, it has borrowed too much money compared to the number of shares it has issued and may not be able to pay the interest on the loans ▸ ˌ**over-ˈleverage** *v.* [T]: *The firm had over-leveraged itself.*

**overload** *v.*, *n.*

• ***v.*** /ˌəʊvəˈləʊd; *AmE* ˌoʊvərˈloʊd/ [T] **1** to put too great a load on sth: *an overloaded truck* **2** to give sb/sth too much of sth: *He's overloaded* ***with*** *responsibilities.* **3** to put too great a demand on an electrical system, a computer, etc., causing it to fail

• ***n.*** /ˈəʊvələʊd; *AmE* ˈoʊvərloʊd/ [U; sing.] too much of sth: *An Internet search can result in* ***information*** *overload.*

**overmanned** /ˌəʊvəˈmænd; *AmE* ˌoʊvərˈm-/ *adj.* (*HR*) having more workers than are needed SYN OVERSTAFFED OPP UNDERMANNED ▸ ˌ**overˈmanning** *n.* [U]

**overnight** *adv.*, *adj.*, *v.*

• ***adv.*** /ˌəʊvəˈnaɪt; *AmE* ˌoʊvərˈn-/ (*Stock Ex.*) since trading ended the day before: *The US Nasdaq fell 2.4% overnight.*

• ***adj.*** /ˌəʊvəˈnaɪt; *AmE* ˌoʊvərˈn-/ **1** an **overnight** delivery of goods arrives the day after you order them **2** (*Stock Ex.*) happening since trading closed the day before: *an overnight fall on Wall Street* **3** (*Finan.*) used to describe a loan that one bank makes to another for a very short period, for example one night: *The central bank kept the overnight rate at 2.75%.*

• ***v.*** /ˈəʊvənaɪt; *AmE* ˈoʊvərn-/ [T] (*AmE*) to send or transport sth during the night so that it arrives the next day: *We overnight fresh fish to restaurants in New York.*

**ˌover-optiˈmistic** *adj.* **1** too confident that sth will be successful: *I'm not over-optimistic about my chances of getting the job.* **2** too high: *over-optimistic sales forecasts*

★ **overpay** /ˌəʊvəˈpeɪ; *AmE* ˌoʊvərˈp-/ *v.* (**-paid**, **-paid** /-ˈpeɪd/) **1** [T] (*often pass.*) to pay sb too much; to pay sb more than their work is worth **2** [T,I] to pay too much for sth; to pay more than sth is worth: *I have been overpaying tax.*
▸ **ˌoverˈpayment** *n.* [C,U]

**overpriced** /ˌəʊvəˈpraɪst; *AmE* ˌoʊvərˈp-/ *adj.* too expensive; costing more than it is worth: *overpriced goods* OPP UNDERPRICED
▸ **ˌoverˈprice** *v.* [T]

**overprint** /ˌəʊvəˈprɪnt; *AmE* ˌoʊvərˈp-/ *v.* [T] **~ A (on B)** | **~ B with A** to print sth on a document, etc. that already has printing on it

**overproduction** /ˌəʊvəprəˈdʌkʃən; *AmE* ˌoʊvərp-/ *n.* [U] the fact that more goods, services, etc. are produced than was planned or than can be sold to make a profit: *overproduction of oil*
▸ **ˌoverproˈduce** /-ˈdjuːs ; *AmE* -ˈduːs/ *v.* [T,I]

**ˌover-reˈport** (*AmE* **overreport**) *v.* [T] (*Account.*) to say that you have earned, sold, etc. more than you actually have: *They admitted over-reporting sales.*

**override** /ˌəʊvəˈraɪd; *AmE* ˌoʊvər-/ *v.* [T] (**-rode** /-ˈrəʊd; *AmE* -ˈroʊd/ **-ridden** /-ˈrɪdn/) **1** to use your authority to reject sb's decision, order, etc: *The chairman overrode the decision.* SYN OVERRULE **2** to be more important than sth: *Safety overrides all other concerns.* **3** to stop a process that happens automatically and control it yourself: *to override a time lock*

**ˌoverriding comˈmission** (*also* **overrider** /ˌəʊvəˈraɪdə(r); *AmE* ˌoʊvərˈr-/) *n.* [C] (*Market.*) a payment earned by a manager of a company's office in another area or country, based on the business created by the agents in that office

**overrule** /ˌəʊvəˈruːl; *AmE* ˌoʊvərˈr-/ *v.* [T] to change a decision or reject an idea from a position of greater power: *The government overruled the decision to block the merger.* SYN OVERRIDE

**overrun** *v.*, *n.*
• *v.* /ˌəʊvəˈrʌn; *AmE* ˌoʊvərˈr-/ [T,I] (**-ran** /-ˈræn/-**run**) to take more time or money than was intended: *The project overran by a month.*
• *n.* /ˈəʊvərʌn; *AmE* ˈoʊ-/ [C] **1** a situation when sth takes more time or money than planned: *the cost of overruns in time or costs* **2** (*AmE*) a quantity of sth produced that is extra or more than you need: *We will buy first-quality overruns.*

★ **overseas** /ˌəʊvəˈsiːz; *AmE* ˌoʊvər-/ *adj.*, *adv.* connected with foreign countries, esp. those that you have to cross the sea or ocean to get to: *overseas trade* ◇ *to live/work/go ~*

**oversee** /ˌəʊvəˈsiː; *AmE* ˌoʊvərˈsiː/ *v.* [T] (**-saw** /-ˈsɔː/-**seen** /-ˈsiːn/) **1** to watch sb/sth and make sure that a job or an activity is done correctly: *My job involves overseeing 120 employees.* SYN SUPERVISE **2** (*Finan.*) to be responsible for the way an amount of money is invested: *a fund that oversees $100 m*

**overseer** /ˈəʊvəsɪə(r); *AmE* ˈoʊvərsɪr/ *n.* [C] **1** a person or an organization that is responsible for making sure that a system is working as it should: *an accounting overseer* **2** (*old-fash.*) a person whose job is to make sure that other workers do their work

**oversell** /ˌəʊvəˈsel; *AmE* ˌoʊvərˈsel/ *v.* (**-sold**, **-sold** /-ˈsəʊld; *AmE* -ˈsoʊld/) **1** (*Comm.*) [T] to sell too much or more of sth than is available: *The seats on the plane were oversold.* **2** (*Market.*) [T,I] to try to make sb buy more of sth than they need: *overselling insurance policies* **3** [T] to exaggerate the quality or importance of sth: *He oversells himself.*
▸ **ˌoverˈselling** *n.* [U]

**overshoot** /ˌəʊvəˈʃuːt; *AmE* ˌoʊvərˈʃ-/ *v.* [T,I] (**-shot**, **-shot** /-ˈʃɒt; *AmE* -ˈʃɑːt/) to spend more money or to do more than you originally planned: *We overshot our sales target by 20%.* ▸ **ˈovershoot** *n.* [C]: *a big budget overshoot*

**oversight** /ˈəʊvəsaɪt; *AmE* ˈoʊvərs-/ *n.* **1** [U] the state of being in charge of sb/sth: *Who has oversight of finance and general policy?* **2** [C,U] the fact of making a mistake because you forget to do sth or you do not notice sth: *Due to an oversight, I have not been paid.*

**oversized** /ˈəʊvəsaɪzd; *AmE* ˈoʊvərs-/ (*also* **ˈoversize**, *less freq.*) *adj.* bigger than the normal size; too big: *oversized packages*

**oversold** /ˌəʊvəˈsəʊld; *AmE* ˌoʊvərˈsoʊld/ *adj.* (*Stock Ex.*) used to describe a situation when the value of shares, a currency, etc. has fallen too far as too many people have been selling

**overspend** /ˌəʊvəˈspend; *AmE* ˌoʊvərˈs-/ *v.* [T,I] (**-spent**, **-spent** /-ˈspent/) to spend too much money or more than you planned: *The company has overspent* **on** *marketing.* ▶ **ˈoverspend** *n.* [C, usu. sing., U] (*esp. BrE*): *a €1 m overspend from last year* **ˌoverˈspending** *n.* [U]

**overstaffed** /ˌəʊvəˈstɑːft; *AmE* ˌoʊvərˈstæft/ *adj.* (*HR*) (about a company, an office, etc.) having more workers than are needed: *The airline was heavily overstaffed.* SYN OVERMANNED ▶ **ˌoverˈstaffing** *n.* [U]

**overstate** /ˌəʊvəˈsteɪt; *AmE* ˌoʊvərˈs-/ *v.* [T] to say that sth is larger than it really is, esp. an amount of money: *The company overstated its revenues by $20 m.* ▶ **ˈoverstatement** /-mənt/ *n.* [C,U]

**overstock** /ˌəʊvəˈstɒk; *AmE* ˌoʊvərˈstɑːk/ *v.* [T,I] (*Comm.*) to buy or make more of sth than you need or can sell: *to overstock inventory* ▶ **ˈoverstock** *n.* [C,U]: *an overstock of summer clothing* **ˌoverˈstocking** *n.* [U]

**overstretch** /ˌəʊvəˈstretʃ; *AmE* ˌoʊvərˈs-/ *v.* [T] to make sb/sth do more than they are capable of; to do more than you are capable of: *The firm overstretched itself by expanding into Asia.* ▶ **ˌoverˈstretched** *adj.*: *an overstretched budget*

**oversubscribed** /ˌəʊvəsəbˈskraɪbd; *AmE* ˌoʊvərs-/ *adj.* **1** (*Finan.*) if new shares, bonds, etc. are **oversubscribed**, too many people want to buy them **2** (*Comm.*) if a service is **oversubscribed**, more people have the right to use it than is possible at the same time ▶ **ˌoversubˈscription** /-ˈskrɪpʃn/ *n.* [U]: *oversubscription of services*

**oversupply** /ˌəʊvəsəˈplaɪ; *AmE* ˌoʊvərs-/ *n., v.*
• ***n.*** [U; C, usu. sing.] (*pl.* **-lies**) more of sth than can be sold: *An oversupply of paper has led to a fall in price.*
• ***v.*** [T,I] (**-lies**, **-lying**, **-lied**, **-lied**) to provide sb/sth with more than they can use or sell: *Coffee is a heavily oversupplied market.*

**overtake** /ˌəʊvəˈteɪk; *AmE* ˌoʊvərˈt-/ *v.* [T] (**-took** /-ˈtʊk/ **-taken** /-ˈteɪkən/) to become greater in number, amount or importance than sth else: *We may be overtaken by our competitors.* SYN OUTSTRIP

**ˌover-the-ˈcounter** *adj.* (*abbr* **OTC**) **1** (*Finan.*) used to describe investments, currencies, etc. that are traded between independent dealers rather than in an organized system such as a stock exchange: *~ shares/stock/trading ◇ OTC markets*
**2** (about medicines) that can be bought without written permission from a doctor ▶ **ˌover the ˈcounter** *adv.* (*abbr* **OTC**): *shares are traded over the counter*

★ **overtime** /ˈəʊvətaɪm; *AmE* ˈoʊvərt-/ *n.* [U] **1** time that you spend working at your job after you have worked the normal hours: *a union ban on overtime*
⊕ *to* ***do/work*** *~* ◆ *to* ***ban/cut*** *~* ◆ *an ~* ***ban***
**2** the money that sb earns for doing **overtime**: *$150 a day plus overtime.*
⊕ *to* ***earn*** *~* ◆ *to* ***pay*** *(sb) ~* ◆ *~* ***earnings/pay/payments***
**3** extra time that a factory operates, esp. to meet orders: *Several plants will* **work** *overtime next week.*

**overtrade** /ˌəʊvəˈtreɪd; *AmE* ˌoʊvərˈt-/ *v.* [T,I] to do more business than you can afford; to produce or buy more of sth than you will be able to sell

**overtrading** /ˌəʊvəˈtreɪdɪŋ; *AmE* ˌoʊvərˈt-/ *n.* [U] (*Finan.*) a situation when a company has increased its business too quickly and does not have enough cash available to pay debts, wages and other expenses

**overturn** /ˌəʊvəˈtɜːn; *AmE* ˌoʊvərˈtɜːrn/ *v.* [T] (*Law*) to officially decide that a legal decision is not correct, and to make it no longer valid: *to ~ a ban/decision/patent/ruling/verdict*

**overvalue** /ˌəʊvəˈvæljuː; *AmE* ˌoʊvərˈv-/ *v.* [T] (*often pass.*) to fix the value of sth at a level that is too high: *The shares are 25% overvalued.*

**overview** /ˈəʊvəvjuː; *AmE* ˈoʊvərv-/ *n.* [C] a general description of sth: *to give you an overview of future plans* SYN OUTLINE
⊕ *to* ***offer/present/provide*** *an ~ (of sth)* ◆ *a* ***broad/detailed/quick*** *~*

**overweight** /ˌəʊvəˈweɪt; *AmE* ˌoʊvərˈw-/ *adj.* (*Stock Ex.*) having more of a particular type of investment or asset in a collection than the index that you are following or than your usual position ▶ **ˌoverˈweight** *v.* [T,I]

**overwork** /ˌəʊvəˈwɜːk; *AmE* ˌoʊvərˈwɜːrk/ *v., n.*
• ***v.*** [T,I] to work too hard; to make sb work too hard: *overworked executives*
• ***n.*** [U] the fact of working too hard: *His illness was brought on by overwork.*

**ovno** *abbr* (*written*) **or very near offer** used in private sales to say that the seller will accept a slightly lower price: *Desk for sale, €75 ovno.*

★ **owe** /əʊ; *AmE* oʊ/ *v.* [T] **~ sth (to sb) (for sth)** | **~ (sb) sth (for sth)** to have to pay sb for sth that you have already received or return money that you have borrowed: *We still owe €5 000 to the bank.* ◇ *We still owe the bank €5 000.* ◇ (*fig.*) *I'm still owed three days' leave.*

**owing** /ˈəʊɪŋ; *AmE* ˈoʊɪŋ/ *adj.* (*BrE*) money that is **owing** has not been paid yet

★ **own** /əʊn; *AmE* oʊn/ *adj.*, *v.*
• ***adj.*** done or produced by and for yourself: *The store has its own product line of organic foods.* → idiom at BEAT
• ***v.*** [T] (*not used in the continuous tenses*) to have sth that belongs to you, esp. because you have bought it: *80% of our customers own a PC.*

**ˌown ˈbrand** (*also* **ˌown ˈlabel**) *n.* [C] (*both BrE*) (*Comm.*; *Market.*) a product or group of products that a shop/store sells with its own name on rather than the name of the company that produced them SYN HOUSE BRAND, STORE BRAND (*AmE*)

**-owned** /əʊnd; *AmE* oʊnd/ *adj.* (*used to form adjs*) having the owner or type of owner mentioned: *state-owned/privately-owned/foreign-owned*

★ **owner** /ˈəʊnə(r); *AmE* ˈoʊ-/ *n.* [C] a person or an organization that owns sth: *the firm's owner* ◇ *the owners of the hotel* ◇ *business owners*
IDM **at (the) owner's ˈrisk** used in formal notices to say that the owner of sth and not anyone else is responsible for any loss or damage: *Cars are parked at the owner's risk.*

**ˌowner of ˈrecord** = SHAREHOLDER OF RECORD

**ˌowner-ˈoperator** *n.* [C] (*AmE*) a person who owns a lorry/truck and runs it as a business

**ˌowners' ˈequity** = NET WORTH

★ **ownership** /ˈəʊnəʃɪp; *AmE* ˈoʊnərʃ-/ *n.* [U] the fact of owning sth; the legal right to own sth: *The restaurant is* ***under*** *new ownership.* ◇ *a growth in home ownership*

**ˌownership in ˈcommon** = COMMON OWNERSHIP

**ˌown-price elasˈticity** = PRICE ELASTICITY OF DEMAND

**oz** *abbr* (*written*) ounce(s): *a 16 oz container*

# Pp

**p** (*also* **p.**) *abbr* /piː/ penny; pence: *The shares closed 1p up at 25p.*

**P2P** (*also* **p2p**, **P-to-P**) /ˌpiː tə ˈpiː/ *adj.* (*IT*) **peer-to-peer** used to describe the situation when one computer can communicate with another directly, without using a central SERVER

**P3** /ˌpiː ˈθriː/ = PUBLIC-PRIVATE PARTNERSHIP

**P45** /ˌpiː ˌfɔːti ˈfaɪv; *AmE* ˌfɔːrti/ *n.* [C] in the UK, a form that you receive from your employer when you stop working for them and that shows how much you earned in the job and how much tax you paid

**PA** /ˌpiː ˈeɪ/ = PERSONAL ASSISTANT, PUBLIC ADDRESS (SYSTEM)

**p.a.** /ˌpiː ˈeɪ/ *abbr* **per annum** per year; for each year

**PABX** /ˌpiː eɪ biː ˈeks/ *abbr* **private automatic branch exchange** an automatic system for transferring telephone calls to the correct part of an organization

**pace** /peɪs/ *n.*, *v.*
• ***n.*** [C,U] the speed at which sth happens or is done: *the slow pace of change*
⊕ ***a brisk/fast/steady*** *~* ♦ *to* ***change/increase/slow*** *the ~ (of sth)*
IDM **keep ˈpace (with sth)** to happen, develop, or act at the same speed as sth else: *to keep pace with your rivals* **put sb/sth through their/its ˈpaces** to give sb/sth a number of tasks to perform so that you can judge what they/it can do **set the ˈpace** to do sth at a particular speed or to a particular standard so that other people are then forced to copy it if they want to be successful: *They set the pace with new technology.*
• ***v.*** [T] **~ yourself** to work at the speed or level of activity that suits you best, so that you can continue without getting too tired

**the Paˌcific ˈRim** *n.* [sing.] the countries around the Pacific Ocean, esp. countries in East Asia, considered as an economic group

★ **pack** /pæk/ *v.*, *n.*
• ***v.*** [T] **~ sth (up) (in/into sth)** to put goods into containers for delivery or sale: *to pack and ship an order* SYN PACKAGE PHR V **ˌpack sth ˈin** (*infml.*) to stop doing sth: *She's packed in her job.* **ˌpack (sth) ˈup** (*BrE*) (*infml.*) to stop doing sth: *I'm ready to* ***pack up*** *and go home.*

• *n.* **1** [C] a container, usu. a small one; a container and its contents: *a ~ of cigarettes/gum* **2** [C] a set of documents or objects inside the same cover: *an information pack* ◇ *a book and CD-ROM pack* **3** [C with sing./pl.verb] the people or things in a particular field or industry; the people or things that are not the leaders: *Two of the supermarket chains are pulling away from the pack.*

★ **package** /'pækɪdʒ/ *n., v.*
• *n.* [C] **1** (*esp. AmE*) = PARCEL **2** (*AmE*) a box, bag, etc. in which things are wrapped or packed; the contents of a box, bag, etc: *Our system allows us to track each package.* **3** (*IT*) a set of programs for a particular type of task which are supplied together: *an accounting package* **4** a set of products or services that are supplied together: *We put together the right package of services for each client.* **5** a set of conditions, proposals, etc. that are offered and must be accepted together; the money involved in them: *a benefits package*
• *v.* [T] **1 ~ sth (up)** to put goods into containers for delivery or sale: *We produce and package the drink here.* ◇ *packaged teas* SYN PACK **2** to combine goods, services, etc. and provide them as a set: *The book is packaged with a CD.* **3** to present services, products, people, etc. in a particular way, esp. in an attractive way: *an attempt to package news as entertainment*

**'package deal** *n.* [C] an agreement to offer a number of things that must all be accepted together

**'packaged goods** *n.* [pl.] goods, esp. food and other things sold in supermarkets, which are already in boxes, bags or packages when customers choose them

**,packaged 'software** *n.* [U] (*IT*) a computer program that is developed for sale to consumers or businesses, generally designed to appeal to more than a single customer

**packager** /'pækɪdʒə(r)/ *n.* [C] a person, machine or company that packs or wraps products ready to be stored, transported or sold

★ **packaging** /'pækɪdʒɪŋ/ *n.* [U] **1** the materials used to wrap or protect goods that are sold in shops/stores; the design of these materials: *a new type of packaging* ◇ *packaging materials*
✪ ***attractive/bright/fancy/glossy ~*** • ***paper/plastic/recyclable ~***
**2** the process of packing goods in containers or covers: *We outsource the packaging and distribution of our products.*
✪ *a ~* ***company/group/plant*** • *~* ***equipment/machinery***
**3** the way that services, people or activities are presented; the way that makes them seem most attractive

**packer** /'pækə(r)/ *n.* [C] a person, machine or company that puts food, goods, etc. into containers to be sold or sent to sb: *The pickers deliver the completed orders to the packers.*

**packet** /'pækɪt/ *n.* [C] **1** (*BrE*) a small container or covering for goods; the container or covering and its contents: *a ~* ***of*** *cornflakes/cigarettes* **2** a small object wrapped in paper or put into a thick envelope so that it can be sent by mail, carried easily or given as a present: *Orders under 2 kg are sent as a small packet.* **3** (*AmE*) a set of documents or objects inside the same cover: *a packet of legal papers* SYN PACK **4** (*AmE*) = SACHET **5** (*IT*) a small amount of data that is separated from other data before being sent. The data is joined together again after it arrives: *packets of Internet data* IDM **cost, lose, make, etc. a 'packet** (*infml.*) cost, lose, make, etc. a very large amount of money

**packing** /'pækɪŋ/ *n.* [U] **1** the act of packing goods for delivery or sale: *labels for use in packing and shipping* **2** material used for wrapping around delicate objects in order to protect them, esp. before sending them somewhere: (*BrE*) *The price includes* ***postage and packing***.

**pact** /pækt/ *n.* [C] an agreement or a promise to do sth: *Chile has signed a free-trade pact* ***with*** *the EU.*

**pad** /pæd/ *n., v.*
• *n.* [C] a number of sheets of paper fastened together along one edge: *a memo pad*
• *v.* [T] (**-dd-**) (*AmE*) to make an amount bigger, esp. dishonestly: *to pad profit margins*

**,padded 'envelope** *n.* [C] an envelope with a layer of soft material in it, used for sending things that might break or tear easily → JIFFY

**page** /peɪdʒ/ *n., v.*
• *n.* [C] **1** a section of a newspaper or magazine that is used for a particular topic: *the business/financial ~s* **2** a section of a website that can be shown on a computer screen at any one time: *The page got a huge number of hits.* **3** a message that sb receives on a PAGER IDM **be on the same 'page** (*esp. AmE*) if two or more people or groups are **on the same**

page, they work together and have the same goal
• *v.* [T] to call sb using a PAGER or by announcing their name in a public place such as an airport: *I **had** him **paged**.* PHR V ˌ**page 'through sth** to go from one page to another in a document or on a computer screen

**'page break** *n.* [C] a symbol on a computer screen that shows where a printer will start a new page in a typed document

**'page imˌpression** = PAGE VIEW

**pager** /ˈpeɪdʒə(r)/ *n.* [C] a small electronic device that you carry around with you and that lets you know when sb is trying to contact you, by showing a message, making a sound, etc.

**'page ˌtraffic** *n.* [U] the number of times that a web page is visited; the number of people who read a particular page in a magazine, newspaper, etc.

**'page view** (*also* **'page imˌpression**) *n.* [C] (*Market.*) one visit to a single web page

★ **paid** /peɪd/ *adj.* **1** (about work, etc.) for which people receive money: *be in paid employment* ◇ *~ leave/vacation* ◇ *a **well-paid** job*
**2** (about a person) receiving money for doing work: ***well-paid** bankers*
**3** (*often used following a n.*) that has been paid: *postage paid*

**ˌpaid-up 'capital** (*also* **ˌpaid-up 'share ˌcapital**) *n.* [U] (*Finan.*) the amount of money that has been received for shares that have been bought and paid for, rather than the money owed to a company from shares that have been bought but not paid for yet

**ˌpaid-up 'policy** *n.* [C] (*Insur.*) a LIFE INSURANCE agreement in which regular payments have stopped before the end of the agreement

**ˌpaid-up 'share** *n.* [C] (*Finan.*) a share whose full value was paid at the time of issue

**ˌpaid-up 'share ˌcapital** = PAID-UP CAPITAL

**'paint shop** *n.* [C] the part of a factory in which goods are painted, esp. in a car factory

**pairing** /ˈpeərɪŋ; *AmE* ˈper-/ *n.* [U,C] two people or things that work together or are put together; the act of putting them together: *the pairing of coffee bars and booksellers*

**P & L** /ˌpiː ənd ˈel/ = PROFIT AND LOSS ACCOUNT

**pallet** /ˈpælət/ *n.* [C] a flat wooden frame used for storing and moving goods; the frame and its contents: *Each pallet contains 60 bags.*

**'palm-size** (*also* **'palm-sized**) *adj.* small enough to hold in your hand: *palm-size PCs*

**palmtop** /ˈpɑːmtɒp; *AmE* -tɑːp/ *n.* [C] a small computer that you can hold in one hand: *a palmtop organizer*

**p. and h.** (*also* **p. & h.**) /ˌpiː ənd ˈeɪtʃ/ *abbr* (*AmE*) **postage and handling** the cost of dealing with an order and sending the package by post

**p. and p.** (*also* **p. & p.**) /ˌpiː ən ˈpiː/ *abbr* (*BrE*) **post(age) and packing** the cost of packing and sending goods: *Add £2 for p. and p.*

**panel** /ˈpænl/ *n.* **1** [C with sing./pl. v.] a group of specialists brought together to give their advice or opinion about sth, discuss sth, decide on sth, investigate sth, etc.
➊ *an **advisory/interview/a selection** ~ • a ~ of **experts/judges** • to **appoint sb to/set up** a ~*
**2** [C with sing./pl. v.] a group of people used to research or test sth
**3** (*Law*) (*also* **'jury ˌpanel**) [C] (*both esp. AmE*) = JURY **4** [C] a flat board in a vehicle or on a piece of machinery where the controls and instruments are fixed: *a control/display ~*

**panellist** (*AmE* **panelist**) /ˈpænəlɪst/ *n.* [C] (*BrE only*) one of the group of people in a PANEL

**'panel truck** *n.* [C] (*AmE*) (*Transpt.*) a small van/truck with a space for storing goods that can be reached from the driver's seat, used for delivering goods, etc.

**'panel van** *n.* [C] (*Transpt.*) (*used mainly in Australian English*) a small van/truck with doors at the back, used for carrying goods, tools, etc.

**ˌpan-Euro'pean** *adj.* relating to, or affecting, the whole of Europe; across the whole of Europe: *pan-European trading*

**paper** /ˈpeɪpə(r)/ *n.* **1** (*Finan.*) [U] assets in the form of shares, BILLS OF EXCHANGE, etc. rather than cash: *a bid made up equally of cash and paper* **2 papers** [pl.] documents: *a stack of work papers* **3 papers** [pl.] official documents that prove your identity, give you permission to do sth, etc: *identification papers* **4** [C] an article on a particular subject: *a consultation paper* **5** [C] a newspaper: *the New York papers* IDM **on 'paper 1** printed or written on paper, rather than in electronic form **2** based on recorded information, rather than on reality → idiom at WORTH *adj.*

**ˈpaper-based** *adj.* **1** using paper rather than electronic means: *a paper-based billing* **system** **2** (*Finan.*) involving payment in shares, rather than in cash: *a paper-based deal*

**paperchase** /ˈpeɪpətʃeɪs; *AmE* -pərtʃ-/ *n.* [C] (*AmE*) **1** the fact of producing too much work on paper **2** a thorough search through books and documents: *the paperchase that uncovered the bank fraud*

**ˌpaper ˈcurrency** = PAPER MONEY

**ˌpaper ˈgain** = PAPER PROFIT

**paperless** /ˈpeɪpələs; *AmE* -pərləs/ *adj.* using computers, telephones, etc. rather than paper, to store and send information: *the paperless office*

**ˌpaper ˈloss** *n.* [C,U] (*Account.*) a loss in value which appears in your accounts, but which may not exist in reality, for example because an asset has become less valuable OPP PAPER PROFIT

**ˌpaper ˈmoney** (*also* **ˌpaper ˈcurrency**) *n.* [U] money in the form of paper, not coins or cards

**ˌpaper ˈprofit** (*also* **ˌpaper ˈgain**) *n.* [C,U] (*Account.*) a profit that has been made but not taken as real money yet, for example shares that have risen in value but have not yet been sold SYN BOOK PROFIT OPP PAPER LOSS

**ˈpaper-ˌpusher** *n.* [C] (*infml.*) a person whose job involves boring or unimportant office work such as keeping records or writing a great deal → PEN-PUSHER

**ˈpaper trail** *n.* [C, usu. sing.] (*esp. AmE*) (*infml.*) a series of documents that show what you have done or what has happened

**paperwork** /ˈpeɪpəwɜːk; *AmE* ˈpeɪpərwɜːrk/ *n.* [U] **1** the documents needed or produced for sth: *How quickly can you prepare the paperwork?* **2** the written work that is part of a job, such as filling in forms or writing letters and reports: *routine paperwork* ◇ *to deal with/do/get through (the) ~*

**par** /pɑː(r)/ *n.* [U] (*also* **ˌpar ˈvalue**, **ˌnominal ˈvalue** [C,U]) (*also* **ˌnominal ˈprice** [C]) (*Finan.*) the value given to a share when it is first made available for sale, which may be greater or smaller than the price paid for it: *The bonds trade at less than 8% of par value.* ◇ *shares trading above/below ~* IDM **below/under/sub ˈpar** less well, good, etc. than is usual or expected: *Performance is sub par.* **on a par with sb/sth** (*also* **on par with sb/sth**, *esp. in AmE*) as good as usual; as good, bad, etc. as sb/sth else: *Prices in Germany are on a par with the UK.*

**parachute** /ˈpærəʃuːt/ *n.*, *v.*
• *n.* [C] (*HR*) money or other benefits that you will receive if you lose your job; an agreement to receive this money or these benefits: *a parachute payment*
• *v.* PHR V **ˌparachute sb ˈin**; **ˌparachute sb ˈinto sth** (*usu. pass.*) to put sb from outside a company into a senior position in the company

**ˈparadigm shift** *n.* [C] a very important and noticeable change in the way sth is done or thought about: *a paradigm shift* **in** *management*

**paralegal** /ˌpærəˈliːɡl/ *n.* [C] (*AmE*) an employee in a law firm who is trained to deal with some types of legal work, but who is not qualified as a lawyer

**parallel** /ˈpærəlel/ *adj.* **1** (*Econ.*) used to describe a system of buying and selling goods that happens outside the official system of the company that produces them. Goods are bought in one country and imported into another where they are sold at a lower price than the official price for that country: *parallel imports* **2** (*IT*) involving several computer operations at the same time: *parallel processing* OPP SERIAL

**the ˌparallel eˈconomy** = SHADOW ECONOMY

**ˌparallel ˈloan** = BACK-TO-BACK LOAN

**ˌparallel ˈmarket** *n.* [C] (*Econ.*) a separate market for goods and currencies that is different from a country's official money market, esp. in countries where the official market is strictly controlled by government

**paralyse** (*AmE* **paralyze**) /ˈpærəlaɪz/ *v.* [T] to prevent sth from working normally: *The port is still paralysed by the truck drivers' strike.*

**parameter** /pəˈræmɪtə(r)/ *n.* [C, usu. pl.] a target or limit which measures or controls an activity: *We have to work within the established parameters.*
➊ *performance/price ~s* ♦ *financial/investment ~s* ♦ *to* **define/set** *~s*

**parastatal** /ˌpærəˈsteɪtl/ *adj.* used to describe an organization, esp. in some African countries, that has some political power and serves the state ▸ **ˌparaˈstatal** *n.* [C]

**ˈpar bond** *n.* [C] (*Finan.*) a share, bond, etc. which is sold at the value it is given when it is first issued, rather than at a higher or lower price

**parcel** /ˈpɑːsl; *AmE* ˈpɑːrsl/ *n.*, *v.*
• ***n.*** [C] **1** (*esp. BrE*) (*AmE usu.* ˈ**package**) something that is wrapped in paper or put into a thick envelope so that it can be sent by mail, etc: *the parcel delivery business* **2** a set of things, for example, a set of investments which are offered, bought or sold together: *parcels of shares* **3** (*Prop.*) a piece of land
• ***v.*** [T] (-ll-, *AmE* -l-) **~ sth (up)** to wrap sth and make it into a **parcel**
PHR V ˌ**parcel sth** ˈ**off** to transfer or get rid of a set of things: *They'll parcel off some of the stores* ***to*** *the other companies.* ˌ**parcel sth** ˈ**out** to divide things into sets, and then offer or transfer them to other people or companies

**pare** /peə(r); *AmE* per/ *v.* [T] **~ sth (back/down)** to gradually reduce the size or amount of sth: *a decision to pare down the workforce*

**parent** /ˈpeərənt; *AmE* ˈper-/ = PARENT COMPANY

**paˌrental** ˈ**leave** *n.* [U] (*HR*) **1** time that the parent of a new baby is allowed to have away from work **2** in Europe and some other countries, time that a parent is allowed to have away from work to look after a child who is below a particular age

★ ˈ**parent** ˌ**company** (*also* ˈ**parent**) *n.* [C] (*Finan.*) an organization that owns and controls another company

**Paˈreto aˌnalysis** /pəˈreɪtəʊ; -ˈriːt-; *AmE* -toʊ/ *n.* [C,U] a method that allows you to identify the main causes of an effect, so that you know where you should aim most of your efforts, for example when dealing with a problem

**Paˌreto-ˈoptimal** /pəˈreɪtəʊ; -ˈriːt-; *AmE* -toʊ/ *adj.* (*Econ.*) used to describe a situation, solution or result that is the best and most efficient possible, because any other situation would make things worse for at least one group

**Paˈreto's ˌprinciple** (*also* **Paˈreto's law/rule**) /pəˈreɪtəʊz; -ˈriːt-; *AmE* -toʊz/ *n.* [sing.] the theory that a small number or amount of sth always creates a large part of the results, problems, value, etc. associated with it: *Pareto's principle tells you that 80 per cent of your sales will come from 20 per cent of your sales staff.* SYN 80/20 RULE

**the** ˈ**Paris Club** *n.* [sing.] the G10 group of countries, whose central banks meet and work together to support the international finance and currency system and who lend money to the IMF

**parity** /ˈpærəti/ *n.* (*pl.* **-ties**) **1** [U] the state of being equal, esp. the state of having equal pay or status: *Part-time workers are demanding pay parity* ***with*** *full-time staff.* **2** (*Econ.*) [U,C] the situation when units of money of two different countries, or units of two different products, have equal value: *The dollar remained near parity* ***with*** *the euro.* **3** (*Econ.*) [C,U] the amount of a foreign currency that is the same as a particular amount of a country's own currency at an established rate of exchange: *a parity of 1.40 pesos to the dollar*

**park** /pɑːk; *AmE* pɑːrk/ *n.*, *v.*
• ***n.*** [C] an area of land used for a particular purpose, esp. for small businesses, office buildings, small factories, etc.
• ***v.*** [T] **1** (*Finan.*) to leave money, shares, etc. with an organization for a period of time: *investors looking for a safe haven to park their cash* **2** (*infml.*) to decide to leave an idea or issue to be dealt with at a later meeting: *Let's park that until our next meeting.*

ˈ**Parkinson's law** /ˈpɑːkɪnsənz; *AmE* ˈpɑːrk-/ *n.* [U] the humorous idea that work will always take as long as the time available for it

**parlay** /ˈpɑːleɪ; *AmE* ˈpɑːrleɪ/ *v.*
PHR V ˈ**parlay sth into sth** (*AmE*) to use or develop sth you have, such as money, a skill, an idea, etc. in order to get sth or make it more successful or valuable: *He was able to parlay his idea into a 70-employee company.*

**part** /pɑːt; *AmE* pɑːrt/ *n.*, *v.*
• ***n.*** [C] a piece of a machine or structure: *a manufacturer of aircraft parts*
IDM **take** ˈ**part (in sth)** to be involved in sth SYN PARTICIPATE
→ idioms at PLAY *v.*, SUM *n.*
• ***v.*** IDM **part** ˈ**company (with/from sb/sth)** to leave sb/sth; to end a relationship with sb

ˌ**part deˈlivery** (*also* ˌ**part** ˈ**shipment**) *n.* [C,U] (*Comm.*) an order that has been only partly completed and delivered

ˌ**part exˈchange** *n.* [U,C] (*BrE*) a way of buying sth, such as a car, in which you give your old one as part of the payment for a more expensive one; the used item itself: *We'll take your old car* ***in*** *part exchange.* SYN TRADE-IN ▶ ˌ**part-exˈchange** *v.* [T]

**partial** /ˈpɑːʃl; *AmE* ˈpɑːrʃl/ *adj.* not complete or whole: *a partial shut-*

*down of the plant ◇ a ~ sale/payment*

**ˌpartial acˈceptance** *n.* [U] (*Finan.*) the act of agreeing to pay part of the value of a BILL OF EXCHANGE

**ˌpartial ˈloss** (*also* ˈ**average**) *n.* [C,U] (*Insur.*) a situation in which only part of a ship or its cargo is damaged and an insurance claim can be made for this

**ˌpartial ˈownership** = PART OWNERSHIP

**ˌpartial ˈpayment** = PART PAYMENT

**participant** /pɑːˈtɪsɪpənt; *AmE* pɑːrˈt-/ *n.* [C] a person who is taking part in an activity or event

★ **participate** /pɑːˈtɪsɪpeɪt; *AmE* pɑːrˈt-/ *v.* [I] **1** to take part in sth: *to participate* ***in*** *global markets* **2** (*Finan.*) to receive part of an amount of money, for example part of the profits of a company you work for: *a right to participate* ***in*** *the profits* ▶ **parˌticiˈpation** /-ˈpeɪʃn/ *n.* [U]: *employee participation* **ˌparˈticipative** /-pətɪv/ *adj.*: *a participative approach to planning*

**parˌticipating ˈpreference share** (*also* **parˌticipating preˈferred share**) *n.* [C, usu. pl.] (*both BrE*) (*AmE* **parˌticipating preˈferred stock, parˌticipating ˈpreference stock** [U,C]) (*Finan.*) a type of PREFERENCE SHARE which also allows the shareholder to receive DIVIDENDS and extra payments

**parˌticipative ˈmanagement** *n.* [U] (*HR*) a way of running a company in which employees who are not managers are involved in making important decisions

**particulars** /pəˈtɪkjələz; *AmE* pərˈtɪkjələrz/ *n.* [pl.] written information and details about a business, job, person, property, etc: *Further particulars are available from…*

**partition** /pɑːˈtɪʃn; *AmE* pɑːrˈt-/ *n., v.*

• *n.* [C] **1** a thin wall or screen that separates one part of a large room from another **2** (*IT*) one of a number of sections that a computer's memory or the place where information is stored can be divided into

• *v.* [T] (*often pass.*) to divide sth into two or more parts **PHR V parˌtition sth ˈoff** to separate one area, one part of a room, etc. from another with a wall or screen

**ˌpartly-ˈowned** *adj.* used to describe a company that is owned partly by another larger company, and also has other owners: *partly-owned subsidiaries*

**ˌpartly paid ˈshares** (*also* **ˌpartly paid-up ˈshares, conˌtributing ˈshares**) *n.* [pl.] (*all esp. BrE*) (*AmE usu.* **ˌpartly paid ˈstock** [U,C]) (*Finan.*) shares for which the investor has paid only part of the price

★ **partner** /ˈpɑːtnə(r); *AmE* ˈpɑːrt-/ *n., v.*

• *n.* [C] **1** one of the people who starts a business by investing in it, and who shares the profits and the risks **2** a member of a group of professional people who work together, own their business and share the profits: *a junior/senior ~* **3** a company that works with another company in a particular area of business: *seeking investment partners* **4** a country that has a political or economic agreement with another country

• *v.* [T,I] **~ sb | ~ (up) with sb** to be sb's **partner** in an investment or business project

★ **partnership** /ˈpɑːtnəʃɪp; *AmE* ˈpɑːrtnərʃɪp/ *n.* **1** [C,U] a relationship between people who own a business together and share the profits and risks; the state of having this relationship: *The office has been set up* ***in partnership with*** *FM Recruitment.* ⊕ *to* ***create/enter into/establish/form*** *a ~* ◆ *to* ***go into/work in*** *~ with sb* ◆ *to* ***dissolve*** *a ~* **2** [C] a business that is owned by a group of professional people who work together and share the profits; the state of being a member of this group: *She was offered a partnership in the law firm.* ⊕ *to* ***establish/join/set up*** *a ~* ◆ *to* ***take sb into*** *~* **3** [C] a relationship between companies or organizations that work together: *a partnership* ***between*** *unions and employers* ⊕ *to* ***create/enter into/establish/form*** *a ~* **4** [C] a relationship between countries that have a political or an economic agreement

**ˌpart ˈorder** *n.* [C] (*Comm.*) an order that has been only partly completed or delivered; an order for a smaller quantity than usual

**ˌpart-ˈowner** *n.* [C] (*Law*) one of two or more people or companies who own part of a business or a piece of property ▶ **ˌpart-ˈown** *v.* [T] **ˌpart ˈownership** *n.* [U]

**ˌpart ˈpayment** (*also* **ˌpartial ˈpayment**) *n.* [U,C] the act of paying part of the total price of sth; the amount paid

**ˌpart ˈshipment** = PART DELIVERY

**ˌpart-ˈtime** *adj., adv.* (*abbr* **PT**) for only part of the day or week during which people normally work: *a part-time job* ◇ *Liz works part-time.*
▸ **ˌpart-ˈtimer** *n.* [C]

**party** /ˈpɑːti; *AmE* ˈpɑːrti/ *n.* [C] (*pl.* **-ties**) **1** (*Law*) one of the people or groups of people involved in a legal agreement or dispute: *The contract can be terminated by either party.* **2** one of the people or organizations who are involved in doing sth together

**ˈparty plan** *n.* [C] (*Market.*) a method of selling goods for the home or for personal use, in which people are invited to a party where they are shown examples of the goods

**ˌpar ˈvalue** = PAR

**Pascal** (*also* **PASCAL**) /ˈpæskl; ˌpæsˈkɑːl; *AmE* ˌpæsˈkæl/ *n.* [U] (*IT*) a language that is used for writing programs for computer systems, and is often used to teach people to write programs

**pass** /pɑːs; *AmE* pæs/ *v., n.*
• *v.* [T] **1** to accept a proposal, law, etc. by voting: *The tax reform was passed by 360 votes to 280.* **2** to become greater than a particular total: *Unemployment has passed the three million mark.* **3** to examine sb/sth and decide that they are/it is good enough or acceptable: *The committee has now passed the final figures.* OPP FAIL IDM **pass a ˈdividend** (*Finan.*) to pay no DIVIDEND in a particular period of time PHR V **ˌpass sth aˈlong (to sb)** (*esp. AmE*) = PASS STH ON (TO SB) **ˌpass sth ˈoff as sth** (*Law*) to dishonestly pretend that something is something different: *Cheaply made goods were passed off as designer clothes.* **ˌpass sth ˈon (to sb)** (*also* **ˌpass sth aˈlong (to sb)**, **ˌpass sth ˈthrough (to sb)**, *both esp. in AmE*) to transfer sth, such as a higher or lower cost, to sb else: *Will the higher wage costs be absorbed or passed on?* SYN HAND STH ON **ˌpass ˈover sb** to not give sb a promotion in a job, esp. when they deserve it or think that they deserve it **ˌpass sth ˈthrough (to sb)** (*esp. AmE*) = PASS STH ON (TO SB)
• *n.* [C] an official document or ticket that shows you have the right to enter or leave a place, to travel, etc: *a visitor's pass*
◐ *a press/security ~* ◆ *a boarding/parking ~* ◆ *to issue/produce/show your ~*

**ˈpass-aˌlong** *n., adj.* (*AmE*)
• *n.* [C,U] (*Econ.*) = PASS-THROUGH (1)
• *adj.* (*Market.*) **1** (*BrE* **ˌpass-ˈon**) used to describe people who read a newspaper or magazine after the person who has bought it: *pass-along readership* **2** used to describe people who pass on an email message or a computer file: *the pass-along rate for an e-zine*

**ˈpass-along ˌreaders** = SECONDARY AUDIENCE (2)

**passenger** /ˈpæsɪndʒə(r)/ *n.* [C] **1** a person who is travelling in a car, bus, train, plane or ship and who is not working on it: *airline passengers* **2** (*infml.*) (*esp. BrE*) a member of a group or team who does not do as much work as the others: *We can't afford to carry passengers.*

**ˌpassing ˈoff** *n.* [U] (*Law*) the act of dishonestly leading customers to think that a product or service is associated with a particular company when it is not

**ˌpassing ˈtrade** *n.* [U] (*Comm.*) customers who come into a shop/store or business because they are going past it and see it

**passive** /ˈpæsɪv/ *adj.* (*Finan.*) **1** used to describe shareholders who do not take part in any management decisions about the company they invest in **2** used to describe a way of investing in which the investor buys a range of shares, bonds, etc. and allows their value to gradually increase as the market rises, rather than buying and selling shares often as the value changes: *passive fund management*

**ˌpass-ˈon** = PASS-ALONG *adj.* (1)

**ˈpass-through** *n.* (*AmE*) **1** (*Econ.*) (*AmE also* **ˈpass-aˌlong**) [U,C] the fact that sth such as a tax or a higher or lower price is transferred to customers: *price pass-through to end-users* **2** (*Finan.*) [U,C] (*also* **ˌpass-through seˈcurity** [C]) a type of investment in which investors lend money to home buyers or businesses through a bank or government agency, and the money paid back passes from the bank or agency back to investors

**password** /ˈpɑːswɜːd; *AmE* ˈpæswɜːrd/ *n.* [C] (*IT*) a series of letters and/or numbers that you need in order to be able to use a computer or computer system: *Enter your username and password.*

**ˌpast ˈdue** *adj., adv.* (*AmE*) after the date when a payment should have been made: *The payment is past due.*

◇ *They often pay invoices 90 days past due.*

**paste** /peɪst/ *v.* [T,I] to copy or move text into a document from another place or another document → idiom at CUT *v.*

★ **patent** /ˈpætnt; *BrE also* ˈpeɪtnt/ *n., v.*

• ***n.*** [C,U] a legal right to be the only person to make, use or sell a product or an invention; a document that proves this: *Edison took out a patent on the light bulb.*

⊕ ***to apply for/file/obtain a ~ • to grant/issue/refuse a ~ • a ~ expires/ lapses***

• ***v.*** [T] to obtain a **patent** for an invention or a process: *The technology was patented in 2001.* ▸ **ˈpatentable** /-əbl/ *adj.* **ˈpatented** *adj.*

**ˈpatent ˌagent** *n.* [C] a person who helps people or companies arrange **patents** for their product, invention, etc.

**ˌpatent apˈplied for** = PATENT PENDING

**ˌpatent ˈdefect** *n.* [C,U] (*Law*) a fault in a product that is obvious enough to be noticed when you buy it → LATENT DEFECT

**patentee** /ˌpætənˈtiː; *BrE also* ˌpeɪt-/ *n.* [C] a person or company that owns the **patent** for a product, an invention, etc.

**ˈpatent ˌoffice** *n.* [C] (*Law*) a government office that deals with and gives **patents**

**ˌpatent ˈpending** (*also* **ˌpatent apˈplied for**) *phr.* words used on a product to show that the maker or seller has applied for a **patent**

**ˈpatent proˌtection** *n.* [U] laws that protect a person or company that has developed a new product, method, etc. from having it copied or used by others

**ˈpatent right** *n.* [C, usu. pl.] the right to make or sell sth that is given to one particular person or company by a **patent**

**paternalistic** /pəˌtɜːnəˈlɪstɪk; *AmE* -ˌtɜːrn-/ *adj.* a **paternalistic** company is one in which people lower down in the organization are looked after very well but are not given much responsibility to make decisions

**paˈternity leave** *n.* [U] (*HR*) a period of time when the father of a new baby is allowed to be away from work: *to take paid paternity leave*

**paˈternity pay** *n.* [U] (*HR*) money paid to the father of a new baby while he is not working

**pathfinder** /ˈpɑːθfaɪndə(r); *AmE* ˈpæθ-/ *n.* [C] a person, company, product, etc. that finds or shows a new way of doing sth: *The firm is a pathfinder in computer technology.*

**ˈpathfinder prosˌpectus** (*AmE also* **ˌred ˈherring**, *infml.*) *n.* [C] (*Stock Ex.*) a document issued by a company that is going to sell shares for the first time, giving details of the company but no details of the price of the shares, etc.

**patron** /ˈpeɪtrən/ *n.* [C] **1** (*Comm., fml.*) a customer of a particular shop/store, restaurant, theatre, etc. **2** a person or company who gives money or support to an organization such as a charity

**patronage** /ˈpætrənɪdʒ; ˈpeɪt-/ *n.* [U] **1** (*Comm.*) the support that customers give to a business by spending money there **2** support, esp. financial support, given to an organization such as a charity by an individual or a company: *her generous patronage of the arts* **3** a system by which an important person gives help or a job to sb in return for their support

**patronize, -ise** /ˈpætrənaɪz; *AmE also* ˈpeɪt-/ *v.* [T] **1** (*Comm.*) to be a customer of a shop/store, restaurant, hotel etc: *The hotel is largely patronized by business travellers.* **2** to treat sb in a way that seems friendly but shows you do not think they are very intelligent, experienced, etc. **3** to help a particular person, organization or activity by giving them money

**pattern** /ˈpætn; *AmE* -tərn/ *n., adj.*

• ***n.*** [C] **1** the way in which sth usu. or repeatedly happens: *Consumer spending follows a regular seasonal pattern.* **2** an excellent example to copy: *The store has **set** the pattern **for** others in customer service.* → idiom at HOLD *v.*

• ***adj.*** (*esp. AmE*) (*HR*) a **pattern** agreement, contract, etc. is based on other agreements or contracts with similar companies

**pawn** /pɔːn/ *v., n.*

• ***v.*** [T] to leave an item with a PAWNBROKER. If the money is paid back within an agreed period of time, the item is returned to the owner, but if not, the item can be sold.

• ***n.*** IDM **in pawn** if sth is in pawn, it has been **pawned out of pawn** if you get or take sth **out of pawn**, you pay back the money you owe and get back the item that has been **pawned**

**pawnbroker** /ˈpɔːnbrəʊkə(r); *AmE* -broʊ-/ *n.* [C] a person who lends money in exchange for items left with them. If the money is not paid back within an agreed period, the **pawnbroker** can sell the item.

**pawnshop** /ˈpɔːnʃɒp; *AmE* -ʃɑːp/ *n.* [C] a **pawnbroker**'s shop

★ **pay** /peɪ/ *v., n.*

• *v.* (**paid, paid** /peɪd/) **1** [T,I] to give sb money for work, goods, services, etc: *How much are people willing to pay **for** your product?* ◇ *Are you paying **in cash** or **by credit card**?* ◇ *My company pays well* (= pays high salaries). ◇ *I'm paid $100 a day.* ◇ ***paying customers*** **2** [T] to give sb money that you owe them: *We don't have enough money to pay our bills.* **3** [I] (about a business, etc.) to produce a profit: *Training is a growth area—you could **make it pay**.* **4** [T,I] to result in some advantage or profit for sb: *It would pay you to hire an accountant.* **IDM** **pay 'dividends** to produce great advantages or profits **pay for it'self** (about a new system, sth you have bought, etc.) to save as much money as it cost **pay its 'way** (about a business, etc.) to make enough money to pay what it costs to keep it going **pay/spend over the 'odds** (*BrE*) (*infml.*) to pay more than you would normally expect **pay through the 'nose (for sth)** (*infml.*) to pay much too much money for sth **pay your 'way** to pay for everything yourself without having to rely on anyone else's money: *She had to pay her way through college.* **PHR V** **ˌpay sb 'back (sth)**; **ˌpay sth 'back (to sb)** to return money that you borrowed from sb: *I'll pay you back next week.* **ˌpay 'down sth** (*AmE*) (*Finan.*) to reduce the amount of a debt by paying some of the money: *The money will be used to pay down their $2.4 bn debt.* **ˌpay sth 'down** (*Comm.*) to give an amount of money as the first payment for sth: *You pay $200 down and the rest in 12 monthly instalments.* **ˌpay sth 'in**; **ˌpay sth 'into sth** to put money into a bank account **ˌpay 'off** (*infml.*) (about a plan or an action) to be successful and bring good results: *Our efforts have paid off and profits have doubled.* **ˌpay sb 'off** to pay sb what they have earned and tell them to leave their job **ˌpay sth 'off** to finish paying money owed for sth: *We've paid off our mortgage.* **ˌpay (sth) 'out** to pay a large amount of money for sth **ˌpay 'up** to pay all the money that you owe to sb, esp. when you do not want to or when the payment is late

• *n.* [U] the money that sb gets for doing regular work: *Her job is hard work, but the pay is good.* ◇ *workers **on** low pay* ◇ (*BrE*) *a pay rise* ◇ (*AmE*) *a pay raise* ◇ *better **pay and conditions*** ◇ *17% pay cuts*

◉ *to get/give (sb)* ~ ◆ ***high/poor*** ~ ◆ ***monthly/weekly*** ~ ◆ ***full/half*** ~

★ **payable** /ˈpeɪəbl/ *adj.* **1** that must be paid or can be paid at a particular time or in a particular way: *The full fee is payable in advance.* **2** when a cheque, etc. is made **payable to** sb, their name is written on it and they can pay it into their bank account

**payables** /ˈpeɪəblz/ *n.* [pl.] (*Account.*) money that a company owes, for example loans to be paid back, etc. → RECEIVABLES

**ˌpayable to 'bearer** *adj.* (*Finan.*) used to describe a cheque, a BILL OF EXCHANGE, etc. that can be signed by the person who holds it and paid to them

**ˌpayable to 'order** *adj.* (*Finan.*) used to describe a cheque, a BILL OF EXCHANGE, etc. that must be paid to the person named on it

**ˌPay and 'File** *n.* [U] a way of paying tax in which a company or a person calculates the tax that they owe and pays it at the same time as they send their TAX RETURN

**ˌpay-as-you-'go** *adj.* connected with a system of paying for a service as you use it or paying costs as they happen, rather than paying one amount before or after, or fixed regular amounts: *pay-as-you-go phones* ▸ **ˌpay as you 'go** *n.* [U]

**payback** /ˈpeɪbæk/ *n.* [C,U] **1** (*Finan.*) the profit that you receive on money that you have invested (esp. when this is equal to the amount that you invested); the time that it takes to get your money back: *a 10-year payback* **2** the advantage or reward that sb receives for sth they have done: *He feels his success is the payback for five years of hard work.*

**'payback ˌperiod** *n.* [C] (*Account.*) **1** the time it will take for the profit from a business project, an asset, etc. to be equal to the amount invested in it **SYN** RECOVERY PERIOD **2** the amount of time over which a loan can be paid back

**'pay ˌcable** *n.* [U,C] (*AmE*) a cable television service for which customers pay an amount of money each month

**ˈpay ˌchannel** *n.* [C] a television channel that you must pay for separately in order to watch it

**ˈpay cheque** (*AmE* **paycheck**) *n.* [C] **1** the cheque that you are given when your wages are paid **2** (*esp. AmE*) a way of referring to the amount of money that you earn: *She earns a huge paycheck.*

**ˈpay claim** *n.* [C] a demand by a group of workers for more pay

**ˌpay comparaˈbility** *n.* [U] (*HR*) similar systems of pay in different companies

**payday** /ˈpeɪdeɪ/ *n.* [U,C] **1** the day on which you get your wages or salary **2** (*infml.*) (*esp. AmE*) a way of referring to an amount of money, esp. money that can be won in a contest: *The way to get the biggest payday is to sell the business by auction.*

**ˈpay determiˌnation** *n.* [U] (*HR*) the process of setting rates of pay, including increases in pay

**paydown** /ˈpeɪdaʊn/ *n.* [C] (*AmE*) (*Finan.*) a payment of part of an amount of money that has been borrowed

**PAYE** /ˌpiː eɪ waɪ ˈiː/ *abbr* **pay as you earn** a British system of paying income tax in which money is taken from your wages by your employer and paid to the government

**payee** /ˌpeɪˈiː/ *n.* [C] (*Finan.*) a person that money or a cheque is paid to

**ˈpay ˌenvelope** = PAY PACKET

**payer** /ˈpeɪə(r)/ *n.* [C] (*Finan.*) a person or an organization that pays or has to pay for sth: *mortgage payers* ◇ *chasing up slow payers* ◇ *a bad/late ~* ◇ *a fast/good ~*

**ˌpay for perˈformance** = PERFORMANCE-RELATED PAY

**ˈpaying ˌagent** *n.* [C] (*Finan.*) a bank or other organization that makes payments to the holders of shares or bonds on behalf of the company that issues them

**ˈpaying bank** (*also* **ˈpaying ˌbanker**) *n.* [C] (*Finan.*) the bank that is responsible for paying a cheque written by sb who has an account there

**ˌpaying-ˈin book** *n.* [C] (*BrE*) a set of PAYING-IN SLIPS fastened together inside a cover

**ˌpaying-ˈin slip** *n.* [C] (*BrE*) a printed form on which you record the amount of money, the date, etc. when you put money into your bank account SYN DEPOSIT SLIP

**payload** /ˈpeɪləʊd; *AmE* -loʊd/ *n.* [C,U] (*Transpt.*) **1** the passengers or goods on a ship or an aircraft for which payment is received: *The new ferries can carry 70% more payload.* **2** goods that a vehicle, such as a ship, a lorry/truck or an aircraft, is carrying

**paymaster** /ˈpeɪmɑːstə(r); *AmE* -mæs-/ *n.* [C] **1** a person or an organization that provides money for another and therefore controls them **2** an official who pays wages in the army or in a factory

★ **payment** /ˈpeɪmənt/ *n.* **1** [U] the act of paying a person, paying a bill or debt, or of being paid: *We accept payment* **by** *cash, cheque, or credit/debit card.* ◇ *payment in advance* ◇ *an electronic payment system* OPP NON-PAYMENT
◉ *to* ***receive/take*** *~* ♦ *to* ***demand/refuse*** *~* ♦ *to* ***defer/delay*** *~* ♦ ***immediate/late/prompt*** *~* ♦ ***full/part/partial*** *~*
**2** [C] a sum of money paid or expected to be paid: *a cash payment* ◇ *monthly mortgage payments*
◉ *to* ***accept/make/receive*** *a ~* ♦ *to* ***keep up/meet/miss*** *~s* ♦ ***credit-card/electronic*** *~s* ♦ *a* ***bonus/lump-sum/one-off/single*** *~* ♦ ***annual/regular*** *~s* ♦ ***dividend/interest/loan*** *~s*

**ˌpayment by reˈsults** *n.* [U,C] (*abbr* **PBR**) (*HR*) a system of paying people in which the amount of money they receive depends on the amount of work they do or the profits made

**ˈpay-off** (*AmE* **payoff**) *n.* [C] (*infml.*) **1** a payment of money to sb to persuade them to leave their job **2** the money you receive from an investment, etc. **3** an advantage or a good result from sth: *The pay-off of the new system shows up in all stages of a project.*

**payout** /ˈpeɪaʊt/ *n.* [C] a large amount of money that is given to sb: *huge payouts to managers*

**ˈpayout ˌratio** *n.* [C] (*Finan.*) the proportion of a company's profits that it pays to its shareholders as DIVIDENDS

**ˈpay ˌpackage** (*also* **ˈsalary ˌpackage**) (*also* **reˌmuneˈration ˌpackage**, *fml.*) *n.* [C] (*HR*) the money that sb gets for doing their job, with other benefits that the company offers: *Your pay package will consist of cash and bonuses.*

**ˈpay ˌpacket** (*also* **ˈwage ˌpacket**) (*both BrE*) (*AmE* **ˈpay ˌenvelope**) *n.* [C] an envelope containing your wages; the amount you earn: *They are demanding larger pay packets.*

**ˈpay-per-** *comb. form* (*Market.*) used to form adjs describing a system in which people pay for a service as they use it: *TV pay-per-play games*

**ˈpay ˌperiod** *n.* [C] (*esp. AmE*) (*HR*) the amount of time for which a worker receives a regular payment: *Submit timesheets for each pay period.*

**ˌpay-per-ˈview** *n.* [U] a system of television broadcasting in which you pay an extra amount of money to watch a particular programme

**ˈpay reˌstraint** = WAGE RESTRAINT

**payroll** /ˈpeɪrəʊl; *AmE* -roʊl/ *n.* (*Account.*; *HR*) **1** [C] a list of people employed by a company showing the amount of money to be paid to each of them: *We have 500 people **on the payroll.*** **2** [C, usu. sing.] the total amount paid in wages by a company: *a monthly payroll of $1 million* **3** [U] the activity of managing a company's payroll: *the cost of payroll training*

**payrolled** /ˈpeɪrəʊld; *AmE* -roʊld/ *adj.* (*HR*) on the **payroll** of a company: *payrolled employees*

**payrolling** /ˈpeɪrəʊlɪŋ; *AmE* -roʊl-/ *n.* [U] (*HR*) the situation when a company chooses staff, esp. temporary staff, but asks an agency to employ them and organize their wages

**ˈpayroll tax** *n.* [U,C] (*Econ.*) a tax that is based on the wages paid to employees and is paid either by employers or partly by employers and partly by employees

**ˈpay scale** *n.* [C] (*HR*) **1** the range of levels of pay that a person can receive in a particular job: *be promoted to the next degree of the pay scale* **2** the range of levels of pay that people receive in different jobs: *the top end of the pay scale*

**payslip** /ˈpeɪslɪp/ (*BrE*) (*AmE* **ˈpay stub**) *n.* [C] a piece of paper given to an employee that shows how much money they have been paid and how much has been taken away for tax, etc.

**ˈpay spine** *n.* [C] (*BrE*) (*HR*) a series of fixed points between a lower and an upper limit that form the basis of a system of pay for groups of workers in some organizations

**ˈpay stub** = PAYSLIP

**ˈpay TˌV** (*also* **ˈpay ˌtelevision**) *n.* [U] a system of television broadcasting in which you pay extra money to watch particular programmes or channels

**PBR** /ˌpiː biː ˈɑː(r)/ = PAYMENT BY RESULTS

**PBT** /ˌpiː biː ˈtiː/ *abbr* (*esp. BrE*) (*Account.*) **profit(s) before tax** the amount of profit that a company makes during a particular period, without taking away the tax that it owes

**PBX** /ˌpiː biː ˈeks/ *abbr* **private branch exchange** a private telephone network used within offices or a company, in which there are a limited number of lines for making calls outside the company, which are shared

★ **PC** /ˌpiː ˈsiː/ *abbr* **personal computer** a small computer that is designed for one person to use at work or at home

**pcm** *abbr* (*BrE*) (*written*) **per calendar month** used to show how much sb must pay each month, esp. for rent

**pct.** *abbr* (*AmE*) a short way of writing **per cent**

**PDA** /ˌpiː diː ˈeɪ/ *abbr* **personal digital assistant** a very small computer that is used for storing personal information and creating documents, and that may include other functions such as telephone, FAX, connection to the Internet, etc.

**PDF** /ˌpiː diː ˈef/ (*also* **ˌPDˈF file**) *abbr* (*IT*) **Portable Document Format** (*used as a countable n.*) a type of computer file that can contain words or pictures. It can be read using any system, can be sent from one computer to another, and will look the same on any computer

**PDR** /ˌpiː diː ˈɑː(r)/ = PRICE-DIVIDEND RATIO

**ˌP/ˈD ˌratio** /ˌpiː ˈdiː/ = PRICE-DIVIDEND RATIO

★ **peak** /piːk/ *n., v., adj.*

• ***n.*** [C, usu. sing.] a period of time when the level, value or rate of sth is at its highest; the best or most successful point: *Inflation has reached its peak.* ◇ *She's **at the peak of** her career.* OPP TROUGH

⊕ *an **all-time**/a **record** ~* ♦ ***above/below** the ~* ♦ *to **hit/rise to** a ~*

• ***v.*** [I] to reach the highest level or value: *The price peaked.*

• ***adj.*** **1** used to describe the highest level of sth: *Property prices have reached peak levels.*

⊕ *a ~ **rate/value*** ♦ *~ **efficiency/performance***

**2** of a time when the greatest number of people are doing sth or using sth, and prices are often higher: *Phone calls are more expensive during peak times.* ◇ *a ~ period/season*

**'peak time** (*also* **,peak 'viewing time**) = PRIME TIME

**peanuts** /'pi:nʌts/ *n.* [pl.] (*infml.*) a very small amount of money: *They work for peanuts.*

**'pecking ,order** *n.* [C, usu. sing.] the order of importance among the members of a group: *Junior officials are too far down the pecking order to influence decisions.*

**peculation** /,pekjə'leɪʃn/ *n.* [U] the act of taking sb else's money for yourself, esp. when they have trusted you to take care of it: *peculation of public funds*

**pecuniary** /pɪ'kju:niəri; *AmE* -ieri/ *adj.* (*Law*) relating to or connected with money: *pecuniary loss*

**peddle** /'pedl/ *v.* [T,I] (*infml.*) to try to sell goods, often by going from place to place ▸ **'peddler** (*BrE also* **pedlar**) *n.* [C]

**peer** /pɪə(r); *AmE* pɪr/ *n.* [C, usu. pl.] **1** a company or product that is similar to others: *We have suffered as bigger peers have cut their prices.* **2** a person who is similar to you in age, social status, etc: *She enjoys the respect of her peers.*

**,peer ap'praisal** = PEER REVIEW

**'peer group** *n.* [C] **1** a group of similar companies or products: *a peer group of 13 global pharmaceutical companies* **2** a group of people of the same age, social status, etc.

**,peer re'view** (*also* **,peer ap'praisal**) *n.* [C,U] (*HR*) a system of asking people who work with sb to give an opinion about them and their work

**,peer-to-'peer** *adj.* (*IT*) (about a computer system) in which each computer can act as a SERVER for the others, allowing data to be shared without the need for a central server

**peg** /peg/ *v.*, *n.*
• ***v.*** [T] (-gg-) **1** (*Econ.*) to fix or keep prices, currencies, etc. at a particular level: *Interest rates will be pegged* ***at*** *4%.* ◇ *They will peg their currency* ***to*** *the dollar.* **2** (*infml.*) (*AmE*) to measure, consider or estimate sth at a particular amount: *Unemployment was above the 400 000 level that economists peg* ***as*** *a weak labour market.* ▸ **'pegging** *n.* [U]
• ***n.*** [C] (*Econ.*) an arrangement to fix or keep prices, currencies, etc. at a particular level: *The country has now abandoned its exchange rate peg to the dollar.*

**,P/'E ,multiple** /,pi: 'i:/ → PRICE-EARNINGS RATIO

**penalty** /'penəlti/ *n.* [C,U] (*pl.* **-ties**) a sum of money to be paid by sb who breaks a rule or contract: *The penalty* ***for*** *late payment of tax is $100.*
➊ *to* ***impose/introduce*** *a ~* ♦ *to* ***face/incur*** *a ~*

**'penalty clause** *n.* [C] (*Law*) part of a contract that states the amount of money to be paid by a person who breaks the contract

**pence** /pens/ pl. of PENNY (1)

**pencil** /'pensl/ *v.* (-ll-, *AmE* -l-)
**PHR V** **,pencil sb/sth 'in** to write down sb's name or details of an arrangement with them that you know might have to be changed later: *We've pencilled in a meeting* ***for*** *Tuesday afternoon.*

**'pencil-,pusher** = PEN-PUSHER

**pending** /'pendɪŋ/ *adj.*, *prep.* (*fml.*)
• ***adj.*** **1** waiting to be decided or settled: *Nine cases are still pending.* **2** going to happen soon: *A crisis is pending in the industry.*
• ***prep.*** while waiting for sth to happen; until sth happens: *He was suspended pending the outcome of the enquiry.*

**penetrate** /'penɪtreɪt/ *v.* [T] (*Market.*) to start selling products or services in a new area or to a new group of customers: *to identify and penetrate new markets*

**penetration** /,penɪ'treɪʃn/ *n.* [U] (*Market.*) **1** the extent to which a product or service is bought in a particular area or by a particular group of people: *a strategy for achieving greater* ***market*** *penetration* **2** the sale of products or services in a new area or to a new group of customers: *London is the target area for penetration.*

**,pene'tration ,pricing** *n.* [U] (*Market.*) the activity of selling a new product at a low price for a short period in order to attract customers

**penny** /'peni/ *n.* [C] (*pl.* **pennies** *or* **pence**) **HELP** In sense 1 **pennies** is used to refer to the coins, and **pence** to refer to an amount of money. In sense 2, the plural is **pennies**.
**1** (*abbr* **p**) a small British coin and unit of money. There are 100 PENCE in one pound (£1): *They cost 20p each.* **2** (*AmE*) a cent coin: *Her change purse is full of pennies and nickels.* **IDM** **,every 'penny** all of the money: *She's on a high salary but she's worth every penny.* **not a 'penny** no money at all: *It didn't cost a penny.*

**'penny-,pinching** *adj.* unwilling to spend money on things

▸ 'penny-ˌpincher *n.* [C] 'penny-ˌpinching *n.* [U]

**ˌpenny 'share** (*BrE*) (*also* **ˌpenny 'stock**, *AmE, BrE*) *n.* [C] (*Stock Ex.*) a share, usu. in a small company, that has a very low price

**'pen-ˌpusher** (*esp. BrE*) (*AmE usu.* **'pencil-ˌpusher**) *n.* [C] (*infml.*) a person with a boring job, esp. in an office, that involves a lot of writing

★ **pension** /'penʃn/ *n., v.*
• ***n.*** [C] an amount of money paid regularly by a government or company to sb who is considered to be too old or too ill/sick to work: *retirement pensions ◇ to take out a private pension*
⊕ *to **draw/pay/receive** a ~ ♦ an **old-age** ~ ♦ a **company/state** ~ ♦ a **basic/generous/good/small** ~*
• ***v.*** **PHR V** **ˌpension sb 'off** (*esp. BrE*) (*usu. pass.*) to allow or force sb to retire and to pay them a **pension**: (*fig., infml.*) *That PC of yours should have been pensioned off years ago.*

**pensionable** /'penʃənəbl/ *adj.* **1** giving sb the right to receive a pension: *an employee of pensionable age ◇ The employment is not pensionable.* **2 pensionable** pay is the part of an employee's pay used for calculating how much pension they will receive

**'pension fund** *n.* [C] an amount of money that is invested and then used to pay **pensions**: *to join/manage/pay into a ~*

**'pension plan** (*BrE also* **'pension scheme**) (*AmE also* **re'tirement plan**) *n.* [C] a system in which you, and usu. your employer, pay money regularly into a PENSION FUND while you are employed. You are then paid a **pension** when you retire

**people** /'pi:pl/ *n.* [pl.] the men and women who work for a particular person or organization: *Our people are all highly trained.*

**ˌpeople-in'tensive** *adj.* needing or employing a lot of people: *Services is a people-intensive business.*

**'people ˌmeter** *n.* [C] (*Market.*) an electronic device used esp. in the US that is attached to a television and used for recording who is watching and what they are watching

**'people skills** *n.* [pl.] the ability to deal with people well

**ˌpeppercorn 'rent** *n.* [C] (*BrE*) (*Law; Prop.*) a very low rent

★ **per** /pə(r)/ *or, in the strong form,* /pɜ:(r)/ *prep.* used to express the cost or amount of sth for each person, number used, distance travelled, etc: *Rooms cost £50 per person, per night.*
**IDM** **'as per sth** following sth that has been decided; according to sth: *The goods were delivered as per contract.*

**ˌP/'E ˌratio** /ˌpi: 'i:/ = PRICE-EARNINGS RATIO

**per capita** /ˌpə 'kæpɪtə; *AmE* ˌpər/ *adj.* for each person: *per capita income* ▸ **ˌper 'capita** *adv.*: *It publishes more books per capita than any other country.*

**perˌceived 'value** *n.* [U] (*Market.*) how much a customer believes sth is worth compared with its price

★ **per cent** (*AmE usu.* **percent**) /ˌpə 'sent; *AmE* ˌpər/ *n., adj., adv.*
• ***n.*** (*pl.* **per cent**, **percent**) one part in every hundred: *Last year sales increased by 8 per cent.*
• ***adj., adv.*** in or for every hundred: *a 7 per cent rise in price*

★ **percentage** /pə'sentɪdʒ; *AmE* pər's-/ *n.* **1** [C with sing./pl. v.; usu. sing.] the number, amount or rate of sth, expressed as part of a total which is 100; a part or share of a whole: *The percentage of sales to Greece has risen. ◇ The figure is **expressed as** a percentage. ◇ Interest rates may rise by one **percentage point** (= 1%).*
⊕ *a **high/large/low/small** ~ ♦ to **calculate/estimate** a ~ ♦ a ~ **gain/growth/increase/loss/rise***
**2** [C, usu. sing.] a share of the profits of sth: *He gets a percentage for every car sold.*

**percentile** /pə'sentaɪl; *AmE* pər's-/ *n.* [C] (*Tech.*) one of the 100 equal groups that a larger group of people can be divided into, according to their place on a scale measuring a particular value: *The 75th percentile represents the pay level higher than 75% of the wages reported.*

**per diem** /ˌpə 'di:em; *AmE* ˌpər/ *n., adj.* (*esp. AmE*)
• ***n.*** [U,C] money paid, for example to employees, for things they need to buy every day: *How much per diem is allowable for my travel?*
• ***adj.*** for each day: *a per diem allowance*

**ˌperfect compe'tition** *n.* [U] (*Econ.*) a situation in which there are enough buyers and sellers of a product, all with full information, to prevent prices being controlled by one person or organization

★ **perform** /pə'fɔ:m; *AmE* pər'fɔ:rm/ *v.* **1** [T] to do sth, such as a piece of work, task or duty: *A computer can perform many tasks at once.* **2** [I] **~ well/badly/poorly** to produce a profit or loss: *Britain's best-*

*performing fund* **3** [I] **~ (well/badly/poorly)** to do sth, work or function well, badly or as expected: *Poorly performing teams will be replaced.*

★**performance** /pəˈfɔːməns; *AmE* pərˈfɔːrm-/ *n.* **1** [C,U] how far a company or an investment makes a profit: *The group reported a strong performance* (= a good profit) *in its telecoms division.*

⊙ *a* ***good/solid*** ~ ♦ *a* ***bad/disappointing/flat/poor/weak*** ~ ♦ ***business/financial/operating/sales/trading*** ~ ♦ *to* ***boost/improve/measure*** ~

**2** [C,U] how well or badly you do sth; how well or badly sth works: *an assessment of your performance*

⊙ ***bad/good/impressive/satisfactory*** ~ ♦ *to* ***evaluate/improve/measure*** ~

**3** (*fml.*) [U; sing.] the act or process of performing a task, an action, etc: *the performance of her duties*

**perˈformance apˌpraisal** = APPRAISAL (1)

**perˈformance asˌsessment** = APPRAISAL (1)

**perˈformance bond** = CONTRACT BOND

**perˈformance evaluˌation** = APPRAISAL (1)

**perˈformance fund** = AGGRESSIVE GROWTH FUND

**perˈformance ˌindicator** *n.* [C] a measure that shows how well or badly sth is working → METRIC *n.*

**perˈformance ˌmanagement** *n.* [U] the process of controlling the performance of employees, for example by setting goals for them, providing training and encouraging them to work as well as they can

**perˌformance-related ˈpay** (*abbr* **PRP**) (*BrE*) (*also* **ˌpay for perˈformance**, **ˌvariable ˈpay**, *AmE*, *BrE*) *n.* [U] (*HR*) an arrangement where the amount sb is paid depends on how well they do their job

**perˈformance reˌview** = APPRAISAL (1)

**performer** /pəˈfɔːmə(r); *AmE* pərˈfɔːrm-/ *n.* [C] **1** an investment or a business, considered from the point of view of how much profit it makes compared with the average shares, businesses, etc: *Toyota was the star performer with record annual profits.*

⊙ *an* ***average***/*a* ***good/solid/strong/top*** ~ ♦ *a* ***bad/weak*** ~

**2** a person who works in the way mentioned

⊙ ***good/high/outstanding/star/top*** ~ ♦ ***bad/low/poor*** ~

**peril** /ˈperəl/ *n.* [C] (*Insur.*) an event that can cause a financial loss, for example a fire or a storm

★**period** /ˈpɪəriəd; *AmE* ˈpɪr-/ *n.* [C] a particular length of time: *You can repay the loan over a period of two years.* ◇ *This week is one of the busiest periods of the year.*

ˈ**period bill** (*also* ˈ**term bill**) *n.* [C] (*Finan.*) a BILL OF EXCHANGE which will be paid at a particular time in the future

**peripheral** /pəˈrɪfərəl/ *adj.*, *n.*

• ***adj.*** **1** not as important as the main aim, part, etc. of sth: *to sell off peripheral businesses* **2** (*IT*) used to describe equipment that is connected to a computer: *a peripheral device*

• ***n.*** [C] (*IT*) a piece of equipment that is connected to a computer

**perishables** /ˈperɪʃəblz/ (*also* **ˌperishable ˈgoods**) *n.* [pl.] types of food that decay or go bad quickly

**perk** /pɜːk; *AmE* pɜːrk/ *n.*, *v.*

• ***n.*** (*also* ˈ**perquisite**, *fml.*) [C, usu. pl.] (*HR*) something you receive as well as your wages for doing a particular job: *Perks offered by the firm include a car and free health insurance.*

• ***v.*** PHR V **ˌperk (sth) ˈup** to increase, or to make sth increase, in value, etc: *Share prices had perked up slightly by close of trading.*

**permanent** /ˈpɜːmənənt; *AmE* ˈpɜːrm-/ *adj.* lasting or staying for a long time: *a permanent job* ◇ *permanent staff* OPP TEMPORARY

**permatemp** /ˈpɜːmətemp; *AmE* ˈpɜːrm-/ *n.* [C] (*HR*) **1** a temporary worker who is employed many times by an organization as this is cheaper than having a permanent employee **2** an agency that supplies temporary employees to an employer

★**permission** /pəˈmɪʃn; *AmE* pərˈm-/ *n.* **1** [U] the act of allowing sb to do sth, esp. when this is done by sb in a position of authority: *The trademark can't be used* **without** *permission.*

⊙ *to* ***ask for/request/seek*** ~ ♦ *to* ***get/obtain/receive*** ~ ♦ *to* ***give/grant*** ~ ♦ *to* ***deny/refuse*** ~

**2** (*Law*) [C, usu. pl.] an official written statement allowing sb to do sth: *You must obtain the necessary permissions to reproduce illustrations.*

**perˈmission ˌmarketing** *n.* [U] a method of advertising products and services to customers through the Internet in which they must first give their permission to receive advertising information

★**permit** *n., v.*

• *n.* /ˈpɜːmɪt; *AmE* ˈpɜːrmɪt/ [C] an official document that gives sb the right to do sth, esp. for a limited period of time: *to apply for/grant (sb)/issue a ~*

• *v.* /pəˈmɪt; *AmE* pərˈm-/ (-tt-) **1** [T] **~ sb/sth (to do sth)** to allow sb to do sth or to allow sth to happen: *The government won't permit the merger of the two companies.* **2** [T,I] **~ (sb/ sth) (to do sth)** to make sth possible: *The password permits access to all files on the network.*

**perˌpetual ˈinventory** = CONTINUOUS INVENTORY

**perquisite** /ˈpɜːkwɪzɪt; *AmE* ˈpɜːrk-/ = PERK

**ˌper-ˈshare** *adj.* (*Account.*) used to describe the amount of income, profit, etc. that a company receives for each one of its shares: *~ earnings/loss/profit/value*

**personal** /ˈpɜːsənl; *AmE* ˈpɜːrs-/ *adj.* **1** belonging to or connected with an individual, not a company or an organization: *personal debt* **2** intended for individuals, not companies or organizations: *cheap personal loans* **3** acting as an individual, not as a company or an organization: *high demand for credit from both corporate and personal customers* **4** connected with a particular person and not with their job or official position: *personal information*

**ˌpersonal ˈaction** *n.* [C] (*Law*) a type of court case in which sb tries to get money from sb who has caused them to suffer injury, damage, etc: *to bring a personal action against sb*

**ˌpersonal alˈlowance** (*BrE*) (*AmE* **ˌpersonal exˈemption**) *n.* [C] the amount of money you are allowed to earn each year before you have to pay tax

**ˌpersonal asˈsistant** *n.* [C] (*abbr* **PA**) a person who works as a secretary or an assistant for one person: *the personal assistant* **to** *the Director*

**ˌpersonal ˈcare** *n.* [U] the activity of keeping your hair, skin and teeth clean and in good condition: *a new range of personal care products*

**ˌpersonal ˈcheque** *n.* [C] a cheque written by an individual using the money that they have in the bank

**ˌpersonal ˈcontract** *n.* [C] (*HR*) a type of contract of employment that is designed for an individual employee rather than for groups of workers

**ˌpersonal ˈcredit** = CONSUMER CREDIT

**ˈpersonal day** *n.* [C] (*HR*) in the US and other countries, a day that you are allowed to be away from work with pay for personal reasons: *I* **took** *a personal day to attend my daughter's graduation.*

**ˌpersonal deˈvelopment** *n.* [U] (*HR*) the process of gaining the knowledge, skills and abilities you need SYN SELF-DEVELOPMENT

**ˌpersonal exˈemption** = PERSONAL ALLOWANCE

**ˌpersonal ˈfinance** *n.* [U] the activity of managing the money belonging to an individual

**ˌpersonal inforˈmation ˌmanager** *n.* [C] (*abbr* **PIM**) a computer program in which you write names, addresses, things you have to do, etc.

**ˌpersonal ˈinjury** *n.* [U] (*Law*) physical injury to a person, rather than damage to property or to sb's reputation: *personal injury claims*

**personality** /ˌpɜːsəˈnæləti; *AmE* ˌpɜːrs-/ *n.* (*pl.* **-ties**) **1** [C] a famous person, esp. one who works in entertainment or sport: *a sports personality* **2** (*Market.*) [C,U] the qualities of a product or an organization that make it interesting and different: *corporate personality* **3** (*Law*) [C,U] an organization which is considered in law to exist separately from the people who own it or run it and to have legal rights and duties

**personalize**, **-ise** /ˈpɜːsənəlaɪz; *AmE* ˈpɜːrs-/ *v.* [T] **1** (*usu. pass.*) to design or change sth so that it is suitable for the needs of a particular person: *a highly personalized service* **2** to mark or change sth in some way to show that it belongs to a particular person: *By choosing your own ringtone, you can personalize your phone.* ▸ **ˌpersonaliˈzation**, **-iˈsation** /-laɪˈzeɪʃn; *AmE* -ləˈz-/ *n.* [U]

**ˌpersonal ˈleave** *n.* [U] (*HR*) time that you are allowed away from work, with or without pay, for personal reasons

**ˌpersonal liaˈbility** *n.* [U] (*Law*) the legal responsibility that an individual has for injury or damage to sb/sth, or for the debts of a company they own

**ˌpersonal ˈorganizer** *n.* [C] a small file with loose sheets of paper in which you write down information, addresses, what you have arranged to do, etc.; a very small computer for the same purpose

**ˌpersonal ˈpension** *n.* [C] an arrangement in which you pay money regularly to an insurance company or a bank, etc. which invests the money and pays you a pension when you retire

**ˌpersonal ˈproperty** (*also* **ˈpersonalty**, *less freq.*) *n.* [U] (*Law*) the assets that sb has, such as money, shares, etc. except for land and buildings

**ˌpersonal repreˈsentative** *n.* [C] (*Law*) a person who is responsible for the assets of sb who has died

**ˌpersonal ˈselling** *n.* [U] (*Market.*) the use of people who are trained to sell a company's goods or services to talk to and persuade a customer to buy sth

**ˌpersonal ˈstatement** *n.* [C] a written description of yourself, your education and working life, your abilities and your goals

**personalty** /ˈpɜːsənəlti/ = PERSONAL PROPERTY

★ **personnel** /ˌpɜːsəˈnel; *AmE* ˌpɜːrs-/ *n.* (*HR*) **1** [pl.] the people who work for an organization: *Key personnel will be appointed by March.*
**o** *qualified/skilled/trained ~* ♦ *marketing/sales/security/technical ~*
**2** [U with sing./pl. v.] the department in a company that deals with employing and training people: *~ is/are reviewing pay scales.* SYN HUMAN RESOURCES

**ˌperson-to-ˈperson** *adj.* **1** happening between two or more people who deal directly with each other rather than through another person: *Technical support is offered on a person-to-person basis.* **2** (*AmE*) (about a telephone call) made by calling the OPERATOR and asking to speak to a particular person. If that person is not available, the call does not have to be paid for: *Person-to-person calls are charged at a higher rate.*

**PERT** /pɜːt; *AmE* pɜːrt/ *abbr* (*Product.*) **Project/Program/Performance Evaluation and Review Technique** a way of managing the tasks involved in a project and showing the order in which they should be completed and how much time is needed for each

**pessimism** /ˈpesɪmɪzəm/ *n.* [U] ~ **(about/for/over sth)** a feeling that bad things will happen and that sth will not be successful; the tendency to have this feeling: *business/economic/investor/market ~*
OPP OPTIMISM ▸ **ˈpessimist** *n.* [C] **ˌpessiˈmistic** /-ˈmɪstɪk/ *adj.* **ˌpessiˈmistically** /-kli/ *adv.*

**ˈPEST aˌnalysis** /pest/ (*also* **ˈSTEP aˌnalysis**) *n.* [C,U] an examination of the political, economic, social and TECHNOLOGICAL aspects of the situation in which a company is operating to see how they will affect its products and markets

**ˈpester ˌpower** *n.* [U] (*infml.*) the ability that children have to make their parents buy things, by repeatedly asking them until they agree

**the ˈPeter ˌPrinciple** /ˈpiːtə(r)/ *n.* [sing.] the theory that employees continue to be given a higher rank in an organization until finally they reach a position where they do not have the ability to do their jobs properly

**petition** /pəˈtɪʃn/ *n.* [C] (*Law*) an official document asking a court of law to take a particular course of action: *One creditor has **filed** a petition for the company to be wound up.*

**petrochemical** /ˌpetrəʊˈkemɪkl; *AmE* ˌpetroʊ-/ *n.* [C] any chemical substance obtained from PETROLEUM oil or natural gas: *the petrochemical industry*

**petrodollar** /ˈpetrəʊdɒlə(r); *AmE* ˈpetroʊdɑːlər/ *n.* [C] (*Finan.*) a unit of money that is used for calculating the money earned by countries that produce and sell oil

**petroleum** /pəˈtrəʊliəm; *AmE* -ˈtroʊ-/ *n.* [U] (often used in the names of companies) mineral oil that is found under the ground or the sea and is used to produce petrol/gas, etc: *BP (British Petroleum)*

**ˌpetty ˈcash** *n.* [U] a small amount of money kept in an office to pay small expenses

**pharma** /ˈfɑːmə; *AmE* ˈfɑːrmə/ *adj.*, *n.* (*infml.*)
• ***adj.*** pharmaceutical: *pharma companies*
• ***n.*** [U] pharmaceutics

**pharmaceutical** /ˌfɑːməˈsuːtɪkl; -ˈsjuː-; *AmE* ˌfɑːrməˈsuː-/ *adj.*, *n.*
• ***adj.*** connected with making and selling drugs and medicines: *the pharmaceutical industry*
• ***n.*** [C, usu. pl.] drugs or medicines: *sales of pharmaceuticals*

**pharmaceutics** /ˌfɑːməˈsuːtɪks; -ˈsjuː-; *AmE* ˌfɑːrməˈsuː-/ *n.* [U] the study and development of the production of drugs and medicine

★ **phase** /feɪz/ *n.*, *v.*
• ***n.*** [C] a stage in a process of change or development: *Our company went through a phase of rapid expansion.*

◊ *the* ***design/development/manufacturing*** *~* ♦ *the* ***growth/start-up*** *~*
• *v.* [T] (*usu. pass.*) to arrange to do sth gradually in stages over a period of time: *The closure of offices was phased over a two-year period.*
PHR V ˌ**phase sth 'down** to reduce sth gradually in stages over a period of time: *phasing down production* ˌ**phase sth 'in/'out** to start/stop using sth gradually in stages over a period of time: *The new tax will be phased in over two years.*

**phishing** /'fɪʃɪŋ/ *n.* [U] (*IT*) the activity of tricking people by getting them to give their identity, bank account numbers, etc. over the Internet or by email, and then using these to steal money from them

★ **phone** /fəʊn; *AmE* foʊn/ *v.* (*esp. BrE*) PHR V ˌ**phone 'in** to make a telephone call to the place where you work: *Three people have* ***phoned in sick*** *today.* ˌ**phone sth 'in** to make a telephone call to the place where you work in order to give sb some information

**'phone book** = TELEPHONE DIRECTORY

**phonecard** /'fəʊnkɑːd; *AmE* 'foʊnkɑːrd/ *n.* [C] **1** (*AmE*) a plastic card with an individual number on it that allows you to use a telephone service, for example to make international calls. The cost of the call is charged to your account and you pay it later. **2** (*esp. BrE*) a plastic card that you can use in some public telephones instead of money

**photocopier** /'fəʊtəʊkɒpiə(r); *AmE* 'foʊtoʊkɑːp-/ (*also* **'copier**, *esp. in AmE*) *n.* [C] a machine that makes copies of documents, etc. by photographing them

**photocopy** /'fəʊtəʊkɒpi; *AmE* 'foʊtoʊkɑːpi/ *n., v.*
• *n.* [C] (*pl.* **-pies**) a copy of a document, etc. made by the action of light on a specially treated surface
• *v.* (**-pies, -pying, -pied, -pied**) **1** [T,I] to make a **photocopy** of sth: *photocopied documents* ◊ *photocopying facilities* **2** [I] **~ well/badly** (about printed material) to produce a good/bad **photocopy**

**physical** /'fɪzɪkl/ *adj.* **1** (*IT*) existing in a form that can be seen or touched, as opposed to electronic: *The website has features that physical stores can't offer.* OPP VIRTUAL
**2** (*Finan.*) used to describe a product or a raw material that can be bought and sold, or used, as opposed to cash, shares or FUTURES: *~ assets/commodities/goods*

ˌ**physical 'capital** *n.* [U] (*Econ.*) items such as land, factories, machinery and materials that are used to produce goods and provide services

ˌ**physical distri'bution** *n.* [U] (*Product.*) the tasks involved in moving finished goods from producers to consumers in the most efficient way and in planning and controlling this

**pick** /pɪk/ *v.* [T] (*Product.*) to collect items that a customer has ordered from the place where they are stored so that the order can be packed and sent: *They claim to be able to pick, pack and ship a large order in only 30 minutes.* ▸ **'picking** *n.* [U]: ***picking and packing*** *staff* IDM **pick up the 'bill/'tab (for sth)** (*infml.*) to pay for sth: *The company picked up the tab for his hotel room.* → idiom at SLACK *n.* PHR V ˌ**pick sth 'off** to take the best people or things from a group and leave the rest ˌ**pick sb/sth 'out** to choose sb/sth carefully from a group of people or things ˌ**pick 'up** to get better, stronger, etc.; to improve: *In the last few weeks sales have started to pick up.* ˌ**pick sth 'up** (*infml.*) to buy sth, esp. cheaply or by chance: *Investors have a chance to pick up some bargains.*

**picket** /'pɪkɪt/ *n., v.*
• *n.* [C] a person or group of people who stand outside the entrance to a building in order to protest about sth, esp. in order to stop people from entering a factory, etc. during a strike; an occasion when this happens: *Five pickets were arrested by police.* ◊ *a mass picket of the factory*
• *v.* [T,I] to stand outside somewhere such as your place of work to protest about sth or to try and persuade people to join a strike: *200 workers were picketing the factory.*
▸ **'picketer** *n.* [C] (*AmE*)

**'picket line** *n.* [C] a line or group of **pickets**: *Fire crews refused to cross the picket line.*

**pickup** /'pɪkʌp/ *n.* **1** [C] an improvement: *a pickup in consumer spending* **2** (*Transpt.*) [C,U] an occasion when sth is collected

**pictogram** /'pɪktəgræm/ *n.* [C] a diagram that uses pictures to represent amounts or numbers of a particular thing

**'piece rate** *n.* [C] (*HR*) an amount of money paid for each thing or amount of sth that a worker produces: *Slow workers on piece rates took home less pay.*

**piecework** /'piːswɜːk; *AmE* -wɜːrk/ *n.* [U] (*HR*) work that is paid

for by the amount done and not by the hours worked
▸ **'pieceworker** *n.* [C]

**'pie chart** (*also* **'pie graph**) *n.* [C] a diagram consisting of a circle that is divided into parts to show the size of particular parts in relation to the whole

**pigeonhole** /'pɪdʒɪnhəʊl; *AmE* -hoʊl/ *v., n.*
• ***v.*** [T] to decide that sb/sth belongs to a particular group or type, often without thinking deeply enough about it: *She never tried to pigeonhole her customers.* SYN CATEGORIZE
• ***n.*** [C] **1** one of a set of small boxes that are fixed on a wall and open at the front, used for putting letters, messages, etc. in **2** a group or type of people or things that sb/sth is put into, that is often too general, unfair or not correct: *Many clients want their advisers to fit into neat pigeonholes.* SYN CATEGORY

**piggyback** /'pɪgibæk/ *v.*
PHR V **'piggyback (sth) on/onto sth 1** to use a system that already exists as a basis for sth else: *Search engines piggyback on one another to provide more complete results.* **2** to use a larger organization, etc. for your own advantage

**pile** /paɪl/ *n.* [C] a large amount of money or debt: *to reduce a debt pile*

**pilfer** /'pɪlfə(r)/ *v.* [T,I] to steal things of little value or in small quantities, esp. from the place where you work ▸ **pilferage** /-ərɪdʒ/ *n.* [U] (*fml.*): *reducing the costs of pilferage by employees* **'pilferer** *n.* [C] **'pilfering** *n.* [U]

**pilot** /'paɪlət/ *n., v., adj.*
• ***n.*** [C] **1** a person who operates the controls of an aircraft, esp. as a job **2** a person with special knowledge of a difficult area of water who guides ships through it **3** a single television programme that is made in order to find out if people will like it and want to watch further programmes
• ***v.*** [T] **1** to fly an aircraft or guide a ship; to act as a **pilot 2 ~ sb/sth (through sth)** to guide sb/sth somewhere, esp. through a complicated place or system: *She has piloted the company through a period of successful growth.* **3** (*Market.*) to test a new product, idea, etc. with a few people or in a small area before it is introduced everywhere: *piloting the software with small businesses*
• ***adj.*** done on a small scale in order to see if sth is successful enough to do on a large scale: *a ~ project/test*

**PIM** /ˌpiː aɪ 'em/ = PERSONAL INFORMATION MANAGER



**PIN** /pɪn/ (*also* **'PIN ˌnumber**) *n.* [C] **personal identification number** a number given to you, for example by a bank, so that you can use a plastic card to take out money from a cash machine

**ping** /pɪŋ/ *v.* [T] (*IT*) **1** to use an Internet program to test whether a computer you are trying to connect with is working properly **2** (*infml.*) to send sb a type of electronic message similar to an email that appears on their screen as soon as it is sent: *We can ping each other questions and requests.* ▸ **ping** *n.* [C] (*infml.*): *I'm busy and I'm not taking pings.*

**ˌpink-'collar** *adj.* (*esp. AmE*) connected with jobs with low pay that are done mainly by women, for example in offices: *pink-collar workers*

**'Pink Sheets™** (*also* **pink sheets**) *n.* [pl.] (*Finan.*) in the US, a list of the latest prices of OVER-THE-COUNTER shares, that is published every day: *The shares closed at 86 cents on the Pink Sheets.*

**ˌpink 'slip** *n.* [C] (*AmE*) (*HR, infml.*) a letter given to sb to say that they must leave their job ▸ **'pink-slip** *v.* [T] (-pp-): *He was afraid he was going to be pink-slipped.*

**'PIN ˌnumber** = PIN

**pioneer** /ˌpaɪə'nɪə(r); *AmE* -'nɪr/ *n., v.*
• ***n.*** [C] a person or an organization that is the first to develop a particular area of knowledge, type of product, etc. that other people or organizations then continue to develop: *a pioneer* **in** *the pharmaceutical field*
• ***v.*** [T] to be one of the first to do, discover or use sth new

**pioneering** /ˌpaɪə'nɪərɪŋ; *AmE* -'nɪr-/ *adj.* introducing ideas and methods that have never been used before: *pioneering research*

**pipeline** /'paɪplaɪn/ *n.* [C] a series of pipes that are usu. underground and are used for carrying oil, gas, etc. over long distances IDM **in the 'pipeline** something that is **in the pipeline** is being discussed, planned or prepared and will happen or exist soon

**piracy** /'paɪrəsi/ *n.* [U] the act of making illegal copies of video tapes, computer programs, books, etc., in order to sell them: *software piracy*

**pirate** /'paɪrət/ *n., v.*
• ***n.*** [C] (*often used as an adj.*) a person who makes illegal copies of video tapes, computer programs, books,

etc., in order to sell them: *software pirates* ◇ *pirate copies of CDs*
• *v.* [T] to copy and use or sell a product without permission and without having the right to do so: *pirated computer games*

**pit** /pɪt/ *n.* [C] **1** (*Stock Ex.*) (*AmE*) the area of a stock exchange or other EXCHANGE where a particular product is traded **2** a coal mine: *pit closures*

**pitch** /pɪtʃ/ *n., v.* (*Comm.; Market.*)
• *n.* [C, usu. sing.] talk or arguments used by a person trying to sell things or persuade people to do sth: *to make its* **pitch** *for a contract*
• *v.* **1** [T] to set sth at a particular level: *They have pitched their prices too high.* **2** [T] to aim or direct a product or service at a particular group of people: *The new software is being pitched* **at** *banks.* **3** [T,I] to try to persuade sb to buy sth, to give you sth or to make a business deal with you: *pitching* **for** *business*

**pitfall** /ˈpɪtfɔːl/ *n.* [C, usu. pl.] a danger or difficulty, esp. one that is hidden or not obvious at first: *how to avoid some of the pitfalls of online banking*

**pittance** /ˈpɪtns/ *n.* [C, usu. sing.] a very small amount of money, esp. paid to sb as wages: *They paid us a pittance.*

**pivotal** /ˈpɪvətl/ *adj.* of great importance because other things depend on it: *The company plays a pivotal role in the local economy.*

**pixel** /ˈpɪksl/ *n.* [C] (*IT*) any of the small individual areas on a computer screen, which together form the whole display

**place** /pleɪs/ *v., n.*
• *v.* [T] **1** to give instructions about sth or make a request for sth to happen: *Placing an ad in the local newspaper cost $250.* ◇ *to place an order* **2** to find a suitable job for sb: *The agency placed about 2 000 office workers last year.* → idiom at RECORD *n.*
• *n.* [C] a building or an area used for a particular purpose: *an online meeting place* ◇ *your place of work*
**IDM** **be 'going places** to be getting more and more successful in your life or career **in 'place** working or ready to work

**placement** /ˈpleɪsmənt/ *n.* [U,C] **1** the act of finding sb a suitable job or place to live: *a job placement service* **2** (*BrE*) (*AmE* **'practicum**) a job, often as part of a course of study, where you get some experience of a particular kind of work: *The third year is spent* **on** *placement in selected companies.* ◇ *work placements* **3** (*Finan.*) (*AmE*) = PLACING

**placing** /ˈpleɪsɪŋ/ (*AmE also* **'placement**) *n.* [C,U] (*Finan.*) an occasion when new shares in a company are made available for sale to particular individuals or institutions

**plaintiff** /ˈpleɪntɪf/ *n.* [C] (*Law*) a person who makes a formal complaint against sb in court → CLAIMANT (3)

★**plan** /plæn/ *n., v.*
• *n.* [C] **1** a set of things to do in order to achieve sth: *They drew up a plan* **for** *reducing costs.* **2** an idea for doing or achieving sth in the future: *We have no plans* **to** *sell the business.* **3** (*Finan.*) (*esp. with other ns*) a way of investing money or making payments: *retirement* **savings** *plans* **4** a detailed drawing of a machine, building, etc. that shows its size, shape and measurements **5** a diagram that shows how sth will be arranged: *a seating plan*
• *v.* [T,I] (-nn-) **1** to make detailed arrangements for sth you want to do in the future: *A meeting has been planned for next week.* **2** ~ **(on sth/ on doing sth)** to intend or expect to do sth: *news of planned job cuts*
**PHRV** **ˌplan sth 'out** to plan carefully and in detail sth that you are going to do in the future: *She has her career all planned out.*

**ˌplanned e'conomy** *n.* [C] (*Econ.*) an economic system that is controlled by the government rather than by the amount of goods available and the level of demand from customers

**planner** /ˈplænə(r)/ *n.* [C] **1** a person whose job is to plan the growth and development of a town **2** a person who makes plans for a particular area of activity: *the country's top economic planner* **3** a book, computer program, etc. that contains dates and is used for recording information, arranging meetings, etc: *a day/ year ~*

★**planning** /ˈplænɪŋ/ *n.* [U] **1** the process of making plans for sth: *Organizing a conference requires a lot of careful planning.*
✪ ***advance/forward ~ • business/ financial ~ • to need ~***
**2** the control of the growth and development of towns and their buildings, roads, etc. so that they can be pleasant and convenient places for people to live in
✪ ***city/town/urban ~ • ~ approval/ consent/permission***

★**plant** /plɑːnt; *AmE* plænt/ *n.* **1** [C] a factory or place where power is produced or an industrial process takes place
○ *an* ***assembly****/a* ***bottling/manufacturing/packing/processing*** *~ ◆ a* ***car/chemical*** *~*
**2** [U] large machinery that is used in industrial processes: *investing in new plant and equipment*

**plastic** /ˈplæstɪk/ (*also* ˌ**plastic ˈmoney**) *n.* [U] (*infml.*) credit cards or other bank cards: *Do they take plastic?*

**plateau** /ˈplætəʊ; *AmE* plæˈtoʊ/ *n., v.*
• *n.* [C] (*pl.* **plateaux** *or* **plateaus** /-təʊz; *AmE* -ˈtoʊz/) a time of little or no change after a period of growth or progress: *Inflation has reached a plateau.*
• *v.* [I] ~ **(out)** to stay at a steady level after a period of growth or progress: *Unemployment has at last plateaued out.*

**platform** /ˈplætfɔːm; *AmE* -fɔːrm/ *n.* [C] **1** a basis on which sth can develop: *a platform* **for** *long-term growth* **2** (*IT*) the technical basis of a system, esp. a computer or broadcasting system **3** a raised structure standing in the sea, built by a company that is taking oil or gas from under the sea: *an oil/production platform*

ˌ**platform-ˈneutral** *adj.* (*IT*) able to work on different technical systems

**platinum** /ˈplætɪnəm/ *n.* [U] a very valuable silver-grey metal used in making expensive jewellery and in industry

**play** /pleɪ/ *v., n.*
• *v.* [I] (*esp. AmE*) to have a particular effect on sb: *Providing good service plays well* **with** *customers.* IDM **have money, time, etc. to ˈplay with** (*infml.*) to have a particular amount of money, time, etc. for doing sth: *We don't have a lot of money to play with.* **play by sb's (own) ˈrules** if sb **plays by their own rules** or makes other people **play by their rules** they set the conditions for doing business **play by the ˈrules** to deal fairly and honestly with people **play ˈcatch-up** (*esp. AmE*) to try to be as good or successful as a competitor: *We're always playing catch-up with them.* **play for high ˈstakes** to be involved in an activity where you can lose a lot if it fails, but gain a lot if it is successful **play the (ˈstock) ˈmarket** to buy and sell shares in order to make a quick profit **play a (key, major, vital, etc.) ˈpart/ˈrole (in sth)**; **have a (key, major, vital, etc.) ˈpart/ˈrole to play (in sth)** to be involved in sth and have an important effect on it **play the ˈsystem** to use a set of rules that control sth in a way that gives you an advantage: *The developers know how to play the planning system.* **play to your ˈstrengths** to give your attention and effort to things that you do well PHRV ˌ**play sth ˈdown** to try to make sth seem less important than it is OPP PLAY STH UP ˈ**play for sth** to try to gain sth; to compete with sb for sth: *There is still 96% of the company to play for.* ˌ**play (itself/themselves) ˈout** to develop or end in a particular way: *Let's make a decision and see how it plays out.* ˌ**play sth ˈup** to try to make sth seem more important than it is OPP PLAY STH DOWN
• *n.* **1** [U] the activity or operation of sth; the influence of sth on sth else: *the free play of market forces* **2** (*Stock Ex., infml.*) [C] an act of investing money in particular shares, bonds, etc: *Although the shares are not cheap, they are a defensive play that won't let you down.* IDM **bring/call sth into ˈplay** to begin to use sth: *More funding will be brought into play.* **come into ˈplay** to begin to be used or to have an effect: *A number of factors come into play when you ask people to work in groups.* **in play** if a company is **in play**, it can be bought by another company **make a ˈplay for sb/sth** to try to obtain or achieve sth: *making a play for the sales manager's job*

**playbook** /ˈpleɪbʊk/ *n.* [C] (*AmE*) a set of plans for achieving an aim: *The business plan is a playbook for everyone in the company.*

**player** /ˈpleɪə(r)/ *n.* [C] an important company or person involved in a particular area of business: *The company is a major player in the London property market.*
○ *a* ***big/dominant/global/key/leading*** *~ ◆ a* ***niche/small*** *~*

ˈ**playing field** *n.* [C, usu. sing.] (*Market.*) used to describe a situation where people are competing with each other: *Do you have the skills to perform on today's corporate playing field?* IDM **a ˌlevel ˈplaying field** a situation where everyone has a fair and equal chance of succeeding: *The tariffs mean that Europe and the US are not competing on a level playing field.* **an ˌuneven ˈplaying field** a situation in which some competitors have an unfair advantage

**plc** /ˌpiː el ˈsiː/ *abbr* (*BrE*) **1** (*usu. written*) (*also* **PLC**) public limited company (used after the name of a company or business): *Lloyd's Bank plc* **2** (*Market.*) **PLC** = PRODUCT LIFE CYCLE

**pledge** /pledʒ/ *v., n.*
• *v.* [T] **1** to formally promise to give or do sth: *Japan has pledged $100 m in aid.* **2** (*Law*) to leave sth valuable with sb to prove that you will pay back money that you owe: *The shares were pledged to the bank as security for loans.*
• *n.* [C] **1** a serious promise: *Management has* ***given*** *a pledge that there will be no job losses this year.* **2** (*Law*) something valuable that you leave with sb to prove that you will pay back money that you owe

**plenary** /ˈpliːnəri/ *adj., n.*
• *adj.* (about meetings, etc.) to be attended by everyone who has the right to attend: *a plenary session*
• *n.* [C] (*pl.* **-ries**) a **plenary** meeting

**ˈPlimsoll line** (*also* **ˈPlimsoll mark**) /ˈplɪmsəl/ = LOAD LINE

**PLM** /ˌpiː el ˈem/ = PRODUCT LIFE CYCLE MANAGEMENT

**plot** /plɒt; *AmE* plɑːt/ *n., v.*
• *n.* [C] a piece of land that is used or intended for a special purpose: *building plots*
• *v.* [T] (**-tt-**) **1** to make a diagram or chart from some information: *The results of the survey were plotted on a chart.* **2** to mark points on a graph and draw a line or curve connecting them

**plough** (*AmE* **plow**) /plaʊ/ *v.*
PHRV **ˌplough sth ˈback (into sth)**; **ˌplough sth back ˈin** to put money made as profit back into a business in order to improve it **ˌplough sth ˈinto sth** to invest a large amount of money in a company or project

**plug** /plʌg/ *v., n.*
• *v.* [T] (**-gg-**) **1** to provide sth that has been missing from a particular situation and is needed in order to improve it: *The cheaper range of products should* ***plug the gap*** *in the market.* **2** (*Market.*) to give praise or attention to a new product, book, CD, etc. in order to encourage people to buy it: *She came on the show to plug her latest album.* SYN PROMOTE
PHRV **ˌplug sth ˈinto sth** (*IT*) to connect a computer to a computer system **ˌplug ˈinto sth 1** (about a piece of electrical equipment) to be able to be connected to the main supply of electricity or to another piece of electrical equipment: *The modem plugs into the USB port.* **2** to become involved with a particular activity or group of people: *The company is plugging into lucrative overseas markets.*
• *n.* [C] praise or attention given to a new product, book, CD, etc. in order to encourage people to buy it
→ idiom at PULL *v.*

**ˌPlug and ˈPlay™** *n.* [U] (*IT*) a system which makes it possible for a user to connect a device such as a printer to a computer and use it immediately

**ˈplug-in** *adj.* **1** able to be connected using a plug: *a plug-in kettle* **2** (*IT*) that can be added to a computer system so that it can do more things: *a plug-in graphics card* ▸ **ˈplug-in** *n.* [C] (*IT*): *a handheld with a dictionary plug-in*

**plummet** /ˈplʌmɪt/ *v.* [I] to fall suddenly and quickly from a high level or position: *Share prices plummeted to an all-time low.* SYN PLUNGE ▸ **ˈplummet** *n.* [C, usu. sing.]

**plunge** /plʌndʒ/ *v., n.*
• *v.* [I] to decrease suddenly and quickly: *Share prices have plunged in recent months.* SYN PLUMMET
PHRV **ˌplunge (sb/sth) ˈinto sth** to experience sth unpleasant; to make sb/sth do this: *The country plunged deeper into recession.*
• *n.* [C, usu. sing.] a sudden decrease in an amount or the value of sth: *a plunge in annual profits* SYN DROP
IDM **take the ˈplunge** (*infml.*) to decide to do sth important or difficult, esp. after thinking about it for a long time

**plus** /plʌs/ *prep., adj., n.*
• *prep.* **1** used when the two numbers or amounts mentioned are being added together: *The book is available at $19.49 plus shipping.* **2** as well as sth/sb; and also OPP MINUS
IDM **plus or ˈminus** used when the number mentioned may be more or less by a particular amount: *They expect to report earnings of $174 m, plus or minus $1 m.*
• *adj.* **1** used to describe an aspect of sth that you consider to be a good thing: *The airline's safety record is a major plus* ***point***. OPP MINUS **2** used after a number to show that the real number or amount is more than the one mentioned: *The profit is expected to be $22 m plus.*
• *n.* [C] **1** (*infml.*) an advantage; a good thing: *One of the pluses of the job is being able to work from home.* **2** (*also* **ˈplus sign**) the symbol ( + ), used in mathematics OPP MINUS

**ˈplus tick** = UPTICK

**ply** /plaɪ/ *v.* [T,I] (**plies, plying, plied, plied**) to travel regularly along a particular route or between two particular places: *airlines plying transatlantic routes* IDM **ply your 'trade** to do your work or business

**PMI** /ˌpiː em 'aɪ/ *abbr* (*Econ.*) **Purchasing Managers' Index** (*used as a singular n.*) a measure of economic activity in the section of the economy that is concerned with the manufacture of goods, published every month: *A PMI over 50% means that manufacturing is expanding.*

**'P-note** = PROMISSORY NOTE

**PO** /ˌpiː 'əʊ; *AmE* 'oʊ/ = POST OFFICE (2), POSTAL ORDER

**POA** /ˌpiː əʊ 'eɪ; *AmE* oʊ/ = POINT OF ACTION

**poach** /pəʊtʃ; *AmE* poʊtʃ/ *v.* [T] to take and use staff, customers, etc. from another company in a dishonest or unfair way ▸ **'poaching** *n.* [U]

**ˌP'O box** (*also* **'post ˌoffice box**) *n.* [C] used as a kind of address, so that mail can be sent to a post office where it is kept until it is collected: *PO Box 155, Irvington*

**pocket** /'pɒkɪt; *AmE* 'pɑːk-/ *n.*, *v.*, *adj.*

• ***n.*** [C, usu. sing.] the amount of money that a person, an organization or a government has available to spend: *London has hotels to suit every pocket.* SYN PURSE IDM **ˌout of 'pocket** (*esp. BrE*) having lost money as a result of sth: *The collapse of the company left investors out of pocket.* → idioms at DEEP *adj.*, DIP *v.*, FILL, HAND *n.*, LINE *v.*

• ***v.*** [T] **1** to earn or win an amount of money: *She pocketed a profit of $6 m from the deal.* **2** to take or keep sth, esp. an amount of money, in an illegal or a dishonest way; to steal sth: *He charges passengers more than the normal fare and pockets the difference.*

• ***adj.*** used to describe sth that is very small or small enough to be put and carried in a pocket: *a ~ pager/dictionary*

**'pocket change** *n.* [U] **1** coins **2** a small amount of money: *$7000 isn't pocket change.*

**'pocket-sized** (*also* **'pocket-size**) *adj.* small enough to fit into your pocket or to be carried easily

**point** /pɔɪnt/ *n.*, *v.*

• ***n.*** **1** [C] a thing that sb says or writes giving their opinion or stating a fact: *She made several interesting points at the meeting.* ◇ *to raise/discuss/prove a ~* **2** *usually* **the point** [sing.] the main or most important idea in sth that is said or done: *I'll come straight to the point: we need more money.* ◇ *to get/miss the ~* **3** [U; sing.] the purpose or aim of sth: *What's the point of this memo?* **4** [C] a particular detail or fact: *a six-point survival guide for new managers* **5** [C] a particular quality or feature that sb/sth has: *good/plus/strong ~s* **6** [C] a particular time, stage or level: *The talks have reached a critical point.* **7** (*Finan.*) [C] a mark or unit on a scale of measurement, esp. a financial index: *Blue-chip stocks were up 87 points.* ◇ *The central bank cut its rates by half a point.* **8** [C] a unit used to measure the quality of sb/sth: *Lending decisions are made on a points system.* **9** [C] a particular place or area: *a meeting point* **10** [C] a small dot that separates a whole number from the part that comes after it: 2.6 (said: 'two point six') IDM **ˌpoint of 'contact** a place where you go or a person that you speak to when you are dealing with an organization **a ˌpoint of de'parture 1** a place where a journey starts **2** an idea, a theory or an event that is used to start a discussion, an activity, etc.

• ***v.*** [T,I] to lead to or suggest a particular development or a logical way to continue an argument: *The evidence seems to point in that direction.*

**pointer** /'pɔɪntə(r)/ *n.* [C] **1** a sign that sth exists; a sign that shows how sth may develop in the future: *Results from the retail sector are key pointers to progress.* **2** (*infml.*) a piece of advice SYN TIP **3** a stick used to point to things on a map or picture on a wall, etc. **4** a small symbol, for example an arrow, that marks a point on a computer screen

**ˌpoint of 'action** *n.* [C] (*abbr* **POA**) (*Market.*) the place or time in a presentation, on a website, etc. when a possible customer has the opportunity and is encouraged to react and to do sth

**ˌpoint of 'purchase** *n.* [C] (*abbr* **POP**) (*Comm.*; *Market.*) the place where a product is bought: *point-of-purchase displays*

**ˌpoint-of-purchase 'advertising** *n.* [U] (*abbr* **POPA**) (*Market.*) advertising at the place where a product is bought

**ˌpoint of 'sale** *n.* [C] (*abbr* **POS**) (*Comm.*; *Market.*) the place where a product is sold: *point-of-sale displays*

**ˌpoint of 'use** *n.* [sing.] the place where or the time when a product or a service is actually used: *Medical care is still free* ***at*** *the point of use.*

**poised** /pɔɪzd/ *adj.* completely ready for sth or to do sth: *The economy is poised **for** recovery.* SYN SET

**ˌpoisoned ˈchalice** *n.* [sing.] (*fml.*) a job or position that seems attractive at first but soon becomes very unpleasant

**ˌpoison ˈpill** *n.* [C] (*Finan., infml.*) a form of defence used by a company when another company is trying to take control of it, in order to make itself less attractive, for example by selling some of its main assets

★ **policy** /ˈpɒləsi; *AmE* ˈpɑːl-/ *n.* (*pl.* **-cies**) **1** [C,U] a plan of action agreed or chosen by a business, an organization or a political party: *the group's accounting policies ◇ policy decisions*

○ *to **adopt/implement/introduce** a ~* ◆ *to **abandon/change/develop** (a) ~*

**2** (*Insur.*) [C] a written statement of a contract of insurance: *Check the terms of the policy before you sign.*

**policyholder** /ˈpɒləsihəʊldə(r); *AmE* ˈpɑːləsihoʊl-/ *n.* [C] (*Insur.*) a person or group that holds a contract of insurance

**ˈpolicy-ˌsetting** *adj.* that decides on plans of action: *a ~ board/committee*

**politics** /ˈpɒlətɪks; *AmE* ˈpɑːl-/ *n.* [U with sing./pl. v.] matters concerned with getting or using power within a particular group or organization: *office politics*

**poll** /pəʊl; *AmE* poʊl/ *n., v.*

• ***n.*** [C] (*also* **oˈpinion poll**) the process of questioning people who represent a larger group in order to get information about the general opinion SYN SURVEY

○ *to **carry out/conduct/take** a ~* ◆ *a ~ **indicates/shows/suggests** sth*

• ***v.*** [T] to ask a large number of members of the public what they think about sth: *60% of those polled said they booked flights online.*

**pollutant** /pəˈluːtənt/ *n.* [C] a dirty or harmful substance that makes land, air, water, etc. no longer pleasant or safe to use

**pollution** /pəˈluːʃn/ *n.* [U] **1** the process of making air, water, soil, etc. dirty; the state of being dirty: *reducing environmental pollution* **2** substances that make air, water, soil, etc. dirty: *A cloud of pollution hangs over the city.*

**polˈlution ˌcredit** = EMISSION CREDIT

**polybag** /ˌpɒliˈbæg; *AmE* ˌpɑːl-/ *n.* [C] (*infml.*) a bag made of strong thin clear plastic material, used for wrapping things

**polystyrene** /ˌpɒliˈstaɪriːn; *AmE* ˌpɑːl-/ (*also* **ˈStyrofoam™**, *esp. in AmE*) *n.* [U] very light soft plastic that is usu. white, used for packing goods or for making containers that prevent heat loss: *polystyrene cups*

**ˈPonzi scheme** /ˈpɒnzi skiːm; *AmE* ˈpɑːnzi/ *n.* [C] (*AmE*) a plan for making money that involves encouraging people to invest by offering them a high rate of interest and using their money to pay earlier investors. When there are not enough new investors, people who have recently invested lose their money.

**pool** /puːl/ *n., v.*

• ***n.*** [C] **1** a supply of things or money that is shared by a group of people and can be used when needed: *a pool of cars used by the sales force ◇ a pool car* **2** a group of people available for work: *a large pool of cheap labour*

• ***v.*** [T] to collect money, information, etc. from different people so that it can be used by all of them: *Departments are beginning to pool resources.*

**POP** /ˌpiː əʊ ˈpiː; *AmE* oʊ/ = POINT OF PURCHASE

**POPA** /ˌpiː əʊ piː ˈeɪ; *AmE* oʊ/ = POINT-OF-PURCHASE ADVERTISING

**ˌpopular ˈprice** *n.* [C] a price that is liked because it is low: *quality at popular prices*

▸ **ˌpopular ˈpricing** *n.* [U]

**population** /ˌpɒpjuˈleɪʃn; *AmE* ˌpɑːp-/ *n.* **1** [C with sing./pl. v.; U] all the people who live in a particular area, city or country; the total number of people who live there **2** [C with sing./pl. v.] a particular group of people living in a particular area: *The textile industry employs a third of the working population.*

**ˈpop-ˌunder** *adj., n.* (*IT; Market.*)

• ***adj.*** appearing on a computer screen quickly to display an advertisement, etc. behind sth that you are looking at on the Internet: *pop-under ads*

• ***n.*** [C] an advertisement that appears in a small window on your computer screen behind sth else that you are looking at

**ˈpop-up** *adj., n.* (*IT; Market.*)

• ***adj.*** appearing on a computer screen quickly to display a list of choices, an advertisement, etc. while you are working on another document: *Select an item from the pop-up menu.*

• ***n.*** [C] an advertisement that appears in a small window on your computer screen while you are looking at sth else

★ **port** /pɔːt; *AmE* pɔːrt/ *n., v.*

• ***n.*** **1** [C] a town or city with a harbour, esp. one where ships load and unload goods **2** [C,U] a place where ships load and unload goods or shelter from storms: *The ship spent four days **in port**.* **3** (*IT*) [C] a device on a computer where you can connect pieces of equipment such as a keyboard or a printer

• ***v.*** [T] (*IT*) to move software from one computer to another one of a different type: *The software can be ported to an IBM RS/6000.*

**portable** /ˈpɔːtəbl; *AmE* ˈpɔːrt-/ *adj., n.*

• ***adj.*** **1** that is easy to carry or to move: *Cellphones are easy to use and portable.* **2** (about computer software) that can be used with different kinds of computers **3** a **portable** pension or loan is one that you can move to another company if you change jobs, banks, etc.

▸ **ˌportaˈbility** /-ˈbɪləti/ *n.* [U]

• ***n.*** [C] a small type of machine that is easy to carry, esp. a computer or a television

**portal** /ˈpɔːtl; *AmE* ˈpɔːrtl/ *n.* [C] (*IT*) a website that is used as a link to the Internet, where information has been collected that will be useful to a person interested in particular kinds of things: *a business/news/shopping ~*

**ˈPorter's geˈneric ˈstrategies** /ˈpɔːtəz; *AmE* ˈpɔːrtərz/ *n.* [pl.] (*Market.*) the possible ways in which a business can achieve a strong position in a particular industry. These are: producing goods at a lower cost than competitors (**cost leadership strategy**), developing products that are different from other similar products and that customers value (**differentiation strategy**) or focusing on a small group of customers (**focus strategy**).

★ **portfolio** /pɔːtˈfəʊliəʊ; *AmE* pɔːrtˈfoʊlioʊ/ *n.* [C] (*pl.* **-lios**) **1** (*Finan.*) a set of investments owned by a particular person or organization: *The group has a property portfolio worth $2.4 bn.*

⊙ *to **build (up)/broaden/expand/have/hold** a ~ • a **balanced/diversified**/an **international**/a **large/strong** ~ • a **bond**/an **equity/investment**/a **share/stock** ~ • a **loan/property** ~*

**2** (*Comm.*) the range of products or services offered by a particular company: *We needed to expand our product portfolio.*

⊙ *to **build up/have/offer** a ~ • a **brand/business** ~ • a **broad/strong/wide** ~*

**portˌfolio caˈreer** *n.* [C] (*HR*) a career that is based on building skills and knowledge in a series of different jobs rather than one based on increasingly senior jobs in one profession

**portˈfolio ˌmanager** *n.* [C] (*Stock Ex.*) someone whose job is to control a group of investments with the aim of making the most profit with the least risk ▸ **portˈfolio ˌmanagement** *n.* [U]

**portion** /ˈpɔːʃn; *AmE* ˈpɔːrʃn/ *n.* [C] **1** one part of sth larger: *The division accounts for only a small portion of total sales.* **2** an amount of food that is large enough for one person: ***portion control** in the food-service industry*

**ˌport of ˈentry** *n.* [C] a place where people or goods can enter a country officially

**POS** /ˌpiː əʊ ˈes; *AmE* oʊ/ = POINT OF SALE

★ **position** /pəˈzɪʃn/ *n., v.*

• ***n.*** **1** [C] a job: *He held a senior position in a large company.* ◇ *to advertise/apply for/fill/have/take up a ~* **2** [C,U] a person or an organization's level of importance or success when compared with others: *the company's dominant position **in** the world market*

⊙ *to **establish/gain/hold/strengthen/use** a ~ • to be in a ~ of **authority/power/strength***

**3** [C, usu. sing.] the situation that sb is in, esp. when it affects what they can and cannot do: *the company's financial position* ◇ *I'm afraid I'm not **in a position to** help you.* ◇ *to achieve/reach/strengthen/weaken a ~* **4** (*Finan.*) [C] the total amount of a particular share, bond, currency, etc. that a dealer or an investor owns, or has sold but needs to buy back in the future

• ***v.*** [T] **1** to put sth/sb in a particular position: *The company is uniquely positioned to compete in foreign markets.* **2** (*Market.*) to advertise a product, service or company in a particular way in a particular part of the market so that it appears different from other products, services or companies: *The magazine has been positioned **as** an educational product.*

**poˈsition ˌaudit** (*also* **poˈsition reˌview**) *n.* [C] **1** a thorough analysis of the current situation of an organization that is done in order to plan for the future **2** (*HR*) an analysis of exactly what is involved in a particular job with a company

**positioning** /pəˈzɪʃnɪŋ/ *n.* [U] (*Market.*) the way a product, service or company is advertised in a particular part of the market so that it appears different from others; the way that people think about a product, service or company: *The market positioning of the two stores is very different.*

**poˈsition reˌview** = POSITION AUDIT

★**positive** /ˈpɒzətɪv; *AmE* ˈpɑːz-/ *adj.*, *n.*

• ***adj.*** **1** greater than zero **2** good or useful: *The news has had a positive effect on our finances.* **3** expressing agreement or support: *We've had a very positive response to the new product.* OPP NEGATIVE ▸ **ˈpositively** *adv.*

• ***n.*** **1** [C] the result of a test or an experiment that shows that a substance or condition is present OPP NEGATIVE **2** [C,U] a good or useful quality or aspect: *We can take several positives from this experience.*

**ˌpositive ˈaction** *n.* [U] (*BrE*) anything that is done to give everyone the same chances of education or employment, esp. by helping groups that are often treated unfairly because of their race, sex, etc.

**ˌpositive discrimiˈnation** (*also* **reˌverse discrimiˈnation**) *n.* [U] (*BrE*) the practice or policy of giving an advantage to people from groups that are often treated unfairly because of their race, sex, etc., for example by making sure that a particular number of jobs are given to people from these groups SYN AFFIRMATIVE ACTION (*AmE*)

**ˌpositive-ˈsum game** *n.* [C] a situation in which both sides involved in a relationship or a piece of business gain an advantage

**ˌpositive ˈterritory** *n.* [U] often used in newspapers to describe a level that is above zero, or above the previous or expected level: *Five stocks ended the day* ***in*** *positive territory.*

**possession** /pəˈzeʃn/ *n.* **1** [U] the state of having or owning sth: *The bank may* ***take possession of*** *the company's assets.* **2** [C, usu. pl.] something that you own or have with you at a particular time: *Please take your possessions away with you.*

**possessor** /pəˈzesə(r)/ *n.* [C] (*fml.*) a person who owns or has sth SYN OWNER

★**post** /pəʊst; *AmE* poʊst/ *n.*, *v.*

• ***n.*** **1** (*BrE*) [U] the official system used for sending and delivering letters, packages, etc: *I'll send it to you* ***by post.*** SYN MAIL **2** (*BrE*) [U] letters, packages, etc. that are sent and delivered: *Have you opened your post yet?* SYN MAIL **3** [U; sing.] (*BrE*) an occasion during the day when letters, etc. are collected or delivered: *The package came in this morning's post.* **4** [C] a job, esp. an important one in a large organization: *She has held the post for three years.* ◇ *15 new full-time posts*

⊙ ***a junior/senior/key/managerial*** ~ • *to* ***apply for/leave/resign from/ take up*** *a* ~ • *to* ***appoint sb to/fill*** *a* ~ • ***vacant*** ~*s*

→ idiom at RETURN *n.*

• ***v.*** [T] **1** (*BrE*) **~ sth (off) (to sb)** | **~ sb sth** to send a letter, etc. to sb by post/mail: *I'll post you the cheque next week.* SYN MAIL **2** (*BrE*) to put a letter, etc. into a public box to be sent SYN MAIL **3** (*usu. pass.*) to send sb to a particular place for a period of time as part of their job: *She's been posted to Washington for two years.* **4** (*often pass.*) to put a notice, etc. in a public place so that people can see it: *The letter was posted on the noticeboard.* **5** (*IT*) to put information or a message on the Internet: *The results will be posted tomorrow.* **6** (*esp. AmE*) to announce sth publicly or officially, esp. financial information or a warning: *The company posted a $1.1 bn loss.* ◇ *to ~ gains/earnings (of…)*

IDM **keep sb ˈposted (about/on sth)** to regularly give sb the most recent information about sth and how it is developing: *I'll keep you posted on his progress.*

**post-** /pəʊst; *AmE* poʊst/ *prefix* (*in adjs, vs, advs and ns*) after; later than: *post-tax income* ◇ *post-date*

**postage** /ˈpəʊstɪdʒ; *AmE* ˈpoʊ-/ *n.* [U] the cost of sending a letter, etc. by post: *an increase in postage rates*

**ˌpostage and ˈpacking** (*also* **ˌpostage and ˈpackaging**) (*both BrE*) (*AmE* **ˌpostage and ˈhandling**) *n.* [U] the cost of wrapping an item and sending it by post: *price £30 + £5.50 postage and packing*

**ˌpostage ˈpaid** *adj.* used to describe sth such as an envelope on which the company has already paid the cost of sending it by post: *a postage-paid questionnaire/label*

**ˈpostage stamp** = STAMP *n.* (1)

**postal** /ˈpəʊstl; *AmE* ˈpoʊstl/ *adj.* connected with the official system for sending and delivering letters, etc: *your full postal address*

**'postal code** = POSTCODE

**ˌpostal 'money ˌorder** = MONEY ORDER

**'postal ˌorder** = MONEY ORDER

**postcode** /'pəʊstkəʊd; *AmE* 'poʊst-koʊd/ (*also* **'postal code**) (*both BrE*) (*AmE* **'zip code**) *n.* [C] a group of letters and/or numbers that are used as part of an address so that post/mail can be separated into groups and delivered more quickly: *postcode: CB11 3AD*

**ˌpost-'date** (*AmE usu.* **postdate**) *v.* [T] **1** to put a later date on a cheque or other document than the date at the time of writing, usu. to delay payment: *a post-dated cheque* **2** (*BrE*) (*usu. pass.*) to make sth, esp. a payment, take effect from a later date: *a 5% post-dated pay rise* OPP BACKDATE

**poster** /'pəʊstə(r); *AmE* 'poʊ-/ *n.* [C] a large notice, often with a picture on it, that is put in a public place to advertise sth: *a ~ advertisement/campaign* IDM **'poster child/boy/girl** (*AmE*) a person or thing that is seen as representing a particular quality or activity: *He's the IT industry's poster boy for success.*

**ˌpost-'Fordism** *n.* [U] (*HR*) a method of management that aims to give workers a large amount of responsibility and freedom ▸ **ˌpost-'Fordist** *adj.* **ˌpost-'Fordist** *n.* [C]

**ˌpost-'free** *adj.* (*BrE*) used to describe sth that you can send by post without having to pay anything ▸ **ˌpost-'free** *adv.*

**posting** /'pəʊstɪŋ; *AmE* 'poʊ-/ *n.* **1** (*HR*) [C] an act of sending sb to a particular place for a period of time as part of their job: *an overseas posting* **2** (*IT*) [C] a message or information put on the Internet **3** (*Account.*) [U,C] the activity of writing figures in a LEDGER; the figures written: *transaction and payment posting* ◇ *correcting routine posting errors*

**'Post-it™** (*also* **'Post-it™ note**) *n.* [C] a small piece of coloured, sticky paper that you use for writing a note on, and that can be easily removed from where you put it

**'post ˌoffice** *n.* **1** [C] a place where you can buy stamps, send letters, etc. **2 the Post Office** [sing.] (*abbr* **PO**) the national organization in many countries that is responsible for the mail

**'post ˌoffice box** = PO BOX

**ˌpost-'paid** (*AmE* **postpaid**) *adj.* (*abbr* **ppd**) that you can send free because the charge has already been paid: *a post-paid envelope* ▸ **ˌpost-'paid** (*AmE* **postpaid**) *adv.*

★ **postpone** /pə'spəʊn; *AmE* poʊ-'spoʊn/ *v.* [T] to arrange for an event, etc. to take place at a later time or date: *We'll have to postpone the meeting until next week.* OPP ADVANCE ▸ **post'ponement** *n.* [U,C]

**'post room** (*BrE*) (*AmE* **'mail room**) *n.* [C] the department of a company that deals with sending and receiving mail

**postscript** /'pəʊstskrɪpt; *AmE* 'poʊst-/ *n.* [C] (*abbr* **PS**) **1** an extra message that you add at the end of a letter after your signature: *PS See you tomorrow.* **2** something extra that is added to sth after it has finished

**potential** /pə'tenʃl/ *adj.*, *n.*

• ***adj.*** that can develop into sth or be developed in the future: *potential customers* ▸ **po'tentially** /-ʃəli/ *adv.*: *a potentially huge market*

• ***n.*** [U] **1** the possibility of sth happening or being developed or used: *The new service has huge market potential.* **2** qualities that exist and can be developed: *We try to help all our employees* ***realize their full potential.***

**POTS** /pɒts; *AmE* pɑːts/ *abbr* (*IT*) **plain old telephone service** used to describe a standard telephone service rather than a very fast one

**pound** /paʊnd/ *n.* **1** [C] the unit of money in the UK and several other countries; £ **2 the pound** [sing.] the value of the British pound compared with the value of the money of other countries: *The euro fell 1% against the pound.* **3** (*abbr* **lb**) [C] a unit for measuring weight, equal to 0.454 of a kilogram

**power** /'paʊə(r)/ *n.*, *v.*, *adj.*

• ***n.*** **1** [U] the ability to control or influence people, things, events, etc: *She has the power* **to** *hire and fire.* **2** [U] (*used to form compound ns*) strength or influence in a particular area of activity: *the growing economic power of women consumers* **3** [C] a powerful country, organization or person that has a lot of influence: *one of the major powers in the world of IT* **4** [U] energy that can be used to operate a machine, to make electricity, etc: *solar power* **5** [U] the public supply of electricity: *There was a power cut.* **6** [U] the ability of a machine, an engine, etc. to do work: *computing power*

• ***v.*** [T] to supply a machine or vehicle with the energy that makes it work: *The aircraft is powered by a jet engine.* PHR V **ˌpower sth 'up** to prepare a

machine to start working by supplying it with electricity, etc: *I need to power up my laptop.*
• *adj.* **1** operated by a motor, electricity, etc: *power tools* **2** used to describe sth that shows you have an important position in a company

**'power brand** *n.* [C] (*Market.*) a very important and well-known brand, for example, one that has a large share of the market or that has been made and sold for a long time

**-powered** /'paʊəd; *AmE* 'paʊərd/ *adj.* (*used in compounds*) using the type of energy mentioned: *battery-powered toys*

**powerhouse** /'paʊəhaʊs; *AmE* 'paʊərh-/ *n.* [C] **1** a group or an organization that has a lot of power: *a media powerhouse* **2** a person who is very strong and full of energy

**'power lunch** *n.* [C] an occasion when business is discussed or deals made during lunch

**'power nap** *n.* [C] a short sleep sb has while they are working in order to get back their energy ▸ **'power-nap** *v.* [I] (**-pp-**)

**ˌpower of at'torney** (*also* **ˌletter of at'torney**) *n.* [U,C] (*pl.* **powers -, letters -**) (*Law*) the right to act as the representative of sb in business or financial matters; a document that gives sb this right

**PowerPoint™** /'paʊəpɔɪnt; *AmE* 'paʊər-/ *n.* [U] a computer program produced by Microsoft™ for creating presentations for an audience: *I did my talk* **on** *PowerPoint?* ◇ *a PowerPoint* **presentation** ▸ **'powerpoint** *v.* [T]: *powerpointed presentations*

**'power ˌstation** (*also* **'power plant**) *n.* [C] a building or group of buildings where electricity is produced

**pp** *abbr* (*written*) **1** (*BrE also* **pp.**) pages **2** (*BrE also* **p.p.**) used in front of a person's name when sb signs a business letter on his/her behalf: *pp Tim Walker*

**ppd** *abbr* (*written*) **1** prepaid **2** post-paid; postpaid: *All CDs cost $12 ppd (US).*

**PPI** /ˌpiː piː 'aɪ/ = PRODUCER PRICE INDEX

**ppm** /ˌpiː piː 'em/ *abbr* **part(s) per million 1** (*Tech.*) a measurement of how much of a substance a liquid or other substance contains: *air with 50 ppm nitrogen dioxide* **2** (*Product.*) a measurement of how efficient a manufacturing process is, which records the number of DEFECTS found in each million parts produced: *We aim for a quality level of 3ppm in our production line.*

**PPP** /ˌpiː piː 'piː/ = PURCHASING POWER PARITY, PUBLIC-PRIVATE PARTNERSHIP

★ **PR** /ˌpiː 'ɑː(r)/ *abbr* (*Market.*)
**1 public relations** the business of giving the public information about a particular organization or person in order to create a good impression: *She's in PR.*
⊕ *a ~* ***agency/company/department/firm*** ♦ *a ~* ***consultant/executive/manager*** ♦ ***good/bad*** *~*
**2** = PRESS RELATIONS

★ **practice** /'præktɪs/ *n., v.*
• *n.* **1** [U] action rather than ideas: ***putting*** *new ideas* ***into*** *practice*
**2** [U,C] a way of doing sth that is the usual or expected way in a particular organization or situation: *guidelines for good practice* ◇ *a review of pay and working practices*
⊕ ***bad*** *~* ♦ ***common/current/standard/usual*** *~* ♦ ***accounting/business/management*** *~s* ♦ ***employment/labour*** *~s* ♦ *to* ***adopt/follow/introduce/use*** *~s*
**3** [C] a thing that is done regularly; a habit or a custom: *the practice of giving workers a say in how their company is run* **4** [U,C] the work or the business of some professional people; the place where they work: *My solicitor is no longer in practice.* ◇ *a successful law practice*
⊕ *a* ***dental/legal/medical*** *~* ♦ *a* ***group/private*** *~* ♦ *to* ***go into/set up in*** *~* ♦ *to* ***run/set up/start*** *a ~* ♦ *to* ***join/leave*** *a ~*
• *v.* (*AmE*) = PRACTISE

**practiced** = PRACTISED

**practicing** = PRACTISING

**'practicing ˌlicense** = PRACTISING CERTIFICATE

**practicum** /'præktɪkəm/ = PLACEMENT (2)

★ **practise** (*AmE* **practice**) /'præktɪs/ *v.* **1** [T] to do sth regularly as part of your normal behaviour: *The company practises Total Quality Management.* **2** [T,I] to work as a doctor, lawyer, etc: *There are over a thousand lawyers practising in the city.*

**practised** (*AmE* **practiced**) /'præktɪst/ *adj.* good at doing sth because you have been doing it regularly: *She is a practised negotiator.*

**practising** (*AmE* **practicing**) /'præktɪsɪŋ/ *adj.* taking an active part in a particular profession, etc: *a practising lawyer*

**'practising cerˌtificate** (*BrE*) (*AmE* **'practicing ˌlicense**) *n.* [C] an official document that proves that a professional person is qualified and has the right to work in their profession

**practitioner** /ˌpræk'tɪʃənə(r)/ *n.* [C] **1** a person who is qualified to work in a profession, esp. medicine or law: *a medical/legal* ~ **2** a person who regularly does a particular activity or follows a particular theory

**pre-** /priː/ *prefix* (*used in vs, ns and adjs*) before: *pretest* ◇ *pre-tax*

**ˌpre-addressed 'envelope** (*also* **preaddressed**, *esp. in AmE*) *n.* [C] an envelope with the address already printed on it that is sent with sth to make it easy to reply

**ˌpre-ap'proach** (*also* **preapproach**, *esp. in AmE*) *n.* [C,U] (*Market.*) the activities that a SALESPERSON does before they meet a possible customer: *What is the objective of your pre-approach?*

**preˌcarious em'ployment** *n.* [U] (*HR*) the situation when sb is working on a temporary contract or has no guarantee that they will keep their job

**precaution** /prɪ'kɔːʃn/ *n.* [C, usu. pl.] something that is done in advance in order to prevent problems or to avoid danger: *safety precautions* ▸ **pre'cautionary** /-ʃənri; *AmE* -ʃəneri/ *adj.*

**precedence** /'presɪdəns/ *n.* [U] the condition of being more important than sb/sth else and therefore coming or being dealt with first: *In the fashion industry, quality **takes precedence over** price.* → PRIORITY

**precedent** /'presɪdənt/ *n.* [C,U] an official action or decision that has happened in the past and that is seen as an example or a rule to be followed in a similar situation later: *The judgement set a precedent for similar legal cases.*
**●** *to **create/establish/provide/serve as** a* ~ • *to **base sth on/follow** a* ~

**precinct** /'priːsɪŋkt/ *n.* [C] (*BrE*) a commercial area in a town where cars cannot go: *a shopping precinct*

**precision** /prɪ'sɪʒn/ *n.* [U] the quality of being exact and accurate: ~ *instruments/tools*

**preˌcision engi'neering** *n.* [U] the activity of designing and making machines, etc. containing parts that need to be made very accurately

**precondition** /ˌpriːkən'dɪʃn/ *n.* [C] sth that must happen or exist before sth else can exist or be done

**predator** /'predətə(r)/ *n.* [C] (in newspapers) a company that uses weaker companies to its own advantage, for example by trying to buy them
▸ **'predatory** /-tri; *AmE* -tɔːri/ *adj.*

**ˌpredatory 'lending** *n.* [U] (*Finan.*) a situation where a financial organization lends money in an unfair or illegal way, for example to people who they know will probably not be able to pay back the debt
▸ **ˌpredatory 'lender** *n.* [C]

**ˌpredatory 'pricing** (*also* **ˌpredatory 'price-cutting**) *n.* [U] (*Econ.*) a situation where a company makes its prices very low, even though this will lose money, so that other companies cannot compete and have to stop selling similar goods or services ▸ **ˌpredatory 'price** *n.* [C]

**predecessor** /'priːdəsesə(r); *AmE* 'pre-/ *n.* [C] **1** a person who did a job before sb else **2** a thing, such as a machine, that has been followed or replaced by sth else

★**predict** /prɪ'dɪkt/ *v.* [T] to say that sth will happen in the future: *Many analysts are predicting a rise in interest rates.* SYN FORECAST

**predictable** /prɪ'dɪktəbl/ *adj.* if sth is **predictable**, you know in advance that it will happen or what it will be like: *Revenues have become less predictable.* ▸ **preˌdicta'bility** /-'bɪləti/ *n.* [U] **pre'dictably** /-bli/ *adv.*: *Prices were predictably high.*

**prediction** /prɪ'dɪkʃn/ *n.* [C,U] a statement that says what you think will happen; the act of making such a statement: *The sales figures confirmed our predictions.*

**pre-empt** (*also* **preempt**, *esp. in AmE*) /pri'empt/ *v.* [T] **1** to prevent sth from happening by taking action to stop it: *A good training course will pre-empt many problems.* **2** to buy goods, shares, etc. before the opportunity is given to other people **3** to do or say sth before sb else does
▸ **pre-'emptive** (*also* **preemptive**, *esp. in AmE*) /-tɪv/ *adj.*: *a pre-emptive right to buy the shares*

**pre-emption** (*also* **preemption**, *esp. in AmE*) /pri'empʃn/ *n.* [U] (*Law*) the opportunity given to one person or group to buy goods, shares, etc. before other people: *Existing shareholders will have pre-emption rights.*

**ˌpre-ex'ceptional** *adj.* (*Account.*) used to describe a company's profits that have been calculated without including unusual items of income or expenses

**pref.** *abbr* (*Finan., written*) (used about a share) preference; preferred

★ **preference** /ˈprefrəns/ *n.* **1** [U; sing.] a greater interest in or desire for sth/sb than sth/sb else: *Investors have a strong preference **for** bonds rather than shares.* **2** [C] a thing that is liked better or best: *consumer preferences* IDM **give (a) preference to sb/sth** to treat sb/sth in a way that gives them an advantage over other people or things: *Preference will be given to candidates with some knowledge of Spanish.*

**ˈpreference ˌcapital** (*also* **ˌpreference ˈshare ˌcapital**) (*both esp. BrE*) (*AmE usu.* **preˌferred ˈcapital**) *n.* [U] (*Finan.*) money that is raised by a company selling PREFERENCE SHARES

**ˈpreference ˌdividend** (*esp. BrE*) (*AmE usu.* **preˌferred ˈdividend**) *n.* [C] (*Finan.*) the fixed DIVIDEND that is paid to holders of PREFERENCE SHARES

**ˈpreference share** *n.* [C] (*esp. BrE*) (*AmE usu.* **preˌferred ˈstock** [U,C]) (*also* **preˌferred ˈshare** [C] *BrE, AmE*) (*Finan.*) a type of share in a company that gives the owner the right to receive DIVIDENDS, but does not usu. give them the right to vote at meetings of shareholders. People who hold them must be paid before owners of all other shares.

**ˌpreference ˈshare ˌcapital** = PREFERENCE CAPITAL

**preferential** /ˌprefəˈrenʃl/ *adj.* giving an advantage to a particular person or group: *Small sugar exporters may lose their preferential access to the EU.*

**ˌpreferential ˈcreditor** *n.* [C] (*Finan.*) a person or company whose debt must be paid before others if a business fails

**preferred** /prɪˈfɜːd; *AmE* -ˈfɜːrd/ *adj.* (*Finan.*) **1** a company's **preferred** investors are those who are paid first if the company has financial difficulties or fails: *a ~ creditor/investor/shareholder* **2** used to describe investments held by these investors or the money they receive from them: *preferred securities*

**preˌferred ˈcapital** = PREFERENCE CAPITAL

**preˌferred ˈdividend** = PREFERENCE DIVIDEND

**preˌferred ˈshare** = PREFERENCE SHARE

**preˌferred ˈstock** = PREFERENCE SHARE

**preˌferred ˈvendor** (*also* **preˌferred supˈplier, apˌproved ˈvendor**) *n.* [C] (*Product.*) a business that has an agreement to supply another business with goods or services, or has met any necessary requirements

**prejudice** /ˈpredʒudɪs/ *n., v.*
• ***n.*** [U,C] an unreasonable dislike of a person or group of people, esp. when it is based on their race, religion, sex, etc: *There is little prejudice **against** workers from other EU states.*
• ***v.*** [T] **1** to influence sb so that they have an unfair or unreasonable opinion about sb/sth: *A poorly written email may prejudice the reader **against** you.* **2** to have a harmful effect on sth: *The long strike is prejudicing the company's future.*
▸ **ˈprejudiced** *adj.*

**preliminary** /prɪˈlɪmɪnəri; *AmE* -neri/ *adj.* happening before a more important action or event: *The figures are preliminary results only.*

**preˌliminary inˈjunction** = INTERIM INJUNCTION

**ˌpre-ˈmarket** (*also* **ˌpre-ˈopen**) *adj.* (*Finan.*) **pre-market** trading takes place before the stock markets open officially ▸ **ˌpre-ˈmarket** *adv.*

**premier** /ˈpremiə(r); *AmE* prɪˈmɪr; -ˈmjɪr/ *adj.* most important or successful: *plans to develop and improve our premier product*

**premises** /ˈpremɪsɪz/ *n.* [pl.] the buildings and land that a business owns or uses: *business/commercial ~* ◇ *The food is made **on the premises**.*

★ **premium** /ˈpriːmiəm/ *n., adj.*
• ***n.*** [C] **1** (*Insur.*) an amount of money that you pay once or regularly for insurance: *a monthly premium of $20* **2** (*Comm.*) an extra payment added to the basic rate: *Customers will pay a premium for superior service.* **3** (*HR*) (*also* **ˈpremium pay** [U]) extra money that is added to employees' basic pay for particular reasons, for example if they work at weekends or away from home
IDM **at a ˈpremium 1** if sth is at a premium, there is little of it available and it is difficult to get: *Parking here is at a premium.* **2 ~ (to sth)** (*Finan.*) at a higher than normal price: *Their shares trade at a premium to most of their rivals.* **put/place/set a premium on sb/sth** to think that sb/sth is particularly important or valuable: *They place a high premium on creativity.*
• ***adj.*** **1** very high and higher than usual: *to charge premium prices* **2** of high quality: *We are positioning the coffee as a premium product.*

**ˈpremium ˌincome** *n.* [U] (*Insur.*) the total amount of money that an insurance company gets from its customers

**ˈpremium pay** = PREMIUM *n.* (3)

**ˌpre-ˈopen** = PRE-MARKET

**ˌpre-ˈowned** *adj.* (*AmE*) that has belonged to or been used by sb else before SYN SECOND-HAND

**ˌpre-ˈpackaged** (*AmE* **prepackaged**) *adj.* **1** (*Comm.*) (*BrE also* **ˌpre-ˈpacked**) **pre-packaged** goods, esp. food, are wrapped before being sent to shops/stores to be sold **2** (*Comm.*) **pre-packaged** services are sold as a whole rather than in separate parts **3** (*Finan.*) **pre-packaged** financial arrangements for a business that is in difficulty are agreed before the business is made officially BANKRUPT

**prepaid** /ˌpriːˈpeɪd/ *adj.* (*abbr* **ppd**) **1** (*Comm.*) paid for in advance: *The prepaid cash card allows customers to order over the Web without a credit card.* **2** a **prepaid** envelope has already had the cost of posting paid

**prepay** /ˌpriːˈpeɪ/ *v., adj.*

• ***v.*** (**-paid, -paid** /-ˈpeɪd/) **1** (*Comm.*) [T,I] to pay for sth before you get it or use it: *Some customers prepay* ***for*** *electricity.* **2** (*Finan.*) [T] if you **prepay** a loan, you pay it back before you have to ▶ **ˌpreˈpayable** /-ˈpeɪəbl/ *adj.* **ˌpreˈpayment** /-mənt/ *n.* [C,U]: *the prepayment of rent*

• ***adj.*** (*BrE*) (*Comm.*) **prepay** goods and services are paid for before you get them or use them: *prepay phones* ▶ **ˈprepay** *n.* [U]

★ **present** /prɪˈzent/ *v.* [T] **1** to show or offer sth for other people to consider: *The business plan will be presented* ***to*** *the board tomorrow.* **2** to give sb a cheque or bill that they should pay: *A cheque presented by Mr Jones was returned by the bank.*

★ **presentation** /ˌpreznˈteɪʃn; *AmE* ˌpriːzen-/ *n.* **1** [C] a talk or speech in which sth, esp. a new product or idea, is shown or explained to a group of people; a meeting when this happens: *the company's annual results presentation*

⊙ *to* ***deliver/give/make/prepare*** *a ~* ♦ *a* ***sales/strategy*** *~*

**2** [U] the way in which sth is offered, shown, explained, etc. to others: *improving the product's presentation* (= the way it is wrapped, advertised, etc.) **3** (*fml.*) [U] the act of presenting or giving sth to sb

**ˈpresent ˈdiscounted ˈvalue** = PRESENT VALUE

**presenteeism** /ˌprezənˈtiːɪzəm/ *n.* [U] (*HR*) staying longer at work than you need to, esp. so that people will think you work very hard

**ˌpresent ˈvalue** (*also* **ˈpresent ˈdiscounted ˈvalue**) *n.* [U,C] (*abbr* **PV**) (*Account.*) the value now of a particular amount of money that you expect to receive in the future, calculated by taking away the amount of interest likely to be earned between now and the future date

★ **president** /ˈprezɪdənt/ (*also* **President**) *n.* [C] **1** (*also* **ˌcompany ˈpresident**) (*both esp. AmE*) the person who leads a company and is responsible for deciding on policy, esp. one who leads a group of people that manage different parts of it, usu. under the authority of a CHIEF EXECUTIVE OFFICER NOTE In some companies the **president** is the same person as the **CEO**. **2** (*esp. AmE*) in some large companies, a person who is responsible for a part of the business: *AOL's ~* ***of/for*** *technology* **3** the person in charge of some organizations, clubs, colleges, etc: *the President of the European Central Bank*

**press** /pres/ *n., v.*

• ***n.*** **1** (*often* **the Press**) [sing. with sing./pl. verb] newspapers and magazines, and the people who work on them: *the financial press* ◇ *The press were invited to the launch.* **2** [U; sing.] the type or amount of reports that newspapers write about sb/sth: *The industry has had a lot of* ***bad press.*** **3** (*Manufact.*) [C] a business that prints and publishes books: *Oxford University Press* **4** (*Manufact.*) [C] a machine for printing books, newspapers, etc.; the process of printing them: *The prices were correct at the time of* ***going to press.***

• ***v.*** **1** [T,I] to make strong efforts to persuade sb to do sth: *The unions are pressing* ***for*** *a 6% pay rise.* SYN PUSH FOR STH **2** [T] to express or repeat sth with force: *to press your claim*

**ˈpress ˌagent** *n.* [C] a person whose job is to supply information and advertising material about a particular company, actor, etc. to newspapers, radio or television

**ˈpress communiˌcations** *n.* [pl.] (*Market.*) information or activities that are intended to make the media more aware of a product, service or company

**ˈpress ˌconference** (*esp. BrE*) (*AmE usu.* **ˈnews ˌconference**) *n.* [C] a meeting at which sb talks to a group of journalists in order to answer their questions or to make an official statement: *to give/hold a ~*

**'press kit** *n.* [C] (*Market.*) a set of documents, photographs, etc. that advertise or give information about a particular product and are given to the media

**'press ˌoffice** *n.* [C] the office of a large organization that answers questions from journalists and provides information ▸ **'press ˌofficer** *n.* [C]

**'press reˌlations** *n.* [U] (*abbr* **PR**) (*Market.*) the process of developing relationships with journalists and other people who work in the media in order to make a company or its products known to the public: *a press relations adviser to the company*

**'press reˌlease** (*also* **'news reˌlease**) (*also* **re'lease**, *less freq.*) *n.* [C] an official statement made to journalists, etc. by a large organization: *to issue/publish/put out a ~*

**'pressure group** *n.* [C] a group of people who try to influence the government, people with power in organizations and the opinions of ordinary people in order to achieve the action they want, for example a change in a law

**prestige** /pre'stiːʒ/ *n., adj.*
• ***n.*** [U] the respect and admiration that sb/sth has because of their success, good quality, or social importance: *the prestige of British industry* ◇ *jobs with* ***low/high*** *prestige* ◇ *to enjoy/have/lack ~* ▸ **prestigious** /pre'stɪdʒəs/ *adj.*: *prestigious clients*
• ***adj.*** **1** admired and respected because of looking important and expensive: *prestige products* SYN LUXURY **2** bringing respect and admiration; important: *a ~ job/project*

**presumption** /prɪ'zʌmpʃn/ *n.* [U,C] (*Law*) the act of supposing that sth is true, although it has not yet been proved or is not certain: *the presumption of innocence*

**ˌpre-'tax** (*also* **pretax**, *esp. in AmE*) *adj.* (*Account.*) before tax has been taken away: *~ earnings/income/losses/profits*

**pretest** /ˌpriː'test/ *v.* [T] to test a product or an advertisement before making it available or using it, to make sure it is safe or effective ▸ **'pretest** *n.* [C] **ˌpre'testing** *n.* [U]

**prevailing** /prɪ'veɪlɪŋ/ *adj.* existing or most common at a particular time: *the prevailing conditions*

**prevalent** /'prevələnt/ *adj.* that exists or is very common at a particular time or in a particular place: *This trend may become more prevalent.* ▸ **'prevalence** /-əns/ *n.* [U]

**ˌpre-'vet** *v.* [T,I] (-tt-) (*often pass.*) the process of finding out information about sb/sth to see if they are suitable before using them/it: *a pre-vetted, or 'approved', contractor* ▸ **ˌpre-'vetting** *n.* [U]

**preview** /'priːvjuː/ = PRINT PREVIEW

**prey** /preɪ/ *n., v.*
• ***n.*** [U; sing.] **1** a person who is harmed or deceived by sb, esp. for dishonest purposes: *Elderly people are* ***easy prey*** *for dishonest salesmen.* **2** (esp. in newspapers) a company that another company wants to buy, esp. when the first one is weak or does not want to be bought: *The group may become prey to a bigger rival.* SYN TARGET COMPANY → PREDATOR IDM **be/fall 'prey to sth** (*fml.*) **1** to be harmed or affected by sth bad: *The rebuilding programme fell prey to cutbacks.* **2** (about a company) to be bought by another company
• ***v.*** PHR V **'prey on/upon sb** to harm sb who is weaker than you, or make use of them in a dishonest way to get what you want: *lenders who prey on people with debt problems*

★**price** /praɪs/ *n., v.*
• ***n.*** [C,U] the amount of money you must pay for sth: *house/retail/share ~s* ◇ *We sold 10 000 units at a price of €15 each.* ◇ *The price charged to customers may be changed.* ◇ *Computers have come down* ***in price.***
✪ *a* ***competitive/high/low/reasonable*** *~* ♦ ***falling/rising*** *~s* ♦ *to* ***increase/put up/raise*** *~s* ♦ *to* ***cut/lower/slash*** *~s*
IDM **at a 'price** costing a lot of money: *You can buy strawberries in the winter, but at a price.* **put a 'price on sth** to say how much money sth valuable is worth → idiom at BALLPARK
• ***v.*** [T] **1** (*Market.*) (*usu. pass.*) to fix the price of sth at a particular level: *The new model will be priced* ***at*** *$10 000–$15 000.* ◇ *attractively/competitively/keenly/reasonably priced* **2** (*Comm.*) **~ sth (up)** to write or stick tickets on goods to show how much they cost: *I spent all day pricing tins of fruit.* **3 ~ sth (up)** to compare the prices of different types of the same thing: *We priced various models before buying this one.* IDM **price yourself/sth out of the 'market** to charge such a high price for your goods, services, etc. that nobody wants to buy them PHR V **ˌprice sth ˌin; ˌprice sth 'into sth** (*Finan.*) to include sth when you are fixing the

price of an item: *The bad news is already priced into the shares.*

**ˈprice compeˌtition** *n.* [U] (*Econ.*; *Market.*) a situation in which companies compete with each other to sell products by trying to keep their prices lower than the prices of similar goods and services produced by other companies

**ˈprice conˌtrol** *n.* [C, usu. pl., U] (*Econ.*) limits that a government or an official organization puts on the amount companies can charge for goods and services

**ˈprice cut** *n.* [C] a reduction in the price of sth ▸ **ˈprice-ˌcutting** *n.* [U]: *a price-cutting war*

**ˈprice discrimiˌnation** *n.* [U] (*Econ.*; *Market.*) the practice of selling the same product to different types of customers at different prices

**ˌprice-ˈdividend ˌratio** *n.* [C] (*abbr* **PDR, P/D ratio**) (*Account.*) the relationship between the present market price of the shares of a particular company and the DIVIDEND for the previous year, used to compare different companies

**ˌprice-ˈearnings ˌratio** (*also* **ˌprice-to-ˈearnings ˌratio**) (*abbr* **P/E ratio**) (*also* **ˌprice-ˈearnings ˌmultiple** *abbr* **P/E multiple**) *n.* [C] (*Account.*) the relationship between the present market price of shares in a particular company and the EARNINGS PER SHARE, used to analyse the company's performance over a period of time or compare it with others

**ˈprice efˌfect** *n.* [C] (*Econ.*) **1** the way in which sth that happens affects the prices of goods: *the price effect of the merger* **2** the way in which a change in the price of a product changes demand for it

**ˈprice elasˈticity of deˈmand** (*also* **ˌprice elasˈticity, ˌown-price elasˈticity**) = ELASTICITY OF DEMAND

**ˈprice-ˌfixing** (*also* **ˌcommon ˈpricing**) *n.* [U] (*Econ.*) the practice of companies agreeing to sell the same goods for the same price, which is illegal in many countries

**ˈprice ˌindex** *n.* [C, usu. sing.] (*Econ.*) a figure that shows the change in the price of sth over a period of time: *a monthly house price index*

**ˌprice-inˈsensitive** *adj.* **1** (*Econ.*) if sales of goods and services are **price-insensitive**, the quantity sold does not change when prices go down or up **2** (*Market.*) **price-insensitive** customers are not influenced by price when buying things OPP PRICE-SENSITIVE ▸ **ˌprice-insensiˈtivity** *n.* [U]



**ˌprice ˈleader** *n.* [C] (*Market.*) a business that is usu. the first to reduce or increase prices ▸ **ˌprice ˈleadership** *n.* [U]

**priceless** /ˈpraɪsləs/ *adj.* extremely valuable or important: *Customer loyalty is a priceless asset.*

**ˈprice ˌlevel** *n.* [C] (*Econ.*) the average prices of goods and services in a country or an area at a particular time

**ˈprice list** *n.* [C] (*Comm.*) a list of prices for goods or services that a business provides for its customers

**ˈprice ˌmechanism** (*also* **ˈmarket ˌmechanism**) *n.* [sing.] (*Econ.*) the way in which changes in prices influence the production of goods and services and those who receive them: *The market relies on the price mechanism to balance supply and demand.*

**ˈprice point** *n.* [C] (*Market.*) the price that a product is sold for, chosen from a range of possible prices: *The product sells at an attractive price point.*

**ˈprice range** *n.* [C, usu. sing.] **1** a group of prices that are close together, often within fixed limits: *the higher/lower/middle* ~ **2** (*Stock Ex.*) the price at which a share is offered for sale: *a price range of $1.25 to $1.52 a share* **3** the amount that a person can afford to pay for something: *This is **out of my price range**.*

**ˈprice ring** = CARTEL

**ˌprice-ˈsensitive** *adj.* **1** (*Econ.*) if sales of goods and services are **price-sensitive**, the quantity sold increases or decreases when prices go down or up OPP PRICE-INSENSITIVE **2** (*Market.*) **price-sensitive** customers are influenced mainly by price when buying things OPP PRICE-INSENSITIVE **3** (*Finan.*) **price-sensitive** information could affect prices, esp. share prices ▸ **ˌprice sensiˈtivity** *n.* [U]

**ˈprice supˌport** *n.* [U] (*Econ.*) a system in which a government helps producers, esp. farmers, by acting to stop the price of goods falling below a particular level

**ˈprice tag** *n.* [C, usu. sing.] **1** a label showing the price of an item that is for sale in a shop/store **2** the cost of sth, esp. when this is high: *The business is for sale with a price tag of more than $50 m.*

**ˌprice ˈtaker** *n.* [C] (*Econ.*) a company or person that has little power over the price at which sth sells

**ˌprice-to-ˈearnings ˌratio** = PRICE-EARNINGS RATIO

**pricey** (*also* **pricy**) /ˈpraɪsi/ *adj.* (**pricier**, **priciest**) (*infml.*) expensive: *At $1 000, the product is too pricey.* SYN DEAR

★ **pricing** /ˈpraɪsɪŋ/ *n.* [U] (*Comm.*; *Econ.*) the prices that a company charges for its products or services; the act of deciding what they should be: *They are trying to win back customers with competitive pricing.* ⊙ *aggressive/fair/unfair ~ • ~ policies/practices/strategies • a ~ structure/system*

**ˈpricing ˌmodel** *n.* [C] (*Comm.*) a system that a company uses to decide what to charge for its products or services

**ˈpricing ˌpower** *n.* [U] (*Econ.*) the effect that a change in the price of a company's products has on the quantity demanded

**pricy** = PRICEY

**primary** /ˈpraɪməri; *AmE* -meri/ *adj.* **1** main; most important: *Their primary business is life insurance.* **2** used to describe sth that is not caused by or based on sth else: *primary source materials* **3** (*Finan.*) relating to shares, bonds, etc. that are being sold for the first time: *the primary bond market* → SECONDARY

**ˌprimary ˈaction** *n.* [U] (*HR*) action such as stopping work that is taken by workers in a factory, company, etc. who are involved in a dispute with their employers

**ˌprimary ˈdata** *n.* [U] (*Market.*) information that a company collects itself, rather than getting from other sources

**ˌprimary ˈdealer** *n.* [C] (*Econ.*) a financial institution that is allowed to deal directly with a country's central bank

**ˌprimary deˈmand** *n.* [U,C] (*Market.*) the desire of consumers for a type of product rather than for a particular brand

**ˈprimary ˌindustry** *n.* [U,C] (*Econ.*) industry that produces and collects things like crops, metals, raw materials, etc.

**ˈprimary ˌmarket** *n.* [C] (*Stock Ex.*) the section of the money market where shares, bonds, etc. are sold for the first time

**ˌprimary ˈmortgage ˌmarket** = MORTGAGE MARKET (1)

**ˌprimary proˈduction** *n.* [U] (*Econ.*) the production and collection of crops and raw materials, rather than making goods from them

**the ˈprimary ˌsector** *n.* [sing.] (*Econ.*) the part of a country's economy that collects or produces crops, raw materials, etc.

**prime** /praɪm/ *adj.*, *n.*, *v.*
• ***adj.* 1** main; most important: *The care of the environment is of prime importance.* SYN PRIMARY **2** of the best quality: *prime office space* **3** typical: *a prime example of the problem*
• ***n.*** IDM **above/below ˈprime** (*AmE*) (*Finan.*) an interest rate that is **above** or **below prime** is higher or lower than the PRIME RATE
• ***v.*** [T] IDM **prime the ˈpump** to encourage the growth of sth such as a new business or a weak economy

**ˌprime conˈtractor** *n.* [C] the **contractor** who has direct contact with the company that needs work done

**ˌprime ˈcost** (*also* **ˌfirst ˈcost**) *n.* [C,U] (*Account.*) the cost of sth calculated by adding the cost of materials used to make it and the cost of paying sb to make it, but not including OVERHEADS SYN DIRECT COST

**ˈprime rate** (*also* **ˌprime ˈinterest rate**, **ˌprime ˈlending rate**) *n.* [C] (*all esp. AmE*) (*Finan.*) the lowest interest rate at which businesses can borrow money from a bank SYN BASE RATE

**ˈprime time** (*BrE also* **ˈpeak time**, **ˌpeak ˈviewing time**) *n.* [U] the time when the largest number of people are watching television or listening to the radio, usu. the middle part of the evening

**principal** /ˈprɪnsəpl/ *n.*, *adj.*
• ***n.* 1** (*Finan.*) [sing; U] an amount of money that is lent or invested to earn interest: *interest and principal payments* **2** (*Law*) [C] a person who is making a business deal or taking part in a legal case, rather than sb who is acting on their behalf **3** [C] an important manager or other person in an organization, who usu. has legal responsibility for what the organization does: *The company's three principals are women.*
• ***adj.* 1** most important; main: *the principal markets for our products* **2** (*Finan.*) relating to an original amount of money that is lent or invested, rather than any interest: *the principal amount*

**ˌprincipal ˈtrading** = PROPRIETARY TRADING

**principle** /ˈprɪnsəpl/ *n.* [C] **1** a law, rule or theory that sth is based on: *the principles of banking* **2** a general or scientific law that explains how sth works or why sth happens: *the principle that heat rises* SYN LAW (5) IDM **in ˈprinciple 1** if sth can be done **in principle**, there is no reason why it should not be done although it has not been done yet **2** in general but not in detail: *They reached an agreement in principle.*

**print** /prɪnt/ *v., n.*

• *v.* **1** [T,I] to produce letters, pictures, etc. on paper using a machine that puts ink on the surface: *to print a copy of a document* ◇ *Click on the icon when you want to print.* **2** [T] to produce books, newspapers, etc. by printing them in large quantities **3** [T] to publish sth in printed form: *Parts of the report were printed in several newspapers.* **4** [T] to write without joining the letters together: *Print your name and address in the box.*
→ idioms at LICENCE, WORTH *adj.*
▸ **ˈprinting** *n.* [U,C]: *the ~ trade/industry* ◇ *None of his books has had a second printing.* PHRV **ˌprint sth ˈoff/ˈout** to produce a document or information from a computer in printed form **ˌprint sth ˈup** to produce sth in printed form, esp. quickly or in large quantities

• *n.* [U] **1** letters, words, numbers, etc. that have been printed onto paper **2** used to refer to the business of producing newspapers, magazines and books: *print and online media*
IDM **in ˈprint/ˌout of ˈprint** (about a book) still available/not available from the company that published it

**ˈprint ˌadvertising** *n.* [U] (*Market.*) the act of using newspapers, magazines, etc. to advertise a company and its products; the advertisements that are used ▸ **ˈprint ad** (*also* **ˈprint adˌvertisement**, *fml.*) *n.* [C]

**printer** /ˈprɪntə(r)/ *n.* [C] **1** a machine for printing on paper, esp. one that is connected to a computer **2** a person or company whose job is printing books, etc.

**printout** /ˈprɪntaʊt/ *n.* [C] a page or set of pages with printing on it produced by a computer

**ˈprint ˌpreview** (*also* **ˈpreview**) *n.* [C,U] (*IT*) a feature of some computer programs that allows you to see how a document or drawing will look when you print it

**prior** /ˈpraɪə(r)/ *adj.* **1** happening or existing before sth else or before a particular time: *Sales grew 8% over the prior year.*
⊕ *~ **approval/knowledge/notice*** ◆ *the ~ **month/quarter/week*** ◆ *a ~ **arrangement/engagement***
**2 ~ to** (*fml.*) before sth: *during the week prior to the meeting*

★ **prioritize, -ise** /praɪˈɒrətaɪz; *AmE* -ˈɔːr-; -ˈɑːr-/ *v.* [T,I] to put tasks, problems, etc. in order of importance, so that you can deal with the most important first: *Use folders to prioritize your work.*

★ **priority** /praɪˈɒrəti; *AmE* -ˈɔːr-; -ˈɑːr-/ (*pl.* **-ties**) *n.* **1** [C] something that you think is more important than other things and should be dealt with first: *Reducing costs is our top priority.*
⊕ *your **first/main/number one** ~* ◆ *a **high/key/low** ~*
**2** [U] the most important place among various things that have to be done or among a group of people: *We give priority **to** training and customer service.* ◇ *to be given/have/take ~ (over sth/sb)* SYN PRECEDENCE

**priˈority claim** *n.* [C] (*Law*) a right that a company or person has to be paid money owed to them by a BANKRUPT company before others

**privacy** /ˈprɪvəsi; *AmE* ˈpraɪv-/ *n.* [U] the right to keep some information private: *Nearly all commercial websites now have a privacy policy.*
⊕ *to **preserve/protect/respect** sb's ~* ◆ *to **invade/violate** sb's ~* ◆ *an **invasion** of ~* ◆ *~ **law/legislation/rules***

★ **private** /ˈpraɪvət/ *adj.* **1** owned, managed or provided by an individual person or an independent company, rather than by the state: *a private law firm* OPP PUBLIC **2** working or acting for yourself rather than for the state or for an organization or a company: *working as a private IT consultant* **3** belonging to or for the use of a particular person or group; not for public use: *This car park is private.* OPP PUBLIC **4** (*Comm.*; *Finan.*) sold only to particular people or organizations; not offered to the public in general to buy: *a private sale of $1.25 billion of shares* OPP PUBLIC **5** intended for or involving a particular person or group of people; not for people in general to attend or know about: *a private meeting* ◇ *The letter was marked 'Private'.* OPP PUBLIC **6** not connected with your work or official position: *You should not make private calls from the office.* SYN PERSONAL ▸ **ˈprivately** *adv.*: *a privately funded organization* ◇ *Can we speak privately?* IDM **go ˈprivate; take a company ˈprivate** (*Finan.*) if a company whose shares are sold on the stock market **goes private**, it becomes independent by buying back shares from shareholders; to make a company independent in this way

**ˌprivate ˈbank** *n.* [C] **1** a bank that offers personal services in managing investments and assets to individuals and families with a lot of money **2** a bank that is not a member of a CLEARING HOUSE **3** a bank that is not owned by the state ► ˌ**private 'banking** *n.* [U]

ˌ**private 'brand** *n.* [C] (*Comm.; Market.*) a product sold by a particular supplier or shop/store with its own name on SYN HOUSE BRAND

ˌ**private 'company** (*also* '**private 'limited 'company**) (*both esp. BrE*) (*AmE usu.* ˌ**private corpo'ration**) *n.* [C] a business that may not offer its shares for sale to the public

ˌ**private 'enterprise** *n.* **1** [U] the economic system in which industry or business is owned by individuals and independent companies and is not controlled by the government **2** [C] a business that is owned by individuals or other companies, not by the government

ˌ**private 'equity** *n.* [U] (*Finan.*) shares that are held by companies or investors in new or small companies whose shares are not available for the public to buy and sell on the stock market

ˌ**private 'income** *n.* [U,C] money that you receive from property or other sources, and do not earn by working

ˌ**private 'label** *n.* [C] (*esp. BrE*) (*Comm.; Market.*) a product or group of products that a shop/store or company sells with its own name on

ˌ**private 'law** *n.* [U] (*Law*) the part of the law that deals with the relationship between individuals and organizations, and not their relationship with the state

'**private 'limited 'company** = PRIVATE COMPANY

ˌ**privately-'held** *adj.* (*Law*) used to describe a company whose shares may not be bought and sold by the public

ˌ**private 'placing** (*BrE*) (*also* ˌ**private 'placement**, *AmE, BrE*) *n.* [C] (*Finan.*) when shares are sold directly to investors rather than to the public on the stock market

'**private-'public 'partnership** = PUBLIC-PRIVATE PARTNERSHIP

ˌ**private 'sale** *n.* [C,U] (*Comm.; Finan.*) when sth such as property is sold by the owner directly to the buyer; when shares, etc. are offered for sale to only a few people and not to the public: *We bought the house by private sale.*

ˌ**private 'sector** *n.* [sing.] (*Econ.*) the part of a country's economy that is not under the direct control of the government, but is owned by individuals and independent companies: *salary increases in the private sector*

ˌ**private 'treaty** *n.* [U,C] (*Law*) an agreement to sell property or a valuable item between its owner and a buyer

**privatize, -ise** /'praɪvətaɪz/ *v.* [T] (*Econ.*) to sell a business or an industry so that it is no longer owned and controlled by the government: *Air traffic control has been privatized.* SYN DENATIONALIZE OPP NATIONALIZE ► ˌ**privati'zation, -i'sation** /-taɪ'zeɪʃn; *AmE* -tə'z-/ *n.* [U,C]

**privilege** /'prɪvəlɪdʒ/ *n.* **1** [C,U] a special right or advantage that a particular person or group of people has **2** (*Law*) [U] a special right that protects sb from being punished if they do or say a particular thing, or refuse to do or say a particular thing, because of their position

**privileged** /'prɪvəlɪdʒd/ *adj.* (*Law*) **privileged** information is known only to a few people and is legally protected so it does not have to be made public SYN CONFIDENTIAL

**privity** /'prɪvəti/ *n.* [U,C] (*pl.* **-ties**) (*Law*) a relationship between two people or groups that is accepted by law, for example the relationship between people who have signed a contract

**prize** /praɪz/ *n., adj.*

• *n.* [C] **1** an award or amount of money given to a person who wins a competition, etc. or who does very good work **2** sth very valuable or important that is difficult to obtain

• *adj.* being a very good or valuable example of its kind: *If she leaves, the team will lose its prize asset.*

**PRO** /ˌpiː ɑːr 'əʊ; *AmE* 'oʊ/ *n.* [C] **public relations officer** a person whose job is to give the public information about an organization or a person in order to create a good impression

**pro** /prəʊ; *AmE* proʊ/ = PROFESSIONAL *n.*

**proactive** /ˌprəʊ'æktɪv; *AmE* ˌproʊ-/ *adj.* controlling a situation by making things happen, rather than waiting for things to happen and then reacting to them: *The company has a proactive approach to recruiting.* ► ˌ**pro'actively** *adv.*

ˌ**proactive 'marketing** *n.* [U] methods of selling a company's products or services in which the company tries to find new ways of finding and attracting customers

**probation** /prə'beɪʃn; *AmE* proʊ-/ *n.* [U] **1** (*HR*) a time of training and testing when you start a new job to see if you are suitable for the work: *a period of probation* **2** a period of time during which a person or company that has not been doing well must improve: *Management was* **on** *probation.* ▸ **pro'bationary** /-ʃnri; *AmE* -ʃəneri/ *adj.*: *a probationary period* **pro'bationer** *n.* [C]

**probe** /prəʊb; *AmE* proʊb/ *n.*, *v.*
• *n.* [C] (used esp. in newspapers) an investigation
• *v.* [T,I] to ask questions in order to find out secret or hidden information about sb/sth: *They have been probing deeply into the way that teams work.*

**probity** /'prəʊbəti; *AmE* 'proʊ-/ *n.* [U] (*fml.*) the quality of being completely honest: *financial probity*

**'problem child** *n.* [C] **1** something such as a product, business, or part of a business that is not very successful or causes particular difficulties for its makers or owners **2** (*Market.*) a product that only has a small share of the market in a market that is growing quickly: *Large investments will be needed for a problem child.* → BOSTON MATRIX

**'problem-ˌsolving** *n.* [U] the act of finding ways of dealing with problems: *developing problem-solving skills* ▸ **'problem-ˌsolver** *n.* [C]

**pro bono** /ˌprəʊ 'bəʊnəʊ; *AmE* ˌproʊ 'boʊnoʊ/ *adj.* used to describe work that is done without charging a fee: *She agreed to take the case on a pro bono basis.* ▸ **ˌpro 'bono** *adv.*: *a lawyer who often works pro bono*

★**procedure** /prə'siːdʒə(r)/ *n.* [C,U] a way of doing sth, esp. the usual or correct way: *You must follow the correct procedure* **for** *hiring staff.* ◇ *court/legal* ~
⊕ *to* ***adopt/use*** ~*(s)* ◆ ***established/normal/proper/standard*** ~*(s)* ◆ ***complaints/emergency*** ~*s*
▸ **pro'cedural** /-dʒərəl/ *adj.*: *the procedural rules for a dismissal*

**proceed** /prə'siːd; *AmE* proʊ-/ *v.*
**PHRV** **pro'ceed against sb** (*Law*) to start a court case against sb

**proceeding** /prə'siːdɪŋ/ *n.* [C, usu. pl.] (*fml.*) a legal process which aims to settle a dispute or deal with a complaint: *costly legal proceedings* ◇ *bankruptcy/extradition* ~*s*

**proceeds** /'prəʊsiːdz; *AmE* 'proʊ-/ *n.* [pl.] money that sb receives, for example when they sell sth; profits: *proceeds* **from** *the sale of assets*

★**process** /'prəʊses; *AmE* 'prɑːses; 'proʊ-/ *n.*, *v.*
• *n.* [C] **1** a series of things that are done in order to achieve a particular result: *the selection process for staff*
⊕ *an* ***approval/evaluation*** ~ ◆ *a* ***consultation/decision-making*** ~ ◆ *to* ***improve/streamline*** *a* ~
**2** a method used in industry for doing or making sth
⊕ *an* ***industrial/****a* ***manufacturing/production*** ~ ◆ *to* ***improve/streamline/use*** *a* ~
**IDM** **be in the process of doing sth** to be continuing sth that you have started: *We are in the process of selling the business.*
• *v.* [T] **1** to treat raw material, food, etc. in order to change it, preserve it, etc: *Bacteria were found in meat processed at the plant.* **2** to deal officially with a document, request, etc: *to process orders* **3** (*IT*) to perform a series of operations on data in a computer: *to process and store information*
▸ **'processing** *n.* [U]: *a processing plant*

**processor** /'prəʊsesə(r); *AmE* 'prɑː-; 'proʊ-/ *n.* [C] **1** a machine or business that processes things: *a food/meat* ~ **2** (*IT*) the part of a computer that controls all the other parts of the system **SYN** CENTRAL PROCESSING UNIT

**'process ˌowner** *n.* [C] the person who is responsible for a process in a business, for how well it works and for improving it

**procurement** /prə'kjʊəmənt; *AmE* -'kjʊrm-/ *n.* [U,C] (*Product.*) the process of obtaining supplies of equipment or raw materials for an organization **SYN** PURCHASING

**pro'curement ˌofficer** = PURCHASING OFFICER

★**produce** *v.*, *n.*
• *v.* /prə'djuːs; *AmE* -'duːs/ [T] **1** to make or grow things to be sold, esp. in large quantities: *The firm produces 25 million tons of steel a year.* **2** to cause a particular result or effect: *The drug can produce some side effects.*
• *n.* /'prɒdjuːs; *AmE* 'prɑːduːs; 'proʊ-/ [U] things that have been made or grown, esp. things connected with farming: *The store buys produce from local farmers.*

★**producer** /prə'djuːsə(r); *AmE* -'duː-/ *n.* [C] a person, company or country that grows or makes food, goods or materials: *The company is a producer of industrial and electronic materials.*

**proˌducer 'price ˌindex** (*also* **Producer Price Index**) *n.* [C] (*abbr* **PPI**) (*Econ.*) a set of figures showing the average change in prices paid to producers and manufacturers for goods over a period of time

★ **product** /ˈprɒdʌkt; *AmE* ˈprɑːd-/ *n.* **1** [C,U] a thing that is manufactured, developed, produced or grown, usu. for sale: *dairy/electrical/software ~s* ◇ *to* ***launch*** *a new product onto the market* ◇ *We need new product to sell* (= a new range of products). **2** [C] a service that people can buy, esp. a way of investing or saving money: *financial/investment ~s* **3** [C] (*with another n.*) sth that is made from the thing mentioned: *paper/steel/wood ~s* **4** [C] a thing produced during a natural, chemical or industrial process: *waste products*

**ˈproduct ˌadvertising** *n.* [U] (*Market.*) advertising that aims to make people notice and want to buy a particular product

**ˌproduct aˈwareness** *n.* [U] (*Market.*) to what extent people know about and are interested in a company's products and their main features

**ˈproduct base** *n.* [C] (*Market.*) the range of goods produced or services provided by a company: *We have a product base of over 60 000 software items.* ◇ *to broaden/deepen/expand the ~*

**ˈproduct ˌcategory** *n.* [C] (*Market.*) a general type of product: *product categories such as gifts and food*

**ˌproduct deˈvelopment** *n.* [U] the process of designing, producing and marketing a new product

**ˌproduct diˈversion** = DIVERSION (2)

**ˈproduct engiˌneer** *n.* [C] a person whose job is to develop new products for a business and be responsible for the design, manufacture and technical aspects of the products

**ˈproduct ˌfamily** *n.* [C] (*Market.*; *Product.*) a group of products made by one manufacturer that are very similar in some way

**ˌproduct innoˈvation** *n.* [U,C] (*Market.*) the process of improving an existing product or creating a new and better product; a new or improved product

★ **production** /prəˈdʌkʃn/ *n.* [U] **1** the process of making goods or materials or growing food, esp. in large quantities; the department in a company that is responsible for this: *Production of the new car will start next month.* ◇ *high production costs* ◇ *to be in/go into/go out of ~* **2** the quantity of goods, materials or food that is produced: *It is important to monitor production levels.* ◇ *a decline/fall/increase/rise in ~* **IDM** **on production of sth** (*fml.*) when you show sth: *Discounts given only on production of your student ID card.*

**proˈduction ˌconcept** *n.* [sing.] (*Econ.*) the theory that consumers prefer products that are easy to obtain and not expensive and therefore companies should produce and deliver goods as efficiently as possible

**proˈduction conˌtrol** *n.* [U] (*Product.*) the activity of checking the process of production to make sure that it is efficient
▸ **proˈduction conˌtroller** *n.* [C]

**proˈduction line** = ASSEMBLY LINE

**proˈduction ˌmanager** *n.* [C] (*Product.*) the person who is in charge of the process of making goods or materials

★ **productive** /prəˈdʌktɪv/ *adj.* **1** making goods or growing crops, esp. in large quantities: *highly productive workers* ◇ *productive farming land* **2** doing or achieving a lot; producing a good result: *We had a very productive meeting.* ▸ **proˈductively** *adv.*: *The funds were used productively.*

★ **productivity** /ˌprɒdʌkˈtɪvəti; *AmE* ˌprɑːd-; ˌproʊd-/ *n.* [U] the rate at which a worker, a company or a country produces goods, and the amount produced, compared with how much time, work and money is needed to produce them: *Wage rates depend on levels of productivity.* ◇ *a productivity bonus* (= extra money for producing more goods)
● ***high/low/lost ~*** ♦ *to* ***boost/improve/increase/raise/reduce ~*** ♦ ***a ~ agreement*** ♦ ***~ gains/growth/improvement(s)***

**productize, -ise** /ˈprɒdʌktaɪz; *AmE* ˈprɑːd-/ *v.* [T] (*Market.*) to present sth such as a process or a service to customers by selling it like a product: *to productize expertise*

**ˈproduct launch** *n.* [C] (*Market.*) the action of making a product available to consumers for the first time; an event when this happens

**ˌproduct liaˈbility** *n.* [U] (*Law*) the fact that a manufacturer or trader is legally responsible for damage, injury or illness caused by a product that is not working or not made correctly

**ˌproduct ˈlife ˌcycle** *n.* [C] (*abbr* **PLC**) (*Market.*) the theory that sales of a product pass through four stages: introduction, when there is a gradual increase in sales; growth, when sales increase rapidly; MATURITY, when sales increase slowly; decline, when sales fall

**ˈproduct ˈlife cycle ˈmanagement** *n.* [U] (*abbr* **PLM**) (*Market.*) the job of organizing and directing the work that is needed to get the most profit from a product during the different stages of its life

**ˈproduct line** = PRODUCT RANGE

**ˌproduct line ˈmanager** = CATEGORY MANAGER

**ˈproduct line ˌstretching** = LINE STRETCHING

**ˈproduct ˌmanagement** *n.* [U] (*Market.*) the process of planning and directing the products that a company produces and the way that they are sold

**ˈproduct ˌmanager** *n.* [C] (*Market.*) a person in charge of planning and organizing the marketing of a particular brand or product

**ˈproduct mix** *n.* [C] (*Market.*) all the products and items that a particular company offers for sale

**ˈproduct orienˌtation** *n.* [C, usu. sing., U] (*Market.*) the situation when a company focuses on the quality of the products that it makes, rather than on what customers want to buy ▸ **ˈproduct-ˌoriented** *adj.*

**ˈproduct ˌplacement** *n.* [C,U] (*Market.*) a type of advertising in which a company pays to have one of its products appear in a film/movie or television programme

**product range** (*also* **ˈproduct line**) *n.* [C] a set of products of a particular type that are made or sold by a company: *The new car is filling a gap in their product range.* ◇ *to broaden/increase/widen the ~*

**product reˈturn** = RETURN *n.* (4)

**product substiˈtution** *n.* [U] (*Market.*) **1** when a company that has a contract to use or provide particular products uses different products instead, esp. ones that do not meet the required standards **2** when consumers buy and use a related but different product from the one they normally buy and use; when producers offer a different product

★ **profession** /prəˈfeʃn/ *n.* **1** [C] a type of job that needs special training or skill, esp. one that needs a high level of education: *She was an engineer **by profession**.* ◇ *people entering the accounting profession* **2 the profession** [sing. with sing./pl. verb] all the people who work in a particular type of **profession**: *The legal ~ has/have always resisted change.* **3 the professions** [pl.] the traditional jobs that need a high level of education and training, such as being a doctor or a lawyer

★ **professional** /prəˈfeʃənl/ *adj., n.*
• ***adj.* 1** connected with a job that needs special training or skill, esp. one that needs a high level of education: *professional development* ◇ *professional associations*
○ *~ qualifications/skills/standards*
• *~ advice/fees/help/services*
**2** (about people) having a job which needs special training and a high level of education: *busy professional couples with two incomes* **3** showing that sb is well trained and extremely skilled: *He dealt with the problem in a highly professional way.* **4** suitable or appropriate for sb working in a particular profession: *~ conduct/misconduct* OPP UNPROFESSIONAL **5** doing sth as a paid job rather than as a hobby: *professional investors*
• ***n.*** [C] (*also* **pro**, *infml.*) **1** a person who does a job that needs special training and a high level of education: *a staff of over 500 IT professionals* **2** a person who has a lot of skill and experience: *This was a job for a real professional.*

**proˌfessional liaˈbility** *n.* [U] (*Law*) the fact that sb such as a doctor, a lawyer, an accountant, etc. is legally responsible for any damage or harm that they cause by the way that they do their job

**proficiency** /prəˈfɪʃnsi/ *n.* [U] the ability to do or use sth well because you have had training and practice: *developing technical proficiency* ▸ **proˈficient** /-ʃnt/ *adj.*: *She's proficient **at** her job.* ◇ *proficient **in** several languages*

★ **profile** /ˈprəʊfaɪl; *AmE* ˈproʊ-/ *n., v.*
• ***n.*** [C] **1** a description of sb/sth that gives useful information: *a profile of our customers and their requirements*
○ *a **company/financial/personal** ~*
• *to **build up/develop** a ~*
**2** the general impression that sb/sth gives to the public and the amount of attention they receive: *raising the company's profile in Europe.*
○ *a **high/low** ~* • *a **corporate/public** ~* • *to **improve** your ~*
• ***v.*** [T] to give or write a description of sb/sth that gives the most important information: *Her career is profiled in this month's journal.*

★ **profit** /ˈprɒfɪt; *AmE* ˈprɑːfɪt/ *n., v.*
• ***n.*** [C,U] the money that you make in business or by selling things, esp. after paying the costs involved: *The*

*company made a profit last year.* ◇ *Profit from exports rose 7.3%.* ◇ *to sell something* ***at a profit.*** OPP LOSS
→ idiom at TURN *v.*

◆ *a* ***big/healthy/record/substantial*** ~ ◆ *a* ***modest/small*** ~ ◆ *an* ***after-tax/*** *a* ***pre-tax/taxable*** ~ ◆ *to* ***bring (in)/ generate/report/show*** *a* ~

• *v.* [T,I] (*fml.*) to get money or sth useful from a situation; to be useful to sb or give them an advantage: *Small businesses are profiting from the new legislation.*

★ **profitable** /ˈprɒfɪtəbl; *AmE* ˈprɑːf-/ *adj.* **1** that makes or is likely to make money: *a highly profitable business* **2** that gives sb an advantage or a useful result: *We had a very profitable meeting.* ▶ **ˌprofitaˈbility** /-ˈbɪləti/ *n.* [U] **ˈprofitably** /-bli/ *adv.*: *to run a business profitably*

**ˌprofit and ˈloss acˌcount** (*also* **ˌprofit and ˈloss ˌstatement**) *n.* [C] (*abbr* **P & L**) (*all BrE*) (*Account.*) an official financial record that gives details of a company's income and expenses for a particular period and shows if it has made a profit or loss SYN EARNINGS REPORT

**ˈprofit ˌcentre** *n.* [C] (*Account.*) a part of a business that is responsible for its own income and for planning and controlling its expenses

**profiteer** /ˌprɒfɪˈtɪə(r); *AmE* ˌprɑːfəˈtɪr/ *n.* [C] a person or an organization that makes a lot of money in an unfair way, for example by asking very high prices for things that are hard to get: *wartime profiteers* ▶ **ˌprofiˈteer** *v.* [I]: *Businesses who tried to profiteer from the new sales tax were fined.* **ˌprofiˈteering** *n.* [U]

**ˈprofit-ˌmaking** *adj.* (about a product, an activity, or an organization) that does or is intended to make a profit: *a profit-making operation* ▶ **ˈprofit-ˌmaker** *n.* [C]: *Not every car they sell is a profit-maker.*

**ˈprofit ˌmargin** *n.* [C,U] (*Account.*) **1** a percentage showing the relationship between the profit a company makes and the money that it obtains from sales: *a very disappointing profit margin of 0.4% of revenue* **2** the difference between the cost of buying or producing sth and the price that it is sold for, calculated as a percentage of the selling price SYN MARGIN

**ˈprofit ˌmotive** *n.* [sing.] (*Econ.*) the desire to make money, which is the reason that most businesses exist

**ˈprofit-ˌsharing** (*also* **profit sharing**) *n.* [U] (*HR*) a system in which employees receive part of the profit the company has made, for example in one year, either in cash or as shares ▶ **ˈprofit-share** *adj.*

**ˈprofit squeeze** (*also* **ˈprofits squeeze**, *less freq.*) *n.* [C] a situation in which profit becomes less over a period of time, because prices fall or costs increase

**ˈprofits ˌwarning** = PROFIT WARNING

**ˈprofit-ˌtaking** *n.* [U] (*Finan.*) the act of selling shares, bonds, etc. that have increased in value, in order to make a profit ▶ **ˈprofit-ˌtaker** *n.* [C]

**ˈprofit ˌwarning** (*also* **ˈprofits ˌwarning**, *esp. in BrE*) *n.* [C] (*Finan.*) a statement by a company that its profits will be lower than expected: *to* ***issue*** *a profit warning*

**pro forma** /ˌprəʊ ˈfɔːmə; *AmE* ˌproʊ ˈfɔːrmə/ *adj.* **1** (about a document) prepared in order to show the usual way of doing sth or to provide a standard method: *a pro forma letter* **2** (*Account.*) used to describe a financial statement that is based on estimated or expected costs, income, etc. before the real figures are known ▶ **ˌpro ˈforma** *n.* [C]

**ˌpro forma ˈinvoice** *n.* [C] (*Account.*) a document sent before goods are supplied, for example to ask for payment from a new customer or to show prices that will be paid

★ **program** /ˈprəʊɡræm; *AmE* ˈproʊ-/ *n.*, *v.*

• *n.* [C] **1** (*IT*) (*also* **comˈputer ˌprogram**) a set of instructions in code that control the operations or functions of a computer

◆ *to* ***load/download/install/uninstall*** *a* ~ ◆ *to* ***run/design/develop/ execute/use/write*** *a* ~

**2** (*AmE*) = PROGRAMME

• *v.* (**-mm-**, *AmE also* **-m-**) **1** (*IT*) [T,I] to give a computer, etc. a set of instructions to make it perform a particular task: *The printer can be programmed to handle any font.*
**2** (*AmE*) = PROGRAMME

**programmable** /ˈprəʊɡræməbl; prəʊˈɡræm-; *AmE* ˈproʊ-; proʊˈɡ-/ *adj.* (*IT*) (about a computer or other machine) able to accept instructions that control how it operates or functions: *programmable machine tools*

★ **programme** (*AmE* **program**) /ˈprəʊɡræm; *AmE* ˈproʊ-/ *n.*, *v.*

• *n.* [C] **1** a plan of things that will be done or included in the development of sth: *a training programme for new staff* ◇ *a programme of reform*

◆ *a* ***building/research*** ~ ◆ *to* ***finance/set up*** *a* ~ ◆ *to* ***carry out/ launch*** *a* ~

**2** sth that people watch on television or listen to on the radio: *news programmes*
⊙ *to* ***broadcast/do/make/show*** *a ~* ◆ *to* ***listen to/see/watch*** *a ~*
• ***v.*** [T] (*usu. pass.*) **1** to plan for sth to happen, esp. as part of a series of planned events: *The project is programmed* ***for*** *completion next month.* **2** to give a machine instructions to do a particular task

**programmer** /ˈprəʊɡræmə(r); *AmE* ˈproʊ-/ (*also* **comˌputer ˈprogrammer**) *n.* [C] (*IT*) sb whose job is to write computer programs

**programming** /ˈprəʊɡræmɪŋ; *AmE* ˈproʊ-/ *n.* [U] **1** (*IT*) (*also* **comˌputer ˈprogramming**) the process of writing and testing programs for computers **2** the planning of which television or radio programmes to broadcast

**ˈprogramming ˌlanguage** = COMPUTER LANGUAGE

**ˈprogram ˌtrading** *n.* [U] (*Finan.*) the automatic buying and selling of large numbers of shares by computer when prices reach a particular level

**progressive** /prəˈɡresɪv/ *adj.* **1** happening or developing steadily: *a progressive reduction in the size of the workforce* **2** in favour of new ideas, modern methods and change: *progressive employers* **3** (*Account.*; *Econ.*) used to describe a tax, usu. on income, in which people who earn more money pay a higher rate or percentage of tax than people who earn less money

**ˈprogress ˌpayment** *n.* [C] a part of a larger payment, paid to a company when they have completed a particular stage in a job

**prohibit** /prəˈhɪbɪt; *AmE also* proʊˈh-/ *v.* [T] **~ sth | ~ sb from doing sth 1** (*often pass.*) to stop sth from being done or used, esp. by law: *rules prohibiting the use of some additives in foods* **2** to make sth impossible: *High costs prohibit many businesses from entering the industry.*

**prohibition** /ˌprəʊɪˈbɪʃn; *AmE* ˌproʊəˈb-/ *n.* **1** [U] the act of stopping sth being done or used, esp. by law: *the prohibition of imports of some types of meat* **2** [C] a law or rule that stops sth being done or used: *prohibitions on price-fixing*

**prohibitive** /prəˈhɪbətɪv; *AmE also* proʊˈh-/ *adj.* **1** (about a price or a cost) so high that it prevents people from buying or doing sth: *a prohibitive tax on imported cars* **2** preventing people from doing sth by law: *prohibitive legislation*
▸ **proˈhibitively** *adv.*: *Car insurance can be prohibitively expensive for young drivers.*

★ **project** *n., v.*
• ***n.*** /ˈprɒdʒekt; *AmE* ˈprɑːdʒ-/ [C] a planned piece of work, often involving many people, that is designed to produce sth new, to improve sth or to find information about sth: *to set up a project to develop a new engine*
⊙ *a* ***large/joint/major*** *~* ◆ *a* ***building/research*** *~* ◆ *to* ***fund/manage/run*** *a ~* ◆ *a ~* ***leader/manager/team***
• ***v.*** [T] /prəˈdʒekt/ **1** (*usu. pass.*) to estimate what the size, cost or amount of sth will be in the future based on what is happening now: *A growth rate of 4% is projected for next year.* SYN FORECAST **2** (*usu. pass.*) to plan an activity, a project, etc. for a time in the future: *The projected merger will go ahead next year.* **3** to present sb/sth/yourself to other people in a particular way, esp. one that gives a good impression: *We need to project ourselves better.*

**ˌproject engiˈneer** *n.* [C] a person with technical knowledge and qualifications whose job is to arrange, organize and control a project

**projection** /prəˈdʒekʃn/ *n.* [C, usu. pl.] an estimate or a statement of what figures, amounts or events will be in the future, or what they were in the past, based on what is happening now: *Sales have exceeded our projections.*
⊙ ***budget/earnings/financial/growth/sales*** *~s* ◆ ***gloomy/optimistic/rosy*** *~s* ◆ *to* ***make/revise*** *~s*

**ˈproject ˌmanagement** *n.* [U] the process of planning, organizing and controlling the tasks, costs, staff and resources of a project so that it is completed successfully in the most efficient way
▸ **ˈproject ˌmanager** *n.* [C]

**projector** /prəˈdʒektə(r)/ = OVERHEAD PROJECTOR

**PROM** /ˌpiː ɑːr əʊ ˈem; *AmE* oʊ/ *n.* [U] (*IT*) **programmable read-only memory** a type of computer memory that can have information and instructions recorded on it once, after which the data cannot be removed

**ˈpromissory note** (*also* **note**) *n.* [C] (*abbr* **P-note**) (*Finan.*) a signed document containing a promise to pay a stated amount of money on or before a particular date

**promo** /ˈprəʊməʊ; *AmE* ˈproʊmoʊ/ *n.* [C] (*pl.* **promos**) (*Market., infml.*) a video, film/movie, etc. intended to advertise a particular product: *a trade promo*

★ **promote** /prəˈməʊt; *AmE* -ˈmoʊt/ *v.* **1** [T] to help sth to happen or develop: *to promote competition in the industry* **2** (*Market.*) [T,I] to help sell a product, service, etc. or make it more popular by advertising it or offering it at a special price: *promoting new products* ◇ *The store has been promoting aggressively.* **3** (*HR*) [T] (*often pass.*) to move sb to a more senior job in an organization SYN UPGRADE OPP DEMOTE **4** (*Finan.*) [T] to move a company to a higher position within a particular system, such as a stock exchange index SYN UPGRADE OPP DEMOTE

**promoter** /prəˈməʊtə(r); *AmE* -ˈmoʊ-/ *n.* [C] (*Market.*) **1** a person or company that tries to persuade others about the value or importance of a product or service **2** a person or company that organizes or provides money for an artistic performance or a sporting event

★ **promotion** /prəˈməʊʃn; *AmE* -ˈmoʊʃn/ *n.* **1** (*HR*) [U,C] a move to a more important job in a company or an organization: *her promotion to Sales Manager* **2** (*Market.*) [U,C] activities done in order to increase the sales of a product or service; a set of advertisements for a particular product or service: *sales and promotion* ◇ *a special promotion of French food* **3 promotions** [U with sing./pl. v.] the part of a company that is responsible for advertising products or services and increasing sales

**promotional** /prəˈməʊʃənl; *AmE* -ˈmoʊ-/ *adj.* (*Market.*) connected with advertising: *~ campaigns/deals*

**prompt** /prɒmpt; *AmE* prɑːmpt/ *adj., n., v.*

• ***adj.*** **1** done without delay: *prompt payment* **2** (about a person) acting without delay; arriving at the right time SYN PUNCTUAL ▸ **ˈpromptly** *adv.*: *pay promptly* **ˈpromptness** *n.* [U]

• ***n.*** [C] (*IT*) a sign on a computer screen that shows that the computer has finished doing sth and is ready for more instructions

• ***v.*** [T] (*IT*) (about a computer) to ask the user for more instructions: *The program will prompt you to update.*

**ˈprompt note** *n.* [C] (*Finan.*) a letter sent to someone to remind them that their payment is due

**ˈproof ˌcopy** *n.* [C] (*also* **proof** [usu. pl.]) (*Product.*) a copy of the pages of a book, magazine or other printed material that a printer produces so that they can be checked and corrected before all the copies are printed

**ˌproof of ˈpurchase** *n.* [C,U] (*Comm.*) a document that shows that you have bought and paid for sth

**prop** /prɒp; *AmE* prɑːp/ *v.*

PHR V **ˌprop sth ˈup** to help or support sth that is having difficulties: *The government is propping up declining industries.*

**prop.** = PROPRIETOR

★ **property** /ˈprɒpəti; *AmE* ˈprɑːpərti/ *n.* (*pl.* **-ties**) **1** [U] a thing or things that are owned by sb; a possession or possessions: *Your PC is the property of the company.* **2** [U] land and buildings: *investing in property*

⊙ ***business/investment/residential ~*** • *to* ***buy/own/sell*** *~*

**3** [C] a building or buildings: *There are some empty properties in the area.*

⊙ *to* ***buy/own/rent/sell*** *a ~* • *a* ***business****/an* ***investment****/a* ***residential*** *~* • *a* ***hotel****/an* ***office****/a* ***retail*** *~*

**ˈproperty bond** *n.* [C] (*BrE*) (*Finan.*) a bond sold by insurance companies, who invest the money in property

**ˈproperty ˌcompany** (*BrE*) (*AmE* **ˈreal estate ˌcompany**) *n.* [C] a company that buys, sells and rents buildings

**ˈproperty deˌvelopment** *n.* **1** [U] the business of building new property or changing existing property **2** [C] a place where new property has been built or is being built ▸ **ˈproperty deˌveloper** *n.* [C]

**ˈproperty loan** (*AmE also* **ˈreal eˌstate loan**) = MORTGAGE

**ˈproperty ˌmanagement** (*AmE also* **ˈreal estate ˌmanagement**) *n.* [U] the business of making sure that sb's property remains in good condition, trying to get a good profit from land or buildings, helping people to rent a property to others, etc. ▸ **ˈproperty ˌmanager** (*AmE also* **ˈreal estate ˌmanager**) *n.* [C]

**the ˈproperty ˌmarket** (*AmE also* **ˈreal estate ˌmarket**) *n.* [C, usu. sing.] the activity of buying and selling buildings and land

**ˈproperty ˌregister** (*also* **Property Register**) *n.* [C] (*BrE*) **1** a list where people can advertise their property for sale, or search for property to rent or buy **2** in the UK, an official list containing details about who owns buildings or land

**ˈproperty tax** *n.* [U,C] tax that is paid on buildings or other things that you own, based on a percentage of their value

★ **proportion** /prəˈpɔːʃn; *AmE* -ˈpɔːrʃn/ *n.* **1** [C, usu. sing.] a part or share of a whole: *A significant proportion of the shares have been bought by overseas investors.* ◇ *a high/large/low/small* ~ **2** [U] the relationship of one thing to another in size, amount, etc: *Shareholders can buy new stock* ***in proportion to*** *the shares they own.* **3 proportions** [pl.] the measurements of sth; the size or shape of sth: *This method divides the task into more manageable proportions.*
→ idiom at INVERSE

**proportional** /prəˈpɔːʃənl; *AmE* -ˈpɔːrʃ-/ (*also* **proˈportionate**) *adj.* increasing or decreasing in size, amount or degree according to changes in sth else: *Salary is proportional* ***to*** *years of experience.*
▸ **proˈportionally** /-nəli/ (*also* **proˈportionately**) *adv.*

**proˌportional ˈtax** = FIXED TAX

**proportionate** /prəˈpɔːʃənət; *AmE* -ˈpɔːrʃ-/ = PROPORTIONAL

★ **proposal** /prəˈpəʊzl; *AmE* -ˈpoʊzl/ *n.* **1** [C,U] a formal suggestion or plan; the act of making a suggestion: *a sales proposal* ◇ *the proposal* ***to*** *raise the retirement age*
⊙ *to* ***draw up/make/put forward/submit*** *a* ~ ◆ *to* ***accept/consider/discuss/reject*** *a* ~
**2** (*Insur.*) [C] a written request for an insurance policy that involves giving information about yourself or your property on a printed form

★ **propose** /prəˈpəʊz; *AmE* -ˈpoʊz/ *v.* [T] **1** to suggest a plan, an idea, etc. for people to think about and decide on: *The union proposed changes to the regulations.* ◇ *He proposed changing the name of the company.* ◇ *the proposed changes* **2** to suggest sth at a formal meeting and ask people to vote on it ▸ **proˈposer** *n.* [C]

**proposition** /ˌprɒpəˈzɪʃn; *AmE* ˌprɑːp-/ *n.* [C] a business idea or plan of action that is suggested: *I'd like to put a business proposition to you.*
⊙ *a* ***commercial/financial*** ~ ◆ *an* ***attractive****/a* ***risky/viable*** ~

**proprietary** /prəˈpraɪətri; *AmE* -teri/ *adj.* **1** (about goods) made and sold by a particular company and protected by a REGISTERED TRADEMARK: *a proprietary brand* **2** used or owned by one particular company **3** relating to an owner or to the fact of owning sth: *proprietary rights*

**proˌprietary ˈtrading** (*also* **ˌprincipal ˈtrading**) *n.* [U] (*Stock Ex.*) trading in shares, bonds, etc. by a financial institution for itself rather than on behalf of its customers

**proprietor** /prəˈpraɪətə(r)/ *n.* [C] (*abbr* **prop.**) **1** the owner of a business, a hotel, land or buildings, etc: *Enquiries must be made to the proprietor.* **2** (*Law*) the owner of a PATENT
▸ **proˈprietorship** /-ʃɪp/ *n.* [U]

**pro rata** /ˌprəʊ ˈrɑːtə; *AmE* ˌproʊ/ *adj.* (about a payment or share of sth) calculated according to how much of sth has been used, the amount of work done, etc: *Leave is calculated on a pro rata basis, according to length of service.* ▸ **ˌpro ˈrata** *adv.*: *Pay is €400 per week pro rata, according to hours worked.*

**prorate** /ˌprəʊˈreɪt; *AmE* ˌproʊ-/ *v.* [T] (*esp. AmE*) (*Account.*) (*usu. pass.*) to divide a payment or share of sth according to how much of sth has been used, the amount of work done, etc: *Bills for less than a complete month's service will be prorated.*
▸ **ˌproˈration** /-ˈreɪʃn/ *n.* [U]

**prosecute** /ˈprɒsɪkjuːt; *AmE* ˈprɑːs-/ *v.* [T,I] to officially accuse sb of a crime and try to prove it in court: *Strikers may be prosecuted.*
▸ **ˈprosecutor** *n.* [C]

**prosecution** /ˌprɒsɪˈkjuːʃn; *AmE* ˌprɑːs-/ *n.* **1** [C,U] the process of trying to prove in court that sb is guilty of a crime; the process of being officially accused of a crime in court: *The company paid the tax it owed in order to avoid prosecution.* **2 the prosecution** [sing. with sing./pl. verb] a person or an organization that **prosecutes** sb in a court, together with the lawyers, etc.

**prospect** *n., v.*
• ***n.*** /ˈprɒspekt; *AmE* ˈprɑːs-/ **1** [U; sing.] the possibility that sth will happen: *to have no immediate prospect of getting a job* **2** [sing.] an idea of what might or will happen in the future: *Starting your own business is a daunting prospect.* **3 prospects** [pl.] the chances of being successful in the future: *What are the company's financial prospects?* **4** [C] a person, company, etc. who is a possible customer: *likely prospects*
• ***v.*** /prəˈspekt; *AmE* ˈprɑːspekt/ [I] to search an area for minerals, gold, etc: *to prospect* ***for*** *oil*
▸ **proˈspector** *n.* [C]

**prospective** /prəˈspektɪv/ *adj.* **1** expected to do sth or to become sth: *a prospective buyer* SYN POTENTIAL **2** expected or likely to happen: *prospective changes in the law*

**prospectus** /prəs'pektəs/ *n.* [C] **1** a document giving information about a company's shares before they are offered for sale **2** a small book giving information about a new company or project, a college, etc.

**prosper** /'prɒspə(r); *AmE* 'prɑːs-/ *v.* [I] to develop in a successful way; to be successful, esp. financially SYN THRIVE ▶ **prosperity** /prɒ'sperəti; *AmE* prɑː's-/ *n.* [U] '**prosperous** /-pərəs/ *adj.*

**prosumer** /ˌprəʊ'sjuːmə(r); *AmE* ˌproʊ'suːmər/ *n.* [C] (*Market.*) **1** a customer who wants very good quality technical products but cannot afford to buy professional equipment **2** a customer who becomes involved in the design and manufacture of products

★ **protect** /prə'tekt/ *v.* **1** [T,I] **~ (sb/sth) (against/from sth)** to make sure that sb/sth is not harmed, injured, damaged, etc: *protecting your computer from viruses* ◇ *to protect the interests of shareholders* **2** (*Insur.*) [T,I] **~ (sb/sth) (against sth)** to provide sb/sth with insurance against fire, injury, damage, etc. **3** (*Econ.*) [T] to help an industry in your own country by taxing goods from other countries so that there is less competition: *a protected industry*

★ **protection** /prə'tekʃn/ *n.* [U] **1 ~ (for/of sb/sth) (against/from sth)** the act of protecting sb/sth; the state of being protected: *legal protection against unfair dismissal* **2** (*Econ.*) the system of helping an industry in your country by taxing foreign goods: *trade protection* **3** (*Insur.*) insurance against fire, injury, damage, etc: *protection* ***against*** *fire and theft*

**protectionism** /prə'tekʃənɪzəm/ *n.* [U] (*Econ.*) the principle or practice of protecting a country's own industry by taxing foreign goods ▶ **pro'tectionist** /-nɪst/ *adj.*

**protective** /prə'tektɪv/ *adj.* **1** providing or intended to provide protection: *protective clothing* **2** (*Econ.*) intended to give an advantage to your own country's industry: *protective tariffs*

**pro tem** /ˌprəʊ 'tem; *AmE* ˌproʊ/ *adv.* for now, but not permanently: *She's our manager pro tem.* ▶ **ˌpro 'tem** *adj.*

**protest** *n., v.*

• ***n.*** /'prəʊtest; *AmE* 'proʊ-/ [C,U] the expression of strong disagreement with or opposition to sth; a statement or an action that shows this: *She resigned* **in protest** *at the decision.*

✪ *a* ***huge/mass/nationwide/public*** *~* ◆ *a* ***peaceful/violent*** *~* ◆ *a* ***flood of/ wave of*** *~* ◆ *to* ***spark/trigger*** *a ~* ◆ *to* ***organize/stage/threaten*** *a ~*

• ***v.*** /prə'test; *AmE also* 'proʊ-/ [T,I] **~ (about/against/at sth)** to say or do sth to show that you disagree with or disapprove of sth, esp. publicly: *protesting against job cuts* ◇ (*AmE*) *They fully intend to protest the decision.*

**protocol** /'prəʊtəkɒl; *AmE* 'proʊtəkɔːl; -kɑːl/ *n.* **1** (*IT*) [C] a set of rules that control the way data is sent between computers **2** [U,C] the rules for the correct way of behaving or of doing sth in a particular situation or organization: *What's the protocol for asking questions at these meetings?*

**prototype** /'prəʊtətaɪp; *AmE* 'proʊ-/ *n.* [C] the first design of sth from which other forms are developed: *They designed and built a working prototype.*

✪ *to* ***develop/test*** *a ~* ◆ *a* ***physical/ virtual*** *~*

★ **provide** /prə'vaɪd/ *v.* [T] **1 ~ sb (with sth)** | **~ sth (for sb)** to give sth to sb or make it available for them to use: *The bank has provided the company with a three-year loan.* SYN SUPPLY **2** (*Law*) **~ that** (about a law or rule) to state that sth will or must happen SYN STIPULATE

PHR V **pro'vide against sth** (*fml.*) to make preparations to deal with sth bad or unpleasant that might happen in the future: *insurance to provide against loss of income* **pro'vide for sth 1** to prepare to deal with sth that is going to happen or that might happen in the future, esp. sth bad or unpleasant: *to provide for your retirement* **2** (*Law*) (about a law, rule, etc.) to make it possible for sth to be done

**provident** /'prɒvɪdənt; *AmE* 'prɑːv-/ *adj.* often used in the names of organizations that help people plan for the future by saving money: *Friends Provident*

**'provident fund** *n.* [C] a system in which you and your employer pay money regularly into an investment fund while you are employed. You are then paid a large sum of money when you retire or when you leave the company.

★ **provider** /prə'vaɪdə(r)/ *n.* [C] an organization that supplies sb with sth they need or want: *an electricity provider*

★ **provision** /prə'vɪʒn/ *n., v.*

• ***n.*** **1** (*Account.*) [C,U] an amount of money that a company keeps for a

particular purpose or to deal with possible problems or expenses in the future: *bad debt provision* SYN RESERVE **2** [U] the act of supplying sb with sth that they need or want: *the provision of health care* **3** (*Law*) [C] a condition or an arrangement in a legal document: *The contract is subject to the provisions of the Supply of Goods and Services Act.*
• *v.* [T,I] (*Account.*) to keep an amount of money for a particular purpose, for example paying taxes: *It is essential to provision **against** the possibility of non-payment.* ▸ **pro'visioning** *n.* [U]: *The bank has increased its provisioning against bad loans.*

**proviso** /prə'vaɪzəʊ; *AmE* -zoʊ/ *n.* [C] (*pl.* **provisos**) a condition that must be accepted before an agreement can be made: *The contract was approved **with the proviso that** amendments were made.* SYN PROVISION

**proxy** /'prɒksi; *AmE* 'prɑ:ksi/ *n.* (*pl.* **proxies**) **1** [U] the authority that a shareholder gives to sb to vote on their behalf: *Many shareholders vote by proxy.* ◇ *proxy votes* **2** [C,U] a person who has been given the authority to vote on behalf of a shareholder: *to **act as** a proxy at a meeting* **3** (*fml.*) [C] **~ for sth** something that you use to represent sth else that you are trying to measure or calculate: *The company is seen as a proxy for the radio industry.*

**'proxy fight** (*also* **'proxy ˌbattle**) *n.* [C] (*Finan.*) a situation in which a company or a group that is planning to take control of a particular company tries to persuade the shareholders of that company to give them their authority to vote for new directors who will support their plans

**'proxy ˌstatement** *n.* [C] information that must be sent to shareholders before they give sb authority to vote on the company's plans

**PRP** /ˌpi: ɑ: 'pi:; *AmE* ɑ:r/ = PERFORMANCE-RELATED PAY

**prudence** /'pru:dns/ *n.* [U] **1** (*Account.*) (*esp. BrE*) (*AmE usu.* **con'servatism**) the principle that a company's financial records must not make the company seem more valuable than it might be **2** care in making judgements and decisions; the practice of avoiding unnecessary risks: *to exercise financial prudence*

**prudent** /'pru:dnt/ *adj.* **1** sensible and careful when you make judgements and decisions; avoiding unnecessary risks: *a ~ businessman/decision* OPP IMPRUDENT **2** (*Account.*) taking care not to make a company seem more valuable in its financial records than it might be ▸ **'prudently** *adv.*

**PS** /ˌpi: 'es/ = POSTSCRIPT

**PSBR** /ˌpi: es bi: 'ɑ:(r)/ = PUBLIC SECTOR BORROWING REQUIREMENT

**PSV** /ˌpi: es 'vi:/ = PUBLIC SERVICE VEHICLE

**psychographics** /ˌsaɪkə'græfɪks/ *n.* [U] (*Market.*) techniques for analysing the values, opinions and attitudes to life of a group of people, in order to understand the best way to advertise to them ▸ **ˌpsycho'graphic** *adj.*

**ˌpsychological 'test** *n.* [C] a type of test used to see if sb has the right skills, interests and personality for a particular job ▸ **ˌpsychological 'testing** *n.* [U]

**psychometrics** /ˌsaɪkə'metrɪks/ *n.* [U] techniques used for measuring mental abilities and processes ▸ **ˌpsycho'metric** *adj.*

**ˌpsychometric 'test** *n.* [C] (*HR*) any test that measures sb's mental abilities, personality, attitudes, etc., often used when choosing sb for a job ▸ **ˌpsychometric 'testing** *n.* [U]

**PT** /ˌpi: 'ti:/ = PART-TIME

**P-to-P** = P2P

**Pty** /ˌpi: ti: 'waɪ/ *abbr* used in the names of some companies in Australia and South Africa

★ **public** /'pʌblɪk/ *adj., n.*
• *adj.* **1** connected with ordinary people in society in general: *Smoking in public places is banned in some cities.* **2** provided, esp. by the government, for the use of people in general: *public transport* OPP PRIVATE **3** connected with the government and the services it provides: *The rail industry is no longer in public ownership.* SYN STATE OPP PRIVATE **4** (*Comm.*; *Finan.*) sold or offered to people in general to buy: *investments and public offerings* OPP PRIVATE **5** known to people in general: *Details of the report have not yet been **made public**.* **6** intended to be seen or heard by people in general: *a public enquiry* OPP PRIVATE **7** where there are a lot of people who can see and hear you: *Can we talk somewhere a little less public?* OPP PRIVATE ▸ **'publicly** /-kli/ *adv.* IDM **go 'public** (*Stock Ex.*) (about a company) to start selling shares on the stock exchange → idiom at COMPANY
• *n.* [sing. with sing./pl. verb] **1 the public** ordinary people in society in general: *The survey sample comprised*

300 members of the public. ◇ The public has/have a right to know what is in the report. **2** a group of people who share a particular interest or who are involved in the same activity: *the music listening public*

**ˌpublic acˈcount** *n.* [C] a bank account in which a national or local government holds money

**ˌpublic adˈdress (ˌsystem)** *n.* [C] (*abbr* **PA**) an electronic system that is used to make music, voices, etc. louder so that they can be heard by everyone in a particular place or building

**publication** /ˌpʌblɪˈkeɪʃn/ *n.* **1** [U,C] the act of printing a book, magazine, etc. and making it available to the public; a book, magazine, etc. that has been published: *The publication date is April 1st.* ◇ *specialist publications* **2** [U] the act of printing sth in a newspaper, report, etc. so that the public knows about it: *the publication of the annual results*

**ˌpublic ˈcarrier** = COMMON CARRIER

**ˌpublic ˈcompany** (*also* **ˌpublicly-owned ˈcompany**) *n.* [C] (*BrE*) a company whose shares can be bought and sold on the stock market

**ˌpublic corpoˈration** *n.* [C] **1** (*AmE*) a company whose shares can be bought and sold on the stock market, etc. **2** a company owned and managed by the government

**ˌpublic ˈdebt** *n.* [U,C] (*Econ.*) the total amount of money owed by a national or local government

**ˌpublic deˈposits** *n.* [pl.] (*Econ.*) money held by national and local governments in bank accounts

**the ˌpublic doˈmain** *n.* [sing.] if sth is in the **public domain**, it is available for everyone to look at, to know, etc.

**ˌpublic emˈployee** *n.* [C] a person who works for the government

**ˌpublic ˈenterprise** *n.* **1** [U] the development of businesses by the government of a country rather than by the people **2** [C] a business owned by the government rather than by individuals or other companies

**ˌpublic ˈholiday** *n.* [C] a day on which most of the shops/stores, businesses and schools in a country are closed, often to celebrate a particular event

**ˌpublic ˈissue** *n.* [C,U] (*Stock Ex.*) an occasion when a company makes shares available for the public to buy for the first time: *The shares were offered through public issue.* SYN IPO

**publicist** /ˈpʌblɪsɪst/ *n.* [C] (*Market.*) a person whose job is to make sth, such as a new product, a book or an event, known to the public

**publicity** /pʌbˈlɪsəti/ *n.* [U] **1** the attention that is given to sth/sb by newspapers, television, etc.
⊙ ***adverse/bad/good/negative/unfavourable*** ~ ♦ *to* ***attract/avoid/generate/get/receive/seek*** ~
**2** (*Market.*) the business of attracting the attention of the public to sth/sb; the things that are done to attract attention: *She works in publicity.*
⊙ *a* ~ ***agent/budget/campaign/department/manager*** ♦ ~ ***material/photos*** ♦ ***to give sth*** ~

**pubˈlicity stunt** *n.* [C] (*Market.*) something that is done to attract people's attention

**publicize, -ise** /ˈpʌblɪsaɪz/ *v.* [T] to make sth known to the public; to advertise sth: *a* ***highly/much/widely*** *publicized event*

**ˌpublic ˈlaw** *n.* [U] (*Law*) the part of law that deals with the relationship between the government of a country and its people

**ˌpublic liaˈbility** *n.* [U] (*Insur.*) when a company is responsible if a member of the public or their property is harmed by one of its products, while in one of its shops/stores, etc: *public liability insurance*

**ˈpublic ˈlimited ˈcompany** *n.* [C] (*abbr* **plc**) in the UK and some other countries, a LIMITED COMPANY whose shares are offered to the public and are bought and sold on a stock exchange

**ˌpublicly-ˈheld** *adj.* (*Law*) used to describe a company whose shares can be bought and sold by the public

**ˌpublicly-owned ˈcompany** = PUBLIC COMPANY

**ˌpublicly ˈtraded** *adj.* **1** if a company is **publicly traded**, its shares are sold to the public **2** if shares are **publicly traded**, they are sold to the public

**ˌpublic ˈoffering** *n.* [C,U] (*Stock Ex.*) a number of shares, bonds, etc. that are offered for sale to the public for the first time

**ˈpublic-ˈprivate ˈpartnership** (*also* **ˈprivate-ˈpublic ˈpartnership**) *n.* [C] (*abbr* **PPP, P3**) an arrangement in which a government organization and a private company invest in a project and work together

★ **ˌpublic reˈlations** *n.* **1** [U] (*abbr* **PR**) the business of giving the public information about a particular

organization or person in order to create a good impression
◐ *a ~ consultant/manager/officer* ◆ *a ~ agency/firm* ◆ *a ~ campaign/exercise/operation*
**2** [pl.] the state of the relationship between an organization and the public: *We had to deal with a public relations crisis.* ◇ *bad/good ~*

**the ˌpublic ˈsector** *n.* [sing.] (*Econ.*) the part of the economy of a country that is owned or controlled by the government: *~ employees/jobs/managers/organizations*

**ˈpublic ˈsector ˈborrowing reˌquirement** *n.* [sing.] (*abbr* **PSBR**) (*Econ.*) the difference between the amount a government spends and the income it receives from taxes in a particular period, which it has to borrow

**ˌpublic ˈservant** *n.* [C] a person who works in or for the government

**ˌpublic ˈservice** *n.* **1** [C] a service such as transport or health care that a government or an official organization provides for people in general in a particular society **2** [U] the government and government departments: *public service workers* **3** [C,U] something that is done to help people rather than to make a profit: *to perform a public service*

**ˌpublic ˈservice ˌvehicle** *n.* [C] (*abbr* **PSV**) a bus or large taxi that is used to carry members of the public, usu. for money

**ˌpublic ˈspending** *n.* [U] the amount of money that is spent by a government or a government organization

**ˌpublic ˈtransport** (*BrE*) (*AmE* **ˌpublic transporˈtation**) *n.* [U] a system for carrying passengers from one place to another by road or rail: *to travel **on/by** public transport*

**ˌpublic ˈwarehouse** *n.* [C] a building where companies can pay to store goods and materials, usu. for a short period of time
▸ **ˌpublic ˈwarehousing** *n.* [U]

**ˌpublic ˈworks** *n.* [pl.] building work, such as that of hospitals, schools and roads, that is paid for by the government: *a programme of public works*

★ **publish** /ˈpʌblɪʃ/ *v.* [T] **1** to produce a book, magazine, CD-ROM, etc. and sell it to the public: *Our catalogue is published in six languages.* **2** to print a letter, an article, etc. in a newspaper or magazine: *We published a full-page ad in today's paper.* **3** to make sth available to the public on the Internet: *to publish a website* **4** to make official information known to the public: *The report will be published on the Internet.*
▸ **ˈpublisher** *n.* [C]: *book/magazine/music ~s* **ˈpublishing** *n.* [U]: *He works in publishing.*

**puff** /pʌf/ *n.* [C,U] (*AmE also* **ˈpuff piece** [C]) (*Market.*) a short piece of writing that exaggerates the quality of a book, product, etc. and is used to advertise it

**pull** /pʊl/ *v., n.*
• *v.* [T] **1** to cancel an event; to stop showing an advertisement, etc: *They pulled the ad after complaints.* **2** to attract the interest or support of sb/sth: *The special offers were pulling **in** shoppers.* **IDM** **pull the ˈplug on sth/sb** (*infml.*) to put an end to sb's project, a plan, etc. **pull sth/a ˌrabbit out of the ˈhat** (*infml.*) to suddenly produce sth as a solution to a problem **pull ˈstrings (for sb)** (*AmE* **pull ˈwires**) (*infml.*) to use your influence in order to get an advantage for sb: *They say his father pulled strings for him.* **pull the ˈstrings** to control events or the actions of other people: *Although he has retired, he is still pulling the strings.* **pull your ˈweight** to work as hard as everyone else in a job, an activity, etc. **pull ˈwires** (*AmE*) (*infml.*) = PULL STRINGS (FOR SB)
**PHR V** **ˌpull aˈhead (of sb/sth)** to start to progress faster than sb/sth: *Japanese firms are now pulling ahead.* **ˌpull ˈback (from sth)** to decide not to do sth that you were intending to do, because of possible problems **ˌpull sth ˈin/ˈdown** to earn the large amount of money mentioned: *Our core software business pulled in $351 m last year.* **ˌpull sth ˈoff** (*infml.*) to succeed in doing sth difficult: *We managed to pull off the deal.* **ˌpull ˈout (of sth)** to move away from sth or stop being involved in it: *The project became so expensive that we had to pull out.* **SYN** WITHDRAW **ˌpull toˈgether** to act, work, etc. together with other people in an organized way: *If we pull together, we can meet this deadline.*
• *n.* **1** [C, usu. sing.] the fact of sth attracting you or having a strong effect on you: *The show is not the pull it once was.* **2** [U] power and influence over other people: *people who have a lot of pull with the media*

**pullback** /ˈpʊlbæk/ *n.* [C,U] a situation where the price of sth suddenly changes after rising or falling steadily for a period of time

**ˈpull date** = SELL-BY DATE

**ˈpull-down** = DROP-DOWN

**ˈpull ˌstrategy** *n.* [C] (*Market.*) a method of marketing that depends on spending a large amount of money on advertising, etc. in order to persuade consumers that they want to buy the product → PUSH STRATEGY

**ˈpull ˌsystem** *n.* [C] (*Product.*) a system of production in which only the quantity of items needed are made, based on a signal of what has just been used or sold. This cuts costs by reducing the need for goods and materials to be stored, and reduces the time in which orders can be delivered → PUSH SYSTEM

**pulsing** /ˈpʌlsɪŋ/ *n.* [U] (*Market.*) a pattern of advertising a product in which periods when there is little or no advertising and periods when there is a lot of advertising follow each other in a regular way

**pump** /pʌmp/ *v.* **1** [T] to make water, air, gas, etc. flow in a particular direction by using a pump, etc. **2** [I] (about a liquid) to flow in a particular direction as if it is being forced by a pump PHR V **ˌpump sth ˈinto sth**; **ˌpump sth ˈin** to put a lot of money into sth: *We pumped millions into the campaign.* **ˌpump sth ˈout** to produce sth in large amounts: *pumping out hundreds of products every year* **ˌpump sth ˈup** to increase the amount, value or volume of sth: *to pump up interest rates*

**ˈpump price** *n.* [C, usu. sing.] the price at which petrol/gas is sold to the public

**ˈpump-ˌpriming** *n.* [U] (*Econ.*) a situation where the government invests money it has borrowed to encourage economic activity ▸ **ˈpump-prime** *v.* [T,I] **ˈpump-ˌprimer** *n.* [C]

**punch** /pʌntʃ/ *v.* [T] to make a hole in sth with a special tool or sharp object: *to punch a time card*
PHR V **ˌpunch ˈin** (*AmE*) = CLOCK IN/ON at CLOCK **ˌpunch ˈout** (*AmE*) = CLOCK OUT/OFF at CLOCK

**punctual** /ˈpʌŋktʃuəl/ *adj.* happening or doing sth at the arranged or correct time; not late: *We made a punctual start at 9 o'clock.* SYN PROMPT ▸ **ˌpunctuˈality** /-uˈæləti/ *n.* [U] **ˈpunctually** /-uəli/ *adv.*

**pundit** /ˈpʌndɪt/ *n.* [C] (*infml.*) a person who knows a lot about a particular subject and who often talks about it in public; an expert

**punitive** /ˈpjuːnɪtɪv/ *adj.* **1** intended as punishment: *imposing punitive tariffs on US imports* **2** very severe and that people find very difficult to pay: *punitive taxes*

**ˌpunitive ˈdamages** (*also* **eˌxemplary ˈdamages**) *n.* [pl.] (*Law*) an amount of money that a court orders a person, company, etc. to pay as a punishment, rather than to pay for the harm or damage they have caused

**punter** /ˈpʌntə(r)/ *n.* [C] (*infml.*) a person who buys or uses a particular product or service; a customer

★ **purchase** /ˈpɜːtʃəs; *AmE* ˈpɜːr-/ *n.*, *v.*
• ***n.* 1** [U,C] the act or process of buying sth: *How many people actually made a purchase?* ◇ *a bulk purchase of 50 PCs* ◇ *an employee share purchase plan*
⊕ ***a cash/credit/online ~* ♦ *big/big-ticket/major/small ~s* ♦ *equipment/house/share/stock ~s***
**2** [C] sth that you have bought: *ways of paying for your purchases*
• ***v.*** [T] (*fml.*) to buy sth
▸ **ˈpurchaser** *n.* [C] (*fml.*): *potential purchasers of the company*

**ˈpurchase aˌgreement** (*also* **ˈsales aˌgreement**, **aˌgreement of ˈsale**) = CONTRACT OF PURCHASE

**ˈpurchase ˌinvoice** *n.* [C] a list of goods bought, that a business receives from a supplier SYN BILL

**ˈpurchase ˌledger** (*also* **ˈbought ˌledger**, *less freq.*) *n.* [C] (*both BrE*) (*Account.*) in a company's financial records, the group of accounts in which amounts owed to suppliers are recorded SYN CREDITORS' LEDGER

**ˈpurchase ˌorder** *n.* [C] (*Comm.*) a formal document requesting the supply of goods or services, giving details of the goods, price, conditions of delivery and payment, etc.

**ˈpurchase price** *n.* [C] (*Comm.*) the amount of money that sb actually pays for sth SYN BUYING PRICE

**ˈpurchase requiˌsition** *n.* [C,U] (*Comm.*) a formal document from one department in a company to the department that buys materials, equipment, etc., giving details of the goods and services they require

**purchasing** /ˈpɜːtʃəsɪŋ; *AmE* ˈpɜːrtʃ-/ *n.* [U] the activity of buying things that a company needs, such as materials, parts, equipment, services, etc.; the department that deals with this: *She is responsible for purchasing worldwide.* ◇ *the purchasing manager* SYN PROCUREMENT

**ˈpurchasing ˌofficer** (*also* **proˈcurement ˌofficer**) *n.* [C] a person whose job is to choose suppliers and agree contracts with them to provide the equipment, materials or services that are used by a company SYN MATERIALS BUYER

**'purchasing ˌpower** (*also* **'spending ˌpower**) *n.* [U] **1** the amount of money that a person or business has available to spend on goods and services **2** (*Econ.*) the amount of goods and services that a currency can buy at a particular time: *the purchasing power of the dollar* SYN BUYING POWER

**'purchasing 'power 'parity** *n.* (*abbr* **PPP**) (*Econ.*) **1** [U] the theory that the rate of exchange between two currencies adjusts so that eventually the cost of a range of goods and services will be the same in both countries **2** [U,C] a rate of exchange that is calculated for two currencies so that the amount paid for a range of goods and services in both countries is the same

**'pure play** *n.* [C] a company that is involved in only one type of business: *newspaper pure plays* ◇ *a pure-play provider of financial services*

**purse** /pɜːs; *AmE* pɜːrs/ *n.* [sing.] the amount of money available to a person, an organization or a government to spend: *We produce a car for every purse.* IDM **ˌtighten/ˌloosen the 'purse strings** to spend less/more money → idiom at HOLD *v.*

**pursue** /pə'sjuː; *AmE* pər'suː/ *v.* [T] (*fml.*) **1** to do sth or try to achieve sth over a period of time: *to pursue a career in law* **2** to continue to discuss or be involved in sth: *She has no interest in pursuing the deal.*

**purveyor** /pə'veɪə(r); *AmE* pər'v-/ *n.* [C] (*fml.*) a person or company that supplies sth, esp. food, services or information: *Brown and Son, purveyors of fine foods* ▶ **pur'vey** *v.* [T]

**push** /pʊʃ/ *v., n.*

• *v.* [T] **1** (*with an adv. or a prep.*) to affect sth so that it reaches a particular level or state: *The rise in interest rates will push prices up.* **2** (*infml.*) to try hard to persuade people to buy sth: *to push a product* **3** to try hard to persuade people to do sth, accept an idea, etc: *No one pushed you to take the job.* **4** to make sb or yourself work hard: *Jack should push himself harder.* IDM **be pushed for 'time** (*infml.*) to have too little time to do sth **push the 'envelope** (*esp. AmE*) (*infml.*) to do more than is usu. considered possible: *pushing the envelope of computer technology* PHR V **ˌpush sth 'back** to make the time or date of a meeting, etc. later than planned SYN POSTPONE **'push (sb) for sth** to repeatedly ask for sth or try to make sth happen SYN PRESS **ˌpush sb 'out** to make sb leave an organization **ˌpush sth 'out** to produce sth in large quantities: *The factory pushes out 20 000 PCs a day.*

• *n.* [C] a determined effort to achieve sth: *a major marketing push* IDM **give sb/get the 'push** (*BrE*) (*infml.*) to dismiss sb/to be dismissed from your job

**'push ˌstrategy** *n.* [C] (*Market.*) a method of marketing that depends on persuading shop/store owners to make a product available and sell it to their customers → PULL STRATEGY

**'push ˌsystem** *n.* [C] (*Product.*) a system of production in which more goods are made than are needed in order to have a BUFFER STOCK in case there is a sudden increase in demand → PULL SYSTEM

★ **put** /pʊt/ *v., n.*

• *v.* (**putting, put, put**) → idiom at RECORD *n.* PHR V **ˌput yourself/sth a'cross/'over (to sb)** to communicate your ideas, feelings, etc. successfully to sb **ˌput sth a'side** (*also* **ˌput sth 'by**, *esp. in BrE*) to save money: *putting money aside for when you retire* **'put sth at sth** to calculate sb/sth to be a particular age, weight, amount, etc: *The damage to the building is put at over $1 m.* **ˌput sth a'way** to save money to spend later **ˌput sth 'back 1** to move sth to a later time or date **2** to cause sth to be delayed: *Poor sales put back plans for expansion.* **ˌput sth 'by** = PUT STH ASIDE **ˌput sth 'down 1** to pay part of the cost of sth: *to put down a deposit* **2** to lower or reduce sth: *putting prices down* **3** to write sth; to make a note of sth **ˌput yourself/sb/sth 'forward** to suggest yourself/sb as a candidate for a job or position **ˌput sth 'forward** to suggest sth for discussion: *to put forward a proposal* **ˌput sth 'in 1** to officially make a claim, request, etc: *The company has put in a claim for damages.* SYN SUBMIT **2** (*also* **ˌput sth 'into sth**) to spend a lot of time or work very hard at doing sth: *She often puts in twelve hours' work a day.* **3** (*also* **ˌput sth 'into sth**) to use or give money: *They put $80 000 of their own money into the business.* **ˌput 'in for sth** (*esp. BrE*) to officially ask for sth: *Perhaps I should put in for a rise.* **ˌput sth 'into sth** = PUT STH IN (2,3) **ˌput sb 'off** to cancel a meeting or an arrangement that you have made with sb **ˌput sth 'off** to change sth to a later time or date **ˌput sth 'on sth** to add an amount of money or a tax to the cost of sth: *The tax puts an*

*extra €70 on the price of a ticket.* ˌ**put sth ˈout 1** to produce sth, esp. for sale: *The plant puts out 500 new cars a week.* **2** to give a job or task to sb outside your company ˌ**put yourself/sb/sth ˈover (to sb)** = PUT YOURSELF/STH ACROSS (TO SB) ˌ**put sth ˈthrough** to continue with and complete a plan or activity: *to put the deal through* ˌ**put sb ˈthrough (to sb/sth)** to connect sb by telephone: *I'll put you through to the accounts department.* ˈ**put sth to sb** to offer a suggestion to sb so that they can accept or reject it ˌ**put sth toˈgether** to create or prepare sth: *They put the report together in two weeks.* ˈ**put sth towards sth** to give money to pay part of the cost of sth ˌ**put sth ˈup 1** to raise or increase sth: *to put up the rent* **2** to provide or lend money: *A syndicate of banks put the money up.* **3** to promise a particular asset to sb who is lending you money if you do not pay back the loan: *to put up your home as collateral* **4** to fix sth in a place where it will be seen: *to ~ up a poster/an ad* SYN DISPLAY
• *n.* [C] (*Finan.*) = PUT OPTION

**ˈput ˌoption** (*also* **put**) *n.* [C] (*Finan.*) a right to sell sth, such as a number of shares in a company or a quantity of raw materials, at a particular price within a fixed period or on a particular date: *to buy/exercise/hold/use a ~* → CALL OPTION

**PV** /ˌpiː ˈviː/ = PRESENT VALUE

**p.w.** *abbr* (*written*) **per week** for each week

**pyramid** /ˈpɪrəmɪd/ *n.* [C] an organization or a system in which there are fewer people at each level as you get near the top
▸ **pyramidal** /pɪˈræmɪdl/ *adj.*

**ˈpyramid ˌselling** *n.* [U] (*Comm.*) a way of selling things by encouraging sb to buy the right to sell a company's goods and a particular amount of stock. They then sell this and a smaller amount of stock to other people, who in turn sell to others and so on.

# Qq

**QA** /ˌkjuː ˈeɪ/ = QUALITY ASSURANCE

**QC** /ˌkjuː ˈsiː/ = QUALITY CONTROL

**QFD** /ˌkjuː ef ˈdiː/ = QUALITY FUNCTION DEPLOYMENT

**qtr** *abbr* a short way of writing **quarter** (a period of three months)

★ **qualification** /ˌkwɒlɪfɪˈkeɪʃn; *AmE* ˌkwɑːl-/ *n.* **1** [C, usu. pl.] (*BrE*) an exam that you have passed or a course of study that you have successfully completed: *What qualifications do you have?*
● *academic/educational/professional/technical/vocational ~s* • *to acquire/gain/get/obtain ~s*
**2** [C] a skill or type of experience that you need for a particular job or activity: *Previous managerial experience is a necessary qualification.*
**3** [U] the fact of passing an exam, completing a course of training or reaching the standard necessary to do a job: *You may be offered employment here following qualification.*

★ **qualified** /ˈkwɒlɪfaɪd; *AmE* ˈkwɑːl-/ *adj.* **1** having passed the exams or completed the training necessary to do a particular job; having the experience to do a particular job: *a list of qualified candidates* ◇ *She's extremely* **well** *qualified* **for** *the job.*
● *a ~ accountant/electrician, etc.* • *~ candidates/staff/workers* • *to be fully/highly/well ~*
**2** having the practical knowledge or skills to do sth: *I don't feel qualified* **to** *advise you.*

ˌ**qualified oˈpinion** (*also* ˌ**qualified reˈport**, *less freq.*) *n.* [C] (*Account.*) used to show that an AUDIT is limited in some way, for example because the information provided was not complete or there is a problem NOTE The words **qualified opinion** may be written on the front of the report.

★ **qualify** /ˈkwɒlɪfaɪ; *AmE* ˈkwɑːl-/ *v.* (**-fies**, **-fying**, **-fied**, **-fied**) **1** [I] to reach the standard of ability or knowledge needed to do a particular job, for example by completing a course of study or passing exams: *How long does it take to qualify?* **2** [T] to give sb the skills and knowledge they need to do sth: *This training course will qualify you* **for** *a better job.* **3** [T,I] to have or give sb the right to do sth: *My credit card qualifies me* **for** *a discount.*

ˈ**qualifying ˌperiod** *n.* [C] (*HR*) the length of time you must have been doing sth in order to be entitled to a particular benefit

**qualitative** /ˈkwɒlɪtətɪv; *AmE* ˈkwɑːləteɪt-/ *adj.* **1** considering sth by examining aspects that cannot easily be measured or expressed as numbers, such as opinions or attitudes: *qualitative research* **2** involving a comparison based on quality: *There is no qualitative difference between these PCs.* → QUANTITATIVE

★ **quality** /ˈkwɒləti; *AmE* ˈkwɑːl-/ *n., adj.*

• ***n.*** (*pl.* **-ties**) **1** [U,C] the standard of sth when it is compared to other things like it; how good or bad sth is: *There has been a decline in quality.*

⊙ *be of (a)* ***good/high/top*** *~* ♦ ***low/poor/varying*** *~* ♦ *~* ***declines/improves/suffers***

**2** [U] a high standard: *We provide quality at reasonable prices.* **3** [C] a thing that is part of a person's character, esp. sth good: *people with the right qualities for the job* **4** [C] a feature or aspect of sth, often one that makes it different from sth else

• ***adj.*** (used esp. by people trying to sell goods or services) of a high standard: *We sell quality cars.*

**ˈquality asˌsurance** *n.* [U] (*abbr* **QA**) (*Product.*) the practice of managing every stage of the process of producing goods or providing services to make sure they are kept at the standard the customer expects

**ˈquality ˌcircle** *n.* [C] (*Product.*) a small group of workers who meet regularly to propose solutions to problems related to work

★ **ˈquality conˌtrol** *n.* [U] (*abbr* **QC**) (*Product.*) a system of keeping high standards in manufactured products by planning carefully, checking and making necessary improvements ▸ **ˈquality conˌtroller** *n.* [C]

**ˈQuality ˈFunction Deˈployment** *n.* [U] (*abbr* **QFD**) (*Market.; Product.*) a method of creating products and services that involves basing design, development and delivery on what customers say they need

**ˈquality ˌmanagement** = TOTAL QUALITY MANAGEMENT

**ˈQuality of ˈWorking ˈLife** (*esp. BrE*) (*AmE usu.* **ˈQuality of ˈWork Life**) *phr.* (*abbr* **QWL**) (*HR*) how happy and satisfied employees feel at work; techniques and methods designed to improve this

**quango** /ˈkwæŋgəʊ; *AmE* -goʊ/ *n.* [C] (*pl.* **quangos**) in the UK, an organization dealing with public matters, started and financed by the government, but working independently and with its own legal powers SYN NDPB

★ **quantify** /ˈkwɒntɪfaɪ; *AmE* ˈkwɑːn-/ *v.* [T] (**-fies**, **-fying**, **-fied**, **-fied**) to describe or express sth as an amount or a number: *The risks are difficult to quantify.* ▸ **ˈquantifiable** *adj.*: *developing quantifiable goals* **ˌquantifiˈcation** /-fɪˈkeɪʃn/ *n.* [U]

**quantitative** /ˈkwɒntɪtətɪv; *AmE* ˈkwɑːntəteɪt-/ *adj.* **1** considering sth by examining aspects that can be measured or expressed as numbers: *quantitative research* **2** involving a comparison based on quantity: *a ~ change/difference* → QUALITATIVE

★ **quantity** /ˈkwɒntəti; *AmE* ˈkwɑːn-/ *n.* (*pl.* **-ties**) **1** [C,U] an amount or a number of sth: *Vast quantities of oil were found in northern Alaska.* ◇ *Materials are cheaper when bought* ***in large quantities.***

⊙ ***huge/massive*** *quantities* ♦ *a* ***large/small*** *~*

**2** [U] the measurement of sth by saying how much of it there is: *The data is limited in terms of both quality and quantity.* **3** [C,U] a large amount or number of sth: *It was the first PC to be manufactured* ***in quantity.***

**ˈquantity surˌveyor** *n.* [C] (*BrE*) a person whose job is to calculate the quantity of materials needed for building sth, how much it will cost and how long it will take ▸ **ˈquantity ˌsurvey** *n.* [C]

**quarantine** /ˈkwɒrəntiːn; *AmE* ˈkwɔːr-; ˈkwɑːr-/ *n.* [U] a period of time when an animal, a food product, etc. entering a country is kept away from others in order to prevent disease from spreading: *agricultural quarantine laws* ▸ **ˈquarantine** *v.* [T]

★ **quarter** /ˈkwɔːtə(r); *AmE* ˈkwɔːrt-/ *n.* [C] (*Account.*) a period of three months, used esp. as a period for which bills are paid or a company's income is calculated

IDM **ˌquarter on ˈquarter** (*Account.*) compared with the last quarter: *Sales rose 20% quarter on quarter.* → YEAR ON YEAR at YEAR

**ˈquarter day** *n.* [C] (*BrE*) (*Finan.*) the fixed day of each **quarter** on which payments must be made, for example at the stock exchange

**quarterly** /ˈkwɔːtəli; *AmE* ˈkwɔːrtərli/ *adj., n.*

• ***adj.*** **1** relating to a period of three months: *quarterly earnings* **2** produced or happening every three months: *quarterly meetings* ▸ **ˈquarterly** *adv.*

• ***n.*** **1** [C] a magazine, etc. published four times a year **2** (*Account.*) **quarterlies** [pl.] in the US, the financial results that large companies publish every three months

**ˈquarter point** *n.* [C] (*Finan.*) one of four equal divisions of one per cent: *a quarter-point cut in interest rates*

**quasi-** /ˈkweɪzaɪ; -saɪ; ˈkwɑːzi/ *comb. form* (*used in adjs and ns*) **1** partly; almost: *The carmaker had a quasi-monopoly position in the mar-*

*ket.* **2** that appears to be sth but is not really so: *The company chose a quasi-official name.*

**quay** /kiː/ *n.* [C] (*Transpt.*) a platform in a harbour where boats come in to load, etc.

★**query** /ˈkwɪəri; *AmE* ˈkwɪri/ *n., v.*
• *n.* [C] (*pl.* **-ries**) a question, esp. one asking for information or expressing a doubt about sth: *Our staff will be happy to answer your queries.*
• *v.* [T] (**-ries**, **-rying**, **-ried**, **-ried**) to express doubts about sth: *We queried the bill as it seemed too high.*

**questionable** /ˈkwestʃənəbl/ *adj.* **1** that you have doubts about because you think it is not accurate or correct: *The assumptions about economic growth are highly questionable.* **2** likely to be dishonest or morally wrong: *questionable accounting*

**questionnaire** /ˌkwestʃəˈneə(r); *AmE* -ˈner/ *n.* [C] a written list of questions that are answered by a number of people so that information can be collected from the answers
⊙ *to* ***complete/fill in/fill out/reply to/respond to*** *a* ~ ♦ *to* ***analyse*** *a* ~

**queue** /kjuː/ *n., v.*
• *n.* [C] **1** (*BrE*) (*AmE* **line**) a line of people, cars, etc. waiting to do sth: *queues at the check-outs* **2** (*BrE*) (*AmE* **line**) a large number of people who want to do or have sth: *a queue of buyers for the company* **3** (*IT*) a list of jobs that a computer has to do in a particular order: *the print queue* **4** if your call is being held in a **queue**, a number of other calls will be dealt with before your call is answered
**IDM** **at the front/back of the ˈqueue** among the first or the last people to do sth or have sth
• *v.* (**queuing** *or* **queueing**) **1** [I] (*BrE*) **~ (up) (for sth)** to wait in a line to do sth, buy sth, go somewhere, etc.; to be one of a large number of people who want to do sth: *Hundreds of shoppers queued from 2 a.m.* **2** (*IT*) [T,I] to arrange jobs in a **queue**

**ˈquick ˌratio** (*also* **ˌquick-ˈassets ˌratio**) = ACID-TEST RATIO

**quiet** /ˈkwaɪət/ *adj.* (**-er**, **-est**) if business, trading, etc. is **quiet**, there is not much activity

**quit** /kwɪt/ *v.* (**quitting**, **quit**, **quit**, *BrE also* **quitting**, **quitted**, **quitted**) **1** (*infml.*) [T,I] to leave your job, esp. because you are angry or unhappy about sth: *Her decision to quit was completely unexpected.* **2** [T] to leave a place or an activity **3** (*IT*) [T] to close a computer program

**quorum** /ˈkwɔːrəm/ *n.* [sing.] the smallest number of people who must be at a meeting before it can begin or decisions can be made
▸ **ˈquorate** /-rət/ *adj.*

**quota** /ˈkwəʊtə; *AmE* ˈkwoʊtə/ *n.* [C] **1** (*Econ.*) the limited number or amount of people or things that is officially allowed: *export quotas* ◇ *a quota system for greenhouse gases*
⊙ *to* ***impose/introduce/lift/set*** ~ ♦ *to* ***increase/raise/reduce*** *a* ~ ♦ *to* ***comply with/exceed*** ~
**2** a fixed amount of sth that sb can receive or must do; a fixed number of people expected or needed: *Our sales quotas were not met last year.*
⊙ *to* ***impose/introduce*** ~ ♦ *to* ***increase/raise/reduce*** *a* ~ ♦ *to* ***achieve/fill/make/reach*** *a* ~

**quotation** /kwəʊˈteɪʃn; *AmE* kwoʊ-/ *n.* [C] **1** (*Comm.*) a statement of how much a particular piece of work will cost
⊙ *to* ***give (sb)/provide (sb with)/submit*** *a* ~ ♦ *to* ***accept/ask for/get*** *a* ~
**2** (*Stock Ex.*) the price of a share on the stock market **3** (*Stock Ex.*) when a company's shares are accepted on a stock exchange and can be bought and sold: *The company does not have a full stock market quotation.*

★**quote** /kwəʊt; *AmE* kwoʊt/ *v., n.*
• *v.* [T] **1** (*Comm.*) **~ sb sth** to tell a customer how much you will charge them for a job, service or product: *We were quoted a price of $9 a metre.* **2** (*Stock Ex.*) to record the name of a company on a stock exchange so that its shares can be bought and sold: *The company is quoted on the NYSE.* **3** (*Finan.*) to give the price of a share on a stock exchange or a currency
• *n.* [C] (*Comm.*) a statement of how much money a particular piece of work will cost

**quoted** /ˈkwəʊtɪd; *AmE* ˈkwoʊt-/ *adj.* (*Stock Ex.*) **quoted** shares are bought and sold on a stock exchange SYN LISTED OPP UNQUOTED

**ˌquoted ˈcompany** *n.* [C] (*Stock Ex.*) a company whose shares are bought and sold on a stock exchange

**QWL** /ˌkjuː dʌbljuː ˈel/ = QUALITY OF WORKING LIFE

# Rr

**ˌrace to the ˈbottom** *n.* [sing.] the idea that economic competition will lead to lower standards, worse conditions for workers, and workers in some countries losing their jobs to lower-paid workers in others

**rack** /ræk/ *v.* PHR V ˌ**rack sth 'up** (*esp. AmE*) to collect sth such as profits or losses, esp. quickly or in large amounts: *The business racked up $205 m in sales in its first year.*

**racket** /'rækɪt/ *n.* [C] a dishonest or an illegal way of getting money

**racketeer** /ˌrækə'tɪə(r); *AmE* -'tɪr/ *n.* [C] a person who makes money through dishonest or illegal activities ▶ ˌ**racke'teering** *n.* [U]

'**rack rate** *n.* [C] (*esp. AmE*) the standard price of a hotel room

★ **R&D** (*also* **R and D**) /ˌɑːr ən 'diː/ *abbr* **research and development** (*used as an uncountable n.*) **1** work that examines new ideas and tries to develop new products and processes: *They spend $5 bn a year on R&D.* **2** the department in a company that tries to develop new products and ideas and improve existing ones: *the R&D division*

**radar** /'reɪdɑː(r)/ *n.* IDM **below/under the 'radar (screen)** if something is **below/under the radar**, people are not aware of it **on/off the 'radar (screen)** used to say that people are aware or not aware of sth, or are thinking or not thinking about it: *This sale was not even on our radar.*

**raft** /rɑːft; *AmE* ræft/ *n.* [C, usu. sing.] a large number or amount of sth: *a raft of economic measures*

**rage** /reɪdʒ/ *n.* [U] (*used with other ns*) anger and violent behaviour caused by a particular situation: *trolley rage in the supermarket* ◇ *air/computer/phone/road/work ~*
IDM **be all the 'rage** (*infml.*) to be extremely fashionable and popular

**raid** /reɪd/ *n.* [C] (*Stock Ex.*) an occasion when a person or company unexpectedly tries to take control of another company by buying a large number of its shares ▶ '**raider** *n.* [C]

**rail** /reɪl/ *n.* [U] railways/railroads as a means of transport: *freight carried* ***by rail*** ◇ *~ services/fares*

ˌ**rail con'signment note** *n.* [C] (*abbr* **CIM**) (*Transpt.*) a document that goes with goods that are sent by rail, stating that the company transporting them has received them in good condition

**rainmaker** /'reɪnmeɪkə(r)/ *n.* [C] (*esp. AmE*) a person who gets a lot of business and income for a company and makes it successful

★ **raise** /reɪz/ *v., n.*
• ***v.*** [T] **1** to increase the amount or level of sth: *to ~ salaries/prices/taxes* ◇ *a campaign to raise awareness of the brand* **2** to bring or collect money together; to manage to get money for sth: *to ~ capital/a loan* **3** to mention sth for people to discuss or for sb to deal with: *I'm glad you raised* ***the subject of*** *money.* SYN BRING STH UP **4** (*Account.*) if you **raise** an INVOICE you write out or print one or ask sb to do this: *Invoices are not raised where immediate payment is required.* **5** if you **raise** a call, you contact sb by telephone, email, etc. to ask for some help with a technical problem → idiom at ANTE
• ***n.*** [C] (*AmE*) = RISE *n.* (2)

**rake** /reɪk/ *v.* PHR V ˌ**rake 'in sth** (*infml.*) to earn a lot of money, esp. when it is done easily: *The store's been* ***raking it in*** *recently.*

★ **rally** /'ræli/ *v., n.*
• ***v.*** [I] (**rallies, rallying, rallied, rallied**) (*Finan.*) to rise in price after a period of falling prices or little activity: *The dollar has rallied sharply.*
• ***n.*** [C] (*pl.* **rallies**) a rise in prices after a period of falling prices or little activity: *The market staged a late rally yesterday.*
◉ ***a market/price/stock ~*** ♦ ***a powerful/sharp/strong ~*** ♦ ***an early/a late ~*** ♦ ***to spark/trigger a ~***

**RAM** /ræm/ *abbr* (*IT*) **random-access memory** computer memory in which data can be changed or removed and can be looked at in any order: *32 megabytes of RAM*

**ramp** /ræmp/ *v.* PHR V ˌ**ramp (sth) 'up** to increase; to make sth increase in amount: *to ramp up production of the new model*

**rampant** /'ræmpənt/ *adj.* (about sth bad) existing or spreading everywhere in a way that cannot be controlled: *~ inflation/unemployment*

**RAN** /ˌɑːr eɪ 'en/ = REVENUE ANTICIPATION NOTE

**random** /'rændəm/ *adj., n.*
• ***adj.*** done, chosen, etc. without sb thinking or deciding in advance what is going to happen, or without any regular pattern: *The information is processed in a random order.*
▶ '**randomly** *adv.*
• ***n.*** IDM **at 'random** without thinking or deciding in advance what is going to happen: *Select a customer at random each month to receive a special gift.*

ˌ**random 'sample** *n.* [C] (*Tech.*) a number of people or things taken from a larger group using a process in which each person or thing has an equal chance of being chosen
▶ ˌ**random 'sampling** *n.* [U,C]

★ **range** /reɪndʒ/ *n., v.*

• ***n.* 1** [C, usu. sing.] a variety of things of a particular type: *a wide range of facilities and services* **2** [C] a set of products of a particular type: *a new range of hair products* SYN LINE **3** [C, usu. sing.] the limits between which sth varies: *the 18–30 age range*

• ***v.*** [I] **1 ~ from A to B | ~ between A and B** to vary between two particular amounts, sizes, etc., including others between them: *Prices range from $20 to $50.* **2 ~ from A to B** to include a variety of different things in addition to those mentioned: *Their products range from coffee to soap.*

**rank** /ræŋk/ *n., v.*

• ***n.* 1** [U,C] the position, esp. a high position, that sb has in an organization: *He holds the rank of CEO.*

◐ *a low/high/middle/top ~ • junior/management/senior ~s*

**2** [sing.] the position that sb/sth has in a list arranged according to quality or importance: *They are in the top rank of financial institutions.* **3 the ranks** [pl.] the members of a particular group or organization: *joining the growing ranks of the unemployed*

IDM **break 'ranks** if members of a group **break ranks**, they refuse to support the group

• ***v.*** [T,I] (*not in the continuous tenses*) to give sb/sth a particular position on a scale according to quality, importance, success, etc.; to have a position of this kind: *The tasks have been ranked in order of difficulty.* ◇ *a* ***top-ranked*** *business school* SYN RATE

**the ˌrank and 'file** *n.* [sing. with sing./pl. verb] the ordinary members of an organization, esp. a trade union: *The rank and file approved the proposals.* ◇ *rank-and-file members*

▸ **ˌrank-and-'filer** *n.* [C]

**ranking** /'ræŋkɪŋ/ *n., adj.*

• ***n.* 1 the rankings** [pl.] an official list showing how good or important people or things are in relation to other similar people or things: *first place in the plant's productivity rankings* **2** [C] the position of sb/sth in this list: *We achieved a four-star ranking.* **3** [U] the action of giving a position in a list to sb/sth: *the annual ranking of fastest-growing companies*

• ***adj.* 1** (*esp. AmE*) having a high or the highest rank in an organization, etc: *our five ranking officers* **2** (*used in compounds*) having the particular rank mentioned: *lower- to middle-ranking staff*

**ratchet** /'rætʃɪt/ *v.* PHR V **ˌratchet (sth) 'up/'down** to increase/decrease by small amounts; to make sth do this: *Overuse of credit cards has ratcheted up consumer debt.*

★ **rate** /reɪt/ *n., v.*

• ***n.*** [C] **1** a fixed amount of money that is charged or paid for sth: *advertising rates* ◇ *a low hourly rate of pay*

◐ *a* ***cheap/competitive/reasonable*** *~ • a* ***good/high*** *~ • a* ***fixed/variable*** *~ • an* ***annual/average*** *~ • to* ***charge/pay/set*** *a ~ (of...)*

**2** a measurement of the speed at which sth happens: *Inflation is running at an annual rate of 4.5 to 5%.* ◇ *the company's current rate of growth*

◐ *a* ***fast/slow/steady*** *~ • to* ***improve/increase/maintain*** *a ~ • to* ***cut/reduce*** *a ~*

**3** a measurement of the number of times sth happens or exists during a particular period: *Local businesses are closing* ***at the rate of*** *three a year.*

◐ *a* ***high/low/rising/falling*** *~ • a* ***drop/rise*** *in the ~ of sth • a* ***failure/success*** *~ • to* ***improve/increase/maintain*** *a ~ • to* ***cut/reduce*** *a ~*

• ***v.* 1** [T,I] **~ sb/sth (as) sth | ~ (as sth)** (*not in the continuous tenses*) to have, or think that sb/sth has, a particular level of quality, value, etc: *They rated him highly as a colleague.* ◇ *highly-rated software* **2** [T] (*usu. pass.*) to place sb/sth in a particular position on a scale in relation to similar people or things: *a top-rated hotel* SYN RANK **3** (*Finan.*) [T] **~ sth (as) sth** to decide if shares, bonds, etc. are a good or bad investment because of the level of risk: *The analysts rate these shares a 'buy'.*

◐ *to ~ sth (as)* ***(a) hold/junk/(a) sell*** *• to ~ sth (as)* ***investment grade/Triple A***

**4** [T] to give a machine, a ship or an electrical device a number, mark, etc. according to how powerful it is, what it can do, etc.

**'rate card** *n.* [C] (*Market.*) a list that shows how much it costs to advertise on television, in a particular newspaper, on a particular website, etc. and gives other important details

**'rate-ˌcutting** *n.* [U] (*Econ.*) the action of reducing the amount of money that people or businesses pay in interest on money they borrow

**ˌrate of depreci'ation** = DEPRECIATION RATE

**ˌrate of ex'change** = EXCHANGE RATE

**ˌrate of 'interest** = INTEREST RATE

**ˌrate of re'turn** *n.* [C] (*Finan.*) the amount of profit that an investment produces, expressed as a percentage of the amount invested: *The*

*average rate of return on assets was 9.3%.*

◆ *a good/high/low/poor ~ ◆ a guaranteed ~ ◆ to earn/offer/provide a ~*

**ratify** /ˈrætɪfaɪ/ *v.* [T] (**-fies, -fying, -fied, -fied**) to make an agreement officially valid by voting for or signing it ▸ **ˌratifiˈcation** /-fɪˈkeɪʃn/ *n.* [U]

★**rating** /ˈreɪtɪŋ/ *n.* **1** [C] a measurement of how good, popular, important, etc. sb/sth is, esp. in relation to other people or things: *The directors' skills were rated and compared to the average rating of all the others.*

◆ *a high/low/poor/top ~ ◆ to achieve/get/have a ~ ◆ to give sth a ~ ◆ a ~ falls/improves/rises*

**2** (*Finan.*) [C,U] = CREDIT RATING **3** (*Finan.*) [C,U] a measurement of whether shares, bonds, etc. are a good or bad investment because of the level of risk

◆ *to have a ~ ◆ to put a ~ on sth ◆ to review/upgrade a ~ ◆ to cut/downgrade/lower a ~*

**4 ratings** [pl.] a set of figures that show how many people watch or listen to a particular television or radio programme, used to show how popular a programme is: *The show has gone up in the ratings.*

◆ *good/poor ~ ◆ to get/have ~ ◆ ~ go down/improve ◆ a ~ battle/war*

**5** (*Insur.*) (*also* **inˈsurance ˌrating**) [C] a measurement of the risk involved in giving sb insurance, used to calculate how much they must pay

◆ *to calculate/have/receive a ~*

**ˈrating ˌagency** (*also* **ˈratings ˌagency**) *n.* [C] (*Finan.*) an organization that analyses how likely a company is to pay back the money that it owes and provides a score for this SYN CREDIT RATING AGENCY

**ˈratings point** *n.* [C] (*Market.*) a way of measuring the size of an audience for a television programme. One **ratings point** is one per cent of all the homes in a particular area watching a programme.

**ratio** /ˈreɪʃiəʊ; *AmE* -oʊ/ *n.* [C] (*pl.* **ratios**) the relationship between two groups of people, things or amounts of money that is represented by two numbers or a percentage showing how much larger one group is than the other: *Ten years ago, the ratio of employees to customers was about 1:10.* ◇ *the ratio of a company's share price to its earnings*

**ˈratio aˌnalysis** *n.* [C,U] (*Account.*) the study of the relationships between various financial numbers or amounts, used to judge a company's financial condition

**rationale** /ˌræʃəˈnɑːl; *AmE* -ˈnæl/ *n.* [C, usu. sing.] (*fml.*) the principles or reasons that explain a particular decision, course of action, etc: *The rationale* **behind** *the merger is clear.*

**rationalize, -ise** /ˈræʃnəlaɪz/ *v.* [T,I] to make changes to a business, an organization, etc. to make it more efficient, esp. by spending less money: *to rationalize production* ▸ **ˌrationaliˈzation, -iˈsation** /-laɪˈzeɪʃn; *AmE* -ləˈz-/ *n.* [U]

**the ˈrat race** *n.* [sing.] (*infml.*) the way of life of people living and working in a big city where everyone competes in an aggressive way to be more successful, earn more money, etc: *to quit the rat race*

**raw** /rɔː/ *adj.* **1 raw** substances are in their natural state and have not yet been changed, used or made into sth else: *~ cotton/steel* **2 raw** data has not yet been organized into a form in which it can easily be used or understood IDM **a raw ˈdeal** the fact of sb being treated unfairly: *Older workers often get a raw deal.*

**ˌraw maˈterial** *n.* [C,U] a natural or basic substance that is used to make sth in an industrial process: *the supply of raw materials to the factory*

**RD** = REFER TO DRAWER

**RDO** /ˌɑː diː ˈəʊ; *AmE* ˌɑːr diː ˈoʊ/ = ROSTERED DAY OFF

**Re** /reɪ/ *abbr* (*Insur.*) **Reinsurance** used in the names of companies: *Munich Re*

**re** /riː/ *prep.* concerning; used in business letters and notes to say what the letter or note is about: *Re your letter of 1 September...*

**re-** /riː/ *prefix* (*used in vs and related ns, adjs and advs*) again: *rebrand* ◇ *re-engineer*

★**reach** /riːtʃ/ *v., n.*

• *v.* [T] **1** to increase to a particular level: *Consumer debt has reached record levels.* **2** to be seen or heard by a particular group of people, esp. when you want them to buy your products: *Daily papers reach a mass audience.* **3** to communicate with sb, esp. by telephone: *I've been trying to reach her all morning.* **4** to achieve a particular aim: *to reach agreement with sb* ◇ *We've reached a final decision.*

• *n.* **1** [sing.] the number of people that can see or hear sth, buy a product, use a service, etc: *The company's reach was 1% of the PC market.*

◆ *a global/massive/wide ~ ◆ to expand/extend/increase your ~*

**2 reaches** [pl.] particular sections of an organization, a system, etc: *the upper reaches of management*
IDM **beyond/out of sb's 'reach; beyond/out of (the) reach of sb** costing more than sb can afford: *Rising prices have put a house beyond the reach of many buyers.* **within sb's 'reach; within (the) reach of sb** costing an amount that sb can afford

**react** /ri'ækt/ *v.* [I] **1** if markets, share prices, etc. **react**, they start to rise or fall as a result of things that happen: *People are waiting to see how the markets react.* **2** if people or organizations **react** to sth, they change or behave in a particular way in response to sth: *Bookings have fallen and several companies have reacted by cutting jobs.* ▸ **re'action** /-kʃn/ *n.* [C,U]: *There was a mixed reaction* **to** *her appointment.*

**reactive** /ri'æktɪv/ *adj.* waiting for things to happen before acting, rather than controlling a situation by planning or by making things happen: *a reactive approach to customer satisfaction* → PROACTIVE

**ˌreactive 'marketing** *n.* [U] methods of selling a company's goods and services that rely on possible customers contacting the company

**readership** /'ri:dəʃɪp; *AmE* -dərʃ-/ *n.* [C, usu. sing., U] the number or type of people who read a particular newspaper, magazine, etc., often compared to the number of people who buy it

**'read-out** *n.* [C] (*IT*) the display of information on a computer screen

**ˌread-'write** *adj.* (*abbr* **RW**) (*IT*) if a file, disk or memory is **read-write**, it allows you to make changes to data: *a CD-RW drive/disk*

**ˌready-'made** *adj.* **1** made in standard types and sizes, rather than for an individual customer: *ready-made clothing* **2** prepared in advance so that you can use it or eat it immediately: *ready-made meals*

**ˌready-to-'wear** *adj.* ready-to-wear clothes are made in standard types and sizes, rather than being made to fit an individual customer

**real** /'ri:əl *BrE usu.* rɪəl/ *adj.* (*Econ.*) including the effects of INFLATION: *GNP contracted 1.2%* ***in real terms*** *in the last quarter.* ◇ *~ costs/earnings/incomes/prices*

**the ˌreal e'conomy** *n.* [sing.] (*Econ.*) the parts of the economy that produce goods and services, rather than the parts involving buying and selling on the financial markets

**'real eˌstate** *n.* [U] (*esp. AmE*) property in the form of land or buildings; the business of buying and selling this: *investing in real estate*

**'real estate ˌagent** *n.* [C] **1** = ESTATE AGENT **2** in the US, a person who has official permission from a state to be an ESTATE AGENT and works for a REAL ESTATE BROKER ▸ **'real estate ˌagency** *n.* [C]

**'real estate ˌbroker** *n.* [C] (*AmE*) a person or business that is given official permission by a state to help people buy and sell houses, other buildings, or land, and often employs REAL ESTATE AGENTS ▸ **'real estate ˌbrokerage** *n.* [C]

**'real estate ˌcompany** = PROPERTY COMPANY

**'real eˌstate loan** = PROPERTY LOAN

**'real estate ˌmanagement** = PROPERTY MANAGEMENT

**the 'real estate ˌmarket** = PROPERTY MARKET

**ˌreal ex'change rate** *n.* [C] (*Econ.*) the relation in value between one currency and another when it has been adjusted for differences in prices between the two countries

**realign** /ˌri:ə'laɪn/ *v.* [T] to change the way a business, an organization, etc. is organized in order to adapt it to a new situation: *realigning our business to lower demand* ▸ **ˌrea'lignment** *n.* [U,C]

**realizable, -isable** /'ri:əlaɪzəbl; *BrE also* 'rɪə-/ *adj.* **1** (*Account.*) **realizable** assets, investments, etc. can be sold quickly to make money available **2** possible to achieve or make happen: *realizable goals*

★**realize, -ise** /'ri:əlaɪz; *BrE also* 'rɪəl-/ *v.* [T] **1** to be sold for a particular amount of money: *The paintings realized $2.5 m at auction.* **2** to make or lose a particular amount of money: *realized gains* **3** (*Finan.*) **~ an asset** to sell things that you own, for example property, in order to get the money that you need for sth SYN LIQUIDATE **4** to achieve sth important that you very much want to do: *realizing your full potential* ▸ **ˌreali'zation, -i'sation** /-laɪ'zeɪʃn; *AmE* -lə'z-/ *n.* [U]

**ˌreal 'time** *n.* [U] (*IT*) used to describe the way in which a computer system can receive information and react to it immediately: *Brokers use real-time data and news to make investment decisions.*

**ˌreal-time 'company** *n.* [C] a company that uses the Internet and other technology so that they can react immediately to information or requests from customers and suppliers

**Realtor™** /ˈriːəltə(r)/ = ESTATE AGENT

**realty** /ˈriːəlti/ *n.* [U] (*AmE*) (often used in the names of companies) land or property: *Kimco Realty*

**ˌreal ˈwages** *n.* [pl.] (*Econ.*) a person's income measured by what it can buy rather than the money received, considering the effects of INFLATION: *Real wages have fallen.*

**ream** /riːm/ *n.* **1 reams** [pl.] a large amount of writing or information: *reams of data* **2** (*Tech.*) [C] five hundred sheets of paper

**reap** /riːp/ *v.* [T] (often used in newspapers) to obtain money or a benefit as a result of sth you have done: *reaping the rewards of cost cuts* ◇ *to ~ benefits/gains/profits*

**reasonable** /ˈriːznəbl/ *adj.* **1** (about a price or the cost of sth) acceptable and appropriate; not too cheap and not too expensive **2** fair, practical and sensible: *It is a reasonable request.* OPP UNREASONABLE **3** fairly good, but not very good: *The sales results were reasonable.* ▸ **ˈreasonableness** *n.* [U]

**rebadge** /ˌriːˈbædʒ/ *v.* (*Market.*) **1** [T] to buy a product or service from another company and sell it as your own: *They could import a small car and rebadge it.* **2** [T,I] to change the name or symbol of a business or one of its products or services

**rebate** /ˈriːbeɪt/ *n.* [C] **1** (*Account.*) an amount of money that is given back to you because you have paid too much: *a tax rebate* **2** (*Comm.*) an amount of money that is taken off the cost of sth before you pay for it: *cash rebates and other discounts* SYN DISCOUNT ▸ **ˈrebate** *v.* [T]

**reboot** /ˌriːˈbuːt/ *v.* [T,I] (*IT*) if you **reboot** a computer or it **reboots**, you switch it off and then start it again immediately

**rebound** *v.*, *n.*
• *v.* /rɪˈbaʊnd/ [I] to rise, increase or become more active again after a difficult period: *The bank's share price fell to $26, before rebounding to $36.*
• *n.* /ˈriːbaʊnd/ [C] a positive reaction that happens after sth negative: *a rebound* **in** *the manufacturing sector*

★**rebrand** /ˌriːˈbrænd/ *v.* [T,I] (*Market.*) to change the image of a company or an organization, or of one of its products or services, for example by giving it a new name, advertising it in a different way, etc. ▸ **rebrand** /ˈriːbrænd/ *n.* [sing.]: *a multi-million-dollar rebrand* **ˌreˈbranding** *n.* [U; sing.]: *a $10m rebranding*

**rebut** /rɪˈbʌt/ *v.* [T] (-tt-) (*fml.*) to say or prove that a statement or criticism is not true: *He rebutted suggestions that the company might be sold.* ▸ **reˈbuttal** /-tl/ *n.* [C,U]: *a 26-page rebuttal of the claims*

**recall** /rɪˈkɔːl/ *v.* [T] **1** (*Comm.*) to ask people to return a product they have bought, usu. because there is sth wrong with it: *They recalled 6.5 million tyres.* SYN CALL STH IN **2** (*not in the continuous tenses*) to remember sth you have seen or heard: *recalling an ad* ▸ **recall** /rɪˈkɔːl; ˈriːkɔːl/ *n.* [C,U]: *a series of product recalls* ◇ *brand recall*

**recap** /ˈriːkæp/ *v.* [T,I] (-pp-) **~ (on sth)** to repeat or give a summary of what has already been said, decided, etc. ▸ **ˈrecap** *n.* [C]

**recapitalize**, **-ise** /ˌriːˈkæpɪtəlaɪz/ *v.* [T,I] (*Finan.*) to put more capital into a business or change the way the capital is held ▸ **ˌreˌcapitaliˈzation**, **-iˈsation** /-laɪˈzeɪʃn; *AmE* -ləˈz-/ *n.* [C,U]: *a recapitalization plan*

**recd** *abbr* (*written*) received

**recede** /rɪˈsiːd/ *v.* [I] to become smaller, weaker, etc: *The market in general is receding.*

★**receipt** /rɪˈsiːt/ *n.*, *v.*
• *n.* **1** (*also* **ˈsales slip**) [C] a piece of paper that shows that goods or services have been paid for: *Can I have a receipt, please?*
◐ *to ask for/file/keep/need a ~* ◆ *to give sb/issue/make out/sign a ~* ◆ *a credit-card/sales ~*
**2** (*Account.*) **receipts** [pl.] money that a business, bank or government receives: *Receipts from tourism fell by about one third.* ◇ *cash/export/tax ~* **3** (*fml.*) [U] the act of receiving sth, or the fact of sth having been received: *to* **acknowledge** *receipt of an order*
• *v.* [T] (*often* **receipted**, *used as an adj.*) **1** to sign or mark a bill to say that it has been paid: *a receipted hotel bill* **2** to give a **receipt** for money or goods: *receipting goods*

**receivable** /rɪˈsiːvəbl/ *adj.* [not usu. before n.] (*Account.*) for which money has not yet been received: *net interest receivable*

**receivables** /rɪˈsiːvəblz/ *n.* [pl.] (*Account.*) money that is owed to a business: *outstanding receivables* → PAYABLES

**receiver** /rɪˈsiːvə(r)/ *n.* [C] **1** (*Law*) (*also* **of͵ficial reˈceiver**) a person who is chosen by a court to manage the financial affairs of a company that is BANKRUPT, to sell its assets in order to pay its debts, and to close it → idiom at CALL *v.* **2** the part of a telephone that you hold close to your mouth and ear

**receivership** /rɪˈsiːvəʃɪp; *AmE* -vərʃ-/ *n.* [U,C] (*Law*) a situation where the financial affairs of a company are being controlled by a **receiver**, because it has no money: *Her company is now* ***in receivership.*** ◇ *to be placed in/go into ~*

**reˈceiving ͵order** *n.* [C] (*Law*) in the UK, an order from a court placing a company in the control of a **receiver**

★**reception** /rɪˈsepʃn/ *n.* **1** [U] (*esp. BrE*) the place inside the entrance of a hotel, an office building, etc. where guests or visitors go first when they arrive: *to meet* ***in*** *reception* ◇ *to leave a message* ***with*** *reception* **2** [C] a formal social occasion to welcome sb or celebrate sth: *an official reception* **3** [sing.] the type of welcome that people give to sb/sth: *The new product got a cool reception from customers.* **4** [U] the quality of radio, television and telephone signals that are broadcast: *bad/good/poor ~*

★**receptionist** /rɪˈsepʃənɪst/ *n.* [C] a person who works in a hotel, an office building, etc. answering the telephone and dealing with people when they arrive

★**recession** /rɪˈseʃn/ *n.* [C,U] (*Econ.*) a difficult period in the economy of a country or group of countries, when there is less trade and industrial activity than usual and more people are unemployed: *The economy is now* ***in recession.***
**◐** *to* ***be hit by/fall into/slip (back) into*** *(a) ~* ◆ *to* ***emerge from/recover from*** *a ~* ◆ *(a)* ***deep/severe*** *~* ◆ *(a)* ***mild/shallow*** *~* ◆ *(a)* ***global/world*** *~*
▸ **reˈcessionary** /-ʃnri; *AmE* -ʃəneri/ *adj.*: *recessionary pressures*

**recharge** /͵riːˈtʃɑːdʒ; *AmE* -ˈtʃɑːrdʒ/ *v.* [T,I] to fill a battery with electrical power; to be filled with electrical power: *to recharge your phone* ▸ **reˈchargeable** *adj.*: *rechargeable batteries* **IDM** **recharge your ˈbatteries** to get back your energy by resting for a while

**recipient** /rɪˈsɪpiənt/ *n.* [C] (*fml.*) a person who receives sth: *email/loan ~s*

**reciprocal** /rɪˈsɪprəkl/ *adj.* involving two people or groups who agree to help each other or behave in the same way as each other: *We have a reciprocal arrangement with another firm that uses the same computing systems.* ◇ *reciprocal trade between the EU and Chile* ▸ **reciprocity** /͵resɪˈprɒsəti; *AmE* -ˈprɑːs-/ *n.* [U]

**reclaim** /rɪˈkleɪm/ *v.* [T] **1** to get back sth that has been taken from you, that you have lost or that is owed to you: *reclaiming markets* ◇ *to reclaim a deposit* **2** to make land that is naturally too wet or too dry suitable to be built on, farmed, etc: *reclaimed land* **3** to obtain materials from waste products so that they can be used again ▸ **reclamation** /͵rekləˈmeɪʃn/ *n.* [U]

★**recognition** /͵rekəgˈnɪʃn/ *n.* [U] **1** (*Market.*) the fact of knowing what sth is when you see it: *You don't need to spend a lot of money to gain recognition of your products.* **2** the ability of a machine to recognize sth: *voice recognition* **3** praise and rewards for the work that sb does: *She gained little recognition for her work.* **4** the act of accepting that sth exists, is true, or is official: *the recognition of trade unions*

**͵recogˈnition test** *n.* [C] (*Market.*) a test done after an advertisement has been shown to find out how well sb can remember it

★**recognize**, **-ise** /ˈrekəgnaɪz/ *v.* [T] (*not used in the continuous tenses*) **1** to know what sth is when you see it or remember who sb is: *a nationally recognized brand* **2** (*often pass.*) to praise and reward people for the work they do; to think of sb/sth as good or important: *Every team member is recognized* ***for*** *their efforts.* **3** to accept sth officially: *recognized qualifications* **4** (*Account.*) to put a particular figure on sth or to show sth in a particular way in a set of financial records: *They recognized a pre-tax gain of $22.4 m.* **5** if a machine **recognizes** sb/sth, it identifies them/it and reacts in the correct way

★**recommend** /͵rekəˈmend/ *v.* [T] **1** to tell sb that they should do sth, esp. because you have expert knowledge: *The report recommended an $11 pay increase.* **2** to tell sb that sth is good and useful: *80% of dentists recommend this product.* ◇ *a highly recommended restaurant* **3** to suggest sb for a particular job or task because you think they would do it well

★**recommendation** /͵rekəmenˈdeɪʃn/ *n.* **1** [C] a suggestion about the best thing to do, esp. by sb with expert knowledge **2** [U] the act of telling sb that sb or sth is good, useful, suitable, etc: *They were appointed* ***on the recommendation of*** *family or friends.* **3** [C] a product that sb says is good: *The book is one of this week's recommendations.*

**recompense** /ˈrekəmpens/ *v.* [T] (*fml.*) to give sb money as payment or because they have suffered in some way SYN COMPENSATE
▸ **ˈrecompense** *n.* [U; sing.] SYN COMPENSATION

**reconcile** /ˈrekənsaɪl/ *v.* [T] (*Account.*) to make one set of financial records or figures agree with another: *reconciling bank statements and cash accounts*
▸ **ˌreconciliˈation** /-sɪliˈeɪʃn/ *n.* [U]

**ˌreconciliˈation ˌstatement** (*also* **ˌreconciliˈation**) *n.* [C] (*Account.*) a document that explains the differences between two sets of accounts

**reconfigure** /ˌriːkənˈfɪɡə(r); *AmE* -ˈfɪɡjər/ *v.* [T] (*IT; Tech.*) to change the way that sth is organized or arranged, esp. computer equipment or a program: *to reconfigure a network*
▸ **ˌreconfiguˈration** /-ˈreɪʃn/ *n.* [C,U]

**reconstruct** /ˌriːkənˈstrʌkt/ *v.* [T] to build or make again sth that has been damaged or that no longer exists: *a reconstructed plant*

**reconstruction** /ˌriːkənˈstrʌkʃn/ *n.* [U] **1** the process of changing or improving the condition of sth or the way it works; the process of putting sth back into the state it was in before: *the economic reconstruction of the country* **2** the process of changing the way a company is organized, usu. because it has financial problems

★ **record** *n., v.*
• *n.* /ˈrekɔːd; *AmE* ˈrekərd/ **1** [C] a written account of sth that is kept so that it can be looked at and used in the future: *You can update your records online.* ◇ *one of the worst years* ***on record***
❶ *to* ***keep*** *a ~ (of sth)* ◆ ***administrative/financial/personnel/tax*** *~s*
**2** [C] the best result or the highest or lowest level that has ever been reached: *record sales*
❶ *to* ***break/hit/hold/set*** *a/the ~* ◆ *a ~* ***high/level/low/number***
**3** [sing.] the facts that are known about sb/sth's past behaviour, character, achievements, etc: *The airline has a good safety record.*
❶ *a* ***bad****/an* ***impressive****/a* ***poor/strong*** *~*
IDM **(just) for the ˈrecord** used to show that you want what you are saying to be officially written down and remembered **ˌoff the ˈrecord** if you tell sb sth **off the record**, it is not yet official and you do not want them to repeat it publicly **put/place sth on (the) ˈrecord; be/go on (the) ˈrecord (as saying ...)** to say sth publicly or officially so that it may be written down and repeated
• *v.* /rɪˈkɔːd; *AmE* rɪˈkɔːrd/ [T] **1** to keep a permanent account of facts or events by writing them down, storing them in a computer, etc: *You should record all your expenses.* **2** to show a particular amount of profit or loss, or a particular number of sth: *The bank recorded a net loss for the year.*

**ˈrecord-ˌbreaking** *adj.* bigger, better, etc. than has ever been done before: *record-breaking sales figures*

**ˈrecord date** *n.* [C] (*Finan.*) the date when a shareholder must own shares in order to be able to vote at a meeting, receive a DIVIDEND, etc.

**reˌcorded deˈlivery** (*BrE*) (*AmE* **ˌcertified ˈmail**) *n.* [U] a method of sending mail in which the sender is given a note to say it has been posted and the person receiving it has to sign a form to say it has been delivered: *to send sth* ***by*** *recorded delivery*

**ˈrecord-ˌkeeping** *n.* [U] the job or process of storing documents, files, information, etc. in an office

**recoup** /rɪˈkuːp/ *v.* [T] to get back money spent or lost: *The company could take seven years to recoup its investment.* SYN RECOVER

**recourse** /rɪˈkɔːs; *AmE* ˈriːkɔːrs/ *n.* **1** (*fml.*) [U; sing.] the fact of using sth that can provide help in a difficult situation; the person or thing that you use for help: *The business was stabilized* ***without recourse to*** (= without using) *external financing.* **2** (*Law*) [U] the legal right to claim money from sb for a loss, an injury, etc. that they have caused: *You have no recourse* ***against*** *the seller if the goods are faulty.*

★ **recover** /rɪˈkʌvə(r)/ *v.* **1** [I] to improve and begin to return to a normal position or level after a period of difficulty: *The market is recovering from its 20-year low.* **2** [T] to get back money that has been spent or lost SYN RECOUP **3** (*Law*) [T] **~ costs/damages** to obtain money by a legal process because of loss or injury that you have suffered **4** [T] to get oil, minerals, etc. from the ground

▸ **re'covery** *n.* [U,C] (*pl.* **-ries**): *a recovery* **in** *consumer spending* ◇ *debt recovery*

**recoverable** /rɪ'kʌvərəbl/ *adj.* **1** used to describe money that can be got back after it has been spent or lost: *recoverable expenses* OPP IRRECOVERABLE **2** (*Law*) used to describe money that can be obtained by sb by a legal process, for example if they have been injured: *recoverable damages* **3 recoverable** oil, minerals, etc. can be taken from the ground

**re'covery ˌperiod** *n.* [C, usu. sing.] (*Account.*) the time it will take for the profit produced by an asset to be equal to the amount invested in it SYN PAYBACK PERIOD

★ **recruit** /rɪ'kru:t/ *v.*, *n.*

• *v.* **1** (*HR*) [T,I] to find new people to join a company or an organization: *to recruit and retain the best people* **2** [T] to persuade sb to do sth, esp. to help you in some way: *He recruited investors to fund the project.*

▸ **re'cruiter** *n.* [C]

• *n.* [C] (*HR*) a person who joins a company or an organization: *attracting graduate recruits*

★ **recruitment** /rɪ'kru:tmənt/ *n.* **1** (*HR*) [U] the act or the process of finding new people to join a company or an organization: *staff recruitment* **2** (*HR*) [C] a person who has been chosen to join a company or an organization; an occasion when sb is chosen: *Ten new recruitments have been carried out so far this year.* **3** [U] the act of persuading sb to do sth for you: *the recruitment of people to take part in market research*

**re'cruitment fair** = JOB FAIR

**recuperate** /rɪ'ku:pəreɪt/ *v.* (*fml.*) **1** [I] to improve and begin to return to a normal position or level after a period of difficulty: *I expect the stock to recuperate soon.* **2** [T] to get back money that has been spent or lost: *to recuperate your investment* SYN RECOVER

**recurring** /rɪ'kɜ:rɪŋ/ *adj.* happening more than once, or a number of times: *~ costs/expenses/profit* → NON-RECURRING

**recycle** /ˌri:'saɪkl/ *v.* [T,I] to put things that have already been used through special processes so that they can be used again: *envelopes made from recycled paper*

▸ **ˌre'cyclable** /-kləbl/ *adj.*: *recyclable packaging* **ˌre'cycling** *n.* [U]: *a recycling plant*

**red** /red/ *n.* IDM **be, remain, etc. in the 'red; move into, return to, etc. the 'red 1** to be operating at a loss; to be spending more than you earn: *They are €70 bn in the red.* **2** (*Stock Ex.*) if markets or shares are **in the red**, they are lower in value than they were previously OPP BE, REMAIN, ETC. IN THE BLACK, MOVE INTO, RETURN TO, ETC. THE BLACK

**ˌred-'circling** *n.* [U] (*HR*) the situation when a job has been moved to a lower grade with a lower rate of pay, but the people who are already doing that work are still paid the old rate ▸ **ˌred-'circle** *v.* [T]

**redeem** /rɪ'di:m/ *v.* [T] **1** (*Finan.*) to pay back the full amount of money that you owe; to pay a debt SYN PAY OFF **2** (*Finan.*) to exchange shares, bonds, etc. for money: *The shares can be redeemed after March 4.* **3** (*Comm.*) to exchange a VOUCHER for goods or services: *The gift certificates can be redeemed at any of our hotels.* **4** to get back a valuable item from sb by paying them back the money you borrowed from them in exchange for the item

▸ **re'deemable** /-əbl/ *adj.*: *~ bonds/securities/shares/stock* ◇ *The points are redeemable for gifts.*

**redefine** /ˌri:dɪ'faɪn/ *v.* [T] to change the nature or limits of sth; to make people consider sth in a new way: *Some jobs might have to change or be redefined.* ◇ *to ~ a brand/business/problem* ▸ **redefinition** /ˌri:defɪ'nɪʃn/ *n.* [U,C]

**redemption** /rɪ'dempʃn/ *n.* [U,C] (*Finan.*) **1** an occasion when money invested in shares, bonds, etc. is paid back to the investor: *£52 bn in bond redemptions* **2** the act of paying back a loan or MORTGAGE

**re'demption date** = MATURITY (1)

**re'demption yield** *n.* [C] (*Finan.*) the amount of money that an investor will get back from a bond if it is kept until the end of its life, usu. expressed as a percentage SYN YIELD TO MATURITY

**redeploy** /ˌri:dɪ'plɔɪ/ *v.* [T] (*fml.*) **1** (*HR*) to give employees a different job to do or move them to a different place of work: *redeploying staff in other roles* **2** (*Finan.*) to use money or resources for a different purpose: *selling assets and redeploying the capital* ▸ **ˌrede'ployment** *n.* [U]

**redesign** /ˌri:dɪ'zaɪn/ *v.* [T] to design a product, service, system, etc. again in a different way

▸ **ˌrede'sign** *n.* [U,C]: *a complete redesign of the website*

**'red-eye** (*also* **,red-eye 'flight**) *n.* [C, usu. sing.] (*infml.*) a flight on a plane at night, on which you do not get enough sleep

**,red 'herring** = PATHFINDER PROSPECTUS

**,red-'hot** *adj.* extremely strong, active, successful, etc: *the red-hot housing market*

**,red 'ink** *n.* [U] (*AmE*) used to talk about a situation in which a business is losing a lot of money, has a lot of debt, etc: *It was the company's third quarter of red ink.*
→ idiom at HAEMORRHAGE *v.*

**redirect** /ˌriːdəˈrekt; -dɪ-; -daɪ-/ *v.* [T] **1** to use money, resources, etc. in a different way or for a different purpose: *We redirected funds to a new marketing campaign.* **2** to send sth such as mail, phone calls, etc. to a different address: *Calls can be redirected to your mobile phone.*

★ **redistribute** /ˌriːdɪˈstrɪbjuːt; ˌriːˈdɪs-/ *v.* [T] (*Econ.*) to share money or resources in a different way: *Raising taxes will redistribute wealth more fairly.* ▸ **,redistri'bution** /-ˈbjuːʃn/ *n.* [U; sing.]

**redistributive** /ˌriːdɪˈstrɪbjətɪv/ *adj.* (*Econ.*) **redistributive** policies or actions use a country's tax system to give a more equal share to poorer people

**redline** /ˈredlaɪn/ *v.* [T] (*AmE*) (*infml.*) to refuse to provide loans, insurance or other financial services to people or businesses in particular areas ▸ **'redlining** *n.* [U]

**redress** *v., n.*
• *v.* /rɪˈdres/ [T] (*fml.*) to correct sth that is unfair or wrong: *They will attempt to redress the budget deficit next year.* IDM **redress the 'balance** to make a situation equal or fair again
• *n.* /rɪˈdres; ˈriːdres/ [U] (*Law*) a legal solution to a problem, esp. sth that you should get for sth wrong that has happened to you or harm that you have suffered: *She is* **seeking** *legal redress* **for** *unfair dismissal.*
SYN COMPENSATION, REMEDY

**,red 'tape** *n.* [U] official rules that seem more complicated than is necessary and prevent things being done quickly SYN BUREAUCRACY

★ **reduce** /rɪˈdjuːs; *AmE* -ˈduːs/ *v.* [T] **~ sth (from sth) (to sth)** | **~ sth (by sth)** to make sth less or smaller in price, quantity, size, etc: *reducing costs* ◇ *Losses were reduced from €4.7 m to €2.7 m.*
SYN CUT OPP INCREASE

**re,ducing 'balance ,method** (*also* **de,clining 'balance ,method, di,minishing 'balance ,method**) *n.* [sing.] (*Account.*) a way of reducing the value of an asset in a company's financial records in which the amount taken from the asset's value decreases each year. The value of the asset is reduced by a fixed percentage each year.

★ **reduction** /rɪˈdʌkʃn/ *n.* **1** [C,U] an act of making sth smaller or less; the state of being made smaller or less: *a $300 m reduction* **in** *costs*
⊙ *a* ***drastic/slight/substantial*** *~* ♦ *to* ***achieve/make/produce*** *a ~*
**2** [C] the amount by which sth is made cheaper to buy: *price reductions to attract buyers*
⊙ ***big/massive*** *~* ♦ *to* ***ask for/get/receive*** *a ~* ♦ *to* ***give/make/offer*** *a ~*

★ **redundancy** /rɪˈdʌndənsi/ *n.* [U,C] (*pl.* **-cies**) (*BrE*) (*HR*) a situation when a person loses their job because there is no more work available for them; jobs lost in this way: *workers facing redundancy* ◇ *There could be up to 32 000 redundancies.*
⊙ *to* ***accept/face/take*** *~* ♦ ***compulsory/voluntary*** *~* ♦ *to* ***announce/avoid/make*** *redundancies* ♦ ***large-scale/mass/sweeping*** *redundancies*

★ **redundant** /rɪˈdʌndənt/ *adj.* (*BrE*) (*HR*) without a job because your employer has no more work available for you: *retraining redundant employees* ◇ *She has just been* **made redundant**.

**,re-engi'neer** (*also* **reengineer**, *esp. in AmE*) *v.* **1** [T,I] to change the structure of a company or an organization in order to make it more efficient: *re-engineering the way we do business* **2** [T] to change the way a product is made so that it works better: *The car was re-engineered for the European market.*
▸ **,re-engi'neering** (*also* **reengineering**, *esp. in AmE*) *n.* [U]

**,re-e'valuate** (*also* **reevaluate**, *esp. in AmE*) *v.* [T,I] to think about sth again, esp. in order to form a new opinion about it: *My job has been re-evaluated and upgraded.*
▸ **,re-evalu'ation** (*also* **reevaluation**, *esp. in AmE*) *n.* [U]

**re-export** (*also* **reexport**, *esp. in AmE*) *n., v.* (*Trade*)
• *n.* /ˌriːˈekspɔːt; *AmE* -ˈekspɔːrt/ [C, usu. pl.] goods that are imported into a country and then exported, often without being changed at all
• *v.* /ˌriːɪkˈspɔːt; *AmE* -ɪkˈspɔːrt/ [T] to import goods into a country and then export them, either in a different

form or without changing them at all ▸ ˌre-exporˈtation /-ˈteɪʃn/ *n.* [U,C]

**ref.** *abbr* a short way of writing **reference** (= a set of letters or numbers that identifies a person, letter, etc.): *our ref. 3498*

**refer** /rɪˈfɜː(r)/ *v.* (-rr-)
**PHR V** **reˈfer to sb/sth 1** to describe or be connected to sb/sth: *The figures referred to data for the previous month.* **2** to look at sth or ask a person for information: *to refer to your notes* **reˈfer to sb/sth (as sth)** to mention or speak about sb/sth: *I refer to your letter of May 26th.* **reˈfer sb/sth to sb/sth** to send sb/sth to sb/sth for help, advice or a decision: *The bids will be referred to the competition commission.*

**referee** /ˌrefəˈriː/ *n., v.*
• ***n.*** [C] **1** (*BrE*) (*also* **ˈreference**, *AmE, BrE*) a person who gives information about your character and ability, usu. in a letter, for example when you are applying for a job: *Please give the names of three referees.* **2** a person who is asked to settle a disagreement: *to* ***act as*** *a referee between the two parties* **3** a person who reads and checks the quality of a technical article before it is published
• ***v.*** [T] **1** to help to settle disagreements between people or groups: *The panel referees all takeover battles.* **2** to read and check the quality of a technical article before it is published

**reference** /ˈrefrəns/ *n., v.*
• ***n.*** [C] **1** (*abbr* **ref.**) a set of letters or numbers that identifies a person, letter, etc: *Please quote reference ZK42.* ◇ *a reference number* **2** a letter written by sb who knows you, giving information about your character and abilities, esp. to a new employer
⊙ *to* ***ask for/follow up/take up*** *~s* ♦ *to* ***give (sb)/write (sb)*** *a ~*
**3** (*esp. AmE*) = REFEREE *n.* (1)
**IDM** **in/with ˈreference to** (*fml., usu. written*) used to say what you are talking or writing about: *With reference to your letter of 2 May...*
• ***v.*** [T] to refer to sth; to provide sth with a **reference** number

**ˈreference group** *n.* [C] **1** a group that gives advice to an organization, the government, etc. on a particular issue: *a marketing reference group* **2** (*Market.*) a group that people compare themselves to and that influences their choices and opinions **3** (*Tech.*) a group that another group is compared with when you are analysing data to study the effects of sth **SYN** CONTROL

**referral** /rɪˈfɜːrəl/ *n.* [U,C] the act of recommending sb or sth; a person or an organization that has been recommended

**reˈferral ˌmarketing** = VIRAL MARKETING

**reˌfer to ˈdrawer** *phr.* (*abbr* **RD**) words written on a cheque when a bank refuses to pay it, usu. because there is not enough money in the account

**refinance** /ˌriːˈfaɪnæns/ *v.* [T,I] (*Finan.*) to borrow money, usu. at a lower rate of interest, in order to pay a debt or loan: *refinancing mortgages at lower interest rates*
▸ ˌ**reˈfinancing** *n.* [U,C]: *debt refinancing*

**refine** /rɪˈfaɪn/ *v.* [T] **1** to make a substance pure by taking other substances out **2** to improve sth by making small changes to it: *The design has been refined.* ▸ **reˈfining** *n.* [U]

**refinery** /rɪˈfaɪnəri/ *n.* [C] (*pl.* **-ries**) a factory where a substance such as oil is REFINED

**refit** /ˌriːˈfɪt/ *v.* [T] (-tt-) to repair equipment, furniture, machinery, etc. in a building, shop/store, ship, etc. or replace with new ▸ **refit** /ˈriːfɪt/ *n.* [C]: *store refits*

**reflate** /ˌriːˈfleɪt/ *v.* [T,I] (*Econ.*) if a government or national bank **reflates** the economy, it increases or brings back economic demand by lowering taxes, increasing government spending, lowering interest rates, etc. ▸ ˌ**reˈflation** /-ˈfleɪʃn/ *n.* [U]: *global reflation* ˌ**reˈflationary** /-ʃənri; *AmE* -neri/ *adj.*: *reflationary policies*

★**reform** /rɪˈfɔːm; *AmE* rɪˈfɔːrm/ *n., v.*
• ***n.*** [U,C] change that is made to an organization, a law, a social system, etc. in order to improve or correct it: *reform of the labour market* ◇ *much-needed reforms in the banking sector*
⊙ ***corporate/economic/financial/structural*** *~s* ♦ ***fundamental/sweeping*** *~s* ♦ *to* ***call for/carry out/introduce*** *~s*
• ***v.*** [T] to improve a system, an organization, a law, etc. by making changes to it: *proposals to reform the tax system* ▸ **reˈformer** *n.* [C]

**refresh** /rɪˈfreʃ/ *v.* [T,I] (*IT*) to get the most recent information, for example on a website or an Internet page: *Click to refresh this document.*

**reˈfresher course** (*also* **reˈfresher**, *esp. in AmE*) *n.* [C] a short period of training to improve your skills or to teach you about new ideas and developments in your job

★**refund** *n., v. (Account.; Comm.)*
• ***n.*** /ˈriːfʌnd/ [C] a sum of money that is paid back to you, esp. because you paid too much or because you returned goods to a shop/store: *a tax refund*
⊙ *to* ***claim/demand/receive*** *a ~* ♦ *to* ***make/offer/pay*** *a ~*
• ***v.*** /rɪˈfʌnd/ [T] **~ sth (to sb)** | **~ sb sth** to give sb their money back, esp. because they have paid too much or because they are not satisfied with sth they bought: *Tickets cannot be exchanged or money refunded.* SYN REIMBURSE ▸ **reˈfundable** *adj.*: *a refundable deposit*

**refunding** /ˌriːˈfʌndɪŋ/ *n.* [C,U] (*Finan.*) the act of borrowing money, usu. at a lower rate of interest, in order to pay a debt or loan

**refurbish** /ˌriːˈfɜːbɪʃ; *AmE* -ˈfɜːrb-/ *v.* [T] to clean and decorate a building, an office, a shop/store, etc. in order to make it more attractive or useful ▸ **ˌreˈfurbishment** *n.* [U,C]: *The hotel is closed for refurbishment.*

**reg** *abbr* used as a short way of writing words such as **regular, regulation, registered**, etc.

**regain** /rɪˈɡeɪn/ *v.* [T] to get back sth you no longer have: *regaining our position in the local market*

**regard** /rɪˈɡɑːd; *AmE* rɪˈɡɑːrd/ *n.* [C] **regards** [pl.] used to send good wishes to sb at the end of a letter: *With kind regards, Yours ...* IDM **in/with regard to sb/sth** (*fml.*) (often used in letters, etc.) concerning sb/sth: *I am writing with regard to your application ...*

**regarding** /rɪˈɡɑːdɪŋ; *AmE* -ˈɡɑːrd-/ *prep.* (often used in letters, etc.) concerning sb/sth; about sb/sth: *I refer to my letter regarding your overdue payment ...*

**regd** *abbr* (*written*) registered

★**region** /ˈriːdʒən/ *n.* [C] a large area of land such as a part of the world or one of the areas that a country is divided into: *the Asia-Pacific region* IDM **in the region of** used when you are giving a number, price, etc. to show that it is not exact: *He earns in the region of €50 000.* SYN APPROXIMATELY

★**regional** /ˈriːdʒənl/ *adj.* **1** used to describe a business or an organization that operates in a particular part of a country rather than the whole country: *a regional bank* **2** connected with a particular part of a country or of the world: *a regional manager* ▸ **ˈregionally** /-nəli/ *adv.*

**ˌregional ˈjet** *n.* [C] (*Transpt.*) a small plane that is mainly used for local flights over short distances

★**register** /ˈredʒɪstə(r)/ *v., n.*
• ***v.*** **1** [T,I] to record your/sb's/sth's name on an official list: *to ~ a company/trademark/design* ◇ *Customers can register online.* **2** [T] to show or record an amount or measurement: *The stock exchange has registered huge losses this week.* **3** [T] to make your interest or opinion known officially: *Two potential buyers have registered an* ***interest***. **4** [T] (*usu. pass.*) to send sth by mail, paying extra money to protect it against loss or damage: *a registered letter*
• ***n.*** [C] **1** an official list or record of names, items, etc.; a book that contains such a list: *a national register of qualified engineers*
⊙ *to* ***compile/draw up*** *a ~* ♦ *to* ***appear/be*** *on a ~* ♦ *to be* ***struck/taken*** *off a ~*
**2** (*Comm.*) (*AmE*) = CASH REGISTER → idiom at RING *v.*

**registered** /ˈredʒɪstəd; *AmE* -tərd/ *adj.* (*abbr* **reg, regd**) **1** included on a legal or an official record: *a registered bank* ◇ *registered customers* **2** (*Finan.*) **~ bond/security/share/stock** that has the name and address of the owner on a central record kept by the company that issued the bond or by its agent

**ˌregistered ˈcapital** *n.* [U] (*Finan.*) the maximum amount of money that a company is allowed to raise by selling shares

**ˌregistered ˈcompany** *n.* [C] **1** in the UK, a company that is on the COMPANIES REGISTER **2** (*Stock Ex.*) (*AmE*) a company that is on the official list of the SECURITIES AND EXCHANGE COMMISSION and is able to issue shares

**ˌregistered ˈmail** (*BrE also* **-ˈpost**) *n.* [U] a method of sending a letter or package in which the person sending it can claim money if it arrives late or is lost or damaged

**ˌregistered ˈoffice** *n.* [C] (*Law*) in the UK, the official address of a company which is recorded on the COMPANIES REGISTER

**ˌregistered ˈpost** = REGISTERED MAIL

**ˌregistered ˈtrademark** *n.* [C] (*Law*) the sign or name of a product, etc. that is officially recorded and protected so that nobody else can use it, shown by the symbol ®

**ˌregister of ˈcompanies** = COMPANIES REGISTER

**ˈregister of diˈrectors' ˈinterests** *n.* [sing.] (*Law*) in the UK, an official record that provides information on the number of shares in the company that each director owns

**ˌregister of ˈmembers** = SHAREHOLDERS' REGISTER

**ˌregister of ˈtransfers** = TRANSFER REGISTER

**registrar** /ˌredʒɪˈstrɑː(r); ˈredʒɪstrɑː(r)/ *n.* [C] a person or an organization whose job is to keep official records

**ˌRegistrar of ˈCompanies** *n.* [C, usu. sing.] the official who is responsible for recording information on all companies in the UK

**registration** /ˌredʒɪˈstreɪʃn/ *n.* [U,C] (*abbr* **reg**) the act of making an official record of sth/sb; a document showing this information: *Online registration is quick and easy.* ◇ *new car registrations*

**regisˈtration ˌstatement** *n.* [C] (*Stock Ex.*) in the US, a document that a company must give to the SECURITIES AND EXCHANGE COMMISSION before it can sell shares, containing financial information that will help investors to judge the value of the company: *to file a registration statement with the commission*

**registry** /ˈredʒɪstri/ *n.* [C] (*pl.* **-ries**) a place or an organization where official information is kept

**ˌRegistry of ˈCompanies** = COMPANIES REGISTRY

**regressive** /rɪˈgresɪv/ *adj.* **1** becoming or making sth less advanced: *The policy is seen as a regressive step.* **2** (*Econ.*) used to describe a tax such as sales tax that has less effect on people with a high income than on people with a low income OPP PROGRESSIVE

**reˈgret ˌletter** = LETTER OF REGRET

**regroup** /ˌriːˈgruːp/ *v.* [T,I] to organize a group, team, etc. in a new way so that it is more efficient and competitive ▸ **ˌreˈgrouping** *n.* [U,C]

**regs** /regz/ *n.* [pl.] (*infml.*) a short form of **regulations**: *rules and regs*

**regular** /ˈregjələ(r)/ *adj.*, *n.*
• ***adj.*** **1** frequent and usu. happening at the same time each day, week, month, year, etc: *to hold regular meetings* ◇ *Back up your work* ***at regular intervals.*** OPP IRREGULAR **2** (about a person) often going to the same place or using the same service: *our regular customers* **3** usual: *my regular duties* **4** (*Comm.*) (*esp. AmE*) of a standard size or type; ordinary: *Regular or large fries?* **5** (*Stock Ex.*) during the usual hours of trading for the stock exchange: *regular NASDAQ trade* **6** lasting for all the normal working hours of the week; working during all the normal working hours: *regular employment* SYN FULL-TIME
• ***n.*** [C] (*infml.*) a customer who often goes to a particular shop/store, restaurant, etc: *He's one of our regulars.*

★ **regulate** /ˈregjuleɪt/ *v.* [T] to control sth by means of rules or laws: *The activities of credit companies are regulated by law.* ◇ *The industry regulates itself.* OPP DEREGULATE

**regulation** /ˌregjuˈleɪʃn/ *n.*, *adj.*
• ***n.*** **1** [C, usu. pl.] (*abbr* **reg**) an official rule made by a government or some other authority: *accounting/safety* ~ ◇ *rules and regulations* **2** [U] controlling sth by means of rules: *the voluntary regulation of the press*
• ***adj.*** that must be worn or used according to the official rules: *regulation uniform*

★ **regulator** /ˈregjuleɪtə(r)/ *n.* [C] **1** a person or an organization that officially controls an area of business or industry and makes sure that it is operating fairly: *a banking/energy* ~ **2** a device that automatically controls sth such as speed, temperature or pressure

★ **regulatory** /ˈregjələtəri; *AmE* -tɔːri/ *adj.* having the power to control an area of business or industry and make sure that it is operating fairly
○ *a* ~ ***agency/authority/body*** • *to get* ~ ***approval/clearance*** • ~ ***hurdles/obstacles***

**ˌregulatory ˈfiling** *n.* [C] an official document such as a financial statement that a company must send to the organization that controls its industry

**reimburse** /ˌriːɪmˈbɜːs; *AmE* -ˈbɜːrs/ *v.* [T] to pay back money to sb which they have spent or lost: *We will reimburse expenses incurred.* SYN REFUND ▸ **ˌreimˈbursement** *n.* [U,C]

**reimport** /ˌriːɪmˈpɔːt; *AmE* -ˈpɔːrt/ *v.* [T] **1** (*Trade*) to bring back into a country finished goods made from materials that have been exported, or goods that have previously been exported **2** (*IT*) **~ sth into sth** to copy a file, data, etc. back into a program ▸ **reˈimport** *n.* [C,U] **ˌreimporˈtation** /-ˈteɪʃn/ *n.* [U]

**rein** /reɪn/ *n.*, *v.*
• ***n.*** **the reins** [pl.] the state of being in control or the leader of sth: *It was time to* ***hand over the reins*** *of power*

(= to give control to sb else).
→ idiom at TIGHT
• *v.* **PHR V** ˌ**rein sb/sth 'back**; ˌ**rein sth 'in** to start to control sb/sth more strictly: *Consumers are reining back spending.*

**reinforce** /ˌriːɪn'fɔːs; *AmE* -'fɔːrs/ *v.* [T] (*Tech.*) to make a structure or material stronger, esp. by adding another material: *reinforced concrete*

**reinstate** /ˌriːɪn'steɪt/ *v.* [T] **~ sb/sth (in/as sth) 1** to give back a job or position that had been taken away from sb: *He was reinstated in his post.* **2** to return sth to its previous position or status: *The 40-hour week is unlikely to be reinstated.* SYN RESTORE ▸ ˌ**rein'statement** *n.* [U,C]

**reinsurance** /ˌriːɪn'ʃɔːrəns; -'ʃʊər-; *AmE* -'ʃʊr-/ *n.* [U] (*Insur.*) the practice of one insurance company buying insurance from another company in order to share the risk of large claims that their clients could make ▸ **reinsure** /ˌriːɪn'ʃɔːr; -'ʃʊər; *AmE* -'ʃʊr/ *v.* [T] ˌ**rein'surer** *n.* [C]

**reinvent** /ˌriːɪn'vent/ *v.* [T] to present yourself/sth in a new form or with a new image: *The company is trying to reinvent itself* **as** *a retailer of casual clothing.* ▸ ˌ**rein'vention** /-'venʃn/ *n.* [C,U] **IDM** **reinvent the 'wheel** to waste time creating sth that already exists and works well

**reinvest** /ˌriːɪn'vest/ *v.* [T,I] **~ (in sth)** to put profits that have been made on an investment back into the same investment or into a new one ▸ ˌ**rein'vestment** *n.* [U,C]

**reissue** /ˌriː'ɪʃuː/ *v.* [T] to make a new supply or a different form of sth available: *The government may reissue the 30-year Treasury bond.* ▸ ˌ**re'issue** *n.* [C,U]

**REIT** /reɪt/ *abbr* **real estate investment trust** (*used as a countable n.*) in the US, a company that invests in and manages property on behalf of a number of investors; a share issued by one of these companies: *to invest in REITs*

★**reject** *v., n.*
• *v.* /rɪ'dʒekt/ [T] **1** to refuse to accept or consider sth: *They rejected the $47-a-share offer.* **2** to refuse to accept sb for a job, position, etc. **3** to decide not to sell or use sth because its quality is not good enough OPP ACCEPT ▸ **re'jection** /-kʃn/ *n.* [U,C]: *a rejection letter* (= telling sb they have not been given a job)
• *n.* /'riːdʒekt/ [C] something that cannot be used or sold because there is sth wrong with it: *factory rejects*

**rejig** /ˌriː'dʒɪg/ *v.* [T] (-gg-) (*BrE*) (*AmE* **rejigger** /ˌriː'dʒɪgə(r)/) (*infml.*) to make changes to sth; to arrange sth in a different way: *We can solve some of the problems by rejigging our assets.* ▸ **'rejig** *n.* [C]: *a management rejig*

**rejuvenate** /rɪ'dʒuːvəneɪt/ *v.* [T] to make sb/sth more confident, more successful, more exciting, etc: *a fresh, rejuvenated brand* ▸ **reˌjuve'nation** /-'neɪʃn/ *n.* [U; sing.]

**relate** /rɪ'leɪt/ *v.* [T] to show or make a connection between two or more things: *Pay increases will be related to productivity.* SYN CONNECT **PHR V** **re'late to sth/sb** to be connected with sth/sb; to refer to sth/sb: *legal action relating to the merger*

**related** /rɪ'leɪtɪd/ *adj.* connected with sth/sb in some way: *salaries and related costs* ◇ *a media-related company* ▸ **re'latedness** *n.* [U]

**reˌlated 'company** *n.* [C] a company that controls or is controlled by another company or is a member of a group of companies, esp. an ASSOCIATE COMPANY

**reˌlated 'party** *n.* [C] an individual, a company, etc. that has the ability to control or influence another organization

**relations** /rɪ'leɪʃnz/ *n.* [pl.] the way in which two people, groups or countries behave towards each other or deal with each other: *US-Europe relations* ◇ *good relations* **with** *the unions*

★**relationship** /rɪ'leɪʃnʃɪp/ *n.* [C] the way in which two people, groups or countries behave towards each other or deal with each other: *building relationships* **with** *customers* ◇ *I have a good* **working** *relationship with my boss.*
⊕ *to* **build/develop/establish/maintain** *a* ~ • *a* **business/contractual/personal** ~

**re'lationship ˌmanagement** = CUSTOMER RELATIONSHIP MANAGEMENT

**re'lationship ˌmarketing** *n.* [U] (*Market.*) marketing activities that concentrate on developing a good relationship with a customer which will last for a long time

**relatively** /'relətɪvli/ *adv.* to a fairly large degree, esp. in comparison to sth else: *The software is relatively cheap.*

**relaunch** /ˌriː'lɔːntʃ/ *v.* [T] (*Market.*) to start or present sth again in a new or different way, esp. a product for sale ▸ **'relaunch** *n.* [C]: *the relaunch of the magazine*

**relax** /rɪ'læks/ *v.* [T] to allow rules, laws, etc. to become less strict

**release** /rɪ'li:s/ *v., n.*

• *v.* [T] **1** to make data, information, a report, etc. available to the public: *The sales figures have not yet been released.* **2** to make a product, esp. a film/movie or a CD, available to the public to buy: *The DVD will be released in April.* **3** to free sb from a duty, responsibility, contract, etc: *releasing employees from their contracts* **4** to make sth available that previously had not been allowed or had been used for another purpose: *They hope to release $1 bn cash by selling the car repair company.*

• *n.* **1** [U; sing.] the act of making sth available to the public such as a new product or new information: *The new software is scheduled for release in January.* **2** [C] a product that is made available to the public to buy, esp. a new CD or film/movie: *new releases* **3** [C] = PRESS RELEASE

**reliable** /rɪ'laɪəbl/ *adj.* **1** that you can trust or rely on: *a ~ machine/worker* **2** that is likely to be correct or true: *reliable information*
▸ **re,lia'bility** /-'bɪləti/ *n.* [U]

**reliance** /rɪ'laɪəns/ *n.* [U; sing.] the state of needing a particular person or thing: *They want to reduce their heavy reliance on foreign capital.* ▸ **re'liant** *adj.*: *businesses reliant on computers*

**relief** /rɪ'li:f/ *n.* **1** [U] if you are given **relief** from a debt, a payment, tax, etc. then you do not have to pay it or you pay it at a lower rate: *interest relief* ***on*** *loan repayments*
⊙ *to give/offer/provide ~* ♦ ***to claim/gain/get/receive ~*** ♦ *to* ***be eligible for/be entitled to/qualify for ~***
**2** [U] help given to a country or people after a war or natural disaster, etc: *emergency/flood ~* **3** [U] (*esp. AmE*) financial help given by the government to people who need it: *state and federal relief funds* **4** [C with sing./pl. v.] (*often used as an adj.*) a person or group of people that replaces another when they have finished working for the day or when they are ill/sick: *relief drivers*

**relieve** /rɪ'li:v/ *v.* [T] to make a problem less serious: *Lower energy prices will relieve the pressure on household finances.* PHR V **re'lieve sb of sth 1** to dismiss sb from a job, position, etc: *She was relieved of her duties.* **2** to help sb by taking away a difficult task or problem

**relocate** /,ri:ləʊ'keɪt; *AmE* ,ri:'loʊk-/ *v.* [T,I] to move, or to move sb/sth, to a new place to work or operate: *We relocated our office to Stanford.* ▸ **,relo'cation** /-'keɪʃn/ *n.* [U,C]: *a relocation allowance*

**remainder** /rɪ'meɪndə(r)/ *n., v.*

• *n.* **1** [sing.] the remaining amount of sth such as money, people, time, etc: *Two-thirds of the job cuts were in the US and the remainder in Europe.* **2** (*Comm.*) [C] a book, CD, etc. that is sold at a reduced price

• *v.* [T] (*Comm.*) (*usu. pass.*) to sell books, CDs, etc. at a reduced price, for example because there are too many left: *remaindered books*

**remarket** /,ri:'mɑ:kɪt; *AmE* ,ri:'mɑ:rk-/ *v.* [T,I] **1** (*Market.*) to sell new or used things that were produced by or belonged to sb else: *The company buys and remarkets IT equipment.* **2** (*Finan.*) to sell shares, bonds, etc. issued by another company ▸ **,re'marketer** *n.* [C] **,re'marketing** *n.* [U]

**remedy** /'remədi/ *n., v.*

• *n.* [C] (*pl.* **-dies**) **1** (*Law*) a legal solution to a problem or disagreement: *a legal remedy* SYN REDRESS **2** a way of dealing with or improving an unpleasant or difficult situation: *There is no simple remedy for unemployment.*

• *v.* (**-dies**, **-dying**, **-died**, **-died**) [T] to correct or improve sth: *This situation is easily remedied.*

**reminder** /rɪ'maɪndə(r)/ *n.* [C] a letter or note informing sb that they have not done sth such as paying a bill: *a ~ invoice/letter*

**remission** /rɪ'mɪʃn/ *n.* [U,C] **1** (*fml.*) an act of reducing or cancelling the amount of money that sb has to pay: *tax remission* **2** a period during which a bad situation improves although it is likely to become bad again: *a brief period of remission*

**remit** *n., v.* (*fml.*)

• *n.* /'ri:mɪt; rɪ'mɪt/ [C, usu. sing.] (*BrE*) the area of activity over which a particular person or group has authority, control or influence: *Such decisions are* ***outside*** *the remit of this committee.*

• *v.* /rɪ'mɪt/ [T] (**-tt-**) **1** (*Finan.*) to send money, etc. to a person or place: *using banks for remitting funds* **2** to cancel or free sb from a debt, duty, punishment, etc: *to remit a fine*

**remittance** /rɪ'mɪtns/ *n.* [C,U] (*Account.*; *Finan.*, *fml.*) a sum of money sent to sb; the act of sending it: *Here is my remittance.* ◇ *Remittance can be made by credit card.*

**remortgage** /ˌriːˈmɔːɡɪdʒ; *AmE* -ˈmɔːrg-/ *v.* [T,I] to arrange a second MORTGAGE on your house or apartment, or to increase or change your first one: *They had to remortgage their home.* ▸ **ˌreˈmortgage** *n.* [C,U] **ˌreˈmortgaging** *n.* [U]

**remote** /rɪˈməʊt; *AmE* rɪˈmoʊt/ *adj.* **1** (*IT*) (about a computer system) that you can connect to from far away, using an electronic link: *remote* **access** *from our branch offices* **2** (*HR*) used to describe the situation when people work for a company from home by using a computer that is linked to the central office computer system: *~ workers/working* ▸ **reˈmotely** *adv.*: *You can access the extranet remotely.*

**removal** /rɪˈmuːvl/ *n.* **1** [U] the act of getting rid of sth or of taking sb/sth away: *the removal of trade barriers* **2** (*HR*) [U] the act of dismissing sb from their job: *the removal of Mr Grant as chief executive* **3** [C] (*BrE*) an act of taking furniture, etc. from one building to another: *a removal company*

**remove** /rɪˈmuːv/ *v.* [T] **1** (*HR*) to dismiss sb from their position or job: *to be removed from office/power* **2** to get rid of sb/sth or to take sb/sth away: *to ~ barriers/objections* ◇ *to be removed from a mailing list*

**remover** /rɪˈmuːvə(r)/ (*BrE*) (*also* **ˈmover**, *AmE, BrE*) *n.* [C, usu. pl.] a company that takes possessions to new offices or homes for people or organizations: *furniture removers*

**remunerate** /rɪˈmjuːnəreɪt/ *v.* [T] (*fml.*) (*usu. pass.*) to pay sb for work that they have done: *She was well remunerated* **for** *her work.* ▸ **reˌmuneˈration** /-ˈreɪʃn/ *n.* [U,C]

**reˌmuneˈration ˌpackage** = PAY PACKAGE

**remunerative** /rɪˈmjuːnərətɪv/ *adj.* (*fml.*) paying a lot of money: *remunerative work*

**render** /ˈrendə(r)/ *v.* [T] (*fml.*) **1** (*Account.*) to present sth such as a bill, financial accounts, etc: *~ accounts/an invoice* **2** to officially give a decision, judgement, etc. about sth: *The judge rendered his decision.* **3** to provide help, a service, etc. to sb: *to render assistance* ◇ *fees for services rendered* **4** (*IT*) to make a computer image appear like a real object: *3D-rendered images* ▸ **ˈrendering** *n.* [U,C]: *a workshop on rendering*

**renege** /rɪˈniːg; rɪˈneɪg/ *v.* [I] (*fml.*) to break a promise, an agreement, etc: *to ~* **on** *an agreement/a commitment/contract/deal*

★**renew** /rɪˈnjuː; *AmE* -ˈnuː/ *v.* **1** (*Comm.*) [T,I] to make sth valid for a further period of time: *to ~ a contract/loan* **2** [T] to begin sth again after a pause or an interruption: *to renew our efforts to attract graduates* **3** [T] to change sth that is old or damaged and replace it with sth new of the same kind

**renewable** /rɪˈnjuːəbl; *AmE* -ˈnuː-/ *adj.* **1** (*Comm.*) (about a contract, licence, loan, etc.) that can be made valid for a further period of time after it has finished: *The work permit is not renewable.* **2** (*Tech.*) (about energy, fuel, resources, etc.) that is replaced naturally or controlled carefully and can therefore be used without the risk of finishing it all OPP NON-RENEWABLE ▸ **reˈnewable** *n.* [C]: *generating electricity by/from renewables*

**renewal** /rɪˈnjuːəl; *AmE* -ˈnuːəl/ *n.* [U,C] **1** (*Comm.*) the act of making a contract, etc. valid for a further period of time after it has finished: *The policy is coming* **up for** *renewal.* **2** a situation in which sth is improved or made more successful: *ongoing product renewal*

**reˈnewal ˌnotice** *n.* [C] (*Comm.*) a warning given in advance that a contract is going to end and that you must make it valid for a further period if you want it to continue

**renminbi** /ˈrenmɪnbi/ *n.* [C] (*pl.* **renminbi**) **1 the renminbi** [sing.] the money system of China **2** the unit of money in China (the **yuan**)

★**renovate** /ˈrenəveɪt/ *v.* [T] (*Prop.*) to repair and decorate an old building, etc. so that it is in good condition again: *a renovated warehouse* ▸ **ˌrenoˈvation** /-ˈveɪʃn/ *n.* [U,C]

★**rent** /rent/ *n., v.*
• *n.* [U,C] **1** an amount of money that you pay regularly so that you can use a property, etc: *office rents* ◇ *The landlord has put the rent up again.* ⊙ *a fair/high/low ~* • *to charge/pay ~* • *to fall behind with/owe ~* **2** (*esp. AmE*) = RENTAL (1) IDM **for rent** (*esp. AmE*) (esp. on printed signs) available to rent
• *v.* **1** [T,I] to regularly pay money to sb so that you can use sth that they own, such as a property, a machine, etc: *rented accommodation* **2** [T] **~ sth (out) (to sb)** to allow sb to use sth that you own in exchange for payment: *They rent office space to an IT company.* **3** [T] (*esp. AmE*) to pay

money to sb so that you can use sth for a short period of time: *We rented a car at the airport.* **4** [I] (*AmE*) to be available for sb to use if they pay a particular amount of money: *The apartment rents for $600 a month.*
▸ **'renter** *n.* [C]

**rental** /ˈrentl/ *n.* **1** (*also* **rent**, *esp. in AmE*) [U;C, usu. sing.] the amount of money that you pay to use sth for a particular period of time: *Telephone charges include line rental.* **2** [U,C] the act of renting sth or an arrangement to rent sth: *a car rental company* SYN HIRE **3** [C] (*esp. AmE*) a house, car, or piece of equipment that you can rent

**'rental fleet** *n.* [C] a group of cars or other vehicles that are owned by a company and rented to customers

**reopen** /ˌriːˈəʊpən; *AmE* -ˈoʊ-/ *v.* (*Finan.*) [T] **~ an issue, etc.** to issue additional amounts of an existing bond, etc. with the same MATURITY date and rate of interest as the original ▸ **ˌre'opening** *n.* [U; sing.]

**reorder** /ˌriːˈɔːdə(r); *AmE* -ˈɔːrd-/ *v.* [T,I] to ask sb to supply you with more of a product ▸ **ˌre'order** *n.* [C]

**re'order point** = ORDER POINT

**reorganization, -isation** /riˌɔːgənaɪˈzeɪʃn; *AmE* -ˌɔːrgənəˈz-/ *n.* [U,C] **1** a change in the way in which sth is organized or done: *a plan for reorganization of the business* **2** (*Law*) in the US, an official change in the way a company is organized because it has gone BANKRUPT
▸ **re'organize, -ise** *v.* [T,I]: *The warehouse is to be reorganized.*

**rep** /rep/ *n., v.* (*infml.*)
• ***n.*** [C] **1** (*Market.*) = SALES REPRESENTATIVE **2** = REPRESENTATIVE *n.* (1,3)
• ***v.*** [T,I] (**-pp-**) to act as a SALES REPRESENTATIVE: *At eighteen she was repping on the road.*

**repackage** /ˌriːˈpækɪdʒ/ *v.* [T] **1** (*Market.*) to put a product in a new container or cover so that people will want to buy it **2** to present sb/sth in a new way so that they/it will become more popular: *repackaging milk as a designer drink*

★**repair** /rɪˈpeə(r); *AmE* -ˈper/ *v., n.*
• ***v.*** [T] to make sth that is broken or damaged in good condition again: *We must get/have the printer repaired.* ▸ **re'pairer** *n.* [C]: *auto repairers*
• ***n.*** [C,U] an act of repairing sth: *to pay the cost of repairs* ◇ *The fax had gone in for repair.*
⊙ *to* ***carry out/do/make*** *~s* ◆ ***emergency/essential/major/minor*** *~s*
IDM **in good/bad re'pair** (*also* **in a good/bad state of re'pair**) in good or bad condition

**repairman** /rɪˈpeəmæn; *AmE* -ˈperm-/ *n.* [C] (*pl.* **-men** /-men/) a person whose job is to repair things

**reparation** /ˌrepəˈreɪʃn/ *n.* [C, usu. pl., U] money that is paid to a person, company, or country for loss, damage, or suffering that has been caused to them

**repatriate** /ˌriːˈpætrieɪt; *AmE* -ˈpeɪt-/ *v.* [T] (*Finan.*) to send money or profits back to your own country: *repatriated earnings/funds*
▸ **ˌreˌpatri'ation** /-ˈeɪʃn/ *n.* [C,U]

★**repay** /rɪˈpeɪ/ *v.* [T] (**-paid, -paid** /-ˈpeɪd/) to pay back money that you have borrowed; to pay back money that has been taken from a person or an organization: *to ~ a debt/loan/mortgage* ◇ *How much you can afford to repay each month?*

**repayable** /rɪˈpeɪəbl/ *adj.* (*Finan.*) that must be paid or can be paid back at a particular time or in a particular way: *The loan is repayable in 2010.*

★**repayment** /rɪˈpeɪmənt/ *n.* **1** [U] the act of paying back money that has been borrowed from a bank or other organization: *The loan is due for repayment by May.* ◇ *The repayment period is five years.*
⊙ *to* ***claim/demand*** *~* ◆ ***debt/loan/mortgage*** *~* ◆ ***early/late*** *~*
**2** [C] a sum of money that is paid regularly to a bank or other organization as part of paying back a loan
⊙ *to* ***keep up/make*** *~s* ◆ *to* ***afford/meet*** *the ~s* ◆ ***monthly/weekly/yearly*** *~s* ◆ ***capital/loan/mortgage/overdraft*** *~s* ◆ *a* ***minimum*** *~*

**repeat** /rɪˈpiːt/ *n.* [C] an event that is very similar to sth that happened before: *a repeat of last year's sales gains* ◇ ***repeat business*** (= when customers return to buy more) ◇ *~ customers/orders*

**reˌpetitive 'strain/'stress ˌinjury** = RSI

★**replace** /rɪˈpleɪs/ *v.* [T] **1** to be used instead of something else: *The new design will replace all existing models.* **2** to take a new job, or to put a new person in a job, instead of sb else: *People leaving are not being replaced.* **3** (*Comm.*) to change sth that is damaged, old, or does not work properly for sth new or better: *The PCs need replacing.*

**replacement** /rɪˈpleɪsmənt/ *n.* **1** [C] a thing that replaces sth that is old, broken, not good enough, not available, etc: *Return the item for a replacement or refund.* **2** [C] a person who replaces another person in an organization, for example by taking their job: *to find a replacement **for** sb* **3** [U] the act of replacing one thing with another, esp. sth that is newer or better: *Our PCs are due for replacement.*

**re'placement cost** (*also* **ˌcost of re'placement, re'placement ˌvalue**) *n.* [U,C] **1** (*Account.*) the cost of replacing an asset, calculated by considering the cost of buying or producing the same item today **2** (*Insur.*) the cost of replacing an item of property with a new one of the same type and quality

★**reply** /rɪ'plaɪ/ *v., n.*
• *v.* [T,I] (**-lies**, **-lying**, **-lied**, **-lied**) to say or write sth as an answer to sth that has been said or written to you: *Over 500 people replied **to** the job ad.*
• *n.* [C,U] (*pl.* **-lies**) something said, written, or done as an answer to sth: *All letters should receive a prompt reply.*
⊙ *get/have a ~* ♦ *give/make a ~*
**IDM** **in re'ply to** used to start a formal letter which is an answer to a letter that you have received: *In reply to your letter of 16 March ...*

**re'ply card** *n.* [C] a printed card or piece of paper, or an electronic form, that a company provides for sb to reply to sth such as an offer, an invitation, or a survey

**reˌply 'paid** *n.* [U] a service in which a company provides a card, an envelope, etc. that a possible customer can use to send a reply. The customer does not have to use a stamp but the company pays only for the replies that are sent back to them: *reply-paid envelopes*

**repo** /'riːpəʊ; *AmE* -poʊ/ *n., v.* (*infml.*)
• *n.* **1** (*Finan.*) [C] = REPURCHASE AGREEMENT **2** [U,C] the act of taking back property or goods from sb who has borrowed money to buy them and not paid it back; the property or goods taken: *specialists in debt recovery and repo* ◇ *house repos*
• *v.* [T] = REPOSSESS

★**report** /rɪ'pɔːt; *AmE* rɪ'pɔːrt/ *n., v.*
• *n.* [C] **1** a spoken or written description of sth, usu. for sb that needs particular information: *a monthly progress report* ◇ *to present/produce/write a ~* **2** an official document written by a group of people who have examined a particular situation or problem: *a report **on** the coal industry* ◇ *to commission/issue/publish a ~* **3** (*Account.*) = ANNUAL REPORT **4** (*IT*; *Product.*) a way of finding particular information, for example about costs, stock, etc., from information that is stored electronically; the information you get: *SAP reports* ◇ *to download/run/use a ~* **5** (*HR*) a person that a particular manager is responsible for: *I have 6 reports.*
• *v.* **1** [T,I] to make a public statement about a company's accounts and its profits and losses: *The company reported record profits this year.* **2** [T,I] to give people information about a subject or an event: *to report **on** research* **3** [I] to tell sb that you have arrived, for example for work or for a meeting: *All visitors must report **to** reception.* **PHR V** **reˌport 'back (on sth) (to sb)** to give sb information about sth that they have asked you to find out about: *She reported back to us on the meeting.* **re'port to sb** (*HR*) (*not in the continuous tenses*) if you **report to** a particular manager in an organization that you work for, they are officially responsible for your work and tell you what to do

**reporting** /rɪ'pɔːtɪŋ; *AmE* -'pɔːrt-/ *n.* [U] **1** the act of giving written or spoken information about sth, esp. the financial position of an organization: *the reporting of figures for non-payment* **2** (*HR*) the system in an organization of having managers who are officially responsible for the work of particular employees

**re'porting line** *n.* [C, usu. pl.] (*HR*) a system in an organization of having managers who are officially responsible for the work of particular employees

**re'porting pay** = CALL-IN PAY

**re'porting ˌperiod** *n.* [C] (*Account.*) the period of time included in a report about sth such as the financial position of a company

**reposition** /ˌriːpə'zɪʃn/ *v.* [T] (*Market.*) to present a product in a new way so that it will attract more or different customers: *We plan to reposition the brand as sportswear.*
▸ **ˌrepo'sitioning** *n.* [U]

**repossess** /ˌriːpə'zes/ (*also* **'repo**) *v.* [T] (*usu. pass.*) to take back property or goods from sb who has borrowed money to buy them but does not pay it back as agreed
▸ **ˌrepos'session** /-'zeʃn/ *n.* [U,C]: *house repossessions*

★**represent** /ˌreprɪ'zent/ *v.* **1** [T] to act or speak officially for a person, a group or an organization: *I represented the HR team at the meeting.* **2**

[T] (*not used in the continuous tenses*) to be a symbol of sth: *Our brand represents high quality.* **3** (*linking v.*) (*not used in the continuous tenses*) to be sth: *This contract represents 20% of the company's annual revenue.* SYN CONSTITUTE

**representation** /ˌreprɪzenˈteɪʃn/ *n.* **1** [U] the fact of having people who will speak or vote on your behalf in official situations; the people who speak for you, etc. in these circumstances: *legal representation* **2** [U,C] the act of presenting sth in a particular way such as financial accounts; something that shows or describes sth: *making false representations about the company's performance* **3 representations** [pl.] (*esp. BrE*) formal statements made to sb in authority, esp. in order to make your opinions known or to protest: *to make representations to the CEO*

★**representative** /ˌreprɪˈzentətɪv/ *n., adj.*

• ***n.*** [C] **1** (*also* **rep**, *infml.*) a person who has been chosen to speak or vote for sb else or on behalf of a group: *Representatives of 31 countries attended the conference.* **2** (*Market.*) = SALES REPRESENTATIVE **3** (*also* **rep**, *infml.*) (*BrE also* **'holiday rep**, *infml.*) an employee of a travel company who stays at a place where customers are on holiday/vacation and helps them with problems, organizes activities, etc.

• ***adj.*** **1** typical of a particular group of people: *Are these people representative of the population?* **2** containing or including examples of all the different types of people or things in a large group: *a representative sample of health workers*

**reprice** /ˌriːˈpraɪs/ *v.* **1** (*Comm.*) [T] to change the price of sth: *Some of the older products have been repriced.* **2** (*Finan.*) [T,I] to change the interest rate: *repricing interest rates*

**reprocess** /ˌriːˈprəʊses; *AmE* -ˈprɑː-; -ˈproʊ-/ *v.* [T] to treat waste material in order to change it or use it again: *reprocessed fuel*

▸ **ˌreˈprocessing** *n.* [U]: *a nuclear reprocessing plant*

**repudiate** /rɪˈpjuːdieɪt/ *v.* [T] (*Law*) to refuse to pay a debt or do sth that a contract requires you to do: *to ~ a contract/debt/document*

▸ **reˌpudiˈation** /-ˈeɪʃn/ *n.* [C,U]

**repurchase** /ˌriːˈpɜːtʃəs; *AmE* -ˈpɜːrtʃəs/ *v.* [T] to buy sth back

▸ **ˌreˈpurchase** *n.* [C]

**reˈpurchase aˌgreement** (*also* **ˌsale and reˈpurchase aˌgreement**) (*also* **ˈrepo**, *infml.*) *n.* [C] (*Finan.*) a way of raising money over a short period in which sb sells shares, bonds, etc. and agrees to buy them back at a particular price at a later date

**reputable** /ˈrepjətəbl/ *adj.* that people consider to be honest and to provide a good service: *to buy from a reputable dealer*

**reputation** /ˌrepjuˈteɪʃn/ *n.* [C,U] the opinion that people have about what sb/sth is like, based on what has happened in the past: *The firm has a reputation* ***as*** *a good employer.*

⊕ *to* ***build/develop/earn/gain*** *a ~* • *to* ***damage*** *sb's ~* • *a* ***good/strong*** *~* • *a* ***bad/poor*** *~*

★**request** /rɪˈkwest/ *n., v.*

• ***n.*** [C] the action of asking for sth formally and politely: *a request* ***for*** *a loan* ◇ *Details are available* ***on*** *request.*

⊕ *to* ***make/put in/submit*** *a ~* • *to* ***agree to/comply with/grant*** *a ~* • *to* ***refuse/reject/turn down*** *a ~*

• ***v.*** [T] (*fml.*) to ask for sth or ask sb to do sth in a polite or formal way: *They requested permission to build houses on the land.*

★**require** /rɪˈkwaɪə(r)/ *v.* [T] (*fml.*) (*not usu. in the continuous tenses*) **1** to make sb do or have sth, esp. because it is necessary according to a particular law or set of rules: *Motorists are required by law* ***to*** *have insurance.* ◇ *Output has fallen below the required level.* **2** to need sth: *The new equipment requires less maintenance.*

★**requirement** /rɪˈkwaɪəmənt; *AmE* -ˈkwaɪərm-/ *n.* **1** [C] something that is needed or asked for by an authority: *In order to be listed on a stock exchange, the company must meet certain requirements.*

⊕ *to* ***fulfil/satisfy*** *~* • *to* ***impose/lay down/set (down/out)*** *~*

**2** [C, usu. pl.] something that sb/sth needs or wants: *a software package to meet your requirements* ◇ *to satisfy/suit ~s*

**requisition** /ˌrekwɪˈzɪʃn/ *n., v.* (*fml.*)

• ***n.*** [C,U] a formal, official written request for sth: *a requisition number for the goods*

• ***v.*** [T] to make a formal, official request or demand for sth: *to requisition an emergency general meeting*

**rerate** (*also* **re-rate**) /ˌriːˈreɪt/ *v.* [T,I] to make a judgement about the quality or value of sth again, esp. the quality or value of a company or its shares: *The bond has been rerated up-*

wards. ▸ ˌre'rating (*also* **re-rating**) *n.* [C,U]

**resale** /'riːseɪl; ˌriː'seɪl/ *n.* (*Comm.*) **1** [U] the sale to another person of sth that you have bought: *The nuts are packaged **for resale**.* **2** [C] something that has been bought in order to sell to sb else ▸ **ˌre'saleable** (*also* **resalable**) /-əbl/ *adj.*

★ **reschedule** /ˌriː'ʃedjuːl; *AmE* ˌriː'skedʒuːl/ *v.* [T] **1** (*Finan.*) to arrange for sb to pay back money that they have borrowed at a later date than was originally agreed

⊙ *to ~ a **debt/loan** ◆ to ~ **payments/repayments***

**2** to change the time at which sth has been arranged to happen, esp. so that it takes place later: *The meeting has been rescheduled for next week.* ▸ **ˌre'scheduling** *n.* [U]: *debt rescheduling*

**rescind** /rɪ'sɪnd/ *v.* [T] (*Law*) to officially state that a law, contract, decision, etc. is no longer valid: *The offer may be rescinded.* SYN REVOKE

**rescue** /'reskjuː/ *n., v.* (*Finan.*)

• ***n.*** [C,U] an occasion when sb/sth is saved from a difficult financial situation: *Who **came to the rescue** of the struggling company?*

⊙ *a ~ **package/plan** ◆ a ~ **attempt/bid/deal***

• ***v.*** [T] to save sb/sth from a difficult financial situation: *A government loan helped rescue the airline.*

★ **research** *n., v.*

• ***n.*** /rɪ'sɜːtʃ; 'riːsɜːtʃ; *AmE* 'riːsɜːrtʃ/ [U] (*also* **researches** [pl.]) a careful study of a subject, esp. in order to discover new facts or information about it: *The company has invested a great deal in research.* ◇ *research **into/on** robotics*

⊙ *to **carry out/conduct/do/undertake** ~ ◆ **extensive/in-depth** ~ ◆ ~ **proves/shows/suggests** sth ◆ a ~ **centre/laboratory/unit** ◆ a ~ **analyst/scientist/team/worker***

• ***v.*** /rɪ'sɜːtʃ; *AmE* -'sɜːrtʃ/ [T,I] **~ (into/in/on sth)** | **~ sth** to study sth carefully and try to discover new facts about it: *They're researching new product ideas.* ▸ **re'searcher** *n.* [C]

**reˌsearch and de'velopment** = R&D

**re'search ˌmanager** *n.* [C] **1** a person at a company who is in charge of developing new products **2** a person in a financial organization who is in charge of studying investments to see how likely they are to make money

**resell** /ˌriː'sel/ *v.* [T] (**-sold**, **-sold** /-'səʊld; *AmE* -'soʊld/) (*Comm.*) to sell sth that you have bought: *He resells the goods at a profit.*

**reseller** /ˌriː'selə(r)/ *n.* [C] (*Comm.*) a company that buys goods from manufacturers and sells them without making any changes to them: *the computer reseller market*

**ˌreser'vation price** *n.* [C] (*Econ.*) the lowest price that a seller will sell their product for or the highest price that a buyer will pay

★ **reserve** /rɪ'zɜːv; *AmE* rɪ'zɜːrv/ *n., v.*

• ***n.*** **1** [C, usu. pl.] a supply of sth that is available to be used in the future or when it is needed: *large gas/oil ~s* ◇ *reserves of capital* **2** (*Econ.*) **reserves** [pl.] the foreign currency, gold, etc. that is held by the central bank of a country: *Russia's gold and foreign currency reserves* **3** (*Account.*) [C, usu. pl.] profits that a company has made and keeps as part of its CAPITAL and does not pay to shareholders **4** (*Account.*) [C] (*esp. AmE*) money that is kept from a company's profits in order to deal with possible problems or expenses in the future SYN PROVISION **5** (*Finan.*) [C, usu. pl.] the amount of money that banks or similar institutions must keep to pay to customers when they ask for it. Most of this money is kept with the central bank. SYN BANK RESERVES **6** (*Comm.*) [C] (*BrE*) = RESERVE PRICE IDM **in re'serve** available to be used in the future or when needed

• ***v.*** [T] **1** to keep sth so that it cannot be used by any other person or for any other reason: *privileges normally reserved **for** executives* **2** to have or keep a particular power: *The company **reserves the right** to check the way employees use the Internet.* ◇ ***All rights reserved*** (= nobody else can publish or copy this material). **3** to not make a decision until you have all the evidence: *I'd prefer to **reserve judgement** until I know all the facts.*

**re'serve bank** = CENTRAL BANK

**re'serve ˌcurrency** *n.* [C, usu. sing.] (*Econ.*) a foreign currency kept by governments and central banks because it is strong and can be used for making international payments

**re'serve fund** *n.* [C] (*Finan.*) the part of an income that is kept for a particular purpose or for unexpected expenses in the future

**re'serve price** (*BrE also* **re'serve**) (*AmE also* **'upset price**) *n.* [C] (*Comm.*) the lowest price that a seller will accept for sth that is sold at

AUCTION: *The item failed to reach its reserve price.*

**re'serve re,quirement** (*also* **re'serve ,ratio**) *n.* [C] (*esp. AmE*) (*Account.*) the percentage of their total assets that banks must keep in cash or in LIQUID assets
SYN CASH RATIO

**reshape** /,riː'ʃeɪp/ *v.* [T] to change the shape or structure of sth: *The merger will reshape the drinks industry.* ▶ **,re'shaping** *n.* [U]

**reshuffle** /,riː'ʃʌfl/ (*also* **'shuffle**, *less freq.*) *v.* [T,I] **1** to change around the jobs that a group of people do: *reshuffle the management team* **2** to organize sth in a different way by giving new positions to the different items in a group: *The index is reshuffled every quarter.* ▶ **'reshuffle** (*also* **,re'shuffling**) *n.* [C]: *a boardroom reshuffle*

**resident** /'rezɪdənt/ *adj., n.*
• ***adj.*** (about a person or company) living or situated permanently in a particular country, esp. when this relates to tax: *to be resident in the UK*
• ***n.*** [C] **1** a person who lives permanently in a particular country or place, or who has their home there: *a resident of the UK* **2** a person who is staying at a particular hotel: *The restaurant is open to residents.*
OPP NON-RESIDENT

**residential** /,rezɪ'denʃl/ *adj.* consisting of homes and houses rather than factories or offices; where people live: *a quiet residential area* ◇ *We deliver electricity to residential and business customers.*
OPP NON-RESIDENTIAL

**residual** /rɪ'zɪdjuəl; *AmE* -dʒu-/ *adj., n.*
• ***adj.*** **1** (*Account.*) (about money, income, etc.) still remaining after other costs such as tax have been taken away **2** still remaining at the end of a process: *a few residual problems*
• ***n.*** (*Account.*) **1** [C, usu. pl.] = RESIDUAL VALUE **2** [C] the money that a company or person receives after particular costs are taken away: *The residual is corporate profits.* **3** [C, usu. pl.] (*esp. AmE*) = RESIDUAL INCOME (2)

**re,sidual 'income** *n.* (*Account.*) [U,C] **1** the part of your income that remains after costs such as tax have been taken off **2** (*also* **re'sidual** [C]) (*both esp. AmE*) money that sb such as a SALESPERSON continues to receive as a result of sth they have done, a customer they have gained, etc. without making any further effort

**re,sidual 'value** *n.* [C,U] (*also* **re'sidual** [C]) (*Account.*) the remaining value of sth after it has been used or when it is no longer useful

★ **resign** /rɪ'zaɪn/ *v.* [T,I] (*HR*) **~ (as/from sth)** | **~ sth** to officially tell sb that you are leaving your job, an organization, etc: *She resigned as manager after eight years.*

★ **resignation** /,rezɪg'neɪʃn/ *n.* (*HR*) **1** [U,C] the act of officially giving up your job or position; the occasion when you do this: *a letter of resignation* ◇ *Further resignations are expected.* **2** [C] a letter, for example to your employers, to say that you are giving up your job or position
○ *to* ***hand in/tender*** *your ~* • *to* ***accept/reject*** *sb's ~*

**resilient** /rɪ'zɪliənt/ *adj.* strong and able to recover quickly from difficulties, losses, problems, etc: *a resilient economy* ▶ **re'silience** /-əns/ (*also* **re'siliency** /-ənsi/ *less freq.*) *n.* [U]: *the resilience of the US economy*

**resistance** /rɪ'zɪstəns/ *n.* [U; sing.] dislike of or opposition to a plan, an idea, etc.; refusal to accept sth: *The proposal has met with resistance.* ◇ *resistance to change*

**reskill** /,riː'skɪl/ *v.* [T,I] (*HR*) to learn or to teach sb new skills for a different job ▶ **,re'skilling** *n.* [U]

★ **resolution** /,rezə'luːʃn/ *n.* **1** [C] a formal statement of an opinion that is decided on by a committee or a council, esp. by means of a vote: *The board opposed the resolution.*
○ *to* ***adopt/carry/pass/reject*** *a ~* • *a* ***draft/formal/special*** *~*
**2** [U; sing.] the act of solving or settling a problem, disagreement, etc: *a swift resolution to the crisis*
○ *to* ***achieve/reach*** *a ~* • *to* ***call for/require*** *a ~* • *an* ***early****/a* ***final/quick/peaceful*** *~*
**3** (*IT*) [U; sing.] the power of a computer screen, printer, etc. to give a clear image, depending on the size and number of dots that make up the image

★ **resolve** /rɪ'zɒlv; *AmE* rɪ'zɑːlv/ *v.* **1** [T] to find an acceptable solution to a problem or difficulty: *to ~ a crisis/dispute/an issue* **2** [I] to reach a decision by means of a formal vote: *The board resolved to accept the offer.*

**resort** /rɪ'zɔːt; *AmE* rɪ'zɔːrt/ *n., v.*
• ***n.*** **1** [C] a place where a lot of people go on holiday/vacation: *beach/ski ~s* **2** [sing.] **the first/last/final ~** the first or last course of action that you should or can take in a

particular situation: *We will only strike* ***as a last resort***.

• *v.* PHR V **re'sort to sth** to make use of sth, esp. sth bad, as a way of achieving sth, often because there is no other possible solution: *We may have to resort to using untrained staff.*

★ **resource** /rɪ'sɔːs; -'zɔːs; *AmE* 'riːsɔːrs; rɪ'sɔːrs/ *n., v.*

• *n.* [C, usu. pl.] **1** a supply of sth such as money, labour, etc. that an organization or a person has and can use: *We need to allocate available resources more effectively.* ◇ *More companies are pooling resources* (= each company is giving sth) *in order to win big contracts.*

⊕ *to* ***have/lack/share*** *~s* ♦ *to* ***manage/use*** *~s* ♦ ***capital/cash/financial/technical*** *~s* ♦ ***limited/scarce*** *~s*

**2** (*Econ.*) a supply of sth such as oil, gas, land, minerals, etc. that a country has and can use, esp. to increase their wealth: *South Africa's natural resources*

⊕ *to* ***be rich in/have/lack*** *~s* ♦ *to* ***develop/manage/use*** *~s*

• *v.* [T] (*usu. pass.*) to provide sth with the money, equipment, labour, etc. that is needed: *The IT department is* ***under-resourced.***

**re'source allo,cation** *n.* [U,C] the way in which the resources of a company are divided and given to different departments, projects, etc.; the act of deciding this

**re,source produc'tivity** *n.* [U] (*Econ.*) the fact of producing more goods using smaller amounts of raw materials and causing less waste; ways of doing this

**respect** /rɪ'spekt/ *n.* IDM **in respect of sth** (*written*) **1** concerning: *A writ was served on the firm in respect of their unpaid bill.* **2** in payment for sth: *money received in respect of overtime worked* **with respect to sth** (*written*) concerning: *The two groups were similar with respect to income.*

**respond** /rɪ'spɒnd; *AmE* rɪ'spɑːnd/ *v.* [I] **1** to give a spoken or written answer to sb/sth: *to ~* ***to*** *an ad/an email enquiry* **2** to react to sth that sb has said or done: *Consumers responded positively* ***to*** *the ad.*

**respondent** /rɪ'spɒndənt; *AmE* -'spɑːnd-/ *n.* [C] **1** (*Market.*) a person who answers questions, esp. in a survey **2** (*Law*) in some legal cases, the person who is accused of sth

**response** /rɪ'spɒns; *AmE* rɪ'spɑːns/ *n.* [C,U] **1** a spoken or written answer: *We received more than 50 responses.* ◇ ***In response to*** *your enquiry...* **2** a reaction to sth that has happened or been said: *The product was developed* ***in response to*** *customer demand.*

**res'ponse rate** *n.* [C] (*Market.*) the percentage of people who reply to a message or an advertisement they are sent by telephone, email, post/mail, etc.

**res'ponse time** *n.* [C,U] the length of time that a person or system takes to react to sth: *a set response time for calls to the help desk*

★ **responsibility** /rɪ,spɒnsə'bɪləti; *AmE* -,spɑːn-/ *n.* (*pl.* **-ties**)

**1** [U] **~ (for sth)** the duty of being in charge of a particular activity, area, department, etc: *She has responsibility for managing the UK business.*

⊕ *to* ***assume/take*** *~ for sth* ♦ *to* ***delegate/share*** *~ for sth*

**2 responsibilities** [pl.] the things that sb deals with, manages or controls in their job: *key job responsibilities and skills*

⊕ *to* ***give up/have/take on*** *responsibilities* ♦ *to* ***assign/delegate*** *responsibilities* ♦ ***day-to-day/heavy/increased*** *responsibilities*

**3** [U; C, usu. sing.] a duty to help or take care of sb/sth because of your job, position, etc: *We have a responsibility* ***to*** *our shareholders.* **4** [U] blame for sth bad that has happened: *to* ***accept/assume/take*** *~* ***for*** *sth*

★ **responsible** /rɪ'spɒnsəbl; *AmE* -'spɑːn-/ *adj.* **1** having the job or duty of dealing with sb/sth, so that it is your fault if sth goes wrong: *Who is responsible for the smooth running of the office?* **2 ~ to sb** to have to report to sb/sth with authority or sb that you work for and explain to them what you have done **3** a **responsible** job or position is an important one that needs sb that you can trust and rely on

**responsive** /rɪ'spɒnsɪv; *AmE* -'spɑːn-/ *adj.* reacting quickly and in a positive way: *fast, responsive customer service* ▶ **res'ponsively** *adv.* **res'ponsiveness** *n.* [U]

**rest** /rest/ *v.* PHR V **'rest with sb (to do sth)** (*fml.*) if a decision, an action, etc. **rests with** sb, they have responsibility for it

**restart** /,riː'stɑːt; *AmE* -'stɑːrt/ *v.* [T,I] to start again; to make sth start again: *Load the software and then restart your PC.*

**restate** /,riː'steɪt/ *v.* [T] (*Account.*) if a company **restates** all or part of its financial results, it publishes them again with some differences, usu. because of changes in the way sth is calculated: *to ~ accounts/earnings/profits/results* ▸ ˌ**re'statement** *n.* [C,U]: *financial restatements*

**restitution** /ˌrestɪ'tju:ʃn; *AmE* -'tu:-/ *n.* [U] (*fml.*) **1** (*Law*) payment for some harm or wrong that sb has suffered: *to make/pay ~* ◇ *He is seeking $100 m* ***in restitution***. **2** the act of giving back sth lost or stolen to its owner: *to claim/demand ~*

**restock** /ˌri:'stɒk; *AmE* -'stɑ:k/ *v.* [T,I] (*Comm.*; *Product.*) to get new supplies to replace those used or sold ▸ ˌ**re'stocking** *n.* [U]

**restore** /rɪ'stɔ:(r)/ *v.* [T] **1** to bring back a situation or feeling that existed before: *restoring investor confidence* **2 ~ sb/sth to sth** to bring sb/sth back to a former condition, place or position: *to restore the industry to financial health*

**restrain** /rɪ'streɪn/ *v.* [T] to stop sth that is growing or increasing from continuing to do so: *restraining spending*

**restraint** /rɪ'streɪnt/ *n.* **1** [C] a rule or an agreement that limits what a person, group, country, etc. can do: *a* ***restraint of trade*** **2** [U] the act of controlling or limiting sth because it is necessary or sensible to do so: *to* ***exercise*** *restraint in pay increases*

**restrict** /rɪ'strɪkt/ *v.* [T] **1** to limit the size, amount or range of sth: *Private investors were restricted* ***to*** *35 shares each.* ◇ *The decline in trade was not restricted to Europe.* **2** to prevent sb from doing sth: *Insiders are restricted* ***from*** *selling their shares for a short period.* ▸ **re'stricted** *adj.*: *a restricted supply*

**restriction** /rɪ'strɪkʃn/ *n.* **1** [C] a rule or law that limits what you can do or what can happen: *There are no restrictions* ***on*** *the amount of money you can withdraw.*

⊕ *to* ***impose/place/put*** *~s on sth* ♦ *to* ***ease/lift/relax/remove*** *~s* ♦ ***export/import/planning/price/trade*** *~s* ♦ ***tight/tough*** *~s*

**2** [U] the act of limiting or controlling sth: *restriction of supply*

**restrictive** /rɪ'strɪktɪv/ *adj.* tightly controlled by rules, in a way that prevents people from doing what they want: *a period of restrictive shopping laws*

**reˌstrictive 'practice** *n.* [C, usu. pl.] (*BrE*) **1** (*HR*) ways of working arranged by one group of workers that limit the freedom of other workers or employers in order to protect people's jobs **2** (*Econ.*) (*also* **reˌstrictive 'trade/'business ˌpractice**) agreements between businesses in an industry or trade that limit or prevent free competition between businesses

★ **restructure** /ˌri:'strʌktʃə(r)/ *v.* **1** [T,I] to organize sth such as a company, an industry, etc. in a different way to make it more efficient: *The company has recently restructured.* **2** (*Finan.*) [T] if a company with problems **restructures** its debts, it agrees with lenders to pay them in a different way from before

▸ **res'tructuring** *n.* [U; C, usu. sing.]

**re'structuring charge** (*also* **re'structuring cost**) *n.* [C, usu. pl.] (*Account.*) **1** the cost to a company, an industry, etc. of organizing itself in a different way in order to become more efficient: *They* ***took*** *a $26 m restructuring charge.* **2** the amount that a company has to pay to organize its debts in a different way

★ **results** /rɪ'zʌlts/ *n.* [pl.] **1** (*also* **fiˌnancial re'sults**) the profits and losses made by a company during a particular period; a report on this that a company prepares: *The company's end-of-year results were better than expected.*

⊕ *to* ***announce/post/report*** *~* ♦ ***annual/first-half****, etc. ~* ♦ ***final/interim/preliminary*** *~* ♦ ***good/strong*** *~* ♦ ***disappointing/weak*** *~*

**2** things achieved successfully: *to* ***achieve/bring/get/produce/show*** *~*

★ **resume** /rɪ'zu:m; *BrE also* -'zju:-/ *v.* [T,I] (*fml.*) if you **resume** an activity or if it **resumes**, it begins again or continues after an interruption: *Production has resumed at the plant.*

▸ **resumption** /rɪ'zʌmpʃn/ *n.* [sing; U]: *a resumption of merger talks*

**résumé** /'rezjumeɪ; *AmE* 'rezəmeɪ/ *n.* [C] (*AmE*) a written record of your education and employment, that you send when applying for a job SYN CV (*BrE*)

**resurgence** /rɪ'sɜ:dʒəns; *AmE* -'sɜ:rdʒ-/ *n.* [sing; U] the return and growth of an activity that had stopped: *a resurgence* ***in*** *consumer confidence* ▸ **re'surgent** *adj.*

★ **retail** /'ri:teɪl/ *n., adj., adv., v.* (*Comm.*)

• ***n.*** [U] the selling of goods to the public, esp. through shops/stores: *a career in retail* ◇ *The store combines food retail with home products.*

→ WHOLESALE

• ***adj.*** connected with selling goods to the public, mainly through shops/stores: *retail outlets*

⊙ *a ~ business/chain/group* ◆ *~ space/stores/units* ◆ *~ consumers/customers* ◆ *the ~ market/sector/trade*

• ***adv.*** being bought and sold to the public: *to buy/sell ~* (= in a shop/store)

• ***v.*** **1** [I] to be sold at a particular price: *The printer retails **for** $299.* **2** [T] to sell goods to the public, usu. in small quantities: *retailing woollen goods*

**'retail ˌaudit** = STORE AUDIT

**'retail ˌbanking** (*also* **con'sumer ˌbanking**) *n.* [U] the part of a bank's business that involves providing services to members of the public
▸ **'retail bank** *n.* [C]

**ˌretail co'operative** *n.* [C] **1** (*Finan.*) = CONSUMER COOPERATIVE **2** (*Comm.*) (*also* **ˌretailer co'operative**) a group of RETAILERS who buy goods together in large quantities so that they can get lower prices

**ˌretail de'posits** *n.* [pl.] (*Finan.*) small amounts of money that a bank's customers deposit in their accounts; money that local individuals or small businesses deposit

**ˌretail distri'bution** *n.* [U] (*Market.*) the process of getting the goods that sb produces into shops/stores so that people will buy them; the shops/stores that sell a particular product: *a nationwide retail distribution system* ◇ *The product doesn't have general retail distribution.*

★ **retailer** /'ri:teɪlə(r)/ *n.* [C] (*Comm.*) a business or person that sells goods directly to the public: *clothing/food ~s* ◇ *a leading high-street retailer* → WHOLESALER

⊙ *a **large/small** ~* ◆ *a **major/top** ~* ◆ *an **independent**/a **speciality** ~* ◆ *an **Internet/online**/a **mail-order** ~*

**ˌretailer co'operative** = RETAIL COOPERATIVE (2)

**retailing** /'ri:teɪlɪŋ/ *n.* [U] (*Comm.*) the business of selling goods to the public, esp. through shops/stores: *career opportunities in retailing* ◇ *music retailing*

**ˌretail in'vestment** *n.* [U;C] (*Finan.*) investment that is made by an individual for themselves, rather than by an institution
▸ **ˌretail in'vestor** *n.* [C]

**'retail ˌmedia** *n.* [U with sing./pl. v.] (*Market.*) ways of advertising products in shops/stores

**'retail park** *n.* [C] a group of large shops/stores with a large car park, usu. on the edge of a town or city

**'retail price** *n.* [C] (*Comm.*) the price that customers pay for goods in a shop/store

**ˌretail 'price ˌindex** *n.* [sing.] (*abbr* **RPI**) (*Econ.*) in the UK, a list of the prices of some ordinary goods and services which shows how much these prices change each month, used to measure the rate of INFLATION SYN CONSUMER PRICE INDEX, COST-OF-LIVING INDEX

**'retail sales** *n.* [pl.] sales to the public rather than to shops or businesses

**'retail store ˌaudit** = STORE AUDIT

**ˌretail 'therapy** *n.* [U] shopping that is done in order to make yourself feel happier rather than because you need things

★ **retain** /rɪ'teɪn/ *v.* [T] (*fml.*) **1** to keep sth; to continue to have sth: *cutting prices to retain customers* ◇ *to retain control of the company* SYN KEEP **2** (*HR*) if a company **retains** people, it continues to employ them: *to hire and retain good people* SYN KEEP **3** to give regular payments or payments in advance to sb with special knowledge such as a lawyer so that they will do work for you: *a retaining fee*

**reˌtained 'earnings** (*also* **reˌtained 'profits**) *n.* [pl.] (*Account.*) the part of the profit made by a company after tax has been paid that is invested in the company rather than being paid to shareholders as DIVIDENDS
SYN UNDISTRIBUTED EARNINGS

**retainer** /rɪ'teɪnə(r)/ *n.* [C,U] an amount of money that is paid to sb to make sure they are available to do work when they are needed: *a monthly retainer of $6 000* ◇ *We have a lawyer **on retainer**.*

**retaliatory** /rɪ'tæliətri; *AmE* -tɔ:ri/ *adj.* intended to punish sb for sth they have done to harm you: *retaliatory action*

**retention** /rɪ'tenʃn/ *n.* **1** (*HR*) [U] the ability of a company to keep its employees; the fact of this happening: *ways to improve recruitment and retention* **2** [U] the fact of keeping sb or sth: *a document retention policy* **3** (*Account.*) **retentions** [pl.] part of the money that is owed to sb for work they have done that is not paid until the work is completed in a satisfactory way

**rethink** /ˌri:'θɪŋk/ *v.* [T,I] (**-thought, -thought** /-'θɔ:t/) to think again about an idea, a plan, etc., esp. in

order to change it: *We need to rethink our whole business strategy.*
▸ **'rethink** (*also* **,re'thinking**) *n.* [sing.]: *a radical rethink of our working practices*

**retire** /rɪ'taɪə(r)/ *v.* **1** (*HR*) [T,I] to stop doing your job, esp. because you have reached a particular age or you are ill/sick; to tell sb they must stop doing their job: *She retired early because of ill health.* ◇ *the official retiring age* ◇ *retired executives* **2** (*Law*) [I] if a JURY **retires**, it goes to a separate room to decide whether sb is guilty or not **3** (*Finan.*) [T] to pay a debt; to say that sb does not have to pay a debt: *They retired $600 m of their loan.*

**retiree** /rɪ,taɪə'riː/ *n.* [C] (*AmE*) a person who has stopped working because of their age

★**retirement** /rɪ'taɪəmənt; *AmE* -'taɪərm-/ *n.* **1** (*HR*) [U,C] the fact of stopping work because you have reached a particular age; the time when you do this: *She* ***took early retirement*** (= retired before the usual age). ◇ *a retirement pension* **2** [U; sing.] the period of your life after you have stopped work at a particular age: *Up to a third of your life could be spent* ***in*** *retirement.* ◇ *to plan for/provide for ~* **3** (*Finan.*) [U] the act of paying back loans completely: *the early retirement of debt*

**re'tirement plan** = PENSION PLAN

**retool** /,riː'tuːl/ *v.* **1** (*Manufact.*) [T,I] to replace or change the machines or equipment in a factory so that it can produce new or better goods: *the costs of retooling the plant* **2** (*infml.*) [T] (*AmE*) to organize sth in a new or different way: *How should we retool our strategy?*
▸ **,re'tooling** *n.* [U; sing.]

**retract** /rɪ'trækt/ *v.* [T,I] **1** to say that sth you have said earlier is not true or correct or that you did not mean it: *She retracted the comment.* **2** to become, or to make sth become, smaller in amount or value: *IT spending retracted last year.* ▸ **re'traction** /-kʃn/ *n.* [U,C]

**retrain** /,riː'treɪn/ *v.* [T,I] (*HR*) to learn, or to teach sb, a new type of work, a new skill, etc.
▸ **,re'training** *n.* [U]

**retreat** /rɪ'triːt/ *v.* [I] **1** to lose value: *Shares retreated 4.4%.* **2** to decide not to do or continue to do sth because the situation has become too difficult: *They are retreating from retail.* ▸ **re'treat** *n.* [C,U]: *a retreat in share prices* ◇ *The business has* ***gone into retreat.*** ◇ *a retreat* ***from*** *e-commerce*

**retrench** /rɪ'trentʃ/ *v.* **1** (*fml.*) [I] (about a business, government, etc.) to spend less money; to reduce costs: *The company is retrenching.* **2** (*HR*) [T] to tell sb that they cannot continue working for you: *The plan is to retrench about 500 people.* SYN LAY OFF ▸ **re'trenchment** *n.* [U,C]

**retrieve** /rɪ'triːv/ *v.* [T] **1** (*IT*) to find and get back data or information that has been stored in the memory of a computer: *to retrieve information from the database* **2** to get back sth that you have lost, lent, etc: *You have a right to retrieve your property* ▸ **re'trievable** /-vəbl/ *adj.*

**retro-** /'retrəʊ; *AmE* -troʊ/ *prefix* back or backwards: *retrospectively*

**retrospective** /,retrə'spektɪv/ (*also* **,retro'active** /,retrəʊ'æktɪv; *AmE* -troʊ-/) *adj.* (about a new law, rule, etc.) intended to take effect from a particular date in the past rather than from the present date: *retrospective pay awards*
▸ **,retro'spectively** (*also* **,retro'actively**) *adv.*

★**return** /rɪ'tɜːn; *AmE* rɪ'tɜːrn/ *v.*, *n.*
• *v.* [T] **1** (*Account.*; *Finan.*) to give or produce a particular amount of money as a profit or loss: *My investments return a high rate of interest.* **2** (*Comm.*) to take or send a product back to the place it came from because you do not want it or because there is sth wrong with it: *How do you process and store returned goods?* **3** to telephone or email sb who has telephoned or emailed you: *We return all calls quickly.*
• *n.* **1** (*Account.*; *Finan.*) [U,C] **~ (on/from sth)** the amount of profit or income that you get from a particular investment: *Equities have produced higher returns than bonds.*
○ *a* ***good/strong*** *~* • *a* ***low/poor*** *~* • *an* ***annual/average*** *~* • *a* ***negative/positive*** *~* • *to* ***show/yield*** *a ~*
**2** [C] an official report or statement that gives particular information about sth to an official body: *a VAT return* ◇ *to do/file/make/submit a ~* **3** (*Account.*) [C] = TAX RETURN **4** (*Comm.*) (*also* **,product re'turn**) [C] goods that a customer has bought or ordered and then returned; the act of returning a product **5** [U] (*also* **re'turn key** [C]) the button you press on a computer when you reach the end of an instruction, or to begin a new line IDM **by re'turn (of 'post)**

(*BrE*) using the next post; as soon as possible: *Please reply by return.*

**returnable** /rɪˈtɜːnəbl; *AmE* -ˈtɜːrn-/ *adj.* **1** that can or must be given back after a period of time: *a returnable deposit* **2** (about bottles, containers, etc.) that can be taken back to a shop/store to be used again

**returner** /rɪˈtɜːnə(r); *AmE* -ˈtɜːrn-/ *n.* [C] (*BrE*) (*HR*) a person who goes back to work after not working for a long time: *courses for adult returners*

**reˈturn key** = RETURN *n.* (5)

**reˌturn on ˈassets** *n.* [U,C] (*abbr* **ROA**) (*Account.*) a measure that is used to see how well a company is using its assets to produce profits. It shows the profits for the year as a percentage of the recent total assets.

**reˌturn on ˈcapital** = RETURN ON CAPITAL EMPLOYED, RETURN ON INVESTMENT

**reˈturn on ˈcapital emˈployed** (*abbr* **ROCE**) (*also* **reˌturn on ˈcapital**) *n.* [U,C] (*Account.*) a measure that is used to see how well a company is using the money invested in its activities to produce profits, often calculated by comparing the company's profits for the year before tax and interest are taken off with the value of its total assets minus its total debts

**reˌturn on ˈequity** *n.* [U,C] (*abbr* **ROE**) (*Account.*) a measure used to see how much profit a company is producing compared to the value of its SHAREHOLDER EQUITY

**reˌturn on inˈvestment** (*abbr* **ROI**) (*also* **reˌturn on ˈcapital**) *n.* [U,C] (*Account.*) a measure of how much profit an investment produces compared with the amount originally invested

**reˌturn-to-ˈbase** *adj.* (*abbr* **RTB**) (*Comm.*) used to describe a GUARANTEE where the buyer must send the product back to where it came from in order to have it repaired or replaced

**revalue** /ˌriːˈvæljuː/ *v.* **1** [T] to estimate the value of sth again, esp. giving it a higher value: *Investors revalued the group's assets.* **2** (*Finan.*) [T,I] to increase the value of a currency in relation to the money of other countries: *The euro is being revalued **against** the dollar.* OPP DEVALUE ▸ **ˌreˌvaluˈation** /-uˈeɪʃn/ *n.* [U; C, usu. sing.]

**revamp** /ˌriːˈvæmp/ *v.* [T] to make changes to the form of sth to improve its appearance, how efficiently it works, etc: *He is revamping the company's web page.* ▸ **ˈrevamp** *n.* [sing.]

★**revenue** /ˈrevənjuː; *AmE* -nuː/ *n.* [U] (*also* **revenues** [pl.]) **1** the money that is received by a business usu. from selling goods or services: *advertising revenue* ◇ *They have annual revenues of around £3 bn.*

○ ***full-year/quarterly*** ~ • ***to bring in/generate/produce/yield*** ~ • ***to boost/grow/increase*** ~ • ***to post/project/report*** ~

**2** the money that is received by the State from taxes

○ ***government/public/tax*** ~ • ***to collect/get/lose/raise*** ~

**ˈrevenue acˌcount** *n.* [C] (*Account.*) a record of all the money that a company has earned and spent in its normal business activities during a particular period

**ˌrevenue anticiˈpation note** (*abbr* **RAN**) (*also* **ˌtax anticiˈpation note** *abbr* **TAN**) *n.* [C, usu. pl.] (*Finan.*) in the US, a type of bond issued by a local government that is paid back using money from taxes and other income that the local government expects to receive in the future

**ˈrevenue bond** *n.* [C] (*Finan.*) in the US, a bond that is issued by a local government in order to finance a public project such as the building of a new hospital, bridge, road, etc. The bond and interest payments are taken from the profits made by the project once it is completed.

**ˌrevenue exˈpenditure** *n.* [U] (*also* **ˌrevenue exˈpense** [C,U]) (*abbr* **revex**) (*Account.*) money spent on the normal activities of a business during a particular period such as the cost of labour, materials, etc.

**ˌrevenue reˈserve** *n.* [C, usu. pl.] (*Account.*) profits that a company has made which are kept so that they can be given to shareholders through a DIVIDEND payment in years when profits are low → CAPITAL RESERVE

**ˈrevenue stamp** *n.* [C] a stamp that is put on sth such as a packet of cigarettes to show that a government tax has been paid

**ˈrevenue stream** (*also* **ˌstream of ˈrevenue**, *less freq.*) *n.* [C] a source of income: *We are looking for new revenue streams.*

**ˈrevenue ˌtariff** *n.* [C] (*Econ.*) a tax on imported products that is intended to raise money for the government rather than protect local businesses from foreign competition

**reverse** /rɪˈvɜːs; *AmE* rɪˈvɜːrs/ *v., n., adj.*
• *v.* [T] **1** to change sth to the opposite of what it was before: *to ~ a process/trend* **2** (*Law*) to change a previous decision, law, etc. to the opposite: *The Court of Appeal reversed the decision.* SYN REVOKE
• *n.* **1** [C] a change, esp. a change from success to failure: *to suffer a reverse* **2 the reverse** [sing.] the opposite of sth that has been mentioned: *We seem to be consuming more, but the reverse is true.* IDM **go/shift into reˈverse; put/send sth into reˈverse** to start to happen, or to make sth happen, in the opposite way: *The share price has gone into reverse.*
• *adj.* opposite to what has been mentioned

**reˌverse ˈauction** *n.* [C] (*Comm.*) a type of **auction** in which prices go down rather than up as suppliers compete for a contract by offering to supply sth at a lower price than their competitors

**reˌverse ˈbilling** *n.* [U] a method of payment on mobile phones/cellphones in which the person receiving a message pays for it

**reˌverse-ˈcharge** *adj.* a reverse-charge telephone call is paid for by the person who receives the call
▸ **reˌverse-ˈcharge** *adv.*: *I had to call reverse-charge.*

**reˌverse discrimiˈnation** = POSITIVE DISCRIMINATION

**reˌverse engiˈneering** *n.* [U] the copying of another company's product after examining it in detail to find out how it is made

**reˌverse loˈgistics** *n.* [U] (*Product.*) the process of handling and storing products returned by a customer or sth that has been used and must now be thrown away
▸ **reˌverse loˈgistic** *adj.*

**reˌverse ˈmerger** (*also* **reˌverse ˈtakeover**) *n.* [C] (*Finan.*) a process in which a PRIVATE COMPANY buys all or most of the shares in a PUBLIC COMPANY so that it can issue shares and trade them on the stock exchange

**reˌverse reˈpurchase aˌgreement** (*also* **reˌverse ˈrepo**, *infml.*) *n.* [C] (*Finan.*) an agreement to buy shares, bonds, etc. from an investor and then sell them back at a higher price at a later date

**reˌverse ˈsplit** (*BrE also* **reˌverse ˈshare split**) (*AmE also* **reˌverse ˈstock split**) *n.* [C] (*Finan.*) a reduction in the number of shares a company trades without any reduction in the total value of all the shares

**reˌverse ˈtakeover** *n.* [C] (*Finan.*) **1** the process in which a smaller company takes control of a larger company **2** = REVERSE MERGER

**reversion** *n., v.*
• *n.* /rɪˈvɜːʃn; *AmE* rɪˈvɜːrʒn/ **1** (*Law*) [U,C] the legal return of sth to sb such as land or property **2** (*fml.*) [sing; U] the act or process of returning to a former state: *a reversion to normal conditions*
• *v.* (*also* **re-version**) /ˌriːˈvɜːʃn; *AmE* ˌriːˈvɜːrʒn/ [T] (*usu. pass.*) to make changes to sth such as TV programme, a film/movie, software, etc. in order to make it more suitable for a particular purpose or a particular market: *The Mac-only CD-ROM was reversioned for PC.*

**revex** *abbr* (*Account.*) a short way of writing **revenue expenditure**

★ **review** /rɪˈvjuː/ *n., v.*
• *n.* **1** [U,C] a careful examination of sth, usu. to see if any changes need to be made: *a pay/salary ~* ◇ *The contract is **under review**.*
➊ *to **carry out/conduct/undertake** a ~ of sth* ◆ *a **financial/spending/strategic** ~* ◆ *an **independent/internal**/a **judicial** ~* ◆ *a ~ **body/panel***
**2** [C] a report on a particular subject: *to publish a review of recent research*
**3** [C] used in the names of magazines that deal with a particular subject or profession: *the Harvard Business Review*
• *v.* [T] to carefully examine or consider sth again, esp. so that you can decide if it is necessary to make changes: *Staff performance is reviewed annually.*

★ **revise** /rɪˈvaɪz/ *v.* [T] (*often with an adv. or a prep.*) to change sth such as a document or an estimate in order to correct or improve it: *a revised estimate* ◇ *Marketing budgets were revised downward.* ◇ *to ~ sth down/higher/up/upwards*
▸ **revision** /rɪˈvɪʒn/ *n.* [C,U]: *a downward/upward ~*

**revitalize**, **-ise** /ˌriːˈvaɪtəlaɪz/ *v.* [T] to make sth stronger, more active or more healthy: *The brand has been revitalized.* ▸ **reˌvitaliˈzation**, **-iˈsation** /-laɪˈzeɪʃn; *AmE* -ləˈz-/ *n.* [U]

**revive** /rɪˈvaɪv/ *v.* **1** [T,I] to become, or to make sb/sth become, strong and active again: *The economy is beginning to revive.* ◇ *reviving falling sales* **2** [T] to bring sth back; to make sth start being used or done again: *She has been trying to revive the debate over equal pay.* ▸ **reˈvival** /-vl/ *n.* [U,C]: *an economic revival*

**revoke** /rɪˈvəʊk; *AmE* -ˈvoʊk/ *v.* [T] to officially cancel sth such as a decision, licence, rule or a particular right to do sth: *to revoke a commercial licence* SYN RESCIND
▶ **revocable** /ˈrevəkəbl/ *adj.* **revocation** /ˌrevəˈkeɪʃn/ *n.* [U,C]

**revolution** /ˌrevəˈluːʃn/ *n.* [C] a great change in conditions, ways of working, beliefs, etc. that affects large numbers of people: *a social/technological ~* ▶ **ˌrevoˈlutionary** /-ʃənri; *AmE* -neri/ *adj.*: *a revolutionary idea* **ˌrevoˈlutionize**, **-ise** /-ʃənaɪz/ *v.* [T]

**revolve** /rɪˈvɒlv; *AmE* rɪˈvɑːlv/ *v.* [T] (*Finan.*) if you **revolve** a debt you do not pay all of it back but carry the remaining debt into a new financial period

**reˌvolving ˈcredit** (*also* **ˌopen ˈcredit**) *n.* [U,C] (*also* **reˈvolving ˈline of ˈcredit, reˌvolving ˈloan** [C]) (*Finan.*) an agreement with a bank, etc. in which sb is allowed to borrow up to a particular amount. If they pay back part of the loan they can then borrow more money up to the agreed limit: *The company has negotiated a €500 m revolving credit facility.*

**reˌvolving ˈdoor** *n.* [sing.]
**1** (*HR*) used to say that the person holding a particular job or position in an organization frequently changes: *revolving-door leadership* **2** a place, an organization or a system where people come in and go out again quickly, often many times: *a revolving-door workplace* (= where people take jobs but leave after a short time) **3** used to talk about a situation in which the same events or problems keep happening: *revolving-door crime*

**reˈvolving ˈline of ˈcredit** = REVOLVING CREDIT

**reˌvolving ˈloan** = REVOLVING CREDIT

★ **reward** /rɪˈwɔːd; *AmE* rɪˈwɔːrd/ *n.*, *v.*
• *n.* [C,U] a thing that you are given or money that you receive for working hard, doing sth good, etc: *The firm offers financial rewards to motivate its employees.*
○ *a big/rich ~* • *to earn/get/win a ~*
• *v.* [T] **~ sb (with sth) (for sth/for doing sth)** to give sth to sb because they have done sth good, worked hard, etc: *We were rewarded with bonuses for reaching our targets.*

**rewarding** /rɪˈwɔːdɪŋ; *AmE* -ˈwɔːrd-/ *adj.* providing benefits such as a feeling of achievement, a lot of money, etc: *a financially rewarding job* (= one that is well paid)

**rework** /ˌriːˈwɜːk; *AmE* -ˈwɜːrk/ *v.* [T] to make changes to sth in order to improve it, correct it or make it more suitable: *We reworked our forecasts for the coming year.*
▶ **reˈworking** (*esp. BrE*) (*AmE usu.* **ˈrework**) *n.* [C,U]: *a reworking of the tax code*

**RFID** /ˌɑːr ef aɪ ˈdiː/ *abbr* **radio frequency ID/identification** (*usu. used as a countable n.*) an electronic device used for identifying sth or for preventing products from being stolen

**ride** /raɪd/ *v.*, *n.*
• *v.* (**rode** /rəʊd; *AmE* roʊd/**ridden** /ˈrɪdn/) IDM **be riding for a ˈfall** to be doing sth that involves risks and that may end in disaster: *The stock markets were riding for a fall.* **be riding ˈhigh** to be successful or very confident **ride (on) the ˈcoattails of sb/sth; ride sb's/sth's ˈcoattails** to benefit from sb else's success **ride a/the ˈwave of sth** to enjoy or be supported by the particular situation or quality mentioned: *We've been riding the wave of the Italian food craze.* PHR V **ˈride on sth 1** to be supported by or to follow a particular situation or change: *Interest rates on loans have been riding on an uptrend.* **2** (*usu. in the continuous tenses*) to depend on sth: *My future is riding on this interview.*
• *n.* [C, usu. sing.] used to describe how easy or difficult a particular process or period of time is for sb/sth: *an easy/a rocky/smooth ~* IDM **take sb for a ˈride** (*infml.*) to cheat or trick sb: *The taxpayer is being taken for a ride.*

**rider** /ˈraɪdə(r)/ *n.* [C] **1** (*Law*) an extra piece of information added to a contract or an official document **2** (*Insur.*) extra information added to an insurance agreement to include items not mentioned in the standard agreement; a form used for this

**rig** /rɪg/ *v.*, *n.*
• *v.* [T] (**-gg-**) (*usu. pass.*) **1** to arrange or influence sth in a dishonest way in order to get the result that you want: *Did the company rig energy prices?* SYN FIX **2 ~ sth (up) (with sth)** to fit equipment somewhere, sometimes secretly: *The lights had been rigged (up).* ▶ **ˈrigging** *n.* [U]: *market rigging*
• *n.* [C] **1** a large piece of equipment that is used for taking oil or gas from the ground or the bottom of the sea:

*a drilling rig* **2** (*infml.*) (*AmE*) a large lorry/truck

**right** /raɪt/ *n.*, *v.*

• *n.* **1** [C,U] a moral or legal claim to have or get sth or to behave in a particular way: *The union has a right to strike on this issue.* ◇ *a right of appeal* ◇ *consumer/employment ~s* **2 rights** [pl.] the legal authority to publish, sell, show, etc. a particular work such as a book, film/movie, etc: *He sold the rights for $2 m.* ◇ *broadcasting/distribution/licensing ~* **3** (*Finan.*) [C, usu. pl.] = STOCK RIGHT

• *v.* [T] to correct sth that is wrong or not in its normal state

**ˌright first ˈtime** *phr.* (*Product.*) used to describe a system of manufacturing aiming to produce products that are perfect from the start rather than quickly producing sth that will need to be corrected later: *right-first-time silicon chips*

**ˌright of first reˈfusal** *n.* [C,U] (*also* **ˌfirst reˈfusal**, *infml.* [U]) (*Law*) the right to decide whether to accept or refuse sth before it is offered to others

**ˈrights ˌissue** *n.* [C] (*Finan.*) an occasion when new shares are offered to existing shareholders, often at a lower price than the current market price: *They aim to raise $2.5 bn through a rights issue.*

**rightsizing** /ˈraɪtsaɪzɪŋ/ *n.* [U,C] (*esp. AmE*) **1** (*HR*) the act of making a company a more efficient size, usu. by reducing the number of employees and cutting costs **2** (*IT*) when an organization changes to a more efficient computer system, usu. by using a smaller, cheaper system to do the same work: *the rightsizing of systems* ▶ **ˈrightsize** *v.* [T,I]

**ˈrights ˌmanager** *n.* [C] a person whose job is organizing contracts and fees for buying, selling and using goods, ideas, designs, etc. in another country or another medium

**ring** /rɪŋ/ *v.*, *n.*

• *v.* [I] (**rang** /ræŋ/**rung** /rʌŋ/) (about a telephone) to make a sound because sb is trying to telephone you: *Your phone's ringing!* **IDM ring the ˈregister; ring the ˈcash register** to sell sth and make a profit **PHR V ˌring ˈin** (*BrE*) to telephone the place where you work: *Two members of staff* ***rang in sick*** *at short notice.* **ˌring sth ˈup** to enter the cost of goods being bought in a shop/store on a CASH REGISTER **ˌring ˈup sth** to record an amount of sales or profits in a particular period of time: *The company rang up sales of $166 m last year.*

• *n.* [C] **1** a group of people who are working together, esp. in a secret or illegal activity **2** (*Stock Ex.*) an area of a stock exchange where a particular product is traded SYN PIT

**ˈring-fence** *v.* [T] (*BrE*) **1** (*Finan.*) to protect a particular amount of money so that it can only be used for a particular purpose: *a ring-fenced bank account* **2** to protect sth by putting restrictions on it so that it can only be used by particular people or for a particular purpose: *You can access the parts of the Intranet that are not ring-fenced.* ▶ **ˈring fence** *n.* [C]: *to put a ring fence around funding for education*

**rip** /rɪp/ *v.* (**-pp-**) **PHR V ˌrip sb ˈoff** (*infml.*) (*often pass.*) to cheat sb, for example by making them pay too much or by selling them sth of poor quality: *We've been ripped off!*

**ˈrip-off** *n.* (*infml.*) **1** [C, usu. sing.] sth that is not worth what you pay for it: *The taxi fare from the airport was a rip-off.* ◇ *rip-off prices* **2** [C] a copy of sth, esp. one that is less expensive or not as good as the original thing

**ˈripple efˌfect** *n.* [C] **~ (on sth)** a situation in which an event or action has an effect on sth, which then has an effect on sth else

**rise** /raɪz/ *n.*, *v.*

• *n.* [C] **1** an increase in an amount, a number or a level: *price rises* ◇ *a 10% rise* ***in*** *sales* ◇ *Credit-card use is* ***on the rise.***

◆ *a* ***dramatic/rapid/sharp/steady/strong*** *~* ◆ *a* ***modest/slight/small*** *~*

**2** (*BrE*) (*AmE* **raise**) an increase in the money you are paid for the work you do: *I'm going to ask for a rise.*

• *v.* [I] (**rose** /rəʊz; *AmE* roʊz/**risen** /ˈrɪzn/) to increase in amount, number or level: *The price of gas rose.* ◇ *Gas rose* ***in price.*** ◇ *Production rose* ***by*** *8%.* ◇ *rising unemployment*

◆ *to ~* ***dramatically/sharply/slightly/steadily*** ◆ *to* ***be expected to/be likely to/be set to*** *~*

**PHR V ˈrise to sth** to show that you are able to deal with an unexpected situation, problem, etc: *How will they rise to the* ***challenge*** *of increased competition?*

★ **risk** /rɪsk/ *n.*, *v.*

• *n.* **1** [C,U] the possibility of sth bad happening at some time in the future: *The high risk deters many investors.* ◇ *There is a risk* ***that*** *the whole deal will fall through.*

◆ *a* ***low/small*** *~* ◆ *a* ***real/serious*** *~ (of sth)* ◆ ***financial/health/personal/security*** *~s* ◆ *to* ***avoid/face*** *~s*

**2** (*Finan.*) [U] the possibility that an asset may rise or fall in value
○ *to carry/take on ~ • high/low ~*
**3** (*Insur.*) [C,U] the possibility of loss or damage that sth is insured against: *to cover (for)/insure against/protect against (a) ~* **4** [C] **a good/bad/poor ~** a person or business considered from the point of view of whether they are likely to pay back money they borrow, have an accident, etc. **IDM** **at 'risk** in danger of being lost or damaged; in danger of losing sth or being injured: *Five thousand jobs are at risk.* **do sth at your ˌown 'risk** to do sth even though you have been warned about the possible dangers and will have to take responsibility for anything bad that happens → idioms at OWNER, RUN *V.*, TAKE *V.*
• *v.* [T] **1** to put sth valuable or important in a dangerous situation, in which it could be lost or damaged: *She risked all her capital in the new business.* **2** to be in a situation in which sth bad could happen to you: *We risk losing our best staff.*

**'risk aˌnalysis** *n.* [C,U] **1** the process of identifying possible risks, developing ways of making their effects less serious, and sharing information about them **2** (*Finan.*) a method of calculating how safe it is to lend money to a person, an organization, etc. or how safe an investment is

**'risk ˌarbitrage** *n.* [U] (*Finan.*) the practice of using differences in prices in a market to try to make a profit, for example by buying shares in a company that is being taken over and at the same time selling shares in the company that is taking it over

**'risk asˌsessment** *n.* [C,U] the part of the process of RISK ANALYSIS that involves identifying possible risks, calculating how likely they are to happen, and estimating what effects they might have

**'risk aˌverse** *adj.* unwilling to do sth if it is possible that sth bad could happen ▶ **'risk aˌversion** *n.* [U]

**'risk ˌcapital** = VENTURE CAPITAL

**'risk ˌmanagement** *n.* [U] the part of the process of RISK ANALYSIS that involves developing plans for making the effects of risks less serious, esp. the risk of losing money

**'risk ˌprofile** *n.* [C] (*Finan.*) **1** an analysis of a possible investment that considers how likely it is to result in a loss: *The company has a high risk profile due to the level of its debts.* **2** the amount of risk that a person, bank, etc. has when they invest or lend money: *Banks are improving their risk profile by reducing the number of loans they make.* **3** how likely a person or company is to pay back money that has been borrowed: *a credit-card holder's risk profile*

**'risk-ˌtaking** *n.* [U] doing things that involve risks in order to achieve sth ▶ **'risk-ˌtaker** *n.* [C]

**risky** /ˈrɪski/ *adj.* (**-kier, -kiest** **HELP** You can also use **more risky** and **most risky**.) involving the possibility of sth bad happening: *a risky investment* ▶ **'riskiness** *n.* [U]

★ **rival** /ˈraɪvl/ *n., adj., v.*
• *n.* [C] a person, company, or thing that competes with another: *This new magazine is a rival to the major news weekly.* **SYN** COMPETITOR
○ *a bigger/larger/smaller ~ • your closest/main/nearest ~(s)*
• *adj.* that competes with another person, company or thing: *a rival bid for the company*
○ *a ~ offer • a ~ business/company/firm/group/operator • ~ products/services/brands*
• *v.* [T] (**-ll-**, *AmE also* **-l-**) to be as good, impressive, etc. as sb/sth else: *This company may soon be rivalling the market leaders.*

**rivalry** /ˈraɪvlri/ *n.* [C,U] (*pl.* **-ries**) **~ (with sb/sth) (for sth) | ~ (between A and B) (for sth)** a state in which two people, companies, etc. are competing for the same thing

**ROA** /ˌɑːr əʊ ˈeɪ; *AmE* oʊ/ = RETURN ON ASSETS

**road** /rəʊd; *AmE* roʊd/ *n.* **IDM** **on the 'road** travelling, esp. for long distances or periods of time: *She spends four days a week on the road.*

**ˌroad conˈsignment note** *n.* [C] (*abbr* **CMR**) (*Transpt.*) a document that goes with goods that are sent by road, stating that the company that is transporting the goods has received them and that they are in good condition

**'road ˌhaulage** *n.* [U] (*BrE*) (*Transpt.*) the business of transporting goods by road

**'road ˌhaulier** *n.* [C] (*BrE*) (*Transpt.*) a company that transports goods by road

**roadshow** (*also* **road show**, *esp. in AmE*) /ˈrəʊdʃəʊ; *AmE* ˈroʊdʃoʊ/ *n.* [C] a series of events in different places to encourage people to invest in a company: *an investor roadshow*

**roaming** /ˈrəʊmɪŋ; *AmE* ˈroʊ-/ *n.* [U] a system that allows you to use local services to connect your computer to the Internet or use your mobile phone/cellphone when you are travelling

**roar** /rɔː(r)/ *v.* [I] (*usu. with an adv. or a prep.*) to act or happen very quickly and in an impressive way: *Sales roared ahead in the second half.*

**roaring** /ˈrɔːrɪŋ/ *adj.* IDM **do a ˈroaring trade (in sth)** (*infml.*) to sell a lot of sth very quickly **a roaring sucˈcess** (*infml.*) a very great success

**ROB** /ˌɑːr əʊ ˈbiː; *AmE* oʊ/ = RUN OF BOOK

**robot** /ˈrəʊbɒt; *AmE* ˈroʊbɑːt/ *n.* [C] a machine used in manufacturing that can do some tasks that a human can do and works automatically or is controlled by a computer

**ROC** = RETURN ON CAPITAL

**ROCE** = RETURN ON CAPITAL EMPLOYED

**ˌrock ˈbottom** *n.* [U] the lowest point or level that is possible: *Interest rates are* **at** *rock bottom.* ▸ **ˌrock-ˈbottom** *adj.*: *rock-bottom prices*

**rocket** /ˈrɒkɪt; *AmE* ˈrɑːkɪt/ *v.* [I] to increase very quickly and suddenly: *Sales rocketed* **by** *110%.* ◇ *rocketing costs*

**ROE** = RETURN ON EQUITY

**ˌrogue ˈtrader** *n.* [C] (*Stock Ex.*) a STOCKBROKER who acts alone and takes a lot of risks, sometimes losing a lot of their company's money ▸ **ˌrogue ˈtrading** *n.* [U]

**ROI** = RETURN ON INVESTMENT

★**role** /rəʊl; *AmE* roʊl/ *n.* [C] the function or position that sb has in an organization, an industry, a group, etc. → idiom at PLAY *v.*

**ˈrole ˌplaying** *n.* [U] (*also* **ˈrole play** [C,U]) a learning activity that is often used in business training in which you behave in the way sb else would behave in a particular situation ▸ **ˈrole-play** *v.* [T,I]

**roll** /rəʊl; *AmE* roʊl/ *v.* IDM **roll up your ˈsleeves** to start to work hard → idiom at HEAD *n.* PHR V **ˌroll sth ˈback** to reduce a tax, price, rate, etc., usu. back to a previous level: *to roll back insurance rates* **ˌroll ˈin** (about money, orders, profits, etc.) to arrive or appear in large quantities: *The orders kept rolling in.* **ˌroll ˈoff sth** (about a product) to be produced, usu. in large numbers, in a factory: *By next year, 60 000 cars will be rolling off its assembly lines.* **ˌroll (sth) ˈout 1** to introduce a new product, service or technology by gradually making it available to more people; to become available in this way: *The new service is to be rolled out next year.* **2** to show a new aircraft or vehicle to the public for the first time; to be seen for the first time: *The new airline rolls out in 2006.* **ˌroll (sth) ˈover** (*Finan.*) if money that has been paid into a fund, an insurance plan, etc. and not spent **rolls over**, or you **roll** it **over**, it is included in a new fund **ˌroll sth ˈover** (*Finan.*) to take an old debt, loan, etc. and include the money that is owed in a new loan agreement: *to roll over €4.2 bn of debt* **ˌroll sth ˈup 1** to buy several smaller companies and then combine their operations to make a more efficient business **2** (*Finan.*) if an amount of money, such as the interest on an investment, is **rolled up**, it is not paid regularly, but added to the investment and paid in one amount at the end

**rollback** /ˈrəʊlbæk; *AmE* ˈroʊl-/ *n.* [C, usu. sing.] (*esp. AmE*) a return of prices, taxes, etc. to a previous state: *a rollback of the tax increases*

**ˈroller ˌcoaster** *n.* [C] a situation or period of time when the prices of shares, currencies, etc. keep going up and down very quickly and by a large amount

**ˌrolling ˈcontract** *n.* [C] (*Comm.*) a contract for a particular period of time that continues to be made valid for further periods of time until one person in the agreement decides to end it: *a one-year rolling contract*

**ˌrolling ˈlaunch** = ROLL-OUT

**ˈrolling stock** *n.* [U] (*Transpt.*) **1** the engines, trains, etc. that a railway/railroad company owns or can use **2** (*AmE*) the vehicles, trucks, etc. that a company that transports goods by road owns and can use

**roll-ˌon roll-ˈoff** *adj.* (*abbr* **ro-ro**) (*BrE*) (*Transpt.*) (about a ship) designed so that cars, trucks, etc. can be driven directly onto it at one end and off it at the other

**ˈroll-out** (*AmE also* **rollout**) *n.* [C,U] (*BrE also* **ˌrolling ˈlaunch** [C]) (*Market.*) an occasion when a company introduces a new product, service or technology by gradually making it available to more people

**rollover** /ˈrəʊləʊvə(r); *AmE* ˈroʊloʊvər/ *n.* [C, usu. sing.] **1** (*Finan.*) the act of allowing an old loan or debt to continue into a new agreement with the same conditions: *a ~ loan/mortgage* ◇ *a debt rollover* **2** (*Finan.*) (*AmE*) when money is moved from one investment to another, often without paying tax **3** (*IT*) (on web pages) an image that changes when the mouse goes over it; a technique for creating this image: *Javascript rollover buttons*

**'roll-up** *n.* [C] a situation where several smaller companies are bought and combined in order to make a more efficient business

**ROM** /rɒm; *AmE* rɑːm/ *n.* [U] (*IT*) **read-only memory** a type of computer memory that contains information and instructions that are permanent and cannot be changed or removed

**RON** /ˌɑːr əʊ 'en; *AmE* oʊ/ = RUN OF NETWORK

**ROP** /ˌɑːr əʊ 'piː; *AmE* oʊ/ = RUN OF PAPER, RUN OF PRESS, RUN OF PUBLICATION

**ro-ro** (*also* **RO/RO**) /'rəʊ rəʊ; *AmE* 'roʊ roʊ/ = ROLL-ON ROLL-OFF

**ROS** /ˌɑːr əʊ 'es; *AmE* oʊ/ = RUN OF SITE

**roster** /'rɒstə(r); *AmE* 'rɑːs-/ *n.* [C] **1** a list of the names of people such as employees, customers, etc. **2** a list of people's names and the jobs that they have to do at a particular time: *the* **duty** *roster*

**ˌrostered day 'off** *n.* [C] (*pl.* **-days off**) (*abbr* **RDO**) (*HR*) esp. in Australia and New Zealand, an arrangement in which, every two or four weeks, employees receive an extra paid day when they do not have to work, if they work longer hours on the other days

**rotate** /rəʊ'teɪt; *AmE* 'roʊteɪt/ *v.* [T,I] if a job **rotates**, or if people **rotate** a job, they regularly change the job or regularly change who does the job: *The EU presidency rotates among the members.* ▸ **ro'tating** *adj.*: *a rotating presidency*

**rotation** /rəʊ'teɪʃn; *AmE* roʊ-/ *n.* [C,U] **1** the act of regularly changing the person who does a particular job: *The meeting is chaired by all the members of the team* **in rotation**. **2** (*Stock Ex.*) = SECTOR ROTATION ▸ **ro'tational** /-ʃənl/ *adj.*

**rough** /rʌf/ *adj.*, *n.*, *v.*

• ***adj.*** (**-er**, **-est**) **1** not exact; not including all details: *a rough estimate of the cost* **2** not finished or corrected: *a rough draft of a report* ▸ **'roughly** *adv.*: *Sales are up by roughly 10%.*

• ***n.*** [C, usu. pl.] (*Tech.*) the first version of a drawing or design that has been done quickly and without much detail: *I've only seen the roughs.*

• ***v.*** **PHR V** **ˌrough sth 'out** to draw or write sth without including all the details: *I've roughed out a few ideas.*

**round** /raʊnd/ *adj.*, *n.*, *v.*

• ***adj.*** a **round** figure or amount is given as a whole number, usu. one ending in 0 or 5: ***In round figures*** (= not the exact amount), *it will cost $1.5 m.*

• ***n.*** [C] a group of events that are part of a longer series: *the latest round of trade talks*

• ***v.*** **PHR V** **ˌround sth 'up/'down (to sth)** to increase or decrease a number to the next highest or lowest whole number

**rounding** /'raʊndɪŋ/ *n.* [U] increasing or decreasing a number to the next highest or lowest whole number

**ˌround 'lot** *n.* [C] (*Stock Ex.*) the standard unit of trading on the stock market that often equals 100 shares

**ˌround 'table** *n.* [C, usu. sing.] a group of people that meet to discuss sth at a conference, etc.; the meeting or discussion that takes place: *a round-table discussion*

**route** /ruːt; *AmE also* raʊt/ *n.*, *v.*

• ***n.*** [C] **1** a fixed way along which a bus, train, plane, etc. regularly travels or goods are regularly sent: *a plane/shipping* ~ **2** (*IT*) the path that a PACKET takes when it is directed from one computer system to another

• ***v.*** [T] (**routing** *or* **routeing**, **routed**, **routed**) **1** (*IT*) to direct information that is received from one computer system to another: *a system that routes messages to the appropriate workers* **2** to send sb/sth by a particular route: *The goods were routed via Lyons.* ▸ **'routing** (*BrE also* **routeing**) *n.* [U]

**Route 128** /ˌruːt ˌwʌn twenti 'eɪt/ *n.* [U] in the US, an area in Massachusetts where there are many companies connected with the computer and electronics industries

**routeing** = ROUTING at ROUTE *v.*

**router** /'ruːtə(r); *AmE also* 'raʊt-/ *n.* [C] (*IT*) a device that directs data from one computer system to another in the shortest possible time: *a wireless router*

**routine** /ruː'tiːn/ *n.*, *adj.*

• ***n.*** **1** [C,U] the things you usu. do every day or at regular intervals and the way you normally do them: *We clean and repair the machines* ***as a matter of routine***. **2** (*IT*) [C] a list of instructions that enable a computer to perform a particular task: *The program contains two assembly code routines.*

• ***adj.*** **1** done as a normal part of a particular job, situation or process;

ordinary and not unusual: ~ *enquiries/tests* **2** ordinary and boring; the same every day: *The work soon becomes routine.* ▸ **rou'tinely** *adv.*

**'routing ˌnumber** = SORT CODE

**royalty** /'rɔɪəlti/ *n.* [C, usu. pl.] (*pl.* **-ties**) (*Comm.*) **1** money that is paid for the right to use the property of another person, such as the owner of a COPYRIGHT OR PATENT. A particular amount is paid each time their book, product, etc. is sold or their work performed: *She received $5 000 in royalties.* ◇ *a 12% royalty*
**2** money that is paid by an oil or mining company to the owner of the land that they are working on

**RPI** /ˌɑː piː 'aɪ; *AmE* ˌɑːr/ = RETAIL PRICE INDEX

**RRP** /ˌɑːr ɑː 'piː; *AmE* ˌɑːr ɑːr/ *abbr* (*BrE*) (*Comm.*) **recommended retail price** the price at which the maker of a product suggests that it should be sold in shops/stores: *RRP €500* SYN MSRP, SRP

**RSI** /ˌɑːr es 'aɪ/ *abbr* **repetitive strain/stress injury** pain and swelling, esp. in the arms and hands, caused by performing the same movement many times in a job SYN OOS

**RSVP** /ˌɑːr es viː 'piː/ *abbr* written at the end of an invitation to ask sb to reply

**RTB** /ˌɑː tiː 'biː; *AmE* ˌɑːr/ = RETURN-TO-BASE

**ˌrubber 'cheque** *n.* [C] (*infml.*) a cheque that a bank does not accept because the person who wrote it does not have enough money in their account

**ˌrubber 'stamp** *n.* [C] **1** a small tool that you use for printing the date, etc. on a document **2** a person or group that automatically gives approval to the actions or decisions of others: *acting as a rubber stamp for the management* **3** automatic approval that is given to sth: *They provided a rubber stamp for the scheme.*
▸ **ˌrubber-'stamp** *v.* [T]: *They refused to rubber-stamp the plans.*

**ruin** /'ruːɪn/ *n.*, *v.*
• ***n.*** [U] the fact of having no money, of having lost your job, etc: *financial ruin* IDM **in 'ruins** destroyed or severely damaged: *Her career was in ruins.*
• ***v.*** [T] **1** to damage sth so badly that it loses all its value, etc.; to spoil sth: *The tourist industry has ruined this area.* **2** to make sb/sth lose all their money, their position, etc: *The scandal ruined him.*

**rule** /ruːl/ *n.*, *v.*
• ***n.*** [C] **1** an official statement of what may, must or must not be done in a particular situation: *the* ***rules and regulations*** *concerning safety equipment* ◇ *The deal was unusual, but didn't break any rules.*
● *to* ***establish/make/set*** *~s* • *to* ***follow/obey/observe*** *the ~s* • *to* ***breach/violate*** *a ~*
**2** a measuring instrument with a straight edge **3** a thin straight line that has been drawn or printed **4** a statement of what you are advised to do in a particular situation: *The first rule is to make eye contact with your customer.* IDM **bend/stretch the 'rules** to change the rules to suit a particular person or situation **the rules of the 'game** the standards of behaviour that most people accept or that actually operate in a particular area of life or business → idioms at PLAY *V.*, WORK *V.*
• ***v.*** **1** [T,I] to give an official decision about sth: *The deal may be ruled illegal.* ◇ *to ~ against/in favour of/on sth* **2** [T] to draw a straight line using sth that has a firm straight edge
PHRV **ˌrule sb/sth 'out 1** to state or decide that sth is not possible or that sb/sth is not suitable: *He would not rule out the possibility of a merger.* **2** to prevent sb from doing sth; to prevent sth from happening: *His age ruled him out* **as** *a candidate.*

**'rule book** *n.* [C] (*often* **the rule book** [sing.]) a set of rules that must be followed in a particular job or organization

**ruling** /'ruːlɪŋ/ *n.* [C] an official decision made by sb in a position of authority, esp. a judge: *The court will make its ruling on the case next week.*

★ **run** /rʌn/ *v.*, *n.*
• ***v.*** (**running**, **ran** /ræn/**run**) **1** [T] to be in charge of a business, etc: *to ~ a business/hotel/factory/store* ◇ *a badly/well-~ company* ◇ *state-run industries* **2** [T] to make a service, a course of study, etc. available to people: *to run a training course* SYN ORGANIZE **3** [T,I] (about a machine, a vehicle, a computer, software, etc.) to operate or work; to make sth do this: *to run a program* ◇ *We keep the machines running.* **4** [I] (*with a prep. or an adj.*) to be at or near a particular level: *Inflation was running* ***at*** *26%.* **5** [I] to operate or be valid for a particular period of time: *The contract runs for 5 years.* **6** [T,I] to show or publish advertisements, stories, television programmes, etc.; to be shown or published: *to run a series of*

*ads on TV* **7** [T] **~ a deficit/surplus** to have or keep a debt/an extra amount of money **8** [T] **~ a test/check (on sth)** to do a test/check on sth **9** [T] to own and use a vehicle or machine **10** [I] (*with an adv. or a prep.*) (*usu. in the continuous tenses*) to happen in the way mentioned or at the time mentioned: *The business is running smoothly.* IDM **run a/the 'risk of (doing) sth** to be or put yourself in a situation in which sth bad could happen to you **run 'late** (*esp. in the continuous tenses*) to do things after the time you planned: *I'm running late for the meeting.* **run out of 'time** to have no more time available **run 'short**; **run 'short (of sth)** if sth **runs short** or you **run short of sth** there is very little left: *Time is running short.* **run a tight 'ship** to organize sth in a very efficient way, controlling other people very closely → idioms at CONTROL *n.*, FOOT *n.*, GROUND *n.*, UP *adj.*
PHR V **,run back 'over sth** to discuss or consider sth again SYN REVIEW **,run sth 'by/'past sb** (*infml.*) to show sb sth or tell sb about an idea in order to see their reaction to it: *Run that past me again.* **,run (sth) 'down 1** to lose power or stop working; to make sth do this: *The battery has run down.* **2** to gradually stop working or become smaller in size or number; to make sth do this: *running down the sales force* **'run into sth 1** to experience difficulties, etc: *Don't run into debt.* **2** to reach a particular level or amount: *Her income runs into six figures.* **,run sth 'off** to copy sth on a machine: *Could you run off twenty copies?* **,run 'out 1** if a supply of sth **runs out**, it is used up or finished: *The money has run out.* **2** if an agreement or a document **runs out**, it becomes no longer valid SYN EXPIRE **,run 'out (of sth)** to use up or finish a supply of sth: *We ran out of cash.* **,run sth 'past sb** = RUN STH BY/PAST SB **,run 'through sth 1** to discuss, repeat or read sth quickly: *Could we run through your report again?* **2** to use up or spend money carelessly **'run to sth** to be of a particular size or amount: *Building costs may run to $1 m.* **,run (sth) 'up** to reach or allow sth to reach a large total: *Some banks have run up huge losses.* **'run with sth** to accept or start to use a particular idea or method: *OK, let's run with that.*
• *n.* **1** [C] a period when good or bad things happen; a series of successes or failures: *We've had a run of poor results.* **2** (*Manufact.*) [C] the amount of a product that a company decides to make at one time: *Our first production run was only 400 units.* **3** (*Econ.*) [C, usu. sing.] **~ on the dollar, yen, etc.** a situation when many people suddenly sell a currency and its value falls **4** (*Comm.*) [C, usu. sing.] **~ on sth** a situation when many people suddenly want to buy sth, often because they are afraid there may not be enough **5** (*Econ.*) [C, usu. sing.] **~ on a bank, etc.** a time when too many people want to take their money out of the banks at the same time, so the banks cannot pay them all: *The crisis started a run on the banks.* **6** (*Finan.*) [C, usu. sing.] a situation when many people want to buy shares, bonds, property, etc. and prices go up: *The market had a tremendous run.* → idioms at LONG RUN, SHORT RUN

**runaway** /ˈrʌnəweɪ/ *adj.* **1** increasing at a very fast rate and not able to be controlled: *fighting runaway inflation* ◊ *~ costs/prices* **2** very successful: *a ~ best-seller/hit*

**rundown** /ˈrʌndaʊn/ *n.* [C, usu. sing.] **1** an explanation or a description of sth: *Can you give me a brief rundown* **on** *each of the applicants?* **2** (*BrE*) a reduction in the amount, size or activity of sth, esp. a business: *a rundown of transport services*

**,run-'down** *adj.* **1** (about a buildings, place, machine, etc.) in very bad condition; that has not been taken care of **2** (about a business, etc.) not as busy or as active as it used to be: *run-down transport services*

**rung** /rʌŋ/ *n.* [C] a level or position in an organization, a system, etc: *moving up the rungs of the corporate ladder*

**running** /ˈrʌnɪŋ/ *n.* [U] the activity of managing or operating sth: *the* **day-to-day** *running of a business* IDM **in/out of the 'running (for sth)** (*infml.*) having some/no chance of succeeding or of achieving sth: *We are in the running for the contract.*

**'running cost** *n.* [C, usu. pl.] the amount of money it costs to operate a machine, vehicle, business, etc.

**,running re'pairs** *n.* [pl.] small things that you do to a vehicle, a machine, etc. to keep it working

**,running 'total** *n.* [C, usu. sing.] the total number or amount of things, money, etc. that changes as you add each new item: *We* **keep** *a running total of how much we spend.*

**,run of 'book** *n.* [U] (*abbr* **ROB**) (*Market.*) when an advertisement is placed anywhere in a newspaper, magazine, etc. and the advertiser has not paid for a particular place

**ˌrun of ˈnetwork** *n.* [U] (*abbr* **RON**) (*Market.*) when an advertisement is placed on pages on some or all websites in an advertising network and the advertiser has not paid for a particular place

**ˌrun of ˈpaper** (*also* **ˌrun of ˈpress**, **ˌrun of publiˈcation**) *n.* [U] (*abbr* **ROP**) (*Market.*) when an advertisement is placed anywhere in a newspaper, magazine, etc. and the advertiser has not paid for a particular place

**ˌrun of ˈsite** *n.* [U] (*abbr* **ROS**) (*Market.*) when an advertisement is placed anywhere on a website and the advertiser has not paid for a particular place

**ˌrun-of-the-ˈmill** *adj.* ordinary or standard, with no special features

**ˈrun-time** *n.* [U,C] (*IT*) **1** the amount of time that a program takes to perform a task **2** the time when a program performs a task

**ˈrun-up** *n.* [C, usu. sing.] **1** a period of time leading up to an important event; the preparation for this: *an increase in spending in the run-up to New Year* **2** (*also* **runup**) an increase in prices that is often sudden: *a sharp run-up in share prices*

**ˈrush hour** *n.* [C, usu. sing., U] the time, usu. twice a day, when the roads are full of traffic and trains are crowded because people are travelling to or from work

**ˌRussell ˈ2000™** /ˈrʌsl/ *n.* [sing.] (*Stock Ex.*) a list of the average of the share prices of 2 000 smaller companies in the US, published by the Russell Company

**ˈrust belt** (*also* **Rust Belt**) *n.* [C, usu. sing.] (*esp. AmE*) an area where there are many old factories which are closed or which no longer make much money

**RW** /ˌɑː ˈdʌbljuː; *AmE* ˌɑːr/ = READ-WRITE

# Ss

**S** /es/ *abbr* (esp. for sizes of clothes) small

**SA** /ˌes ˈeɪ/ *abbr* (*written*) used in the name of some companies in French- and Spanish-speaking countries: *Renault SA*

**sabbatical** /səˈbætɪkl/ *n.* [C,U] a period of time when an employee is allowed to stop their normal work in order to study or travel: *to take a six-month sabbatical* ◇ *sabbatical leave*

**sabotage** /ˈsæbətɑːʒ/ *v.* [T] **1** to damage or destroy sth deliberately to prevent sb from using it, or to protest about sth **2** to prevent sth from being successful or being achieved: *The rise in interest rates sabotaged any chance of the firm's recovery.*
▸ **ˈsabotage** *n.* [U]: *an act of industrial sabotage*

**sachet** /ˈsæʃeɪ; *AmE* sæˈʃeɪ/ (*BrE*) (*AmE* **ˈpacket**) *n.* [C] a closed plastic or paper packet that contains a very small amount of liquid or a powder

**sack** /sæk/ *n.*, *v.*
• *n.* **1** [C] a large bag with no handles, made of strong rough material or strong paper or plastic, used for storing and carrying things in: *The rice is sold in 20kg sacks.* **2** (*AmE*) [C] a strong paper bag for carrying shopping: *a grocery sack* **3** [C] the contents of a **sack**: *a sack of flour* **4 the sack** [sing.] (*BrE*) (*infml.*) being told by your employer that you can no longer work for a company, etc., usu. because of sth that you have done wrong: *She* **got** *the sack for being late every day.*
• *v.* [T] (*BrE*) (*infml.*) to dismiss sb from a job: *The CEO may be sacked.*

**sae** (*also* **SAE**) /ˌes eɪ ˈiː/ *abbr* (*BrE*) **stamped addressed/self-addressed envelope** (*used as a countable n.*) an envelope on which you have written your name and address and put a stamp so that sb else can use it to send sth to you

**safe** /seɪf/ *n.* [C] a strong metal box or cupboard with a complicated lock, used for storing money or valuable things in

**ˈsafe deˌposit** (*also* **ˈsafety deˌposit**) *n.* [U,C] the action of putting important documents or valuable items in a strong room or metal box, for example in a bank, to keep them safe; a place that offers this service: *items on safe deposit at the bank* ◇ *a safe-deposit box*

**ˌsafe ˈhaven** (*also* **ˌsafe ˈharbour**) (*AmE* - **harbor**) *n.* [C] a place where sb/sth can go to be safe from danger or risk: *a safe-haven stock*

**safety** /ˈseɪfti/ *n.* [U] **1** the state of not being dangerous: *The plant has been closed for safety checks.* ◇ *The airline has an excellent safety* **record**. ◇ *The* **safety culture** *of a plant is critical.*

**⊙** *to check/improve* ~ ◆ *a* ~ *assessment/inspection* ◆ ~ *requirements/rules/standards* ◆ ~ *procedures*

**2** the state of being safe and protected from danger or harm: *The safety of employees is our main concern.*
⊙ *passenger/personal/public* ~ ♦ *to ensure/guarantee* ~
**3** used to describe sth designed to prevent injury or damage: ~ *devices/equipment/features/glasses*

**'safety de,posit** = SAFE DEPOSIT

**'safety net** *n.* [C] an arrangement that helps to prevent disaster if sth goes wrong: *a financial safety net*

**'safety stock** *n.* [U,C] (*Product.*) the smallest extra supply of goods, raw materials, etc. that a company tries to have at all times in case more than expected is ordered or new stock arrives late

**'safety valve** *n.* [C] a device that lets out steam or pressure in a machine when it becomes too great

**S & L** /,es ənd 'el/ *abbr* (*AmE*) savings and loan association

**salable** = SALEABLE

**sa'lami ,slicing** *n.* [U] the act of removing sth gradually by small amounts at a time: *Local rail services have been withdrawn by a process of salami slicing.*

**salaried** /'sælərid/ *adj.* **1** (about a person) receiving a salary: *a salaried employee* **2** (about a job) for which a salary is paid

★ **salary** /'sæləri/ *n.* [C] (*pl.* **-ries**) money that employees receive for doing their job, esp. professional employees or people working in an office, that is usu. paid every month: *an annual salary of $40 000* ◇ *She's on a salary of €33 000.*
⊙ *to earn/receive a* ~ ♦ *to cut/increase/pay a* ~ ♦ *a monthly/starting* ~ *(of...)* ♦ *an average/a big/competitive/high/low/modest* ~

**salaryman** /'sælərimæn/ *n.* [C] (*pl.* **-men** /-men/) a word used esp. in Japan to refer to a man who has an ordinary job in an office: *the year-end exchange of gifts between salarymen and their superiors*
NOTE **Salarywoman** is also used, but less often.

**'salary ,package** = PAY PACKAGE

**'salary scale** *n.* [C] (*HR*) **1** (*BrE also* **'salary prog,ression**) the range of levels of pay that a person can receive in a particular job within an organization: *The salary scale of the next grade is €28 500 to €37 000.*
**2** the range of levels of pay that people receive in different jobs within an organization: *They are only hiring people at the lower end of the salary scale.*

★ **sale** /seɪl/ *n.* **1** [U,C] an act or the process of selling sth: *The sale of assets raised €100 000.* ◇ *I haven't made a sale all week.* ◇ *to close/complete/lose a* ~ **2** [C] an occasion when a shop/store sells its goods at a lower price than usual: *the January sales* ◇ ~ *items/goods* ◇ *to have/hold a* ~ **3** [C] an occasion when goods are sold, esp. an AUCTION: *an art sale*
IDM **for 'sale** available to be bought: *The group has* **put** *its book business* **up** *for sale.* **on ,sale 1** available to be bought, esp. in a shop/store: *The latest model* **goes on sale** *next week.* **2** being offered at a reduced price

**saleable** (*AmE also* **salable**) /'seɪləbl/ *adj.* **1** that can be sold; good enough to be sold: *a saleable product* **2** that sb will want to buy: *the company's most saleable asset*
▸ **,salea'bility** (*AmE also* **salability**) /-'bɪləti/ *n.* [U]

**,sale and 'leaseback** *n.* [U] (*Finan.*) the process of selling a building, machinery, etc. to sb and then continuing to use it by renting it from the buyer

**,sale and re'purchase a,greement** = REPURCHASE AGREEMENT

**,sale as 'seen** *phr.* (*Comm.*) if used goods are advertised as **sale as seen**, the buyer must examine them carefully as there is no promise that they are suitable or in good condition

**,sale by des'cription** *phr.* (*Comm.*) a situation in which a buyer cannot see goods for sale, but must rely on a description of them

**,sale by 'sample** *phr.* (*Comm.*) a situation in which a buyer sees only a small amount or piece of sth before buying it and must assume that the quality of the rest will be the same

**,sale or re'turn** *phr.* (*BrE*) (*abbr* **S/R**) (*Comm.*) if goods are supplied (on) **sale or return**, there is an agreement that any item that is not sold can be sent back without having to be paid for: *We supply goods* **on a** *sale-or-return* **basis**.

**'sale price** *n.* [C] **1** the price at which sth is offered for sale or is sold **2** a special low price that an item is sold at for a period of time when a shop/store reduces its prices

**saleroom** /'seɪlruːm; -rʊm/ (*BrE*) (*AmE* **'salesroom**) *n.* [C] (*Comm.*) a room where goods are sold at an AUCTION

★ **sales** /seɪlz/ *n.* **1** [pl.] the amount of goods or services sold: *The com-*

*pany reported sales of $190 m.* ◇ *Retail sales fell by 2%.*
◘ *annual/full-year/like-for-like* ~ • *global/national* ~ • *to boost/generate* ~ • ~ *growth/performance* • ~ *charts/figures/quotas/targets*
**2** [U] the business of selling things; the department of a company that is responsible for selling things: *one of the sales staff* ◇ *He works* **in** *sales.*
◘ *a* ~ *department/director/manager/team* • ~ *methods/presentations/techniques*

**'sales ac,count** *n.* [C]
**1** (*Account.*) a financial record in which total sales for cash or credit during a particular period are recorded **2** a company that is a customer of another company and buys goods or services from them

**'sales a,greement** = CONTRACT OF PURCHASE

**'sales a,nalysis** *n.* [C,U] (*Market.*) a detailed examination of a company's sales records in order to measure and improve its performance

**,sales and 'marketing** *n.* [U; U with sing./pl. v.] the business of advertising and selling goods or services; the department of a company that is responsible for this

**'sales ,area** *n.* [C] **1** (*Market.*) (*also* **'sales ,territory**) an area, a part of a market or a group of products that a SALES REPRESENTATIVE or a team is responsible for: *My sales area covers eight states and 60 customers.*
**2** (*Comm.*) the part of a store where customers can buy things: *a retail sales area of more than 2 000 sq feet*

**'sales as,sistant** (*BrE*) (*AmE* **'sales clerk, clerk**) *n.* [C] a person whose job is to serve customers in a shop/store SYN SHOP ASSISTANT

**'sales ,budget** *n.* [C] (*Account.*) a plan for a particular period of time of how much money a company is likely to receive from the sale of goods and services

**'sales cam,paign** *n.* [C] (*Market.*) a series of planned activities that are intended to sell a particular product or increase sales of a product

**'sales ,channel** = CHANNEL *n.* (3)

**'sales charge** *n.* [C] (*Finan.*) a fee you pay when you buy sth such as shares, insurance, etc. from a BROKER

**'sales check** = SALES SLIP

**'sales clerk** (*also* **salesclerk**) = SALES ASSISTANT

**'sales ,concept** = SELLING CONCEPT

**'sales ,conference** *n.* [C] (*Market.*) an event at which members of a company's sales team from different offices meet to discuss and plan ways of selling the company's goods

**'sales drive** *n.* [C] (*Market.*) an attempt to increase a company's sales

**'sales force** *n.* [C with sing./pl. v.] all the people who are involved in selling a company's goods or services: *a 6 000 strong sales force*

**'sales ,history** *n.* [C] (*Market.*) a record of how many of a particular product have been sold since it was first produced

**'sales in,centive** *n.* [C] (*Market.*) a reward offered to SALESPEOPLE to encourage them to sell more

**'sales ,invoice** *n.* [C] (*Account.*) a list of goods that have been sold, that is given to the customer to show what they must pay and when

**'sales ,ledger** *n.* [C] (*BrE*) (*Account.*) in a company's financial records, a group of accounts that is used to record the amounts owed by particular customers

★ **salesman** /'seɪlzmən/, **saleswoman** /'seɪlzwʊmən/ *n.* [C] (*pl.* **-men** /-mən/-**women** /-wɪmɪn/) a man or woman whose job is to sell goods, for example, in a shop/store: *a car salesman*

**salesmanship** /'seɪlzmənʃɪp/ *n.* [U] the methods and skills involved in selling things: *aggressive/slick/successful* ~

**'sales mix** *n.* [sing.] (*Market.*) the way that a company's total sales are divided among all their products: *Sports cars are likely to make up about 35% of our sales mix.*

**'sales ,office** *n.* [C] a part of a company that sells a company's products in a particular area: *Contact your local sales office for a list of prices.*

**'sales orien,tation** *n.* [U] (*Market.*) used to describe a way of doing business where a company competes mainly by developing its methods for selling products, rather than by producing better ones

★ **salesperson** /'seɪlzpɜːsn; *AmE* -pɜːrsn/ *n.* [C] (*pl.* **-people** /-piːpl/) (*Market.*) a person whose job is to sell a company's goods or services: *a strong team of salespeople*

**'sales pitch** *n.* [C] (*Market.*) talk or arguments used by a person trying to sell things

**'sales pro,motion** *n.* [U,C] (*Market.*) activities done in order to increase the sales of a product or service: *to run a sales promotion*

★ **'sales repre,sentative** (*also* **'sales rep, rep**, *infml.*) (*also*

ˌrepreˈsentative, ˈtrade repreˌsentative) *n.* [C] (*Market.*) a person who sells a company's goods or services by visiting possible customers, usu. receiving a COMMISSION on what they sell: *You can request a sample or a rep visit.*

**ˈsales reˌsistance** *n.* [U] (*Market.*) when someone is unwilling to buy a product, esp. as a result of aggressive selling techniques

**ˈsales reˌturns** *n.* [pl.] (*Account.*) goods that a customer has bought and then returned: *We monitor our sales returns.* ◇ *the ~ account/book*

**ˈsales ˌrevenue** *n.* [U] (*also* **sales revenues** [pl.]) (*esp. in AmE*) (*Account.*) the total income that a company receives from sales of goods and services in a particular period of time SYN TURNOVER (1)

**salesroom** /ˈseɪlzruːm; -rʊm/ = SALEROOM

**ˈsales slip** (*also* **ˈsales check**) = RECEIPT (1)

**ˈsales subˌsidiary** *n.* [C] a company that is owned by a larger company whose products it sells

**ˈsales tax** *n.* [U,C] tax that must be paid on many goods and services when you buy them → VAT

**ˈsales ˌterritory** = SALES AREA (1)

**ˈsales ˌturnover** *n.* [C, usu. sing., U] (*Account.*) the total value of goods or services sold by a company during a particular period of time

**ˈsales ˌvolume** *n.* [C, usu. sing., U] (*Account.*) the total number of units of a product sold by a company during a particular period of time

**salvage** /ˈsælvɪdʒ/ *v., n.*

• ***v.*** [T] to save goods or a ship from being completely destroyed in an accident or a disaster

• ***n.*** [U] **1** the act of saving goods or a ship from being completely destroyed in an accident or a disaster: *a ~ company/operation* **2** the things that are saved from a disaster or an accident: *The stock was only slightly damaged and was sold as salvage.*

**ˈsalvage ˌvalue** (*also* **ˈscrap ˌvalue**) *n.* [C,U] **1** (*Account.*) the value of an asset at the end of its useful life **2** (*Insur.*) the value of sth that has been damaged in an accident, etc., such as goods or a ship

**ˈsalvage yard** *n.* [C] (*AmE*) a place where old machines, cars, etc. are broken up so that the metal can be sold or used again

**ˌsame-ˈday** *adj.* used to refer to a service that is provided on the same day you order it: *same-day delivery*

**ˌsame-store ˈsales** (*also* **ˌcomparable-store ˈsales**) *n.* [pl.] (*Account.*) used to refer to the change in the value of sales in a company or group's stores compared to the same stores in the previous year, used as a way of measuring the performance of the company as a whole: *July same-store sales were up 6%.*

★ **sample** /ˈsɑːmpl; *AmE* ˈsæmpl/ *n.* [C] **1** a small amount or example of sth that can be looked at or tried to see what it is like: *free samples of shampoo* ◇ *samples of your work* ◇ *to offer/provide a ~* **2** (*Tech.*) a number of people or things taken from a larger group and used in tests to provide information about the group: *We did a survey of a random sample of 1 000 workers.* ◇ *a large/representative/small ~* **3** (*Tech.*) a small amount of a product that is looked at or tested in order to see what the rest is like: *A sample of parts are inspected for quality.* ◇ *to analyse/test a ~*
▸ **ˈsample** *v.* [T]: *You can sample the service for two weeks.* ◇ *12% of the people sampled use a dictionary.*

**sampler** /ˈsɑːmplə(r); *AmE* ˈsæm-/ *n.* [C] a collection that contains typical examples of sth, so that people can try or experience them: *a sampler of our designs*

**sampling** /ˈsɑːmplɪŋ; *AmE* ˈsæm-/ *n.* **1** (*Tech.*) [U] the process of taking a sample: *statistical sampling* **2** [C] a small part, number or amount of sth that has been taken or chosen as a sample: *a sampling of the price ranges*

**ˈsampling ˌfraction** *n.* [C] (*Market.*) the relationship between the part of a group that is chosen to take part in a survey and the size of the whole group: *We used a sampling fraction of 1 in 100.*

**ˈsampling frame** *n.* [C] (*Market.*) the list of people or things that form the group from which a sample is chosen

**sanction** /ˈsæŋkʃn/ *n.* [C, usu. pl.] an official order that limits trade, contact, etc. with a particular country, in order to make it do sth, such as obeying international law
○ *to* ***apply/impose/lift*** *~s* ♦ ***economic/financial/trade*** *~s*

**s and h** (*also* **s & h**) /ˌes ənd ˈeɪtʃ/ = SHIPPING AND HANDLING

**ˈsandwich board** *n.* [C] (*Market.*) **1** a pair of boards with advertisements on them that sb wears at the front and back of their body as they walk around in public

2 a wooden frame in two parts, joined at the top, that stands on the ground and has advertisements on each side

**'sandwich course** *n.* [C] (*BrE*) a course of study which includes periods of study and periods of working in business or industry

**ˌS&P '500™** /ˌes ən 'pi:/ = STANDARD & POOR'S 500 INDEX

**SARL** /ˌes eɪ ɑ:r 'el/ *abbr* (*written*) used in the name of some companies in French-speaking countries: *KeeBoo SARL*

**SASE** /ˌes eɪ es 'i:/ *abbr* (*AmE*) **self-addressed stamped envelope** (*used like a countable n.*) an envelope on which you have put your name and address and a stamp so that sb else can use it to send you sth

**satellite** /'sætəlaɪt/ *n.* [C] **1** an electronic device that is sent into space, and is used for communicating by telephone, radio, television, etc. and for providing information: *making a call to a satellite phone* **2** an organization, a town or a country that is controlled by and depends on another larger or more powerful one: *our satellite office in Hong Kong*

**satisfaction** /ˌsætɪs'fækʃn/ *n.* [U] **1** the good feeling that you have when you are happy with sth that you have done, that you have bought, that has happened, etc: *She had the satisfaction of seeing her book become a best-seller.* **2** an acceptable way of dealing with a complaint, a debt, an injury, etc: *a payment of $5 000 in full satisfaction of the debt*

**satisfactory** /ˌsætɪs'fæktəri/ *adj.* good enough for a particular purpose; acceptable: *A bonus is paid on satisfactory completion of the contract.*

**saturate** /'sætʃəreɪt/ *v.* [T] (*Market.*) (*often pass.*) to supply so much of a product in a particular market that few new customers can be found: *The cellphone market is becoming saturated.* ▸ **ˌsatu'ration** /-'reɪʃn/ *n.* [U]: *The market for this product is reaching* ***saturation point****.*

★ **save** /seɪv/ *v.* **1** [T] to avoid wasting sth or using more than necessary: *to save energy costs* ◇ *Book early and save €100!* **2** [T,I] **~ (sth) (up) (for sth)** to keep money instead of spending it: *I've been saving $200 a month for years.* **3** [T,I] to make a computer keep work, for example by putting it on a disk: *Save the file* **to** *your hard drive.* IDM **save (sb's) 'face** to avoid or help sb avoid embarrassment: *She was fired, but she saved face by saying she'd resigned.* → LOSE FACE at LOSE

**saver** /'seɪvə(r)/ *n.* [C] **1** a person who saves money and puts it in a bank, etc. for future use **2** (*often with another n.*) something that helps you spend less money or use less of the thing mentioned: *The program is a real time-saver.*

★ **saving** /'seɪvɪŋ/ *n.* **1** [C] an amount of sth such as time or money that you do not need to use or spend: *With the new heating we can make big savings on fuel bills.* **2 savings** [pl.] money that you have saved, esp. in a bank, etc. **3** (*Econ.*) [U] the situation when income is greater than money spent; the process of spending less than income: *a drop in household saving* **4 -saving** (*in adjs*) that reduces the amount used of the thing mentioned; preventing waste of the thing mentioned: *time-saving devices*

**'savings acˌcount** *n.* [C] a bank account that receives interest on the money put into it

**ˌsavings and 'credit coˌoperative** = CREDIT COOPERATIVE

**ˌsavings and 'loan associˌation** (*abbr* **S & L**) (*also* **ˌbuilding and 'loan associˌation**) (*both AmE*) *n.* [C] an organization like a bank that issues shares to people who deposit money and lends the money to people who want to buy a home
SYN THRIFT INSTITUTION

**'savings bank** *n.* [C] a bank that pays interest on money you save but does not offer other services

**savvy** /'sævi/ *n., adj.* (*infml.*)
• *n.* [U] practical knowledge or understanding of sth: *business savvy*
• *adj.* (*infml.*) (*esp. AmE*) having practical knowledge or understanding of sth: *Are you IT savvy?*

**SBU** /ˌes bi: 'ju:/ = STRATEGIC BUSINESS UNIT

**scab** /skæb/ *n.* [C] (*infml.*) an offensive way of referring to a worker who refuses to join a strike or who works instead of sb on strike
SYN BLACKLEG

**scalable** /'skeɪləbl/ *adj.* (*IT*) **1** used to describe a computer, a network, software, etc. that can be adapted to meet greater needs in the future **2** designed to work on a large or small scale, as needed: *scalable graphics*
▸ **ˌscala'bility** /-'bɪləti/ *n.* [U]

**scale** /'skeɪl/ *n., v.*
• *n.* **1** [sing; U] the size or extent of sth, esp. when compared with sth

else: *The sales figures reveal the full scale of the crisis.* **2** [C] a range of levels or numbers used for measuring sth: *a five-point pay scale ◇ a ~ of fees/charges* **3** [C, usu. sing.] the set of all the different levels of sth, from the lowest to the highest **4** [C,U] the relation between the actual size of sth and its size on a map, diagram or model that represents it: *a scale model ◇ a scale of 1:10 000* **5** [C, usu. pl.] an instrument for weighing people or things
• *v.* [T] (*Tech.*) to change the size of sth: *Text can be scaled from 4 points to 108 points without losing quality.*
**PHR V** ˌ**scale sth 'down** (*AmE also* ˌ**scale sth 'back**) to reduce sth in number, size or extent: *scaling down our training programmes ◇ a scaled-down version* ˌ**scale sth 'up** to increase sth in number, size or extent

ˌ**scaled 'question** *n.* [C] (*Market.*) a type of question used to get data on people's opinions, behaviour, etc., where a range of possible answers are shown and people choose the one that is closest to their own opinion, behaviour, etc. Each answer is represented by a number which shows its position in the range, so that people's answers can easily be compared and measured.

ˌ**scale e'conomy** = ECONOMY OF SCALE

**scalp** /skælp/ *n., v.*
• *n.* [C] a symbol of the fact that sb has been defeated or punished: *The crisis has claimed the scalp of the firm's CEO* (= he has lost his job).
• *v.* [T] to make a quick profit by buying tickets for concerts, sports events, etc. and selling them for a much higher price

**scalper** /'skælpə(r)/ = TOUT *n.*

**scam** /skæm/ *n.* [C] (*infml.*) a clever and dishonest plan for making money: *an insurance scam ◇ to operate/pull/set up a ~*

**scan** /skæn/ *v., n.*
• *v.* [T] **1** (*Comm.*) to use a SCANNER to read the information on a BAR CODE, etc. **2** (*IT*) to change a document, picture, etc. into a form that can be stored or processed on a computer, using a SCANNER **3** to look quickly but not very carefully at a document, etc: *I scanned the list quickly for my name.* ▶ **'scannable** /-əbl/ *adj.* **PHR V** ˌ**scan sth 'into sth**; ˌ**scan sth 'in** (*IT*) to change a document, picture, etc. into a form that can be stored or processed on a computer, by using a SCANNER
• *n.* **1** (*IT*) [C] an image of sth produced on a computer screen by a special machine **2** [sing.] the act of looking quickly but not very carefully at a document, etc: *have a quick scan of the report*

**scanner** /'skænə(r)/ *n.* [C] **1** a device that uses a narrow line of strong light for reading the information on sth such as a credit card, BAR CODE, etc. **2** (*IT*) a machine for changing a document, picture, etc. into a form that can be stored or processed on a computer

**scarce** /skeəs; *AmE* skers/ *adj.* (**scarcer**, **scarcest**) if sth is **scarce**, there is not enough of it and it is only available in small quantities: *scarce resources* ▶ **'scarcity** /-səti/ *n.* [U,C] (*pl.* **-ties**)

**'scarcity ˌvalue** *n.* [U,C] (*Econ.*) a situation where the price of sth rises because there is not enough of it available

**'scatter ˌdiagram** (*also* **'scatter chart**, **'scatter graph**, **'scatter plot**) (*also* **scattergram** /'skætəgræm; *AmE* -tərg-/) *n.* [C] a type of graph that shows the relationship between two values, numbers or quantities by creating a pattern of dots

**SCC** /ˌes siː 'siː/ = SINGLE COLUMN CENTIMETRE

**SCEM** /ˌes siː iː 'em/ = SUPPLY CHAIN EVENT MANAGEMENT

**scenario** /sə'nɑːriəʊ; *AmE* sə'nærioʊ/ *n.* [C] (*pl.* **-rios**) a description of how things might happen in the future: *the* ***worst-case scenario*** (= the worst possible thing that could happen)

★**schedule** /'ʃedjuːl; *AmE* 'skedʒuːl/ *n., v.*
• *n.* **1** [C,U] a plan that lists all the work that you have to do and when you must do each thing: *I have a very busy schedule for the next few days. ◇ Work began* **on schedule** (= at the planned time).
**o** *a* ***heavy/hectic*** *~* • *a* ***strict/tight*** *~* • *a* ***production/work*** *~* • *to* ***draw up/plan*** *a ~* • *to* ***keep to/work to*** *a ~* • *to* ***be/run ahead of*** *~* • *to* ***be/fall/slip behind*** *~*
**2** [C] (*AmE*) a list showing what time particular events happen: *a bus/train ~* **SYN** TIMETABLE **3** [C] a formal written list of things, for example prices, rates or conditions: *a price schedule* **4** (*Insur.*) [C] a list that describes what is covered by a particular insurance policy
• *v.* [T] **1** (*esp.* **be scheduled**) to arrange for sth to happen at a particular time: *The meeting is scheduled for Friday afternoon.* **2** (*fml.*) to include

sth in an official list of things: *The substance has been scheduled as a poison.* ▶ **'scheduler** *n.* [C]: *programme schedulers* **'scheduling** *n.* [U]

**scheme** /skiːm/ *n.* [C] **1** (*BrE*) a plan or system for doing or organizing sth: *a training scheme* ◇ *a scheme for recycling plastic* ◇ *to design/devise/draw up/introduce/operate/propose a ~* **2** a plan for getting money or some other advantage for yourself, esp. one that involves deceiving other people: *a scheme to avoid taxes*

**ˌscheme of arˈrangement** *n.* [C] (*BrE*) (*Law*) a legal arrangement reached between a company that is unable to pay all its debts and its CREDITORS and shareholders, in which the company will pay what it can

**SCI** /ˌes siː ˈaɪ/ → SINGLE COLUMN CENTIMETRE

**SCM** /ˌes siː ˈem/ = SUPPLY CHAIN MANAGEMENT

**ˌscorched-ˈearth ˌpolicy** *n.* [C] (*Finan.*) a situation in which a company makes itself less attractive, for example by selling its assets, in order to prevent sb else taking control of it

**scrap** /skræp/ *n.*, *v.*

• ***n.*** [U] things that are not wanted or cannot be used for their original purpose: *~ metal/iron*

• ***v.*** [T] (**-pp-**) (*often pass.*) to cancel or get rid of sth that is no longer practical or useful: *Plans for a new store have been scrapped.*

**ˈscrap ˌvalue** = SALVAGE VALUE

**scratch** /skrætʃ/ *v.*, *n.*

• ***v.*** IDM **ˈyou scratch ˈmy back and ˈI'll scratch ˈyours** used to say that if sb helps you, you will help them, even if this is unfair to others

• ***n.*** IDM **from ˈscratch** without any previous preparation or knowledge: *The prototype was built from scratch in a month.* **up to ˈscratch** as good as sth/sb should be; satisfactory: *His work simply isn't up to scratch.*

**screen** /skriːn/ *n.*, *v.*

• ***n.*** [C] the flat surface at the front of a television, computer, mobile phone/cellphone, etc. on which you see pictures or information

• ***v.*** [T] **1** (*HR*) to find out information about people who work or who want to work for you, in order to make sure that they are suitable or can be trusted **2** to check sth to see if it is safe or suitable to be used, seen, etc: *An antivirus program screens attachments.* SYN VET ▶ **ˈscreening** *n.* [U]

PHR V **ˌscreen ˈout sb/sth** to reject sb/sth: *The program screens out spam.*

**ˈscreen-based** *adj.* used to describe an activity that is done using a computer: *screen-based advertising*

**ˈscreening ˌinterview** *n.* [C] (*AmE*) (*HR*) a first short interview for a job, used to identify who is suitable for the company and who is not

**ˈscreen ˌsaver** *n.* [C] an image that appears on the computer screen when the computer has not been used for a time, originally to stop the screen from being damaged; the program that does this

**scrip** /skrɪp/ *n.* (*Finan.*) **1** [C,U] one of a group of extra shares that a company gives to shareholders instead of a DIVIDEND; the set of shares given **2** [C] a certificate showing that sb owns shares or bonds

**ˈscrip ˌdividend** (*esp. BrE*) (*AmE usu.* **ˈstock ˌdividend**) *n.* [C] (*Finan.*) an amount of the profits that a company pays to shareholders in the form of new shares

**ˈscrip ˌissue** (*also* **ˈfree ˌissue**) *n.* [C] (*BrE*) (*Finan.*) a situation in which a company uses its RESERVES to create new shares, which are then given free to the shareholders in proportion to the number of shares that they already own SYN BONUS ISSUE, CAPITALIZATION ISSUE

**script** /skrɪpt/ *n.*, *v.*

• ***n.*** **1** [C] words that are prepared for sb to say: *a script for a TV ad* **2** (*IT*) [C,U] a list of instructions or a simple program for a computer; the language that is used to write these

• ***v.*** [T] (*often pass.*) **1** to prepare words for sb to say: *scripted interviews* **2** (*IT*) to write computer **script**

**scroll** /skrəʊl; *AmE* skroʊl/ *v.* [T,I] (*IT*) (*often used with an adv. or a prep.*) to move text up or down on the screen of a computer, a mobile phone/cellphone, etc. so that you can read different parts of it: *Scroll down to the bottom of the document.*

**ˈscroll bar** *n.* [C] (*IT*) a strip at the edge of a computer screen that you use to **scroll** through a file with, using a mouse

**ˈscroll key** *n.* [C] a key on a computer, a mobile phone/cellphone, etc. that allows you to **scroll** through information

**scrutinize**, **-ise** /ˈskruːtənaɪz/ *v.* [T] to look at or examine sb/sth carefully ▶ **scrutiny** /ˈskruːtəni/ *n.* [U]: *The policy has come under scrutiny.*

**SCSI** /ˈskʌzi; ˈseksi; ˌes siː es ˈaɪ/ *n.* [C,U] (*IT*) **Small Computer System Interface** a system used for connecting a computer to another device

**SD card** /ˌes 'di: kɑ:d; *AmE* kɑ:rd/ *n.* [C] (*IT*) **Secure Digital card** a very small card containing memory that can be used in electronic devices such as cameras, mobile phones/ cellphones, etc.

**seal** /si:l/ *v., n.*
• *v.* [T] **1** to close PACKAGING so that the contents cannot get out: *Heat is applied to seal the shrink-wrap.* **2** to close an envelope by sticking the edges of the opening together **3** to make sth definite and final, so that it cannot be changed or argued about: *to seal a deal* → idiom at SIGN *V.*
• *n.* **1** [C] a substance, strip of material, etc. used to fill a crack so that air, liquid, etc. cannot get in or out **2** [C] a piece of paper, metal, etc. placed across the opening of sth such as a letter, a box, etc., that has to be broken before the letter or box can be opened **3** [C] an official design or mark, stamped on a document to show that it is genuine and has the authority of a particular person or organization **4** [sing.] a thing that makes sth definite: *The CEO has given the project his* ***seal of approval.***
IDM **under 'seal** (*Law, fml.*) (about a document) that cannot be copied or made available to the public

**ˌsealed 'bid** *n.* [C] a **bid** that is kept in a sealed envelope and therefore remains secret until all other bids have been received when they are opened all together

**SEAQ** /'si:æk/ *n.* [U] (*Stock Ex.*) **Stock Exchange Automated Quotation System** a system used by the London Stock Exchange to show the latest prices of shares on computers around the world

**searchable** /'sɜ:tʃəbl; *AmE* 'sɜ:rtʃ-/ *adj.* (*IT*) that can be searched: *a searchable database*

**'search ˌengine** *n.* [C] (*IT*) a computer program that searches the Internet for information, esp. by looking for documents containing a particular word or group of words

**'search firm** *n.* [C] a company that provides the service of finding managers for other companies

**ˌsearch unem'ployment** = FRICTIONAL UNEMPLOYMENT

**season** /'si:zn/ *n.* [C,U] **1** a period of time each year when a particular activity takes place or particular conditions exist: *Plane tickets are most expensive* ***at the height of*** *the season.*
⊙ *the* ***holiday/tourist*** ~ • *the* ***autumn/spring/summer/winter*** ~ • *the* ***earnings/reporting*** ~



**2** a period of time during one year when a particular style of clothes, hair, etc. is popular and fashionable: *This season's look is cool and feminine.*
IDM **con'fessional ˌseason/ ˌperiod** (*esp. AmE*) (*Stock Ex.*) a period of time during the year when companies warn that their profits will be lower than expected **in 'season** (about fruit or vegetables) easily available and ready to eat because it is the right time of year for them **out of 'season 1** at the times of year when few people go on holiday/vacation **2** (about fruit or vegetables) not easily available because it is not the right time of year for them

**seasonal** /'si:zənl/ *adj.* happening or needed during a particular season; varying with the seasons: *Seasonal workers are used to pick fruit.* ◇ *the hotel's seasonal rates*
▸ **'seasonally** /-nəli/ *adv.*: *The unemployment figures are seasonally adjusted* (= do not include the changes that always happen in different seasons).

**ˌseasonal unem'ployment** *n.* [U] (*Econ.*) a rise in the number of people who are not working at particular times of the year as a result of the jobs that can only be done at other times

**'season ˌticket** *n.* [C] a ticket that you can use many times within a particular period, for example on a regular train or bus journey, that costs less than paying separately each time: *a monthly season ticket* ◇ *a season ticket holder*

**seat** /si:t/ *n.* [C] **1** an official position as a member of a committee, council, Parliament, etc: *seats* ***on*** *the board* **2** (*Stock Ex.*) (*esp. AmE*) if you have a **seat** on a stock exchange, you are a member of the exchange and are allowed to buy and sell shares **3** a place where you pay to sit on a plane, in a theatre, etc: *to book seats online*
→ idioms at BACK, DRIVE *V.*

**SEC** /ˌes i: 'si:/ = SECURITIES AND EXCHANGE COMMISSION

**Sec.** (*AmE also* **Secy.**) *abbr* a short way of writing **secretary**

**second**[1] /'sekənd/ *v., n.*
• *v.* [T] to state officially at a meeting that you support another person's idea, suggestion, etc. so that it can be discussed and/or voted on: *Any proposal must be seconded by two other members.* ▸ **'seconder** *n.* [C]
• *n.* (*Comm.*) [C, usu. pl.] an item that is sold at a lower price than usual be-

cause it is not perfect: *These shoes are slight seconds.*

**second**[2] /sɪˈkɒnd; *AmE* -ˈkɑːnd/ *v.* [T] (*esp. BrE*) (*HR*) **~ sb (to sth)** (*usu. pass.*) to send an employee to another department, office, etc. to do a different job for a short period of time ▶ **seˈcondment** *n.* [U,C]: *She is on secondment overseas.*

**secondary** /ˈsekəndri; *AmE* -deri/ *adj.* **1** less important than sth else: *secondary airports* **2** used to describe sth that happens as a result of sth else: *a secondary product of farming* **3** (*Finan.*) used to describe the buying and selling of existing shares, bonds, etc. rather than new ones: *secondary trading* → PRIMARY ▶ **secondarily** /-drəli; *AmE* -ˈderəli/ *adv.*

**ˌsecondary ˈaction** *n.* [U] (*HR*) action such as stopping work that is taken by workers in a factory, company, etc. not directly involved in a dispute in order to support workers who are involved

**ˌsecondary ˈaudience** *n.* [C] (*Market.*) **1** the people who are not the main people that your product, advertising, report or presentation is aimed at **2** (*also* **ˈpass-along ˌreaders** [pl.]) people who read a particular newspaper or magazine but who do not buy it

**ˌsecondary ˈboycott** *n.* [C] a situation when people refuse to buy the goods of, or do services for, a company that is not directly involved in a dispute in order to persuade them not to do business with a company that is involved

**ˌsecondary ˈdata** *n.* [U] (*Market.*) information that was originally collected for a particular purpose and is then also used for another purpose or project

**ˈsecondary ˌindustry** *n.* [U,C] (*Econ.*) industry that uses raw materials to make goods to be sold or to make machines, etc. that are used to make goods

**ˈsecondary ˌmarket** *n.* [C] (*Stock Ex.*) a market in which investors buy and sell existing shares, bonds, etc. rather than new ones

**ˌsecondary ˈmortgage ˌmarket** = MORTGAGE MARKET (2)

**ˌsecondary ˈoffering** *n.* [C] (*Stock Ex.*) a time when an important shareholder, or a group, sells their shares in a company to the public

**ˌsecondary ˈpicketing** *n.* [U] (*BrE*) the act of preventing workers who are not involved in a strike from working or supplying goods to the company where the strike is held

**ˌsecondary proˈduction** *n.* [U] (*Econ.*) the process of manufacturing goods for sale from raw materials and the activity of building houses, bridges, roads, etc.

**the ˈsecondary ˌsector** *n.* [sing.] (*Econ.*) the part of a country's economy that manufactures goods for sale from raw materials. Sometimes construction is also included.

**ˌsecond ˈclass** *n.* [U] **1** a way of travelling on a train or ship that costs less and is less comfortable than FIRST CLASS **NOTE** In the UK this is now called **standard class**. **2** in the UK, the class of mail that costs less and takes longer to arrive than FIRST CLASS **3** in the US, the class of mail used for newspapers and magazines ▶ **ˌsecond ˈclass** *adv.*: *to travel second class*

**ˌsecond-geneˈration** *adj.* **1** used to describe technology, a product, etc. that has been developed and improved since it first appeared **2** (*abbr* **2G**) used to describe mobile telephone networks without wires that were the first to use DIGITAL technology

**ˌsecond ˈhalf** (*also* **ˌfiscal second ˈhalf**, *esp. in AmE*) *n.* [C, usu. sing.] **1** (*Account.*) the second six months of a company's FINANCIAL YEAR **2** the period of six months between 1 July and 31 December

**ˌsecond-ˈhand** *adj.* not new; owned by sb else before: *second-hand cars* SYN USED, PRE-OWNED (*AmE*) ▶ **ˌsecond-ˈhand** *adv.*

**ˌsecond ˈsection** *n.* [sing.] (*Stock Ex.*) the part of the Tokyo Stock Exchange on which the shares of smaller and less successful companies are traded: *second-section companies*

**ˌsecond ˈtier** *n.* [C, usu. sing.] the second level of sth or a less important level than the first: *the second tier of management*

**ˌsecond-tier supˈplier** *n.* [C] (*Product.*) a company that delivers raw materials or goods to a FIRST-TIER SUPPLIER, who will then make them ready for the customer and deliver them

★**secretary** /ˈsekrətri; *AmE* -teri/ *n.* [C] (*pl.* **-ries**) **1** a person who works in an office, working for another person, dealing with letters and phone calls, typing, keeping records, arranging meetings, etc. **2** = COMPANY SECRETARY ▶ **secretarial** /ˌsekrəˈteəriəl; *AmE* -ˈter-/ *adj.*

**section** /ˈsekʃn/ *n.* [C] **1** a department in a company, an organization, etc: *director of the finance section* SYN DIVISION **2** a separate part of a document, book, website, etc: *the business section of the newspaper* **3** (*Stock Ex.*) a group of companies on the Japanese stock markets

★ **sector** /ˈsektə(r)/ *n.* [C] (*Econ.*) a particular area of activity or business; a part of a country's economy: *the banking/financial/IT ~* ◇ *service-sector jobs* ▸ **ˈsectoral** /-rəl/ (*also* **secˈtorial** /-ˈtɔːriəl/) *adj.*: *a sectoral study*

**ˈsector roˌtation** (*also* **roˈtation**) *n.* [C,U] (*Stock Ex.*) the movement of money from one area of the market or **sector** to another

★ **secure** /sɪˈkjʊə(r); *AmE* səˈkjʊr/ *v., adj.*

• *v.* [T] **1** (*fml.*) **~ sth (for sb/sth)** | **~ sb sth** to obtain or achieve sth, esp. when this means using a lot of effort: *They have secured the contract for the project.* **2** (*Finan.*) (*usu. pass.*) to legally agree to give sb who lends you money particular property or goods if you do not pay the money back: *The loan was fully secured* ***on/against*** *properties the company owned.* **3** to protect sth and make it safe: *The investment will secure 577 jobs.*

• *adj.* **1** safe and likely to continue or be successful for a long time: *a ~ job/income* **2** safe and protected so that it cannot be harmed or affected by sth/sb: *a secure network*

**secured** /sɪˈkjʊəd; *AmE* səˈkjʊrd/ *adj.* (*Finan.*; *Law*) **1** if a loan, debt, etc. is **secured**, the borrower agrees to give the lender particular property or goods if they do not pay the money back: *~ credit/debt/lending/loans* **2** used to describe a person, company, etc. that lends money to sb on the agreement that if the borrower does not pay back the money they will give the lender particular property or goods: *~ creditors/lenders*

**the Seˌcurities and Exˈchange Coˌmmission** *n.* [sing.] (*abbr* **SEC**) in the US, a government organization that is responsible for controlling how shares, bonds, etc. are traded to make sure that this is done in an honest way in order to protect investors

**the Seˌcurities and ˈFutures Auˌthority** *n.* [sing.] (*abbr* **SFA**) in the UK, an organization that controls the buying and selling of shares, bonds, etc. and protects investors, now part of the Financial Services Authority

**seˈcurities ˌmarket** (*also* **seˈcurities exˌchange**) *n.* [C] (*Stock Ex.*) a place where shares, bonds, etc. are bought and sold; the business activity involved in this

**securitize, -ise** /sɪˈkjʊərətaɪz; *AmE* səˈkjʊr-/ *v.* [T] (*Finan.*) to change a financial asset such as a loan into bonds that can be bought and sold in order to raise cash ▸ **seˌcuritiˈzation, -iˈsation** /-taɪˈzeɪʃn; *AmE* -təˈz-/ *n.* [U; C, usu. sing.]: *mortgage securitization*

★ **security** /sɪˈkjʊərəti; *AmE* səˈkjʊr-/ *n.* (*pl.* **-ties**) **1** [U] the activities involved in protecting a country, building or person against attack, danger, etc: *airport/hotel ~* ○ ***lax/strict/tight*** *~* • *to* ***improve/strengthen/tighten*** *~* • *a ~* ***alert/check/system*** • *a ~* ***guard*** **2** [U with sing./pl. v.] the department of a large company or organization that deals with the protection of its buildings, equipment and staff **3** [U] protection against sth bad that might happen in the future: ○ ***economic/financial*** *~* • *to* ***give (sb)/have/offer (sb)/provide (sb with)*** *~* **4** (*Finan.*; *Stock Ex.*) **securities** [pl.] a financial asset such as a share or bond; the certificate that shows you own this: *to buy high-yield securities* ○ *to* ***hold/sell*** *~* • *to* ***deal in/issue*** *~* • *a ~* ***business/company/dealer/firm/house*** **5** (*Finan.*; *Law*) [U,C] a valuable item that you agree to give to sb if you are unable to pay back the money that you have borrowed: *to give/offer/pledge sth as ~*

**seˈcurity deˌposit** *n.* [C] (*Comm.*) a first amount of money that a seller asks a buyer to give them in case the buyer does not complete the business

**seˌcurity of emˈployment** = EMPLOYMENT SECURITY

**seˈcurity ˌrating** *n.* [C, usu. sing.] **1** (*Finan.*) a measurement of the risk involved in investing in a particular company: *Triple-A is the highest form of security rating.* **2** (*IT*) a measurement of how well a computer or computer system protects data from being read or changed by sb without permission: *a network with a C2 security rating* **3** a measurement that shows if sth is safe or dangerous: *an airport with a low security rating*

**Secy.** = SEC.

**seed** /siːd/ *n., v.*

• *n.* **1** (*Finan.*) [U] **~ capital, money, etc.** money that is used to start a new business, project, etc. that will bring profits in the future: *He raised only $150 000 in seed capital.* **2** (*Market.*) (*also* '**decoy**) [C] a name that is added to a MAILING LIST to check how the list is being used

• *v.* [T] **1** (*Finan.*) to provide the money or other resources that are needed to start a new business, project, etc: *a venture capital company that seeds tech start-ups* **2** (*Market.*) to add one or more names to a MAILING LIST to check how the list is being used

**seedcorn** (*also* **seed corn**, *esp. in AmE*) /'si:dkɔ:n; *AmE* -kɔrn/ *n.* [U] (*esp. BrE*) ~ **(for sth)** money, people, etc. that will bring success or profit in the future

**seek** /si:k/ *v.* (**sought**, **sought** /sɔ:t/) [T] (*fml.*) (often used in newspapers) to try to obtain or achieve sth: *a small rise in the number of people seeking work* ▸ '**seeker** *n.* [C]

★ **segment** *n.*, *v.*

• *n.* /'segmənt/ [C] **1** a part or division of sth such as an economy, a market, a social group, etc: *Small businesses are the fastest-growing segment of the economy.* ◇ *the lower-priced segment of the market*

⊕ *the* ***business/industrial/retail/services/technology*** *~* • *the* ***energy/food/health-care/insurance*** *~* • ***core/key/profitable/target*** *~s* • *the* ***low-priced/luxury/mid-priced*** *~*

**2** a part or section of sth such as a chart

• *v.* /seg'ment/ [T,I] (*often pass.*) to divide sth into different parts; to divide into different parts: *Customers are segmented* ***into*** *4 basic groups.* ▸ ˌ**segmen'tation** /-'teɪʃn/ *n.* [U,C]: *the segmentation of work*

**seigniorage** (*also* **seignorage**) /'seɪnjərɪdʒ/ *n.* [U] (*Econ.*) the profit that is made by a government from issuing BANKNOTES, coins, etc.

**seize** /si:z/ *v.* [T] **1** to take goods away from sb officially or legally: *The bank has the right to seize your assets if you fail to repay the loan.* **2** to take control of a place or situation, often very suddenly: *to seize* ***control*** *of the business* ▸ **seizure** /'si:ʒə(r)/ *n.* [U,C]: *the seizure of assets/funds*

**select** /sɪ'lekt/ *v.*, *adj.*

• *v.* **1** [T,I] ~ **sb/sth (as/for sth)** | ~ **(sb/sth) (from sth)** to choose sb/sth from a group of people or things, usu. according to a system: *Customers can select from thousands of products.* ◇ *Available at selected stores only.* **2** (*IT*) [T] to mark sth on a computer screen; to choose sth from a list: *Select 'New Mail' from the 'Send' menu.*

• *adj.* carefully chosen as the best out of a larger group of people or things: *a select group of customers*

**selection** /sɪ'lekʃn/ *n.* **1** [U] the process of choosing sb/sth from a group of people or things, usu. according to a system: *the selection of board members* ◇ *the selection process* **2** [C] a number of people or things that have been chosen from a larger group: *You can make a selection and pay online.* **3** [C] a collection from which sth can be chosen: *a* ***wide*** *selection of cars* SYN CHOICE

**selective** /sɪ'lektɪv/ *adj.* **1** affecting only a small number of people or things from a larger group: *selective price cuts* ◇ *a selective mailing* **2** careful about what or who you choose ▸ **se'lectively** *adv.* **selectivity** /səˌlek'tɪvəti/ *n.* [U]

**seˌlective at'tention** (*also* **seˌlective per'ception**) *n.* [U] (*Market.*) a process in which consumers only notice or become aware of some pieces of information in an advertisement, etc.

**seˌlective de'mand** *n.* [U,C] (*Market.*) the desire of consumers for a particular brand of product

**seˌlective distri'bution** *n.* [U] (*Market.*) when a product is made available in a limited number of shops/stores, etc. in an area

**seˌlective per'ception** = SELECTIVE ATTENTION

**self** /self/ *pron.* written on a cheque or other document to refer to the person who has signed it

ˌ**self-actuali'zation**, **-i'sation** *n.* [U] (*HR*) the fact of using your skills and abilities and achieving as much as you can

ˌ**self-ad'dressed** *adj.* if an envelope is **self-addressed**, sb has written their address on it

ˌ**self-ad'hesive** *adj.* covered on one side with a sticky substance so that it can be stuck to sth without using glue, etc.

ˌ**self-ap'praisal** *n.* [U,C] (*HR*) the process of judging your own work; your opinion about your work

ˌ**self-as'sembly** *adj.* (about furniture, etc.) bought in several pieces that you must put together yourself: *self-assembly cupboards* ▸ ˌ**self-as'sembly** *n.* [U]: *furniture ready for self-assembly*

ˌ**self-as'sessment** *n.* [U,C] **1** a system of paying tax in which you calculate yourself how much you should pay; a form with this information: *a self-assessment tax return* **2** (*HR*) the process of judging your own work, skills, etc.; your opinion about this

**ˌself-corˈrecting** *adj.* if a system, machine, etc. is **self-correcting**, it corrects or adjusts itself without outside help if it begins to go wrong ▸ **ˌself-corˈrect** *v.* [I] **ˌself-corˈrection** *n.* [U]

**ˌself-ˈdealing** *n.* [U] (*Law*) when sb uses their influence in an organization to make money for themselves: *He was accused of self-dealing.*

**ˌself-deˈvelopment** *n.* [U] (*HR*) the process of gaining the knowledge, skills and abilities you need SYN PERSONAL DEVELOPMENT

**ˌself-diˈrected** *adj.* not controlled by sb else; making your own decisions: *self-directed teams*

**ˌself-emˈployed** *adj.* working for yourself and not employed by a company, etc: *a self-employed designer* ◇ *retirement plans for* **the self-employed** (= people who are self-employed) ▸ **ˌself-emˈployment** *n.* [U]

**ˌself-ˈfinancing** (*also* **ˌself-ˈfinanced**) *adj.* a **self-financing** company, project, etc. produces enough money to pay its own costs and does not need financial support

**ˌself-ˈliquidating** *adj.* (*Finan.*) **1** used to describe a debt or loan that buys sth that will earn enough money to pay back the loan **2** used to describe a project, deal, etc. that makes enough profit to pay its costs

**ˌself-ˈmade** *adj.* having become rich and successful through your own hard work rather than having had money given to you

**ˌself-ˈmailer** *n.* [C] a printed sheet or card that is designed to be sent without an envelope

**ˌself-ˈmanaged** *adj.* making your own decisions and not receiving instructions from sb else: *self-managed teams* ▸ **ˌself-ˈmanagement** *n.* [U]

**ˌself-ˈpowered** *adj.* used to describe sth that can produce its own energy and does not need energy from another source

**ˌself-ˈregulating** *adj.* **1** (*also* **ˌself-ˈregulatory**) (about an organization, a system, etc.) that is not controlled by the government but decides on its own rules and makes sure they are obeyed: *The profession is largely self-regulating.* **2** (about a machine, system, etc.) that controls and adjusts itself: *self-regulating heating products* ▸ **ˌself-reguˈlation** *n.* [U]

**ˌself-ˈseal** *adj.* used to describe an envelope, etc. that will close and stick when you press the two open edges together

**ˌself-ˈservice** *adj.* a self-service shop/store, restaurant, etc. is one in which customers serve themselves and then pay for the goods: *self-service check-in at the airport* ◇ *self-service banking* ▸ **ˌself-ˈservice** *n.* [U]

**ˌself-ˈstarter** *n.* [C] a person who is able to work on their own and make decisions without needing anyone to tell them what to do

**ˌself-sufˈficient** *adj.* able to do or produce everything that you need without the help of other people: *The country is no longer self-sufficient* **in** *oil.* ▸ **ˌself-sufˈficiency** *n.* [U]

**ˌself-supˈporting** *adj.* having enough money to be able to operate without financial help from other people

**ˌself-susˈtaining** *adj.* able to continue in a successful way without outside help

★**sell** /sel/ *v.*, *n.*

• *v.* (**sold**, **sold** /səʊld; *AmE* soʊld/) **1** [T,I] **~ sth (to sb) (at/for sth)** | **~ sb sth (at/for sth)** | **~ (sth)** to give sth to sb in exchange for money: *We sold the hotel to private investors for $365 m.* ◇ *Did you sell him the car?* ◇ *They sold the business* **at a profit/loss**. ◇ *Shareholders were advised not to sell.* **2** [T] to offer sth for people to buy: *Do you sell stamps?* **3** [T,I] to be bought by people usu. in the way or in the numbers mentioned; to be offered at the price mentioned: *DVD players now sell* **for** *only $80.* ◇ *The book is selling well.* ◇ *The magazine sells 300 000 copies a week.* **4** [T,I] to make people want to buy sth: *It is quality that sells our products.* **5** [T] **~ sth/yourself (to sb)** to persuade sb that sth is a good idea, service, product, etc.; or that you are the right person for a job, etc: *Now we have to sell the idea to management.* ◇ *You have to sell yourself at an interview.*

▸ **ˈsellable** /-əbl/ *adj.*: *sellable securities* IDM **sell/go like hot ˈcakes** to sell quickly or in great numbers → idiom at BULK *n.* PHR V **ˌsell (sth) ˈinto sth** (*Finan.*) to sell shares, bonds, etc. when the situation mentioned exists: *to sell into a falling market* **ˌsell sth ˈoff 1** to sell all or part of an industry, a company, etc. often at a low price in order to get rid of it **2** to sell things cheaply because you want to get rid of them or because you need the money: *to sell off old stock* **ˌsell sth ˈon** to sell to sb else sth that you have bought not long before **ˌsell ˈout (to sb/sth)** to sell your business or a part of your business **,sell 'out (of sth)** (*Finan.*) to sell particular shares, bonds, etc. that you own, often because they no longer seem to be a good investment **,sell 'out; be ,sold 'out** to be all sold: *A hot product can sell out within 24 hours.* **,sell 'out (of sth); be ,sold 'out (of sth)** to have sold all the available items: *I'm sorry, we've sold out.* **,sell 'through** if items in a shop/store **sell through** they are sold to customers: *A really good guitar will sell through fast.* **,sell (sth) 'up** (*esp. BrE*) to sell your home, possessions, business, etc., usu. because you are leaving the country or retiring: *They plan to sell up and retire.* • *n.* **1** [C] an act of selling sth or of trying to sell sth: *Luxury goods can be a **tough** sell* (= difficult to sell). **2** [C, usu. sing.] an act of trying to persuade sb that sth is a good idea, product, service, etc. **3** (*Stock Ex.*) [U; sing.] = SELL RATING **4** (*Stock Ex.*) [C] = SELL ORDER

**'sell-by date** (*AmE also* **'pull date**) *n.* [C] the date, printed on a container or package, that advises a shop/store how long it should offer a particular item of food or drink for sale. Items can usu. be used after this: *a packet of hot dogs past its sell-by date*

★ **seller** /'selə(r)/ *n.* [C] **1** a person or company that sells sth: *a clothing/software ~* ◇ *a **big/leading/top** ~ of sth* ◇ *The law protects both the buyer and the seller.* **2** a product that is sold in the amounts or the way mentioned: ***big/hot/strong/top** ~s*

**,seller's 'market** *n.* [C, usu. sing.] a situation in which people selling sth have an advantage, because there is not a lot for sale, and prices can be kept high OPP BUYER'S MARKET

**selling** /'selɪŋ/ *n.* [U] **1** the act of giving sb sth in exchange for money: *steady selling of shares* **2** the job, skill, study, etc. of persuading people to buy things: *a career in selling* **3** **-selling** used to describe a product that sells in the way mentioned: *a best-selling chocolate bar*

**'selling ,concept** (*also* **'sales ,concept**) *n.* **1** (*Market.*) [C] an idea for the way to sell a product **2** (*Econ.*) **the selling concept, the sales concept** [sing.] the approach to business that emphasizes persuading customers to buy products that you already have, rather than producing new ones that they may want

**'selling cost** *n.* [C, usu. pl.] the amount that a company spends on advertising and selling a product

**'selling ,order** = SELL ORDER

**'selling point** *n.* [C] (*Market.*) a feature of sth that makes people want to buy or use it: *The price is one of the main selling points.* → USP

**'selling price** *n.* [C] the price at which sth is sold

**'sell limit ,order** *n.* [C] (*Stock Ex.*) an order to a BROKER to sell a number of shares, bonds, etc. at a particular price or higher: *to execute/place a ~*

**'sell-off** *n.* [C] **1** the sale of all or part of an industry, a company, etc., esp. at a low price to get rid of it: *a major sell-off of assets* **2** (*Finan.*) (*esp. AmE*) the sale of a large number of shares, bonds, etc., after which their value usu. falls: *The sell-off **in** tech stocks is slowing down.*

**'sell ,order** (*also* **sell**, **'selling ,order**) *n.* [C] (*Stock Ex.*) an order to a BROKER to sell a number of shares, bonds, etc.

**'sell-out** *n.* [C, usu. sing.] a product that has sold very well so that there are none left; an event for which all the tickets have been sold: *The book was a sell-out.* ◇ *a sell-out tour*

**'sell ,rating** *n.* [C] (*also* **sell** [U; sing.]) (*Stock Ex.*) a statement made by a bank, a dealer, etc. that investors should sell a particular company's shares: *to put a sell rating on the stock*

**'sell ,signal** *n.* [C] (*Stock Ex.*) a situation where the pattern of recent movements in a share price indicates that it is a good time to sell shares: *to generate/give a ~*

**'sell-through** *n.* (*Market.*) **1** [U,C] the number of items of a particular product that a shop/store manages to sell to customers compared to the number it bought to sell: *The average sell-through rate for these magazines is 35-38%.* **2** [C] an item, esp. a video/DVD, that you can buy rather than hire ▸ **'sell-through** *adj.*

**semi-** /'semi/ *prefix* (*in adjs and ns*) **1** half; partly: *semicircular* ◇ *semi-professional* **2** happening twice during the period mentioned: *a semi-annual review*

**,semi-'durable** *adj.* (*Econ.; Market.*) (about clothes, furniture, etc.) not expected to last for more than a few years: *semi-durable fabrics* ▸ **,semi-'durable** *n.* [C, usu. pl.]

**,semi-'finished** *adj.* partly made; ready to be made into a finished product

**seminar** /'semɪnɑː(r)/ *n.* [C] a meeting for discussion or training: *a one-day management seminar* ⊙ *to **conduct/hold/run** a ~* ♦ *to **attend** a ~* ♦ *a **business/training** ~*

ˌ**semi-'skilled** *adj.* having or needing some special training or qualifications: *semi-skilled jobs*

ˌ**semi-structured 'interview** *n.* [C] (*Market.*) an informal way of finding out the opinion of a person or group by asking some fixed questions as well as others that seem suitable

**send** /send/ *v.* [T] (**sent**, **sent** /sent/) **1 ~ sth (to sb)** | **~ sb sth** to make sth go or be taken to a place, esp. by post/mail, email, etc: *to ~ a package/cheque/fax* ◇ *She sent the letter by airmail.* ◇ *All the staff were sent the email.* **2** to tell, or arrange for, sb to go somewhere or do sth: *to be sent on a training course* **3** to make sth move quickly or suddenly; to make sb act quickly: *The news sent shares 3% higher.* PHRV ˌ**send a'way (to sb) (for sth)** = SEND OFF (FOR STH) ˌ**send sth 'back** to return sth to a place ˌ**send sth 'in** to send sth by post/mail to a place where it will be dealt with: *to send in an application form* ˌ**send 'off (for sth)**; ˌ**send a'way (to sb) (for sth)** to write to sb and ask them to send you sth by post/mail: *I've sent off for details of the job.* ˌ**send sth 'off** to send sth to a place by post/mail ˌ**send sth 'on (to sb) 1** to send a letter, email, etc. that has been sent to you to sb else SYN FORWARD **2** to send a letter that has been sent to sb's old address to their new address SYN FORWARD **3** to send sth from one place/person to another ˌ**send sth 'out** to send sth to a lot of different people or places SYN MAIL STH OUT

**sender** /'sendə(r)/ *n.* [C] a person who sends sth

★**senior** /'si:niə(r)/ *adj., n.*

• ***adj.* 1** having a higher rank in an organization or a profession than others: *~ analysts/bankers* ◇ *He is senior* **to** *me.* ◇ *the most senior person present*

○ *a ~* ***employee/executive/manager/official/vice-president*** • *~* ***management/staff*** • *a ~* ***associate/partner*** • *a ~* ***position/post***

**2** (*Finan.*) used to describe a debt that must be paid before all other debts if the borrower has financial problems

○ *~* ***debentures/debt/loans/notes*** • *~* ***creditors/lenders***

• ***n.*** [C] **1** a person with a higher level of job or status than others: *her colleagues and her seniors* OPP JUNIOR **2** (*esp. AmE*) = SENIOR CITIZEN

ˌ**senior 'citizen** (*also* **'senior**, *esp. in AmE*) *n.* [C] an older person, esp. sb over 65 years old who has retired from work

**seniority** /ˌsi:ni'ɒrəti; *AmE* -'ɔ:r-; -'ɑ:r-/ *n.* [U] **1** the fact of being older or of a higher rank than others: *a position of seniority* **2** the rank you have in a company because of the length of time you have worked there: *Promotion is based on seniority.*

**sensitive** /'sensətɪv/ *adj.* **1 ~ (to sth)** reacting quickly to sth or to small changes: *Sales at larger stores are more sensitive to changes in consumer spending.* ◇ *a sensitive instrument* **2** (about information) not to be shared or given to other people; secret **3 ~ (to sth)** aware of and able to understand other people and their feelings: *sensitive to the needs of employees* ▸ **'sensitively** *adv.* ˌ**sensi'tivity** /-'tɪvəti/ *n.* [U]: *increased price sensitivity among consumers* ◇ *the high sensitivity of the data*

**sensi'tivity aˌnalysis** *n.* [C,U] a study of how much a project, system, etc. would be affected by a change in one of its elements, such as sales, costs, etc.

**sentiment** /'sentɪmənt/ *n.* **1** [U] a measure of how people, esp. investors or financial experts, feel about the economy, esp. about whether it will get better: *a decline in business sentiment* SYN CONFIDENCE

○ ***investor/market*** *~* • *to* ***boost/improve//lift*** *~* • *to* ***damage/depress/hit/hurt/undermine*** *~* • ***bearish/bullish/positive/negative*** *~*

**2** [U,C] what a group of people feel or think about sth: *Sentiment about the new CEO was mixed.*

**separation** /ˌsepə'reɪʃn/ *n.* [U,C] (*AmE*) (*HR*) when sb stops working for a company either because they retire or because they lose their job: *voluntary separation* ◇ *a $4 m separation package*

**sequential** /sɪ'kwenʃl/ *adj.* (*fml.*) **1** following in order of time or place; following in a logical order: *four sequential stages* **2** (*Account.*) compared with the most recent similar accounting period: *a slight sequential decline in revenue* ▸ **se'quentially** /-ʃəli/ *adv.*

**seˌquential 'sampling** *n.* [U] (*Tech.*) a process of **sampling** that continues until enough data has been collected

**sequester** /sɪ'kwestə(r)/ *v.* [T] (*Law*) **1** to keep a group of people, esp. a JURY, away from other people **2** = SEQUESTRATE

**sequestrate** /ˈsiːkwəstreɪt; sɪˈkwes-/ (*also* **seˈquester**) *v.* [T] (*Law*) to take control of sb's property or assets until a debt has been paid ▶ ˌ**sequeˈstration** /-ˈstreɪʃn/ *n.* [U,C] ˈ**sequestrator** *n.* [C]

**serial** /ˈsɪəriəl; *AmE* ˈsɪr-/ *adj.* **1** (*IT*) sending data one BIT at a time: *the serial transmission of data* OPP PARALLEL **2** (*Tech.*) arranged in a series: *tasks carried out in serial order* **3** doing the same thing in the same way several times: *a ~ claimant/ entrepreneur* ▶ ˈ**serially** /-əli/ *adv.*

ˌ**serial ˈbonds** *n.* [pl.] (*Finan.*) a set of bonds that a company or local government, etc. issues that become due for payment at regular times over a period of time

ˈ**serial ˌnumber** *n.* [C] a number put on a product to identify it

**series** /ˈsɪəriːz; *AmE* ˈsɪr-/ *n.* [C] (*pl.* **series**) **1** a range of similar products produced by one company: *a popular series of video games* **2** (*Finan.*) a group of shares, bonds, etc. that have the same rules and guarantees about the rights of the owners, payment of interest, etc: *Series A shares and Series B shares* **3** several events or things of a similar kind that happen one after the other: *a series of meetings*

**serve** /sɜːv; *AmE* sɜːrv/ *v.* **1** [T] to provide an area or a group of people with a product or service: *These firms serve local markets.* ◇ *The area is well served with major road links.* **2** [T] to deal with people, esp. customers, and give them what they need: *serving our customers better and faster* **3** [T,I] to give sb food or drink, for example at a restaurant: *Breakfast is served from 7 a.m.* **4** [T,I] (*esp. BrE*) to help a customer or sell them sth in a shop/store: *Are you being served?* **5** [T,I] to spend a period of time in a particular job, esp. a senior one, or training for a job: *He has served* **as** *CEO since 2004.* **6** (*Law*) [T] to give sb an official document or instruction, esp. one that orders them to appear in court: *to ~ a writ/summons on sb*

IDM **serve ˈnotice (on/upon sb) (that ...)** (*Law*) to officially inform sb, often in writing, that you will do sth or that they must do sth

PHR V ˌ**serve sth ˈout** to continue working until a previously agreed period of time has been completed

**server** /ˈsɜːvə(r); *AmE* ˈsɜːrv-/ (*also* ˈ**file ˌserver**) *n.* [C] (*IT*) a computer program that controls or supplies information to computers connected in a network; the main computer on which this program is run

ˈ**server farm** *n.* [C] (*IT*) a business with a large number of SERVERS in one place that provide computer services for many different organizations

★ **service** /ˈsɜːvɪs; *AmE* ˈsɜːrv-/ *n.*, *v.*, *adj.*

• *n.* **1** [C,U] a business whose work involves doing sth for customers but not producing goods; the work that such a business does: *the development of new* **goods and services** ◇ *a service industry*

○ *to* **offer (sb)/provide (sb with)** *a ~* • **financial/marketing/security/ travel** *~s*

**2** [U] help and advice given to customers in hotels, restaurants, shops/ stores and businesses: *10% will be added to your bill for service.*

○ *to* **give (sb)/offer (sb)** *~* • **efficient/ good/quick** *~* • **bad/poor/slow** *~*

**3** [C] a system that provides sth that the public needs, organized by the government or a private company: *the ambulance/bus ~*

○ *to* **offer (sb)/provide (sb with)** *a ~* • **education/health/social** *~s* • *an* **essential**/*a* **vital** *~*

**4** [C] an organization or a company that provides sth for the public or does sth for the government: *a debt counselling service* **5** [C, usu. sing.] a system of regular buses, trains, planes, etc. that goes to a particular place; a bus, train, plane, etc. that regularly goes at a particular time: *There is an air service to the island.* ◇ *the 10.15 service to Glasgow* **6** [U] the work that sb does for an organization, etc., esp. when it continues for a long time or is admired very much: *25 years' service with the company* **7** [C, usu. pl.] the particular skills or help that a person is able to offer: *You need the services* **of** *a good lawyer.* **8** [U] the use that you can get from a vehicle or machine; the state of being used: *That PC gave us very good service.* **9** [C] an examination of a vehicle or machine followed by any work that is necessary to keep it operating well: *a service engineer*

IDM **be of ˈservice (to sb)** (*fml.*) to be useful or helpful → idiom at ENTER

• *v.* [T] **1** (*Finan.*) **~ a debt/loan** to pay interest on money you have borrowed **2** (*Finan.*) **~ a loan** to collect and manage the regular payments made to pay back a loan **3** (*fml.*) to do sth for people or provide them with help or with sth they need, such as shops/stores, or a transport system: *The city is serviced by six airlines.*

**4** to examine a vehicle or machine and repair it if necessary so that it continues to work correctly
• ***adj.*** used only by people who work in a building or who are delivering sth to a building: *a service elevator*
▸ **'servicing** *n.* [U]: *debt servicing*

**'service a,greement** = SERVICE CONTRACT

**'service ,bureau** *n.* [C] (*IT*) a business that sells a variety of computing or printing services or allows people to pay to use their computers or printers

**'service ,centre** *n.* [C] **1** a place that checks or repairs machines and equipment and provides parts for them **2** a place (**garage**) where vehicles are repaired and where you can buy parts for vehicles **3** a place where a company provides help and information for customers who have bought or are using its products

**'service ,charge** *n.* [C] **1** a charge for work that sb does for you that is usu. extra to the main bill **2** (*BrE*) an amount of money added to a bill in a restaurant that goes to pay for the work of the staff **3** an amount of money that is paid to the owner of an apartment building for services such as putting out rubbish/ garbage, cleaning the stairs, etc.

**'service ,contract** (*also* **'service a,greement**) *n.* [C] **1** (*HR*) a formal agreement about employment made between a company and an employee, usu. one with special conditions that is given to a senior manager, etc. **2** an arrangement with a company in which the company will check and repair equipment for a fixed price for a particular period of time **3** an agreement with a company providing mobile phone/cellphone services in which a customer pays a fixed fee each month for a period of time

**'service e,conomy** *n.* [C, usu. sing.] (*Econ.*) an economy in which most of the workers and businesses are involved in providing services rather than manufacturing or producing things; all the businesses that provide services: *the shift from a manufacturing to a service economy*

**'service ,handbook** = SERVICE MANUAL

**'service ,industry** = TERTIARY INDUSTRY

**,service level a'greement** = SLA

**'service ,manual** (*also* **'service ,handbook**) *n.* [C] a book that describes how to check and repair a vehicle or a machine

**'service pack** *n.* [C] (*IT*) a set of additional software elements that corrects any errors in the software or makes improvements to it

**'service pro,vider** *n.* [C] (*IT*) a business that provides a service to customers, esp. one that connects customers to the Internet

**'service road** (*AmE also* **'frontage road**) *n.* [C] a small road that runs parallel to a main road, that you use to reach houses, shops/stores, etc.

**,service 'sector** = TERTIARY SECTOR

**session** /'seʃn/ *n.* [C] **1** (*Stock Ex.*) (*also* **'trading ,session**) a period of trading on the stock exchange, usu. from when it opens to when it closes on a particular day: *a session of heavy trading* **2** a period of time that is spent doing a particular activity: *a training session* **3** a formal meeting or series of meetings

**SET** /,es iː 'tiː/ *abbr* (*E-comm.*) **secure electronic transfer** a safe and private way of ordering goods and paying for them on the Internet

★**set** /set/ *v., n., adj.*
• ***v.*** [T] (**setting, set, set**) **1** to arrange or fix sth; to decide on sth: ~ *a date/price for sth* SYN FIX **2** to fix sth so that others copy it or try to achieve it: *to set a standard* **3** to give sb a piece of work, a task, etc: *set targets* NOTE Idioms containing **set** are at the entries for the nouns or adjectives in the idioms. PHR V **,set sth ('off) a'gainst sth** (*Account.*) to use one cost or payment, or one group, in order to cancel or reduce the effect of another: *to set capital costs off against tax* **,set sth a'side 1** to save or keep money or time for a particular purpose: *We set a certain amount aside for emergencies.* **2** (*Law*) to state that a decision made by a court is not legally valid **,set sth/sb 'back** to delay the progress of sth/sb by a particular time **,set sb 'back sth** (*not in the pass.*) to cost sb a particular amount of money: *The repairs set us back over €20 000.* **,set sth 'down** to give sth as a rule, principle, etc: *Building regulations are set down by the government.* **,set sth 'out** to present ideas, facts, etc. in an organized way, in speech or writing **,set sb 'up** (*Finan.*) to provide sb with the money that they need in order to do sth: *to set sb up in business* **,set sth 'up 1** to make a piece of equipment or a machine ready for use **2** to arrange for sth to happen: *to set up a meeting* **3** to create or start a company or a business: *to set up your own business* ◇ *setting-up costs* **4** to start a

process or a series of events ˌ**set (yourself) 'up (as sth)** to start a new business: *He set himself up as a consultant.*

• ***n.*** [C] a group of similar things that belong together in some way: *a set of accounts*

• ***adj.*** **1** planned or fixed: *Tasks are performed in a set order.* ◇ *a set price* **2** (esp. in newspapers) likely to do sth; ready for sth or to do sth: *Interest rates look set to rise again.*

**setback** /'setbæk/ *n.* [C] **1** a difficulty or problem that delays or prevents sth, or makes a situation worse: *The delay in receiving parts was a temporary setback.*

✪ *a **big/major/serious** ~* ♦ *to **recover from/suffer** a ~*

**2** (*Stock Ex.*) (used esp. in newspapers) a fall in prices: *a 6.7% setback*

✪ *to **recover from/suffer** a ~*

**'set-off** *n.* [C,U] **1** (*Account.*) a cost or payment, or a group, used to cancel or reduce the effect of another **2** (*Law*) an occasion when sb reduces the amount that they owe sb else because the other person also owes them money

**settle** /'setl/ *v.* **1** [T] to pay money that you owe: *to ~ your account/debt* **2** [T,I] to put an end to an argument or a disagreement: *to settle a dispute* **3** [T] (*often pass.*) to decide or arrange sth finally **4** [I] if prices, etc. **settle**, they stop rising or falling and stay the same for a period of time **5** [I] to sink slowly down: *The contents may settle in transit.* **PHRV** **'settle for sth** to accept sth that is not satisfactory but is the best that is available: *They wanted a 5% pay increase, but had to settle for 3%.* **'settle on sth** to choose or make a decision about sth after thinking about it ˌ**settle 'up (with sb)** to pay sb the money you owe them

★**settlement** /'setlmənt/ *n.* **1** [C] an official agreement that ends an argument between two people or groups: *The management and unions have reached a settlement.*

✪ *to **agree/negotiate/offer** a ~* ♦ *a **financial/global**/an **industry-wide** ~* ♦ *a **pay/wage** ~*

**2** [U] the action of reaching an agreement: *the settlement of a dispute* **3** [U] the action of paying money that you owe: *a cheque **in settlement** of a bill* **4** (*Finan.*; *Stock Ex.*) [U] the action of paying money that you owe for investments, etc: *the settlement system for securities*

**'settlement date** (*also* **'settlement day**) (*BrE also* **'settling day**, *less freq.*) *n.* [C] (*Finan.*; *Stock Ex.*) the date by which shares, bonds, etc. must be paid for and must be passed to the buyer

**'set-up** (*also* **setup**, *esp. in AmE*) *n.* **1** [C, usu. sing.] a way of organizing sth; a system: *I don't understand the set-up here yet.* **2** [C, usu. sing.] the act of starting a company or making an official arrangement: *set-up costs* **3** [C] a business: *He runs his own set-up.* **4** [C, usu. sing., U] the act of preparing machines and organizing a system in a factory in order to make a particular product: *Set-up only takes a few minutes.* **5** [C] the equipment needed for a particular task or purpose: *a recording set-up*

**severally** /'sevrəli/ *adv.* (*Law or fml.*) separately: *The directors are **jointly and severally** responsible for paying debts.*

**severance** /'sevərəns/ *n.* [sing; U] **1** (*HR*) the act of ending sb's contract of employment: *voluntary severance* ◇ *severance pay* **2** the act of ending a connection or relationship: *the severance of relations*

**sew** /səʊ; soʊ/ *v.* (**sewed, sewn** /səʊn; *AmE* soʊn/ *or* **sewed, sewed**) **PHRV** ˌ**sew sth 'up** (*infml.*) **1** to arrange sth in a satisfactory way: *We need to sew up the deal today.* **2** to be in complete control of sth: *They have the computer games market sewn up.*

**sexism** /'seksɪzəm/ *n.* [U] the unfair treatment of people, esp. women, because of their sex; the attitude that causes this
▸ **'sexist** *n.* [C] **'sexist** *adj.*

**'sex ˌtyping** *n.* [U] the belief that particular behaviour is more typical of either men or women; the belief that particular roles or jobs are more suitable for either men or women

**SFA** /ˌes ef 'eɪ/ *abbr* **1** = SECURITIES AND FUTURES AUTHORITY **2 sales force automation** software that deals with the whole process of selling goods and services

**sgd** *abbr* (*written*) signed

**shadow** /'ʃædəʊ; *AmE* -doʊ/ *v.* [T] (*HR*) to be with sb who is doing a particular job, so that you can learn about it: *New employees shadow other members of the department as part of their training.*

**the ˌshadow e'conomy** (*also* **inˌformal e'conomy**, ˌ**parallel e'conomy**) *n.* [sing.] (*Econ.*) illegal work, trade or business activities that are done without the knowledge or

approval of the government
→ BLACK ECONOMY

**ˌshadow ˈmarket** *n.* [sing.] illegal trade in sth → BLACK MARKET

**shady** /ˈʃeɪdi/ *adj.* (**-dier**, **-diest**) seeming to be dishonest or illegal: *a ~ businessman/deal*

**shake** /ʃeɪk/ *v.* [T] (**shook** /ʃʊk/ **shaken** /ˈʃeɪkən/) **~ hands (with sb) (on sth)** | **~ sb's hand** to take sb's hand and move it up and down to say hello or to show that you agree about sth: *We shook hands on the deal.* **PHRV** **ˌshake ˈdown** to begin to work well in a situation, esp. a new one: *The new employees are shaking down well.* **ˈshake on sth** to shake hands in order to show that sth has been agreed: *They shook on the deal.* **ˌshake sth ˈup** to make important changes in an organization, a profession, etc. to make it more efficient: *The whole industry needs shaking up.*

**shakedown** /ˈʃeɪkdaʊn/ *n.* [C] (*AmE*) (*Manufact.*) a test of a vehicle, piece of equipment, etc. to see if there are any problems before it is used generally

**ˈshake-out** (*also* **shakeout**, *esp. in AmE*) *n.* [C] **1** a big change that takes place in an industry, in which people lose their jobs and one or more competing companies may disappear **2** = SHAKE-UP

**ˈshake-up** (*also* **shakeup**) (*also* **ˈshake-out**) *n.* [C] a situation in which a lot of changes are made to an organization to improve the way in which it works: *a management shake-up*

**shaky** /ˈʃeɪki/ *adj.* (**-kier**, **-kiest**) not seeming very successful; likely to fail: *The business is looking shaky.*

**shape** /ʃeɪp/ *v.* **IDM** **shape ˌup or ship ˌout** (*AmE*) (*infml.*) used to tell sb that if they do not improve, work harder, etc. they will have to leave their job, position, etc.
**PHRV** **ˌshape ˈup (as sth) 1** to develop in a particular way, esp. in a good way: *Our plans are shaping up nicely* (= showing signs that they will be successful). **2** to improve your behaviour, work harder, etc.

★**share** /ʃeə(r); *AmE* ʃer/ *n., v.*
• ***n.*** [C] **1** (*Finan.*) any of the units of equal value into which a company is divided and sold to raise money. People who own **shares** become owners of the company and receive part of the company's profits: *shares in British Airways* ◇ *They will issue 24 million new shares worth €3 bn.*
⊙ *to* ***acquire/buy/have/hold/own/sell*** *~s* ♦ *to* ***allocate/allot*** *~s* ♦ *to* ***deal in/invest in/trade in*** *~s* ♦ *to* ***float*** *~s*
**2** one part of sth that is divided between two or more people, businesses, etc: *to have a bigger share of the market* ◇ *a growing/an increased/a large/small ~* **3** the part that sb has in a particular activity that involves several people: *Everybody has done their share of the work.*
**IDM** **ˌshare of ˈmind** (*Market.*) how aware people are of a particular brand or product compared with other brands or products of the same type
• ***v.*** **1** [T,I] to have or use sth at the same time as sb else: *I share an office with two other people.* **2** [T] **~ sth (out)** to divide sth between two or more people

**ˈshare appliˌcation** (*also* **appliˌcation for ˈshares**) *n.* [C] (*both BrE*) (*Finan.*) a request to buy some of the shares that a company is issuing

**ˈshare ˌbuyback** (*BrE*) (*AmE* **ˈstock ˌbuyback**) *n.* [C,U] (*Finan.*) a situation when a company buys its own shares from shareholders

**ˈshare ˌcapital** *n.* [U] (*BrE*) (*Finan.*) the money that investors put into a company when they buy shares, which the company uses to continue its activities

**ˈshare cerˌtificate** (*BrE*) (*AmE* **ˈstock cerˌtificate**) *n.* [C] (*Finan.*) a legal document given to a shareholder, containing details of the shares that they own

**ˈshare ˌdividend** *n.* [C] (*Finan.*) **1** = DIVIDEND **2** an amount of profits that a company pays to its shareholders in the form of shares rather than cash

★**shareholder** /ˈʃeəhəʊldə(r); *AmE* ˈʃerhoʊ-/ (*esp. BrE*) (*AmE usu.* **ˈstockholder**) *n.* [C] (*Finan.*) a person or group that owns shares in a company or business: *a shareholders' meeting*
⊙ *a* ***big/large/leading/major/substantial*** *~* ♦ *the* ***controlling/main/principal*** *~*

**ˌshareholder ˈequity** (*also* **ˌshareholders' ˈequity**) (*both esp. BrE*) (*AmE usu.* **ˌstockholder ˈequity**) *n.* [U] (*Account.*) the value of a company as shown in its financial records, which is its assets minus its LIABILITIES **SYN** BOOK VALUE

**ˌshareholder ˈfunds** (*also* **ˌshareholders' ˈfunds**) *n.* [pl.] (*both BrE*) (*Account.*) the value of a company's assets minus its LIABILITIES, which legally belongs to its shareholders SYN NET WORTH

**ˌshareholder of ˈrecord** (*esp. BrE*) (*AmE usu.* **ˌstockholder of ˈrecord**) (*also* **ˌholder of ˈrecord, ˌowner of ˈrecord**, *AmE, BrE*) *n.* [C] the person, company, etc. that is in a company's records as a holder of shares. Only **shareholders of record** can receive DIVIDENDS and other payments.

**ˌshareholders' ˈequity** = SHAREHOLDER EQUITY

**ˌshareholders' ˈfunds** = SHAREHOLDER FUNDS

**ˌshareholders' ˈregister** (*also* **ˈshare ˌregister, ˌregister of ˈmembers**) (*all BrE*) *n.* [C] (*Law*) a legal document that contains a list of all the people or companies that own shares in a business

**ˌshareholder ˈvalue** (*esp. BrE*) (*AmE usu.* **ˌstockholder ˈvalue**) *n.* [U,C] the financial benefits that a company's shareholders have, in the form of DIVIDENDS and the value of their shares if they sell them

**shareholding** /ˈʃeəhəʊldɪŋ; *AmE* ˈʃerhoʊ-/ (*esp. BrE*) (*AmE usu.* **ˈstockholding**) *n.* (*Finan.*) **1** [C] a share of the ownership of a company; the value of shares in a company that a particular shareholder owns: *The agency has a 21% shareholding in Telecall.*

◯ ***to acquire/build up/increase/reduce/sell** your ~ ◆ **a controlling/majority/minority** ~*

**2** [C, usu. pl.] a number of shares that a company, fund, etc. owns as an asset: *details of the company's shareholdings at the end of last year*

**ˌshare inˈcentive plan** (*BrE*) (*AmE* **ˌstock inˈcentive plan**) *n.* [C] (*abbr* **SIP**) (*Finan.; HR*) a system in which a company gives its employees shares, or allows them to buy shares, so that when the company makes a profit they will receive part of it

**ˈshare ˌindex** (*BrE*) (*AmE* **ˈstock ˌindex**) *n.* [C] (*Stock Ex.*) a list of the average price of a particular set of shares, that can be easily compared with the average price on a previous date and used to show whether the value of shares in general is rising or falling

**ˈshare ˌissue** (*also* **ˈshare ˌoffer**) (*both BrE*) (*AmE* **ˈstock ˌissue**) *n.* [C] (*Finan.*) an occasion when a company offers a number of new shares for sale to existing shareholders or to other investors or members of the public; the shares that it offers

**ˈshare ˌoffer** (*BrE*) (*AmE* **ˈstock ˌoffer**) *n.* [C] (*Finan.*) **1** = SHARE ISSUE **2** an occasion when one company tries to buy another by offering its own shares rather than money

**ˌshare of ˈvoice** *n.* [U; sing.] (*abbr* **SOV**) (*Market.*) the amount of money that one company spends on advertising a brand in a particular period compared with other companies selling similar products

**ˈshare ˌoption** (*BrE*) (*AmE* **ˈstock ˌoption**) *n.* [C] **1** (*Finan.; HR*) a right that is given to employees to buy shares in the company at a low price: *a ~ plan/scheme/package* **2** (*Finan.*) a right, which can be bought and sold, to buy or sell shares in a company at a fixed price by or on a particular date

**ˈshare-out** *n.* [C, usu. sing.] (*BrE*) an act of dividing sth between two or more people; the amount of sth that one person receives

**shareowner** /ˈʃeərəʊnə(r); *AmE* ˈʃeroʊ-/ *n.* [C] (*Finan.*) a person or company that owns shares in a business SYN SHAREHOLDER

**ˈshare ˌpremium** *n.* [C] (*BrE*) (*Finan.*) the difference between the value stated on shares that a company issues and the higher amount it receives for them

**ˈshare price** (*BrE*) (*AmE* **ˈstock price**) *n.* [C] (*Stock Ex.*) the price at which a company's shares are bought and sold at a particular time

**ˈshare ˌregister** = SHAREHOLDERS' REGISTER

**ˌshares outˈstanding** = OUTSTANDING SHARES

**ˈshare split** *n.* [C] (*BrE*) (*Finan.*) an occasion when a company divides its SHARE CAPITAL into more shares in order to lower the price of each share. People who already have shares are given a number of new ones according to how many they hold: *The bank is planning a four-for-one share split.* SYN STOCK SPLIT

**shareware** /ˈʃeəweə(r); *AmE* ˈʃerwer/ *n.* [U] (*IT*) software that is available free for a user to test, after which they must pay if they wish to continue using it

**shark** /ʃɑːk; *AmE* ʃɑːrk/ *n.* [C] (*infml.*) **1** a person who is dishonest in business, esp. sb who gives bad advice and gets people to pay too much for sth **2** a company that tries to take over another company that does not want to be taken over

**ˈshark reˌpellent** *n.* [U,C] (*esp. AmE*) (*infml.*) action that a company takes to make it less attractive as the object of a takeover

**'shark ˌwatcher** *n.* [C] (*esp. AmE*) (*infml.*) a person or company whose job is to warn and help a company if sb has bought a lot of its shares and may try to take it over

**sharp** /ʃɑːp; *AmE* ʃɑːrp/ *adj.* (**-er**, **-est**) **1** (esp. about a change in sth) sudden and rapid: *There was a sharp increase in sales in July.* **2** (about people or their minds) quick to notice or understand things or to react: *He has a sharp business brain.* **3** (about a person or their way of doing business) clever but possibly dishonest: ***sharp practice*** *from competing companies* ▸ **'sharply** *adv.* **'sharpness** *n.* [U,C] IDM **the 'sharp end (of sth)** (*BrE*) (*infml.*) the place or position of greatest difficulty or responsibility: *a salesman working at the sharp end of the business*

**shed** /ʃed/ *v.*, *n.*

• *v.* [T] (**shedding, shed, shed**) (*often used in newspapers*) **1** to get rid of sth that is no longer wanted: *shedding jobs* **2** (about shares) to lose value: *The shares shed 6%.*

• *n.* [C] (*BrE*) a large industrial building used for working in or keeping equipment

**sheet** /ʃiːt/ *n.* [C] **1** a piece of paper for writing or printing on, etc., usu. in a standard size: *an information sheet* **2** a flat thin piece of any material, normally square or similar in shape: *a ~ of glass/steel* IDM **ˌsing from the same 'hymn sheet/'song sheet** to show that you are in agreement with each other by saying the same things in public

**'sheet feed** *n.* [C] a device that pushes pieces of paper into a printer separately

**shelf** /ʃelf/ *n.* [C] (*pl.* **shelves** /ʃelvz/) a flat board, made of wood, metal, glass, etc. fixed to the wall or forming part of a piece of furniture for things to be placed on: *The book was on the top shelf.* ◇ *stores with well-stocked shelves* ◇ *to fill/refill/restock/stack the shelves* ◇ *competition for tight shelf space in supermarkets* IDM **fly/leap/walk off the 'shelves** to sell extremely well **off the 'shelf** that can be bought immediately and does not have to be specially designed or ordered: *off-the-shelf software packages*

**'shelf ˌcompany** (*also* **ˌoff-the-'shelf ˌcompany**) *n.* [C] a company that has been formed but not used, so that it can be sold to sb who wants to start a company immediately or to give the impression that their company has existed for a few years

**'shelf-ˌfiller** = SHELF-STACKER

**'shelf life** *n.* [C, usu. sing.] (*Comm.*) **1** the length of time that a product remains in good condition after it is made and can be sold: *Canned food has a shelf life of two years or more.* **2** the length of time that people will buy a product after it is first available

**'shelf ˌoffering** *n.* [C] (*Finan.*) in the US, an occasion when a company offers for sale some of the shares, bonds, etc. that have already been prepared in a SHELF REGISTRATION

**'shelf regisˌtration** *n.* [C] (*Finan.*) in the US, an arrangement in which larger companies can get permission to issue shares, bonds, etc. at some time within a two year period if they need money

**'shelf-ˌstacker** (*also* **'shelf-ˌfiller**) *n.* [C] a person whose job is to fill shelves with goods to be sold, esp. in a supermarket

**'shelf ˌtalker** (*also* **'shelf ˌwobbler**) *n.* [C] (*Market.*, *infml.*) a printed advertisement hung over the edge of a shelf in a shop/store to make people notice a particular product

**shell** /ʃel/ *n.*, *v.*

• *n.* [C] **1** a structure that forms a hard outer frame: *the body shell of a car* **2** = SHELL COMPANY

• *v.* PHR V **ˌshell (sth) 'out (for sth)** (*infml.*) to pay a lot of money for sth SYN FORK OUT

**'shell ˌcompany** (*AmE also* **'shell corpoˌration**) (*also* **shell**, **'cash shell**, *BrE*, *AmE*) *n.* [C] a company that has been formed but does not really do any business, often for legal reasons. It can be used by its owners to do some business deals or sometimes to hide illegal activities.

**shelving** /'ʃelvɪŋ/ *n.* [U] shelves; material for making shelves

**'sheriff's sale** *n.* [C] (*AmE*) (*Law*) an occasion when a court orders that sb's property should be sold to the public because they have not paid money that they owe

**shift** /ʃɪft/ *n.*, *v.*

• *n.* **1** [C] a change in position or direction: *the shift from a manufacturing to a service economy* ⊙ *a* ***dramatic/fundamental/major*** *~* ♦ *a ~* ***away from/towards*** *sth* **2** (*HR*) [C] a period of time worked by a group of workers who start work as another group finishes: *to be on/do the day/night ~* ◇ *to work eight-hour shifts* ◇ *We work* **in** *shifts.* ⊙ *the* ***early/evening/late*** *~* ♦ *to* ***change*** *~s* ♦ *a ~* ***supervisor/worker***

**3** (*HR*) [C with sing./pl. v.] the workers who work a particular **shift**: *What time does the day shift come on?*
**4** [C,U] (*also* **'shift key** [C]) a key on a computer keyboard that allows capital letters or a different set of characters to be keyed
• *v.* **1** (*infml.*) [T] to move sth from one position or place to another: *They are shifting their production to China.* **2** [I] (about a situation, an opinion, a policy, etc.) to change from one state, position, etc. to another: *Consumer tastes are constantly shifting.* **3** [T] to change your opinion of or your attitude towards sth; to change the way that you do sth
**4** (*Comm., infml.*) [T] to sell goods, esp. goods that are difficult to sell: *They cut prices to try and shift stock.*

**'shift key** = SHIFT *n.* (4)

**shingle** /'ʃɪŋgl/ *n.* [C] (*AmE*) a sign outside a doctor's or lawyer's office that gives their name, etc.

★**ship** /ʃɪp/ *n., v.*
• *n.* [C] a large boat that carries people or goods by sea: *Goods are placed **on board ship** by the seller.*
⊕ *to **load (sth onto)/unload (sth from)** a ~ • a ~ **loads/unloads** (sth)*
*• a **cargo/container/merchant** ~*
IDM **abandon/jump 'ship** to leave an organization suddenly or unexpectedly because you think it is going to fail → idiom at RUN *v.*
• *v.* (-pp-) **1** (*Transpt.*) [T] to send or transport sth by ship: *We ship goods all over the world.* **2** (*Comm.; Transpt.*) [T,I] to send goods by air, road or rail: *Goods can be shipped or collected from the store.* **3** (*Comm.*) [T,I] to be available, or to make sth available, to be bought: *The software will be shipping next month.*
▸ **ˌshipper** *n.* [C]: *The shipper will pay transportation costs.*
→ idiom at SHAPE

**shipbuilder** /'ʃɪpbɪldə(r)/ *n.* [C] a person or company that builds ships
▸ **'shipbuilding** *n.* [U]

**'ship date** *n.* [C] (*Product.*) the date on which goods must be sent to a customer

★**shipment** /'ʃɪpmənt/ *n.* (*Comm.; Transpt.*) **1** [C] a load of goods that are sent from one place to another: *You can track your shipment online.*
SYN CONSIGNMENT
⊕ *to **deliver/send** a ~ • to **accept/receive/sign for** a ~*
**2** [U] the process of sending goods from one place to another: *The goods are ready for shipment.* ◇ *~ charges/costs*

**shipping** /'ʃɪpɪŋ/ *n.* [U] **1** (*Comm.; Transpt.*) the activity of carrying goods from one place to another by ship or by air, road or rail: *We offer free shipping for orders over $99.*
⊕ *a ~ **company/group/line** • ~ **charges/costs/rates** • a ~ **clerk***
**2** (*Transpt.*) ships in general or considered as a group: *The canal is open to shipping.*

**ˌshipping and 'forwarding ˌagent** *n.* [C] (*Transpt.*) a person or company that arranges for goods to be sent from one country to another by sea, air, rail or road, arranges insurance and prepares the necessary documents

**ˌshipping and 'handling** *n.* [U] (*abbr* **s and h**) (*Comm.; Transpt.*) the packing and transport of goods; the charge for this: *$20 plus $4 s and h*

**'shipping ˌdocuments** *n.* [pl.] (*Trade; Transpt.*) the documents that are needed when goods are sent from one country to another, including a BILL OF LADING or an air WAYBILL, an insurance certificate, a commercial INVOICE, an export licence, etc.

**'shipping note** *n.* [C] (*abbr* **S/N**) (*Transpt.*) a document prepared and signed by an exporter when sending goods by sea, giving details of the goods

**shoot** /ʃu:t/ *v.* [I] (**shot, shot** /ʃɒt; *AmE* ʃɑ:t/) (*with an adv. or a prep.*)
**1** to increase very quickly: *Profits shot up 40% last year.* **2** to become important, powerful, famous, etc. suddenly or quickly: *She will shoot to the top of the company.*
PHRV **'shoot for sth** (*AmE*) to try to achieve or get sth, esp. sth difficult: *shooting for a pay raise*

★**shop** /ʃɒp; *AmE* ʃɑ:p/ *n., v.*
• *n.* [C] **1** (*esp. BrE*) a building or part of a building where you can buy goods or services: *a chain of electrical shops* ◇ *airport retail shops*
⊕ *a **high-street/local** ~ • to **have/own/run/set up** a ~ • to **close (down)/open (up)/shut (down)** a ~ • a ~ **closes (down)/opens (up)/shuts (down)***
**2** (*esp. with other ns*) a place where things are made or repaired, esp. part of a factory where a particular type of work is done: *a repair shop* ◇ *a paint shop* (= where cars are painted) SYN WORKSHOP **3** (*infml.*) [usu. sing.] (*BrE*) an act of going shopping, esp. for food and other items needed in the house: *We do a weekly shop at the supermarket.* IDM **mind the 'shop** (*BrE*) (*AmE* **mind the 'store**) to be in charge of sth for a short time while sb is away **ˌset up 'shop** to

start a business → idioms at SHUT *v.*, TALK *v.*

• *v.* (-**pp**-) **1** [I] to buy things in shops/stores: *shopping for food* ◇ *to shop at the local market* **2 go shopping** [I] to spend time going to shops/stores and looking for things to buy **3** [T] (*AmE*) to buy things at a particular shop/store: *Thank you for shopping Land's End.* **4** [T] (*AmE*) to try to sell sth such as a company by talking about it to people who might buy it: *The owner is shopping the company.* **PHRV** ˌ**shop aˈround** to compare the quality or prices of goods or services that are offered by different shops/stores, companies, etc. so that you can choose the best: *Shop around for the best deal.*

**ˈshop asˌsistant** *n.* [C] (*BrE*) a person whose job is to serve customers in a shop/store **SYN** ASSISTANT, SALES ASSISTANT

**shopfitting** /ˈʃɒpfɪtɪŋ; *AmE* ˈʃɑːp-/ *n.* [U] the business of putting equipment and furniture into shops/stores ▸ **ˈshopfitter** *n.* [C]

**the ˌshop ˈfloor** *n.* [sing.] **1** the area in a factory where the goods are made: *to work **on** the shop floor* **2** (*HR*) the workers in a factory, not the managers ▸ **ˈshop-floor** *adj.*

**shopfront** /ˈʃɒpfrʌnt; *AmE* ˈʃɑːp-/ *n.* [C] (*BrE*) **1** the front of a shop: *a shopfront sign* **2** (*E-comm.*) (*also* ˌ**web ˈshopfront**) a website that a company uses to sell goods or services

**shopkeeper** /ˈʃɒpkiːpə(r); *AmE* ˈʃɑːp-/ (*esp. BrE*) (*AmE usu.* **ˈstorekeeper**) *n.* [C] sb who owns or manages a shop/store, esp. a small one

**shoplifting** /ˈʃɒplɪftɪŋ; *AmE* ˈʃɑːp-/ *n.* [U] the crime of stealing goods from a shop/store by deliberately leaving without paying ▸ **ˈshoplift** *v.* [T,I] **ˈshoplifter** *n.* [C]

**shopper** /ˈʃɒpə(r); *AmE* ˈʃɑːp-/ *n.* [C] a person who buys goods from shops/stores: *big savings for shoppers* ⊙ ***home/last-minute/online*** ~s ◆ ***to attract/draw in/lure/woo*** ~s ◆ ~s ***buy/choose/look for/pay for*** *sth*

**shopping** /ˈʃɒpɪŋ; *AmE* ˈʃɑːp-/ *n.* [U] **1** the activity of going to shops/stores and buying things: (*BrE*) *to do the/your* ~ ⊙ *a* ~ ***bag/basket/cart/trolley*** ◆ ***catalogue/Internet/online*** ~ ◆ *a* ~ ***expedition/spree/trip*** **2** (*esp. BrE*) the things that you have bought from shops/stores: *to put your shopping away*

**ˈshopping bot** (*also* **ˈshopping ˌagent**) *n.* [C] (*E-comm.*) a piece of software that searches for products that are being sold on the Internet and compares prices

**ˈshopping ˌcentre** *n.* [C] (*esp. BrE*) a group of shops/stores built together, sometimes under one roof

**ˈshopping goods** (*also* **ˈshopping ˌproducts**) *n.* [pl.] (*Comm.*) items that people do not buy very frequently, such as furniture and clothes, and like to compare in quality and price before they buy

**ˈshopping list** *n.* [C] a list that you make of all the things that you need to buy when you go shopping: (*fig.*) *The group has put the supermarket chain on its shopping list* (= it wants to buy the company).

**ˈshopping mall** (*also* **mall**) (*both esp. AmE*) *n.* [C] a large group of shops/stores, restaurants, etc. built together under one roof and closed to traffic

**ˈshopping ˌproducts** = SHOPPING GOODS

**ˈshop-soiled** (*BrE*) (*AmE* **ˈshop-worn**) *adj.* (*Comm.*) **shop-soiled** goods are dirty or not in good condition because they have been in a shop/store for a long time

**ˌshop ˈsteward** *n.* [C] (*esp. BrE*) (*HR*) a person who is elected by members of a union in a factory or company to represent them in meetings with managers

**shopworn** /ˈʃɒpwɔːn; *AmE* ˈʃɑːpwɔːrn/ = SHOP-SOILED

**shore** /ʃɔː(r)/ *v.* **PHRV** ˌ**shore sth ˈup** to help to support sth that is weak or going to fail: *They had to sell assets to shore up the balance sheet.*

★ **short** /ʃɔːt; *AmE* ʃɔːrt/ *adj., adv., v.*

• *adj.* **HELP** The forms **shorter** and **shortest** are not usu. used in these meanings. **1** ~ **of sth** not having enough of sth: *She never seems to be short of cash!* **2** not easily available; not supplying as much as you need: *Time is getting short.* **3** (*infml.*) ~ **on sth** lacking or not having enough of a particular quality: *The industry is short on good leadership.* **4** ~ **(of sth)** less than the number, amount, weight, etc. mentioned or needed: *We're still two people short on the project.* **5** ~ **(for sth)** being a shorter form of a name or word: *'Co' is short for 'company'.* **6** (*Finan.*; *Stock Ex.*) relating to the situation when sb sells shares, currencies, etc. that they do not yet own, in the hope that their price will fall and they will make a profit by buying them later at a lower price: *investors who are **short on stock*** **OPP** LONG **IDM** **at short ˈno-**

tice (*AmE also* **on short 'notice**)**at a moment's 'notice** not long in advance; without much warning or time for preparation: *The meeting was called at very short notice.* **in ˌshort sup'ply** if something is **in short supply** there is not enough of it available **on short 'notice** (*esp. AmE*) = AT SHORT NOTICE → idiom at SHORT RUN

• ***adv.*** **HELP** The forms **shorter** and **shortest** are not usu. used in these meanings. **1** if you **go/run short of** sth, you do not have enough of it **2** (*Finan.; Stock Ex.*) if you **sell** sth **short** or **go short** (on sth), you sell shares, currencies, etc. that you do not yet own, hoping that their price will fall and you will make a profit by buying them later at a lower price → idioms at FALL *V.*, RUN *V.*

• ***v.*** [T,I] (*Finan.; Stock Ex.*) to agree to sell shares, currencies, etc. that you do not yet own, in the hope that their price will fall and you will make a profit by buying them later at a lower price: *You have to be able to borrow shares to short them.*

★**shortage** /'ʃɔːtɪdʒ; *AmE* 'ʃɔːrt-/ *n.* [C,U] a situation when there is not enough of the people or things that are needed: *a ~ of funds/space* OPP GLUT

⊕ *an* ***acute***/*a* ***chronic/serious/severe*** *~ • a* ***cash/parts/labour/skills*** *~ • to* ***face/suffer*** *a ~ • to* ***cause/create/lead to*** *a ~ • to* ***ease/prevent*** *a ~*

**ˌshort-'change** *v.* [T] (*often pass.*) **1** to give back less than the correct amount of money to sb who has paid for sth with more than the exact price: *I've been short-changed!* **2** to treat sb unfairly by not giving them what they have earned or deserve: *Poor after-sales service can leave customers feeling short-changed.*

**ˌshort 'covering** *n.* [U] (*Stock Ex.*) the process of sb borrowing or buying shares, bonds, etc. in order to replace the ones that they have sold or agreed to sell but did not own

**shortfall** /'ʃɔːtfɔːl; *AmE* 'ʃɔːrt-/ *n.* [C] if there is a **shortfall in** sth, there is less of it than you need or expect: *They are selling assets to make up a shortfall in profits.*

⊕ *to* ***compensate for/cover/meet*** *a ~ • a* ***funding/profit/revenue*** *~ • an* ***order***/*a* ***production*** *~ • a* ***big/significant/small*** *~*

**shorthand** /'ʃɔːthænd; *AmE* 'ʃɔːrt-/ *n.* **1** (*AmE also* **ste'nography**) [U] a quick way of writing using special signs or short forms of words, used esp. to record what sb is saying: *to take sth down* **in** *shorthand* **2** [U,C] **~ (for sth)** a shorter way of saying or referring to sth

**ˌshort-'handed** *adj.* [not usu. before n.] not having as many workers or people who can help as you need SYN SHORT-STAFFED

**ˌshorthand 'typist** (*BrE*) (*also* **ste'nographer**) (*also* **'steno**, *infml.*) (*both AmE*) *n.* [C] a person whose job is to write down what sb says using **shorthand**, then write it on a computer or type it

**'short-haul** *adj.* that involves transporting people or goods over short distances: *~ flights/trucking*

**shorting** /'ʃɔːtɪŋ; *AmE* 'ʃɔːrt-/ = SHORT SELLING

**shortlist** /'ʃɔːtlɪst; *AmE* 'ʃɔːrt-/ *n.*, *v.* (*HR*)

• ***n.*** (*AmE also* **short list**) [C] a small number of candidates for a job who have been chosen from all the people who applied: *to draw up a shortlist*

• ***v.*** (*AmE also* **short-list**) [T] (*usu. pass.*) to put sb/sth on a **shortlist**

**'short poˌsition** *n.* [C] (*Finan.; Stock Ex.*) a situation in which an investor sells or agrees to sell shares, currencies, etc. that he/she does not own yet, hoping that the price will fall and they will make a profit by buying them later at a lower price: *to take/cover a ~* SYN BEAR POSITION

**ˌshort-'range** *adj.* connected with a short period of time in the future: *short-range plans*

**ˌshort 'run** (*also* **ˌshort 'term**) *n.* [sing.] (*Econ.*) the period during which a business or an industry can change the quantity of some of the things that are needed in order to produce goods or services, but at least one is fixed **IDM** **in the 'short run**; **in the 'short term** concerning the immediate future: *A deal is unlikely in the short term.*

**'short-run** = SHORT-TERM (1)

**shorts** /ʃɔːts; *AmE* ʃɔːrts/ *n.* [pl.] (*Finan.*) **1** investments such as bonds that are due to be paid back in a short time, usu. less than five years **2** shares that a dealer has borrowed and sold but does not yet own

**ˌshort 'selling** (*also* **'shorting**) *n.* [U] (*Finan.; Stock Ex.*) the act of selling or agreeing to sell shares, currencies, etc. that you do not yet own, hoping that the price will fall and you will make a profit by buying them later at a lower price ▶ **ˌshort 'sale** *n.* [C] **ˌshort 'seller** *n.* [C]

**ˌshort-'staffed** *adj.* [not usu. before n.] having fewer members of staff than you need or usu. have SYN SHORT-HANDED

**ˌshort ˈterm** = SHORT RUN

**ˈshort-term** *adj.* **1** (*also* **ˈshort-run**) lasting a short time; lasting only for a short period of time in the future: *short-term contracts* **2** (*Finan.*) (about money) that is borrowed, lent or invested for a short period of time, usu. one year SYN NEAR-TERM

**ˌshort-ˈtermism** *n.* [U] a way of thinking or planning that is concerned with the advantages or profits you could have now, rather than the effects in the future

**ˌshort-term liaˈbilities** = CURRENT LIABILITY

**ˌshort ˈtime** *n.* [U] (*BrE*) (*HR*) a situation in which workers work fewer hours than usual when there are not enough orders, materials, etc., so that they can keep their jobs: *Staff have been put* ***on*** *short time.*

**ˌshort ˈton** (*abbr* **st.**) (*also* **ˌnet ˈton**) (*both esp. AmE*) *n.* [C] a unit of weight equal to 907.18 kilograms or 2 000 pounds

**shovelware** /ˈʃʌvlweə(r); *AmE* -wer/ *n.* [U] (*IT*) content that is taken from, for example, printed material, and put on a website as quickly as possible without changing it to suit the Internet

**show** /ʃəʊ; *AmE* ʃoʊ/ *n.* [C,U] an occasion when people, businesses, etc. show and sell their goods and services: *a trade show* IDM **show of ˈhands** a way of voting in which people at a meeting raise their hands to show if they agree with sth or are against it

**showcase** /ˈʃəʊkeɪs; *AmE* ˈʃoʊ-/ *n.* **1** [C, usu. sing.] an event that presents sb's abilities or the good qualities of sth in an attractive way: *The exhibition is a showcase* ***for*** *young designers.* **2** [C] a box with a glass top or sides used for showing objects in a shop/store, etc. ▶ **ˈshowcase** *v.* [T]: *to showcase new products*

**showroom** /ˈʃəʊruːm; -rʊm; *AmE* ˈʃoʊ-/ *n.* [C] a large shop/store in which goods for sale, esp. cars and electrical goods, are displayed

**shred** /ʃred/ *v.* [T] (**-dd-**) to cut sth into small pieces: *We shred old documents.* ▶ **ˌshredder** *n.* [C]: *We bought a document shredder.*

**shrewd** /ʃruːd/ *adj.* (**-er, -est**) **1** clever at understanding and making judgements about a situation: *a shrewd businesswoman* **2** showing good judgement and likely to be right: *a shrewd guess* ▶ **ˈshrewdly** *adv.* **ˈshrewdness** *n.* [U]

**shrink** /ʃrɪŋk/ *v.* [T,I] (**shrank** /ʃræŋk/**shrunk** /ʃrʌŋk/ *or* **shrunk**, **shrunk**) to become or to make sth smaller in size or amount: *The market for these cars is shrinking.*

**shrinkage** /ˈʃrɪŋkɪdʒ/ *n.* [U] **1** the process of becoming smaller in size; the amount by which sth becomes smaller: *The T-shirts are sized to allow for shrinkage.* **2** (*Comm.*) (*also* **ˈleakage**) the amount of goods that a business loses because they have been damaged, stolen, etc.

**ˈshrink-wrap** *v.* [T] to wrap sth tightly in a thin plastic covering: *Cans come shrink-wrapped in packs of six.* ▶ **ˈshrink-wrap** *n.* [U]: *The book and CD are packaged in shrink-wrap.* **ˈshrink-ˌwrapping** *n.* [U]

**SHRM** /ˌes eɪtʃ ɑːr ˈem/ = STRATEGIC HUMAN RESOURCE MANAGEMENT

**shuffle** /ˈʃʌfl/ = RESHUFFLE

**shut** /ʃʌt/ *v., adj.*

• ***v.*** [T,I] (**shutting, shut, shut**) **1** when a shop/store, restaurant, etc. **shuts** or when sb **shuts** it, it stops being open for business and you cannot go into it: *We shut at six.* **2** when a business **shuts** or when sb **shuts** it, it stops operating as a business: *We have had to shut several factories.* IDM **shut up ˈshop** (*BrE*) (*infml.*) to close a business permanently or to stop working for the day

PHR V **ˌshut ˈdown** (about a factory, shop/store, etc. or a machine) to stop opening for business; to stop working **ˌshut sth ˈdown** to stop a factory, shop/store, etc. from opening for business; to stop a machine from working **ˌshut ˈoff** (about a machine, tool, etc.) to stop working: *The engines shut off automatically.* **ˌshut sth ˈoff 1** to stop a machine, tool, etc. from working **2** to stop a supply of electricity, gas, etc. from flowing or reaching a place: *Have you shut off the power?*

• ***adj.*** not open for business: *Is the bank shut?*

**shutdown** /ˈʃʌtdaʊn/ *n.* [C,U] **1** the act of closing a factory or business: *factory shutdowns* **2** the act of stopping a computer or large machine from working: *My PC freezes on shutdown.*

**shuttle** /ˈʃʌtl/ *n.* [C] a plane, bus or train that travels regularly between two places: *a shuttle service*

**SI** /ˌes ˈaɪ/ *abbr* International System (used to describe units of measurement): *SI units such as the metre*

**SIBOR** /ˈsiːbɔː(r)/ *abbr* **Singapore Inter-Bank Offered Rate** the rate at which banks lend money to other banks in Singapore, which is used as a measure of LENDING RATES in Asia

**sick** /sɪk/ *adj.* **1** ill: (*BrE*) *to be* ***off sick*** (= away from work because you are ill) ◇ (*AmE*) *to be* ***out sick*** ◇ *to* ***call in sick*** (= phone to say you are ill and will not be coming to work) **2** (about an organization, a system, etc.) having serious problems: *a sick economy*

**ˌsick ˈbuilding ˌsyndrome** *n.* [U] a set of physical conditions that are not caused by a known illness but seem to be caused by spending time in a particular building

**ˈsick day** *n.* [C] (*HR*) a day when an employee does not work because they are ill/sick

**sickie** /ˈsɪki/ *n.* [C] (*BrE*) (*infml.*) a day when you say that you are ill/ sick and cannot go to work when it is not really true: *to* ***have/pull/take/ throw*** *a* ~

**ˈsick leave** *n.* [U] (*HR*) permission to be away from work because of illness; the period of time spent away from work: *to be* ***on*** *sick leave*

**ˈsickness ˌbenefit** *n.* [U,C] money paid by the government to people who are away from work because they are sick/ill

**ˈsick note** (*BrE*) (*AmE* **exˈcuse**) *n.* [C] (*HR*) a letter that an employee gets from a doctor to say that they are or have been too ill/sick to go to work

**ˈsickout** (*also* **sick-out**) /ˈsɪkaʊt/ *n.* [C] (*AmE*) (*HR*) an occasion when workers protest against sth by staying away from work and saying they are ill/sick when really they are not: *Bus drivers are staging a sickout.*

**ˈsick pay** *n.* [U] (*HR*) pay given to an employee who is away from work because of illness

**side** /saɪd/ *n.* [C] **1** one of the two or more people or groups taking part in an argument, a discussion, etc: *an agreement acceptable to all sides* **2** one of the opinions, attitudes or positions held by sb in a business arrangement, an argument, etc: *Will they keep their side of the bargain?* **3** (*infml.*) a particular aspect of a job or a company's business: *He works on the sales and marketing side.* **4** one of the two parts of a financial account: *the credit/debit* ~

**sidebar** /ˈsaɪdbɑː(r)/ *n.* [C] (*IT*) a narrow section on the left side of a web page

**sideline** /ˈsaɪdlaɪn/ *n.* [C] an activity that sb does as well as their main activity in order to earn extra money

**SIG** /sɪg/ *abbr* (*IT*) **special interest group** a place in a computing system, esp. the Internet, where people can discuss a particular subject and exchange information about it

**ˈsig file** *n.* [C] (*IT, infml.*) **signature file** a short personal message that can be automatically added at the end of emails showing who has sent it

**ˈsight bill** *n.* [C] (*Finan.*) a BILL OF EXCHANGE that must be paid immediately

**ˈsight deˌposit** (*also* **deˈmand deˌposit**) *n.* [C, usu. pl.] (*Finan.*) money kept in a bank on the basis that it can be taken out at any time

**ˈsight draft** *n.* [C] (*Finan.*) a **draft** that must be paid immediately

**ˌsight unˈseen** *adv.* (*Comm.*) if you buy sth **sight unseen**, you cannot see it before you buy it

**sign** /saɪn/ *n., v.*

• ***n.*** [C] **1** a piece of paper, wood, metal, etc. that has writing or a picture on it that gives you information, instructions, a warning, etc: *flashing neon signs* ◇ *a sign board* **2** a mark used to represent sth: *a euro/ dollar* ~ *(€/$)*

• ***v.*** [T,I] to write your name on a document, letter, etc. to show that you have written it, that you agree with what it says, or that it is genuine: *Sign here, please.* ◇ *to* ~ *a cheque/contract/deal* **IDM** **ˌsigned and ˈsealed**; **ˈsigned, ˈsealed and deˈlivered** definite, because all the legal documents have been signed **sign on the dotted ˈline** (*infml.*) to sign a document to show that you have agreed to do sth or buy sth **PHR V** **ˈsign for sth** to sign a document to show that you have received sth **ˌsign (sb) ˈin/ˈout** to write your name or the name of a guest when you arrive at or leave an office **ˌsign (sth) ˈoff** to end a letter, etc: *I usually sign off with 'regards'.* **ˌsign sth ˈoff** to give your formal approval to sth, by signing your name: *to sign off the accounts* **ˌsign ˈoff on sth** (*AmE*) (*infml.*) to express your approval of sth formally and definitely **ˌsign ˈon** (*BrE*) (*infml.*) to sign a form stating that you are unemployed so that you can receive payment from the government **ˌsign (sb) ˈon/ˈup** to sign a form or contract which says that you agree to work for sb, do a deal, etc.; to persuade sb to sign a form or contract like this **ˌsign (sb) ˈout** → SIGN (SB) IN/OUT **ˌsign (sb) ˈup (for sth)** **1** to arrange to receive or do sth: *Sign up for our monthly email newsletter.* **2** = SIGN (SB) ON/UP: *She's signed up with an employment agency.*

**signage** /ˈsaɪnɪdʒ/ *n.* [U] a sign or signs that advertise a product, show the name of a shop/store, etc.

**signatory** /ˈsɪɡnətri; *AmE* -tɔːri/ *n.* [C] (*pl.* **-ries**) (*fml.*) **~ (to/of sth)** a person, a country or an organization that signs an official agreement

**signature** /ˈsɪɡnətʃə(r)/ *n.* **1** [C] your name as you usu. write it, for example at the end of a letter: *The cheque requires two signatures.* **2** [U] (*fml.*) the act of signing sth: *The contract will be sent to you for signature.* **3** [C, usu. sing.] a particular quality, product, phrase, etc. that makes sth different from other similar things and makes it easy to recognize: *the company's signature shoes and bags*

**ˈsignature brand** *n.* [C] (*Market.*) **1** a range of products that is the most famous thing made by a particular company **2** a product or range of products that have the name of a famous person on them: *Calvin Klein signature brand sunglasses*

**ˈsignature loan** *n.* [C] (*Finan.*) money that is lent to sb without any SECURITY except that the borrower signs a document

**ˈsign-up** *n.* **1** [U] the act of saying that you want to join sth, receive sth, etc. by adding your name to a list **2** [C] a person who adds their name to a list in order to join sth, receive sth, etc: *new sign-ups for the service*

**ˌsilent ˈpartner** = SLEEPING PARTNER

**silicon** /ˈsɪlɪkən/ *n.* [U] a chemical element that is used in making TRANSISTORS and glass

**ˌSilicon ˈAlley** *n.* [U] an area of New York where many Internet companies started in business in the 1990s

**ˌsilicon ˈchip** *n.* [C] a very small piece of **silicon** used to carry a complicated electronic CIRCUIT

**ˌSilicon ˈValley** *n.* [U] an area in California where there are many computer and HIGH-TECH companies

**ˌsilver ˈmarket** = GREY MARKET (3)

**ˌsilver ˈsurfer** *n.* [C] (*infml.*) an older person who spends a lot of time using the Internet

**sim** /sɪm/ *n.* [C] (*infml.*) a computer or video game that SIMULATES an activity such as flying a plane or managing a business

**ˈSIM card** /sɪm/ *n.* [C] a plastic card inside a mobile phone/cellphone that stores personal information

**ˌsimple ˈinterest** *n.* [U] (*Account.*) interest that is calculated only on the original amount of money lent or borrowed, and not on any interest that it has earned

**simulation** /ˌsɪmjuˈleɪʃn/ *n.* [C,U] a situation in which a particular set of conditions is created artificially in order to study or experience sth that could exist in reality: *a business simulation* ◇ *a computer simulation of the new building*
▸ **ˈsimulate** /-leɪt/ *v.* [T]

**simulˌtaneous engiˈneering** = CONCURRENT ENGINEERING

**sincerely** /sɪnˈsɪəli; *AmE* -ˈsɪrli/ *adv.* **IDM** **Yours sincerely** (*BrE*) (*AmE* **Sincerely (yours)**) used at the end of a formal letter before you sign your name, when you have addressed sb by their name

**sinecure** /ˈsɪnɪkjʊə(r); ˈsaɪn-; *AmE* -kjʊr/ *n.* [C] (*fml.*) a job that you are paid for even though it involves little or no work

**sine die** /ˌsɪneɪ ˈdiːeɪ; ˌsaɪni ˈdaɪiː/ *adv.* (*Law or fml.*) without a future date being arranged

**sine qua non** /ˌsɪneɪ kwɑː ˈnəʊn; ˌsaɪni; *AmE* ˈnoʊn/ *n.* [sing.] (*fml.*) something that is essential before you can achieve sth else

**ˌsingle column ˈcentimetre** (*AmE* **- centimeter**) (*abbr* **SCC**) (*also* **ˌsingle column ˈinch** *abbr* **SCI**) *n.* [C] a unit used for measuring advertising space in a newspaper or magazine

**ˌsingle ˈdigits**, **ˌsingle-ˈdigit** = SINGLE FIGURES

**ˌsingle-entry ˈbookkeeping** *n.* [U] (*Account.*) a way of keeping a company's financial records, in which each amount spent, received, etc. is recorded in only one account

**ˌsingle ˈfigures** (*esp. BrE*) (*AmE usu.* **ˌsingle ˈdigits**) *n.* [pl.] a number less than ten: *Inflation is down to single figures.* ▸ **ˌsingle-ˈfigure** (*esp. BrE*) (*AmE usu.* **ˌsingle-ˈdigit**) *adj.*

**ˌsingle-ˈhanded** *adv.* on your own with nobody helping you: *She runs the company single-handed.*
▸ **ˌsingle-ˈhanded** *adj.* **ˌsingle-ˈhandedly** *adv.*

**ˌsingle ˈmarket** (*also* **inˌternal ˈmarket**) *n.* [C, usu. sing.] (*Econ.*) a group of countries that have few or no restrictions on the movement of goods, money and people between the members of the group

**ˈsingle ˈminute exˈchange of ˈdies** *phr.* (*abbr* **SMED**) (*Product.*) a technique for reducing the time needed to prepare a machine or a piece of equipment for a new task

**ˌsingle ˈsourcing** *n.* [U] **1** (*Product.*) the practice of buying all of a company's supplies of a particular item from one supplier **2** (*IT*) the use of information stored in one file to produce many different types of documents ▸ **ˌsingle-ˈsource** *v.* [T]: *Most of our raw materials are single-sourced.*

**ˌsingle ˈtax** *n.* [C] (*Econ.*) a system in which there is tax on only one kind of thing, for example on the value of land

**ˌsingle-ˈuse** /ˈjuːs/ *adj.* made to be used once only: *single-use cameras*

**sink** /sɪŋk/ *v.* (**sank** /sæŋk/**sunk** /sʌŋk/) *or, less frequent* (**sunk**, **sunk**) **1** [T,I] if a ship **sinks** or sb/sth **sinks** it, it is damaged and goes below the surface of the sea **2** [I] to decrease in amount, volume, strength, etc: *The pound has sunk to a new low.* **PHRV** **ˌsink sth ˈinto sth** to spend a lot of money on a business: *We sank all our savings into the venture.*

**ˈsinking fund** *n.* [C] (*Finan.*) money that a company keeps and adds to regularly in order to pay debts, pay for equipment, etc. at a fixed date in the future

**ˈsin tax** *n.* [C,U] (*infml.*) a tax on goods or services that many people consider bad, for example cigarettes and alcohol

**SIP** /ˌes aɪ ˈpiː; sɪp/ = SHARE INCENTIVE PLAN

**SIS** /ˌes aɪ ˈes/ = STRATEGIC INFORMATION SYSTEM

**ˈsister ˌcompany** *n.* [C] a company that is part of the same group, with the same PARENT COMPANY

**ˈsit-down** *n.* [C] **1** a strike or protest in which people sit down to block a road or the entrance to a building: *to hold/stage a ~* **2** a more formal meeting to discuss things: *to have a sit-down* ▸ **ˈsit-down** *adj.*: *a ~ strike/meeting*

**site** /saɪt/ *n., v.*

• *n.* [C] **1** a place where sth has been or will be built: *Hard hats must be worn* ***on site****.*

⊕ *a* ***good/prime/suitable*** *~ (for sth)* ♦ *a* ***brownfield/greenfield/protected*** *~* ♦ *a* ***building/construction*** *~*

**2** a place where a particular type of work takes place: *We will repair the machine* ***on site****.* ◇ *an industrial/ a manufacturing ~* **3** (*IT*) a place on the Internet where an organization puts information

⊕ *to* ***access/browse/search/visit*** *a ~* ♦ *to* ***build/create/host/set up*** *a ~*

• *v.* [T] (*often pass.*) to build or place sth in a particular position: *The plant will be sited close to the port.*

**ˈsit-in** *n.* [C] (*HR*) a protest in which a group of workers refuse to leave their place of work: *to hold/stage a ~*

**situˌational ˈinterview** *n.* [C] (*HR*) a type of interview for a job in which sb is asked what they would do in particular situations

**ˌsituˈation aˌnalysis** (*also* **ˌsituˈation ˌaudit**) *n.* [C,U] (*Market.*) the first stage in the process of planning marketing, in which an organization collects information and examines its strengths and weaknesses, the opportunities it has and the threats it faces

**ˌSituations ˈVacant** *n.* [U] (*BrE*) (*HR*) a section in a newspaper, on a website, etc., where jobs are advertised: *putting an ad in Situations Vacant*

**ˌSituations ˈWanted** *n.* [U] (*BrE*) (*HR*) a section in a newspaper, on a website, etc., where people who are looking for a job can advertise

**ˈsix-pack** *n.* [C] a set of six bottles or cans sold together

**ˌsix ˈsigma** (*also* **Six Sigma**) /ˈsɪgmə/ *n.* [U] (*Product.*) a system that aims to improve production processes so that almost all products are of perfect quality

**size** /saɪz/ *n., v.*

• *n.* [C] **1** one of a number of standard measurements in which clothes, shoes and other goods are made and sold: *What size do you* ***take****?* ◇ *I need a bigger/smaller ~.* ◇ *The glass can be cut* ***to size*** *for you.* **2** (*also* **-sized**) (in adjs) having the size mentioned: *a pocket-size camera* ◇ *a medium-sized market* **IDM** **ˌone size fits ˈall** **1** used to describe an item of clothing that can be worn by people of most sizes and shapes **2** used to describe a situation where one action, policy, solution, etc. is considered suitable for everybody

• *v.* [T] (*usu. pass.*) **1** to mark the size of sth; to give a size to sth: *The screws are sized in millimetres.* **2** to change the size of sth

**skeleton** /ˈskelɪtn/ *n.* [C] **1** the main structure that supports a building: *the concrete skeleton of the factory* **2** (*used as an adj.*) used to describe the smallest number of people, things or parts that you need to do sth: *a skeleton staff*

**skid** /skɪd/ *n.* [C] (*esp. AmE*) a raised wooden base onto which goods are loaded so that they can be easily moved or transported, esp. by a FORKLIFT

★**skill** /skɪl/ *n.* **1** [U] the ability to do sth well: *She manages her team **with** great skill.*
⊙ *to **need/require/take** ~ • to **have/lack** ~ (at/in sth)*
**2** [C] a particular ability, esp. one that needs training and experience to do well: *learning a practical skill ◇ a new set of skills ◇ a serious **skill shortage** in the industry*
⊙ ***business/social** ~s • **communication/interpersonal/management** ~s • **computer/technical** ~s • to **have/lack/possess** ~s • to **acquire/develop/improve/learn** ~s*

**skilled** /skɪld/ *adj.* **1** having the ability, experience and knowledge to be able to do sth well: *a ~ engineer/negotiator ◇ a shortage of **skilled labour*** **2** (about a job) needing special abilities or training

**'skill set** *n.* [C] a range of skills

**skim** /skɪm/ *v.* [T] (**-mm-**) **1** (*infml.*) to steal small amounts of money frequently over a period of time: *skimming money from the store's accounts* **2** (*infml.*) to illegally copy information that is stored electronically on a credit card in order to use it without the owner's permission: *I think my credit card was skimmed at a gas station.* IDM **skim the 'market** (*Market.*) to set the price for a new product high at first in order to make as much profit as possible and then lower it gradually to attract more customers PHR V **,skim sth/sb 'off** to remove the most valuable part of sth for yourself, often in an unfair way: *to skim off profits*

**skimming** /'skɪmɪŋ/ *n.* [U] **1** (*Market.*) (*also* **,market-skimming 'pricing**) the practice of setting the price for a new product high at first in order to make as much profit as possible and then lowering it gradually to attract more customers **2** (*Finan., infml.*) the illegal practice of not telling the government about part of your profits in order to avoid paying tax **3** (*infml.*) the illegal practice of copying information that is stored electronically on a credit card in order to use it without the owner's permission

**skive** /skaɪv/ *v.* [T,I] (*BrE*) (*infml.*) **~ (off)** to avoid work by pretending to be ill/sick or leaving early: *Have you been skiving again?* ▶ **'skiver** *n.* [C]

**SKU** /skjuː; ,es keɪ 'juː/ (*also* **'SKU ,number**) *n.* [C] (*Comm.*) **stock-keeping unit** a number or a group of numbers and letters used to identify a particular product that a shop/store sells; a product that has its own number

**'skunkworks** (*also* **skunk works**) /'skʌŋkwɜːks; *AmE* -wɜːrks/ *n.* **1** [C with sing./pl. v.] (*pl.* **skunkworks**) a part of a company that has the freedom to develop new products without being closely controlled by the company **2** [pl.] projects that this part of a company works on

**,sky-'high** *adj., adv.* extremely high; too high: *sky-high prices*

**skyrocket** /'skaɪrɒkɪt; *AmE* -rɑːk-/ *v.* [I] to go up very high and very fast: *Prices have skyrocketed.*

**skyscraper** /'skaɪskreɪpə(r)/ *n.* [C] a very tall building in a city

**SLA** /,es el 'eɪ/ *abbr* (*Comm.; IT*) **service level agreement** a written agreement between a supplier of a service and a customer stating what the supplier will provide, when it will be provided, the quality of what is provided, what it will cost, etc.

**slack** /slæk/ *adj., n., v.*
• ***adj.*** (**-er, -est**) **1** (about a business) not having many customers; not busy: *a slack period* **2** (about a person) not putting enough care, attention or energy into sth and so not doing it well enough ▶ **'slackly** *adv.* **'slackness** *n.* [U]
• ***n.*** [U] people, money, time or space that a company is not using fully: *There's very little slack in the budget.* IDM **pick/take up the 'slack** to do sth, supply sth, etc. that is needed but is not being done or supplied: *As desktop PC sales have fallen, laptops have taken up the slack.*
• ***v.*** [I] to work less hard than you usu. do or should do: *I've been slacking this week.* PHR V **,slack 'off (on sth)** to do sth more slowly or with less energy than before

**slacken** /'slækən/ *v.* [T,I] **~ (sth) (off)** to gradually become, or to make sth become, slower, less active, etc: *We've been busy, but things are starting to slacken off now.*
▶ **'slackening** [U]: *a slackening of demand for steel*

**slash** /slæʃ/ *v., n.*
• ***v.*** [T] (*often pass.*) (often used in newspapers) to reduce sth by a large amount: *to ~ costs/prices*
• ***n.*** [C] the symbol (/)

**sleeper** /'sliːpə(r)/ *n.* [C] (*esp. AmE*) (*infml.*) a share or sth such as a book or film/movie that is not successful immediately but then is suddenly a success

**,sleeping 'partner** (*BrE*) (*AmE* **,silent 'partner**) *n.* [C] sb who has invested money in a new company and has a right to a share of the profits but does not take part in managing it

**slice** /slaɪs/ *n.* [C] (*infml.*) a part or share of sth: *a 17% slice of the market* → idiom at ACTION

**slick** /slɪk/ *adj.* (**-er**, **-est**) **1** done in a way that is clever and efficient but is often not sincere or lacks important ideas: *a slick sales pitch* **2** (about a person) good at persuading people but probably not sincere **3** done, or doing things, quickly and with great skill: *a ~ deal/presentation*
▸ **'slickly** *adv.* **'slickness** *n.* [U]

**slide** *v., n.*
• *v.* [I] (**slid**, **slid** /slɪd/) **1 ~ (from ...) (to ...)** to become gradually lower or of less value: *Shares slid to a 10-year low.* **2** to move gradually into a worse situation: *The industry has slid* ***into*** *decline.*
• *n.* **1** [C, usu. sing.] a change to a lower value or worse condition: *a downward slide in the price of oil*
✪ *a* ***dramatic/sharp/steady/steep*** *~* ♦ *to* ***halt/prevent/stop*** *a ~*
**2** [C] a small piece of film held in a frame that can be shown on a screen when you shine a light through it: *a slide show* **3** [C] a single screen of information that is part of a presentation given using a computer: *Press F5 to run the slide show.*

**ˌsliding 'peg** = CRAWLING PEG

**ˌsliding 'scale** *n.* [C] a system of taxes, wages, etc. in which amounts paid increase or decrease in relation to changes or differences in sth else: *a sliding scale of charges based on frequency of use*

**slim** /slɪm/ *adj., v.*
• *adj.* (**slimmer**, **slimmest**) **1** very small; not as big as you would like: *Airlines run on very slim margins.* **2** (about a business or an organization) reduced to a smaller and more efficient size: *a smaller and slimmer company*
• *v.* [T,I] (**-mm-**) **~ (sth) (down)** to make a company or an organization smaller, usu. in order to make it more efficient; to become smaller in this way: *a slimmed down company*

**slip** /slɪp/ *v., n.*
• *v.* [I] (**-pp-**) **1** to fall to a lower level; to become worse: *The Nikkei slipped 0.67%.* **2** (*used with an adv. or a prep.*) to pass into a particular state or situation, esp. a difficult or an unpleasant one: *slipping* ***into*** *recession*
**PHR V** **ˌslip 'up** (*infml.*) to make a careless mistake: *The agency had slipped up badly.*
• *n.* [C] **1** an occasion when sth becomes worse or falls to a lower level: *a 0.6% slip in profits* **2** a small piece of paper, esp. one with sth printed on it: *a credit-card slip* **3** a small, careless mistake

**slippage** /'slɪpɪdʒ/ *n.* [U; C, usu. sing.] **1** a slight or gradual fall in the amount, value, etc. of sth: *a slippage* ***in*** *prices* **2** failure to achieve an aim or complete a task by a particular date or to a particular standard **3** (*Finan.*) the difference between an amount that you have estimated and the actual amount

**'slip-up** *n.* [C] a careless mistake

**slogan** /'sləʊgən; *AmE* 'sloʊ-/ (*BrE also* **'strapline**, *less freq.*) *n.* [C] (*Market.*) a phrase or sentence that is easy to remember, used for example in advertising to attract people's attention and make them remember a product **SYN** TAG LINE

**slot** /slɒt; *AmE* slɑːt/ *n.* [C] **1** a time when something is arranged to happen, as part of a series of similar things; a position in a list: *take-off and landing slots at Heathrow* **2** a job, esp. a senior one: *the top slot*

**slow** /sləʊ; *AmE* sloʊ/ *adj., v.*
• *adj.* (**-er**, **-est**) **1** not happening quickly: *slow growth in Brazil* **2** not very busy; with little action: *Sales are slow.* **3 ~ to do sth** | **~ (in) doing sth** not doing sth immediately; not happening immediately: *The industry has been slow to react.* ▸ **'slowly** *adv.* **'slowness** *n.* [U]
• *adv.* **IDM** **go 'slow (on sth)** to show less enthusiasm for achieving sth: *going slow on tax reforms*
• *v.* [T,I] **~ (sth/sb) (down/up)** to go at a slower speed; to be less active; to make sb/sth do this: *The market shows little sign of slowing down.*

★**slowdown** /'sləʊdaʊn; *AmE* 'sloʊ-/ *n.* [C, usu. sing.] **1** a reduction in speed or activity: *a slowdown* ***in*** *economic growth*
✪ *a* ***gradual/marked/rapid/sharp/slight*** *~* ♦ *a* ***consumer****/an* ***economic*** *~* ♦ *a* ***global/worldwide*** *~*
**2** (*HR*) (*AmE*) = GO-SLOW

**sluggish** /'slʌgɪʃ/ *adj.* happening more slowly than is usual; not very active: *Sales are sluggish.*
▸ **'sluggishly** *adv.* **'sluggishness** *n.* [U]

★**slump** /slʌmp/ *n., v.*
• *n.* [C] **1** a sudden fall in sales, prices, etc: *a sharp slump* ***in*** *share prices* **SYN** DECLINE
✪ *a ~ in* ***demand/profits/sales/spending*** ♦ *a* ***bad/deep/dramatic/prolonged*** *~*

**2** (*Econ.*) a period when a country's economy or a business is doing very badly: *Tourism is in a slump.* OPP BOOM

○ *an economic/industry/a stock market ~* • *a bad/deep/global/ prolonged ~*

• *v.* [I] **~ (from sth) (to sth)** | **~ (by sth)** to fall in price, value etc. suddenly and by a large amount: *The share price slumped from £3 to £1.*

**'slush fund** *n.* [C] (*also* **'slush ˌmoney** [U]) money that is kept secretly for making illegal payments

**'small ad** (*AmE* **'want ad**) = CLASSIFIED ADVERTISEMENT

**'small and 'medium-sized 'enterprise** *n.* [C] (*abbr* **SME**) a business that does not have a large number of employees or sell a large amount of goods and services, and is often run by a family

**ˌsmall 'business** *n.* [C,U] a business that has a small number of employees; these businesses in general: *to encourage investment and promote small business*

**'small cap** *n.* [C] (*Stock Ex.*) a company that has a small total value of shares on the stock exchange: *small caps that trade on the NYSE*

**ˌsmall 'claim** *n.* [C] (*BrE*) (*Law*) a court case involving a small amount of money, esp. one brought by a consumer over goods or services that are not satisfactory: *the small claims court*

**ˌsmall 'company** *n.* [C] a business that sells goods or services worth less than a fixed amount, has assets below a particular amount and/or has less than 50 employees

**ˌsmall in'vestor** *n.* [C] a person who invests small amounts of money

**the 'small print** (*esp. BrE*) (*AmE usu.* **'fine print**) *n.* [U] part of a document, esp. a contract, that is printed in small type and may contain important information that is easy to miss: *Read all the small print before signing.*

**ˌsmall-'scale** *adj.* (about an organization or activity) not large in size or extent; limited in what it does: *a ~ test/study* OPP LARGE-SCALE

**'small self-ad'ministered ('pension) 'scheme** = SSAS

**ˌsmall 'shopkeeper** *n.* [C] (*esp. BrE*) a person who owns or manages a small shop/store

**'small-sized** (*also* **'small-size**) *adj.* small; smaller than medium and large: *small-sized companies*

**ˌsmall 'stock** *n.* [C,U] (*Stock Ex.*) shares in a company that has only a small total value of shares on the stock exchange

**'small talk** *n.* [U] polite conversation about unimportant things: *making small talk*

**SMART** /smɑːt; *AmE* smɑːrt/ *abbr* (*HR*) **Specific, Measurable, Agreed, Realistic and Timed** used in a formal system of APPRAISAL to describe the aims that a business or an employee is trying to achieve

**smart** /smɑːt; *AmE* smɑːrt/ *adj.* (**-er, -est**) **1 smart** design, technology, etc. is very advanced and usu. uses computers: *Smart phones can handle email.* NOTE **Smarter, smartest** are not used in this meaning. **2** intelligent; very clever in business matters: *smart investors* **3** (about clothes) clean, neat and often formal

**'smart card** *n.* [C] a small plastic card that contains information stored in electronic form SYN CHIP CARD

**the 'smart ˌmoney** *n.* [U] **1** money that is invested or bet by people who have expert knowledge: *The smart money is no longer invested in insurance.* **2** used to say what people who know a lot think will happen: *The smart money says that prices will fall.*

**SME** /ˌes em 'iː/ = SMALL AND MEDIUM-SIZED ENTERPRISE

**SMED** /smed; ˌes em iː 'diː/ = SINGLE MINUTE EXCHANGE OF DIES

**ˌsmoke and 'mirrors** *n.* [U] something that is deliberately intended to attract people's attention so that they will not notice sth else: *a piece of accounting smoke and mirrors*

**smokestack** /'sməʊkstæk; *AmE* 'smoʊk-/ *n.* [C] a tall chimney that takes smoke away from factories: *traditional smokestack industries*

**SMP** /ˌes em 'piː/ = STATUTORY MATERNITY PAY

**SMS** /ˌes em 'es/ *n.*, *v.*

• *n.* **1** [U] **short message service** a system for sending short written messages from one mobile phone/cellphone to another **2** [C] a message sent by **SMS** SYN TEXT MESSAGE

• *v.* [T,I] to send a message to sb by **SMS**: *You can email or SMS.* SYN TEXT

**smuggle** /'smʌgl/ *v.* [T] to take, bring or send goods or people secretly and illegally into or out of a country: *smuggling fake goods into the EU*
▸ **'smuggler** *n.* [C] **'smuggling** *n.* [U]

**S/N** = SHIPPING NOTE

**'snail mail** *n.* [U] (*infml.*) a humorous name for ordinary mail, used by people who use email

**snap** /snæp/ *v.* [T] (-pp-) (used in newspapers) to break a pattern of rising or falling prices: *The Nasdaq snapped a six-week losing streak.* PHR V **,snap 'back** if markets, currencies or prices **snap back**, they recover quickly **,snap sb 'up** to act quickly in order to employ a person: *He was snapped up by a rival bank.* **,snap sth 'up** to buy sth quickly, for example because it is cheap or you think it will increase in value: *Shoppers have been snapping up bargains.*

**snapback** /'snæpbæk/ *n.* [C] a situation when markets, currencies or prices are recovering quickly: *a snapback in car sales*

**sneakernet** /'sni:kənet; *AmE* 'sni:kər-/ *n.* [U] (*IT, infml.*) used in a humorous way to talk about the way in which electronic information is passed from one computer to another by being physically carried, stored on a disk, CD, etc.

**snip** /snɪp/ *n.* [sing.] (*BrE*) (*infml.*) a thing that is cheap and good value: *The phone is a snip at $50.* SYN BARGAIN

**snow** /snəʊ; *AmE* snoʊ/ *v.* IDM **be snowed 'under (with sth)** to have more work than you are able to deal with: *We're completely snowed under at the moment.*

**'snowball ,sampling** *n.* [U] (*Market.*) a method of finding people to take part in research by finding a few and then asking them to find others ▸ **'snowball ,sample** *n.* [C]

**soar** /sɔ:(r)/ *v.* [I] if the value, amount or level of sth **soars**, it rises very quickly: *Unemployment has soared to 18%.* ◇ *soaring prices*

**Soc.** /sɒk; *AmE* sɑ:k/ *abbr* (*usu. written*) Society: *Coventry Building Soc.*

**social** /'səʊʃl; *AmE* 'soʊʃl/ *adj.* **1** connected with society and the way it is organized: *social and economic reform* **2** connected with your position in society: *social class* **3** connected with activities in which people meet each other for pleasure: *The job needs good social skills.*

**,social 'capital** *n.* [U] (*Econ.; HR*) the people who work for a company or live in a society, their knowledge and skills, considered as an asset: *organizations rich in social capital*

**,social 'cost** *n.* [C] (*Econ.*) the total cost of a business activity to a business and to everyone in society or in a particular area: *the social costs of polluting the environment*

**,social in'surance** *n.* [U] (*Econ.*) a system in which people pay money to the government when they are working and receive payments from the government when they are too old or ill/sick to work

**socialism** /'səʊʃəlɪzəm; *AmE* 'soʊ-/ *n.* [U] a set of political and economic theories based on the belief that everyone has an equal right to a share of a country's wealth and that the government should own and control the main industries ▸ **'socialist** *n.* [C] **'socialist** *adj.*

**,social 'market** *n.* [C, usu. sing.] (*Econ.*) an economic system based on a FREE MARKET but with help from the state for those who are old, ill/sick, unemployed, etc.

**,social se'curity** *n.* [U] **1** (*BrE*) (*also* **'welfare**, *AmE, BrE*) money that the government pays regularly to people who are poor, ill/sick, unemployed, etc: *people living **on** social security* ◇ *to apply for/be eligible for/claim ~* **2** (*abbr* **SS**) a system in which people pay money to the government when they are working and receive payments from the government when they are too old or ill/sick to work

⊙ *to **pay/pay into ~*** ◆ *~ **contributions/payments/tax***

**societal** /sə'saɪətl/ *adj.* (*Tech.*) connected with society and the way it is organized: *We considered the personal and societal costs of cutting jobs.*

★**society** /sə'saɪəti/ *n.* (*pl.* **-ties**) **1** [C] (*abbr* **Soc.**) (used esp. in names) a group of people who join together for a particular purpose: *the Society of Motor Manufacturers and Traders* SYN ASSOCIATION **2** [U] people in general, living together in communities: *the roles of men and women in today's society* **3** [C,U] a particular community of people who share the same customs, laws etc: *We live in a consumer society.*

**soft** /sɒft; *AmE* sɔ:ft/ *adj.* (**-er, -est**) **1** going down or likely to go down in price, value, amount, etc: *The dollar was softer against the euro.* OPP FIRM **2** (*HR*) **soft** skills are the abilities that people have to communicate well and work with other people OPP HARD

**,soft 'benefit** *n.* [C] (*HR*) advantages and rewards that employees receive that are not money: *soft benefits, such as childcare services*

**,soft com'modity** *n.* [C, usu. pl.] (*Finan.*) goods other than metals that are traded in the COMMODITY MAR-

KETS, for example coffee, grains and sugar: *soft commodity prices* SYN SOFTS

**'soft costs** *n.* [pl.] (*Account.*) money spent on items other than physical equipment, for example labour, transport, software, etc.

**ˌsoft 'currency** *n.* [C] (*Econ.*) money whose value often falls so is not easy to exchange for money from another country

**ˌsoft 'data** *n.* [U] information that cannot be measured or proved: *soft data, such as customer satisfaction*

**soften** /'sɒfn; *AmE* 'sɔːfn/ *v.* **1** [I] if prices, markets or the economy **soften**, prices stay the same or start to fall **2** [T] to make sth less severe or unpleasant: *trying to* ***soften the blow*** *of job cuts* ▸ **'softening** *n.* [sing; U]: *a softening of demand*

**'soft goods** *n.* [pl.] (*Comm.*) goods made of cloth such as sheets or clothes

**ˌsoft HR'M** *n.* [U] (*HR*) an approach to managing people that regards them as assets that must be looked after, trained and developed in order to get the best out of them

**ˌsoft 'landing** *n.* [C, usu. sing.] (*Econ., infml.*) a situation in which the economy, or part of it, slows down gradually after a period when it has been growing rapidly, without causing problems such as unemployment: *a soft landing for the economy*

**ˌsoft 'loan** *n.* [C] (*Finan.*) a loan that is made to a person or country on conditions that are good for the borrower, such as a very low rate of interest or the chance to pay it back in a SOFT CURRENCY

**ˌsoft 'market** *n.* [C] (*Finan.*) a situation in which the prices of particular goods or services are falling because there are more people selling them than people wanting to buy them SYN BUYER'S MARKET

**softs** /sɒfts; *AmE* sɔːfts/ *n.* [pl.] (*Finan., infml.*) goods other than metals traded in the COMMODITY MARKETS SYN SOFT COMMODITY

**ˌsoft 'sell** *n.* (*Market.*) **1** [sing; U] a way of selling sth to sb by persuading them gently rather than using pressure or aggressive methods: *a soft-sell approach* **2** [sing.] (*AmE*) a product that is easy to sell: *The new toy is a soft sell.* ▸ **ˌsoft-'selling** *n.* [U] **ˌsoft-'selling** *adj.*

★**software** /'sɒftweə(r); *AmE* 'sɔːftwer/ *n.* [U] (*IT*) the programs, etc. used to operate a computer: *Will the software run on my machine?* ◇ *software applications for business*

✪ ***accounting/business/financial/investment*** *~* ◆ *to* ***design/develop/write*** *~* ◆ *to* ***download/install/load/run/use*** *(a piece of) ~* ◆ *a ~* ***company/developer/firm***

**'software engiˌneer** *n.* [C] a person whose job is writing computer programs ▸ **'software engiˌneering** *n.* [U]

**SOHO** /'səʊhəʊ; *AmE* 'soʊhoʊ/ *abbr* **small office/home office** a small business, esp. one that is run from sb's home, or a person who works at home; a room in sb's home that is used as an office: *new software products for the growing SOHO market*

**ˌsold as 'seen** *adj.* (*Comm.*) (about goods) offered for sale with no promise that they are suitable or in good condition

**sole** /səʊl; *AmE* soʊl/ *adj.* **1** only: *The company is the sole supplier in many areas.* **2** belonging to one person or group; not shared: *She has sole responsibility for the project.*

**ˌsole pro'prietorship** *n.* [U,C] (*esp. AmE*) (*Law*) a business that is owned and run by one person ▸ **ˌsole pro'prietor** *n.* [C]

**ˌsole 'trader** *n.* [C] (*esp. BrE*) (*Law*) a person who owns and runs a business and is the only person who is legally responsible for it: *The business is run on a sole trader basis.*

**solicitor** /sə'lɪsɪtə(r)/ *n.* [C] (*BrE*) a lawyer who prepares legal documents, advises people on legal matters and represents them in some courts: *a firm of solicitors*

**solid** /'sɒlɪd; *AmE* 'sɑːl-/ *adj.* good and steady: *solid growth in sales*

★**solution** /sə'luːʃn/ *n.* [C] a way of solving a problem or dealing with a difficult situation: *software solutions for small businesses* (= software for business activities)

✪ *a* ***creative****/a* ***good/practical/simple*** *~* ◆ *a* ***long-term/quick-fix*** *~* ◆ ***business/financial*** *~s* ◆ *to* ***find/look for/propose*** *a ~ (to sth)*

**solvency** /'sɒlvənsi; *AmE* 'sɑːl-/ *n.* [U] (*Account.*) the state of not being in debt: *There are doubts about the company's solvency.* OPP INSOLVENCY

**'solvency ˌmargin** *n.* [C] (*Account.*) the money that a business has in addition to the amount that it needs to pay its usual bills. It can be in the form of cash or assets that can be sold easily.

**'solvency ˌratio** *n.* [C] (*Account.*) a method used to calculate how safe a company is and if it can pay all the money it owes

**solvent** /ˈsɒlvənt; *AmE* ˈsɑːl-/ *adj.* (*Account.*) **1** a **solvent** company has more assets than LIABILITIES **2** having enough money to pay your debts OPP INSOLVENT

**SOP** /ˌes əʊ ˈpiː; *AmE* oʊ/ = STATEMENT OF PRINCIPLES, STANDARD OPERATING PROCEDURE

**sort** /sɔːt; *AmE* sɔːrt/ *v., n.*
• ***v.*** [T,I] to arrange things in groups or in a particular order according to their type: *sorting the mail*
• ***n.*** [sing.] (*IT*) the process by which a computer puts data into a particular order: *to do a sort*

**ˈsort code** (*BrE*) (*AmE* **ˈrouting ˌnumber**) (*also* **ˌbank identifiˈcation ˌnumber**, *BrE, AmE less freq.*) *n.* [C] the set of numbers, found on a cheque, etc., that identifies a particular bank: *Do you have your sort code and account number?*

**sound** /saʊnd/ *v., adj.*
• ***v.*** → idiom at STRIKE *v.*
PHR V **ˌsound sb ˈout (about/on sth)**; **ˌsound sth ˈout** to try to find out from sb what they think about sth, often in an indirect way: *Did you sound him out about working for us?*
• ***adj.*** **1** sensible; that you can rely on and that will probably give good results: *The data provides a sound basis for making decisions.* **2** good and thorough: *a sound knowledge of network software* **3** in good condition; not damaged

**sour** /ˈsaʊə(r)/ *v.* [T,I] to change and become more difficult or less pleasant or friendly; to make sth do this: *Weak job prospects soured spirits.*
IDM **go/turn ˈsour** to become unpleasant or bad; to fail: *The deal started to go sour.*

**source** /sɔːs; *AmE* sɔːrs/ *n., v.*
• ***n.*** **1** [C] a place, person or thing that you get sth from: *renewable energy sources* ◇ *a source of income* **2** [C, usu. pl.] a person, book or document that provides information about sth IDM **at ˈsource** (*Account.*) used to show that money is taken from sb's income before they receive it: *Tax is **deducted** at source.*
• ***v.*** [T] (*Comm.; Product.*) (*often pass.*) to get materials, parts or products from a particular place: *The steel will be sourced **from** abroad.*
▸ **ˈsourcing** *n.* [U]: *local sourcing of parts*

**ˈsource code** *n.* [U] (*IT*) a computer program, written in the form of text, that must be translated into MACHINE CODE before it can be run on a computer

**ˌsource crediˈbility** *n.* [U] (*Market.*) how much people believe or trust a person, an advertisement, etc.

**SOV** /ˌes əʊ ˈviː; *AmE* oʊ/ = SHARE OF VOICE

**sovereign** /ˈsɒvrɪn; *AmE* ˈsɑːvrən/ *adj.* connected with a national government: *sovereign debt*

**ˌsovereign ˈrisk** = COUNTRY RISK

**SpA** /ˌes piː ˈeɪ/ *abbr* used in the names of some Italian companies: *Unicredito Italiano SpA*

**space** /speɪs/ *n.* [U] an amount of an area or of a place that is empty or available for use: *500 000 square feet of new factory floor space* ◇ *to make/take up/use ~* ◇ *disk/storage ~*

**ˈspace bar** *n.* [C] a bar on the keyboard of a computer that you press to make a space between words

**spam** /spæm/ *n.* [U] (*IT, infml.*) advertising material sent by email to large numbers of people who have not asked for it: *Filters block spam from your inbox.*
▸ **spam** *v.* [T,I] (-mm-) **ˈspammer** *n.* [C] **ˈspamming** *n.* [U]

**ˌspan of conˈtrol** *n.* [C] (*HR*) the number of people that a manager is responsible for: *a wide/narrow ~*

**ˌspare ˈpart** *n.* [C, usu. pl.] a new part that is bought and kept to replace an old or broken part of a machine, vehicle, etc: *spare parts makers*

**spawn** /spɔːn/ *v.* [T] to cause sth to develop or be produced, esp. quickly or in large numbers: *Silicon Valley is still spawning new companies.*

**SPC** /ˌes piː ˈsiː/ = STATISTICAL PROCESS CONTROL

**-speak** /spiːk/ *comb. form* (*in ns*) the language used by a particular group of people, esp. when this is difficult for other people to understand: *business-speak* ◇ *management-speak*

**speakerphone** /ˈspiːkəfəʊn; *AmE* -ərfoʊn/ *n.* [C] a telephone that you can use without holding it to your ear: *a desktop speakerphone*

**spearhead** /ˈspɪəhed; *AmE* ˈspɪrhed/ *v.* [T] to begin or lead an activity or a change: *spearheading a campaign to boost sales*

**spec** /spek/ *n., v.* (*Manufact., infml.*)
• ***n.*** [C] (*esp. BrE*) (*AmE usu.* **specs** [pl.]) **1** a detailed description of a product, esp. the design and materials needed to produce it: *a design spec* ◇ *engineering specs* **2** the particular set of features that a machine or a vehicle has: *What specs do you want for your PC?* SYN SPECIFICATION

• ***v.*** [T] (**-cc-**) (*esp. BrE*) to design and make sth to a particular standard or with particular features: *The camera is well specced at the price.*

**special** /ˈspeʃl/ *adj., n.*
• ***adj.*** **1** not ordinary or usual: *They are running a special promotion this week.* **2** appointed or created for a particular purpose: *A special committee will consider the bids.*
• ***n.*** [C,U] (*esp. AmE*) (*infml.*) a price for a particular product in a shop/store or restaurant that is lower than usual: *There's a special* ***on*** *sugar this week.*

**ˌspecial deˈlivery** *n.* [U] a service that delivers a letter or parcel/package faster than usual: *to send sth* ***by*** *special delivery*

**ˌspecial ˈdividend** (*also* **ˌextra ˈdividend**) *n.* [C] (*Finan.*) money or shares given to shareholders in addition to the normal **dividend**

**specialism** /ˈspeʃəlɪzəm/ *n.* [C] an area of business where a person or company has a lot of knowledge and experience: *Sales and advertising are separate specialisms.* SYN SPECIALITY

★**specialist** /ˈspeʃəlɪst/ *n., adj.*
• ***n.*** [C] a person or company that has a lot of knowledge and experience in a particular area of business: *a tax specialist with a major bank* ◇ *a firm of recruitment specialists*
• ***adj.*** **1** a **specialist** business operates in a particular area of activity: *~ shops/stores* **2** involving or having a lot of knowledge and experience in a particular subject: *~ skills/advice*

**speciality** /ˌspeʃiˈæləti/ (*BrE*) (*also* **ˈspecialty**, *AmE, BrE*) *n., adj.*
• ***n.*** [C] (*pl.* **-ties**) **1** an area of business in which a person or company has a lot of knowledge and experience: *Mergers and acquisitions are the firm's speciality.* SYN SPECIALISM **2** a type of food or product that a restaurant or a place is famous for: *local specialities*
• ***adj.*** **1** **speciality** products are designed for a particular purpose: *speciality chemicals* **2** a **speciality** shop/store sells a small range of special or unusual products

★**specialize**, **-ise** /ˈspeʃəlaɪz/ *v.* [I] **1** to be involved in one particular area of business: *a firm specializing* ***in*** *charter flights* **2** to become an expert in one particular area of business: *She specialized* ***in*** *media sales.*
▸ **ˌspecialiˈzation**, **-iˈsation** /-laɪˈzeɪʃn; *AmE* -ləˈz-/ *n.* [U,C] **ˈspecialized** *adj.*: *highly specialized firms*

**ˌspecial ˈleave** *n.* [U] (*HR*) a period of time when an employee is allowed to be away from work, either with or without pay, because of personal or family circumstances

**ˌspecial ˈoffer** *n.* [C,U] **1** a product or service that is sold at less than its usual price, to encourage people to buy it; the act of offering goods or services in this way: *a special offer* ***on*** *suits* ◇ *What is* ***on*** *special offer?* **2** an extra item that is given free or at a low cost with a product or service to encourage people to buy it

**ˌspecial poˈsition** *n.* [C] (*Market.*) a particular advertising space in a newspaper or magazine that advertisers must pay more to use

**ˌspecial resoˈlution** *n.* [C] a **resolution** that must be accepted by 75% of shareholders

**ˌspecial situˈation** *n.* [C, usu. pl.] (*Finan.*) a company that seems a good investment because its shares are likely to rise in value for a particular reason: *a special situation stock*

**specialty** /ˈspeʃəlti/ (*pl.* **-ties**) = SPECIALITY

**specific** /spəˈsɪfɪk/ *adj.* **1 -specific** (*used with a n.*) done, made, produced, etc. for the purpose or people mentioned; connected with the thing mentioned: *market-specific products* **2** (about a tax) calculated at a fixed amount for each unit of the goods, using number, weight or volume, rather than on the value of the goods: *a ~ duty/tariff/tax*

★**specification** /ˌspesɪfɪˈkeɪʃn/ *n.* **1** (*Manufact.*) [C, usu. pl., U] detailed information about how sth is or should be designed or made: *the technical specifications of the new car* ◇ *The part will perform exactly* ***to specification*** (= as it is supposed to).
⊕ ***design/product ~*** • ***to agree/change/set ~*** • ***to comply with/conform to/meet ~***
**2** (*Manufact.*) [C] the particular set of features that a machine or a vehicle has **3** [C,U] an act of giving detailed information about what sb wants or expects from sth: *a clear specification of objectives* → SPEC

**speˌcific ˈrisk** = UNSYSTEMATIC RISK

★**specify** /ˈspesɪfaɪ/ *v.* [T] (**-fies**, **-fying**, **-fied**, **-fied**) to state or explain sth, giving an exact measurement, time, exact instructions, etc: *You can specify a date and time for delivery.* ◇ *to buy shares at a specified price*

**ˌspecimen ˈsignature** *n.* [C] an example of your signature that you give to a bank, etc. so that they can compare it with the signature on cheques and other documents

**specs** /speks/ = SPEC *n.*

**speculate** /ˈspekjuleɪt/ *v.* [I] (*Finan.*) **~ (in/on sth)** to buy shares, property, goods, etc. hoping to make a profit when you sell them, but with the risk of losing money: *He made thousands (of dollars) speculating in property.* ▸ **ˈspeculative** /-jələtɪv; *AmE also* -jəleɪtɪv/ *adj.*: *~ investments/traders* **ˈspeculator** *n.* [C]: *property/currency ~s*

★ **speculation** /ˌspekjuˈleɪʃn/ *n.* [U,C] (*Finan.*) the activity of buying shares, property, goods, etc. in the hope of making a profit when you sell them, but with the risk of losing money: *speculation* ***on*** *the currency markets* ◇ *financial/property ~*

**ˌspeculative appliˈcation** *n.* [C] a request that you send to a company for a job, although they have not advertised one

**ˈspeech recogˌnition** = VOICE RECOGNITION

**speed** /spiːd/ *n.* IDM **up to ˈspeed (on sth)** (*infml.*) **1** (about a person, company, etc.) performing at the rate or level that is expected: *getting new employees up to speed* **2** having the most recent and accurate information or knowledge: *up to speed on the latest developments*

**spellcheck** (*AmE* **spell-check, spell check**) /ˈspeltʃek/ *v.* [T] to use a computer program to check the spelling in a text ▸ **ˈspellcheck** *n.* [C]: *The text needs a spellcheck.*

**spellchecker** (*AmE* **spell-checker, spell checker**) /ˈspeltʃekə(r)/ (*also* **ˈspellcheck, ˈspelling ˌchecker**) *n.* [C] **1** a computer program that checks the spellings in a text: *Always use a spellchecker.* **2** a small computer that you can use to check spellings: *a handheld spellchecker*

★ **spend** /spend/ *v., n.*

• ***v.*** [T] (**spent, spent** /spent/) **1** to give money to pay for goods, services, etc: *Shoppers spent $17.1 bn in April.* ◇ *The company spends* ***a fortune*** (= a very large amount of money) *on salaries.* **2** to use time for a particular purpose; to pass time: *We spend a lot of time getting to know our customers.*

• ***n.*** [sing.] (*infml.*) the amount of money spent for a particular purpose or over a particular length of time: *a $2.5 m marketing spend* ◇ *the average spend* ***on*** *leisure activities*

★ **spending** /ˈspendɪŋ/ *n.* [U] the amount of money that is spent by a person, a government or an organization: *a sharp drop in business spending* ***on*** *technology* ◇ *high street ~* ❶ ***consumer/corporate/government ~*** • ***~ drops/falls/increases/rises***

**ˈspending ˌmoney** *n.* [U] money that you spend for your own pleasure or entertainment rather than on things you need

**ˈspending ˌpower** = PURCHASING POWER

**spendthrift** /ˈspendθrɪft/ *n.* [C] a person who spends too much money or who wastes money ▸ **ˈspendthrift** *adj.*

**ˈspider food** *n.* [U] (*IT, infml.*) words or phrases placed on a web page to attract SEARCH ENGINES

**spiff** /spɪf/ *n., v.* (*AmE*) (*infml.*)

• ***n.*** [C] (*also* **spif**) a special reward that a SALESPERSON receives for selling a particular product: *Spiffs were offered for selling unpopular PCs.*

• ***v.*** PHR V **ˌspiff sth ˈup** to improve sth by making it more attractive, more efficient, etc: *spiffing up the website*

**spike** /spaɪk/ *v.* [I] (*esp. AmE*) (*infml.*) (used esp. in newspapers) to rise quickly and reach a high value: *The US dollar spiked to a new high.* ▸ **spike** *n.* [C, usu. sing.]: *a spike* ***in*** *oil prices*

★ **spin** /spɪn/ *v.* (**spinning, spun, spun** /spʌn/) PHR V **ˌspin (sth) ˈoff (from sth)** to happen or to produce sth as a new or unexpected result of sth that already exists: *products spinning off from favourite books* **ˌspin sth ˈoff (from sth)** (*Finan.*) (*usu. pass.*) to form a new and independent company from part of an existing one by selling or giving new shares to shareholders: *The company was spun off from its parent group last year.* **ˌspin (sth) ˈout (of/from sth)** (*Finan.*) (*usu. pass.*) to form a new and independent company from part of an existing one by selling or giving new shares to shareholders: *a newly spun out company*

**spinner** /ˈspɪnə(r)/ *n.* [C] (*Market.*) a piece of equipment that usu. stands on the floor and can be turned in a circle, used in a shop/store for displaying books, etc.

**ˈspin-off** (*AmE also* **spinoff**) *n.* [C] **1** (*Finan.*) (*also* **ˈspin-out**, *esp. in AmE*) the act of forming a new, independent company from part of an existing one; a company formed in this way: *the proposed spin-off of the group's restaurants* ◇ *Three of our spin-offs may go public.* **2** an unexpected but useful result of an activity designed to produce sth else: *commercial spin-offs from medical research* **3** a book, a film/movie, a television programme, or an object based on one: *The magazine is a spin-off from the TV show.*

**'spin-out** *n.* [C] (*esp. AmE*)
**1** (*Finan.*) a company that is formed to develop and use the results of research done at a university or college
**2** = SPIN-OFF (1)

**spiral** /'spaɪrəl/ *n.*, *v.*
• ***n.*** [C] a continuous harmful increase or decrease in sth, that gradually gets faster: *a downward spiral* ***in*** *share prices* ◇ *an inflationary spiral*
• ***v.*** [I] (-**ll**-, *AmE usu.* -**l**-) (*usu. used with an adv. or a prep.*) to increase rapidly: *spiralling costs/debts*
**PHR V** **ˌspiral 'down/'downwards** to decrease rapidly

★**split** /splɪt/ *v.*, *n.*
• ***v.*** (**splitting, split, split**) **1** [T] **~ sth (between sb/sth)** | **~ sth (with sb)** to divide money, property, etc. into two or more parts and share it between different people: *The five executives will split $44 m between them.* **2** [T,I] **~ (sth) (into sth)** to divide into two or more parts; to make sth do this: *The group will be split into four divisions.* **3** [T,I] **~ (sth) (from sth)** to leave a company or group and become an independent company; to make part of a company do this: *The firm's European operations split from the US business.* **4** (*Finan.*) [T] if a company **splits** shares, it divides its capital into more shares so that each share has a lower value: *They split shares two-for-one.* **IDM** **split sth 50-'50** to divide sth so that each person gets or pays half **split the 'difference** (when discussing a price, etc.) to agree on an amount that is exactly half way between the two amounts that have been suggested **PHR V** **ˌsplit (sth) 'up** to divide sth into two or more parts; to make sth do this: *We didn't want to split up the group.*
• ***n.*** [C] **1** a way of dividing sth: *a 50-50 split between shares and bonds*
**2** (*Finan.*) = STOCK SPLIT

**ˌsplit 'run** *n.* [C] (*Market.*) a newspaper, magazine or web page which is produced in different versions, with different advertisements in each, usu. to see how successful the advertising is

**ˌsplit 'share** *n.* [C] (*Finan.*) one of a number of new shares with a lower value that a group of shares has been divided into

**ˌsplit 'shift** *n.* [C] (*HR*) two periods of work with a long break in between that sb works in a day

**ˌsplit 'stock** *n.* [U] (*Finan.*) the new shares that a group of shares has been divided into in order to lower the price

**spokesman** /'spəʊksmən; *AmE* 'spoʊ-/, **spokeswoman** /'spəʊkswʊmən; *AmE* 'spoʊ-/ *n.* [C] (*pl.* **-men** /-mən/**-women** /-wɪmɪn/) a person who speaks on behalf of a group or an organization: *a spokeswoman* ***for*** *the union*

**spokesperson** /'spəʊkspɜːsn; *AmE* 'spoʊkspɜːrsn/ *n.* [C] (*pl.* **-persons** *or* **-people** /-piːpl/) a person who speaks on behalf of a group or an organization: *A spokesperson* ***for*** *the company confirmed that it would be opening 20 new stores.*

★**sponsor** /'spɒnsə(r); *AmE* 'spɑːn-/ *n.* [C] **1** (*Market.*) a person or company that helps pay the costs of sth such as a special event, a sports team or a project, usu. to advertise their products: *They are the main sponsors of the conference.*

⊙ *a* ***big/major*** *~* ◆ *a* ***corporate/*** *an* ***industrial/*** *a* ***private*** *~*

**2** (*Market.*) (*esp. AmE*) a person or a business that pays for a radio or TV programme or part of a website by buying advertising time: *Click here to visit our sponsors.* **3** a person or company that supports sb by paying for their training or education **4** a person who agrees to be officially responsible for another person
▸ **'sponsor** *v.* [T]: *The company has sponsored the team for seven years.* **'sponsorship** *n.* [U,C]: *a $50 m sponsorship deal*

**'sporting goods** (*also* **'sports goods**) *n.* [pl.] clothes and equipment used for sport

**spot** /spɒt; *AmE* spɑːt/ *n.* **1** (*Finan.*) [sing.] (*used with ns*) connected with a system of trading where goods are delivered and paid for immediately after sale: *spot trades* ◇ *spot gas sales to Britain* **2** (*Market.*) [C] a television advertisement: *a 30-second spot* **3** [C] a position in a competition: *competing for* ***top spot*** *in the market*

**'spot ˌadvertising** *n.* [U] (*Market.*) **1** advertising that is done using television or radio advertisements **2** advertising that is done in a particular place or area, not everywhere ▸ **'spot adˌvertisement** (*also* **'spot ad**, *infml.*) *n.* [C]

**'spot cash** *n.* [U] (*Comm.*) payment for goods made as soon as they are delivered: *a spot cash payment*

**ˌspot 'check** *n.* [C] a check made suddenly and without warning on a few things from a group to see that everything is satisfactory: *doing spot checks **on** accounts*
▶ **'spot-check** *v.* [T]

**'spot ˌcolour** *n.* [C,U] (*Market.*) one colour that is used in a black-and-white advertisement to make people notice sth

**'spot deˌlivery** *n.* [U,C] (*Finan.*; *Trade*) when goods are delivered and paid for immediately rather than in the future

**ˌspot ex'change rate** (*also* **'spot rate**) *n.* [C] (*Finan.*) the rate at which one currency can be exchanged for another at the present time rather than at a future date

**'spot ˌmarket** (*also* **'cash ˌmarket**) *n.* [C] (*Finan.*) the buying and selling of goods, currencies, etc. that are available to be delivered immediately: *steel sold **on** the spot market*

**'spot price** (*also* **'cash price**) *n.* [C] (*Finan.*) the price of sth that is available to be delivered immediately, esp. a COMMODITY

**'spot rate** = SPOT EXCHANGE RATE

**SPP** /ˌes piː 'piː/ = STATUTORY PATERNITY PAY

★**spread** /spred/ *v.*, *n.*
• ***v.*** **1** [T] **~ sth (out) (over sth)** to separate sth into parts and divide them between different times or people: *The payments are spread over a year.* **2** [T,I] to affect or make sth affect, be used by, etc. more and more people: *The virus spread across the world in hours.* **3** [T,I] (*with an adv. or a prep.*) to cover, or make sth cover, a large area: *Our stores are spread throughout the country.*
• ***n.*** **1** [U] an increase in the amount or number of sth, or in the area affected by sth: *the spread of wireless technology* **2** [C, usu. sing.] a range or variety of people or things: *a broad spread of topics* **3** [sing.] the area that sth exists in or happens in: *The company has a good spread of hotels here.* **4** [C] two opposite pages in a newspaper or magazine; an article or advertisement that covers two opposite pages: *a **double-page** spread* **5** (*Finan.*) [C] the difference between two rates or prices: *the spread between the list price and the market price of the car* **6** (*Finan.*) [C] the difference between the interest rate that a bank pays for borrowing money and the rate at which it is prepared to lend it **7** (*Finan.*) = BID-OFFER SPREAD

★**spreadsheet** /'spredʃiːt/ *n.* [C] (*IT*) a computer program used, for example, when doing financial or project planning. You enter data in rows and columns and the program calculates costs, etc. from it: *to store data **in/on** a ~ ◇ to create/fill in/ update a ~*

**springboard** /'sprɪŋbɔːd; *AmE* -bɔːrd/ *n.* [C, usu. sing.] something that helps you start to do or become sth: *Her job was a springboard **to** a successful career.*

**spurt** /spɜːt; *AmE* spɜːrt/ *n.* [C] a sudden increase in speed, effort, activity, etc. for a short period of time: *a spurt **in** sales ◇ If we **put on a spurt** we'll finish this job today.* ▶ **spurt** *v.* [I]

**sq.** (*also* **sq**, *esp. in AmE*) *abbr* (in writing measurements) square: *2 000 sq metres of office space*

**SQC** /ˌes kjuː 'siː/ = STATISTICAL QUALITY CONTROL

**squander** /'skwɒndə(r); *AmE* 'skwɑːn-/ *v.* [T] to waste money, time, etc. in a stupid or careless way: *squandering millions **on** legal battles*

**square** /skweə(r); *AmE* skwer/ *adj.*, *n.*, *v.*
• ***adj.*** **1** used before a unit of measurement to express an area equal to a square with sides of the length mentioned: *Office rental is €290 per square metre.* **2** (*abbr* **sq.**) used after a number to give a measurement of area: *15 000 square metres* **3** (*infml.*) **(all) ~** if two people are **square**, neither of them owes money to the other
• ***n.*** **IDM** **back to square 'one** used to describe a situation when you are forced to return to the beginning of a project, task, etc., and have therefore made no real progress
• ***v.*** [T] (*Stock Ex.*) to make the total number of shares bought and sold equal: *Investors are squaring their short positions.* **PHR V** **ˌsquare 'up 1 ~ (to sb/sth)** to face a difficult situation and deal with it in a determined way: *to square up to the challenges* **2 ~ (to sb/sth)** to face sb as if you are going to fight them: *small stores squaring up to supermarkets* **3** (*infml.*) **~ (with sb)** to pay sb the money you owe them **'square (sth) with sth** to make two amounts, facts, etc. agree with each other; to agree with another amount, fact, etc: *squaring invoices with purchase orders* **'square sth with sb** to ask permission or check with sb that they ap-

prove of what you want to do: *I'd like to come, but I'll have to square it with my boss.*

**ˌsquare cut ˈfolder** *n.* [C] a folded piece of thin brown card used for keeping loose papers together, often in a FILING CABINET

**the ˌSquare ˈMile** *n.* [sing.] (*infml.*) a name for the City of London where there are many banks and financial businesses

**squeeze** /skwi:z/ *v.*, *n.*
• ***v.*** [T] **1** to strictly limit or reduce the amount of money that sb/sth has or can use: *We have had our profits squeezed this year.* **2** to get as much as you can from sb/sth, usu. with difficulty: *The bank is trying to squeeze more money out of us.* IDM **ˌsqueeze sb ˈdry** to get as much money, information, etc. out of sb as you can PHR V **ˌsqueeze sb/sth ˈin** to give time to sb/sth, although you are busy: *Can you squeeze in a short meeting today?* **ˌsqueeze sb/sth ˈout (of sth)** to prevent sb/sth from continuing to do sth or be in business: *Supermarkets are squeezing out small shops.*
• ***n.*** [C, usu. sing.] a reduction in the amount of money, number of jobs, etc. available; a difficult situation caused by this: *Smaller magazines are **feeling the squeeze**.*
⊕ *a **cash/job/pay** ~ • a ~ **on credit/jobs/manufacturing/pay/profits***

**S/R** = SALE OR RETURN

**SR** /ˌes ˈɑ:(r)/ = SUPPLIER RATING

**SRDS™** /ˌes ɑ: di: ˈes; *AmE* ɑ:r/ = STANDARD RATE AND DATA SERVICE

**SRP** /ˌes ɑ: ˈpi:; *AmE* ɑ:r/ *abbr* (*Comm.*) **suggested retail price** the price at which the maker of a product suggests that it should be sold to customers in shops/stores SYN MSRP, RRP

**SS** /ˌes ˈes/ = SOCIAL SECURITY (2)

**SSAS** /es ˌes eɪ ˈes/ *abbr* **small self-administered (pension) scheme** a PENSION FUND organized by the main shareholders of a small company

**SSL** /ˌes es ˈel/ *abbr* (*E-comm.*) **secure sockets layer** a safe and private way of making payments on the Internet

**SSP** /ˌes es ˈpi:/ = STATUTORY SICK PAY

**st.** *abbr* (*written*) short ton

★**stability** /stəˈbɪləti/ *n.* [U] the quality or state of being steady and not changing: *the firm's financial stability*
⊕ ***economic/price** ~ • to **create/give/maintain/provide** ~*

**stabilize, -ise** /ˈsteɪbəlaɪz/ *v.* [T,I] to become, or to make sth become, steady and unlikely to change: *government measures to stabilize prices* ▸ **sˌtabiliˈzation, -iˈsation** /-laɪˈzeɪʃn; *AmE* -ləˈz-/ *n.* [U]: *stabilization in the job market*

★**stable** /ˈsteɪbl/ *adj.* firmly fixed; not likely to move, change or fail: *Exports have remained stable.* ◇ *stable prices* SYN STEADY ▸ **ˈstably** /-bli/ *adv.*

**stack** /stæk/ *n.*, *v.*
• ***n.*** [C] **1** a pile of sth, usu. neatly arranged: *a stack of boxes* **2** (*infml.*) (*esp. BrE*) a lot of sth: *I've got stacks of work to do.* **3** (*IT*) a way of storing information in a computer in which the most recently stored item is the first to be RETRIEVED
• ***v.*** **1** [T,I] **~ (sth) (up)** to arrange objects neatly in a pile; to be arranged in this way: *The boxes are stacked up in the warehouse.* **2** [T] to fill sth with piles of things: *staff stacking shelves in the supermarket* PHR V **ˌstack ˈup** to keep increasing in quantity until there is large pile, a long line, etc. waiting to be dealt with **ˌstack ˈup (against sb/sth)** (*esp. in questions or negative sentences*) to compare with sb/sth else: *How does their latest model stack up against ours?*

★**staff** /stɑ:f; *AmE* stæf/ *n.*, *v.*
• ***n.*** [C with sing./pl. v.; usu. sing.] all the people who work for a company or an organization HELP In the singular, **staff** is often used with a plural verb, esp. in BrE: *We have a staff of 25.* ◇ *We have 25 people **on the staff**.* ◇ *Five **staff members** moved to London.* ◇ *companies with small technical staffs*
⊕ ***full-time/part-time/permanent/temporary** ~ • **administrative/office/sales** ~ • to **hire/recruit/take on** ~ • to **dismiss/fire/lay off** ~ • ~ **development/training** • ~ **shortages/turnover***
• ***v.*** [T] (*usu. pass.*) to provide people to work in a company: *We are now fully staffed.* ▸ **ˈstaffing** *n.* [U]: *staffing levels*

**ˈstaff ˌagency** = EMPLOYMENT AGENCY

**ˈstaff associˌation** *n.* [C] (*HR*) an organization, similar to a union, for employees of a company or for people who do the same job

★**stage** /steɪdʒ/ *n.*, *v.*
• ***n.*** [C] **1** a period or state that sth passes through as it develops: *This technology is still **in its early stages**.* ◇ *The product is at the design stage.* **2** a separate part that a process, etc.

is divided into: *the first stage of the cost-cutting process*

• *v.* [T] **1** to organize an event: *to ~ a conference/an exhibition/event* **2** to organize and take part in action that needs careful planning, esp. as a public protest: *to ~ a protest/stoppage/strike* **3** to make sth happen: *to ~ a comeback/rally/recovery*

**'stage-gate** *adj.* (*Market.*) used to describe a way of developing a new product where the process is divided into separate stages. At the end of each stage managers must make a decision about whether and how to continue: *a ~ process/review/system*

**stagflation** /stæg'fleɪʃn/ *n.* [U] (*Econ.*) an economic situation where there is high INFLATION but no increase in the jobs that are available or in business activity

**stagger** /'stægə(r)/ *v.* [T] to arrange for events that would normally happen at the same time to start or happen at different times: *staggered working hours*

**stagnant** /'stægnənt/ *adj.* not developing, growing or changing: *a stagnant economy*

**stagnate** /stæg'neɪt; *AmE* 'stægneɪt/ *v.* [I] to stop developing or making progress: *Demand has stagnated and profits are down.* ▶ **stag'nation** /-'neɪʃn/ *n.* [U]

★ **stake** /steɪk/ *n., v.*

• *n.* **1** (*Finan.*) [C, usu. sing.] money that sb invests in a company: *The group has a 40% stake **in** the airline.* ⊙ *a **controlling/majority/minority** ~ (in sth)* ♦ *to **acquire/buy/sell/take** a ~ (in sth)* ♦ *to **cut/increase/raise/reduce** your ~ (in sth)* ♦ *to **hold/own** a ~ (in sth)*

**2** [C] something that you risk losing, esp. money, when you try to predict the result of a race, etc. or when you are involved in an activity that can succeed or fail: *How much was the stake* (= how much did you bet)? ◇ *When you start a new business, **the stakes are high**.* **3** [sing.] an important part or share in a business, plan, etc. that is important to you and that you want to be successful: *The workers **have** a personal stake **in** the wage negotiations.* IDM **at 'stake** that can be won or lost, depending on the success of a particular action: *Hundreds of jobs are at stake.* → idiom at PLAY *v.*

• *v.* [T] to risk money or sth important on the result of sth: *We are staking our future **on** the success of this product.* IDM **stake (out) a/your 'claim (to/for/on sth)** to say or show publicly that you think sth should be yours

**stakeholder** /'steɪkhəʊldə(r); *AmE* -hoʊld-/ *n.* [C] a person or group that is involved in and can be affected by a particular organization, project, system, etc., for example directors, employees, shareholders and customers

**stall** /stɔːl/ *n., v.*

• *n.* [C] a table or small shop that people sell things from, esp. in a market SYN STAND

• *v.* **1** [I] to try to avoid doing sth or answering a question so that you have more time: *They are stalling **on** the deal.* **2** [T,I] to stop growing or making progress; to make sth do this: *The economy seems to be stalling.*

**stallholder** /'stɔːlhəʊldə(r); *AmE* -hoʊld-/ *n.* [C] a person who sells things from or owns a **stall** in a market, etc.

**stamp** /stæmp/ *n., v.*

• *n.* [C] **1** (*also* **'postage stamp**, *fml.*) a small piece of paper with a design on it that you buy and stick on an envelope or a parcel/package before you post it **2** a tool for printing the date or a design or mark onto a surface **3** a design or words made by **stamping** sth onto a surface: *a passport with a visa stamp*

• *v.* [T] **1 ~ A on B | ~ B with A** (*often pass.*) to print letters, words, a design, etc. onto sth using a special tool: *The box was stamped with the maker's name.* **2** (*usu. pass.*) to stick a stamp on a letter or package

**'stamp duty** (*BrE*) (*AmE* **'stamp tax**) *n.* [U] a tax that must be paid when land, buildings or shares are sold. A stamp is fixed to the legal document to show that the tax has been paid.

**stand** /stænd/ *v., n.*

• *v.* IDM **stand 'pat** to stay the same and not change; to refuse to change: *The unemployment rate stood pat at 4%.* **stand the test of 'time** to prove to be successful, popular, etc. over a long period of time

PHRV **,stand 'by** to be ready for action: *We have an IT engineer standing by in case the system crashes.* **,stand 'down** to leave a job or position: *He stood down **as** chairman after ten years.* **,stand 'in (for sb)** to take sb's place: *My boss couldn't go to the conference so I stood in for her.* SYN DEPUTIZE

• *n.* [C] **1** a table or a vertical structure that goods are sold from, esp. in the street or at a market: *a hamburger/newspaper ~* SYN STALL **2** (*esp. BrE*) a table or a vertical structure where things are displayed or advertised, for example at an exhibition: *a display/an exhibition ~* ◇ *Two reps will man the stand.* **3** (*often with another n.*) a piece of equipment or furniture that you use for holding a particular type of thing: *a floor stand for a TV*

**'stand-alone** *adj.* that exists or functions on its own: *Their retail branch is now run as a stand-alone company.*

★ **standard** /'stændəd; *AmE* -dərd/ *n.*, *adj.*

• ***n.*** **1** [C,U] a level of quality that is expected or required: *This vehicle set new standards for safety.* ◇ *We offer the highest standard of customer care.* ⊙ *to establish ~* • *to **achieve/meet/reach** a ~* • *to **improve/raise** ~* • *a **low/minimum** ~*
**2** [C] an official rule used when producing sth; an official unit of measurement: *For measuring shipments, the international standard is TEU.* ◇ *to **apply/enforce/set/tighten/use** a ~*
**3** [C] something that most people who do a particular job use: *The manual is the industry standard for health and safety.* ◇ *The wages are low **by** today's **standards**.*

• ***adj.*** **1** average or normal: *Our standard terms and conditions apply.* ◇ *The wireless mouse comes **as standard**.* **2** following a particular standard that is set, for example, by an industry: *standard sizes of clothes* **3** used by most people who are studying a particular subject: *the standard book on marketing*

**'Standard & 'Poor's '500 ˌindex** /ˌstændəd ən 'pɔːz; *AmE* ˌstændərd ən 'pɔːrz/ (*also* **'Standard and 'Poor's '500 'stock ˌindex**) *n.* [sing.] (*abbr* **S&P 500™**) an average of the share prices of five hundred US companies, used to measure changes in the US market

**ˌstandard 'costing** *n.* [U] (*Account.*) a method of calculating and controlling the costs of producing goods by comparing the usual or estimated costs and income with the actual ones

▸ **ˌstandard 'cost** *n.* [C,U]

**ˌstandard devi'ation** *n.* [C,U] (*Tech.*) the amount by which measurements for members in a group vary from the average for the group: *A survey of 100 people shows that they spend an average of £52 on books per year, with a standard deviation of £12.*

**ˌstandard-form 'contract** *n.* [C] (*Law*) a contract that a seller or an employer, etc. uses in the same form for many different cases

**ˌstandard 'issue** *n.* [U] **1** sth given to everybody who does a particular job, works for a particular company, etc: *the company's standard-issue business card* **2** a typical example of sth with no unusual features: *standard-issue office furniture*

★ **standardize**, **-ise** /'stændədaɪz; *AmE* -dərd-/ *v.* [T] to make objects or activities of the same type have the same features or qualities; to make sth standard: *standardized tests/systems*

▸ **ˌstandardi'zation**, **-i'sation** /-daɪ'zeɪʃn; *AmE* -də'z-/ *n.* [U]

**ˌstandard of 'living** *n.* [C] the money and level of comfort that a person or group has

**ˌstandard 'operating proˌcedure** *n.* [C,U] (*abbr* **SOP**) the official or accepted way that particular things are done in a company or an industry

**'Standard 'Rate and 'Data ˌService™** *n.* [sing.] (*abbr* **SRDS™**) (*Market.*) in the US, a book published every month that contains information about all the newspapers, magazines and other media that have advertising

**ˌstandard-'rated** *adj.* used to describe goods or services on which a normal level of a particular tax is charged: *Pet food is standard-rated for VAT.*

**'standard time** *n.* [U] the official time of a country or an area

**standby** /'stændbaɪ/ *n.*, *adj.*

• ***n.*** [C] (*pl.* **standbys**) sth/sb that can always be used if needed: *I have a laptop as a standby in case my computer crashes.* **IDM** **on 'standby** ready to do sth immediately if needed or asked: *We are on standby to increase production if demand increases.*

• ***adj.*** **1** ready to be used if needed: *Leave the PC in standby mode.*
**2** (*Econ.*) used to describe an arrangement by which a country can borrow extra money from the IMF in an emergency: *a $16 bn standby agreement with the IMF*

**'standby 'letter of 'credit** *n.* [C] (*Finan.*) a written document that a bank can provide for a customer in which the bank agrees to pay a bill, pay back a loan, etc. if the customer does not do so

**standing** /'stændɪŋ/ *adj.*, *n.*

• ***adj.*** existing or arranged without a time limit, not formed or made for a particular situation: *a standing arrangement to share printing facilities*

• ***n.*** [U] **1** the position or reputation of sb/sth within a group of people or in an organization: *efforts to improve* *the firm's weak financial standing* (= it does not have much money) SYN STATUS **2** the period of time that sth has existed: *the firm's head of many years' standing*

**ˌstanding ˈorder** (*also* **ˌbanker's ˈorder**) *n.* [C,U] (*both BrE*) an instruction that you give to a bank to pay sb a fixed amount of money from your account on the same day each week, month, etc: *to set up a standing order* ◇ *to pay by standing order*

**ˌstanding room ˈonly** *phr.* (*Market.*) a technique in which sb trying to sell a product or service suggests that the customer should buy immediately as they may not have another chance in the future because so many people want to buy it

**standout** /ˈstændaʊt/ *n.* (*esp. AmE*) (*Market., infml.*) **1** [C] sb/sth that is very noticeable because they are better, more impressive, etc. than others: *Their new minidisc player is a standout.* **2** [U] the ability to be noticed very easily: *to achieve standout* ◇ *standout features*

**standstill** /ˈstændstɪl/ *n.* [sing.] a situation in which all activity or movement has stopped: *The strike **brought** production **to a standstill**.*

**ˈstandstill aˌgreement** *n.* [C] (*Law*) a contract in which both sides agree to leave the current situation as it is for a period of time

**staple** /ˈsteɪpl/ *adj., n., v.*

• ***adj.*** forming a basic, large or important part of sth: *the price of rice, fuel and other staple goods*

• ***n.*** [C] **1** a small piece of wire that is used in a STAPLER and is used to fasten pieces of paper together **2** (*Econ.*) something that is produced by a country and is important for its economy: *Copper is a staple of the local economy.* **3** a large or important part of sth: *Business clients are the staple of luxury hotels* (= their main customers).

• ***v.*** [T] to attach pieces of paper together using a **staple**: *Staple the invoice to the receipt.*

**ˈstaple gun** *n.* [C] a device for fixing paper to walls, etc. using **staples**

**stapler** /ˈsteɪplə(r)/ *n.* [C] a small device for putting **staples** into paper

**star** /stɑː(r)/ *n.* [C] **1** a mark that tells you how good sth is in sb's opinion: *This printer had a top rating of five stars from the magazine.* **2** a thing or person that is the best of a group: *The company is the star of its sector.* **3** in the BOSTON MATRIX, a product that has a large market share in a market that is growing very quickly

★ **start** /stɑːt; *AmE* stɑːrt/ *v., n.*

• ***v.*** **1** [I] (*with an adv. or a prep.*) to begin at a particular level: *Prices start at about $100.* **2** [T,I] **~ (sth/sb) (up)** to begin to exist; to make sth begin to exist: *There are a lot of small business starting up in the area.* **3** [T,I] **~ (out/off) (sth) (as sth)** to begin in a particular way that changes later: *We started out with just 2 employees.* **4** [T,I] when you **start** a machine or a vehicle or it **starts**, it begins to operate PHR V **ˌstart ˈout 1** to begin to do sth, esp. in business or work: *to start out in business* **2** to have a particular intention when you begin sth: *I started out **to** fix a bug but I ended up writing a new program.* **ˌstart ˈover** (*esp. AmE*) to begin again **ˌstart (sth) ˈup** to begin working, happening, etc.; to make sth do this: *My computer won't start up.*

• ***n.*** **1** [C, usu. sing.] the point at which sth begins: *the start of the year* **2** [sing.] the act or process of beginning sth: *I've **made a start on** the accounts.* **3** [C, usu. sing.] the opportunity that you are given to begin sth in a successful way: *The job gave him his start in publishing.* **4** [C, usu. pl.] a business, project, etc. that has just begun: *a large number of new business starts*

→ idioms at FIT *n.*, HEAD *n.*

★ **ˈstart-up** (*also* **startup**) *n.* **1** [U] the action or process of starting or making sth start: *the start-up of a new pension plan* **2** [C] a new company: *business start-ups* ▸ **ˈstart-up** *adj.*: *~ costs/companies*

**starve** /stɑːv; *AmE* stɑːrv/ *v.* PHR V **ˈstarve sb/sth of sth** (*AmE also* **ˈstarve sb/sth for sth**) (*usu. pass.*) to prevent sb/sth from having sth they want or need: *The firm was starved for cash when it started up.*

★ **state** /steɪt/ *n., adj., v.*

• ***n.*** **1** [C, usu. sing.] the good or bad conditions that exist in an economy, a market, an industry, etc. at a particular time: *a report on the state of the economy* ◇ *the dire state of the steel industry*

◐ *a **buoyant/healthy** ~* • *a **depressed/poor/precarious/weak** ~*

**2** [C, usu. sing.] the condition that a thing or person is in: *The factory is in a poor **state of** repair.*

◐ *a **good/healthy** ~* • *a **bad/run-down/terrible/untidy** ~*

**3** (*also* **State**) [C] a country considered as an organized political community controlled by one government: *EU member states* **4** (*also* **State**) [C] an organized political

community forming part of a country: *the southern States of the US* **5** (*also* **the State**) [U; sing.] the government of a country: *The airline is 53% state-owned.*
• *adj.* (*also* **State**) **1** controlled or provided by the government of a country: *the state airline* **2** connected with a particular state of a country, esp. in the US: *a ~ bank/tax*
• *v.* [T] **1** to formally write or say sth: *The facts are clearly stated in the report.* **2** (*usu. pass.*) to fix or announce the details of sth, esp. on a written document: *You must arrive at the time stated.*

**ˌstate ˈbenefit** *n.* [U,C] in the UK, money provided by the government to people who need financial help because they are unemployed, ill/sick, etc.

★ **statement** /ˈsteɪtmənt/ *n.* [C] **1** a printed record of money paid, received, etc: *My bank sends me monthly statements.* **2** sth that you say or write that gives information or an opinion: *Some of the statements in the brochure are misleading.* **3** sth that is written and then made public: *a press statement*

**ˌstatement of acˈcount** *n.* [C] (*Account.*) a list that a company sends to a customer giving details of the amounts of money paid and still owed for goods or services

**ˌstatement of afˈfairs** *n.* [C] (*Account.*) a list that shows the assets and the debts of a company or person that has become or is about to become BANKRUPT

**ˌstatement of ˈclaim** *n.* [C] (*Law*) a written statement made by a person or company that is making a legal claim against sb, giving details of why they are doing so, etc.

**ˌstatement of ˈearnings** (*also* **ˈearnings ˌstatement**) *n.* [C] (*AmE*) (*Account.*) a record that a company publishes of its income and expenses for a particular period
SYN EARNINGS REPORT

**ˌstatement of ˈprinciples** *n.* [C] (*abbr* **SOP**) **1** a statement in which a company or an organization describes its aims and beliefs: *a five-point statement of principles* **2** (*Account.*) **Statement of Principles** an official set of rules for recording a company's finances

**ˌstatement of ˈpurpose** = MISSION STATEMENT

**ˌstate of the ˈart** *adj.* using the most modern techniques or methods; as good as it can be at the present time: *state-of-the-art equipment*

**statewide** /ˈsteɪtwaɪd/ *adj., adv.* happening or existing in all parts of a state of the US

**static** /ˈstætɪk/ *adj.* not moving, changing or developing: *Pre-tax profits have* ***remained*** *static.*

**station** /ˈsteɪʃn/ *n.* [C] **1** a place in a room where a particular worker does their job **2** a place or building where a special type of work is done or a service is prepared: *the assembly station on the production line* ◇ *a petrol/gas ~* **3** a radio or television company and the programmes it broadcasts

**stationery** /ˈsteɪʃənri; *AmE* -neri/ *n.* [U] materials for writing and for using in an office: *office stationery*

★ **statistic** /stəˈtɪstɪk/ *n.* **1 statistics** (*also* **stats**, *infml.*) [pl.] a collection of information shown in numbers: *economic/employment ~*
⊙ ***current/new/official*** *~* ♦ ***accurate/gloomy/surprising*** *~* ♦ *to* ***analyse/collect*** *~* ♦ *~* ***indicate/prove/show*** *sth*
**2 statistics** (*also* **stats**, *infml.*) [U] the science of collecting and analysing **statistics**: *She has a background in statistics.* **3** [C] a piece of information shown in numbers: *The key statistic used to price TV ads is the number of viewers.*
⊙ *an* ***important/a vital*** *~* ♦ *a* ***simple/startling*** *~* ♦ *to* ***release/use*** *a ~*
▸ **staˈtistical** /-ɪkl/ *adj.*: *a statistical analysis* **staˈtistically** /-ɪkli/ *adv.*

**staˌtistical ˈprocess conˌtrol** *n.* [U] (*abbr* **SPC**) (*Product.*) the use of STATISTICS to analyse data and to study a process continuously over a period of time in order to control its quality and how efficient it is

**staˌtistical ˈquality conˌtrol** *n.* [U] (*abbr* **SQC**) (*Product.*) the use of STATISTICS to study data about processes and products in order to make sure that the quality of items produced always meets the required standard

**statistician** /ˌstætɪsˈtɪʃn/ *n.* [C] a person who works with or studies STATISTICS

**stats** /stæts/ = STATISTICS

**status** /ˈsteɪtəs; *AmE also* ˈstætəs/ *n.* **1** [U; C, usu. sing.] the situation at a particular time: *the current status of orders* ◇ *a status report* **2** [U; C, usu. sing.] the legal or official position of a company, person, country, etc: *The legal status of the firm is limited company.* **3** [U; C, usu. sing.] the level or position of sb/sth in relation to others: *low status jobs* **4** [U] high rank or social position: *The job has status and a high salary.* ◇ *A Porsche is still a* ***status symbol.***

**'status di,vide** *n.* [C, usu. sing.] (*HR*) a difference in the way one group of employees is treated or considered compared with another group: *a status divide between office and factory workers*

**'status en,quiry** *n.* [C] (*BrE*) a request made to a bank to give a report about whether a customer is likely to be able to pay back a loan, pay rent, etc.; the report that the bank gives

**statute** /'stætʃuːt/ *n.* **1** [C,U] a law that is passed by a parliament, council, etc. and formally written down **2** [C] a formal rule of an organization or institution: *company statutes*

★**statutory** /'stætʃətri; *AmE* -tɔːri/ *adj.* fixed by law; that must be done by law: *The employers failed to carry out their statutory duties.* ◇ *the statutory retirement age*
◉ *~ obligations/rights* ♦ *~ powers/procedures/requirements*
▸ **'statutorily** *adv.*

**,statutory 'books** *n.* [pl.] (*Law*) a set of records that a company must keep by law, giving details of the directors, shareholders, meetings, etc.

**,statutory 'company** *n.* [C] in the UK, a company formed by a government law to provide a public service, such as supplying gas or water

**,Statutory Ma'ternity Pay** (*abbr* **SMP**), **,Statutory Pa'ternity Pay** (*abbr* **SPP**) *n.* [U] (*HR*) in the UK, the amount of money that a working mother or father is legally allowed when they take time away from work when they have a baby, if they meet particular conditions

**,statutory re'port** *n.* [C] (*Law*) a report that a company must publish by law, esp. the annual financial report

**,Statutory 'Sick Pay** *n.* [U] (*abbr* **SSP**) (*HR*) in the UK, money an employer must pay for a period of time to an employee who is ill/sick

**stay** /steɪ/ *v.* **PHRV** **,stay 'on** to continue working, etc. somewhere for longer than expected or after other people have left: *He was due to retire but decided to stay on for another year.* **,stay 'out** (about workers) to continue to be on strike → idiom at AHEAD OF

**'stay-at-home** *adj.* a stay-at-home mother or father is one who stays at home to look after their children instead of going out to work

**'staying ,power** *n.* [U] the ability to continue doing sth even when it becomes difficult: *Internet companies with staying power* (= that last longer than others)

**STD** /,es tiː 'diː/ *abbr* **subscriber trunk dialling** a system of making direct telephone calls over long distances

**std.** *abbr* (*written*) standard

**steady** /'stedi/ *adj., v., adv.*
• *adj.* (**-dier, -diest**) **1** developing, growing, etc. gradually and in an even and regular way: *a ~ increase/decline in sales* **2** not changing and not interrupted: *She has a steady job with a good salary.* **SYN** REGULAR, STABLE ▸ **'steadily** *adv.*: *Sales have grown steadily.*
• *v.* [T,I] (**-dies, -dying, -died, -died**) to stop, or to make sth stop, changing and become regular again or stay at the same level: *The yen steadied against the dollar.*
• *adv.* in a way that does not change: *Their shares* ***held*** *steady at €1.5.*

**steal** /stiːl/ *v., n.*
• *v.* [T,I] (**stole** /stəʊl; *AmE* stoʊl/ **stolen** /'stəʊlən; *AmE* 'stoʊ-/) to take sth from a person, shop/store, etc. without permission and without intending to return it or pay for it: *I* ***had*** *my credit card* ***stolen.*** ◇ (*fig.*) *We will steal business from our competitors.* **IDM** **steal a 'march (on sb)** (*not in the pass.*) to gain an advantage over sb by doing sth before them
• *n.* [sing.] (*esp. AmE*) something that is for sale at an unexpectedly low price: *The stock was* ***a steal*** *at $2.20.*

**'stealth ,marketing** *n.* [U] a method of advertising your products without letting people realize that you are trying to make them buy sth

**steel** /stiːl/ *n.* [U] **1** a strong hard metal that is made of a mixture of iron and CARBON **2** the industry that produces steel: *steel workers*

**steelmaker** /'stiːlmeɪkə(r)/ *n.* [C] a company that makes steel
▸ **'steelmaking** *n.* [U]

**steelworks** /'stiːlwɜːks; *AmE* -wɜːrks/ *n.* [C with sing./pl. v.] (*pl.* **steelworks**) a factory where steel is made

**steep** /stiːp/ *adj.* (**-er, -est**) **1** (about a rise or fall in an amount) sudden and very big: *a steep increase in prices* **2** (*infml.*) (about a price or an expense) very high; too high: *the steep cost of hiring and training staff*
▸ **'steeply** *adv.*

**'steering com,mittee** (*also* **'steering group**) *n.* [C with sing./pl. v.] a group of people who are not directly involved in a project, but who are responsible for such things as making sure that it fits with the company's policy and aims, and that each stage is completed within the agreed time and cost

**stellar** /'stelə(r)/ *adj.* (often used in newspapers) excellent: *The company has achieved stellar growth.*

**steno** /'stenəʊ; *AmE* -noʊ/ = STENOGRAPHER, STENOGRAPHY

**stenographer** /stə'nɒgrəfə(r); *AmE* -'nɑːg-/ = SHORTHAND TYPIST

**stenography** /stə'nɒgrəfi; *AmE* -'nɑːg-/ (*also* **'steno**) = SHORTHAND

**step** /step/ *n., v.*

• *n.* [C] one of a series of things that you do in order to achieve sth or to solve a problem: *an important step towards achieving our goal* IDM **in/out of 'step (with sb/sth)** thinking or doing sth in the same way as/in a different way from other people: *They have raised their prices in step with other airlines.* **keep 'step with sb/sth** to be aware of changes that are taking place and be ready to change too if necessary: *keeping step with key trends* **one step a'head (of sb)** in a better position than sb: *to stay one step ahead of the competitors*

• *v.* (-pp-) IDM **step into the 'breach** to do sb's job or work when they are suddenly or unexpectedly unable to do it **step into sb's 'shoes** to continue a job or the work that sb else has started PHRV **,step a'side/'down** to leave an important job or position and let sb else take your place: *He will step down as chairman next year.* **,step 'in** to help sb in a dispute or difficult situation: *The bank stepped in to rescue the company.* **,step sth 'up** to increase the amount, speed, etc. of sth: *We stepped up production.*

**'STEP a,nalysis** /step/ = PEST ANALYSIS

**'step change** *n.* [C, usu. sing.] a big change or improvement in sth: *a step change in production levels*

**'step-up** *n.* [sing.] an increase or improvement in sth: *a step-up in consumer spending*

★ **sterling** /'stɜːlɪŋ; *AmE* 'stɜːrlɪŋ/ *n.* [U] the money system of the UK, based on the pound: *We accept payment in US dollars or pounds sterling.*

**stevedore** /'stiːvədɔː(r)/ (*also* **'longshoreman**) *n.* [C] (*both AmE*) a person whose job is moving goods on and off ships SYN DOCKER (*BrE*) ▸ **'stevedore** *v.* [T,I]

**stewardship** /'stjuːədʃɪp; *AmE* 'stuːərd-/ *n.* [U] the act of taking care of or managing sth, for example an organization, property or money: *The business has grown* ***under*** *her stewardship.*

**stick** /stɪk/ *v.* (**stuck**, **stuck** /stʌk/) **1** [T] (*used in the form* **be stuck**) to stay at the same level, value, etc.; to fail to improve: *Sales are stuck at $200 000.* **2** [I] to stay at the same level, value, etc: *Unemployment is sticking at around 12%.* IDM **stick to the/your 'knitting** to continue to do what you know and can do well: *Their success is based on sticking to the knitting.*

**sticker** /'stɪkə(r)/ *n.* [C] a sticky label with information, pictures, etc. on ▸ **'sticker** *v.* [T]: *stickered items*

**'sticker price** = LIST PRICE

**'sticker shock** *n.* [U] an unpleasant feeling that you get when you see that sth is much more expensive than you expected

**sticky** /'stɪki/ *adj., n.*

• *adj.* (-**kier**, -**kiest**) **1** (about paper, labels, etc.) with glue on one side so that you can stick it to a surface **2** (*IT*) (about a website) that makes people want to stay for longer than usual or visit more often **3** (*Econ.*) (about prices or wages) slow to change or react to change: *Inflation remains sticky.* ▸ **'stickiness** *n.* [U]: *a website's stickiness*

• *n.* [C] (*pl.* -**kies**) (*also* **'sticky note**) a small piece of sticky paper that you use for writing a note on, and that can easily be removed SYN POST-IT

**stiff** /stɪf/ *adj., v.*

• *adj.* (-**er**, -**est**) **1** more difficult or severe than usual: *stiff competition* **2** (*infml.*) (about a price, etc.) high or too high: *a stiff $30 entrance fee* **3** firm and difficult to bend or move: *stiff cardboard* SYN INFLEXIBLE

• *v.* [T] (*AmE*) (*infml.*) **~ sb (on/for sth)** to cheat sb or not pay them what you owe them or what they expect: *He said they had stiffed him on his fee.*

★ **stimulate** /'stɪmjuleɪt/ *v.* [T] **1** to make sth develop or become more active: *to stimulate demand* **2** to make sb interested and excited about sth: *Are you stimulated by your work?* ▸ **'stimulating** *adj.*: *I don't find the work very stimulating.* **,stimu'lation** /-'leɪʃn/ *n.* [U] **'stimulative** /-lətɪv/ *adj.*

**stimulus** /'stɪmjələs/ *n.* [C, usu. sing., U] (*pl.* **stimuli** /-laɪ; -liː/) **~ (to/for sth)** something that helps sb/sth to develop better or more quickly: *the use of interest rate policies as a stimulus to economic growth*

**sting** /stɪŋ/ *v.* (**stung**, **stung** /stʌŋ/) [T] (*infml.*) **1** to charge sb more money than expected: *We got stung for a large bill.* **2** to make sb lose money: *They were stung by a collapse in the share price.*

**stipend** /ˈstaɪpend/ *n.* [C] (*esp. AmE*) a fixed amount of money that is paid regularly to sb as wages or money to live on: *a stipend for attending board meetings*
▸ **stiˈpendiary** /-diəri; *AmE* -dieri/ *adj.*: *stipendiary training* (= you receive a fixed amount of money while you do it) **stiˈpendiary** *n.* [C] (*pl.* **-ries**)

**stipulate** /ˈstɪpjuleɪt/ *v.* [T] (*fml.*) (in a contract, etc.) to state clearly that sth must be done, or how it must be done: *A delivery date is stipulated in the contract.* ▸ ˌ**stipuˈlation** /-ˈleɪʃn/ *n.* [C,U]

**stk.** (*also* **STK**) *abbr* a short way of writing **stock** (= goods or shares)

★ **stock** /stɒk; *AmE* stɑːk/ *n.*, *v.*, *adj.*
• *n.* **1** (*Comm.*; *Product.*) [U,C] the goods that a business has for sale at a particular time: *a fast turnover of stock* ◇ *That model is not* ***in stock.*** ◇ *I'm afraid we're* ***out of stock.*** ◇ *We carry a large stock of office stationery.* SYN INVENTORY
● *to* ***order/replenish*** *~* ◆ *to* ***have/hold/keep*** *(a) ~ (of sth)* ◆ *to* ***control/get rid of/reduce*** *~*
**2** (*Account.*; *Product.*) [U,C] (*esp. BrE*) goods owned by a company, such as raw materials or parts, products being made and finished products: *Just-in-time manufacturing allows firms to reduce their stock levels and so cut storage costs.* SYN INVENTORY
● *to* ***build (up)/maintain/order/replenish/store*** *~* ◆ *to* ***control/get rid of/reduce/run down/sell (off)*** *~*
**3** [C,U] a quantity of a particular raw material, product, supply, etc. that is available to be used if needed: *global ~s of cereals/fossil fuels* ◇ *selling off surplus stocks*
● *to* ***build up/maintain/replenish*** *~* ◆ *to* ***control/run down*** *~*
**4** (*Finan.*) [U] (*esp. AmE*) all the shares a company can make available; the value of those shares: *He owns 32% of the stock.* ◇ *The value of the company's stock has risen.* ◇ *to issue stock* SYN CAPITAL STOCK
**5** (*Stock Ex.*) [C, usu. pl., U] a number of shares in a company that one investor holds: (*AmE*) *She sold her large* ***block of stock*** *in the company* ◇ *to buy/have/hold ~s* **6** (*Stock Ex.*) [pl.] the shares of a particular company, type of company or industry: *blue-chip/technology ~s* ◇ *to buy/hold/invest in/sell ~s* **7** (*Finan.*) [U,C] (*BrE*) a type of bond with a fixed rate of interest that a government sells in order to borrow money: (*BrE*) *to invest in* ***stocks and shares*** ◇ *to buy/have/hold/invest in/sell (government) ~* IDM **on the ˈstocks** in the process of being made, built or prepared: *The new model is on the stocks.* → idiom at TAKE *v.*
• *v.* [T] **1** (about a shop/store, etc.) to keep a supply of a particular type of goods to sell: *We stock a wide range of laptops.* **2** (*often pass.*) to have a supply of sth ready to be used: *a well-stocked bookstore* PHR V ˌ**stock ˈup (on/with sth)** to buy a lot of sth so that you can use it later: *Consumers are stocking up on T-shirts and shorts.*
• *adj.* usu. available for sale in a shop/store: *stock sizes*

**stockbroker** /ˈstɒkbrəʊkə(r); *AmE* ˈstɑːkbroʊ-/ (*also* **ˈbroker**) *n.* [C] (*Stock Ex.*) a person or an organization that buys and sells shares for other people

**stockbrokerage** /ˈstɒkbrəʊkərɪdʒ; *AmE* ˈstɑːkbroʊk-/ *n.* (*Stock Ex.*) **1** [C] an organization that buys and sells shares, bonds, etc. for other people: *He works for a stockbrokerage.* **2** [U] = STOCKBROKING

**stockbroking** /ˈstɒkbrəʊkɪŋ; *AmE* ˈstɑːkbroʊ-/ (*also* **ˈstockbrokerage**) *n.* [U] (*Stock Ex.*) the activity of buying and selling shares, bonds, etc. for other people as a business; the business of a STOCKBROKER: *a stockbroking business*

**ˈstock ˌbuyback** = SHARE BUYBACK

**ˈstock cerˌtificate** = SHARE CERTIFICATE

**ˈstock ˌcompany** *n.* [C] (*AmE*) a company owned by people who have shares in it

**ˈstock conˌtrol** (*also* **ˈstock ˌmanagement**) *n.* [U] (*both esp. BrE*) (*Comm.*; *Product.*) the process of making sure that a suitable quantity of goods, materials or parts are stored and available at any time while keeping the costs of doing this as low as possible; the department in a company responsible for this: *stock control software* ◇ *She works in stock control.* SYN INVENTORY CONTROL
▸ **ˈstock conˌtroller** (*also* **ˈstock ˌmanager**) *n.* [C]

**ˈstock count** *n.* [C] (*esp. BrE*) (*Account.*) an act of checking how many items a shop/store or business has available for sale
SYN INVENTORY COUNT

**'stock ˌdividend** = SCRIP DIVIDEND

★ **'stock exˌchange** *n.* [C, usu. sing.] (*often* **Stock Exchange**) a place where shares in companies are bought and sold; all of the business activity involved in doing this: *The firm trades* **on** *the London Stock Exchange.* ◇ *a stock exchange listed company*

**stockholder** /'stɒkhəʊldə(r); *AmE* 'stɑːkhoʊldər/ = SHAREHOLDER

**ˌstockholder 'equity** (*also* **ˌstockholders' 'equity**) = SHAREHOLDER EQUITY

**ˌstockholder of 'record** = SHAREHOLDER OF RECORD

**ˌstockholders' 'equity** = STOCKHOLDER EQUITY

**ˌstockholder 'value** = SHAREHOLDER VALUE

**stockholding** /'stɒkhəʊldɪŋ; *AmE* 'stɑːkhoʊldɪŋ/ = SHAREHOLDING

**ˌstock in'centive ˌplan** = SHARE INCENTIVE PLAN

**'stock ˌindex** = SHARE INDEX

**ˌstock in 'hand** *n.* [U] (*BrE*) (*Account.*; *Comm.*) the materials, parts, finished products, etc. that a company holds ready to be used: *value of stock in hand at year end*

**ˌstock-in-'trade** *n.* [U]
**1** (*Account.*) (*also* **'trading stock**) the goods that a business owns at a particular time, including raw materials or parts, products being made and finished products SYN INVENTORY **2** the normal work of a business: *Convenience is their stock-in-trade.*

**'stock ˌissue** (*also* **'stock ˌoffer**) = SHARE ISSUE

**stockist** /'stɒkɪst; *AmE* 'stɑːk-/ *n.* [C] (*BrE*) a shop/store that regularly sells a particular brand of product: *Click to find your nearest stockist.*

**'stock-ˌkeeping** *n.* [U] (*Comm.*; *Product.*) the activity of checking that a shop/store or business has the right amount of goods available to sell

**stocklist** /'stɒklɪst; *AmE* 'stɑːk-/ *n.* [C] (*BrE*) (*Comm.*) a list published by a company of the products that it has available for sale to the public, and their prices

**'stock ˌmanagement** = STOCK CONTROL

★ **'stock ˌmarket** (*also* **'market**) *n.* [C] (*usu.* **the stock market**) the business of buying and selling shares in companies and the place where this happens; a stock exchange: *The company was* **floated on** *the stock market* (= its shares were sold to the public) *in 2004.* ◇ *to* **invest in** *the stock market* ◇ *falling stock markets* ◇ *a stock market slump*

**'stock ˌoffer** = SHARE OFFER

**'stock ˌoption** = SHARE OPTION

**'stock-out** (*AmE* **stockout**) *n.* [C] (*Comm.*) a situation in which a company or shop/store has no more examples of a particular item available: *to avoid/minimize/prevent ~s*

**'stock ˌpicking** *n.* [U] (*Stock Ex.*) the activity of choosing which shares to buy, sell or hold

**stockpile** /'stɒkpaɪl; *AmE* 'stɑːk-/ *n.*, *v.*
• *n.* [C] a large supply of sth, esp. sth that is kept to be used in the future if necessary: *an emergency oil stockpile* ◇ *stockpiles of unsold goods*
• *v.* [T] to collect and keep a large supply of sth: *They stockpiled goods in case of a strike.*

**'stock price** = SHARE PRICE

**'stock right** (*also* **right**) *n.* [C, usu. pl.] (*Finan.*) a right offered to existing shareholders to buy more shares at a particular price by a particular date

**stockroom** /'stɒkruːm; -rʊm; *AmE* 'stɑːk-/ *n.* [C] a room for storing things in a shop/store, an office, etc.

**'stock split** (*also* **split**) *n.* [C] (*AmE*) (*Finan.*) an occasion when a company divides its SHARE CAPITAL into more shares in order to lower the price of each share. Shareholders are given new shares according to how many they already hold.
SYN SHARE SPLIT

★ **stocktaking** /'stɒkteɪkɪŋ; *AmE* 'stɑːk-/ *n.* [U] (*esp. BrE*) (*Account.*) the process of making a list of all the goods or materials that a company, shop/store, etc. has stored and available for use or sale; the time when this is done: *The warehouse is closed for stocktaking.* ◇ *We* **do** *the end-of-year stocktaking in March.*
▸ **'stocktake** *n.* [C] **'stocktaker** *n.* [C]

**'stock ˌticker** *n.* [C] (*Stock Ex.*) an electronic display that shows the current price of shares

**ˌstock 'turnover** (*also* **ˌstock 'turn**) *n.* [C,U] (*also* **ˌstock 'turnover ˌratio** [C]) (*all BrE*) (*Account.*) the relationship between the value of goods a business sells in a particular period, usu. 12 months, and the average value of the goods it has available to sell: *If this product does fewer than 12 stock turns a year, it is overstocked.* SYN INVENTORY TURNOVER

**ˌstock valuˈation** *n.* [U,C] (*Account.*) **1** the process of calculating the value of all the goods, finished or not finished, and materials that a company, shop/store, etc. has stored and available for use or sale at the end of a particular period; the value that is calculated **2** the activity or process of calculating how much shares in a company are worth

**stop** /stɒp; *AmE* stɑːp/ *v., n.*
• *v.* [T] (-pp-) **1** (*also* **ˈcancel**) to prevent money from being paid: *to stop a cheque* (= tell the bank not to pay it) **2** if you **stop** an account, you will no longer supply goods or services to a particular customer
• *n.* **1** [C] an act of preventing money from being paid: *to put a stop on a cheque* **2** [U,C] a situation when a business will no longer supply a customer with goods or services: *We have put your account* ***on stop.***

**ˌstop-ˈgo** *adj.* **1** used to describe sth that does not continue smoothly, but stops and starts: *stop-go negotiations* **2** (*Econ.*) (*BrE*) used to describe the policy of first restricting and then encouraging economic activity and growth: *the damaging stop-go economic cycle*

**stoppage** /ˈstɒpɪdʒ; *AmE* ˈstɑːp-/ *n.* [C] (*HR*) a situation in which people stop working as part of a protest or strike: *a number of 24-hour stoppages ◇ to call/join/organize/stage a ~*

**ˌstoppage in ˈtransit** (*also* **ˌstoppage in tranˈsitu** /ˈtraenzətuː; ˈtraensə-/) *n.* [U] (*Comm.*) a situation in which a seller discovers that a buyer is unable to pay for goods already sent out, and so stops them from being delivered

**ˈstop-work ˌmeeting** *n.* [C] (*HR*) in Australia and New Zealand, a type of strike in which workers stop their work in order to attend a meeting to discuss working conditions

★ **storage** /ˈstɔːrɪdʒ/ *n.* [U] **1** the process of keeping sth in a particular place until it is needed; the space where things can be kept: *The goods are* ***in storage.*** *◇ ~ costs/space*
**○** ***long-term/short-term ~*** ♦ ***a ~ depot/facility***
**2** (*IT*) the process of keeping information on a computer; how it is kept: *data storage ◇ 50 MB of storage space*
**○** ***computer/document ~*** ♦ ***~ devices/hardware/media/software***

★ **store** /stɔː(r)/ *n., v.*
• *n.* **1** [C] a large shop that sells many different types of goods: *a department store* **2** [C] (*esp. AmE*) a shop, large or small: *a retail store ◇ a clothing store ◇ an online store* **3 stores** [pl.] goods of a particular kind or for a particular purpose: *fuel/medical ~s* **4** [C] (*often* **stores** [pl.]) a place where goods of a particular kind are kept: *a frozen food store* **5** [C] a quantity or supply of sth that is available to use: *a store of information*
→ idiom at SHOP *n.*
• *v.* [T] **1** to put sth somewhere and keep it there to use later: *The goods are stored in warehouses.* **2** (*IT*) to keep information in a computer

**ˌstore-and-ˈforward** *adj.* (*IT*) using or relating to an electronic system in which messages are collected in one place and then sent to another

**ˈstore ˌaudit** (*also* **ˈretail ˌaudit, ˈretail store ˌaudit**) *n.* [C] (*Market.*) the process of calculating how many of a particular product have been sold in different shops/stores

**ˈstore brand** (*also* **ˈstore ˌlabel**) *n.* [C] (*both AmE*) (*Comm.; Market.*) a product that a shop/store sells with its own name on: *lower-priced store brands* SYN OWN BRAND

**ˈstore card** *n.* [C] a plastic card that you can use to buy things in one particular shop/store and pay for them later

**ˈstore deˌtective** *n.* [C] a person employed by a large shop/store to watch customers and make sure they do not steal goods

**storefront** /ˈstɔːfrʌnt; *AmE* ˈstɔːrf-/ *n.* [C] (*AmE*) **1** the front of a shop/store **2** a room at the front of a shop/store: *a storefront office* **3** (*E-comm.*) (*also* **ˌweb ˈstorefront**) a website that a company uses to sell goods or services

**storekeeper** /ˈstɔːkiːpə(r); *AmE* ˈstɔːrk-/ = SHOPKEEPER, STOREMAN

**ˈstore ˌlabel** = STORE BRAND

**storeman** /ˈstɔːmən; *AmE* ˈstɔːr-/ *n.* [C] (*pl.* **-men** /-men/) (*BrE*) (*also* **ˈstorekeeper**, *AmE, BrE*) a person in charge of the goods or materials stored in a shop/store, factory, etc.

**storeroom** /ˈstɔːruːm; -rʊm/ *n.* [C] a room used for storing things

**ˈstore ˌtraffic** *n.* [U] (*Market.*) the number of people who visit a shop/store

**storyboard** /ˈstɔːribɔːd; *AmE* -bɔːrd/ *n.* [C] (*Market.*) a series of drawings or pictures that show the outline of the story of a television advertisement, a film/movie, etc.

**ˌstraight-ˈline ˌmethod** *n.* [sing.] (*Account.*) a way of reducing the value of an asset in a company's financial records in which the value is reduced by the same amount each year. This amount is the difference between the original value of the asset and the final value, divided by a particular number of years.

**ˌstraight ˈrebuy** *n.* [C] (*Market.*) when a person or a business orders exactly the same product again from the same supplier

**stranglehold** /ˈstræŋglhəʊld; *AmE* -hoʊld/ *n.* [sing.] complete control over sth that makes it impossible to develop in a normal way: *The company has a complete stranglehold **on** the market.*

**strapline** /ˈstræplaɪn/ = SLOGAN

**strapped** /stræpt/ *adj.* (*infml.*) having little or not enough money: *Many companies are **strapped for cash**.* → CASH-STRAPPED

★**strategic** /strəˈtiːdʒɪk/ (*also* **strategical** /strəˈtiːdʒɪkl/ *less freq.*) *adj.* related to a business's efforts to gain an advantage or achieve a particular purpose: ~ *goals/objectives* ◇ *The merger was a sound strategic move.* ▸ **straˈtegically** /-kli/ *adv.*

**straˌtegic alˈliance** *n.* [C] an arrangement in which companies work together in order to gain an advantage or achieve a particular purpose

**straˌtegic aˈnalysis** *n.* [U,C] the process of examining the current situation of a company, its markets, the economy, etc. and of predicting future changes to develop a plan which will allow the company to gain as much advantage as possible

**straˌtegic ˈbusiness ˌunit** *n.* [C] (*abbr* **SBU**) a part of a business, for example a particular range of products or a division, that has its own customers and competitors and is allowed to operate independently and develop business plans

**straˌtegic ˈfit** *n.* [sing.] the extent to which an action that a company may take would help it achieve its aims

**straˈtegic ˈhuman reˈsource ˌmanagement** *n.* [U] (*abbr* **SHRM**) (*HR*) the process of a company organizing and using its employees in the way that best helps it achieve its aims

**straˌtegic ˈindustry** *n.* [C] an industry that is considered to be extremely important to the economy or the defence of a country or region

**straˌtegic inforˈmation ˌsystem** *n.* [C] (*abbr* **SIS**) a computer system used in an organization to help it plan how to achieve a particular purpose or gain an advantage

**straˌtegic ˈmanagement** *n.* [U] the process of predicting the opportunities, difficulties, etc. that a company will have in the future and planning how the company can gain as much advantage as possible

**straˌtegic ˈmarketing** *n.* [U] the process of a company planning where and how to sell its products most effectively

**straˌtegic ˈpartner** *n.* [C] another company that a business works with in order to gain an advantage or achieve a particular aim ▸ **straˌtegic ˈpartnering** *n.* [U]

**straˌtegic ˈplanning** *n.* [U] the activity of analysing the progress of a company or an organization and deciding what it must do in order to be successful in the future

**straˌtegic ˈvalue** *n.* [U] the benefits that a business would bring to another company if that company bought it

**strategist** /ˈstrætədʒɪst/ *n.* [C] **1** sb whose job involves developing a plan which will allow the company to gain as much advantage as possible: *a market strategist* **2** sb who is good at analysing a situation and making plans: *She's a great strategist.*

★**strategy** /ˈstrætədʒi/ *n.* [C,U] (*pl.* **-gies**) a plan that is intended to achieve a particular purpose; the process of planning sth: *We need to develop a global marketing strategy.* ◇ *a change/shift in* ~

⊕ *to **build/devise/plan** a ~* • *to **follow/implement** a ~* • *a **clear/good/winning** ~* • *a **broad/core** ~* • *a **long-term/medium-term/short-term** ~* • *a ~ **director/group/team***

**ˌstratified ˈsampling** *n.* [U] (*Market.*) a method of research in which people from different groups of the population are used in tests to find information about the whole population ▸ **ˌstratified ˈsample** *n.* [C]

**streak** /striːk/ *n.* [C] a series of successes or failures: *The company has been on a **winning streak** recently.*

**stream** /striːm/ *n.* [C] a continuous flow of sth: *a **steady** stream of orders* **IDM** **be, come, go on ˈstream**; **bring sth on ˈstream** to be in operation or available; to make sth be in operation or available: *The new plant will come on stream next May.*

**streamline** /ˈstriːmlaɪn/ *v.* [T] **1** to make a system, an organization, etc. work better, esp. in a way that saves money: *We streamlined the production process.* **2** (*often* **stream-**

**lined**, *used as an adj.*) to give sth a smooth even shape so that it can move quickly and easily through air or water: *a more streamlined design* ▶ **'streamlining** *n.* [C,U]: *The airline needs a major streamlining.*

**ˌstream of 'revenue** = REVENUE STREAM

**'street price** *n.* [C] (*esp. AmE*) the price at which a product is sold in shops/stores SYN RETAIL PRICE

★ **strength** /streŋθ/ *n.* **1** [U] how strong a country's currency is in relation to others: *the continuing strength of the dollar against the yen* **2** [U] the power and influence that sb/sth has: *The new base will boost the airline's strength in Europe.* **3** [C] a quality or an ability that sb/sth has that gives them an advantage: *The plan has both* ***strengths and weaknesses.*** **4** [U] the ability that sth has to resist force or hold heavy weights without breaking or being damaged: *Carbon fibre has superior strength.* **5** [U] the number of people in a group, a team or an organization: *The board is now up to* ***full strength*** (= with all the members it needs). IDM **go from ˌstrength to 'strength** to become more and more successful **on the strength of sth** because sb has been influenced or persuaded by sth: *I got the job on the strength of your recommendation.* → idiom at PLAY *v.*

★ **strengthen** /'streŋθn/ *v.* [T,I] to become stronger; to make sth/sb stronger: *The yen has strengthened against the dollar.*

**stress** /stres/ *n., v.*

• *n.* **1** [U,C] pressure or worry caused by the problems in sb's life or work: *The course teaches you to handle workplace stress.* ◇ *the* ***stresses and strains*** *of running a firm* ◇ *stress management* (= dealing with stress)
⊙ *to* ***be under/suffer (from)/have*** ~ • *to* ***cause/increase*** ~ • *to* ***avoid/reduce/relieve*** ~ • *to* ***cope with/deal with/manage*** ~
**2** [U,C] pressure that is put on sth that can harm it or cause problems: *Funding problems were placing stress* ***on*** *the project.*
⊙ *to* ***be under/put sth under*** ~ • ***economic/financial/market*** ~
**3** [U] special importance given to sth: *to lay/place ~ on sth*

• *v.* [T] to emphasize a fact, an idea, etc: *She stressed the importance of meeting the deadline.*

**stressed** /strest/ *adj.* **1** (*also* **ˌstressed 'out**) too worried and tired to be able to relax **2** that has a lot of pressure on it: *financially stressed companies*

**stressful** /'stresfl/ *adj.* causing a lot of anxiety and worry: *a ~ job/lifestyle/situation*

**'stress ˌpuppy** *n.* [C] (*AmE*) (*infml.*) a person who enjoys stress but complains about it all the time

**stretch** /stretʃ/ *v., n.*

• *v.* **1** [I] (*in negative sentences and questions about an amount of money*) to be enough to buy or pay for sth: *Our budget won't stretch* ***to*** *a new server.* **2** [T] to make money last longer or buy more than planned: *tips for stretching your training budget* **3** [T] to make use of all your money, supplies, time, etc. so that there is little left: *The extra orders have stretched us* ***to the limit.*** **4** [T] to make use of all sb's skill, intelligence, etc: *My job really stretches me.* **5** (*Market.*) [T] if a company **stretches** a brand, they use a successful brand name to sell new types of products or services → idiom at RULE *n.*

• *n.* IDM **at full 'stretch** using as much energy as possible, or the greatest possible amount of supplies: *working at full stretch*

**ˌstrict lia'bility** *n.* [U] (*Law*) a situation where a person or company is responsible for the harm or injury that their actions, products, etc. cause, even though they did not intend to cause the harm or had tried to act carefully

**strife** /straɪf/ *n.* [U] (used esp. in newspapers) angry disagreement between two groups of people: *industrial strife* (= strikes)

★ **strike** /straɪk/ *n., v.*

• *n.* [C] (*HR*) a period of time when an organized group of employees of a company stops working because of a disagreement over pay or conditions: *a 48-hour strike by production workers* ◇ (*BrE*) *The workforce threatened to* ***come out*** *on strike.* ◇ *to take strike action*
⊙ *to* ***call (for)/have/hold*** *a* ~ • *to* ***be (out)/go*** *on* ~ • *to* ***call sb out*** *on* ~

• *v.* **1** (*HR*) [I] to refuse to work, as a protest: *to strike* ***for*** *a pay increase* ◇ *striking workers* **2** [T] to make an agreement with sb: *to ~ a bargain/contract/deal* ▶ **'striker** *n.* [C] (*HR*): *He listened to the strikers' demands.*
IDM **strike a 'balance (between A and B)** to manage to find a way of being fair to two opposing things: *You need to strike a balance between your work and your personal life.*
**strike/sound a cautious, optimistic, etc. 'note/'tone; strike/sound a note of 'caution, 'optimism,**

**etc.** to express feelings or opinions of a particular kind **strike 'gold** to find or do sth that brings you a lot of success or money: *They struck gold with fat-free ice cream.* → idiom at HARD *adj.* **PHR V** **ˌstrike sb/sth 'off** to remove sb/sth's name from sth, such as the list of members of a professional group **ˌstrike 'out** **1** to start being independent: *She decided to strike out on her own and form her own company.* **2** (*AmE*) to fail

**'strike-bound** *adj.* that cannot function or move because of strikes: *strike-bound airports*

**'strike-ˌbreaker** (*AmE* **strikebreaker**) *n.* [C] (*HR*) a person who continues working or is employed to work while others are on strike, and therefore makes the strike less successful ▸ **'strike-ˌbreaking** (*AmE* **strikebreaking**) *n.* [U]

**'strike pay** *n.* [U] (*HR*) money that a union pays to its members when they are on strike

**'strike price** = EXERCISE PRICE

**'striking price** = EXERCISE PRICE

**stringent** /'strɪndʒənt/ *adj.* **1** (about a law, rule, etc.) very strict and that must be obeyed: *Licences are only granted under the most stringent conditions.* **2** (about financial conditions) difficult and very strictly controlled because there is not much money: *stringent cost controls* ▸ **'stringency** /-ənsi/ *n.* [U]: *financial stringency* **'stringently** *adv.*

**strip** /strɪp/ *v., n.*
• *v.* [T] (-pp-) **1** **~ sth from sb/sth | ~ sb/sth of sth** to remove sth from sth/sb: *Three directors were stripped of their posts after the scandal.* **2** (*Finan.*) to remove the right to interest payments from a bond so that they can be sold separately from the bond **PHR V** **ˌstrip (sth) 'down** to remove parts from sth in order to make it smaller, simpler, etc: *Many companies are stripping down to the essentials.* **ˌstrip sth 'down** to separate a machine, etc. into parts so that they can be cleaned or repaired **ˌstrip sth 'out (of sth)** **1** to remove or not include sth: *When South America is stripped out of the total, the sales figures are good.* **2** (*BrE*) to take parts out of a machine so that they can be cleaned or repaired
• *n.* [C] **1** (*AmE*) a street that has many shops/stores, restaurants, etc. along it: *Sunset Strip* **2** (*Finan.*) the right to interest payments on a bond that is sold as a separate investment

**'strip mall** *n.* [C] (*AmE*) a set of shops/stores, restaurants, etc. that are built together along a main road

★**strong** /strɒŋ; *AmE* strɔːŋ/ *adj.* (**-ger** /-gə(r)/**-gest** /-gɪst/) **1** (about a business or an industry) in a safe financial position: *one of the strongest banks in Europe* **2** (about prices, an economy, etc.) having a value that is high or increasing: *The euro is getting stronger against the dollar.* ◇ *strong share prices* **3** firmly established; difficult to defeat or destroy: *building a strong brand* **4** likely to succeed or happen: *There is a strong* ***possibility*** *that the business will fail.* **5** having a lot of power or influence: *strong management* **6** good at sth: *Design is not my* ***strong point*** (= I am not very good at it). **7** used after numbers to show the size of a group: *a 50-strong workforce* **8** not easily broken or damaged; made well: *a ~ cable/glue* OPP WEAK ▸ **'strongly** *adv.*: *The business was performing strongly.* **IDM** **be 'strong on sth** **1** to be good at sth **2** to have a lot of sth: *The report was strong on criticism, but short on ideas.* **be sb's 'strong suit** to be a subject that sb knows a lot about and does well

**strongbox** /'strɒŋbɒks; *AmE* 'strɔːŋbɑːks/ *n.* [C] a strong metal box for keeping valuable things in

**strongroom** /'strɒŋruːm; -rʊm; *AmE* 'strɔːŋ-/ *n.* [C] a room, for example in a bank, with thick walls and a strong solid door, where valuable items are kept

**structural** /'strʌktʃərəl/ *adj.* connected with the way in which sth is built or organized: *The building had several structural defects.* ▸ **'structurally** /-rəli/ *adv.*

**ˌstructural a'nalysis** *n.* [U,C] (*Tech.*) a careful examination of sth to see how its parts function together: *~ of a company*

**ˌstructural 'deficit** *n.* [C] (*Econ.*) the difference by which the amount of money a government would spend in average economic conditions is greater than the money it would receive

**ˌstructural engi'neering** *n.* [U] the activity of applying scientific knowledge to the design and construction of buildings, bridges, etc. ▸ **ˌstructural engi'neer** *n.* [C]

**ˌstructural in'flation** *n.* [U] (*Econ.*) the rate at which the prices of goods and services in a particular country naturally rise because of the government's MONETARY POLICY

**ˌstructural 'surplus** *n.* [C] (*Econ.*) the difference by which the amount of money a government would spend in average economic conditions is less than the money it would receive

**ˌstructural unemˈployment** *n.* [U] (*Econ.*) a reduction in the amount of paid work available as a result of a fall in demand for a product, changes in technology, etc. and not because of the temporary effects of the time of year, events, etc.

★ **structure** /ˈstrʌktʃə(r)/ *n., v.*

• *n.* **1** [U,C] the way in which the parts of sth are connected together, arranged or organized; a particular arrangement of parts: *changes in the structure of the company* ◇ *a pay structure* **2** [U,C] the state of being well organized or planned with all the parts linked together; a careful plan: *His presentation lacked structure.* **3** [C] a thing that is made of several parts, esp. a building: *steel structures*

• *v.* [T] (*usu. pass.*) to arrange or organize sth into a system or pattern: *a highly structured recruitment process*

**struggle** /ˈstrʌgl/ *v.* [I] **1** to have a lot of difficulties or problems while trying to achieve sth: *a struggling company* ◇ *We are still struggling along.* **2** to fight against sb/sth in order to prevent a bad situation or result: *The industry is struggling* ***with*** *weak demand.* **3** to compete with sb, esp. in order to get sth: *struggling* ***for*** *market share* ▸ **ˈstruggle** *n.* [C]: *a bitter struggle for control of the company* ◇ *the struggle* ***against*** *corruption* ◇ *It is a struggle to cope with the workload.*

**stub** /stʌb/ *n.* [C] the part of a cheque, ticket, etc. that you keep as a record when you give the other part to sb: *cheque stubs*
SYN COUNTERFOIL

**study** /ˈstʌdi/ *n., v.*

• *n.* (*pl.* **-dies**) **1** [U] the activity of learning: *scientific study* **2** [C] a piece of research: *We are conducting a study of how people use our products.* ◇ *to carry out/do/make/undertake a ~* **3 studies** [pl.] a particular person's learning activities: *I worked for a year before continuing my studies.* **4 studies** [U with sing./pl. v.] used in the names of some academic subjects: *Business Studies* **5** [U] the act of considering or examining sth in detail: *The proposal deserves careful study.*

• *v.* (**-dies, -dying, -died, -died**) **1** [T,I] to spend time learning about a subject: *studying* ***for*** *a business qualification* **2** [T] to examine sth carefully in order to understand it or find out sth: *We will study the proposals.*

**stump** /stʌmp/ *v.* PHR V **ˌstump ˈup (sth) (for sth)** (*BrE*) (*infml.*) (used esp. in newspapers) to pay money for sth: *Investors could be asked to stump up as much as $1 bn.*

**style** /staɪl/ *n.* **1** [C,U] the particular way in which sth is done: *She has an informal management style.* **2** [C] a particular design of sth, esp. clothes

**stylus** /ˈstaɪləs/ (*pl.* **styluses** *or* **styli** /ˈstaɪlaɪ; -liː/) (*also* **ˈstylus pen**) *n.* [C] (*IT*) a device like a pen that you can use to write text or draw an image on a special computer screen

**Styrofoam™** /ˈstaɪrəfəʊm; *AmE* -foʊm/ = POLYSTYRENE

**subagent** /ˈsʌbeɪdʒənt/ *n.* [C] a person or company who is paid to work for or represent an agent ▸ **ˈsubagency** /-dʒənsi/ *n.* [C] (*pl.* **-cies**)

**subcommittee** /ˈsʌbkəmɪti/ *n.* [C with sing./pl. v.] a group of people who do a particular part of the work of a committee

**subcomponent** /ˈsʌbkəmpəʊnənt; *AmE* -poʊn-/ *n.* [C] a part of one of the parts of sth

**subcontract** *v., n.*

• *v.* /ˌsʌbkənˈtrækt; *AmE* ˌsʌbˈkɑːntrækt/ [T] **~ sth (to sb)** | **~ sb (to do sth)** to pay a person or company to do some of the work that you have been given a contract to do: *We subcontracted the work* ***to*** *a small engineering firm.* ▸ **subcontracting** /ˌsʌbkənˈtræktɪŋ; *AmE* -ˈkɑːn-/ *n.* [U] **subcontractor** /ˌsʌbkənˈtræktə(r); *AmE* -ˈkɑːn-/ *n.* [C]

• *n.* /ˌsʌbˈkɒntrækt; *AmE* -ˈkɑːn-/ [C] a contract to do part of the work that has been given to another person or company

**subdivision** *n.* **1** /ˌsʌbdɪˈvɪʒn/ [U] the act of dividing a part of sth into smaller parts: *the subdivision of tasks* **2** /ˈsʌbdɪvɪʒn/ [C] one of the smaller parts into which a part of sth has been divided **3** (*Prop.*) /ˈsʌbdɪvɪʒn/ [C] (*AmE*) an area of land divided up for building houses on

**subject** /ˈsʌbdʒekt; -dʒɪkt/ *adj.* **~ to sth 1** depending on sth in order to be completed or agreed: *The deal is subject to approval by shareholders.* **2** likely to be affected by sth, esp. sth bad: *All flights today are subject to delay.* **3** under the authority of sth: *subject to EU laws*

**ˈsubject line** *n.* [C] the words in the space at the top of an email that describe what the email is about

**sub judice** /ˌsʌb ˈdʒuːdəsi; -seɪ; -keɪ/ *adj.* [not usu. before n.] (*Law*) if a legal case is **sub judice**, it is being discussed in a court and it is therefore illegal to talk about it in newspapers, on the television, etc.

**sublease** /ˈsʌbliːs/ (*also* **ˈsublet**) *n.* [C] (*Prop.*) **1** an agreement in which sb rents all or part of a property from sb who rents it from the owner **2** an agreement in which sb who rents property from the owner rents all or part of it to sb else
▸ **ˌsubˈlease** *v.* [T,I] = SUBLET *v.*

**sublet** /ˌsʌbˈlet/ *v.* [T,I] (**subletting, sublet, sublet**) (*also* **ˌsubˈlease**) (*Prop.*) **1** to rent to sb else all or part of a property that you rent from the owner: *They rented land and sublet it* ***to*** *a hotel for car parking.* **2** to rent all or part of a property from sb that rents it from the owner: *They sublet office space* ***from*** *a major airline.*
▸ **ˈsublet** *n.* [C] = SUBLEASE *n.*

**subliminal** /ˌsʌbˈlɪmɪnl/ *adj.* affecting your mind even though you are not aware of it: *~ advertising/messages*

★**submit** /səbˈmɪt/ *v.* (**-tt-**) **1** [T] to give a document, proposal, etc. to sb in authority so that they can study or consider it: *Completed projects must be submitted by 10 March.* **2** [T,I] to accept the authority or control of sb/sth; to agree to sth because of this: *to submit the dispute to arbitration* **3** (*Law or fml.*) [T] to say or suggest sth ▸ **subˈmission** /-ˈmɪʃn/ *n.* [U,C]: *the submission of proposals*

**suboptimal** /ˌsʌbˈɒptɪməl; *AmE* -ˈɑːp-/ *adj.* of less than the highest standard or quality: *There was a suboptimal performance of all the test shoes on wet surfaces.*

**suboptimization, -isation** /ˌsʌbɒptɪmaɪˈzeɪʃn; *AmE* -ɑːptɪməˈz-/ *n.* [U] a situation where individual parts of a business consider only the aims and benefits of their own departments, without considering other departments or the business as a whole

★**subordinate** *adj., n., v.*
• ***adj.*** /səˈbɔːdɪnət; *AmE* -ˈbɔːrd-/ **1** having less power or authority than sb else in a group or an organization: *The Project Manager is subordinate* ***to*** *the Product Manager.* **2** less important than sth else: *All other issues are subordinate* ***to*** *this one.*
• ***n.*** /səˈbɔːdɪnət; *AmE* -ˈbɔːrd-/ [C] a person who has a position with less authority and power than sb else in an organization
• ***v.*** /səˈbɔːdɪneɪt; *AmE* -ˈbɔːrd-/ [T] to treat sth/sb as less important than sth/sb else: *Safety considerations were subordinated to commercial interests.*

**subordinated** /səˈbɔːdɪneɪtɪd; *AmE* -ˈbɔːrd-/ *adj.* (*Finan.*) used to describe a debt that will only be paid after all other debts have been paid if the borrower has financial problems: *~ bonds/debentures/debt/notes* SYN JUNIOR

**subpar** /ˌsʌbˈpɑː(r)/ *adj.* below an average or expected level: *subpar performance*

**subpoena** /səˈpiːnə/ *n.* [C] (*Law*) a written order for sb to attend a court as a witness to give evidence or for documents to be brought as evidence: *He was served with a subpoena.* ▸ **ˌsubˈpoena** *v.* [T]: *The court subpoenaed the firm's records.*

**subrogation** /ˌsʌbrəˈgeɪʃn/ *n.* [U] (*Insur.*) the right of an insurance company to claim back money it has paid out to sb from the person, company, etc. who caused the loss, damage or injury

★**subscribe** /səbˈskraɪb/ *v.* [I] **~ (to sth)** **1** (*Stock Ex.*) to apply or agree to buy shares in a company: *to subscribe to the share offer* ◇ *The issue is* ***fully*** *subscribed.* **2** (*Comm.*) to ask or pay to receive a service, regular copies of a magazine, etc.

**subˌscribed ˈcapital** = ISSUED CAPITAL

★**subscriber** /səbˈskraɪbə(r)/ *n.* [C] **1** (*Comm.*) a person who asks or pays to receive a service, regular copies of a magazine, etc: *subscribers* ***to*** *broadband services* **2** (*Law*) a person who signs the MEMORANDUM OF ASSOCIATION for a new company and who joins with other members of the company in paying for a particular number of shares, appointing the first directors, etc.

★**subscription** /səbˈskrɪpʃn/ *n.* [C,U] **1** an amount of money that you pay to receive a service, regular copies of a magazine, etc.; the act of paying this money: *an annual subscription of £500* ◇ *Copies are available* ***by*** *subscription.*
⊙ *to* ***buy/pay/take out*** *a ~ (to sth)* • *to* ***cancel/renew*** *a ~* • *a ~* ***charge/fee/price/rate***
**2** (*Stock Ex.*) the act of applying for or agreeing to buy shares in a company: *a subscription list for shares*
⊙ *the ~* ***price/period*** • *~* ***rights***

★**subsidiary** /səbˈsɪdiəri; *AmE* -dieri/ *adj., n.*
• ***adj.*** **1** (about a company) owned or controlled by another company: *to*

*sell off subsidiary businesses* **2** connected with sth but less important than it: *the firm's subsidiary activities*
• *n.* [C] (*pl.* **-ries**) a company owned or controlled by another company

**subsidize, -ise** /ˈsʌbsɪdaɪz/ *v.* [T] to give money to sb or an organization to help pay for sth; to give a **subsidy**: *Their online service is subsidized by advertising.* ▸ **ˈsubsidized** *adj.*: *heavily subsidized imports*

**subsidy** /ˈsʌbsədi/ *n.* [C,U] (*pl.* **-dies**) money paid by a government or an organization to reduce the costs of services or of producing goods so that their prices can be kept low: *agricultural/export subsidies* ◇ *public subsidy* **of** *aviation*
⊙ *to* ***get/qualify for/receive*** *a* ~ • *to* ***give/grant/pay/provide*** *a* ~ *(on sth)*

**subsistence** /səbˈsɪstəns/ *n.* [U] the state of having just enough money or food to stay alive: *a subsistence wage*

**subˈsistence alˌlowance** *n.* [C] (*esp. BrE*) **1** a small amount of money for food and other expenses that is paid to an employee who has to travel somewhere for their work **2** an ADVANCE paid to a new employee so that they can live until they receive their first pay

**ˌsubstance over ˈform** *phr.* (*Account.*) the important idea that a company's financial records should show what has actually happened, including what it actually owns or is owed, not just the legal form of pieces of business

**ˈsubstitute goods** *n.* [pl.] (*Econ.*) similar products or services for which an increase (or fall) in demand for one, due to a change in price, leads to a fall (or increase) in demand for the other

**ˌsubstiˈtution efˌfect** *n.* [sing.] (*Econ.*) the change in demand for a product or service that happens when its price changes relative to similar products or services

**subtotal** /ˈsʌbtəʊtl; *AmE* -toʊtl/ *n.* [C] the total of a set of numbers which is then added to other totals to give a final number

**subtract** /səbˈtrækt/ *v.* [T] **~ A (from B)** to take a number or an amount away from another number or amount OPP ADD ▸ **subˈtraction** /-ˈtrækʃn/ *n.* [U,C]

**succession** /səkˈseʃn/ *n.* **1** [C, usu. sing.] a number of things or people that follow each other in time or order; a series: *Interest rates have risen for the third month* **in succession**. **2** (*HR*) [U] the act of taking over an official position or title; the right to take over an official position or title: *He became chairman* **in succession to** *Eric Main.*

**sucˈcession ˌplanning** *n.* [U] (*HR*) the process of training and preparing employees in a company or an organization so that there will always be sb to replace a senior manager who leaves or retires
▸ **sucˈcession plan** *n.* [C]

**successor** /səkˈsesə(r)/ *n.* [C] a person or thing that comes after sb/sth else and takes their/its place: *a potential successor* **to** *the CEO*

★ **sue** /suː; *BrE also* sjuː/ *v.* [T,I] to make a claim against sb in a court about sth that they have said or done to harm you: *They threatened to sue if the work was not completed.*

**suit** /suːt; *BrE also* sjuːt/ *n.* [C] **1** a set of clothes made of the same fabric, including a jacket and trousers/pants or a skirt: *a business suit* **2** (*infml.*) [usu. pl.] sb with an important job as a manager in an organization, esp. sb concerned with financial matters: *We can leave the detailed negotiations to the suits.* **3** = LAWSUIT → idiom at STRONG

**suite** /swiːt/ *n.* [C] **1** a set of rooms, esp. in a hotel or an office building: *a hotel* ~ ◇ *a suite of offices* **2** (*IT*) a set of related computer programs

**suitor** /ˈsuːtə(r); *BrE also* ˈsjuː-/ *n.* [C] a company that wants to buy another company: *a hostile suitor*

★ **sum** /sʌm/ *n., v.*
• *n.* **1** [C] an amount of money: *a large sum of money* ◇ *policies for savers with small sums to invest*
⊙ *a* ***considerable/substantial*** ~ • *a* ***huge/vast*** ~ • *a* ***modest/nominal*** ~
**2** [C, usu. sing.] the number you get when you add two or more numbers together: *the sum of exports and imports* ◇ *to calculate/find/work out the* ~ *(of sth)* **3** [C] a simple problem that involves calculating numbers: *If we've* ***got our sums right****, we should soon be profitable.* **4** (*also* **ˌsum ˈtotal**) [sing.] all of sth: *The sum of all these small changes has had a huge effect.* IDM **be greater/more than the ˌsum of its ˈparts** to be better or more effective as a group than you would think just by looking at the individual members of the group **in ˈsum** used to introduce a short statement of the main points of a discussion or speech
• *v.* (**-mm-**) PHR V **ˌsum (sth) ˈup** to state the main points of sth in a short and clear form: *To sum up, there are*

*three ways of tackling the problem ...* SYN SUMMARIZE

**ˌsum inˈsured** (*also* **ˌsum asˈsured**) *n.* [C] (*Insur.*) the maximum amount that a company will pay for a particular claim

**summarize, -ise** /ˈsʌməraɪz/ *v.* [T,I] to give the main points of sth: *Can you summarize what was said in the meeting?* SYN SUM UP

★ **summary** /ˈsʌməri/ *n., adj.*
• ***n.*** [C] (*pl.* **-ries**) a short statement that gives only the main points of sth: *a two-page summary of the report*
• ***adj.*** **1** giving only the main points of sth: *a summary financial statement* **2** done immediately, without paying attention to the normal process that should be followed: *summary* (= instant) *dismissal* ▸ **summarily** /ˈsʌmərəli; *AmE* səˈmerəli/ *adv.*

**ˌsumming-ˈup** *n.* [C] (*pl.* **ˌsummings-ˈup**) **1** (*Law*) a statement that the judge makes for the JURY near the end of a trial in a court **2** an occasion when sb states the main points of an argument, etc.

**summons** /ˈsʌmənz/ *n., v.* (*Law*)
• ***n.*** [C] (*pl.* **-ses** /-zɪz/) an order to appear in a court
• ***v.*** [T] to order sb to appear in a court: *She has been summonsed.*

**ˌsum of the ˈdigits ˌmethod** (*also* **ˌsum of the ˌyears' ˈdigits ˌmethod**) *n.* [sing.] (*abbr* **SYD**) (*Account.*) a way of reducing the value of an asset in a company's financial records in which the amount taken from the asset's value decreases each year. The value of the asset is reduced at a rate that gets smaller each year.

**ˌsum ˈtotal** = SUM *n.* (4)

**sundry** /ˈsʌndri/ *adj.* various; not important enough to be named separately: *sundry expenses*
▸ **ˈsundries** *n.* [pl.]: *You can claim up to £20 a day for sundries.*

**ˌsundry ˈdebtor** *n.* [C, usu. pl.] (*Account.*) one of the companies or people who owe a relatively small amount of money to a company for services or goods usu. not connected with the main work of the company

**ˈsunk cost** *n.* [C] (*Account.*) an amount of money that a company has already spent and cannot now get back

**ˈsunrise ˌindustry** *n.* [C] (*Econ.*) a new growing industry, using new technology

**ˈsunset clause** = SUNSET PROVISION

**ˈsunset ˌindustry** *n.* [C] (*Econ.*) an old industry, using old technology, that has started to become less successful: *Shipbuilding is a classic sunset industry.*

**ˈsunset proˌvision** (*also* **ˈsunset clause**) *n.* [C] (*Law*) part of a law, a rule, an agreement, etc. that states that it will stop being effective on a particular date

**sunshine** /ˈsʌnʃaɪn/ *adj.* (*esp. AmE*) used to describe laws, rules, etc. that are introduced to make government organizations do business in an open way, so that the public can attend meetings, etc. and check that nothing dishonest or illegal is happening: *The sunshine laws were introduced to curb corruption.*

**super-** /ˈsuːpə(r)/ *comb. form* **1** (*in adjs, advs and ns*) extremely; more or better than normal: *super-advanced* ◇ *a superstore* **2** (*in ns and vs*) above; over: *superstructure*

**superannuation** /ˌsuːpərˌænjuˈeɪʃn/ *n.* [U] (*esp. BrE*) (*HR*) a pension that you get, usu. from your employer, when you retire and that you pay for while you are working; the money that you pay for this: *a ~ fund/scheme* ◇ *to contribute to/pay/receive ~*

**supercomputer** /ˈsuːpəkəmpjuːtə(r); *AmE* ˈsuːpərk-/ *n.* [C] (*IT*) one of the most powerful computers that exist at a particular time

**superette** /ˌsuːpəˈret/ *n.* [C] (*AmE*) a small supermarket

**superhighway** /ˌsuːpəˈhaɪweɪ; *AmE* ˌsuːpərˈh-/ = INFORMATION SUPERHIGHWAY

**superintend** /ˌsuːpərɪnˈtend/ *v.* [T] to be in charge of sth and make sure that everything is working, being done, etc. as it should be: *Who superintended the building work?* SYN SUPERVISE

**superior** /suːˈpɪəriə(r); *AmE* suːˈpɪr-/ *adj., n.*
• ***adj.*** **1** better in quality than sb/sth else; greater than sb/sth else: *This model is technically superior* ***to*** *its competitors.* ◇ *investments with* ***vastly*** *superior returns* **2** (esp. in advertisements) of very good quality; better than other similar things: *superior apartments* **3** higher in position, importance or rank: *superior status*
• ***n.*** [C] sb of higher position, status or rank: *my immediate superior*

**supermarket** /ˈsuːpəmɑːkɪt; *AmE* ˈsuːpərmɑːrkət/ *n.* [C] a shop/store that sells food, drinks and goods used in the home. People choose what they want from the shelves and pay for it as they leave: *the UK's*

*largest supermarket chain* ◇ *The new range will hit supermarket shelves* (= will go on sale) *next month.*
→ GROCERY (1)
**○** *a* ***high-street/leading*** *~* • *a ~* ***giant/group/operator/retailer*** • *~* ***aisles/checkouts/trolleys***

**superstore** /ˈsuːpəstɔː(r); *AmE* ˈsuːpərs-/ *n.* [C] **1** a very large supermarket that sells a wide variety of goods
**○** *an* ***edge-of-town/out-of-town*** *~* • *a ~* ***chain/giant/group/operator/retailer***
**2** a large shop/store that sells a wide variety of one type of goods, often at lower prices than normal
**○** *a* ***computer/DIY/an office*** *~* • *a* ***discount*** *~*

**supertanker** /ˈsuːpətæŋkə(r); *AmE* ˈsuːpərt-/ *n.* [C] (*Transpt.*) a very large ship for carrying oil, etc.

**supertax** /ˈsuːpətæks; *AmE* ˈsuːpərt-/ *n.* [U,C] (*esp. BrE*) an extra tax on sth that has already been taxed, esp. a higher rate of tax that is paid by companies or people who earn more than a particular amount SYN SURTAX

★**supervise** /ˈsuːpəvaɪz; *AmE* ˈsuːpərv-/ *v.* [T,I] to be in charge of sb/sth and make sure that everything is done correctly, safely, etc: *Trainees are* ***closely*** *supervised.* SYN OVERSEE
▸ **ˌsuperˈvision** /-ˈvɪʒn/ *n.* [U]: *You will work* ***under the supervision of*** *a manager.* **ˈsupervisor** *n.* [C] **ˌsuperˈvisory** *adj.*: *to have a supervisory role*

**ˈsupervisory board** *n.* [C with sing./pl. v.] in some countries, a group of directors who represent a company's shareholders, advising the directors who manage the company and checking that everything is done correctly

**ˌsupervisory ˈmanagement** *n.* [U; C with sing./pl. v.] (*HR*) the lowest level of managers in a company who are directly responsible for the work of a group of employees; the work that the managers do

**supplement** *n., v.*
• *n.* /ˈsʌplɪmənt/ [C] **1** a thing that is added to sth else to improve it or make it more complete: *a supplement* ***to*** *government funding* **2** an amount of money that you pay for an extra service or item: *a supplement of €30 for a single room* **3** something that you eat in addition to what you usu. eat, esp. to stay healthy: *vitamins and dietary supplements* **4** an extra section that comes with a newspaper or a book, report, etc: *a supplement to the main report*
▸ **ˌsuppleˈmentary** /-ˈmentri/ (*esp. BrE*) (*AmE usu.* **ˌsuppleˈmental** /-ˈmentl/) *adj.*: *a ~ charge/income*
• *v.* /ˈsʌplɪment/ [T] to add sth to sth else in order to improve it or make it more complete: *Salaries are supplemented by performance bonuses.*

★**supplier** /səˈplaɪə(r)/ *n.* [C] **1** a company that provides raw materials or pieces of equipment to companies that make goods; a company that provides finished goods, for example for other companies to sell to the public: *suppliers* ***to*** *the catering industry* ◇ *a building supplier* (= supplying materials for building) ◇ *a big/key/leading ~ (of sth)* ◇ *our* ***supplier base*** (= the number of companies that supply us) SYN VENDOR **2** a company that supplies gas, water or electricity: *an energy supplier*

**supˈplier ˌrating** = VENDOR RATING

★**supply** /səˈplaɪ/ *n., v.*
• *n.* (*pl.* **-lies**) **1** [U] the act of providing sth or making it available to be used: *a delay in the supply of parts* ◇ *a reliable* ***supply base*** (= the companies that supply materials, etc.) **2** [C, usu. sing.] an amount of sth that is provided or available to be used: *We have a 64-day supply of vehicles.* ◇ *a plentiful supply of labour* ◇ *gas supplies*
**○** *a* ***large/small/steady*** *~ (of sth)* • ***to get/produce/provide*** *a ~* • ***to disrupt/increase/reduce*** *a ~*
**3** [U] the amount of sth that is offered for sale: *to match supply with demand* ◇ *a global steel supply glut* (= too much steel is available) ◇ *a supply crunch* (= there is not enough of sth available)
**○** *to* ***exceed/outstrip*** *~* • *~* ***falls/increases***
**4 supplies** [pl.] basic things that are needed for a particular purpose: *office supplies*
**○** ***limited/plentiful*** *supplies* • ***to lay in/provide*** *supplies* • *supplies* ***run low/run out***
→ idiom at SHORT *adj.*
• *v.* [T] (**-lies**, **-lying**, **-lied**, **-lied**) **1** to provide raw materials, equipment, etc. to companies, esp. in large quantities; to provide goods or services: *We supply Internet-based services* ***to*** *businesses.* **2** to provide sb/sth with sth that they need or want: *Can you supply a list of recent customers?*

**supˌply and deˈmand** *n.* [U] (*Econ.*) the relationship between the amount of goods or services available and the amount that people want to buy, esp. when this controls prices: *the laws of supply and demand*

★**sup'ply chain** *n.* [C] (*Product.*) the whole series of processes, companies, places, etc. that are involved in making and selling a product, including the supply of raw materials and parts and the processes of manufacturing, storing, transporting and selling the product to the customer: *every link/point/stage in the ~ ◇ supply-chain costs*
**o** *to* ***improve/streamline*** *the ~* ◆ *to* ***shorten/tighten*** *the ~* ◆ ***along/down/in/through/up*** *the ~*

**sup,ply chain e'vent ,management** (*abbr* **SCEM**) (*also* **e'vent ,management**) *n.* [U] (*Product.*) a system for predicting, controlling and dealing with unexpected events in any part of the SUPPLY CHAIN, for example when customers order more of a product than usual

**sup'ply chain ,management** *n.* [U] (*abbr* **SCM**) (*Product.*) the control of all the materials, money and information in the whole series of processes involved in making, selling and delivering a product

**sup'ply price** *n.* [C] (*Econ.*) the lowest price that sellers are willing to accept for providing a particular amount of a product or service

**sup'ply side** *n.* [sing.] (*usu.* **the supply side**) (*Econ.*) the part of an economy relating to the production and supply of goods and services
▸ **sup'ply-side** *adj.*: *supply-side policies* (= to increase the supply of goods and services and create jobs)

★**support** /sə'pɔːt; *AmE* -'pɔːrt/ *v.*, *n.*
• ***v.*** [T] **1** to help and encourage sb/sth by saying or showing that you agree with them/it: *Managers are supporting the plan.* **2** to help sth/sb by giving it/them money: *Two major companies supported the project.* **3** to give or be ready to give help to sb/sth if they need it: *We still support customers using older versions of the software.* **4** to prevent sth from failing; to help sth continue: *supporting oil prices* **5** to help to show that sth is true or correct: *The decision cannot be supported by the data.* **6** (*IT*) (about a piece of computer software or equipment, etc.) to allow a particular type of software, equipment or data to be used with it: *The program supports HTML formatting.*
• ***n.*** [U] **1** help and encouragement that you give to sb/sth: *support* ***for*** *union leaders ◇ There is strong support for the merger* ***from*** *shareholders. ◇ The CEO has our* ***full*** *support.*
**o** ***broad/unanimous*** *~* ◆ *to* ***give/lend/withdraw*** *your ~* ◆ *to* ***gain/receive/win*** *~*
**2** money given to sth/sb to help it/them become successful: *financial support*
**o** *to* ***give/provide*** *~* ◆ *to* ***look for/receive/seek*** *~*
**3** help that is given to sb/sth or available if needed: *providing after-sales support to customers* **4** the act of preventing sth from failing or helping sth to continue: *There will be no official support* ***for*** *the dollar.* **5** evidence that helps to show that sth is true: *support* ***for*** *our theory*

**sup'port staff** *n.* [C, usu. sing., U] (*HR*) the people in a company who help it to operate, but who are not directly involved in the company's business **HELP** In the sing., **support staff** is often used with a pl. verb, esp. in BrE.: *Our ~ is/are based in our London office.*

**suppress** /sə'pres/ *v.* [T] **1** to prevent sth from growing or developing: *laws that suppress demand for tobacco* **2** to prevent sth from being published or made known: *to suppress a report*

**supranational** /ˌsuːprə'næʃnəl/ *adj.* involving more than one country: *supranational institutions*

★**surcharge** /'sɜːtʃɑːdʒ; *AmE* 'sɜːrtʃɑːrdʒ/ *n.* [C] an extra amount of money that you must pay in addition to the usual price: *a surcharge* ***on*** *some flights ◇ to add/impose/pay a ~* ▸ **'surcharge** *v.* [T]

**surf** /sɜːf; *AmE* sɜːrf/ *v.* [T,I] to look at many different websites: *surfing the Internet/Net/Web* ▸ **'surfer** *n.* [C]: *Internet surfers* **'surfing** *n.* [U]

**'surface mail** *n.* [U] letters, etc. carried by road, rail or sea, not by air: *to send sth (by) surface mail*

**'surface ,transport** *n.* [U] the activity of carrying goods or of travelling by road, rail or sea, not by air; the vehicles used

**surge** /sɜːdʒ; *AmE* sɜːrdʒ/ *v.*, *n.*
• ***v.*** [I] to suddenly increase in value: *Share prices surged.* **PHR V** **,surge a'head** to increase or improve quickly, by a large amount, and often more than other prices, companies, etc.
• ***n.*** [C] a sudden increase in the amount or number of sth; a large amount of sth: *a power surge ◇ a surge* ***in*** *consumer spending*

**surpass** /sə'pɑːs; *AmE* sər'pæs/ *v.* [T] to be or do better than sth/sb: *Sales have surpassed expectations.*

★ **surplus** /ˈsɜːpləs; *AmE* ˈsɜːrp-/ *n.*, *adj.*
• ***n.*** [C,U] **1** an amount that is extra or more than you need: *a surplus of housing* ◇ *Skilled workers are* ***in surplus*** *in the region.* SYN GLUT OPP SHORTAGE **2** (*Account.*; *Econ.*) the amount by which money that a government or business receives is greater than the amount of money spent in a particular period of time: *a huge budget surplus* ◇ *The balance of payments is* ***in surplus.*** → DEFICIT
• ***adj.*** more than is needed or used: *~ cash/funds* ◇ *The items are* ***surplus to requirements*** (= not needed).

**surrender** /səˈrendə(r)/ *v.* **1** (*Insur.*) [T] if you **surrender** a life insurance agreement you end it before its official end date and receive back part of the money you have paid **2** (*Finan.*) [T] (usu. used in newspapers) if a share, an index, etc. **surrenders** a particular amount, its value falls by that amount **3** [T,I] to give up sth when you are forced to: *to surrender control of a company to sb else* ▸ **surˈrender** *n.* [C,U]: *the* ***surrender value*** *of a policy* ◇ *a ~ charge/fee/penalty* ◇ *the surrender of your passport*

**surtax** /ˈsɜːtæks; *AmE* ˈsɜːrt-/ *n.* [U,C] (*esp. AmE*) an extra tax on sth that has already been taxed, esp. a higher rate of tax that is paid by companies or people who earn more than a particular amount SYN SUPERTAX

★ **survey** *n.*, *v.*
• ***n.*** /ˈsɜːveɪ; *AmE* ˈsɜːrv-/ [C] **1** an investigation of the opinions, behaviour, etc. of a particular group of people, which is usu. done by asking them questions: *The report is based on a survey of 5 000 households.*
○ *to* ***carry out/conduct/do*** *a ~* ◆ *to* ***respond to/take part in*** *a ~* ◆ *a ~* ***finds/reveals/shows*** *sth*
**2** a general study or description of sth: *a survey of safety conditions in factories*
○ *to* ***carry out/commission/conduct/do*** *a ~* ◆ *to* ***issue/publish*** *a ~* ◆ *a ~* ***finds/reports/shows*** *sth*
**3** the act of examining and recording the measurements, features, etc. of an area of land or of a building
○ *to* ***carry out/do/make*** *a ~* ◆ *a* ***full/geological/structural/valuation*** *~*
• ***v.*** /səˈveɪ; *AmE* sərˈv-/ [T] **1** to investigate the opinions or behaviour of a group of people by asking them a series of questions **2** to study and give a general description of sth: *The websites of the major stores were surveyed.* **3** to measure and record the features, etc. of an area of land or of a building

**surveyor** /səˈveɪə(r); *AmE* sərˈv-/ *n.* [C] **1** sb whose job is to examine and record the details of a piece of land **2** (*BrE*) (*AmE* **inˈspector**) sb whose job is to examine a building to make sure it is in good condition: *a surveyor's report* **3** (*BrE*) an official whose job is to check that sth is accurate, of good quality, etc: *the surveyor of public works*

**suspend** /səˈspend/ *v.* [T] **1** to officially stop sth for a time; to prevent sth from being active, used, etc. for a time: *to ~ payments/production/talks* **2** to delay sth; to arrange for sth to happen later than planned **3** (*HR*) (*usu. pass.*) to officially prevent sb from doing their job for a time: *He was suspended on full pay.*

**susˈpense acˌcount** *n.* [C] (*Account.*) a temporary account in which a company records items until they can be put into the correct or final account

**suspension** /səˈspenʃn/ *n.* [U,C] **1** (*HR*) the act of officially removing sb from their job for a period of time, usu. as a punishment: *the temporary suspension of five employees* **2** the act of delaying sth for a period of time: *the suspension of talks*

**susˈpension file** *n.* [C] a file made of stiff card with metal edges that hangs in the drawer of a FILING CABINET

**sustain** /səˈsteɪn/ *v.* [T] **1** to make sth continue for some time without becoming less: *a period of sustained economic growth* **2** to experience sth bad: *They sustained massive losses.* **3** to provide evidence to support an opinion, a theory, etc: *to sustain an argument* **4** (*Law*) to decide that a claim, etc. is valid

★ **sustainable** /səˈsteɪnəbl/ *adj.* **1** that can continue or be continued for a long time: *sustainable increases in sales* **2** involving the use of natural products and energy in a way that does not harm the environment: *a source of sustainable energy*
▸ **suˌstainaˈbility** /-ˈbɪləti/ *n.* [U]

**swamp** /swɒmp; *AmE* swɑːmp/ *v.* [T] to make sb/sth have more of sth than they can deal with: *to be swamped* ***with*** *work* ◇ *The market has been swamped* ***by*** *cheap imports.*

★ **swap** (*also* **swop**) /swɒp; *AmE* swɑːp/ *n.* [C] **1** an act of exchanging one thing or person for another: *Let's do a swap. You work Friday night and I'll do Saturday.* **2** (*Finan.*) an exchange of different types of payments between two companies, for example payments in different currencies or with different interest rates **3** (*Finan.*) an act of exchanging one investment or asset for another, instead of for money ▸ **swap** *v.* [T,I] (**-pp-**): *to swap ideas* **with** *colleagues* ◇ *I'm swapping my car* **for** *a smaller model.* → SWITCH

**swatch** /swɒtʃ; *AmE* swɑːtʃ/ *n.* [C] a small piece of fabric used to show what a larger piece would be like

**'sweat ˌequity** *n.* [U] (*infml.*) the work, rather than money, that the owners of a new business invest in it and for which they receive shares

**sweatshop** /ˈswetʃɒp; *AmE* -ʃɑːp/ *n.* [C] a place where people work for low wages in poor conditions

**sweeping** /ˈswiːpɪŋ/ *adj.* having an important effect on a large part of sth: *sweeping* **changes**

**the sweeps** /swiːps/ *n.* [pl.] (*AmE*) (*infml.*) a time when television companies examine their programmes to find out which ones are the most popular, esp. in order to calculate advertising rates: *the May sweeps*

**sweeten** /ˈswiːtn/ *v.* [T] to make sth more pleasant or acceptable: *The group has sweetened its offer* (= offered more money) *for the store.*

**sweetener** /ˈswiːtnə(r)/ *n.* [C] (*infml.*) sth that is given to sb to persuade them to do sth: *accepting sweeteners from suppliers* → BRIBE

**'sweetheart deal** *n.* [C] a private agreement between two groups or organizations which benefits one or both of them but is often unfair to other people who are involved

**S.W.I.F.T.™** /swɪft/ *abbr* **Society for Worldwide Interbank Financial Telecommunciations** a computer network that allows member banks in all parts of the world to move money from one to another safely

**swindle** /ˈswɪndl/ *v.* [T] to cheat sb in order to get sth, esp. money, from them: *He swindled customers* **out of** *millions of dollars.* ▸ **'swindle** *n.* [C, usu. sing.]: *an insurance swindle* **'swindler** *n.* [C]

**swing** /swɪŋ/ *v., n.*

• *v.* (**swung, swung** /swʌŋ/) **1** [T,I] to change or make sb/sth change from one level, situation, opinion, etc. to another: *Food prices can swing widely from month to month.* **2** [T] to succeed in getting or achieving sth, sometimes in a slightly dishonest way: *Large companies can swing these deals.*

• *n.* [C] a change from one level, situation or opinion to another; the amount by which sth changes: *huge price swings*

**'swing shift** = BACK SHIFT

**swipe** /swaɪp/ *v.* [T] to pass a plastic card through a special machine that can read the information stored on it: *Rooms have* **swipe cards** *instead of keys.*

**switch** /swɪtʃ/ *n., v.*

• *n.* [C] **1** a small device used to turn a light or piece of electrical equipment on and off **2** a change from one thing to another, esp. when this is sudden and complete: *to* **make the switch** *from full- to part-time work*

• *v.* **1** [T,I] **~ (sth) (over) (from sth) (to sth) | ~ (between A and B)** to change or make sth change from one thing to another: *We're switching over to a new system of invoicing.* **2** [T,I] **~ (sth) (with sb/sth) | ~ (sth) (over/around/round)** to exchange one thing for another: *to switch desks/shifts with sb* SYN SWAP

PHR V **ˌswitch (sth) 'off/'on** to turn a light, machine, etc. off/on by pressing a button or switch

**switchboard** /ˈswɪtʃbɔːd; *AmE* -bɔːrd/ *n.* [C] the central part of a telephone system used by a company, etc., where calls are answered and connected to the appropriate person or department; the people who work this equipment: *a switchboard operator* ◇ *Call the switchboard and ask for extension 410.*

**swop** = SWAP

**SWOT** /swɒt; *AmE* swɑːt/ *n.* [U] a method used to study an organization and plan how it can change and grow, by analysing its strengths and weaknesses, the opportunities it has and the threats it faces: *a SWOT analysis*

**SYD** /ˌes waɪ ˈdiː/ *abbr* (*Account.*) **sum of the year's digits** a short way of referring to the SUM OF THE DIGITS METHOD

**symbol** /ˈsɪmbl/ *n.* [C] **1** a sign, number, letter, etc. that has a particular meaning: *The company's symbol is a lion.* **2** a company, a person, an object, an event, etc. that represents a more general quality or situation: *Fiat was a symbol of Italy's economic success.* **3** (*Stock Ex.*) = TICKER SYMBOL

**'sympathy strike** (*also* **ˌsympa'thetic strike**, *less freq.*) *n.* [C] (*HR*) an occasion when a group of workers stop work in order to show support for another group who have stopped work

**symposium** /sɪm'pəʊziəm; *AmE* -'poʊ-/ *n.* [C] (*pl.* **-sia** /-ziə/ *or* **-siums**) a meeting at which experts have discussions about a particular subject: *an international symposium on the environment*

★**syndicate** *n., v.*
• ***n.*** /'sɪndɪkət/ [C] (*Finan.*) a group of people or companies who work together to achieve a particular aim: *a 24-strong syndicate of banks*
• ***v.*** /'sɪndɪkeɪt/ **1** (*Finan.*) [T] (*usu. pass.*) to control or manage sth as a **syndicate**: *a syndicated credit facility* **2** [T,I] to form a **syndicate**: *syndicated lenders* ▶ **ˌsyndi'cation** /-'keɪʃn/ *n.* [U]

★**synergy** /'sɪnədʒi; *AmE* -ərdʒi/ *n.* [C,U] (*pl.* **-gies**) the extra power, success, profits, etc. achieved by two or more groups, people, companies, etc. working together instead of on their own: *The combined companies aimed to achieve synergies of €300 m a year by 2009.*
⊕ *to* ***create/deliver/generate*** *synergies* ◆ ***cost/merger/operational*** *synergies* ◆ *~* ***benefits/savings***
▶ **ˌsyner'gistic** /-'dʒɪstɪk/ *adj.*: *a synergistic merger*

**synthesize, -ise** /'sɪnθəsaɪz/ *v.* [T] **1** to combine separate ideas, styles, pieces of information, etc: *The results are synthesized in the report.* **2** (*Tech.*) to produce a substance by means of chemical or other processes: *synthesized drugs* **3** (*Tech.*) to produce sound by electronic methods: *a computer-synthesized voice*

**synthetic** /sɪn'θetɪk/ *adj., n.*
• ***adj.*** artificial; made by combining chemical substances rather than being produced naturally: *skin products with no synthetic ingredients*
▶ **syn'thetically** /-kli/ *adv.*
• ***n.*** [C] an artificial substance or material

★**system** /'sɪstəm/ *n.* [C] **1** an organized set of ideas or theories, or a particular way of doing sth: *We are changing our system of recruitment.* ◇ *the tax system* **2** a group of things, pieces of equipment, etc. that are connected or work together: *a computer/transport ~* → idiom at PLAY *v.*

**systematic** /ˌsɪstə'mætɪk/ *adj.* done according to a system or plan, in a thorough, efficient or determined way: *We need to handle customer feedback in a more systematic way.* ▶ **ˌsyste'matically** /-kli/ *adv.*

**ˌsystematic 'risk** (*also* **ˌmarket 'risk**) *n.* [U,C] (*Finan.*) risk that affects the price of all investments of a particular type (shares, bonds, etc.), for example the possible effects of political or economic change

**systemic** /sɪ'stemɪk; sɪ'sti:mɪk/ *adj.* (*Tech.*) affecting or connected with the whole of a system: *systemic weaknesses in the network*
▶ **sy'stemically** /-kli/ *adv.*

**sysˌtemic 'risk** *n.* [U,C] (*Finan.*) risk that can cause serious problems for a whole system, esp. the risk that a problem in one market can lead to very serious problems for the whole market

**'system ˌintegrator** = INTEGRATOR (1)

**'systems ˌanalyst** (*also* **'systems ˌarchitect, ˌbusiness 'systems ˌanalyst**) *n.* [C] (*IT*) a person whose job is to analyse the needs of a business organization and then design processes for working efficiently using computer programs SYN COMPUTER ANALYST
▶ **'systems aˌnalysis** (*also* **'systems ˌarchitecture, ˌbusiness 'systems aˌnalysis**) *n.* [U]

**'systems ˌintegrator** = INTEGRATOR (1)

**'systems ˌprogrammer** *n.* [C] (*IT*) a person who writes computer programs for a company's computer system

# Tt

**t/a** *abbr* (*esp. BrE*) (*written*) a short way of writing **trading as** in the name of a business, esp. one owned by a SOLE TRADER: *Jo Wilmot, t/a Jo's Supplies*

**tab** /tæb/ *n., v.*
• ***n.*** [C] **1** (*infml.*) a bill for goods or services; the price or cost of sth: *to* ***pick up the tab*** (= pay the cost) *for sth* **2** a record of the items ordered in a bar or restaurant: *Can I put it on my tab?* **3** a small piece of paper, fabric, metal, etc. attached to the edge of sth, used to give information about it or to help you find sth; a similar device on information shown on a computer screen: *colour-coded tabs* **4** = TAB STOP
• ***v.*** (**-bb-**) **1** [T] to mark sth with a **tab**: *tabbed pages* **2** [T] (*esp. AmE*) to say that sb is suitable for a particular job or role or to describe them in a particular way: *He has been tabbed* **as** *the next CEO.* **3** [I] to use TAB STOPS

★**table** /ˈteɪbl/ *n., v.*
• *n.* [C] a list of facts or numbers arranged in a special order, usu. in rows and columns: *The table shows sales in each main market.* IDM **on the ˈtable 1** (*BrE*) (about a plan, suggestion, etc.) offered to people so that they can consider or discuss it **2** (*esp. AmE*) (about a plan, suggestion, etc.) not going to be discussed or considered until a future date
• *v.* [T] **1** (*BrE*) to present sth formally for discussion: *to table a motion to shareholders* **2** (*esp. AmE*) to leave an idea, a proposal, etc. to be discussed at a later date: *to table a proposal until a later meeting*

**ˈtab stop** (*also* **tab**) *n.* [C] a fixed position in a line of a document that you are typing that shows where a piece of text or a column of figures, etc. will begin

**tabular** /ˈtæbjələ(r)/ *adj.* presented or arranged in rows and columns: *tabular data*

**tabulate** /ˈtæbjuleɪt/ *v.* [T] to arrange facts or figures in columns or lists so that they can be read easily
▸ **ˌtabuˈlation** /-ˈleɪʃn/ *n.* [U,C]

**T-acˌcount** *n.* [C] (*Account.*) a simple way of recording financial TRANSACTIONS, consisting of a DEBIT column and a credit column

**tachograph** /ˈtækəgrɑːf; *AmE* -græf/ *n.* [C] (*Transpt.*) a device used in vehicles such as large lorries/trucks to measure their speed, how far they have travelled and when the driver has stopped to rest

**ˌtacit ˈknowledge** (*also* **imˌplicit ˈknowledge**) *n.* [U] (*HR*) knowledge that sb gains from working in an organization and becoming familiar with the equipment, procedures, customers, etc.

**tack** /tæk/ *v.* PHR V **ˌtack sth ˈon; ˌtack sth ˈonto sth 1** to add sth to sth that is already there: *An update has been tacked on at the end of the manual.* **2** (*Stock Ex.*) (*esp. AmE*) if a share price **tacks on** an amount, it increases by that amount: *U.S. Electric tacked on 3 per cent to $20.95.*

**tactic** /ˈtæktɪk/ *n.* [C, usu. pl.] the particular method you use to achieve sth: *What strategies and tactics have they used to improve their operations?*

**tactical** /ˈtæktɪkl/ *adj.* **1** connected with the particular method you use to achieve sth: *~ discussions/planning* **2** carefully planned in order to achieve a particular aim: *a tactical move to get a better price*

**tag** /tæg/ *n., v.*
• *n.* [C] **1** (*often used in compounds*) a small piece of paper, fabric, plastic, etc. attached to sth to identify it or give information about it: *name tags* **2** (*Comm.*) an electronic device that is attached to sth so that it can be checked, for example to stop people stealing it: *security tags* **3** (*IT*) a set of letters or symbols that are put before and after a piece of text or data in order to identify it or show how it is to be treated: *XML tags*
• *v.* [T] (**-gg-**) **1** (*Comm.*) to fasten a tag onto sth: *All goods are electronically tagged.* **2** (*IT*) to add a set of letters or symbols to a piece of text or data to identify it or show that it is to be treated in a particular way

**ˈtag line** *n.* [C] (*esp. AmE*) (*Market.*) a phrase or sentence that is easy to remember, used for example in advertising to attract people's attention and make them remember a product: *The company uses the tag line 'leaders in the lighting world'.* SYN SLOGAN

**tailor** /ˈteɪlə(r)/ *v.* [T] to make or adapt sth for a particular purpose, a particular person, etc: *We tailor our training courses* **to** *the client's needs.*

**ˌtailor-ˈmade** *adj.* made for a particular purpose or person, and so very suitable: *tailor-made courses*

★**take** /teɪk/ *v., n.*
• *v.* [T] (**took** /tʊk/ **taken** /ˈteɪkən/) **1** to earn a particular amount of money by selling goods or services: *The store took $100 000 last week.* **2** (*with an adv. or a prep.*) to remove sth/sb from somewhere: *The sign must be taken down.* ◇ *They have been taking market share away from their rivals.* **3** to get control of sth/sb: *Creditors will* **take control of** *the company.* **4** to choose, buy or rent sth: *I'll take the grey jacket.* **5 ~ A (away) from B | ~ A away** (*not in the continuous tenses*) to reduce one number by the value of another: *Take costs away from sales income and what is left is profit.* SYN SUBTRACT **6** (*not usu. in the continuous tenses or in the pass.*) to accept or receive sth: *Do you take credit cards?* IDM **have (got) what it ˈtakes** to have the quality, ability, etc. needed to be successful: *He doesn't have what it takes to lead such a large team.* **take adˈvantage of sb/sth** to make use of sb/sth well **take adˈvice (from sb)** to ask sb with special knowledge or skill for information or help in a difficult situation: *to take advice from accountants* **take a ˈbath** (*AmE*) (*slang*) to lose a lot of money, for example on an investment **take a ˈbite out of sth** to reduce sth by a large amount **take a ˈdive** (*infml.*) to suddenly get worse:

*Profits took a dive last year.* **take sth on 'board** to accept and understand an idea or a suggestion **take a 'risk; take 'risks** to do sth even though you know that sth bad could happen as a result **take some 'doing** (*infml.*) to be very difficult to do: *The new system will take some getting used to.* **take 'stock 1** (*Account.*) (*esp. AmE*) to count the items for sale in a shop/store **2** to stop and think carefully about the way in which a particular situation is developing in order to decide what to do next: *to take stock of progress* **take time 'out (of/from sth) (to do sth)** to spend some time away from your usual work or activity in order to rest or do sth else **take a (heavy/terrible) 'toll (on sb/sth); take its/their 'toll (on sb/sth)** to have a bad effect on sb/sth; to cause a lot of damage, suffering, etc. **take a (dramatic, unexpected, etc.) ˌturn (for the 'worse/'better)** to suddenly start getting worse/better: *The economy is taking a turn for the better.* → idioms at EFFECT, RIDE *n.*

**PHRV** **ˌtake sth a'part** to separate a machine, etc. into the different parts that it is made of **ˌtake sth 'back** if you **take** sth **back** to a shop/store, or if a shop/store **takes** sth **back**, you return sth that you have bought there, for example because it is the wrong size or does not work **ˌtake sth 'forward** to work with sth in order to develop it and make it successful: *She is the right person to take this company forward.* **ˌtake sth 'in 1** (*esp. AmE*) to earn a particular amount of money: *The business took in $9 m last year.* **2** to accept new people, etc: *The EU will take in more new members next year.* **ˌtake 'off** (about a product, an idea, etc.) to become successful or popular very quickly or suddenly: *The new magazine has really taken off.* **ˌtake sth 'off** to have a period of time as a break from work: *I'm taking tomorrow off.* **ˌtake sth 'off sth** to remove an amount of money in order to reduce the total: *They have taken 10% off their prices.* **ˌtake sb 'on 1** to employ sb: *We have taken on 25 new staff this year.* **2** to compete or fight against sb: *The company is already taking on established companies.* **ˌtake sth/sb 'on** to decide to do sth; to agree to be responsible for sth/sb: *This is the largest project we have ever taken on.* **ˌtake sth 'out** to obtain an official document or service: *to take out insurance* **ˌtake sth 'out (of sth)** to remove money from a bank account **ˌtake sth 'out of sth** to remove an amount of money from a larger amount, esp. as a payment: *About 20% is taken out of salaries as tax.* **ˌtake (sth) 'over (from sb)** to begin to have control of or responsibility for sth, esp. in place of sb else: *Mazza will take over from Mudu as chairman.* **ˌtake sth 'over** (*Finan.*) to gain control of a company, esp. by buying shares: *The supermarket chain was taken over by a rival.* **ˌtake sth 'up 1** to start or begin sth such as a job: *She takes up her new position next month.* **2** to accept sth that is offered or available: *He took up the redundancy offer.* **ˌtake sth 'up with sb** to speak or write to sb about sth that they may be able to deal with or help you with: *She took up her complaint with the union.*

• *n.* [C, usu. sing.] (*esp. AmE*) (*Account., infml.*) the amount of money earned by a business during a particular period: *Last year's take totalled $10.2 m.* **IDM** **be on the 'take** (*infml.*) to accept money from sb for helping them in a dishonest way

**'take-home pay** *n.* [U] the amount of money that you earn after you have paid tax, etc.

**'take-off** *n.* [U,C] **1** the moment at which an aircraft leaves the ground OPP LANDING **2** the moment at which sth suddenly becomes very successful: *The economy is poised for take-off.*

**'takeout ˌfinancing** *n.* [U] (*Finan.*) loans that are used to replace BRIDGING loans

★ **takeover** /'teɪkəʊvə(r); *AmE* -oʊ-/ *n.* [C,U] (*Finan.*) an act of taking control of a company by buying most of its shares: *The airline has announced details of the planned takeover of its rival.* ◇ *to reject a $3.5 bn takeover offer*

⊕ *a* ***failed/successful/*** *an* ***unsuccessful*** *~* ◆ *to* ***accept/contest*** *a ~* ◆ *an* ***all-share/****a* ***cash*** *~* ◆ *a ~* ***attempt/battle*** ◆ *a ~* ***target***

**'takeover bid** (*also* **ˌoffer to 'purchase**, *less freq.*) *n.* [C] (*Finan.*) an offer made to the shareholders of a company to buy their shares at a particular price in order to gain control of the company: *The shareholders voted against acceptance of the takeover bid.*

⊕ *to* ***launch/make*** *a ~ (for sth)* ◆ *to* ***accept/defeat/reject*** *a ~* ◆ *a* ***friendly/hostile*** *~*

**'takeover code** *n.* [C] (*Finan.*) a set of rules that companies agree to follow, designed to make sure that **takeovers** take place in a fair way

**ˈtakeover ˌpanel** *n.* [C] (*Finan.*) a group of people in the UK and some other countries who are given the job by the government of making sure that all **takeovers** obey the laws and rules that exist

**taker** /ˈteɪkə(r)/ *n.* [C, usu. pl.] **1** (*often with* **few**, **no**, **not many**, *etc.*) a person, company, etc. who is willing to accept or buy sth: *So far there are no takers for the business.* **2** (*often in compounds*) sb who takes or receives sth: *Shares were down 4% as profit takers moved in.*

**ˈtake-up** *n.* [U; sing.] the rate at which people accept sth that is offered or made available to them: *high levels of broadband take-up* ◇ *a slow take-up of new TV services* ◇ *high/low/poor/widespread ~*

**takings** /ˈteɪkɪŋz/ *n.* [pl.] (*Account.*) the amount of money that a business such as a shop/store, etc. receives from selling goods or services over a particular period of time: *Takings are up on last year.* ◇ *banking the day's takings*

★**talent** /ˈtælənt/ *n.* **1** [C,U] a natural ability to do sth well: *She showed considerable talent as an organizer.* **2** [U,C] people or a person with a natural ability to do sth well: *recruiting top talent*

**talk** /tɔːk/ *v., n.*

• *v.* IDM **talk ˈshop** to talk about work with other people you work with, esp. when you are with people who are not connected with your work: *Let's not talk shop.* **ˌtalk the ˈtalk** (*infml.*) to be able to talk in a confident way that makes people think you are an expert: *You can talk the talk, but can you walk the walk?* **talk ˈturkey** (*infml.*) (*esp. AmE*) to talk about sth honestly and directly → idioms at LANGUAGE, MONEY, WALK *v.* PHR V **ˌtalk sth/sb ˈdown** to make sth/sb seem less important or successful than it really is: *Don't talk down your achievements.* **ˌtalk ˈdown to sb** to speak to sb as if they were less important or intelligent than you: *Don't talk down to your audience.* **ˌtalk sb ˈthrough sth** to describe or explain sth to sb so that they understand it: *Talk me through your plan.* **ˌtalk sth/sb ˈup** to describe sb/sth in a way that makes them sound better than they really are

• *n.* **1 talks** [pl.] formal discussions between organizations or governments: *pay/merger/trade ~* **2** [C] a speech or lecture on a particular subject: *He's **giving** a talk **on** TQM.*

**ˈtalking point** *n.* [C] **1** a subject that is talked about or discussed by many people: *The losses were the day's main talking point.* **2** (*AmE*) an item that sb will speak about at a meeting, often one that supports a particular argument **3** (*AmE*) a new or special feature of a product that is used in advertising to interest people or persuade them to buy the product

**ˈtalking shop** *n.* [C] a place where there is a lot of discussion and argument but no action is taken

**tall** /tɔːl/ (**-er**, **-est**) *adj.* used to describe an organization where there are many levels between the top and the bottom

**tally** /ˈtæli/ *n., v.*

• *n.* [C] (*pl.* **-lies**) a record of the number or amount of sth, esp. one that you can keep adding to: *What was the final tally of job cuts this year?*

• *v.* (**-lies**, **-lying**, **-lied**, **-lied**) **1** [I] to be the same as or to match another set of figures, another person's account of sth, etc: *The two sets of figures don't tally.* **2** [T] to calculate the total number, cost, etc. of sth: *The final figures have not yet been tallied.*

**tamper** /ˈtæmpə(r)/ *v., comb. form*

• *v.* PHR V **ˈtamper with sth** to make changes to sth in a way that could damage it or make it dangerous: *The phone had been tampered with.*

• ***comb. form*** used in adjs to describe a device that is designed to prevent people from using, stealing, breaking, etc. sth: *The drug is sold in a **tamper-proof** container.*

**TAN** /ˌtiː eɪ ˈen/ = TAX ANTICIPATION NOTE

**tangible** /ˈtændʒəbl/ *adj., n.*

• *adj.* **1** that can be clearly seen to exist: *~ benefits/progress/results* ◇ *~ proof/signs* **2** that you can touch and feel: *tangible goods* OPP INTANGIBLE ▸ **ˈtangibly** /-bli/ *adv.*

• *n.* **1** [C] a thing that exists physically and is not just an idea **2** (*Account.*; *Finan.*) [C] = TANGIBLE ASSET **3** (*Finan.*) **tangibles** [pl.] physical things that you can invest in, rather than financial investments: *investing in tangibles like antiques* OPP INTANGIBLE

**ˌtangible ˈasset** (*also* **ˈtangible**) *n.* [C, usu. pl.] (*Account.*; *Finan.*) a physical thing that is owned by a company or person, such as goods, machines, buildings and cash

**ˌtangible ˌnet ˈworth** *n.* [U] (*Account.*) the total value of a company's TANGIBLE ASSETS minus its LIABILITIES

**tank** /tæŋk/ *n., v.*

• ***n.*** [C] **1** a large container for holding liquid or gas **2** the contents of a tank or the amount it will hold **IDM** **in the 'tank** (*AmE*) (*Finan., infml.*) (about the price of shares, bonds, etc.) falling quickly: *Tech stocks are doing well, but others are in the tank.*

• ***v.*** [I] (*AmE*) (*Finan., infml.*) (about prices) to fall quickly: *The company's shares tanked on Wall Street.*

**tanker** /'tæŋkə(r)/ *n.* [C] (*Transpt.*) a ship or lorry/truck that carries oil, gas or petrol in large quantities: *an oil tanker* ◇ *a tanker driver*

**tap** /tæp/ *v., n.*

• ***v.*** (**-pp-**) **1** [T,I] to make use of a source of energy, knowledge, money, etc. that already exists: *to tap the skill of our staff* ◇ *tapping shareholders for new cash* ◇ *to tap* ***into*** *a large market* **2** [T] (*AmE*) (*usu. pass.*) to choose sb for a particular role or job: *She has been tapped* ***for*** *the top job.*
**PHRV** **,tap sth 'in/'out** (*infml.*) to put information, numbers, letters, etc. into a machine by pressing buttons

• ***n.*** [C] a device for controlling the flow of liquid or gas from a pipe or container: *a gas tap* **IDM** **on 'tap** (*infml.*) **1** available to be used at any time: *We have technicians on tap.* **2** (*AmE*) likely to happen at the planned time; planned and ready to happen: *The report is on tap* ***for*** *Friday.*

**'tape ma,chine** = TICKER (1)

**tare** /teə(r); *AmE* ter/ *n.* [U; sing.] (*Transpt.*) **1** the weight of a container or vehicle used to transport goods, without its load: *The max. weight allowed is 20 tons including tare.* **2** the weight of the materials used for wrapping and protecting goods

★**target** /'tɑːgɪt; *AmE* 'tɑːrgɪt/ *n., v.*

• ***n.*** [C] **1** a result that a business or an organization tries to achieve: *The company has set a target of 20% sales growth.* ◇ *We are* ***on target*** *to break even by 2008.* ◇ *Production was well* ***below*** *target.* ◇ *The* ***target date*** *for the rollout is mid 2008.*

➊ *to* ***lower*** *a ~* ◆ *to* ***exceed/meet/miss/reach*** *a ~* ◆ ***earnings/performance/price/sales*** *~s*

**2** (*Finan.*) a company that another more powerful company wants to buy: *potential acquisition targets* **SYN** TARGET COMPANY **3** (*Finan.*; *Market.*) the price at which a company or person aims to sell or buy sth: *The bank's target for the shares is €150.* **IDM** **(be/make) an easy 'target (for sb/sth)** (to be) open to attack or not able to defend yourself: *Is your computer system an easy target for hackers?*

• ***v.*** [T] (**targeting, targeted, targeted**) **1 ~ sb/sth | ~ sth at/to sb/sth** (*often pass.*) to try to have an effect on a particular group of people or a particular area: *Their campaigns* ***specifically*** *target young people.* ◇ *magazines targeted at teens* **SYN** AIM **2** to choose to attack sb/sth or treat sb/sth in a particular way: *a list of products targeted* ***for*** *sanctions*

**'target ,audience** *n.* [C, usu. sing.] (*Market.*) the group of people that an advertisement, a programme or a product is aimed at

**'target ,buyers** = TARGET MARKET

**'target ,company** *n.* [C] (*Finan.*) a company that another company wants to buy or get control of **SYN** TARGET

**'target ,customers** = TARGET MARKET

**,Target Group 'Index** *n.* [sing.] (*abbr* **TGI**) (*Market.*) a regular report, based on the answers to QUESTIONNAIRES, that provides information about the types of products and services, newspapers and TV programmes, etc. that are popular

**'target ,market** *n.* [C, usu. sing.] (*also* **'target ,buyers, 'target ,customers** [pl.]) (*Market.*) the group of people that you want to sell your products to: *Our target market* ***for*** *this drink is teenagers.* ◇ *to identify/reach your ~*

▸ **'target ,marketing** *n.* [U]

**tariff** /'tærɪf/ *n.* [C] **1** (*Trade*) a tax paid on goods coming into or going out of a country: *High tariff barriers protect domestic industry.*

➊ *to* ***impose/set*** *a ~* ◆ *to* ***place*** *a ~* ***on*** *sth* ◆ *to* ***abolish/eliminate*** *a ~* ◆ ***low/punitive*** *~s*

**2** (*Comm.*) a list of fixed prices charged by a company for a particular service, or by a hotel or restaurant for rooms, meals, etc.

★**task** /tɑːsk; *AmE* tæsk/ *n.* [C] **1** a piece of work that sb has to do: *Our first task is to set up a communications system.*

➊ *to* ***carry out/complete/do/perform/undertake*** *a ~* ◆ *to* ***give sb/set (sb)*** *a ~* ◆ *a* ***big***/*an* ***important/urgent*** *~* ◆ *a* ***difficult/hard***/*an* ***impossible*** *~*

**2** (*IT*) an item of work which is processed by a computer as a single unit: *to do/execute/perform a ~* **SYN** JOB

**'task force** (*also* **'task group**) *n.* [C] a group of people who are brought together to deal with a particular problem
**⊕** *to **form/put together/set up** a ~ (on sth)* ◆ *to **chair/head/lead** a ~*

**'task-ˌoriented** (*also* **'task-ˌorientated**, *esp. in BrE*) *adj.* **1** used to describe a method of doing sth that is designed for a particular task rather than for all tasks **2** used to describe a style of management where performing tasks is the main aim rather than trying to improve how workers feel and relate to each other

★ **tax** /tæks/ *n., v.*
• ***n.*** [C,U] money that you have to pay to the government so that it can pay for public services: *I pay over €10 000 a year **in** tax.* ◇ *profits **before/after** tax* ◇ *a tax **on** cigarettes*
**⊕** ***high/low** taxes* ◆ *to **introduce/impose/levy** a ~* ◆ *to **abolish/cut/remove** (a) ~* ◆ *to **increase/raise** taxes* ◆ *to **avoid/evade** ~* ◆ *~ **cuts/increases*** ◆ *a ~ **advisor/consultant*** ◆ *a ~ **authority/office***
• ***v.*** [T] to put a tax on sb/sth; to make sb pay tax: *You will be taxed **on** all your income.* ◇ *Companies are **heavily** taxed.*

**'tax aˌbatement** *n.* [U] an arrangement that allows a business to pay less tax than usual for a period of time

**taxable** /'tæksəbl/ *adj.* (*Account.*) (about money, etc.) that you have to pay tax on OPP NON-TAXABLE
▸ **ˌtaxa'bility** /-'bɪləti/ *n.* [U]

**'tax acˌcounting** *n.* [U] the branch of accounting that prepares financial information so that tax can be calculated and aims to make sure that a company or person does not pay more tax than necessary

**'tax alˌlowance** (*esp. BrE*) (*AmE usu.* **'tax exˌemption**) *n.* [C,U] an amount of money that you are allowed to earn or receive before you start paying tax

**ˌtax antici'pation note** = REVENUE ANTICIPATION NOTE

**'tax asˌsessment** *n.* [U,C] the act of calculating how much tax sb must pay; the amount that has been calculated and that must be paid: *appeals against tax assessments* ▸ **'tax asˌsessor** *n.* [C] (*esp. AmE*)

★ **taxation** /tæk'seɪʃn/ *n.* [U] **1** money that has to be paid as taxes: *low levels of taxation* **2** the system or the act of collecting money by taxes: *Any profits made are exempt from taxation.*

**'tax aˌvoidance** *n.* [U] (*Account.*) ways of paying only the smallest amount of tax that you legally have to → TAX EVASION

**'tax band** *n.* [C] (*BrE*) **1** = TAX BRACKET **2** a range of properties of different values on which the same rate of tax must be paid

**'tax base** *n.* [C, usu. sing.] (*Econ.*) all the things that tax is paid on in a particular country, region, etc: *to broaden/cut/protect/widen the ~*

**'tax bite** *n.* [C] (*infml.*) the part of a particular amount of money that is taken as tax: *The new law will increase the tax bite on small companies.*

**'tax ˌbracket** (*also* **'bracket**) (*BrE also* **'tax band**, *less freq.*) *n.* [C] a range of different incomes on which the same rate of tax must be paid: *My salary increase means I'm now **in** the highest tax bracket.*

**'tax break** *n.* [C] (*esp. AmE*) an advantage or a reduction in taxes that the government gives to particular people or organizations, often to encourage them to do sth: *tax breaks for companies that use environmentally-friendly technology*

**'tax ˌcredit** *n.* [C,U] a reduction in the amount of tax that you have to pay, allowed to companies or people in particular situations

**'tax declaˌration** *n.* [C] (*Account.*) a formal statement made by a company or person giving details of all the money they have received so that the amount of tax they have to pay can be calculated: *to file/make/submit a ~*

**'tax deˌduction** *n.* [C] (*Account.*) an expense that is allowed to be taken off the total amount of money earned or received before the amount of tax that must be paid is calculated: *tax deductions for new equipment such as computers and machinery* ◇ *to claim/enjoy/get/take a ~*
▸ **ˌtax-de'ductible** *adj.*: *Legal fees are not tax-deductible.*

**ˌtax-de'ferred** *adj.* (*AmE*) (*Account.*) if an amount of money earned or received is **tax-deferred**, you pay tax on it at a later time than when you earn or receive it, for example after you retire

**'tax depreciˌation** *n.* [U] (*Account.*) the total amount of money invested in new buildings, machinery, etc. that a company can take away from profits before calculating its tax

**ˌtax-ef'ficient** *adj.* **1** (*Account.*) used to describe a way of organizing assets that allows a person or company to pay the lowest possible amount of tax: *a tax-efficient structure for the acquisition and development of the company* **2** (*Finan.*) (*BrE*) used to describe an investment whose profits are taxed less than others ▸ **ˌtax efˈficiency** *n.* [U]

**ˈtax eˌvasion** *n.* [U] (*Account.*) the crime of deliberately not paying all the taxes that you should pay → TAX AVOIDANCE ▸ **ˈtax eˌvader** *n.* [C]

**ˌtax exˈemption** *n.* (*Account.*) **1** [U,C] (*BrE*) a situation in which a person or a company does not have to pay tax **2** [C] (*esp. AmE*) = TAX ALLOWANCE

**ˈtax ˌexile** *n.* **1** [C] a rich person who has left their own country and gone to live in a place where the taxes are lower **2** [U] the situation when a rich person lives in another country as a **tax exile**: *He's now living in tax exile in Monaco.*

**ˈtax-ˌfavored** *adj.* (*AmE*) (*Finan.*) used to describe an investment whose profits are taxed less than other investments: *tax-favored life insurance*

**ˈtax form** *n.* [C] a document on which a company or person gives details of the amount of money that they have earned so that the government can calculate how much tax they have to pay

**ˌtax-ˈfree** *adj.* (about money, goods, etc.) that you do not have to pay tax on ▸ **ˌtax-ˈfree** *adv.*

**ˈtax ˌhaven** *n.* [C] a place where taxes are low and where people choose to live or officially register their companies because taxes are higher in their own country: *an offshore tax haven*

**ˈtax ˌholiday** *n.* [C] (*Account.*) a period during which a company does not have to pay tax or pays less tax

**ˈtax inˌcentive** *n.* [C] a reduction in tax that encourages companies or people to do sth: *The government is offering tax incentives to companies who move to the region.*

**ˈtax inˌspector** = INSPECTOR OF TAXES

**ˈtax ˌinvoice** *n.* [C] (*Account.*) esp. in Australia and New Zealand, a document that a business provides when it sells goods or services to another company, giving details of the tax that has been paid

**ˈtax liaˌbility** *n.* (*Account.*) **1** [C] the amount of tax that a company or person must pay: *a $1.5 bn tax liability* ◇ *I need to minimize my tax liabilities.* **2** [U,C] the fact of having to pay tax on sth: *No tax liability arose from the sale of the company.*

**ˈtax lien** *n.* [C] (*AmE*) (*Law*) the right of authorities who collect taxes to claim assets from a person or company if they do not pay tax

**ˈtax loss** *n.* [C] (*Account.*) **1** a loss that a company makes which reduces the amount of tax it has to pay **2** a situation where a government receives less tax than it should because of illegal trading

**taxman** /ˈtæksmæn/ *n.* (*pl.* **-men** /-men/) **1** (*Account.*) [sing.] a way of referring to the government department that is responsible for collecting taxes **2** (*infml.*) [C] (*esp. BrE*) a person whose job is to collect taxes SYN INSPECTOR OF TAXES

**ˈtax obliˌgation** *n.* [C] the amount of tax that a person or company owes

★ **taxpayer** /ˈtækspeɪə(r)/ *n.* [C] a person who pays tax to the government, esp. on the money that they earn: *a basic-rate/higher-rate/standard-rate/top-rate ~*

**ˈtax proˌvision** *n.* [C,U] (*Account.*) an amount of money that a company keeps in order to pay tax at the end of the year

**ˈtax rate** *n.* [C] the percentage of an amount of money or of the value of sth that has to be paid as tax: *a low corporate tax rate*

**ˈtax reˌlief** *n.* [U] (*Account.*) a reduction in the amount of tax you have to pay: *Small companies can claim tax relief* **on** *R&D expenditure.*
⊙ *to* ***get/qualify for*** *~* ◆ *to* ***give/offer/provide*** *~* ◆ *to* ***abolish/end*** *~*

**ˈtax reˌturn** (*also* **reˈturn**) *n.* [C] (*Account.*) a statement of how much money a company or person has earned and their expenses, used by the government to calculate how much tax they have to pay; the form on which this statement is made: *a tax return for the year 2007–8*
⊙ *to* ***file/make/send in*** *a ~* ◆ *to* ***complete/do/fill in/fill out*** *a ~*

**ˈtax sale** *n.* [C] (*AmE*) (*Law*) when a property is sold by a government because the owner has not paid their taxes

**ˈtax ˌshelter** *n.* [C] (*Account.*) a way of using or investing money so that you can legally avoid paying tax on it ▸ **ˈtax-ˌsheltered** *adj.*: *tax-sheltered savings plans*

**ˈtax ˌsubsidy** *n.* [C,U] a reduction in the amount of tax that a company pays, given by the government for a particular purpose: *tax subsidies to encourage firms to create new jobs*

**'tax take** *n.* [C] (*esp. AmE*) (*infml.*) the amount of money that is taken as tax: *a high tax take* **on** *earned income*

**'tax ˌthreshold** (*also* **'threshold**, *less freq.*) *n.* [C] the level of income above which a company or person starts to pay income tax: *The corporate tax threshold for small businesses is to be raised to €500 000.*

**'tax year** *n.* [C] (*esp. BrE*) (*Account.*) the period of 12 months over which the taxes of a company or a person are calculated

**t.b.** (*also* **TB**) /ˌtiː 'biː/ = TRIAL BALANCE

**T.B.A** /ˌtiː biː 'eɪ/ *abbr* (used in notices about events, etc.) to be arranged, to be announced, to be advised, to be agreed: *Meeting Tuesday 2.30, venue t.b.a.*

**'T-bill** = TREASURY BILL

**'T-bond** = TREASURY BOND

**TCN** /ˌtiː siː 'en/ = THIRD-COUNTRY NATIONAL

**TCO** /ˌtiː siː 'əʊ; *AmE* 'oʊ/ = TOTAL COST OF OWNERSHIP

**'t-ˌcommerce** *n.* [U] **1** the buying and selling of products through INTERACTIVE television **2** the buying and selling of products by telephone

★ **team** /tiːm/ *n.*, *v.*

• *n.* [C with sing./pl. v.] a group of people who work together: *A team of experts has/have been called in.* ◇ *a team meeting* ◇ *a ~ leader/member* ⊙ *to* ***build/form*** *a ~* ♦ *to* ***head (up)/ lead/manage/run*** *a ~*

• *v.* **1** [I] **~ (up) (with sb)** to join with another person or group in order to do sth together: *The two companies teamed up to launch an online service.* **2** [T] **~ sb/sth (up) (with sb/sth)** to combine or match two or more things or people: *We teamed up our designer with a software engineer.*

**'team ˌbuilding** *n.* [U] the process of getting people to work together on a particular job: *team-building activities/exercises*

**teaming** /'tiːmɪŋ/ *n.* [U] the practice of working as a team: *good ~*

**teammate** /'tiːmmeɪt/ *n.* [C] a person who works in the same team as yourself

**ˌteam 'player** *n.* [C] a person who is good at working as a member of a team: *He is not a team player.*

**teamster** /'tiːmstə(r)/ *n.* [C] (*AmE*) a person whose job is driving a truck

**teamwork** /'tiːmwɜːk; *AmE* -wɜːrk/ *n.* [U] the activity of working well together as a team: *Trust is essential for successful teamwork.*

**teamworking** /'tiːmwɜːkɪŋ; *AmE* -wɜːrk-/ *n.* [U] (*HR*) a way of organizing work in which employees work together in groups and are trained to do a range of tasks

**teaser** /'tiːzə(r)/ *n.* [C] (*Market.*) **1** = TEASER AD **2** (*AmE*) an advertisement that offers sth free to attract customers

**'teaser ad** (*also* **'teaser**) *n.* [C] (*Market.*) a short or strange advertisement that is used to increase the public's interest in a product, esp. one that is not yet available

**'teaser rate** *n.* [C] (*Market.*) a low rate of interest that is offered for a period of time to attract people to use a credit card or arrange a loan

**tech** /tek/ *n.*, *adj.* (*infml.*)

• *n.* [C, usu. pl.] (*also* **'technical**) (used esp. in newspapers) a technology company

• *adj.* technology; technological; technical: *tech companies*

**'tech-ˌheavy** (*also* **'tech-ˌladen**) *adj.* (*infml.*) (*also* **tech'nology-ˌheavy**) (*Stock Ex.*) (about a stock market) with mainly technology companies: *the tech-heavy Nasdaq index*

**techie** (*also* **techy**) /'teki/ *n.* [C] (*pl.* **-ies**) (*infml.*) a person who knows a lot about or is very interested in technology, esp. computing: *a group of bright young techies*

**'tech-ˌladen** = TECH-HEAVY

**techMARK™** /'tekmɑːk; *AmE* -mɑːrk/ *n.* [sing.] (*Stock Ex.*) a group of technology companies that have their own section on the London Stock Exchange: *the FTSE TechMARK*

**technical** /'teknɪkl/ *adj.*, *n.*

• *adj.* **1** connected with the practical use of machinery, methods, etc: *Younger employees have good technical know-how.* ◇ *We had technical difficulties with our email distribution list.* ⊙ *a ~* ***fault/glitch/hitch*** ♦ *a ~* ***breakthrough*** ♦ *~* ***capabilities/ developments***

**2** connected with a particular subject and therefore difficult to understand if you do not know about that subject: *~ jargon/terms* **3** connected with the exact details of official laws, rules, etc: *the technical definition of a recession* ◇ *~ grounds/reasons/rules*

▸ **'technically** /-kli/ *adv.*

• *n.* **1** (*Stock Ex.*) **technicals** [pl.] (*also* **ˌtechnical 'indicator** [C]) measurements, such as the price of shares and the number bought and sold, that are used to predict what will happen to a stock market in the future: *I follow the market technicals.* **2** [C, usu. pl.] = TECH *n.*

**ˌtechnical ˈanalyst** (*also* **ˈchartist**) *n.* [C] (*Stock Ex.*) sb who studies investments and uses charts and computer programs to analyse how the share prices of particular companies have risen and fallen in the past. These patterns are then used to see what might happen in the future. ▸ **ˌtechnical aˈnalysis** *n.* [U,C]

**ˌtechnical efˈficiency** *n.* [U] (*Manufact.*; *Product.*) a situation in which a machine or a business produces the highest possible amount or quality of goods or services with a particular amount of resources SYN X-EFFICIENCY OPP TECHNICAL INEFFICIENCY

**ˌtechnical ˈindicator** = TECHNICAL *n.* (1)

**ˌtechnical ˌinefˈficiency** *n.* [U] (*Manufact.*; *Product.*) a situation in which a machine or a business could produce more or better goods or services with a particular amount of resources SYN X-INEFFICIENCY OPP TECHNICAL EFFICIENCY

**ˌtechnical supˈport** (*also* **ˌtech supˈport**) *n.* [U] help from experts that is available to people who use computers, machines, etc.; the department in an organization that provides this

**technician** /tekˈnɪʃn/ *n.* [C] a person whose job is keeping a particular type of equipment or machinery in good condition: *lab/computer ~s*

★ **technological** /ˌteknəˈlɒdʒɪkl; *AmE* -ˈlɑːdʒ-/ *adj.* connected with the practical use of scientific knowledge in industry

⊙ *~ capabilities/know-how* ◆ *~ advances/developments/innovations*
▸ **ˌtechnoˈlogically** /-kli/ *adv.*

★ **technology** /tekˈnɒlədʒi; *AmE* -ˈnɑːl-/ *n.* (*pl.* **-gies**) **1** [U,C] scientific knowledge used in practical ways in industry, for example in designing new machines: *recent advances in medical technology* ◇ *new digital technologies* ◇ ***technology-based** products* **2** [U] machinery or equipment designed using **technology**
▸ **techˈnologist** *n.* [C]: *a food technologist*

**techˈnology-ˌheavy** = TECH-HEAVY

**technophile** /ˈteknəfaɪl; *BrE also* -nəʊf-/ *n.* [C] a person who is very interested in new technology

**technophobe** /ˈteknəfəʊb; *BrE also* -nəʊf-; *AmE* -foʊb/ *n.* [C] a person who does not like using new technology

**ˌtech supˈport** = TECHNICAL SUPPORT

**techy** = TECHIE

**tel** *abbr* a short way of writing **telephone** before a telephone number: *tel: 556768*

**telco** /ˈtelkəʊ; *AmE* -koʊ/ *n.* [C] (used esp. in newspapers) a TELECOMMUNICATIONS company

**tele-** /ˈteli/ *comb. form* (*in ns, vs and adjs*) **1** over a long distance; far: *teleworking* **2** connected with television: *teletext* **3** done using a telephone: *telesales*

**telecast** /ˈtelikɑːst; *AmE* -kæst/ *n.* [C] (*esp. AmE*) a broadcast on television ▸ **ˈtelecast** *v.* [T] (**-cast**, **-cast**) (*usu. pass.*): *The game will be telecast live.* **ˈtelecaster** *n.* [C]

**telecentre** (*AmE* **telecenter**) /ˈtelisentə(r)/ *n.* [C] (*HR*) a building, usu. in the country, filled with computer equipment so that people can work there instead of travelling to an office in a town or city

**telecom** /ˈtelikɒm; *AmE* -kɑːm/ *n.* **1** [C] (often used in names) a telecommunications company: *France Telecom* **2** [U] (*infml.*) telecommunications: *telecom equipment*

**telecommunication** /ˌteləkəˌmjuːnɪˈkeɪʃn/ (*also* **ˈtelecom**, *infml.*) *n.* [U] telecommunications: *telecommunication services*

★ **telecommunications** /ˌtelikəˌmjuːnɪˈkeɪʃnz/ (*also* **ˈtelecoms**, *infml.*) *n.* [pl.; U] the technology of sending messages over long distances by radio, telephone, television, SATELLITE, etc.

⊙ *a ~ business/carrier/company/operator/provider* ◆ *the ~ industry/market/sector* ◆ *~ equipment* ◆ *a ~ infrastructure/network/system*

**telecommuting** /ˌteləkəˈmjuːtɪŋ/ *n.* [U] the activity of working for a company from your home and communicating with your office, colleagues and customers by computer and telephone, etc. SYN TELEWORKING ▸ **ˌtelecomˈmute** *v.* [I] **ˌtelecomˈmuter** *n.* [C]

**telecoms** /ˈtelikɒmz; *AmE* -kɑːmz/ = TELECOMMUNICATIONS

**teleconference** /ˈtelikɒnfərəns; *AmE* -kɑːn-/ *n.* [C] a meeting, discussion, etc. between two or more people in different places, using phones, television or computers: *to conduct/have/hold/participate in a ~* ▸ **ˈteleconferencing** *n.* [U] **ˈteleconference** *v.* [I]

**telecottage** /ˈtelikɒtɪdʒ; *AmE* -kɑːt-/ *n.* [C] (*BrE*) (*HR*) a building, usu. in the country, filled with computer equipment for people who live in the area to use for work or pleasure ▸ **ˌteleˈcottaging** /-ɪdʒɪŋ/ *n.* [U]

**telegram** /ˈtelɪɡræm/ *n.* [C] a message sent by TELEGRAPH, then printed and given to sb

**telegraph** /ˈtelɪɡrɑːf; *AmE* -ɡræf/ *n.* [U] a system for sending messages over long distances, using wires that carry electrical signals
▸ **ˈtelegraph** *v.* [T,I]

**ˌtelegraphic ˈtransfer** = WIRE TRANSFER

**telemarketing** /ˈtelimɑːkɪtɪŋ; *AmE* -mɑːrk-/ (*also* **ˈtelephone ˌselling**) *n.* [U] (*BrE also* **ˈtelesales** [U; pl.]) (*Market.*) a method of selling goods and services and taking orders for sales by contacting possible customers by telephone
▸ **ˈtelemarketer** *n.* [C]

**telematics** /ˌteliˈmætɪks/ *n.* [U] (*IT*) the branch of INFORMATION TECHNOLOGY that deals with using computers to send information over long distances: *We use telematics to track the position of our vehicles.*
▸ **ˌteleˈmatic** *adj.*

**ˈtelephone diˌrectory** (*also* **ˈtelephone book**, **ˈphone book**) *n.* [C] a book that lists the names, addresses and telephone numbers of people and/or businesses in a particular area

**ˈtelephone ˌselling** = TELEMARKETING

**telephonist** /təˈlefənɪst/ = OPERATOR (3)

**telephony** /təˈlefəni/ *n.* [U] the business or process of sending messages and signals by telephone: *a mobile telephony business*
○ ***cable/fixed-line/voice/wireless*** *~*
♦ *a ~* ***company/operator/provider***

**telesales** /ˈteliseɪlz/ = TELEMARKETING

**teletext** /ˈtelitekst/ *n.* [U] a service providing written news and information using television

**ˈtelevision ˌrating** *n.* [C] (*abbr* **TVR**) (*Market.*) the number of people who watch a particular programme on television, compared with the total number of people available to watch, used to measure how popular the programme is: *The World Cup final had a record television rating of 48.3%.*

**teleworking** /ˈteliwɜːkɪŋ; *AmE* -wɜːrk-/ (*also* **ˈtelework**) *n.* [U] (*HR*) the activity of working for a company from your home and communicating with your office and colleagues by computer and telephone, etc. SYN TELECOMMUTING
▸ **ˈtelework** *n.* [U] **ˈtelework** *v.* [I] **ˈteleworker** *n.* [C]

**telex** /ˈteleks/ *n.* **1** [U] an international system of communication in which messages are typed on a special machine and sent by the telephone system **2** [C] a message sent or received by **telex**; a machine for doing this
▸ **ˈtelex** *v.* [T,I]: *Can you telex the order today?*

**teller** /ˈtelə(r)/ *n.* [C] **1** = BANK TELLER **2** a machine that pays out money automatically SYN ATM

**temp** /temp/ *n.* [C] (*HR*) a temporary employee in an office: *a temp agency* SYN CASUAL
▸ **temp** *v.* [I] (*infml.*): *I've been temping for 3 months.*

**template** /ˈtempleɪt/ *n.* [C] **1** a thing that is used as a model for producing other similar examples: *a basic email template for orders* **2** a shape cut out of a hard material, used as a model for producing exactly the same shape many times in another material

**temporary** /ˈtemprəri; *AmE* -pəreri/ *adj.* lasting or intended to last only for a short time; not permanent: *More than half the staff are temporary.* ◇ *workers on temporary contracts* OPP PERMANENT

**ˌtemporary ˈhelp ˌagency** *n.* [C] (*HR*) a business that provides workers for other businesses for limited periods of time

**tenancy** /ˈtenənsi/ *n.* (*pl.* **-cies**) (*Law; Prop.*) **1** [C,U] the right to live or work in a building or on land that you rent: *a tenancy agreement*
○ *to* ***get/give up/take (over)/hold/surrender*** *a ~* ♦ *to* ***grant/offer/renew/terminate*** *a ~*
**2** [C] a period of time that you rent a house, land, etc. for
○ *a* ***life/fixed-term/long-term/short-term*** *~* ♦ *a ~* ***expires/lapses***

**tenant** /ˈtenənt/ *n.*, *v.* (*Law; Prop.*)
• ***n.*** [C] a person or company that pays rent for the use of a building, land, room, etc. to the person or company that owns it: *The shopping mall has 115 tenants.*
• ***v.*** [T] (*usu. pass.*) to work or live in a place as a **tenant**: *a tenanted farm*

**ˌtenant at ˈwill** *n.* [C] (*pl.* **tenants -**) (*Law*) a **tenant** that can be forced to leave a property, piece of land, etc. without any warning

★**tender** /ˈtendə(r)/ *n., v.*
• ***n.*** [C,U] **1** (*Comm.*) a formal offer to supply goods or do work at a stated price: *We submitted the lowest tender.* ◇ *Cleaning services have been* ***put out to (competitive) tender.***
⊙ *to* ***invite/request*** *~s (for sth)* • *to* ***accept/award/issue*** *a ~* • *to* ***apply for/bid for/win*** *a ~*
**2** (*Finan.*) an offer to buy shares, etc. at a stated price: *The shares are being sold by tender.*
• ***v.*** **1** (*Comm.*) [T,I] to make a formal offer to supply goods or do work at a stated price: *to tender* ***for*** *a project* ◇ *competitive tendering* **2** (*Finan.*) [I] to make a formal offer to buy shares, etc. at a stated price, esp. in order to gain control of a company **3** (*Finan.*) [T] to make a formal offer to sell shares, etc. at a stated price **4** (*fml.*) [T] to offer money as payment: *Enter the amount tendered.* **5** (*fml.*) [T] to offer or give sth to sb: *to tender your resignation* ▸ **ˈtenderer** *n.* [C]

**ˈtender ˌoffer** *n.* [C] (*Finan.*) **1** an invitation to the existing shareholders of a particular company to sell some of their shares at a particular price either to the company itself or to another company **2** the act of offering to buy new shares at a particular price

**tenner** /ˈtenə(r)/ *n.* [C] (*infml.*) **1** (*BrE*) £10 or a ten-pound note **2** (*AmE*) ten dollars

**tenor** /ˈtenə(r)/ *n.* [sing.] (*Finan.*) the length of time stated on a BILL OF EXCHANGE, etc. before it becomes due for payment: *the tenor of the bill* SYN TERM

**tentative** /ˈtentətɪv/ *adj.* **1** (about an arrangement, agreement, etc.) not definite or certain because you may want to change it later: *a tentative agreement with sb* **2** not behaving with confidence; not done with confidence: *I'm no longer tentative about online shopping.*
▸ **ˈtentatively** *adv.* **ˈtentativeness** *n.* [U]

**tenure** /ˈtenjə(r)/ *n.* [U] **1** the period of time when sb holds an important job: *The company grew under his tenure as CEO.* **2** (*HR*) the right to stay permanently in your job, esp. as a teacher at a university: *It's still difficult to get tenure.* **3** (*Law*) the legal right to live in a house or use a piece of land: *to have* ***security of tenure***

**tepid** /ˈtepɪd/ *adj.* (used esp. in newspapers) lower in level, less successful, less good, etc. than expected: *Their sales rose a tepid 0.4%.*

★**term** /tɜːm; *AmE* tɜːrm/ *n., v.*
• ***n.*** **1** [C] a word or phrase used as the name of sth, esp. one connected with a particular type of language: *business/legal/scientific/technical ~s* **2** [C, usu. sing.] a period of time for which sth lasts; a fixed or limited time: *the full term of the loan* ◇ *a five-year term of office* **3** [sing.] the end of a particular period of time, esp. one for which an agreement, etc. lasts: *to reach the term* **4** (*Finan.*) [sing.] the length of time stated on a BILL OF EXCHANGE, etc. before it becomes due for payment: *the term of the bill* SYN TENOR IDM **in/over the ˈlong/ˈmedium/ˈshort/ˈfar/ˈnear term** used to describe what will happen in a long, short, etc. time in the future
• ***v.*** [T] to use a particular name or word to describe sb/sth: *The meetings were termed 'crisis talks'.*

**ˈterm asˌsurance** (*BrE*) (*also* **ˈterm inˌsurance**, *AmE, BrE*) *n.* [U] a type of life insurance that only lasts for a fixed time and does not pay money if the insured person dies after that time

**ˈterm bill** = PERIOD BILL

**ˈterm deˌposit** = TIME DEPOSIT

**terminal** /ˈtɜːmɪnl; *AmE* ˈtɜːrm-/ *n., adj.*
• ***n.*** [C] **1** a building or set of buildings at an airport where air passengers arrive and leave **2** (*IT*) a piece of equipment, usu. consisting of a keyboard and a screen that joins the user to a central computer system
• ***adj.*** **1** certain to get worse and come to an end: *The industry is* ***in terminal decline.*** **2** at the end of sth: *the terminal bonus on a policy*

**ˈterminal ˌmarket** *n.* [C] **1** (*Finan.*) a place where COMMODITIES, FUTURES, etc. are bought and sold that is in a trading centre such as London or New York rather than in the country where the goods are produced **2** (*Comm.*) (*AmE*) a central place, usu. near an important town or city, where goods, esp. agricultural goods, are brought from many different areas to be bought and sold

★**terminate** /ˈtɜːmɪneɪt; *AmE* ˈtɜːrm-/ *v.* **1** [T,I] to end; to make sth end: *Your contract terminates in May.* **2** (*HR*) [T] (*esp. AmE*) to remove sb from their job: *terminated employees*
▸ **ˌtermiˈnation** *n.* [U,C]

**ˌtermiˈnation charge** *n.* [C, usu. pl.] the fee for making a call to a mobile phone/cellphone from another system

**ˌterm inˈsurance** = TERM ASSURANCE

**ˈterm loan** *n.* [C] (*Finan.*) a loan for a fixed period of time, usu. from a bank to a company, that is repaid in regular amounts

★**terms** /tɜːmz; *AmE* tɜːrmz/ *n.* [pl.] **1** the conditions that people offer, demand or accept when they make an agreement: *The Board has now agreed the terms of the deal.* ◇ *A payment is due* ***under the terms of*** *the contract.* ◇ *the* ***terms and conditions*** *of employment*

⊙ *to* ***accept/negotiate*** ~ ◆ *to* ***offer/set*** ~ ◆ ***better/favourable*** ~

**2** (*Comm.*) conditions that you agree to when you buy, sell, or pay for sth; a price or cost: *attractive credit terms* ◇ *Our terms are 30 days* (= payment must be made in 30 days).

⊙ ***easy/favourable*** ~ ◆ ***cash/payment/trade*** ~

**3** a way of saying sth or of expressing yourself: *to explain sth* ***in simple terms*** IDM **in terms of sth; in ... terms** used to show what aspect of a subject you are talking about: *Success is not just measured in financial terms.* **on your own ˈterms; on sb's ˈterms** according to the conditions that you or sb else decides: *I'll only take the job on my own terms.* → idiom at EQUAL

**ˌterms of ˈreference** *n.* [pl.] the limits that are set on what an official committee or report has been asked to do

**ˌterms of ˈtrade** *n.* [pl.] (*Econ.*) the average price of a country's imports compared with the average price of its exports

**terrestrial** /təˈrestriəl/ *adj.* (used about television and broadcasting systems) operating on earth rather than from a SATELLITE

**territory** /ˈterətri; *AmE* -tɔːri/ *n.* [C,U] (*pl.* **-ries**) **1** an area of a town, a country or the world that sb has responsibility for in their work **2** an area of knowledge or activity: *Legal problems are Andy's territory* (= he deals with them).

**tertiary** /ˈtɜːʃəri; *AmE* ˈtɜːrʃieri; -ʃəri/ *adj.* third in order, rank or importance → PRIMARY, SECONDARY

**ˈtertiary ˌindustry** (*also* **ˈservice ˌindustry**) *n.* [C,U] (*Econ.*) a business whose work involves doing sth for customers but not producing goods; these businesses as a group

**ˈtertiary ˌsector** (*also* **ˈservice ˌsector**) *n.* [sing.] (*Econ.*) the part of a country's economy connected with providing services rather than manufacturing or producing things

★**test** /test/ *n., v.*

• ***n.*** [C] **1** an experiment to discover whether or how well sth works, or to find out more information about it: *Market tests showed that €80 was too high a price.* ◇ *a test version of the software*

⊙ *to* ***conduct/do/run*** *a* ~ ◆ *a* ~ ***proves*** *sth*

**2** an examination of sb's knowledge or ability, consisting of questions for them to answer or activities for them to do

⊙ *to* ***do/sit/take*** *a* ~ ◆ *to* ***fail/pass*** *a* ~

**3** a situation or an event that shows how good, strong, etc. sb/sth is: *Sales of the new model will be a key test of customer loyalty.*

⊙ *a* ***good/tough*** ~ ◆ *an* ***important/the ultimate*** ~

IDM **put sb/sth to the ˈtest** to put sb/sth in a situation which will show what their true qualities are → idiom at STAND *v.*

• ***v.*** **1** [T] **~ sth (out)** to use or try sth to find out how well it works or to find out more information about it: *They opened one store in Europe to test out the market.* **2** [T,I] to examine sb's knowledge or ability by asking them questions or giving them activities to do **3** [T] to be difficult and therefore need all your ability, strength, etc: *The talks really tested my French.* PHR V **ˈtest (sth) for sth** to examine sth to see if a particular substance is present: *to test software for viruses*

**ˈtest case** *n.* [C] (*Law*) a legal case or other situation whose result will be used as an example when decisions are being made on similar cases in the future

**ˈtest deck** *n.* [C] (*Tech.*) a small amount of data, material, etc. that is used as a basis for testing a project

**ˈtest drive** *n.* [C] an occasion when you drive a vehicle or use a piece of equipment, etc. to see how well it works and if you like it and want to buy it ▸ **ˈtest-drive** *v.* [T]

**tester** /ˈtestə(r)/ *n.* [C] **1** a person or thing that tests sth: *a code tester for a software firm* **2** a small amount of a product that you can try to see if you like it

**testimonial** /ˌtestɪˈməʊniəl; *AmE* -ˈmoʊ-/ *n.* [C] **1** (*Market.*) a formal written statement about the quality of sth: *customer testimonials* **2** (*HR*) a formal written statement, often by a former employer, about sb's abilities, qualities and character: *She got a* ***glowing*** *testimonial from her former boss.* SYN RECOMMENDATION

★**testing** /ˈtestɪŋ/ *n.* [U] the activity of trying or using sth in order to find sth out, see if it works, etc: *The product is still* **in** *testing.* ◇ *to undergo testing*
⊕ ***consumer/market*** ~ ♦ *to* ***carry out/do/undertake*** ~

**ˈtest ˌmarket** *n.* [C] (*Market.*) an area, a country, etc. where a product is sold in order to test it before it is sold in other places: *several test-market cities* ▸ **ˈtest-ˌmarket** *v.* [T]: *The product is being test-marketed.* **ˈtest ˌmarketing** *n.* [U]

**ˈtest run** *n.* [C] (*Market.*) an occasion when a product is tested: *We gave the software packages a test run.*

**TEU** /ˌtiː iː ˈjuː/ *abbr* (*Transpt.*) **twenty-foot equivalent unit** (*used as a countable n.*) a standard container for transporting goods that is approximately six metres long: *a ship with a capacity of over 6 000 TEU*

**text** /tekst/ *n., v.*
• ***n.* 1** [U] the words of a book, web page, etc., not the pictures, notes, etc: *text and graphics* **2** [U] any form of written material **3** [C] = TEXT MESSAGE **4** [C] the written form of a speech, an article, etc.
• *v.* [T,I] **~ (sb) (sth)** to send sb a written message using a mobile phone/cellphone: *I texted him the details.* SYN SMS ▸ **ˈtexting** *n.* [U]

**textile** /ˈtekstaɪl/ *n.* **1** [C] any type of fabric made by weaving or knitting: *a range of textiles* ◇ *the textile industry* **2 textiles** [pl.] the industry that makes fabric: *a job in textiles*

**ˈtext ˌmessage** (*also* **text**) *n.* [C] a short written message sent to sb using a mobile phone/cellphone SYN SMS ▸ **ˈtext ˌmessage** *v.* [T,I] **ˈtext ˌmessaging** *n.* [U]

**ˌtext-to-ˈspeech** *adj.* (*IT*) used to describe the technology that allows a computer to change data into spoken words ▸ **ˌtext-to-ˈspeech** *n.* [U]: *to install text-to-speech*

**TGI** /ˌtiː dʒiː ˈaɪ/ = TARGET GROUP INDEX

**T-group** (*also* **ˈtraining group**) *n.* [C] (*HR*) a small group of people who meet, with a leader, and talk and think in order to improve their skills in dealing with people

**theory** /ˈθɪəri; *AmE* ˈθɪri; ˈθiːəri/ *n.* (*pl.* **-ries**) **1** [C,U] a formal set of ideas intended to explain why sth happens or exists: *the boom and bust theory of British economics* **2** [U,C] the principles on which a particular activity is based: *management theory* **3** [C] an opinion or idea that sb believes is true but may in fact be wrong: *The theory* **is** *that CEOs get rich only when shareholders get rich.*
IDM **in ˈtheory** used to say that a particular statement is supposed to be true but may in fact be wrong: *This sounds fine in theory, but would it work in practice?*

**ˌtheory of conˈstraints** *n.* [sing.] (*abbr* **TOC**) (*Product.*) a way of improving production by finding and improving the things or people that are limiting the amount or speed of production

**ˌTheory ˈX** /ˈeks/ *n.* [sing.] (*HR*) a way of managing people based on the idea that most workers do not enjoy working for a company and do not want responsibility, so they need to be watched carefully, given a lot of instructions and be threatened with punishments

**ˌTheory ˈY** /ˈwaɪ/ *n.* [sing.] (*HR*) a way of managing people based on the idea that most workers enjoy work and want responsibility, so they should be given freedom to deal with difficult problems and be promised rewards

**ˌTheory ˈZ** /ˈzed; *AmE* ˈziː/ *n.* [sing.] (*HR*) a way of managing people, developed from Japanese styles of management, based on the idea that employees work best when they feel they are trusted and that they are an important part of the company

**think** /θɪŋk/ *v.* IDM **think on your ˈfeet** to be able to think and react to things very quickly and effectively without any preparation **think out of/outside the ˈbox** to think in a new or different way in order to solve a problem: *people who are paid to think outside the box*

**ˈthink tank** *n.* [C] a group of experts who provide advice and ideas on political, social or economic issues ▸ **ˈthink-ˌtanker** *n.* [C]

**ˌthin ˈmarket** (*also* **ˌnarrow ˈmarket**) *n.* [C] (*Finan.*) a market in which there is not much buying and selling, and small changes in supply or demand can have a great effect on the prices of shares, bonds, etc.

**ˌthird-country ˈnational** *n.* [C] (*abbr* **TCN**) (*HR*) an employee of an international organization who does not come from the country in which the organization has its main base, or from the country in which they are working

**ˌthird-geneˈration** *adj.* **1** (*abbr* **3G**) used to describe technology that has been developed to send data to mobile phones/cellphones, etc. at much higher speeds than were possible before **2** used to describe any technology being developed that is more advanced than the earlier two stages

**ˌthird line ˈforcing** *n.* [U] (*Econ.*) the illegal practice of a company refusing to allow a customer to have a product or service that they want unless they also buy sth that they do not want

**ˌthird ˈparty** *n.* [C] (*Insur.; Law or fml.*) an organization, a person, etc. that is involved in a situation in addition to the two main people or groups: *The company might be bought back by its parent or sold to a third party.* ◇ (*BrE*) ***third party, fire and theft*** *car insurance* (= that covers you if you injure sb or damage another car, or if yours is burnt or stolen)

**ˌthird-party interˈvention** *n.* [U] (*HR*) when an outside person or organization becomes involved in a dispute between employers and employees in order to try to end it

**ˌthird-party ˈsoftware** *n.* [U] (*IT*) computer programs which add to the range of functions that existing programs can perform, that are developed or supplied by a different company from the one that develops or supplies the existing software: *third-party plug-ins*

**the ˌthird ˈsector** *n.* [sing.] (*Econ.*) the part of the economy of a country that involves organizations that do not aim to make a profit and whose employees may work without being paid

**the ˌThird ˈWorld** *n.* [sing.] a way of referring to the poor or developing countries of Africa, Asia and Latin America, which is sometimes considered offensive → DEVELOPING

**thirtysomething** /ˈθɜːtisʌmθɪŋ; *AmE* ˈθɜːrti-/ *n.* [C] (*infml.*) a person who is between thirty and thirty-nine years old: *thirtysomethings with no children* → TWENTYSOMETHING

**thrash** /θræʃ/ *v.* **PHR V** **ˌthrash sth ˈout** to discuss a situation or problem thoroughly in order to decide sth: *thrashing out the details*

**ˌthree-ˈway** *adj.* involving three people, groups, processes or directions: *a ~ battle/deal/merger*

**threshold** /ˈθreʃhəʊld; *AmE* -hoʊld/ *n.* [C] (*Account.*) **1** the level at which sth starts to happen, change or have an effect: *Assets had fallen below a key threshold.* ◇ *a pay/salary/wage threshold* **2** = TAX THRESHOLD

**ˈthreshold efˌfect** *n.* [C, usu. sing.] **1** (*Market.*) the way in which advertising for a product has to reach a particular level before sales begin to increase **2** (*IT*) the way in which, as new technology, such as the phone, becomes familiar, people no longer think of it as technology

**ˈthreshold price** *n.* [C] (*Econ.*) a minimum price set for a product

**thrift** /θrɪft/ *n.* **1** [U] the habit of not spending too much money **2** [C] (*AmE*) = THRIFT INSTITUTION

**ˈthrift instiˌtution** (*also* **thrift**) (*both AmE*) *n.* [C] an organization like a bank that issues shares to people who deposit money and lends the money to people who want to buy a home **SYN** SAVINGS AND LOAN ASSOCIATION

**thrive** /θraɪv/ *v.* [I] to become, and continue to be, successful, strong, healthy, etc: *an environment where small businesses can thrive* **SYN** FLOURISH ▶ **ˈthriving** *adj.*

**throughput** /ˈθruːpʊt/ *n.* [U; C, usu. sing.] **1** (*Product.*) the amount of work done, or the number of people dealt with, in a particular period of time: *Our throughput has increased by 40%.* ◇ *the airport's passenger throughput* **2** (*IT*) the amount of data that passes through a piece of equipment or a system in a particular period: *The network will have to withstand high throughput.*

**throw** /θrəʊ; *AmE* θroʊ/ *v.* (**threw** /θruː/ **thrown** /θrəʊn; *AmE* θroʊn/) **IDM** **throw good money after ˈbad** to spend more money on sth, when you have wasted a lot on it already **throw your ˈmoney about/around** (*infml.*) to spend money in a careless and obvious way **throw ˈmoney at sth** to try to deal with a problem or improve a situation by spending money on it **throw your ˈweight about/around** (*infml.*) to use your position of authority or power in an aggressive way in order to achieve what you want → idioms at DEEP *adj.*, MONEY

**PHR V** **ˌthrow sth aˈway 1** (*also* **ˌthrow sth ˈout**) to get rid of sth that you no longer want: *He throws away his phones after three months.* **2** to fail to make use of sth; to waste sth: *to ~ away a chance/an opportunity* **ˌthrow sth ˈin** to include sth with what you are selling or offering, without increasing the price **ˌthrow sth ˈout 1** = THROW STH AWAY (1) **2** to decide not to accept a proposal, an idea, etc. **ˌthrow sth ˈup 1** to produce sth; to make people notice sth: *A Web search threw up a couple of* useful pages. **2** to leave your job: *She'e decided to throw up her job.* **3** to build or make sth in a hurry

**throwaway** /ˈθrəʊəweɪ; *AmE* ˈθroʊ-/ *adj.* (about goods, etc.) produced cheaply and intended to be thrown away after use

**ˌthumbs ˈup/ˈdown** *n.* [sing.] used to show that sth has been accepted/rejected or that it is a success/failure: *The latest model has got the thumbs down from consumers.*

**tick** /tɪk/ *v., n.*
• ***v.*** (*BrE*) (*AmE* **check**) [T] to put a mark (✓) next to an item on a list, an answer, etc., usu. to show that it has been dealt with or is correct **IDM have ˌticks in all the right ˈboxes** (*infml.*) to be doing the right things to achieve a particular result **PHR V ˌtick sb/sth ˈoff** (*BrE*) (*AmE* **ˌcheck sb/sth ˈoff**) to put a mark (✓) beside a name or an item on a list to show that sth has been dealt with **ˌtick ˈover** (*BrE*) (*usu. in the continuous tenses*) (about a business, a system, an activity, etc.) to keep working slowly without producing or achieving much: *Just keep things ticking over while I'm away.*
• ***n.*** [C] **1** (*BrE*) (*AmE* **ˈcheck mark, check**) a mark (✓) put beside a sum or an item on a list, usu. to show that it has been checked or done or is correct **2** (*Finan.*) (*also* **ˈtick point**) the smallest amount by which the price of shares, FUTURES, etc. can change, often 0.01% of the NOMINAL VALUE: *The gilt futures price closed 67 ticks up.* **3** (*Finan.*) an upward or downward movement in the price of a share, bond, COMMODITY, etc.

**tickbox** /ˈtɪkbɒks; *AmE* -bɑːks/ = CHECKBOX

**ticker** /ˈtɪkə(r)/ *n.* [C] (*Stock Ex.*) **1** (*also* **ˈticker-tape maˌchine, ˈtape maˌchine**) a machine that prints data on a strip of paper, esp. information about prices of shares on a stock market; an electronic device that shows information of this type **2** = TICKER SYMBOL

**ˈticker ˌsymbol** (*also* **ˈticker, ˈsymbol**) *n.* [C] (*Stock Ex.*) esp. in the US, a set of usu. three or four letters that identifies a share, etc. on a stock exchange

**ˈticker tape** *n.* [C] a strip of paper on which data is recorded by a ticker; a similar strip on a computer screen: *A ticker tape scrolls across the screen with breaking news.*

**ˈticker-tape maˌchine** = TICKER (1)

**ticket** /ˈtɪkɪt/ *n., v.*
• ***n.*** [C] **1** a printed piece of paper that gives you the right to travel on a particular plane, train, etc. or to go into a theatre, etc.
⊕ *to* ***book/buy/reserve/sell*** *~s* ◆ *a* ***non-refundable*** *~* ◆ *~* ***prices/sales*** ◆ *a ~* ***agent/counter/machine/office***
**2** a label attached to sth in a shop/store giving details of its price, size, etc: *10% off the price on the ticket*
• ***v.*** [T] to produce and sell tickets for an event, a trip, etc.; to give sb a ticket: *Passengers can now be ticketed electronically.* ▶ **ˈticketing** *n.* [U]: *ticketing systems*

**ˈticket tout** = TOUT *n.*

**ˈtick point** = TICK *n.* (2)

**tie** /taɪ/ *v., n.*
• ***v.*** [T] (**ties, tying, tied, tied**) **1** (*usu. pass.*) to connect or link sb/sth closely with sb/sth else: *Pay increases are tied* ***to*** *inflation.* **2** (*usu. pass.*) to restrict sb and make them unable to do everything they want to: *be tied* ***to*** *a contract* **IDM tie the ˈknot (with sb/sth)** (*infml.*) (esp. in newspapers) to join together with sb/sth else in order to form a single organization: *to tie the knot with a rival company* **PHR V ˌtie ˈin (with sth)** to match or agree with sth **ˌtie (sth) ˈin (with sth)** to link sth or be linked to sth: *A magazine was produced to tie in with the event.* **ˌtie sb ˈinto sb/sth** to restrict sb to a particular situation, person, organization, etc: *They were tied into an agreement to buy from particular suppliers.* **ˌtie sb ˈup** (*usu. pass.*) to keep sb busy so that they have no time for other things: *I'm tied up in a meeting until 3.* **ˌtie sth ˈup 1** (*often pass.*) to invest money so that it is not easily available for use: *His money is all tied up in the company.* **2** (*usu. pass.*) to connect or link sth to sth else **3** to deal with all the remaining details of sth: *to tie up a deal* ◇ *tying up* ***loose ends*** (= remaining small jobs) **4** to keep sth in use so that it cannot be used for other things: *I was using the Internet, so the phone line was tied up.* **ˌtie ˈup with sb/sth** to be linked to sth such as another company and work together on sth
• ***n.*** [C] **1** [usu. pl.] a strong connection between people or organizations: *We have* ***close*** *ties* ***with*** *a Japanese firm.* **2** (*AmE also* **ˈnecktie**) a long narrow piece of fabric worn around the neck, esp. by men, with a knot in front: *wearing a* ***suit and tie*** ◇ *a* ***collar and tie***

**ˌtied ˈagent** *n.* [C] (*Finan.*; *Insur.*) a person who represents one particular company and gives people advice only about its products and services

**ˌtied ˈloan** *n.* [C] (*Econ.*) money lent to one country by another on condition that it is spent on goods or services from the country that provided the money

**ˈtie-in** *n.* [C] (*Comm.*; *Market.*) **1** a product such as a book or toy that is connected with a film/movie, television programme, etc: *tie-in products* **2** the act of advertising or selling a product or service that is closely related to the main product or service being advertised or sold: *Selling nail polish at the beauty salon is a great marketing tie-in.* **3** when two or more companies work together, for example to try to sell their products: *a tie-in* **with** *an American giant* **4** (*esp. AmE*) a way of selling sth in which two or more products must be bought together; a product that is sold in this way: *tie-in deals* **5** a contract or an agreement that limits what you can do or makes you do sth for a fixed period of time

**tier** /tɪə(r); *AmE* tɪr/ *n.* [C] **1** one of several levels in an organization or a system: *the top tier of management* ◇ *a two-tier pay structure* **2** one of several levels of quality

**ˌTier ˈ1 ˌcapital** *n.* [U] (*Finan.*) the main part of a bank's funds that comes from the money that shareholders have invested and spare profits it has kept
SYN CORE CAPITAL

**ˈtie-up** *n.* [C] **~ (with sb)** | **~ (between A and B)** an agreement between two companies to join together

**tiger** /ˈtaɪɡə(r)/ *n.* [C] (*Econ.*) (esp. in newspapers) a country whose economy is growing very fast

**tight** /taɪt/ *adj.* (**-er**, **-est**) **1** (about time or money) difficult to manage, because there is not enough: *We have a very tight budget.* **2** very strict and firm: *tight control over costs*
IDM **keep a tight ˈrein on sb/sth** to control sb/sth carefully or strictly: *to keep a tight rein on costs/spending*
→ idiom at RUN *v.*

**tighten** /ˈtaɪtn/ *v.* [T] **~ sth (up)** to make sth become stricter; to increase control over sth: *to ~ policy/rules/security* ▸ **ˈtightening** *n.* [U; sing.]: *a tightening of safety standards*
IDM **tighten your ˈbelt** to spend less money because there is less available → idiom at PURSE
PHRV **ˌtighten ˈup (on sth)** to become stricter or more careful: *steps to tighten up on tax evasion*

**ˌtight ˈmoney** *n.* [U] (*Econ.*) a situation when money is difficult to borrow and can only be borrowed at a high rate of interest: *a tight money policy* SYN DEAR MONEY

**TIL** /ˌtiː aɪ ˈel/ *abbr* (*BrE*) (*HR*) time in lieu

**till** /tɪl/ *n.* [C] **1** (*BrE*) a machine used in shop/stores, restaurants, etc. that has a drawer for keeping money in, and that shows and records the amount of money received for each thing sold SYN CASH REGISTER **2** (*BrE*) the place where you pay for the things that you are buying in a large shop/store: *Please pay at the till.* SYN CHECKOUT **3** (*esp. AmE*) the drawer where the money is put in a CASH REGISTER
→ idiom at CATCH *v.*

**timber** /ˈtɪmbə(r)/ *n.* [U] **1** trees grown to be used in building or for making things: *the timber industry* **2** (*esp. BrE*) (*AmE usu.* **ˈlumber**) wood that is prepared for use in building, etc: *a timber merchant*

**ˈtime acˌcount** = DEPOSIT ACCOUNT

**ˌtime and a ˈhalf** *n.* [U] (*HR*) a rate of pay that is 50% more than the normal rate, which a worker gets for working outside normal hours

**ˌtime-and-ˈmotion ˌstudy** *n.* [C] a detailed study of how a person, a department, a company, etc. works, the results of which are used to find ways to make them/it more efficient

**ˈtime card** *n.* [C] (*HR*) a card that is marked with the time when an employee arrives and leaves

**ˈtime ˌcharter** *n.* [C,U] (*Transpt.*) the hire of ship or an aircraft and the people to operate it for a fixed period of time

**ˈtime clock** (*also* **ˈtime reˌcorder**) *n.* [C] (*HR*) a machine in a place of work, esp. a factory, that records the exact times when employees arrive or leave by marking cards

**ˈtime deˌposit** (*also* **ˈterm deˌposit**) *n.* [C] (*Finan.*) a type of account at a bank or other financial institution in which money is left for a fixed period of time with a fixed rate of interest

**ˈtime frame** *n.* [C] the length of time that is used or available for sth: *We expect to complete the project within a fairly short time frame.*

**ˌtime in ˈlieu** = TIME OFF IN LIEU

**timekeeping** /ˈtaɪmkiːpɪŋ/ *n.* [U] a person's ability to arrive in time for things, esp. work: *good/poor ~*

▸ **'timekeeper** *n.* [C]: *good time-keepers*

**'time lag** (*also* **lag**, **'time lapse**) *n.* [C] the period of time between two connected events: *a time lag between invoicing a customer and getting paid*

**'time ˌlimit** *n.* [C] the length of time within which you must do or complete sth: *We have to set a time limit for the work.*

⊙ *to* ***impose/put*** *a ~ on sth* ◆ *to* ***extend/relax*** *a ~* ◆ *to* ***go over/overrun*** *a ~* ◆ *the ~* ***expires***

**timeline** /ˈtaɪmlaɪn/ *n.* [C] a line representing when the different stages of an event, a project, etc. happen: *They have not yet* ***set*** *a timeline* ***for*** *the merger.*

**'time ˌmanagement** *n.* [U] organizing your working time in the most efficient way

**ˌtime 'off** *n.* [U] a period when you are away from work because you are ill/sick, taking a holiday/vacation, etc: *to ask for/get/have/take ~*

**ˌtime off in 'lieu** /luː; *BrE also* ljuː/ (*abbr* **TOIL**) (*also* **ˌtime in 'lieu** *abbr* **TIL**) (*both BrE*) *n.* [U] (*HR*) extra time away from work that employees can have if they have worked extra hours SYN COMP TIME (*AmE*)

**timeout** /ˈtaɪmaʊt/ *n.* [C] (*IT*) an occasion when an action takes too long to be completed and is automatically cancelled

**'time rate** *n.* [C] (*HR*) an arrangement where people are paid for the number of hours they work rather than for the items they produce

**'time reˌcorder** = TIME CLOCK

**timescale** /ˈtaɪmskeɪl/ *n.* [C] the period of time that it takes for sth to happen or be completed: *What's the timescale for this project?*

**'time ˌseries** *n.* [C] (*Tech.*) a series of values of a quantity obtained over a period of time, often with equal amounts of time between them: *You can use time series data to monitor sales trends over a period of years.*

**'time-ˌserver** *n.* [C] used in a disapproving way to describe sb who does as little work as possible in their job because they are just waiting until they leave for another job or finish work completely
▸ **'time-ˌserving** *adj., n.* [U]

**'time sheet** *n.* [C] (*HR*) a piece of paper on which the number of hours that sb has worked is recorded: *to fill in/fill out/keep/submit a ~*

**timetable** /ˈtaɪmteɪbl/ *n., v.*
• ***n.*** [C] **1** a plan of when you expect particular events to happen: *I have a busy timetable this week.*
⊙ *a* ***detailed/strict/tight*** *~* ◆ *to* ***draw up/set*** *a ~* ◆ *to* ***keep to/stick to*** *a ~*
**2** a list showing what time particular events happen: *a bus/train ~*
→ SCHEDULE
• ***v.*** [T] (*esp. BrE*) (*usu. pass.*) to arrange for sth to take place at a particular time: *a timetabled meeting*
→ SCHEDULE ▸ **'timetabling** *n.* [U]

**'time-ˌtested** *adj.* that has been used for a long time and has been proved to be successful

**ˌtime to 'market** *n.* [U; sing.] (*abbr* **TTM**) (*Market.*; *Product.*) the amount of time from when a company starts to develop a new product until the product goes on sale: *to achieve a fast time to market*

**'time 'value of 'money** *n.* [U] (*Account.*) the idea that the value of an amount of money received today is worth more than the same amount of money received in the future, as it can be invested to earn interest

**timing** /ˈtaɪmɪŋ/ *n.* **1** [U,C] the act of choosing when sth happens; a particular point or period of time when sth happens or is planned: *The timing of the announcement took attention away from the lay-offs.* **2** [U] the skill of doing sth at exactly the right time: *The success of a new product depends on good timing.*

**tip** /tɪp/ *n., v.*
• ***n.*** [C] **1 ~ (on/for sth)** a small piece of advice about sth practical or about what is likely to happen: *investment/share ~s for 2007*
⊙ *to* ***give (sb)/pass on*** *~s* ◆ *to* ***get/pick up*** *~s* ◆ ***good/helpful/money-saving/practical*** *~s*
**2** a small amount of extra money that you give to sb, for example sb who serves you in a restaurant: *We get rather poor tips on weeknights.*
⊙ *a* ***generous/large/small*** *~* ◆ *to* ***give/leave*** *(sb) a ~*
IDM **the tip of the 'iceberg** only a small part of a much larger problem
• ***v.*** (**-pp-**) **1** [T] **~ sb/sth (as/for sth)** to say in advance that sb/sth will be successful or that sth will happen: *She was widely tipped for the top job.*
**2** [T,I] to give sb an extra amount of money to thank them for sth they have done for you as part of their job: *How much should I tip?*

**TIR** /ˌtiː aɪ ˈɑː(r)/ *abbr* (*Transpt.*) **transport international routier** *or* **transports internationaux routiers** an organization that makes rules and sets standards for international road transport in Europe

**tirekicker** = TYREKICKER

**tissue** /ˈtɪʃuː; *BrE also* ˈtɪsjuː/ (*also* ˌ**tissue ˈpaper**) *n.* [U] very thin paper used for wrapping and packing things that break easily

**titanium** /tɪˈteɪniəm/ *n.* [U] a strong light expensive metal

**title** /ˈtaɪtl/ *n.* **1** [C] the name of a book, an article, etc. **2** [C] a particular book or magazine: *We publish twenty new titles a year.* **3** [C] the name of a job: *My **job title** is 'Senior Financial Analyst'.* **4** [C] a word in front of a person's name to show their rank or profession, whether or not they are married, etc: *Give your name and title* (= Mr, Miss, Ms, Dr, etc.). **5** (*Law*) [U,C] the legal right to own sth, esp. land or property; the document that shows you have this right: *Do you have **proof of title**?*

ˈ**title deed** *n.* [C, usu. pl.] (*Law*) a legal document proving that sb is the owner of a particular piece of land, house, etc: *the title deeds **to** a house*

ˈ**title-ˌholder** (*also* **titleholder**) *n.* [C] (*AmE*) (*Law*) the legal owner of property

ˈ**title inˌflation** *n.* [U] (*HR*) the practice of giving an employee a more important name to describe their job although the job does not change

**TLD** /ˌtiː el ˈdiː/ = TOP-LEVEL DOMAIN

**TM** /ˌtiː ˈem/ *abbr* a short form of the word TRADEMARK, shown by the symbol ™

**TNA** /ˌtiː en ˈeɪ/ = TRAINING NEEDS ANALYSIS

**TOC** /ˌtiː əʊ ˈsiː; *AmE* oʊ/ = THEORY OF CONSTRAINTS

**to-do** /təˈduː/ *adj.* used to describe things that need to be done: *a to-do list*

**toehold** /ˈtəʊhəʊld; *AmE* ˈtoʊhoʊld/ *n.* [C] a position in a place or an activity which you hope will lead to more power or success: *a toehold in the American market* ◇ *to establish/gain/get a* ~

**TOIL** /ˌtiː əʊ aɪ ˈel; *AmE* oʊ/ = TIME OFF IN LIEU

**token** /ˈtəʊkən; *AmE* ˈtoʊ-/ *n., adj.*
• ***n.*** [C] **1** a piece of paper that you can collect when you buy a particular product and then exchange for sth **2** a round piece of metal or plastic used instead of money to operate some machines or as a form of payment: *a parking token* **3** (*BrE*) a piece of paper that you pay for and that sb can exchange for sth in a shop/store: *a book/gift* ~ **4** something that is done, given, etc. as a symbol of how strongly sb feels about sth: *a token of gratitude*
• ***adj.*** **1** involving very little effort or feeling and intended only as a way of showing other people that you think sb/sth is important, when really you are not sincere: *The company made a token effort to improve facilities for staff.* **2** done as a symbol: *a token one-hour strike* (= to show that workers feel strongly about sth)

**tokenism** /ˈtəʊkənɪzəm; *AmE* ˈtoʊ-/ *n.* [U] the fact of doing sth only in order to do what the law requires or to satisfy a particular group of people, but not in a sincere way

**toll** /təʊl; *AmE* toʊl/ *n., v.*
• ***n.*** **1** [C] money you pay to use a particular road, bridge or area: *motorway tolls* **2** [C] (*AmE*) a charge for a telephone call calculated at a higher rate than a local call: *toll calls* **3** [sing.] the amount of damage that sth causes: *the emotional toll of running a company* → idiom at TAKE *v.*
• ***v.*** [T,I] to charge for the use of a road, bridge, transport, etc: *a new tolling scheme on a public road*

ˈ**tolling aˌgreement** *n.* [C] (*Manufact.*) an agreement to process a particular amount of a raw material at a particular factory

**ton** /tʌn/ *n.* [C] (*pl.* **tons** *or* **ton**) **1** a unit for measuring weight, in the UK 2 240 pounds or 1016.04 kilograms (**long ton**) and in the US 2 000 pounds or 907.18 kilograms (**short ton**) **2** a unit for measuring the size of a ship. One ton is equal to 100 CUBIC feet

**tonnage** /ˈtʌnɪdʒ/ *n.* [U,C] (*Transpt.*) **1** the size of a ship or the amount it can carry, expressed in tons: *a large amount of new tonnage—268 new ships this year* **2** the total amount that sth, esp. cargo, weighs: *rail freight tonnage*

**tonne** /tʌn/ (*pl.* **tonnes** *or* **tonne**) = METRIC TON

★**tool** /tuːl/ *n., v.*
• ***n.*** [C] **1** an instrument that you hold in your hand and use for making things, repairing things, etc: *a cutting tool* ◇ *power tools* ◇ *a tool kit* **2** a thing that helps you to do a job or to achieve sth: *research tools such as questionnaires* ◇ *an essential/a key/powerful* ~ **3** a computer program that performs a particular function: *design/desktop publishing/interactive* ~*s* IDM **the tools of your ˈtrade** the things that you need to do your job → idiom at DOWN *v.*

• *v.* **PHR V** ˌ**tool 'up**; ˌ**tool sb/sth 'up** to get or provide sb/sth with the equipment that is necessary to do or produce sth

**toolbar** /'tu:lbɑ:(r)/ *n.* [C] (*IT*) a line of symbols on a computer screen that show the different things that the computer can do when you click on one of them

**tooling** /'tu:lɪŋ/ *n.* [U] (*Manufact.*) the activity or process of making special tools or machines for a factory; the tools themselves: *a supplier of machines and precision tooling*

**toolmaker** /'tu:lmeɪkə(r)/ *n.* [C] (*Manufact.*) a person or business that makes tools and machines for the manufacturing industry and keeps them in good condition ▸ **'toolmaking** *n.* [U]

**'tool shop** *n.* [C] (*Manufact.*) the part of a factory where special tools and machines are made

**top** /tɒp; *AmE* tɑ:p/ *n.*, *adj.*, *v.*
• *n.* [sing.] the highest or most important position or rank: *She's at the top of her profession.* ◇ *This decision came from the top.* **IDM** **at the top of the 'tree** in the highest position or rank in a profession or career **from the top 'down** starting with the most important people in a company or an organization OPP FROM THE BOTTOM UP **get on 'top of sth** to manage to deal with or control sth: *We're struggling to get on top of all the work we've got.* **on 'top 1** in a leading position or in control **2** in addition **on 'top of sth 1** in control of a situation; knowing about a situation: *to stay on top of technological changes* **2** in addition to sth ˌ**top of 'mind** (*Market.*) = FRONT OF MIND at FRONT *n.*
• *adj.* highest in position, rank or degree: *top management* ◇ *top-quality goods*
• *v.* [T] (-pp-) **1** to be higher than a particular amount: *Their market share topped 20% in May.* **2** to be in the highest position on a list because you are the most successful, important, etc: *The company topped the list of best performers.* **3** to do or say sth that is better, etc. than sth that sb else did or said: *Another company has topped our offer* (= offered more money). **PHR V** ˌ**top 'out (at sth)** if sth **tops out** at a particular price, speed, etc. it does not rise any higher: *Sales topped out at a record $10 bn.* ˌ**top sth 'up** to increase the amount of sth to the level you want or need

ˌ**top 'brass** (*also* **brass**, *esp. in AmE*) *n.* [sing. with sing./pl. verb] (*infml.*) the people who are in the most important positions in a company or an organization: *All the top brass was/were there.*

ˌ**top 'dog** *n.* [C, usu. sing.] (*infml.*) a person or group that is better than all the others, esp. in a situation that involves competition: *He used to be top dog in the company.*

ˌ**top 'dollar** *n.* [U] (*esp. AmE*) (*infml.*) a high price; the highest price: *Customers will **pay** top dollar for same-day deliveries.*

ˌ**top-'down** *adj.* **1** starting from or involving the people who have higher positions in an organization: *~ decision-making/management* **2** (about a plan, project, etc.) starting with a general idea to which details are added later OPP BOTTOM-UP

ˌ**top-'end** *adj.* among the best, most expensive, etc. examples of sth: *top-end phones* ◇ *top-end business travellers* (= with most money to spend)

ˌ**top 'flight** *n.* [C, usu. sing.] the best or most successful of a particular group: *They have kept their place in the market's top flight.* ▸ ˌ**top-'flight** *adj.*: *a top-flight sales force*

ˌ**top-'grossing** *adj.* (about a product) that has earned more money than any other

ˌ**top-'heavy** *adj.* (about an organization) having too many senior staff or managers compared with the number of workers

ˌ**top-'level** *adj.* involving the most important people in an organization: *a top-level meeting*

ˌ**top-level do'main** *n.* [C] (*abbr* **TLD**) (*IT*) the end of a name which identifies a website or a group of websites, for example '.com'

ˌ**top 'line** *n.* [sing.] (*Account.*) the amount of money that a company receives from sales: *We are hoping our new product will boost our top line.* SYN REVENUE → BOTTOM LINE ▸ **'top-line** *adj.*: *~ growth/revenue*

ˌ**top-'notch** *adj.* excellent; of the highest quality: *They provide a top-notch service.*

ˌ**top-of-the-'line** *adj.* (*AmE*) used to describe the most expensive of a group of similar products: *a top-of-the-line MP3 player*

ˌ**top of the 'range** *n.* [C] (*BrE*) the most expensive of a group of similar products: *This car is the top of the range.* ▸ ˌ**top-of-the-'range** *adj.*: *a top-of-the-range model*

**topple** /'tɒpl; *AmE* 'tɑ:pl/ *v.* [T] to make sb lose their position of power

**ˌtop-ˈranked** *adj.* considered to be the best or most popular of a number of similar things: *the top-ranked business schools* SYN TOP-RATED

**ˌtop ˈranking** *n.* [C,U] **1** the highest or most important position in an organization, an industry, etc: *The airline has earned top ranking for customer service.* **2** (*IT*) a high, or the highest, position in the list of websites given by a SEARCH ENGINE ▸ **ˌtop-ˈranking** *adj.*

**ˌtop-ˈrated** *adj.* **1** considered to be the best or most popular of a number of similar products or people: *the top-rated brand of soft drinks* SYN TOP-RANKED **2** that has received a high score for the measurement of a particular quality: *The top-rated bonds are 'investment grade'.*

**ˌtop-ˈselling** *adj.* (about a product) that has sold more than others

**ˌtop-ˈtier** *adj.* considered to be one of the best: *top-tier companies in the printer and copier markets*

**ˈtop-up** *n.* [C] an extra amount of money that is added to the original amount so that there is enough: *a ~ loan/payment*

**ˈtop-up card** *n.* [C] a card which allows you to make more calls from your mobile phone/cellphone to the value of the card or the money you pay

**torrid** /ˈtɒrɪd; *AmE* ˈtɔːr-; ˈtɑːr-/ *adj.* (in newspapers) very difficult: *a torrid period on the stock market*

**tort** /tɔːt; *AmE* tɔːrt/ *n.* [C,U] (*Law*) something wrong that sb does to sb else that is not criminal, but can lead to action in a civil court: *tort law*

**total** /ˈtəʊtl; *AmE* ˈtoʊtl/ *adj., n., v.*
• ***adj.*** **1** being the amount or number after everyone or everything is counted or added together: *The total number of jobs is now over 3 000.* ◇ *the grand total* (= the final total of the totals) **2** complete; including everything: *a total ban on smoking*
• ***n.*** [C] the amount you get when you add several numbers or amounts together; the final number of people or things when they have all been counted: *The chain closed 170 out of a total of 420 stores.* ◇ *The bank employs 80 000 staff **in total**.*
• ***v.*** [T] (-ll-, *AmE also* -l-) **1** to reach a particular total: *debts totalling $4 bn* **2** to add up the numbers of sth/sb and get a total: *Balances were totalled daily.* **3** (*infml.*) (*esp. AmE*) to damage a car very badly, so that it is not worth repairing it

**ˈtotal ˈcost of ˈownership** *n.* [U] (*abbr* **TCO**) (*Account.*) a method of calculating the costs involved in buying and using a product or service which includes the cost of buying it and other costs such as delivering, keeping it in good condition, etc.

**ˈtotal proˈductive ˈmaintenance** *n.* [U] (*abbr* **TPM**) (*Product.*) a way of improving how a factory's machines and equipment are used by continuously making sure that they are working as efficiently as possible

**ˈTotal ˈQuality ˈManagement** (*also* **total quality management**) (*abbr* **TQM**) (*also* **ˈquality ˌmanagement**) *n.* [U] a system of management that considers that every employee is responsible for keeping the highest standards in every aspect of the company's work in order to meet customers' needs; the techniques used for controlling and checking quality: *to institute total quality management*

**ˈtotal ˈshareholder reˈturn** *n.* [U,C] (*abbr* **TSR**) (*Finan.*) a measure of the profit gained from investing in the shares of a particular company over a fixed period of time, usu. expressed as a percentage over one year

**touch** /tʌtʃ/ *v., n.*
• ***v.*** [T] to reach a particular level, etc: *Shares in the company touched a two-year low of €7.6.* IDM **touch ˈbase (with sb)** (*infml.*) to make contact with sb again: *She travels to Boston every other week to touch base with her home office.* **touch ˈbottom** to reach the worst or lowest state: *The recession has now touched bottom.*
• ***n.*** [C, usu. sing.] an act of putting your hands or fingers on sth: *All this information is available **at the touch of a button*** (= by simply pressing a button). IDM **be, get, keep, etc. in ˈtouch (with sb)** to communicate with sb, esp. by writing to them or telephoning them: *I'll be in touch again next week.* **be, keep, etc. in ˈtouch (with sth)** to know what is happening in a particular subject or area: *It's vital to keep in touch with the latest innovations.*

**ˈtouch screen** *n.* [C] (*IT*) a computer screen which you touch with your finger or with a special pen in particular places in order to give instructions to the computer: *a handheld with a touch screen and stylus* ◇ *touch-screen monitors*

**ˈtouch-type** *v.* [I] to type without looking at the keys of the keyboard

**ˌtough ˈlove** *n.* [U] (*HR*) **1** used to describe decisions made by senior managers that benefit the organization but may not help the employees **2** used to describe the situation when managers make employees aware of the fact that they are not working well and make them responsible for improving

**ˌtough-ˈminded** *adj.* **1** used to describe a person who makes firm decisions and does not easily change their mind: *tough-minded leaders* **2** used to describe a decision, situation, etc. connected with this type of person: *a tough-minded strategy*

**ˈtour ˌcompany** = TOUR OPERATOR

**tourism** /ˈtʊərɪzəm; ˈtɔːr-; *AmE* ˈtʊr-/ *n.* [U] the business activity connected with providing accommodation, services and entertainment for people who are visiting a place for pleasure: ***mass/package~*** ◇ *the tourism industry* ▶ **ˈtourist** *n.* [C]

**ˈtour ˌoperator** (*also* **ˈtour ˌcompany**) *n.* [C] a company that arranges visits to places for pleasure

**tout** /taʊt/ *v., n.*

• *v.* **1** [T] to try to persuade people that sb/sth is important or valuable by praising them/it: *She is being touted **as** the next CEO.* **2** [T,I] (*esp. BrE*) to persuade people to buy your goods or services, esp. by going to them and asking them directly: *companies publicly touting **for** investors*

• *n.* (*also* **ˈticket tout**) (*both BrE*) (*AmE* **ˈscalper**) [C] a person who buys tickets for concerts, sports events, etc. and then sells them to other people at a much higher price

**Toˌyota Proˈduction ˌSystem** *n.* [sing.] (*abbr* **TPS**) (*Product.*) a system of manufacturing developed by the Toyota Motor Corporation in Japan that aims to improve production by wasting as little time, money, etc. as possible and being able to change quickly to deal with new situations

**TPM** /ˌtiː piː ˈem/ = TOTAL PRODUCTIVE MAINTENANCE

**TPS** /ˌtiː piː ˈes/ = TOYOTA PRODUCTION SYSTEM

**TQM** /ˌtiː kjuː ˈem/ = TOTAL QUALITY MANAGEMENT

**trace** /treɪs/ *v., n.* (*Product.*)

• *v.* [T] to follow the movements of materials, goods, stocks, etc. through a complete process: *These systems track and trace inventory through the supply chain.* ▶ **ˌtraceaˈbility** /-əˈbɪləti/ *n.* [U]: *inventory traceability* **ˈtraceable** /-əbl/ *adj.*

• *n.* [C, usu. sing.] the process of following the movements of materials, goods or stocks of items: *We'll **put a trace on** the shipment.*

**track** /træk/ *n., v.*

• *n.* [C] a path or direction that sb/sth is moving in: *a career track*

IDM **ˌback on ˈtrack** going in the right direction again after a mistake, failure, etc: *The project is now back on track.* **be on ˈtrack** to be doing the right thing in order to achieve a particular result: *The group is on track **to** achieve its growth targets.* **keep/lose ˈtrack of sth/sb** to have/not have information about what is happening or where sth/sb is **be on the right/wrong ˈtrack** to be thinking or doing sth in the right/wrong way in order to achieve sth

• *v.* **1** [T] to follow the progress or development of sth/sb: *the system for tracking sales* **2** [T,I] to move in a particular direction; to move in the same direction as sth: *Tech stocks were tracking higher.* **3** (*Product.*) [T] to follow the movements of goods and stocks of items: *Her job involved tracking inventory.* ▶ **ˌtrackaˈbility** /-əˈbɪləti/ *n.* [U]: *Bar codes provide complete trackability of each package.* **ˈtrackable** /-əbl/ *adj.*

**ˈtracker fund** (*BrE*) (*also* **ˈindex fund**, *AmE, BrE*) *n.* [C] (*Finan.*) a type of investment fund, consisting of some of the shares in a particular SHARE INDEX, whose value always follows the market

**ˈtracking poll** = TRACKING STUDY

**ˈtracking stock** *n.* [C,U] (*Stock Ex.*) shares in one part of a company's activities that represent the value of that part rather than the company as a whole

**ˈtracking ˌstudy** (*also* **ˈtracking poll**) *n.* [C] (*Market.*) a study in which people are asked the same questions at different times, in order to find out how opinions, tastes, needs, etc. change

**ˈtrack ˌrecord** *n.* [C] the past achievements, successes or failures of a person or an organization: *He has a proven track record in sales.*

**tradable** (*also* **tradeable**) /ˈtreɪdəbl/ *adj.* that you can easily buy and sell or exchange for money: *~ goods/securities/shares*

★**trade** /treɪd/ *n., v.*

• *n.* **1** [U] the activity of buying and selling or of exchanging goods or services between people or countries: *Trade between the two countries has increased.* ◇ *global trade **in** electronic equipment* ◇ *unfair trade practices*

**2** [C] a particular type of business: *the retail trade* ◇ *the building/tourist* ~ **3 the trade** [sing. with sing./pl. verb] a particular area of business and the people or companies connected with it: *In the trade, this is called 'success'.* **4** [U] the amount of goods or services that you sell: *Trade was very good last month.* **5** [U,C] a job, esp. one that involves working with your hands and that requires special training and skills: *to learn a trade* **6** (*Stock Ex.*) [U,C; usu. pl.] buying and selling on a stock exchange; one act of doing this: *The share price fell in afternoon trade.* ◇ *daily trades on the stock exchange* → idioms at PLY, ROARING

• *v.* **1** [I] ~ **(with sb)** to buy and sell things: *companies that trade* ***in*** *chemicals* **2** [I] ~ **(as sb/sth)** to exist and operate as a business or company: *The firm has now ceased trading.* **3** (*Stock Ex.*) [T,I] to be bought and sold, or to buy and sell sth, on the stock exchange: *Shares were trading* ***at*** *half their usual value.* **4** [T] to exchange sth that you have for sth that sb else has: *I wouldn't trade* ***places*** *with him.* PHR V **'trade at ...** (*AmE*) to buy goods or shop at a particular store **,trade 'down** to spend less money on things than you did before: *to trade down to cheaper brands* **,trade sth 'in (for sth)** to give sth you have used as part of the payment for sth new: *People can trade in their old PCs for the latest model.* **,trade sth 'off** to balance two things or situations that are opposed to each other: *You need to trade price off* ***against*** *quality.* **,trade 'up 1** to sell sth in order to buy sth more expensive **2** to give sth you have used as part of the payment for sth more expensive

**tradeable** = TRADABLE

**'trade ,advertising** *n.* [U] (*Market.*) the act of making a product or service known to the people who will sell it to customers

**'trade a,greement** (*also* **com,mercial 'treaty**) *n.* [C] (*Econ.*) an arrangement between two or more countries in which they agree to special conditions when buying from and selling to each other

**'trade associ,ation** *n.* [C] (*Econ.*) an organization for companies in the same industry, that provides advice, information and other services for its members SYN INDUSTRY ASSOCIATION

**'trade ,balance** = BALANCE OF TRADE

**'trade ,barrier** *n.* [C] (*Econ.*) an action by a government that makes free trade between its own country and other countries more difficult or impossible, for example TARIFFS
◆ *to* ***create/erect/raise*** *~s* ◆ *to* ***dismantle/lower/reduce/remove*** *~s*

**'trade bill** (*also* **com'mercial bill**) *n.* [C] (*Trade*) a BILL OF EXCHANGE that is used to pay for goods

**'trade ,buyer** *n.* [C] (*Finan.*) a company that buys another company, esp. one in the same business

**'trade ,counter** *n.* [C] (*BrE*) (*Comm.*) a part of a factory, WAREHOUSE or website where a business can buy goods at reduced prices

**'trade ,credit** *n.* [U,C] (*Account.*) an arrangement by which one company allows another company a period of time in which to pay for goods after it has received them
▸ **'trade ,creditor** *n.* [C]

**'trade ,cycle** *n.* [C] (*esp. BrE*) (*Econ.*) the usual pattern of a country's economy, with periods of success and periods of difficulty happening regularly one after another SYN BUSINESS CYCLE

**'trade debt** = BUSINESS DEBT

**'trade ,deficit** (*also* **'trade gap**) *n.* [C, usu. sing.] (*Econ.*) a situation in which the value of a country's imports is greater than the value of its exports; the amount by which the two values are different: *a trade deficit of $1.5 bn*
◆ *to* ***post/run/suffer*** *a ~* ◆ *to* ***cut/reduce*** *a ~* ◆ *a* ***widening/worsening*** *~*

**'trade dele,gation** *n.* [C] a group of manufacturers or suppliers who visit another country in order to increase business with that country

**,trade des'cription** *n.* [C] (*BrE*) (*Law*) something that describes all or some features of goods, for example their quantity, size, time or place of origin, method of manufacture, price, etc: *The firm was accused of false trade descriptions.*

**,Trade Des'criptions Act** *n.* [sing.] in the UK, a law stating that all information given about goods must be true and clear

**,trade 'discount** *n.* [C] (*also* **'trade terms** [pl.]) (*Comm.*) an amount of money taken off the usual cost of goods or services when one company sells them to another

**'trade dis,pute** *n.* [C] **1** (*HR*) a disagreement between employers and employees about pay, working conditions, etc. SYN INDUSTRIAL DISPUTE **2** (*Econ.*) a disagreement between countries or companies in different countries about trade

**ˈtrade exhiˌbition** = TRADE SHOW

**ˈtrade fair** = TRADE SHOW

**ˈtrade ˌfigures** *n.* [pl.] (*Econ.*) figures that show the value of a country's imports compared with the value of its exports

**ˈtrade gap** = TRADE DEFICIT

**ˈtrade-in** *n.* [C,U] a method of buying sth by giving a used item as part of the payment for a new one; the used item itself: *the trade-in value of the old car*
SYN PART EXCHANGE (*BrE*)

**ˈtrade magaˌzine** (*also* **ˈtrade journal**) *n.* [C] a magazine that is published regularly with news and articles about a particular industry

★ **trademark** /ˈtreɪdmɑːk; *AmE* -mɑːrk/ *n.* [C] **1** (*abbr* **TM**) a name, symbol or design that a company uses for its products and that cannot be used by anyone else: *a registered trademark* ◇ *trademark infringement* (= illegal use of another company's trademark) **2** sth special that is typical of sb/sth and makes them/it easily recognized: *He was wearing his trademark white suit.* ▸ **ˈtrademark** *v.* [T]: *trademarked names*

**ˈtrade ˌmission** *n.* [C] **1** a group of government officials or business people who go to another country to encourage trade **2** an office of one country in another, which encourages trade between the two

**ˈtrade name** *n.* [C] **1** a name used by a particular company **2** a name that a company gives to a product: *The drug is sold* ***under the trade name*** *Lipitor.* **3** a word that is used for sth within a particular industry but is not well known outside it

**ˈtrade-off** *n.* [C] the act of balancing two things that are opposed to each other: *a trade-off* ***between*** *increased production* ***and*** *a reduction in quality*

**ˈtrade press** *n.* [sing. with sing./pl. verb] magazines and newspapers published for a particular industry

**ˈtrade price** = WHOLESALE PRICE

★ **trader** /ˈtreɪdə(r)/ *n.* [C] **1** (*Comm.*) a person or company that buys things and sells them at a profit: *small market traders* ◇ *commodity traders* **2** (*Finan.*; *Stock Ex.*) (*AmE*) = DEALER (2)

**ˈtrade repreˌsentative** *n.* [C] (*abbr* **ˈtrade rep**) **1** (*Market.*) = SALES REPRESENTATIVE **2** a person or an organization that represents a country in matters relating to trade

**ˈtrade sale** *n.* [C] **1** (*Comm.*) [usu. pl.] sales that a company makes to another business **2** (*Finan.*) when a company is sold to another company, usu. in the same industry

**ˌtrade ˈsecret** *n.* [C] a piece of information, for example the method of making a product, that a company does not want other companies to know

**ˈtrade show** (*also* **ˈtrade exhiˌbition**, **ˈtrade fair**) *n.* [C] (*Market.*) an event at which many different companies producing related products show and sell their products

**tradesman** /ˈtreɪdzmən/, **tradeswoman** /ˈtreɪdzwʊmən/ *n.* [C] (*pl.* **-men** /-mən/*pl.* **-women** /-wɪmɪn/) **1** a skilled person, esp. one who makes or repairs sth: *tradesmen such as carpenters and electricians* **2** a person who buys and sells goods, esp. on a small scale: *market tradesmen*

**tradesperson** /ˈtreɪdzpɜːsn; *AmE* -pɜːrsn/ *n.* [C] (*pl.* **-people** /-piːpl/ *or, esp. in formal use,* **-persons**) **1** a skilled person, esp. one who makes or repairs sth **2** a person who buys and sells goods, esp. on a small scale

**ˌtrades ˈunion** = TRADE UNION

**the ˌTrades Union ˈCongress** = TUC

**ˌtrades ˈunionist** = TRADE UNIONIST

**ˈtrade ˌsurplus** *n.* [C, usu. sing.] (*Econ.*) a situation in which the value of a country's exports is greater than the value of its imports: *a trade surplus of $2.2 bn* OPP TRADE DEFICIT

**ˈtrade terms** = TRADE DISCOUNT

★ **ˌtrade ˈunion** (*also* **ˌtrades ˈunion**) (*both BrE*) (*AmE* **ˈlabor ˌunion**) (*also* **ˈunion**, *BrE, AmE*) *n.* [C] an organization of workers, usu. in a particular industry, that exists to protect their interests, improve conditions of work, etc: *a trade union representing car workers* ◇ *the trade union movement*
● *to* ***belong to/form/join*** *a ~* ♦ *a ~* ***leader/member/representative***
▸ **ˌtrade ˈunionism** *n.* [U]

**ˌtrade ˈunionist** (*also* **ˌtrades ˈunionist**) (*both BrE*) (*also* **ˈunionist**, *AmE, BrE*) *n.* [C] a member of a trade union

**ˈtrade war** *n.* [C] a disagreement between countries in which they take action to damage each other's trade: *a bitter/damaging/fierce/full-scale ~*

**ˈtrade-ˌweighted** *adj.* (*Econ.*) that shows the value of a country's currency, compared with that of other countries that it trades with:

*The dollar has fallen nearly 5% **on a trade-weighted basis**.*

★**trading** /ˈtreɪdɪŋ/ *n.* [U] **1** the activity of buying and selling things: *The group has been hit by tough trading conditions.* ◇ *oil/diamond ~*
◆ ***illegal/poor/strong ~*** ◆ ***Internet/online ~***
**2** (*Finan.*; *Stock Ex.*) the activity of buying and selling shares, currencies, etc: *a day of hectic trading* ◇ *fast electronic trading of futures*
◆ ***heavy/light/quiet ~*** ◆ ***commodity/currency/share/stock ~***

**ˈtrading acˌcount** *n.* [C] (*Account.*) a statement of the money that a company has spent on making or buying goods and of the money received from selling those goods, so that the TRADING PROFIT can be calculated

**ˈtrading ˌcompany** *n.* [C] (*Comm.*) a company that exists to buy and sell goods

**ˈtrading esˌtate** = INDUSTRIAL ESTATE

**ˈtrading floor** (*BrE also* **ˈdealing floor**) *n.* [C, usu. sing.] (*Stock Ex.*) an area in a stock exchange where dealers meet and buy and sell shares

**ˈtrading loss** (*also* **ˌgross ˈloss**) *n.* [C] (*Account.*) the amount by which money received from the sale of goods or services is less than the cost of producing or providing them, calculated before OVERHEADS, interest and tax are taken off

**ˈtrading ˌpartner** *n.* [C] **1** (*Econ.*; *Trade*) a country or company that another country or company buys goods from or sells goods to **2** (*IT*) a company that is involved in exchanging electronic information with another company using EDI

**ˈtrading ˌperiod** = ACCOUNTING PERIOD

**ˈtrading post** *n.* [C] **1** (*E-comm.*) a website where people can buy and sell things **2** (*Trade*) a small place a long way from any town, used as a centre for buying and selling goods

**ˈtrading ˌprofit** (*also* **ˌgross ˈprofit**) *n.* [C] (*Account.*) the amount by which money received from the sale of goods or services is greater than the cost of producing or providing them, calculated before OVERHEADS, interest and tax are taken off

**ˈtrading ˌsession** = SESSION (1)

**ˌTrading ˈStandards** *n.* [pl.; U] (*Law*) in the UK, the process of making sure that laws protecting consumers are obeyed; the government department responsible for this

**ˈtrading stock** = STOCK-IN-TRADE (1)

**traffic** /ˈtræfɪk/ *n.*, *v.*
• ***n.*** [U] **1** the vehicles on a road at a particular time **2** the movement of ships, trains, aircraft, etc. along a particular route: *air/rail/sea ~* ◇ *domestic/international ~* **3** the movement of people or goods from one place to another: *the traffic of goods between one country and another* **4** (*Market.*) the number of people who come to a place or use a service in a particular period: *customer/mall/walk-in ~* **5** (*IT*) information that travels across a computer system in a particular period: *email/Internet/network ~* **6** illegal trade in sth: *traffic **in** drugs*
• ***v.*** (**-ck-**) PHR V **ˈtraffic in sth** to buy and sell sth illegally
▸ **ˈtrafficker** *n.* [C] **ˈtrafficking** *n.* [U]

**trail** /treɪl/ *v.*, *n.*
• ***v.*** **1** [T,I] (*esp. in the continuous tenses*) to be less successful than other companies, people, etc: *Their sales are trailing **behind** other superstores.* **2** [T] to advertise a plan, product, film/movie, etc. in advance: *the company's **heavily/widely** trailed plans* **3** [T] to follow behind sb/sth: *New orders may trail a recovery by several months.* PHR V **ˌtrail ˈoff** (*esp. BrE*) to gradually become less: *Advertising revenue has trailed off.*
• ***n.*** IDM **be/go on the ˈtrail of sb/sth; be/go on the ... trail** to be following or trying to find sb/sth: *The company is on the acquisition trail.* **blaze a/the ˈtrail** to be the first to do or discover sth that others follow

**trailblazer** /ˈtreɪlbleɪzə(r)/ *n.* [C] a person or company that is the first to do or discover sth and so makes it possible for others to follow

**trailer** /ˈtreɪlə(r)/ *n.* [C] **1** (*Transpt.*) a truck, or a container with wheels, that is pulled by another vehicle **2** (*esp. BrE*) a series of short scenes from a film/movie or television programme, shown in advance to advertise it

**ˌtrailing ˈspouse** *n.* [C] a husband or wife who gives up their job to follow their partner to a new place where they have a job

★**train** /treɪn/ *v.* (*often used as an adj.* **trained**) **1** [T,I] to teach a person the skills for a particular job or activity; to be taught in this way: *highly trained sales personnel* ◇ *She trained **as** a lawyer.* **2** [T] to develop a natural ability or quality so that it improves: *a trained eye*

**trainee** /ˌtreɪˈniː/ *n.* [C] (*HR*) sb who is being taught how to do a particular job: *a management ~* ◇ *a trainee manager*
▶ **ˌtraiˈneeship** *n.* [C]

**ˌtrainee soˈlicitor** (*also* **ˌarticled ˈclerk**, *old-fash.*) (*both BrE*) *n.* [C] (*Law*) the title for sb employed by a group of lawyers while being trained to become a qualified SOLICITOR

★**training** /ˈtreɪnɪŋ/ *n.* [U] the process of learning the skills that you need to do a job: *He had no formal training* ***in*** *design.* ◇ *in-house training* ◇ *a* ***training and development*** *budget*
○ *to* ***do/receive*** *~* ◆ *to* ***give/provide*** *~* ◆ ***corporate/staff*** *~* ◆ ***hands-on*** *~* ◆ ***job/management/vocational*** *~* ◆ *a ~* ***course/manual/session***

**ˈtraining group** = T-GROUP

**ˈtraining needs aˌnalysis** *n.* [C, usu. sing.; U] (*abbr* **TNA**) (*HR*) a method of calculating what training is required to give a company's employees all the skills and knowledge that they need for the company to be successful

**ˈtraining ˌtransfer** = TRANSFER OF TRAINING

**tranche** /trɑːnʃ/ *n.* [C] (*Finan.*) a part of a loan, a payment, an investment or other large amount of money: *the first tranche of the fee*

**transact** /trænˈzækt/ *v.* [T,I] to do business with a person or an organization: *transacting* ***business*** *online*

★**transaction** /trænˈzækʃn/ *n.* **1** [C] a piece of business done between people, esp. an act of buying or selling: *transactions* ***between*** *companies* ◇ *a financial transaction tax*
○ *a* ***business/financial*** *~* ◆ *to* ***complete/conduct/do/make*** *a ~*
**2** [U] the process of doing sth: *the transaction of business*
▶ **tranˈsactional** /-kʃənl/ *adj.*

**tranˈsactional costs** = TRANSACTION COSTS

**tranˌsactional ˈleadership** *n.* [U] (*HR*) a way of managing people by setting them clear tasks and rewarding them for good performance

**tranˈsaction costs** (*also* **tranˈsactional costs**) *n.* [pl.] (*Econ.*) the amount of effort, time and money (not including the cost of buying sth) that it takes to arrange a piece of business

**tranˈsaction ˌprocessing** *n.* [U] **1** (*IT*) a type of computer system in which the computer responds immediately to a request made by a user. Each request is a **transaction**. **2** (*Comm.*) a method of dealing with a piece of business

**transcontinental** /ˌtrænzˌkɒntɪˈnentl; ˌtræns-; *AmE* -ˌkɑːn-/ *adj.* crossing a continent: *transcontinental flights*

★**transfer** /trænsˈfɜː(r)/ *v.* (**-rr-**) **1** [T,I] to move, or to move sb/sth, from one place to another: *The containers are transferred* ***to*** *trains at the port.* **2** [T,I] to pass money, shares, property, etc. from one owner to another; to pass money from one place to another: *The money has been transferred abroad.* **3** [T,I] to move from one job, situation, etc. to another; to arrange for sb to move: *He's been transferred* ***to*** *Sales.* **4** [T] to officially arrange for sth to belong to sb else or for sb else to control sth **5** [T] to copy information, music, etc. from one method of recording or presenting it to another: *The digital images can be transferred* ***to/onto*** *disk.* **6** [T,I] to change from one vehicle to another when travelling **7** [T] to pass a phone call to another phone, person, etc: *Let me transfer you.*
▶ **transfer** /ˈtrænsfɜː(r)/ *n.* [U,C]: *fast transfer of information* ◇ *I've applied for a transfer.* ◇ *transfer* ***from*** *the airport* ***to*** *the hotel*

**transferable** /trænsˈfɜːrəbl/ *adj.* that can be moved from one person, place or use to another: *The licence is not transferable.* ◇ *transferable* ***skills*** (= that can be used in different jobs) OPP NON-TRANSFERABLE

**ˈtransfer book** = TRANSFER REGISTER

**ˈtransfer deed** (*also* **ˌdeed of ˈtransfer**) *n.* [C] (*Law*) a legal document that shows that the owner of shares or property has changed

**transferee** /ˌtrænsfɜːˈriː/ *n.* [C] (*Law*) a person to whom property, shares, rights, etc. are transferred

**ˈtransfer ˌincome** (*also* **ˈtransfer ˌpayment**) *n.* [C,U] (*Econ.*) money received from a government in the form of pensions, UNEMPLOYMENT BENEFIT, etc., which comes from taxes

**ˌtransfer of ˈtraining** (*also* **ˈtraining ˌtransfer**, *less freq.*) *n.* [U] (*HR*) the practical use in your work of skills learned in a training course

**ˌtransfer of underˈtaking** *n.* [C,U] (*Law*) when a business passes from one owner to another

**transferor** /trænsˈfɜːrə(r)/ *n.* [C] (*Law*) a person who transfers property, shares, rights, etc. to another

**'transfer price** *n.* [C] (*Account.*) the price at which part of a company sells goods or services to another part ▸ **'transfer ˌpricing** *n.* [U]

**'transfer ˌregister** (*also* **ˌregister of 'transfers, 'transfer book**, *less freq.*) *n.* [C] (*Finan.*) a book in which all movements of a company's shares from one owner to another are recorded

★ **transform** /træns'fɔːm; *AmE* -'fɔːrm/ *v.* [T] **1** to completely change the character or appearance of sth, esp. so that it is better: *It has been transformed from a teen shop* ***into*** *a high-fashion store.* **2** to change the form of sth ▸ **ˌtransfor'mation** /-fə'meɪʃn; *AmE* -fər'm-/ *n.* [C,U] **ˌtransfor'mational** /-ʃənl/ *adj.*

**ˌtransforˌmational 'leadership** *n.* [U] a way of managing people and producing change by making people enthusiastic and willing to work hard for the company, and by providing a personal example

**transformative** /træns-'fɔːmətiv; *AmE* -'fɔːrm-/ *adj.* able to completely change and improve the character of sth: *transformative deals that move companies into new lines of business*

**tranship** = TRANS-SHIP

**transient** /'trænziənt; *AmE* 'trænʃənt/ *adj.* **1** continuing only for a short time **2** staying or working in a place for only a short time: *a transient workforce* ▸ **'transience** *n.* [U]

**transistor** /træn'zɪstə(r); *AmE* -'sɪst-/ *n.* [C] a small electronic device used in computers, radios, televisions, etc. for controlling an electric current as it passes along a CIRCUIT

**transit** /'trænzɪt; -sɪt/ *n.* [U] **1** (*Transpt.*) the process of being moved or carried from one place to another: *goods damaged* ***in*** *transit* **2** the act of going through a place on the way to somewhere else: *the transit lounge at an airport* ◇ *transit passengers* **3** (*AmE*) a system for carrying people from one place to another using vehicles: *the city's public transit system*

**translate** /træns'leɪt; trænz'leɪt/ *v.* [T,I] to change sth, or to be changed, into a different form: *a system that translates Web data* ***into*** *phone data* ◇ *Our hard work will translate into profits.*
▸ **translation** /-'leɪʃn/ *n.* [C,U]

**transmit** /træns'mɪt; trænz'mɪt/ *v.* (**-tt-**) **1** [T,I] to send an electronic signal, radio or television broadcast, etc: *to transmit data* **2** [T] to pass or send sth from one person, place or thing to another: *Big banks control the way money is transmitted around the system.* ▸ **trans'mission** /-'mɪʃn/ *n.* [U,C]: *transmission rights for the World Cup*

**transnational** /ˌtrænz'næʃnəl; ˌtræns'næʃnəl/ *adj.* operating or existing in or between many different countries, without being based in any particular one: *~ companies*

★ **transparency** /træns'pærənsi/ *n.* (*pl.* **-cies**) **1** [U] the quality of sth, such as glass, that allows you to see through it **2** [U] the fact of sth being easy to understand and not being secret: *transparency* ***in*** *company dealings* **3** (*also* **ˌOH'T**) [C] writing or a picture on a piece of film that you can see through, that can be shown on a screen by shining light through the film ▸ **trans'parent** *adj.*: *a transparent and fair system of voting*

**transport** /'trænspɔːt; *AmE* -spɔːrt/ *n., v.*
• ***n.*** [U] (*esp. BrE*) (*AmE usu.* **ˌtranspor'tation**) **1** a system for carrying people or goods from one place to another using vehicles: *to travel* ***on/by*** *public ~*
○ ***air/freight/passenger/rail/road ~*** ◆ *~* ***networks/infrastructure/links*** ◆ *a ~* ***company/operator*** ◆ *the ~* ***industry/sector*** ◆ *a ~* ***plan/policy***
**2** a vehicle or method of travel: *Will transport be provided?* **3** the activity or business of carrying goods from one place to another using lorries/trucks, trains, etc: *goods damaged during transport* ◇ *transport costs*
• ***v.*** [T] to take sth/sb from one place to another in a vehicle: *The chemicals are transported by road.*
▸ **trans'portable** /-əbl/ *adj.* [not usu. before n.]

**transportation** /ˌtrænspɔː'teɪʃn; *AmE* -pɔːr't-/ = TRANSPORT *n.*

**transporter** /træn'spɔːtə(r); *AmE* -'spɔːrt-/ *n.* [C] **1** a large vehicle used for carrying heavy objects, for example other vehicles: *a car transporter* **2** a company that moves goods from one place to another: *a large gas transporter*

**trans-ship** (*also* **tranship**) /trænz'ʃɪp/ *v.* [T] (**-pp-**) to move goods from one ship or other form of transport to another ▸ **trans-'shipment** (*also* **transhipment**) *n.* [C,U]

**'travel ˌagency** *n.* [C] a company that arranges travel and/or accommodation for people going on a holiday/vacation or journey ▸ 'travel ˌagent *n.* [C] 'travel ˌagent's *n.* [C] (*pl.* **travel agents**): *She works in a travel agent's.*

**'traveller's cheque** (*AmE* **traveler's check**) *n.* [C] a cheque for a fixed amount, sold by a bank or TRAVEL AGENT that can be exchanged for cash in foreign countries

**treasurer** /'treʒərə(r)/ *n.* [C] sb who is responsible for the money and accounts of an organization or a club

**Treasuries** /'treʒəriz/ = TREASURY BOND

★**treasury** /'treʒəri/ *n.* [sing. with sing./pl. verb] **the Treasury** in the UK, the US and some other countries, the government department that controls public money

**Treasury bill** (*also* **T-bill**) *n.* [C] (*Finan.*) in the UK and the US, a form of borrowing by the government for short periods of time, on which no interest is paid. **Treasury bills** are bought at less than their value.

**Treasury bond** (*also* **T-bond**) *n.* [C] (*also* **Treasuries** [pl.]) (*Finan.*) in the US, a bond issued by the government for a long period of time, that pays interest

**'treasury ˌmanagement** = CASH MANAGEMENT

**Treasury note** *n.* [C, usu. pl.] (*Finan.*) in the US, a form of government borrowing for between one and ten years, that pays interest

**'treasury stock** *n.* [U] (*Finan.*) shares a company has issued but has bought back from public investors

**treat** /tri:t/ *v.* [T] **1** to behave in a particular way towards sb/sth: *Treat your customers **with** respect.* **2** to deal with or discuss sth in a particular way: *These forecasts should be treated **with** caution.* **3** to use a chemical substance or process to clean, protect, preserve, etc. sth: *wood treated **with** preservative* ▸ **'treatment** *n.* [U,C]: *equal treatment for all staff* ◇ *water treatment*

**treaty** /'tri:ti/ *n.* [C] (*pl.* **-ties**) a formal agreement between two or more countries

★**trend** /trend/ *n.* [C] a general direction in which a situation is changing or developing: *There is a growing trend **towards** shorter contracts.* ◇ *current trends **in** advertising* ◇ *This car **set** a trend **for** smaller vehicles.*

⊕ ***business/industry/market** ~s* ◆ *a **downward**/an **upward** ~* ◆ ***future/long-term/recent** ~s* ◆ *a **general/global** ~* ◆ *to **break with/reverse** a ~*

▸ **trend** *v.* [I] (*esp. AmE*): *Unemployment has been trending upwards.*

**'trend line** (*also* **trendline**) *n.* [C] the general direction in which sth is changing or developing, shown, for example, by a line on a chart connecting high or low points

**trial** /'traɪəl/ *n.*, *v.*

• *n.* **1** [C] the process of testing the quality or performance of a product
⊕ ***early-stage/late-stage/mid-stage** ~s* ◆ ***drug/safety** ~s* ◆ *to **conduct/run/take part in/undergo** ~s*
**2** [C,U] the process of using a product or service, employing a person, etc. for a short period before you make a decision about it/them: *You can **give** the service a trial before you make up your mind.* ◇ *She agreed to employ me for **a trial period**.* ◇ *We had the machine **on trial** for a week.*
**3** [U,C] a formal examination of evidence in a court by a judge and often a JURY, to decide if sb accused of a crime is guilty or not
⊕ *to **go on/stand** ~* ◆ *to **come to/go to** ~*

• *v.* [T] (-ll-, *AmE* -l-) (*esp. BrE*) to test the quality or performance of a product: *They trialled the product **with** 20 customers.* ▸ **'trialling** *n.* [U]

**ˌtrial 'balance** *n.* [C, usu. sing.] (*abbr* **t.b.**) (*Account.*) a list of all the BALANCES in a company's accounts at a particular date, used to check that DEBITS and CREDITS are equal and that everything has been recorded accurately

**ˌtrial 'offer** *n.* [C] the opportunity to use a product or service free or at a low cost for a short period before you decide if you want to buy it

**tribunal** /traɪ'bju:nl/ *n.* [C] a type of court with the authority to deal with a particular problem or disagreement: *She took her case to a tribunal.*
⊕ *an **appeals/arbitration/employment** ~* ◆ *to **bring sth before/go to/refer sth to** a ~*

**trickle** /'trɪkl/ *v.*, *n.*

• *v.* [I] (*with an adv. or a prep.*) to go, or to make sth go, somewhere slowly or gradually: *Orders are trickling in.*
PHR V **ˌtrickle 'down (to sb/sth)** (esp. about money) to spread from rich to poor people through a country's economic system

• *n.* [C, usu. sing.] a small amount or number of sth, coming or going slowly: *a steady trickle of customers*

**'trickle-down** *n.* [U] **1** (*Econ.*) (in an economic system) the way in which the poorest people benefit as a result of the increasing wealth of the richest **2** used to describe a process where people at the bottom level of an organization or a system eventually start to have or do sth that people at a higher level had or did first

**trigger** /ˈtrɪɡə(r)/ *n., v.*
• *n.* [C, usu. sing.] something that is the cause of a particular reaction or development, esp. a bad one: *the trigger* ***for*** *the strike*
• *v.* [T] **1** to make sth happen suddenly: *The news triggered a fall in the share price.* **2** to cause a device to start functioning: *to trigger an alarm*

**ˈtrigger point** *n.* [C] a level or rate that is reached, or an event that happens, which causes action to be taken

**trim** /trɪm/ *v.* [T] (**-mm-**) to make sth smaller by cutting parts from it: (*fig.*) *20% of staff are to be trimmed.*
IDM **trim (the) ˈfat** if a business **trims the fat**, it reduces or removes unnecessary expenses, for example by cutting jobs

**trip** /trɪp/ *n.* [C] **1** a journey to a place and back again for business or pleasure: *Bill's away* ***on*** *a trip this week.* **2** a journey to or back from a place: *the outward/return ~*

**ˌtriple-ˈA** *adj.* (*abbr* **AAA**) (*Finan.*) used to describe a company that is considered one of the safest to lend money to: *The company has a triple-A credit rating.*

**triplicate** /ˈtrɪplɪkət/ *n.* IDM **in ˈtriplicate 1** done three times: *Each sample was tested in triplicate.*
**2** (about a document) copied twice, so that there are three copies in total: *Fill out the forms in triplicate.*

**ˌTrojan ˈhorse** /ˈtrəʊdʒən; *AmE* ˈtroʊ-/ *n.* [C] **1** a person or thing that is used to deceive an enemy in order to achieve a secret purpose: *The move by supermarkets into banking is a Trojan horse. Banks may soon no longer exist.* **2** (*IT*) a computer program that seems to be helpful but that is, in fact, designed to destroy data, etc.

**troll** /trəʊl; *AmE* troʊl/ *v.* [T,I] (*infml.*) **1** to search for sth, esp. on the Internet: *trolling Internet sites for information* **2** (*Market.*) to try to get new customers by telephoning or visiting people you do not know: *trolling for customers*

**ˈtrophy wife** *n.* [C] (*infml.*) a young attractive woman who is married to an older senior businessman and is thought of as sth that shows that the man is successful

**troubled** /ˈtrʌbld/ *adj.* (often used in newspapers) having a lot of problems: *troubled companies*

**troubleshoot** /ˈtrʌblʃuːt/ *v.* [T,I] (**-shot**, **-shot** /-ʃɒt; *AmE* -ʃɑːt/) **1** to try to solve problems that sb/sth has: *She troubleshoots problems with clients.* **2** (*IT*) to find and solve problems in a mechanical or an electronic system ▸ **ˈtroubleshooter** *n.* [C] **ˈtroubleshooting** *n.* [U] (*IT*)

**trough** /trɒf; *AmE* trɔːf/ *n., v.*
• *n.* [C] a period of time when the level of sth is low, esp. a time when a business or the economy is not growing: *The rate fell to a trough of 3% last year.*
• *v.* [I] if a price, a rate, etc. **troughs**, it reaches its lowest level: *Interest rates have troughed at 4%.* OPP PEAK

**truck** /trʌk/ *n., v.*
• *n.* [C] **1** a large motor vehicle for carrying heavy loads by road: *a ten-ton truck* ◇ *a commercial/heavy-duty/refrigerated ~* SYN LORRY (*BrE*)
**2** (*BrE*) an open railway vehicle for carrying goods or animals **3** a vehicle that is open at the back, used for carrying goods, animals, etc. **4** a vehicle for carrying things, pulled or pushed by hand
• *v.* [T] to take sth somewhere by truck: *The goods are trucked from Oslo to Karasjok.* ▸ **ˈtrucking** *n.* [U]

**truckage** /ˈtrʌkɪdʒ/ *n.* [U] (*Transpt.*) **1** the movement of goods by road: *a truckage company* **2** the charge made for this

**truckload** /ˈtrʌkləʊd; *AmE* -loʊd/ *n.* [C] the amount of sth that fills a truck (often used to mean a large amount): *20 truckloads of building materials*

**ˌtrue and fair ˈview** *phr.* (*Account.*) in the UK, words that AUDITORS use to show that they have checked a company's accounts and think that they give accurate information about its financial state

**trump** /trʌmp/ *v.* [T] (*infml.*) to beat another company's product or action by producing sth or doing sth even better: *Their $55 m offer was trumped by a rival bidder.*

★**trust** /trʌst/ *n.* **1** (*Finan.*; *Law*) [C,U] an arrangement in which TRUSTEES have legal control of money or property for another person or group; an amount of money or property controlled in this way: *He* ***set up*** *a trust for his children.* ◇ *money held in trust* **2** (*Finan.*) [C] an organization or a group of people that invests money given or lent to it: *to create/establish/manage/set up a ~* ◇ *a trust board/manager* **3** (*Econ.*) [C] (*esp. AmE*) a group of companies that work together illegally to reduce competition: *antitrust laws*

**trustbuster** /'trʌstbʌstə(r)/ *n.* [C] (*esp. AmE*) (*Law*) a person or an organization that works to prevent groups of companies from working together illegally
▸ **'trustbusting** *n.* [U]

**'trust deed** (*also* **ˌdeed of 'trust, 'trust ˌinstrument**) *n.* [C] (*Law*) a legal document that creates a **trust** and gives details of the TRUSTEES and BENEFICIARIES, and how the trust must be run

★**trustee** /trʌ'sti:/ *n.* [C] (*Law*) a person or an organization responsible for managing money or property for another person or group: *a board of trustees* SYN FIDUCIARY

**trusˌtee in 'bankruptcy** *n.* [C] (*Law*) a person chosen by a court to manage the affairs of a BANKRUPT company or person, sell its/their property and pay its/their debts where possible

**trusteeship** /trʌ'sti:ʃɪp/ *n.* [U,C] (*Law*) the job of being a **trustee**; a situation where money or property is controlled by a **trustee**

**'trust fund** *n.* [C] (*Finan.*) money, property and other assets that are held for sb by an organization or a group of people

**'trust ˌinstrument** = TRUST DEED

**'trust reˌceipt** *n.* [C] (*Finan.*) a document given to a bank by a company that has accepted goods but cannot pay for them at that time, to say that the bank owns the goods. The bank pays for the goods and the company pays back the money later.

**the ˌTruth in 'Lending Act** *n.* [sing.] a law in the US that protects consumers by saying that companies who lend money must give full information about the cost of the loan and the annual rate of interest

**TSR** /ˌti: es 'ɑ:(r)/ = TOTAL SHAREHOLDER RETURN

**TTM** /ˌti: ti: 'em/ = TIME TO MARKET

**TUC** /ˌti: ju: 'si:/ *abbr* **Trades Union Congress** in the UK and some other countries, an organization to which many trade unions belong

**tumble** /'tʌmbl/ *v.* [I] to fall rapidly in value or amount: *Shares tumbled 8 per cent.* ▸ **'tumble** *n.* [C]: *Shares **took** a sharp **tumble**.*

**tune** /tju:n; *AmE* tu:n/ *n.*, *v.*
• *n.* IDM **to the tune of sth** used to emphasize how much money sth has cost: *loans to the tune of $92 m* → idiom at CALL *v.*
• *v.* [T] **1 ~ sth (up)** to adjust sth so that it works more efficiently: *to tune up our after-sales service* **2** to prepare or adjust sth so that it is suitable for a particular situation: *products **finely tuned to** customers' needs*

**turbine** /'tɜ:baɪn; *AmE* 'tɜ:rb-/ *n.* [C] a machine or an engine that receives its power from a wheel turned by the pressure of water, air or gas

**turn** /tɜ:n; *AmE* tɜ:rn/ *v.*, *n.*
• *v.* [T,I] to change into a particular state; to make sth do this: *The loss has been turned **into** a profit.*
IDM **turn a (small, modest, $10 m, etc.) 'profit** (*infml.*) to make a profit in business **turn sth on its 'head** to change sth completely: *The magazine's low price has turned the usual pricing process on its head.* **turn your 'back on sth** to reject sth/sb that you were previously connected with: *Investors are now turning their backs on Internet start-ups.* → idioms at HOSTILE, SOUR
PHRV **ˌturn (sth) a'round/'round** if a business, an economy, etc. **turns around** or sb **turns** it **around**, it starts being successful after it has failed to be successful for a time **ˌturn sth a'round/'round** to do a piece of work that you have been given and return it: *They try to turn any repair around in 72 hours.* **ˌturn 'down** to become weaker or less active, make less money, etc. → DOWNTURN **ˌturn sb/sth 'down** to reject or refuse to consider an offer, a proposal, etc. or the person who makes it: *The bank turned us down **for** a loan.* **ˌturn 'in sth** to achieve a particular performance, profit, etc: *Our UK division turned in a strong performance.* **ˌturn sb 'on (to sth)** to make sb become interested in sth or use sth for the first time: *turning Internet users on to broadband* **ˌturn sth 'out** to produce sth/sb: *The firm turns out 75 000 bicycles a year.* **ˌturn 'over sth** to do business worth a particular amount of money in a particular period of time: *We turn over £3.5 m a year.* **ˌturn sth 'over** (*Comm.*) (about a shop/store) to sell goods and replace them: *A supermarket turns over its stock very quickly.* **ˌturn sth 'over to sb/sth** to give the control of sth to sb else: *He turned the business over to his daughter.*
• *n.* [C] **1** a change in what is happening: *a downward turn in the company's fortunes* **2** (*Finan.*) the difference between the buying and selling price of shares or other finan-

cial products; the profit made: *making a quick turn on the shares* → idiom at TAKE *v.*

**turnaround** /ˈtɜːnəraʊnd; *AmE* ˈtɜːrn-/ (*BrE also* **ˈturnround**) *n.* [C, usu. sing.] **1** the amount of time it takes to do and return a piece of work: *a 2-day turnaround for small printing jobs* **2** a situation in which sth changes from bad to good: *a dramatic turnaround **in** the company's fortunes* **3** the amount of time it takes to unload a ship or plane at the end of one journey and load it again for the next one

**ˈturnaround ˌmanagement** (*BrE also* **ˈturnround -**) *n.* [U] the act of making changes to a failing company in order to make it more successful; the study of this subject

**turndown** /ˈtɜːndaʊn; *AmE* ˈtɜːrn-/ *n.* [C] **1** a fall in the amount of business done; a time when the economy becomes weaker: *market turndowns* SYN DOWNTURN **2** a refusal; not being accepted for a job, etc.

**turnkey** /ˈtɜːnkiː; *AmE* ˈtɜːrn-/ *adj.* **1** (*IT*) used to describe a product or service, esp. a computer system, that is supplied in a complete form, ready for the buyer to use: *turnkey systems* **2** (*Comm.*) used to describe a large project that one company designs, builds and provides equipment for on behalf of another, so that it is completely ready to use at the end of the contract: *a **turnkey contract** to build an airport terminal*

★**turnover** /ˈtɜːnəʊvə(r); *AmE* ˈtɜːrnoʊ-/ *n.* [C, usu. sing., U] **1** (*Account.*) the total value of goods or services sold by a company during a particular period of time: *The firm has an annual turnover of $75 m.* SYN SALES REVENUE

⊙ ***daily/first-half/full-year*** ~ ◆ ***an overall/a total*** ~ ◆ ***a high/low*** ~

**2** (*HR*) the rate at which employees leave a company and are replaced by other people: *The factory has a high turnover of staff.* ◇ *employee/labour/staff* ~ **3** (*Account.*; *Comm.*) the rate at which goods are sold in a shop/store and replaced by others: *a fast turnover of stock* ◇ *the stock turnover rate* **4** (*Stock Ex.*) the total value of the business done on a stock exchange during a particular period of time; the total number of shares bought and sold: *Market turnover was 2.6 billion shares.* ◇ *heavy/light* ~

**ˈturnover ˌratio** *n.* [C, usu. sing.] (*Finan.*) the relationship between the value of shares, bonds, etc. that a fund buys or sells in a particular period and the average total value that it holds during the period

**ˈturnover tax** *n.* [U; sing.] (*Econ.*) tax a company pays on the money received from the sale of goods

**turnround** /ˈtɜːnraʊnd; *AmE* ˈtɜːrn-/ = TURNAROUND

**ˈturnround ˌmanagement** = TURNAROUND MANAGEMENT

**TVR** /ˌtiː viː ˈɑː(r)/ = TELEVISION RATING

**twentysomething** /ˈtwentisʌmθɪŋ/ *n.* [C] (*infml.*) a person who is between twenty and twenty-nine years old

**ˌtwo-ˈtier** *adj.* (about a system) having two levels: *a two-tier system of interest rates*

**ˌtwo-ˈway** *adj.* **1** moving, or allowing sth to move, in two different directions: *two-way trade* **2** involving two people or groups: *a two-way battle for the company* **3** with each person or side playing an equal role: *a two-way dialogue with customers*

**tycoon** /taɪˈkuːn/ *n.* [C] a person who is successful in business or industry and has become rich and powerful: *a media/property* ~

**type** /taɪp/ *v.*, *n.*

• *v.* [T,I] to write sth using the keyboard of a computer, etc: *Type the url **into** the address box.* ▸ **ˈtyping** *n.* [U]: *typing errors* **ˈtypist** *n.* [C]

PHRV **ˌtype sth ˈup** to type sth that was written by hand, often in the form of notes

• *n.* [U] letters that are printed or typed: *The warning is written **in** small type on the packet.*

**typeface** /ˈtaɪpfeɪs/ *n.* [C] a set of letters, numbers, etc. of a particular design, used in printing

**typescript** /ˈtaɪpskrɪpt/ *n.* [C,U] a copy of a text or document that has been typed

**typewritten** /ˈtaɪprɪtn/ *adj.* written using the keyboard of a computer, etc.

**tyrekicker** (*AmE* **tirekicker**) /ˈtaɪəkɪkə(r); *AmE* ˈtaɪərkɪkər/ *n.* [C] (*Market.*, *infml.*) a possible customer who asks a lot of questions about a product but never buys anything → idiom at KICK

# Uu

**UK SIC** /juː keɪ ˌes aɪ ˈsiː/ *abbr* **United Kingdom Standard Industrial Classification of economic activities** in the UK, a system in which industries and services are given a code to show which type of economic activity they are involved in, for reference and research purposes

**ˌultimate conˈsumer/ˈcustomer** *n.* [C] (*Market.*) the person who actually buys or uses a particular product SYN END-USER

**ultimatum** /ˌʌltɪˈmeɪtəm/ *n.* [C] (*pl.* **-tums** *or* **-ta** /-tə/) a final warning to a person, group or country that if they do not do what you ask, you will take action against them: *to issue an ultimatum to sb*

**ultra vires** /ˌʌltrə ˈvaɪriːz/ *adj.* (*Law*) (about the action of a person, company or government) beyond legal or official powers: *an ultra vires transaction* ▸ **ˌultra ˈvires** *adv.*: *to have acted ultra vires*

**u/m** *abbr* a short way of writing undermentioned

**umbrella** /ʌmˈbrelə/ *n.* [C] a thing that contains many parts or elements: *22 companies operate* **under the umbrella of** *SRC Holdings Corp.* ◇ *an ~ brand/group*

**UMTS** /ˌjuː em tiː ˈes/ *abbr* **Universal Mobile Telecommunications System** a system for sending information between mobile phones/ cellphones

**unacˈcounted for** *adj.* a thing that is **unaccounted for** is missing, for example from an account or an amount of money, and people cannot explain why: *$30 000 of the money is still unaccounted for.*

**unachievable** /ˌʌnəˈtʃiːvəbl/ *adj.* that you cannot manage to reach or obtain: *unachievable sales targets*

**unadjusted** /ˌʌnəˈdʒʌstɪd/ *adj.* (about data) that has not been changed to make it more suitable or more accurate: *the unadjusted unemployment figure*

**unanimous** /juːˈnænɪməs/ *adj.* **1** if a decision or an opinion is **unanimous**, it is agreed or shared by everyone in a group **2** if a group of people are **unanimous**, they all agree ▸ **uˈnanimously** *adv.*

**unaudited** /ˌʌnˈɔːdɪtɪd/ *adj.* (*Account.*) (about financial accounts) that have not been examined by an AUDITOR

**unauthorized, -ised** /ˌʌnˈɔːθəraɪzd/ *adj.* without official permission: *unauthorized use of the computer system*

**unbalanced** /ˌʌnˈbælənst/ *adj.* **1** (*Account.*) (in a set of financial accounts) where the total of the DEBITS is not equal to the total of the CREDITS, because a mistake has been made **2** (*Account.*) (about a budget, etc.) where the money going out is greater than the money coming in **3** giving too much importance to one part or aspect of sth: *an unbalanced and inaccurate report*

**unbundle** /ˌʌnˈbʌndl/ *v.* [T] **1** to divide a group of businesses into individual parts, esp. in order to sell the less important parts: *The group was unbundled after a year of heavy losses.* **2** (*Market.*) to supply a product, a service or a piece of equipment separately and not with any other ▸ **ˌunˈbundling** *n.* [U,C]

**ˌuncalled ˈcapital** *n.* [U] (*Account.*) the difference between the value of the shares a company has issued and the amount shareholders have paid so far

**uncashed** /ˌʌnˈkæʃt/ *adj.* (about a cheque/check, etc.) that has not been exchanged for money

**uncompetitive** /ˌʌnkəmˈpetətɪv/ *adj.* not cheaper or better than others and therefore not able to compete equally: *~ industries/prices*

**unconditional** /ˌʌnkənˈdɪʃənl/ *adj.* without any conditions or limits: *an unconditional offer* ▸ **ˌunconˈditionally** /-nəli/ *adv.*

**ˌunconditional ˈtakeover bid** *n.* [C] (*Finan.*) an offer to buy any number of a company's shares at a particular price with no special conditions

**unconsolidated** /ˌʌnkənˈsɒlɪdeɪtɪd; *AmE* -ˈsɑːl-/ *adj.* **1** (*Account.*) (about financial results, accounts, etc.) not combined into one set of figures **2** (about businesses, etc.) not joined into one group

**uncontested** /ˌʌnkənˈtestɪd/ *adj.* without any opposition, argument or competition: *an uncontested bid for the television company*

**ˌuncrossed ˈcheque** = OPEN CHEQUE

**undated** /ˌʌnˈdeɪtɪd/ *adj.* **1** without a date written on it: *an ~ cheque/letter* **2** (*Finan.*) (about an investment) that has no fixed date when it will be repaid: *undated bonds*

**underbid** /ˌʌndəˈbɪd; *AmE* -dərˈb-/ *v.* [T,I] (**-bidding, -bid, -bid**) (*Comm.*) to make a lower **bid** than sb else, for example when trying to win a contract

**undercapitalized**, **-ised** /ˌʌndəˈkæpɪtəlaɪzd; *AmE* -dərˈk-/ *adj.* (*Finan.*) (about a business) not having enough money to be able to operate normally, pay debts and grow

**undercharge** /ˌʌndəˈtʃɑːdʒ; *AmE* -dərˈtʃɑːrdʒ/ *v.* [T,I] to charge too little for sth, usu. by mistake: *Customers had been undercharged* **by** *$100.* ▸ **ˈundercharge** *n.* [C]: *an undercharge of $8*

**undercut** /ˌʌndəˈkʌt; *AmE* -dərˈk-/ *v.* [T] (**-cutting**, **-cut**, **-cut**) **1** to sell goods or services at a lower price than your competitors: *The bank will undercut rivals' rates and services.* **2** to make sth weaker or less likely to be effective: *The laws undercut workers' rights.*

**underdeveloped** /ˌʌndədɪˈveləpt; *AmE* -dərd-/ *adj.* **1** (about a country, society, etc.) having few industries and a low standard of living NOTE 'Developing countries' is now the usual term used. **2** not developed to a very high level or standard ▸ **ˌunderdeˈvelopment** *n.* [U]

**underemployed** /ˌʌndərɪmˈplɔɪd/ *adj.* not having enough work to do; not having work that makes full use of your skills

**underestimate** /ˌʌndərˈestɪmeɪt/ *v.* [T] **1** to think or guess that the amount, cost or size of sth is smaller than it really is: *They* **grossly** *underestimated the costs involved.* **2** to not realize how good, strong, determined, etc. sb really is: *Don't underestimate our rivals.* ▸ **underestimate** /ˌʌndərˈestɪmət/ *n.* [C] **ˌunderˌestiˈmation** /-ˈmeɪʃn/ *n.* [C,U]

**underfunded** /ˌʌndəˈfʌndɪd; *AmE* -dərˈf-/ *adj.* (*Finan.*) (about an organization, a project, etc.) not having as much money as it needs: *The pension plan was underfunded by $2 m.* ▸ **ˌunderˈfunding** *n.* [U]

**the ˌunderground eˈconomy** = BLACK ECONOMY

**underinsured** /ˌʌndərɪnˈʃɔːd; -ˈʃʊəd; *AmE* -ˈʃʊrd/ *adj.* (*Insur.*) **1** (about a person) not having enough insurance **2** (about a thing) insured for less than it is worth ▸ **ˌunderinˈsurance** *n.* [U]

**ˌunder-inˈvestment** *n.* [U] (*Finan.*) the fact of less money being invested in sth than is needed: *under-investment* **in** *plant and people* ▸ **ˌunder-inˈvest** *v.* [I] **ˌunder-inˈvested** *adj.*: *Many funds are under-invested.*

★**underlying** /ˌʌndəˈlaɪɪŋ; *AmE* -dərˈl-/ *adj.* **1** important in a situation but not always easily noticed or stated clearly: *The underlying cause of the crisis was a lack of investment.* **2** (*Econ.*; *Finan.*) used to describe basic figures, rates, etc. excluding any special effect, event or payment: *Underlying sales growth rose 4.5%.* **3** (*Finan.*) used to describe the items that particular types of investments are based on: *The value of derivatives depends on the value of an underlying security.*

**ˌunderlying inˈflation** *n.* [U] (*Econ.*) the rate at which the prices of goods and services rise over a period of time, measured without considering prices that go up and down frequently, esp. the costs of MORTGAGES

**undermanned** /ˌʌndəˈmænd; *AmE* -dərˈm-/ *adj.* (*HR*) not having enough people working and therefore not able to function well SYN UNDERSTAFFED ▸ **ˌunderˈmanning** *n.* [U]

**undermentioned** /ˌʌndəˈmenʃənd; *AmE* -dərˈm-/ *adj.* (*abbr* **u/m**) (*written*) used to refer to sth that appears below or in a later part of a document

★**underpay** /ˌʌndəˈpeɪ; *AmE* -dərˈp-/ *v.* (**-paid**, **-paid** /-ˈpeɪd/) **1** [T] (*often pass.*) to pay sb too little money, esp. for their work: *I'm overworked and underpaid.* **2** [T,I] to pay too little for sth; to pay less than sth is worth: *The acquirer has underpaid* **for** *the firm.* ▸ **ˌunderˈpayment** *n.* [C,U]

★**underperform** /ˌʌndəpəˈfɔːm; *AmE* ˌʌndərpərˈfɔːrm/ *v.* **1** [T,I] to not make as much money as expected or as sb/sth else: *The company has underperformed its rivals this year.* ◇ *underperforming stores* **2** [I] to be less successful in your job than expected: *underperforming managers* ▸ **ˌunderperˈformance** /-məns/ *n.* [U] **ˌunderperˈformer** *n.* [C]: *The stock is a market underperformer.*

**underpin** /ˌʌndəˈpɪn; *AmE* -dərˈp-/ *v.* [T] (**-nn-**) **1** to provide a strong financial basis for sth **2** to support or form the basis of an argument, a claim, etc: *The report is underpinned by extensive research.*

★**underpriced** /ˌʌndəˈpraɪst; *AmE* ˌʌndərˈp-/ *adj.* cheap; costing less than it is worth: *underpriced exports* OPP OVERPRICED ▸ **ˌunderˈprice** *v.* [T]

**underproduction** /ˌʌndəprəˈdʌkʃən; *AmE* ˌʌndərp-/ *n.* [U] the fact that fewer goods, services, etc.

are produced than are needed or planned: *Underproduction results in lost sales.* ▶ **ˌunderproˈduce** /-ˈdjuːs; *AmE* -ˈduːs/ *v.* [T,I]

**ˌunder-reˈport** (*AmE* **underreport**) *v.* [T] (*Account.*) to state a smaller amount of money, etc. than the real amount, esp. for dishonest reasons: *They under-reported earnings by €100 m.*

**undersell** /ˌʌndəˈsel; *AmE* -dərˈsel/ *v.* [T] (**-sold**, **-sold** /-ˈsəʊld; *AmE* -ˈsoʊld/) **1** (*Comm.*) to sell goods or services at a lower price than your competitors: *Foreign companies are underselling us.* **2** (*Comm.*) to sell sth at a lower price than its real value: *They were underselling their PCs.* **3** to make people think that sth is not as good or as interesting as it really is: *Don't undersell yourself.* IDM **ˌnever ˌknowingly underˈsold** (*Comm.*) used by stores to advertise their policy of selling their products at lower prices than other stores. If you find the same product at a lower price somewhere else, the store will lower its own price to match.

**undershoot** /ˌʌndəˈʃuːt; *AmE* -dərˈʃ-/ *v.* [T,I] (**-shot**, **-shot** /-ˈʃɒt; *AmE* -ˈʃɑːt/) to fail to reach a target: *Tax revenues undershot by $7 bn.* ▶ **ˈundershoot** *n.* [C]

the **undersigned** /ˌʌndəˈsaɪnd; *AmE* -dərˈs-/ *n.* [C] (*pl.* **the undersigned**) (*written*) the person who has signed that particular document: *We, the undersigned, agree to ...*

**underspend** /ˌʌndəˈspend; *AmE* -dərˈs-/ *v.* [T,I] (**-spent**, **-spent** /-ˈspent/) to spend less than the amount that you can or should spend: *We have underspent our IT budget this year.* ▶ **ˈunderspend** *n.* [C, usu. sing., U]: *a £5 m underspend* **ˌunderˈspending** *n.* [U]

**understaffed** /ˌʌndəˈstɑːft; *AmE* ˌʌndərˈstæft/ *adj.* (*HR*) (about a company, an office, etc.) not having enough people working and so not able to function well: *The office was seriously understaffed.* SYN UNDERMANNED ▶ **ˌunderˈstaffing** *n.* [U]

**understate** /ˌʌndəˈsteɪt; *AmE* -dərˈs-/ *v.* [T] (*Account.*) to report a smaller amount of money, etc. than the real amount in official records: *The accounting methods understated the company's liabilities.* ▶ **ˈunderstatement** /-mənt/ *n.* [C,U]

**undersubscribed** /ˌʌndəsəbˈskraɪbd; *AmE* -dərs-/ *adj.* (*Finan.*) (about a sale of shares, bonds, etc.) not having enough buyers

★ **undertake** /ˌʌndəˈteɪk; *AmE* -dərˈt-/ *v.* (**-took** /-ˈtʊk/ **-taken** /-ˈteɪkən/) **1** [T] to make yourself responsible for sth and start doing it ⊕ *to ~ a* ***project/task*** • *to ~ an* ***analysis/investigation/a study*** • *to ~* ***reforms/research/work*** **2** [I] to agree or promise that you will do sth: *He undertook* ***to*** *finish the job by Friday.*

**undertaking** /ˌʌndəˈteɪkɪŋ; *AmE* -dərˈt-/ *n.* **1** [C] a task or project, esp. one that is important and/or difficult: *a huge/major/massive ~* **2** [C] a business: *failing commercial undertakings* **3** [C,U] **~ (to do sth)** an agreement or a promise to do sth: *to break/give/honour an ~*

**undervalue** /ˌʌndəˈvæljuː; *AmE* -dərˈv-/ *v.* [T] (*usu. pass.*) **1** to give sth a value that is less than its real value: *The currency is undervalued* ***against*** *the dollar.* **2** to not recognize sth/sb as being as good or as important as it/he/she, etc. really is: *She feels undervalued.*

**underweight** /ˌʌndəˈweɪt; *AmE* -dərˈw-/ *adj.* (*Stock Ex.*) having less of a particular type of investment or asset in a collection than the index you are following or than your usual position: *The fund is underweight in both stocks.* ▶ **ˌunderˈweight** *v.* [T,I]

**underwrite** /ˌʌndəˈraɪt/ *v.* [T] (**-wrote** /-ˈrəʊt; *AmE* -ˈroʊt/**-written** /-ˈrɪtn/) **1** (*Finan.*) to agree to pay for an activity and accept financial responsibility for any losses it may make: *to underwrite new business* **2** (*Insur.*) to accept responsibility for an insurance policy so that money will be paid if loss or damage as stated in the policy happens: *the company underwriting the risk* **3** (*Stock Ex.*) to agree to buy shares that are not bought by the public when new shares are offered for sale, at a fixed price and on a particular day: *an underwriting group/syndicate* ▶ **ˈunderwriting** *n.* [U]

**underwriter** /ˈʌndəraɪtə(r)/ *n.* [C] **1** (*Insur.*) a person whose job is to estimate the risks involved in a particular activity, decide if it can be insured and how much sb must pay for insurance **2** (*Insur.*) a person or an organization that **underwrites** insurance policies, esp. for ships **3** (*Stock Ex.*) a bank or another organization that promises to buy the shares that are not sold when new shares are offered for sale

**undeveloped** /ˌʌndɪˈveləpt/ *adj.* **1** (about land) not used for farming, industry or building **2** (about a country) without modern industries, and with a low standard of living

**undifferentiated** /ˌʌndɪfəˈrenʃieɪtɪd/ *adj.* (*Market.*) used to describe products or services that are aimed at the largest number of people of all types

**ˌundischarged ˈbankrupt** *n.* [C] (*Law*) a person officially stated to be BANKRUPT by a court but who has to keep paying back money and is not allowed to do business

**undisclosed** /ˌʌndɪsˈkləʊzd; *AmE* -ˈkloʊzd/ *adj.* not made known or told to anyone: *The company sold its shipping arm for an undisclosed sum.*

**ˌundisˌtributable reˈserve** = CAPITAL RESERVE (1)

**ˌundisˌtributed ˈearnings** (*also* **ˌundisˌtributed ˈprofits**) *n.* [pl.] (*Account.*) profits that are invested back into a company rather than paid to shareholders
SYN RETAINED EARNINGS

**undue** /ˌʌnˈdjuː; *AmE* ˌʌnˈduː/ *adj.* (*fml.*) more than is thought to be reasonable or necessary: *~ delay/pressure/risk*

**ˌunearned ˈincome** *n.* [U] (*Account.*) money that you receive but do not earn by working
OPP EARNED INCOME

**uneconomic** /ˌʌniːkəˈnɒmɪk; ˌʌnek-; *AmE* -ˈnɑːm-/ *adj.* **1** = UNECONOMICAL **2** not making a profit: *Prices have been fixed at uneconomic levels.* SYN UNPROFITABLE

**uneconomical** /ˌʌniːkəˈnɒmɪkl; ˌʌnek-; *AmE* -ˈnɑːm-/ (*also* **ˌunecoˈnomic**) *adj.* using too much time or money, or too many materials, and therefore not likely to make a profit: *The old system was uneconomical to run.* OPP ECONOMICAL
▸ **ˌunecoˈnomically** /-ɪkli/ *adv.*

**unemployable** /ˌʌnɪmˈplɔɪəbl/ *adj.* lacking the skills or qualities that you need to get a job

★ **unemployed** /ˌʌnɪmˈplɔɪd/ *adj.* **1** without a job although able to work: *How long have you been unemployed?* ◇ *an unemployed engineer* SYN OUT OF WORK **2** (*usually* **the unemployed**) *n.* [pl.] people who are **unemployed**: *helping the unemployed find jobs*

★ **unemployment** /ˌʌnɪmˈplɔɪmənt/ *n.* [U] **1** the fact of a number of people not having a job; the number without a job: *an area of high unemployment* ◇ *a rising/falling ~ rate* **2** the state of not having a job: *long-term unemployment*

**ˌunemˈployment ˌbenefit** *n.* [U,C] money paid by the government to sb who is unemployed

**ˌunemˈployment compenˌsation** *n.* [U] (*AmE*) money paid regularly from a government or union plan to sb who has recently become unemployed

**ˌunemˈployment inˌsurance** *n.* [U] a system where workers pay a regular amount of money, so that if they lose their job they receive a regular payment

**ˌunemˈployment line** = DOLE QUEUE

**unethical** /ʌnˈeθɪkl/ *adj.* not morally correct or acceptable
▸ **unˈethically** /-kli/ *adv.*

**unexpired** /ˌʌnɪkˈspaɪəd; *AmE* -ˈspaɪərd/ *adj.* (about an agreement, a contract, etc) still valid and not yet having come to an end

★ **unfair** /ˌʌnˈfeə(r); *AmE* -ˈfer/ *adj.* not giving every group or person the same opportunity to do sth; not right or fair: *The new pension plans are unfair to older workers.* OPP FAIR
▸ **ˌunˈfairly** *adv.*: *Some employees claim they were treated unfairly.*

**ˌunfair disˈmissal** (*also* **ˌwrongful disˈmissal**) *n.* [U,C] (*HR*) an occasion when sb is removed from their job without a good reason: *She is **suing** the company **for** unfair dismissal.*

**unfavourable** (*AmE* **unfavorable**) /ʌnˈfeɪvərəbl/ *adj.* **1** (about conditions, situations, etc.) not good and likely to cause problems or make sth more difficult: *unfavourable market conditions* **2** showing that you do not approve of or like sb/sth: *an unfavourable report* ▸ **unˈfavourably** (*AmE* **unfavorably**) *adv.*: *This year's results **compare unfavourably with** last year's.*

**unˌfavourable ˈbalance** *n.* [C] (*Account.*) an amount of debt shown on an account
SYN ADVERSE BALANCE

**unˌfavourable ˈtrade ˌbalance** (*also* **ˌunfavourable ˌbalance of ˈtrade**) *n.* [sing.] (*Econ.*) when a country spends more on imports than it earns from exports
SYN ADVERSE TRADE BALANCE

**unfriendly** /ʌnˈfrendli/ = HOSTILE

**unfulfilled** /ˌʌnfʊlˈfɪld/ *adj.* that has not been completed, achieved or satisfied: *an ~ contract/order* ◇ *~ potential/targets*

**ungeared** /ʌnˈɡɪəd; *AmE* -ˈɡɪrd/ *adj.* (*Finan.*) not using borrowed money; with no debt: *ungeared investments*

**unˌhappy ˈcamper** *n.* [C] (*infml.*) a customer, an employee, etc. who has complaints

**ˌuniform ˈprice ˌauction** = DUTCH AUCTION (2)

**ˌunilateral ˈcontract** *n.* [C] (*Law*) an agreement in which only one side promises to do sth, or promises to do sth only if sb does a particular thing

**uninstalled** /ˌʌnɪnˈstɔːld/ *adj.* (*AmE*) (*HR, infml.*) used to describe an employee who has been removed from their job

**uninsurable** /ˌʌnɪnˈʃɔːrəbl; -ˈʃʊər-; *AmE* -ˈʃʊr-/ *adj.* (*Insur.*) **1** (about a thing or person) that cannot be insured **2** (*also* **ˌnon-inˈsurable**) (about an event) that cannot be insured against because it is impossible to calculate possible losses exactly: *Earthquakes are an* ***uninsurable risk***.

**uninsured** /ˌʌnɪnˈʃɔːd; -ˈʃʊəd; *AmE* -ˈʃʊrd/ *adj.* (*Insur.*) **1** without insurance: *an uninsured driver* **2** (about an event) that is not insured against: *uninsured losses*

★**union** /ˈjuːniən/ *n.* **1** [C] = TRADE UNION **2** [C] a group of states or countries that have the same central government or that agree to work together: *the European Union* ◇ *to create/dissolve/form/join a ~* **3** [sing; U] the act of joining two or more things together; the state of being joined together: *economic and monetary union*

**ˈunion-ˌbashing** *n.* [U] (*HR, infml.*) active or spoken opposition to trade/labor unions

**ˈunion ˌbusting** *n.* [U] (*AmE*) (*HR*) the act or process of trying to stop trade/labor unions from having any power

**unionist** /ˈjuːniənɪst/ = TRADE UNIONIST

**unionize, -ise** /ˈjuːniənaɪz/ *v.* [T,I] (*HR*) to organize people to become members of a trade union: *a unionized workforce/industry*
▶ **ˌunioniˈzation, -iˈsation** /-naɪˈzeɪʃn; *AmE* -nəˈz-/ *n.* [U]

**ˈunion shop** = CLOSED SHOP

**unique** /juːˈniːk/ *adj.* **~ (to sb/sth)** being the only one of its kind; very special or unusual

**uˌnique ˈselling propoˌsition** (*also* **uˌnique ˈselling point**) = USP

**uˌnique ˈvisitor** *n.* [C] (*IT; Market.*) a person who visits a website in a particular period of time and can be identified, usu. by the address of their computer, used as a measure of how popular the website is: *800 000 unique visitors a month*

**ˌunissued ˈcapital** (*also* **ˌunissued ˈshare ˌcapital**) *n.* [U] (*Finan.*) shares that a company can officially issue but has not yet issued

★**unit** /ˈjuːnɪt/ *n.* [C] **1** a single item of the type of product that a company sells: *The game's selling price was $15 per unit.* **2** a part of a company that does a particular activity or that is not divided into smaller parts: *business units* **3** a fixed quantity, etc. that is used as a standard measurement: *a ~ of time/length* **4** (*Finan.*) a single share, bond, etc. **5** a small machine that has a particular purpose or is part of a larger machine **6** a building on an INDUSTRIAL ESTATE: *The workshop is in unit 20.*

**ˈunitary tax** *n.* [C,U] a form of CORPORATION TAX used in some states of the US, which calculates the amount a company must pay according to their total income, and not on their income in just one state

**ˈunit cost** *n.* [C, usu. sing.] (*Account.*) the cost of producing, buying or providing one item: *The more goods produced, the lower the unit cost.*

**ˌunit-ˈlinked** *adj.* (*Finan.*) used to describe LIFE INSURANCE, etc. in which money is invested in a UNIT TRUST

**ˌunit of acˈcount** *n.* [C] (*Account.; Econ.*) **1** money when it is used to measure the value of goods or services and to keep financial records **2** the standard system of money that is used in a particular country **3** a special system of money that is created only for accounting

**ˌunit of ˈcurrency** *n.* [C] (*Econ.*) the money that is used in a particular country SYN MONETARY UNIT

**ˈunit price** *n.* [C] (*Account.*) the price of a single item

**ˈunit sales** *n.* [pl.] (*Market.*) the number of items of a particular product that have been sold

**ˈunit share** *n.* [C] (*Market.*) the UNIT SALES of a particular product compared with the total sales of all similar products

**ˌunit ˈtrust** (*BrE*) (*AmE* **ˈmutual fund**) *n.* [C] (*Finan.*) an organization that manages a fund that is invested in a wide range of shares, bonds, etc. The fund is divided into small units which are bought and sold, usu. by people who only invest a small amount of money.

**universal** /ˌjuːnɪˈvɜːsl; *AmE* -ˈvɜːrsl/ *adj.* done by, involving, etc. all the people in the world or in a particular group: *The books have universal appeal* (= they are liked by all types of people in all places).

**ˌuniversal ˈbank** *n.* [C] a bank that combines INVESTMENT BANKING and COMMERCIAL BANKING
▸ **ˌuniversal ˈbanking** *n.* [U]

**universe** /ˈjuːnɪvɜːs; *AmE* -vɜːrs/ *n.* [sing.] **1** (*Market.*) a complete group of people, companies, etc. that have the same features or qualities: *the universe* (= number of possible readers) *for men's magazines* SYN POPULATION **2** an area of activity; the people and companies involved in it: *the investment universe*

**unladen** /ˌʌnˈleɪdn/ *adj.* without a load: *unladen aircraft* ◇ *the unladen weight of a vehicle*

**unlawful** /ʌnˈlɔːfl/ *adj.* not allowed by law: *unlawful trading*
▸ **unˈlawfully** /-fəli/ *adv.*

**unlicensed** /ʌnˈlaɪsnst/ *adj.* without a **licence**: ~ *software/cabs*

**unˌlimited ˈcompany** *n.* [C] a company whose shareholders are responsible for all its debts if it fails → LIMITED COMPANY

**unˌlimited liaˈbility** *n.* [U] the legal duty of the shareholders of an UNLIMITED COMPANY to pay all its debts → LIMITED LIABILITY

**unlisted** /ʌnˈlɪstɪd/ *adj.* **1** (*Finan.*) (*also* **unˈquoted**) not bought and sold on a stock exchange: ~ *companies/securities* **2** (*esp. AmE*) (about a telephone number) not listed in the public telephone book, at the request of the owner of the telephone SYN EX-DIRECTORY

**unload** /ˌʌnˈləʊd; *AmE* ˌʌnˈloʊd/ *v.* **1** [T,I] to remove things from a vehicle or ship after it has taken them somewhere: *ships waiting to unload* **2** (*infml.*) [T] to get rid of or sell sth, esp. sth illegal or of bad quality

**unlock** /ˌʌnˈlɒk; *AmE* ˌʌnˈlɑːk/ *v.* [T] to allow sth to start being used that has existed but not been available for use: *The group is selling stores to try to* **unlock value** *for shareholders.*

**unmanageable** /ʌnˈmænɪdʒəbl/ *adj.* difficult or impossible to control or deal with: *unmanageable debt*

**unmetered** /ˌʌnˈmiːtəd; *AmE* -tərd/ *adj.* (about the use of a service) not being measured, for example by a METER

**unmoved** /ˌʌnˈmuːvd/ *adj.* (about the value of sth) not having changed: *The FTSE 100 was unmoved for much of the day.*

**unnerve** /ˌʌnˈnɜːv; *AmE* -ˈnɜːrv/ *v.* [T] (in newspapers) to make sb feel nervous or lose confidence: *The news has unnerved investors.*

**unofficial** /ˌʌnəˈfɪʃl/ *adj.* **1** that does not have permission or approval from sb in authority: *Unofficial estimates put the loss at over $2 m.* **2** that is not part of sb's business: *an unofficial visit*
▸ **ˌunofˈficially** /-ʃəli/ *adv.*

**ˌunofˌficial ˈstrike** *n.* [C] (*HR*) a strike that does not have the approval or permission of an accepted trade union

**unpaid** /ˌʌnˈpeɪd/ *adj.* **1** (*Account.*) not yet paid: *unpaid bills* **2** (about work, etc.) done without payment: *to take unpaid leave* **3** (about people) not receiving payment for work that they do

**unpredictable** /ˌʌnprɪˈdɪktəbl/ *adj.* if a situation, an event, a price, etc. is **unpredictable**, you cannot be sure what will happen because it changes a lot or depends on too many different things
▸ **ˌunpreˌdictaˈbility** /-ˈbɪləti/ *n.* [U] **ˌunpreˈdictably** /-bli/ *adv.*

**unproductive** /ˌʌnprəˈdʌktɪv/ *adj.* not producing very much; not producing good results: *unproductive use of resources* ◇ *an unproductive meeting*

**unprofessional** /ˌʌnprəˈfeʃənl/ *adj.* not reaching the standard expected in a particular profession: *unprofessional conduct*
▸ **ˌunproˈfessionally** /-nəli/ *adv.*

**unprofitable** /ʌnˈprɒfɪtəbl; *AmE* -ˈprɑːf-/ *adj.* **1** not making enough financial profit: *unprofitable product lines* SYN UNECONOMIC **2** not bringing any advantage
▸ **unˈprofitably** /-bli/ *adv.*

**unquoted** /ˌʌnˈkwəʊtɪd; *AmE* -ˈkwoʊ-/ = UNLISTED (1)

**unrealized**, **-ised** /ˌʌnˈriːəlaɪzd; *BrE also* -ˈrɪəl-/ *adj.* **1** not achieved or done: ~ *potential/projects* **2** (*Finan.*) (about a profit, loss, etc.) that has been made but not turned into real money yet

**unreasonable** /ʌnˈriːznəbl/ *adj.* not fair; expecting too much: *Her boss is making unreasonable demands.* ◇ *My fee is not unreasonable.*

**unrecoverable** /ˌʌnrɪˈkʌvərəbl/ *adj.* **1** (about money that has been lent or lost) that you will never be able to get back: *unrecoverable loans* **2** (*IT*) (about information on a computer) that cannot be found again: *an unrecoverable file* **3** (*IT*) (about an error in a computer program) that cannot be corrected

**unredeemed** /ˌʌnrɪˈdiːmd/ *adj.* **1** (*Finan.*) if something given as SECURITY on a loan is **unredeemed**, it can be kept by the person, etc. who made the loan because the money has not been paid back **2** (*Comm.*) not exchanged for cash or goods: *unredeemed frequent-flier miles*

**unregulated** /ˌʌnˈregjuleɪtɪd/ *adj.* not controlled by rules or laws: *a free, unregulated market*

**ˌunreported ˈincome** *n.* [U] money that sb has earned and should pay tax on but has not mentioned to the tax authorities

**unscrupulous** /ʌnˈskruːpjələs/ *adj.* without moral principles; not honest or fair: *unsrupulous lenders* ▸ **unˈscrupulously** *adv.* **unˈscrupulousness** *n.* [U]

**unsecured** /ˌʌnsɪˈkjʊəd; *AmE* -səˈkjʊrd/ *adj.* (*Finan.*; *Law*) **1** if a loan, debt, etc. is **unsecured**, nothing is given as SECURITY **2** used to describe a person, company, etc. that has lent money with no SECURITY

**unskilled** /ˌʌnˈskɪld/ *adj.* **1** (about a person) not having special skills or training: *unskilled manual workers* **2** (about a job) not needing special abilities or training

**unsocial** /ˌʌnˈsəʊʃl; *AmE* ˌʌnˈsoʊʃl/ *adj.* (*also* **unsociable** /ʌnˈsəʊʃəbl; *AmE* -ˈsoʊ-/ *less freq.*) (*both BrE*) outside the normal times of working: *to work* ***unsocial hours***

**unsold** /ˌʌnˈsəʊld; *AmE* ˌʌnˈsoʊld/ *adj.* not bought by anyone: *The store cut its prices to get rid of unsold stock.*

**unsolicited** /ˌʌnsəˈlɪsɪtɪd/ *adj.* not asked for and sometimes not wanted: *~ calls/email* ◇ *an ~ (takeover) bid/offer* ◇ *~ advice*

**unsubscribe** /ˌʌnsəbˈskraɪb/ *v.* [T,I] (*IT*) **~ (from sth)** to remove your address from an Internet MAILING LIST

★ **unsustainable** /ˌʌnsəˈsteɪnəbl/ *adj.* that cannot continue or be continued for a long time: *unsustainable levels of debt*

**ˌunsystematic ˈrisk** (*also* **ˌnonsystematic ˈrisk, speˌcific ˈrisk**) *n.* [U] (*Finan.*) risk that affects the price of a particular investment or a small number of shares, bonds, etc., for example the possible effects of a strike in a company or of a company going out of business

**untapped** /ˌʌnˈtæpt/ *adj.* available but not yet used: *~ demand/markets* ◇ *~ resources/talent*

**unveil** /ˌʌnˈveɪl/ *v.* [T] (in newspapers) to show or introduce a new plan, product, etc. to the public for the first time

**unwind** /ˌʌnˈwaɪnd/ *v.* (**-wound, -wound** /-ˈwaʊnd/) **1** [T,I] (esp. in newspapers) to undo or change sth; to change or be undone: *Several takeovers that had been agreed are now being unwound.* **2** (*Finan.*) [T] **~ a long/short position** to sell or buy shares, currencies, etc. in order to gradually end the POSITION you are in **3** [I] to stop thinking about work and start to relax SYN WIND DOWN ▸ **unˈwind** *n.* [C] **ˌunˈwinding** *n.* [U]: *the unwinding of the agreement*

**unzip** /ˌʌnˈzɪp/ *v.* [T] (**-pp-**) (*IT*) to return computer files to their original size after they have been made smaller SYN DECOMPRESS OPP ZIP

**up** /ʌp/ *adv., adj., v., n.*

• ***adv.*** to or at a higher level: *Total sales were* ***up by*** *7%.* OPP DOWN IDM **up for sth 1** on offer for sth: *The house is up for sale.* **2** being considered for sth: *She's up for re-election next year.*

• ***adj.*** (*IT*) (of a computer system) working: *Our system should be up again by this afternoon.* OPP DOWN IDM **ˌup and ˈrunning** (about a system, for example a computer system) working; being used

• ***v.*** [T] (**-pp-**) to increase the price or amount of sth: *The group upped its bid from $10 to $30 a share.* SYN RAISE → idiom at ANTE

• ***n.*** IDM **on the ˈup** increasing or improving: *Business confidence is on the up.* **on the ˌup and ˈup** (*BrE*) (*infml.*) becoming more and more successful **ˌups and ˈdowns** the mixture of good and bad things in a particular situation: *Every business has its ups and downs.*

**upbeat** /ˈʌpbiːt/ *adj.* (*infml.*) positive and enthusiastic; making you feel that the future will be good: *She's was upbeat* ***about*** *the firm's prospects.* OPP DOWNBEAT

**UPC** /ˌjuː piː ˈsiː/ *abbr* (*Comm.*) **Universal Product Code** a pattern of thick and thin lines printed on things that you buy in a shop/store, that contains information that a computer can read SYN BAR CODE

**upcoming** /'ʌpkʌmɪŋ/ *adj.* going to happen soon: *upcoming events*

★**update** /ˌʌp'deɪt/ *v.* [T] **1** to make sth more modern by adding new parts, etc: *updated software* **2** to give sb the most recent information about sth; to add the most recent information to sth: *Our records are regularly updated.* ▶ **'update** *n.* [C]: *to provide regular updates*

**upfront** /ˌʌp'frʌnt/ *adj., adv.*
• ***adj.*** (*Comm.*) paid in advance, before other payments are made: *There will be an upfront fee of 4%.*
• ***adv.*** (*usu.* **up front**) as payment in advance: *We'll pay you half the money up front.*

★**upgrade** /ˌʌp'greɪd/ *v.* **1** [T,I] **~ sth** | **~ (to sth)** to make a piece of machinery, computer system, etc. more powerful and efficient; to start to use machinery or systems of this type: *upgraded computers* **2** (*Finan.*) [T] **~ sth (to sth)** to give sth a higher grade, value or status: *The Bank has upgraded its rating on the stock* **to** *'buy'.* SYN PROMOTE **3** (*HR*) [T] **~ sb (to sth)** to give sb a more important job; to make a job more important SYN PROMOTE **4** [T,I] **~ sb (to sth)** to give sb a better seat on a plane, room in a hotel, etc. than the one they have paid for **5** [T] to improve the condition of a building, etc. in order to provide a better service ▶ **'upgrade** *n.* [C]: *installing an upgrade* ◇ *rating upgrades* **ˌup'grading** *n.* [U,C]

**upkeep** /'ʌpki:p/ *n.* [U] the cost or process of keeping sth in good condition: *the upkeep of a building* SYN MAINTENANCE

**uplift** *n., v.*
• ***n.*** /'ʌplɪft/ [C] (esp. in newspapers) the fact of sth being raised or of sth increasing: *a sales uplift of 18% over the year*
• ***v.*** /ˌʌp'lɪft/ [T] (*esp. BrE*) (*fml.*) to collect passengers, luggage or goods

★**upload** /ˌʌp'ləʊd; *AmE* -'loʊd/ *v.* [T,I] (*IT*) to move data to a larger computer system from a smaller one; to be moved in this way: *upload an image from a digital camera* OPP DOWNLOAD ▶ **upload** /'ʌpləʊd; *AmE* -loʊd/ *n.* [U,C]: *access other users' uploads*

**upmarket** /ˌʌp'mɑ:kɪt; *AmE* -'mɑ:rk-/ (*AmE also* **'upscale**) *adj.* **1** designed for or used by people who belong to a high social class; expensive and of good quality: *an ~ brand/product/store* **2** used to describe people who have more money and can afford expensive products and services: *upmarket customers* ▶ **ˌup'market** *adv.*: *The company has moved upmarket.*

**upselling** /'ʌpselɪŋ/ *n.* [U] (*Market.*) the technique of persuading customers to buy more products or a more expensive product than they originally intended ▶ **'upsell** *v.* [I]

**'upset price** = RESERVE PRICE

**upside** /'ʌpsaɪd/ *n.* **1** (*Econ.*; *Finan.*) [sing; U] the possibility that sth will increase in price or value: *The plan has high* ***upside potential*** (= opportunity for making high profits). **2** (*Finan.*) [sing; U] an increase in profits or share prices: *a 50% upside for shareholders* **3** [sing.] the more positive aspect of a situation that is generally bad

**upsize** /'ʌpsaɪz/ *v.* [T,I] **1** (*IT*) to move from a smaller computer system to a larger one: *to upsize* **to** *a larger system* **2** (*HR*) to increase the size of a company by employing more people: *28% of plants upsized.* ▶ **'upsizing** *n.* [U]

**upskill** /'ʌpskɪl/ *v.* (*HR*) **1** [T,I] to teach sb new skills; to learn new skills: *upskilling the workforce* **2** [T] to change a job so that it needs more skills to do it: *upskilled tasks/jobs* ▶ **'upskilling** *n.* [U]

**upstart** /'ʌpstɑ:t; *AmE* -stɑ:rt/ *n.* [C] a company or person that is new in a business, but may already be becoming important → START-UP

**upstream** /ˌʌp'stri:m/ *adj.* (*Econ.*; *Product.*) at or connected with an early stage in an industrial or commercial process: *~ assets/business/operations* ▶ **ˌup'stream** *adv.*

**upsurge** /'ʌpsɜ:dʒ; *AmE* -sɜ:rdʒ/ *n.* [C, usu. sing.] a sudden large increase in sth: *a big upsurge* **in** *demand for new cars*

**upswing** /'ʌpswɪŋ/ = UPTURN

**uptick** /'ʌptɪk/ (*also* **'plus tick**, *less freq.*) *n.* [C, usu. sing.] (*both AmE*) (*Finan.*; *Econ.*) a small increase in sth, esp. in the price of shares: *an uptick* **in** *manufacturing activity*

**uptime** /'ʌptaɪm/ *n.* [U] (*IT*) the period of time when a machine, esp. a computer, is working and can be used

**ˌup to 'date** *adj.* **1** having or including the most recent information: *keeping staff ~* ***on/with*** *sth* ◇ *up-to-date records* **2** modern; fashionable: *up-to-date equipment*

**ˌup to the 'minute** *adj.* **1** having or including the most recent information: *The accounts must always*

*be up to the minute.* **2** modern; fashionable: *up-to-the-minute designs*

**uptrend** /ˈʌptrend/ *n.* [sing.] (*esp. AmE*) a situation in which business activity or performance increases or improves over a period of time: *The euro is* **on** *an uptrend.*

**upturn** /ˈʌptɜːn; *AmE* -tɜːrn/ (*also* **ˈupswing**) *n.* [C, usu. sing.] a situation in which sth improves or increases over a period of time: *a sustained upturn* **in** *trade*

**ˌupwardly ˈmobile** *adj.* moving towards a higher social position, usu. in which you become richer
► **ˌupward moˈbility** *n.* [U]

**URL** /ˌjuː ɑːr ˈel/ *abbr* (*IT*) **uniform/universal resource locator** the address of a web page: *The URL is http://www.oup.com.*
SYN WEB ADDRESS

**usability** /ˌjuːzəˈbɪləti/ *n.* [U] (*Market.*) how easy sth is to use, esp. a website: *a usability consultant*

**usance** /ˈjuːzəns/ *n.* [U; C, usu. sing.] (*Finan.*) the time that is allowed for the payment of foreign BILLS OF EXCHANGE

**USB** /ˌjuː es ˈbiː/ *abbr* (*IT*) **universal serial bus** a device in a computer that allows other devices such as printers and SCANNERS to be connected to it: *The PC has 2 USB ports.*

**ˈuse-by date** *n.* [C] the date by which you must use some types of food or drink, printed on the container or package. It may not be safe to use the items after this date.

**used** /juːzd/ *adj.* that has belonged to or been used by sb else before: *a website for selling used goods* SYN PRE-OWNED (*AmE*), SECOND-HAND

**ˌuseful ˈlife** *n.* [C, usu. sing.] (*Account.*) the period of time that you can use an asset such as a machine or a vehicle before it is worth buying a new one to replace it
SYN ECONOMIC LIFE

**user** /ˈjuːzə(r)/ *n.* [C] a person or thing that uses sth: *heavy users of IT* ◇ *software for the average user*

**ˈuser fee** *n.* [C] (*AmE*) a tax on a service that is provided for the public

**ˌuser-ˈfriendly** *adj.* easy for people who are not experts to understand and use
► **ˌuser-ˈfriendliness** *n.* [U]

**username** /ˈjuːzəneɪm; *AmE* -zərn-/ *n.* [C] (*IT*) the name you use in order to be able to use a computer program or system

**USP** /ˌjuː es ˈpiː/ *abbr* (*Market.*) **unique selling proposition/point** a feature of a product or service that makes it different from all others: *Many of the best slogans are simple statements of USPs.*

★ **utility** /juːˈtɪləti/ *n.* (*pl.* **-ties**) **1** [C, usu. pl.] a service provided for the public, for example an electricity, water or gas supply: *public utilities* **2** [C] a company that provides such a service **3** (*IT*) [C] a piece of computer software that performs a particular task: *an anti-virus utility* **4** (*Econ.*) [U] the amount of benefit or satisfaction that sb gets from using a product or service: *Water has high utility but low commercial value.*

**utilization, -isation** /ˌjuːtəlaɪˈzeɪʃn; *AmE* -ləˈz/ *n.* [U] **1** (*Product.*) the relationship between the amount that a factory, etc. produces and the amount that it is designed to produce: *capacity/machine/plant ~* **2** the process of using sth, esp. for a practical purpose: *the utilization of equipment*

**ˌutmost good ˈfaith** *phr.* (*Insur.*) a basic condition of insurance in which the person wishing to be insured must provide all the necessary facts and information, even if they are not asked for them

**UW** (*also* **uw, U/W, U/w**) *abbr* (*Insur.*) a short way of writing **underwriter**

# Vv

**v** (*AmE* **v.**) *abbr* (*written*) versus

**vacancy** /ˈveɪkənsi/ *n.* [C] (*pl.* **-cies**) **1** (*HR*) a job that is available for sb to do: *We've filled the vacancy* **for** *a designer.* ◇ *a ~ arises/exists/occurs* **2** a room that is available in a hotel: *No vacancies.*

**ˈvacancy rate** *n.* [C] **1** (*Prop.*) the percentage of buildings, offices, etc. available to be sold or rented at a particular time **2** (*HR*) the percentage of jobs available to be filled

**vacant** /ˈveɪkənt/ *adj.* **1** (*HR*) if a job in a company is **vacant**, nobody is doing it and it is available for sb to take: *We had difficulty filling the vacant post.*
⊕ *a ~* ***job/position/post/situation*** ♦ *to* ***become/be left/fall/remain*** *~*
**2** empty; not being used
⊕ *a ~* ***lot/property/room/seat*** ♦ *to* ***become/be left/remain*** *~*

**vacate** /vəˈkeɪt; veɪˈk-; *AmE also* ˈveɪkeɪt/ *v.* [T] (*fml.*) **1** (*HR*) to leave a job, position of authority, etc. so that it is available for sb else **2** to leave a building, seat, room, etc., esp. so that sb else can use it

**vacation** /və'keɪʃn; veɪ'k-/ *n.* **1** [U,C] (*AmE*) a holiday or a period when people are not working: *You should **take** a vacation.* ◇ *to be **on** vacation* **2** [C] in the UK, one of the periods of time when universities or courts of law are closed; in the US, one of the periods of time when schools, colleges, universities or courts of law are closed → HOLIDAY

**vacillate** /'vasɪleɪt/ *v.* [I] if a price, a currency, etc. **vacillates**, it goes up and down frequently, but only by a small amount each time

★**valid** /'vælɪd/ *adj.* **1** legally or officially acceptable: *a valid passport* ◇ *a valid claim* **2** (*IT*) accepted by the system: *a valid password* OPP INVALID ▶ **'validly** *adv.*

**validate** /'vælɪdeɪt/ *v.* [T] **1** to check or prove that sth is accurate, true, useful or of an acceptable standard: *to validate invoices* **2** to make sth legally valid: *to ~ a contract/credit card* OPP INVALIDATE ▶ **ˌvali'dation** /-'deɪʃn/ *n.* [U,C]

**validity** /və'lɪdəti/ *n.* [U] the state of being legally or officially acceptable: *the period of validity of the agreement*

**valuable** /'væljuəbl/ *adj.* **1** worth a lot of money: *valuable assets* **2** very useful or important: *a valuable employee* OPP WORTHLESS

**valuables** /'væluəblz/ *n.* [pl.] things that are worth a lot of money, esp. small personal things such as jewellery, etc.

**valuation** /ˌvælju'eɪʃn/ *n.* [C,U] **1** (*Finan.*) a professional judgement about how much money sth is worth; the estimated value of sth: *Surveyors carried out a valuation of the property.* ◇ *A valuation of almost $1 bn was put on the company.* **2** a judgement about how useful or important sth is; the estimated importance of sth

★**value** /'vælju:/ *n., adj., v.*

• ***n.*** **1** [U,C] how much sth is worth in money or other goods for which it can be exchanged: *What is the current value of the company?* ◇ *Investments can decrease in value.*

⊙ *to **fall/increase/rise** in ~* ◆ *the **long-term/potential/present/short-term** ~ of sth* ◆ *a **high/low** ~* ◆ *to **place/put/set** a ~ on sth*

**2** [U] (*esp. BrE*) how much sth is worth compared with its price: *This service offers the best **value for money**.*

⊙ ***bad/excellent/poor** ~* ◆ *to **give/provide/represent** ~*

**3 values** [pl.] beliefs about what is right and wrong and what is important in life: *the eight **core** values on which company policy is based*

• ***adj.*** (about a product) produced and sold cheaply: *our value range of toiletries*

• ***v.*** [T] **1** to decide how much money sth is worth: *The company has been valued **at** €2 bn.* **2** to think that sb/sth is important: *valued customers/employees*

**ˌvalue 'added** *n.* [U] **1** (*Econ.*) the amount by which the value of a product increases at each stage of the production process, not including the cost of the basic materials SYN ADDED VALUE **2** (*Market.*) the extra value that a company adds to a basic product or service, for example by adding extra features, before it is sold to the consumer SYN ADDED VALUE **3** (*Market.*) the extra features that a product or service has that a customer is willing to pay more for ▶ **ˌvalue-'added** *adj.*: *~ products/services* ◇ *~ engineering/processes*

**ˌvalue-added ˌmanu'facturing** *n.* [U] the production of goods in which processes increase the value of the materials used and the price that they can be sold for: *high/low ~ industries*

**ˌvalue-added 'reseller** *n.* [C] (*abbr* **VAR**) (*Comm.*) a company that adds extra features or improvements to another company's product or service, esp. computers and software, before it is sold to the consumer

**'value aˌnalysis** *n.* [U,C] (*Product.*) a way of trying to reduce the cost of a product while keeping the same quality by examining all the things the product does for the customer and the production cost of each

**'value-based ˌpricing** = VALUE PRICING (1)

**'value chain** *n.* [C] (*Market.; Product.*) **1** the series of stages involved in the design, manufacture, marketing and support of a product, each of which adds value to it **2** a series of companies that includes the company that makes a product and those that add extra features to it before it is sold to the customer

**'valued ˌpolicy** *n.* [C] (*Insur.*) a type of insurance policy in which the value of the items insured, and the amount that will be paid if a claim is made, is agreed in advance

**ˈvalue engiˌneering** *n.* [U] (*Product.*) the process of designing a product or service so that it gives as much value as possible to customers without unnecessary costs

**ˌvalue for ˈmoney ˌaudit** *n.* [C] an official examination of the records of a business that does not aim to make a profit in order to check that it is using the money that it spends in the best way

**ˈvalue inˌvestor** *n.* [C] (*Finan.*) an investor who buys shares that they believe are being traded at less than their real value and whose price will probably soon rise

**ˈvalue judgement** *n.* [C,U] a decision about how good or important sth is, based on personal opinions rather than facts

**ˈvalue ˌpricing** *n.* [U] (*Market.*) **1** (*also* **ˈvalue-based ˌpricing**) a way of deciding the price of a product based on its value to the customer rather than on the cost of producing it **2** the practice of selling a product at a lower price, while keeping its value to the customer the same

**valuer** /ˈvæljuːə(r)/ *n.* [C] a person whose job is to estimate how much property, land, etc. is worth

**ˈvalue share** *n.* [C] (*Market.*) the share of a market that a particular product has in terms of the money it makes

**ˈvalue-stream aˌnalysis** *n.* [U,C] (*Product.*) a method of analysing which parts of the production process add to the value of the product and which parts do not

**vanilla** /vəˈnɪlə/ *adj.* (*infml.*) ordinary; not special in any way: *plain vanilla cellphones*

**vapourware** (*AmE* **vaporware**) /ˈveɪpəweə(r); *AmE* -pərwer/ *n.* [U] (*IT, infml.*) software that is being advertised but is not yet available and may never be developed and sold: *from vapourware to product*

**VAR** /ˌviː eɪ ˈɑː(r)/ = VALUE-ADDED RESELLER

★ **variable** /ˈveəriəbl; *AmE* ˈver-; ˈvær-/ *adj.*, *n.*

• ***adj.*** **1** often changing; likely to change: *variable rates of interest* **2** able to be changed: *a tool with variable speed control*

• ***n.*** [C] a situation, number or quantity that can vary or be varied and affect a situation in different ways: *Weather is one of the variables that affect the profits of clothing stores.*

**ˌvariable ˈbudget** *n.* [C] (*Account.*) an amount of money available to a company, person, etc. that can be increased or decreased as necessary

**ˌvariable ˈcost** *n.* [C] (*Account.*) an amount of money used to produce goods that varies according to the quantity made: *Fuel consumption is a variable cost.*

**ˌvariable ˈcosting** (*also* **diˌrect ˈcosting**) *n.* [U] (*Account.*) a method of calculating the cost of a unit of a product that includes only costs that often change, such as the cost of materials and workers SYN MARGINAL COSTING

**ˌvariable ˈpay** = PERFORMANCE-RELATED PAY

**variance** /ˈveəriəns; *AmE* ˈver-; ˈvær-/ *n.* [U,C] **1** (*fml.*) the amount by which sth changes or is different from sth else: *testing for any variance **in** quality* **2** (*Account.*) the difference between the levels of costs or income that have been planned for an activity and the actual costs or income: *adverse/favourable/positive/unfavourable variance*

★ **variation** /ˌveəriˈeɪʃn; *AmE* ˌver-/ *n.* [C,U] a change, esp. in the amount or level of sth; a difference: *wide variations **in** interest rates* ◇ *The new drinks are a variation **on** their best-selling products.*

⊙ ***considerable/marked/significant/substantial*** *~(s)* ◆ ***minor/slight/small/subtle*** *~(s)* ◆ ***regional/seasonal/year-to-year*** *~(s)*

**varied** /ˈveərid; *AmE* ˈverid; ˈvær-/ *adj.* **1** of many different types: *stores with varied merchandise* **2** not staying the same, but changing often: *She's had a varied career.*

**variety** /vəˈraɪəti/ *n.* (*pl.* **-ties**) **1** [C] a type of a thing, for example a plant or product, that is different from the others in the same general group: *They sell seven varieties **of** apple/apples.* **2** [C, usu. sing.] several different sorts of the same thing: *He resigned for a variety of reasons.* **3** [U] the quality of not being the same or not doing the same thing all the time: *I like variety **in** my work.*

**vaˈriety store** *n.* [C] (*AmE old-fash.*) a shop/store that sells a wide range of goods at low prices

**vary** /ˈveəri; *AmE* ˈveri; ˈværi/ *v.* (**varying**, **varied**, **varied**) **1** [I] (about a group of similar things) to be different from each other in size, shape, etc: *Laptops vary considerably in size and weight.* **2** [I] to change or be different according to the situation: *Marketing methods vary **with** market size.* **3** [T] to make changes to sth to make it slightly different: *I can vary the hours I work.*

★ **VAT** /ˌviː eɪ ˈtiː; væt/ *n.* [U] **value added tax** a tax that is added to the price of many goods and services: *Prices include VAT.*

**VATman** /ˈvætmæn/ *n.* (*pl.* **-men** /-men; -mən/) (*infml.*) **1 the VATman** [sing.] (*BrE*) a way of referring to the government department responsible for collecting VAT **2** [C] a person whose job is to check that a company has paid VAT

**vault** /vɔːlt/ *n.* [C] a room with thick walls and a strong door, esp. in a bank, used for keeping valuable things safe

**ˈvault cash** *n.* [U] (*AmE*) (*Finan.*) the paper money and coins kept at a bank at a particular time

**VDT** /ˌviː diː ˈtiː/ *abbr* (*esp. AmE*) (*IT*) **video/visual display terminal** a computer MONITOR

**VDU** /ˌviː diː ˈjuː/ *abbr* (*esp. BrE*) (*IT*) **video/visual display unit** a computer MONITOR: *a VDU screen*

**vehicle** /ˈviːəkl; *AmE also* ˈviːhɪkl/ *n.* [C] **1** a car, bus, lorry/truck, etc: *a fleet of vehicles*
⊕ *a* ***commercial/delivery/(heavy) goods*** *~* ◆ *~* ***makers/manufacturers/producers*** ◆ *to* ***hire/lease*** *a ~*
**2** sth used as a way of achieving sth or to express your ideas or feelings : *The intranet provides a vehicle* ***for*** *teams to share information.*

**veˌlocity of circuˈlation** *n.* [sing.] (*Econ.*) the average number of times that a unit of money is passed from person to person in an economy in a particular period

**vendee** /ˌvenˈdiː/ *n.* [C] (*Law*) a person who is buying a house or other property

**vender** = VENDOR

**vending** /ˈvendɪŋ/ *n.* [U] (*Comm.*) the activity of selling small items, esp. food or drink, from a STALL or a machine

**ˈvending maˌchine** *n.* [C] a machine from which you can buy cigarettes, drinks, etc. by putting coins into it

★ **vendor** (*AmE also* **vender**) /ˈvendə(r)/ *n.* [C] (*fml.*) **1** (*Comm.*) a company or person that sells sth: *a software vendor* ◇ *street vendors* **2** (*Product.*) a company that supplies raw materials or pieces of equipment to companies that make goods SYN SUPPLIER **3** (*Law*) a person who is selling a house or other property

**ˈvendor ˌrating** (*abbr* **VR**) (*also* **supˈplier ˌrating** *abbr* **SR**) *n.* [U,C] (*Product.*) a system of recording and ranking how well a supplier does what they agree to do, the quality of the goods they supply, etc.; the score that they receive: *We were keen to get the highest vendor rating possible.*

★ **venture** /ˈventʃə(r)/ *n.*, *v.*
• *n.* [C] a business project or activity, esp. one that involves taking risks SYN ENTERPRISE
⊕ *a* ***business/commercial/corporate****/an* ***Internet*** *~* ◆ *to* ***create/form/set up/start*** *a ~* ◆ *to* ***invest in/finance/fund*** *a ~*
• *v.* **1** [I] to go somewhere or become involved in sth even though it may be a risk to do so: *They are about to venture* ***into*** *the hotel business.* **2** [T] to risk losing sth valuable or important if you are not successful at sth: *He ventured his financial security on the deal.*

**ˈventure ˌcapital** (*also* **ˈrisk ˌcapital**) *n.* [U] (*Finan.*) money invested in a new company to help it develop or expand, which may involve a lot of risk but can bring good profits
⊕ *to* ***attract/look for/raise*** *~* ◆ *~* ***backing/funding*** ◆ *a ~* ***firm/group/investor***

**ˈventure ˌcapitalist** *n.* [C] (*Finan.*) a private investor or a financial business that invests money in new companies, which may involve a lot of risk and bring good profits

**venue** /ˈvenjuː/ *n.* [C] a place where people meet for an organized event: *The hotel is a popular venue for conferences.*

**VER** /ˌviː iː ˈɑː(r)/ = VOLUNTARY EXPORT RESTRAINT

**verbal** /ˈvɜːbl; *AmE* ˈvɜːrbl/ *adj.* **1** spoken, not written: *a verbal agreement* **2** relating to words: *good verbal skills* ► **ˈverbally** *adv.*

**verdict** /ˈvɜːdɪkt; *AmE* ˈvɜːrd-/ *n.* [C] **1** a decision that you make or an opinion that you give about sth, after you have tested it or considered it carefully: *to deliver/give/issue your ~ (on sth)* **2** (*Law*) a decision made by a judge, a JURY, etc. in a court, stating if sb is considered guilty of a crime or of doing sth wrong or not: *to reach/record/return a ~*

**ˌverification of ˈassets** *n.* [U] (*Account.*) the process of checking what buildings, machinery, investments, etc. a company has and calculating their value

★ **version** /ˈvɜːʃn; -ʒn; *AmE* ˈvɜːrʒn/ *n.* [C] a form of sth that is slightly different from or newer than the original thing: *the latest version of the* *software* ▶ **'version** *v.* [T]: *The games are versioned for the local market.*

**versus** /'vɜːsəs; *AmE* 'vɜːrsəs/ *prep.* (*abbr* **v**, **vs**) **1** used to compare two different ideas, choices, etc: *It's time versus money.* **2** (*Law*) used to show that two sides are against each other in a legal case: *the State versus Ford*

**vertical** /'vɜːtɪkl; *AmE* 'vɜːrt-/ *adj.* **1** having a structure in which there are top, middle and bottom levels: *a vertical flow of communication* **2** (about a line, etc.) going straight up or down: *the vertical axis of the graph* → HORIZONTAL

**ˌvertical disinteˈgration** *n.* [U] (*Econ.*) a situation where a company stops producing some goods or parts itself and starts to buy them from an outside supplier

**ˌvertical 'equity** *n.* [U] (*Econ.*) the principle that people with different characteristics should be treated in different ways, for example that the rate of tax people pay should vary according to their income

**ˌvertical inteˈgration** (*also* **ˌvertical exˈpansion**) *n.* [U] (*also* **ˌvertical 'merger** [C]) (*Econ.*) a situation where a company buys one of the companies which supplies it with goods or which buys goods from it

**ˌvertical 'loading** *n.* [U] (*HR*) the fact of giving sb more responsibility in their job, more power to make decisions, etc.

**ˌvertical 'merger** = VERTICAL INTEGRATION

**ˌvertical segreˈgation** *n.* [U] (*HR*) used to describe a situation where some types of people, for example women, have less chance of getting jobs at a high level in a company, an industry, etc.

**vessel** /'vesl/ *n.* [C] a large ship or boat: *a cargo/commercial ~*

**vest** /vest/ *v.* (*Finan.*) **1** [T,I] (about shares in a company, esp. ones given to employees) to come to the end of an agreed period after which their owner has the right to sell them: *The CEO's share option will vest/become vested after four years.* **2** [I] to agree to keep your shares in a company for at least a particular period of time: *Even the directors had to vest as a guarantee to investors.* **PHR V** **'vest in sb/sth** (*Law*) to be controlled by sb/sth legally: *The property shall vest in the trustee.* **'vest sth in sb/sth; 'vest sb with sth** (*Law*) (*usu. pass.*) **1** to give sb the legal right or power to do sth: *Overall authority is vested in the Supreme Council.* **2** to make sb the legal owner of land or property

**vested** /'vestɪd/ *adj.* (*AmE*) (*Law*) (about an employee) having the right to receive a particular amount of benefits after working for a fixed number of years: *I haven't worked here long enough to be fully vested.*

**ˌvested 'interest** *n.* [C] **1** a personal reason for wanting sth to happen, esp. because you get some financial advantage from it: *The bank has a vested interest* **in** *seeing your business succeed.* **2** a group of people who have a personal reason of this kind for wanting sth to happen: *the vested interests that have the power*

**vesting** /'vestɪŋ/ *n.* [U] (*AmE*) (*Law*) the process of an employee getting the right to receive full pension or other benefits

**vet** /vet/ *v.* [T] (**-tt-**) **1** (*HR*) (*esp. BrE*) to find out about a person's past life and career in order to decide if they are suitable for a particular job: *All candidates are carefully vetted.* **2** to examine sth carefully to make sure it is correct, suitable, legal, etc: *The document was vetted and approved.* SYN SCREEN ▶ **'vetting** *n.* [U]

**veto** /'viːtəʊ; *AmE* -toʊ/ *n.*, *v.*
• *n.* (*pl.* **-toes**) **1** [C,U] the right to refuse to allow sth to be done, esp. the right to stop a law from being passed or a decision from being taken: *They have a final veto* **on/over** *business decisions.* ◇ *She used her veto to block the proposal.* ◇ *to have the power/right of ~* **2** [C] an occasion when sb refuses to allow sth to be done: *a veto* **on** *employing new staff*
• *v.* [T] (**-toes**, **-toing**, **-toed**, **-toed**) **1** to stop sth from happening or being done by using your **veto**: *The takeover was vetoed by the EC.* **2** to refuse to accept or do sth

**viable** /'vaɪəbl/ *adj.* that can be done, used, achieved, etc.; likely to be successful: *They could not get a large enough share of the market to make the business viable.*
**o** *a ~* ***alternative/option/solution*** • ***commercially/economically/ financially*** *~*
▶ **ˌvia'bility** /-'bɪləti/ *n.* [U]

**viˌcarious liaˈbility** *n.* [U] (*Law*) the fact of sb having legal responsibility for the actions of sb else, for example a company being responsible for the actions of its employees

**vice-** /vaɪs/ *comb. form* (*in ns and related adjs*) next in rank to sb and able to represent them or act for them: *the vice-director of the group*

**ˌvice-ˈpresident** *n.* [C] (*esp. AmE*) (*abbr* **VP**) a person in charge of a particular part of a company: *vice-president of marketing*

**videoconferencing** /ˌvɪdiəʊˈkɒnfərənsɪŋ; *AmE* ˌvɪdioʊˈkɑːn-/ *n.* [U] a system that enables people in different places to have a meeting by watching and listening to each other using computers, video cameras, etc: *to use videoconferencing*
▸ **ˈvideoconference** *n.* [C,U]: *to talk **via** videoconference*

**videophone** /ˈvɪdiəʊfəʊn; *AmE* -oʊfoʊn/ *n.* [C] a type of telephone with a screen that allows you to see the person you are talking to

**viewer** /ˈvjuːə(r)/ *n.* [C] **1** a person watching television: *to attract/bring in/draw/lure ~s* **2** a device or computer program that allows you to look at pictures: *a graphics viewer*

**viewership** /ˈvjuːəʃɪp; *AmE* ˈvjuːər-/ *n.* [U] the number of people who watch a particular programme or channel on television

**violate** /ˈvaɪəleɪt/ *v.* [T] **1** to go against or refuse to obey a law, an agreement, etc: *violating the company's rules* **2** to disturb or not respect sb's PRIVACY, etc.
▸ **ˌvioˈlation** /-ˈleɪʃn/ *n.* [U,C]: *You're **in violation of** the agreement.*

**ˈviral ˌmarketing** (*also* **reˈferral ˌmarketing**) *n.* [U] (*Market.*) a way of advertising and selling in which information about a company's products or services is spread by people telling other people or sending on emails SYN BUZZ MARKETING

★ **virtual** /ˈvɜːtʃuəl; *AmE* ˈvɜːrtʃ-/ *adj.* **1** almost or very nearly the thing described, so that any slight difference is not important: *The company has a virtual monopoly in this area.* **2** (*IT*) existing only on computer; using computers as the means of communication: *the success of the virtual bookstore* OPP PHYSICAL

**ˌvirtual ˈmemory** (*also* **ˌvirtual ˈstorage**) *n.* [U] (*IT*) a way of providing extra memory for a computer by moving data between the computer's memory and a disk

**ˌvirtual ˈoffice** *n.* [C] (*HR*) a place for work that is not a physical building but consists of people working in different places, such as their homes, using computer equipment, telephones and other technology

**ˌvirtual organiˈzation** *n.* [C] a group of companies, employees, suppliers, etc. that work together using computer equipment, telephones and other technology in order to provide a service or product

**ˌvirtual reˈality** *n.* [U,C] (*abbr* **VR**) (*IT*) images with sound of places, objects, etc., created by a computer, that appear to surround the person looking at them and seem almost real

**ˌvirtual ˈstorage** = VIRTUAL MEMORY

**virus** /ˈvaɪrəs/ *n.* [C] (*IT*) instructions that are hidden inside a computer program and are designed to cause faults or destroy data: *anti-virus (detection) software*
⊙ *a ~ **alert/attack*** ◆ *to **detect/import/spot/spread** a ~*

**visibility** /ˌvɪzəˈbɪləti/ *n.* [U] **1** how easily sth/sb is seen or noticed by the public: *The ads increased the company's visibility in the marketplace.* **2** (*Account.*) the fact that it is possible to see the activities and the financial state of a company from its accounts

**ˌvisible ˈbalance** = BALANCE OF TRADE

**visibles** /ˈvɪzəblz/ *n.* [pl.] (*Econ.*) imports and exports that are goods not services → INVISIBLES

**ˌvisible ˈtrade** *n.* [U] (*Econ.*) goods, not services, that are sold to or bought from other countries

**vision** /ˈvɪʒn/ *n.* **1** [C] an idea of how the future will be: *a common/corporate/shared/strategic ~* **2** [U] the ability to think about or plan the future with great imagination and intelligence: *lack of vision*

**visioning** /ˈvɪʒənɪŋ/ *n.* [U] the process of senior managers or directors thinking about and planning what they would like the future of their organization to be

**ˈvision ˌstatement** *n.* [C] an official statement of how an organization would like to be in the future

**ˌvisual ˈaid** *n.* [C, usu. pl.] a picture, video, etc. used in teaching or giving talks

**vocation** /vəʊˈkeɪʃn; *AmE* voʊ-/ *n.* [C] a type of work or way of life that you believe is esp. suitable for you: *He has a vocation **for** teaching.*

**vocational** /vəʊˈkeɪʃənl; *AmE* voʊ-/ *adj.* connected with the skills, knowledge, etc. that you need to have in order to do a particular job: *~ courses/qualifications/training*

**voicemail** (*also* **voice mail**) /ˈvɔɪsmeɪl/ *n.* **1** [U] an electronic system for storing telephone messages: *We have voicemail after business hours.* **2** [C,U] a message stored on this system: *I left a voice mail.*

**ˈvoice-ˌover** *n.* [C] (*Market.*) information or comments in a television advertisement, etc. that are given by a person who is not seen on the screen: *doing voice-overs for TV ads*

**ˈvoice recogˌnition** (*also* **ˈspeech recogˌnition**) *n.* [U] (*IT*) a system that allows you to give a computer spoken instructions

**void** /vɔɪd/ *adj.*, *v.* (*Law*)
• ***adj.*** (about a contract, an agreement, etc.) not valid or legal: *The agreement was declared void.*
• ***v.*** [T] to state officially that sth is no longer valid: *to void a contract* SYN NULLIFY ▶ **ˈvoidable** /-əbl/ *adj.*: *a voidable contract*

**vol.** *abbr* (*written*) volume

**volatile** /ˈvɒlətaɪl; *AmE* ˈvɑːlətl/ *adj.* **1** likely to change suddenly in value, state, etc: *Food prices are* ***highly*** *volatile* (= they rise or fall very suddenly). **2** (*Tech.*) (about a substance) that changes quickly into a gas: *Petrol is a volatile substance.* ▶ **ˌvolaˈtility** /-ˈtɪləti/ *n.* [U]

★**volume** /ˈvɒljuːm; *AmE* ˈvɑːl-; -jəm/ *n.* [U,C] **1** the amount of space that an object or a substance fills; the amount of space in a container: *Liquid fuels are sold* ***by*** *volume.* ◇ *The barrel has a volume of ten cubic metres.* **2** the amount of sth: *The volume of trade decreased last year.* ◇ *Sales have doubled* ***in*** *volume.* ◇ *a high/low/large/substantial ~ (of sth)* **3** (*Stock Ex.*) the total number of shares bought and sold on a stock exchange on a particular day: *(a) brisk/heavy/light/low/strong ~ (of sth)* IDM **in ˈvolume** in large quantities: *bikes that sell in volume*

**ˈvolume ˌbusiness** *n.* [U] (*Comm.*) trade in very large quantities of goods: *discounts for volume business*

**ˈvolume ˌdiscount** *n.* [C,U] (*Comm.*) a reduction in the price of goods offered to sb who buys a large amount SYN BULK DISCOUNT

**voluntary** /ˈvɒləntri; *AmE* ˈvɑːlənteri/ *adj.* **1** done willingly, not because you are forced: *Redundancy should be* ***on a voluntary basis.*** OPP COMPULSORY, INVOLUNTARY
**2** (about work) done by people who choose to do it without being paid
**3** (about a person or an organization) doing a job without wanting to be paid for it: ***the voluntary sector*** (= organizations which help people and which do not make a profit)

**ˌvoluntary arˈrangement** *n.* [C] (*BrE*) (*Law*) a legal arrangement made between a failing company and the people it owes money to, to pay its debts and solve its financial problems without stopping business

**ˌvoluntary ˈbankruptcy** *n.* [U,C] (*Law*) a situation in which a person or company asks to be officially declared BANKRUPT

**ˌvoluntary ˈexport reˌstraint** (*abbr* **VER**) (*also* **ˌvoluntary reˈstraint aˌgreement**) *n.* [C] (*Econ.*) an agreement between two or more countries that limits the number of exports of particular goods that the exporting country can make to the importing country/countries

**ˌvoluntary liquiˈdation** (*also* **ˌvoluntary ˌwinding ˈup**) *n.* [U,C] (*Law*) a situation where a company's owners decide that it should stop doing business, sell its assets and pay its debts

**ˌvoluntary reˈstraint aˌgreement** = VOLUNTARY EXPORT RESTRAINT

**ˌvoluntary ˌwinding ˈup** = VOLUNTARY LIQUIDATION

★**vote** /vəʊt; *AmE* voʊt/ *n.*, *v.*
• ***n.*** **1** [C] a formal choice that you make in an election or at a meeting in order to choose sb or decide sth: *72% of the votes* ***cast*** *were in favour of a strike.* **2** [C] an occasion when a group of people vote on sth: *Let's* ***take*** *a vote* ***on*** *the issue.* **3** [C] the right to vote: *Only individual policyholders have a vote.* **4** [sing.] the total number of votes in an election: *She obtained 40% of the vote.*
• ***v.*** **1** [T,I] to show formally by marking a paper, raising your hand, or using a special machine, etc. which person you want to win an election, or which plan or idea you support: *Did you vote* ***for*** *or* ***against*** *her?* **2** [T] (*usu. pass.*) to choose sb for a position or an award by voting: *She was voted designer of the year.* **3** [T] to agree to give sb/yourself sth by voting: *The directors have just voted themselves a pay rise.* PHRV **ˌvote sb/sth ˈdown** to reject or defeat sb/sth by voting for sb/sth else **ˌvote sb ˈin**; **ˌvote sb ˈinto/ˈonto sth** to choose sb for a position or as a member of sth by voting: *She was voted onto the board of governors.* **ˌvote sb ˈout**; **ˌvote sb ˈout of/ˈoff sth** to dismiss sb from a position by voting: *He was voted out of office.* **ˌvote sth ˈthrough** to approve of sth by voting

**ˌvote of ˈconfidence** *n.* [C, usu. sing.] **1** an act that shows that people trust sb/sth: *Financial markets have* ***given*** *the new currency a vote of confidence* (= its value on the markets has risen). **2** a formal vote to show whether people support a leader, a political party, an idea, etc.

**ˌvote of no ˈconfidence** *n.* [C, usu. sing.] **1** an act that shows that people do not trust sb/sth **2** a formal vote to show that people do not support a leader, a political party, an idea, etc.

**ˈvoting rights** *n.* [pl.] (*Finan.*) the right of shareholders to vote at company meetings: *to **exercise** your voting rights*

**ˈvoting shares** *n.* [pl.] (*BrE*) (*AmE* **ˈvoting stock** [U]) (*Finan.*) shares that give the people who hold them the right to vote at company meetings

**voucher** /ˈvaʊtʃə(r)/ *n.* [C] **1** (*BrE*) a printed piece of paper that can be used instead of money to pay for sth, or that allows you to pay less than the usual price of sth: *vouchers for free flights* **2** (*Account.*) a document that shows that money has been paid for sth, or that explains why an amount has been recorded in a financial account: *payment/sales ~s*

**vouching** /ˈvaʊtʃɪŋ/ *n.* [U] (*Account.*) the responsibility of an AUDITOR or an accountant to examine and approve all documents such as VOUCHERS and INVOICES when checking financial records

**ˈvoyage ˌcharter** *n.* [C,U] (*Transpt.*) the hire of a ship or space on a ship for one or more journeys rather than for a fixed period of time

**VP** /ˌviː ˈpiː/ = VICE-PRESIDENT

**VR** /ˌviː ˈɑː(r)/ = VENDOR RATING, VIRTUAL REALITY

**VRA** /ˌviː ɑː(r) ˈeɪ/ = VOLUNTARY RESTRAINT AGREEMENT

**vs** *abbr* a short way of writing **versus**

# Ww

★ **wage** /weɪdʒ/ *n.* [sing.] (*also* **wages** [pl.]) a regular amount of money that you earn, usu. every week, for work or services: *wages of €500 a week ◇ You will receive a basic weekly wage of €500 plus bonuses. ◇ a wage claim for a 9% rise*

⊕ *an **average**/a **high/low** ~ • **hourly/regular** ~s • to **earn/pay** a ~ • to **increase/raise** ~s • ~s **increase/rise** • ~ **bargaining/negotiations** • a ~ **agreement/rise** • a ~ **cut/freeze***

**ˈwage bill** (*also* **ˈwages bill**, *less freq.*) *n.* [C] the total amount of money that an organization or an industry pays to its employees

**waged** /weɪdʒd/ *adj.* **1** (about a person) having regular paid work: *waged workers* **2** (about work) that you are paid for: *waged employment* **3 the waged** *n.* [pl.] people who have regular paid work

**ˈwage diffeˌrential** *n.* [C] (*Econ.*) the difference in rates of pay between different groups of workers, esp. the difference between workers with similar jobs in different industries, or between workers with different skills in the same industry

**ˈwage drift** *n.* [U] (*Econ.*) the situation when the average level of wages earned rises faster than the rates of pay that have been agreed at a national level: *Wage drift consists of such things as overtime, bonuses, etc.*

**ˈwage ˌearner** *n.* [C] a person who earns money, esp. a person who works for **wages**: *a high/low/top ~*

**ˈwage gap** *n.* [C] the difference in rates of pay between one group of people and another: *the male-female wage gap ◇ the ~ narrows/widens*

**ˈwage inˌflation** *n.* [U] (*Econ.*) a general rise in the rates of pay in a particular industry, country, etc.

**ˈwage ˌpacket** = PAY PACKET

**ˌwage-ˈprice ˌspiral** *n.* [sing.] (*Econ.*) the idea that a general rise in prices causes levels of pay to rise, which then causes prices to rise again, and so on

**ˌwage-ˈpush inˌflation** *n.* [U] (*Econ.*) a rise in prices caused by a general rise in levels of pay that makes goods cost more to produce

**ˈwage reˌstraint** (*also* **ˈpay reˌstraint**) *n.* [U,C] (*esp. BrE*) (*Econ.*) the process of controlling the amount by which pay can rise: *dealing with high inflation through wage restraint*

**ˈwages bill** = WAGE BILL

**ˈwage scale** *n.* [C] (*HR*) **1** the range of levels of wages that a person can receive in a particular job **2** the range of levels of wages that people receive in different jobs: *people at the bottom end of the wage scale*

**ˈwages clerk** *n.* [C] a person whose job is to calculate and arrange payment for a company's employees

**ˈwage slave** *n.* [C] (*infml.*) a person who depends completely on the money they receive each week from their job, esp. sb who has a boring or hard job

**ˌwait-and-ˈsee** *adj.* used to describe a situation where you wait to see what happens before making a decision: *We're taking a wait-and-see attitude to m-commerce.*

**waive** /weɪv/ *v.* [T] to choose not to demand sth in a particular case, even though you have a legal or official right to do so: *to ~ your claim/fee/right*

**waiver** /ˈweɪvə(r)/ *n.* [C] (*Law*) a situation in which sb gives up a legal right or claim; an official document stating this: *A waiver of the licence fee may be made for educational events.*

**ˈwake-up call** *n.* [C] **1** the service that hotels provide of telephoning guests to wake them up at the time they ask **2** a sudden warning that you need to take action: *The shocking figures were a wake-up call to the sales team.*

**walk** /wɔːk/ *v., n.*
• *v.* IDM **walk off the ˈjob** (*AmE*) to stop working and go on strike **walk the ˈplank** (*infml.*) to be forced to leave your job **ˌwalk the/your ˈtalk** (*infml.*) to start to do the things that you talk about: *Managers are walking the talk about encouraging new ideas.* **ˌwalk the ˈwalk** (*infml.*) to do sth rather than just talk about ideas and plans for doing it: *Don't talk the talk unless you can walk the walk.* → idiom at SHELF PHR V **ˌwalk ˈout** (*HR, infml.*) to stop working and go on strike **ˌwalk ˈout (of sth)** to leave a meeting, etc. suddenly, esp. to show your disapproval **ˌwalk ˈout (on sth)** to stop doing sth that you have agreed to do, before it is completed: *I never walk out on a job half done.*
• *n.* IDM **a walk of ˈlife** a person's job or position in society: *She has friends from all walks of life.*

**ˈwalking ˌpapers** *n.* [pl.] (*AmE*) (*HR, infml.*) the letter or notice dismissing sb from a job: *She's just been given her walking papers.*

**walkout** /ˈwɔːkaʊt/ *n.* [C] **1** a sudden strike by workers: *to call/call off/hold/stage/threaten a ~* **2** the act of suddenly leaving a meeting as a protest: *a walkout by angry delegates*

**wall** /wɔːl/ *n.* IDM **go to the ˈwall** if a company **goes to the wall**, it fails because of lack of money → idiom at HIT *v.*

**wallchart** /ˈwɔːltʃɑːt; *AmE* -tʃɑːrt/ *n.* [C] a large piece of paper containing information that is put up on a wall, for example in an office, so that people can look at it

**ˈWall Street** *n.* [U] **1** (*without* **a** *or* **the**) the financial centre and stock exchange in New York City; the business that is carried out there: *Share prices fell on Wall Street today.* ◇ *Wall Street responded quickly to the news.* **2** used to refer to large companies in the US as a group: *Foreign investors are pulling out of Wall Street.*

**WAN** /wæn/ *abbr* (*IT*) **wide area network** a number of computers and other devices that are far apart but are connected together so that equipment and information can be shared → LAN

**want** /wɒnt; *AmE* wɑːnt; wɔːnt/ *n.* [C, usu. pl.] sth that you need or want: *satisfying customers' wants*

**ˈwant ad** = SMALL AD

**WAP** /wæp/ *abbr* (*IT*) **wireless application protocol** a standard system for sending information between HAND-HELD pieces of equipment and other electronic sources of information without using wires. It enables people, for example, to use a mobile phone/cellphone to look at the Internet: *~ phones/technology*

**war** /wɔː(r)/ *n.* [C,U] a situation in which there is aggressive competition between groups, companies, countries, etc. over a period of time ❶ *a* ***bidding/price/sales ~*** ♦ ***to lose/wage/win*** *a ~*

**ˈwar chest** *n.* [C] (used in newspapers) an amount of money that a company or a government has available to spend on a particular plan, project, etc.

**ware** /weə(r); *AmE* wer/ *n.* **1** [U; pl.] (*in compounds*) objects used for the purpose or in the room mentioned: *a retailer of home wares* **2** [U; pl.] (*in compounds*) objects made of the material or in the way or place mentioned: *ceramic ware* **3 wares** [pl.] things that sb is selling: *selling your wares over the Internet*

★ **warehouse** /ˈweəhaʊs; *AmE* ˈwer-/ *n.* [C] a building where large quantities of goods are stored, esp. before they are sent to shops/stores to be sold ▸ **ˈwarehouse** *v.* [T]: *to warehouse surplus stock* **ˈwarehousing** /-haʊzɪŋ/ *n.* [U]: *~ costs/systems*

**ˈwarehouse club** *n.* [C] (*AmE*) an organization that operates from a large store, usu. outside a town, and sells goods cheaply in large amounts to customers who must pay to be members: *shopping at a discount warehouse club* → CASH AND CARRY

**warehouseman** /ˈweəhaʊsmən; *AmE* ˈwer-/ (*pl.* **-men** /-mən/) (*also* **ˈwarehouse ˌkeeper**) *n.* [C] a person who works in, manages or owns a **warehouse**

**ˌwarehouse reˈceipt** (*also* **ˌwarehouse ˈwarrant**, *less freq.*) *n.* [C] (*Trade*) a document that proves that goods exist and shows where they are stored and who owns them. In financial markets it is often given to sb who buys goods instead of actually delivering the goods to them.

**'warehouse store** *n.* [C] a large simple store that sells a limited variety of food and other items for the home very cheaply

**ˌwarehouse 'warrant** = WAREHOUSE RECEIPT

**warning** /'wɔːnɪŋ; *AmE* 'wɔːrn-/ *n.* **1** [C,U] a statement, an event, etc. telling sb that sth bad or unpleasant is possible or might happen: *They ignored warnings of increasing costs.*
⊙ *a **blunt/clear/dire/grim/stark** ~* ◆ *to give sb **adequate/advance** ~*
**2** [C] a statement telling sb that they will be punished if they continue to behave in a particular way: *Employees must receive two written warnings before being dismissed.*
⊙ *a **final/formal**/an **official** ~* ◆ *an **oral**/a **verbal** ~*
▸ **'warning** *adj.*: ***warning signs***

**warrant** /'wɒrənt; *AmE* 'wɔːr-; 'wɑːr-/ *n., v.*
• ***n.*** [C] **1** (*Finan.*) a type of investment that gives you the right to buy shares at a fixed price on or by a particular date: *the issue of warrants for equity shares* **2** (*Law*) a legal document signed by a judge that gives the police authority to do sth: *an arrest warrant* ◇ *to get/issue a ~*
• ***v.*** [T] (*Comm.*; *Law, fml.*) (*usu. pass.*) to promise that a statement is true, or that sth is genuine or in good condition: *The goods were warranted to be in perfect condition.*

**warrantee** /ˌwɒrən'tiː; *AmE* 'wɔːr-; 'wɑːr-/ *n.* [C] (*Comm.*; *Law*) a person that a WARRANTY is given to

**warrantor** /'wɒrəntɔː(r); *AmE* 'wɔːr-; 'wɑːr-/ *n.* [C] (*Comm.*; *Law*) a person or company that provides a WARRANTY

★ **warranty** /'wɒrənti; *AmE* 'wɔːr-; 'wɑːr-/ (*pl.* **-ties**) *n.* [C,U] (*Comm.*; *Law*) a written agreement in which a company selling sth promises to repair or replace it if there is a problem within a particular period of time: *The TV comes with a full two-year warranty.* ◇ *Is the car still **under warranty**?* SYN GUARANTEE

**wastage** /'weɪstɪdʒ/ *n.* [U] **1** the fact of losing or destroying sth, esp. because it has been used or dealt with carelessly; the amount of sth that is wasted: *a new production method aimed at minimizing wastage* **2** (*HR*) (*BrE*) = NATURAL WASTAGE

★ **waste** /weɪst/ *v., n., adj.*
• ***v.*** [T] **1** to use more of sth than is necessary or useful: *We don't want to waste money **on** equipment that we won't use much.* **2** (*usu. pass.*) to not make good or full use of sb/sth: *His talents are wasted in that job.*
• ***n.*** **1** [U; sing.] the act of using sth in a careless or unnecessary way, so that it is lost or destroyed: *the department's waste of resources* **2** [sing.] a situation in which it is not worth spending time, money, etc. on sth: *These meetings are a **waste of time**.* **3** [U] (*also* **wastes** [pl.]) materials that are no longer needed and are thrown away: *household/industrial/toxic ~*
• ***adj.*** no longer needed for a particular process and therefore thrown away: *waste water*

**wasteful** /'weɪstfl/ *adj.* using more of sth such as money or resources than is necessary; not saving or keeping sth that could be used: *The process is wasteful and inefficient.*

**ˌwaste 'product** *n.* [C] (*Manufact.*) a useless material or substance that is produced while sth else is being made: *to break down/dispose of/recycle ~s*

**ˌwasting 'asset** *n.* [C] (*Account.*) a thing of value that a company owns that will only last or be useful for a fixed period of time, for example, a lease or a piece of equipment

**watchdog** /'wɒtʃdɒg; *AmE* 'wɑːtʃdɔːg; 'wɔːtʃ-/ *n.* [C] a person or group of people whose job is to check that companies are not doing anything illegal and to protect people's rights
⊙ *a **competition/financial**/an **industry**/a **pollution/safety** ~* ◆ *a **government**/an **independent/official** ~*

**ˌwatching 'brief** *n.* [C] the task of watching and reporting on the progress of sth on behalf of sb else: *The Network Manager has a watching brief **on** security issues.*

**'watch list** *n.* [C] **1** (*Finan.*) a list of investments that are being studied very carefully because people think sth unusual or interesting will happen to them: *a watch list of 50 companies that may do well this year* **2** a list of people, organizations, etc. that are being studied carefully because people think that they are doing sth dishonest or illegal

**'water ˌcooler** *n.* [C] **1** a machine, for example in an office, that cools water and supplies it for drinking **2** (*infml.*) (*esp. AmE*) (*used as an adj.*) used to describe any informal conversation among office workers of the type that takes place around the **water cooler**: *water-cooler chats/ gossip*

**watershed** /ˈwɔːtəʃed; *AmE* ˈwɔːtərʃed; ˈwɑːt-/ *n.* **1** [C] an event or a period of time that marks an important change **2** [sing.] in the UK, the time before which programmes not considered suitable for children must not be shown on television

**WATS** /wɒts; *AmE* wɔːts/ *abbr* (*AmE*) (*IT*) **Wide Area Telecommunications Service** a service that allows companies to make and receive large numbers of phone calls to and from places that are far away at a low cost

**wave** /weɪv/ *n.* [C] **1** a sudden increase in a particular activity or feeling: *a wave of investment* **2** (*Tech.*) the form that some types of energy such as heat, sound, light, etc. take as they move → idiom at RIDE *v.*

**waybill** /ˈweɪbɪl/ *n.* [C] (*abbr* **WB**) (*Transpt.*) a document that gives information about goods being transported, where they are going and who they must be delivered to

**WDV** /ˌdʌbljuː diː ˈviː/ = WRITTEN-DOWN VALUE

★**weak** /wiːk/ *adj.* (**-er**, **-est**) **1** not very great: *a weak market share* ◇ *weaker-than-expected results* **2** not financially strong or successful: *a weak company* **3** (about prices, markets, etc.) moving towards a lower level; falling: *falling demand and weaker prices* ◇ *the weak dollar*
OPP STRONG ▸ **ˈweakness** *n.* [U,C]

**weaken** /ˈwiːkən/ *v.* [T,I] **1** to make sb/sth less strong or powerful; to become less strong or powerful: *The recession has weakened demand for luxury goods.* **2** to make a currency, market etc. move towards a lower level; to fall: *The yen is weakening.*

★**wealth** /welθ/ *n.* **1** [U] a large amount of money, property, etc. that a person or country owns; how much money, etc. a person or a country has: *His personal wealth is around $100 m.* ◇ *the country's mineral wealth* ◇ *The purpose of industry is to create wealth.*
✪ ***household/national/private ~*** ◆ ***economic/financial/industrial ~*** ◆ ***to distribute/generate/manage ~*** ◆ ***~ creation/management***
**2** [sing.] a large amount of sth worth having: *The new manager brings a wealth of experience to the job.* ◇ *a ~ of detail/information/talent*

**ˈwealth efˌfect** *n.* [sing.] (*Econ.*) an increase in the amount of money that consumers spend when the value of their investments and assets rises: *the wealth effect of rising house prices*

**ˈwealth tax** *n.* [U,C] a tax that only very rich people have to pay

**wealthy** /ˈwelθi/ *adj.* (**-thier**, **-thiest**) **1** rich; having a lot of money, possessions, resources, etc: *the world's wealthiest software company* **2 the wealthy** *n.* [pl.] people who are rich

**wear** /weə(r); *AmE* wer/ *n.* [U] **1** (*usu. in compounds*) used esp. in shops/stores to describe clothes for a particular purpose or occasion: *children's wear* ◇ *sportswear* **2** the fact of wearing sth: *casual clothes for everyday wear* **3** the amount or type of use that sth has over a period of time: *carpets that give years of wear* **4** the damage or loss of quality that is caused when sth has been used a lot: *The machines are checked for signs of wear.* IDM **ˌwear and ˈtear** the damage to objects, furniture, property, etc. that is the result of normal use

**wearout** /ˈweəraʊt/ *n.* [U] **1** the process of sth becoming no longer useful or able to be used because it has been used for a long time: *wearout and failure in car engines* **2** (*Market.*) the situation when an advertisement has been shown so many times that it is no longer useful as people are now bored or annoyed with it: *advertising wearout*

**ˌweather ˈworking days** *n.* [pl.] (*abbr* **WWD**) (*Transpt.*) days on which work can be done if the weather is good: *The contract allowed two weather working days for the ship to be unloaded.*

★**the Web** /web/ = WORLD WIDE WEB

**ˈweb adˌdress** *n.* [C] (*IT*) the address of a web page SYN URL

**ˌweb-based ˈseminar** = WEBINAR

**webcast** /ˈwebkɑːst; *AmE* -kæst/ *n.* [C] (*IT*) a live broadcast that is sent out on the Internet ▸ **ˈwebcast** *v.* [T] **ˈwebcasting** *n.* [U]

**ˈweb deˌsign** *n.* [U] (*IT*) the art or process of arranging the information in websites ▸ **ˈweb deˌsigner** *n.* [C]

**ˈweb deˌvelopment** *n.* [U] (*IT*) the art or process of making websites

**ˈweb-eˌnabled** *adj.* (*IT*) designed to be used on the WORLD WIDE WEB; able to use the Internet for business: *web-enabled mobile phones*

**ˈweb ˌhosting** (*also* **web-hosting**) *n.* [U] (*IT*) the service of keeping websites on a SERVER so that they

can be looked at by people using the Internet
◘ *a ~ business/group* ◆ *~ services*

**webinar** /ˈwebmɑː(r)/ (*also* ˌ**web-based** ˈ**seminar**) *n.* [C] (*IT*) a meeting, talk, lesson, etc. that is broadcast on the Internet, in which the people taking part can talk to each other: *to participate/take part in a ~*

ˈ**web log file** *n.* [C] (*IT*) a computer file that records information about the people that visit a website, the pages that they look at, any technical problems, etc.

**webmaster** (*also* **Webmaster**) /ˈwebmɑːstə(r); *AmE* -mæs-/ *n.* [C] (*IT*) a person who is responsible for particular pages of information on the World Wide Web

ˈ**web page** *n.* [C] (*IT*) a document that is connected to the WORLD WIDE WEB and that anyone with an Internet connection can see, usu. forming part of a website

ˌ**web** ˈ**shopfront** = SHOPFRONT (2)

★ **website** (*also* **web site**) /ˈwebsaɪt/ *n.* [C] (*IT*) a place connected to the Internet, where an organization puts information on the WORLD WIDE WEB: *Customers can visit our website to see the progress of their orders.*
◘ *to log into/log onto/look at a ~* ◆ *to build/create/design/develop/make/set up a ~*

ˌ**web** ˈ**storefront** = STOREFRONT (3)

**webzine** /ˈwebziːn/ *n.* [C] a magazine published on the Internet, not on paper

**weekday** /ˈwiːkdeɪ/ *n.* [C] any day except Saturday or Sunday: *The bus runs on weekdays.* ▶ ˈ**weekdays** *adv.*

**weekend** /ˌwiːkˈend; *AmE* ˈwiːkend/ *n.* [C] **1** Saturday and Sunday: (*BrE*) *The office is closed* ***at*** *the weekend.* ◇ (*esp. AmE*) *The office is closed* ***on*** *the weekend.* **2** Saturday and Sunday, or a slightly longer period, as a holiday/vacation: *a weekend break*

**WEF** /ˌdʌbljuː iː ˈef/ = WORLD ECONOMIC FORUM

**weighbridge** /ˈweɪbrɪdʒ/ *n.* [C] a machine for weighing vehicles and their loads, usu. with a platform that the vehicle is driven on to

**weight** /weɪt/ *n.*, *v.*
• *n.* **1** (*abbr* **wt**) [U,C] how heavy sb/sth is, which can be measured in, for example, kilograms or pounds: *It is about 70 kilos* ***in*** *weight.* ◇ *Bananas are sold* ***by*** *weight.* ◇ *a weight of just 4 kilos* ◇ *Meat must be marked with its* ***net weight****, excluding packaging.* **2** [U] the fact of being heavy: *The pillars have to support the weight of the roof.* **3** [C] an object that is heavy: *Lifting heavy weights can damage your back.* **4** [C,U] a unit or system of units by which weight is measured: *imperial/metric ~* **5** [U] importance, influence or strength: *His opinion* ***carries weight*** *with the boss.* → idioms at PULL *v.*
• *v.* [T] **1** to give different values to things to show how important you think each of them is compared with the others: *The results of the survey were weighted to allow for variations in the sample.* **2** (*usu. pass.*) to arrange sth in such a way that a particular person or thing has an advantage or a disadvantage: *The new pay levels are weighted* ***against*** *part-time workers.*

ˌ**weighted** ˈ**average** *n.* [C] (*Tech.*) an average value for a number of things that is calculated by first giving a value to each thing according to how important it is compared with others: *The Retail Price Index is a weighted average of the prices of a number of selected goods.*

ˌ**weighted** ˈ**index** *n.* [C] (*Econ.*; *Finan.*) an index that considers the value of each item according to how important it is compared with others: *A price-weighted index counts changes in the prices of high-priced shares more than changes in the prices of low-priced shares.*

**weighting** /ˈweɪtɪŋ/ *n.* **1** (*HR*) [U] (*BrE*) extra money that you are paid for working in a particular area because it is expensive to live there: *Do you get London weighting?* SYN ALLOWANCE **2** (*Tech.*) [C,U] a value that you give to each of a number of things to show how important it is compared with the others

ˈ**weight note** *n.* [C] (*Trade*) a document that says how much goods weigh when they are taken off a ship

**welfare** /ˈwelfeə(r); *AmE* -fer/ *n.* [U] **1** the general health, happiness and safety of a person, a country, etc. **2** (*HR*) the physical and mental health of employees and practical help provided for people that need it: *an employee welfare plan* **3** practical or financial help provided, often by the government, for people that need it: *a social welfare programme* **4** (*esp. AmE*) = SOCIAL SECURITY (1)

ˈ**welfare** ˌ**benefit** *n.* [C, usu. pl., U] money that is given to people who are unemployed or who cannot work because they are ill/sick, or to their family if they die

**ˌwelfare to ˈwork** *n.* [U] a government policy of helping unemployed people find work, for example by training them or by giving companies money to employ them

**ˈwellness ˌprogram** *n.* [C] (*AmE*) (*HR*) benefits, activities or training that a company offers to improve and develop the physical and mental health of its employees

**ˌwell ˈoff** *adj.* (**better off**) **1** having a lot of money; rich: *tax reductions for the less well off* **2** in a good situation: *You'd be better off looking for a new job.* **3** having plenty of sth: *We're much better off for storage space in our new offices.*

**ˈwet goods** (*also* **ˈwet comˌmodities**) *n.* [pl.] (*Trade*) liquids; goods from which water or other liquid may come out, for example, soap or fish → DRY GOODS

**ˈwet lease** *n.* [U,C] (*Transpt.*) an arrangement that allows a company to use another company's aircraft and the people who fly them for a period of time
▸ **ˈwet-lease** *v.* [T] → DRY LEASE

**wharf** /wɔːf; *AmE* wɔːrf/ *n.* [C] (*pl.* **wharves** /wɔːvz; *AmE* wɔːrvz/ *or* **wharfs**) a flat structure built beside the sea or a river where boats can be tied up and goods unloaded: *a warehouse on the wharf*

**wharfage** /ˈwɔːfɪdʒ; *AmE* ˈwɔːrf-/ *n.* [U] (*Transpt.*) **1** a place at a **wharf** for loading, unloading or storing goods: *a harbour with two miles of wharfage* **2** a charge that is made for using this place

**wharfinger** /ˈwɔːfɪndʒə(r); *AmE* ˈwɔːrf-/ *n.* [C] the person or company in charge of a **wharf**

**ˌwhat-ˈif** *n.* [C] (*infml.*) a situation or an event that might happen in the future and that you need to think about now: *a what-if brainstorming session*

**ˈwheelchair ˌaccess** *n.* [U] a way of entering or leaving a place, a vehicle, etc. for sb who uses a chair with wheels because they cannot walk

**ˌwheeling and ˈdealing** *n.* [U] (*infml.*) very complicated, sometimes dishonest, business deals: *A lot of wheeling and dealing is done over lunch.* ▸ **ˌwheel and ˈdeal** *v.* [I] **ˌwheeler-ˈdealer** (*also* **ˌwheeler and ˈdealer**) *n.* [C]

**ˈwhistle-ˌblower** *n.* [C] (esp. in newspapers) a person who informs people in authority or the public that the company they work for is doing sth wrong or illegal
▸ **ˈwhistle-ˌblowing** *n.* [U]

**whiteboard** /ˈwaɪtbɔːd; *AmE* -bɔːrd/ *n.* [C] **1** a large board with a smooth white surface that you can write on with special pens when giving a talk, etc. **2** (*IT*) an area on a computer screen that several people at different computers can use to exchange information, often used in a TELECONFERENCE

**ˌwhite-ˈcollar** *adj.* working in an office rather than in a factory, etc.; connected with work in offices: ~ *workers/jobs*

**ˌwhite ˈelephant** *n.* [C, usu. sing.] a thing that is useless and no longer needed, although it may cost a lot of money to keep it

**ˈwhite goods** *n.* [pl.] (*Comm.*) large pieces of electrical equipment in the home: *washing machines and other white goods*

**ˌwhite ˈknight** *n.* [C] (*Finan.*) a person or an organization that rescues a company from being bought by another at too low a price

**ˌWhite ˈPages** *n.* [pl.; U] in the US and some other countries, the part of a telephone book that has white pages and gives a list of individuals and companies with their telephone numbers, arranged in alphabetical order

**ˈwhite sale** *n.* [C] (*esp. AmE*) (*Comm.*) an occasion when a shop/store sells goods at a much lower price than usual

**ˈwhizz-kid** (*AmE usu.* **whiz kid**) *n.* [C] (*infml.*) a person who is very good and successful at sth, esp. at a young age: *a computer/financial ~*

**ˌwhole-ˈlife** *adj.* (*Account.*; *Insur.*) lasting until a person dies or until a product can no longer be used: *a whole-life insurance policy* ◇ *the whole-life cost of a vehicle*

★ **wholesale** /ˈhəʊlseɪl; *AmE* ˈhoʊl-/ *n.*, *v.* (*Comm.*)
• ***n.*** [U] the buying and selling of goods in large quantities, esp. to businesses, so that they can be sold again to make a profit: *I used to work in wholesale.* → RETAIL
• ***v.*** [T] to sell goods in large quantities to businesses, so that they can be sold again to make a profit: *They import tea and wholesale it to retail stores.* → RETAIL ▸ **ˈwholesale** *adj.*: *a wholesale business* ◇ *wholesale goods* ◇ *the wholesale market* **ˈwholesale** *adv.*: *We buy the materials whole-*

sale. ˈ**wholesaling** *n.* [U]: *Their core business is the wholesaling of healthcare products to pharmacists.* ◇ *a wholesaling business*

ˈ**wholesale bank** *n.* [C] a bank that provides services for other banks and large businesses and not to individual customers or small businesses ▸ ˌ**wholesale ˈbanking** *n.* [U]

ˌ**wholesale coˈoperative** *n.* [C] (*Comm.*) a **cooperative** that buys goods in large quantities to sell to the cooperatives that own it and to others

ˈ**wholesale price** (*also* ˈ**trade price**) *n.* [C] (*Comm.*) the price that a RETAILER pays for goods from a manufacturer or **wholesaler**

★ **wholesaler** /ˈhəʊlseɪlə(r); *AmE* ˈhoʊl-/ *n.* [C] (*Comm.*) a person or business that buys goods in large quantities and sells them to businesses, so they can be sold again to make a profit: *fruit and vegetable wholesalers* → RETAILER

ˌ**wholly-ˈowned** *adj.* used to describe a company whose shares are all owned by another company: *a wholly-owned* ***subsidiary*** *of sth*

ˌ**wide area ˈnetwork** = WAN

**widget** /ˈwɪdʒɪt/ *n.* [C] (*infml.*) **1** used to refer to any small device that you do not know the name of **2** (*Manufact.*) a product that does not exist, used as an example of the typical product of a manufacturer, esp. when accounting or financial processes are being explained: *Calculate the total cost per widget.*

**Wi-Fi** /ˈwaɪ faɪ/ *n.* [U] (*IT*) technology without wires that allows several computers to share the same fast Internet connection in a small area such as an office or shop/store

ˈ**wild card** *n.* [C] **1** sb or sth whose behaviour or effect is difficult to predict **2** (*IT*) a symbol that has no meaning of its own and can represent any letter: *a wild-card search*

**wildcat** /ˈwaɪldkæt/ *adj.*, *n.*, *v.* (*infml.*)

• ***adj.*** **1** (*HR*) a **wildcat** strike happens suddenly and without the official support of a trade union **2** (about a business or project) that has not been carefully planned and that will probably not be successful; that does not follow normal standards and methods: *a wildcat scheme* ◇ *wildcat stocks*

• ***n.*** [C] **1** (*AmE*) an oil or gas well made in an area where oil or gas has not yet been found **2** a business or project that will probably not be financially successful

• ***v.*** [I] (*AmE*) to look for oil where nobody has looked for it before: *wildcatting for oil* ▸ ˈ**wildcatter** *n.* [C]

**will** /wɪl/ *n.*, *v.*

• ***n.*** [C] a legal document that says what is to happen to sb's money and property after they die: *Have you made a will?*

• ***v.*** [T] **~ sth (to sb)** | **~ sb sth** to formally give your property or possessions to sb after you have died, by means of a **will**

**win** /wɪn/ *v.*, *n.*

• ***v.*** (**winning, won, won** /wʌn/) **1** [T,I] to be the most successful in a competition, etc: *Who is winning the battle for the German market?* **2** [T] to get sth as the result of a competition, etc: *The company has won a contract to build 500 trucks.* **3** [T] to achieve or get what you want, esp. by your own efforts: *to win new customers* ▸ ˈ**winner** *n.* [C]: *The new software package is a winner.*

PHR V ˌ**win sb aˈround/ˈover/ˈround (to sth)** to get sb's support or approval by persuading them that you are right: *The new model hasn't won over consumers.* ˌ**win sb/sth ˈback** to get or have again sb/sth that you had before: *How can we win our customers back?*

• ***n.*** [C] a victory in a competition

**wind** /waɪnd/ *v.* (**wound, wound** /waʊnd/) PHR V ˌ**wind ˈdown** **1** (about a business, piece of machinery, etc.) to go slowly and then stop: *The market is winding down ahead of the holidays.* **2** to stop thinking about work and start to relax: *to wind down after a long day at work* SYN UNWIND ˌ**wind sth ˈdown** to bring a business, an activity, etc. to an end gradually over a period of time: *The bank is winding down its involvement in the venture.* ˌ**wind (sth) ˈup** to bring sth such as a meeting or a speech to an end: *Let's wind up the discussion.* ˌ**wind sth ˈup** (*Law*) to stop running a business and close it completely: *The business will be wound up or sold.* SYN LIQUIDATE

**windfall** /ˈwɪndfɔːl/ *n.* [C] money that sb/sth wins or receives unexpectedly: *~ gains/profits*

ˈ**windfall tax** *n.* [C] a tax on profits that is paid once only, not every year

**wind farm** /ˈwɪnd/ *n.* [C] an area of land on which there are a lot of TURBINES for producing electricity from wind

**winding up** /ˌwaɪndɪŋ ˈʌp/ *n.* [U,C] the process of closing a com-

pany, selling its assets and paying its debts SYN LIQUIDATION
⊙ *to vote for/order ~* ◆ *a winding-up order/petition/sale* ◆ *winding-up* ***proceedings*** ◆ *~ occurs/takes place*

**window** /ˈwɪndəʊ; *AmE* ˈwɪndoʊ/ *n.* [C] **1** (*IT*) an area with a frame on a computer screen, in which a particular program is operating or in which information of a particular type is shown **2** the glass at the front of a shop/store and the area behind it where goods are shown to the public: *items* ***in the window*** ◇ *a window display* **3** a small area that you can see through: *the window of the envelope* **4** a time when there is an opportunity to do sth, although it may not last long: *Do you have a window to discuss the project with me?*

**ˈwindow ˌdressing** *n.* [U] **1** the art of arranging goods in shop/store windows in an attractive way **2** the fact of doing, saying or presenting sth in a way that creates a good impression but does not show the real facts **3** (*Stock Ex.*) trade on a stock market at the end of a FINANCIAL YEAR or part of a year that is intended to make a collection of investments look more successful

**ˈwindow-ˌshopping** *n.* [U] the activity of looking at the goods in shop/store windows, usu. without intending to buy anything
▶ **ˈwindow-shop** *v.* [I] (**-pp-**)

**winning** /ˈwɪnɪŋ/ *adj.* **1** that wins or has won a competition, etc: *They developed a winning strategy.* **2** successful or likely to be successful: *a winning product*

**ˌwin-ˈwin** *adj.* used to describe a situation in which everybody involved gains sth

**WIP** /ˌdʌbljuː aɪ ˈpiː/ = WORK IN PROGRESS

**wipe** /waɪp/ *v.* PHRV **ˌwipe sth ˈoff sth** to reduce the value of sth, esp. shares: *Billions of pounds were wiped off share prices today.* **ˌwipe sth ˈout** (*often pass.*) to destroy or remove sb/sth completely: *Last year's profits were virtually wiped out.*

**wire** /ˈwaɪə(r)/ *n., v.*
• ***n.*** **1** [U,C] metal in the form of a thin thread **2** [U,C] a piece of wire used to carry an electric current or signal: *telephone wires* **3** (*infml.*) [U] (*AmE*) the system of sending messages by TELEGRAM; a TELEGRAPH
IDM **go, come, etc. (right) down to the ˈwire** (*infml.*) if you say that a situation goes **down to the wire**, you mean that the result will not be decided or known until the very end → idiom at PULL *v.*
• ***v.*** [T] **1 ~ sth (up)** to connect a building, piece of equipment, etc. to an electricity supply using wires: *a wrongly wired plug* **2 ~ sb/sth (up) (to sth)** to connect sb/sth to a piece of equipment, esp. a computer system: *All schools will soon be wired up to the Internet.* **3 ~ sth (to sb) | ~ sb sth** to send money from one bank to another using an electronic system: *We will wire the money to you today.* **4** (*infml.*) (*AmE*) **~ sth (to sb) | ~ sb sth** to send sb a TELEGRAM

**wireless** /ˈwaɪələs; *AmE* ˈwaɪərləs/ *adj.* without wires; using radio signals rather than wires: *wireless access to the Internet* ▶ **ˈwirelessly** *adv.*: *to connect wirelessly to the Internet*

**ˌwireless ˈInternet** (*also* **ˌwireless ˈWeb**) *n.* [U; sing.] (*IT*) a system that enables people to communicate with the Internet using a mobile phone/cellphone or other device that is not connected to anything by wires

**wireline** /ˈwaɪəlaɪn; *AmE* ˈwaɪərl-/ *adj., n.*
• ***adj.*** used to describe a system, device or technology that uses telephone wires: *wireline networks*
• ***n.*** **1** [C] a telephone wire **2** [U] technology that uses telephone wires: *Some telecoms companies only have wireline.*

**ˈwire ˌservice** *n.* [C] (*esp. AmE*) a company that sends news to newspapers, television stations, people's computers, etc.

**ˌwire ˈtransfer** (*also* **ˌcable ˈtransfer, ˌtelegraphic ˈtransfer**) *n.* [C,U] a quick way of moving money from one bank to another anywhere in the world by phone, computer, etc.

**wiring** /ˈwaɪərɪŋ/ *n.* [U] the system of electrical connections, cables and wires in a building, machine, etc: *faulty wiring*

**ˈwish list** *n.* [C] (*infml.*) all the things that you would like to have, buy or do, or that you would like to happen

**withdraw** /wɪðˈdrɔː; wɪθˈd-/ *v.* (**-drew** /-ˈdruː/ **-drawn** /-ˈdrɔːn/) **~ (from sth) 1** [T] to take money out of a bank account, etc: *You can withdraw money from cashpoints all over the world.* SYN DRAW OPP DEPOSIT **2** (*Comm.*) [T] to stop giving or offering sth to sb: *The drug was withdrawn from sale.* **3** [T,I] to stop, or to stop sb/sth, taking part in an activity or being a member of an organization: *Will Britain withdraw from the EU?* SYN PULL OUT

**withdrawal** /wɪð'drɔːəl; wɪθ'd-/ *n.* **~ (from sth) 1** [C,U] the act of taking an amount of money out of your bank account, pension plan, etc.; the amount of money that you take out: *You can **make** withdrawals of up to €250 a day.* OPP DEPOSIT **2** (*Comm.*) [U,C] the act of moving or taking sth away or back: *the withdrawal of an offer ◇ a product withdrawal* → RECALL **3** [U] the act of no longer taking part in sth or being a member of an organization

**withhold** /wɪð'həʊld; wɪθ'h-; *AmE* -'hoʊld/ *v.* [T] (**-held, -held** /-'held/) (*fml.*) to refuse to give sth to sb: *to withhold payments*

**with'holding tax** *n.* [C,U] **1** in the US, an amount of money that an employer takes out of sb's income as tax and pays directly to the government **2** an amount of money that a financial institution takes out of the interest or DIVIDENDS that sb earns on an investment and pays directly to the government

**with,out en'gagement** *adj., adv.* (*Comm.*) used to show that a seller has the right to change a stated price, delivery date, etc: *All prices are without engagement.*

**with,out 'prejudice** *adj., adv.* (*Law*) words on a document that mean that the information it contains does not affect legal rights that already exist or any claim that sb has

**with,out-'profit** (*also* **with,out-'profits**) *adj.* (*BrE*) (*Finan.; Insur.*) used to describe an insurance policy or an investment where the amount paid does not include a share in the company's profits

**with,out re'course** *adj., adv.* (*Law*) words written on a BILL OF EXCHANGE that mean that money cannot be claimed from the person who prepared or sold it if the money is not paid

**,with-'profits** (*also* **,with-'profit**) *adj.* (*BrE*) (*Insur.*) used to describe a type of insurance or an investment where an amount of money related to the profits that the company has made is added each year to the amount invested or is paid separately

**witness** /'wɪtnəs/ *n., v.*
• ***n.*** [C] **1** a person who gives evidence in a court: *to appear as/be called as a ~* **2** a person who is present when an official document is signed and who also signs it to prove that they saw this happen: *She signed the document **in front of** a witness.*
• ***v.*** [T] to be present when an official document is signed and sign it yourself to prove that you saw this happen: *to ~ a contract/signature*

**wizard** /'wɪzəd; *AmE* -ərd/ *n.* [C] **1** a person who is esp. good at sth: *a financial wizard* **2** (*IT*) a part of a computer program that helps the user do a complicated task by providing instructions or asking a series of simple questions

**wk** *abbr* (*pl.* **wks**) (*written*) week

**womenswear** /'wɪmɪnzweə(r)/ *n.* [U] (esp. in shops/stores) clothes for women

**woo** /wuː/ *v.* [T] (esp. in newspapers) to try to attract or get the support of a person, a group, an organization, etc: *to woo younger consumers*

**wording** /'wɜːdɪŋ; *AmE* 'wɜːrd-/ *n.* [U; C, usu. sing.] the words that are used in a piece of writing or speech, esp. when they have been carefully chosen: *the wording of the contract*

**,word of 'mouth** *n.* [U] the process of people telling each other about sth: *word-of-mouth marketing*

**'word ,processing** *n.* [U] (*abbr* **WP**) the use of a computer to create, store and print a piece of text, such as letters, reports, etc.

**'word ,processor** *n.* [C] (*abbr* **WP**) a computer that runs a WORD PROCESSING program

**,words and ,figures 'differ** (*also* **,words and ,figures do not a'gree**) *phr.* (*written*) words written on a cheque to show that the amount written on it in words is different from the amount written in figures SYN AMOUNTS DIFFER

★ **work** /wɜːk; *AmE* wɜːrk/ *v., n.*
• ***v.* 1** [I] to have a job: *Both my parents work. ◇ to ~ full-time/part-time ◇ Who does she work **for**? ◇ He works **as** a programmer.* **2** [T,I] **~ (on/at sth)** to do sth that involves physical or mental effort, esp. as part of your job: *My boss works very long hours. ◇ What project are you working **on**?* **3** [I] to make efforts to achieve sth: *We're working hard **to** find a solution.* **4** [T] to make yourself/sb work, esp. very hard: *She works her staff hard and pays them well.* **5** [T] to manage or operate sth in order to gain benefit from it: *Some of the sales reps work a very large area.* **6** [I] to function; to operate: *My phone isn't working. ◇ The article examines how companies work.* **7** [T] to make a machine, device, etc. operate: *The machine is worked by wind power.* **8** [I] to have the result or effect that you want: *The new appraisal system works well.*

**9** [I] to have a particular effect: *His inexperience could work **against** him.* **10** [T,I] to move or pass to a particular place or state, usu. gradually: *She **worked her way** up to senior manager.* IDM **'work it/things** (*infml.*) to arrange sth in a particular way, esp. by being clever: *I managed to work it so that I could leave early.* **work to 'rule** to follow the rules of your job in a very strict way in order to cause delay, as a form of protest against your employer → idioms at GROUND *n.*, LONG PHR V **,work 'out** to develop in a successful way: *My first job didn't work out.* **,work 'out (at sth)** if sth **works out** at sth, you calculate that it will be a particular amount: *It works out cheaper to fly.* **,work sth 'out 1** to calculate an amount or the cost of sth **2** to find the answer to sth; to solve sth **3** to plan or think of sth: *Have you worked out the best way to do it?* SYN FIGURE STH OUT **'work to sth** to follow a plan, TIMETABLE, etc: *to work to a budget* **'work towards sth** to try to reach or achieve a goal **,work sth 'up** to spend time developing sth: *to work up a business plan*

• ***n.*** **1** [U] the job that a person does: *I'm looking for work.* ◇ (*BrE*) *the number of people **in work*** ◇ *What **line of work** are you in?* SYN EMPLOYMENT

⊕ ***full-time/part-time/permanent/regular/temporary*** ~ • ***paid/unpaid/voluntary*** ~ • ***badly paid/well-paid*** ~ • *to **find/get/seek*** ~ • *to **give up/go back to/return to/start*** ~

**2** [U] (*without* **the**) the place where you do your job: *I go to work at 8 a.m.* ◇ *health and safety at work* ◇ *to leave work* ◇ *to (be) at/off* ~ **3** [U] the duties that you have and the activities that you do as part of your job: *Do you enjoy your work?* ◇ *the day-to-day work of the department*

⊕ ***administrative/clerical/factory/office/secretarial*** ~ • *to **do/take on*** ~ • *to **begin/finish/start/stop*** ~

**4** [U] tasks that need to be done: *We **have** a lot of work **on** at the moment.* ◇ *to take on/do/have/undertake* ~ **5** [U] materials needed or used for doing work, esp. books, papers, etc: *She often brings work home.* **6** [U] activity that uses physical strength or mental power in order to do or make sth: *She got her promotion through sheer hard work.*

⊕ *to **carry out/put in*** ~ • *to **complete/halt/start/stop*** ~

**7** [U] a thing or things that are produced as a result of work: *She did her best work before she was 30.* ◇ *The analysis is an impressive **piece of work**.* ◇ *bad/major/outstanding* ~ **8** [U] the result of an action; what is done by sb: *The report was the work of the production manager.* **9 works** [pl.] (*often with other ns*) activities involving building or repairing sth: *engineering works* ◇ *roadworks* **10 works** [C with sing./pl. v.] (*pl.* **works**) (*often with other ns*) a place where things are made or industrial processes are carried out: *an engineering works*

⊕ *a **cement/chemical/gas/steel*** ~ • *the* ~ ***canteen/foreman***

**11 the works** [pl.] (*infml.*) the moving parts of a machine, etc. SYN MECHANISM IDM **at 'work (on sth)** busy doing sth: *Everybody is hard at work.* **get (down) to/set to 'work** to begin; to make a start **in the 'works** something that is **in the works** is being discussed, planned or prepared → idioms at DIRTY, LIGHT

**workaholic** /ˈwɜːkəˈhɒlɪk; *AmE* ˈwɜːrkəˈhɔːlɪk; -ˈhɑːl-/ *n.* [C] (*infml.*) a person who works very hard and finds it difficult to stop working and do other things

**workday** /ˈwɜːkdeɪ; *AmE* ˈwɜːrk-/ = WORKING DAY

★**worker** /ˈwɜːkə(r); *AmE* ˈwɜːrk-/ *n.* [C] **1** (*often in compounds*) a person who works, esp. one who does a particular kind of work: *The plant has 1 400 workers.*

⊕ ***assembly-line/factory/production*** ~s • ***full-time/part-time/temporary*** ~s • ***blue-collar/manual/white-collar*** ~s • ***semi-skilled/skilled/unskilled*** ~s

**2** a person employed to do physical work rather than organizing things or managing people: *talks between workers and management* **3** (*usu. after an adj.*) a person who works hard or who works in a particular way: *a good/hard/quick* ~

**,worker di'rector** *n.* [C] (*HR*) an employee who has a place on the BOARD OF DIRECTORS to represent the ordinary workers

**,worker partici'pation** = EMPLOYEE PARTICIPATION

**,workers' co'operative** = COOPERATIVE

**'work ex,perience** *n.* [U] **1** the work or jobs that you have done in your life so far: *to have little/no work experience* **2** a period of time that a young person, esp. a student, spends working in a company as a form of training: *a work experience placement*

**workfare** /ˈwɜːkfeə(r); *AmE* ˈwɜːrkfer/ *n.* [U] in the US, a system in which unemployed people have to do some work or training in order to get money for food, rent, etc. from the government

★ **workforce** (*also* **work force**, *esp. in AmE*) /ˈwɜːkfɔːs; *AmE* ˈwɜːrkfɔːrs/ *n.* [C with sing./pl. v.] **1** all the people who work for a particular organization: *a 1 000-strong workforce* ◇ *Two-thirds of the ~ is/are women.* SYN STAFF **2** all the people in a country or an area who are available for work: *A quarter of the local ~ is/are unemployed.* ◇ *a skilled/trained ~* SYN LABOUR FORCE

**working** /ˈwɜːkɪŋ; *AmE* ˈwɜːrk-/ *adj., n.*

• *adj.* **1** having a job for which you are paid: *the working population* SYN EMPLOYED **2** connected with your job and the time you spend doing it: *~ conditions/hours* **3** having a job that involves hard physical work rather than office work, studying, etc: *an ordinary working man* **4** a **working** breakfast or lunch is one at which you discuss business **5** used as a basis for work, discussion, etc. but likely to be changed or improved in the future: *a working hypothesis of what caused the accident* **6** if you have a **working** knowledge of sth, you can use it at a basic level: *a working knowledge of Spanish* **7** the **working** parts of a machine are the parts that move to make it function → idiom at ORDER *n.*

• *n.* [C] (*usually* **workings** [pl.]) the way in which a machine, a system, an organization, etc. works: *the internal workings of the company*

**ˌworking ˈcapital** (*also* **ˌcirculating ˈcapital**) *n.* [U; sing.] (*Account.*) the money, stocks of goods, etc. that are used to run a business, pay employees and produce and sell more goods

**ˌworking ˈday** *n.* [C] (*BrE*) **1** (*also* **ˈworkday**, *AmE, BrE*) a day on which you usu. work or on which most people. work: *Thousands of working days were lost through strikes last year.* ◇ *Allow two working days* (= not Saturday or Sunday) *for delivery.* **2** (*AmE* **ˈworkday**) the part of a day during which you work: *an 8-hour working day*

**ˈworking group** (*BrE also* **ˈworking ˌparty**) *n.* [C] a group of people given the task of studying a subject and producing a report on it: *a working group* **on** *alternative sources of energy*

○ *to* ***form/set up*** *a ~* • *to* ***head/lead*** *a ~* • *a ~* ***recommends sth/reports (on sth)*** • *a ~* ***looks at sth/studies sth***

**ˈworking hours** *n.* [pl.] the time during the day when most people are at work and when shop/stores and offices are open

**ˌworking ˈinterest** *n.* [C] a share in a property, esp. one that produces oil, gas, etc., that gives the owner the right to develop it and to receive a share of the profits from what is produced

**ˌworking ˈlife** *n.* [C,U] **1** the part of a person's life that they spend working **2** the total time that a machine, a factory, etc., operates

**ˈworking ˌpaper** *n.* **1** [C] a report written by a group of people chosen to study an aspect of law, education, health, etc., for people to discuss **2 working papers** [pl.] in the US, an official document that enables sb under 16 years old or born outside the US to have a job

**ˌworking ˈpartner** = ACTIVE PARTNER

**ˈworking ˌparty** = WORKING GROUP

**ˌWorking Time Diˈrective** *n.* [sing.] (*HR*) European Union rules that limit the number of hours most employees can work to 48 a week, and say how much rest and holiday/vacation they should have

**ˌworking ˈweek** (*AmE also* **ˈworkweek**) *n.* [sing.] the total number of hours or days worked in a week: *The working week will be 35 hours.*

**ˌwork in ˈprogress** (*esp. BrE*) (*AmE usu.* **ˌwork in ˈprocess**) *n.* [C,U] (*abbr* **WIP**) **1** (*Account.*) products that are only partly manufactured at the end of an accounting period, valued at the cost of the materials, labour and some regular costs **2** a piece of work that may be shown to people or discussed with them but is not finished

**ˌwork-life ˈbalance** (*also* **work/life -**) (*also* **ˌlife-work ˈbalance**, *less freq.*) *n.* [C, usu. sing., U] (*HR*) a situation when a person manages to spend the right amount of time at work and on their personal life

★ **workload** /ˈwɜːkləʊd; *AmE* ˈwɜːrkloʊd/ *n.* [C] the amount of work that has to be done by a particular person, organization or machine: *a heavy workload* ◇ *to ease/increase/share a ~*

**workman** /ˈwɜːkmən; *AmE* ˈwɜːrk-/ *n.* [C] (*pl.* **-men** /-mən/) **1** a man who is employed to do physical work **2** (*used with an adj.*) a person who works in the way mentioned: *a good/bad/poor ~*

**workmanlike** /ˈwɜːkmənlaɪk; *AmE* ˈwɜːrk-/ *adj.* done, made, etc. in a skilful and thorough way: *They've done a workmanlike job.*

**workmanship** /ˈwɜːkmənʃɪp; *AmE* ˈwɜːrk-/ *n.* [U] the skill with which sb makes sth, esp. when this affects the way it looks or works: *bad/faulty/good/poor ~*

**ˈwork ˌmeasurement** *n.* [U] (*Product.*) a system for calculating how long a piece of work would take if done by an average qualified or trained person

**ˌwork ˈoverload** *n.* [U] when a person has too much work

**ˈwork ˌpermit** *n.* [C] an official document that gives a person the right to work in a foreign country

★ **workplace** /ˈwɜːkpleɪs; *AmE* ˈwɜːrk-/ *n.* [sing.] (*often* **the workplace**) the office, factory, etc. where people work: *introducing new technology into the workplace*

**ˌworkplace ˈbargaining** (*also* **ˌenterprise ˈbargaining**) *n.* [U] (*HR*) discussions between employers and employees about pay, conditions, rules, etc. in a particular office, factory, etc. with the aim of reaching an agreement

**ˌworkplace ˈlearning** *n.* [U] **1** an arrangement where students spend time in a company in order to learn to use their knowledge and skills in a real work situation **2** training or lessons that employees receive while they are at work

**ˌwork psyˈchology** *n.* [U] (*HR*) the study of how people behave at work and what influences their attitudes and behaviour

**ˈwork-reˌlated** *adj.* connected with the work that you do: *a work-related injury*

**workroom** /ˈwɜːkruːm; -rʊm; *AmE* ˈwɜːrk-/ *n.* [C] a room in which work is done, esp. work that involves making things

**works** = WORK *n.* (9,10,11)

**ˈwork ˌsampling** *n.* [U] **1** (*Product.*) (*also* **acˈtivity ˌsampling**) a technique of watching the activities of a group of people or machines in a workplace at particular moments over a period of time, in order to calculate how much time is spent on each activity **2** (*HR*) a method of finding out if a candidate for a job has the necessary skills and abilities by asking them to do a task that is an important part of the job or by looking at examples of work that they have already done

**ˈworks ˌcouncil** *n.* [C with sing./pl.verb] (*esp. BrE*) (*HR*) a group of employees who are elected to represent all the employees at a factory, etc. and meet with employers to discuss pay and conditions

**ˈwork ˌshadowing** *n.* [U] (*HR*) an arrangement that allows a student to find out about a particular type of work by spending some time with sb while they are doing their job

**ˈwork-ˌsharing** = JOB-SHARING

**worksheet** /ˈwɜːkʃiːt; *AmE* ˈwɜːrk-/ *n.* [C] a piece of paper recording work that is being done or that has been done

**workshop** /ˈwɜːkʃɒp; *AmE* ˈwɜːrkʃɑːp/ *n.* [C] **1** a room or building in which things are made or repaired using tools or machinery **2** a period of discussion and practical work on a particular subject, in which a group of people share their knowledge and experience: *They run a two-day workshop on marketing techniques.* ◇ *to conduct/do/hold a ~* ◇ *to attend/take part in a ~*

**ˈwork-shy** *adj.* (*BrE*) unwilling to work

**ˌwork simplifiˈcation** *n.* [U; sing.] (*Product.*) the process of making tasks, for example in manufacturing, as simple as possible so that they can be completed quickly and costs can be reduced

**worksite** /ˈwɜːksaɪt; *AmE* ˈwɜːrk-/ *n.* [C] (*Manufact.*) an area where a factory, etc. has been built or where work is done

**workspace** /ˈwɜːkspeɪs; *AmE* ˈwɜːrk-/ *n.* [C,U] **1** an area that is designed for sb to work in: *a bright, open workspace* **2** (*IT*) the area on a computer screen on which you can work in a particular program; the way this is arranged

**workstation** /ˈwɜːksteɪʃn; *AmE* ˈwɜːrk-/ *n.* [C] **1** the area where one person works, esp. a desk with a computer **2** (*IT*) a computer that is more powerful than a personal computer and is used for very technical work or design **3** (*IT*) a computer and a screen that are connected to a central computer system and use data from there **4** (*Product.*) an area in a factory where a particular process or task is done

**ˈwork ˌstructuring** *n.* [U] **1** (*HR*) the process of arranging important parts of employees' jobs, such as their hours of work and their duties, in the most efficient way **2** (*Product.*) the process of arranging the steps in making a product so that everything happens quickly and efficiently

**ˈwork ˌstudy** *n.* [U] (*BrE*) (*HR; Product.*) a system of analysing the way work is done in an organization in order to improve it

**ˈwork-ˌstudy** *adj.* (*AmE*) used to describe an arrangement that allows a person to work part-time at the same time as studying

**ˌwork-to-ˈrule** (*esp. BrE*) (*AmE usu.* **ˌwork-to-ˈcontract**) *n.* [C, usu. sing.] (*HR*) a situation in which workers refuse to do any work that is not in their contracts, in order to protest about sth: *to be on/go on/call for/stage a ~*

**workwear** /ˈwɜːkweə(r); *AmE* ˈwɜːrkwer/ *n.* [U] (*AmE*) clothes that are worn for work, esp. to do MANUAL work

**workweek** /ˈwɜːkwiːk; *AmE* ˈwɜːrk-/ = WORKING WEEK

**the ˌWorld ˈBank** *n.* [sing.] a group of financial organizations, established in 1946 and linked with the United Nations, that provides loans for developing countries to help with their economic development

**the ˌWorld Ecoˌnomic ˈForum** *n.* [sing.] (*abbr* **WEF**) an international organization that works with politicians and leaders from business, education, etc. to encourage economic growth and social progress and does not aim to make a profit

**the ˌWorld ˈTrade Organiˌzation** *n.* [sing.] (*abbr* **WTO**) an international organization, formed in 1995, that encourages and controls international trade and economic development

★ **worldwide** /ˈwɜːldwaɪd; *AmE* ˈwɜːrld-/ *adj.* in or affecting all parts of the world: *an increase in worldwide sales* ▸ **ˌworldˈwide** *adv.*: *She travels worldwide.*

★ **the ˌWorld Wide ˈWeb** (*also* **the Web**) *n.* [sing.] (*abbr* **WWW**) (*IT*) a system for finding information on the Internet in which documents are connected to other documents using HYPERTEXT links: *to browse a site* ***on*** *the World Wide Web*

**ˌworst-perˈforming** *adj.* producing the worst results: *our worst-performing stores*

★ **worth** /wɜːθ; *AmE* wɜːrθ/ *adj., n.*
• ***adj.*** (*usu. used like a prep.*) **1** having a value in money, etc: *The deal is worth about $28 m.* **2** used to recommend the action mentioned because you think it may be useful, enjoyable, etc: *Their website is worth a look.* **3** important, good or enjoyable enough to make sb feel satisfied, esp. when some difficulty or effort is involved: *I took a salary cut when I changed jobs, but it was worth it.*
**IDM** **not worth the paper it's ˈwritten/ˈprinted on** (*infml.*) (about an agreement or official document) having no value, esp. legally, or because one of the people involved has no intention of doing what they said they would → idiom at JOB *n.*
• ***n.*** [U] **1 ten dollars', €40, etc. ~ of sth** an amount of sth that has the value mentioned **2 a week's, month's, etc. ~ of sth** an amount of sth that lasts a week, etc: *3 months' worth of stock* **3** the financial, practical or moral value of sb/sth: *a personal net worth of $10 m*

**worthless** /ˈwɜːθləs; *AmE* ˈwɜːrθ-/ *adj.* having no practical or financial value: *~ currency/shares* **OPP** VALUABLE ▸ **ˈworthlessness** *n.* [U]

**wow factor** /ˈwaʊ ˌfæktə(r)/ *n.* [C, usu. sing.] (*Market.*) the ability of a product to make people feel surprised and impressed when they see or use it for the first time: *The latest model still lacks the wow factor.*

**WP** /ˌdʌbljuː ˈpiː/ = WORD PROCESSOR, WORD PROCESSING

**wpm** *abbr* (*written*) words per minute: *My typing speed is 55 wpm.*

**wrap** /ræp/ *v., n.*
• ***v.*** [T] (-pp-) **~ A (up) (in B) | ~ B round/around A** to cover sth completely in paper or other material: *individually wrapped chocolates*
**PHR V** **ˌwrap sth ˈup** (*infml.*) to complete sth such as an agreement or a meeting in a satisfactory way: *That just about wraps it up for today.*
• ***n.*** [U] paper, plastic or other material that is used for wrapping things in: *a box covered with plastic wrap*
**IDM** **under ˈwraps** (*infml.*) being kept secret until some time in the future: *The development of the new machine was kept under wraps.*

**wrapper** /ˈræpə(r)/ *n.* [C] a piece of paper, plastic, etc. that is wrapped around sth, esp. food, when you buy it in order to protect it and keep it clean: *a plastic wrapper*

**wrapping** /ˈræpɪŋ/ *n.* [U] (*also* **wrappings** [pl.]) paper, plastic, etc. used for covering sth in order to protect it: *~ paper/material*

**wreckage** /ˈrekɪdʒ/ *n.* [U] the parts of a vehicle, building, etc. that remain after it has been badly damaged or destroyed: (*fig.*) *They tried to save something from the wreckage of the bankrupt company.*

**writ** /rɪt/ *n.* [C] (*Law*) a legal document from a court telling sb to do or not to do sth: *to serve sb with a writ*

**write** /raɪt/ *v.* (**wrote** /rəʊt/**written** /ˈrɪtn/) **1** [T,I] to produce a document, an article or a piece of software: *We wrote a business plan for the new company.* ◇ *He writes* **about/on** *business issues.* ◇ *to ~ code/programs* **2** [T,I] to put a request or some information in a letter or an email and send it to sb: *I am writing to inform you ...* ◇ *to write a memo* **3** [T] **~ sth (out) (for sb)** | **~ sb (out) sth** to complete a cheque or other form with the necessary information: *I wrote (out) a cheque for €100.* **4** (*IT*) [T] **~ sth to sth** to transfer or copy information from a computer's memory to sth that stores it in a more permanent form: *to write data to a disk* → idiom at WORTH *adj.*
**PHR V** ˌ**write sth** ˈ**back** (*Account.*) (*usu. pass.*) to include an item in a company's accounts that had deliberately not been included before, when calculating the company's profits ˌ**write sth** ˈ**down 1** to write sth on paper, esp. in order to remember or record it **2** (*Account.*) to reduce the value of an asset in a company's accounts OPP WRITE STH UP ˌ**write sth** ˈ**off** (*often pass.*) **1** (*Account.*) to reduce the value of an asset in a company's accounts over a period of time: *Goodwill was written off over 5 years.* **2** (*Account.*) to remove a debt from a company's accounts because the money cannot be collected; to remove an asset that has no value: *to write off bad loans* **3** (*Insur.*) (*BrE*) to accept that sth is so badly damaged that it cannot be repaired: *The car was written off.* ˌ**write sth** ˈ**up 1** to record sth in writing in a full and complete form, often using notes that you made earlier: *to write up the minutes of a meeting* **2** (*Account.*) (*AmE*) to increase the value of an asset in a company's accounts or give it a value that is too high OPP WRITE STH DOWN

ˈ**write-back** *n.* [C,U] (*Account.*) a situation where money that had been kept to deal with a possible loss or expense is no longer needed; an amount of money entered in the profit side of financial records because of this

ˈ**write-down** *n.* [C,U] (*Account.*) a situation where an asset loses some value; an amount of money entered in the accounts because of this: *a €550 m write-down of assets*

ˈ**write-off** *n.* **1** (*Account.*) [C,U] a situation where an asset loses some or all of its value; an amount of money entered in the financial records because of this: *Last year's losses were due to bad debt write-offs.* **2** (*Finan.*) [C,U] a decision that a debt need not be paid back: *countries qualifying for a debt write-off* **3** [C] (*BrE*) a vehicle that has been so badly damaged in an accident that it is not worth spending money to repair it: *The car was a write-off.*

ˌ**write-pro**ˈ**tect** *v.* [T] (*IT*) to protect a computer file or disk so that its contents cannot be changed or removed ▶ ˌ**write-pro**ˈ**tected** *adj.*

**writer** /ˈraɪtə(r)/ *n.* [C] (*Finan.*) a person or business that sells an OPTION contract

ˈ**write-up** *n.* [C,U] **1** (*Account.*) a situation where the value of an asset increases; an amount of money entered in the accounts because of this **2** an article in a newspaper, magazine, etc. in which sb gives information and their opinion about a new product, book, etc: *The site includes company write-ups.* **3** an act of recording sth in a full and complete form: *Do the write-ups of your books monthly.*

ˌ**writ of exe**ˈ**cution** *n.* [C] (*Law*) a legal document that makes sure that what has been decided by a court is done

ˌ**written-down** ˈ**value** = BOOK VALUE (1)

**wrongful** /ˈrɒŋfl; *AmE* ˈrɔːŋ-/ *adj.* not fair, morally right or legal: *fraud and other wrongful conduct*

ˌ**wrongful dis**ˈ**missal** = UNFAIR DISMISSAL

**wt** *abbr* a short way of writing **weight**: *average net wt 120 g*

**Wtd.** *abbr* a short way of writing **warranted** to show that sth is guaranteed to be what it says it is: *Wtd. 100% pure*

**WTO** /ˌdʌbljuː ˌtiː ˈəʊ; *AmE* ˈoʊ/ = WORLD TRADE ORGANIZATION

**wunderkind** /ˈwʊndəkɪnd; *AmE* -dərk-/ *n.* [C] (*pl.* **-kinder** /-kɪndə(r)/ *or* **-kinds**) (*infml.*) a person who is very successful at a young age: *a wunderkind of investment banking*

**WWD** /ˌdʌbljuː ˌdʌbljuː ˈdiː/ = WEATHER WORKING DAYS

**WWW** /ˌdʌbljuː dʌbljuː ˈdʌbljuː/ (*also* **www**) *abbr* (*IT*) a short way of writing and saying World Wide Web, used in the addresses of websites: *www.oup.com*

**WYSIWYG** /ˈwɪziwɪg/ *abbr* (*IT*) **what you see is what you get** what you see on your computer screen is exactly the same as what will be printed or seen on other computers: *a ~ display/editor*

# Xx

**ˌx-efˈficiency** *n.* [U] the ability of a company to use the people, machines, etc. that it has in the best way in order to produce as much as possible quickly and at a low cost: *to achieve x-efficiency* SYN TECHNICAL EFFICIENCY OPP X-INEFFICIENCY ▸ **ˌx-efˈficient** *adj.*

**Xerox™** /ˈzɪərɒks; *AmE* ˈzɪrɑːks/ *n.* [U,C] a process for producing copies of documents using a special machine; a copy made using this process: *a Xerox machine* ◊ *She kept Xeroxes of the letters.* ▸ **ˈxerox** *v.* [T]: *to xerox a letter*

**ˌx-inefˈficiency** *n.* [U] the amount by which a company does not use the people, machines, etc. that it has in the best way in order to produce as much as possible quickly and at a low cost: *The factory had a 25% x-inefficiency.* SYN TECHNICAL INEFFICIENCY OPP X-EFFICIENCY ▸ **ˌx-inefˈficient** *adj.*

**xtn** *abbr* (*written*) extension: *call xtn 216*

# Yy

**yard** /jɑːd; *AmE* jɑːrd/ *n.* [C] **1** (*usu. with other ns*) an area of land used for a special purpose or business: *a boat yard* ◊ *a freight yard* **2** (*abbr* **yd**) a unit for measuring length, equal to 3 feet or 0.9144 of a metre

**yardstick** /ˈjɑːdstɪk; *AmE* ˈjɑːrd-/ *n.* [C] a standard used for judging how good or successful sth is: *GDP is not the only yardstick of economic success.*

**yd** *abbr* (*written*) yard

**year** /jɪə(r); jɜː(r); *AmE* jɪr/ *n.* [C] (*abbr* **yr**) **1** the period from 1 January to 31 December, divided into 12 months: *The project ends early next year.* **2** a period of 12 months, measured from a particular time: *In the UK, the tax year runs from April to April.* ◊ ***year-earlier** levels* (= levels at the same time the year before) IDM **car, product, manager, etc. of the ˈyear** a thing or person that people decide is the best in a particular field in a particular year **ˌyear on ˈyear** (*Account.*) (used esp. when talking about figures, prices, etc.) compared with the figures, prices, etc. a year earlier: *Spending has increased year on year.* ◊ *a year-on-year increase* **ˌyear over ˈyear** (*Account.*) compared with the same period a year earlier: *Sales have declined 9% year over year.*

**yearbook** /ˈjɪəbʊk; *AmE* ˈjɪrbʊk/ *n.* [C] a book published once a year, giving details of what happened the previous year in a particular company, country or area of activity

**ˌyear ˈend** (*AmE also* **ˌyear's ˈend**) *n.* [U; sing.] **1** the end of the FINANCIAL YEAR: *the financial position at year end* ◊ *year-end targets* **2** the end of December

**ˌyear-ˈlong** (*AmE also* **yearlong**) *adj.* continuing for a whole year: *a year-long downward trend*

**yearly** /ˈjɪəli; ˈjɜːli; *AmE* ˈjɪrli/ *adj.* **1** happening once a year or every year: *Pay is reviewed on a yearly basis.* **2** paid, valid or calculated for one year: *your yearly income* ▸ **ˈyearly** *adv.*: *The committee meets twice yearly.*

**ˌyear's ˈend** = YEAR END

**ˌyear to ˈdate** *n.* [sing.] (*abbr* **YTD**) (*Account.*) this year as far as today: *Our turnover has risen 50% in the year to date.* ▸ **ˌyear-to-ˈdate** *adj., adv.*: *year-to-date revenues*

**ˌYellow ˈPages™** *n.* [pl.; U] a book with yellow pages that gives a list of companies and organizations and their telephone numbers, arranged according to the type of services they offer: *Look in the Yellow Pages.*

**ˈYellow Sheets™** (*also* **yellow sheets**) *n.* [pl.; U] (*Finan.*) in the US, a list of the latest prices of bonds and other information about them, that is published every day

**yen** /jen/ *n.* (*pl.* **yen**) **1** [C] the unit of money in Japan; ¥: *a net loss of 110 m yen* **2 the yen** [sing.] the value of the **yen** compared with the value of the money of other countries: *The yen has fallen/risen against the dollar.*

★**yield** /jiːld/ *n., v.*

• ***n.*** [C,U] **1** (*Finan.*) the total amount of profits or income that you get from an investment or a business: *This will give a yield of 10% on your investment.* **2** the total amount of sth produced: *a high crop yield*

• ***v.*** [T] to produce or provide a profit, an income, a result, a crop or a product: *These accounts yield good returns.* ◊ *The oil field has yielded over 3 m barrels.*

**ˌyield to maˈturity** *n.* [C] (*pl.* **yields** -) (*abbr* **YTM**) (*Finan.*) the amount of money that an investor will get from a bond if it is not paid back until the end of its life, usu. expressed as a percentage SYN REDEMPTION YIELD

**yours** /jɔːz; *AmE* jərz; jɔːrz; jʊrz/ *pron.* (*usually* **Yours**) used, usu. in phrases, at the end of a letter before signing your name: (*BrE*) ~ *sincerely/faithfully* ◇ (*AmE*) *Sincerely yours* ◇ (*AmE*) *Yours truly*

**yr** (*AmE usu.* **yr.**) *abbr* (*written*) **1** year **2** your

**yrs** (*AmE usu.* **yrs.**) *abbr* (*written*) **1** years **2** **Yrs** a short way of writing Yours at the end of letters

**YTD** /ˌwaɪ tiː ˈdiː/ = YEAR TO DATE

**YTM** /ˌwaɪ tiː ˈem/ = YIELD TO MATURITY

# Zz

**ZBB** /ˌzed biː ˈbiː; *AmE* ˌziː/ = ZERO-BASED BUDGETING

**zero** /ˈzɪərəʊ; *AmE* ˈzɪroʊ; ˈziː-/ *number, v.*

• ***number*** (*pl.* **zeros** *or* **zeroes**) **1** (*esp. AmE*) the number 0 SYN NOUGHT (*BrE*) **2** the lowest possible amount or level; nothing: *zero growth*

• ***v.*** **(zeroes, zeroing, zeroed, zeroed)**

PHR V **ˌzero ˈin on sb/sth** to fix all your attention on the person or thing mentioned: *They zeroed in on the key issues.*

**ˌzero-based ˈbudgeting** *n.* [U] (*abbr* **ZBB**) (*Account.*) a system of planning a company's budget where each department is not automatically given all the money it spent the previous year, but instead must give reasons why it needs all the money it is asking for

**ˌzero ˈdefects** *n.* [pl.] (*Product.*) used to describe a system of quality management which aims to make products with almost no faults

**ˌzero-ˈrated** *adj.* used to describe goods or services on which a particular tax is not charged: *These goods are zero-rated for VAT.* ▸ **ˌzero-ˈrate** *v.* [T] **ˌzero ˈrating** *n.* [U]

**ˌzero-ˈsum game** *n.* [C] a situation in which what is gained by one person or group is lost by another

**zip** /zɪp/ *v.* [T] (-pp-) (*IT*) **~ sth (up)** to make a computer file smaller in order to send it or store it SYN COMPRESS OPP UNZIP

**ˈzip code** (*also* **ZIP** -) = POSTCODE

**ˈzip file** *n.* [C] (*IT*) a computer file that has been made smaller in order to be sent or stored

★ **zone** /zəʊn; *AmE* zoʊn/ *n., v.*

• ***n.*** [C] **1** an area or a region with a particular feature or use: *an industrial zone* **2** one of the areas that a larger area is divided into for the purpose of organization: *postal charges to countries in zone 2*

• ***v.*** [T] (*usu. pass.*) **1** to keep an area of land to be used for a particular purpose: *The town centre was zoned for office development.* **2** to divide an area of land into smaller areas

▸ **ˈzoning** *n.* [U]

**ˈZ-score** *n.* [C] (*Finan.*) a measure of how likely a business is to fail

# Useful phrases

## 1. Phrases for telephoning

### Calling a company

Good morning/afternoon.
  This is.... from....
I'd like to/Could I speak to..., please.
Could you put me through to..., please?
Extension..., please.
Can I leave a message?
OK, I'll call back later.
Could you ask her to call me back?

### Taking a call

Good morning/afternoon. Smith and Black Ltd. How can I help you?
Certainly Sir/Madam. I'll put you through.
I'll try to connect you.
Can you hold the line/hold on, please?
I'll put you on hold.
Please bear with me for a moment.
I'm afraid she's in a meeting/out of the office at the moment.
Can I take a message?
Could you call back later?
Could she call you back?
Thank you for calling. Goodbye.

### Dealing with problems

I think you've got the wrong number.
Could you repeat that, please – it's a bad line.
I'm sorry, I didn't catch that.
Could you spell that, please?
I'm sorry – we got cut off.

### Automated messages that you may hear

Thank you for holding - your call is in a queue/line.
All our operators are busy at present. Please call back/try again later.
You are being redirected to voicemail.
Leave a message after the tone.
Your call may be recorded for training purposes.
Please listen carefully to the following options.
Enter your credit card number, followed by the hash key/pound sign.
If you don't have a touch tone phone, please hold to be connected to a customer service adviser.

## 2. Phrases for meetings

### Arranging a meeting

I'm trying to fix/arrange a meeting for next week.
A meeting of the management team has been called.
A special board meeting has been convened. (*Formal*)
We have a meeting in an hour.
Everyone must attend.
The meeting has been postponed until tomorrow.

### Informal meetings

I think we're all here – let's start.
I'd like to start the meeting by...
The first item on the agenda is....
Let's move on to the next item.
Shall we park that until the next meeting?
Shall we put that on the agenda for the next meeting?
Is there anything else?
Let's wind up/end the meeting there.

### More formal meetings

We have a quorum so we can start.
Apologies have been received from...
The minutes of the previous meeting have been circulated.
Can this be recorded in the minutes?
I'd like to propose the motion that...
Can we take a show of hands?
All those in favour? Against?
Is there any other business?
I'll close the meeting there.
We will adjourn until tomorrow.

### Asking questions and making points

I'd like to ask something/a question.
I'd like to raise an issue.
Can I bring something up?
I'd just like to say...
I can't go along with that.
That's a good idea/
a good point.
I agree/I don't agree.
I agree/don't agree
with Jane.
I agree that we should find
out more about this.